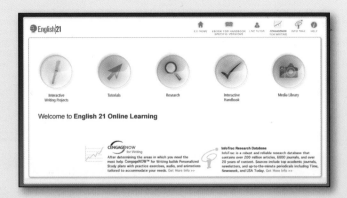

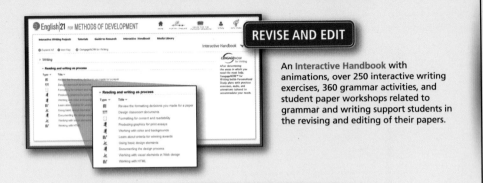

REVISE AND EDIT

An **Interactive Handbook** with animations, over 250 interactive writing exercises, 360 grammar activities, and student paper workshops related to grammar and writing support students in the revising and editing of their papers.

EXPLICATE

An extensive **Media Library**, featuring over 700 multimedia assets, includes a wealth of audio clips (42), video clips (32), stories (11), poems (389), plays (8), essays (58), and images (203). To help students annotate works and generate evidence for their papers, all media can be read through Wadsworth's unique note-taking tool, the *Explicator*.

Unlike traditional note-taking, the *Explicator* empowers students with a state-of the art analysis tool that allows them to examine and annotate both traditional texts as well as non-traditional texts, including images, video clips, and audio clips, acting as a bridge between reading and writing.

Also available: English21 *Plus*

English21 *Plus* includes all of the features mentioned above plus access to Wadsworth's **InSite for Writing and Research™**, a groundbreaking, all-in-one electronic portfolio and peer review application. **InSite** also includes an originality checker powered by **Turnitin®**, a rich assignment library, and an electronic grademarking system.

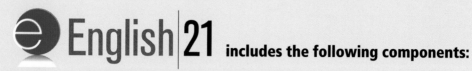 **English|21** includes the following components:

ANALYZE

Interactive Writing Projects contain professionally written paper-length assignments that engage students with multimedia tutorials and a series of interactive activities. The guided steps in each assignment thread students' analyses together to encourage deeper synthesis in their papers.

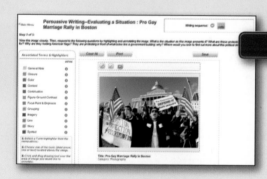

WRITE

More than 150 interactive **Tutorials** span subjects from rhetorical to literary concepts to support students as they construct their papers—each with brief instruction, animated examples, and interactive activities.

RESEARCH

A comprehensive **Guide to Research** contains animations, more than 50 interactive research exercises, and student paper workshops related to research—as well as desktop access to **InfoTrac® College Edition**, a research database that contains links to over 6,000 journals and periodicals and over 20 years of content—to support students' research activities.

THE POP CULTURE ZONE

WRITING CRITICALLY ABOUT POPULAR CULTURE

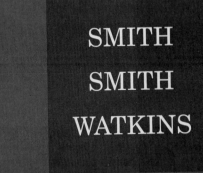

SMITH

SMITH

WATKINS

THE POP CULTURE ZONE

WRITING CRITICALLY ABOUT POPULAR CULTURE

ALLISON D. SMITH
Middle Tennessee State University

TRIXIE G. SMITH
Michigan State University

STACIA RIGNEY WATKINS
Middle Tennessee State University

 WADSWORTH
CENGAGE Learning™

Australia • Brazil • Japan • Korea • Mexico • Singapore • Spain • United Kingdom • United States

The Pop Culture Zone: Writing Critically about Popular Culture
Smith, Smith, Watkins

Publisher: Lyn Uhl

Development Editor: Laurie K. Runion

Senior Editorial Assistant: Megan Power

Associate Development Project Manager: Emily Ryan

Executive Marketing Manager: Mandee Eckersley

Senior Marketing Communications Manager: Stacey Purviance Taylor

Content Project Manager: Jessica Rasile

Senior Art Director: Cate Rickard Barr

Senior Print Buyer: Betsy Donaghey

Text Permissions Manager: Scott Bragg

Text Permissions Researcher: Karyn Morrison

Senior Image Manager: Sheri Blaney

Photo Researcher: Jill Engebretson

Production Service/Compositor: Lachina Publishing Services

Cover/Text Design: Yvo Riezebos Design

For product information and technology assistance, contact us at
Cengage Learning Academic Resource Center, 1-800-423-0563

For permission to use material from this text or product,
submit all requests online at **www.cengage.com/permissions.**
Further permissions questions can be e-mailed to
permissionrequest@cengage.com.

Library of Congress Control Number: 2008926771

ISBN-13: 978-1-4282-0506-2

ISBN-10: 1-4282-0506-3

Wadsworth Cengage Learning
25 Thomson Place
Boston, MA 02210
USA

Cengage Learning products are represented in Canada by Nelson Education, Ltd.

For your course and learning solutions, visit **academic.cengage.com.**

Purchase any of our products at your local college store or at our preferred online store, **www.ichapters.com.**

We have made every effort to trace the ownership of all copyrighted material and to secure permission from copyright holders. In the event of any question arising as to the use of any material, we will be pleased to make the necessary corrections in future printings.

Printed in the U.S.A.
4 5 6 7 8 16 15 14 13

Contents

CHAPTER 5
writing about film 177

Test Your Pop Culture IQ: Film 178

***Asterisks indicate student essays.*

CHAPTER 6
writing about groups, spaces, and places 255

Test Your Pop Culture IQ: Groups, Spaces, and Places 256

YOU AND GROUPS, SPACES, AND PLACES 258

WHY WRITE ABOUT GROUPS, SPACES, AND PLACES? 259

PREPARING TO WRITE ABOUT GROUPS, SPACES, AND PLACES 260

Terms to Know 261

Researching and Documenting 261

***Asterisks indicate student essays.

CHAPTER 7
writing about music 355

Test Your Pop Culture IQ: Music 356

YOU AND MUSIC 358

WHY WRITE ABOUT MUSIC? 359

PREPARING TO WRITE ABOUT MUSIC 359

WRITING ABOUT MUSIC 364

Music Reviews or Review Essays 365

***Asterisks indicate student essays.

CHAPTER 8
writing about popular literature 449

Test Your Pop Culture IQ: Popular Literature 450

YOU AND POPULAR LITERATURE 452

WHY WRITE ABOUT POPULAR LITERATURE? 453

PREPARING TO WRITE ABOUT POPULAR LITERATURE 453

WRITING ABOUT POPULAR LITERATURE 457

CHAPTER ⑨

writing about sports and leisure 573

Test Your Pop Culture IQ: Sports and Leisure 574

YOU AND SPORTS AND LEISURE 576

WHY WRITE ABOUT SPORTS AND LEISURE? 576

PREPARING TO WRITE ABOUT SPORTS AND LEISURE 578

***Asterisks indicate student essays.*

CHAPTER 10
writing about television 643

***Asterisks indicate student essays.*

***Asterisks indicate student essays.

PART III
THE RESEARCH ZONE

CHAPTER 11
researching and documenting in the pop culture zone 739

Rhetorical Contents

*** Asterisks indicate student essays.*

REVIEW

REVIEW ESSAY

***Asterisks indicate student essays.*

***Asterisks indicate student essays.

A = Analysis
R = Review
RE = Review Essay
R/R = Reflection/Response
S = Synthesis

Thematic Contents

***Asterisks indicate student essays.*

***Asterisks indicate student essays.

***Asterisks indicate student essays.*

CONSUMERISM

***Asterisks indicate student essays.*

EDUCATION

****Asterisks indicate student essays.*

ENVIRONMENT/LOCATION

FAITH

GOVERNMENT/POLITICS

***Asterisks indicate student essays.*

IDENTITY

***Asterisks indicate student essays.

TECHNOLOGY/SCIENCE

***Asterisks indicate student essays.

Preface for Instructors

WHY WE WROTE *THE POP CULTURE ZONE: WRITING CRITICALLY ABOUT POPULAR CULTURE*

Our own search for a first-year composition (FYC) textbook that utilized pop culture for its content proved frustrating. Although we found textbooks that included cultural or pop cultural readings, most did not include the focus on writing that we wanted for our freshmen or our new instructors or teaching assistants. We needed a textbook that used pop culture as a starting point—a point where teachers could meet their students, reflect on personal preferences and review different aspects of pop culture together, and use all of this as a transition to the critical analysis and writing that we wanted our freshmen to do.

The Pop Culture Zone: Writing Critically about Popular Culture focuses on pop culture because it is something that first-year college students know and can get passionate about. Pop culture is the bridge between their lives and the critical reading, thinking, and writing that are part of freshman composition. *The Pop Culture Zone* focuses on the relationship students have with pop culture and how this relationship can help them become more critical readers and writers.

ABOUT *THE POP CULTURE ZONE*

Often, FYC classes or their textbooks are so focused on questioning or mastering the content in a reader that the primary goal of improving writing is weakened or lost entirely. The overriding purpose of an FYC class is to improve student writing, and the textbooks, readings, and assignments used in such a course should all be aimed at reaching this goal. The reading selections and writing assignments in *The Pop Culture Zone* are included to get students thinking critically as they read, respond, analyze, and criticize the pop culture of today and yesterday. We use decades to organize the reading selections and to show readers that pop culture is not just what is happening now, but also includes the current connections we make to popular media of the past. The book's primary focus is getting students to think more critically about the pop culture world around them and to write critically about their thoughts and reactions.

We use pop culture as a contact zone where students can engage with pop culture elements, readings, and their classmates. The pop culture zone approach is influenced by Mary Louise Pratt's theoretical model of the contact zone, a place where students are encouraged to make choices, disagree with readings, and argue with their peers and others about interpretations and the importance of pop culture. *The Pop Culture Zone* meets students where they are and then asks them to do what they already do when they choose to watch a particular television show or read multiple books in the same pop literature series—critique, review, and then present supporting evidence. Students tell personal stories and explain their reactions, analyzing not only the pop culture element but also themselves and others as they do so.

Bringing pop culture into the composition classroom allows students not only to learn the discourse of academia. It also allows them to use the familiar forms of persuasion that are often already present in student discourse as the bridge to the critical reasoning and writing that occur in a college writing course. Students learn to listen to viewpoints that differ from their own, summarize their views effectively, compare and contrast, and present their ideas in a way that creates a continuing conversation of ideas.

Our text provides sections called The Reading Zone, where students meet ideas through reading and connect those ideas to their own culture, and Contemplations and Collaborations in the Pop Culture Zone, where students connect their ideas with others inside and outside the class through cooperative and collaborative discussions and writing assignments. These zones are needed to decode texts, connect the author culture to the student culture, and provide opportunities for discussion that lead to collaborative and/or individual writing. The readings used can trigger warm reflections or heated debates on issues related to student lives and their identities, including topics related to power, gender, sexuality, race, and culture. Students and instructors can also bring their own theories and methods of analysis to the various texts and genres of writing. *The Pop Culture Zone* uses an approach that focuses more on a critical analysis of the self in relation to popular culture rather than just an analysis of pop culture or culture itself. This critical analysis provides the pedagogical apparatus for students to write review, reflection or response, analysis, and synthesis essays.

FEATURES OF THE BOOK

The Parts

The Pop Culture Zone is divided into three main parts: introductory chapters, content chapters, and a research and documentation chapter. Chapter 1, The Pop Culture Zone, gives an overview of the text's features. Chapter 2, Writing in the Pop Culture Zone, provides a writing apparatus, something that might not be available in their current popular culture or other reader. Part I ends with Chapter 3, Defining Popular Culture, which introduces students to the broad scope of popular culture. Part II consists of seven content chapters devoted to a variety of media or themes encountered in popular culture, including advertisements, pop lit, and television. The third part, Chapter 11, Researching and Documenting in the Pop Culture Zone, ends the book with an overview of the researching processes, especially in connection to popular culture. As experienced teachers, we recognize that many instructors may not find it necessary to use the writing or research chapters, but new teachers may appreciate the support that these chapters provide. Experienced teachers can also expand and modify these chapters to use with their beginning writers.

The Chapters

Each chapter begins with a trivia quiz to get students thinking and talking about the pop culture unit coming up. These informal quizzes are provided as conversation starters to the chapter. Following the quiz, each chapter provides a description of what writing in this field or this medium looks like, why people write about it or may want to, and then discusses how to write about this medium or theme, including presentations of related content and techniques. For example, the chapter on film introduces students to concepts and terms such as "mise-en-scène," "cinematography," and "character." This introductory section in each chapter also includes a sample annotated essay, which calls attention to writing and analysis techniques, followed by about ten other readings, including a student essay, organized into sections: 1970s, 1980s, 1990s, 2000s, and Across the Decades.

The reading selections in each chapter are preceded by Tackling Topics, prereading questions designed to get students thinking and conversing before they read the selections. The Reading Zone, a collection of essay selections, follows the prereading questions. Each of the individual essays is preceded by Considering Ideas—questions that can be used for journaling, blogging, or in-class writing. Each is followed by Decoding the Text and Connecting to Your Culture questions, which ask students to analyze the text and then connect the ideas from the reading selection to their own lives. At the end of The Reading Zone, questions given in the sections entitled Contemplation in the Pop Culture Zone and Collaboration in the Pop Culture Zone are used to stimulate critical thinking and subsequent discussion and writing. These chapters close with several wide-ranging essay ideas in the section Start Writing Essays About [the pop culture element].

Range of Readings

We include a wide range of selected readings in each chapter gathered from a variety of disciplines, including student essays, online film or music reviews, newspaper articles, and more sophisticated analysis and synthesis essays from academic journals. Each chapter includes student and professional writers and also includes examples of review, reflection or response, analysis, and synthesis essays. The readings were selected to encompass multiple viewpoints and perspectives: liberal and conservative, biased and unbiased, pro and con.

The Case Studies

In thematic chapters, some readings are grouped together in case studies, which provide a variety of perspectives on smaller topics related to the same overall theme. Having your students read the essays as a case study encourages them to investigate complex, multifaceted issues and to share their thoughts with others in class and in writing.

Student Writers *Are* Writers

In an effort to empower and encourage students, we treat student writers in our text equally to professional writers by providing the same apparatus for both student and professional readings. Student essays are sometimes annotated as samples or offered as regular reading selections. Student essays are indicated by asterisks (***) in the table of contents.

Visuals

Because pop culture often includes visual rather than just written text, we include approximately 130 photos and visuals throughout our text. Some reading selections are primarily visual essays, including the color insert on Coca-Cola images. In addition, we also offer visual essays as alternative assignments for students to create.

Assistance in the Writing and Research Process

Our text includes a writing instruction apparatus both in Chapter 2, Writing in the Pop Culture Zone, and also at the beginning of each content chapter. This assistance is often missing from pop culture readers. *The Pop Culture Zone* also includes a sample annotated essay for each content area—a feature unique to this market—to help students see what makes for good organization or good detail when pop culture is the subject. In Chapter 11, Researching and Documenting in the Pop Culture Zone, we provide guidelines for connecting research around specific pop culture media and themes—another feature unique to this market. The book itself uses MLA documentation throughout; however, both MLA and APA documentation styles are introduced, including many examples of popular culture documentation often left out of basic overviews.

Test Your Pop Culture IQ

As a form of metacognitive blueprinting, we provide a short pop culture quiz at the beginning of each chapter to remind students how much they do (or don't) know about the content area. The quizzes are an amusing way to jump-start students' critical thinking, help them make connections to pop culture, and create the cognitive dissonance that can lead to active engagement and learning. Not meant to be graded, the trivia quizzes may be used by students and teachers as a fun way to start discussing the medium or theme. Additional ideas for using the quizzes are available in the Instructor's Manual.

Grappling with Ideas

Each chapter includes Grappling with Ideas boxes that ask students to think critically about their own experiences. Teachers and students can use these questions as triggers for student discussion, journal writing, blogging, or other low-risk class assignments.

Alternative Tables of Contents

We recognize that teachers sometimes want to take an alternative approach when using pop culture reading selections, so we provide both a rhetorical and a thematic table of contents at the front of the text to help you plan possible alternative teaching units using themes or rhetorical strategies.

ANCILLARIES

Companion Website

The Pop Culture Zone has a companion website—academic.cengage.com/english/SmithPopCulture—which offers examples of the media being discussed and provides author biographies that are linked to other works or similar topics. Reading quizzes and additional sample essay assignments are also included. In addition, the website gives links to online sources that are useful for researching in the various areas of pop culture and offers additional tables of content that group the readings by decade or type of media.

Instructor's Manual

Especially useful for new teachers, the Instructor's Manual (IM) provides insights into how to use particular essays and general pop culture topics effectively as content. The IM also provides reading questions, alternative prewriting and discussion topics, and additional writing assignments. Expanded information on the trivia quiz answers is available, and a bibliography of resources on teaching pop culture, writing, and the contact zone is also provided. In addition, the IM includes additional tables of content that are organized around the decades approach and on the type of media discussed in essays.

Teaching in the Pop Culture Zone: Using Popular Culture in the Composition Classroom, edited by Allison D. Smith, Trixie G. Smith, and Rebecca Bobbitt

A Cengage Learning professional development textbook that offers insights and strategies about using pop culture in the writing classroom is also available. The edited volume includes essays by instructors, who share details of their most effective class ideas and writing assignments.

ACKNOWLEDGMENTS

From all of us, we say thank you to these people who helped us at various times throughout this project. We cannot say enough, but many thanks to all of you: Dianna Baldwin, Kirsten Boatwright, Becky Bobbitt, Katrina Byrd, Jimmie Cain, Andy Coomes, Matt Cox, Chris Driver, English 6560/7560 students, English 6570/7570 students, Jaime Espil, Mark Francisco, the Graduate College at MTSU, Stephanie Harper, Qingjun Li, Jessica McKee, Star McKenzie Burruto, Tanya McLaughlin, Dickson Musselwhite, Rachel Robinson Strickland, Hillary Robson, Michael Rosenberg, Tom Strawman, Ben Strickland, Holly Tipton, and Karen Wright. We also want to express our appreciation to Brad Walker, who took on the enigmatic task of creating the Index.

We also give our utmost thanks to all those who assisted us in the editorial, permissions, production, and marketing process: Lyn Uhl, Publisher; Laurie Runion, Development Editor; Megan Power, Editorial

Assistant; Jessica Rasile, Content Project Manager; Mandee Eckersley, Executive Marketing Manager; Sheri Blaney, Senior Image Manager; Jill Engebretson, Photo Researcher; Scott Bragg, Rights Acquisitions Account Manager; Karyn Morrison, Text Permission Researcher; Kelli Strieby, Assistant Editor; Anne Pietromica and Jennifer Bonnar, Project Managers at Lachina Publishing Services; Sona Lachina, Compositor; Pam Connell, Artist; and Melissa Higey, Assistant Editor at Lachina Publishing Services.

—Allison, Trixie, Stacia

First, thank you to both Trixie and Stacia for their collegial company as we progressed through the writing of this book. It took many meetings, discussions, and jokes to get to the final product, and I could not think of anyone else whom I would have wanted to work with on this pop culture project. In addition, our two colleagues—Dianna Baldwin and Becky Bobbitt—were instrumental in collecting essays, trying out ideas, working on the supplements, and keeping us on track. An additional thank you to Becky for the time she spent as my research assistant—you are both a first-rate researcher and assistant. Laurie Runion, you helped keep us to deadline but also knew when we needed more time; thanks for your insight and never-ending support. Each year, forty or so teaching assistants show me new ways to teach and new pop culture to investigate—thanks to all of them for keeping me up to speed. In fact, this book took flight as a project in my English 6560/7560 and 6570/7570 courses, and I thank all those freshman students and graduate teaching assistants who helped with the brainstorming. Also, thanks to Bill Connelly, Tom Strawman, and the Graduate College at MTSU for support both financially and academically; this kind of teaching scholarship cannot happen without administrators who understand the need for it. I also give kudos to Trixie Smith, Stacia Watkins, Rachel Strickland, Jimmie Cain, and Karen Wright; sharing administrative duties with you helped me do other things, so thanks for giving me that extra time each day. On the home front, I thank my family and friends for always being supportive of my need to do some writing or grading or watching films and television (for this book or not). I give special thanks to Lynne Murphy, one of my first academic writing partners, for always giving good advice and support. And finally, my part of this book is dedicated to my mother, Mary Anne Smith, who always encouraged me and my interests in reading, writing, and education.

—Allison

First and foremost, I would like to thank my coauthors, Allison and Stacia, for the time, energy, and laughs that went into this project; I'm especially grateful for their willingness to think creatively and brainstorm new ideas. Likewise, I'm thankful for the invaluable help from a number of research assistants at both MTSU and MSU who helped locate articles and images, create and test quizzes, and track down sources—Dianna Baldwin, Becky Bobbitt, and Matt Cox. There were also a number of students, TAs, and writing center consultants who willingly shared experiences, assignments, feedback, writings, and their love of pop culture to help make this text a reality; thank you. Likewise, thanks to my faculty writing group at MSU. Finally, thanks to my friends and family members who have always believed in me and have always given their support for my various endeavors: Mom and Jerry, Dad and Annie, Melanie, Pam, James, Teresa and family, and my niece Tabitha who was even willing to clean house and wash clothes during her summer vacation so I could attend one more book meeting.

—Trixie

Thank you to my family, especially my parents, John and Sandra Rigney, and my grandmother, Marcia Rigney, for their guidance during this project and all of the other life moments that happened throughout the writing process; to Rachel Strickland for being my personal and academic co-conspirator; to Drs. Michael and Sarah Dunne for inspiring my love of pop culture in academics; to Jennifer Stephens Block for instigating and encouraging my love of pop culture; to Allison and Trixie for inviting me to be a part of the text; and to my husband, Cody, for loving me, supporting me, and teaching me more every day. Chapter 7, on music, is devoted to him. My desire to use popular culture to teach writing is inspired by everything I enjoy from Wilco, to *The Simpsons,* to *GoodFellas,* to the Kentucky Derby, to Jimmy Carter's politics. I hope you and your students, too, can find your loves represented in this text.

—*Stacia*

And finally, thank you and much appreciation to our reviewers. Your insights and comments helped us refine both the readings and the framework, and we truly appreciate your time in assisting us with this project.

Amy Braziller, *Red Rocks Community College*

James Burns, *University of Delaware*

Pamela Childers, *The McCallie School*

Earnest Cox, *University of Arkansas at Little Rock*

Samantha A. Morgan-Curtis, *Tennessee State University*

Silver Damsen, *University of Illinois, Urbana–Champaign*

Sahara Drew, *Tufts University*

Anthony Edgington, *University of Toledo*

Carolyn Embree, *University of Akron*

William Etter, *Irvine Valley College*

Brooke Eubanks, *Central Arizona College*

Stephen Evans, *University of Kansas*

Africa Fine, *Palm Beach Community College*

Karen Fitts, *West Chester University of Pennsylvania*

Kathryn Fitzgerald, *Utah State University*

Christy Friend, *University of South Carolina*

Katheryn Giglio, *University of Central Florida*

Gwendolyn Hale, *Savannah State University*

Stephanie Harper, *Nashville Christian School*

Chris Harris, *University of Louisiana at Monroe*

Kevin Haworth, *Ohio University*

Bruce Henderson, *Fullerton College*

Craig Hergert, *Minneapolis Community and Technical College*

Michael Howarth, *University of Louisiana–Lafayette*

John Hyman, *American University*

Tobi Jacobi, *Colorado State University*

Karen Jacobson, *Valdosta State University*

Michelle Jimmerson, *Louisiana Tech University*

June Joyner, *Georgia Southern University*

Marjorie Justice, *Governors State University*

Sarah Lanius, *Michigan State University*

Katherine Lee, *Indiana State University*

John Levine, *University of California, Berkeley*

Jacquelyn Lyman, *Anne Arundel Community College*

Leanne Maunu, *Palomar College*

Lei Lani Michel, *University of Washington*

Lindee Owens, *University of Central Florida*

Merry G. Perry, *West Chester University of Pennsylvania*

Tamara Powell, *Louisiana Tech University*

Zach Pugh, *Palomar College*

Hillary Robson, *Middle Tennessee State University*

Brooke Rollins, *Louisiana State University*

Laura Gray-Rosendale, *Northern Arizona University*

Cynthia Ryan, *University of Alabama at Birmingham*

Lisa Schneider, *Georgia Institute of Technology*

Aaron Shapiro, *Middle Tennessee State University*

Marsha Elyn Wright, *Garden City Community College*

COVER PHOTOS

From local nightclubs to Studio 54 in New York City, people disco danced their way through the '70s.

Reggae singer, songwriter, and activist Bob Marley in a 1979 performance.

No longer your grandmother's hobby, knitting became a hip leisure activity in the '00s. "Pocket Pups" also became quite popular after Paris Hilton and her Chihuahua, Tinkerbelle, became celebs on *The Simple Life*.

Popular author J. K. Rowling at the launch of *Harry Potter and the Deathly Hallows* at The Natural History Museum in London in 2007.

SMITH

SMITH

WATKINS

From stock cars to state-of-the-art ultramodern machines, NASCAR has become one of America's favorite spectator sports.

Once only seen on sailors and bikers, tattoos have become a mainstream form of body art and a marker of group identity.

DJs, a subculture of the club scene, focus on the music they spin, as well as how they remix tracks to create the most energy and the best dance vibe.

Actress Tippi Heddrin in Alfred Hitchcock's Academy Award-winning film *The Birds* (1963).

American Idol judges Randy Jackson, Paula Abdul, and Simon Cowell.

The introduction of the Apple iPod shuffle revolutionized the way we acquire and listen to music.

A Monday Night Football game between the Indianapolis Colts and Jacksonville Jaguars on Oct. 22, 2007.

THE POP CULTURE ZONE

WRITING CRITICALLY

ABOUT POPULAR

CULTURE

the pop culture zone

"When I say essay, I mean, essay. I do not mean a single word repeated a thousand times."

—From *The Breakfast Club*

© Columbia/Revolution Studios/The Kobal Collection

1 Match the film title to the discipline being taught.

1. *Dead Poets Society*
2. *Harry Potter and the Sorcerer's Stone*
3. *Stand and Deliver*
4. *Mona Lisa Smile*
5. *Election*

a. Art
b. Literature
c. Political science
d. Math
e. Herbology

TEST YOUR POP CULTURE IQ: EDUCATION AND POP CULTURE

2 Match the fictional president to the actor who plays him or her.

1. President Thomas J. Whitmore in *Independence Day*
2. President Mackenzie Allen in *Commander in Chief*
3. President Josiah "Jed" Bartlet in *The West Wing*
4. President Laura Roslin in *Battlestar Galactica*
5. President Andrew Shepherd in *The American President*

a. Mary McDonnell
b. Martin Sheen
c. Michael Douglas
d. Bill Pullman
e. Geena Davis

3 Place these children's educational series in order of when they began.

a. *Zoom*
b. *Reading Rainbow*
c. *Sesame Street*
d. *Bill Nye, the Science Guy*
e. *Schoolhouse Rock!*

4 In which song do hordes of students chant the mantra, "We don't need no education/ We don't need no thought control"?

a. "Jeremy," Pearl Jam
b. "School," New Edition
c. "Centerfold," The J. Geils Band
d. "Another Brick in the Wall," Pink Floyd
e. "School's Out," Alice Cooper

5 Which of these films is based on a book and was also made into a TV series?

a. *Freedom Writers*
b. *Clueless*
c. *The Breakfast Club*
d. *Legally Blonde*
e. *10 Things I Hate About You*

Chapter opener photo © Universal/The Kobal Collection

6 What 1980s TV series about college life featured guest appearances by Jada Pinkett-Smith, Gladys Knight, and Bill Cosby?

    a. *A Different World*
    b. *Head of the Class*
    c. *Square Pegs*
    d. *Beverly Hills, 90210*
    e. *Coach*

7 Which of these children's books has *not* been made into a film?

    a. *Mrs. Frisby and the Rats of Nimh*
    b. *Harriet the Spy*
    c. *Howl's Moving Castle*
    d. *The Secret Garden*
    e. *The Boxcar Children*

8 Which politician-turned-actor played a teacher on *The Wonder Years*, hosted his own game show from 1997 to 2002, and hosted *America's Most Smartest Model* in 2007?

    a. Pat Sajak
    b. Jeff Foxworthy
    c. Ben Stein
    d. Penn Jillette
    e. Regis Philbin

9 Which of these TV series does not focus on students and their coach?

    a. *Friday Night Lights*
    b. *The White Shadow*
    c. *Beverly Hills, 90210*
    d. *Hangin' with Mr. Cooper*
    e. *Hang Time*

© Roberts Mikel/CORBIS SYGMA

10 In what year did companies begin advertising products within school systems via *Channel One News*?

    a. 1988
    b. 1990
    c. 1982
    d. 1997
    e. 2001

ANSWERS

1 *1. b. Literature 2. e. Herbology 3. d. Math 4. a. Art 5. c. Political science* **2** *1. d. Bill Pullman 2. e. Geena Davis 3. b. Martin Sheen 4. a. Mary McDonnell 5. c. Michael Douglas* **3** *c. Sesame Street a. Zoom e. Schoolhouse Rock! b. Reading Rainbow d. Bill Nye, the Science Guy* **4** *d. "Another Brick in the Wall," Pink Floyd* **5** *b. Clueless* **6** *a. A Different World* **7** *e.* The Boxcar Children **8** *c.* Ben Stein **9** *c.* Beverly Hills, 90210 **10** *b. 1990*

"All objects, all phases of culture are alive. They have voices. They speak of their history and interrelatedness. And they are all talking at once!"

—Camille Paglia

"Like other secret lovers, many speak mockingly of popular culture to conceal their passion for it."

—Mason Cooley

WHY WRITE ABOUT POP CULTURE?

Pop culture is your culture. It is what you watch, read, listen to, take part in, and enjoy each and every day of your life. Pop culture is *The Office* and *Lost*, Beyoncé and Mary J. Blige, *Borat* and *Braveheart*. It is Timbaland and Justin Timberlake, Second Life and Grand Theft Auto, fandom sites about NASCAR and *Star Wars*. You can even make money exhibiting your knowledge of pop culture at local trivia contests held across the country or on the national World Series of Pop Culture, sponsored by *Entertainment Weekly* and VH1. Pop culture crosses time and also changes with time since pop culture icons can disappear as quickly as they become popular, return with a wave of nostalgia, or stay around for decades. Pop culture is a

powerful part of all our lives. You are an expert when it comes to your own pop culture; you know what appeals to you and what does not, and you know why. Because critical thinking and writing both rely on the writer's interest in and knowledge about the topic, pop culture is a surprisingly interesting and uncomplicated way to begin the journey of thinking, reading, and writing critically. Pop culture itself is the content that you will read about, observe, grapple with, discuss, and write about. In the pop culture zone, the term "content" is often synonymous with "text," which refers to the different types of pop culture available for studying. Be sure to read Chapter 3, Defining Popular Culture, to help you figure out what pop culture means to you.

The reading and writing assignments in *The Pop Culture Zone* revolve around how you read, respond to, analyze, and criticize pop culture, using what is familiar to you as a bridge to the writing you do in an academic setting. The questions related to the reading selections and the writing assignments ask you not only to critique pop culture but also to analyze and describe the relationship you and others around you have with it. Your knowledge of and familiarity with pop culture are at the center of everything you read and write about in *The Pop Culture Zone*, and this is why writing about pop culture can help you begin or expand both your critical thinking and writing.

WHAT IS THE POP CULTURE ZONE?

The pop culture zone is where you can meet with other students in class or writers of the essays in the book to investigate, discuss, and sometimes argue about your personal responses to pop culture in a critical way. The pop culture zone approach is influenced by the contact zone theoretical model presented first by Professor Mary Louise Pratt in her talk at a Modern Language Association conference and published in *Profession* in 1991. The title of her talk, "Arts of the Contact Zone," refers to those places where students and instructors are free to "meet, clash, and grapple with each other, often in contexts of highly asymmetrical relations of power." (A highly asymmetrical relationship is one in which a person has more power due to social status or socioeconomic level.) Pratt proposes the contact zone model to emphasize the idea that members within any community are not always the same in their thinking or actions.

The Pop Culture Zone takes this model and applies it to the writing classroom, assuming that all students in the class community are enlightened and knowledgeable about the topic in question—pop culture—and that all members of the class can feel free to discuss, argue, and clash with others about their views in the pop culture zone. However, we are not trying to take away or change the enjoyment you have in your own pop culture choices, and we expect that you are also free to express your ideas in what Pratt calls the "safe house," a place where you can meet with others who share your opinions and experiences. Sometimes, you will find this safe house in collaborative projects or the writing you do in class, but most often, you will find it where you have always found it, with your friends or others who enjoy and make the same pop culture choices you do.

WHAT ARE SOME OF THE BOOK'S SPECIAL FEATURES?

Test Your Pop Culture IQ

Each chapter begins with a trivia quiz that provides an opening to the contents of the chapter. Getting all the answers correct is not the goal; using the quizzes as a conversational starting point is. See how many of these pop culture questions you know, and compare your answers with your classmates or test your friends. Once the conversation gets around to pop culture, see how many people become interested in what you are doing in your writing course.

Grappling with Ideas

Throughout the book, you will find Grappling with Ideas boxes that ask you to think more deeply about the information in that portion of the book or in a section that follows. Your instructor may ask you to answer these questions in a journal, a blog, or some other type of informal writing. Use these questions as a way to reflect on your own thoughts and opinions before you encounter the thoughts and opinions of your classmates, your instructor, or the essay authors in this book.

> **grappling with ideas**
>
> Be sure to take the pop culture IQ trivia quiz at the beginning of this chapter.
> - How well did you do on the quiz?
> - What answer(s) surprised you the most? The least? Why?
> - What other television programs, films, songs, or popular books have focused on the educational experience?

Think about and share some of your favorite pop culture "texts."

- What types of advertisements make you want to purchase a product? Why?

- What are three of your favorite films? Why do you think these are your favorites?

- What are some of the groups—formal or informal—that can call you a member? Where do these groups meet? Is there any special language usage you share with the groups?

- What are some of your favorite songs? Do these songs have anything in common?

- What kinds of books did you enjoy reading when you were five? Ten? Now?

- What are your favorite sports or leisure activities? Do these have anything in common?

- What kinds of television programs do you enjoy the most? Has your taste changed over your lifetime? If so, in what way?

Annotated Sample Essays

We provide annotated sample essays in each chapter to highlight features that combine to create interesting and effective writing. Many of these samples are written by students who use their personal interest in pop culture to help them create essays that fit into the chapter topic. Read these essays, check out the features that are highlighted, and use the essays as examples of how to write about pop culture.

The Reading Zone

The Reading Zone in each chapter is a place—a contact zone— where you meet new ideas through the readings and the reactions these readings generate in yourself and your classmates. The reading selections in The Reading Zone provide topics that you can investigate, discuss, or argue with; these selections also provide models for writing review, reflection or response, analysis, and synthesis essays—the types of essays that are later asked for in the writing assignment sections of the chapters.

Sometimes, it is easier to be critical about the things that are not so close to us. *The Pop Culture Zone* is not focused on you picking apart the things you like; it also allows some distance for those who want or need it by looking at pop culture in other time periods. In addition, to appeal to all students and to show that pop culture is not just something that is happening now, but also can be what happened in an earlier time, the essay selections are organized into the last four decades and a final section that goes across the decades. The chapters that are organized into the 1970s, 1980s, 1990s, and 2000s include essays about pop culture items during that time period and/or essays that were written during that time. Being able to see how pop culture affected others will help you investigate how it may be affecting you as well. Since some pop culture icons never go out of style—The Beatles or Elvis, for instance—and some go out and come back over and over again—like Madonna or Prince—being able to place your pop culture in the overall continuum sometimes helps you take a backseat look at what is driving the pop culture of your time.

The Reading Zone is not a place where one idea, one analysis, or one argument is expected to be the only one. At the beginning of The Reading Zone, you are invited to see how much you know about the coming topics with the Tackling Topics questions. Before you read the essays, you can share your ideas in Considering Ideas questions, which are provided to get you thinking about the topics and sharing your prereading ideas about the specific essay topics as you write in journals or blogs or have conversations with your classmates. After you read, you are asked to analyze the readings in Decoding the Text questions and to analyze and share reactions to readings in the

Connecting to Your Culture questions. Throughout The Reading Zone section, you are invited to share your own pop culture favorites, as you contemplate and react to the pop culture mentioned in the reading selections.

© Michael Ochs Archives/Getty Images

After you and others grapple with, share, and possibly argue about your reactions and analyses of the readings and how they relate to your own culture, you are invited to connect the chapter readings or unite with your classmates in the Contemplations in the Pop Culture Zone sections. Here you investigate how the pop culture medium or type affects you personally, and you look for connections across readings in the chapter or across chapters or topics throughout the book. Possibly, you can figure out what topic you may be interested in writing about for your next essay. You can then use the Collaborations in the Pop Culture Zone questions to share your ideas with your classmates, looking for things you have or do not have in common and considering topics in preparation for writing. The Collaborations questions can also help you expand on your knowledge about class topics by helping you investigate websites, conduct interviews, or discuss class topics with your friends, family, or colleagues.

Writing and Research Advice

Each chapter is set up using the same format for both reading selections and the questions that follow. Beginning with a Why Write About section, each chapter discusses the importance of reading and writing critically about the pop culture in question and then gives guidance in preparing to write and the types of essays that could be written. Although there are many ways to write about pop culture, *The Pop Culture Zone* focuses on four types of essays that are useful for evaluating and writing about pop culture: reviews or review essays, reflection or response essays, analysis essays, and synthesis essays.

Reviews or Review Essays

We all find it easy to applaud or criticize songs or films or websites; however, detailing out why we like or do not like something is a much tougher task. The Reading Zone selections and the questions that precede and follow them can help you begin to think about the structure or influence pop culture has on you; they can also help you critically analyze which parts of a film or song are leading you to your opinions or arguments. Each chapter describes how to write reviews or review essays specifically about the pop culture media or item in question.

In general, a review, such as a song or film review, is an evaluation that describes whether you find something interesting or of value for yourself or others. Like the reviews found in newspapers or on websites, reviews are usually rather short because they focus on the evaluation of one song or film or other piece of pop culture. You may be asked to review the same item as your classmates, or you may be allowed to choose your own item from pop culture to review. Either way, reviews usually follow a somewhat conventional format, giving a short synopsis or description first and then a judgment or evaluation that is supported with details from the piece or relevant material from outside the piece. Each chapter has a set of key questions to help you write reviews or the longer review essays, which can focus on multiple items or ask you to delve a bit more deeply into the history of a pop culture time period or style.

Reflection or Response Essays

When we react to pop culture, we are not only reacting to the item or experience in front of us or around us, but we are also reacting to how that item or experience fits in with other experiences we have had. Writing reflection or response essays allows you to write critically about pop culture but from your own personal viewpoint; in other words, you examine your reaction, asking yourself key questions that are given in each chapter, and then write critically about your response or reflection to the pop culture being studied. Since pop culture helps you reflect on your life, your choices, and your opinions, reflection and response essays usually use the pop culture item or experience as a starting point, not as the focus of the entire essay.

Analysis Essays

An analysis essay may be the essay you are more likely to associate with academic writing. When you write an analysis essay, you are presenting an argument or an in-depth discussion about a pop culture item or experience and then supporting your position with details drawn from the pop culture item or experience. For instance, you may suggest that certain types of pop literature appeal to a particular gender due to the way genders are socialized in the United States. You would offer your opinion, most likely your thesis, and then support it with details drawn from the pop lit type and possibly from outside sources if your essay assignment requires research. Being analytical and critical is at the center of writing a strong analysis essay. Analysis requires more than just a description of pop culture; it needs you to have strong opinions or arguments that are supported by observations you have made about the pop culture item and possibly the observations of others that you have gathered through research.

Synthesis Essays

Pop culture does not occur in a vacuum, and this means that sometimes you have multiple ways of evaluating and writing about pop culture. A synthesis essay is often the best choice for writing about pop culture. Synthesis essays allow you to bring narration often associated with reflection and response essays into the more analytical writing you might want to do. If you have a very strong argument or opinion that can be supported not only by your own personal experiences but also by outside research or sources, you may want to consider writing a synthesis essay. Different instructors and classes focus on different types of rhetorical strategies, so be sure to look over your assignment carefully to determine which type of essay or type(s) of rhetorical strategies might work best for organizing and writing about the topic of your choice. If you use a mixture of essay strategies, you can look at the key questions in each chapter for review, reflection and response, and analysis to help you make confident and effective choices.

The Writing and Research Process

Writing and research advice is offered throughout the content chapters and is also available in Chapter 2, Writing in the Pop Culture Zone, and Chapter 11, Researching and Documenting in the Pop Culture Zone. Because writers craft their essays in many different ways, these chapters give you an overview of various predrafting and composing strategies. Writers are usually quite familiar with the pop culture that surrounds them but may not be that familiar with their own writing strategies and process. Chapter 2 also allows you to investigate your usual writing process and try out strategies that you may not normally use.

Not all students using *The Pop Culture Zone* will be asked to do outside research about their essay topics; however, if you are asked to research or decide that it is needed to strengthen your essay, Chapter 11 introduces some general research strategies, along with some particular to researching about the areas of pop culture presented in this book. You can also find tips on using Internet search engines and library portals, documenting sources, and avoiding plagiarism.

Companion Website

You are invited to visit the Companion Website for *The Pop Culture Zone* at http://academic.cengage.com/english/SmithPopCulture. Online, you will find author biographies that are linked to sites with more information about authors, essay topics, or related content. If you are asked to develop or choose your own essay topic, the site also has an Assignment Bank, which provides possible topics other than those given in the textbook. In addition, if you need to do some research with online library databases, assistance is available through the Companion Website.

FINDING IDEAS FOR YOUR ESSAYS

At the end of each chapter, *The Pop Culture Zone* offers a Start Writing Essays About section that offers various suggestions for essay topics separated into review, reflection or response, analysis, and synthesis essays. You may find the topic you want to write about in these offerings, or you might want to return to other questions offered throughout each chapter to help you narrow down your topic. For instance, look for essay topics in the Grappling with Ideas blocks throughout the chapter or the Considering Ideas questions before each reading selection. You might also look back again at the questions asked in the Connecting to Your Culture at the end of each reading or the Contemplations or Collaborations you discussed or wrote about at the end of each chapter. Just remember, pop culture is yours, and the topic you choose to write about should be something that interests you and inspires you to write the best essay you can.

THE READING ZONE

CONSIDERING IDEAS

1. What is your own definition for "essay writing"?

2. How is essay writing different from other types of writing?

3. Do you read comics, cartoons, or graphic novels? If so, what are some of your favorites? Why do they appeal to you?

Ben Strickland *currently teaches composition and literature at Middle Tennessee State University. He has published a few articles and essays, including one in* Saving the World: A Guide to *Heroes. Ben also composes regular comic strips for Fountainhead Press.*

"Synthesis" was composed for The Pop Culture Zone *to show how images and words can illustrate various ideas and relationships. Strickland claims that the first "Synthesis" image that came to mind became the second frame of the cartoon—a strategic combination of ideas that presents one single concept.*

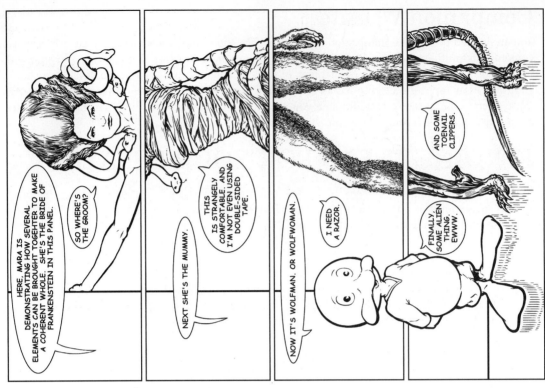

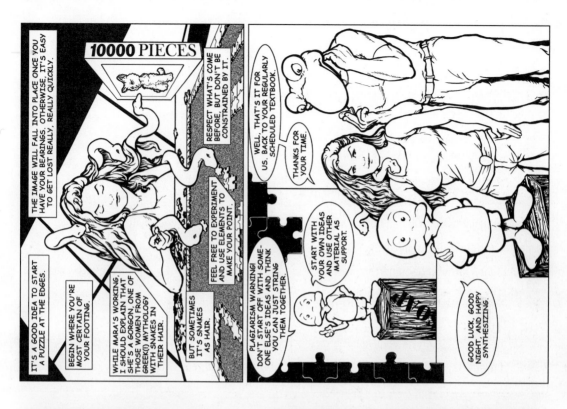

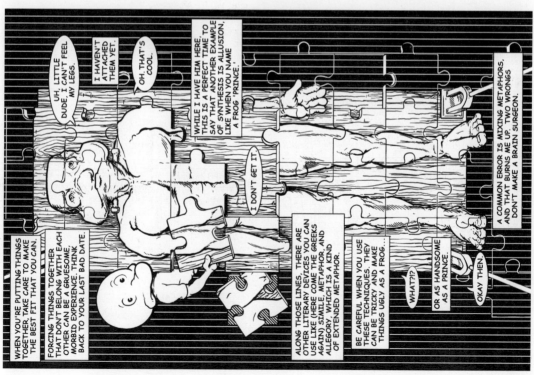

1. How does Strickland define the term synthesis in this visual essay?

2. How does he illustrate synthesis with his images?

3. How do the words and images interact with each other? Was one method more effective than the other? Why or why not?

1. Can you name or describe any other visual forms of synthesis? What does synthesis look like in movies or sound like in music?

2. Why might synthesis be important when writing about pop culture? How does it fit with academic writing?

3. Look at the images on the front cover of this text. What do they tell you about the content of the text? How do they inform your reading of the text?

4. An old cliché says, "Don't judge a book by its cover." Do you agree with this? Why or why not?

FOR FURTHER READING

Eisner, Will. *Graphic Storytelling and Visual Narrative.* Tamarac, FL: Poorhouse Press, 1996.

Gravett, Paul. *Graphic Novels: Everything You Need to Know.* New York: Collins Design, 2005.

Jenkins, Henry, ed. *Hop on Pop: The Politics and Pleasures of Popular Culture.* Durham, NC: Duke U Press, 2002.

Kress, Gunther. *Reading Images: The Grammar of Visual Design.* New York: Routledge, 1996.

Mirzoeff, Nicholas. *An Introduction to Visual Culture.* New York: Routledge, 2000.

Storey, John. *Cultural Theory and Popular Culture: An Introduction.* Athens, GA: U of Georgia Press, 2006.

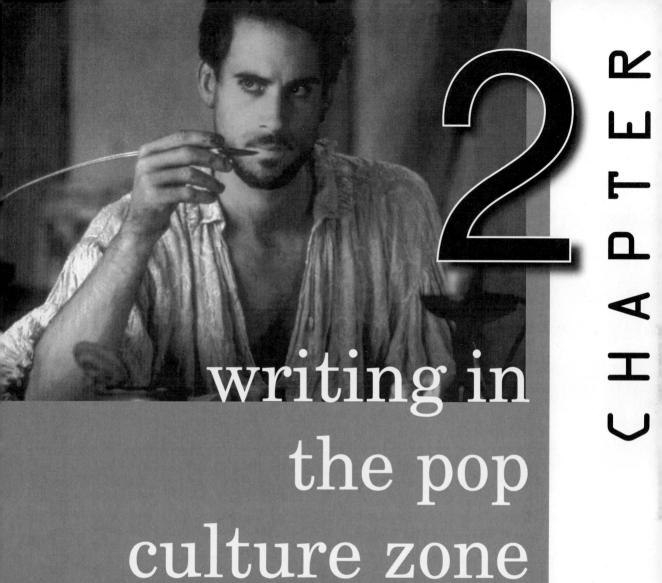

writing in the pop culture zone

William Shakespeare: "I have a new play."

Christopher Marlowe: "What's it called?"

William Shakespeare: "Romeo and Ethel the Pirate's Daughter."

Christopher Marlowe: "What is the story?"

William Shakespeare: "Well, there's this pirate . . . In truth I have
not written a word."

—**From** *Shakespeare in Love*

1 Many of Stephen King's characters were writers. Can you name any of his characters who were writers? Or list any of his books or films that featured writers? Name as many as you can.

© James Devaney/WireImage/Getty Images

2 Match the TV character writer with the appropriate television show.

1. Ray Barone
2. Jessica Fletcher
3. Maya Gallo
4. Carrie Bradshaw
5. Oscar Madison

a. *Sex and the City*
b. *Everybody Loves Raymond*
c. *The Odd Couple*
d. *Murder, She Wrote*
e. *Just Shoot Me*

3 Who has received the most Academy Award nominations for writing?

a. Oliver Stone
b. Woody Allen
c. Billy Wilder
d. Federico Fellini

4 E. B. White, the author of *Charlotte's Web*, cowrote what popular writing guide used often in writing classes?

a. *Fun with Style*
b. *The Writer's Guide*
c. *The Elements of Style*
d. *A Fun Guide to Writing*

5 Match these writers with their publications.

1. Lois Lane
2. Nina Van Horn
3. Peter Parker
4. Murray Slaughter

a. *Blush*
b. WJM-TV News
c. *The Daily Planet*
d. *The Daily Bugle*

6 What pseudonym does best-selling romance novelist Nora Roberts use when she's writing sci-fi suspense?

a. Anne Rice
b. J. D. Robb
c. Elizabeth Lowell
d. Sherrilyn Kenyon

Chapter opener photo © CORBIS/SYGMA

7 Who has received the most Academy Awards for writing?

    a. Billy Wilder
    b. Francis Ford Coppola
    c. Charles Brackett
    d. Paddy Chayefsky

8 Match these musicians with their autobiographies.

1. Melissa Etheridge	a. *The Facts of Life: And Other Dirty Jokes*
2. Willie Nelson	b. *The Music of Silence: A Memoir*
3. Jerry Lewis	c. *The Truth Is . . . : My Life in Love and Music*
4. Andrea Bocelli	d. *Dean and Me (A Love Story)*

9 In fall 2006, MySpace reported growth by how many million writers/users a month?

    a. 2 million
    b. 5 million
    c. 7 million
    d. 9 million

10 The word *celebutante* was added to the *Oxford English Dictionary* in 2006 with the following example sentence: "_____ and _____, the swanky yet skanky . . . celebutantes." Fill in the blanks.

ANSWERS

1 *Paul Sheldon*—Misery, *Ben Mears*—Salem's Lot, *Jack Torrance*—The Shining, *Mike Noonan*—Bag of Bones, *Scott Landon*—Lisey's Story, *Thad Beaumont/George Stark*—The Dark Half, *Mort Rainey*—Secret Window, *John Marinville*—Desperation, *Gordon Lachance*—"The Body," *William Denbrough*—It, *Michael Enslin*—"1408," *Reg Thorpe*—"The Ballad of the Flexible Bullet," *Richard Hagstrom*—"Word Processor of the Gods," *Stephen King himself*—Song of Susannah and The Dark Tower
2 *1. b.* Everybody Loves Raymond, *2. d.* Murder, She Wrote, *3. e.* Just Shoot Me, *4. a.* Sex and the City, *5. c.* The Odd Couple
3 *b.* Woody Allen   **4** *c.* The Elements of Style   **5** *1. c.* The Daily Planet, *2. a.* Blush, *3. d.* The Daily Bugle, *4. b.* WJM-TV News
6 *b. J. D. Robb*   **7** There's a four-way tie with three each: *a.* Billy Wilder, *b.* Francis Ford Coppola, *c.* Charles Brackett, *d.* Paddy Chayefsky   **8** *1. c.* The Truth Is . . . : My Life in Love and Music, *2. a.* The Facts of Life: And Other Dirty Jokes, *3. d.* Dean and Me (A Love Story), *4. b.* The Music of Silence: A Memoir   **9** *b. 5 million*   **10** *Paris Hilton and Nicole Richie*

People write for all kinds of reasons. Students, like you, write for class assignments—essays, lab reports, test answers, class notes—but also to send e-mails to friends, post entries on Facebook, and make lists for the grocery store. You may write notes for your child to take to school, letters to the editor of the local newspaper, and annotations in your Bible on Sunday mornings. In your work life, you may find yourself writing memos to your employees, presentations for potential clients, reports for your boss, and remarks on drafts for fellow team members. Of course, you may also write to document your daily activities in a blog or journal, to compose original poetry, or to record amusing anecdotes. Whatever your reasons for writing, you are more likely to achieve your purposes and communicate your message if your writing is easy to read and clearly addresses your intended audience and purpose.

Of course, clear and concise writing does not happen by accident. It is a process that takes work. The same is true for writings about pop culture, the kinds of writings you are asked to compose in this textbook. Although writing about pop culture is a good way to explore your own thoughts and feelings about the various media around you, it doesn't necessarily come naturally or effortlessly. However, the purpose of this chapter, as well as all of the hints and guidelines in the other chapters, is to help the process move more smoothly for you and to help you come up with more interesting ideas for your writing.

Writing about pop culture can serve a variety of diverse purposes and audiences and can utilize many different formats: Reviewing, responding or reflecting, analyzing, and synthesizing are just a few of the possibilities. In the freshman composition class, this writing might be completed in class or out of class. When you learn more about and practice the recursive or overlapping steps of the writing process, all of these types of assignments can become more successful and less frustrating. Rather than letting your writing assignment sit on your desk or in your bag for days or weeks as the deadline looms closer and closer, you can take control of both your time and assignment and enjoy the composing process along the way. Follow all of the hints given, and you will be able to turn in a text that is more thoughtful and probably better composed than those written at the last minute.

There are several key steps to becoming a successful writer who clearly communicates his or her purpose or answers the problem that has been posed. In this chapter, you will find explanations of these key steps in the writing process. Of course, writing is a messy endeavor, circular in nature, and sometimes never-ending. The following steps are presented in a linear format, an approach to writing that is often not seen in real writing since you often revise as you plan and draft or go back to brainstorming when you get stuck as you write. However, these steps should help you begin to evaluate your current writing process and possibly improve it in some way.

- *Brainstorming:* This is what you can do to find an interesting and comfortable topic, propose a problem to be solved, or create a persuasive argument, as well as figure out how to support what to say about the topic, problem, or argument.
- *Planning and Drafting:* In this step, you organize and create your first draft.
- *Revising:* At this stage, you write additional drafts, rethink or resee your thesis, and improve content, organization, support, and word choice.
- *Editing:* In this step, you double-check grammar and mechanics and proofread.

Attempt all of the various revision and editing steps or tips given in this chapter for your first out-of-class essay and then adopt the ones that most improve your writing for the quicker in-class essays and for later out-of-class assignments in all of your classes. The additional time you spend on your writing process, whether alone or with your peers, should help your writing be more successful. Taking control of your writing and your writing process is an important step in becoming a skilled writer, and the guidelines in this section will help you get on the right track.

WHAT IS WRITING?

In its most basic definition, writing is a process that allows you to communicate thoughts to an audience by managing symbols—usually words and images. Your writing can serve a variety of purposes and achieve a number of different goals. For example:

Writing supports

- insight, giving you an outlet for your internal discussion.
- discovery, offering a visual space to prepare your ideas for public view.
- creative expression, allowing you to construct and compose thoughts.

Writing communicates

- thoughts to yourself and to others in a formal as well as an informal setting.
- imagination, making it visible to others.
- identity, as choice of words, punctuation, and mode of writing unite to reveal facets of your individuality.

Writing manages

- ideas, for clarification.
- symbols, enabling you to manipulate alphabetic characters to create words and meaning.
- language, allowing you to gain power and authority by learning how to control language so that it concisely conveys your message.
- people, by guiding, stimulating, exciting, and placating human beings.

Many people do not consider themselves actors, yet we do, in fact, act every day. Just as an actor's performance is shaped by an audience, our behavior changes depending on the setting and/or the audience. When in an informal setting, we might perform in a manner not considered appropriate in a more formal setting.

Likewise, most people do not consider themselves writers; however, each day, our lives, as mentioned earlier, may include such informal writing tasks as composing e-mail or writing in a personal journal or blog or the more formal writing required for an office memo, a résumé, or an essay for school. Similar to an individual's performance as an actor, a writer also must consider such issues as setting and audience when shaping his or her performance on the page or on the computer screen.

Shaping a Written Performance

While many factors ultimately determine the final performance for an actor or the final product for a writer, several factors are crucial to both. The *rhetorical triangle*, sometimes called the *communication triangle*, illustrates these key factors to consider when shaping a written performance.

Writer: Although it may seem obvious, the writer is the person who writes. The writer explores, explains, and/or expresses his or her knowledge of a subject in writing, which leads the writer to ask, "What do I, as the writer, know about this subject?"

Subject: A writer thinks about the subject of the text and what information about or connected to that subject the audience, or reader, needs to know, which leads the writer to ask, "What about this subject do I want my reader to know?"

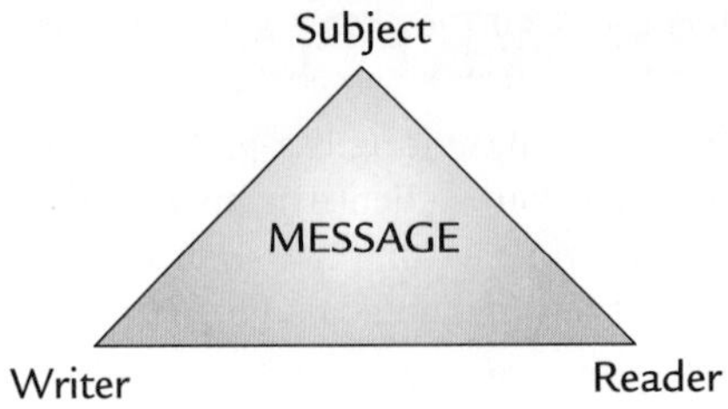

FIGURE 2.1

                                    Subject

                              MESSAGE

                    Writer   Reader

Reader: A writer also thinks about his or her reader or audience—the person or people being
               addressed through the text. Considering the audience leads the writer to ask, "Who is
               my reader (or audience), and what do they want to know or need to read?"

Message: The message is the product of the writer's consideration of the answers to the preceding
               questions; in other words, the message is the writer's main idea or thesis and is the
               result of considering what the writer knows about the subject and the reader.

grapplingwithideas

- Reminisce about a first experience in your life: your first day of school, your first crush, your first kiss, your first day of driving all by yourself.
- Where were you? Who was around? How did it feel physically? Emotionally?
- Now record this same experience in a letter to a friend or a family member. How does your language change? Your content? The details?

Consider how you convey knowledge to the reader. For example, think about how you set up a personal page on Facebook or MySpace and then think about the different ways you set up your own personal blog on Blogger or how you might write in a personal paper journal. With Facebook, you are publishing your information, but you can still control who sees it by limiting your friends list. Consequently, you are writing for a limited audience of friends. With most blogs, however, anyone can access your space and read what you have written. So while you may treat your blog as a personal journal, you are always aware that you are writing for a large, public audience. In both examples, the writer is the subject of his or her own text, but the distinct differences in purpose and audience result in a much more personal, and possibly informal, tone in Facebook writing than in blog writing. Of course, both of these are probably less formal than an essay you would write for a class.

Think about your own writing. How might the writing describing your experiences in a personal journal or in an e-mail to a friend differ from the writing you might use to compose a cover letter to a potential employer or a personal narrative written for an essay assignment? Again, in both situations, the writer is the subject, but each has a clearly different purpose and audience.

WHAT IS BRAINSTORMING?

We write best when we write about topics we are interested in and are familiar with. Finding these topics and what you want to write about them through brainstorming is the first key step to improving your writing process. You can come up with ideas for essays in many ways, which include responding to and questioning the world around you and the model essays in this textbook. If, however, you are stuck and cannot find a topic, brainstorming, as part of your prewriting, can help narrow down general ideas into a focused topic and then help you decide what to use as supporting detail. You may already have your own style of prewriting; however, experiment with different methods to find what best suits your style.

Freewriting

Freewriting is a no-holds-barred type of brainstorming. When you freewrite, begin by allotting yourself a specific amount of time, such as ten to fifteen minutes. This technique is more constructive when you already have an idea for your topic. However, freewriting can be used to generate ideas for topics. Begin by simply writing. Write whatever comes into your mind. Do not be concerned with punctuation, grammar, or complete sentences. Use symbols or question marks in place of words that you cannot come up with automatically. If you cannot think of anything to write, simply jot down the phrase "I don't know" until you begin writing other words. Remember, this does not have to make sense to anyone else. Freewriting should be as stress-free as possible.

EXAMPLE

Topic: Freewrite for seven minutes about the picture you brought in today, a peer or family picture that triggers memories associated with being part of a group or association. (Harper, "Freewrite")

Me and Lyndsey—my favorite pic. My first pic of us was when she was born. In this picture she is 13. We were at homecoming. Her sister and brothers also went. It was at the U of Mobile. I can't believe how much those kids ate. The boys liked the air toys and the fishing for those really small prizes. Too much money. L and I got our faces painted, but the boys didn't. I don't know why. Lyndsey's face—she got a cherry painted on it. I didn't know why. But then someone in the crowd told us it looked just like the Pac-Man game. No wonder then. The '80s was the theme of homecoming. The T shirt for homecoming also had a pacman on it. I ended up buying Lyndsey a T shirt anyway with the pac-man because she was cold and she kept on bugging me about buying one so she could get warm. My face has a flower. I think it was orange, but the picture doesn't look like it. I love this picture. We look at our face art, we smile at each other. It's a great picture because it shows love. Our face art wasn't the point of the picture. It was the love. And the smiles. L gave me the picture in a great frame for Christmas. I'm pretty sure that she sees the picture and thinks of me and that time and the smiles and the love. Think think think. It's a great sign—it's small—but it's great. Our relationship is important to both of us. We have a close one. I can't think of a time when we weren't close. We talk on the phone—Cingular is great. She calls me about tests and boys and her parents and her sister and her brothers and her parents, and I'm glad we have cell phones or I'd miss a lot of the great conversations we've had. It's me she wants to stay with every summer. We have a great relationship. We have been together for a lot of things—a lot of things important to her and me. Her first bra fittings, her 8th grade dress, my trips home . . . I've always tried to be there for her. I was even in the delivery room when my sister delivered her. My sister wasn't breathing. I was worried about the baby and her getting some/ enough oxygen. My sister cracked me up when she said, "The baby can come out and get its own damn oxygen." She did come out and became my best friend. And I'm hoping that I am. . . .

Once your time is up, sit back, and look at what you have written. Separate out the promising phrases, organize these ideas, and then expand them. Go back and read your paragraph again, underlining potential topics and subtopics.

Looping

Looping is a variation of freewriting. It can be a more constructive brainstorming exercise for those who need a little more focus than freewriting provides. This technique works best when you already have a general topic in mind. For example, if you have been assigned to write on the general topic of "war and the media," you could take out several sheets of paper and begin to freewrite as defined earlier. When time is up, read over what you have written and try to pinpoint a central idea that has emerged from what you have written. Perhaps it is the idea that you liked best for whatever reason or an idea that stands out to you. Put this thought or idea in one sentence below the freewriting; this is called your "center of gravity" statement and completes loop number one.

To begin loop number two, begin freewriting from the previous center of gravity statement. Freewrite for another ten minutes. Upon completion of this freewriting session, you will once again assess what you have written and extract a compelling or important idea that emerged from your writing. Write this main idea below your freewriting; this is your second center of gravity statement. You can now begin freewriting from the second center of gravity statement.

EXAMPLE

Loop Number 1
Is the media biased? Liberal? Conservative? Patriotic? Anti-American? Whatever it is we all question it during times of war. While some newspapers receive praise for accurate, timely, honest reporting, others are seen as bad, evil, villains. Unfortunately, these labels have less to do with the media than with those reading or seeing the messages offered.

Loop Number 2
Whatever it is we all question it during times of war. While Americans choose media outlets for a variety of reasons, few willingly watch, read, or listen to media that offer opinions, stories, or programming contrary to their personal views. During the height of the Vietnam War, network news outlets aired graphic taped footage of the death and destruction of war. However, while the violence displayed might be the same, viewers maintained that only network "A" or network "B" presented it without bias.

You can continue this looping process until you are satisfied and comfortable with the topic you have generated.

Journaling

Sometimes, instructors will lead you toward a topic or problem by assigning journals—handwritten in class, on a personal blog, or through a class discussion board. These are informal writings that allow you to take a vague idea and write about it. These journals allow you to follow an idea or a hunch without worrying about penalty; you can think of these journals as a more controlled version of freewriting. Once you complete a journal entry or a Grappling with Ideas section, you can set it aside for a time and come back to it later when you are rested and ready to approach the topic once again. You may even have new ideas or a different take than you initially had.

Example—Writing Case Study, Draft 1

Journal Assignment: Pick a character from *Se7en*. List major ethical decisions that he or she makes in the movie. (Tipton, "Journal")

Ethical Decisions

Erin Halcott
Feb. 26

Good to have a few quotes to help support ideas.

Mills

• gets cliff notes • gets coffee for Somerset on 1st day • makes fun of every crime and crime scene • apologizes to Tracy when he cusses in front of her • is upset when he can't remember the name of his friend who was shot • gets caught up in emotion • acts on emotion • knocks camera away • impatient to work • dismisses John Doe as a lunatic • kicks in Doe's door • pays a homeless lady to be a "witness" • even though he doesn't agree with what Somerset had to say, he thanks him for his advice • goes with Doe to get confession • calls John Doe a freak • fiercely questions and argues with Doe • keeps referring to Doe as a P. O. S. • becomes #7 – wrath • has a flash of Tracy (• kills Doe)

• career over family • selfish
• decided to move into the city eventhough he knew Tracy didn't want to
• shot the criminal who killed his friend

Somerset

• tries to get Mills off the case b/c of "integrity of the scene" • wanted to finish a case before retirement • didn't want the Doe case • didn't think it should be Mills' first case • called the 1st crime scene the "obesity murder scene" not "fat boy case" • respects the victims • integrity • takes the time to really research • creates reading list to help Mills • always carries a switch blade • divorces himself from emotion in crimes • meets Tracy to talk • tells Tracy that if she chooses not to keep the baby, she should never tell Mills about the pregnancy

① shows he REALLY cares – careful

→ trying to Google protect Mills research detective maybe

protect & serve

uphold the law

Look up seven deadly sins, for extra research, maybe wikipedia 7 deadly sins

Inferno by Dante start @ Wikipedia... look @ recommended books

• kills Tracy – the only victim to not commit a sin

• Smacked Doe when Doe told Mills about the pregnancy

• a long time ago, convinced his girlfriend not to keep his baby • knows he made the right decision but wishes he chose the other option • tells Tracy that if she keeps the baby to spoil it every chance she gets • tells Mills not to dismiss Doe as a lunatic • pays $50 for a secret, illegal library list • doesn't kick in Doe's door • throws the metronome • throws switchblade at target • decides to retire AFTER case is closed • goes with Doe to get confession to "finish it" • shows restraint with Doe in the car • leaves Mills with Doe and goes to stop the white van • tells Mills not to shoot Doe • tells Mills that if he shoots Doe, Doe wins • tells cop to accommodate Mills with anything he needs • seems to have new respect for Mills

Tracy cite imdb & movie! (crime drama)

• calls Mills at work to invite Somerset to dinner • tries to get Somerset and Mills to see each other as David and William • stays in city and doesn't tell Mills she is miserable • doesn't want to be a burden • calls Somerset sounding upset, wanting to talk in the morning • doesn't tell Mills about her pregnancy

John Doe

• kills innocent strangers • takes on non-identity • patient with killings • beats but doesn't kill Mills • calls the apartment to declare admiration • turns himself in • calm • will take Mills $ Somerset to last 2 scenes • or will plead insanity • delusions of grandeur • knows just how to rouse Mills • wants to be shot for his sin of envy, #6

From this journal entry, you can revisit the topic after possibly utilizing other brainstorming exercises or even after discussion with your instructor and other classmates; you can see notes on this journal entry from the instructor and classmates. To get you thinking and to jump-start your writing ideas, *The Pop Culture Zone* has numerous journal ideas scattered throughout, including the Grappling with Ideas and Considering Ideas sections.

Clustering or Mapping

Another technique you can use for brainstorming is clustering, sometimes referred to as mapping. You can cluster in two different ways.

- Start with possible topic ideas and then cluster them by drawing circles around them and organizing them into clusters.
- Start with a clustering grid and then fill in the circles with ideas.

Whatever way you decide to cluster, start by putting your general topic in the middle of a blank page. If you want to use the first clustering method,

- Jot down possible subtopics and details all around the central circle.
- After you have written down as many subtopics or details as you can, locate the more general subtopics, circle them, and attach these circles to the middle circle that holds the general topic.
- After this, find details that will support the subtopics, circle them, and attach these circles to the subtopic circles.
- When you have circled enough subtopics and details to start outlining or writing your paper, erase or cross out all the extra or unconnected information.

If you want to try the second clustering method,

- Write your general topic in the middle of a blank page and draw lines from this circle to five or six circles (these will hold your subtopics).
- Then, draw lines from the subtopic circles to three or four other circles (these will be your supporting details).

Regardless of the clustering method you choose, you should allot between ten and twenty minutes for this brainstorming process. What you end up with might look something like the cluster/map on the next page that uses the movie *Fight Club* as the general topic.

Cubing

Yet another way to generate ideas is cubing. Imagine a cube with six sides, or use a die from a game set you have around your home. Next, imagine the following questions or methods of interrogation, written on each side of the cube, or in the alternative, use the numbers of the actual die to help you choose from the numbered questions below. Here are the questions to visualize on your cube or to match the numbers on the die you roll.

1. **Describe it:** What does the subject look like? Sound like? Engage all five senses if possible.
2. **Compare and contrast it:** What is the subject similar to? What is it different from? How so?
3. **Free-associate with it:** What does the subject remind you of? Any particular memories?
4. **Analyze it:** How does it work? What is its significance?
5. **Argue for or against it:** What advantages and disadvantages does it have?
6. **Apply it:** What are the uses of your subject? What can you do with it?

Write whatever comes to your mind for ten minutes or so. When you have finished cubing, take the topics and subtopics you have generated and organize them by clustering or outlining them. (More on outlining on page 26.)

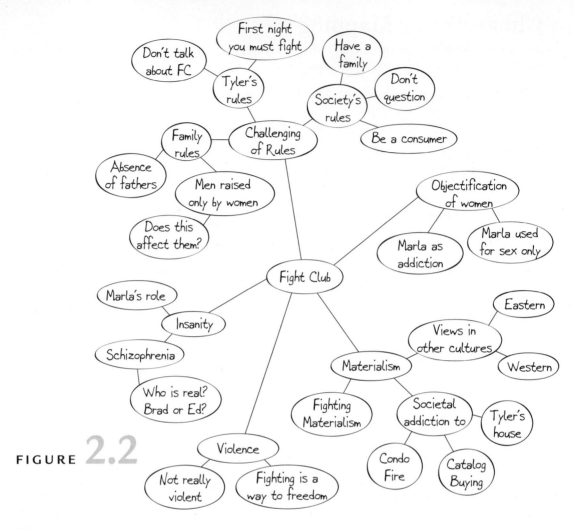

FIGURE 2.2

Listing

Another way to brainstorm is to simply jot down any ideas or questions that pop into your head for about ten minutes. After you have finished your list, look for connections between ideas, or look for one main idea that encompasses several small ones. Here is an example for the general topic of television.

EXAMPLE

ENTERTAINING	USUALLY THIRTY- OR SIXTY-MINUTE PROGRAMS
INFORMATIVE	MEDIA
CORRUPTING	LISTEN
POISONING	CORPORATE SPONSORSHIP
NEWS	MUSIC TELEVISION
COMEDY	HOME SHOPPING

DRAMA	"BOOB TUBE"
SPORTS	GAME SHOWS
EDUCATIONAL	REMOTE CONTROL
BIASED	MIND-NUMBING
COMMERCIALS	WEIGHT GAIN
PEOPLE	POSSIBLE CONTRIBUTOR TO "DUMBING DOWN" OF SOCIETY?

After examining the list, do you make any connections? Does anything stand out that you might want to write about? If so, try clustering or outlining the idea to see if it can be developed further.

Interviewing and Discussing

Sometimes, we have an idea that is unclear in our minds; however, once we begin talking about this topic with others, our idea becomes clearer, or the other person may be able to offer a perspective that you had not thought about before. Think about your subject or topic while a classmate or friend asks you questions about the subject—questions that would naturally come up in conversation. Also, your "interviewer" might ask you what are termed "journalism questions," such as

Who?	Who believes X? Who is involved?
When?	When did it happen? When did you change?
Why?	Why did X do Y? Why is this interesting?
What?	What happened? What did you do?
Where?	Where did it happen? Where were you?
How?	How did you become involved? How is it interesting?

Make sure you listen to what you are saying as you are being "interviewed," or consider jotting down some notes as you answer. Was there a particular part of the subject that you were most interested in talking about? If so, why? You may find that you have discussed your way into an interesting topic. However, this may not have given you all of the information you need for an interesting essay. If you are still without a clear subject by the end of the interview session, ask your classmates or friends questions. If they had to write an essay based on the information you had just discussed, what would they write about? Why?

Questioning

Sometimes, no one is available to interview you. If this type of brainstorming works best for you, try questioning yourself about the subject. Think of your favorite attorney on television or in books—How would he or she cross-examine a witness? Model your cross-examination of yourself in this manner; ask yourself a million questions about your subject. However, here is a list of five categories to help you start narrowing your subject.

- **Definition:** How does the dictionary define the word or subject? How does the majority define it? How do your friends or family members define it? What is its history? Where did it come from? Give some examples.
- **Compare and contrast:** What is it similar to? What is it different from? Think also along the lines of similar terms (synonyms) and opposites (antonyms).
- **Relationship:** What are its causes and effects? What subjects are connected to this one?

- **Circumstance:** Is it possible or impossible? When has it happened before? Are there any ways to prevent it?
- **Testimony:** What do people say about it? What has been written about it? Have you had any experience with it? Has any relevant research been done on the subject?

Outlining

Outlining can help you brainstorm for subtopics, or it can be used as a method for organizing the material that other invention techniques have helped you generate. Either way, the value of the outline is its ability to help you plan, see logical connections between your ideas, and see obvious places to add new ideas and details.

An informal outline can be just a map of paragraphs that you plan to use. For example, here is a short, informal outline for the topic "women in music videos."

Body paragraphs, topic one: discussion of female pop stars
Body paragraphs, topic two: discussion of women in rap videos

EXAMPLE

I. Female pop stars
    A. Jessica Simpson
    B. Beyoncé
        a. Destiny's Child
        b. Solo career
    C. Fergie
        a. Black Eyed Peas
        b. Solo career
    D. Gwen Stefani
        a. No Doubt
        b. Solo career
II. Rap videos
    A. Female rappers
        a. Missy Elliott
        b. Lil' Kim
        c. Eve
        d. Salt-N-Pepa
        e. Mary J. Blige
    B. Backup dancers/singers for male rappers

Note that this is not a formal outline, which would have strictly parallel parts and might be expressed in complete sentences. Follow the outline form you find most useful or that has been assigned. An informal or working outline helps you get to the drafting stage, but it should not restrict you from changing subtopics or details to make your essay topic stronger.

You can also see by looking at this outline that you may have more information than you need for one paper. You could choose to focus on just female pop stars and develop it a bit more, perhaps adding other artists like Britney Spears, Ciara, or Kelly Clarkson. This brief outline also points out the possibility of looking at women who used to front various bands or groups and then broke out on their own. You could choose to focus on just female rappers, possibly even adding others like Queen Latifah and MC Lyte. You would have to do more brainstorming if you wanted to write about women in the videos of male rappers.

Brainstorming, no matter which technique you use, is just the beginning of your writing process. These invention strategies can help you discover what you want to say and how you are going to support or illustrate your ideas. Of course, they do not necessarily tell you how to say it; writing or drafting is the next stage, when you take your ideas and put them into the desired form for your audience and purpose. As you write, you will also find yourself continuing to freewrite, make lists, ask questions, and use other prewriting techniques to expand your ideas or come up with additional supports because writing is a recursive and messy process that rarely happens in linear form.

- What kind of brainstorming techniques have you tried in the past?
- After trying all of the ideas just described, which one(s) works best for you?
- Do you have another technique or method your classmates should try?
- Have you observed a writer in a film, television show, or novel that you want to copy?

WHAT IS DRAFTING?

Drafting is taking the ideas that you have generated through brainstorming and outlining and constructing a rough draft or perhaps two or three different rough drafts. As you write, go back to the rhetorical triangle (on page 18) and think about your audience, purpose, and subject. Who are you writing to? What language and style are appropriate for this audience? What is the topic of your essay? What is the purpose of your essay? Are you reviewing a new CD? Narrating your personal reaction to a film? Analyzing an advertisement for gender bias? Comparing and contrasting two different places where you like to hang out? What question are you answering or what problem are you solving? As you consider audience and purpose, consider what format will help you reach your readers. Also think about what approach will make you most believable or credible to your audience. At times, your format or genre may be assigned, but if you have a choice, consider alternatives to the traditional essay. Letters, memos, websites, songs, videos, liner notes, or reviews for newspapers and magazines can be just as valid as the academic essay.

No matter what format you choose, your text will need to have a central idea or topic, otherwise known as the *thesis* or *thesis statement*. Your thesis answers the question, "so what?" Why should a reader be interested in your review, narrative, or analysis? What is the point of what you are writing? Your thesis can also serve as an organizing device because in your text you will want to include examples, anecdotes, details, descriptions, illustrations, pictures, and other forms of evidence that support your thesis and make your essay interesting and convincing for your reader. You may also include outside support or references to the media you are discussing. When you use other texts in your paper, you will want to make sure you document your materials in your essay and with a Works Cited page to validate your sources and your credibility and to avoid plagiarism (read more about plagiarism as well as how to create a Works Cited page in Chapter 11).

When composing your draft(s), you will also want to keep in mind the three main parts of most essays: the introduction, the body, and the conclusion.

INTRODUCTION: Although you may not actually write your introduction first (yes, it is okay to write your introduction last), at some point you will want to include an introduction that gets your readers' attention and makes them want to read more. In fact, the introduction generally has three main purposes: to capture your readers' attention, to give them background information, and to give them an idea of what is to come. This preview may come from the thesis or from a more general overview if your thesis will be located elsewhere in the essay. For example, an essay may build up to the main idea; in that case, the thesis will be closer to the end of the essay. In some essays, the thesis is even implied, so while the writer has a clear point and uses it to guide his or her writing, the thesis might not show up as a specific sentence in the essay.

Keep in mind that introduction does not necessarily mean introductory paragraph. Your introduction may require more than one paragraph to adequately interest and inform your reader. A longer introduction will also push your thesis further into the paper and not necessarily at the end of the first paragraph, as you may have done in the past.

BODY: The body of the essay will be the longest and most important part of your text because it is here that you will use many of the ideas generated in prewriting, as well as those that come to you as you begin to write, rewrite, and revise. It is also in the body paragraphs that you will support or illustrate your thesis. As you decide how to organize your body paragraphs, go back to the rhetorical triangle and consider your subject, audience, and purpose; likewise, consider the conventions of the genre you have been assigned or the format you have chosen for your essay. For instance, are you composing a traditional essay, writing a letter, or creating a website? In *The Pop Culture Zone*, you will be asked to write in four different broad genres: a review or review essay, a personal reflection or response essay, an analysis essay, or a synthesis essay, which utilizes at least two different rhetorical strategies or genres. These strategies can be presented in a variety of ways: traditional essays, letters, brochures, websites, and visual essays, just to name a few. See Chapter 1 for more information about the four types of essays used in *The Pop Culture Zone*, as well as writing instructions in each of the individual chapters on various media or topics.

CONCLUSION: Finally, you will need a conclusion that indicates you have come to the end of your essay but that still leaves your reader with something to think about and possibly reflect on. The conclusion is a place to reinforce your key ideas, pull all of your points together, and leave your reader wanting more. It is a time to point out the significance and effectiveness of your thesis and how you have proven or illustrated it. The conclusion is also where you can call your reader to action or ask for a response—watch this movie, check out this television program, learn more about this group of people, or avoid this badly written book.

Now, let us go back to one of our earlier brainstorming activities and turn it into a rough draft that is ready for peer commenting and then revision.

Example—Writing Case Study, Draft 2

Assignment: For this essay, you will engage with a film that deliberates an ethical dilemma. This will require you to consider the complexity of the film's characters and the quandaries that they face and require you to go beyond the movie, the characters, and the circumstances as just pure entertainment. Your essay will be an investigation, analysis, and evaluation of the ethical issues in *Se7en*. This means you will analyze and evaluate one, several, or all characters in the film and the ethical choices they make. (Tipton, "Ethical")

Erin Halcott
English 1020-028
Prof. Tipton
March 02, 2008

Somerset's Ethical Decisions

In 1995, David Fincher directed a movie called *Se7en* (imdb). It
follows mainly two detective, David Mills (Brad Pitt) and William Somerset
(Morgan Freeman) on a hunt to catch a serial killer, John Doe (Kevin
Spacey) (*Se7ve*). Detective Mills, unlike Somerset, is harsh and impatient.
Somerset's decisions show that he is a calm, collective, and calculating
individual.

Throughout the movie, Somerset really takes his time to research
before he makes decisions. He is the kind of person who wants to know
everything before he acts. Unlike Milss, Somerset does not get caught up
in the moment and make rash decision. He takes his time to collect all he
knows.

Somerset also seems to have respect John doe's victims. At the
first crime scene, all of the associates make fun of the victim by labeling
the crime scene "the fat boy scene." Somerset takes a higher road and
calls it the "obesity murder scene." Instead of making light of the victim
and scene, Somerset shows his maturity by dealing with the crimes
professionally.

He also shows great restraint when he, Mills, and John Doe are in the
car on the way to the "last two murder scenes." As Mills fiercely questions
and mocks Doe, Somerset asks questions respectively. Detective Mills
passes Doe off as a crazy lunatic, but Somerset sees differently. He has
more respect for Doe. He sees him as more than a crazy lunatic.

*Consider combining the
first two sentences (to
condense).*

*What is your thesis?
Are you comparing
Somerset's ethics with
Mills's ethics? I take
from your title that
you're going to focus
on Somerset.*

*Can you provide any
scenes from the film
as evidence for these
assertions?*

*Great examples here of
Somerset's ethics!*

Somerset seems to have a certain respect for Doe, and instead of mocking him, he tries to understand him and why he did the things he did. Instead of wasting his time irritating Doe, he uses his time to learn all he can about him.

Good use of your own ethical system here to analyze the characters' ethics.

All of Somerset's decisions make a lot of sense to me. By knowing all the information before hand, you avoid making decisions in the heat of the moment that you might regret later on. Take, for example, when Mills and Somerset go to John Doe's apartment. Mills is ready to kick in the door, but Somerset warns him otherwise. Somerset thought about how they found the apartment in the first place and knew that they could get in serious trouble. Mills, on the other hand, kicks in the door anyway, deciding to worry about it later.

It seems as though this essay focuses mostly on Somerset, but there is enough of Mills in there for me to think that you also want to analyze his actions. Do you intend to further analyze Mills's ethical decisions? Consider expanding your essay's reach.

Detective Somerset choose to learn as much about the murders as possible before acting. By knowing everything, he was able to make sound judgement and was guaranteed to not regret any rash actions. As Somerset sarcastically told Mills, "It's impressive to see a man feeding off his emotions," (imdb).

WHAT IS REVISING?

When you draft, you get your ideas out on the paper or the screen. But this is not the end of the process; it is really just the beginning. Once you have a rough draft, you are ready to start rereading and rewriting—you are ready for revision. *Revision* literally means to resee or look at again, and this is what you do when you revise your writing. Many writers confuse revision and editing, but they are really two different parts of the writing process, even when writers and instructors try to group them together or refer to the two processes with one label such as rewriting, revision, redrafting, editing, or proofreading. However, revision is one of the creative parts of the writing process rather than a time to correct your grammar or spelling—that is for the editing process.

Revision is what writing specialists consider the **global** process of redrafting. Global characteristics of writing focus on overall issues, such as content, thesis, organization, word choice, and word use. When you edit, you focus on what writing specialists call **local** issues of editing, such as grammar, sentence variety, mechanics, spelling, and formatting.

Often, writers try to revise and edit at the same time; however, this is not a good idea. The focused attention to minute parts of words and sentences when editing often distracts a writer from thoroughly developing ideas. Thus, instructors and skilled writers recommend that all writers try to separate revision and editing into two activities. In many freshman composition classes, instructors purposely divide revision from editing by using separate peer workshop days and by giving different grades or grade percentages for these activities as part of an overall paper grade.

Why Revise?

When writers revise, they often discover and develop new or better ideas through the revision process. Revision is changing the paper, ideally for the better. Most professional or skilled writers view revision as a necessary part of their writing because it is useful for generating new ideas, focusing and reorganizing ideas, and polishing the overall paper. As mentioned earlier, a draft is a work in progress, and it is a good idea to write multiple drafts for each essay to write the best paper and get the best grade possible. In Chapter 3, we discuss several strategies for critically reading and viewing popular culture; these same strategies can be applied to your own essays and to the writings of your peers.

You can add, delete, and substitute material during the revision process. For example, if a point is unclear, you can add details to clarify your point, delete ambiguous words or phrases, or substitute new examples that have more clarity. Sometimes, you will find it necessary to cut material you like but that does not fit your point, or you will find that you have gone in a different direction and need to start over. Do not feel bad—this is just part of the drafting and revising process. When you revise, you focus on content, organization, and word choice, global issues that can be found at all of the different levels of your essay. The next few sections will help you revise on all of these levels: the overall essay, paragraphs, sentences, and words. It is best to divide these levels of revision and to work on them separately because a good revision plan includes investigation of all these levels.

Revising at the Essay Level

When you revise at the essay level, focus on large-scale changes that will improve the overall essay. Here is a list of essay-level concerns to consider each time you write and revise an essay.

- *Look first at the central idea of the essay.* If all sentences in the essay do not support this main idea, consider revising the main idea or revising the support in the essay. Although it is not necessary to have an explicit or stated thesis statement, it is a good idea to include one in a college essay, so you have a clearly defined central idea that will help you write the essay and help guide your reader through it.
- *Make sure that you have an audience in mind when writing and revising the essay.* If a reader cannot see himself or herself as the audience or you cannot envision the audience, then pay more attention to the audience of the essay when you revise.
- *Check the introduction and the rest of the essay for your underlying purpose in writing the essay.* If any of the support given throughout the essay does not support your purpose, you can cut what does not fit and add the support that is missing.
- *Review the overall organization of the essay.* Does each body paragraph support the central idea of the essay? Are the paragraphs ordered in a way that will make sense to the reader?
- *Check the balance inside the essay.* Are any of the supporting paragraphs out of balance with the rest of the essay? If so, check whether or not large paragraphs can be split or short paragraphs can be reorganized together.
- *Make sure that your essay flows well.* Use transitional words such as *however, next,* or *finally* and phrases such as *in comparison* or *on the other hand* between body paragraphs, so your reader will not get confused when you change topics.
- *Review your central idea if it is an argument, making sure that you have addressed counterarguments at some point in the essay.* You will lose some of your credibility with your reader if you do not acknowledge what others have to say about your topic, especially those who disagree. Showing that you know and can even counter the opposing arguments will make your argument that much stronger.
- *Be sure to use an interesting title that will encourage your reader to take the time to read your essay.* The title is your first chance to gain your reader's attention, so make it catchy as well as informative.

Revising at the Paragraph Level

After revising on the essay level, you will want to check whether the paragraphs in your essay are effective. Here is a list of paragraph-level concerns to consider each time you write and revise an essay.

- *Reread the introductory paragraph(s).* Does it include an effective lead-in to the central idea? Will the introductory material capture your readers' interest? Perhaps an interesting anecdote, vivid description of the pop culture topic, or a set of startling statistics will capture your readers' attention. Be sure to stay away from overused introductory strategies, such as providing a dictionary definition or general statements like *today's society.*
- *Focus on topic sentences or main ideas.* Can you put into one sentence what each paragraph says? Do you have one sentence within each paragraph that gives a good indication of the central idea of the paragraph? Does the supporting evidence work with this topic or main idea?
- *Add more examples and details to weakly developed paragraphs.* Stay away from only giving generalizations. For example, instead of writing, "Comic book sales are on the rise," write,

"In 2007, comic book sales in North America topped $429.9 million," and cite the source of the information.

- *Check summarized, paraphrased, or quoted material that you use for support.* Make sure you have accurately represented your source materials and that you have acknowledged your sources. See Chapter 11 for more information about citing sources.
- *Check for coherence within body paragraphs, making sure all of the pieces of the paragraph fit together and make sense.* If you provide multiple supporting sentences, use transitions to join them together. Review and perhaps rewrite the introduction and conclusion.
- *Reread your concluding paragraph(s).* In addition to reinforcing key ideas from the body of the essay, try to end in a way that makes your reader want to read more. Make a prediction or invite a response from your readers, but be careful not to introduce new information. You can also call attention to the significance of your argument or what the reader should do with the information provided.

Revising at the Sentence Level

Writers often check sentences for grammar and punctuation errors and forget to check for sentence-level changes that would clarify content or organization. Here are some sentence-level strategies to use when you revise your essays.

- *Check sentences for clarity.* Does each sentence make sense? Check for ambiguity. For instance, a sentence such as "Filming crews can be fun" has multiple meanings and needs clarification. Changing this sentence to "The crews who shoot films for a living often have a great sense of humor and fun" or "I like to film people while they're working" will clear up the ambiguity.
- *Try not to use long introductory phrases or clauses.* These usually distract the reader from what you are trying to emphasize in the sentence. A sentence such as "Before I got to work and had to fix the copy machine and spilled my Starbucks Caramel Macchiato on my new shirt, I won tickets to the Sheryl Crow concert" has a long unnecessary introductory clause that de-emphasizes the main point of the sentence.
- *Use sentence-combining techniques to provide more sentence variety in the essay.* Readers get bored reading the same structure over and over again. Balancing short, simple sentences with compound or complex sentences usually works best. Refer to the next section on editing for more information on how to do this.

Revising at the Word Level

Choosing your words well helps your reader understand the central point more easily. Not only will revising word-level problems improve the content of your essay, but it will also improve the way the paper flows. Here are some word-level strategies you can use when revising your essay.

- *Look for wordiness.* Cut empty phrases, such as *there are, it is, I feel that, I know that, you will understand that, I think, in today's society.*
- *Use concrete nouns for subjects and avoid overusing pronouns, especially at the beginning of sentences.* For example, instead of generalizing about all films, let your reader know that you are referring to horror films based on Stephen King novels.
- *Ask your instructor about his or her policy on using first person* (I, me, my) *and second person* (you, your, yours). Some instructors prefer that students write only in third person, which can give a paper a more objective tone, while others may ask students to consider which approach is most appropriate for a given format, topic, or audience.

- *Be sure to use* you *appropriately if you use it. You* can only be used if the reader is actually the *you* referent, or the person you are talking to. For example, when writing directions, the writer is talking directly to the reader and often directly addresses the reader.
- *Change passive verbs to active ones, unless the passive form serves a specific purpose in your essay.* Passive verbs, which use a form of the verb *to be*, conceal who did what or who is responsible for the action in the sentence. Look at this sentence for example: "Women are portrayed in negative ways in some rap music." This passive form, "are portrayed," doesn't tell the readers who is portraying women in this negative way; it doesn't tell us who is responsible for this negativity. If you rewrite it with an active verb, you will have to name the actor, or the person responsible. The new sentence might say, "T. I. often portrays women in negative ways through his song lyrics." In a few instances you might actually want to conceal the responsible party or divert blame for something; in this case you might consciously choose to use the passive voice. For example, "The payment for the birthday party was delayed."
- *Use the literary present tense.* When you write an essay that reviews, reflects on, responds to, or analyzes literature, music, film, or television, use the literary present tense. For example, when describing a scene that you are reflecting on, write "Homer Simpson grins smugly and then leaves the barber shop" instead of "Homer Simpson grinned smugly and then left the barber shop." However, if you are writing a research paper focused on a historical event, past tense is more appropriate.
- *Read aloud for unnecessary repetition.* Replace overused words with synonyms, but be careful that you clearly understand how to use words you borrow from a thesaurus.
- *Check the tone of your essay since word choice plays a role in creating the overall tone.* If your instructor asks you to use academic tone, do not use contractions such as *can't* or *won't* or conversational-type word choices, such as, "Well, I then went to the bus stop on the corner and then got on the bus and then took it downtown" or "I was chillin' in my crib."
- *Review transition use throughout the essay.* Pay particular attention to using transitions between body paragraphs and within body paragraphs when switching from one supporting point to another.

Revision Helpers

The person most invested in helping you revise is *you*. Be sure to include enough time for a thorough revision in your writing process, and focus on the essay, paragraph, sentence, and word levels one at a time.

Next, find someone else who is in your class or who is taking a writing class with the same instructor because this person is the most familiar with your assignments. You can also ask your roommate, friend, work colleague, or family member to help you revise; however, these revisers will probably need instruction in what revision really is. It will not help you if they focus on editing when you need to be focusing on revision. In addition, be careful not to have anyone rewrite your words or write sections of your paper. Your revisers need to make suggestions, but you are the only one who can put those suggestions on paper because having someone else rewrite your words is a type of plagiarism.

The best way to find people to help you revise is to participate fully in your peer revision workshop. Finish a rough draft of your paper and revise it thoroughly yourself. Then, bring this revised draft to your class revision workshop. Incorporate any changes that your peer reviewer suggests if the change improves your paper. If your school has a writing center, the writing assistants, tutors, or consultants there can also help with revision. Again, be sure to incorporate those suggestions that you feel will improve your essay.

Questions for Peer Reviewers

(Check lists and examples throughout this chapter for further explanations.)

1. Is there a title? Is it interesting? If you answered "no" to either of these questions, suggest a title to the writer after you read the entire essay.
2. Does the introductory material work well as an attention getter for you as a reader?
3. How well does the writer keep his or her audience in mind? What does the writer's purpose seem to be? How could it be clarified?
4. Read the beginning of the essay and then pause. What is the main idea of the entire essay? Is there a clear and well-written thesis? <u>Underline it.</u> Provide information on how to make the thesis and/or the introduction better or more effective.
5. Read only the topic sentences of the body paragraphs in order. Do they give a general outline of the paragraphs on their own? Does each paragraph have a topic sentence that relates directly to the thesis or main point?
6. Look at each of the body paragraphs individually now. Does each paragraph have enough support/specific detail? Does each paragraph support the topic sentence given at the beginning of the paragraph?
7. Does the writer use transitions to move the reader from one idea to another (between body paragraphs and within body paragraphs)?
8. Should the writer expand on any points? Go to the essay and mark three places with an X where you think the writer needs to provide more developed and effective details to support the main idea. Next to these, offer suggestions to help the writer revise for more effective support.
9. Look at the word level now. Are there word-choice problems?
10. What do you like best about the entire essay?

Peer revision, whether it is inside or outside class, gives you a chance to hear from an immediate audience rather than from an instructor. This midstep allows you to improve your paper without negatively impacting your grade, and when you exchange papers with someone else, it is usually a win-win situation. Getting immediate feedback is also a plus since using this strategy will help you develop your essay more before it gets turned in for evaluation.

Working with other writers can also help boost your confidence about an essay. If your peer reader enjoys your essay and gives you good advice, you feel better about the essay and, in turn, will probably work harder on it. In addition, peer workshops allow you to see firsthand that other writers also struggle with the same things you do; most first drafts are less than excellent essays, and you will feel better about your own in-process essay by being aware of this. Peer revision, most importantly, gets you into the habit of working collaboratively, something you will do in other classes and in the workplace after you leave the freshman writing classroom.

ten steps to help you revise

1. Put aside your rough or first draft for a time before you start your revision.
2. Print your draft and read it slowly, making notes as you go.
3. Revise on the essay level.
4. Revise on the paragraph level.
5. Revise on the sentence level.
6. Revise on the word level.
7. Ask someone to read your essay for revision purposes only.
   It is best to find someone who understands the difference between revision and editing and who will comment only on global concerns.
8. Incorporate changes from 7.
9. Participate in a peer-revision workshop in class if available.
10. Incorporate changes from 9 and then begin the editing stage.

When you ask for revision help, you often need to give feedback in return on your peer's work. Sometimes, it is difficult for students to participate in peer revision; it takes time to feel comfortable incorporating this step into the writing process. Here are some good strategies when participating in peer revision.

- *Work to get over your shyness about sharing your work with others.* Understand that all writers are in the same boat when it comes to sharing their work; it is difficult to let others see a work in progress, but sharing your writing and receiving feedback improve your writing.
- *Be an interested reader and give good comments and critiques.* As you respond to your peers' writing, you will also be modeling for them the kinds of responses you want to receive about your own writing. The comments "That's good" or "I like it" aren't really very helpful when revising.
- *Use peer revision forms to help you give advice: one provided by your instructor, the one located on* The Pop Culture Zone's *companion website, or the one in the box on page 35.* Answer all the questions on the forms with full answers that will help the writer revise later when you are not present.
- *Never apologize for your first draft.* Do the best you can in your rough draft and your revised draft, and then turn the essay over to your peer reviewer.
- *Throw your ego out the window.* Peer reviewers are helping you improve your writing and your grade; if they were not available and the essay went directly to the instructor for grading, your grade would probably be lower.
- *Focus on global concerns only.* Save any comments on grammar, mechanics, spelling, and formatting for the editing review or workshop.
- *Pick and choose what you want to use from your peer reviewer's comments.* You might not want to change everything mentioned; however, be sure to consider everything your peer reviewer suggests. Sometimes, others can see what we cannot see ourselves, and they can help us get out of an ineffective writing rut.

You can also ask your instructor for revision help during his or her office hours. You can make the most of such a conference if you have specific questions ready when you go. Make a list of things that you found difficult to revise when you did your thorough revision or questions that came up as you rewrote. Some instructors allow students to submit papers electronically for revision help; however, before you do this, check with your instructor about his or her policy. Most instructors like to have you and your paper present when they discuss possible global changes to the paper.

When to Stop Revising

Nearly all good writing is revised often and in a thoughtful manner, so taking time and making a substantial effort are important if you want to improve your writing and your writing grades. Most competent writers can become excellent writers if they take the time to revise their writing significantly before turning it in for evaluation. Multiple drafts are important because each time you draft, you have the opportunity to learn something new, clarify an idea for your readers, or make your language more accessible and interesting. Plus, doing significant revision that is separate from significant editing improves all writing; even professional writers do it.

Although an essay is never really finished, it may be ready to turn in when

- It follows all instructions in the writing assignment.
- It says what you want it to say in the most effective way.
- It looks right on the page—it follows your assignment guidelines as well as the expectations for the chosen format or genre.
- It has content and a central theme that are fully developed.
- It is well organized.
- It has effective word choice.
- It has been edited well.

Revising in a Timed Writing Situation

In-class writing sometimes does not allow time for massive revision; however, you can and should build time into any writing assignment for revision. If given an in-class essay, break the time allowed into short blocks that resemble the parts of the process for an out-of-class essay. If you have sixty minutes, use five to ten minutes to brainstorm and outline, thirty to forty minutes to write the first draft, five to ten minutes to revise for global concerns, and five to ten minutes to edit for local concerns. If you are writing on a computer, print a copy of the paper, if possible, to revise and edit offline. Then, add changes, correct spelling and typos, and print your final draft. Even in a tight writing situation, it pays to always make time for revision and editing.

Example—Writing Case Study, Draft 3

This draft shows a combination of comments made by peer reviewers and the instructor.

Halcott 1

Erin Halcott
English 1020-028
Prof. Tipton
March 9, 2008

I like the new title! Have you expanded your essay topic then? · · · · · · · · · · · · · · · · Crossing Ethical Lines

Good work on combining this into one sentence. Could it still be condensed a little more?

The movie *Se7en*, directed by David Fincher in 1995, follows mainly two detectives, David Mills, played by Brad Pitt, and William Somerset, played by Morgan Freeman, who are on a hunt to catch a serial killer, John Doe, who is played by Kevin Spacey (imdb). Although the movie mainly focuses on the murders themselves, there is an emphasis on several ethical

Have you expanded your analysis to include Somerset, Mills, and Doe? Cool! This is a good group to analyze together.

dilemmas. Each of the three main characters, Somerset, Mills, and Doe,

This is a great analysis of just what "ethics" is and some of the issues it brings up.

Good analysis, but a few more examples from the film could help prove your point.

struggle with their own ethical decisions. The biggest thing all three of them struggle with is deciding what is considered ethical for them in their minds. What is ethical for Somerset is not ethical for Mills or Doe and vice versa any way. Many times, it is hard for each of hem to decide what is ethical and what is not. We too, are a lot like the characters. We have a hard time deciding what is ok and what is considered wrong. We struggle with holding ourselves to the same standards as we hold other people.

Detective Somerset is a man who lives by the book. He plays by the rules and never steps out of line. He thinks about every move before he makes it and every word before he says it. So it's not too surprising that he rarely fights to act within his own ethical system. His beliefs tell him that breaking into an apartment is wrong, but when Detective Mills kicks in the door, Somerset walks in with no hesitation. As long as Somerset didn't break his ethics physically, he is ok with whatever happens and easily walks into that apartment.

Somerset also believes that murder is wrong. He took his job as an investigator to keep people safe, not to harm anyone. In the last scene of the movie, as Mills is being driven away in the police car for shooting and killing John Doe, Somerset is talking to a near-by policeman. He tells him to make sure that they really take care of Mills and give him anything he needs. To me, that shows that even though Somerset knows murder is wrong, he does not look down on Mills for killing John Doe. I think he understands why Mills acted unethically and let Doe get the best of him. Even though Somerset believes that murder is wrong, he does not judge Mills for killing John Doe. He doesn't extend his ethical beliefs to those around him.

Detective Mills is very different than Somerset. Mills doesn't worry about the consequences of his actions. He acts first and worries about it later. He knows that breaking into the apartment is wrong, so he gets around it by paying off a homeless woman to tell the police man that Mills and Somerset should search the apartment. He sneaked around his ethics and ended up doing what he knew he wanted to do anyway.

Is there another example you could add here to help illustrate Mills's rashness?

In the climax of the movie, Mills faces the biggest ethical struggle of the whole movie when he is deciding whether or not to kill John Doe. You can easily see on his face the internal struggle he is going through. He obviously believes that murder is wrong, but he also obviously believes in revenge. He can't just turn his head when he finds out that Doe has just killed his wife, Tracy, but he knows that the only way to get even is to kill him. So he fights with himself. Does he kill Doe and show his true wrath, or does he let Doe live, and never avenge Tracy's murder? You can easily see that he know murder is wrong, otherwise, he would have just killed Doe right away. Instead, he goes back and forth with himself. Can he break his own ethics? Yes. In the end, Mills has a flash of Tracy and kills Doe. It was the only way Mills could make things right in his mind.

Excellent analysis!

John Doe's ethics are so askew, but in his mind, he is perfectly sane. He believes that what he is doing is fine, because he does not see his actions as murder. He sees himself as teaching a lesson to society. He is preaching. The only sin he sees himself committing is envy. He is able to overlook his own sin of murder, but he does not overlook his victims' sins. We see his victims as innocent civilians, but Doe sees them as filthy sinners, and he believes that by killing the sinners, he is doing a good thing. His ethics tell him that he is ridding the world of evil.

Can you use any example here from the film as evidence for these claims? Perhaps an analysis of one of Doe's victims could help?

As crazy as it may sound, I see a lot of us in John Doe. It is so easy for us to point out everyone else's sin and flaws but go around as if we are totally innocent. We walk around all day making judgements about the people we encounter but never stop to think that we are no better. Say, for example, that you're in class. You hear two girls talking behind you about one of their friends. They call her various names, say more bad things about her, and you begin to think, "They are so mean to be saying those things." But wait- haven't you talked bad about somebody behind their back? Of Cource you have! Everybody has. But it doesn't matter. It is so much easier to focus on the flaws of others thatn it tis to examine ourselves and our own ethics.

Everyone has their own set of ethics, and at some point, everyone has broken their own code of ethics. Just as Somerset disregards the fact that Mills killed Doe, just as Mills finally crossed his line and killed Doe, and just as Doe himself ignores his own crime, so have we crossed our own lines. So next time you feel yourself beginning to hate John Doe, just remember how similar we really are.

Works Cited

The Internet Movie Database. 2007. <http://www.imdb.com>.
Se7en. Dir. David Fincher. 1995.

Great work here! You are honest about your own ethics and the ethics you see in use around you— this lends personal credibility to your argument. The collective "everybody" makes the reader an active part of your analysis. The tone, however, might be read as a little too informal in view of the rest of your essay.

Good conclusion, but could you include more analysis of John Doe's ethical decisions?

WHAT IS EDITING?

Editing is usually one of the last steps in the writing process. As you learned in the last section, many students make the mistake of focusing on error correction and proofreading before taking the time to develop, clarify, and organize ideas fully through drafting and revision. Although the parts of the writing process are not finite and oftentimes do overlap, editing is a separate activity designed to address local issues, such as grammar, sentence variety, mechanics, spelling, and formatting. Resources such as dictionaries and grammar handbooks, whether in print or online, may help at this stage. In fact, if you do not understand any of the concepts in the editing lists that follow, check with a handbook, your instructor, or a tutor at your local writing center.

When to Edit

Editing should begin after you feel confident about the choices you have made in content, organization, and style. You might compare editing and proofreading to washing, waxing, and polishing your car—it would be absurd to take the time to do these things to a vehicle that does not run! Drafting and revising ensure that your writing is first fine-tuned; then, you edit to make it shine on the surface.

Different Levels of Editing

- Paragraphs
- Sentences
- Words
- Proofreading
  — Punctuation
  — Spelling
  — Capitalization and italics
  — Formatting (this can also be considered the essay level)

Paragraph-Level Editing

Think of paragraphs as larger forms of punctuation that broaden the connections shown by traditional punctuation marks, such as commas, semicolons, periods, and question marks. Paragraph indentations and lengths provide readers with visual guidance to relationships and connections between major ideas.

When you begin editing at the paragraph level, consider the following:

1. *What does each paragraph say (main idea) and do (introduce, provide proof or support, give an example, illustrate, connect, conclude)?*

   - Did you begin a new paragraph for each new idea?
   - Is the order of the paragraphs logical?
   - Look at what the paragraphs do, like introducing new material and providing support for the main idea, and then question the usefulness or purpose of each.

2. *Are sentences within paragraphs unified and consistent?* Check for

   - Unrelated ideas within the paragraph; paragraphs should focus on one main idea at a time.
   - Illogical sequences and series, such as when a car blows up before it crashes into the eighteen-wheeler in a TV show or film.

- Mixed metaphors and/or confusing comparisons, for example, "A leopard can't change his stripes" (Bozell).
- Mismatched subjects and verbs, for example, *butter reads* or *books believe*.
- Transitional words or phrases.

Sentence-Level Editing

Using a mixture of sentence types makes your writing more interesting and does not distract readers, unlike when you use the same sentence type repeatedly. There are four main sentence patterns from which you can choose, including simple sentences, compound sentences, complex sentences, and compound-complex sentences. Punctuation marks relate directly to the kind of sentence you use and indicate pauses, relationships, and connections within and between sentences. Be sure to proofread for punctuation when you use a variety of sentences.

A *simple sentence* is made up of a subject-main verb combination: "*The Godfather* is my favorite film." The subject can be conjoined, as in "*The Godfather* and *Carlito's Way* are my two favorite films," or the verb can be combined, as in "Al Pacino stars in both and steals the films." Simple sentences may have many optional elements, such as prepositional phrases ("In the first film, Pacino plays Michael Corleone") or adverbials ("Pacino plays his character effectively").

A *compound sentence* combines at least two simple sentences. The new sentence can be joined with a semicolon ("Julia Roberts is Vivian Ward; Richard Gere is Edward Lewis") or with a comma and coordinator ("Julia Roberts is Vivian Ward, and Richard Gere is Edward Lewis"). If the two sentences are closely related, and the right side of the sentence gives more specific information about the left side, a colon can be used to coordinate both sentences together ("Julia Roberts has played many interesting parts: she was a hooker in *Pretty Woman*, a fairy in *Peter Pan*, and a spider in *Charlotte's Web*").

A *complex sentence* is made up of a simple sentence plus one or more subordinate clauses. Complex sentences can use subordinators (such as *after, although, as, because, before, if, since, when, where*) to join two or more sentences together: "After I saw *The Godfather*, I realized that Al Pacino was a great actor." They can also be joined with relative pronouns (such as *that, who, whom, which, what*): "Julia Roberts, who starred in *Pretty Woman*, had her break-out role in *Mystic Pizza*."

A *compound-complex sentence* is made up of two or more simple sentences (this is the compound part) and one or more subordinate clauses (this is the complex part): "Julia Roberts, who is in *Ocean's Eleven* and *Ocean's Twelve*, and Al Pacino, who is in *Ocean's Thirteen*, never made a film together; however, Julia Roberts and George Clooney have made several together."

When you begin editing on the sentence level, ask yourself

1. *Are the connections between ideas communicated effectively through your sentence construction and variety?* Check for

   - **Short, choppy sentences,** especially a group of simple sentences that all begin with a subject: "I enjoyed *The Simpsons Movie*. Homer was unusually funny. The audience laughed a lot."
   - **Excessively long, hard-to-follow sentences:** "Drawn into the Pygmalion-like story of Vivian and Edward and suspending a firm grasp of reality for two hours, the audience, taken away from their everyday humdrum lives, enjoys *Pretty Woman* as a modern-day fairy tale about a modern-day relationship between a businessman and a prostitute and their adventures inside and outside an expensive hotel located in Beverly Hills."
   - **Unclear emphasis due to faulty or excessive subordination:** "Julia Roberts, who had an early role on *Crime Story* (1987) and who also had her break-out role in *Mystic Pizza* (1988), and Al Pacino, who had an early role on *N.Y.P.D.* (1968) and who also had his break-out role in *The Panic in Needle Park* (1971), had surprisingly similar arcs to their careers."

2. *Are individual sentence structures clear and easy to follow?* Check for

- **Misplaced or unclear descriptions:** "Although she has been nominated for an Oscar three times, Julia Roberts only has won one." (**Corrected:** "Although she has been nominated for an Oscar three times, Julia Roberts has won only one.")
- **Modifiers (such as verb phrases, adjectives, or adverbs) that have no referent in the sentence:** "Nominated for an Oscar for *Into the Wild*, the audience was excited to see Sean Penn at the Academy Awards." (**Corrected:** "Nominated for an Oscar for *Into the Wild*, Sean Penn attended the Academy Awards.")
- **Modifiers that are too far from the words they modify:** "The audience enjoyed the three songs from the film *Enchanted* that were nominated for Oscars." (**Corrected:** "The audience enjoyed the three *Enchanted* songs that were nominated for Oscars.")

3. *Are ideas balanced through the use of parallel elements?* Check for

- **Lists that do not have parallel parts of speech,** such as all nouns or all verbs: "I enjoy adventure films, action television shows, and watching NASCAR." (**Corrected:** "I enjoy adventure films, action television shows, and NASCAR.")
- **Phrases and clauses that do not have the same grammatical structures,** such as all prepositional phrases or subordinate clauses within one sentence or a list within a paragraph: "The Academy Awards usually broadcast when I am on vacation or how I like to see award shows." (**Corrected:** "The Academy Awards usually broadcast when I am on vacation or when I am working on a paper for school.")

4. *Are there any sudden shifts in grammatical structures, tone, or style?* Check for

- **Inconsistent use of verb tense;** be sure to write all present tense or all past tense unless there is a reason for the shift: "Ferris Bueller plays a tape of his mother's voice when the principal called." (**Corrected:** "Ferris Bueller plays a tape of his mother's voice when the principal calls.")
- **Inconsistency or lack of agreement in person and number;** be sure to put plural nouns (antecedents) with plural pronouns, or singular verbs with singular nouns: "Every princess in Disney films has their prince charming." (**Corrected:** "Every princess in Disney films has her prince charming.")
- **A tone or style that is not unified;** in a formal essay, for example, maintain the formal tone throughout the whole essay: "When visiting the Florida Keys, tourists often get trashed at local bars." (**Corrected:** "When visiting the Florida Keys, tourists often stay up late drinking at local bars.")

5. *Are sentences concise, free of deadweight or unnecessary words?* Check for

- **Placeholders like *there, it, this,* and *these,*** which often serve no purpose in the sentence: "There is another movie that also shows King's love of abused authors." (**Corrected:** "*Misery* also shows King's love of abused authors.")
- **Excessive use of forms of the verb "to be";** replace with strong, specific verbs: "In *Misery*, Kathy Bates is wonderful, and James Caan is remarkable." (**Corrected:** "In *Misery*, Kathy Bates superbly depicts obsessed fan Annie Wilkes, and James Caan remarkably portrays vulnerable author Paul Sheldon.")
- **Overuse of passive verb forms,** such as "is hit" or "has been improved"; replace with strong, specific active verbs: "George Michael's song 'Faith' was improved by Limp Bizkit when the vocals were changed to be more aggressive and the music speed was made faster." (**Corrected:** "Limp Bizkit improved on George Michael's version of 'Faith' by making the vocals more aggressive and speeding up the music.")

- **Lengthy phrases that can be replaced with one or two words** such as "because" rather than "for the purpose of": "Harry Potter fights Voldemort repeatedly for the purpose of saving the world due to him being the hero." (**Corrected:** "Harry Potter fights Voldemort repeatedly because Harry portrays the hero.")

Word-Level Editing

When you edit for word choice, ask yourself

1. *Are any words vague?* Check for . . .
   - **General nouns** and replace with specific or concrete nouns such as *Dell PC* instead of *computer* or *Friends* instead of *a sitcom.*
   - **General verbs** and replace with specific, active verbs, such as *argues* instead of *says* or *sprinted* instead of *ran.*
   - **General adjectives or modifiers,** where more specific words can be used to give a more concrete image: "The nice tones of Tori Amos's voice on her *American Doll Posse* album are beautiful and nice." (**Corrected:** "The lovely honeyed tones of Tori Amos's voice on her *American Doll Posse* album juxtaposed with the political undertones create a powerful statement.")

2. *Are any words or phrases overused?* Check for . . .
   - **Repeated words at beginnings of sentences:** "The Marlboro Man appears in many types of advertisements. He appears in billboards. He appears in magazines. The Marlboro Man also used to appear on television commercials." (**Corrected:** "The Marlboro man appears in many types of advertisements, including billboards, magazine ads, and television commercials.")
   - **Use of clichés:** "In her song 'Bitch,' Meredith Brooks hit the nail on the head about female stereotypical roles." (**Corrected:** "In her song 'Bitch,' Meredith Brooks sings truthfully about female stereotypical roles.")

3. *Has redundancy been cut?* Check for . . .
   - **Unnecessary words:** "In Stephen King's novel *Salem's Lot*, Ben and his friends fight and kill bloodsucking vampires who bite the necks of victims." (**Corrected:** "In Stephen King's novel *Salem's Lot*, Ben and his friends kill vampires.")

4. *Does the vocabulary reflect sensitivity to audience, purpose, and context?* Check for . . .
   - **The use of stereotypes:** "The audience for chick flicks is always crying into their Kleenexes." (**Corrected:** "*The Holiday* with Cameron Diaz and Kate Winslet made me cry.")
   - **Biased language** based on gender, race, ethnicity, sexuality, religious affiliation, age, or social class: "In *Death Proof*, stuntman Mike (Kurt Russell) whimpers like a little girl when he is shot." (**Corrected:** "In Tarantino's *Death Proof*, stuntman Mike [Kurt Russell] cries out in pain when he is shot.")
   - **Connotations associated with words.** When using a thesaurus, make sure you understand how the word is used and the nuances of meaning associated with the word in various contexts or cultures. Consider the difference in meaning for these two sentences: "In *Working Girl*, Tess McGill ruthlessly works her way to the top." vs. "In *Working Girl*, Tess McGill ambitiously works her way to the top."
   - **Jargon,** making sure technical words are defined or explained. For example, in an episode from *Buffy the Vampire Slayer*, the older, highly educated Giles says, "There is a fringe theory held by

a few folklorists that some regional stories have actual very literal antecedents." Oz, the teenage werewolf, summarizes this same idea without jargon when he says, "Fairy tales are real."

5. *Does your tone (attitude toward the subject) engage your readers or alienate them?* Check for . . .
   - **A hostile tone:** "*Fantastic Four* is a horrible movie that sucks eggs, and all the actors could not act their way out of a paper bag." (**Corrected:** "The slack-jawed and unrealistic acting in *Fantastic Four* is disappointing.")
   - **Assumptions about the readers or their beliefs:** "No one could possibly blame Erica Bain (Jodie Foster) for becoming a vigilante in *The Brave One*." (**Corrected:** "Many people can understand and condone the actions taken by Erica Bain [Jodie Foster] in *The Brave One*.")
   - **The use of** *you,* which should only be used when speaking directly to the reader: "When you see *Cloverfield*, you'll be really surprised." (**Corrected:** "*Cloverfield* surprises its audiences.")

Proofreading: Punctuation

When you edit for punctuation, ask yourself . . .

1. *Do sentences have the correct closing punctuation?* For example, do statements end with periods and questions end with question marks?
2. *Are commas, semicolons, dashes, apostrophes, and other internal punctuation marks used correctly?* Use a handbook if needed to check the rules; likewise, refer to previous explanations of commas splices and fused sentences.
3. *Are quotations correctly introduced, punctuated, and carefully cited? Are quotation marks turned the right way—toward the quoted material?* Refer to Chapter 11 for additional guidelines about incorporating direct quotes.
4. *Are in-text citations correctly punctuated?* Refer to Chapter 11 for additional guidelines about punctuating in-text citations.

Proofreading: Spelling

When you edit for spelling, ask yourself . . .

1. *Are all words spelled correctly?* Remember that spell-checkers are not always foolproof! Check for commonly confused words.
2. *Have you used the correct forms?* Double-check any abbreviations, contractions, or possessive nouns.
3. *Have you used hyphens correctly?* Double-check any hyphenated adjectives.

Proofreading: Capitalization and Italics

When you edit for capitalization and italics, ask yourself . . .

1. *Are words capitalized appropriately?*
2. *Are quotations capitalized correctly?*
3. *Are proper names and titles distinguished with appropriate capitalization and punctuation?*
4. *Are titles punctuated correctly with italics or quotation marks?* (See Chapter 11 on researching and documenting for some of these guidelines.)

Proofreading: Formatting

Formatting correctly shows that you care about the presentation of all your hard work. However, looks can be deceiving, and a paper that looks good can still contain serious errors. Computers have made it much easier to produce a professional-looking document, but editing is still essential. When you edit for formatting, ask yourself

1. *Have you followed all of your instructor's directions about formatting?*
2. *Are the margins correct?*
3. *Is the spacing correct between words, sentences, and paragraphs?*
4. *Is the assignment block present and correct? Does it contain all of the required information in the correct order and form?*
5. *Do you have a title that is centered and spaced correctly—and not underlined, italicized, bolded, in quotation marks, or in a different font?*
6. *Do you have a header with your name and page numbers?*
7. *Does your paper follow the citation guidelines required: Modern Language Association, American Psychological Association, or something else?*

Suggestions for Peer Editors

Paragraphs
1. On a separate sheet of paper, write a sentence summarizing what each paragraph says and does.
2. Mark any places within paragraphs where sentences lack consistency in thought, language, or style.

Sentences
1. Mark any places where sentences are unclear, incorrectly constructed, or indirect.
2. Note any unnecessary repetition in sentence lengths and structures.
3. Underline any agreement errors or illogical shifts—subjects-verbs, pronouns-antecedents, verb tense, or point of view.

Words
1. Circle or bold any words that are unclear, vague, or unnecessary. Suggest two replacements for each.
2. Mark any places where words and tone do not reflect sensitivity to audience, context, or purpose. Explain these responses to the writer.
3. Circle or bold any words that are repetitive, overused, or clichéd. Suggest a replacement for each.

Proofreading
1. Place square brackets around any missing or misused commas, semicolons, colons, dashes, apostrophes, quotations marks, or end punctuation marks.
2. Underline any misspelled words or incorrect/confused forms.
3. Place square brackets around any missing or misused capitalization and/or italics.
4. Note any places in the paper where the formatting fails to follow the instructor's directions.

Example—Writing Case Study, Draft 4

This is a final edited draft of the essay. Notice that the final instructor and peer suggestions have been considered, and the commas and spelling errors have been cleaned up. The citations in the Works Cited are also more complete. The author of this essay is ready to turn it in, but notice from the questions and suggestions in the annotations that the author could still revise at least one more time to make the paper stronger.

Excellent expansion and revision of your introductory paragraph. Your thesis is clearer.

Halcott 1

Erin Halcott
English 1020-028
Prof. Tipton
March 13, 2008

Crossing Ethical Lines

The movie *Se7en*, directed by David Fincher in 1995, follows two detectives, David Mills, played by Brad Pitt, and William Somerset, played by Morgan Freeman, who are on a hunt to catch a serial killer, John Doe, who is played by Kevin Spacey (imdb). Although the movie mainly focuses on the murders themselves, there is an emphasis on several ethical dilemmas. Each of the three main characters, Somerset, Mills, and Doe, struggles with his own ethical decisions. To me, ethics is what is believed to be right and wrong for each person. Different people in society have different ethics. The biggest thing all three main characters struggle with is deciding what is considered ethical for them in their minds. What is ethical for Somerset is not ethical for Mills or Doe and vice versa. Many times, it is hard for each of them to decide what is ethical and what is not. We too, are a lot like Somerset, Mills and John Doe. We struggle with deciding what is right and what is wrong, and we also struggle with holding ourselves to the same standards as we hold other people.

Detective Somerset is a man with very strong ethics. He lives by the book, plays by the rules, and never steps out of line. He thinks about every move before he makes it and every word before he says it. Instead of getting caught up in the emotions of every crime scene, Somerset really takes his time to research everything so that he knows all he can before he makes any decisions. He doesn't mind spending the extra time to prepare. During late nights, he is found in the library looking up everything he can about the seven deadly sins, so that maybe he can understand John Doe that much better. So it's not too surprising that he rarely fights to act within his own ethical system. About halfway through the movie, though, Somerset begins to cross the line of his own ethics. His beliefs tell him that breaking into an apartment is wrong, but when Detective Mills kicks in the door, Somerset walks in with no hesitation. As long as Somerset didn't break his ethics physically, he is OK with whatever happens and easily walks into that apartment.

You used more examples from the film here—great!

Somerset also believes that murder is wrong. He took his job as an investigator to keep people safe, not to harm anyone. In the last scene of the movie, as Mills is being driven away in the police car for shooting and killing John Doe, Somerset is talking to a nearby policeman. He tells him to make sure that they really take care of Mills and give him anything he needs. To me, that shows that even though Somerset knows murder is wrong, he does not look down on Mills for killing John Doe. I think he understands why Mills acted unethically and let Doe get the best of him. Even though Somerset believes that murder is wrong, he does not judge Mills. He doesn't extend his ethical beliefs to those around him. Somerset understands that what is right for him may not be right for everyone. On the other hand, Detective Mills is very different than Somerset.

Mills doesn't worry about the consequences of his actions. He acts first and worries about it later. I believe his disposition has a lot to do with his youth. Mills is much younger than Somerset. He thinks he knows everything, and he is just ready to get out into the field and work. He really doesn't want to spend the time to research. He would rather be out working and believes that he can make his decisions when faced with the problem. He doesn't believe he needs a set plan. He knows that breaking into an apartment is wrong, so he gets around it by paying off a homeless woman to tell the policeman that Mills and Somerset should search the apartment. He sneaked around his ethics and ended up doing what he knew he wanted to do anyway.

You've clarified your analysis of Mills, which is good. But it still seems to need evidence from the film to support your argument.

In the climax of the movie, Mills faces the biggest ethical struggle of the whole movie when he is deciding whether or not to kill John Doe. He just learned that Doe killed his wife out of envy. Doe also tells Mills that his wife was pregnant, a fact that Mills didn't know. Can you imagine what must have been going through his mind? You can easily see on his face the internal struggle he is going through. He obviously believes that murder is wrong, but he also obviously believes in revenge. He can't just turn his head when he finds out that Doe has just killed his wife, Tracy, but he knows that the only way to get even is to kill him. So he fights with himself. Does he kill Doe and show his true wrath, or does he let Doe live, and never truly avenge Tracy's murder? You can easily see that he knows murder is wrong, otherwise, he would have just killed Doe right away. Instead, he goes back and forth with himself. As an investigator, his job is to help people, and he has a hard time deciding whether or not to uphold his job's ideals. John Doe killed his wife. She is all he had in the city. Could he turn from the job he is so passionate about and avenge Tracy's death?

Can he break his own ethics? Yes. In the end, Mills has a flash of Tracy and kills Doe. It was the only way Mills could make things right in his mind.

John Doe's ethics are so askew, but in his mind, he is perfectly sane. He believes that what he is doing is fine, because he does not see his actions as murder. He sees himself as teaching a lesson to society. He is preaching. He doesn't see his victims as victims of murder. Instead, he only sees the sin that they have committed. To him, they are nothing more than sinners. God gave him the mission of getting rid of sin in the world, and his victims are nothing more than a job he is completing. They mean nothing. He doesn't see that he is committing murder. Instead, he is doing a great work for God. The only sin he sees himself committing is envy. He is able to overlook his own sin of murder, but he does not overlook his victims' sins. We see his victims as innocent civilians, but Doe sees them as filthy sinners, and he believes that by killing the sinners, he is doing a good thing. He believes that God told him to do it, so that makes it OK. His ethics tell him that he is ridding the world of evil, just as God told him to do. In his mind, he is doing nothing wrong. He is completely blind to his own sin.

Very good analysis of Doe! Could you use any scenes or lines from the film to help illustrate Doe's ethical beliefs?

As crazy as it may sound, I see a lot of society in John Doe. It is so easy for people in society today to point out everyone else's sins and flaws but go around as if they are totally innocent. They walk around all day making judgments about the people they encounter but never stop to think that they are no better. By only focusing on everyone else's flaws, somehow society forgets about its own. They get so caught up in everyone else's business that they never have to worry about their own ethics. It's the same with John Doe. He gets so caught up worrying about what everybody else is doing that he completely disregards the fact that he has killed six people. By only worrying about what other people are doing wrong, society has become blind to its own ethics. It needs to stop being a John Doe and begin being itself again.

Everyone has their own ethics, and at some point, everyone has broken their own code of ethics. Just as Somerset disregards the fact that Mills killed Doe, just as Mills finally crossed his line, and just as Doe himself ignores his own crime, so have we crossed our own lines. When people think that they are so much better than John Doe, they should remember how similar they really are.

It is easy to see that each main character has a unique set of ethics. Somerset's ethics tell him to take his time and really absorb all the information he can. Mills, on the other hand, believes that his job is better done in the field instead of from behind a book. He is very eager to go out to the crime scenes without knowing very much about them at all. Finally, John Doe has his own unique set of ethics too. While the society doesn't understand why he did the things he did, the murders made perfect sense to John Doe. It's because of his ethical system that he was able to commit six murders with a sound mind.

The point is, what is right for one person may not be right for all people. As long as no harm is done, I believe that every person is entitled to their own set of beliefs. Society should quit worrying about others' shortcomings and begin worrying about their own. The book of Matthew, chapter seven, verse three of the *New International Version of the Bible* says it perfectly when it states, "Why do you look at the speck of sawdust in your brother's eye and pay no attention to the plank in your own eye?"

Works Cited

The Internet Movie Database. 2007. 27 Feb 2007 <http://www.imdb.com>.

New International Version Bible. Anaheim: Foundation, 1997.

Se7en. Dir. David Fincher. 1995.

Good job revising here. You've expanded your analysis of ethics in general and interwoven Doe's decisions into this part of your argument. You've used a much more formal tone here than in your last draft, but this suits the rest of your paper much better.

Good summary of your arguments. Interesting use of a Bible quote in your conclusion, given the nature of Doe's ethical beliefs.

ten steps to help you edit

1. Set the work aside for a time after revising.
2. Participate in editing workshops if available in your classes.
3. Use your resources: previous papers, the Writing Center, and your instructor.
4. Know your problem areas.
5. Read aloud, to yourself or to another person, to avoid self-correcting or thinking you have written the correct form because your mind automatically puts in the correct form when you read to yourself.
6. Read backward, starting with the last sentence, to ensure a focus on editing, not revision.
7. Learn tricks, such as acronyms like FANBOYS (coordinating conjunctions: for, and, nor, but, or, yet, so) and THINTIC (conjunctive adverbs: therefore, however, indeed, nevertheless, thus, in fact, consequently), to help you remember rules or common lists.
8. Use your tools. Keep your dictionary, thesaurus, grammar handbook, class notes, and handouts nearby when editing.
9. Have someone else read your work for proofreading errors, clarity, and sensitivity to audience.
10. Know that you will always have to edit your writing or work. You cannot depend on others to do it for you.

FOR FURTHER READING

Glenn, Cheryl, and Loretta Gray. *The Writer's Harbrace Handbook*, 3rd ed. Boston: Heinle, 2006.

King, Stephen. *On Writing.* New York: Pocket Books, 2002.

Lamott, Anne. *Bird by Bird: Some Instructions on Writing and Life.* New York: Anchor Books, 1995.

Strunk, William, Jr., E. B. White, and Roger Angell. *The Elements of Style*, 4th ed. Boston: Allyn and Bacon, 1999.

Truss, Lynne. *Eats, Shoots and Leaves: The Zero Tolerance Approach to Punctuation.* New York: Gotham Books, 2006.

Zinsser, William K. *On Writing Well: The Classic Guide to Writing Nonfiction.* New York: Collins, 2006.

defining
popular culture

Matt: "You've covered presidential campaigns, you've covered presidents, you've covered wars, what are you writing about a TV show for?"

Martha: "I'm writing about it because what happens here is important. . . . I think popular culture in general and this show in particular are important."

Tom (to Matt): "Excuse me. Wardrobe wanted you to approve this."

Matt: "Yeah, it's good." (pause) "Hang on. It's supposed to be a lobster costume, right?"

Tom: "Yeah."

Matt: "Yeah, then it's fine."

Tom: "Great."

—From *Studio 60 on the Sunset Strip*

1 **Writing About Pop Culture:** What founder of *Ms. Magazine* claimed, "I don't like to write. I like to have written"?

    a. Jane Fonda
    b. Debbie Stoller
    c. Gloria Steinem
    d. Betty Friedan

TEST YOUR POP CULTURE IQ: WHAT IS POP CULTURE?

2 **Defining Pop Culture:** Who boasted to *The Source* in 1994, "I AM Hip-Hop"?

    a. Tupac
    b. L. L. Cool J
    c. Ice-T
    d. Dr. Dre

3 **Advertisements:** Which television advertisement was voted best of all time by *TV Guide*?

    a. "Hare Jordan" Nike (1992)
    b. "1984" Apple Computers (1984)
    c. "Where's the beef?" Wendy's (1984)
    d. "Brilliant!" Guinness (2003)

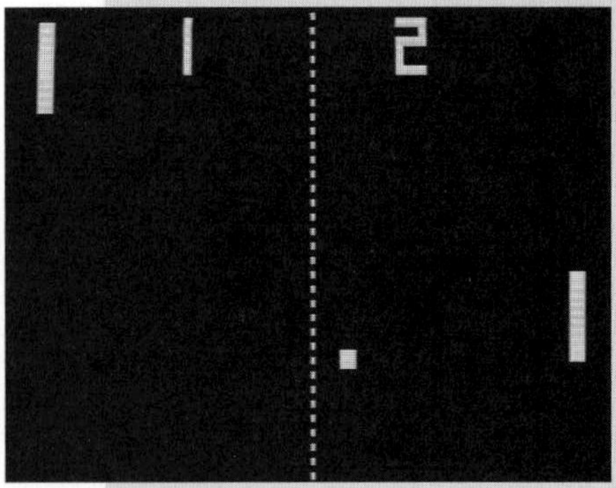

4 **Sports and Leisure:** Which 1972 PC game imitated the sport of tennis?

    a. Pong
    b. Galaga
    c. Pac Man
    d. Defender

© 2003 Jeremy English

5 **Groups, Spaces, and Places:** In March 2006, the Hells Angels Motorcycle Club sued which group for copyright infringement?

    a. The Rolling Stones
    b. The Los Angeles Police Department
    c. The Walt Disney Company
    d. The American Motorcyclist Association

6 **Music:** The now defunct New York club CBGB Omfug, opened by Hilly Kristal and operating from 1973–2006, stands for

    a. City Boys and Girls Boogie
    b. City Bands Groove in the Bowery
    c. Currently Booking Great Bands
    d. Country, Bluegrass, Blues

7 **Popular Literature:** What 1986 book became the fastest-selling hardcover book of all time, spending more than half of its fifty weeks on *The New York Times* Best-Sellers List as number 1?

    a. Bill Cosby's *Fatherhood*
    b. Tom Clancy's *Clear and Present Danger*
    c. Jackie Collins's *Hollywood Wives*
    d. Priscilla Presley's *Elvis and Me*

8 **Film:** How many film versions of *Romeo and Juliet* have been produced?

    a. Two
    b. Six
    c. Ten
    d. More than ten

9 **Television:** Which of these animated series is a spin-off?

    a. *Daria*
    b. *King of the Hill*
    c. *Beavis and Butthead*
    d. All of the above

© MTV/The Kobal Collection

10 **Researching and Documenting Pop Culture:** Who said that he did not sample Queen and David Bowie's "Under Pressure" in a 1990 song because Queen and Bowie's version was "Ding, ding, ding, dingy, ding, ding" and his was "Ding, ding, ding, ding, dingy, ding, ding"?

    a. Snow
    b. Vanilla Ice
    c. Eminem
    d. Marky Mark

ANSWERS

1 *c. Gloria Steinem* **2** *b. L. L. Cool J* **3** *b. "1984" Apple Computers* **4** *a. Pong* **5** *c. The Walt Disney Company*
6 *d. Country, Bluegrass, Blues* **7** *a. Bill Cosby's* Fatherhood **8** *d. More than ten* **9** *d. All of the above* **10** *b. Vanilla Ice*

> "Bruce Springsteen, Madonna
>
> Way before Nirvana
>
> There was U2 and Blondie
>
> And music still on MTV (woohoohoo)
>
> Her two kids in high school
>
> They tell her that she's uncool
>
> 'Cause she's still preoccupied
>
> With 19, 19, 1985"
>
> **—From "1985" by Bowling for Soup**

In their 2004 hit, Bowling for Soup sings about a mother who is still living in the pop culture of her teens and the teenage children who are embarrassed by their mother's inability to adapt to contemporary pop culture (see the lyrics above). Like these teens, many people think that popular culture is only what is happening right now immediately around them; however, popular culture bridges generations, decades, and levels of significance. It is the Afro from the 1970s, Madonna singing "Like a Virgin" from the 1980s, and our nation's reaction to the collapse of the World Trade Center in the 2000s. Popular culture stretches across time to influence and create our language, our interests, our activities, our environment, our beliefs, our opinions, and our identities.

Popular culture became an academic subject in 1967 when Ray B. Browne first conceived the idea for *The Journal of Popular Culture*, and its initiation into the university environment continues today. Popular culture has been defined in many different ways by those who study it. Basically, though, popular culture includes any product (Sarah Jessica Parker's clothing line, *Bitten*), lifestyle (snowboarding), environment (Radio City Music Hall), idea (the creation of a character in an role-playing game), or event (the Super Bowl) that is widely known or received by many people. More often than not, the general population accepts this piece of popular culture. At a deeper and sometimes controversial level, popular culture includes the cultural patterns within a population, such as those items and ideas that appeal more commonly to the working class or the majority culture. Examples may be as varied as the use of grassroots politics and web campaigning to reach a broader audience in presidential elections or the requirement for women to wear head scarves in certain cultures. Finally, although those who study popular culture in academia would probably not agree, popular culture is often considered "low culture" compared to what is sometimes called "high art" or "high culture." Low culture is Lil' Kim; high culture is Josh Groban. Low culture is *The Jerry Springer Show*; *The Sopranos* is the high art of TV. Low culture is NASCAR; high culture is lacrosse. If popular culture is considered the opposite of high culture, then that suggests that a traditional opera such as *La Boheme* is a more valid means of cultural expression than a rock opera such as *Jesus Christ Superstar* or that *Miss Saigon* is a more authentic theater production than *Seussical the Musical*. These definitions—some very broad and others narrower—are obviously controversial because of the biases for or against popular culture that they suggest.

Like some scholars, you might think that the term *popular culture* is a contradiction. To many of us, "culture" often means the most impressive or important contributions to a civilization, such as the construction of the Sears Tower or the composition of George Gershwin's "Rhapsody in Blue." "Popular," on the other hand, often refers to something that is common, ordinary, or generally accepted among the masses, such as "Mother" tattoos and Laffy Taffy candy. Due to this discrepancy, early scholars of popular culture used the term *mass culture*, though this term is not generally used today because it is considered insulting, as it seems to refer to people as groups or masses of unthinking participants or users of non-elite culture. Just as artifacts of high culture are produced for an audience's pleasure, appreciation, and education, so, too, is popular culture.

Trends and History

In fact, many aspects of high art were once a part of popular culture. The most common example is the writing of William Shakespeare. When writing in the sixteenth century, Shakespeare was a popular poet and playwright enjoyed by both commoners and royalty. Because they were so well liked, Shakespeare's company of players became the King's Men, who both wrote and performed for King James I. Shakespeare, however, was not considered a poet of high stature in the Renaissance, as was Philip Sidney or Edmund Spenser, who was granted a high political position because of his popularity. Of course, today, Shakespeare is considered a part of the literary canon taught to all and a representative of high culture.

Other areas of popular culture may also make the switch from what is considered low culture to high culture. For example, fusion cuisine, the combination of traditional culinary products (such as grits, collard greens, and country ham in the South) with gourmet techniques and ingredients (such as caviar and crème fraiche or techniques such as sushi rolling or the use of organic farming), has become increasingly popular. Whereas grits were once considered a food of the common person because of economics and availability, now they are being incorporated into foods served in upscale restaurants that may be inaccessible to the original consumers because of location, reputation, or cost.

The opposite of this trend may occur as well when elements of high culture modify their presentation or composition to appeal to a wider audience. For example, Cirque du Soleil attempted to break into popular culture through its run on Bravo network, its new theatrical production in Las Vegas, and its incorporation of music from The Beatles in the production *Love*.

Convention + Invention = Popular Culture

Because popular culture is a combination of the likes and needs of millions of consumers, each specific aspect of it can be considered. A variety of questions can be asked, such as why a product or event was created, who produced it, who its target audience is, what similarities or differences it has with other major cultural artifacts, and why this specific combination of attributes is successful. Typically, a popular culture event or artifact is comprised of conventional elements and an element of invention to make it new. For example, *The Flintstones* was a combination of the successful television show *The Honeymooners* and Hanna-Barbera children's cartoons.

What/Who Defines American Popular Culture?

American popular culture is defined by consumers—those who watch *El Mariachi*, purchase MP3s of Martina McBride, wear Maurice Malone fashions, go to the Monster Jam Truck Rally, and eat at McDonald's. These consumers are often discriminating, which explains why every song is not a hit, every film is not a blockbuster, and some television series do not even stay on the air until midseason. However, American popular culture is also defined by the corporations that back the production and dissemination of a certain product, adver-tisement, or event. To explain further, if Interscope Records spends $13 million to produce

grappling with ideas

- Is there such a thing as high culture? If so, what is it?
- Are blockbuster films treated differently in academic circles from indie films?
- Does this film example also translate to advertising? Popular literature?
- Can consumers give value to a text, whether it is a television series, a film, and a piece of popular fiction?
- Is there inherent value in a television series or a film without fans to watch it?

Guns N' Roses' new album, the company will more than likely demand a return on its investment. The band will be expected to tour, appear on MTV, be interviewed for *Spin* or *Rolling Stone*, and behave in such a way that they will become "news." The hype around a new album is not inconsequential; it is the way that a band's future studio work is decided. Many sophomore albums, a band's second effort, are promoted heavily by both the record company and the band because of the rarity of matching the success of a first hit recording. "Selling out" is also a concern of many sophomore efforts because fans often turn on a band that spends more time on promoting itself than on making music.

The benefit of corporate promotion is that it creates a national popular culture, which can unite teenagers in southern California with those in upstate New York through their common interests. Fortunately, though, many consumers are becoming more aware that they are seen only as potential consumers and are vulnerable to corporate, political, and even personal marketing strategies through their access to Facebook, television channels, and sporting events. Corporate promotion of popular culture raises valid concerns about censorship. If one CEO is deciding what music will be played on thousands of radio stations, television soundtracks, and advertisements, then millions of other songs and artists are censored by not having the opportunity to be played or to gain an audience. The Internet, with its ability to reach millions of potential consumers, can assist in the limitations of corporate promotion.

What/Who Defines American Popular Culture Studies?

The study of popular culture is defined by both the scholars of the field and the members of the associations who contribute to the scholarship. The Popular Culture Association (PCA) in conjunction with the American Culture Association (ACA) includes people who enjoy the study of relevant areas of popular culture such as film, television, music, and gaming, and less studied areas of academia like motorcycling, food culture, and the tarot. Both organizations also sponsor resources and publications in the field, the most well-known being *The Journal of Popular Culture*, as well as an annual conference where members and nonmembers gather to present their most recent research in the field.

Regional branches of PCA/ACA also provide insight into the field with their annual conferences and publications. The PCA/ACA has thousands of members internationally, and because of this, the area of study has become increasingly relevant in a number of academic fields. For example, the largest of these regional organizations, the Popular Culture Association of the South (PCAS), produces the journal *Studies in Popular Culture*. Many online journals have also contributed to popular culture studies, like *Americana: The Journal of American Popular Culture*, *Images: A Journal of Film and Popular Culture*, and more specialized journals, including *Slayage: The Online International Journal of Buffy Studies*. Any of these publications are appropriate sources for research into popular culture or appropriate models for learning to write about popular culture for an academic audience.

The Popular Culture Divide

Popular culture is a branch of cultural studies. According to scholar John Storey, cultural studies is more broadly defined as the study of a "particular way of life, either of a people, a period or a group" (*Cultural* 2). American popular culture is obviously a part of American culture;

grapplingwithideas

- Our population is expanding, so our popular culture is as well. However, many people look back to the past and regret this expansion of the popular. Were there really "good ol' days" when life was easier?

- Should the popularity of a book, an advertisement, or a video game make it important for study? Why or why not?

- Is popularity often viewed as a negative aspect of a film or television series? Can this opinion be justified?

however, there is much more included in cultural studies that is not necessarily a part of what is popular. For example, religious hymns, opera, underground rap, and classical music are not always a part of popular culture, though these boundaries can be blurred. These cultural ideas and artifacts can be divided into various categories.

Counterculture or subculture, folk culture, and high culture are not typically considered a part of popular culture, though their study often bleeds into the field. Counterculture or subculture is the cultural development, advancement, or achievement that can take place outside popular culture but also often crosses over into popular culture. Typically, this includes movements such as the rise of rap in the 1970s, the increased marketing of independent films in the 1980s, or the grunge fashion trends of the 1990s. For example, Latin pop music is rooted in Latin American folk cultures and subcultures that are centuries old. However, artists such as Los Lobos, Gloria Estefan, and the Barrio Boyzz helped to popularize Latin pop music in the American music scene. Then, in the late 1990s, the American Music Awards added a category for Favorite Latin Artist, and in 2000, the Latin Grammy Awards were broadcast internationally, signifying the fame of Ricky Martin, Jennifer Lopez, and Shakira for a broader and younger audience. Remnants of what was once only a part of Latin American culture can now be seen, and have been seen, on television screens, in movie theaters, and on iPods across the United States.

grappling with ideas

- What role do American subcultures play within your everyday life?

- Think about your own interests: your favorite film, your appointment television series (the one you make sure to watch weekly), the magazines you subscribe to, and the songs you listened to on the way to class. Do your interests fit into the definition of popular culture? Subculture? Folk culture?

- What about your parents' interests? Your grandparents'?

Folk culture is the lifestyles, artifacts, and traditions—typically determined by locale—of a specific group of people. This culture is usually passed down orally and varies greatly by region. Folk culture can, as it is passed from generation to generation, grow in both its appeal and its appreciation. Bluegrass music and quilt making are good examples of how folk traditions can bleed over into popular culture.

Classical music, art, and literature are often considered branches of high culture. As discussed previously, this distinction should not be seen as a hierarchy. The terms *high* and *low* come from traditional definitions and have nothing to do with the legitimacy of the subjects. However, the difference in these cultures is often determined by money and history. High culture most often merges with popular culture through the use of allusions or references to commonly known works, such as a reference to Biblical passages in *The Da Vinci Code*. Almost every cultural artifact can be viewed through the lens of popular culture because anything that is available to the public eye is popular culture.

Popular Culture Is Academic

Popular culture consumers and participants are valuable to academia because their choices create culture, which impacts and influences future fields of study. Some scholars of popular culture view its study as their social responsibility; to understand a culture, the commonly known, enjoyed, and consumed artifacts, ideas, and events must be studied for their relevance. Others study the influence and impact of popular culture on individuals, on families, and on social institutions such as religion, capitalist structures, and academia itself. Still, many scholars view popular culture as a distraction from more important responsibilities of citizenship and study it from a more critical vantage point; however, since the study of popular culture is relatively new, its own influence and impact are difficult to determine even though the influence of popular culture and popular culture studies on academia is undeniable.

Popular culture researcher Ray B. Browne writes, "Society is dominated by the hard sell of reality, both on campus and off. Popular culture studies urge us to reach out into the world around us and do a more effective job for the intro- duction and understanding of everyday culture. Those students who best understand and participate in their every- day cultures develop into the most useful citizens. The world should not be artificially divided into everyday and 'intellectual' life. Both mix and coextend and are part and parcel of each other" (*Popular* 4).

- Should you separate your academic interests from your cultural interests? What advantages might that give you? What disadvantages might that cause?

- How does popular culture apply to your major area of interest or study?

The field of popular culture also contributes to many forms of art or media, which are often seen as academic. Film, music, television production, and advertising are major contributors to the art world. These forms of expression have surpassed art exhibitions and performances in their appeal and availability. Even visual art exhibits show the influence of popular culture and pop art. One example of this is how photographer David LaChapelle's work has been featured everywhere from Burger King commercials to the cover of *Rolling Stone* to the VH1 fashion awards to small galleries in the Chelsea neighborhood of Manhattan. Another example is how filmmaker Spike Lee's work can be seen on Nike commercials, HBO documentaries, feature-length films, music videos, and an Ecko clothing collection inspired by the film *40 Acres and a Mule*.

Popular Culture in Academics

Popular culture is most often studied in the field of liberal arts. As cultural studies become more popular, many universities are devel- oping separate coursework in the field; however, most commonly, popular culture and cultural studies are currently incorporated into several departments: English, communications, music, fine arts, his- tory, philosophy, women's studies, film, and folklore. Each of these departments may use a different approach to the field of study and may only study a portion of the field. For example, in English, pop culture—even that which is not printed—is studied as a text. A film, song, or dachshund race is analyzed in the same way as a novel, poem, or short story. English scholars look for both the internal and exter- nal meanings of the "text." They may look at the actual subject mat- ter, such as Jay Gatsby's relationship with Daisy, or how the cultural context surrounding the text relates to the subject matter, such as how extramarital affairs were accepted in "The Jazz Age." They may also delve into how actions in the text represent a commonplace example, such as Nick's caution in dealing with Jay and Daisy's relationship. In addition, English scholars often explore how other texts from the time period treat the subject matter—this is referred to as the inter- textuality. In this case, they may look at how other works from the 1920s handle extramarital affairs. And, finally, they may look at the purpose F. Scott Fitzgerald had in writing about this particular rela- tionship. Just as with studying literature as text, all of these internal or external investigations can be applied to the texts of pop culture.

Business colleges may also investigate popular culture. Economics and business departments often offer courses on the big business of popular culture. Blockbuster films, top forty albums, and the Clio Award winners for the best television commercial advertising campaigns often generate large amounts of money for both American and international corporations. These patterns of income are important for study and are important for students to use as models of successful business practices, especially for students in marketing programs. The representation of the business world in popular culture is important for student discussion, as well as the use of popular culture by professors to keep classroom material relevant and contemporary. Students interested in these fields may also study the spread of popular culture through the technology of the Information Age.

Basic and applied sciences, with departments such as anthropology, sociology, psychology, health, and geography, use popular culture to update their models, research, and class investigations. Some would argue that popular culture cannot be studied without some application of these methodologies. Audience studies, regional diversity of what is popular, and the study of what is significant in our (and historical) times all add to the importance of clinical studies in popular culture.

The value of popular culture in education is increasingly understood and accepted. As professors and teachers realize the attraction and relevance of using popular culture to reach their students, more areas of popular culture are being used as classroom resources. Not only can students learn from popular culture, but professors and teachers may use popular culture to bridge the gap between their students' frames of reference and their own. This textbook is an example of how popular culture can increase classroom discussion and debate without requiring extensive knowledge of the subject.

Your Place in Popular Culture/ Popular Culture's Place in You

You are a participant in popular culture. The television shows you watch, the movies you rent, the games you play, the music you listen to on the radio, the online communities you belong to, and the magazines you read are all choices that impact popular culture and that impact you. You are probably more familiar with all of these than the last book you read in high school or the history of traditions in your hometown. Popular culture can be explored on many different levels, but to truly understand or appreciate an artifact of popular culture, you must do more than memorize facts or trivia. Through this exploration, you may find common ground with your friends or family who enjoy television shows, films, or music that you currently do not watch or listen to. Popular culture is aptly named for its wide appeal; however, as you are impacted by popular culture, popular culture is also formed by your choices. Corporations and individuals who produce popular culture need to understand you—your likes and dislikes—to understand how to produce goods that will interest you, goods on which you will spend hard-earned money. Even when you were in grade school, your disposable income was of great interest to these producers. You are a valued consumer and have been considered one since you were a child.

You are also an outsider of popular culture. Think about the following list of words from pop culture with definitions recently added to dictionaries: Bollywood, crackberry, crunk, d'oh, dead

grappling with ideas

Cultural critic John Storey argues, "Our dominant view . . . in discussions of globalization and popular culture is to see it as the reduction of the world to an American 'global village' . . . in which everyone speaks English with an American accent, wears Levi jeans and Wrangler shirts, drinks Coca-Cola, eats at McDonald's, surfs the net on a computer overflowing with Microsoft software, listens to rock or country music, watches a mixture of MTV and CNN news broadcasts, Hollywood movies and reruns of *Dallas*, and then discusses the prophetically named World Series, while drinking a bottle of Budweiser or Miller and smoking Marlboro cigarettes" (*Cultural* 153).

- Is there one representative American culture?

- Are cultures determined nationally or within divisions of race, gender, sexual orientation, and class?

- Is a culture's success driven only by economic expansion? Is America the only country that exports culture?

keytips

- Question everything; nothing should be taken at face value:
  - What topics are being addressed?
  - Who produced this text?
  - Who is the intended audience? How do you know?
  - How is this audience addressed?
  - Does the text have a single author? A corporate authorship?
  - What do you know about the author(s)?
- Be honest with yourself and your judgments; if you do (or do not) enjoy a text, ask why.
- Find connections in the content. What does the text remind you of? Are there allusions to other texts in or out of popular culture?
- Conquer confusion; "I don't know" isn't an answer, but it may lead to interesting questions.
- Do not let the message manipulate you; again, always questioning is the answer!
- Find evidence to support your judgments; always back yourself up with facts from the text.
- Do not depend on those who are paid to make judgments—be an independent thinker. Often, media outlets that review a film are owned by the same company that produced the film. Are their judgments always going to be critical and valid?

presidents, dumpster diving, DVR, fanboy, Frankenfood, ginormous, gray literature, headbanger, java jacket, LOL, longneck, McJob, mouse potato, muggle, podcasting, soul patch, spoiler, straightedge, supersize, telenova, wiki. How many can you define? Do you know where each word originated? It is impossible for any individual to be familiar with all popular films, songs, advertisements, organizations, or sporting events. Although you may be an expert in any one or two of these areas, it would take a great deal of time and devotion to keep up with all popular culture as it is currently produced, marketed, and consumed. For example, to familiarize yourself with the back catalogs of advertising alone would take years of careful research and study. Therefore, many areas of popular culture are left to be explored. Perhaps your study of this textbook could lead you to a film, organization, or television show—that is new or new to you—to spark a pursuit in an area of popular culture that you were previously unaware of. Talking to those who were born or who grew up in a different time than you may also help you find artifacts of past popularity to discuss and explore. Although it is nice to have a background of popular culture interests as your frame of reference, to apply your prior knowledge about pop culture to an unfamiliar subject might encourage critical thinking and an adaptation of these new thinking and writing skills throughout your college career.

Critical Reading and Viewing of Popular Culture

All popular culture can be considered a text. A film, an advertisement, or a sporting event may all be mainly visual texts, whereas most music and radio advertising is an auditory text. Even an organization can be considered a text by looking at its history, traditions, and agendas. To analyze popular culture as an academic text, remember a few tips. Do not take anything you read or view at face value. Often, in popular culture, the main argument of a text may be hard to identify; it may be hidden beneath comedy, new trends, or interesting characters. However, this does not mean that the argument is any less important. It is significant to determine what is being conveyed to a mass audience, whether consciously or subconsciously, and to examine how American culture is being portrayed.

In *The Pop Culture Zone*, popular culture is connected to composition because of its controversy, its relationship to you—the reader—and its significance in society. While composing your thoughts about texts within popular culture, use your frame of reference and your new experiences with these texts by asking the Grappling with Ideas questions and considering their answers.

Reseeing Popular Culture

The Pop Culture Zone uses the contact zone theoretical model to help you think critically about the impact and influences of pop culture. By using this model, the text asks for personal reflection and analysis from you, your classmates, and your instructor to engage in discussion about how American popular culture impacts you. See Chapter 1, The Pop Culture Zone, for more information on how this approach can help you as you progress through your academic career.

Popular culture is reviewed and analyzed in a variety of resources, from magazines to online journals to satires, such as *Saturday Night Live, In Living Color,* and *MadTV.* Television series and magazines are often in the unique position of both responding to popular culture and creating popular culture at the same time. For this reason, critical thinking and viewing are incredibly important, and a minimal amount of research may often be involved to find where a trend began, how cultural critics are responding to a text, or to get basic facts about a text's production. The Internet is typically the most effective way to research contemporary popular culture, although more and more texts are being published and produced to help with your study. Internet research, once considered an ineffective method of investigation, is now essential to keep up to date with current cultural texts. It is important, though, for you to make sure that the information you find on the Internet is from a reputable source. Pay close attention to the guidelines in Chapter 11, Researching and Documenting in the Pop Culture Zone, for more information.

Areas of Study from the Popular Culture Association/American Culture Association

The following list from the Popular Culture Association/American Culture Association demonstrates the variety of subject areas that are considered American popular culture. Take a minute to peruse these subject areas and think about your major interests within popular culture. This list may help you when brainstorming for essay topics. For more help in prewriting activities, see Chapter 2, Writing in the Pop Culture Zone.

ACADEMIC CULTURE

Academics ACA
Collegiate Culture: Higher Ed & Pedagogy PCA
Language Attitudes & Popular Linguistics PCA
Popular Culture & Education/ Teaching & History PCA
Popular Culture, Rhetoric & Composition PCA
Technical Communication PCA
Two-Year Colleges PCA

BUSINESS & PROFESSIONAL CULTURE

Business/Corporate Culture PCA
Professional Placement PCA
Technical Communication PCA

ENTERTAINMENT & TRAVEL CULTURE

Automobile Culture PCA
Celebrity Culture PCA
Circuses & Circus Culture PCA
Festivals & Faires PCA
Travel and Tourism PCA
World's Fairs & Expositions PCA

ETHNIC STUDIES & CULTURE

African-American Culture PCA
American Indian Lit. & Cultures ACA
Asian Popular Culture PCA
Black Music Culture PCA/ACA
Caribbean & Latin American Literature & Culture PCA
Chicana/o Culture: Literature, Film, Theory PCA

From Popular Culture Association/ American Culture Association

(continued)

FILM, TELEVISION, & RADIO CULTURE

Adaptation (Film, TV, Lit. & Electronic Gaming
   ACA
Adolescence in Film & Television ACA
Children's Television PCA
Documentary PCA
Film & History PCA
Film Adaptation PCA
Film and Media Studies PCA
Film PCA
Humanities & Popular Cultures PCA/ACA
Musicals, Stage & Film PCA
Radio PCA
Shakespeare on Film and Television PCA
Slapstick Comedy/Early TV PCA
Soap Opera PCA
Television PCA
The Vampire in Literature, Culture & Film PCA/ACA
Westerns & the West PCA

GENDER CULTURE

Cultural Conflict & Women PCA/ACA
Gay & Lesbian Studies PCA/ACA
Gender & Media Studies PCA
Gender Studies PCA
Masculinities ACA
Masculinities PCA
Men/Men's Studies PCA
Sports PCA/ACA
Women's Lives & Literature PCA
Women's Studies ACA

GEOGRAPHIC CULTURE

Appalachian Studies ACA
Border Culture (Political, Cultural,
   Geographical) PCA/ACA
Geography PCA
Midwest Culture ACA
New England Studies ACA
Vietnam PCA
Westerns & the West PCA
World Popular Culture PCA

HISTORIC & FOLK CULTURE

Appalachian Studies ACA
Baby-Boomer Culture PCA/ACA
Cemeteries & Gravemarkers ACA
Civil War & Reconstruction PCA/ACA
Film & History PCA
Festivals & Faires PCA
Folklore PCA
Medieval Popular Culture PCA

Popular Culture in the Age of Theodore
   Roosevelt PCA
Popular History in American Culture PCA
Postcolonial Studies ACA
The Sixties PCA
Sports PCA/ACA
World Popular Culture PCA

HUMOR CULTURE

Comedy and Humor ACA
Slapstick Comedy/Early TV PCA
Sports PCA/ACA

INTERNATIONAL CULTURE

Asian Popular Culture PCA
British Popular Culture PCA
Caribbean & Latin American Literature
   & Culture PCA
European Literature & Culture (excl. UK
   and Germany) PCA
German Literature and Culture PCA
World Popular Culture PCA

LITERATURE & LITERARY CULTURE

Adaptation (Film, TV, Lit. & Electronic
   Gaming) ACA
American Literature PCA
Arthurian Legends PCA
Biographies PCA
Children's Lit. & Culture PCA
Contemporary American Prison Writing PCA
Creative Fiction Writing PCA
Detective & Mystery Fiction PCA/ACA
Dime Novels/Pulps/Juvenile Series Books PCA
Eros, Pornography & Popular Culture PCA
Gothic Literature PCA
Heinlein Studies PCA
Horror (Fiction, Film) PCA
Humanities & Popular Cultures PCA/ACA
Jack London's Life & Works PCA
Literature & Society ACA
Literature & Visual Arts PCA
Literature and Politics ACA
Literature and Science ACA
Madness in Literature PCA
Medieval Popular Culture PCA
Motorcycling Culture and Myth PCA/ACA
Non-Fiction Writing PCA
Poetry Studies PCA
Poetry, Creative PCA
Popular American Authors PCA/ACA
Romance PCA

(continued)

Science Fiction/Fantasy PCA
Sea Literature PCA/ACA
Shakespeare & the Elizabethan Age in Popular
    Culture PCA
Southern Creative Writing (reflects Southern
    Culture & Tradition) PCA
Southern Literature and Culture PCA
Sports PCA/ACA
Stephen King PCA/ACA
The Vampire in Literature, Culture, & Film
    PCA/ACA
Women's Lives & Literature PCA

MATERIAL CULTURE

Automobile Culture PCA
Collecting & Collectibles PCA
Fashion, Appearance, & Consumer ID
    PCA/ACA
Food in Popular Culture PCA
Libraries, Archives, & Popular Culture Research
    PCA
Material Culture ACA
Motorcycling Culture and Myth PCA/ACA
Senior Culture: Seniors and Aging PCA

MEDIA CULTURE

Advertising PCA
Gender & Media Studies PCA
Journalism & Media Culture ACA
Journalism PCA
Media Bias & Distortion PCA
Film and Media Studies PCA

MUSIC CULTURE

Black Music Culture PCA/ACA
Hip Hop Culture (Black Music Culture) PCA/
    ACA
Music PCA
Music ACA
Musicals, Stage & Film PCA
Rock, Film & Contemp. Arts ACA

PHYSICAL & HEALTH CULTURE

The Body and Physical Difference PCA
Fashion, Appearance & Consumer Identity
    PCA/ACA
Fat Studies PCA
Health & Disease in Popular Culture PCA
Senior Culture: Seniors and Aging PCA
Sports PCA/ACA

POLITICS, LAW, & POLITICAL CULTURE

Literature and Politics ACA
Motorcycling Culture and Myth PCA/ACA
Politics in a Mediated World ACA
Politics, Law & Popular Culture PCA

RELIGION & RELIGIOUS CULTURE

Culture & Religion PCA
Jewish Studies PCA

SOCIAL ISSUES & CULTURE

Animal Culture PCA
Collective Behavior: Panics, Fads & Hostile
    Outbursts PCA
Ecology and Culture ACA
Protest Issues & Actions PCA
Senior Culture: Seniors and Aging PCA

TECHNOLOGY CULTURE

Adaptation (Film, TV, Lit. & Elec. Gaming) ACA
Automobile Culture PCA
Digital Games PCA
Electronic Communication & Culture PCA
Internet Culture PCA
Technical Communication PCA

THEORY, MYTH, & CULTURAL BELIEFS

Conspiracy Theory/Claims for the Paranormal
    PCA
Memory & Representation PCA
Mythology in Contemporary Culture PCA
Philosophy and Popular Culture PCA

VISUAL CULTURE & THE ARTS

American Art & Architecture ACA
Comic Art & Comics PCA
Dance Culture PCA/ACA
Eros, Pornography & Popular Culture PCA
Humanities & Popular Cultures PCA/ACA
Literature & Visual Arts PCA
Musicals, Stage & Film PCA
Popular Art, Architecture & Design PCA
Tarot PCA
Theatre PCA/ACA
Visual Culture PCA/ACA

WAR & CULTURE

Civil War & Reconstruction PCA/ACA
Vietnam PCA
World War I & II PCA

The following reading is a sample essay on a general topic in popular culture: Oprah's influence on almost every subject in this text from the obvious, television, to Broadway music, popular literature, film, advertising, and leisure activities. This essay should encourage you to practice your critical thinking skills while preparing for the more specified readings in the following chapters.

Reading Selection: Defining Popular Culture

CONSIDERING IDEAS

1. How does television's popularity and easy access affect other areas of popular culture, such as popular literature, film, and music?
2. Does Oprah Winfrey's gold thumb signify a positive or a negative attribute of American culture?
3. Could the rise of Internet advertising, podcasting, or web viewing interrupt Winfrey's media dominance?

Carmen Wong Ulrich *is a Dominican American from New York City. She has written for several magazines, including* Essence *and* Health, *and she is a former editor of both* Latina *magazine and* Money *magazine. Her most popular book,* Gener@tion Debt: Take Control of Your Money—A How-to Guide, *focuses on money management strategies for young adults. "The Oprah Effect" was published in* Essence *in 2006.*

THE OPRAH EFFECT

Carmen Wong Ulrich

Lisa Price was at a crossroads. By 2002, Carol's Daughter, the bath and beauty products business she had founded in her Brooklyn kitchen, had hit $2 million in sales. "We were trying to decide whether to scale back to keep control of costs or find investors to keep growing," she recalls. Twenty minutes later, the phone rang. It was a producer from *The Oprah Winfrey Show* asking Price to come on the program.

The effect of Price's appearance was astounding: the Carol's Daughter Web site nearly crashed from the high volume of orders that came in after Oprah raved about the products. "What it did was give us a stamp of approval," Price says. The company easily attracted new investors such as Jada Pinkett Smith, celebrity endorsements from Mary J. Blige and mass market distribution in stores like Sephora.

Such is the power of Oprah. She arguably holds more sway in making—or breaking—an individual (James Frey, anyone?), a business (Carol's Daughter and hundreds more), a book (too many to mention) or an industry (the beef brouhaha in 1998) than anyone, ever, in this country—and maybe even the world. She's our $1.4 billion woman—and that's just with her sprawling media empire. Factor in her ability to subtly endorse products without ever appearing in a commercial or an ad, and her economic impact magnifies. She has made her mark on the retail landscape, seemingly fueled the exponential growth of online shopping, transformed the book industry, made giving to charity a priority for millions, and exposed new audiences to Broadway. Consider this: If every one of her 49 million viewers and 2.4 million magazine readers bought just one Oprah-sanctioned item a month, for say $10, that would equal a whopping $6.168 billion a year pumped into America's economy. That's about how much Starbucks made last year, worldwide.

TELEVISION

The Oprah Winfrey Show, now 20 years old, has been No. 1 for 19 seasons. Before Oprah decided to stop submitting the show for Emmy consideration, it won 35 Emmy Awards. It is her most popular showcase, and it's broadcast to 122 countries.

The show (Harpo Productions) is the platform for her business, Harpo, Inc., which has grown and diversified. Harpo, Inc., now includes Harpo Films (*Beloved, Tuesdays With Morrie, Their Eyes Were Watching God*), Harpo Radio (a $55 million deal with XM satellite radio for the new Oprah & Friends channel) and Harpo Print

The Oprah Magazine and O at Home with Hearst), as well as a deal with Oxygen Media and the Oxygen network.

BOOKS

In a 2004 study, Brigham Young University found that Winfrey's book club recommendations had a greater influence on book sales than anything else in the history of modern publishing. Says Sara Nelson, editor-in-chief of *Publishers Weekly*, "Oprah is getting people who were not particularly reading, to read."

It's her 59-and-counting book club picks that usually get the most press, but Oprah gets thousands of books moving in other ways. From April 2005 to April 2006, 162 books got a plug on her show. Kerry McCloskey went on the show in early April 2006 touting her research on sex and passion as the best slim-down plan in her book, *The Ultimate Sex Diet* (True Courage Press). According to Nielsen Bookscan, the week after her appearance, McCloskey's book sales shot up 1,260 percent. Harville Hendrix, Ph.D., also got a lot of love when he appeared on the show twice in April 2006, pushing sales of his *Getting the Love You Want* (Owl Books) up 849 percent.

MAGAZINES

O, The Oprah Magazine was the most successful magazine launch in publishing history: It has a circulation of 2.4 million, it reaches 16.3 million total readers each month, and it's now available in a South African edition. Her magazines are also a lush outlet of product love, lining the coffers of thousands of vendors and retailers. Each issue of *O* features celebrities and experts and books and products that just

ache to be purchased. The spring 2006 issue of *O at Home,* for example, showcased 71 products in one story.

PRODUCT PICKS

She doesn't do traditional endorsements. You'll never see Oprah's name on sneakers or clothes. Instead, her interest is in spreading her passions. Oprah likes to promote what she thinks is important and useful. We follow—and spend in droves. "She influences the purchase of 20 to 25 percent of all goods. I think Oprah is actually underestimated," says Michael Silverstein, coauthor of *Treasure Hunt: Inside the Mind of the New Consumer* (Portfolio). Oprah's product bacchanal hits its pinnacle with "Oprah's Favorite Things—The Holiday Edition." This list of items has included everything from Burberry coats to computers and chocolate.

For every several thousand of Oprah "blessings," a few turn out not so rosy. Though her 2005 audience giveaway of brand-new Pontiac G6's was trumpeted as the epitome of successful product placement, the automotive press was not all convinced. "It was great for Oprah, but I didn't see much on Pontiac. I didn't hear her say, 'This is a Pontiac kind of day,'" said Lincoln Merrihew, managing director of automotive practice at Compete Inc., in *WardsAuto.com*.

Still, for most vendors, there is nothing like an Oprah blessing, says Rob Walker, the consumer columnist for *The New York Times Magazine*. "If you have a product, there's no better environment to be in than on *Oprah*. You're being treated as almost a religious artifact," he says.

Large retailers, such as Sony, see a nice jump in sales, but Oprah also picks small vendors like Pamela Fitzpatrick. Her $39.99 tub of oatmeal raisin cookie dough from Chicago's gourmet grocery Fox & Obel was chosen as a Favorite Thing for holiday 2005. "It was really like winning the Academy Award," Fitzpatrick says, adding that the first 220 sales came 45 minutes into the show. They then sold around 600 tubs in the first two weeks after the show aired, and over the holidays they sold three times that many.

PHILANTHROPY

Oprah's desire to help those in need has been a lifeline to many charities and nonprofits. The Reverend Gloria White-Hammond, chairperson of the Million Voices for Darfur campaign, was certainly pleased. "Oprah's impact on the Save Darfur Coalition's effort was nothing short of tremendous," she says. According to the Coalition, donations went up 1,200 percent in the three days after Oprah highlighted their efforts on her show, and 1,600 percent more donors signed up in the same time. Translation: Many lives were saved in Darfur.

What seems to bolster her featured charities and retailers most is the limitless resource that is oprah.com. "When Oprah does something, there is an immediate 'click' impact," says Heather Dougherty, senior analyst at Nielsen/Net Ratings. For example, take the month that the Save Darfur Coalition was featured on *The Oprah Winfrey Show*. According to Dougherty, oprah.com had 2.2 million unique visitors. "She has a very deep site. The deeper the site, the better the engagement," Dougherty says. "Other compara-

ble sites are so small [number of visitors], we don't measure them."

F.O.O.'S: FRIENDS OF OPRAH

Oprah's protégés serve both as brand extensions and as a fire under her seat. Dr. Phil's success has been its own phenomenon—he now has the second-highest-rated talk show and eight best-selling books, is the new spokesperson for Match.com, and has prime-time TV specials and the Dr. Phil Foundation. Others who've benefited include her crowned boy wonder, interior designer Nate Berkus, with his own home line at Linens 'n Things; Bob Greene, Oprah's personal trainer and fitness guru; Suze Orman, money diva; Mehmet Oz, M.D., health guru; and her two newest additions, Robin Smith, love and relationship psychologist, and Rachael Ray, the smiley TV chef (whose new show is produced by Harpo Productions) and magazine powerhouse in her own right. And, of course, there's Gayle King—Oprah's BFF and editor-at-large of *O, The Oprah Magazine*, who, at press time, was still churning in the rumor mill as a possible cohost to join ABC talkfest *The View*.

ETC., ETC., ETC.

What's left? Ah yes, Broadway. Ms. Winfrey's producer credit for Alice Walker's *The Color Purple* on Broadway surely had something to do with its outrageous opening ticket sales—$16 million in two months—and possibly its 11 Tony nominations. But, more than the bursting moneybags and accolades for the show (this in a business with a 75 percent failure rate), what's significant is, as with her book club, Ms. Winfrey has brought new audiences to Broadway.

With every venture, Oprah somehow finds more to do, more needs to fill, and more ways to make and use her money—and her power. The Live Your Best Life speaking tour and online multimedia workshop is a standing-room-only event every year. She's released a six-disc DVD set of her Twentieth Anniversary Celebration with all pro-ceeds going to the Angel Network, her charitable foundation that has raised $50 million in five years and $10 million for Hurricane Katrina victims. And in October 2005 she launched a Child Predator Watch List that has captured four sexual predators and has rewarded those who located them with $100,000. It is undeniable. Oprah has the Midas touch.

So what will Her Highness turn into gold next? We're all watching.

DECODING THE TEXT

1. What is the author's purpose in describing Winfrey's control on the whole of popular culture?

2. Does the author make a judgment on whether Winfrey's significance benefits the African-American community? Why does she make a judgment or refrain from making a judgment?

CONNECTING TO YOUR CULTURE

1. Has Winfrey impacted your purchases? Have you read a book from her book club, subscribed to her magazine, or bought one of her "favorite things"?

2. If so, why did you make the choice to purchase the goods? If not, why are you exempt from her endorsements?

3. How does product placement affect your other purchasing decisions? How does it affect the decisions of your family and friends?

FOR FURTHER READING

Belton, John, ed. *Movies and Mass Culture.* New Brunswick, NJ: Rutgers UP, 1996.

Bright, Brenda Jo, and Liza Bakewell, eds. *Looking High and Low: Art and Cultural Identity.* Tucson: U of Arizona P, 1995.

Browne, Ray B., ed. *Mission Underway: The History of the Popular Culture Association/American Culture Association and the Popular Culture Movement, 1967–2001.* Bowling Green, OH: PCA/APA, 2002.

Fiske, John. *Television Culture.* London: Routledge, 1987.

Freccero, Carla. *Popular Culture: An Introduction.* New York: NYUP, 1999.

Giroux, Henry A. *Disturbing Pleasures: Learning Popular Culture.* NY: Routledge, 1994.

Hebdige, Dick. *Subculture: The Meaning of Style.* London: Routledge, 1981.

Storey, John. *An Introduction to Cultural Theory and Popular Culture.* Athens: U of Georgia P, 1998.

——. *Inventing Popular Culture.* Malden, MA: Blackwell, 2003.

writing about advertisements

"After earning the highest accolades of the advertising industry—
GOT MILK? has not only helped sell millions of gallons of milk, it's
become an all-American icon."

—From "Got Milk? Turns 10"

1 Which product played an important role in the film *Men in Black?*

    a. Armani suits
    b. Ray-Ban sunglasses
    c. Smith and Wesson shotgun
    d. Play-Doh

TEST YOUR POP CULTURE IQ: ADVERTISEMENTS

2 Match the following product to its catchphrase.

1. LifeCall	a. "Can you hear me now?"
2. Burger King	b. "I've fallen and I can't get up!"
3. Dr. Scholl's	c. "Are you gellin'?"
4. Verizon	d. "Have it your way."

3 The BMW 3Z Roadster was featured in which of the following films?

    a. *The Italian Job*
    b. *Gone in 60 Seconds*
    c. *GoldenEye*
    d. *Cars*

4 The MINI Cooper was featured in which of the following films?

    a. *The Italian Job*
    b. *Gone in 60 Seconds*
    c. *GoldenEye*
    d. *Cars*

5 Name the original product or company being parodied in the adjacent ad.

Joe CHEMO

TOBACCO FREE WASHINGTON 298-4479

THE SURGEON GENERAL WARNS THAT SMOKING IS A FREQUENT CAUSE OF WASTED POTENTIAL AND FATAL REGRET.

© AP Photo/Elaine Thompson

6 What brand of candy saw a boost in sales after it was eaten by the alien E.T. in the film *E.T.?*

    a. M&Ms
    b. Snickers
    c. Reese's Pieces
    d. Skittles

7 What company is being spoofed in this subvertisement?

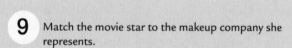

pmsn
Why do you keep bothering me?

© Michael Kovalchick

8 Match the following characters to their products.

    1. Tony the Tiger   a. Froot Loops
    2. Snap, Crackle, and Pop   b. Crunch Berries
    3. Toucan Sam   c. Frosted Flakes
    4. Cap'n Crunch   d. Rice Krispies

9 Match the movie star to the makeup company she represents.

    1. Estée Lauder   a. Penelope Cruz
    2. Elizabeth Arden   b. Gwyneth Paltrow
    3. Cover Girl   c. Queen Latifah
    4. L'Oréal   d. Catherine Zeta-Jones

10 "Dr. McDreamy," Patrick Dempsey, has signed on to represent what cosmetics company, including the design of his own fragrance?

ANSWERS

1 *b. Ray-Ban sunglasses*   2 *1. b. "I've fallen and I can't get up!" 2. d. "Have it your way." 3. c. "Are you gellin'?" 4. a. "Can you hear me now?"*   3 *c. GoldenEye*   4 *a. The Italian Job*   5 *Camel cigarettes*   6 *c. Reese's Pieces*   7 *MSN*   8 *1. c. Frosted Flakes 2. d. Rice Krispies 3. a. Froot Loops 4. b. Crunch Berries*   9 *1. b. Gwyneth Paltrow 2. d. Catherine Zeta-Jones 3. c. Queen Latifah 4. a. Penelope Cruz*   10 *Avon*

YOU AND ADVERTISEMENTS

Market researchers and analysts estimate that the average American is bombarded with 3,000 to 5,000 ads a day (Yankelovich) from a variety of media and sources—television, radio, films, newspapers, magazines, billboards, direct mailings, telemarketers, and Internet banners and pop-ups, as well as fliers on our windshields, bulletin boards, paintings on cars and buses, posters on the sidewalk or the back of a bathroom stall, and ads on your cell phone. We find many of these ads entertaining or visually and aurally stimulating; others we find annoying and perhaps manipulative. When taken at face value, advertisements are about selling us a product, a service, a cause, or even a person, especially during election times; however, in reality, most ads are selling much more than that. Many critics such as Anthony Cortese claim that advertisers are selling consumers a way of life, a worldview, or a system of values, and that we may not even realize the messages that are really being sold to us. Of course, advertising could also be about art and imagination, especially for the graphic artists, copywriters, music composers, cinematographers, and others who do all of the work that goes into advertisement design and creation.

Advertising is a multibillion-dollar business that underwrites most mass media in the United States. In 2008, a thirty-second commercial during the Super Bowl cost $2.7 million, or $90,000 per second (http://www.superbowl-ads.com). Pregame media hype for the two months leading up to the Super Bowl can cost as much as $200,000 plus commercial airtime. While Super Bowl advertising is the extreme of television commercials, this price gives a general idea of how much many companies are willing to spend, especially now that these big ads are archived online for viewers. Is it the amount of money spent that makes an ad effective, or are there other factors involved? How do these factors affect you as a consumer? What products are you being sold? What cultural ideas are you buying? How can you tell? These are some of the questions you will investigate in this chapter. Your answers to these and other questions you ask about advertisements will give you a starting point for writing about advertisements and their roles in your life and culture as well as the world at large. The reading and writing assignments provided will help you see how others have questioned the messages of advertisements and get you started asking your own probing questions and writing your own answers.

WHY WRITE ABOUT ADVERTISEMENTS?

Although we might think we do, we really do not give much thought to advertisements. We believe that we are too smart and independent to be influenced by the ads we see. Postmodern advertising has helped establish this view by making fun of or parodying its own techniques and purposes. Yet, advertising has become one of the most influential texts we encounter. People drive quickly past billboards, use television commercial time to go to the bathroom, or spend only a few seconds glancing over the advertisements before flipping to the next page of a magazine or newspaper. Therefore, advertisers must effectively use those few seconds to grab the viewer's attention. Advertising agencies spend a great deal of time and money tailoring each ad to appeal to a specific target audience and to achieve a specific purpose. Even the simplest and most direct ads can carry subtle and powerful messages for select groups of people. Evaluating and studying advertisements are important activities that will help shape your understanding of the world we live in. Ads can be very powerful and complex to work on the consumers' subconscious. Ads try to persuade consumers through carefully selected words, images, or symbols; therefore, it is important to develop a strong critical eye for the images and sounds you encounter. Writing about advertisements will help you develop this critical stance.

PREPARING TO WRITE ABOUT ADVERTISEMENTS

Advertisements are a pervasive part of our culture; they entertain, they inform, they argue, they sell, and they ask us to think. When you look at or listen to ads for a class or a writing assignment, you will need to view the ads in a way that is probably different from how you normally view them, a way that is a bit more systematic.

As you will discover, there are many different reasons to write about advertisements and many ways to present your writing. Likewise, there are many different methods of experiencing an ad, all of which may influence your overall impression; there are many different questions you can ask yourself about the ad itself as well as your reaction to it. What follows are some different approaches or ideas for you to consider as you dissect an ad.

Examining Advertisements

As you know, advertisements come in a variety of forms, but most share similar elements for you to examine. Radio ads don't have images to look at, but you can still consider all of the pieces that go together to create what you hear. Print ads don't have background music or particular voices for you to hear, but the written text, including images, they present will have a voice or style for you to examine. These questions should get you started analyzing all types of ads, no matter where you encounter them. Use the Got Milk ads at the beginning of this chapter or the Volkswagen ads at the end of the chapter to help you apply the tools that follow; you may also want to use the images in the Coca-Cola case study (see color insert).

Look at the details to determine what the images or people say.

- Who appears in the ad? Is it a famous person or an average person? What effect can a celebrity have on an ad? An average person?

grappling with ideas

In the 1970s and '80s, consumer spending dramatically increased; consequently, the spending on advertisements increased exponentially. At the same time, the United States was feeling the effects of social and political movements in the 1960s and '70s, such as the Civil Rights movement and the push for women's equality.

- What impact did the civil rights movement have on advertisements in the 1960s and '70s? What about the women's movement?

- What cultural phenomena have led to changes in advertising in your lifetime? How do you feel about these changes?

- What are the people's races, ethnicities, genders, classes, abilities, ages, sexualities? How can you tell? What does their presence or absence tell you about the advertisement or advertisers?
- What are their expressions? Body angles? Gestures? Connections to each other and/or the product?
- What props are used? Product images? Models? Puppies? An image of the shampoo bottle or a model with a perfectly styled head of hair? Is the model carrying or holding anything in the ad?
- What is the setting or background of the ad? What can the product placement tell you?
- How does the advertisement speak to you through images? Does the image imply that you, too, can be popular or that this product will get you a date?
- What do the images symbolize? What intended and unintended meanings are attached to the symbols?
- What story does the advertisement tell? According to this ad, will your children love you if you bring home this snack? Will your clothes fit better if you eat this kind of cereal?

Look at the placement of text as well as what it says.

- Are there headlines, subheads, written descriptions? What is said? Where are the words placed on the page, screen, or billboard?
- What is the message being communicated? Does it appeal to the viewers' emotions? Sense of logic? Both?
- Is there a double meaning? What is actually said? What is implied? What are you being asked to assume?
- What does the ad not say? What is left out?
- Does the ad use "weasel words"—words that are intended to mislead or manipulate the reader or viewer? If a product is *new and improved*, what was it before? If this product is *faster*, does the ad tell you what it is faster than? Most cereals are *part* of a healthy breakfast, and most toothpaste brands *help* prevent tooth decay.
- Are there any facts and figures? What do these contribute to the ad and your reading of it?

Look closely at the artistic elements of the ad.

- How do contrasting colors, fonts, and text sizes highlight specific objects and words? What is the effect of these choices?
- What color combination is used? Why? Are there any cultural associations with these colors?
- Does the ad use photographic images or drawn images? What is the effect of this choice?
- If it uses photographs, how does the photo lighting affect the ad's message?

If available, look at marketing factors for the ad.

- What is the source of the ad?
- Who is the target audience of the ad? What is the audience's race or ethnicity? Age range? Gender? Sexuality? Socioeconomic status? Is the ad aimed at a special interest group or subculture?
- What is the date of the ad? Is it a seasonal ad (back to school, Mother's Day, Halloween)? Where is the ad placed? What part of the magazine or newspaper (back cover, inside front cover, next to the "Dear Abby" column)? What businesses are near the billboard? Which Internet sites feature this ad? What television shows run this commercial? What time of day is this commercial run?
- How long have the advertisers been running this ad? Is it part of a bigger campaign? What is its history?

Appealing to Consumers

Advertisements are designed to appeal to our fantasies, needs, or desires. Many critics would say that ads are also creating specific desires and needs or at least the illusion of such. Again, look at the Got Milk ads at the beginning of the chapter, the Volkswagen ads at the end of the chapter, or others in magazines and online. Then consider which of these needs underlie each of the ads.

1. The desire for love, romance, and/or sex: plays on personal attraction, both the desire for others and the need to be desired.
2. The desire for popularity or affiliation: links thousands of products and services to the consumer's desires to be in good company and to be respected; also connects to the bandwagon or everyone-has-it appeal and a desire for prominence.
3. The desire for elegance or luxury, also known as snob appeal: creates feelings of envy and a desire for the best product or name brand.
4. The desire for perfect looks: tells or shows consumers that they are too fat, too thin, too black, too white, too short . . . too imperfect to fit in or be accepted; also referred to as the desire for transfer (that is, use our product and the qualities in our models will transfer to you).
5. The desire to be aggressive: taps the viewer's or reader's feelings of anger.
6. The desire for adventure, high achievement, or escape: focuses on the viewer's ambitions, dreams, wishes, and hopes, often for something new and different.
7. The desire to dominate: appeals to the wish to be powerful and in control.
8. The desire for youth: use our product and you will look and feel younger.
9. The desire for attention: concentrates on the difference in how you are seen now versus how you will be noticed after using the ad's product.
10. The desire for autonomy: focuses on the need to be independent.
11. The desire to nurture: cultivates the caring and compassionate responses of a viewer; this appeal is also tied to the consumer's emotions.
12. The desire for plain folks or a slice of life: uses ordinary people to recommend products.
13. The desire for celebrity or prestige: uses stars and celebrity spokespersons to recommend products.
14. The need to feel safe: appeals to the desire for security; the consumer does not want to be intimidated, menaced, or battered.
15. The need for aesthetic sensations: causes advertisers to make their products visually appealing or arresting.
16. The desire for statistics and scientific facts: piques the consumer's interests through trivia, percentages, scientific studies, or question–answer formats.
17. The desire for humor: appeals to the desire to laugh and enjoy a product.
18. Physiological needs: focuses on the basic requirements of food and shelter.
19. The desire for health: appeals to those who want to be or appear healthy.
20. The desire for convenience: appeals to those who need things quickly or fast.

Subvertising

Subvertising is a method of subverting mainstream ads. It uses well-known ad campaigns, both images and wording, to either speak against the original product or to promote an unrelated value or idea. For example, PETA (People for the Ethical Treatment of Animals) has subverted the Got Milk campaign with its own Got Soy campaign, and Lactaid brand milk substitute has launched its own Miss Milk? campaign. In addition, you can find Got Jesus and Got MLK

campaigns that use the well-known ads to promote their own ideas. Subvertising is often used by social and political movements to gain wider recognition and appeal. Ad parodies can also fall into this category.

Researching and Documenting Advertisements

When writing about advertisements, you will always have to find the specific ad or ads you are discussing; this will be your primary source. Besides the ad itself, you may also want to explore the source of the advertisement, such as the magazine, newspaper, website, or billboard location. At times, you may also want to supplement your primary source(s) with secondary or outside sources; reading what others have to say on your topic or primary source may help you write a more balanced and believable review or analysis of an advertisement. (See Chapter 11 for more on research and documentation.)

Areas of research may include the following:

- The history of the product
- The history of the ad campaign, including budget figures
- Market figures for the ad and the product being sold
- Ads for similar and competing products
- The history or development of techniques used in the ad
- The evolution of particular types of advertising or approaches to ads
- The cultures or subcultures represented in the ad
- How the ad was received by others

Whether or not you conduct outside research may depend on your assignment and/or your research question. What do you want or need to know to complete your essay about a given ad or advertising campaign? Go back to your initial reading of the ad. What do you need to fill in? How do you want to narrow your focus? As you conduct your research, be open to new ideas and interpretations that may arise but still proceed with some type of plan or questions to be answered. While conducting your research or once you have completed it, you may want to study the advertisement again and look for additional examples to support your argument or test your theories about the ad, its design, or its purpose.

As mentioned previously, your first source is usually the advertisement itself. The availability of commercials and radio spots on the Internet has made it easier to access these types of ads, but you must keep in mind that you may not be viewing the ad as it was intended to be seen, so consider whether or not the format has been changed or distorted in some way. You may also come across ads in a variety of print and online sources, as well as on billboards, sidewalk signs, the sides of buses, fliers on your windshield, and other such random locations (see The Reading Zone for a case study about the ubiquitous nature of modern advertising).

Places online to check for copies of ads and commercials include the following:

Commercial Closet Association	http://www.commercialcloset.org
IFilm	http://www.ifilm.com/channel/commercials
Super Bowl Commercials	http://www.superbowl-ads.com
Television Commercial Database	http://clipland.com/index_tvc.shtml
YouTube	http://www.youtube.com

grappling with ideas

Consider the various techniques companies use to get you to buy their products.

- Has an ad ever prompted you to buy something you really didn't need?

- When you go to the store and are confronted with numerous brands of the same product, how to you decide which one to buy?

- How does the product packaging affect you?

- Do advertisements for the products ever pop into your head? How do you feel about that?

You can also search for commercials on websites for particular companies and on many online archives and museums devoted to specific products and services.

Likewise, secondary sources can be found in a variety of places, such as your library's holdings and electronic databases, and through an array of sources, including books, articles, and websites. You may find information about your particular ad, an ad campaign, or a specific genre of ads, such as alcohol or tobacco ads, as well as sources about how to create advertisements or sell products. Consider databases and indexes related specifically to marketing and advertising, as well as those connected to language and rhetoric or perhaps sociology and anthropology, which discuss ads and their impact on our lives and consumer habits.

Although the traditional sources just mentioned are often helpful, with popular culture you sometimes have to look at more contemporary or mainstream sources for additional information. Many of these sources can be found on the Internet, but you will want to evaluate the sources for reliability and trustworthiness. The milk industry will only have good things to say about their Got Milk ad campaign, which has been going strong since 1994, but the PETA group that advocates drinking soy milk instead of dairy has a different take on the campaign. Medical doctors who want to argue with some of the claims of the recent Got Milk ads, especially in regard to losing weight with milk, have yet another point of view about the ad campaign.

When conducting research, remember to record the bibliographic information you will need for your Works Cited page and for your in-text citations. Record information about the advertisements and where they come from as well as any books, articles, and websites you read; you may need to get back to these resources as you write or extend your research. See Chapter 11 for specific guidelines, and see the Works Cited at the end of essays in this chapter for citation examples.

WRITING ABOUT ADVERTISEMENTS

Advertisements can be analyzed and written about in a variety of ways. You may want to look at the images presented, at what the words say, at the colors and arrangements on the page, at where and when the ad appears, at how this ad works with or against other ads for similar products, or at how the product packaging serves as another advertisement. For instance, the Got Milk ads at the start of this chapter, as well as their parodies, are part of the same campaign, but the individual ads have specific audiences in mind and, therefore, are arranged in particular ways, including who is and is not in the ad, what the text of the ad says, and how all of it is arranged on the page, as well as where the specific ad appears. Although there are many ways to write about advertisements, this chapter focuses on four of the main assignments given in most composition classes: advertisement reviews, reflection or response essays, analysis essays, and synthesis essays, which can be a combination of any of the preceding types.

keyquestions

Key Questions for an Advertisement Review Essay

- Have you given the reader an overall description of the ad?
- Who is the audience? How can you tell? What assumptions do the advertisers make about the audience?
- Is this a straightforward, political, satirical, or humorous advertisement? How can you tell? What traditions or standards does it rely on to be understood in these terms? For example, is it set up like a David Letterman Top 10 List? Does it use a common slogan such as "four out of five dentists surveyed said . . ."?
- In what ways is the ad designed to manipulate you into buying the product? What emotions and desires does it play upon? What appeals are used?
- Have you begun the review with an attention-grabbing opening? Have you concluded with your final thoughts about the ad being reviewed?

© Warner Bros./The Kobal Collection

Advertisement Reviews or Review Essays

An advertisement review essay is a close examination of an individual ad or a series of ads for one product. This type of essay primarily describes the components of the ad being reviewed, but it might also express an opinion about what is interesting or valuable about the ad. Evaluation is the main focus. You are giving a judgment about the quality and purpose of the ad, backed up with enough information to indicate that your judgment is sound and can be supported by the actual advertisement. These close readings of ads may be found in newspapers, in magazines, and on most news websites discussing new ads and their success, particularly in media and business circles. For a class, your review will most likely be about an advertisement you were either given in class or asked to bring in.

An advertisement review will usually analyze three or four key issues about the ad. Your overall evaluation of the ad can be phrased as the thesis of the essay and may come at the beginning or end of the essay. The essay often describes the key features and important details of the ad, creating a visual for the reader. The essay will also identify the audience for the ad and explain how the intended audience is made clear (or not) in the ad. Your essay might then discuss how the ad is designed to appeal to the audience identified. Finally, your essay will explain the implicit and explicit messages presented in the ad. During all of these steps, you will want to refer to specific images or text in the ad you are reviewing to support your opinions.

You might also compare the advertisement to other ads for the same product, to ads for competing products, or to other ads by the same company. In the brief and visual review shown here, the author compares an image of Jessica Simpson as Daisy Duke in a television commercial to her image in the film *The Dukes of Hazzard*, where she portrayed Daisy Duke. This approach will help you show your reader that you are familiar with a wide range of advertisements so that your opinion is taken seriously and credibly.

Reflection or Response Essays

Although reflection or response essays will include some description of the advertisement(s), the main purpose is to use the ad as a starting point for your own reflection or response. The writer usually reflects on his or her own feelings that have arisen through critically watching, looking at, or listening to an advertisement, or the writer can respond to some personal issue or emotion that has arisen during the encounter with an advertisement or a series of ads. This essay will be mostly personal narrative, although it can also include evidence and description from the ad(s) that sparked the personal response. Consider what aspect of the advertisement grabs your attention, sparks your interest in the product, or, perhaps, triggers your anger or disgust. Then consider what you would like to say to your readers about the ad and about your own response. Finally, consider using a concrete thesis statement to explain the purpose of the essay and to keep you on track with your reflection.

Analysis Essays

An analysis essay includes more detailed and extensive descriptions, accompanied by an explanation of their significance, than a review essay does. When you analyze an advertisement, you are defending a view about the ad and how its different elements work or do not work. As with any argumentative paper, you want to offer an idea you have about the advertisement and support it with evidence from the ad itself and possibly outside sources as well. When writing an analysis essay, you will probably want to work from a tentative thesis that explains your overall judgment or argument about the ad. Your essay will explain and support this thesis. Similar to the thesis in a review, it offers your opinion, but in addition, it helps other viewers understand the ad: how it functions, why it was created in a certain way, how it affects viewers or listeners, what it means. You can support your thesis with specific evidence and examples from the ad and possibly from outside resources. Remember that analysis requires more than just observations or descriptions; analysis looks critically at what the advertisement is doing and presents your supported evaluation of this action.

When analyzing advertisements, remember that there may be many valid interpretations for any given ad. For credibility purposes, you need to support your interpretation with specific details about the ad's images, text, colors, and arrangement as well as its production, placement, and use of appeals. You may also need to support it with research about the ad's cost, impact, designers or producers, and the target audience, especially as it connects to the particular medium used to disseminate the ad. Likewise, you might also consider these factors in similar or competing ads to help determine why the advertisers have taken a particular approach in this ad or series of ads.

Synthesis Essays

The synthesis essay is a mixture of different rhetorical styles and writing purposes. It is a way of combining review with reflection or using personal response to support analysis. For example, you may have come across an ad on a bus or car, like the one pictured here.

keyquestions

Key Questions for a Reflection or Response Essay

- Have you clearly indicated how you used the advertisement as a springboard for your thesis?
- Have you expressed your personal response to one aspect of the advertisement(s)?
- Does your introduction direct your audience into your response?
- Does your concluding paragraph include some reflection on both the ad and your response?
- Are your essay's intentions clear?

Key Questions for an Analysis Essay

- Do you have a clearly stated or implied thesis?
- Do you have a series of reasons supporting the thesis? Are these arranged in a logical and convincing order?
- Are your supporting reasons backed up? Do you provide specific evidence and examples from the ad for each reason you offer?
- Does your introduction orient your reader to the direction of your argument?
- Is your concluding paragraph summative and/or thought provoking without introducing completely new ideas?

© Bill Mowery

You may have had a personal response to this ad that will be a good opener for your essay, but this response may have led you to use the analysis questions to really dissect what the ad was doing or why it affected you the way it did. You may have even decided to do some research about the company or the history of ads on buses, including images that show the progression of such ads. When you put all of these rhetorical approaches—personal response, analysis, visual arguments, and research—together, you have created a synthesis essay.

This type of essay may be assigned by your instructor, or you may find that this synthesis of approaches is the best way to answer your research question or support your evaluation. When writing for a class, look over the assignment carefully and speak to you instructor if you are unsure as to whether or not the synthesis essay fits the directions for the assignment. Because the synthesis essay utilizes a variety of rhetorical approaches and allows writers to make decisions based on what seems best for the topic being written about, many instructors and student writers prefer it. When you decide to use a mixture of strategies, be sure to look over the key questions for all of the types of essay strategies you are using in your writing.

SAMPLE ANNOTATED ESSAY

CONSIDERING IDEAS

1. What do you know about the women's movement of the 1970s? Gloria Steinem and *Ms. Magazine*?

2. What kinds of ads would you expect to see in a feminist magazine?

3. How do you think the women's movement affected methods of advertising?

Cathleen McBride, *a mother of three teenage children, returned to Middle Tennessee State University after a twenty-year break to pursue her degree in nursing. For this class essay, McBride focuses on advertising images of women through the years and compares them to the way women are targeted today.*

ADVERTISING

Keeping Sexism Alive

Cathleen McBride

I read Gloria Steinem's article "Sex, Lies and Advertising," in which she describes the difficulties she had in getting advertisers for *Ms. Magazine* in the nineteen seventies and eighties. In reading her description of the challenges she faced, I discovered several disturbing indications of how advertisers see women as consumers and as people. Unfortunately, some of the outdated stereotypes of women used back then are still hanging around today.

Steinem needed to both secure advertising to keep her magazine self-supporting and profitable, and to present products to her readers that fit the overall view of *Ms. Magazine*'s readers as consumers. This was no easy task, as the magazine and its readers were breaking new ground. *Ms. Magazine* was present at the birth of the feminist movement that was changing the views that women had of themselves, and the views the world had of women. As a child during this time, I experienced the conflicting views of the mainstream media and women close to me. My mother explained that feminism meant that women were just as good as men and deserved to be treated equally, such as in getting equal pay for equal work. Television told me that feminists were man-hating bra-burners who wanted to abandon their homes and families to selfishly entertain themselves by stealing good jobs from men, and I can still see traces of this image in popular media today. Women craved more freedom and more choices than simply being "his wife" and "their mother."

When Steinem attempted to redirect the efforts of advertisers to reach her audience that no longer saw themselves as merely housewives, she met both resistance and hostility. Women wanted to see advertising that showed them more than laundry soap and makeup; they needed information on financial products,

Writer has a clear thesis to let you know what the essay is about.

Begins with a summary of the advertising article being reviewed and responded to.

Uses personal experience to connect to the article and to the reader.

"Advertising: Keeping Sexism Alive" by Cathleen McBride. Written for Expository Writing at Middle Tennessee State University with Professor Dianna Baldwin, 2006.

Writer gives a specific example of a recent ad to illustrate her argument.

Writer acknowledges benefits of the women's movement but then shows how this "benefit" really worked against women.

Another illustrative example. Would it help if you knew what brand insurance she was discussing?

cars and electronics. Advertisers felt it was silly to market these traditionally "masculine" products to women, and this trend continues. In our modern advertising we see that women need food, cleaning products and shoes, and men want power tools, lawnmowers and electronics. There are, of course, exceptions to these trends, usually just as sexist. For example, women who don't feel powerful or in control are now offered a new solution through advertising. When her son was bullied on the playground, one woman in a recent ad fixed the situation by dragging her son to the Hummer dealership where she bought one of the largest vehicles on the planet. Women are now free to compensate for their inadequacies just like men by buying a new car—hardly an empowering suggestion. Another traditionally male market sector, NASCAR teams and sponsors realize women are their fastest-growing fan base, and they have created some rather puzzling ad campaigns as a result. For example, I know that if I am too busy daydreaming about my favorite driver and how cute he is to watch where I am driving, my insurance company will cover the damages when I crash into a big sign and knock it over. Women drivers! When will we ever learn? These examples illustrate how the gender-specific advertising we see today has changed very little from the images of the early seventies. Or is it that these actually are changes in advertising? Are the advertisers finally offering the same level of stupidity to both women and men?

However, some changes in advertising forced by the women's movement had unexpected consequences. When advertisers finally began to target women who worked outside the home, they were depicted as power-suited executives who delivered gourmet meals and looked like models at all times, creating the unattainable, anti-feminist Superwoman stereotype. It is possible to be a worker and a homemaker and a parent but it isn't possible to do them all perfectly; there simply aren't enough hours in the day, and women everywhere agonize over their inadequacies. Advertisers traditionally used women that were white, blonde, thin and under thirty, bombarding us with images that made the markets for hair color, diet products and wrinkle creams explode. Maybe increased sales of these products were the intended consequences all along.

In her article, Steinem shows us how advertisers control the editorial content of magazines by demanding that their ads should be placed close to certain types of articles, or they will pull the ads that keep the magazine financially solvent. Advertisements for food should accompany recipes, and makeup ads should match fashion "editorials" telling about the newest age-defying foundation and long-lasting lipstick. Women should look pretty, and women's magazines should look pretty and tell women how to look pretty. Television isn't much different, and we see a parade of women who buy pretty clothes and cars and cook pretty food and keep their houses and children clean and pretty. We haven't come very far from the days when June Cleaver did all her housework wearing pearls. A truly insulting ad for Swiffer Carpet Flick shows me that rather than stupidly dragging my full-size vacuum cleaner up the stairs while it's still plugged in, I should buy their small plastic carpet-cleaning device. It's little and cute and you can carry it right up the stairs. Wow! I gotta have that!

Advertisers basically see the buying public as sheep to be enticed to buy their products, and we should keep this in mind. A commercial I saw recently illustrates this concept perfectly. A herd of sheep is cowering in a pen, and one black sheep walks away from the herd, wriggles under the fence and takes off across a field. Other black sheep soon join him, leading to a growing herd of black sheep parading down the road. They reach a town where we see a sign reading "Welcome Harley Riders," and as the sheep head down Main Street they are joined by hundreds of black sheep,

© Adbusters Media Foundation

Uses personal response to once again support her opinion and to bring her essay to a close.

as far as the eye can see, framed on both sides by rows of Harley Davidson motorcycles. I laughed and laughed at this ad and then had to explain myself to the kids; black sheep were once a bad thing but now are a good thing, just like tattoos and Harleys, and they should band together. But when everyone starts doing something, like riding a Harley, is it still cool? At least the ad didn't show bleached blonde black sheep in halter-tops on the backs of the bikes. Times have changed but advertising is still following the same old herd ideas of sexist advertising used in decades past. Whether black or white, mainstream or alternative, male or female, to the advertisers, we are still sheep.

Works Cited

Steinem, Gloria. "Sex, Lies, and Advertising." *Gender, Race, and Class in Media: A Text-reader.* 2nd ed. Ed. Gail Dines and Jean M. Humez. Thousand Oaks, CA: Sage, 2002. 223–29.

DECODING THE TEXT

1. What is the author's main idea? How does the author support this idea?

2. Which illustrations do you find the most authoritative?

3. The author compares the general population to a herd of sheep. Is this analogy convincing? Why or why not?

CONNECTING TO YOUR CULTURE

1. Do you think women want more from commercials and print ads?

2. Do you think some commercials are insulting? Or are they just humorous?

3. Have you ever laughed out loud at a commercial? What makes a commercial funny?

4. Is humor a good selling point? Why or why not?

THE READING ZONE

TACKLING TOPICS

1. What makes you like an ad? Do you want recognizable music? Catchy jingles? Celebrity spokespersons? Artistic images? Do you have a favorite ad?

2. When looking at ads, do you notice how women and men are dressed or undressed? Do you ever wonder what the model has to do with the product or service being sold? Explain your reactions to the use of sex to sell products from cars to tobacco to toothpaste.

3. How are characters like Tony the Tiger used in advertisements? How many commercial characters like Tony can you name? Do you buy the products associated with these characters? Why or why not?

4. Where do you encounter the most ads? On the Internet? Television? Magazines? Newspapers? Have you ever encountered an ad in a place you didn't expect? Describe the place and the ad. How did you react to this ad?

5. Do you see people like yourself in the ads you encounter? Do you see people like your friends? Do you ever think about who is not seen in commercials? Do you ever want to be like the people you see in ads? In what ways?

READING SELECTIONS

The readings that follow are organized into five sections: 1970s, 1980s, 1990s, 2000s, and Across the Decades. This decades organization will be used to organize all content chapters for this textbook and to give a broader picture of what popular culture is and how it affects our daily lives. The readings in each of the sections are not isolated to that decade or section because pop culture is not only what happened at the time but also how the same item or idea is received or remembered later on. Accordingly, in the '70s section, James B. Twitchell discusses Philip Morris's effective ad campaign for Marlboro cigarettes, including how they succeeded despite the 1971 ban on television advertising for cigarettes, while John Seabrook shares his personal response to name-brand clothing, T-shirts that advertise, his own "bad '70s" style, and his father's obsession with the image of clothes. In the '80s section, Leon F. Wynter, author of *American Skin: Pop Culture,*

Big Business, and the End of White America, discusses the movement of black entertainers and athletes into the realm of "pop" and, consequently, the realm of advertising and "coolness," and Murray L. Bob argues against the new late '80s trend of putting ads in books. The '90s saw even more diversity in advertising; thus, Beth A. Haller and Sue Ralph are able to discuss the incorporation of people with disabilities and images of disability into mainstream advertisements, and Anthony J. Cortese, author of *Provocateur: Images of Women and Minorities in Advertising,* looks at sexism—against both men and women—in advertising. A case study about the ubiquitous nature of advertisements makes up the '00s section; various authors report on new outlets as advertisers look for innovative markets and additional ways to bombard us with ads. In the final Across the Decades section, Barbara J. Phillips asks you to examine the role of trade characters in advertisements, and Lawrence C. Rubin looks at the marketing of mental health drugs.

The readings in this chapter are presented as a way for you to become more versed in investigating and analyzing advertisements as both makers and reflectors of pop culture; however, they are also offered as samples of writing reviews, reflections or responses, analyses, and synthesis essays about advertisements and the advertising industry.

Reading Selections: the '70s

CONSIDERING IDEAS

In 1971, the Federal Communications Commission banned television ads about smoking and strengthened regulations concerning the portrayals of cigarette smoking on television programming. The hope was that smoking would decrease. Instead, smoking increased.

1. Why do you think this increase happened?

2. In what other ways has the government, as well as society, attempted to regulate smoking since the early 1970s? Is it working?

3. Do you smoke? How many people do you know who smoke? Why do you or they smoke?

4. Do you think people are enticed by cigarette ads to smoke? Why or why not?

James B. Twitchell *teaches in both the English and advertising departments of the University of Florida. He often compares advertising to religion and thinks it important for people to study the history of a practice that exerts such influence over our lives. Recent books include* Shopping for God: How Christianity Went from In Your Heart to In Your Face, Branded Nation: The Marketing of Megachurch, College Inc., *and* Museumworld, *and* Where Men Hide. *The following essay about the Marlboro Man campaign comes from* Twenty Ads That Shook the World: The Century's Most Groundbreaking Advertising and How It Changed Us All.

THE MARLBORO MAN

The Perfect Campaign

James B. Twitchell

Although advertising agencies love giving themselves prizes, there has been no award for the perfect campaign. If there were, Marlboro would win. Suffice it to say that this brand went from selling less than one quarter of one percent of the American market in the early 1950s to being the most popular in the entire world in just twenty years. Every fourth cigarette smoked is a Marlboro. Leo Burnett's brilliant campaign made Marlboro the most valuable brand in the world.

First, let's dispense with the politics of the product. We all know that cigarettes are the most dangerous legal product in the world. They kill more people each year than do guns. And yes, it is dreadful that the myth of independence is used to sell addiction. But never forget as well that it is exactly this danger that animates the Marlboro Man. He came into being just as smoking became problematic and, ironically, as long as anxiety exists, so will he.

And second, cigarettes, like domestic beer and bottled water, build deep affiliations that have absolutely nothing to do with taste. As David Ogilvy said, "Give people a taste of Old Crow and *tell* them it's Old Crow. Then give them another taste of Old Crow, *but tell them it's Jack Daniel's.* Ask them which they prefer. They'll think the two drinks are quite different. *They are tasting images* (Ogilvy 1985, 87).

In fact, it was the cigarette companies that found this out first. In the 1920s they blindfolded brand-dedicated smokers and put them into dark rooms. Then they gave them Luckies, Pall Malls, Chesterfields, and Camels, as well as European smokes, and asked the smokers to identify "their own brand"—the one they were sure they knew. By now we all know the results. Taste has basically little or nothing to do with why people choose specific brands of cigarettes.

Just as we drink the label, we smoke the advertising. So what's so smokable, so tasty, about this ad?

First, everything fits around the dominant image. The heading and the logotype fall naturally in place. Product name mediates between visual and verbal. Let's start with the name, *Marlboro*. Like so many cigarette brand names, it is English and elegant and, like its counterpart Winston, deceptively vague. Like the joke about how there's gotta be a pony in there somewhere, there's gotta be prestige in here somewhere. (Oddly enough, Marlboro was first created in Victorian England, then transported to the States as a cigarette for women.) The ersatz PM crest at the apex of the "red roof" chevron on the package hints of a bloodline, and the Latin motto "Veni, Vidi, Vici" (!) conveys ancient warrior strength. Clearly, the power is now both in the pack and in the buckaroo.

The buckaroo is, of course, the eponymous Marlboro Man. He is what we have for royalty, distilled manhood. (Alas, the Winston man barely exists. What little of him there is is opinionated, urbane, self-assured—and needs to tell you so.) The Marlboro Man needs to tell you nothing. He carries no scepter, no gun. He never even speaks. Doesn't need to. The difference between Marlboro and Winston is the difference between myth and reality. Winston needed to break the rules publicly to be independent ("Winston tastes good *like* a cigarette should"), the Marlboro Man has already been there, done that. Little wonder the Viceroy man ("a thinking man's filter, a smoking man's taste") couldn't even make the cut.

Generating prestige *and* independence is a crucial aspect of cigarette selling. If you are targeting those who are just entering the consumption community, and if the act of consumption is dangerous, then you do not need to stress rebellion—that's a given. What you need to announce is initiation into the pack.

When R.J. Reynolds tested Marlboro on focus groups, they found that it was not rugged machismo that was alluring to young Marlboro smokers, but separation from restraints (the tattoo) *and* a sense of belonging (Marlboro Country). This "secret" RJR report, now available on the World Wide Web, is one reason why the "I'd walk a mile for a Camel" man was subsumed into the more personable, intelligent, and independent "Cool Joe" Camel.

Let's face it, the Camel man was downright stupid. In the most repeated of his ill-fated "walk a mile" ads he is shown carrying a tire (instead of rolling it) across the desert (with no canteen), wearing no shade-providing hat. That he seemingly forgot the spare tire is as stupid as his choosing to smoke. Little wonder Cool Joe pushed him aside. A camel seems intelligent in comparison.

The Marlboro Man's transformation was less traumatic, but no less meaningful. In fact, it is a reversal of the most popular tabloid story of the 1950s. It was to be, as David Ogilvy would say, one of the "riskiest decisions ever made" and one "which fewer advertisers would take." Here's the cultural context on a thumbnail, and what Phillip Morris did about it:

On February 13, 1953, George Jorgenson went to Denmark and returned as Christine. The idea that one could change one's sex was profoundly unsettling to American culture. Once back at home, she uttered the perhaps apocryphal testament to his journey: "Men are wary of me and I'm wary of the ones who aren't."

At almost the same time, another repositioning was occurring. Now, as any modern ten-year-old can tell you, objects have sexual characteristics, too. Philip

Morris had a female cigarette, Marlboro, that wouldn't sell. So they sent her up to Chicago to be regendered by Leo Burnett. Miss Marlboro was a "sissy smoke . . . a tea room smoke," Burnett said. Although she had been in and out of production for most of the century, in her most recent incarnation she had a red filter tip (called the "beauty tip," to hide lipstick stains) and a long-running theme: "Mild as May." Men wouldn't touch her, nor would many women.

In December 1954, Burnett took Miss Marlboro out to his gentleman's farm south of Chicago and invited some of his agency cohorts over to brainstorm. Something had to be done to put some hair on her chest, to change her out of pinafores and into cowboy chaps, anything to get her out of the suffocating tea room.

"What is the most masculine figure in America?" Burnett asked. "Cab driver, sailor, marine, pilot, race car driver" came the replies. Then someone simply said, "Cowboy." Bingo! Copywriter Draper Daniels filled in the blank: this smoke "Delivers the Goods on Flavor."

But these admen were not thinking of a real cowboy, not some dirty, spitting, toothless, smelly wrangler. They were city boys who knew cowboys in bronzes and oils by Frederic Remington, or in oils and watercolors by Charles Russell, or in the purple prose of Owen Wister's *The Virginian* or in the pulp of Zane Grey's countless novels. Philip Morris and Leo Burnett now love to tell you that the Marlboro Man was always a "real cowboy." Just don't remind them that almost half of the real cowpunchers were black or Mexican.

No matter, Leo Burnett had just the image in mind. He remembered seeing one C. H. Long, a thirty-nine-year-old foreman at the JA Ranch in the Texas panhandle, a place described as "320,000 acres of nothing much," who had been heroically photographed by Leonard McCombe for a cover of *Life* magazine in 1949. In other words, this Marlboro cowboy was a real/reel cowboy, something like what Matt Dillon, played by James Arness, was on television. A slightly roughed-up, *High Noon* Gary Cooper, a lite-spaghetti Clint Eastwood.

To get to this image, the Leo Burnett Company tried out all manner of wind-blown wranglers, some professional models, some not. Then, in 1963, just as the health concerns about lung cancer really took hold, they discovered Carl "Big-un" Bradley at the 6666 Ranch in Guthrie, Texas. Carl was the first real cowboy they used, and from then on the Marlboro Men were honest-to-God cowboys, rodeo riders, and stuntmen.

One look at him and you know: no Ralph Lauren jeans, no 401(k) plans, no wine spritzers, nothing with little ducks all over it, just independence, pure and simple. He doesn't concern himself with the Surgeon General. He's his own sheriff. To make sure he stayed that way, all background was airbrushed out. Later he got a grub-stake in Marlboro Country.

Even today the Philip Morris Company receives letters from all over the world, mostly at the beginning of the summer, from travelers wishing to know how to get to Marlboro Country.

But there's more to the ad than the free-ranging cowboy. That package with the insignia, built truck-tough as a flip-top *box*, was a badge. With its hearty red, white, and black lettering, the smoker pinned it to his chest on the average of twenty-three times a day. This *vade mecum* of a package was designed by Frank Gianninoto and carefully tested through consumer surveys by Elmo Roper & Associates and the Color Research Institute. Now the *Veni, Vidi, Vici* starts making sense. With this package you are the decorated conqueror. You burn bridges, bust broncos, confront stuff like lung cancer.

Sure, the girlie filter was there for the women (incidentally, the famous Marlboro red came from the lipstick red of the orignal "beauty filter"), but it was battled by the box, the medallion—the manliness of it all.

Should you still not be convinced, there was always the brand, the literal brand— the tattoo. Remember, this was the 1950s, when tattoos were not a fashion accessory, but an unambiguous sign of antisocial "otherness." But this brand was not on the biceps to signify Charles Atlas manliness; rather it was on the back of the smoking hand, or on the wrist. A strange place for a tattoo, to be sure, but appropriate.

Although research departments may cringe to hear this, the tattoo was not the result of motivational research showing that the image would be super macho. Leo Burnett supposedly thought the tattoo would "say to many men that here is a successful man who used to work with his hands," while "to many women, we believe it will suggest a romantic past."

But there is another story that also may be true. Alas, it doesn't emphasize virility and romance but the bugaboo of interpretation, namely, happenstance. It seems someone at the agency had scribbled on the hand of the *Life* magazine cowboy that there was no copyright clearance for this particular image. The agency sent this

image in a paste-up to Philip Morris and then made another version from another cowboy photo to avoid copyright problems. It, too, went to the client. Back came the reaction: "Where's the tattoo on the second cowboy?" Perplexed agency people dug up the original photo and saw the warning scribbled across the wrist (McGuire 1989, 23).

No matter what the story, the tattoo stuck, not because of any massive testing but because everyone knew the branding itself was compelling. You are what you smoke.

When a campaign "works," every part seems compelling. In fact, in great ads, as in great works of art, the sum of the parts is always more than the whole. The visual and verbal rhetoric is so strong that they seem to have always been in place. They seem indestructible. In truth, however, often the greatest act of creativity is knowing when to leave well enough alone. "I have learned that any fool can write a bad ad," Burnett says in one of his pithy *100 Leo's*, "but that it takes a real genius to keep his hands off a good one" (Burnett 1995, 53).

Most of the tinkering with this campaign has been by the government. For instance, many people thought that by removing the Marlboro Man from television in the early 1970s the feds would send him into the sunset. No such luck. You can take down all the billboards and remove him from magazines. "Just a little dab" of this rhetoric "will do ya."

When Philip Morris attempted to introduce brand extension—Marlboro Light— after all the advertising bans were in place, all they did was unsaddle the cowboy and foreground the horse. Now that even mentioning the cigarette by name is becoming taboo, they are mining the original campaign by making Marlboro Country into Marlboro Unlimited and selling lots of logo'd stuff to smokers, calling it Gear Without Limits. By selling annually some 20 million T-shirts, caps, jackets, and other items bearing Marlboro logos, Philip Morris was, for a time, the nation's third-largest mail-order house.

This attempt to get around the fear of legal restrictions on advertising is called "sell-through," and you see it happening with almost all the major cigarette and beer brands. So Smokin' Joe, the super-cool Camel musician, appears on a host of nontobacco products like clothing, beach towels, baseball caps, while at the same time he also appears on the hit list of the FTC as a public nuisance.

And so what is Gear Without Limits for people who want to go to the Land That Knows No Limits? Well, what about products from the Marlboro Country Store like Snake River Fishing Gear ("An outfit made to go where the cold rivers run"), the Marlboro Folding Mountain Bike, a Mountain Lantern in Marlboro red, and the Marlboro Country Cookbook (complete with their green salsa recipe for couch cowpokes). Marlboro has so captured the iconography of cowboydom that they now have ads in mass-circulation magazines consisting *only* of recipes for such grub as Huevos Rancheros, Barkeeper's Burgers, and Whiskey Beef Sandwiches.

My favorite Marlboro ad, however, is an English one in which a Harleyesque motorcycle is set out in the bleak Western plains. The only color in the bleached scene is on the bike's gas tank—Marlboro red. In art lingo, this trope is called *metonymy*.

Metonymy transfers meaning because the host image, the Marlboro cowboy, is imbedded so deep not just in American culture but in world culture that we close the circuit. Ironically, slow learners are helped by the appearance of the warning box telling you that smoking is dangerous! The Marlboro Man may indeed be Dracula to his foes, but he is still the perfect icon of adolescent independence.

Ironically, the greatest danger faced by the Marlboro Man is not from lawmen armed with scientific studies, but from some wiseguy MBA in Manhattan who will try to earn his spurs by tinkering with the campaign. This almost happened on April 22, 1993, as Michael Miles, CEO of Philip Morris, thought he could play chicken with the generics who were rustling his customers. Overnight, Miles cut the price of Marlboro by sixty cents a pack.

But the only critter he scared was the stock market, which lopped 23 percent off the price of PM stock in a single day. This day, still called "Marlboro Friday," will live in infamy as it seemed for a moment that other advertisers might follow. The whole point of branding is to make sure the consumer *pays* for the advertising by thinking that the interchangeable product is unique. He knows this when he pays a premium for it. When *Forbes* magazine (February 2, 1987) offered Marlboro smokers their chosen brand in a generic brown box at half the price, only 21 percent were interested. Just as the price of Marlboro is what economists call "inelastic," so is the advertising. Michael Miles lost his job and the company lost $13 billion in shareholder equity, but marketers learned a lesson: you don't fool with Mother Nature or a great campaign.

1. According to Twitchell, how did the Marlboro Man campaign make Marlboro the most popular brand in the world?

2. Twitchell makes a connection between the changing of Marlboro's image and the groundbreaking sex change operation for George "Christine" Jorgenson. Is this comparison believable in the text? Why or why not?

3. Which of the two stories about the Marlboro Man's tattoo do you find most plausible? What are your reasons for this belief?

CONNECTING TO YOUR CULTURE

1. How does the history lesson in this essay connect to you and your views on smoking?

2. How do you think it connects to your peers? Your family?

3. Twitchell says, "even mentioning the cigarette by name is becoming taboo." What is the reason behind this change? How has it affected smokers? Nonsmokers? What other products have been affected in the same way? Do these products have anything in common with cigarettes?

4. What do you think about antismoking ads such as those put out by TheTruth.com? These campaigns may have actually increased smoking; why do you think that is?

CONSIDERING IDEAS

1. What name-brand clothes do you wear? Are the brands important to you?

2. Do you dress like your mother or father or some other relative?

3. Describe clothing or fashion styles you've witnessed or even been a part of. Where did these trends or fads come from?

John Seabrook *is a journalist with an avid interest in popular culture. His first book,* Deeper: My Two-Year Odyssey in Cyberspace, *deals with his first two years of experience on the Internet in the early 1990s. Further writings by the author can be found in such publications as* Booklist, Economist, Fortune, The New Yorker, *and* Time, *just to name a few.* "My Father's Closet" *is an excerpt from his 2001 book-length commentary* Nobrow: The Culture of Marketing, the Marketing of Culture.

MY FATHER'S CLOSET

John Seabrook

When a man of my father's age lies down on an operating table there's always a chance that he may never get up again. But there he was at the breakfast table, two weeks after bone chips were removed from his spine, not only out of bed but dressed in one of his beautiful bespoke British suits, which must have been painful to put on. My father looked pleased with himself. He had cheated mortality again, and now he felt frisky and ready for argument.

"What are you advertising today?" he asked.

He nodded across the breakfast table at my Chemical Brothers T-shirt. There was a slightly supercilious smile on his face, which was intended to annoy me. My father thought it was in poor taste to wear logos or brand names or words of any kind on the outside of clothing. (The T-shirt said DANÜCHT on the back, which means "da new shit" in hip-hop.) A word on a shirt was like a mayonnaise jar at the dining table: an unsightly intrusion of commerce into what should be uncommercial space. You'd never see so much as an alligator or a polo player on his chest, much less a word.

I said, "It's a Chemical Brothers T-shirt."

Silence. Click of a small silver knife on a butter plate, having spread marmalade (removed from its container and placed in a glass jam server with a silver top) on toast (homemade, not store-bought bread).

"And who are the Chemical Brothers?" Slight emphasis on the "who."

"They're a techno group from England. I went to their show last month and bought this T-shirt."

No reply, just raised eyebrows and a slight, courtly bob of my father's head—mock thanks for passing this *terribly* interesting information along to him.

My father took this sort of thing seriously. You start wearing T-shirts with words on them at the breakfast table, and pretty soon you're amusing yourself by watching daytime TV, or smoking. When I was growing up, Seabrooks did not do such things. On a special occasion the Seabrook children might be allowed to watch television—*The Wonderful World of Disney* on Sunday night, say—but never during the week. "You'll thank me one day," my father would say when I would complain about not having anything to talk to the kids on the school bus about. But, in fact, I would not thank him. I missed a valuable opportunity to learn empathy from TV. Fortunately, when we were being minded by Mrs. Hiles, who came in to do the laundry, clean, cook, and look after us after school, the TV was on and I at least got to see *Gilligan's Island* and *Star Trek*.

It was not that my father thought the Seabrooks were really any different from Mrs. Hiles's family, who were our neighbors. He knew how little difference between the Hileses and the Seabrooks there really

Chapter 2: "My Father's Closet" from NOBROW by John Seabrook, copyright © 2000 by John Seabrook. Used by permission of Alfred A. Knopf, a division of Random House, Inc.

was—which was precisely why these cultural distinctions were so important. This was true all over America. No one wanted to talk about social class—it's in poor taste, even among the rich—so people used High-Low distinctions instead. As long as this system existed, it permitted considerable equality between the classes. Strip away that old cultural hierarchy, and social relations between different socioeconomic levels were harsher, because they were only about money.

I could have tried to explain to my father that in my world, two hours up the New Jersey Turnpike, there was an important distinction between a T-shirt that says, say, BUDWEISER or MARLBORO and a Chemical Brothers T-shirt that says DANÜCHT. In a system of status that values authenticity over quality, a Chemical Brothers T-shirt will get me further in many places than my father's suit. (The danüchtians are doing very hip parties for Puffy right now.) But the cultural choices at my parents' house out of which I made an identity for myself in the city seemed so unreal. Anyway it was too early and I felt irritable and tired, and the house was too hot, and I would probably lose if I attempted to mount an argument like this against the Silver Fox (as Dad used to be known in his CEO days). So I said nothing and ended up feeling a little like a traitor for not trying harder to keep the commercialism of my city existence out of the quieter, genteeler spaces of life down here on the farm.

My father was a famously flashy dresser. When I think back over his long and eventful life my mind's eye fills up with his silhouette at different times over the years, as defined by his beautifully tailored suits. I see the closet where his suits hung. Viewed from his dressing room, my father's closet appeared to be the ordinary, well-appointed closet of a successful businessman. It wasn't until you stuck your head inside that you became aware of a much larger collection of suits, hanging on a motorized apparatus, the kind you'd see at a dry cleaner's, extending up through the ceiling of the second floor and looming into the attic, which was mostly filled with a lifetime of his clothes. As with most bespoke suits, each jacket had the exact day, month, and year it was ordered marked on the inside pocket. You could stand in the doorway downstairs, press a button, and watch as the history of my father, in the form of suits from all the different eras of his life, moved slowly past you.

Next to this master closet were other closets. One held shirts made by Sulka or Lesserson or Turnbull & Asser, another a silken waterfall of neckties of every imaginable hue. Still another held the shoe racks, starting at the bottom with canvas-and-leather newmarket boots and then rising in layers of elegance, through brown ankle-high turf shoes, reversed calf-quarter brogues, medallion toe-capped shoes with thick crepe soles, and black wing tips with curved vamp borders to the patent-leather dancing pumps at the top.

This wardrobe was in some respect my father's inheritance from his father. Not the clothes themselves, but the lesson that a custom-made English suit, worn properly, was a powerful engine of advancement up the status hierarchy. Without his clothes, my grandfather was an uneducated man who had spent his early years working in dirt, more or less. (The expression "dirt farmer" was still used sardonically by farmers down here to describe their profession, as though the dirt itself were the product.) But dressed in his Savile Row suits, my grandfather was a man of substance, grace, and good taste.

My father was more of a fashion innovator. He was the Duke of Edinburgh as played by Douglas Fairbanks Jr. In his youth he experimented with elements of both the Brooks Brothers style, which he encountered as an undergraduate at Princeton, and his father's Edward, Prince of Wales look, hitting upon his own synthesis around 1950: double-breasted, high-waisted suits with wide lapels, snug in the body but with deep vents in the back. The cut of the clothes was still that of the sensible establishmentarian, but within those controlled contours you'd get flashes of purple and pink in the wide spread-collared shirts, polka dots in the ties, and a bold green chalk stripe of imagination in the suits, signifying the American tycoon.

Out of these pinstripes and houndstooths and windowpane checks my father created a whole world. There were drape suits, lounge suits, and sack suits, in worsted, serge, and gabardine; white linen suits for Palm Beach and Jamaica before the invention of air-conditioning; glen plaids and knee-length loden coats for brisk Princeton-Harvard football games, and a raccoon coat for Princeton-Dartmouth, which was later in the season. Suits for a variety of business occasions, from wowing prospective underwriters with a new offering (flashy pinstripes) to mollifying angry shareholders whose stock was diluted by the offering (humble sharkskin). Then, as the life-is-clothes approach succeeded at the office, suits for increasingly rarefied social events, from weddings at eleven and open-casket "viewings" at seven, to christenings, confirmations, and commencements, culminating in the outfits needed for my father's rarefied hobby, four-in-hand driving, in which four horses are harnessed to a carriage—a sport that presents one with a daunting range of wardrobe challenges, determined by what time of day the driving event is taking place, whether it's in the country or in town, whether one is a spectator or a participant, or a member or a guest of the club putting it on. Three-quarter-length cutaway coats, striped trousers, fancy waistcoats, top hats: This was the part of my father's closet that bordered on pure costume.

The '60s burst against his solid shoulders of English wool and receded, leaving only one very interesting trace behind: a blue Velvet Nehru smoking jacket, decorated with light-blue-and-navy flower-and-ivy psychedelia, and matched with midnight-blue velvet pants. The suit was made by Blades of London, and dated April 25, 1968, a period when the Nehru was enjoying a brief vogue in the popular culture, thanks mainly to Lord Snowdon's wearing a Nehru-style dinner jacket in a famous *Life* magazine photograph in the '60s.

When he wasn't dressed up, my father was either in pajamas (sensible cotton pajamas like the ones Jimmy Stewart wore in *Rear Window*) or naked. He was often naked. He embarrassed not a few of my friends by insisting on swimming naked in the pool when they were using it. But his nakedness was also a form of clothes, in the sense that it was a spectacle. Dressing without regard to clothes at all, occupying that great middle ground between dressed and undressed—dressing just to be warm or comfortable, which is the way most people wear clothes—did not make sense to him.

Where did the information necessary to create this haberdasherical embodiment of an Anglo-American aristocrat come from? Much of it came from popular culture—from magazines and books and movies about the British aristocracy, from Noël Coward plays, from the Cecil Beaton outfits in *My Fair Lady*, from Cary Grant in *The Philadelphia Story* and Grace Kelly in *High Society*, from *The New Yorker*. This was one of the secrets of the American aristocracy: the degree to which its idea of itself was based on fictions created by wanna-be elites themselves—the Jewish studio bosses, writers like F. Scott Fitzgerald and Preston Sturges, and editors like William Shawn, son of Jackknife Ben Chon, a Chicago knife salesman.

One day back in the mid-'80s, while I was visiting my parents, I found my father contemptuously tearing Ralph Lauren ads out of a magazine. This was around the time that Ralph was making his move from denim into sportswear and "complete lifestyle marketing" (home furnishings, linens, interior design products). Magazines were carrying small ad portfolios primed with a message from Ralph himself, which said in part, "There is a way of living that has a certain grace and beauty. It is not a constant race for what is next, rather, an appreciation of what has come before. There is a depth and quality of experience of what is truly meaningful. . . . This is the quality of life that I believe in. . . ."

"Ralph Lauren *offends* me," my father said, with withering scorn, almost disgust, ripping out another page. The vehemence of his response surprised me. After all, Ralph Lauren's sentiments were not inconsistent with my father's own views on value in culture. Dad did not object to having some of his most elaborate four-in-hand outfits featured in the "Man and the Horse" show at the Met—a show partly underwritten by Ralph Lauren. But after I had thought about it for a while it made perfect sense. In making images of horsey, aristocratic-looking people like my father available to everyone, Ralph Lauren was a threat to my father's identity as an American aristocrat—an identity that he, like Ralph Lauren, had invented out of whole cloth, as it were. Of course, my father would never *ever* wear Ralph Lauren, because he had gone Ralph Lauren one better. This was his distinction in the sand.

As for me, being that much closer to Nobrow, I tended to see Ralph Lauren ads as a validation of my identity, not a threat to it. When I was in my second year at Princeton, for example, someone came down to the crew boathouse looking for models to participate in a Ralph Lauren fashion shoot. The idea was that preppy-looking rowers like us would be seen horsing around on the crew dock wearing Ralph Lauren clothes that suggested rowing (horizontal-striped jerseys, crewneck sweaters, etc.). You might think that since we were all real preppy rowers we would not care about being in a Ralph Lauren ad depicting preppies like us, but of course you would be dead wrong about that. Almost every member of the crew signed up. Being to the manor born couldn't compete with being chosen because you fit the commercial culture's image of you. When I wasn't chosen I tried to console myself with the thought that only fake preppies were picked, but it was hard to swallow.

* * *

My father used his clothes to pass along culture to me. I, in turn, used clothes to resist his efforts. When I was growing up, I had a lot of nice clothes, which my parents got for me, and I did almost everything I could to avoid wearing them. Without really intending to, I managed to rip the silk lining in the beautiful camel's-hair coat Dad bought me, lose buttons off the Brooks Brothers suit, tear the seams around the pockets of the evening clothes. "You're so hard on your clothes," my mother would say, and she was right. My boyhood closet was a riot of misplaced anger exhibited toward innocent garments. Inside the little lord's scrubbed and Etonian exterior there seemed to be a dirt farmer struggling to get out. My brother, on the other hand, seemed effortlessly to acquire my father's ability with clothes. His closet was like an Eagle Scout's version of my father's. Mine was the Anticloset.

When I was fully grown, and turned out to be more or less my father's shape and size, there was rejoicing in my parents' household. Naturally my father was pleased. He had never spent much time with me as a boy, being so busy providing all the advantages that we enjoyed. We never threw a ball together or went camping—even if he'd had the time, he didn't have the clothes for it. But in the art of dressing for success in the adult world he would gladly be my adviser and my friend.

My mother was also pleased. Having grown up without money, she could never reconcile herself to her husband's clothing purchases, to the point where my father had to smuggle new clothes into the house. Now, at least, his reckless extravagance would have a practical outcome: I would never have to buy any clothes of my own.

I could just start wearing my father's, beginning with the earliest items in his wardrobe and working my way along the endless mechanical circle.

Not long after I moved to my first apartment in New York, my father took me to his New York tailor, Bernard Weatherhill, to have a couple of his old suits refitted on me. The shop was upstairs on a midtown street, nothing flashy, just a nameplate on a wall you'd pass every day in the city without giving it a second glance. The man who measured me up was an elderly white-haired Englishman, whose slightly stooped posture was like an unparsable synthesis of class-based deference and the physical toll of years of bending down to measure the bodies of young gentlemen like me. His tremendous discretion seemed to suck all the oxygen out of the air.

The jackets fitted almost perfectly. A little big in the body, but the length in the sleeves was beautiful. My father and the tailor beamed with pleasure. The pants, however, needed taking in; the tailor asked me to "stand naturally" as he marked them up. But for some strange reason I had suddenly forgotten how to stand naturally. It was as if I'd lost the concept of posture.

"Why are you standing like that?" my father said. "Knock it off."

Later he took me to A-Man Hing Cheong, his Hong Kong tailor, to be "measured up" for a few "country" suits (a glen plaid and a windowpane check) and, presumably, many others in the future. ("Big men can wear bolder plaids and more details without appearing to be fairies," Dad once advised me.)

"Which side?" the tailor asked; he spoke a bit of English.

He was kneeling in front of me, pointing at my crotch and waggling his forefinger back and forth.

"He wants to know which side you wear your pecker on," my father said.

"Yeh yeh, ha ha ha, yar peck-ah!"

But all my father's efforts to clothe me in the style of the young gentleman he hoped I would become were almost entirely unsuccessful. Around the house I wore jeans and T-shirts with words of all kinds on them—TV shows, brand names, sports, *Star Wars,* MTV, Ralph Lauren, Calvin Klein, *Jesus Christ Superstar.* Insofar as I had a style it was bad '70s—lots of brown colors, bell-bottoms, cords, and polyester shirts. In some dim inchoate way I perceived that T-shirts with words were *my* culture, and that was the only way out of the larger cage of hegemony in which my father's houndstooth and windowpane checks had me trapped.

DECODING THE TEXT

1. What is the author's reaction to his father's obsession with clothes?

2. How does the author show his feelings to the reader?

3. Can you picture the father? The son (author)?

4. What is the author trying to say with his personal narrative?

5. He calls his style "bad '70s." What do you think this looks like?

CONNECTING TO YOUR CULTURE

1. Have you ever used clothing or a fashion trend as a form of rebellion? As a way to conform?

2. Have you ever witnessed someone else use fads or trends as rebellion or conformity? Describe one of these instances.

3. Did the clothing achieve your, or someone else's, desired goal? In what ways?

Reading Selections: the '80s

Leon E. Wynter, *a journalist and radio commentator, created the "Business and Race" column for the* Wall Street Journal *and has published articles in* The Washington Post *and* The New York Times. *He is also a commentator on National Public Radio. His most recent book is entitled* . . . And I Haven't Had a Bad Day Since. *"Marketing in Color" is an excerpt from his 2002 book* American Skin: Pop Culture, Big Business, and the End of White America.

MARKETING IN COLOR

New Niches Flow into the Mainstream

Leon E. Wynter

In the spring of 1999, shortly after securing the freedom of three American soldiers captured by the Yugoslavian Army during the NATO miniwar on Yugoslavia over Kosovo, the Reverend Jesse Jackson paid a call on the headquarters of PepsiCo in the bucolic New York suburb of Purchase. Still basking in the glow of his latest free-lance foreign policy coup, Jackson's mission was to press top executives to throw more corporate-securities-underwriting work toward certain black- and minority-owned firms. With a small entourage in tow, Jackson's very presence in the mostly empty halls of the secluded corporate campus caused a bigger stir than most anybody in the well-starched head office of the perennial number-two cola maker could remember. It remained for one older employee, a black maintenance man, to put the pagentry of the sales call into context.

"'This is the most excitement since the day Don King came up here,'" said Pepsi marketing executive Maurice Cox, quoting the maintenance man's words. Indeed, everyone involved with selling Pepsi seemed to remember the fall 1983 day when the already-legendary, if not infamous, boxing promoter's humongous white stretch limosine, "big—like the kind they have today, only it was back then," parked on the cobblestone path before Pepsi's executive suite. The day Don King brought Pepsi the then-outrageous proposal of a $5 million sponsorship deal for the twenty-three-year-old "soul singer" Michael Jackson and his brothers was memorable enough to merit a chapter, just two years later, in Pepsi president Roger Enrico's 1986 book on the 1980s cola wars.

Many important personages have come to PepsiCo headquarters . . . none of them made the entrance King did. A land yacht of a limo pulled up, and out stepped this man in a white fur coat that had to cost as much as the car. King's pearly gray hair had been freshly electrocuted and was reaching the sky. Around King's neck was a blindingly shiny necklace, on which hung his logo, a crown with "DON" on top, just in case you might forget he is the king.

Such a man did not come quickly through the halls.

"Hi, everybody, I'm Don King," he told one and all.

Enshrining the moment was the least Enrico could do, because his decision to take a deal that only Don King would think of proposing to a *Fortune* 100 firm back then fixed the word *legendary* before the former PepsiCo chairman's name and secured his place in marketing history. It was a meeting that no one doing marketing at Coke's Atlanta headquarters would forget, either. For decades Pepsi had been desperate to gain a marketing edge over Coke. Enrico, who had just become president of the Pepsi-Cola division, was determined to do whatever it took to pull Coke, still the most hallowed American brand name, down to earth. Beyond the theatrics of the messenger, Don King's message was that Michael Jackson was about to shatter previously shatterproof barriers between black entertainers and mainstream popular culture. But even King's bombast failed to anticipate the

financial records Jackson would also break along the way on the strength of the *Thriller* album. Released early in 1983, it had already topped the charts with nearly 10 million copies sold by the time King came to Pepsi. *Thriller* went on to quadruple that number and became the biggest-selling album in history. Guinness actually held the presses on the 1984 edition of the *World's Records* book (a first in itself) to include *Thriller* as the top seller of all time, passing Carole King's 1970 *Tapestry,* when the industry-shaking album had still hit only 25 million in sales. The $5 million sponsorship deal Pepsi announced in December 1983 was also a Guinness record; it lasted until Jackson signed a $15 million personal endorsement deal with Pepsi two years later.

The awards, concert attendance, television ratings, and the like connected with Jackson during the mid-1980s, summed up by the term *Michaelmania,* could make up a book by themselves. So could the impact of the "Jackson phenomenon," as it was also called, on the very foundations of media-driven commercial culture. It spawned an orgy of "who is he and who are we as a society" journalistic navel-gazing not seen over a performing act since the Beatles landed in the States in 1964. In one week in March 1984, culture critics at both *Time* magazine and the *Washington Post* vainly exhausted more than six thousand words trying to plumb the connection between the Jackson persona and our collective psyche. Writing right after Jackson took eight out of a possible ten awards at the 1984 Grammys (another record) and searching for meaning, the authors seemed to be drowning in the sea of statistics (1 million albums sold per week for over twenty-four weeks and still counting), in the flood of celebrity swells (Jane Fonda, Elizabeth Taylor, Katharine Hepburn, Brooke Shields, Steven Spielberg) attached to the Jackson tide, and in the wave of historical icon comparisons (Babe Ruth, Al Jolson, Elvis, Howard Hughes, the Beatles).

All they really knew for sure was what the *Post's* Richard Harrington asserted:

The combined evidence of the bottom line, the hard listen and the long view is difficult to resist: Jackson is the biggest thing since the Beatles. He is the hottest single phenomenon since Elvis Presley. He just may be the most popular black singer ever.

And still they missed it.

Harrington was to the point in noting that the breathtakingly styled music of *Thriller* wasn't a breakthrough in itself, and that "Michael Jackson is far more popular than influential (again more like Elvis, rather than the Beatles)." But *Time's* Jay Cocks came closer to the pith of the moment in observing that:

Thriller brought black music back to mainstream radio, from which it had been effectively banished after restrictive "special-format programming" was introduced in the mid-'70s. Listeners could put more carbonation in their pop and cut their heavy-metal diet with a dose of the fleetest soul around. "No doubt about it," says composer-arranger Quincy Jones, who produced *Off the Wall* and *Thriller* with Jackson. "He's taken us right up there where we belong. Black music has [had] to play second fiddle for a long time, but its spirit is the whole motor of pop. Michael has connected with every soul in the world."

But neither analysis detected the fault lines deep in the crust of popular culture that happened to intersect with the frail black performer's mercurial rise. Michael Jackson the earthquake struck where the emerging entertainment-information economy met the mother-seam of color at the core of American popular culture. At the epicenter, on the surface, was the thing called pop.

Pop, as a music-industry (as opposed to musical) category, had always been a euphemism for *white* until Michael unleashed "the power of *Thriller.*" For example, Chuck Berry, for all his classic hit songs and unimpeachable claim to rock and roll's paternity, landed only one number-one pop single in his career, and that was at the end, with the novelty tune "My Dingaling" in 1972. In the 1960s and 1970s, the biggest Motown acts, the Bacharach-David-produced Dionne Warwick hits, and a few black bands like Earth, Wind and Fire garnered black performers their first significant "crossover" spots on the pop charts, but most black acts could aspire only to *Billboard's* rhythm-and-blues chart. As part of the Jackson Five, Michael Jackson had been one of the exceptions to the industry practices that limited black access to the pop charts. Between 1970 and 1976, the group had landed seven singles in the pop top ten.

Yet for nonwhite performers, even holding precious slots on the pop charts did not a pop star make. Until *Thriller* the unofficial "King" or "Queen of Pop" had always been white, no matter how many records a black artist sold or how much airplay it got.

American pop, as it turned out, is more than an industry chart. True pop icon status, at the very top, is a state of grace that approaches divine right over one's consumer-subjects in the marketplace. It's a cross between being royalty and being in the top management of mainstream affinity, complete with rituals of respect, ceremonies of adoration, and titles. Pop is what Elvis was after he stopped his initial blues shouting and let Colonel Parker make him the perfect (but not too perfect) heartthrob for white teenage girls as the 1950s became the 1960s. He was the "King." Pop is the firm Sinatra controlled before Elvis, and for many Americans over a certain age, he remained the "Chairman" until the day he died. By the time your parents could be seen nodding in agreement with their peers that "I Want to Hold Your Hand" was really classically inspired, it was the Beatles, one of whom (Paul McCartney) was actually knighted by the queen. Pop is the universal white blue-collar factory that Bruce Springsteen ran in the late 1970s and into the 1980s. He was "the Boss."

To be sure, there were titles enough to go around in the marginal kingdoms of R&B and soul and gospel and Latin music: Aretha Franklin—Queen, James Brown—Godfather, Celia Cruz—Queen of Salsa, and so on. Still, no nonwhites needed to apply for mainstream pop music honorifics as the 1970s became the 1980s. Ditto, with a few notable exceptions, pop positions in television, movies, and (significantly) fashion and style. Bill Cosby, Coke's primary general-market pitchman in the 1970s, also sold well for Jell-O and Ford. O. J. Simpson broke entirely new ground for retired black professional athletes with his ubiquitous Hertz commercials. But neither man would be recognized or recognizable as a pop icon until the early 1990s, and not just because they had yet to star in their respective hit televison

shows. Until Michael Jackson and *Thriller,* marketers simply assumed that no matter how successful a nonwhite performer might be, whiteness was an indispensable requirement for the exaggerated state of mass identification that constitutes "pop stardom."

Then Roger Enrico bet the farm on Michael Jackson and *Thriller*—and won.

As the 1980s began, the business of whiteness-centered pop was, as usual, lurching between cyclical feast and famine. But by the decade's end, the same forces that brought *Thriller's* eruption would move whiteness from indispensable to merely useful in the business of pop, *permanently,* while raising the influence, the reach, and most important, the aggregate profitability of pop entertainment to unimagined heights. By 1990 America's collective pop culture, bonded to the cutting edge of a revolution in telecommunications and information technology, had assumed the lead role in the world's most powerful global economy. Think about it: In 1980 the business of pop could not have imagined the multidimensional marketing star power of Michael Jackson, Michael Jordan, Whitney Houston, or Eddie Murphy. It hadn't seen the platinum branding of predominantly nonwhite professional basketball, football, and baseball or the "Nike-ization" of marketing that attended it. It hadn't even seen a hint of the multibillion-dollar music-fashion-style-literature industry called hip-hop. In other words, in 1980 American commercial popular culture hadn't seen nothing yet.

*   *   *

Imposing a time frame on such a retrospective analysis is always arbitrary, but I place the first moment during a time-out for a Coke commercial in Super Bowl XIV in January 1980. Today the expense, production, and entertainment values of Super Bowl ads rival those of the game itself, but that Sunday in 1980 marked the unintended debut of the first blockbuster Super Bowl commercial. The unlikely star was a big, fierce black man stooping to kindness toward a little white boy. The one-minute ad, which was immediately acclaimed by media and marketing critics, went on to win numerous awards and remains a fixture on "top commercials of all time" lists to this day. Jack Rooney, a former account executive with Foote, Cone and Belding who later headed marketing for Miller Brewing, echoed the response of every advertising or marketing professional I interviewed when I mentioned the commercial. He said he remembered it "like it happened yesterday." "The big joke in the industry was that something like seventy people claimed responsibility for it," he said.

(Scene: Down the tunnel leading from the football field, Pittsburgh Steeler linebacker Joe "Mean Joe" Greene, battered and bruised, fairly limps toward the locker room. A small white boy with a bottle of Coke follows.)

Boy: Mr. Greene—Mr. Greene . . . do you—do you need any help?
Greene: Unh-Unh.
Boy: I just want you to know—I think—I think—you're the best ever!
Greene: Yeah, sure.
Boy: You want my Coke? It's okay—you can have it.
Greene: No, no.
Boy: Really—you can have it.
Greene: (sighs) Okay—thanks.

(Music swells: "A Coke and a smile . . . makes me feel good. . . .")

(Greene downs the Coke in a ten-second-long gulp, then turns toward the locker room.

The boy, dejected, starts walking back to the stands.)

Boy: See ya around.

(Greene turns back.)

Greene: Hey, kid . . . (tosses his soiled jersey to the boy)
Boy: Wow! Thanks, Mean Joe!

True, O. J. Simpson had already been the star of a long-running (no pun intended) Hertz campaign for some time when the Joe Greene Coke commercial made its debut. But unlike Simpson's smiling, clean-shaven re-creation of his evasive gridiron maneuvers—in a business suit—"Hey, Kid," as the spot was dubbed by the ad agency that created it, was the first major commercial to harness, if not confront, the fearful stereotypes of black maleness that American political culture had built for centuries and that mass culture had always emasculated or avoided altogether, to make a positive selling point. Here's Joe Greene, a big (six foot four, 260 pounds), belligerent, bearded black warrior-athlete featured in an unguarded (i.e., out of sight of authority) moment of pain and frustration when, presumably, his animal instincts could lash out against an unspecting white innocent. No levity or dancing was employed to divert the viewer from the almost primal tension building in each moment until Greene accepts the offering of the Coke. When he throws his head back and opens his throat, and the feel-good music swells, all the power in the scene is focused on the magic in the act of sharing this all-American beverage. As the energy of racial tension in the one-minute drama was gathered and then dispelled, the desired main effect was to move the viewer toward having a Coke. But the more powerful side effects flowed from the momentary cathartic relief of race-related tension.

Among them is a benign repression of awareness that the tension had anything to do with Joe Greene's racial persona. Any initial consciousness of the source of the tension is washed away in the wave of joy that follows Greene's jersey into the arms of "the Kid."

Repeated exposure to the ad compounds this repression effect into a long-term deracialization (not the same as deracination) of Joe Greene himself. Perhaps a better term is *humanization*. As the psychological dynamic of cognitive dissonance comes into play over time, the mind finds it uncomfortable to simultaneously hold the specter of Greene as an undifferentiated black brute and the image of the man who shares this special bond of trust and adoration with "the Kid." To reconcile the dissonance, the viewer must embrace one understanding of Greene and abandon the other. Former Coke executive Chuck Morrison joined Coca-Cola's marketing team in 1981, when the Joe Greene ad was still fresh in the beverage industry's mind. As he explained to me when I interviewed him:

What's interesting about it is it also changed the image of "Mean Joe" Greene. What most people forget is that prior to the commercial Joe Greene was [seen as] one of the dirtiest players in the NFL. Vicious, mean . . . I mean, he wasn't called Mean Joe Greene because his college team was called the Mean Greenes. He was a mean sucker! After the commercial Joe Greene became this curmudgeonly, accepted character—which shows you the power of the Coca-Cola brand.

Or rather, it shows the power of archetypes in popular culture, skillfully manipulated by advertising professionals and massively propagated with the resources of a major multinational marketer.

Association with the Coke brand made Greene into a new kind of all-American icon, but only through the exploitation of his images—of the man himself and of his racial persona. Greene, now a coach with the NFL's Arizona Cardinals, says the net effect of the exchange was "liberating." Where once he was seen as unapproachable and depicted in posters in opposing-team cities as "grotesque," the commercial "softened the image and made me more approachable, not just to people who might like football but to young kids, grandmothers, grandfathers, and mothers. To talk not about football but about the commercial, or just to say hello—I enjoyed that very much."

The dynamic elements of "Hey, Kid" the commercial set a pattern that, with ever-evolving variations, could also describe the later mainstreaming of athletes and entertainers of color into commercial pop culture. But at the time, the team at McCann Erickson Worldwide that created the ad were thinking only about selling soda. At first, when interviewed, the commercial's writer, Penny Hawkey, told me the role of race in marketing was the furthest thing from their minds as they set about casting the spot. All they wanted in the athlete was a contrast with "the Kid," and in theory any large, tough, star football player would have done. White quarterbacks naturally headed the list of candidates at the time. The only rules they sought to break were those of then-current soda-jingle conventions; their ambition was to create a one-minute drama. But after thinking it through in hindsight, Hawkey said she realized they ended up casting Greene because they needed the power of race to boost a creative leap.

The rules we were breaking weren't race but the dull wallpaper jingles. It wasn't that he was black, it was that it was a Coke commercial that had never been done before with dialogue. We said, "Hey, what about dialogue, people's real relationship with this drink," recapturing the moment when a Coke is a normal part of the day.

Race wasn't a factor . . . it was juxtaposition. The first candidate [we] had in mind was Terry Bradshaw. But he wasn't big enough. . . . I guess, well now that I think about it—*he wasn't black enough.*

Greene, inducted into the NFL Hall of Fame in 1987 for his on-field prowess, has enjoyed his "liberation" from the precommercial "Mean Joe" image for twenty years. But he told me he never thought much about exactly what prison he was liberated from, or the mechanism by which his freedom was wrought.

I always said "a large black man and the small white kid—it was the contrast." But I didn't delve into the social ramifications. If you start to dissect them, there's probably some truth [to the notion of racial alchemy in the power of the ad], in that this imposing black man, with a reputation to go along with the size, look, and color, became a person. That's how it affected me personally.

Hawkey, who is now executive creative director with Medicus Communications in New York, said, "We didn't realize we were breaking into new racial territory or opening doors. We didn't realize it would have the impact it did." But the conscious, semiconscious, and unconscious use of racial and ethnic notes to achieve creative and commercial breakthroughs would become a repeated theme as marketers navigated the American dreamscape of color in the 1980s.

Coca-Cola did not create Joe Greene's Hall of Fame success or his style on the football field. And Coke had nothing to do with the racial archetypes that fueled the drama; indeed, its creators were barely conscious of the chemicals they were mixing. But what Coke did do, with its investment of marketing resources, was validate a deeper social trend by giving it expression in commercial popular culture. Baby boomers who came of age during the civil rights movement had been cheering black athletes like Joe Greene on the plantations of our national pastimes for over a decade, without being given permission to idolize them in that most American way: to buy products associated with their names. Coke, however unintentionally, sucessfully exploited that unvalidated desire to embrace nonwhite hero athletes *in all their nonwhiteness* to sell soda. Four years later, as the NBA was figuring out how to position its product to satisfy and stoke a similar unmet, ineffable desire for something new and exciting, the same unvalidated potential brimmed in popular culture at large.

Maybe it was coincidence, but 1984 just *happened* to be the year that Vanessa Williams broke the color line at the Miss America pageant; that Eddie Murphy starring in *Beverly Hills Cop* virtually tied *Ghostbusters* for the number-one grossing movie ($234 million worldwide, back when a million dollars was a million dollars); and Bill Cosby's *The Cosby Show* debuted as the number-one-rated show on television. And maybe it was a fluke that the artist who was known in 1984 as Prince grossed $58 million that summer playing a black rock star in an interracial romance in *Purple Rain*, while selling out dozens of big-city arena concert dates within hours after the tickets went on sale.

Roger Enrico and Pepsi didn't create Michael Jackson's talent or music, and they certainly didn't create the central place that African-Americans occupy in American pop culture. All Pepsi did, by leading the procession to crown the first black "King of Pop," was to validate what the mass market had already decided. It simply associated brand Pepsi with a fact on the ground that even the music industry hadn't yet recognized, to sell soda. Enrico's moves were all the more radical because, by all accounts, they were unhesitating and virtually unimpeded by deliberation over Michael Jackson's color, which at the time was still unambiguously brown. One result: Pepsi was one of the first major marketers to catch the pop wave beneath a black artist well before it crested, maximizing the return on its investment. It would not be the last.

Enrico acted on his intuition about where the culture was going without regard to race. It hardly seems revolutionary, in retrospect, but it was way-out-of-the-box thinking at the time.

Coke, the Joe Greene commercial not-withstanding, certainly didn't see it. The preeminent soda marketer had three opportunities to get in on the Michael Jackson *Thriller* phenomenon, and it passed each time. The first chance came in the studio in December 1982, right before the album was shipped. Chuck Morrison, then head of Coke's "ethnic" marketing, met with Michael Jackson, Jackson's father and then manager Joe Jackson, and album producer Quincy Jones. Michael really wanted to represent Coke, Morrison told me, and assumed that a preview of the *Thriller* album would seal the deal.

I'll never forget, Michael looked at me and said, "What can I do for you?". . . And I said, "Nothing: The question is what can I do for you? Because I'm gonna sell Coke whether you do it or not." Joe [Jackson] asked for a million dollars, which was unprecedented at the time. I took it back to management at Coke, and they flat said no. They weren't interested in being tied into a personality like Michael. It wasn't that he was black; he just wasn't Cosby to them.

Six months later Jackson electrified a worldwide audience with a now-legendary performance of "Billie Jean" during the television special saluting Motown Records' twenty-fifth anniversary. "Michael gives that performance of a lifetime . . . but they still say no," Morrison recalled. Coke's last chance was the day before Jackson signed with Pepsi. Don King called Morrison "and says, 'Chuck, Michael has said to us take another run at Coke'—but now the price is five million. I go back up, and Coke says no again. The next day he signs the deal with Pepsi."

Coke bottlers "went nuts" the day after it was announced. Marketing chief Sergio Zyman tracked Morrison down in a Los Angeles restaurant, ordered him back to Atlanta, and authorized a $7 million counteroffer, Morrison said, "but the deal was done."

And the rest was history. That summer of '84 Michael Jackson takes $2.4 billion to the bottom line of Pepsi-Cola. Six share points, just like that, gone. He was absolutely that hot. It was a whole phenomenon; I'd never seen anything like it. It was absolutely brilliant, because it killed two or three birds with one stone. Obviously it was a boon for them with African-Americans, but Michael Jackson was *everybody*. White teenagers loved this boy. Latinos. It was

A Visual Case Study:
Seeing the World of Coca-Cola

Best motion picture.

Just for the taste of it.

diet Coke

DECODING THE TEXT

1. What senses does this advertisement appeal to?

2. Can you really experience Coca-Cola like this? Why or why not?

3. What does the NutraSweet label tell you about this ad? What is the purpose behind that label?

CONNECTING TO YOUR CULTURE

1. How does this image make you feel?

2. Why do you think Coca-Cola chose to associate itself with motion pictures? Does this make Coca-Cola more appealing to you? Your friends?

3. Do you remember the campaign "Just for the taste of it"? What was the purpose behind this campaign? What is its appeal? What does it mean to you? To others?

4. Do you drink Coca-Cola at the movies? At other social events? Why or why not?

© Paul J. Sutton/Duomo/CORBIS

DECODING THE TEXTS

1. Look at the placement of the Coca-Cola logo at these two sporting events. How does the placement of the ad at the event affect the impact of the ad? What about the size of the ad?

2. Does the ad or the product affect the sport? The players? The fans? The television viewing audience?

3. Who else might be affected by these ads?

CONNECTING TO YOUR CULTURE

1. What are the connections between Coca-Cola and sports? In what way do both of these connect to you? Your friends?

2. What do these two sports have in common? What are their differences? Who are their audiences? What products do you think are sold at these two sporting events?

3. Have you seen these kinds of ads at sporting events? What events? What did the ads look like? Did these ads have any effect on you? Why or why not?

4. If you were going to create an ad for a sporting event, what sporting event would you choose? What would your ad look like? Where would you place the ad?

DECODING THE TEXT

1. What do you see first when you look at this image? What items or people catch your attention? Why do you think this is?

2. Why are people's faces cut off? How does this affect your reading of the images?

3. Where do you think this photo was taken? What clues are you reading?

CONNECTING TO YOUR CULTURE

1. Who do you think is responsible for this image? What is the author's/photographer's purpose behind this image?

2. How do the characters in this image compare to those in the sports images across the page? What different images of Coca-Cola do these texts represent?

3. Would Coca-Cola put out an ad with this image? Why or why not? If not, how do you think Coca-Cola would change this image?

There's no disguising the real thing.

Coke Is It.

DECODING THE TEXT

1. Where do you think this Coca-Cola advertisement ran? Who was the intended audience for this ad? How can you tell?

2. How do the words in the ad work with (or against) the image?

3. What details of this image suggest that it is not from the '00s? How would this advertisement (with the same audience and purpose you determined above) look today?

CONNECTING TO YOUR CULTURE

1. If the print references to Coke or Coca-Cola were removed from this ad, would you still get the message? Why or why not?

2. What ideas or even ideals do you associate with the image of the flag? Are these the ideas you associate with Coca-Cola? How do the two compare or contrast?

DECODING THE TEXT

1. Who might the intended audience for this ad be? Given your idea of the audience, where would you place this ad? Where would it have the most impact?

2. Does the line "a world of refreshment" go with the image? Why or why not?

3. Discuss how the color red works with, or against, the rainbow image.

CONNECTING TO YOUR CULTURE

1. What ideas or ideals do you associate with the rainbow image? Are these the ideas you associate with Coca-Cola?

2. How does this bottle compare to the flag bottle on the opposite page?

3. Does Coca-Cola represent both of these ideas? Why or why not?

4. Why do think Coca-Cola choose red as its signature color? What significance does the color red have in your culture?

DECODING THE TEXT

1. What kind of effect do you think was intended by combining American presidents/Mt. Rushmore and Diet Coke? Is the combination effective?
2. What kind of play on language is used in the ad? Is this effective as well?

CONNECTING TO YOUR CULTURE

1. This ad ran in the 1980s; why might that be important in your analysis of it? Would this ad be as effective today?
2. Coca-Cola uses a familiar "monumental" place here with which to associate itself. What are some other places that might be effective for Coca-Cola to use when it wants to market to you? Your friends? How would you design the ad?
3. Coca-Cola, like other companies, also often uses familiar celebrity endorsements, in addition to familiar places. Who are some celebrities you would choose to represent Coca-Cola? Why? How would you design the ad?

DECODING THE TEXT

1. Describe this image of Santa. How does it compare to other images of Santa?

2. What role has Coca-Cola played in shaping our American image of Santa?

3. What are the other items in this text? What role(s) do they play?

CONNECTING TO YOUR CULTURE

1. Do you consider Santa a celebrity endorsement for Coca-Cola? How does this compare to endorsers like Bill Cosby, Mean Joe Greene, Jennifer Lopez, or the *American Idol* judges (see front cover)?

2. Do endorsements make you want to buy a product? Why or why not?

3. Why does Coca-Cola want to be associated with the tradition of Christmas? What other Coca-Cola Christmas ads have made a lasting impression on our culture? On you?

4. Does Coca-Cola play a role in your holiday celebrations? If so, describe this role.

5. What do you think about Coca-Cola tying itself to a traditionally Christian holiday?

6. Do you associate Coca-Cola with any other holidays or annual celebrations? Why or why not?

DECODING THE TEXTS

1. What do you think is the intended message of these visual texts? What is the message that comes through to you personally?

2. Both of these images show collections of objects. How does the arrangement of these objects affect the tone of the image? The message of the image?

3. How does the space or location of these collections affect the message?

4. What do the words within the image tell you literally? Is anything implied through these same words? Why or why not? If so, how?

CONNECTING TO YOUR CULTURE

1. What do these different images say about the effects or influences of Coca-Cola or its place in our culture?

2. Why is collecting Coca-Cola memorabilia such a large business? What draws people to it? Do you know any collectors of Coca-Cola products? Have you ever collected Coca-Cola memorabilia?

3. Do you collect other types of memorabilia? Why or why not?

4. What do you know about labor unions or teamsters? How do you know this information?

5. Have you ever been a part of a strike? What were you protesting?

6. How do these two images fit together? Contrast with each other?

a brilliant stroke, as brilliant as Joe Greene had been for Coke five years before.

Pepsi's success with Jackson opened Coke's eyes to the idea of the browning mainstream. Indeed, in the spring of 1984, singer-songwriter Lionel Richie's single "Hello" topped the pop charts. It was no fluke: six other Richie-penned songs, most sung by Richie (he also gave Kenny Rogers and Diana Ross their biggest hits with "Lady" and "Endless Love," respectively) had reached number one in the previous three years. Suddenly, after Pepsi signed the Jackson deal, Coke could see Lionel Richie as a pop star. It pursued the former Commodores lead singer and was about to sign a deal with Richie's manager, Ken Kragen, Morrison recalled. Then Pepsi found out.

We were supposed to fly to Las Vegas on a Friday to sign the deal. Kragen says Roger Enrico found out, flew to Las Vegas, and put a contract on the table for $8.3 million. But the deal was he had to sign it now, or it's off the table. What do you think Kragen did? Called us and said, "Love you guys—'bye."

The bidding war coincided with *Washington Post* critic Richard Harrington's insightful observation that Richie's success, like Jackson's, represented a quality of crossover for black performers that hadn't been seen before.

In any other year but this one belonging to Michael Jackson, Richie would be the biggest story in the business. At 10 million copies and counting, his *Can't Slow Down* album is living up to its name. He's just begun a forty-city tour expected to gross $12 million. . . . He was the first black entertainer to host a major awards show alone—the recent American Music Awards. Richie's concerts now attract predominantly white audiences, reflecting the appeal he developed in his last few years

with the Commodores. . . . Richie is also more popular with white record buyers than black.

Again, it's not that black acts hadn't overcome the record industry barriers to the top of the pop charts before. In fact, as Harrington went on to point out, where some thirty-five songs performed by black acts crossed over to reach number one in the early 1970s, only thirteen had done so in a similar period in the early 1980s. But the categorical difference with Richie, as it would continue to be with Jackson, was that no major marketers competed hammer and tongs to project those black 1970s acts, performers like Stevie Wonder and Barry White, as genuine pop stars. After Richie, Coke went after Tina Turner the same way, for Diet Coke, but lost her to Diet Pepsi. "Pepsi took Lionel *and* Tina; Enrico wanted to keep his foot on Coke's neck," Morrison told me. "That's how we ended up with Whitney Houston."

Houston, in Morrison's recollection, was a "dowdy looking" newcomer with a "mediocre hit" in "Saving All My Love for You" and considerable record industry hype about her musical family pedigree.

We signed her for Diet Coke, and Lintas Advertising glamorized her, put her in this black dress, bought her some hair, and put $22 million worth of general market media behind her. Two months later Whitney Houston was the darling of this country.

Morrison may be overstating the power of Coke's sponsorship at the expense of Houston's considerable talent. Dowdy or not, she had already been featured as a fashion model in the mainstream magazines *Glamour, Seventeen,* and French *Vogue.* But Morrison's larger point rings true. In the age or rather the moment of *Thriller,* major corporate marketers were now willing to do for Whitney Houston what they would not have considered doing for her cousin, the once-incomparable Dionne Warwick, in the 1960s. Early in her run as "Queen of Pop," Whitney Houston was actually packaged as America's sweetheart. She played the role well enough to carry a major movie with it. In *The Bodyguard,* opposite no less a white romantic leading man than the then-red-hot Kevin Costner, Houston played an international pop diva whose appeal far transcends race. It's hard to say whether it was art finally imitating a life like that of Diana Ross or Donna Summer or Tina Turner in the 1970s or merely an extension of the new Houston icon from music videos to feature film. Audiences apparently had little trouble suspending disbelief. Powered in part by her top-selling sound track, the 1992 film took in $411 million worldwide.

*   *   *

According to [Bill] Katz [president of BBDO New York, the powerful advertising agency], the flow of color into the 1980s cultural mix was so natural, so obviously right and normal that it penetrated beneath the public consciousness of the politics of race. Consciousness is focused on the entertainment experience and then, hopefully, on the product, not on race, which is exactly where marketers want it.

Take when Michael Jackson had his hair burned up. People will say, "I remember this moment in life when the Jackson brothers were dancing for Pepsi-Cola—and Pepsi burned his hair up by mistake." They won't say, "I remember when for the first time ever a black group was in the most popular commercials in America, front-lining for one of the most popular soft drinks." It was secondary that there were five black entertainers. People don't say, "Did you see that commercial with five black people?" What

they remember is the commercial, not the phenomenon of a black person in the commercial. That's the beauty of advertising. Because it only works if it entertains you. You remember the "Mean Joe Greene" commercial because it entertained. It had a compelling emotion attached to it.

The peculiar dynamic by which racial identification is almost magically stripped from nonwhite performers and cultural forms as they pass into the mainstream presents an obstacle to finding the larger meaning of all these developments for race and commercial culture. The measure of that obstacle will be taken at length in the conclusion of this book. But there is another nagging question to be raised here and, I hope, to be put to rest. If Ray Charles had already been a living legend for forty years, why did it take so long for marketers and their ad agencies to recognize and exploit it? Why didn't Ray Charles have a national commercial like that in the 1970s? When I asked Katz, he recalled my hypothetical anecdote about what would have happened to the ambitious record executive who, in 1954, set out to put a Little Richard poster on the bedroom wall of every teenage girl in America.

Why no "Uh-huh" in the 1970s?

Because that guy who was gonna haul the record executive of the 1950s in front of Joe McCarthy still influenced society more than he does today. Because society was not prepared to embrace that. It wasn't until society at large was prepared . . . that advertising could take its cue from that [readiness] and portray it.

The first part of Katz's answer is straightforward enough. Corporate American mass media and marketing had been gaining the power and autonomy to ignore the values and biases of the American social and political establishment since the day the first radio station went on the air. If that power and autonomy could be plotted on a graph, said Katz, it would be an upward curve that finally crossed the social and political color line in the 1980s, not the 1970s. If Katz's argument is consistent, the triumph of Madison Avenue over Capitol Hill was primarily enabled by what was real in the culture, not by the size of Pepsi's checkbook or the power of the new technologies it employed. But Katz, and most other observers I interviewed, was utterly at a loss to explain how we as a culture suddenly became ready to accept what we did, when we did. The difference between advertising and the cultural environment in which it operates, said Katz, is that the culture "just happens"—you can't pick out a moment in life where you say, "I remember when I decided it was okay to be multicultural or multiracial.' In the end the *how* and *when* is for the sociologists and historians to ponder. All marketers focus on is the fact that 'it' happened, and that 'it' superseded or obliterated any issue of race."

Pepsi said, "I want an entertainer to represent my product. I want to be part of the biggest thing in entertainment since the Beatles. I want . . . the imagery Michael Jackson represents to a new generation of constituents out there. I want the fashion associated with Michael Jackson and his brothers. I want *THAT*. I don't want black; I want that." *At some point, it was no longer that cool was represented by black. It was that cool was cool. And I want cool.*

DECODING THE TEXT

1. Which celebrities does the author name as groundbreakers in black advertising?

2. What does the author mean when he says Michael Jackson became "pop," and what did it matter that he moved into that particular field?

3. Do you remember any of the commercials or ads mentioned in this essay?

CONNECTING TO YOUR CULTURE

1. What black celebrities make commercials and pose in ads today?

2. Are these ads part of mainstream advertisements or are they aimed at niche audiences?

3. The author claims that racial identification was stripped from ads in the 1980s. Do you agree with him? Why or why not?

1. How do you define censorship?

2. If authors are pressured to write in certain ways or about particular topics, do you see this as censorship? Why or why not?

3. What role does advertising play in censoring the media?

Murray L. Bob, *now deceased, was a librarian and author as well as a guest lecturer at the University of Illinois. He contributed articles to professional journals, national magazines, and newspapers. He also wrote* A Contrarian's Dictionary: 2,000 Damnable Definitions for the Year 2000. *This editorial, "Keep Ads Out of Books," appeared in a 1989 issue of* Library Journal.

KEEP ADS OUT OF BOOKS

Paid Advertisements in Books Will Undermine Our Freest Vehicle of Expression

Murray L. Bob

Whittle Communications recently caused a stir with its proposal to bring commercial television into the classroom—as if kids don't watch enough TV at home! Now Whittle has a new target for exploitation. Its latest venture is books that include advertising.

The company intends to pay several big-name authors $60,000 each to write 100-page hardcover books on timely topics. The books will contain ads throughout and be distributed free to 150,000 "opinion leaders"—just the sort of folks who can't afford to buy books. The company expects eventually to sell the books in stores.

Those of us who grew up thinking of the book as somehow sacred are appalled. Now that books have been used for discreet payoffs by the Speaker of the House and the House Minority Whip, one can't help wondering if bookmaking hasn't suddenly become the exclusive province of bookies.

It may just be a question of what one considers a book. The exudations of Messrs. Wright and Gingrich barely qualify on several scores. And given their 100-page limit, it is hard to resist referring to Whittle's proposed tomes as "half-whits." Unfortunately, not everyone will make such fine distinctions.

Pressure on Writers

Whittle's idea raises a number of questions that should be of concern to all book lovers: Will the advertisers try to influence content and style? Will advertising become the chief source of revenue—unlike the present arrangement whereby the reader is king—and affect what is written and how it is written? Self-censorship and pre-censorship on the grounds of possible advertisers' reactions are hardly unknown in the mass media.

Video and audio media are notoriously subject to, indeed shaped and reshaped by, advertising pressure. Pressure groups influence advertisers, who influence agencies, who influence networks and/or stations, who influence producers, who influence writers.

Most general magazines carry advertising and seem relatively unpressured. But periodicals, containing a large number of essays on a wide variety of topics, may be better able to defuse, deflect, and resist interference than single-author, single-subject books, subsidized by advertisers. Moreover, the ominous spread in magazines of deceptive "advertorials"—matter in which text and ad are virtually indistinguishable—makes one less sanguine about the prospect of letting advertising jam a foothold in book publishing.

Tampering with Ideals

Authors, perhaps romantically, have hitherto been regarded as "free lances." Will they become "hired guns" instead, working for sponsors? Won't their reputation for independence and thus their credibility suffer as a result? One may say that's their problem. But it isn't only their problem. The book, where it is still honorably and independently written, published, and distributed, is the freest vehicle of expression we have—which is why we abhor attempts to bowdlerize it.

Most books are, fortunately, not like the mass media—yet. This is partly a matter of tradition. The history of Western culture is replete with glorious examples of men and women who resisted censorship and suffered imprisonment and other egregious penalties for expressing their ideas in books. Precisely because of their independence from commercial pressures, books make their unique contribution to our civilization: comprehensive, thoughtful, careful, balanced, and unhurried weighing of ideas, free of astriction.

It seems a shame to take a chance on compromising a book in order to make a buck. Ideas are not like other commodities. They are vital to the functioning of a democracy in a way shaving cream is not. And the recipe for keeping ideas vital, yeasty, controversial, and independent shouldn't be as lightly tampered with as shaving cream formulas.

You Call This Progress?

It is difficult to see anything progressive about Whittle's gimmick, unless any additional way to make money represents progress. Some contend that ads may reduce the cost of the books. A laudable aim, but surely of less consequence than maintaining their integrity. It remains to be seen whether half-whits will be all that cheap. Since it will cost something to advertise in a little whittle, companies will certainly pass that cost on to consumers.

There are other ways to restrain book prices. Whatever the publishing industry and regular retailers may say about remaindering, it represents an important way for the public to buy books for less. Whatever publishers say, they do work ever more closely with remainder houses. As for regular retailers, discounting is not exactly unknown, even to them. Paperback originals, such as Saul Bellow's latest book, constitute yet another check on book prices. And if the idea is to get books to people, how about more money for library book budgets?

Ads in books are not a new idea. They have been tried several times before—and have failed. In this case, at least, there are some of us who hope that history will repeat itself.

DECODING THE TEXT

1. The author mentions the romantic notion of the author as well as the great Western tradition of authorship; he also labels books as sacred. What is he talking about? Does he support this idea in his text?

2. Can you find examples of weasel words in this essay?

CONNECTING TO YOUR CULTURE

1. Bob claims that magazines do not seem to be pressured by their advertisers, whereas video and audio outlets are often controlled by their advertisers. Can you find examples to either support or disprove his two arguments?

2. Do you ever feel pressured to write about certain topics or to avoid topics you would really like to explore? If so, how do you address this pressure?

Reading Selections: the '90s

CONSIDERING IDEAS

1. Would you feel uncomfortable if most of the ads you saw had images of people with disabilities in them? Why or why not?

2. What if ads only featured minority models or images?

3. What do you know about disability rights and legislation? How does this affect advertising?

Beth A. Haller *is an associate professor in the Mass Communication Department at Towson University. She has written numerous articles for professional journals as well as coauthored* An Introduction to News Reporting: A Beginning Journalist's Guide. *She is also coeditor of* Disability Studies Quarterly, *the journal where this essay first appeared in its entirety, and she has received several writing and reporting awards, including the 2003 National Rehabilitation Association Excellence in Media Award.*

Sue Ralph *is the program director for the Master of Education in Communications, Education, & Technology at The University of Manchester as well as a senior lecturer. Her primary areas of research include media and disability and the identification and management of stress in teachers. She has contributed many articles to academic journals and edited three books, including* Anarchy or Diversity. *She also serves as editor for* JORSEN (Journal of Research in Special Educational Needs).

PROFITABILITY, DIVERSITY, AND DISABILITY IMAGES IN ADVERTISING

Beth A. Haller and Sue Ralph

The disabled consumer is coming of age. Companies in the United States and Great Britain are seeing the profitability of including disabled people in their advertising. But what are the implications of the images produced in these advertisements? Are they moving away from the pity narratives of charity? Are they creating acceptance and integration of disabled people?

* * *

Advocates for disabled people in the US have long known the importance of the "disabled consumer market." Carmen Jones of EKA Marketing (1997) says: "Few companies have enjoyed the profitability that results in targeting the consumer who happens to have a disability. . . . I believe if the business community were educated about the size and potential of the market, then advertising programs with the disabled consumer in mind" would be created (p. 4). In the new millennium, advertisers are realizing that disabled people buy soap, milk, socks, jewelry, makeup, home improvement goods, use travel services, live in houses, and enjoy nice home furnishings. There is some evidence that the disabled consumer is very much more brand loyal than other consumers (Quinn, 1995). For example, the hotel chain Embassy Suites found out that becoming sensitive to the needs of disabled people led to more business. And a study by the National Captioning Institute found that 73 percent of deaf people switched to a brand that had TV ad captioning (Quinn, 1995).

British companies are still more hesitant in including disabled people in their advertisements due to both different advertising methods and societal attitudes. Although print ads are just as frequent in British publications, ads on British television are much less prevalent and more restricted than in the US where about 12 minutes of each half hour of commercial TV are advertisements. In the UK "the total amount of spot advertising in any one day must not exceed an average of nine minutes per hour of broadcasting" (ITC, 1998, p. 1).

However, some companies in both countries were slow to learn what accurate and non-stigmatizing advertising images were. For example, in 1990 a Fuji TV ad for film on British television that featured a man with learning disabilities being "improved" by a photograph of him smiling at the end was criticized by disabilities scholar Michael Oliver for its "medical model" approach (Deakin, 1996, Sept. 20, p. 37). The TV ad was interpreted as the Fuji film offering a type of "cosmetic surgery" on the disabled man through the advertisement. Ironically, the ad agency that created the Fuji ad consulted the British charity Mencap, but as Scott-Parker pointed out, "the perceptions and interests of a disability charity are not always synonymous with those of the disabled consumer" (Dourado, 1990, p. 27). Because of early faux pas like this, "disability is still an area in which few advertisers dare to deal" in Great Britain (Deakin, 1996, p. 37).

Excerpt of article "Profitability, Diversity, and Disability Images in Advertising in the United States and Great Britain," from DISABILITY STUDIES QUARTERLY by Beth Haller and Sue Ralph. Spring 2001. Reprinted by permission of the Society for Disability Studies.

In both countries, new disability rights legislation—the US Americans with Disabilities Act (ADA) and Work Incentives Improvement Act (WIIA) and the UK Disability Discrimination Act (DDA)—made the business community more aware of disabled consumers and that there are large numbers of them. These legislative acts have also given businesses an understanding that disabled people want to find more and better employment and in turn purchase more consumer goods. Some policy analysts actually called the ADA a mandate for marketers to begin to recognize the formerly invisible disabled market (Stephens and Bergman, 1995). In addition, the WIIA would provide a $1,000 tax credit to help people with severe disabilities cover work-related expenses. President Clinton pushed for the Act with an inclusive society perspective: "As anyone with a disability can tell you, it takes more than a job to enter the work force. Often, it takes successful transportation, specialized technology or personal assistance" (Clinton, 1999).

These types of legislative acts have made the US and the UK more receptive to accommodating disabled people in terms of architecture and communication so more will have the ability to make purchases and become part of each society's "consumer culture." For example, in the US, 48.5 million disabled people who are age 15 and over had an estimated total discretionary income of $175 billion (Prager, 1999, Dec. 15). In the UK, there are 6.5 million disabled people who represent a 33 billion pound market, which will increase (Deakin, 1996).

* * *

Cultural Meaning of Disability Images in Advertising

Disability studies scholar Harlan Hahn (1987) wrote a seminal article about the role of advertising in culturally defining, or not defining, disabled people. His work creates the framework we will use for analyzing subsequent ads that include disabled people. There is much literature about other societal groups' representation in advertising (Hall, 1997), but we will be focusing specifically on the unique case of advertising's disability images.

Hahn argues generally that advertising's emphasis on beauty and bodily perfection has led to exclusion of disabled people in the images. In addition, the nondisabled audience members' fears of becoming disabled and viewing images of disability meant businesses were hesitant to use disabled people as models.

Apparently the common difficulty of disabled people in gaining acceptance as human beings even permitted the belief that a male seated in a wheelchair was not really a man. Advertising and other forms of mass imagery were not merely designed to the increase sale of commodities; they also comprised a cultural force with an influence that has permeated all aspects of American life. From this perspective, issues of causation, such as whether advertising simply reflected widespread sentiments about disability or whether it contributed to implanting such feelings, become less critical than the assessment of contexts and effects (Hahn, 1987, p. 562).

The context Hahn discusses is disabled people's "inability" to ever fit within a context of beautiful bodies and they are therefore rendered invisible. He points out that advertising promotes a specific "acceptable physical appearance" that then reinforces itself. These advertising images tell society who is acceptable in terms of appearance and that transfers to who is acceptable to employ, associate with, communicate with, and value.

However, Hahn did see signs of hope in changing societal perceptions of disabled people through advertising and other forms of mass communication. He cites many historical examples in which physical appearances/attributes that were once prized were later seen as deviant or unattractive. Bogdan (1988) explained this phenomenon in his study of American freak shows, in which many disabled people were honored as celebrities; however, later people with the same disabilities were institutionalized.

In the modern understanding of diversity as a profitable undertaking for businesses, we argue that the cultural meaning of disability imagery in advertising is changing for the better. As Hahn predicted, some social attitudes are changing and advertising that features disabled people is being associated with profitability, both because of the newfound power of the disabled consumer and general audiences' desire to see "real life" in images. As discussed in the example of the Target advertising campaign, they received several thousand letters of positive feedback and sold products modeled by disabled people at a much higher rate.

Another study done in preparation for the 1996 Atlanta Paralympics illustrated that both households with (49%) and without a disabled person (35%) valued accurate advertising images of disabled people and were likely to buy products and services that showed sensitivity to disabled people's needs (Dickinson, 1996).

In terms of demographics, disabled people in the US and the UK are now seen as "consumers able to buy." With 6.4 million disabled people in the UK and about 50 million disabled people in the US, businesses are recognizing the vast consumer potential (Precision Marketing, 1997, p. 15). Therefore, the cultural meanings of disability advertising imagery in the UK and the US are capitalistic profitability from a huge consumer base and a thrust to better represent the general diversity of society, which general audiences want. Although there is still discomfort among some nondisabled people in seeing disability imagery, it seems to have much diminished in the US. With equalizing legislation such as the ADA, . . . companies and their advertising agencies are realizing what disability activist and former *Mainstream* magazine publisher Cyndi Jones said in 1992: "Portraying disabled consumers in ads 'is just good business'. . . because most places people go to work or to play have 'one if not a multitude of people who are disabled'" (Goerne, 1992 Sept. 14, p. 33).

However, the UK has only begun to try to convince British businesses with a campaign about the profitability of the disabled consumer in 2000 with the Cheshire Foundation's VisABLE campaign established in May 1999. UK Secretary of State for Education and Employment, David Blunkett, said that VisABLE was "a lead we should all follow" and said government departments would be encouraged to use more disabled people in their advertising (Connect, 1999, p. 5). The campaign was launched to encourage mainstream advertising companies to include more disabled people in their advertising material. The campaign, which coincides with the government initiatives to raise awareness about disability issues and the implementation of the Disability Discrimination Act, was created in conjunction with the National Disability Council (Stirling, 2000).

After an analysis of U.S. advertising practices using disabled people and a National Opinion Poll in the UK, Britain found its citizens open to inclusion of disabled people in advertising. One article in *The Guardian* explained how the VisABLE campaign followed some US companies' lead: "There's concrete evidence from the US of the commercial effectiveness of the enlightened approach," mentioning Target stores' pioneering approach to including disabled people in their print ads from 1990 on (Hilton, 1999, May 30). The opinion poll especially confirmed this trend toward a desire for enlightened advertising with its findings that "80 percent of the general public would welcome more disabled people in advertising. Seventy percent said they would not assume an advert featuring disabled people was directed specifically at disabled people rather than the general public as a whole" (Stirling, 2000, p. 9).

The VisABLE campaign did not ask advertising firms to spend money, but to plan their campaigns to include disabled models. In order to do this businesses needed access to disabled models. Rosemary Hargreaves, press and public relations officer for the Leonard Cheshire Charity for disabled people, which created VisABLE, said, "ad agencies and businesses claim there are no disabled models available, so we set out to challenge this perception by finding a pool of disabled models" (Stirling, 2000, p. 11). A modeling competition was launched as part of the campaign and attracted 500 disabled entrants. The two winners were a deaf woman and a wheelchair using man, who subsequently appeared in Marks and Spencer's chain store print ads selling women's tights and men's casual wear (*M&S Magazine*, 2000, p. 32, 45). The winners received a modeling contract

with VisABLE models, an agency created by Louise Dyson in cooperation with the campaign. The competition is meant to be an annual event and has attracted support from seven leading corporate partners—B&Q, British Telecom, Co-operative Bank, HSBC Hong Kong and Shanghai Banking Corp., Marks and Spencer, McDonald's, and One2One—all of whom have made a commitment to use disabled models in the future.

One company specifically took its own initiative to use the disabled people already in its employ. B&Q, which is a do-it-yourself home improvement chain store, already used its own employees in adverts and for the VisABLE campaign asked its disabled employees to volunteer to be in its ads. The B&Q diversity coordinator explained the policy of using disabled people in this way "is not only good for promoting B&Q as a diverse employer, but is good for raising the profile of all disabled people" (B&Q Talking Shop, 2000, p. 8).

Similar to the US, the VisABLE campaign is helping businesses recognize the power of the disabled consumer market. With 8 million disabled people with an estimated annual spending power of 40 billion pounds, "yet they are an untapped customer source," according to the VisABLE campaign (Stirling, 2000, p. 9). B&Q Diversity Manager Kay Allen points out that in addition to profit reasons and legal reasons such as the Disability Discrimination Act, businesses have "obvious moral reasons. It's absolutely right that companies should cover disability as a diversity issue" (Stirling, 2000, p. 10).

However, not all businesses or advertising agencies have come on board for the VisABLE campaign. Some still associate images of disabled people with charity concerns and inspiration (Ralph and Lees, 2000). Other business people admit that disabled people in advertising is an "alien concept" and that advertisers are not used to taking those kinds of risks ("Tonight," 2000). One advertising firm surveyed said including disabled people in advertising smacks of "tokenism" (Ralph and Lees, 2000).

As mentioned, the positive cultural meanings of profitability and diversity in advertising images do not solve all potential problems with disability imagery. As with all advertising images, the beautiful and least disfigured disabled people are depicted. As mentioned, many early TV ads in the US used primarily deaf people. Good-looking and sports-minded wheelchair users are another important visual category. But this does not truly represent the diversity within the disability community. As a disability publication editor said: "Not every person with a disability is young and beautiful and athletic, just like all women aren't size 10, and all African Americans don't have degrees from Harvard. . . . I know people with disabilities who aren't pretty. They drool. They scare the average person. So do we do more harm than good showing this cute little girl with CP?" (McLaughlin, 1993 Aug. 22, p. 31).

Some Current Disability Imagery in Advertising

As mentioned, Target chain stores began a trend by including disabled children and teens in their print ad circulars in 1990. Though hesitant at first, the advertising was a rousing success and the corporate office received 2,000 letters of support early in the campaign.

First, the images are well used because of the way they naturalize disability rather than stigmatize it. In fact, many times it takes several looks at the circulars to actually find the disabled children, whose disabilities are visable, because they are part of scenes of groups of children or a number of images on one page. The way Target uses disabled people in their ads fits squarely within the cultural meaning of diversity in advertising imagery. In fact, in 1994 a circular ad depicted a Latina disabled girl in a wheelchair interacting with a nondisabled Caucasian girls to sell girls pants sets. The ad is even more significant in that it depicts actual interaction between the children, rather than two girls staring at the camera. They are handing something to each other in a kitchen setting. This type of depiction sends several messages: That people of color have disabilities, too, and that interaction between disabled and nondisabled children is quite normal.

In another ad in 1994 for Target, a young blonde woman in a wheelchair is used to advertise women's T-shirts. Although she is alone in the picture and is a typical smiling, blonde model with a peaches and cream complexion, the interesting aspect to this ad is that she is wearing jeans shorts, which show her legs. As a person with a mobility disability her legs are not as muscular as a nondisabled person's might be and this is apparent in the photo. However, the image is not grotesque or disturbing. Once again, it just shows reality and the natural appearance of a wheelchair user's lower body.

In a 1995 Target ad, two teens are featured in an ad for women's cotton T-shirts. They are both smiling, fresh-faced blondes and one is a wheelchair user. The wheel-chair is partially obscured by examples of the T-shirt embroidery at the bottom of the photo so only a corner of a wheelchair peeks out. Again, this very subtle approach erases any stigma and makes the wheelchair using teen the equal of her blonde counterpart in the ad. The nondisabled teen is bent down near to the disabled teen so there is less height difference between the standing and sitting teens.

Finally, Target's ad campaigns realized that wheelchair use is not the only disability or even the most prevalent: In 1995, a circular depicted a boy with a walker in their ad for Power Ranger underwear sets. The walker, however, is placed behind him, possibly so the clothing was not covered in the picture. The boy stands up straight in his walker and is next to a girl modeling Power Ranger underwear for girls. The boy's tanned, smiling appearance is vigorous and healthy and really has little connection to a "medical model" depiction (Clogston, 1990), even with a walker in the scene. Another Target circular in Spanish advertised school uniform wear and featured a young model with a single crutch. She strikes a typical model pose with a sweater slung over her shoulder. She, too, has a healthy appearance and the illustration shows no misshapen extremities. In fact, her only "flaw" is one that normalizes her as a child—she is missing a front tooth. The only possible concern with this image is that it is shot from above her and looks down upon her completely. Finally, a Target promotional flier on tourist spots in Chicago features a child who appears to be blind interacting with two other children and a large bat at The Field Museum. Again, the interaction among the children and the lack of signification about her blindness normalizes the photo and presents no stigma to the viewer.

* * *

The sporting goods company Nike has used disabled athletes in a number of their advertisements. It should be noted that as media researchers of disability images we are concerned that many ads use disabled athletes which we believe to be an extension of the Supercrip image (Clogston, 1990; Covington, 1989). However, because of Nike's product line, all their advertising images are always of superathletes or athlete "wannabes."

Nike's TV ads have a mixture of the incidental use of disabled models and one featured disabled athlete, Craig Blanchette, who held two world records in wheelchair racing in 1989. The Blanchette spot is called "Cross training with Craig Blanchette" and no scene or mention of his disability is made in the first 27 seconds of the 30-second commercial. He is referred to as a 1988 Olympic bronze medalist. The ad seethes with macho images, first of Blanchette lifting weights, then aggressively playing basketball and tennis. The scenes are intensely athletic, and Blanchette is seen reaching for and making difficult shots. Although he is the focus of the ad, he is not alone. Other male athletic types, both young and old, black and white, are depicted in the background of the weight room, and Blanchette smilingly tosses a basketball to another young man in one scene. Blanchette appears muscular with his massive arms and rugged with his scruffy beard. Only in the last few seconds is it revealed that Blanchette is a wheelchair athlete when the camera pans down and he says:

"So I never quit" and turns his back to the camera and races down the track in his sports wheelchair.

Nike officials said it was not relevant to them that Blanchette is a wheelchair-using double amputee. Their VP of marketing explained, "He's a great athlete, which ties to our usual strategy . . . and he's a really motivating guy to be around. The fact that he was handicapped was secondary" (Lipman, 1989 Sept. 7, p. 1). But profitability from disabled athletes or consumers was likely a strong motivation. As a *Wall Street Journal* article says, the Blanchette Nike ad is an example of commercial advertising becoming "increasingly enchanted with the disabled" (Lipman, 1989 Sept. 7, p. 1). Nike also illustrates general inclusiveness in two other TV ads, one of which, "Heritage U.S. Update," has an image of an African American wheelchair racer and concludes with a triumphant white wheelchair user winning a race with "There is no finish line" superimposed in the background. Another Nike ad called "Hope" focuses almost entirely on men and women athletes of color and includes two fast images of wheelchair races and then a concluding image of a wheelchair racer who pulls open his shirt to reveal the "Superman" emblem.

Conclusion and Discussion

This analysis illustrates that companies in the US and the UK are seeing the profitability of including disabled people in their advertising and understanding the benefits of diverse images in advertising. The implication of the images produced in these advertisements is that advertising not only includes disabled people for capitalistic reasons, but realizes these must be accurate images to earn any profit from their use. This means compa-nies have learned, due to their own desire for profits, to move away from the past pity narratives of charity. Our analyses illustrate that corporate America and Britain can create good disability images in advertising that are sensitive and accurate and just represent disability as another slice of life.

However, we recognize that disability images in advertising are not perfect. There is almost total focus on two disabilities: wheelchair use and deafness. For example, McDonald's admitted early in advertising campaigns to taking the path of ease to show disabled people by just including wheelchair users in shots of "hordes of customers" (Dougherty, 1986, p. D26). Ironically, their "easy way out" actually became the best way to depict disability in ads—an incidental use of disability among a variety of people illustrates diversity in a very salient and accurate way. Although the incidence of wheelchair use is actually quite low when compared to other types of disabilities, it is also understood that advertising is a visual medium which needs the equipment cues such as wheelchairs to denote disability as part of the diversity depicted. Disabled screen writer Marc Moss explained that he was initially concerned about how wheelchair users were used in advertising as "proof of corporate soul." However, he does agree "that with varying degrees of finesse, they (advertisers) juggle two points: Their products or services are worthy, and so are people who can't walk" (Moss, 1992 June 19, p. A8).

Of course, as with all advertising, only "pretty people" can become models. This is the area in which many disabled people still have concern about the images of disability in advertising. "It would be nice to have a severely disabled person depicted instead of your superjock 'crip,'" says David Lewis, a quadriplegic who is community relations coordinator for the Center for Independent Living, a non-profit support group for the disabled based in Berkeley, California. "Usually disabled people in commercials look like able bodied people in wheelchairs'" (Lipman, 1989 Sept. 7, p. 1). However, some disabled people applaud finally being visible in ads or being presented as anything other than a charity case. As one disabled actor said, "the Adonis in a wheelchair is better than the whimpering victim in a corner" (McLaughlin, 1993 Aug. 22, p. 31). Therefore, due to the nature of media effects, we believe that these disability advertising images, even if they tend to focus primarily on beautiful deaf people or wheelchair users, can enhance more acceptance and integration of disabled people into society. Several past studies of the potential for attitude changes toward disabled people through use of media images have confirmed this phenomenon (Farnall & Smith, 1999; Panol & McBride, 1999; Farnall, 1996).

Finally, the better and more prevalent use of disabled people in advertising we believe can be tied to important anti-discrimination legislation in the US and the UK. The ADA kicked off a renewed awareness of disability rights which can be seen in the growing number of disabled people in ads from 1990 on and a better understanding of the disabled consumer market. It can be hoped that the Disability Discrimination Act of 1995 in the UK will lead to the same kind of inclusion of diverse disability in British advertising. The VisABLE campaign is an outgrowth of the consultation around the anti-discrimination legislation.

Historically, this article has documented the changing cultural meanings of disability imagery in advertising. Currently, business concerns see profitability in disability imagery and have found diversity to be good business practice. This is quite a shift from the pre-Rehabilitation Act and pre-ADA days. A National Easter Seals Society executive explained that in the mid-1970s she tried to persuade a Minneapolis company to use a disabled person in a promotional photo: "They were horrified at the idea. . . . They told me they would lose sales, it would scare people—they even used the word disgusting" (Sagon, 1991, Dec. 19, p. B10). By 1992 the same Easter Seals spokesperson praised companies like Kmart when they began a new TV ad campaign using a wheelchair-using actress to portray a customer. "Those of us in the nonprofit world have tried for years to change the way disabled people are perceived," Sandra Gordon of Easter Seals said. "Now it seems the for-profit world is finally lending a hand" (Roberts and Miller, 1992, p. 40).

Works Cited

B & Q (2000, June 8). It all adds up. *B & Q Talking Shop*, p. 116.

Blunkett, D. (1999). VisABLE campaign attracts companies and launches modelling competition. *Connect*, 5, Autumn, p. 5.

Bogdan, R. (1988). *Freak Show: Presenting Human Oddities for Amusement and Profit.* Chicago: University of Chicago Press.

Clinton, W. J. (1999, January 13). Remarks by the President on disability initiative. [White House press release].

Clogston, J. (1990). *Disability Coverage in 16 Newspapers.* Louisville: The Advocado Press.

Covington (1989). The stereotypes, the myth, and the media. Washington DC, The news media and disability issues. The news media education national workshop report, pp. 1–2.

Deakin, A. (1996, September 20). Body language. *Marketing Week*, 19 (26), p. 37.

Dickinson, R. J. (1996, May I5).The power of the paralympics. *American Demographics*, p. 15.

Dougherty, P. H. (1986, May 14). Advertising: TV spot for deaf viewers. *New York Times*, p. D26.

Dourado, P. (1990, August 16). Parity not charity. *Marketing*, pp. 26–27.

Farnall, O. (1996). Positive images of the disabled in television advertising: Effects on attitude toward the disabled. Paper presented at the annual meeting of the Association for Education in Journalism and Mass Communication, Anaheim, CA.

Farnall, O. & Smith, K. A. (1999). Reactions to people with disabilities: personal contact versus viewing of specific media portrayals. *Journalism and Mass Communication Quarterly*, 76(4), 659–672.

Goerne, C. (1992, September 14). Marketing to the disabled: New workplace law stirs interest in largely untapped market. *Marketing News*. 26(19), pp. 1, 32.

Granada Television. (2000). *Tonight*. [Television late night news program].

Hahn, H. (1987). Advertising the acceptably employable image: Disability and capitalism. *Policy Studies Journal*, 15: 3, 551–570.

Hall, S. (ed.) (1997) *Representation: Cultural representations and signifying practices*. Milton Keynes: Open University Press.

Hilton, S. (1999, May 30). Snatching defeat from the jaws of a publicity victory. *The Guardian*.

Independent Television Commission. (1998. Autumn). *ITC Rules on the Amount of Scheduling of Advertising*. London: ITC.

Jones, C. (1997). Disabled consumers. [Letter to the Editor]. *American Demographics*. 19(11), p. 4.

Lipman, J. (1989, September 7). Disabled people featured in more ads. *Wall Street Journal*, p. 1.

M&S Magazine (2000). Models with a message. May/June, p. 115.

McLaughlin, P. (1993, August 22). Roll models. *Philadelphia Inquirer*, p. 31.

Moss, M. J. (1992, June 19). The disabled 'discovered.' *Wall Street Journal*, p. A8.

Nike. (1989). Craig Blanchette. [Television advertisement].

Nike. (1990). Heritage U.S. Update. [Television advertisement].

Nike. (1994). Hope. [Television advertisement].

Panol, Z. & McBride, M. (1999). Print advertising images of the disabled: Exploring the impact on nondisabled consumer attitudes. Paper presented at the Association for Education in Journalism and Mass Communication annual conference, New Orleans, LA.

Prager, J. H. (1999, December 15). People with disabilities are next consumer niche—companies see a market ripe for all-terrain wheelchairs, computers with 'sticky keys.' *Wall Street Journal*, p. B1, 2.

Precision Marketing. (1997, May 12). *Life: Disabled people*. pp. 15–16.

Quinn, J. (1995). Able to buy. *Incentive*, 169 (9), p. 80.

Ralph, S. M. & Lees, T. (2000). Survey of London advertising agencies. Unpublished.

Roberts, E. & Miller, A. (1992, February 24). This ad's for you. *Newsweek*, p. 40.

Sagon, C. (1991, December 19). Retailers reach to the disabled; Stores see profit in underserved market. *Washington Post*, p. B10.

Stephens, D. L. & Bergman, K. (1995). The Americans with disabilities act: A mandate for marketers. *Journal of Public Policy and Marketing*, 14 (1) Spring, pp. 164–173.

Stirling, A. (2000). Making disability visible. *Compass*, 3, pp. 8–11.

VisABLE Campaign. (2000). [Video]. Produced by the Co-Operative Bank.

DECODING THE TEXT

1. What is the purpose of this essay?

2. According to Haller and Ralph, how has the for-profit advertising industry aided the nonprofit industry in changing the "way disabled people are perceived"?

3. Why do the authors say this image or perception needs to be changed?

4. According to the authors, what businesses have been the most helpful? In what ways?

CONNECTING TO YOUR CULTURE

1. How familiar are you with the advertising campaigns and images mentioned in the text?

2. Can you think of other ads that could now be added to the list?

3. Do you know of disabled groups that are still left out of mainstream advertising? Do you want to see them in ads? Why or why not?

CONSIDERING IDEAS

Flip through a couple of different magazines and discuss what kinds of ads you see.

1. How are the women portrayed? What do they look like? What are they wearing? What are they selling?

2. How are the men portrayed?

3. Is there any difference between the way the men and women are presented?

4. How do these ads make you feel about your own appearance or possessions?

Anthony J. Cortese, *a professor of sociology at Southern Methodist University, has research interests in social problems, policy, and ethics; ethnic and race relations; media and gender; and sociological theory. He is a prolific writer with four published books and numerous journal articles. The following essay is an excerpt from the chapter "Constructed Bodies, Deconstructing Ads: Sexism in Advertising" in his text* Provocateur: Images of Women and Minorities in Advertising.

CONSTRUCTED BODIES, DECONSTRUCTING ADS

Sexism in Advertising

Anthony J. Cortese

Feminist efforts to redefine gender ideals for advertisers . . . met with disbelief, resistance and downright hostility.

— Gail Dines and Jean M. Humez,
Gender, Race, and Class in Media

This chapter focuses on gender representations in advertising. Ad deconstruction reveals a pattern of symbolic and institutionalized sexism. *Sexism* is any attitude, behavior, institutional arrangement, or policy that favors one gender over another. Advertising sells much more than products; it sells values and cultural representations, such as success and sexuality, as we have seen.

Gender Representations

What kind of representations does advertising produce? It creates a mythical, WASP-oriented world in which no one is ever ugly, overweight, poor, toiling, or physically or mentally disabled (un-less you count the housewives who talk to little men in toilet bowls) (Kilbourne 1989).

Advertising has a great deal to say about gender identity. Ads use visual images of men and women to grab our attention and persuade. They are really projecting gender display—the ways in which we *think* men and women behave—not the ways they actually do behave (Goffman 1976). Such portrayals or images are not reflective of social reality. In advertising, for example, women are primarily depicted as sexual objects or sexual agents.

Because traditional gender roles are so easily recognized by consumers, they figure conspicuously in the imagery of mass media. Gender images hit at the heart of individual identity. What better place to choose than an arena of social life that can be communicated at a glance and

Excerpt of Chapter 3, "Constructed Bodies, Deconstructing Ads: Sexism in Advertising," from the book PROVOCATEUR: IMAGES OF WOMEN AND MINORITIES IN ADVERTISING, 2nd ed. by Anthony J. Cortese, pp. 51–55, 62–68. Reprinted by permission of Rowman & Littlefield.

that reaches into the core of individual identity (Jhally 1990)?

In tracing the evolution of ad campaigns over time in relation to changing social developments and patterns of intergroup tensions, we are actually discerning the cultural codes of gender, class, and race. It is important to expand media literacy in order to endure the invasion of media images, messages, and displays that is flooding our senses.

Advertising images provide culturally sanctioned ideal types of masculinity and femininity. Advertisers targeting women consumers subscribe to very limited notions of what constitutes femininity (e.g., dependency, concern with superficial beauty, fixation on family and nurturance, fear of technology) and, consequently, "feminine" buying patterns (Kilbourne 1989; Steinem 1990). "Feminist efforts to redefine gender ideals for advertisers in the 1970s and 1980s met with disbelief, resistance and downright hostility" (Dines and Humez 1995, 73).

Advertisers sometimes attempt to control the editorial content of the media by trying to censor feature stories that might conflict with their interests. For example, an episode of *Little House on the Prairie* that featured a pack of wild dogs threatening children was pulled when the sponsor, a leading dog food manufacturer, objected. This shows the lengths to which advertisers will go to protect their financial stake in their products and services.

Two general patterns seem to emerge concerning gender and advertising. First, ads tell us that there is a big difference between what is appropriate or expected behavior for men and women, or for boys and girls. Second, advertising and other mass media inculcate in consumers the cultural assumption that men are dominant and women are passive and subordinate. Moreover, while the masculine gender role is valued, the feminine counterpart is disregarded or devalued. . . . Ads portray women as sex objects or mindless domestics pathologically obsessed with cleanliness (Kilbourne 1989).

Perfect Provocateur: Young, Beautiful, and Seductive

Her face was white and perfectly smooth . . . every blemish or flaw she ever had gone away, though what those flaws had been I couldn't have told you. She was perfect now. . . . She had the fullness of young womanhood.
—Anne Rice, *The Vampire Lestat*

Advertisers have an enormous financial stake in a narrow ideal of femininity that they promote, especially in beauty product ads (Kilbourne 1989). The image of the ideal beautiful woman may perhaps be captured with the concept of the *provocateur* (an ideal image that arouses a feeling or reaction). The exemplary female prototype in advertising, regardless of product or service, displays youth (no lines or wrinkles), good looks, sexual seductiveness (Baudrillard 1990), and perfection (no scars, blemishes, or even pores) (Kilbourne 1989).

The provocateur is not human; rather, she is a form or hollow shell representing a female figure. Accepted attractiveness is her only attribute. She is slender, typically tall and long-legged. Women are constantly held to this unrealistic standard of beauty. If they fail to attain it, they are led to feel guilty and ashamed. Cultural ideology tells women that they will not be desirable to, or loved by, men unless they are physically perfect. An ad for Bijan, whose product line includes menswear, perfume, and jewelry, displays a fantasy: a nude obese woman is considered beautiful (the title of the ad is Bella) and worthy of an artist's careful work.

This ultimate image is not real. It can only be achieved artificially through the purchase of vast quantities of beauty products (Kilbourne 1989). The perfect provocateur is a mere façade. Even the models themselves do not look in the flesh as impeccable as they are depicted in ads. The classic image is constructed through cosmetics, photography, and airbrushing techniques.

Although the feminist movement challenged this "beauty myth" (Wolf 1991), the beauty industries (i.e., cosmetics, fashion, diet, and cosmetic surgery) countered with a multidimensional attack. First, they simply increased the number of commercial beauty images to which women are exposed. More than $1 million is spent every hour on cosmetics. Most of that money is spent on advertising and packaging (Kilbourne 1989). Only eight cents of the cosmetics sales dollar goes to pay for ingredients; the rest goes to packaging, promotion, and marketing (Goldman 1987, 697).

Through advertising, the face becomes a mask (something you put on) and the body becomes an object.

Women spend a huge amount of money on cosmetics because of the "structural realignments in gender relations, as women [assume] a more public identity than [has] been accorded them in the past" (Twitchell 1996, 149). This reinterpreta-tion of the meaning of being female in the United States was signaled by suffrage, the birth control movement, the new conception of motherhood, and the development of new frameworks of opportunity for women beyond the confines of the home. It is only within the context of this fundamental change in the perception of the woman's place—the conditional acceptance of the "New Woman"—that the cult of feminine beauty becomes comprehensible (Vinikas 1992, xv).

*   *   *

Muscularity as Masculinity

This omnipresent cult of the body is extraordinary. It is the only object on which everyone is made to concentrate, not as a source of pleasure, but as an object of frantic concern in the obsessive fear of failure or substandard performance.

—Jean Baudrillard, *America*

Baudrillard (1990) states that only women are seducers, but empirical evidence on advertising suggests otherwise. Men, too, are seducers—a male version of the perfect provocateur. The ideal man in ads is young, handsome, clean-cut, perfect, and sexually alluring. Today's man has pumped his pecs and shoulders and exhibits well-defined abs. He has tossed away his stuffy suit and has become a most potent provocateur.

Not many years ago, the slick and refined look defined fashion's ideal man. Now the muscular guy dominates the runways and magazine pages. The male provocateur is the image of the perfect athletic physique. He is the most recent model of manhood to appear in advertisements, films, musical artists, and fashion. Even in children's action figures, the muscular, athletic look has replaced the moderately lean figure. One only needs to compare the G.I. Joe of the early 1980s to the well-defined and brawny superhero action figures of today to see this pattern.

This contemporary warrior has become chic—not accidentally—as fashion has discovered a fresh male lead in the blue-collar man. Fashion photographers help create and capture this ultramasculine image. In fact, 90 percent of male models are working class—rough around the edges and beefy, not as frail, thin, or chiseled as their predecessors.

The new ideal look displays muscularity, athleticism, and a blue-collar background. Some musical artists regularly do strength and aerobic training to maintain a lean, muscular physique and endurance for performing. Shirtlessness is part of a trend that corresponds to the rise of the beefy male model. Designers have embraced the garb of the blue-collar man. For example, Italian designers have presented European blue-collar industrial boots, sweaters, and overcoats. In the same vein are the bold fashions of the late Gianni Versace, who pioneered a tight tank top or vest over the exposed chest.

This ultramasculine look from Italy and other parts of Europe has immigrated to the United States. It has been successfully marketed in stores such as the Gap, Banana Republic, and Old Navy that primarily sell cotton clothing. Out went the preppy look and in came lumberjack plaid and denim shirts and lug-sole shoes. The blue-collar man's wardrobe became mainstream fashion.

The male provocateur has become a symbol of our times. The rise of the blue-collar man has stimulated a return to an emphasis on a muscular, athletic body build. Advertising agencies and fashion photographers have seized the ultramasculine look, marketed it, and propelled its success in popular culture.

The beefy, muscular look has found a receptive audience in everything from beer commercials to clothing ads. It may have evolved as a need to compensate for the widespread violence in postmodern society. An overdeveloped body has traditionally been viewed as a sign of vanity (Morris 1996). Now men (and women) may be bodybuilding to produce a strong physical image or give the illusion of invincibility in hopes of being less vulnerable to random acts of violence. A strong physical image may compensate for a lack of economic security and control over one's work. In other words, a physically powerful look validates masculine identity and provides a dominating image for safety and protection.

The increased popularity of bodybuilding has been associated with male insecurity (Klein 1993). There is an interesting parallel between the anorexic waif look in females and the muscular and athletic look in males. At the extreme of both is obsessive-compulsive behavior, which is believed to be due to a chemical imbalance in individuals. In addition to this biological chemical imbalance, cultural, gender, and subcultural forces guide and shape individuals as part of the processes of socialization and acculturation.

In females, obsessive-compulsive behavior may result in anorexia nervosa, in which girls and women starve themselves in an attempt to reach unrealistic cultural standards of feminine beauty. Similarly, in obsessive-compulsive men we may see a condition called muscle dysmorphia. These men are obsessed with achieving an unrealistic cultural standard of muscularity as masculinity. Like the anorexic who sees herself as fat and unattractive despite her emaciated appearance the man suffering from muscle dysmorphia sees himself as scrawny and inadequate despite his bulging muscles. Many of these men have made lifting weights the most important activity in their lives, at the expense of family, relationships, and career.

Anorexia nervosa in women and muscle dysmorphia in men are sad reminders of the debilitating dysfunctions of gender roles in postmodern society. In contemporary culture, muscles reflect more than merely men's functional ability to perform heavy labor or defend themselves, their loved ones, and their private property. Muscles are waymarks that distinguish men from each other as well as from women (except for female athletes and bodybuilders).

The discussion of muscles as a sign of power involves not only working-class men but also middle- and upper-class males (Katz 1995). Muscularity and strength are highly valued within the male sports subculture by men of all races and social classes. Muscularity as masculinity is a motif in ads that target upper-income men as well as those on the lower range of social stratification. Advertisers often use representations of physically rugged or muscular male bodies to masculinize goods and services aimed at elite male consumers.

Bodybuilding may be men's reaction to compensate for an increase in women's economic, political, and social power. It is the intimidation factor. If men can no longer dominate women economically, politically, and socially, they are developing their bodies to be even bigger and stronger than women's. Men are reconceptualizing their images as they lose control or influence over the wives, girlfriends, mothers, sisters, and secretaries who used to purchase most of their clothes. Now men are designing an image for themselves. There appear to be two key points. First is a strong interest in clothing styles. Second is the beefy image, a type of exhibitionism. The provocateur exhibits himself either by showing his body or by displaying his fashion sense.

Beefy male models understand that they have a look that is currently very marketable. Sexual allure sells everything from cars, clothing, calendars, and cologne to music. After years of depicting women as sex objects and troubled bimbos, advertising is applying those stereotypes to men (Foote 1988). Contrary to Baudrillard's (1990) contention, it is clear that advertising also portrays men as provocateurs or seducers.

As part of my research on advertising, I immersed myself in the acting and modeling industry. I modeled on runways and in print media, played minor roles on several television series and commercials, and was a stand-in for a CEO in another commercial. Despite an emphasis on muscularity, thinness is still demanded of male models. The norm for fashion runway models is a very narrow range: six feet to six feet two inches in height and approximately 160 to 170 pounds. My agent, a former model of Asian descent, stood six feet tall and weighed only 160 pounds. He was so thin that he covertly wore thigh pads in his trousers to simulate muscular quadriceps.

Now in postmodern advertising, it is the man's turn to be the sex object—stripped and moist, promoting everything from underwear to women's fashion. Feminist theory and the women's movement have made it politically incorrect to portray women as potent provocateurs or desperate dullards. Public consciousness has raised awareness in advertising of how women can be delineated. The insertion of men into these traditional roles is good business.

The most noticeable archetypes of the male provocateur are in advertising. Men are depicted in ads as incompetent and sometimes as objects of ridicule, rejection, anger, and violence. Predictably, men's-rights activists have protested the use of these types of images for commercial exploitation. The image of men as incompetent fathers, unfortunately, is consistent with the way men actually have been treated in divorce courts and child custody hearings.

Consumer surveys (Langer, in Foote 1988) have shown that some women simply delight in seeing foolish men in ads and commercials. The portrayal of men as foolish and incompetent has possible connections with general cultural presuppositions about men and women (Elliott and Wootton 1997). This is a better explanation for the images than conspiracy theories that claim that it is female ad execs retaliating for decades of ads that exploited females as sex objects. Typically, women, as an aggregate, are not yet in power positions as advertisers or clients to determine such marketing strategy.

Advertising images of women from sexpots to airheads not only sold brand products and services but also helped to shape social attitudes on relationships and on the roles and status accorded to women. It follows that these images of men confirmed that some women increasingly view men as sex objects, jerks, or nerds. Yet if women were the target audiences for such ads, it made them seem malicious, indignant, and unjust. Advertisers realized that they had gone too far and toned down the male image from the blatant sex object to a more affectionate view.

Men appear to have a mixed reaction to the provocateur image, which is a definite change from the old-fashioned protector and provider images. In fact, partial nudity within a romanticized context of fatherhood has become a convincing marketing device. The hunky dad image—especially the seminude hunky dad—has been cited as among the most positive portrayals of men in advertising (Foote 1988). Men also have reacted favorably to images of vulnerability. However, they seem to be most annoyed by the kitchen-klutz syndrome.

How long will the beefy look be hot? It has thrived for twenty years in a rapidly changing industry. Advertisers must shock us, it seems, to get our attention. We have become numb to their shock tactics. That is why postmodern advertising has sacrificed even its sacred brand logos to get our attention. Images of hunky but sensitive men cause us to pay attention. The postfeminist male in postmodern advertising hauntingly reminds us of the prefeminist female in modern advertising.

The Intrinsic Defect

The promise of the commercial is not just "You will have pleasure if you buy our product," but also (and perhaps more important), "You will be happy

because people will envy you if you have this product."
The spectator of the commercial imagines herself
transformed by the product into an object of envy for
others—an envy which will justify her loving herself.
The commercial images steal her love of herself as she
is, and offer it back to her for the price of the product.
—John Berger

To be successful, an ad must be persuasive on two levels. First, it should raise your anxiety level. It should persuade you that you need something; it should make you feel guilty, inferior, or somehow "less than." Second, an ad must provide the solution. If an ad captures you on both these levels, you are generally hooked.

Advertisers are constantly bombarding consumers, especially women, with the message that they are inherently flawed—that what they are or what they have is not enough, too much, or not good enough (Kilbourne 1989). One ad, for example, says, "Introducing the eyes you wish you had been born with." Women need change—specifically, eliminating what is wrong with them. There is an assumption, often explicit, that there is something wrong with their physical appearance, dress, or body odor. "Where did such widespread afflictions as body odor, halitosis, iron poor blood, gray hair, water spots, vaginal odor, dish pan hands, various small glands and muscles, and split ends come from?" (Twitchell 1996, 32).

Advertisers have cleverly poked fun at the way their own industry portrays women as needing substantial physical changes. A Michelob Light ad balances a group of exhortations to self-improvement with "Relax. You're OK. Improve your beer." This use of self-deprecation has been highly successful and has also come to characterize postmodern advertising, which no longer tries to come across as authoritative.

Ads also sometimes portray men as inherently flawed. There is plenty of room for improvement for men as well as women, the ads say. But advertisers don't seem to be as hard on men as they are on women. Nevertheless, ads target men's physical prowess in two areas especially, stressing a lean and muscular body and a healthy, thick head of hair, without any gray, of course.

DECODING THE TEXT

1. The original text was accompanied by numerous images and sample advertisements. Would seeing these images help or hinder your understanding of the author's argument? In what ways?

2. What is Cortese's main idea? How does he support his ideas?

3. Does the text appeal to your sense of logic? Emotions? Both?

1. Cortese says that ads should raise your anxiety level and then provide the solution. Can you describe ads that do this? Are they effective? Do they make you want to buy certain products?

2. Do you trust ads that are self-deprecating or make fun of the advertising industry?

3. How do you want to see men and women portrayed in advertisements?

Reading Selections: A Case Study from the '00s

CONSIDERING IDEAS

1. Take a day to consciously acknowledge every ad, including logos, you see. Count how many you see in a day.

2. Do you see more in particular areas or when performing particular activities?

3. Do you ever get tired of seeing ads? Do you ignore the ads?

4. How do you feel about Internet pop-ups? Commercials before the movie starts? Prominent name brands used in television shows and movies?

Kathryn Balint *is a staff writer for* The San Diego Union-Tribune, *where this article first appeared. She has more than 200 articles with the newspaper. Her other articles dealing with consumerism that the reader might find interesting are "S.D. Company Helping eBay, Others Reach Niche Audiences with Online Radio" and "Consumers Group Files Suits Against Phone Companies."*

ADS AD NAUSEAM?

Kathryn Balint

Coming soon to your cell phone: advertising, lots of advertising.

- Ads—already staples of TV and the Internet—are appearing on the third screen this year in several formats:

- Video ads. Toyota sponsored Fox Mobile Entertainment's "Prison Break: Proof of Innocence" mobisode for cell phones. A 10-second ad for the carmaker's new U.S. subcompact Yaris appeared at the beginning of the show.

- Banner ads. The newspaper *USA Today* is among advertisers who have opted for advertisements that are stripped across the top of a cell phone screen while users surf for information.

- Product placement in video games and "advergaming," which promotes a product throughout a game.
     CoverGirl, a makeup brand from Procter & Gamble, offered a $1 discount on the $5.99 cell phone game Girls' Night Out Solitaire—featuring "virtual girlfriends"—to customers who entered a product code from a mascara package. CoverGirl received product placement within the game from Menlo Park–based LimeLife.

- Coupons. In one example, a visitor to Mission Bay searching for food using San Diego–based Astroleap's new cell phone directory service can obtain a deal for 10 percent off the bill at Sportsmen's Seafood.

Advertisers are ready to move ahead with cell phone ads—even if customers are wary of mobile marketing and the industry is still debating how to keep from alienating consumers with unwelcome pitches.

"Advertising has dominated the first two screens, television and the Internet. It's natural that the next screen of advertising monetization is going to be the mobile screen," said Craig Hagopian, co-chief executive and president of V-Enable, the San Diego maker of a voice-activated directory assistance service for cell phones to be available early next year.

In 2007, cell phone ad revenue is expected to double to $1.5 billion, according to The Shosteck Group, a market research firm in Silver Spring, Md. Worldwide spending on cell phone advertising could reach more than $11 billion annually by 2011, London-based Informa Telecoms & Media predicted earlier this month.

"Ads Ad Nauseam? Advertising on Cell Phones is on the Increase—But Not Everyone Is Delighted About the Idea" by Kathryn Balint, from the SAN DIEGO UNION-TRIBUNE, September 24, 2006. Reprinted by permission.

Almost 90 percent of 50 brand-name companies surveyed earlier this year by London-based Airwide Solutions said they will advertise on cell phones by 2008. In five years, more than half of the companies expect to spend between 5 percent and 25 percent of their total marketing budgets on cell phone advertising.

Advertising on cell phones has been around since 2001, but only recently has it gathered steam because of technological advances and advertisers growing disenchanted with the effectiveness of traditional media.

In the last month, there have been a flurry of announcements. Among them:

Sprint Nextel said it will become the first wireless carrier to start running banner ads on user's screens. The venture, done in conjunction with New York–based Enpocket, a mobile marketing firm, is set to begin in October.

Amp'd Mobile said it will offer ads for Herbal Essences shampoo, sponsored by Procter & Gamble, on its video-on-demand service.

Other wireless carriers are quietly testing various forms of advertising.

The medium is so new that advertising prices are still shaking out, but some are flat rates, while others are pay-per-click.

"Since this is still a new area for the industry, we're still researching it from different perspectives," said Ken Muche, spokesman for Verizon Wireless. "At the end of the day, the customer's experience with this, or any of our products or services, is paramount, so we've been carefully measuring our customer's reception to the idea of mobile advertising and how it could function."

Advertisers see cell phones as a way to target customers who would be most interested in their products. The potential recipients of the ads, though, might not be all that receptive.

"I like advertising, but not on cell phones," said Ozge Hakimian, 24, of Kearny Mesa. "Ads on cell phones are useless for me, and they bother me. Ads on TV, radio, magazines, that's fine. But a cell phone is something to communicate with."

In a survey of 1,001 Americans earlier this year by Toronto market researcher RBC Capital Markets, 58 percent said mobile advertisements are a nuisance and should be prohibited.

In other research, Informa Telecoms & Media found that cell phone users are "not at all willing" to receive advertising via text messages. But the researcher found that users are generally willing to accept advertising in return for free TV shows, games, music and other services on their cell phones.

One reason why consumers seem to generally dislike the idea of ads on cell phones is that they think it will invade their privacy.

"Let's say you're walking past a coffee shop and you get a text ad saying, 'Step on in, and we'll give you $1 off an espresso drink,'" said Beth Givens, director of the San Diego–based Privacy Rights Clearinghouse. "I have a concern about that, the intrusiveness of combining a marketing message with location information.

There's the creepiness factor here. Someone knows where you are, and they're sending you a message based on your location."

Consumers also are jaded by unwanted spam messages in their computer e-mail accounts and don't want it on their cell phones. One in six cell phone users has received spam text messages from advertisers on their handsets, according to Telephia, a San Francisco market researcher.

In one case, a wireless carrier sent commercial text messages—then charged subscribers for them.

The Utility Consumers' Action Network, a San Diego–based consumer advocacy group, complained to the state Public Utilities Commission in July 2005 after Sprint, now Sprint Nextel, sent customers text messages advertising itself and then charged them for the messages.

Sprint Nextel and UCAN have reached a settlement in which the wireless carrier has agreed to reimburse customers who were billed for the ads and to stop the practice. The settlement is awaiting approval from the PUC.

"We wanted to send a message to the industry: Don't try advertising to customers and then charging them to receive the advertisement," said UCAN Executive Director Michael Shames.

In the settlement agreement, Sprint Nextel said it was unaware that customers had been billed for the ads until UCAN brought it to the company's attention.

"The industry is trying to learn from the Internet, with its obtrusive ads and pop-ups," said Dan Novak, vice president of programming and advertising for San Diego–based MediaFLO USA, a Qualcomm subsidiary that is building a nationwide network to broadcast TV shows to cell phones.

"Our job is to balance the overarching consumer experience with the advertising opportunity," Novak said. "I don't think they're mutually exclusive at all. I think the advertising can add value to the consumer experience."

The Mobile Marketing Association, a trade group of 400 companies involved in the wireless industry and advertising, is developing ground rules for the industry that will address some consumers' rights. For instance, the association disapproves of unsolicited messages and recommends that customers opt in to receive commercial text messages.

"We are establishing these guidelines and best practices in advance of mass deployment so we can ensure we're doing this the right way," said association Executive Director Laura Marriott. "Again, consumer opt-in is critical."

By regulating itself, the industry hopes to avoid government regulations on mobile advertising, she said.

Consumers don't hate all ads—just the ones that are meaningless to their lives, said MediaFLO's Novak. He said the key is to personalize the ads so that the wares being peddled are something the customer is interested in buying.

"If you're in the market for a car and the commercials are relevant to that, they're not intrusive at all," Novak said.

Astroleap Eurekamobile, a free directory service that launched on Cingular earlier this month, was created with the idea of offering ads that directly relate to the cell phone user's search.

Someone searching for a nearby spa comes across a coupon for $50 off on an initial visit to All About Me Medical Day Spa in Rancho Peñasquitos, while someone searching for business services in San Diego is shown a shipping discount coupon for PostalAnnex.

"We've chosen to advertise with Astro-leap because we're excited about the new channel of advertising to our customers," said Steve Goble, director of marketing communications for PostalAnnex. "We think the service they provide is especially relevant to many of our customers who are looking for where to ship a package at the last moment, for instance."

Astroleap co-founder Dan Bailey said the service puts users in control. "We've taken the approach that the user is going to tell us what they want, when they want it," he said. "It's an opt-in system. You won't be walking down the street and get zapped with an ad. You have to actively punch in your search."

Jane Zweig, chief executive of The Shosteck Group, said that it's important for adver-tisers to give cell phone users the chance to opt in—or out—of advertisements.

"We are very much in the early days in terms of successful deployments of ads on cell phones," she said. "There is a lot of potential for mobile advertising. But how it will play out and how revenue distribu-tion and revenue share play out are the big question marks. And no one has really figured out whether end users want this on their cell phones."

Lenore Skenazy *is a contributing editor for the* New York Sun *and* Advertising Age, *as well as a syndicated columnist who works in television, radio, and print. She has appeared on CNBC, The Food Network, and the Bravo reality show* Tabloid Wars; *National Public Radio often features her commentaries on everyday life. This newspaper article first appeared in 2003 in the* New York Daily News, *where Skenazy worked as a columnist for eighteen years.*

THERE'S NO ESCAPE FROM ADS, EVEN IN THE BACKSEAT

Lenore Skenazy

In bathroom stalls, elevators and now even the backseats of taxis, they just can't stop doing it. How disgusting! Have they no shame?

I'm speaking, of course, about advertisers. They're sticking ads everywhere, even in hitherto virgin territory.

"We've done urinal mat advertising," says Marcie Brogan, managing partner of Brogan & Partners in Detroit. Her competition, Flush Media of the Bronx, places ads discreetly above the urinals—as well as in bathroom stalls and smack-dab in health club shower rooms. What exactly do they advertise there? Soap? Shampoo? Liposuction?

"It has reached way past the point of silliness," says Scott Donaton, editor in chief of *Advertising Age*, musing on the ubiquity of marketing messages. "The question these days is, where isn't there advertising?"

His magazine has reported on the European fad of painting ad slogans on live cows—presumably, not for Big Macs. And then there's the Amsterdam ad agency offering free pre-printed strollers to parents who don't mind pushing Precious in a billboard on wheels. Advertisers are placing ads on movie ticket stubs, shopping carts and—how could they resist?—ATM screens. As long as you're waiting for your money, they might as well tell you how to spend it!

Commercials blare, too, from checkout counters and computer screens. They're playing in movie theater lobbies and again before the film. There's even a Florida company that has started placing ads inside golf holes. For what? Roof repair? In case you got (ahem) a hole in one?

But personally, Donaton most resents the ad invasion of his office building's elevator, where a nonstop TV broadcasts news, commercials and trivia. "I work on the second floor. God forbid I have five seconds to myself to have an independent thought," he mutters.

My most recent and vexing ad assault came Christmas Day, when my family was taking a taxi to a friend's apartment.

"Welcome to our world of toys!" sang the TV—yes, TV!—embedded in the backseat. We couldn't turn it off, which meant the kids sat glued to a smarmy toy soldier pitching the magic of the season—i.e., overpriced presents—even as the winter wonderland of a real live white Christmas passed by their windows, unnoticed.

Thank goodness, taxi TVs might not be here to stay. Right now, they're in just about 120 of the city's 12,187 cabs, says Taxi & Limousine Commission spokesman Allan Fromberg. Seven companies have placed them there as part of a year-long pilot project.

Some of the TVs are interactive, providing listings of restaurants and museum exhibits. But some, like the one I saw, are simply a mind-numbing loop of ads mixed with so-called public service announcements advising us to do things like buckle our seat belts. It's enough to make you—and the agonized driver—pine for Elmo. Our cabbie said he gets $100 a month to endure the pain, and it's not worth it.

The public is invited to register its enthusiasm or gigantic lack thereof at nyc.gov/taxi. "If it's good and useful and the public likes it," says Fromberg, the TVs will stay, incorporating the features that consumers enjoy most.

But the feature I enjoy most is called my sanity. With ads blaring from every nook, its meter is running out.

Iain S. Bruce *is the technology editor for Scotland's award-winning* Sunday Herald, *where this article first appeared in 2006. Bruce is also a broadcaster, and he has worked with the national media in places like the United States, United Kingdom, and Scandinavia.*

THE BATTLE FOR ADVERTISING

Internet Giants Get Ready for Full Combat

Iain S. Bruce

There is a battle taking place for the heart of the advertising industry. The risks are high, the stakes are huge, and the price of getting it wrong could end careers, devastate brands and bring about the demise of entire companies.

With the announcement that it intends to launch a context-sensitive display service that embeds relevant adverts in web pages, eBay has injected fresh impetus into the online advertising sector.

Using similar techniques to the Google AdWords technology that has become an almost ubiquitous presence on computer users' screens over the past year, the GBP4.2 billion web-auction leviathan's

"The Battle for Advertising: Internet Giants Get Ready for Full Combat" from the SUNDAY HERALD by Iain S. Bruce, June 18, 2006. Used by permission of the author.

planned AdContext system has reawakened traditional media fears that the digital bogeyman is about to seize a huge chunk of its revenues.

No wonder: paid search advertising of the kind being offered by eBay and Google proved to be the fastest-growing format of 2005, with the total spend increasing by 78.8 per cent to GBP768.4 million, according to the Internet Advertising Bureau (IAB), in a year when the combined spend on all other media fell by about GBP200m.

For sales teams in radio stations, newspapers and regional television broadcasters across the globe, these are very scary times. Total UK online ad spend grew by 65.6 per cent to total GBP1.366bn last year and, according to the IAB, is now chasing national newspaper advertising—worth GBP1.9bn—having already outstripped radio, consumer and outdoor advertising.

Increasingly, clients are trying to get under the skin of the Google generation.

"They are where the action is at," says Alistair Brodie, online director at Glasgow-based agency Curious Group.

"Advertisers are a lot more savvy these days. They want targeted exposure, transparency and an absolute measure of the return they get for their investment, and the web is the only medium that can deliver this."

Responsible for handling the digital spend for companies such as Dell, Clydeport and Croner, Brodie pitches online advertising as the platform that does what it says on the tin.

Billing on a pay-per-click basis means that buyers only have to shell out for what they use, while every consumer who follows a banner advert through can be logged, delivering the sort of detailed information on a campaign's effectiveness that cannot be gleaned from newspaper or television campaigns.

"There will always be a place for newspaper advertising, but all our research indicates that within a couple of years, the majority of all marketing budgets will be spent online," he says.

Yet, while it is true the economics of internet advertising are changing, many argue that this is not the whole story.

For advertisers, search advertising offers large numbers of surfers who are looking for specific products. AOL's Brand New World research indicated that 74 per cent of online consumers have personally researched a product or service online before making a purchase. Google reaches more than 80 per cent of the UK internet audience and has become the biggest media owner on the planet as a result of its simple but effective service.

"For agencies that act as intermediaries for that advertising expenditure by placing advertisers on search engines, search has produced a good source of revenue that has allowed many to get through the bursting of the dotcom bubble five years ago. It has also encouraged the birth of a number of specialist search agency players," says Richard Dance, head of strategy at Unique Digital.

"But to say it has made the internet the only viable medium is misleading, given that the end revenue is concentrated among about four major players and at least 60 per cent of advertising is not search related.

"Competition for search advertising budgets is reducing profit margins for online agencies, and bid costs in many sectors are stabilising."

The problem is that most people use the internet for communication, not buying CDs or car insurance. E-retailers' standards group the IMRG says that in 2005 more than GBP25bn was spent online, which though impressive, is only 10 per cent of all retail sales. Moreover, much of this is produced in the run-up to Christmas rather than across the year.

Although the infrastructure developed by the likes of Google and eBay is significant, it has not yet had a major impact on the way other online advertising media are traded. While some media owner inventory management systems prioritise the highest spending advertisers, this is only really applicable to direct response advertising, whereas a growing proportion of online advertising is trying to raise awareness of brand or products rather than producing an immediate sale.

To achieve this, internet advertising has been forced to look to its traditional competitors and emulate them, selling displays on a per thousand page impression basis that strips the medium of its interactive advantages.

"Of far greater threat to newspapers is the potential loss of classified and recruitment advertising revenues," says Dance. "A quarter of online advertising is in this sector, which experienced a 62.4 per cent increase in 2005, and this is already starting to hurt the traditional press, which saw a 5.1 per cent drop in classified spend."

Yet, the fact is that for all its bluster, the internet sector remains a major advertising customer for the traditional media. AOL still spends more on radio advertising than it does online, devoting in the region of 70 per cent of its marketing budget to offline platforms, and as matters stand, the company sees no reason to abandon this stance.

"Yes, it is true that companies like Sainsbury and Lever Brothers are beginning to carry out brand awareness campaigns online, but then the web is such an important communications channel now that they could hardly ignore it," says Giles Ivy, AOL's European sales director and former head of advertising at Virgin Radio.

"There will be readjustments, of course, but to suggest that television and newspapers are about to be wiped out as an advertising force is simply rubbish."

Ivy argues that rather than getting its knickers in a twist and arguing the toss over which platform is likely to end up the biggest, Britain's advertising industry needs to concentrate on its ability to deliver effective campaigns across all of them.

"Stop thinking about specific media because the lines are already being blurred. If someone watches the news online, is that the internet or is it television?

"The answer is that it doesn't really matter," he says.

"No matter whether you're a newspaper, a broadcaster or an online blog, if you concentrate on delivering what consumers want, then the advertising revenues will inevitably follow."

All of these essays report on the pervasive use of ads—on the Internet, on your cell phone, in the movies, even in the back of taxi cabs.

1. Do the various authors see this practice as good or bad? How can you tell?

2. Does the intended publication for the essay, newspaper versus journal, affect the writing style of the author? If so, in what ways?

CONNECTING TO YOUR CULTURE

1. How much time do you spend on the Internet? What kinds of advertisements have you encountered? Do they interrupt your time online?

2. Do you use a cell phone? Have you ever received an ad on your phone?

3. Where else have you encountered ads? Do they interfere with your sanity as Skenazy claims?

4. Do you think product placement in movies makes them more realistic? Can you describe an example of this placement?

Reading Selections:
Across the Decades

CONSIDERING IDEAS

According to *Advertising Age*, "some of the best-loved ad images of the 20th century have names like Tony, Betty and Ronald. Others, like the Marlboro Man, may not be as beloved, but grew to have tremendous worldwide impact as an instant identifier of Philip Morris Co.'s Marlboro cigarettes."

1. How many of these characters can you name?

2. Have you ever bought posters, signs, or clothing with any of these images on them?

Barbara J. Phillips *is a professor of marketing at the University of Saskatchewan. Her main research interest focuses on the influence of visual images in advertising on consumer response. She has published several journal articles on the topic, and she received the Best Article award in 2005 from the* Journal of Advertising. *The essay "Defining Trade Characters and Their Role in American Popular Culture" first appeared in the anthology* The Journal of Popular Culture.

DEFINING TRADE CHARACTERS AND THEIR ROLE IN AMERICAN POPULAR CULTURE

Barbara J. Phillips

Trade characters have been used as successful advertising tools in the United States for over one hundred years. American popular culture has quietly become inhabited by all sorts of talking animals and dancing products that are used as a communication system by advertisers. In 1982, a research study found that commercials with advertising developed characters who became associated with a brand scored above average in their ability to change brand preference (Stewart and Furse). It appears, then, that society is getting the message. However, although popular with advertisers and consumers, trade characters have been largely ignored in the study of advertising and popular culture. Through a review of the relevant literature, this paper will determine what trade characters are, and how they are employed in modern advertising practice to communicate to consumers in society.

Trade Characters: What They Are

Little attention has been given to defining the term "trade character." In a perusal of dozens of advertising textbooks, only a few offer an explicit definition of the term. The rest are silent on the subject, or focus exclusively on what a trade character does as opposed to what a trade character is. Of the authors who define "trade character," several offer vague explanations such as "a character created in association with a product" (Norris). There is

little consensus among the remaining definitions; many of the more insightful contradict each other. Therefore, this paper will develop an explicit definition of the term "trade character" that considers four areas of contention: animate versus inanimate characters, non-trademarked versus trademarked characters, fictional versus real characters, and trade versus celebrity characters.

Animate Versus Inanimate Characters

Some of the current definitions of "trade character" are very broad, identifying a trade character as any visual symbol that is associated with a product (Dunn and Barban). By including all visual symbols, these authors classify inanimate objects such as the Prudential rock as trade characters. On the other hand, several definitions specify that a trade character must be an animate being or an animated object (Wright, Warner, and Winter; Mandell) thereby excluding the Prudential rock (unless it is made to sing or dance).

There are two reasons why trade characters should be restricted to animate beings or animated objects. The first is that the word "character," defined by Webster's dictionary to mean "person," implies a living personality. This personality is the focal point of the trade character, whether the character is animate by nature, like Betty Crocker, or animated

"Defining Trade Characters and Their Role in American Popular Culture" by Barbara J. Phillips from THE JOURNAL OF POPULAR CULTURE, Spring 1996, Vol. 29, No. 4, pp. 143–158. Reprinted by permission of Wiley-Blackwell Publishing.

by design, like Mr. Peanut. The second reason for limiting trade characters to animate beings is to eliminate from the category characterless visual symbols such as corporate logos, and inanimate objects associated with the product through advertising such as oranges for Tropicana orange juice. Neither of these types of visual symbols functions as a trade character. Thus, the first condition used to define a trade character is that it be animate or animated. This includes people, animals, beings (monsters, spacemen, etc.) and animated objects.

Non-trademarked Versus Trademarked Characters

Another contentious issue is the matter of trademarks. Some authors insist that a trade character must necessarily be a legal trademark (Presbrey; Cohen). Other authors disagree (Ulanoff). To resolve this issue, the role of trademarks and trade characters must be briefly addressed.

A trademark is a name, word, or symbol that is protected by law. It is used to identify the source of the product and to guarantee consistency of quality (Morgan). When consumers see the trademark "Coca-Cola" on a bottle, they know who makes it and how it tastes. In comparison, most definitions agree that a trade character is used primarily as a device around which to build promotional programs (Wright, Warner, and Winter; Ulanoff; Mandell; Bohen). Trade characters can appear on product packaging, in advertisements, in sales promotions, or in other related areas.

Although most trade characters are registered trademarks, limiting the definition only to trademarks would eliminate from the category some characters that have

been created for promotional use. This is especially true of characters created for advertising campaigns that do not appear on the product package such as the Marlboro cowboy, the Maytag Repairman, and Raid's cartoon bugs. Because these characters are used in the same way as trademarks such as Tony the Tiger or Poppin' Fresh, the Pillsbury Dough Boy, it is difficult to draw a distinction between them. Therefore, another stipulation for the definition of "trade character" is that a trade character does not necessarily have to be a legal trademark. However, it must be used for promotional purposes.

Fictional Versus Real Characters

Another issue that relates to the role played by the trade character is the inclusion of real life (i.e., non-fictional) humans in some definitions (Kleppner; Kaufman). By including real people, the definition of trade character could be stretched to cover celebrity spokespeople such as George Burns and even the "common man" found in testimonial advertising. The individuals in these two much-studied genres of advertising are used in a very different way from trade characters. Their value lies in their credibility as realistic spokespeople. On the other hand, the target audience suspends disbelief when entering the fantasy world of a trade character (Baldwin) such as a vegetable-growing giant or a dancing raisin. In advertising that uses real people, the target audience must identify with (testimonial advertising) or aspire to (celebrity advertising) the spokesperson. This is not the case when using trade characters. Instead, the target audience relates to a trade character as a symbolic representation of the product. For example, the Marlboro cowboy is a white male, yet he is used successfully to advertise to women and minorities. It appears that these groups do not view the character as a real person speaking for the brand (Ramirez). Therefore, another definitional requirement is that trade characters be fictional. Note that although human actors play the parts of such trade char-acters as the Marlboro cowboy and Mr. Whipple, these characters are still fictional.

Trade Versus Celebrity Characters

Finally, in their work on animation, Callcott and Alvey draw a distinction between "celebrity" and "non-celebrity" spokes-characters. Celebrity characters are those that originated from a source other than advertising (i.e., cartoons, T.V., etc.) for purposes distinct from advertising. Examples of celebrity characters inclue Mickey Mouse and Snoopy. Advertisers frequently license these characters to cash in on a celebrity's current popularity, such as Bart Simpson's endorsement of the Butterfinger chocolate bar. In fact, these characters function as any other celebrity spokesperson (Callcott and Alvey 1) and therefore play a different role than the characters created by the advertising trade, as discussed above. Thus, they should be excluded from the definition of "trade character."

A definition of trade character can be developed by combining the conditions discussed above. *A trade character is a fictional, animate being or animated object that has been created for the promotion of a product, service, or idea.* A trade character does not have to be a legal trademark.

Trade Characters: How They Communicate

Occasionally, a successful trade character is developed by accident. This was

the case in 1904 when the Campbell Kids were added to streetcar advertisements as a visual element that might appeal to women. Campbell's managers professed themselves to be mystified by the Kids' appeal and subsequent success (Scott). It is much more common, however, for advertisers to carefully deliberate over the creation of a trade character and its message. There are three ways that trade characters are used to communicate with consumers: by creating product identification, by promoting a brand personality, and by providing promotional continuity.

Product Identification

One of the fundamental ways that trade characters communicate with consumers is by creating product identification. A trade character can forge a link between the product, the packaging, and the advertising in the minds of consumers. The use of trade characters for product identification has its roots in the development of trademarks for branded products.

The explosion of trademarks into use as a general marketing tool took place at the beginning of the twentieth century. "In the course of 60 years, from 1860 to 1920, factory-produced merchandise in packages largely replaced locally produced goods sold from bulk containers" (Morgan 9). The product package became the focus of efforts by manufacturers to differentiate their products from the competition. Trademarks were used to help highlight the differences between brands. Even if actual product differences did not exist, consumers who remembered the trademark or the look of the package could still ask for a specific brand by name (Strasser). In this way, the trademark helped the consumer to recognize the brand in a purchase situation.

Manufacturers encouraged trademark recognition by creating promotions that required consumers to cut trademarks from packages and send them to the manufacturer to receive a prize (Strasser). As trade characters were developed for advertising use, many assumed the trademark's role of product identifier by appearing on the label. For example, the trade character Mr. Clean is displayed on the bottle as a pictorial representation of the brand name. By viewing the trade characters on the product package, consumers may be able to recognize the product even if the brand name has been removed (Wallace). Recent research has shown a strong link between trade characters and the products that they identify. Animated non-celebrity (i.e. trade) characters elicited a favorable 71.7% correct product recall in respondents (Callcott and Alvey).

The use of trade characters for product identification surpasses the trademark's traditional function of identifying the package. The strength of trade characters lies in their ability to form a bond between the product, the packaging, and the advertising (Kleppner). A successful trade character connects the advertising message to the product so that consumers recall the message when they view the package. The Jolly Green Giant and the Little Green Sprout are examples of trade characters who have achieved a successful product-packaging-advertising link. These characters appear on product labels, in T.V. and print advertising, and in sales promotions such as coupons and premiums. The two characters tie all of these promotional activities together into a cohesive unit that communicates the message of product quality.

Trade characters do not have to appear on the package to create a strong connection between the advertising message and the brand. When the Marlboro cowboy, who does not appear on the package, was used to advertise cigarettes on television, 95% of respondents could identify the sponsor in the first five seconds, as compared to only 16% for the average commercial (McMahan). Currently, in some Marlboro print advertisements, the Marlboro cowboy is shown without mentioning the product name (Ramirez). Because of the strong product-advertising link, the trade character is considered sufficient to identify the brand.

Personality
The trade character's message, however, goes beyond product identification. Trade characters also communicate through their personalities. A trade character's personality can fulfill two functions; it can give meaning to the brand by symbolizing its character, and it can lend emotional appeal to the brand by personifying the product. These two operations, which may be the paramount functions of a trade character, will be discussed below.

Trade characters with distinct personalities were first created during the 1920s. At that time, advertising practitioners uncovered a public desire to be addressed personally by and to receive advice from the media (Marchand). As traditional sources of information such as the family, the church, and the community became less meaningful to consumers, they turned to advertising to enlighten them regarding their role in society. Thus, advertising took on a cultural role that has continued to the present time. Advertising "seeks to render otherwise incomprehensible social situations meaningful, so as to make it possible to act purposively within them" (Sherry 448).

The new trade characters of the 1920s were developed to fill the informational void. These characters were fictional "people" passed off as real personal advisers and confidantes for everything from etiquette to cooking to personal hygiene. The longest-lived of these characters is Betty Crocker, who was invented in 1921 to sign replies to contest questions at General Mills, and stayed to lend her name to their entire product line.

As fictional "personal adviser" trade characters grew in popularity and became commonplace, the next step became personalization of the product itself. "*Printers Ink* praised new techniques of bringing the ingredients of products to life by depicting them as 'little characters with names' and . . . called on copywriters to find the 'face' that lay embedded in every product" (Marchand). Thus, the modern trade character, complete with a distinct personality, was born.

A. Meaning

The first function of the trade character's personality is to give meaning to the brand by symbolizing the brand's character. The trade character does this by transferring its own cultural meaning to what can be an otherwise meaningless product.

Because the manufacturing process is complex and removed from consumers' daily lives, products have lost the cultural meaning that they once possessed (Jhally). All advertising, in general, functions to assign meaning to a product by linking the product to a representation of the cultur-

ally constituted world (McCracken). This cultural representation is an image that elicits a cluster of ideas and emotions that are commonly associated with that image. "It is . . . the merchandising of a metaphor which will speak to and be understood by the collective imagination of the culture" (Lohof 442). A consumer connects the image with the product, and thereby transfers the meaning of the image to the product (McCracken). A formerly empty product comes to mean something to a group of consumers. By changing the cultural image that is paired with the product, a product can be made to take on almost any meaning (Kleine and Kernan).

The trade character is one cultural image that advertisers use to elicit meaning. Trade characters express meaning through the communication system known as myth. Myth uses visual symbols to send a message (Barthes) that indirectly addresses human concerns (Levy). Trade characters are archetypes, actors in the myth that embody those factors that matter to individuals and society (Hirschman).

All trade characters use their personalities as symbols to elicit and transfer meaning to the brand. Mr. Peanut is sophisticated, Poppin' Fresh is lovable, and Betty Crocker is reliable. In this way, trade characters establish a desired product image by visually representing the product attributes (Zacher) or the advertising message (Kleppner). An example of the link between the personality of the character and the personality of the product is illustrated by Chester Cheetah, the trade character used to promote Chee-tos cheese puffs. "Chester Cheetah reflects characteristics of Chee-tos puffs themselves. Chee-tos puffs are orange and 'go fast'; Chester Cheetah is orange and 'goes fast.' Chee-tos puffs are cheesy and lovable; Chester Cheetah is cheesy and lovable too" (Wells, Burnett, and Moriarty 450). It is apparent that Chester has been created to embody the attributes of his brand.

However, the creation of a symbolically meaningful trade character is not sufficient to ensure its effectiveness. The consumer must correctly decode the trade character's meaning before it can have an impact (McCracken). Therefore, advertisers must communicate through a vocabulary of readily understood signs so that consumers can correctly interpret the signs' meaning (Morgan and Welton). Trade characters have to express their meanings quickly and effortlessly if they hope to compete in the cluttered media environment. Thus, "the signifiers that will be used most often will be those that are judged to be at once appealing, communicative, normative, proper, and easily-understood in a particular moment" (Scott). The use of these types of signifiers to develop meaningful trade characters will lead to the correct decoding of the trade character's message.

As a result, advertisers frequently use animal trade characters because they are standard mythical symbols of human qualities. For example, "everyone" knows that a bee is industrious, a dove is peaceful, and a fox is cunning (Robin). These stereotypical animal symbols are used to express common hopes, aspirations, and ideals (Neal). Advertisers link these animals to their products because consumers intuitively know what the animals "mean" and can therefore transfer that cultural meaning to the brand.

It is their unambiguous meaning that makes trade characters popular with consumers. The characters are predictable and constant; they always "mean" the same thing. As a result, consumers view them as trustworthy and reliable spokespeople in a constantly changing media environment (Callcott and Alvey).

B. Emotional Appeal

Note that Chester Cheetah is also described as "fun" and "cool" (Wells, Burnett, and Moriarty 450). The second function of a trade character's personality is to give emotional appeal to the brand. A trade character can accomplish this by symbolizing an emotional benefit that is transferred to the product. Also, a trade character lends the warmth of an actual personality to the product (Kleppner) and thereby creates an emotional tie between the consumer and the character (Zacher). This emotional tie is crucial to the per-suasive ability of the trade character, especially when the consumer has low involvement with the product category. An advertising executive asks "How do you personalize a message that seems miles away, months apart and mostly relevant to wild animals? Make a bear beg. When Smokey says 'Please,' you feel that he means it" (Nieman A-10).

By association, the character can create an emotional tie between the consumer and the brand, and even between the consumer and the manufacturer. This is because the trade character, through its personality, humanizes the product (Wells, Burnett, and Moriarty) and gives it a conscience (Levy) that makes the product trustworthy. Consumers may not trust Grand Metropolitan, but they trust Poppin' Fresh (PR Newswire). The emotional tie created by the trade character sells the symbolism it represents.

The two functions of the trade character's personality, meaning and emotional appeal, work together to create a successful character. McMahan calls this interplay Visual Image/Personality. It is important that both personality aspects are present, as evidenced by a famous trade character, the Jolly Green Giant. The personality of the Green Giant is full of meaning; he symbolizes nature (Cohen), healthy produce (Zacher), and the size and strength of his company. However, a giant is necessarily large and remote, and perhaps lacks emotional appeal. This could be one reason why, in the 1970s, he received a sidekick, the Little Green Sprout, who is outgoing and enthusiastic (Kapnick). Both characters work together to fulfill the personality functions. The Giant provides meaning and the Sprout provides emotional appeal.

A second example that highlights the importance of synergy between the two personality roles is the extreme care taken by RCA in naming their new trade character, Chipper. RCA's longtime trade character, Nipper, had all but retired by 1990. In his place, RCA created advertisements that attempted to dazzle consumers with technology. However, these ads were found to be confusing and incomprehensible to the target audience. As a result, Nipper was revived as a symbol of tradition and reliability, and a puppy was chosen as a symbol of growth and change. After careful deliberation, the puppy was named Chipper because the name had four associations (Elliott):

1. a computer chip (symbolizing technology),
2. a chip off the old block (symbolizing trust),
3. the definition of "chipper" as "happy and upbeat" (suggesting a positive

emotional response), and
4. Chipper rhymes with Nipper (promoting a connection between the two characters).

In choosing this name, RCA ensured that their new trade character's personality would give meaning and emotional appeal to their product line.

The linking together of myth and emotion gives an added advantage to the trade character; it is very difficult for consumers to pronounce a trade character or the claims the character makes "false." Barthes states that myth is a pure ideographic system, that is, it is a system that suggests an idea without specifically naming it. Because trade characters communicate through myth, they represent ideas and attributes that are never explicitly stated, and therefore are less likely to be rejected. For example, the Jolly Green Giant is a symbol of health and nature, but conveys this message without verbalizing it. His message may therefore be accepted without thought. In contrast, an advertisement that proclaims "Our vegetables are healthy and natural" might be met with skepticism and counterargumentation, since canned vegetables can be far from either. Trade characters make puffery palatable (Baldwin). By entering into the trade character's fantasy world, the consumer gives the character permission to exaggerate.

This puffery effect is enhanced by the emotion elicited by a trade character. As discussed above, a trade character can symbolize an intangible emotional benefit that is transferred to the product. However, a trade character's offer of fun (Kool-Aid Man), friendship (Ronald McDonald), or excitement (Joe Camel) is not easily quantified or measured. Therefore, these "soft" benefits are free from restrictions and regulations, and can successfully persuade without explicitly promising anything. Through the use of myth and emotion, trade characters are free to suggest product attributes and benefits that could not be expressly stated.

Promotional Continuity

The third message that trade characters communicate is promotional continuity. Trade characters can create promotional continuity across advertising campaigns, across brands in a product line, and over time.

A. Advertising Continuity

By appearing in each advertisement, a trade character connects the ads into a meaningful campaign (Bohen). The trade character, in its role of product identifier, signals to the consumer that the ad is for a specific brand. An example of a trade character used for advertising continuity is Little Caesar's Roman. Whether he is the star of the commercial, or appears at the end as a visual tagline, he unites widely dissimilar promotional campaigns by using his presence and his cry of "Pizza! Pizza!" to identify the sponsor.

B. Product Line Continuity

Trade characters can also provide continuity across brands in a product line. The value of using one trade character for several brands is the resulting cumulative publicity; each product connects to and helps to sell the others (Strasser). In addition, each product takes on the attributes symbolized by the character. The Keebler Elves are used in this way. Advertisements show the Elves manufacturing everything in the Keebler line from crackers to cookies to chips. The Elves' magic can link these products together in the minds of

consumers and affirm that each is made with Keebler quality.

C. Continuity Over Time

Also, trade characters can provide continuity over time (Wright, Warner, and Winter): Many currently-used trade characters have an impressive longevity: RCA's Nipper was created in 1901, Mr. Peanut in 1916, Snap! Crackle! and Pop! in 1932, and Borden's cow, Elsie, in 1936. Live-action characters can also provide continuity; the Maytag Repairman celebrates his twenty-fifth birthday this year. By using these characters for years or even decades, advertisers build invaluable brand equity (Berger).

There are several advantages to using these characters over many years. Because consumers have prior experience with the trade character, its role as a product identifier is enhanced. Over time, consumers learn to recognize trade characters and the brands that they represent. At first, consumers attributed Eveready's Energizer Bunny to Duracell. However, the longer the commercials ran, the better the consumers became at identifying the sponsor (Liesse). Because consumers already know that a character represents a certain brand, they will be able to easily identify the advertiser when viewing a specific ad.

Another advantage to using a character for many years is that advertisers are able to build on an image that already exists in the mind of the consumer. Once consumers understand a trade character's meaning and link it to the brand, future advertising can focus on reinforcing this connection instead of trying to establish a new one. As a result, the advertising message is usually clear and easily-understood.

When consumers see Tony the Tiger in an ad, they know that Tony's message will be that Frosted Flakes are "grrreat."

There is an added advantage for advertisers who use their trade characters for many years—the characters may become the objects of nostalgia. Nostalgia is a positive feeling toward some part of a person's past life (Davis). Because of geographic, occupational, and social mobility, nostalgia for a relatively permanent geographic locale (home) has been replaced by nostalgia for media products rooted in a certain time. This time is usually childhood and adolescence (Davis). Therefore, many consumers have strong emotional ties to trade characters that were advertised in their youth. If these characters are still in use, the comfortable, positive, loyal feelings that consumers have towards them can be transferred to the brand (Horovitz).

There are several reasons why trade characters can be used and reused over time. One reason is that trade characters are created to symbolize relatively permanent product attributes or consumer benefits. The Maytag Repairman represents reliability, and Snuggle, the fabric softener bear, represents softness. As long as these basic benefits remain valuable to the target audience, these characters can continue to embody them. Also, because trade characters are advertising creations, the advertiser has complete control over them. They do not grow old, change their meaning, or demand a raise. The creators of Spot, the 7-Up trade character, state "Every dollar we invest in Spot over the long term comes right back to the 7-Up company because he is ours. And Spot is not going to wind up on the front page of *USA Today* for adultery or drug abuse"

(Davis). Finally, trade characters are flexible. They can appear on labels, in advertising, on coupons, on promotions, or "in person." By appearing in different promotional areas, a character's life can be extended. An example is Ronald McDonald, who in addition to appearing in all of the standard promotional areas, will also be used for a nontraditional promotion. He will appear in a video game aimed at reaching the best fast food customers—adolescents (Smith).

D. Limitations of Continuity

There are several limiting factors when using the same trade character for a long time. The character may become dated, may no longer be able to personify the advertising message, or may acquire an undesirable meaning (Cohen). As styles and fashions change, characters can become dated. They can be kept fresh and effective by modernizing them (Berger). Usually, the inner meaning of the character remains the same, but the outward appearance and trappings are changed. For example, Betty Crocker has had her hairstyle and clothing modified many times over the years, and Poppin' Fresh has learned how to rap.

If the advertising message changes, the existing trade character will no longer be able to symbolize its meaning. At that point, the trade character usually has to be retired. Qantas Airways recently abandoned its humorous koala bear trade character for more sophisticated imagery when its focus changed from tourist to business travellers (Porter). In another example, advertisers deemed Smokey Bear unsuitable for use in hard-hitting ads that warned the public about jail terms for setting forest fires. The advertisers wanted to keep Smokey's soft, warm, fuzzy image intact for future soft-sell promotions (United Press International).

As social and political changes take place over time, a benign trade character may acquire an undesirable meaning. This was the case with the Exxon Tiger, who was introduced to convey the concept of smooth, silent power (Rawstone). The character was discontinued in the 1970s because its imagery took on a "wasteful" quality during the austerity of the oil crisis (Levy). However, the tiger was reintroduced in the late 1980s once the oil crisis faded and cultural values shifted again.

The biggest cultural meaning shifts that have affected trade characters are those that stereotype humans, especially minorities. It is important to note that a stereotype is not necessarily negative. All trade characters are based on the skillful manipulation of stereotypes (Morgan and Welton); advertisers use a dove to "mean" peace regardless of a dove's actual behavior in the wild. However, stereotypes have a subtle and persuasive influence that gains power through repetition (Boskin). Once a stereotype of a *group* is imbedded in folklore, it can affect an individual's thoughts and actions (Kern-Foxworth). Therefore, if an accepted stereotype of a group is essentially negative, this negative view of the group will be perpetuated. Because of shifting social values, some stereotypical trade characters from the past now convey unacceptable negative meanings to consumers.

Two trade characters who have the dubious distinction of contributing to negative stereotyping of humans are Sambo (and his "brother" Golliwog in the U.K.) and Aunt Jemima. These two characters were popular and accepted for decades, and since many consumers had no personal experience with blacks, they came to stand for the generic black man and black woman. "The chief problem with stereotypes of ethnic . . . groups is that one character . . . is allowed to stand for a whole diverse collection of human beings" (Kern-Foxworth 56). Unfortunately, the attributes that these characters presented were largely negative (MacGregor). Blacks were presented as childish, comical, subservient, docile, and servile (Boskin; Kern-Foxworth). Over decades of common use, consumers never consciously considered the ramifications of the myth that they were accepting.

Over time, as cultural values changed, society began to examine these trade characters more closely. MacGregor found that the social significance of these symbols had gone far beyond their original intent, and they had become images laden with negative stereotypical cultural meaning. Eventually, the Golliwog came to be perceived as a racist symbol by a substantial portion of British society (MacGregor), and the trade character Sambo faded out of use. In 1968, the Quaker Oats Company scrambled to "update" Aunt Jemima into an acceptable image. She "suddenly lost over 100 pounds, became 40 years younger and her red bandanna was replaced by a headband;" in 1990, she was changed even further, into a "black Betty Crocker" (Kern-Foxworth 63). These major changes in imagery and meaning were necessary to Aunt Jemima's continuance as an acceptable trade character. Thus, it is apparent that shifting cultural values may limit a character's use and effectiveness over time.

Conclusion

In this paper, a trade character has been defined as a fictional, animate being or animated object that has been created for the promotion of a product, service, or idea. Trade characters have become a common element in American popular culture because of their use as advertising tools. In this role, they can communicate in three ways: by creating product identification, by promoting a brand personality, and by providing promotional continuity. It appears, then, that by effectively fulfilling their advertising functions, trade characters have become an easily-understood and accepted communication system between advertisers and consumers. This will ensure that trade characters continue to be an important and enduring part of American popular culture.

Works Cited

Baldwin, Huntley. *Creating Effective TV Commercials.* Chicago: Crain, 1982.

Barthes, Roland. *Mythologies.* New York: Hill, 1957.

Berger, Warren. "A Cult of Personality." *Advertising Age* 1 July 1991: 19-C.

Bohen, William H. *Advertising.* New York: John Wiley & Sons, 1981.

Boskin, Joseph. "Sambo: The National Jester in the Popular Culture." *Race and Social Difference Selected Readings.* Eds. Paul Baxter and Basil Sansom. Penguin, 1972.

Callcott, Margaret F., and Patricia A. Alvey. "Toons Sell . . . and Sometimes They Don't: An Advertising Spokes-Character Typology and Exploratory Study." *1991 American Academy of Advertising Conference Proceedings.* Ed. Rebecca Holman.

Cohen, Dorothy. *Advertising.* Glenview, IL: Scott, 1988.

Davis, Fred. *Yearning for Yesterday: A Sociology of Nostalgia.* New York: The Free Press, 1979.

Davis, Tim. "What Ever Happened to 'Be a Pepper'?" *Beverage World* April 1989: 26–28.

Dunn, S. Watson, and Arnold Barban. *Advertising Its Role in Modern Marketing,* 6th edition. Dryden, 1986.

Elliott, Stuart (1991). "RCA Stresses Ease of Use In Electronics Campaign." *The New York Times* 25 September 1991: D8.

Hirschman, Elizabeth C. "Movies as Myths: An Interpretation of Motion Picture Mythology." *Marketing and Semiotics New Directions in the Study of Signs for Sale.* Ed. Jean Umiker-Sebeok. New York: Mouton de Gruyter, 1987.

Horovitz, Bruce. "Famous Logos Brought to Life to Revive Sales." *Los Angeles Times* 7 May 1991: D6.

Jhally, Sut. "Advertising as Religion: The Dialect of Technology and Magic." *Cultural Politics and Contemporary America.* Ian Angus and Sut Jhally (eds.) New York: Routledge, 1989: 217–29.

Kapnick, Sharon. "Commercial Success: These Advertising Figures Have Become American Icons." *Austin American-Statesman* 25 April 1992: D1.

Kaufman, Louis. *Essentials of Advertising.* New York: Harcourt, 1980.

Kern-Foxworth, Marilyn. "Plantation Kitchen to American Icon: Aunt Jemima." *Public Relations Review* 16.3 (1990): 55–67.

Kleine, Robert E., and Jerome B. Kernan. "Contextual Influences on the Meanings Ascribed to Ordinary Consumption Objects." *Journal of Consumer Research* 18 (1991): 311–23.

Kleppner, Otto. *Advertising Procedure.* 5th edition. Englewood Cliffs, NJ: Prentice, 1966.

Levy, Robert. "Play It Again, Sam." *Dun's Review* March 1980: 108–11.

Levy, Sidney J. "Interpreting Consumer Mythology: A Structural Approach to Consumer Behavior." *Journal of Marketing* 45 (1981): 49–61.

Liesse, Julie. "Bunny back to battle Duracell." *Advertising Age* 17 Sept. 1990: 38.

Lohof, Bruce A. "The Higher Meaning of Marlboro Cigarettes." *Journal of Popular Culture* 3.3 (1969): 443–50.

MacGregor, Robert M. "The Golliwog: Innocent Doll to Symbol of Racism." *Advertising and Popular Culture: Studies in Variety and Versatility.* Ed. Sammy R. Danna. Bowling Green, Ohio: Bowling Green State University Popular Press, 1992.

Marchand, Roland. *Advertising and the American Dream: Making Way For Modernity, 1920–1940.* California: U of California P, 1985.

Mandell, Maurice I. *Advertising.* 3rd edition. Englewood Cliffs, NJ: Prentice, 1980.

McCracken, Grant. "Culture and Consumption: A Theoretical Account of the Structure and Movement of the Cultural Meaning of Consumer Goods." *Journal of Consumer Research* 13 (1986): 71–84.

McMahan, Harry Wayne. "Do Your Ads Have VI/P?" *Advertising Age* 14 July 1980: 50.

Morgan, Hal. *Symbols of America.* New York: Viking, 1986.

Morgan, John, and Peter Welton. *See What I Mean? An Introduction to Visual Communication.* London: Edward Arnold, 1986.

Neal, Arthur G. "Animism and Totemism in Popular Culture." *Journal of Popular Culture* 19.2 (1985): 15–24.

Nieman, John. "As Creatives Rate Them." *Advertising Age* 11 Nov. 1991: A-10.

Norris, James S. *Advertising.* 3rd edition. Reston, VA: Reston, 1984.

Porter, Jeni. "Worldwise Qantas Airline Drops Koala for Mature Int'l Image." *Advertising Age* 21 Oct. 1991: 36.

PR Newswire. "Oh Boy! Pillsbury Doughboy Turns 25!" 20 Sept. 1990.

Presbrey, Frank. *The History and Development of Advertising.* New York: Greenwood, 1929.

Ramirez, Anthony. "Times Change; the Man Rides On." *The New York Times* 8 March 1990: D-1.

Rawstone, Philip. "Marketing and Advertising; The Tiger That Filled Up the Petrol Tank." *The Financial Times* 16 June 1988: 1-12.

Robin, P. Ansell. *Animal Lore in English Literature.* London: John Murray, 1932.

Scott, Linda Marie. *The Rhetoric of the Commercial Cannon.* Unpublished doctoral dissertation. The University of Texas at Austin, 1991.

Sherry, John F., Jr. "Advertising as a Cultural Symbol." *Marketing and Semiotics New Directions in the Study of Signs for Sale.* Ed. Jean Umiker-Sebeok. New York: Mouton de Gruyter, 1987.

Smith, Martin J. "Games Visible Feast for Kids, Companies." *The Chicago Tribune* 19 April 1992: 8.

Stewart, David W., and David H. Furse. *Effective Television Advertising: A Study of 1000 Commercials.* Lexington, MA: Lexington, 1986.

Strasser, Susan. *Satisfaction Guaranteed: The Making of the American Mass Market.* New York: Pantheon, 1989.

Ulanoff, Stanley M. *Advertising in America: An Introduction to Persuasive Communication.* New York: Hastings, 1977.

United Press International. "Keeping Smokey a Softie." 25 April 1985.

Wallace, David. "Myths and Folklore Add More to Labels Than Meets the Eye." *Philadelphia Business Journal* 8.41 (1989): 1.

Wells, William, John Burnett, and Sandra Moriarty. *Advertising Principles and Practice.* Englewood Cliffs, NJ: Prentice, 1989.

Wright, John S., Daniel S. Warner, and Willis L. Winter, Jr. *Advertising.* 3rd edition. McGraw, 1971.

Zacher, Robert Vincent. *Advertising Techniques and Management.* Homewood, IL: Irwin, 1967.

1. Phillips uses review and classification to support her general thesis. Identify these rhetorical strategies in the text.
2. Are there other strategies as well?
3. Which of these strategies help her argument? In what ways?

CONNECTING TO YOUR CULTURE

1. Phillips mentions that one limitation of trade characters is their tendency to become dated. Can you think of any characters in use now that are in need of updating? How would you update the character?
2. If you had to create a new trade character for a product, what product would you pick and what character would you create?
3. What factors will you need to consider as you create your trade character?

CONSIDERING IDEAS

1. Describe a recent commercial you've seen about the symptoms of depression or treating depression.
2. How many different ads have you seen on television, read in magazines, or heard on the radio?
3. What do you think about the recent practice of providing coupons for free trials of new medications (with a doctor's prescription)?
4. Do you request specific medications from your doctor or ask about taking something you have seen in an advertisement?

Lawrence C. Rubin *is an associate professor of counselor education at St. Thomas University. His primary research interest is the intersection of popular culture and psychology. Rubin received the 2006 Ray and Pat Browne Book Award for his text entitled* Psychotropic Drugs and Popular Culture: Essays on Medicine, Mental Health, and the Media. *In 2006, he also published* Using Superheroes in Counseling and Play Therapy. *This essay first appeared in 2004 in* The Journal of Popular Culture.

MERCHANDISING MADNESS

Pills, Promises, and Better Living through Chemistry

Lawrence C. Rubin

Nearly a half-century ago, the drug Thorazine was introduced to ease the suffering of the mentally ill and those who cared for them. Since then, pharmaceutical companies have laid the fruits of science and technology before us through advertising text and images that explicitly or implicitly promise some form of psychological "better living through chemistry."[1] Given our seeming preoccupation with one-stop shopping, ultrafast communication, and the quick fix, there appears to be a wholesale cultural acceptance of this promise as truth—so much so that of the billions of dollars spent annually on prescription drugs over the last several years—those designed to quickly and effectively combat depression, anxiety, and psychosis—consistently rank in the top ten ("Drug Monitor Report"; "US Physicians"; "Top 10 Therapeutic"; "Latest 12 Month").

This dynamic rise in psychotropic drug spending is due in large part to the combined success of the advertising, pharmaceutical, and psychiatry industries in commodifying mental illness. Commodification in this context refers to the blurring of boundaries between discomforts of daily living and psychiatric symptomatology to the point that both can be equally and efficiently remedied through mass-marketed products (i.e., psychotropic medication). And in our free-market, capital-driven society, advertising is the engine that shapes and runs this market-ing. Further, as competition for market shares increases in this highly competitive and lucrative arena, "communication forms that abbreviate and truncate meaning systems" into familiar signs and symbols—that is, dramatic, eye-catching images and seductive text—ascend to the status of popular and powerful cultural icons (Goldman and Montagne, 1047). Who is not familiar with Pfizer's promotional antidepressant campaign featuring a despondent anthropomorphized egg that is transformed through its close encounter of a Zoloft kind?

This blurring of boundaries between the normal and pathological experience of anxiety and depression is continually made evident to television viewers, magazine and newspaper readers, Internet surfers, and medical professionals in the form of advertisements that pathologize and sometimes exaggerate the incidence of these conditions (Vedanram). Capitalizing on the turbulent effect of current events, including terrorism, unemployment, and economic disasters, as well as the disquieting influence of daily pressures, including parenting, noise pollution, and overcrowding, the alluring promises of psychotropic drug ads is often inescapable. People who struggle with the very common problems of shyness, sadness, nervousness, malaise, and even suspiciousness are offered refuge under the umbrella of drug-assisted well-being. Exemplifying this point is a 2000

"Merchandising Madness: Pills, Promises, and Better Living through Chemistry" by Lawrence C. Rubin, 2004, pp. 369–383 in THE JOURNAL OF POPULAR CULTURE. Reprinted by permission of Wiley-Blackwell Publishing.

Bristol-Myers Squibb ad in *Reader's Digest* for the anxiety drug BuSpar. It depicts a smiling young woman triumphantly sitting atop a mountain of words that spell our daily complaints: "I can't sleep . . . I'm always tired . . . so anxious."

Although it has even been argued that temporary emotional discomfort can be instructive, adaptive, and motivational (Kramer 93), Americans readily accept this sacrifice for the benefit of instant equilibrium to the tune of $10.4 billion spent in 2000-2001 on the four top-selling antidepressants alone: Zoloft, Paxil, Wellbutrin, and Celexa (Stefanova; "Antidepressants").

Historical Foundation
The first major push in print psychotropic drug advertising in this country came in the late 1940s, to help manage the rigors of daily life and assist a wounded population recovering from the collective trauma of war. Early ads in professional medical journals promised restful sleep, relief from the psychoneurotic symptoms of depression and anxiety, an improved outlook, and even aid to the unfortunate housewife managing both an ailing husband and returning war veteran son [who was] "a drunkard too weak to support himself."[2] The introduction of the major tranquilizer Chlorpromazine (Thorazine) in 1954 simultaneously heralded the era of deinstitutionalization of the mentally ill and the institutionalization of psychotropic drug advertising.

Thorazine, along with its soon-to-arrive competitors Desbutal, Miltown, Serpasil, Sandil, and Desoxyn, to name a few, picked up the pace with added promises of "counteracting the extremes of emotion, eliminating bizarre behavior prob-

lems, facilitating psychiatric treatment and dispelling shadows."[3] Throughout the rest of the 1950s, the push continued to advertise medications that were aimed not just at the everyday person, but at those unfortunate previously hospitalized mental patients who were now trying to piece together lives outside institutional walls. Images of contented former patients working productively were contrasted with those of their distraught, isolated, and deranged counterparts depicted "peering over the edge of a house of cards"—or, as in a 1956 ad for the antidepressant Serpanry, turned away from the portal to an idyllic pastoral setting. By the end of that first decade of advertising psychotropic drugs, families were depicted in various phases of reunion, men returned successfully to work and women to their domestic responsibilities. Sociocultural equilibrium was to be found in a jar.

Although it has been argued that the subsequent explosion of psychotropic drug advertising fostered psychiatric stereotypes of men, women, children, and the elderly, it can just as easily be argued that they simply held up a mirror to a culture that already defined its population on the basis of these stereotypes. Over the next several decades and into the present, the power of these ad campaigns has rested as much on the delivery as in the deliverables themselves. Masterfully in touch with the climate of the times and the pressures of the day, advertising companies have known exactly when to refocus their campaigns and on what target audience: males, females, young, old, workers, and homebodies.

Common to all of the advertising campaigns was their ability to capitalize, if not prey, on deeply entrenched popular culture archetypes such as the beleaguered housewife, the struggling bread-winning husband, the lonely and disengaged senior citizen, and the child isolated from family and friends by seemingly intractable behavioral and emotional disturbances. The presumption of these ads was that if a drug could "fix" a problem, its origin must have been illness. This equating of problems in daily living with mental (or medical) illness fueled the legitimacy of psychotropic medicine (Kleinman and Cohen 870) that promised to heal the pain of the world, or "Weltschmertz" (Neill 336). The culture was being primed to accept the notion that there was a "pill for every ill." Pill, person, patient, and illness would indistinguishably merge, as depicted in an early 1960s ad for SmithKline-Beecham's Thorazine in which the pill, rather than a person, rested comfortably on the psychoanalyst's leather couch. There wasn't even a psychiatrist in the traditional chair behind it.

Over the next several decades and into the present, the advertising industry honed its ability to capture, if not direct, popular and professional attention to the promises of psychotropic drugs. Capitalizing on the time-tested techniques of repetition, emotional evocation, simplification, and the "picture superiority effect" (Singh et al. 3), the ads for psychiatric panaceas made bold statements, both explicit and implicit. For example, an early 1970s ad for the antipsychotic Stelazine makes an implicit comparison between the philosophical and musical genius of Plato and Beethoven and that of the drug by featuring their busts above the advertising text. In another, a frightening African tribal mask is used to depict the primitive destructive nature of mental illness. Implied in the latter ad is that the advertised drug can resocialize the sufferer.

Advertisements for various other psychotropic drugs have utilized images and icons of popular culture. An ad for Celltech Medeva's stimulant for children with Attention Deficit Hyperactivity Disorder (ADHD) utilizes the Batman genre: a beacon shining a glowing "M" on the clouds calling out for its "champion." Earlier advertisements for Elavil, a mood stabilizer, feature historic physicians Philippe Pinel and Benjamin Rush to suggest that the product user, and the product by association, is imbued with inherent wisdom and strength. Another advertisement for a stimulant drug features a blaring alarm clock that suggests to the reader that the "time has come" to do the right thing— that is, take the advertised medication. What is not suggested is that our society's preoccupation with speed, deadlines, and warning signals probably plays as much a contributing role in the disorder treated by that very same medication. This latter ad highlights one of the marketing strategies called decontextualization, which is addressed below.

Marginalization and Decontextualization
The success of psychotropic advertising in assuring people that well-being is just a pill away has depended on effective use of cliché, metaphor, seductive images, and suggestive text that capitalize on binary oppositions such as "then and now" and "before and after." However, the true backbone of the advertising industry's success in promoting their vision of well-being lay in its two-pronged strategy of marginalization and decontextualization. The process of marginalization involves

simplifying the physician's role to that of a technician primed to dispense pills according to scripted cultural stereotypes. Decontextualization refers to elimination of the personal, social, and cultural contexts of peoples' lives from the explanatory equation, and by doing so, reducing the complexities of living to predictable, manageable, and ultimately medically treatable symptoms.

Marginalization of the Physician

At the 1971 United Nations convention, signatories (the United States included) agreed to prohibit the advertising of psychotropic drugs directly to the public. Up until 1997, when the Food and Drug Administration (FDA) modified its policy to allow direct-to-consumer advertising (DTCA), promotional campaigns for psychotropic drugs targeted physicians through professional medical journals. Through teaser ads and bold product claims, the pharmaceutical industry capitalized on entrenched social stereotypes cloaked in medicalized jargon to convince physicians that symptom reduction and/or elimination was just a prescription away. By merging patients with their problems in dramatic promise-laden ads, the process of "diagnosis at a glance" (Stimson 158) was implied as a substitute for traditional comprehensive assessment. Further, reliance on nonrational appeals, puns, and sympathetic patient depictions (Smith and Griffin 410)—as well as misleading claims and underuse of factual information (Bell, Wilkes, and Kravitz 1093)—began to replace the physician with the drug.

Ostensibly, the ads educated and empowered physicians by undermining alternative treatments, entrenching the medicalization of nonmedical problems, and promoting

lack of confidence in personal health. This elevated the disease model, and with it, the physician (Medawar; Mintzes et al). Early ads prominently featured well-clad officious professionals tending to distressed, disheveled, and disoriented patients. Insidiously, however, the physician became far less prominent in psychotropic drug advertisements, a mere bystander in this conflict for the collective soul of the suffering masses. A 1960s ad for the antipsychotic drug Trilafon depicts a beleaguered and despondent patient sitting across the desk from his psychiatrist; clearly, both are allies in the treatment. In contrast, and in a recent ad for the antipsychotic agent Zyprexa, a disheveled man reaches desperately upward to the outstretched hand of a physician. Upon closer inspection, the viewer notices that the likelihood that the two will reach each other is made possible only by virtue of the patient standing on a rock in the shape of the stylized "Z" associated with the name Zyprexa.

How ironic that in a culture that has historically deified the medical professional—placing him in the central healing role—the very ads that rely on them for profitability eventually chip away at that centrality. The early ads of the 1950s were designed to show physicians how helpful these wonder drugs could be in freeing the mentally ill from institutional life. Drug and doctor were partners in liberation. Medicines were touted for their ability to "help keep more patients out of mental hospitals."[4] Wonderfully artistic and dramatic images reminded physicians that Thorazine and related drugs were the way to avoid the historically barbaric treatment of the mentally ill, and by association, to avoid the failures of his professional ancestors.

As deinstitutionalization of psychiatric patients progressed in the late 1950s and 1960s, psychotropic medicines were promoted as adjunctive aids to physicians who could now better reach their patients through psychotherapy. Nevertheless, those ads also made it quite clear that psychotherapy was not possible without the assistance of the medication that it was attempting to sell. Poignant and emotionally evocative images with captions such as "the therapeutic alliance"[5] and "removing the bars between patient and psychiatrist"[6] reminded both patient and physician that they had a friend. But the implied message was that they could no longer do their jobs alone. Few ads capture this process of physician marginalization better than a current one for the antipsychotic Geodon, in which a tangle of musical notes emerges from blackness into vivid color on a perfectly ordered musical staff. It features neither the patient nor the physician. It is the drug and the drug alone that retrieves the melody of life from the chaos of mental illness. Another ad, this time for the antidepressant Celexa, depicts a brilliantly colored flower sprouting victoriously from the parched and barren desert of depression.

Actual response from physicians regarding the impact of pharmaceutical advertising in both professional and lay venues has varied. A survey of midwestern physicians in both urban and rural settings (Petroshius, Titus, and Hatch) suggests that satisfaction with DTCA is mixed, with greater perceived utility of these ads among younger and urban practitioners. Older and rural practitioners were more resistant to the idea of DTCA, and by association, to their marginalization. A related survey of consumers in a western metropolitan area (Everett 44)

suggested that DTCA could stimulate doctor-patient conversations about appropriate prescriptions. A survey of 199 physicians by *Psychiatric News* suggested that few physicians felt particularly pressured to prescribe medications suggested by their patients ("Direct to Consumer" 2), and that many regarded the phenomenon of DTCA to be at worst benign. What is clear is that as advertising campaigns shifted from professionals to the consuming public, the assault on the bastion of psychiatry and medicine gained even greater momentum.

Decontextualization

The central premise behind decontextualization is as follows: It isn't overcrowding, aging, parenting, terrorism, global warming, recession, unemployment, or even the pressure of being a man or woman that is responsible for the epidemic of anxiety and depression in our culture. It is the individual's failure to adequately respond to these challenges for reasons of emotional and/or psychological inadequacy. Symptoms for which people seek relief through psychotropic medication and to which the pharmaceutical ads appeal are thus reinterpreted as personal failures and then recontextualized as illness. This in turn justifies the need for a medical solution. By localizing pathology within the person rather than in the external factors that give rise to them, decontextualization "serves to reinforce and legitimize social attitudes and relations [such as sexism and alienating working conditions] which may actually contribute to the problems these [medical] products target" (qtd. in Kleinman and Cohen 873). The promoted psychotropic agent may indeed help the harried housewife, disgruntled worker, disenfranchised teen, or painfully shy salesperson muddle through their daily rigors. However, the seductive advertisements implicitly undermine self-help, alternative forms of treatment, and the need to remedy the inequities, injustices, and discomforts that gave rise to the problem in the first place.

By playing to and preying upon weakness, psychotropic drug advertisements make the moral assertion that people who struggle unsuccessfully under these pressures are of a lesser god, and as a result, need the help of the psychiatric establishment. In a sense, the success of decontextualization rests in its power to victimize and dehumanize those who are ostensibly unsuccessful at living. This process was presaged in the early 1960s by psychiatrist Thomas Szasz, who in his treatise *The Myth of Mental Illness* suggested that "We don't expect everyone to be a competent swimmer, chess player or golfer, and we don't regard those who can't play as sick. Yet, we expect everyone to play at his own life game competently, and when they don't, we call them sick—mentally ill!" (35). In his later volume, *Ideology and Insanity,* Szasz reflected on the ethics and morality inherent in calling people mentally ill, noting, "The notion of mental symptom is inextricably tied to the social and particularly ethical context in which it is made, just as the notion of bodily symptom is tied to an anatomical and genetic context" (14).

Consider a 1960s ad for the tranquilizer Prolixin that offers relief from the stresses of the day. The intentionally blurred image of the crowded metropolis literally and metaphorically shifts the reader's focus away from the relatively faceless denizens. We are not asked to consider the context (i.e., the opprobrious rat-race conditions of urban living that results in emotional stress), nor are we asked to consider the humanity of the people caught in it. Instead, we are drawn to the oasis of clarity found in the promissory advertising text that zeroes in on the medicalized symptoms of the emotional stress.

Fast forward to 2001 and the social, emotional, and cultural upheaval following the attacks of September 11. In the twelve-month period between October 2000 and October 2001, national sales for the top three antidepressants—Prozac, Paxil, and Zoloft—rose 20%, or $499 million. Pfizer, maker of Zoloft, spent $5.6 million on TV and magazine advertisements in October of that year, while Glaxo spent $16.5 million on ads for Paxil in that same period, up significantly from spending in October of the previous year ("US Physicians"). Although these statistics do not speak directly to the issue of decontextualization as a driving force in the advertising of psychotropic drugs, the implication is that medication had a role to play in recovery from those events. Pfizer's advertisements for Zoloft during that painful period featured flags, candles, firemen, and referenced the $10 million spent by the company on relief funds. Advertising text such as, "We wish we could make a medicine that could take away the heartache, but until we can, we will continue to do everything we can to help" (qtd. in Parpis 2), suggested that although they could not heal the nation from this tragic event, ultimately it would be their responsibility to do so. Here again, as in the 1963 advertisement for Prolixin, it was not the sociopolitical antecedents of the stressor, which in this case was terrorism that required attention; it was

Freshen! Cleaner!

NEW IMPROVED LIFE!

Better Than Ever!

#1 America's selling Drug!

Prozac

MOOD BRIGHTENER

Wash Your Blues Away!

© Adbusters Media Foundation

an otherwise helpless, anxiety-ridden, victimized, and psychologically impaired populace that required medical assistance. Context had been stripped from the event so that a wounded population could be sold on the merits of modern medication.

Perhaps the most heavily documented example of decontextualization in psychotropic advertising has focused on gender construction. It has been demonstrated that the disproportionate representation of women in ads for antidepressants and antianxiety drugs has perpetuated gender stereotypes (Nikelly 233; Hansen and Osborne 130). Advertising companies took (and take) full advantage of cultural expectations with regard to the gender imbalance inherent in psychiatric epidemiology rates. A 1960s antipsychotic ad for Navane features a mother looking

lovingly at her young, who sits atop a kitchen counter amongst the groceries. It was Navane that brought her home to the bliss of domesticity and parenthood. Another depicts a young woman chatting with her female friend over breakfast, with a pastel-colored early morning sky in the window behind them. A 1980s antidepressant ad for Asendin depicts a woman's face in a crumpled divorce decree, suggesting that the medication will liberate her from this decontextualized nightmare of divorce. A more recent ad for Zoloft shows a mother in a business suit joyfully running through the park with her two young, soccer-clad sons; the ad talks about the power of the medication to provide this. Each of these suggests that relief from the stresses of parenting, domesticity, and even divorce is just a pill away. Once liberated from the grips of disease rather than from the cultural dictates of their role, women are freed to return to that prescribed role, or an idealized version of it.

With regard to the decontextualization of men's issues, psychotropic advertisements have typically focused on the power of the pill to return the man to work by freeing him and those around him from the threat of his aggressive nature, or to re-establish the romantic bond with his partner. In these ways, the flaws of masculinity—or at least the stereotypical limitations of the masculine role—are reduced, as in the case of women, to treatable psychiatric symptoms. In this context, a 1960s ad for Thorazine shows a man in mid-rage against a woman. The text talks about the control of agitation. A later ad, which discusses the power of the drug to return sufferers to reality, depicts a man whose image is cut in half.

On the left is a robotic shell that is being reconstructed square by square. On the right is the man fully restored, including hair and suit. A more recent ad for Remeron, an anti-depressant, shows a sixty-something couple embracing each other, with the man holding a brilliant bouquet of flowers behind the woman. As in the case of advertisements targeting women, the pharmaceutical industry is holding up a mirror to our entrenched cultural attitudes and expectations about men—that is, their violent tendencies, their fulfillment through work, and their potential for grace and compassion (with medication).

Pitching the Pill in the Late 90s: Direct-to-Consumer Advertising

Consider the implications of the following. In the four-year period following the FDA's removal of restrictions on DTCA, national spending on pharmaceutical promotion rose from $791 million to $2.4 billion (Kreling, Motta, and Wiederholt 31). No longer dependent on physicians as their primary audience, advertisers pointed their promises and pills directly at the American public. With estimates that one dollar spent on television and magazine advertising translates into $1.69 and $2.51 in drug sales, respectively ("Europe on the Brink" 2), the potential profit in marketing directly to the public becomes inescapable. In 2001, $16.4 billion was spent on drug promotion, $2.6 billion of which went into DTCA ("In the Six Months" 2). Of that latter amount, $184.5 million was spent solely on marketing only some of the more popular medications for depression, insomnia, and anxiety (O'Connell and Zimmerman 11).

Over the last five years, psychotropic drug ads have found their way into a wide array of popular magazines (*Parents, Reader's Digest, TV Guide, Better Homes & Gardens, Time,* and *Redbook*), newspapers, prime-time television commercials, radio spots, public transportation kiosks, billboards, and the Internet. It is not uncommon to hear references to Prozac in daily conversations or in movie dialogue, and the expression "taking a Prozac moment" has become idiomatic in our culture. Several years ago, the books *Listening to Prozac* by Peter Kramer and *Prozac Nation* by Elizabeth Wurtzel were runaway best-sellers that brought the battle for the American psyche into bold relief. Each year, an astronomical number of prescriptions are written for psychotropic medications by psychiatric and nonpsychiatric physicians: almost 70 million for Paxil, Prozac, and Zoloft alone in 2000 (Kreling, Motta, and Wiederholt 32). Recent research suggests that "patients who request particular brands of drugs after seeing advertisements are nearly nine times more likely to get what they ask for than those who simply seek a doctor's advice" (qtd. in Lewis 20).

It is difficult to overstate the importance of an educated consumer, and DTCA, by all credible accounts, is having just that effect. But while the "hard sell" is ostensibly on the merits of psychotropic medication, destigmatization of mental illness, and consumer empowerment, the driving force behind that "sell" rests in the undeniable truth that there is "gold in them thar pills"! Money and medical promises make for not only strange but also highly unlikely bedfellows who toss and turn in attempts to win over a restless culture seemingly bent on self-stimulation, self-sedation, or both. However, the most restless and that with the greatest stake in the "merchandising of mind mechanics" (Goldman 1047) is the pharmaceutical industry, in its ongoing quest to create new niches from which to market its products.

Quoted in the journal *Advertising Age*, Barry Brand, Paxil's product director, noted that "Every marketer's dream is to find an unidentified or unknown market and develop it. That's what we were able to do with social anxiety disorder" (Vedantam 3). In this context, Brand refers to the marketing success behind the promotion of Paxil, with its "Your life is waiting" campaign. Supporters argue that social anxiety disorder is a legitimate psychiatric condition necessitating medical treatment. Detractors contend that pharmaceutical companies are medicalizing shyness to sell drugs. A related phenomenon occurred in the recent advertising campaign for Serafem, a Prozac clone for treating the depressive component of premenstrual dysphoric disorder (PMDD). In anticipation of Prozac's patent expiration, Lilly spent $14 million in DTCA of Serafem, which in its first six months on the market garnered $33 million in sales. In this case, the controversy centered not so much on the legitimacy of PMDD as a psychiatric condition, but to the morality of expanding the boundaries of the condition to include depression that could then be medicated with the new drug.

In addition to the metaphors, images, and promises that have formed the foundation of these powerful and profitable advertising campaigns, pharmaceutical companies have saturated the professional and popular landscape with a plethora of palpable promotionals. The range of psychotropic pharmaceutical merchandise is breathtaking (Findlay 4). It is not uncommon to find friends and colleagues drinking from a Zoloft mug, writing with a Seroquel pen, squeezing a Paxil sponge ball-brain, relaxing to a Prozac waterfall, eating popcorn and Pop-Tarts in Resperdal packaging, wiping away tears with Librium tissues, or telling time from a Geodon clock. Bombardment is the more apt term for this facet of the psychotropic advertising campaign in its attempt to remind stressed men, women, and children that better living is within quick reach. In a culture that turns both to superheroes and science, what could be a more fitting reminder of the power of the advertising industry than the promotional campaign for Metadate, a stimulant medication used to treat ADHD? With the promising power of their superhero Metadate-Man, the pharmaceutical industry has in a single bound come full circle.

Conclusion

Advertising is so much a part of our culture that it is hard to imagine a day without being sold something in some form by someone. Advertising slogans are part of our language. Their symbols are a part of our visual landscape, and their metaphors reveal and inform our social constructions. We are influenced through every conceivable medium by pitches and promises of products and services ostensibly designed to make our lives easier, richer, and more fulfilling. Of the plethora of products on the market designed to enrich life, psychotropic medication stands prominently. The massive annual dollar amount spent on advertising and purchasing these products is a testament to our willingness to embrace these promises—a culture stricken with "mental pillness."

It is appealing to attribute this phenomenon solely to the joint effort of the advertising and pharmaceutical industries to commodify mental illness, and through doing so, to create products with which to cure it. It can and has been argued that these industries capitalize on the vulnerabilities, perceived powerlessness, and naïveté of the consuming public—and on those of the prescribing professional, on whom both industries depend. Equally, if not more compelling, however, is the possibility that this so-called "merchandising madness" is of our own making, born out of cultural impatience with, among other things, traffic, noise, aging, weight gain, sexual decline, fear, stress, and in the context of this article, emotional pain. The true madness underlying the merchandising of psychotropic medication may be a symptom of our cultural preoccupation with expedience, deification of science, and a collective outward search for salvation.

Notes

1. From advertising motto of the E.I. Dupont Corporation, "Better things for better living through chemistry."

2. Advertising text for Mebaral, Allonal, and Dexamyl appearing in the *American Journal of Psychiatry* between 1945 and 1954.

3. Taken from ads appearing in the *American Journal of Psychiatry* between 1954 and 1956.

4. Taken from a 1955 ad for Thorazine in the *American Journal of Psychiatry*.

5. Taken from a 1970s ad for Haldol in the *American Journal of Psychiatry*.

6. Taken from a 1960s ad for Trilafon in the *American Journal of Psychiatry*.

Works Cited

"Antidepressants." *IMS Health*. 2002. IMS Health. 15 Sept. 2002 (http://www.imshealth.com/public/structure/dispcontent12779,1203-1203-133808,00.html).

Bell, Robert, Michael Wilkes, and Richard Kravitz. "The Educational Value of Consumer Targeted Prescription Drug Promotion Advertising." *Journal of Family Practice* 14.12 (2000): 1092–98.

"Direct to Consumer Ads Have Their Positive Side." *Psychiatric News* 4 Feb. 2000: 1–3.

"Drug Monitor Report." *IMS Health*. 2002. IMS Health. 17 Sept. 2002 (http://www.imshealth.com/public/structure/dispcontent/12779,1000-1000-144319,00.html).

"Europe on the Brink of Direct to Consumer Advertising." *The Lancet* 18 May 2002: 2.

Everett, Stephen. "Lay Audience Responses to Prescription Drug Advertising." *Journal of Advertising Research* 31.2 (1991): 43–50.

Findlay, Steven. "Prescription Drugs and Mass Media Advertising." *NICHM Foundation—Washington* 3 Sept. 2000: 1–8.

Goldman, Robert, and Michael Montagne. "Marketing Mind Mechanics: Decoding Antidepressant Drug Advertisements." *Social Science and Medicine* 22.10 (1986): 1047–58.

Hansen, Finy, and Dawn Osborne. "Portrayal of Women and the Elderly in Psychotropic Drug Ads." *Women & Therapy* 16.1 (1995): 129–41.

"In the Six Months Since 9/11, the Psychiatric Drug Industry Cashes In." *SCI News*. 5 March 2002. MindFreedom Online. 16 Oct. 2002 (http://www.mindfreedom.org/mindfreedom/911.html).

Kleinman, Daniel, and Lawrence Cohen. "The Decontextualization of Mental Illness: The Portrayal of Work in Psychiatric Drug Ads." *Social Science and Medicine* 32.8 (1991): 867–74.

Kramer, Peter. *Listening to Prozac*. New York: Penguin, 1993.

Kreling, David, David Motta, and Joseph Wiederholt. *Prescription Drug Trends: A Chatbook Update of the Kaiser Family Foundation*. Madison: U of Wisconsin P, 2001.

"Latest 12 Month Global Retail Sales." *IMS Health*. 2002. IMS Health. 4 Oct. 2002 (http://www.imshealth.com/public/structure/dispcontent/12779,1000-1000-144238,00.html).

Lewis, Carol. "Selling Your Cure on the Telly." *New Statesman* 24 June 2002: R20–R21.

Medawar, Charles. "Because You're Worth It." *Health Matters* 43 (Winter 2000/2001): 1–4.

Mintzes, Barbara, Ariminee Kazanjian, Ken Bassett, Robert Evans, and Steve Morgan. "An Assessment of the Health System Impacts of DTC Advertising of Prescription Medicines (DTCA)." *Centre for Health Services and Policy Research-University of British Columbia* Feb. 2002: 1–48.

Neill, John. "A Social History of Psychotropic Drug Advertising." *Social Science and Medicine* 28 (1989): 333–38.

Nikelly, Arthur. "Drug Advertising and the Medicalization of Unipolar Depression." *Healthcare for Women International* 16 (1995): 229–42.

O'Connell, Vanessa, and Rachael Zimmerman. "Mood Altering Drug Pitches Resonate with an Edgy Public." *Asian Wall Street Journal* 15 Jan. 2002: 11–12.

Parpis, Eleftheria. "Fear Factor." *Adweek* 12 Nov. 2001: 2.

Petroshius, Susan, Phillip Titus, and Kathryn Hatch. "Physician Attitudes Toward Pharmaceutical Drug Advertising." *Journal of Advertising Research* 35.6 (1995): 35–41.

Sing, Surendra, Parker Lessig, Dongwook Kim, Reetika Gupta, and Mary Ann Hocutt. "Does Your Ad Have Too Many Pictures?" *Journal of Advertising Research* 40.1 (2000): 11–27.

Smith, Mickey, and Lisa Griffin. "Rationality of Appeals Used in the Promotion of Psychotropic Drug Ads: A Comparison of Female and Male Models." *Social Science and Medicine* 11 (1977): 409–14.

Stefanova, Kristina. "FDA is Probing Higher Drug Sales and Advertising." *Washington Times* 10 May 2001: B9.

Stimson, G. "The Message of Psychotropic Drugs Ads." *Journal of Communication* (Summer 1975): 153–66.

Szasz, Thomas. *The Myth of Mental Illness.* New York: Hoeber-Harper, 1961.

———. *Ideology and Insanity.* New York: Anchor, 1970.

"Top 10 Therapeutic Classes by US Population Sales in 2001." *IMS Health.* 2002. IMS Health. 11 Nov. 2002 (http://www.imshealth.com/public/structure/dispcontent12779,1203-1203-1440055,00.html).

"US Physicians' Response to Patient Requests for Brand Name Drugs." *IMS Health.* 2002. IMS Health. 12 Oct. 2002 (http://www.imshealth.com/public/structure/dispcontent/12779,1203-1203-144020,00.html).

Vedantam, Shankar. "Drug Ads Helping Anxiety Make Some Uneasy." *Washington Post* 16 July 2001: A1.

Author's note: The visual ads described in this article are compelling, and the reader is invited to browse through psychiatric and popular journals and magazines, old and new, to garner their full impact.

1. Rubin says the metaphors of advertising "reveal and inform our social construction." What metaphors does he bring into this text to help make his point? What is his point?

2. What does Rubin say is different about the way psychotropic drugs are pitched to men and the way they are pitched to women? Do you think this difference is accurate?

1. Although the Prozac subvertisement shown on page 164 is meant to be funny, could the slogan actually be true? How would Rubin react to this ad?

2. What do you use to wash your blues away? What do those around you do to combat depression?

3. Rubin mentions several stereotypes of those who suffer from depression or take psychotropic medications. Do these stereotypes still exist today? Support your answer with specific examples.

contemplations in the pop culture zone

1. Take a minute to reflect on some current ads for specific women's and men's products. How well do these ads reflect the lives of men and women today? How well do they reflect your life? The demographics of your school or town?

2. *Advertising Age* created the following top ten advertising icons list:

   1. The Marlboro Man—Marlboro cigarettes
   2. Ronald McDonald—McDonald's restaurants
   3. The Green Giant—Green Giant vegetables
   4. Betty Crocker—Betty Crocker food products
   5. The Energizer Bunny—Eveready Energizer batteries
   6. The Pillsbury Dough Boy—assorted Pillsbury foods
   7. Aunt Jemima—Aunt Jemima pancake mixes and syrup
   8. The Michelin Man—Michelin tires
   9. Tony the Tiger—Kellogg's Frosted Flakes
   10. Elsie—Borden dairy products

   Do you agree with this list? Create your own top ten list for icons or some other characteristic (best music in a commercial, top ten food jingles, top ten ways to sell shampoo).

3. Have you ever tried to sell something (a product, a service, your own skills)? What words and/or graphics did you use? What colors and layout? What image of your product were you trying to convey?

4. Make a list of ads you've seen for recent movies or television shows. How can you tell the intended audience(s) of the ad? Does it match the intended audience(s) of the movie or TV show itself? Why would advertisers advertise to more than one audience? How do they make these decisions? How do they make the ads different for the different audiences?

collaborations in the pop culture zone

1. In a small group, discuss your opinions about the ethical and legal obligations of advertisers—both the ad agencies that create the advertisements and the companies that hire them. Should advertisers have to give the public an accurate and unbiased reflection of themselves? Should advertisers be held responsible if they do not show women and minorities positively? Do advertisers have to be politically correct? If you were to flip through a magazine or glance at the billboards along the highway, would it be a problem if all of the ads only showed young, upper-class, white models?

2. Discuss why some celebrities choose to make commercials only in other countries—for example, Bill Murray's character in the film *Lost in Translation* or Matt LeBlanc's character, Joey, in the TV sitcom *Friends*. Why would they make such a choice? Does this affect the person's status in the United States? Should it? Now that the Internet makes so many of these foreign commercials available to U.S. consumers, do you think some celebrities will change their policies?

3. As a group, select a particular type of product or service: MP3 players, deodorant, beer, insurance. Then look at a variety of different types of magazines and newspapers to find multiple examples of ads for your chosen product. Compare the ads from various sources. Can you guess the audience for the magazine by looking at the ad? What ad characteristics serve as clues (or not)? Are there ads you would change to better address different populations?

4. Product packaging is another form of advertising, even though many may not think about it in that way. As a group, collect packaging for several different brands of the same type of product. What information does the packaging include? How is it set up? Is one package more appealing than another? Why or why not? Does the packaging include a trade character? Celebrity endorsement? Other types of images? What difference do things like directions or nutrition information make? What types of regulations govern this information?

start writing essays about advertisements

Reviews or Review Essays

1. Using an ad in this text or one of your own choosing, write a review of the advertisement. To help you get started, you may want to look at some additional ad reviews in business and marketing magazines as well as texts that take a sociological or interdisciplinary approach. Choose a specific publication to help you begin.
2. Choose an ad that you really like or one that you really hate. Write a letter to the advertising agency that developed the ad; share with the agency executives your review of the advertisement and why you like or dislike the ad. Be sure to give specific details from the ad to support your opinion.
3. Choose a subvertisement created by a social or political agency, like Adbusters, PETA, or TheTruth.com. Review this ad and explain whether or not you think the subvertisement is a good idea and achieves it purpose. What makes the ad work (or not)? Give specific details from the actual ad.

Reflection or Response Essays

1. In "Licensed to Shill," David Browne reports that musicians may be selling out:

   > Last year's [2000] flirty intermingling of pop music and Madison Avenue will go down in the history books, but not for the reasons you think. Yes, it was disconcerting to see Sting shill for Jaguar or 'N Sync have it their way with Burger King; "selling out" now seems a quainter notion than a less-than-$50 concert ticket. But in reality, rock stars have been pitchmen before: In the '80s, Eric Clapton pimped for beer as Michael Jackson moonwalked for soda.

   Do you consider it selling out when musicians sign over their music for radio and television commercials? Have you ever bought an artist's CD because you heard his or her music in an ad? What about when you heard a new artist on a television show or in a movie? Is this the same thing as using a song in a commercial?
2. In his essay about his dad, John Seabrook discusses the role films and television played in selling his dad an image of what a properly dressed man looked like as well as what brands he wore. Do films and television shows today still exert this power? Have you ever been influenced to dress a certain way or buy a particular product because of what you saw on the screen? How did this advertising affect your life?
3. When you look at print ads or television commercials, do you see yourself and your life represented? If yes, describe an advertisement that represents you and explain how this makes you feel. If no, why not? Are you not looking hard enough or are the advertisers leaving you out? Why do you think this is happening? What would an ad that represents you look like?

4. Have you ever had a radio jingle stick in your head? What about the jingle appealed to you or made the sound and words stick with you? What would you consider the best jingles you've heard? What made these jingles memorable?

5. As James Twitchell mentions, the Marlboro Man campaign spawned a whole line of Marlboro and cowboy products, including clothes, camping gear, and cookbooks. People have spent a lot of their own money to further advertise the Marlboro name. Coca-Cola has done the same thing with a variety of images and campaigns. What do you think about this pattern or approach to advertising? Do you think it was part of the original marketing plan? Have other brands and companies done the same thing? Do you spend your money to advertise brands for others?

Analysis Essays

1. Choose a trade character from a single advertisement or an ad campaign and write a profile of that trade character. Does your character meet the characteristics delineated by Barbara Phillips? What is the purpose of your trade character? What appeals or needs are being met by this character? Would you change anything about this character?

2. Examine three or four different magazines and look at the ads targeted specifically to men (for example, cologne or clothing ads) or kids (for example, toys or music). Do these ads show any new trends in the way advertisers attempt to appeal to specific consumers? Discuss any trends that you observe. What do you think is the reason behind these trends?

3. Visit a few of your favorite websites and notice the web banners. What kinds of products do different types of websites promote? Are there any common features among web banners? How effective must a banner be to sell the intended product or service? How do you define "effective"? How do web banners compare to other types of advertisements? Use specific examples to support your analysis.

4. Choose a product or service that is advertised in multiple ways, perhaps in print and in television commercials. Compare and contrast the two or more types of ads. What changes do the advertisers have to make when they move from one type of advertisement to another? Is one medium more effective than another? Why or why not?

© Bill Aron/PhotoEdit

5. Create a billboard slogan for yourself. What does the text below your slogan or catch phrase say? What does it look like? What images? What colors? Remember that billboards have to be taken in quickly as people are driving down the road.

Synthesis Essays

1. Imagine you are part of a citizens' group working to improve the quality of advertising in your community. What kinds of local ads do you see and hear? What recommendations would you make, and what standards would you want to see enforced? Be specific. Illustrate your argument with local ads you find that meet or fall below your expectations.

2. Create a new mascot for a product you are familiar with. It is your job to convince readers and company executives that your mascot is the best way to sell their product. Your essay will include a visual element as well as a written version of your sales pitch. What form(s) will you choose to introduce your new mascot? Magazine ads, television commercials, radio spots, billboards, web banners, or other forms and venues? Who is the audience for this new mascot? What appeals will you use to sell your new mascot and the product the mascot is supporting?

3. As mentioned previously, *Advertising Age* has created a top ten advertising icons list; they also created lists for the top slogans, jingles, and ad campaigns. Use your own criteria to create a top ten list. Explain your criteria and your top ten choices. If you want, you can create a sort of anti-top ten list in the style of David Letterman. Be sure to use specific examples to illustrate your criteria and your choices.

4. Compile a list of local media outlets that sell advertising space. Contact some of them, from a variety of different media, and request their sales information: rate cards, demographics, sample ads or ad guidelines, whatever they have to offer. Then decide on a social issue that is important to you and that you'd like to inform others about. Compare the costs and benefits of the various media and discuss which outlet would give you the best value for your advertising money. You may stop here or go to the next step of designing and proposing an ad campaign; don't forget the budget for your campaign.

5. Analyze the ads shown from the various Volkswagen ad campaigns from the last 50 years (pages 174–175). Do the ads appear to be targeting particular audiences? What magazines do you think the various ads appeared in? What television shows ran the commercials the stills are taken from? What appeal is each ad using? Can you distinguish the subvertisements from the advertisements? How can you tell? How do you think Volkswagen responds to the parodies of their ads? Create your own subvertisement for Volkswagen (or some other product).

It's money in the bank...

Volkswagen

Volkswagenwerk GmbH

Your very own Love Bug.

At a special, low $2499,* it's a sweetheart of a deal.

Now you can own your very own
Love Bug, from Volkswagen.
The Love Bug comes in two romantic
colors. Red hot red. And luscious lime green.
It has lovely racing type wheels.
And cute black trim.
But at only $2499*, we can't afford
to be too generous.
So if you want one, you'd better
hurry. A love like this won't
last forever.

The Love Bug
Limited Edition

® Volkswagen of America, 1974. *Love Bug East Coast P.O.E., Suggested Retail Price (West Coast) Slightly Higher). Local Taxes and Any Other Dealer Charges, If Any, Additional.

RABBIT. THE #1 SELLING IMPORT IN JAPAN.

The Japanese obviously know a good thing when they see one. And so more people in Japan are buying Volkswagen Rabbits than any other imported car. Fascinating. But not astonishing.

The Rabbit has more total room than any Japanese car in its class. The Rabbit hops from 0 to 50 mph in 8.3 seconds.

Most Japanese cars don't.

If you're interested in superior handling and maneuverability, you'll get them in a Rabbit, because the Rabbit has front-wheel drive.

Most Japanese cars don't.

If you're interested in economy, a VW Rabbit with a diesel engine got the highest mileage of any car in America for 1978: 53mpg on the highway, 40mpg in the city.

The gasoline Rabbit is no slouch, either, with 38mpg on the highway, 25mpg in the city.

(EPA estimates, with standard transmission. Your own mileage may vary, depending on how and where you drive, your car's condition and optional equipment.)

In short, the Rabbit delivers precisely what thoughtful people anywhere want in a car: performance, room, handling, economy.

So next time you have a yen for a terrific sukiyaki dinner, drive to the restaurant in a Rabbit. And enjoy the best of both worlds.

VOLKSWAGEN DOES IT AGAIN

1980 RABBIT DIESEL NEW YORK TO WASHINGTON ON ONLY 10 GALLONS

AND BACK!

No, we're not kidding. You could actually zip from Lincoln Center all the way to the Lincoln Memorial and back (about 466 miles), on just 10 gallons with a Rabbit Diesel.

Rabbit Diesels are the top two mileage cars in the country. In fact, the 5-speed version gets an EPA estimated [42] mpg, 56 estimated highway. The 4-speed gets an enviable [40] estimated mpg, 52 estimated highway.

(Use "estimated miles per gallon" for comparisons. Your actual mileage may vary with speed, weather and trip length. Highway mileage will probably be less.)

And don't forget, a Rabbit comes with traditional Volkswagen craftsmanship, front-wheel drive, loads of room for people and things, and also happens to be the least expensive Diesel you'll find anywhere.

All that, plus the #1 mileage record in the country.

Add it up, and not only is the Diesel the choicest candidate of the year, the Rabbit is the choicest Diesel.

So the next time you're considering trading Fifth Avenue for Pennsylvania Avenue, consider doing it in a 1980 Rabbit Diesel.

It'll get you something no other car available in the country can get you on only 10 gallons. Home.

VOLKSWAGEN DOES IT AGAIN

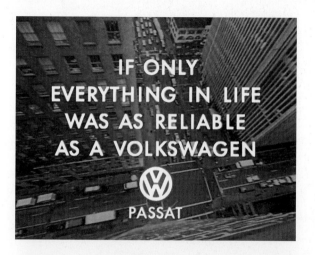

IF ONLY
EVERYTHING IN LIFE
WAS AS RELIABLE
AS A VOLKSWAGEN

PASSAT

Volkswagen recycling

Volkswagen. Wie anders?

The New Beetle Cabriolet.

Less cars, more world. Drivers wanted.®

Small but tough. Polo.

Images at top left, center left, bottom left, and top right all © Volkswagen of America, Inc. Courtesy of The Advertising Archives. Image at bottom right © Adbusters Media Foundation.

FOR FURTHER READING

Adbusters. <http://www.adbusters.org>.

Advertising Age. <http://www.adage.com>.

The Advertising Age Encyclopedia of Advertising. Ed. John McDonough and Karen Egolf. New York: Routledge, 2002.

Cronin, Anne M. *Advertising Myths: The Strange Half-lives of Images and Commodities.* London: Routledge, 2004.

Encyclopedia of Major Marketing Campaigns. Ed. Thomas Riggs. Detroit: Gale Group, 2000.

Encyclopedia of Major Marketing Campaigns, Vol. 2. Ed. Thomas Riggs. Detroit: Gale Cengage, 2006.

Freccero, Carla. *Popular Culture: An Introduction.* New York: NYUP, 1999.

Gender, Race, and Class in Media: A Text-reader, 2nd ed. Ed. Gail Dines and Jean M. Humez. Thousand Oaks, CA: Sage, 2002.

Kilbourne, Jean. *Killing Us Softly* (1, 2, and 3). [Video Series]. Northampton, MA: Media Education Foundation, 1979, 1987, 2000.

Mierau, Christina. *Accept No Substitutes: The History of American Advertising.* Minneapolis, MN: Lerner Publishing, 2000.

Sports, Culture and Advertising: Identities, Commodities and the Politics of Representation. Ed. Steven Jackson. New York: Routledge, 2004.

Twitchell, James B. *Twenty Ads That Shook the World: The Century's Most Groundbreaking Advertising and How It Changed Us All.* New York: Three Rivers Press, 2000.

writing about film

"Life goes by pretty fast. If you don't stop and look around once in awhile, you could miss it."

—**From *Ferris Bueller's Day Off***

Choose the film that features each quote.

1 "What is thy bidding, my master?"

    a. *The Lord of the Rings: The Two Towers*
    b. *Bram Stoker's Dracula*
    c. *Star Wars: Episode IV*
    d. *The Rocky Horror Picture Show*

TEST YOUR POP CULTURE IQ: FILM

© 20th Century Fox/The Kobal Collection

2 "To infinity, and beyond!"

    a. *Independence Day*
    b. *Star Trek*
    c. *Top Gun*
    d. *Toy Story*

3 "Men are rats. Worse than that, they're fleas on rats. Worse than that, they're amoebas on fleas on rats."

    a. *Mean Girls*
    b. *Sleepless in Seattle*
    c. *Jerry Maguire*
    d. *Grease*

4 "You can be my wingman anytime."

    a. *Star Wars: Episode IV*
    b. *Top Gun*
    c. *The Aviator*
    d. *Saving Private Ryan*

5 "You're gonna need a bigger boat."

    a. *Jaws*
    b. *Pirates of the Caribbean: Curse of the Black Pearl*
    c. *Titanic*
    d. *Raiders of the Lost Ark*

6 "The rules of hair care are simple and finite. Any *Cosmo* girl would have known."

    a. *Clueless*
    b. *Legally Blonde*
    c. *Mean Girls*
    d. *The Devil Wears Prada*

© Paramount/The Kobal Collection

7 "I'm the king of the world!"

    a. *Titanic*
    b. *Spider-Man*
    c. *Grease*
    d. *Toy Story*

8 "And you know this, man."

    a. *Dazed and Confused*
    b. *Rush Hour*
    c. *Friday*
    d. *Half Baked*

9 "You do too much—college, a job, all this time with me. You're not Superman, you know."

    a. *Road Trip*
    b. *Batman Begins*
    c. *Legally Blonde*
    d. *Spider-Man*

10 "It rubs the lotion on its skin or else it gets the hose again."

    a. *Silence of the Lambs*
    b. *Saw*
    c. *Texas Chainsaw Massacre*
    d. *Kiss the Girls*

ANSWERS

1 *c.* Star Wars: Episode IV   **2** *d.* Toy Story   **3** *d.* Grease   **4** *b.* Top Gun   **5** *a.* Jaws   **6** *b.* Legally Blonde
7 *a.* Titanic   **8** *c.* Friday   **9** *d.* Spider-Man   **10** *a.* Silence of the Lambs

YOU AND FILM

On the surface, films entertain us and allow us to escape from our everyday lives; we can laugh with Jim Carrey and cry with Meryl Streep and finish a film with a sense of completion. However, films can do more than just entertain us; they can also represent us and inform us. Sometimes, all we want from a film is mindless entertainment, and sometimes, we use films to provoke us into action. Often, we do not think deeply about the content of a film or the way the film was made, but certain films just beg us to take that step into deep thought, discussion, and action. The readings and writing assignments in this chapter represent the many ways films are part of our lives.

Films are usually made for artistic or monetary reasons or a combination of both. The film industry makes billions of dollars in profits annually from films shown in theaters and even more from DVD sales and marketing tie-ins. It is an unusual film that qualifies as both artistic and as a moneymaker, but this does not stop the engine behind artistic or independent filmmaking. What makes a film artistic? Is it the direction, the cinematography, the costumes, the acting, the content, the marketing? What makes a film a blockbuster? Is it just the money a film makes, or is it the way a film connects in some way to us or our culture? Why do we call *Walk the Line* a film but *Shrek* a movie? Why are some films more appealing across age groups or genders? Why are some films awarded artistic awards while others become that year's highest grossing films? These are some of the questions you will investigate in this chapter; the answers to these and other questions you create will help you focus on film as a starting point to writing. The readings and writing assignments provided will help you figure out which questions are important to you, and the introductory information in this chapter will help you write about those questions and your own individual answers.

WHY WRITE ABOUT FILM?

Writing about film teaches you to see something familiar in a new and different way. Although some critics argue that writing about individual scenes of a film destroys the beauty of the whole for the viewer, analyzing films allows you to become aware of film elements that you may not have appreciated before. It teaches you to be aware of and look for certain characteristics that you might value in films that you watch. Sometimes, focusing on film at a deep and critical level can be difficult, but with the availability of DVDs, film has become much easier to study. Many writers find that analyzing film increases and enhances their later film-watching experiences.

PREPARING TO WRITE ABOUT FILM

Films are an important part of our culture, a way to bring people together, to entertain, to inform, and to stimulate critical thinking. However, when you watch films for a class or a writing assignment, you will need to view the films in a way that is probably different from how you normally view them.

Watching and Thinking

As you have already discovered, there are many different reasons to write about film. Likewise, there are many different methods of experiencing a film, all of which may influence your overall impression: Where and when did you see it—big screen, DVD, stadium seating, art house? How much did it cost you? Who watched the film with you? Why did you see the film? Is the film genre, director, or lead actor or actress one of your favorites?

When you view a film specifically for the purpose of writing about it, you can prepare beforehand. Ask questions about the film: What are people saying about it? What do you already know about the film? How does the film connect to your interests? Consider your expectations going in, especially with regard to technology, budget, genre, intended audience, actor reputation, or director reputation. Take some preliminary notes about what you know and your expectations for the film; you will then have them to compare to your reactions after seeing it.

As you watch the film, question what you see and hear and respond to it. Look and listen for key moments in the film, such as Ferris Bueller singing on the parade float. Also look and listen for key patterns and images, such as the feather slowly drifting down in *Forrest Gump*. Think about what seems unfamiliar or different within the film.

When possible, it is best to watch the film once for the full effect without taking any notes and then to take notes on subsequent viewings. However, sometimes you cannot watch a film more than once, and you'll have to take notes as you watch. Develop your own form of shorthand or system of abbreviations, so you can take notes without missing parts of the film. It is especially important to note technical aspects of the film you may want to come back to. The first time you watch *Hairspray*, for example, you may jot down the names of the different dances the characters do or at least take down a short description of them so you can go back later and analyze particular camera movements during different dances. You can also annotate or sketch key scenes by taking down short bursts of dialogue or noting character dress for a key scene. What would the ending of *Grease* be without Sandy changing to uncharacteristic clothing? This is an example of something that pops out at you in your first viewing. Shortly after your viewing, fill in your notes. As you elaborate, you will be able to make

Many disciplines use film in their instruction and education. Scientists record hours of data for experimental purposes, and musicians use long-format music videos to visually express their sound.

- What role has film played or could play in your role as a student?
- How about in your current job or in jobs you have had in the past?
- How about in your future occupation?

keyquestions

Key Questions for Film Viewing

- When was the film made? Check the closing credits or a film biography.

- Are you familiar with the time period(s) the film represents?

- Where was the film made? Check the closing credits or a film biography.

- What settings or locations are represented in the film?

- Who are the main characters? Secondary characters? Seemingly nonessential characters?

- Are there any scenes, props, or locations that are unfamiliar or unique?

- How does the title relate to the location, storyline, or characters?

- How are the opening credits formatted and revealed to the viewer?

- How does the first scene begin? What is the transition between the credits and this first scene?

- Is this film similar to or different from other films you have watched for class or outside class?

- Did you notice anything about the camera movements? Are there particular scenes that have zoomed in or jumpy images? Are there camera angles that highlight certain characters, locations, or props?

- How does the soundtrack contribute to the film?

- What is the concluding scene or image in the film?

additional connections to other parts of the film and add examples to key points or patterns.

After the film, you can also reflect on what you have seen or heard and on what you have noted. You can even compare these to your previewing notes. As you reflect, think about how your previous viewing experiences affected this viewing, how your belief or value systems affect your viewing, and how your politics affect your viewing.

As you reflect and make connections in your notes, you can also consider the context of the film itself and do some research: What is the historical background of the film? What were the politics of the time? What were the film regulations of the time? Likewise, consider the film's use or abuse of standard storyline conventions. Again, consider how you experienced the film: Were you reading subtitles or listening to a dubbed audio? Was it on DVD or on your iPod and formatted to fit your screen? Was the theater too hot or cold? Was your neighbor's cell phone ringing throughout the film? Were people talking—to each other, to the characters in the film? Were you disturbed by others text messaging?

Asking questions and reflecting on your viewing experience will help you select and describe relevant details related to key points or elements in the film. Use these details to build your interpretation or analysis of the film. You may also find the need to conduct outside research as you build your argument and support your thesis.

Watching, Analyzing, and Understanding

As you begin to write about film, you might find it helpful to know the language of film production and analysis. In the following sections, you will find brief summaries of the key elements, along with lists of technical terms that you may find useful. Of course, this is not an exhaustive list or description; if you want to know more, see one of the many texts devoted to film criticism and analysis.

CHARACTERS

It is quite common for writers to focus on the development or description of *characters* when writing about film. What would *Independence Day* be without Will Smith's character? A close reading of a major or minor character can provide many supporting examples for an analysis or synthesis essay or can be the starting point for establishing connections between the character and the writer for a reflection or response essay. Writers often focus on the chronological story of the character's life, referred to as the *arc* of a character or story. In both *Rambo* and *Pretty Woman*, for example, the arc of the character's life has important information about the character's past. How Rambo became a mercenary fighter and how Vivian became a prostitute are key to understanding their characters. Writers who analyze characters deeply usually look at how realistic or stereotypical the character or the character's story is, how the backdrop or clothing or lighting helps define the character, how the character fits in with other characters in the story, and whether the character experiences some kind of change during the progression of the storyline.

CINEMATOGRAPHY

Cinematography concerns how the film that viewers see is produced. The cinematographer works with the director and makes decisions about types of lenses, camera positions, and lighting to provide a unique and memorable design for each particular film. The cinematographer also chooses the type of film to be used because different types of film, along with different filming speeds, can affect how the film looks and indicate mood or atmosphere. Consider the Nicolas Cage film *8MM*, where the focus of the entire film is the juxtaposition of the main storyline with the pornographic 8mm film his character is investigating. Pay attention to the use of light and shadow and the lighting of certain scenes or characters at different times; it is the cinematographer's job to manipulate light and shadow based on how the director wants the scene to look. Also look at how the camera is used. How are close-ups used? Are there scenes when the camera zooms in or zooms out? Are there scenes when camera angles—or points of view—help create the mood or help develop a character? Is the entire film in black and white, or are there particular scenes where the color changes to black and white, as in *Pleasantville*? Look for any slight changes that might be deliberate, and investigate what these manipulations might mean.

COMPOSITION

Composition refers to the use of space or the shape of an image on film, including how the images are affected by light, how they are positioned in relation to each other and the setting, and how they are positioned in relation to the frame of the film. For example, in *Walk the Line*, Joaquin Phoenix takes up the entire screen when he is singing, and in *Little Miss Sunshine*, the camera pulls away from the van each time the family returns to the road after a rest stop. When writing about composition, you may want to look at the screen width or depth of characters, locations, or props. Consider how characters or props are placed in the foreground or background of scenes, and look at how the director angles the camera to highlight characters, locations, or props. You can also consider whether or not you are seeing the whole picture—you are not if the film has been formatted to fit your screen. You may also consider the purpose behind techniques such as split screens and reflected subjects in windows, mirrors, television screens, and so forth. Ask yourself whether or not the arrangement before you on the screen has any special significance: Why is the character always to the left side of the screen? Why are the objects in the foreground out of focus? Why are we watching the character's actions through the window? Why are we looking at the characters from above?

CRITICAL OR IDEOLOGICAL APPROACH

When you write an analysis essay, your instructor might introduce a *critical or ideological approach* to help you view and dissect a film. For example, she might focus on an approach that utilizes political and social theories, perhaps looking for the postcolonial influence in the latest Bollywood film from India. Film analysis might also utilize historical approaches that consider the social and political climate of the culture and time period presented in a film or the climate of the film as it was produced, such as looking at the presentation of gay characters after the Stonewall riots in 1969. Such a historical perspective might also consider the history or biography of the director, as well as the history of his or her body of work.

This biographical method could lead you to auteur criticism, which looks at the director or actor as the author or responsible party of a film and then looks for patterns from a director throughout his or her body of work. When you say that you always enjoy Spike Lee, Judd Apatow, or Meryl Streep films, you are looking at each of these directors or actors as an auteur—you are noting how each embodies his or her own style. Other critical lenses that may be used to examine the content and purpose of a film include psychoanalytic models and theories, feminist and queer theories, and cognitive models. Any of the critical lenses used in other disciplines may be brought to bear on a film and its production. Ask yourself if history has been distorted in some way. Ask yourself how this film was influenced by the politics of the time or what message the director is trying to convey. Ask yourself how minority characters are portrayed in this film. Ask yourself what cinematic and editorial choices were made to conform to the rating codes of the time period.

EDITING

Editing is another key element of film production. A film editor works with the director and producers to add or cut frames or scenes to preserve the storyline and to create the final form of a film. How fast scenes change, how one scene makes its transition into the next, and the use of fade-in or fade-out shots, especially at the beginning and ending of a film, can carry meaning. Look for how your reaction to the entire film or particular scenes is influenced by how the film was edited. Also look for montages, which are scenes built out of many brief shots; montages can signify that an important theme is being emphasized. In *The Breakfast Club*, the fast cutaway scenes in the hallway as the students are trying to get away from the principal give an added urgency to the viewer. Editing can tell you important things about the characters, point of view, theme, symbols, or setting, so be sure to look at how the film is put together. A good way to see the importance of editing is to compare a director's cut of a film to the original offering; *Blade Runner, Apocalypse Now*, and many other films have directors' versions available for you to investigate.

GENRE

Genre, which means "kind" in French, is another important element of film production and film analysis, as it helps viewers identify common patterns. Genre sets up audience expectations and helps audiences believe in what is presented. For instance, in action films, the bad guys are always poor shots while the good guy has almost perfect aim, and viewers usually accept this within the genre of the action film. Genre films usually have familiar or stock characters (the tobacco-chewing cowboy in westerns), filming techniques (the suspenseful music in horror films or non-stop motion in action films), themes (destructive crises or disasters in action films), or settings (historical time periods in dramas). All of these are genre film *conventions*, those recognizable features that each genre exhibits. Genre films can also be subdivided into subgenres; for instance, musical subgenres include comedy musicals (*High School Musical*), dance films (*Step Up*), concert films (*Woodstock*), and Broadway hits brought to film (*Dreamgirls*). Ask yourself if this film is following its generic conventions as *Saw* does—what would *Saw* be without its suspenseful music, its killer brought back to life, or its perceived killer not being the real killer? Or does the film have mixed genres as *Blazing Saddles* does when it combines the conventions of westerns and comedies together? Or does it try to avoid genre conventions or poke fun at them—perhaps commenting on genres themselves, such as in the film *Scream*? Sometimes, directors and producers use genre to target specific audiences, such as those who like sports or who have an interest in history. Filmmakers often also combine genres to bring a film to a wider audience.

Established genres and subgenres include the following films from recent decades:

Film Genres	Sub-genres	Examples
Action/Adventure	Alien Invasion	*Independence Day*
	Buddy Cops	*Lethal Weapon*
	Epic Adventure	*Gladiator*
	Disaster	*Towering Inferno*
	Revenge	*Kill Bill Vol. I & II*
Comedy	Teen Comedy	*Ferris Bueller's Day Off*
	Mock-umentary	*Best in Show*
	Parody	*Scary Movie*
	Fish-Out-of-Water	*She's the Man*
Crime/Gangster	Film Noir	*L.A. Confidential*
	Organized Crime	*Scarface*
	Prison	*The Shawshank Redemption*
	Caper	*Ocean's Eleven*
Drama	Coming of Age	*Harry Potter and the Goblet of Fire*
	Social Problem	*Hotel Rwanda*
	Sports	*Remember the Titans*
	Biography	*Ray*
Epic/Historical	Biblical	*Passion of the Christ*
	Greek	*Troy*
	Historical	*Cold Mountain*
	Medieval	*King Arthur*
Horror	Slasher	*Texas Chainsaw Massacre*
	Zombie	*Dawn of the Dead*
	Teen Terror	*Scream*
	Psychological	*Saw*
Musical	Comedy Musical	*Hairspray*
	Dance Film	*Shall We Dance?*
	Broadway Hit	*Grease*
	Concert Film	*Awesome, I F**kin' Shot That*
	Musical Biography	*Walk the Line*
Romance	Coming of Age	*Pretty in Pink*
	Historical	*Tristan and Isolde*
	Romantic Comedy	*Sleepless in Seattle*
	Star-Crossed	*Romeo and Juliet*
Science Fiction	Alien Encounters	*War of the Worlds*
	Disaster	*The Day After Tomorrow*
	Dystopia	*The Matrix*
	Outer Space	*Serenity*
War	Civil War	*Glory*
	Revolutionary War	*The Patriot*
	Aerial Combat	*Top Gun*
	Action Combat	*Black Hawk Down*
Western	Epic Western	*Dances with Wolves*
	Outlaws	*Young Guns*
	Cattle Drive	*City Slickers*
	Spoof Westerns	*Blazing Saddles*

We all have our personal favorites when it comes to films or movies. Think about those you have really enjoyed and answer the following questions.

- What is your favorite film genre?
- What are some of your favorite films that make up that genre?
- What is it about these films that you enjoy? Give examples.

MISE-EN-SCÈNE

Mise-en-scène (meez ahn sen) refers to the items put before the camera, and the way they are placed, as the director prepares for filming. These items include the setting and subjects and the composition of both. Mise-en-scène, also known as production design, is a very important element of film production. Choices made about setting (the jungle for *Rambo*), subjects (Bo Derek's braided hair in *10*), and composition (the distance between white and black dancers in *Hairspray*) can make political and/or social comments. Likewise, they can pay tribute to other films or film techniques—even through parody, as in the *Scary Movie* franchise. However, some choices are more economic, as props and costumes can be used to promote businesses, products, and skills. Consider the choices of the Wilson soccer ball in *Cast Away*, the Aston Martin cars in James Bond movies, or Reese's Pieces in *E.T., the Extra-Terrestrial*. Just think of how many times you have seen a film character drinking from a can of Coke or Pepsi. Of course, this capitalistic characteristic of filmmaking can be another area for research and analysis in the field of film criticism.

SETTING

Setting is where the filmed action occurs and may include a manufactured set in a studio or a natural location. The setting includes the props used for the background and action, the colors of the props and the background, and the arrangement of the props. This setting may be realistic or imaginary and may be digitally enhanced after filming. The setting usually implies time, space, and place and may enhance style, character, mood, and meaning. The setting may even become or be symbolic of a character in the film. Ask yourself whether or not the objects and the props in the setting carry particular meanings or significance: Why does he carry a cane? Why are the buildings dark with sharp edges? Why is it always raining? Why do the subjects seem to be floating in space?

SOUND

Sound also serves numerous functions in a film. It can set the scene, add emotions, serve as background filler, cover for weak acting, create continuity from scene to scene, and direct attention or emphasize climaxes. The soundtrack itself can have four components: spoken words, which include dialogues, monologues, and narration; sound effects, which are sounds made by objects or people—such as the sounds of walking or background sound like the wind blowing; music, which can be instrumental, vocal, or a combination of the two; and silence. Some of these four types of sound can be overlapped or distorted for a special effect that a director is seeking. Additionally, the soundtrack can be created with commercial value in mind, sometimes more than its value to the film. Ask yourself how the sound affects your experience of the film. If possible, watch part of it without any sound and see how it affects you.

SUBJECT

The term *subject* refers to actors, as well as animals or other personified objects such as robots, that are seen in the film. As in literature, film characters may be fully described or mysterious, either by the director's choice or because of writing and acting styles. As you look at film subjects, you can learn about them as characters and as agents in the film from their actions, reactions, manner of speaking, and appearance—including their possessions (type of clothes, car, house, and so on). Ask yourself why a character is presented in a certain way: What does her hairstyle mean? What does it mean that she constantly bites her nails? Why does he always wear black? Why are his teeth dirty or missing? Why does she drive a VW instead of a Ford Focus?

Watching, Researching, and Documenting

If you are writing a reflection or response essay, you may not be required to do any outside research. However, you may want to do some outside research to write a convincing and well-supported review or analysis of a film.

Areas of research may include the following:

- The author's/director's life
- The author's/director's body of work
- The historical background of the movie itself, of the events portrayed in the film, film-production codes at the time, technology at the time the film was made, and so forth
- The culture represented or presented in the film
- How others received the film
- The economic history or budget of the film
- The original source for the screenplay
- The history or development of techniques
- The evolution of particular genres or conventions

Of course, the type of research you will do depends on the questions you want answered, so start there: What do you want or need to know to complete your analysis of a given film or group of films? Go back to your preliminary notes and observations. What do you need to fill in? How do you want to narrow your focus? As you conduct your research, be open to new ideas and interpretations that may arise, but still proceed with some type of plan or questions to answer. Once you have completed your research, you may want to view the film again and look for additional examples to support your claims or test the ideas you have read about and want to incorporate in your analysis.

Your research can lead you to a variety of primary and secondary sources; for more information on using sources in your writing about film, see Chapter 11: Researching and Documenting in the Pop Culture Zone. Naturally, your first source is the film itself. Films are available in many ways—on DVD, DVR, cable, Netflix, or online—and this has made it easier to access many films, even older films. However you view the film, you need to keep in mind that you may not be viewing the film as it was intended to be seen and that changes in format can distort the quality of the film, including its size, clarity, and color, as well as distorting the soundtrack or even the final cut. Furthermore, you do not get the same experience when you watch a film on a television in your home as you do when you watch it on a large screen in a theater. Of course, the ability to stop and start films can aid in the close analysis process. Published scripts, and sometimes unpublished scripts if you can find a cooperative production company, can also help with the research process, especially if they contain director notes or interviews and other such extraneous information. Many films on DVD also have commentary from directors, producers, actors, and others associated with the film.

As with any research project, secondary sources can be found in a number of places, usually only limited by what has actually been published and by your imagination. You may find books, articles, and websites about your film, the director, the genre, the techniques used, and other aspects of the film. Make sure you check out your library's holdings as well as the electronic databases available through your school or public libraries, such as InfoTrac College Edition, LexisNexis, JSTOR, or the MLA International Bibliography. You may also want to check out the databases and indexes (many only available in print) specifically related to film, such as *The International Film Index, 1895–1990*, or other reference sources such as dictionaries and encyclopedias devoted to film: *The Film Encyclopedia* or *The Complete Film Dictionary*, for example. Use the tables of contents and the indexes in the sources you find to make sure they have relevant information.

As with many pop culture topics, you often have to look outside the traditional sources for additional information. The Internet has numerous worthwhile sites, but remember to evaluate the site and its purpose before you trust it as a reliable source. Of course, Miramax or Disney will only have good things to say about their latest blockbuster, but a site with an educational or analytical focus will probably give a more balanced review and provide more actual analysis. Some sites to check out, whether for basic facts, reviews, archives, or analysis, include the following:

The American Film Institute	http://www.afi.com
Film Studies—University of Alberta	http://www.humanities.ualberta.ca/english/
Independent Film Channel	http://www.ifc.com
The International Federation of Film Archives	http://www.fiafnet.org
The Internet Movie Database	http://www.imdb.com
Rotten Tomatoes	http://www.rottentomatoes.com
Screensite	http://www.screensite.org
Sundance Film Festival	http://festival.sundance.org

With all primary and secondary sources, remember to always record the citation information you will need for your Works Cited page and for your in-text citations. Record information about the film, any books or articles you read, and any websites you review. You should always know where you found your information and how to get back to it if you need to. See Chapter 11 for specific guidelines, and see the Works Cited at the end of each sample essay for examples of citations for specific sources.

WRITING ABOUT FILM

Film is an artistic medium and can be analyzed in a variety of ways, many of which you have already used to critique other media, such as advertisements or popular literature. Writing about film can include a focus on different aspects of the storyline or film process or any of the genres or categories of film, such as student films, blockbusters, independent films, foreign films, documentaries, or animated films. Although there are many types of film writing, there are four main assignments given in most composition or film classes: film reviews, reflection or response essays, analysis essays, or synthesis essays, which can be a combination of any of the preceding types.

Film Reviews or Review Essays

In the film review, evaluation is the focus. You are giving a judgment about the quality of the film, backed up with enough information to indicate that your judgment is based on good reasoning. These are the types of articles found in newspapers, in magazines, and on most news websites discussing films that are currently in theaters or newly released on DVD. For a class, your review will most likely be about a film that you watched in class or one that you are required to watch outside class.

Remember that most good films are not perfect, and even the worst films have good points. Some film reviews are balanced and concentrate on both the positives and negatives of the film, whereas other reviews are intentionally slanted toward an overwhelmingly positive or negative point of view. Your overall evaluation of the film is usually phrased as the thesis or argument of the essay. For example, your thesis might look like this: "Although the Disney princess in *Mulan* shares many of the same traits as most other Disney princesses, the film's accurate depiction of Chinese culture makes *Mulan* one of the most impressive Disney animated features ever."

Film reviews follow certain conventions. Typically, a brief plot synopsis tells the main conflicts and a little about character development. The essay is usually written in present tense (for example, "*Brokeback Mountain* is one of Ang Lee's finest films" instead of "*Brokeback Mountain* was one of Ang Lee's finest films"), and you do not assume that your reader is extremely familiar with the film. Reviewers hardly ever give away the ending, but if they do, they give a spoiler alert, a warning to readers that information that might spoil viewing the film is coming up. You can mention striking aspects of the film, such as impressive sets or costumes, notable visual aspects like color design or music, and acting.

You can also compare the film to other movies in the same genre, to ones made by the same filmmaker or starring members of the cast, or to ones that have similar themes. You can show that you are familiar with a wide range of films so that your opinion is taken seriously and credibly.

Reflection or Response Essays

Although reflection or response essays will include some description of the film, the main purpose is to use the film as a starting point for your own discussion. The name of this type of essay explains the purpose fairly well. The writer can reflect on his or her own feelings that have arisen through critically watching a film, or the writer can respond to some personal issue or emotion that has arisen during the viewing of the film. Although it is important to use evidence from the film to explain why you are making your specific point, the essay mostly will be personal writing.

Writing a reflection or response essay begins when you decide what aspect of the film sparks your attention. Using this spark, you then decide what you would like to say to your audience. A solid thesis statement explaining the purpose of the essay will help keep you on track with the film and not on a rant about the issue you are considering.

Analysis Essays

Like the film review, an analysis essay includes descriptions, but these descriptions are more detailed and extensive, and they also include an explanation of their significance. When you analyze a film, you are attempting to defend your view about how the parts of the film work (or don't work) together. As with any argumentative paper, you want to offer an idea you have about the film and support it with evidence from the film as well as outside sources.

keyquestions

Key Questions for a Film Review Essay

- Have you clearly indicated your judgment of the film's quality?
- Have you provided a brief plot synopsis while avoiding plot summary?
- Have you mentioned specific elements of the film that support your judgment? Have you described these quickly and vividly, using both metaphors and concrete language?
- Have you defined yourself as a credible source? Do you mention that you have seen other films by the same director or actor? Or have you cited secondary sources, if asked to do this type of research?
- Have you qualified your judgment with both positive and negative aspects of the film?
- Have you begun the review with an attention-grabbing opening? Have you concluded it with a memorable sentence or idea?
- Did you write in present tense?

keyquestions

Key Questions for a Reflection or Response Essay

- Have you clearly indicated how you used the film as a springboard for your thesis?

- Have you expressed your personal response to one aspect of the film?

- Did you avoid plot summary?

- Does your introduction direct your audience into your response?

- Does your concluding paragraph include some reflection on both the film and your response?

- Did you write about the film in present tense but use past tense for things that happened in the past?

- Are your essay's intentions clear?

Key Questions for an Analysis Essay

- Do you have a strong thesis or argument?

- Do you have a series of reasons supporting the thesis? Are these arranged in a logical and convincing order?

- Are your supporting reasons backed up? Do you provide specific evidence and examples from the film for each reason you offer?

- Does your introduction orient your reader to the direction of your argument?

- Does your concluding paragraph reiterate your thesis and provide a vivid ending?

- Did you write in literary present tense?

- Did you avoid plot summary?

To write an analysis essay, you must first come up with a thesis. This is the statement that your essay will explain and support. Similar to the thesis in the film review, it offers your opinion, but it also helps other viewers understand the film. Typically, in a film analysis, your thesis will say something about why and how a film is made or its meaning. You also must support your thesis throughout the paper with specific evidence and examples from the film and outside resources. Analysis requires more observations about the film than description from within the film.

When analyzing film, remember that there may be many valid interpretations. You need to support your interpretation with specific scenes, details, or elements from the film. You may also need to support it with research about the director, the context of the film's production, or the history of the film or the film's subject matter.

Synthesis Essays

Sometimes, using personal reflections in a film review essay or using reviews or reflections in an analysis essay can make your writing much more effective. A synthesis essay can be partly one type of writing and partly another; this type of essay can be assigned by your instructor, or you can decide to mix types of writing to create the strongest essay possible. If you are writing for a class, be sure to look over the assignment and speak to the instructor if this type of mixture does not fit strictly into the directions for the assignment. Many instructors and student writers prefer the openness of a synthesized essay, which allows students to make decisions based on what is needed for point of view, argument, support, or interest. When you choose to use a mixture of strategies, be sure to look over the key questions for the types of essay strategies you are including in your essay.

This introduction to writing about film has included ideas that may be new to you. To process them, read over the sample essay provided to see how the writing and film analysis techniques have been used.

SAMPLE ANNOTATED ESSAY

1. Do you enjoy sci-fi? Why or why not?

2. If you've seen at least a few sci-fi films, what are some of their characteristics?

3. Do sci-fi films have a built-in audience because of their popularity in many social circles? How could this affect their production? Their budget? Their casting?

4. Are sci-fi audiences stereotypical or stereotyped?

Chris Driver *is a former staff writer for Nashvillezine.com and Popshot.net. His writings on film, music, and composition studies have been published in* Magazine Americana: The American Popular Culture Online Magazine, Southern Discourse, *and* COMPbiblio: Leaders and Influences in Composition Theory and Composition *(2007). He wrote the following essay while he was a student at Middle Tennessee State University.*

1968 RESONATES IN 2004

2001: A Space Odyssey and the Devolution of the Science Fiction Film

Chris Driver

Note how the introduction grabs the attention of the reader. What strategies does Driver use?

According to the original trailer for Ridley Scott's *Alien* (1979), "In space, no one can hear you scream." Accepting this logic, one would assume that in space, no one can hear the roaring engines of space cruisers, the percussive blasts of explosions, or the metallic screams of eroding exteriors on too-rapidly descending space ships, but this is not the case in the *Alien* "quadrilogy" of films. Why should series directors Scott, Cameron, Fincher and Jeunet have concerned

"1968 Resonates in 2004: 2001: A Space Odyssey and the Devolution of the Science Fiction Film" by Chris Driver. Written for Stanley Kubrick Films with Dr. David Lavery at Middle Tennessee State University, 2004.

themselves with details such as these? Why nitpick over continuity or technical details that probably fail to condemn these modern films but nonetheless nudge them farther from the science and closer to the fiction?

Details can often make or break a film, and science fiction directors of the past two decades have often embraced new technologies while simultaneously adopting a lazy attitude towards realism, content to allow the technology to do all the work and to cover all the details. With his 1968 masterpiece, *2001: A Space Odyssey,* Stanley Kubrick redefined the scope and potential of science fiction film. For several pronounced reasons including Kubrick's meticulous mise-en-scène, his breakthrough approach to the passage of time in space, his use of detailed models, and his incorporation of broad philosophical themes, *2001* remains a powerful, influential work that easily trumps the majority of genre works that have followed it.

2001 creates a convincing, detailed, outer-space milieu by comprising every aspect of every shot with stunning visuals, like the sun rising over a vast, empty, prehistoric landscape, a gently rotating space station, gliding along the edge of the earth's glowing atmosphere, or an astronaut's porcelain face, reflecting rainbow colored lights from a blinking control panel. All of these intense visual scenes become unforgettable images, even after a single viewing. Kubrick utilizes a minimum of sound effects, adding to the realism of every scene, but especially to the shots of the astronauts free-floating outside the ship. When Dave ventures out (in his space suit) to retrieve the antenna that HAL has predicted will malfunction, the viewer hears nothing but Dave's rhythmic, internalized breathing, as he floats away—a single swath of bright red in a sea of blackness—along the bone-white, elongated spinal column that is the ship *Discovery*'s bow. The absence of sound effects or even music adds to the dramatic tension and creates a realism that envelops the viewer, and we too feel isolated, vulnerable and claustrophobic. Kubrick spent a lot of time deciding on every element that makes up every shot, and it shows, but he didn't have the option that some directors have taken

Clearly stated thesis that works as a road map for the rest of the essay.

Note the specific examples from the film.

Focuses on sound effects with specific examples drawn from the film.

advantage of more recently—the option of digitally creating complete environments for their actors, an option which often results in a marked lack of realism. Two examples of this disappointing loss of realism that often accompanies the application of new, computer-based filmmaking technology to science fiction film are the most recent installments of the indefatigable *Star Wars* series. *The Phantom Menace* (1999) and *Attack of The Clones* (2002) rely so heavily on an almost entirely digitized environment (even digitally rendered characters—see the abhorrent, computer-generated Jar Jar) that realism is sacrificed, and the viewer's ability to become lost in a fantastic world is significantly compromised. Admittedly, Kubrick did not have access to the technology that made the recent *Star Wars* films possible, and one wonders what may have happened to the genre if he had. *2001* remains special, largely because of its fantastic, yet precise rendition of a believable space environment.

Another aspect of Kubrick's realistic interpretation of outer space that contributes to every viewer's absorption in *2001* is his use of intricately detailed models for all of his space cruiser scenes involving astronauts and motion. The current trend in science fiction film is to create spaceships digitally, relying completely on computer programs to create a flying, spinning, shooting star cruiser that often looks less than convincing. Films featuring this shortcut to effects are numerous; some of them include *Independence Day* (1996), *Wing Commander* (1999) and both recent *Star Wars* films, in which the space ships do not look as detailed or as realistic because of their lack of physical reality. A close look at many of these computer-generated ships reveals a pronounced lack of textural features and depth, a problem typical of a large portion of computer-created spaceships. Witnessing these computer-animated spaceships cruising across the screen has considerably less impact on the viewer, immediately prompting comments about how "fake" everything looks, and when a viewer cannot become absorbed into the fabricated reality of any film, specially a science fiction film, the movies inevitably fail. Each of Kubrick's pods and ships in *2001* are memorable because they are precisely rendered, down to

Compares *2001: A Space Odyssey* to more modern films a reader might be more familiar with.

Discusses importance of detailed props with specific examples from the film.

the control panels, lights, buttons and knobs, a level of intricacy reminiscent of the B-52 interiors from *Dr. Strangelove* (1963). His miniatures are so detailed that when the enormous ships cruise by on the big screen, they look like entirely realistic, futuristic landscapes of technology, and disbelief is more than adequately suspended.

Kubrick was never really in much of a hurry, often spending several years preparing for a new project (five years passed between *Dr. Strangelove* and *2001;* twelve years passed between *Full Metal Jacket* and *Eyes Wide Shut*), and his films' chronological progression and editing style are clear reminders of his steady, persistent, yet unhurried approach to filmmaking. Much has been said about Americans and their short attention spans; living in a television culture, the land of Attention Deficit Disorder (ADD) and the soundbyte newscast, we want what we want and we want it now. Kubrick was interested in slowing things down, in capturing an essence; he worked in stark contrast to the frenetic, fractured, rapid-fire editing styles of contemporary science fiction directors like Danny Boyle (*28 Days Later*) and Paul Anderson (*Resident Evil*). In *2001*, during Dr. Floyd's space travels, the details of his journey are meticulously laid out for the viewer. As he flies farther away from earth, we witness his loss of control: as he sleeps, his pen floats aimlessly in the cabin, his arm floating next to it; we watch the stewardess' careful steps in her Velcro shoes, and we note Floyd's "phone call" to his daughter, his examination of the "zero-gravity toilet" instructions, and his careful consumption of what amounts to baby food. Kubrick spares no detail, revealing for the viewer, in long, smooth tracking shots (one of his undeniable trademarks) what it is like to navigate a space station on foot, just how a smaller space ship manages to dock into a larger one, how each person on board station and cruiser meticulously performs his or her duty, and much more. Rather than assaulting the viewer with a montage of editing, Kubrick achieves a thorough, even slow, attentive shoot that focuses on the minutia. Eventually all of these smoothly edited and gently paced scenes clue the viewer in to what space travel must really feel like.

A science fiction film that truly makes an impact for generations is one that does more than create an entirely believable visual milieu. As a viewer, being able to dive into a fabricated world and actually accept its reality is a huge step, but it is only the first step required of *legendary* films. These films must be about more than space ships; they must be about ideas—they must force the viewer to think about the human condition. Kubrick did not intend to make a movie about space monsters, dogfights, and laser blasts. His themes incorporate larger philosophical questions, rather than taking an easy road and focusing on the struggle between good and evil (aliens vs. humans, Skywalker vs. Vader, etc.). Kubrick assumes a certain level of intelligence within his audience, and typically chooses not to serve up a didactic moral or ethical allegory on a silver platter. The best science fiction is patently aware of the issues, struggles and questions that consume a human intellectual. *2001* succeeds because it speculates over human history, ponders the present, and asks questions about the future. What will human kind evolve into, and what characteristics will endure? How much of our fears, jealousies, insecurities, fallibilities, and egos will we impart to our electronic "offspring" (i.e., HAL), and what will the consequences bring? Too many modern science fiction films fail to ask questions like these, and rapidly descend into "good versus evil," slasher, hard-boiled detective, or other predictable genre fare.

Addresses the theme of the film and the director's intent.

Stanley Kubrick's *2001: A Space Odyssey* will no doubt be analyzed and debated for years to come; this effort has barely scratched its many varied surfaces. Critics and film historians will have no shortage of material to discuss and debate when considering his monumental work. What this author hopes is that *2001*'s legacy will begin to have more of a profound and pronounced effect on the few modern directors who share an attraction to the science fiction genre. It is too late for George Lucas, but perhaps younger directors like Paul Anderson, whose *Alien Vs. Predator* is to debut this August, will learn something from a few more looks at a milestone classic like *2001,* realizing that there is so much more to a great science fiction film than computer-generated effects, artificial environments, and scary monsters.

Conclusion pulls the entire essay together and looks toward the future.

Works Cited

28 Days Later . . . Dir. Danny Boyle. 20th Century Fox, 2002.

2001: A Space Odyssey. Dir. Stanley Kubrick. MGM, 1968.

Alien. Dir. Ridley Scott. [original trailer] 20th Century Fox, 1979.

AVP: Alien Vs. Predator. Dir. Paul W. S. Anderson. 20th Century Fox, 2004.

Dr. Strangelove, Or: How I Learned to Stop Worrying and Love the Bomb. Dir. Stanley Kubrick. Columbia Pictures, 1964.

Eyes Wide Shut. Dir. Stanley Kubrick. Warner Bros, 1999.

Full Metal Jacket. Dir. Stanley Kubrick. Warner Bros, 1987.

Independence Day. Dir. Roland Emmerich. 20th Century Fox, 1996.

Resident Evil. Dir. Paul W. S. Anderson. Sony Pictures Entertainment, 2002.

Star Wars: Episode I—The Phantom Menace. Dir. George Lucas. 20th Century Fox, 1999.

Star Wars: Episode II—Attack of The Clones. Dir. George Lucas. 20th Century Fox, 2002.

Wing Commander. Dir. Chris Roberts. 20th Century Fox, 1999.

DECODING THE TEXT

1. How does the author connect many sci-fi films into one essay?

2. What is the purpose of using so many films in a relatively short essay?

3. Is this purpose met? How does it strengthen the essay?

4. Does the author consider the elements of a sci-fi film in the essay? How is this addressed?

CONNECTING TO YOUR CULTURE

1. What is the purpose of sci-fi filmmaking?

2. Does this purpose connect to the real world in any way? To your life?

3. How is sci-fi combined with other film genres to appeal to a wider audience? To appeal to you specifically?

TACKLING TOPICS

1. What makes you want to see a movie? The commercials? Previews of coming attractions? Word of mouth? Reviews? Big-name stars? Directors?

2. What are you looking for in a movie? Explain the kind of experience you want.

3. How is music used in film? Do you ever buy soundtrack recordings? What functions does music have in films?

4. Some films are about serious subjects, such as capital punishment (*Dead Man Walking*), and others are strictly for entertainment (*Reno 911!*). What serious subjects have been dealt with in films before? Were some of these films also entertaining? Why or why not?

5. Make a list of your favorite or most-watched films and organize them into categories based on their level of seriousness.

READING SELECTIONS

The readings that follow are organized into five sections: 1970s, 1980s, 1990s, 2000s, and Across the Decades. The familiar decades organization that underpins all content chapters for this textbook is used, and the readings in each of the sections are not isolated to that decade or section because pop culture is not only what happened at the time but also how the same item or idea is received or remembered later on. Thus, in the '70s section, we have an essay on how modern fans of *Star Wars* are creating their own movies that Clive Thompson, the author of "May the Force Be with You, and You, and You . . . ," considers just as good as, if not better than, the recent films from George Lucas in the *Star Wars* franchise. Jay Cocks gives a brief review of *The Godfather*, and Todd Berliner argues that *The Godfather, Part II*, only gets better with age. In the '80s selection, Steve Almond suggests that *Ferris Bueller's Day Off* is one of the most sophisticated teen movies of that era, comparing it to other teen films across the decades. Spike Lee and Ralph Wiley, writing on how Lee's direction of *Malcolm X* and real-life politics coincided one day in the '90s, give a fine example of how pop culture and other aspects of culture come into contact each day. Also included in the '90s section is Roger Ebert's review of *Scream*, explaining how a film can have more than just a surface meaning. A case study of three film reviews for *Fahrenheit 9/11* makes up the '00s section, illustrating how film reviews can be balanced or slanted depending on who the author is and where the piece is published. And in the final Across the Decades section, Kathi Maio investigates the makeup of Disney's heroines from 1937's *Snow White and the Seven Dwarfs* to more current Disney films, Stanley Kauffmann shares the life of a film critic in "Why I'm Not Bored," and Alan Vanneman shares a visual essay on "Alfred Hitchcock: A Hank of Hair and a Piece of Bone."

The readings here are presented as a way for you to become more versed in investigating film as pop culture; however, they are also offered as samples of writing reviews, reflections or responses, analyses, and synthesis essays about films.

Reading Selections: the

CONSIDERING IDEAS

The *Star Wars* film franchise began in 1977 with what is now called Episode IV.

1. Have you seen this 1977 episode or any of the other films in the series?

2. If you have seen the 1977 episode and the more recent films that make up the first to third episodes, how can you compare the earlier films to the later ones?

3. Do the earlier films seem dated now? Or do you think other aspects of the more recent films are better or worse than the older ones?

4. If you've never seen a *Star Wars* film, what has held you back?

Clive Thompson *writes about science, technology, and culture. He is a contributing writer for* The New York Times Magazine *and also regularly writes for* Wired, Discover, *and* Wired News. *His blog is located at http://www.collisiondetection.net.* "May the Force Be with You, and You, and You . . ." *was published at http://www.slate.com in April 2005.*

MAY THE FORCE BE WITH YOU, AND YOU, AND YOU . . .

Clive Thompson

Good news, *Star Wars* buffs. There's a new movie out this spring—and it *isn't* by George Lucas. The 40-minute, fan-made *Star Wars Revelations* cost a mere $20,000. It's also just as good as—and often quite better than—the cringe-inducing *Star Wars* movies of recent years. Indeed, it's so artistically successful that it suggests a radical idea: Maybe Lucas should step aside and let the fans take over.

Our most cherished sci-fi franchises are in a creative trough. Lucas' movies have spiraled into unwatchability; Paramount has so exhausted its ideas for *Star Trek* that it's folding up its tent and going home. The fans, in contrast, still give a damn: The director of *Revelations,* Shane Felux, is clearly more knowledgeable about the strengths and weaknesses of the material than Lucas himself. Felux's movie retains the funky vibe of the original *Star Wars,* down to the kitschy, '70s-style wipes, the obligatory scene in an alien bar, and Darth Vader's throat-choking technique. Better yet, it jettisons Lucas' most loathed innovations—neither Jar Jar Binks nor any Ewoks make an appearance. Fans may be pointy-headed and obsessed with useless trivia, but they have excellent bullshit detectors.

The fans can also give Industrial Light and Magic a run for its money. When it comes to special effects, *Revelations* is nothing short of astonishing. Early on, there's a jaw-dropping chase scene in which the heroes' ship darts like a nimble fish through a cluttered space-yard, a fleet of TIE fighters in hot pursuit. Later, a stunning attack on an Empire Destroyer left me laughing in sheer surprise.

How could Felux produce scenes this good? Because desktop animation and editing programs like Bryce and Adobe Premiere Pro allow anyone to blow up a CGI spacecraft on a garage-band budget. What's more, Felux relied on the techniques of open-source design. Hundreds of people worldwide offered small bits of work, purely for the love of the project—and a chance to brag about their contribution. Felux wrangled free labor from over 30 CGI artists, including one supremely talented 16-year-old kid who lists his occupation as "being awesome." For live-action shots, Felux convinced unpaid actors and crew members to drive out to weekend shoots. When he needed uniforms for Storm Troopers and X-wing pilots, he borrowed them from fans who made their own.

Fan-made art is also easier to distribute than ever before. The proliferation of broadband in the past few years means that a movie doesn't have to open on 3,000 screens to get seen by millions of eyeballs. In only one week online, an estimated 1,000,000 people have already downloaded *Star Wars Revelations*. You can get the movie for free from various online sites or by using BitTorrent—don't worry, it's a legal download. BitTorrent in par-ticular is so efficient in its use of bandwidth that I downloaded the entire 252-megabyte movie in around 12 minutes. (That's probably because 99 percent of the geeks who are into fan-created sci-fi are using BitTorrent.)

George Lucas has always encouraged *Star Wars*-inspired fan movies, so long as the wannabe auteurs didn't try to make a profit. (That's the case with Felux—he isn't selling his movie or any associated merchandise.) Lucas should do more, though. Once he stops polluting the world with prequels, he should slap a liberal "Creative Commons" copyright license on the *Star Wars* franchise. That would explicitly allow any fan to remix an existing movie, or create a new one in homage, so long as there's no profit involved. Everyone wins: Movies like *Revelations* keep the fan base alive, and Lucas can continue selling figurines until the sun explodes.

This open-source method won't work for every defunct cultural property. Fan art works best when it feeds off of dweeby universes that are jam-packed with characters. It would be easy to create amateur, offshoot films based on *Lord of the Rings* or *The Twilight Zone,* and possibly even a show with a revolving-door cast like *Law & Order.* Shows or movies that rely on a single, charismatic actor—like Sarah Michelle Gellar in *Buffy the Vampire Slayer*—aren't as easy to replicate. But *Buffy* fans could simply create spinoffs, the way *Buffy*'s creator churned out a series of comic books starring other teen slayers.

All fan-created movies still face two big stumbling blocks: scriptwriting and acting. Even something as polished as *Revelations* is occasionally marred by a boilerplate plot and wooden acting. (Though that might make the homage all the more authentic given the hollowness of Hayden Christensen and Natalie Portman in *Attack of the Clones*.) The amateurs, it seems, cannot escape the artistic trap that ensnares big-budget sci-fi auteurs. When you fall in love with CGI effects, sometimes you forget how to deal with those quaint, un-animated properties we call "actors."

1. How many films and TV shows are mentioned in the essay?

2. Why does the author mention more than just *Star Wars*?

3. What is Thompson's main argument? How does he support it? Do you think the support he provides is effective?

CONNECTING TO YOUR CULTURE

1. How does the topic of this essay connect to you and your viewing habits? To your age demographic?

2. Even if you have never made or watched a fan movie, do you have any ways to connect or comment on films?

3. What other technological ways are available for you to join the fan culture of a particular film?

CONSIDERING IDEAS

1. Why are film directors and viewers so drawn to films about Mafia, gangster, or gangsta characters and plots?

2. What are some of the more famous films in this genre?

3. What is it about the life of these people that attracts us?

Jay Cocks *is a former film critic for publications such as* Rolling Stone, Time, *and* Newsweek. *After turning to film writing, he received Best Writing Oscar nominations for* The Age of Innocence *(1993) and* Gangs of New York *(2002). "What Is* The Godfather *Saying?" was published in* Time *on April 3, 1972.*

WHAT IS *THE GODFATHER* SAYING?

Jay Cocks

After the first hurrahs for *The Godfather*, critical reaction to the movie has snagged on a few key questions. Does it revel in Hollywood gangster melodrama? Does it sentimentalize the Mafia? Does it present the Mob as a metaphor for all business or politics? One of *Time*'s cinema critics gives his assessment:

"I believe in America."

Those opening words, heard over a black screen, are a testament and a plea—not so much a pledge of allegiance to an adopted country as an obeisance to a shadow government of profound power. An Italian immigrant funeral director has a daughter who has been dishonored. Because of a lack of evidence, the courts offer him no justice. In the tradition of his native land, he turns to a man who understands such matters and who will be able to give him satisfaction. In return he owes the man a service. And he must respectfully call him "Godfather."

No American film before *The Godfather* has ever caught so truly the texture of an ethnic subculture. Director Francis Ford Coppola knows his subject so well that he imparts an almost visceral understanding that does not permit easy judgments. Coppola gets it all down, and gets it right: the Don dancing proudly with his daughter on her wedding day; the informal ritual of family dinner, and the whole preoccupation with food. Even the dialogue has the unmistakable cadence of the street, as when a Corleone lieutenant describes

an untraceable revolver as "cold as they come." The characters become neither stock villains nor national stereotypes, because Coppola has set them in a world of careful complexity.

But the fact that Coppola scrupulously humanizes his characters does not mean that he sentimentalizes the Mafia. The men are racists and hypocrites. They form a society closed to women, who are indulged, protected, finally depersonalized. One may admire the Godfather for his refusal to traffic in dope, but his reasons are practical, not moral: he stands to lose all his political contacts, because they—not he—consider narcotics "a dirty business."

In this world, "business" becomes the ultimate morality, the final and irrefutable excuse for the most insidious disloyalty and the most brutal slaughter. During the wedding that opens the film, the Don metes out favors and punishments; during the christening that ends it, his son and successor Michael pledges faith in God and renounces the devil while gunmen, acting on his instructions, murder rivals all over the city. "Today," says Michael, "I took care of all family business."

Coppola extends this moral masquerade even further, using the Mafia as a metaphor not only for corruption in business, but for corruption in all centers of power, emphatically including government. "My father is no different from any other powerful man," Michael tells his WASPish girl

"What Is *The Godfather* Saying?" by Jay Cocks from TIME, 3 April 1972.

friend Kay. She says, "You're being naive. Senators and Congressmen don't have people killed." Replies Michael: "Who's being naive now, Kay?" When the Don expresses regret that Michael could not have been "a Senator, a Governor," the son promises him, "We'll get there, Pop." As the film would have it, he will.

Although it is nominally about crime, *The Godfather* has no more in common with the razzle-dazzle Warner Bros., gangster yarns of the '30s than *The Wild Bunch* had with *Shane*. *The Godfather*'s primary concern is not bullets and murders but dynasties and power. In the cool savagery of its ironies, expressed within a traditional framework, it is much closer to, say, Bertolucci's *The Conformist*. In its blending of new depth with an old genre, it becomes that rarity, a mass entertainment that is also great movie art.

DECODING THE TEXT

The author argues that *The Godfather* is both great movie art and mass entertainment at the same time.

1. What are some of the specific examples he uses to support this argument?

2. Do you agree with him?

3. According to Cocks, how is the film different from the gangster genre?

CONNECTING TO YOUR CULTURE

The Godfather represents an American ethnic subculture that does not represent the entire ethnic group of Italian Americans.

1. What are some films that represent your ethnic background but do not represent you because of their focus on the characteristics of a subculture that is not part of your life?

2. How do you feel about that representation?

3. Some films about ethnic subcultures intend to promote understanding and acceptance of those cultures. Have you become aware of an ethnic subculture because of a film?

1. Are sequels usually as good as the original films?

2. What is your favorite sequel? What makes it your favorite?

3. What is the worst sequel you have ever seen? What makes it the worst?

Todd Berliner *is associate professor of film studies at the University of North Carolina, Wilmington. His interests include film history, aesthetics, and American cinema. He has been published in* Style, Cinema Journal, *and* Film Quarterly. *"The Pleasures of Disappointment" was published in the* Journal of Film and Video *in 2001.*

THE PLEASURES OF DISAPPOINTMENT

Sequels and *The Godfather, Part II*

Todd Berliner

Film critics normally view sequels as exploitative products that cash in on the popularity of earlier blockbusters, invariably inferior to the original films. However, most critics today consider the 1974 sequel to *The Godfather* not only better than the first movie but one of the best movies of the decade. This fact seems even more surprising when one considers that the first *Godfather* is one of the most beloved films of all time and was, for a brief period, the greatest blockbuster in film history. When *The Godfather* debuted in 1972, it shattered all the major box office records. It made $8 million in its opening week in national release. It brought in a million dollars a day for twenty-six days and $2 million a week for 23 consecutive weeks. In less than six months, it surpassed *Gone with the Wind* to become the biggest box-office grosser in history, earning $86,275,000 in rentals by the end of its first year in release. The critics loved it too, on the whole, except that many thought it romanticized and glamorized the Mafia.

The astounding success of *The Godfather* surprised everyone involved with the picture, especially the executives at Paramount, who immediately began badgering director Francis Ford Coppola for a sequel. If the sequel had only a fraction of the financial success of the original movie, it would mean enormous profits. *The Godfather,* they reasoned, was a formula for success, and plagued by financial troubles, Hollywood studios in the early seventies coveted successful formulas.

In the late sixties and early seventies, theater attendance dropped to record lows. In 1946, 90 million Americans attended the movies each week. That figure dropped

The Pleasures of Disappointment: Sequels and The Godfather, Part II, pp. 107–123 by Todd Berliner from JOURNAL OF FILM AND VIDEO, Summer/Fall 2001. Reprinted by permission of Todd Berliner.

to 47 million per week in 1956, and by 1967 attendance fell to a mere 17.8 million, finally hitting a historic low of 15.8 million in 1971, the year before *The Godfather*'s release (Steinberg, 371). Commentators blamed television, the high cost of movie tickets, and the poor quality of the films. Whatever the cause, Hollywood studios in the sixties recorded their worst financial losses in history. Scrambling for audiences, studio execu-tives hardly understood what people wanted from the movies. As a result, studios in the seventies banked on the successes of earlier hits by producing strings of horror movies and disaster movies and whatever else they hoped would please the public. *The Godfather* spawned a litter of Mafia movies (such as *The Don is Dead* [1973], *Lucky Luciano* [1974], *The Black Godfather* [1974], and *Lepke* [1975]) just as *Bonnie and Clyde* (1967) and *Easy Rider* (1969) had engendered movies about sympathetic outlaws and what had come to be called youth culture (*Little Fauss and Big Halsey* [1970], *Getting Straight* [1974], *Dirty Mary Crazy Larry* [1974], *The Sugarland Express* [1974]). Sequels to popular movies had an almost guaranteed audience, typically earning two-thirds of the profits of the original films (Chown, 103). Not surprisingly, Hollywood loved them, even though the critics did not, and the 1970s saw the greatest incidence of film sequels in Hollywood's history to that time. *They Call Me Mr. Tibbs* (1970 sequel to *In the Heat of the Night*), *Ben* (1972 sequel to *Willard*), *Shaft's Big Score* (1972) and *Shaft in Africa* (1973, both sequels to *Shaft*), *The Trial of Billy Jack* (1974 sequel to *Billy Jack*), *Herbie Rides Again* (1974) and *Herbie Goes to Monte Carlo* (1977, both sequels to *The Love Bug*), *Airport '75, '77*, and *'79, Sounder: Part 2* (1976), *Exorcist II: The Heretic* (1977), *Damien—Omen 2* (1978), and *Beyond the*

Poseidon Adventure (1979) exemplify a small number of sequels that made it to theaters in the seventies, critical assassination notwithstanding. Hollywood was taking few chances.

Most of these sequels have not seen an audience since their first runs, whereas *The Godfather, Part II* has had several re-releases and regularly plays on network and cable TV, and, as we shall see, many film critics regard it as the best movie of the period. Examining first the aesthetics of sequelization and, in particular, the disappointment with which audiences normally greet sequels, this article sets out to explain why *The Godfather, Part II* is so much more admired and beloved than the numerous other film sequels released around the same time, probably more admired and beloved than any other sequel in film history. As with most sequels, *Godfather II* disappoints its audience, but it does so in a peculiarly extravagant way. The film's conspicuous refusal to satisfy paradoxically serves as a source of audience pleasure. Taking an inventive approach to sequelization, the film incorporates into its plot the very nostalgia, dissatisfaction, and sense of loss that sequels traditionally generate in their viewers, thereby giving thematic resonance to audiences' inevitable disappointment with movie sequels.

In order to understand what makes *Godfather II* an unusually impressive sequel, we must first understand the exigencies with which film sequels contend and the typical ways in which filmmakers approach the burdens of sequel making.

Sequels, Spectacle, and Loss
Scholarship has hardly addressed the phenomenon of film sequelization, and

the few critical treatments that exist focus almost exclusively on the horror film series that began inundating theaters in the late seventies and haven't tapered off since. One full-length book has been devoted to literary and film sequels, *Part Two: Reflections on the Sequel*, a chronologically organized collection of essays, mostly by period specialists, which begins by examining epic sequels of the Greek Bronze Age and ends by looking at Hollywood sequels of the 1980s and '90s. It will come as no surprise that the theme common to the essays is that sequels consistently let their audiences down. The essayists normally treat audience disappointment as an unavoidable consequence of publishers' and movie studios' attempts to profit quickly on the successes of earlier hits by churning out invariably inferior products (although several of the essays look at some notable exceptions to this rule). Paul Budra and Betty Schellenberg, in the introduction to *Part Two: Reflections on the Sequel*, also note "the inevitably changed [historical] conditions which make it impossible to achieve a precise repetition of the experience" of the original work (5). In their treatments of the sequel, however, the essayists deal only in passing with perhaps the most pertinent historical fact when considering audiences' common dissatisfaction with sequels: the prior experience of the original popular work. Even if the sequel were every bit as good as the original, and experienced by an otherwise identical culture in equivalent historical circumstances, it would nonetheless disappoint audiences because nothing can equal one's first experience of something great.

In a book on eighteenth-century English literature that also touches on literary sequels, Terry Castle suggests that "sequels inevitably seem to fail us in some obscure yet fundamental way" (133). Her remarks, directed at Samuel Richardson's sequel to his novel *Pamela*, pertain just as well to film sequels. As with Budra and Schellenberg, Castle focuses principally on the socioeconomic reasons for the inevitable disappointment of sequels (especially on the profit motives of publishers and authors); however, she also considers aesthetic causes when she suggests that the readers of literary sequels "are motivated by a deep unconscious nostalgia for a past reading pleasure" (134):

A sequel can never fully satisfy its readers' desire for repetition, however; its tragedy is that it cannot literally reconstitute its charismatic original. Readers know this; yet they are disappointed. Unconsciously they persist in demanding the impossible: that the sequel be different, but also exactly the same. Their secret mad hope is to find in the sequel a paradoxical kind of textual doubling—a repetition that does not look like one, the old story in a new and unexpected guise. They wish to read the "unforgettable" text once more, yet as if they had forgotten it. (134)

The almost inescapable failure of sequels results from the fact that, at the same time a sequel calls to mind the charismatic original, it also recalls its absence, fostering a futile, nostalgic desire to reexperience the original aesthetic moment as though it had never happened. Hence, the experience of a sequel differs fundamentally from that of rewatching a beloved movie. Although in both cases we enjoy something that reminds us of our initial pleasure, second viewings of a movie *restore* the original film to us—even enabling us to relish new insights and details missed on the first viewing. Sequels, by contrast, can only *remind* us of the original film, and continually and conspicuously fail to reinvoke that initial pleasure.

To compensate for the sequel's inherent sense of absense and loss, the maker of a movie sequel tends to supply excessive amounts of whatever audiences seemed to have liked most about the first movie. *Magnum Force* has three times the violence of *Dirty Harry*. Rocky wins in *Rocky II*. *Airport* involved the hijacking of a standard jetliner; ten years, three sequels, and dozens of stars later, Universal released *Airport '79: The Concord*. The shark in *Jaws II* is even bigger than the first; *Jaws III* is in 3-D. The escalation of violence and thrills in sequels seems to occur at a rate higher than that in movies generally, an understandably excessive evolution considering that a sequel must compete not only with other films in its genre but also with the original film it imitates. Though it can be exciting to enjoy the souped-up version of the initial experience, once the closing credits start to roll, one might feel somewhat exploited, as though all the oohhing and aahhing were evoked too cheaply.

Lianne McLarty suggests that, from one perspective, the sequel "marks the end of originality and results in the triumph of surface over depth, spectacle over meaning and history" (201). A movie sequel not only banks on the spectacular profitability of its predecessor; it often takes spectacle for its subject matter, hence the tendency of sequels to overdo the most spectacular elements of the original movie, such as violence, special effects, and stars. In fact, a movie sequel is almost invariably a version of the original movie *as* spectacle, a lavish display of the mere surface of the prior work. Even plots and characters turn into spectacles in a sequel. When C-3PO and R2-D2 make

narratively gratuitous reappearances in George Lucas's prequels to the initial *Star Wars* trilogy, the prequels attempt not only to reinspire the audience's affection for the characters but to call up the *spectacle* of C-3PO and R2-D2 by superficially reiterating their connection to the prior films we loved. Or consider Coppola's extraordinary efforts to include in *The Godfather, Part III* as many of the actors from the first two movies as he could work in. It is understandable why audiences would want to see Al Pacino again, but why should we care about seeing Al Martino as Johnny Fontane or Richard Bright as Al Neri? The sequel makes these characters spectacles for us, banking on their association with the original *Godfather* movies and on our excitement for their bare presence here. The familiar faces also help maintain continuity with the first film; their reappearance eases us into the new movie, reinforces the existence of a world we remember, and strengthens our sense that we have reentered a milieu that continues to function according to consistent and recognizable patterns.

* * *

Several events in *Part II* seem to repeat events from the original picture. Both movies introduce their characters to us at religious celebrations, for example. *The Godfather* begins at Connie's wedding reception at the Corleone home in New York as the don sits in his study granting favors to visitors. Although the first scene in *Part II* shows us a flashback of young Vito as he escapes the Sicilian Mafia and emigrates to America, ten minutes later the movie switches to its first modern-day scene: the first communion of Michael's son, Anthony. During the celebration at Michael's compound in Lake Tahoe, the don conducts business, as did his father before him, sitting in his study, receiving visitors. Jeffrey Chown notes that in both films "bright outdoor action [is] contrasted through cuts with the dark inner sanctums in which the respective dons conduct business" (106). However, Anthony's celebration has none of the familial feeling or ethnic flavor of Connie's wedding. Only respectful Italians visited Vito in his study. Michael's visitors include the aggressively anti-Italian Senator Geary, who tries to bully the don. Later, a garishly dressed Connie and her fiancé, Merle (played by the WASPish Troy Donahue) visit Michael, wanting only money from him, not his blessing. At the party, we are also reintroduced to Fredo, now married to the blonde and drunken Deanna. Frankie Pentangeli remarks that "out of 30 professional musicians, there isn't one Italian in the group" and none can play a tarantella. The festivity looks eerily lifeless and businesslike, designed to look respectable. No Johnny Fontanes appear. No family members sing "Che Le Luna." Instead, Senator Geary introduces the Sierra Boys Choir, "as a special added attraction," who perform "Mr. Wonderful" on behalf of Michael Corleone (the senator mispronounces the name) for having made a "magnificent endowment" to the University. Professional dancers perform a tango. Whereas in the first movie the Corleones seemed defiantly against the establishment, in the second they have entered it.

Even the murders in *Part II* let us down. One could hardly forget the vivid image from *The Godfather* of Captain McCluskey shot in the throat in Louis' restaurant, or of Luca Brasi garroted, a knife through his hand, but how many viewers remember that in *Part II* Michael's bodyguard strangles Johnny Ola with a coat hanger (if they remembered that Ola is killed at all) or that the same bodyguard is shot by Cuban soldiers? These murders sound graphic, but the movie treats them so nonchalantly that the result is forgettable. The murder of Hyman Roth makes a stronger impression, but is not very thrilling. The assassination happens at the airport after Israel, Argentina, and Panama refuse the old man asylum. When Rocco shoots him, Roth looks ailing and frail, not in the least threatening to anyone; it's hard to get excited about his murder. The most memorable murders in the movie occur when Vito shoots Don Fanucci through the cheek and mouth, and when he disembowels Don Ciccio in Sicily, but they both occur in flashback. Scholars have remarked that both *The Godfather* and *The Godfather, Part II* present murder ritualistically, contrasting it with religious ceremony, and that toward the end of each film Michael stages a series of murders depicted in montage; however, though the murders in *Part II* echo those in *The Godfather,* they are also a disappointing reminder of the more exciting violence we saw before.

The editing of the two films' climactic murder montages also indicates the tendency of the sequel to, on the one hand, call to mind corresponding elements of the first movie, and on the other, leave out the original film's most thrilling aspects. An elementary comparison of the editing shows us that, though both montages last roughly four minutes, the montage sequence in *Part II* has 17 cuts and combines three scenes (four deaths total), whereas the comparable sequence in *The Godfather* has 68 cuts and combines six scenes (depicting eight deaths and the baptism of Connie's son). The montage in the first film, then, averages about 17 cuts per minute—as compared to about four cuts per minute in the sequel—giving it a tremendous sense of momentum, especially toward the end as the cuts speed up.

The Godfather's murder montage uses graphic matches and other repeated imagery in order to link the various shots to one another, and most of the echoed images are characterized by physical movement: a swift panning shot of the priest's hand, moving from holy water to the baby's forehead, matches a similar shot of a barber's hand, as he moves from the shaving cream dispenser to the face of a Corleone assassin, Willy Cicci; Rocco and Neri are both seen preparing guns; the image of Neri using a cloth to wipe sweat off his face echoes that of Clemenza making the same gesture as he climbs a staircase: Clemenza, Cicci, and Don Barzini all quickly move up or down stairs; five doors swing open dramatically during the 45 seconds in which the shootings occur (an elevator door opens to reveal a mob boss as Clemenza shoots him; another gangster is shot in a revolving door; assassins burst through a hotel door firing machine guns at a mob leader in bed with a woman; Moe Green's assassin is also seen barging through a door, just before he shoots Green through the eye; the door of a speeding car opens in order to allow Neri's quick escape after he shoots Barzini and two others on the church steps). The images of murder are intercut with those of the baptism and edited to the tempo of dramatic organ music, the baptismal liturgy, and the screams of the infant.

By contrast, what unites most of the images and sounds in the comparable sequences in *Part II* is their sluggishness: Roth's feeble walk and the deadpan speech he gives to the press; the subtle rise and fall of the lake on which Fredo fishes, his body perfectly still; a bloodied Pentangeli motionless in a bathtub. The sequence, moreover, has little of the dramatic tension of the montage in the first movie. Except for Moe Green, each victim in *The Godfather* recognizes his imminent death and vainly fights against it, whereas the victims in the sequel never resist: Roth merely slumps into the arms of the police, and Neri shoots Fredo from behind. Pentangeli isn't murdered at all—his death is a suicide, a somewhat disappointing revelation because the sequence leads us to expect assassins will barge in on him. In fact, we don't even see the deaths of Fredo and Pentangeli, both of which occur off screen. The most visually exciting killing is that of Rocco, Roth's assassin, shot twice by police as he tries to escape. But Rocco is part of the Corleone Family, his death a narrative side-bar; it's hard to feel thrilled by it. Throughout the sequel's murder montage, slow and somber theme music plays, instilling none of the anxious excitement of the organ's dramatic crescendos in *The Godfather*.

The Pleasures of Disappointment

Far from trying to outdo *The Godfather,* the sequel deliberately falls short of the original. It courts our disapproval. However, at the very moment we condemn the movie for being inferior to its predecessor, we can enjoy witnessing the parallels between the two films and the pattern of deterioration. That pleasure—the pleasure of noticing something—does not, by itself, provide a very rich experience. *The Godfather, Part II,* however, enriches and complicates our pleasure by anticipating our judgments and thematizing them. Our own feelings of disappointment and deprivation as we watch the movie reflect those very elements within the story itself. To put this point another way, our experience of *The Godfather, Part II* mirrors prominent elements of the movie's subject matter: loss, nostalgia, and deterioration.

Works Cited

Aigner, Hal, and Michael Goodwin. "The Bearded Immigrant from Tinsel Town." *City* June 1974: 12–25.

Biskind, Peter. *The Godfather Companion*. New York: HarperCollins, 1990.

Bookbinder, Robert. *The Films of the Seventies*. Secaucus, NJ: Citadel Press, 1982.

Budra, Paul. "Recurrent Monsters: Why Freddy, Michael, and Jason Keep Coming Back." *Part Two: Reflections on the Sequel*. Paul Budra and Betty A. Schellenberg, Eds. Toronto, Canada: University of Toronto Press, 1998.

Budra, Paul, and Betty A. Schellenberg, Eds. *Part Two: Reflections on the Sequel*. Toronto, Canada: University of Toronto Press, 1998.

Canby, Vincent. " 'Godfather, Part II' is Hard to Define." Rev. of *The Godfather, Part II, New York Times* 13 December 1974: 58.

———. " 'The Godfather, Part II': One Godfather Too Many." Rev. of *The Godfather, Part II, New York Times* 22 December 1974: 1119.

Castle, Terry. *Masquerade and Civilization: The Carnivalesque in Eighteenth-Century English Literature and Fiction*. Stanford, CA: Stanford University Press, 1986.

Chown, Jeffrey. *Hollywood Auteur: Francis Coppola*. New York: Praeger, 1988.

Clover, Carol. *Men, Women and Chainsaws: Gender in the Modern Horror Film*. Princeton, NJ: Princeton University Press, 1992.

Coleman, John. "Family Snaps." Rev. of *The Godfather, Part II, New Statesman* 16 May 1975: 669.

Crist, Judith. "All in the Family." Rev. of *The Godfather, Part II, New York Magazine* 23 December 1974: 70–71.

Denby, David. "The Grandfather." Rev. of *The Godfather, Part III, New York Magazine* 7 January 1991: 57ff.

Dika, Vera. *Games of Terror: Halloween, Friday the 13th, and the Films of the Stalker Cycle*. London and Toronto, Canada: Associated University Press, 1990.

Felber, Lynette. "Trollope's Phineas Diptych as Sequel and Sequence Novel." *Part Two: Reflections on the Sequel*. Paul Budra and Betty A. Schellenberg, Eds. Toronto, Canada: University of Toronto Press, 1998.

Godfather, The, Part II. Paramount Pictures, dir. Francis Ford Coppola. Perfs. Al Pacino, Robert De Niro, 1974.

Goodwin, Michael, and Naomi Wise. *On the Edge: The Life and Times of Francis Coppola*. New York: William Morrow and Company, 1989.

Haskell, Molly. "The Godfather Part II: The Corleone Saga Sags." Rev. of *The Godfather, Part II, The Village Voice* 23 December 1974: 88–89.

Hess, John. "Godfather II: A Deal Coppola Couldn't Refuse." *Movies and Methods, Volume 1*. Bill Nichols, Ed. Berkeley, CA: University of California Press, 1976: 81–90.

Kael, Pauline. "Fathers and Sons." Rev. of *The Godfather, Part II, The New Yorker* 23 December 1974: 63–66.

Lewis, Jon. *Whom God Wishes to Destroy—Francis Coppola and the New Hollywood*. Durham, NC, and London: Duke University Press, 1995.

Mast, Gerald. *A Short History of the Movies* (4th ed.). New York: Macmillan Publishing Company, 1986.

McLarty, Lianne. " 'I'll Be Back': Hollywood, Sequelization, and History." *Part Two: Reflections on the Sequel*. Paul Budra and Betty A. Schellenberg, Eds. Toronto, Canada: University of Toronto Press, 1998.

Monaco, James. *American Film Now*. New York: New American Library, 1984.

Murf. "The Godfather, Part II." [Rev. of *The Godfather, Part II*.] *Variety* 11 December 1974: 16.

Murray, William. "Playboy Interview: Francis Ford Coppola." *Playboy* 22 July, 1975: 53ff.

Nowlan, Robert A., and Gwendolyn Wright Nowlan. *Cinema Sequels and Remakes 1903–1987*. Jefferson, NC: McFarland Co., 1989.

Rich, Frank. "Beyond the Corleones." Rev. of *The Godfather, Part II. New Times* 27 December 1974: 56–58.

Schickel, Richard. "The Final Act of a Family Epic." Rev. of *The Godfather, Part II, Time* 16 December 1974: 70–73.

Simon, John. "The Godfather, Part III." Rev. of *The Godfather, Part III, National Review* 28 January 1991: 65.

Steinberg, Cobbett. *Reel Facts: The Movie Book of Records*. New York: Vintage Books, 1978.

Thomas, Barbara. " 'Gambler' Tops Thomas' 10 Best." *Atlanta Journal* 5 February 1975: E10.

Walsh, Moira. "The Godfather, Part II." Rev. of *The Godfather, Part II, America* 15 February 1975: 116.

Zimmerman, Paul D. "Godfathers and Sons." Rev. of *The Godfather, Part II, Newsweek* 23 December 1974: 78–79.

DECODING THE TEXT

1. What are some of the reasons Berliner gives for the early disappointment but later success of *The Godfather, Part II*?

2. How does he support his arguments?

3. Berliner includes several statistics about sequels. Do these contribute to the effectiveness of the essay?

CONNECTING TO YOUR CULTURE

1. Have you ever met someone who left a very bad impression on you for some reason but then turned out to be a better (funnier, friendlier, smarter) person than you originally thought?

2. What goes into the first impressions we have of people? Of films? Of books?

3. What things sometimes make us change our minds?

Reading Selection: the '80s

"John Hughes Goes Deep: The Unexpected Heaviosity of *Ferris Bueller's Day Off*" by Steve Almond, from THE VIRGINIA QUARTERLY REVIEW ONLINE, Summer 2006, pp. 277–283. Reprinted by permission of the author.

CONSIDERING IDEAS

John Hughes directed many teen movies from the '80s, such as *Pretty in Pink* and *The Breakfast Club*, which continue to be popular.

1. What teen movies have been made in the last few years?

2. Why do both the classic teen movie and more current versions continue to be popular?

3. How have teen movies changed over the years, or have they changed?

Steve Almond *is a prolific fiction writer and journalist. He is the author of three books, including* The New York Times *best-seller* Candyfreak: A Journey Through the Chocolate Underbelly of America *(Algonquin, 2004). His website is at http://www.stevenalmond.com. "John Hughes Goes Deep" was first published in* The Virginia Quarterly Review Online *(http://www.vqronline.org) in 2006.*

JOHN HUGHES GOES DEEP

The Unexpected Heaviosity of *Ferris Bueller's Day Off*

Steve Almond

I missed *Ferris Bueller's Day Off* on the first pass, so I never quite understood what all the hubbub was about. And, as generally happens when I miss out on all the hubbub, I took it personally and thus bore a senseless grudge against the film, which I would routinely malign whenever people tried to explain how terrific it was. More often than not, I am really just a very big asshole.

Notwithstanding this, last winter I got sick, so sick I was reduced to raiding my landlord's DVD collection. He had about forty movies, most of which were thrillers of the sort that feature a European secret agent babe who takes her shirt off and a picturesque decapitation. He also had *Ferris Bueller.*

I watched the film in a state of growing astonishment. It was, without a doubt, the most sophisticated teen movie I had ever seen. I wasn't entirely sure it qualified as a teen movie at all. It featured a number of techniques that I recognized from other, later films: direct addresses to the camera, on-screen graphics, the prominent use of background songs to create de facto music videos, the sudden exhilarating blur of fantasy and reality.

More than this, though, Hughes performed an astounding ontological feat. He lured viewers into embracing his film as an escapist farce, then hit them with a pitch-perfect exploration of teen angst. He snuck genuine art past the multiplex censors.

I needn't labor the basic plot—kid fakes being sick, outwits dopey grownups, gallivants around Chicago with pals. Hughes is, like any decent Aristotelian, more concerned with character.

Ferris himself (Matthew Broderick, unbearably young) comes across as a charming manipulator utterly devoted to his own enjoyments. We initially encounter him playing sick on his bed. It is a pathetically stagy performance and he seems mildly disappointed when his doting parents fall for it. We get a few scenes of him mugging for the camera, and the introduction of his inept nemesis, the dean of students, Ed Rooney.

The scene shifts to a sleek, modern home, propped up on stilts and perched at the edge of a bluff. We cut to a dark, sarcophagus-like bedroom, littered with medicine bottles and crumpled Kleenex. A figure lies obscured under a blanket, like a mummy, while an electronic dirge plays in the background.

This is our introduction to Cameron Frye (Alan Ruck), Ferris's best friend. The phone by the bed rings and a hand appears and slowly clicks on the speakerphone. It is Ferris demanding that Cameron come over and spend the day with him. Meaning, essentially, chauffeur him around.

Cameron declines in a froggy voice. He is sick. Ferris repeats his demand and hangs up.

"I'm dying," Cameron whispers. The phone rings again and Ferris mutters, "You're not dying. You just can't think of anything good to do."

We now see Cameron from above. His expression is one of resignation, giving unto despair. And then, fabulously, he begins to sing.

"When Cameron was in Egypt's land . . ."

A rich, somber chorus of voices joins him.

"Let my Cameron go!"

The invocation of the old spiritual is at once strange and revelatory. It has no business, really, in what has been—to this point—smarter-than-average teenybopper fare. But then, neither does Cameron Frye.

Hughes could have simply cast him as a straight man for Ferris. But he does something far more compelling: he renders the pair as a psychological dyad. Ferris is fearless, larger-than-life. He has internalized the unconditional love of his parents and skips through his days in a self-assured reverie. He is what every teenage guy dreams of being: a raging, narcissistic id who gets away with it. Cameron is an actual teenager: alienated from his parents, painfully insecure, angry, depressed.

It is the tension between these two that drives the action. Ferris dances around the house (accompanied by the theme from *I Dream of Jeannie*). Dad calls from work and Ferris plays him like a Stradivarius. Then he turns to the camera and, with a look of indignation, says: "I'm so disappointed in Cameron. Twenty bucks says he's sitting in his car debating about whether he should go out or not."

Cut to Cameron, at the wheel of a white junker, his long, rubbery face cast in a morbid posture. He sniffs. He stares ahead. He squinches up his eyes and growls, "He'll keep *calling* and *calling* and *calling*. . . ." He puts the key in the ignition, starts the car. He shakes his head and yanks the key out of the ignition. Then, with no warning, he starts to pound the passenger seat. These are vicious blows. "Goddamn it," he screams. The camera backs off to a midrange shot. We hear the car start again and the engine revs and we hear a primal scream at the exact same pitch. Then the car goes dead. "Forget it," Cameron says. "That's it." He flings himself out of the car and stomps back to his empty house. We cut to a close-up of the empty driver's seat. Birds tweet. Suddenly, we hear the crunch of his penny loafers on gravel and a blurry image of Cameron's hockey jersey through the rear window. He is stomping back toward the car. We think: *Ah, he's given in.* Just then he stops and begins jumping up and down and throwing punches at some invisible adversary.

The sequence lasts barely a minute. It is an astonishing piece of physical humor, an emotional ballet worthy of Chaplin. Hell, it's one of the best pieces of acting I've ever seen, period. Because it's not just funny, it's heartbreaking. We are watching a kid utterly crippled by his own conflicted impulses, torn between outrage and obedience.

In a very real sense, he needs someone to take charge. Ferris is more than willing. Within a few minutes, he has kidnapped Cameron, along with the prize Ferrari convertible Cameron's father keeps in the garage. Next, he rescues his dishy girlfriend, Sloane, from school and the trio tear off toward downtown.

Ruck is tall, blue-eyed, big-jawed, movie-star handsome. Broderick looks like a nebbish by comparison. If the film had been made today, and by a lesser director, you can bet your Milk Duds that their roles would be reversed. (Such are the mandates of the beauty gradient.) But Hughes clearly had a feel for his actors. And they so inhabit their roles that you wind up focused on their effect, not their cheekbones.

Hughes has long been hailed as the clown prince of teen angst. Whether it's Molly Ringwald getting felt up by her grandpa (*Sixteen Candles*) or Ally Sheedy teasing her dandruff into a snowfall (*The Breakfast Club*), he knows how to put across the exquisite humiliation of adolescence. Still, most of his films play to formula. Ferris Bueller has its share. We know, for instance, that Ferris will prevail over Rooney in the end, and that he will make it home in time to fool his benighted parents.

But the film, as a whole, is a looser, more improvisatory affair. It has a dreamy, superannuated quality. There are all these odd, unexpected moments. A secretary pulls a pencil from her bouffant hairdo. Then a second. And a third. As a teacher drones on about the Smoot-Hawley Tariff Act, Hughes shows us a series of stark close-ups of students. These are actual teens—zits, bad hair, gaping mouths—and their expressions convey actual teen imprisonment: boredom, bewilderment, homicidal intent.

Even a character like Ed Rooney (played with transcendent unction by Jeffrey Jones) is granted his own impregnable sense of logic. He knows Ferris Bueller is making a mockery of his authority, and the educational mission, and that Ferris's popularity makes him the ideal target for Rooney's jihad on truancy. "I did not achieve this position in life," he sneers, "by having some snot-nosed punk leave my cheese out in the wind."

There is no line in the universe that more succinctly conveys the Rooney gestalt.

Or consider what Hughes does with a visit by our heroes to the Art Institute of Chicago. Backed by a soft, symphonic score, he offers us lengthy shots of the most beautiful paintings in the world: Hoppers, Modiglianis, Pollocks. There is no ulterior plot motive; he is simply celebrating the majesty of the work. We see Cameron, Ferris, and his dishy girlfriend Sloane stand before a trio of Picassos, transfixed.

As the music crescendoes, we see Cameron standing before Georges Seurat's pointillist masterpiece, *A Sunday Afternoon on the Island of La Grande Jatte*. We cut to a shot of Ferris and Sloane, the happy couple, necking in the blue light of a stained-glass window, then back to Cameron, alone, staring at the Seurat. Another one of these magical things happens: the camera begins zooming in on the little girl in white at the center of the canvas. We cut back to Cameron, closer now. Then back to the little girl. We see his growing anguish as he realizes that her mouth is wide open, that, in fact, she is wailing.

Okay, good enough: Cameron recognizes himself in the figure of this little girl whose mother is holding her hand but making no effort to comfort her. Got it.

But then Hughes takes us even deeper. He gives us an extreme close-up of Cameron's eyes, then cuts back to the canvas, to the girl's face, then to her mouth, then to the specks of paint that make up her mouth, until we can no longer resolve those specks into an image; they are just splotches of color on coarse fabric. This is the true nature of Cameron's struggle: his anxieties have obliterated his sense of identity.

We then cut, somewhat abruptly, to a German street parade. Cameron is fretting. He needs to get his dad's Ferrari back to the house. Ferris objects. He wants to have more fun. But he also knows that his friend needs to loosen up, to conquer his fear and experience life.

The next time we see Cameron, he and Sloane are hurrying along the parade route. Ferris has ditched them. We cut to a float. Ferris has commandeered a microphone. "This is one of my personal favorites and I want to dedicate it to a young man who doesn't think he's seen anything good today. Cameron Frye, this one's for you." He begins a campy lip-synch of the old torch song, "Danke Schoen." Then he launches into a raucous version of "Twist and Shout." The crowd goes nuts. Ferris has induced mass hysteria in downtown Chicago. This could never happen in real life. It is a Walter Mitty–esque diversion. Which is precisely the point: Ferris has staged this adolescent fantasy of omnipotence expressly for his best friend.

By definition, the adults in a Hughes film are beyond hope of transformation. But it is his central and rescuing belief that teens are capable of change—even the ones who seem to be stock characters. I am thinking here of Jeanie Bueller (Jennifer Grey) who plays the overlooked younger sister and spends most of the film in a snit of sibling rivalry. She is so eager to bust her brother that she winds up in a police station, next to a spaced-out drug suspect (an excellent Charlie Sheen) who slowly chips away at her defenses to reveal the sweet, needy kid living beneath her bitterness.

The prime example, of course, is the relationship between Ferris and Cameron. It is without a doubt the most convincing *therapeutic narrative* in his oeuvre. After all, as much as we may want to suspend our disbelief, is there anyone out there who *really* believes that the Molly Ringwald character in *The Breakfast Club* is going to give Judd Nelson the time of day once they're back in school?

Ferris himself is, for the most part, a fabulous cartoon—half James Bond, half Holden Caulfield. But he understands the very real crisis Cameron is facing and takes it as his role to push his friend into emotional danger.

But Ferris, of course, leads a charmed life. His existentialism comes cheap. For Cameron (as for the rest of us) the experience of pleasure is an ongoing battle against anxiety. Ferris and Sloane can treat the day as just another glorious idyll. For Cameron, it comes to assume the weight of a reckoning.

Toward dusk, he, Ferris, and Sloane return to his house with the precious Ferrari intact. Ferris has a plan: they can run the accrued miles off the car's odometer by jacking the car's rear tires off the ground and running the car in reverse.

As they sit outside the garage, Cameron comes clean about his anxieties. "It's ridiculous," Cameron announces. "Being afraid, worrying about everything, wishing I was dead, all that shit. I'm tired of it." He looks at his friends. "That was the best day of my life," he says. "I'm going to miss you guys next year."

The standard teen film would probably end on his upbeat note. Hughes is just getting started. Cameron heads into the garage to check on the car. Ferris's plan is not working. For a moment, Cameron appears panic-stricken.

Ferris suggests they crack open the glass and adjust the odometer.

But Cameron shakes his head.

"No," he says. "Forget it. Forget it. I gotta take a stand." His tone takes a sudden detour into self-loathing. "I'm bullshit. I put up with everything. My old man pushes me around. I never say anything." He is shouting now. "Well, he's not the problem. I'm the problem. I gotta take a stand. I gotta take a stand against him." As he leans over the hood of the Ferrari, his voice drops to a menacing register: "I am not going to sit on my ass as the events that affect me unfold to determine the course of my life. I gotta take a stand and defend it, right or wrong."

He kicks the car. "I am so sick of his shit! Who do you love? You love the car, you son of a bitch!" He continues to kick at the car: the rear bumper, the trunk, the taillights. These are not gentle little movie kicks. They are charged with a real violence of intent. Thanks to some clever crosscutting, we can see that Cameron has nearly knocked the car off its jack. He is nearly in tears; his entire body is tossed by the savagery. And thus it becomes clear what he's really been afraid of all along: his own murderous rage.

"Shit," Cameron says, "I dented the shit out of it." He laughs, in a manner throttled by regret. Ferris and Sloane—like the viewer—are watching this meltdown in a state of shock. After all, this is supposed to be just a funny little teen movie. But something has happened on the way to the happy ending: a much darker, more authentic psychological event. A catharsis.

"Good," Cameron says finally, in a voice of forced assurance. "My father will come home and see what I did. I can't hide this. He'll have to deal with me. I don't care. I really don't. I'm just tired of being afraid. Hell with it. I can't wait to see the look on the bastard's face."

Cameron sets his foot on the beleaguered rear fender, which, of course, sends the car tumbling off the jack. The rear wheels hit the ground with a skid and the car crashes through a plate glass window and off the bluff.

There is a long, gruesome moment of silence, as the three kids try to grasp the magnitude of what's just happened.

"Whoa," Cameron says. "Oh shiiiit."

Ferris immediately insists on taking the blame. This doesn't feel particularly momentous, given the state Cameron is in. But it does mark a profound transfor-

mation in the Bueller weltanschauung. He has risen above his happy-go-lucky solipsism—probably for the first time in his life—and offered to sacrifice himself.

Cameron has undergone an even more radical change. He has developed what my students often refer to, admiringly, as sack.

"No," he says. "I'll take it. I'll take it. I want it. If I didn't want it, I wouldn't have let you take out the car this morning . . . No, I want it. I'm gonna take it. When Morris comes home he and I will just have a little chat. It's cool. No, it's gonna be good, thanks anyway."

I hate trying to convey the power of this scene by setting down the dialogue alone, because Ruck is doing so much as an actor the whole time, with his body, his eyes, his voice. It will seem an audacious comparison, but I was reminded of those long, wrenching soliloquies at the end of *Long Day's Journey into Night*.

I have no idea who won the Oscar for Best Supporting Actor in 1986. It is painful—given the photographic evidence of my wardrobe—for me to even think about that grim era. But I can tell you that Alan Ruck deserved that statue. His performance is what elevates the film, allows it to assume the power of a modern parable.

Look: John Hughes made a lot of good movies. I've seen most of them and laughed in all the right spots and hoped for the right guy to the get the right girl and vice versa and for all the *troubled kids* to find *hope*. I've given myself over to the pleasant surrender of melodrama. But Hughes made only one film I would consider true art, only one that reaches toward the ecstatic power of teendom and, at the same time, exposes the true, piercing woe of that age.

People will tell you they love *Ferris Bueller* because of all the clever lines, the gags. That's what people need to think. They don't want to come out of the closet as drama queens. It's not a kind age for drama queens. The world is too full of absent parents and children gone mean. But the real reason they keep returning to the film is because John Hughes loved those kids enough to lay them bare, and he transmitted that love to us.

Bless him.

DECODING THE TEXT

1. How does the author show his appreciation for the film *Ferris Bueller's Day Off* and its director? What is Almond's main argument?

2. What kind of evidence does he use to support his position?

3. Why is Almond writing about this film twenty years after it was made? Could this have been written when the film just came out?

CONNECTING TO YOUR CULTURE

1. Who watches teen films?

2. Why are these types of films often a guilty pleasure, a pleasure that some viewers hide from others?

3. Are there gender differences in how films are made or how they appeal to certain audiences?

Reading Selections: the

1. What do you know about the Cannes Film Festival or other film festivals in the United States and abroad?
2. What kinds of films are usually shown at film festivals?
3. What do you know about the Rodney King arrest and trial?
4. Can you see any connection between Cannes and the Rodney King trial?

Spike Lee *is the critically acclaimed director of several films, including* When the Levees Broke: A Requiem in Four Acts *(TV),* 4 Little Girls, Malcolm X, *and* Do the Right Thing. *In addition, Lee directs music videos, markets his own promotional material, and publishes accounts of his experiences in film.*

Ralph Wiley, *a journalist and book author, wrote for various publications, including* Sports Illustrated, *the* Oakland Tribune, GQ, Premiere, *and* National Geographic. *Wiley also wrote several books before his death in 2004, including* Why Black People Tend to Shout *and* A Boxing Memoir.

"Revelations" is an excerpt from Lee and Wiley's 1992 book By Any Means Necessary: The Trials and Tribulations of the Making of *Malcolm X.*

REVELATIONS

Spike Lee and Ralph Wiley

I have a certain instinct, and it's maybe my one and only God-given ability. I sometimes see things that haven't quite materialized, haven't quite happened yet. But, sooner or later, these things become obvious to everybody, I seem to have an eye for these things, and I can take no credit for it.

Two of my favorite touches in *Malcolm X* are the opening, a full-frame of the American flag, which then burns down to an American red-white-and-blue X; and near the end, when Denzel-as-Malcolm is taking that fateful drive from the New York Hilton hotel to the Audubon Ballroom, on February 21, 1965. The music behind him is of Sam Cooke singing "A Change Is Gonna Come." I love that song, love the way Sam Cooke interpreted it. I've always loved it, and knew one day the way to use it would make itself known to me.

Those were two of my favorite moments in *Malcolm X* because they are so evocative of what it truly means to be an African-American in this country today. There's our reality, and then there's the hope inside that reality. The reality was that it was now May 4, and I was screening *X* for the second time to the suits at Warner Brothers in Hollywood. This time what we saw was a three-hour, eighteen-minute version of *X*. South-central L.A. was burning as I got up in front of everybody and said, "This film is needed now, more than ever." And not only South-central was burning, but some of the rest of the City

of Angels. It was getting warm on the Left Coast, and it wasn't summer yet. This was on a Thursday, the day after the infamous Rodney King verdict came down from Ventura County, California, north of the basin. It was a bad day to be an American, and maybe the perfect day to think of and reflect on the man they'd called "Brother Minister." We all sat there watching *Malcolm X* in the dark as the light flickered the image onto the screen and hopefully indelibly into the viewers' minds.

This is what it was like. Outside, the switch had been thrown on chaos, pandemonium. Gunfire, burning, looting, murder—a breakdown on all sides of the "law," and all because a jury from Simi Valley, California, one of those suburban lily white Steven Spielberg communities if there ever was one (*Jaws, Close Encounters, Poltergeist, E.T., Always,* and *Hook*), decided that L.A.'s Gestapo, the police trained and led by Daryl "Sieg Heil" Gates, had not been beating a man, a human being, when they viciously and cowardly beat Rodney King. The jury's verdict of not guilty meant they actually believed the police were beating an animal. Why, that bear, that linebacker, that piece of shit, that "gorilla in the mist," he was damn lucky the police didn't put him to sleep permanently with a choke hold, right then and there. This is what the jury of good white folks was saying, no matter how it's sugar-coated for you otherwise. That jury said no matter how you brutalize a Black man, you aren't really brutalizing him,

"Revelations" from BY ANY MEANS NECESSARY: THE TRIALS AND TRIBULATIONS OF THE MAKING OF *MALCOLM X* by Spike Lee, pp. 159–167. New York: Hyperion, 1992.

because he's not a man, because he is not human. Some white people would rather save whales or snail darters, spotted owls and the Amazonian rain forest than get off Black people's asses. It's true; as true as the day is long. Some white people implement programs to save these animals, and at the same time they'll stand by and watch programs implemented to destroy the minds, bodies, and souls of Black folk.

When you tell people their lives mean nothing, they very quickly find a way to make you realize you're wrong about that.

A change is gonna come. Oh yes it will. One way or another.

On the way to the airport, the limo went down La Brea, along the outer, western edges of the community known as South-central Los Angeles, a community made up of Latinos and whites as well as the African-Americans who get all the bad ink. I noticed a bank had been completely torched on one corner. It looked as though somebody had made a building frame out of giant burned matches, like in a Daffy Duck cartoon, and that charred frame was all that was left of it except for one thing—the massive safe, sitting in the middle of the ruins and surrounded by concrete. Just down the street, the Baldwin Hills Theater was completely untouched, just absolutely undamaged. This is the only Black-owned theater that I know of in the U.S.A. I'd heard that the next week the owners allowed free admission to all showings of all films to all patrons for a few days at the Baldwin, as one gesture of thanks that their business wasn't torched. I thought about the name of the theater. The Baldwin. My man, James.

I also heard that a lot of businesses were burned down by the owners themselves, trying to collect on their insurance, and that most of the deaths were the result of the National Guard and the police shooting people in those seventy-two hours of hell after that deadly verdict came down, when there was total anarchy on the streets of L.A., when everybody in America had to face what had been created in America, what many Republicans of Reagan and Bush stripes, and Democratic liberals alike, had tried to deny for so long. The American system was one of injustice, not justice. And everywhere you went, if you watched any sort of electronic media, the images were there. You saw the last five seconds of Rodney King being handcuffed, after the serious, sadistic beating was over, and then you saw a white truck driver named Reginald Denny, who was being beaten up after being pulled out of his truck on the corner of Florence and Normandie. No way are these two images of an equal weight to me.

Later on, police arrested four brothers and charged them with attempted murder and set their bails at an average of $185,000, dressed them in those orange coveralls, and jailed them. They said they were looking at possible life sentences, and we started hearing what terrible people they were—bad men. So where was the justice in all that? People said, yes, what they did was bad, what they did was wrong—but it was more wrong for Rodney King to be beaten in the first place, because he was beaten while he was being electrocuted by *police officers sworn to uphold the law.* And they never did a day in jail, the police. They weren't even touched by law. They were acquitted of all charges, by law.

So, then, what is the law, here in America, after all? What did the law mean? Did it mean death to Black people? Was that the law? We had to ask ourselves these questions now. Was that early, angry Malcolm X right after all as he said it in his righteous anger, right in saying that you, if you are a Black person, would never have peace here, would never have security here, that you would spend a thousand years listening to and being tricked by the lies and false promises of the white man, who doesn't want you to be a law-abiding citizen, who wants you to be a law-breaker, who wants you to be immoral, so he'll have an excuse to come in and bust you upside your head with his clubs?

These were things to think about. The same goddamn videotape that gets ignored so that four policemen can walk is probably going to send four Black men to prison for life. If those young Black men end up getting heavy jail terms, nothing's changed.

I just beat the curfew out of L.A.

No justice, no peace. No justice, no peace.

I went to Cannes for about ten days right after this happened, for the film festival. I had already seen *The Player,* one of the year's entries for the Palme d'Or, the Cannes version of Best Picture. Robert Altman's film was about the madness that can occur in this business, and I thought it was excellent and funny, and that Tim Robbins, who was kind enough to work with me in a small role in *Jungle Fever,* rocked the house as the lead character, a big-time studio executive named Griffin Mill, kind of the way Anthony

Hopkins had rocked the year before as the cannibalistic psychiatrist Hannibal Lecter in *The Silence of the Lambs.* I saw Tim in Cannes, hanging out, and gave him some dap. He and Denzel should be up for the big honor, Best Actor, in '93.

I had a news conference in Cannes, and ripped right into the Simi Valley jury and George Bush. Even my friend Stevie Wonder, who is blind, could have seen what was on that videotape! If you are Black, it looks like you have no rights in America. And George Bush should have been right in there as soon as it happened, flown in on Air Force One, instead of waiting to see what the political landscape might [be] like in a few days. In South Africa, the day before the King verdict, the white government had sentenced a white policeman to death for killing four Black South African people. The operative word is *people.* I never thought South Africa would be ahead of the U.S. in the matter of human rights for Black people. I wish *Malcolm X* could be released tomorrow.

I had just shot some commercials for Nike a couple of weeks before the L.A. uprising, to promote Air Raid sneakers. One of the spots we shot had a *Do The Right Thing* feel to it, a tension between races, represented with some teenagers getting ready to hoop at Spike's "Urban Jungle Gym" by hollering racial insults at each other. Then I came on with the peace sign saying if we're going to live together, we gotta play together. I just had seen that. Felt it. At Cannes, I was asked by a French journalist whether or not *Do The Right Thing* had predicted the revolt, and I told him on the contrary, that film had been taken from events that had already happened in New York City, many times over, the anger left after a deadly session of racist police brutality. I was calling it like it already had been in this case, not as it might be. I was later told that Mickey Rourke was quoted somewhere as saying John Singleton and I were responsible for the riots in L.A. because of the kind of films we'd made. I suggested that just because the French adore his films didn't mean Mickey was an expert on Black folks. I suggested Mickey take a shower and a shave and shut the fuck up. Later on his publicist called and said Mickey had been misquoted.

Anyway, I was in Cannes doing interviews with foreign journalists and having a decent time of it as always, but I couldn't keep my mind off the States, and off *Malcolm X.* But I'll always come to Cannes. This is where *She's Gotta Have It* first broke out in '86. People always want to know how I feel about awards, since I bitched and groaned about *sex, lies and videotape* beating out *Do The Right Thing* for the Palme d'Or, the grand prize at Cannes, back in 1989, and when *Barton Fink* beat out *Jungle Fever* in '91. Well, what I'm trying to do is broaden my market overseas, the entire international scope of my market, get it? I don't think there's a better way of doing that in film than having your work recognized at the Cannes Film Festival. It's like winning an Oscar in the States. What it means is that the studio will run another little marketing campaign for your film, and it will mean more revenue for the picture, by far. That is my position on awards, other than the fact that I think Black people should also have our own, because very often lack of merit ain't the reason you might not get recognized. That's the reason the Black Achievement Awards, the Essence

Awards, the Black Filmmakers Awards, and the Soul Train Awards are very important to me, as well. These awards are important because we have to honor our own, if we want to be honored at all. An example of this is Stevie Wonder. I thought he got jerked last year for his songs for *Jungle Fever.* He didn't even get an Academy Award nomination. But he was honored by the Black Oscars. That's an event they have every year, hosted by the actor Bernie Casey, where they honor the Black Academy Award nominees.

Sometimes the best award is like what Sam Jackson is getting now, after finally being recognized for Gator in *Jungle Fever.* What Sam is getting right now, and will continue to get, is work. Work, good work, meaningful work, quality work, well-paid work, is the best award I know about. As for *Malcolm X,* I don't know what kind of awards we'll be up for behind it, I haven't thought about it but some of the few people who have seen it say it should be up for four or five or six Academy Awards. We'll see. I don't know anything but this: The Academy won't be able to deny Denzel Washington. Denzel rocks the world with this performance.

While all this is going on, my Knicks had beaten the Detroit Pistons in a hard five-game set in the NBA playoffs and now faced the world champs, Mike and the Chicago Bulls.

Nobody gave the Knicks a chance, but they went in and beat the Bulls in the first game at Chicago Stadium. I'd seen two games at Chicago Stadium already in this season, but I missed this one. However, I wasn't going to miss any more at home. I got on the plane from Cannes and beat it back to New York, to the Garden, for games three and four—we lost the first, but won the second and the best-of-seven set was tied at two games apiece. My plane back to France left at 10:00 P.M., and the game was over at 9:00. I made it. I went back to Cannes and hung out for a little while doing more interviews, picking up what scuttlebutt I could that might be of some use to me later as I try to expand my horizons in film. Again, we had gone $5 million over budget. Bette Smith and the Completion Bond Co. were trying to cut their losses. They felt it was unfair for them to take the full hit. They wanted Warner Brothers to absorb some of the overage. Warner Brothers wasn't having it. Their position was this: This is your job, we paid you for a service, the film went over budget, it's not our concern, later for you.

This was the dilemma I was in. The Bond Company had fired my editors, Warner Brothers legally said they couldn't fund me or they would be in breach, and I myself was tapped. I got paid 3 million bananas for X; 2 million of those went directly back into the film, so I didn't have it either. I couldn't ask the editors to work for free, they had to be paid. I was up the creek without a paddle or a boat. I was in the water and I can't swim, I was going down. I prayed on it, then drew on *Malcolm X* for inspiration. I had been studying him for two years doing this film. Malcolm always talked about, DO FOR SELF. The BLACK MAN has to learn to stand on his own two feet. DO FOR SELF. I took a page out of the MALCOLM MANUAL. I know BLACK FOLKS with money. I would appeal directly to their BLACKNESS, to their sense of knowing how important this film is. How important MALCOLM X is to us. How

important it is that this film succeed. I got down and came up with a list of all the people I knew that I should contact. Let the record state, the first call went out to Bill Cosby. I was in L.A. at the time staying at the Chateau Marmont. Luckily, I was able to track him down in New York. I was straight with him. I told him the deal. At first, Bill said he was tapped. I think he thought I was asking for a million, which I wasn't. Bill said, "How much you need?" I said the amount, he said call my accountant, the check will be at your hotel that night. It was simple as that. Even though I knew what had to be done, it was still nonetheless a hard thing to ask people for money, especially, the type of money I was asking for. When I approached everyone I told them it wasn't to be considered a loan, nor an investment, this was a gift. The only thing I've ever asked Michael Jordan for is for some tickets, that's it. I didn't feel good asking him, begging him, if you will, for the bread, but I had no choice. What's great is that folks responded. Not everyone I approached gave. A lot more said yes than no but it's important to emphasize the positive. Bill, Oprah Winfrey, Michael Jordan, Janet Jackson, Prince, Magic Johnson, Tracy Chapman, and Peggy Cooper-Cafritz didn't have to give me shit, not a red cent but they chose to. Too often we hear and too often we believe that Black folks never get together, never come together, never are unified, well this wasn't the case with *Malcolm X*. Here was a group, A WHO'S WHO, all African-Americans, all have much bank and all gave their money. These folks saved *Malcolm X*. It was their money that kept us to continue to work on the film. Before things were finally worked out between Warner Brothers and the Completion Bond Co. two months elapsed. For two whole months, we were alone, stranded, cut-off, no funding, no money, and it was prominent African-Americans that financed this film. There has been a lot of speculation about how much I was able to get, well, you can guess all you want. I'm not telling.

With our "Black" money, we got on the good foot, still editing the picture. Warner Brothers and the Completion Bond Co. knew we were still proceeding but they had no idea who was paying for it. I got the idea to announce this whole thing on May 19, on what would have been Malcolm's sixty-eighth birthday. We held a press conference at the Schomburg Library in Harlem, all the major press was invited and it became a big news story. It was definitely a historic event, it was a precedent, this had never been done before, and the world needed to be told. We can do for ourselves, here was a concrete example of it. Who's to say the next time I don't go directly to the same individuals to finance my next film, bypassing Hollywood. Who's to say that these individuals or other people like them don't get together and start pooling their wealth, pooling their resources and talents. It can be done. I don't and I'm not waiting on white folks. If you know only one thing about Malcolm, that should be it.

Malcolm X will be the sixth film we've done in seven years, and, frankly, I'm tired. I'm whipped! It is a physically and mentally draining effort, making films. I'll still direct in the future, no question about that, but right now I think what I want to do most is executive produce some projects that I have in mind. If all goes well, I've got an agreement I'll enter into with my old friends at Universal, a contract that

will allow me to be executive producer on any number of projects.

Universal always was my favorite shop among the Hollywood studios that I worked with, and my experience with *Malcolm X* at Warner Brothers (the Plantation) has done nothing to change the studio rankings in my mind. It should be a good year for Warner Brothers, though. They've got *Lethal Weapon 3* with Danny Glover and Mel Gibson and Joe Pesci ready for release, and despite how I might feel about the film itself, I know it will make money for Warner Brothers. Then *Batman Returns* opens in June. Then, to cap it off, *Malcolm X* opens the weekend before Thanksgiving. Warner Brothers should have no complaints about their 1992. But I hope my deal and my new home will be at Universal. I also want to make sure we get Forty Acres and a Mule Musicworks off the ground running, and I've already put in some promotional appearances with some of the talent we have on the label. I'm looking forward to that as well. I'm just looking forward. The future isn't set in stone, but these are the things I'd really like to get down on.

The sixth game of the Knicks-Bulls series at the Garden was a throw down. Patrick Ewing came off the bench on an injured leg, a bad ankle sprain, sort of the way Willis Reed had played on a bad knee in 1970 against the Lakers. Patrick scored 27 points. The Knicks ran the Chicago Bulls out of New York, 100–85, before the Bulls ran the Knicks back to New York in a seventh-game blowout at Chicago Stadium to end the series in Chicago's favor, four games to three. I went to both games. It had been a good run.

I'd run with the bulls myself, the Pamplona bulls that is, in Pamplona, Spain, in the ritual running of the bulls, the spring before this. I'll tell you, my life sometimes seems like a long jolt of ironies, character establishments, and foreshadowings and turnabouts and plot twists and fighting wars and battles—sometimes it's like a movie itself. I'm constantly rewriting scenes in it. Right now, I'm working on an ending. A somewhat happy ending. Somewhat. I want to and will continue to make films for the rest of my life. I've been blessed. I'm doing what makes me the happiest. Nothing in this world gives me the feeling I get from cinema.

DECODING THE TEXT

1. How do Spike Lee and Ralph Wiley connect the film *Malcolm X* to events that occur both inside and outside the film?

2. Who is the intended audience for this essay?

3. How do Lee and Wiley use language and images to appeal to that audience?

CONNECTING TO YOUR CULTURE

1. How familiar are you with the events that Lee and Wiley describe in their essay? The Rodney King trial and decision? The cultural and political aftermath of that decision?

2. How does this essay connect to you and life in the community you live in or the larger community of the United States?

3. Do you agree with Lee and Wiley about a film's ability to affect society? To challenge prejudice?

In the United States today, horror films are even more popular and prolific than they were decades ago.

1. Why do you think people watch horror films?

2. What are some common characters?

3. What are some common scenes?

4. If you're a fan of horror films, what are some recent ones that you've seen? Why did you pick these films to see?

Roger Ebert *has been* The Chicago Sun-Times' *film critic since 1967. Ebert also cohosts the weekly television show* Ebert & Roeper. *He is the author of more than fifteen books on film, including* Roger Ebert's Movie Yearbook, *published annually. In 1975, Ebert won the Pulitzer Prize for criticism. His film reviews may be found online at http://rogerebert.suntimes.com and http://www.ebertandroeper.tv. Ebert's review of* Scream *was published December 20, 1996, at http://rogerebert.com.*

SCREAM

Roger Ebert

Wes Craven's *Scream* violates one of the oldest rules in movie history: It's about characters who go to the movies. They've even heard of movie stars. They refer by name to Tom Cruise, Richard Gere, Jamie Lee Curtis. They analyze motivations ("Did Norman Bates have a motive? Did Hannibal Lecter have a reason for wanting to eat people?") True, they went to the movies in *The Last Picture Show*, and the heroes of *Clerks* worked in a video store. Even Bonnie and Clyde went to the movies. But those movies were about the *act* of going to the movies. *Scream* is about *knowledge* of the movies: The characters in *Scream* are in a horror film, and because they've seen so many horror films, they know what to do, and what not to do. "Don't say 'I'll be right back,'" one kid advises a friend, "because whenever anybody says that, he's *never* right back." In a way, this movie was inevitable. A lot of modern film criticism involves "deconstruction" of movie plots. "Deconstruction" is an academic word. It means saying what everybody knows about the movies in words nobody can understand. *Scream* is self-deconstructing; it's like one of those cans that heats its own soup.

Instead of leaving it to the audience to anticipate the horror clichés, the characters talk about them openly. "Horror movies are always about some big-breasted blond who runs upstairs so the slasher can corner her," says a character in *Scream*. "I hate it when characters are that stupid." The movie begins, of course, with a young woman (Drew Barrymore) at home alone. She gets a threatening phone call from an evil Jack Nicholson soundalike. She is standing in front of patio doors with the dark night outside. She goes into a kitchen where there are lots of big knives around. You know the drill.

Later, we meet another young woman (Neve Campbell). Her father has left for the weekend. Her mother was murdered . . . why, exactly a year ago tomorrow! Her boyfriend climbs in through the window. At high school, rumors of cult killings circulate. The killer wears a spooky Halloween costume named "Father Death." There are more phone calls, more attacks. The suspects include the boyfriend, the father, and a lot of other people. A nice touch: The high school principal is The Fonz.

All of that is the plot. *Scream* is not about the plot. It is about itself. In other words, it is about characters who *know* they are in a plot. These characters read *Fangoria* magazine. They even use movie-style dialogue: "I was attacked and nearly filleted last night." The heroine has been rejecting her boyfriend's advances, and just as well: As another character points out, virgins are never victims in horror films. Only bad boys and girls get slashed to pieces. Realizing they're in the midst of a slasher plot, the characters talk about who could play them: "I see myself as sort of a young Meg Ryan. But with my luck, I'll get Tori Spelling." The movie itself, for all of its ironic in-jokes, also functions as a horror film—a bloody and gruesome one, that uses as many clichés as it mocks.

One old standby is the scene where someone unexpectedly enters the frame, frightening the heroine, while a sinister musical chord pounds on the soundtrack. I love these scenes, because (a) the chord carries a message of danger, but (b) of course the unexpected new person is always a harmless friend, and (c) although we can't see the newcomer because the framing is so tight, in the real world the frightened person would of course be able to see the newcomer all the time.

The movie is also knowledgeable about the way TV reporters are portrayed in horror films. The reporter this time, played by Courteney Cox of *Friends*, asks wonderful questions, such as "How does it feel to almost be the victim of a slasher?" Savvy as she is, she nevertheless suggests to a local deputy that they shouldn't drive to an isolated rural setting when it's a nice night to walk down a deserted country road in the dark while a slasher is loose.

What did I think about this movie? As a film critic, I liked it. I liked the in-jokes and the self-aware characters. At the same time, I was aware of the incredible level of gore in this film. It is *really* violent.

Is the violence defused by the ironic way the film uses it and comments on it? For me, it was. For some viewers, it will not be, and they will be horrified.

Which category do you fall in? Here's an easy test: When I mentioned *Fangoria*, did you know what I was talking about?

1. How does Ebert set up his review?

2. Does he use a structure that is familiar to you? If so, what is that structure?

3. What words or phrases does Ebert use to show his like or dislike for the film?

CONNECTING TO YOUR CULTURE

1. Why do you think horror films are so popular?

2. What is the difference between watching a horror movie and one that is labeled as mystery/ suspense?

3. What kind of music is often played during horror movies? Why?

Reading Selections: A Case Study from the '00s

CONSIDERING IDEAS

1. Where do you go to find information about films you may want to see?

2. How often do you read film reviews?

3. How often do you watch or listen to film reviews rather than reading them?

4. Is there a difference between a written film review and an oral or visual one?

5. Do you always trust what others (for example, your friends, your family, paid film reviewers) say in their film reviews?

6. Are there film reviewers you just never trust?

Peter Travers *is the film critic and senior editor for film at* Rolling Stone. *His reviews have been broadcast on CNN and published in anthologies. He is a member of the National Society of Film Critics and the New York Film Critics Circle. His review of* Fahrenheit 9/11 *was published in* Rolling Stone *(http://www.rollingstone.com) in June 2004.*

FAHRENHEIT 9/11

Review

Peter Travers

Rumor has it that Michael Moore needs to get his Bush-bashing documentary out pronto (with the DVD following close behind) because his film will pass its sell-by date on Election Day. That would reduce the brilliant battering ram that is *Fahrenheit 9/11* to propaganda with no resonance as cinema, history, humanism or entertainment. Nuts to that. Getting Bush out is just part of Moore's agenda. Political hypocrisy, across all party lines, is on trial in this broadside from the director of *Roger and Me* and *Bowling for Columbine*.

Disney found the film too explosive to release it through its Miramax subsidiary, so Miramax bought it back and found other distribution. At Cannes, the film won the Palme d'Or, the top prize. The ovation that followed was dismissed by cynics as European anti-Americanism. Nuts to that, too.

What Moore does in *Fahrenheit 9/11*, besides drubbing Dubya and his family's ties to Saudi Arabia, is to measure the human toll that U.S. foreign policy after 9/11 and the war in Iraq are taking on the disenfranchised. Moore likes to rile folks up, which he does with sharp humor. Did I mention that *Fahrenheit 9/11* is ferociously, cathartically funny? In one pointedly hilarious scene, Moore rallies members of Congress to get their own children to enlist in the Marines. No chance. Moore isn't above a cheap laugh at the expense of a pro-war Britney Spears, John Ashcroft warbling a patriotic ditty or Deputy Defense Secretary Paul Wolfowitz vainly prepping for a TV interview. But he steps aside more often than not to let America speak for itself, whether it's GIs in Iraq, the mother of a dead soldier or the unemployed being recruited in his hometown of Flint, Michigan.

Images of the dead and wounded, and of U.S. soldiers abusing Iraqi prisoners, aren't new. But Moore has marshaled what's on the record and off into a stinging indictment of where we're going. In a multiplex filled with Hollywood cotton candy, we need him more than ever.

"Fahrenheit 9/11: Review" by Peter Travers from ROLLING STONE Magazine, 16 June 2004.

Michael Wilmington *is the chief movie critic for the* Chicago Tribune. *His work has appeared in many news outlets and film journals. He has also taught courses for the University of Southern California and the University of Chicago Continuing Education Program. He is a board member of the National Society of Film Critics and the Chicago Film Critics. His review of* Fahrenheit 9/11 *was published in the* Tribune *(http://metromix.chicagotribune.com) in June 2004.*

FAHRENHEIT 9/11

Movie Review

Michael Wilmington

Among the movies everyone should see this year—whatever your film taste or your political bent—Michael Moore's incendiary documentary *Fahrenheit 9/11* heads the list.

Fahrenheit may provoke, delight or divide its audience. But no one will react indifferently to this shocking, sad and funny look at the Bush administration's handling of terrorism and the Iraqi war.

It's another howitzer blast of heartland humor and journalistic chutzpah from director-writer Moore—his cheekiest, gutsiest, most hilarious assault yet on the halls of the rich and mighty.

Fahrenheit is, of course, not the last word on President George W. Bush or Iraq. It's Moore's word. This movie, the subject of controversy, is a defiantly personal statement on what the war really is—laced with that now-familiar *Roger and Me* mix of homespun wit, pop culture playfulness, populist heart twisting and "gotcha" guerilla film-making tactics.

From beginning to end, *Fahrenheit 9/11* is told in Moore's unmistakable voice: the deceptively casual tones of a wisecracking gadfly never happier than when he faces down or questions some person of great power or wealth whom he feels, knowingly or not, betrayed the public trust.

Like, in this case, George W. Bush. Using archival footage, cannily edited and narrated, the film shows Bush sometimes as an attractive, determined politician and likable, boyishly charming guy. But it also savages him with wicked satire, depicting Bush as a lightweight opportunist, swayed by privileged upbringing and moneyed pals and, to some extent, trapped in the whirlwind of events.

So strangely attractive is the subject and so amusing the portrait, that Bush quickly becomes the comic star of *Fahrenheit 9/11* with Moore as his straight man. But it's very dark comedy, soaked in tragedy. At times it wrenches your heart.

That's the strength of *Fahrenheit 9/11*: the way it attacks emotions and stings us to laughter, anger and sorrow.

Movie Review: Fahrenheit 9/11 by Michael Wilmington. From METROMIX, 25 June 2004 (Chicago Tribune). Reprinted by permission of The Permissions Group, Inc. on behalf of TMS Reprints.

In his trademark Andy Rooney-gone Zap Comix style, Moore comments on the disputed Florida election, the Bush family's close ties to Saudi Arabian oil interests, the President's frequent pre-9/11 vacation-time romps and his pained bewilderment on 9/11. Then Moore relentlessly presents his own take on Iraq, a conflict that in his eyes is born of fear, deception and confusion and realized in blood, death and tears, diminishing the American dream it purported to defend. Moore pointedly questions the premises, goals and "selling" of the war, its relevance to 9/11 and, most of all, its fearsome costs both in national resources and human lives. The film isn't objective, nor does it ever pretend to be. Moore keeps mockingly overstepping the boundaries while imagining what Bush is thinking, playing up the president's humor (both conscious and unconscious) and, at one point, superimposing Bush into the *Bonanza* TV title scene, along with fellow "Cartwrights" Dick Cheney, Donald Rumsfeld and Tony Blair.

This is a movie often much closer to David Letterman, *Saturday Night Live* or *Dr. Strangelove*—or a Rush Limbaugh satiric tirade—than to Ken Burns or *60 Minutes*. There's a human voice behind every scene: joking or occasionally—as in the scenes with bereaved war mother Lila Lipscomb or Moore's moving paean to America's preponderantly working-class fighting forces—rising to unexpected heights of grief and eloquence.

Fahrenheit 9/11 is not unassailable journalism or history, though it's almost always *superb moviemaking. Moore's thesis that* oil money and geo-politics primarily drove the war, rather than nuclear fear or compassion for the Iraqi masses, will be rejected by many.

For some audiences *Fahrenheit 9/11* will seem propaganda and for others a fiery modern *J'Accuse*. But one doesn't have to share Moore's views to be entertained by him. Last May, *Fahrenheit 9/11* received both the first prize (Palme d'Or) and the longest continuous standing ovation in the history of the Cannes Film Festival (25 minutes)—and it wasn't because of some clichéd French antipathy to America.

Fahrenheit 9/11 takes its title from Ray Bradbury's Orwellian novel about a futuristic book-burning society, *Fahrenheit 451* (the temperature at which book paper burns). And in the end, both liberals and conservatives—and some political extremes—will be amused and edified by the film. Conservatives, in fact, may especially respond to Moore's evocations of American ideals, national spirit and tradition he sees as being trampled on.

Yet, whatever its ultimate validity as history or its effect on the electorate, this is obviously one of the movies of the year. Moore's ability to kick off a debate—even a vicious one—remains priceless, as do his gifts for ridicule, for wringing laughs, shock and tears from his subjects and for shedding a spotlight on ordinary Americans.

What's more, there's a ferocious candor in his commentary that puts Moore in the classic Mark Twain tradition of American humorous skepticism. And, here, his comic game—playing the common schmo trying to confront the powerful people you can't reach—hits its highest peak. "Behave yourself, will you?" Bush himself jokes with Moore part way through this movie, adding impishly, "Go find real work!" Indisputably, he has.

Glenn Lovell *is a member of the San Francisco Film Critics Circle. His reviews have been published in* Daily Variety *and the* San Jose Mercury News. *He also regularly appears on KGO AM 810 and teaches film courses at colleges in the Bay Area. "Sub-par Propaganda" was first printed in June 2004 in the* Mercury News.

SUB-PAR PROPAGANDA

Glenn Lovell

Obviously all that lovely *Bowling for Columbine* green has gone to Michael Moore's head. How else to explain *Fahrenheit 9/11*, a film so sloppy, illogical and formulaic that it begs the questions: Can a hatchet job actually elicit sympathy for its sitting-duck target? Can it cause, if not a change of heart, at least feelings of regret over missed opportunities to inflict real damage?

Though a huge fan of *Bowling*, Moore's powerful plea for gun control, I found this all-out assault on Bush and his response to the terrorist attacks of Sept. 11 to be so smug in its position, so cavalier in its documentation, that I left feeling more hoodwinked than enlightened.

Moore's charge that Bush, Cheney, Rumsfeld and British Prime Minister Tony Blair—whose faces are superimposed over the hard-riding Cartwrights of *Bonanza*—used the attacks as a justification to in-vade Iraq is incendiary but it's hardly revelatory. Nor are Moore's charges of conflict of interest and shameful exploitation of the poor to fight a war that's really about oil, arms contracts and personal revenge.

What is new is the fervor with which Moore launches his preemptive counter-attack. In his rush to portray Bush as both con artist and boob, he leaves no conspiracy theory unaired, no cheap shot untaken. The cumulative picture is that of a menace to peace and democracy who can't think on his feet.

Moore opens with the "stolen election" of 2000, once again connecting the dots between the contested Florida vote, brother/Gov. Jeb Bush and Republican appointees to the Supreme Court.

He segues to Bush's first days in office. The new president is depicted as bone lazy, unprepared for and finally paralyzed by the events of Sept. 11. During a visit to a Florida classroom, he is told about one plane, then another. He purses and nibbles his lips as a digital clock in the corner of the screen ticks off the seconds, then minutes between when he is alerted and when he reacts.

Cheap shot? Regardless of whether you voted against the man, it certainly feels that way. Might Bush simply have delayed running from the room to keep from panicking the kids?

It'll Make You Squirm

There's a lot more here that's guaranteed to make you squirm, as much over what

"Sub-par Propaganda" by Glenn Lovell from SAN JOSE MERCURY NEWS, 25 June 2004.

it says about Moore as for what it says about Bush. From the president seemingly frozen in fear, Moore moves on to possible collusion as he recounts how Saudis and members of Osama bin Laden's family—some of whom had business dealings with George Senior—were flown out of the country.

To pound home what he sees as outrageously lax police work, Moore throws in a lengthy insert from TV's *Dragnet*, with Jack Webb (a right-wing propagandist if ever there was one) gathering "Just the facts, ma'am."

To come is a slew of accusations about illegal-sounding arms contracts, George Senior's "private" trips to Saudi Arabia and the civil-liberties-busting Patriot Act. Again, the material comes at us so fast and is so hastily "substantiated" that the first term that leaps to mind isn't "exposé" but "necktie party."

How will *Fahrenheit 9/11* (which takes its title from the Ray Bradbury classic about book-burning) fare at the box office? Given all the advance hype, it should do better than *Bowling*, which took in $21 million (or $10 million less than *DodgeBall* got just on its opening weekend).

But will it attract many who are not predisposed to its message? Unlikely. Bush lovers won't want to line their sworn enemy's pockets. Meanwhile, Bush-bashers will just swap chummy punches in the arm and "I told you so" winks.

What of those discerning students of great (read: more balanced) documentaries, from *Harlan County, USA* to *Fog of War*? This group should be as offended by this crock-doc as they are shocked. They'll praise Moore's discreet handling of the terrorist attacks (screams against a blank screen) but grimace as he resorts to the ambush tactics that served him so much better in *Columbine*.

Absurd Gambit
Here, playing recruiter, he approaches members of Congress with pamphlets and asks them to volunteer their own children to serve in Iraq. The politicians run from the camera—at least, those politicians who made the final cut. Any who may have seen through the absurdity of Moore's gambit and responded, "Sure, I'll share this with my kids. They're old enough to make up their own minds about these things," is nowhere to be found.

Moore's parting shot is of a hopelessly flummoxed Bush trying to recall an adage that begins "Fool me once, shame on you. . . ." The footage is meant as further proof of what a buffoon our current president is. It boomerangs, and makes America's most famous documentarian look facile and petty, and unworthy of a most worthy opponent.

All three reviewers saw the same film and reviewed it, but they have different reactions and responses.

1. How do their interpretations and reactions to the film differ? Is there any overlap?

2. Which review is the most positive? The most negative? The most balanced?

3. Why did the authors choose to present their views in the manner they did?

4. Does the place where the review was published determine or influence how the author reacted or responded to the film or wrote the review?

CONNECTING TO YOUR CULTURE

1. What percentage of the films you see each year are documentaries?

2. What is usually the purpose behind making a documentary?

3. Is this purpose something you like to connect with in your film viewing?

4. What's your favorite documentary? Why?

Reading Selections:
Across the Decades

CONSIDERING IDEAS

How many Disney animated films have you seen in your lifetime? List them.

1. What do these films have in common?

2. What were the storylines?

3. How were the primary characters depicted? The secondary characters?

4. How did the filmmakers use music for the film?

Kathi Maio *has been a film columnist for* The Magazine of Fantasy and Science Fiction *since the early 1990s. She is the author of two books,* Feminist in the Dark *and* Popcorn & Sexual Politics, *and is the former editor of* Sojourner: The Women's Forum. *Maio is currently assistant director for reference services at the Milfred F. Sawyer Library at Suffolk University in Boston. "Disney's Dolls" was first published in* New Internationalist *in December 1998.*

DISNEY'S DOLLS

Kathi Maio

It is more than a little ironic that the Walt Disney Company's current animated feature, *Mulan*, retells an age-old legend about the Chinese successfully fighting off a foreign invasion. The American media giant chose to make this particular story into its 36th animated feature precisely because it was the perfect vehicle for a strategic incursion into the Chinese film market.

The legendary woman warrior, Hua MuLan, who bravely fought off alien onslaughts has now herself become an agent of a US conglomerate's ambition to dominate the culture of Asia—and the entire globe.

It's a heavy burden for one young, doe-eyed heroine to bear. But so it is for all of the young women Disney has co-opted for the screen. They aren't simply cartoons. They are symbols of the times— and one company's measurement of how their target audiences want to see women.

Disney's first animated feature, *Snow White and the Seven Dwarfs* (1937), set a standard for full-length animation and established a pattern for later Disney heroines to follow. Snow White is young, virginal, pretty, sweet-natured and obedient. Domestic drudgery doesn't faze her since she is sure that a handsome owning-class chap will, someday soon, come and save her.

Meanwhile, when faced with danger she runs away on tiny high-heeled shoes and then falls in a weeping heap. She finds a shelter in a dusty and dishevelled cottage and immediately feels compelled to clean it from top to bottom (since the owners, a group of full-grown, if quite short, miners, obviously don't have a "Mother" to clean for them).

Snow White's one adversary is her wicked and powerful stepmother, the Queen. Like most Disney crones, the Queen is eventually destroyed. But not before feeding her lovely step-daughter a poisoned apple that places her in a death-like coma. Snow White is lovingly waked by her house-mates who place her on a bier. But she is awakened only when Prince Charming comes and plants one on her rosy lips. Back among the living, Snow White rides away with her new boyfriend, with nary a second thought for her short friends.

It's prototypical Disney. Young women are natural-born happy homemakers who lie in a state of suspended animation until a man gives them a life. Older women are the enemy, especially if they seek power. And the working class (hardworking, but dirty and uncivilized) are there to serve the rich and privileged, never questioning their subordinate position.

Although the Disney team made use of different fairytales over the years, the basic formula for telling women's stories through animated features changed very little from *Snow White* to *Cinderella* (1950) to *Sleeping Beauty* (1959).

"Disney Dolls" by Kathy Maio from NEW INTERNATIONALIST, December 1998, pp. 12–14.

Then came the sixties: Uncle Walt died in 1966. And Disney's animation teams fell into years of disarray and second-rate work. Some felt the Disney studio would never again produce a "classic." They were wrong. Several years after management of the studio was assumed by Michael Eisner the company made an impressive comeback with *The Little Mermaid* (1989). With its vibrant animation and music *The Little Mermaid* proved that the Disney studio still knew how to make a first-rate cartoon feature. The movie also proved that old attitudes towards women die hard. Looking at the film you'd never know that the women's movement ever happened.

Disney's take on Hans Christian Andersen is the "same old, same old." Except, for the first time, there is a new nymphet quality to the virginal heroine. Above her green tail Disney's Ariel wears only a string bikini top made from a couple of sea shells. And as innocent, wide-eyed and flipper-tailed as she is, there is something distinctly sexy about her too. Her image may not be informed by feminism, but it has most certainly been informed by the eroticizing of the pubescent female, so common in Western advertising and popular culture.

Like Disney heroines before her, Ariel is looking for a romantic solution to the yearning in her heart. (Andersen's mermaid looks for human love only as a means of achieving her true desire: an immortal soul. Disney's mermaid sees a cute fella as her be-all and end-all.) Ariel will do anything to have the bland handsome Prince fall in love with her. She'll disobey her stern but loving father, King Triton. She'll even make a bargain with the devil—played by a corpulent, white-haired seawitch named Ursula. Again, the older, powerful woman (representing evil) must be annihilated. The young Prince, who embodies a healthier form of (inherited patriarchal) power, finishes the witch off. But not before she makes big trouble for our lovelorn heroine.

Ursula gives Ariel a set of shapely legs, but takes her voice in trade. Hence, in *The Little Mermaid*, we are given a female protagonist who is literally silenced by her desperate need for male approval. "Shut up and be beautiful," the movie seems to tell young girls. (Books like *Reviving Ophelia* have argued that this is a message preteen girls constantly get from their society. Why not from their cartoons?)

Since *The Little Mermaid* is a Disney flick, Ariel gets her voice back and she gets the guy. But she is nevertheless forced to abandon completely her sea world (her family and friends) for the land-locked kingdom of her Prince. In the end, Ariel is a woman without a social support system, investing her entire life in a romance. Not a situation that I've ever found to have "happily ever after" written all over it.

And many women agreed. Stung by the criticism, Disney promised to show more sensitivity towards gender issues in their next movie, a re-telling of *Beauty and the Beast* (1991). The company hired a woman, Linda Woolverton, as screenwriter. And they put their PR department into over-drive—promoting their new heroine, Belle, as "modern," "active" and even "feminist."

It worked with most critics. But, as far as I could tell, the most feminist thing about Disney's Belle was that she liked to read. Like the eighteenth-century folktale's

Beauty, this Belle remains a self-sacrificing daughter of a silly and cowardly father (switching places with her papa when the Beast takes him prisoner). Still, Disney's idea of an "independent" woman didn't bother me half as much as their concept of a male romantic hero.

The original fairy tale (and all the retellings I've ever read or seen, from Cocteau's 1946 movie masterpiece to the cult late-1980s American TV show) portrayed the "Beast" of the story as a big teddy bear. He looked fierce and strange, but was really kind, tender—and hopelessly devoted. The moral: Don't judge a book by its cover. An ugly exterior can hide a loving heart.

But Disney admitted that they went out of their way to create a hero with a "very serious problem." Their Beast is, well, beastly. He terrorizes his household staff. And he intimidates his lovely prisoner, as well. Although he isn't violent with Belle, that always seems a distinct possibility. It is her poise and exquisite beauty that tame his savagery.

The problem? Disney's reworking of the old fable implies that women are responsible for controlling male anger and violence. If a woman is only pretty and sweet enough, she can transform an abusive man into a prince—forever. If only it were true. But this is a blame-the-victim scenario waiting to happen. In a realistic sequel, Belle would seek refuge at the village's battered women's shelter.

No matter its sexual politics, Disney's *Beauty and the Beast* was an international hit, spawning an equally successful stage musical. Disney's cartoon features were back in the groove and they proved it again with 1992's *Aladdin*. It's hardly worth mentioning the portrayal of women in this translation of an "Arabian Nights" tale. The only significant female character is Princess Jasmine, who is nothing more than a comely pawn bandied back and forth between the hero Aladdin, the evil vizier and the sultan who just happens to be her foolish father.

More interesting is the obvious racism and ethnic stereotyping in the story. The dastardly characters (like Jafar, the vizier) are decidedly Arabic looking. While the hero, Aladdin, looks and sounds ("Call me Al") like a fresh-faced American. And then there were the song lyrics, the most insulting of which went like this: "I come from a land . . . where they cut off your ears, if they don't like your face. It's barbaric, but hey, it's home."

Obviously, Disney never means to offend anyone. That would be bad business. But even animators and songwriters internalize racism. And the "imagineers" at Disney obviously look to reinforce cultural assumptions and push a few buttons in their audience members, if for no other reason than it's the most efficient way to tell a story. Boyish Tom Cruise look = Good guy. Swarthy, hook-nosed Basil Rathbone look = Villain. Most audience members don't even notice when this happens. It is simply the undertow of the "Disney Magic."

Some of that same undertow can be felt in the most successful animated feature of all time, a Hamlet fable in fur called *The Lion King*. Here, despite the African locale, the young hero is voiced by All-American white actors (Jonathan Taylor Thomas, Matthew Broderick), while disloyal, vicious hyena baddies are given street-jive dialogue and voiced by actors like Whoopi Goldberg and Cheech Marin.

Women don't fare well in this story either. Although Simba's childhood playmate, Nala, can kick his butt in a mock fight, when Simba runs away Nala and the other lionesses are powerless to resist the oppressive rule of Scar (a crypto-homosexual villain, another Disney favorite).

With the tremendous success (over $766 million in worldwide box office) of *The Lion King*, Disney plunged wholeheartedly into its own "Wonderful World of Multiculturalism." The next animated feature, *Pocahontas*, blended their traditional all-for-love Princess tale with a true story from Native American history. And there lies the outrage: Pocahontas is not a fictional character to be casually re-interpreted. She was a real woman, who deserved better than the cartoon portrait Disney painted of her.

There's no room in this article to list all the inaccuracies in this 1995 film. Suffice it to say that Disney's buckskin Barbie bears little resemblance to the pre-pubescent girl who first met John Smith. Her real name was Matoaka and her "saving" of Smith from "execution" was probably nothing more than a tribal adoption ceremony. There was no romance between the two. She called him "father" when she met him again, years later.

In an attempt to put a cheery spin on what amounts to genocide, Disney ends their film with peace achieved between the natives and colonists. No mention is made of the eventual decimation of the Powhatan nation. And neither in this movie, nor its 1998 straight-to-video hit sequel, *Pocahontas II: Journey to a New World*, is any mention made of the fact that Pocahontas was kidnapped, held hostage, forcibly "civilized" and converted to Christianity, then married off to a colonist who viewed her origins as "accursed."

Later, as a publicity gimmick for the Virginia colony, she was taken to England where she sickened and died. It's hard to make two upbeat cartoon adventures out of such a tragic story. So Disney didn't try. Instead, they drew a barefoot babe and gave her cute, comical animal sidekicks and a penchant for falling in love with hunky anglos. Sadly, millions of people around the world saw *Pocahontas* not only as a colorful cartoon but as a palatable history lesson.

In the newest animated film, *Mulan*, Disney has laid claim to a Chinese hero who, although real, lived so long ago that her story has passed into myth. The basic legend tells of a young woman who—to protect her disabled veteran father—enters the imperial army, fighting bravely for many years. As you'd expect, Disney has declared its good intentions and its sincere respect for this Chinese national hero. In fact the distortion level in Disney's *Mulan* equals that of *Pocahontas*.

In Disney's version the woman warrior is discovered after she is injured in battle and sentenced to die. But her handsome commanding officer, Shang (a Disney invention), cannot kill her. Instead, he expels her from the army. In the legend, Hua MuLan isn't discovered until after the war when her comrades visit and find her in women's attire. In the Disney version, Shang (Mulan's would-be executioner) shows up after the war to court his former buddy—to the delight of her family and her. The real Mulan had no interest in romance.

So, even though Mulan is a brave, strong hero, her motivation for entering the army has nothing to do with her own ambitions and everything to do with serving patriarchy (represented by her father and her emperor). Disney makes it clear that men still command Mulan and they always retain the power of life-and-death over her. But not to worry, all they really want to do is marry her and turn her into a Disney happy homemaker.

By looks alone, kick-boxing Mulan would seem to have little in common with dainty Snow White. But looks are deceiving. Disney has changed only the trappings and in recent cases the skin color of its heroines. At heart, they all still identify with male authority instead of seeking their own empowerment. And in the end a good-looking boyfriend remains the truest measure of feminine happiness and success.

As I write this, the Chinese Government has still not given its permission for a mainland theatrical release for *Mulan* (although the film is already a hit in Taiwan, Hong Kong and other Asian markets). Chinese officials are engaged, as the *Sunday Telegraph* put it, in a "wider struggle to suppress foreign-backed interpretations of the country's literary heritage."

More power to their struggle. But there may just be no stopping the cultural tsunami called the Walt Disney Company.

DECODING THE TEXT

1. What overall argument does the author make?

2. How does she use and connect many Disney animated films into this one essay?

3. How strong is her supporting evidence?

4. Does she make you believe or at least seriously consider her argument?

CONNECTING TO YOUR CULTURE

1. What was the first animated film from Disney that you saw? How old were you?

2. Do you think your interpretation of or response to the film would change if you viewed it again?

3. What movies or TV shows did you enjoy as a child? How did those movies or shows depict genders?

1. Before you read the following essay, consider the life and work of a film critic.

2. How do you think a film critic organizes his or her day?

3. How many times do you think critics view a film that they write about?

4. What do you think film critics look for in the films that they view?

5. How influential do you think film critics are in U.S. culture?

Stanley Kauffmann *is a renowned film critic, theater critic, and author. He has written for* The New Republic *since 1958 and is the author of several books on film criticism, including* Albums of Early Life *(1980) and* Regarding Film: Criticism and Comment *(2001). Kauffmann has taught film and theater at several schools and has received many awards for criticism and teaching, among them the George Polk Award for Criticism. "Why I'm Not Bored" was first published in* The New Republic *in 1974.*

WHY I'M NOT BORED

Stanley Kauffmann

The two most frequent questions are: "How many films do you see a week?" and "Don't you get bored with going to films?" I've been writing about them in *The New Republic* since 1958, with one intermission of a year and a half, have heard each of these questions at least once a week in that time, and am always pleased by them. As for the first, the number has varied sharply from none to twelve—usually it's about three—but the point is that most weeks it wouldn't have been less even if I weren't a critic. (And, grown gray in the ranks, I still get a thrill out of getting in free.) Once in a great while there have been too many. On two separate occasions there were two successive days in which I had to see four films each day—no kind of record but sickening to me. After each of these pairs of days it was a week before I could see another picture. But most of the time when I'm asked the question, I can't really remember how many times I've gone in the previous week or two, it all seems so natural. And therefore pleasant.

As to the second and more interesting question, the answer is a firm no. A happy no. To salute the obvious, this doesn't mean that I never see boring films or that I am unborable. On the contrary, I'm somewhat more acutely borable—by reason, I tell myself, of professional acuteness—than most of my friends. But the *idea* of going to films is never boring.

The former editor of *The New Republic* once generously suggested that I also write about television from time to time. The prospect of merely crossing the living room to switch on television dramas was numbing. But even when I have to leave the house to see the most unpromising of films (and I limit myself to those with as least some sort of promise), there is something beyond the specifics of the film that tingles and attracts.

To begin with, there is the elemental kinetic aspect. As with billions of people throughout the world since 1900, the mere physical act of filmgoing is part of the kinesis of my life—the getting up and going out and the feeling of coming home, which is a somewhat different homecoming feeling from anything else except the theater (and which is totally unavailable from television). When I am not going out, rather frequently, to films (as a New Yorker this is also true for me of the theater), it's because I'm ill or sore beset with work or isolated somewhere in the country. To have my life unpunctuated by the physical act of filmgoing is almost like walking with a limp, out of my natural rhythm.

Past that there is the community, also known to billions, of being in a group dream, a group reality. This is true of the theater as well, but with films there is a paradox: because of the greater darkness there is, even in the middle of a group, the sense of private ownership of the occasion. That ownership has attachments. No one goes to a film theater—or a press screening-room—without taking with him all of his filmgoing past, including his initial fear. (For years students have been writing papers for me on their recollections of their very first film experiences,

and more often than not, that first experience had included a feeling of fear.) That fear is never quite lost, perhaps, though gradually it is understood, is used to underpin and nourish other responses. No one can go to a film theater without taking with him his parents and childhood friends and the first grapplings of romance in the balcony. And no one can sit in a film theater without acknowledging, however secretly, that this is where some part of his psyche originated. Messenger boy or mogul, peasant or Pope, there can hardly be anyone alive whose secret fantasies, controlled and uncontrolled, have not in some measure been made by film. This has never been so widely true of any other art. My guess is that it is not yet true of television, may never be true in quite the same way. The size of the film screen in itself plays a part in its sacerdotal function; it ministers down to us while the television screen paws upward, smaller than we are, vulnerable to dials and switches. (If films ever really become principally available through television cassettes, as has been prophesied sporadically for years, whole psychic orders will have to be redeployed.)

All this exercise and enjoyment before we even touch matters of art, discrimination, esthetics! Once we get to the question of specific films rather than generic experience, the specter of boredom raises its threat. Some films turn out to be just as boring as feared, though not so many as the fulfilled dreads in the theater and not many more than with new fiction. No one assumes that a literary critic gets bored, yet, having worked in both kinds of criticism, I know that the rewards of poor films are more savorable, more certain, than those of poor novels.

In Westerns, however feeble, there are horses, the creak of leather, the reach of landscape. In any film there are likely to be attractive women or, if you prefer, attractive men. For myself, heterosexually straitened though I am, I get a kick out of seeing O'Toole and Newman and Redford, just as I did with Cooper and Grant and March. Then there are syntactical rewards. Richard Lester's maritime thriller *Juggernaut* missed the boat, but its editing and photography were in themselves thrilling. Visconti's *Ludwig* was drear, but the costumes were sumptuous. The music in *Once Upon a Time in the West* was like a Puccini sauna. I don't suggest that anyone go to see those films for those reasons: I'm just answering the once-a-week question.

There are other, greater things. Direction, for instance. Joseph Sargent, out of television, has done a really crisp job with *The Taking of Pelham One Two Three*. I enjoyed the way he used the subway tunnels and the racing through the streets and the compact arena of the hijacked subway car in a picture that, as a whole, was fading before it finished. (I couldn't read the novel.)

And in some dismal pictures one can often find bright spots of acting. A thriller called *11 Harrowhouse* is laden with Charles Grodin and Candice Bergen and a finale that was apparently devised by a moron on LSD; but James Mason plays an aging diamond expert, dying of cancer, who revenges himself on his niggardly employers by collaborating with thieves, and he creates a whole man, quietly in the middle of roaring nonsense. Jon Voight has the leading role in a more notoriously inane thriller, *The Odessa File,* and presents the young German journalist he

is supposed to be, even to a beautifully precise accent. (Obeying that hilarious convention under which Germans in Germany, speaking English to one another in English-language films, have German accents.)

It would be easy to put together a large bouquet, a garden, several hothouses of flowers culled from poor pictures. They don't quite compensate for their pictures, not even for the waste of themselves in those pictures, still they are rewards not easily accessible in poor examples of other arts. Theater performances, yes, when they stand out from a bad script and/or a bad company. As for other matters, although the theater's symbolic systems are just as "real" as film's, they are less intensely packed to the square millimeter, and when one is forced away from the foreground by tedium, the theater's supportive symbols are less varied, less continuingly interesting. Boris Aronson's beautiful settings for *Company* didn't *continue* to make up for a dullish evening as Tonino delli Colli's cinematography almost did for Pasolini's *Decameron.*

But that's enough of scrounging, of beggarly gratitude for edible scraps amidst the swill. The chief reason for never being bored with the idea of film is that boredom is incompatible with hope, and hope is more of a constant in film than in virtually any other art in America. Fiction and poetry and dance and theater performance (as against playwriting) are in good estate, with good prospects but (say the experts I've met) this is not true of painting or sculpture or musical composition or architecture. And no art is more persistently, almost irritatingly, pulsing with prospects than the film.

Distribution of films is in difficulties, but it always was: only the type of trouble changes. The vulgar and the violent are more popular than the good; so what else is new? Nothing rotten that happens in film—and most of what does happen is rotten—can negate the fact that it is still an avenue of possibilities, an expanding nebula of esthetic mysteries, a treasury of aptness for our time.

In 1966 I published an essay called "The Film Generation" that is now sometimes knocked because the size of the audience has not much increased, has not returned to anything like the size of the mid-1940s, and worse, because some of the best pictures that come along—works by Bresson and Bellocchio, for instance—have short first-run lives. But I wouldn't alter much in that essay today. (Except for one addition: I've learned since writing it, by a lot of travel around the country and through four years" service on the Theater Panel of the National Endowment for the Arts, that theater appetite among young people is lesser only in size, not in urgency, to film appetite.) The film audience is smaller than it used to be because, obviously, free movies are available at home, as well as free vaudeville; but the fact that the film audience has not completely disappeared in the face of that situation is itself proof of that audience's vitality. Far from disappearing, that audience is now increasing. And if the television-threat argument were valid, there ought now to be no film theaters at all.

Blacks flocking to cheap "blaxploitation" films, yes. Kung-fu kooks, yes. Hard and soft porno for hard and soft fans, yes. But if statistics prove that those types account for a lot, statistics prove other things as well. *Somebody* is taking those thousands of film courses in those 1000-plus universities and colleges that offer them; *somebody* is buying those film books and magazines that continue to flood out, attending those festivals that continue to spring up and those film societies and campus and community series. It's not quite a nation of Bazins and Agees as yet, but to argue that the smaller audience has not improved qualitatively is either a confusion of cynicism with taste or a fear of improvement, a nostalgia for Hedda Hopper's Hollywood. The fact that Ozu doesn't run very long in the nation's biggest city doesn't prove any more about the status of the art and its audience than the fact *Boesman and Lena* didn't break the *Hello, Dolly!* record or that Berryman's *Dream Songs* doesn't outsell Rod McKuen.

Film is in money trouble these days because of inflation, but so is everything, including book publishing. Relatively, money doesn't control the making of films much more than it does the publication of poetry and fiction: if film investments are higher, so are possible profits. The money squeeze is not new: finance has always worked cruelly in the film world even when money seemed to be more free (true of publishing, too) distribution has always been tyrannical, you've always been just as successful as your last picture, the putrid ones have always seemed to be surging up to our nostrils, and still the good ones have been made here and abroad—where the difficulties are different only in nomenclature or proportion—and the less ones have had their compensations.

To me this combination of views is hardheaded, with no touch of Pollyanna—unless there is also a touch of Pollyanna in the human race's general insistence on survival. Concurrent with our lives runs this muddied, quasi-strangulated, prostituted art, so life-crammed and responsive and variegated and embracing, so indefinable no matter how far one strings out phrases like these, that to deny it seems to me to deny the worst and the best in ourselves, a chance to help clarify which is which, and which is in the ascendant on any particular day. No matter how much I know about a film's makers or its subject before I go, I never *really* know what it's going to do to me: depress me with its vileness, or just roll past, or change my life in some degree, or some combination of all three, or affect me in some new way that I cannot imagine. So I like being asked whether the filmgoing gets boring: it makes me think of what I don't know about the next film I'm going to see.

DECODING THE TEXT

1. What strategy does the author include in the introduction to set up the entire essay?

2. How effective are his supporting examples for his argument(s)?

3. Is the essay's title effective? What tone does it set for the essay?

CONNECTING TO YOUR CULTURE

1. Do you think you would become bored with viewing films if your job was to do so every day?

2. If you could be a film critic and get paid, which publication would you like to work for? Why?

3. Do you read film reviews before you see a film? Have you ever written a review for a website such as Amazon or Netflix?

CONSIDERING IDEAS

Essays can be written, but they can also include or be made up entirely of multimedia components, such as sounds or visuals, when the essays are presented in digital form.

1. What types of multimedia varieties are acceptable to you or your instructor for composing essays for your class?

2. How does this acceptability vary depending on field, discipline, or publication type?

3. When an author uses both written and visual texts, what are some of the reasons the essay might need to be set up or organized differently?

Alan Vanneman *writes for* Bright Lights Film Journal *and its companion blog,* Bright Lights After Dark. *He has also published two novels,* Sherlock Holmes and the Giant Rat of Sumatra *and* Sherlock Holmes and the Hapsburg Tiara. *"Alfred Hitchcock: A Hank of Hair and a Piece of Bone" was originally published in* Bright Lights Film Journal *in November 2003 and is available online at http://www.brightlightsfilm.com/42/hitch.htm.*

ALFRED HITCHCOCK

A Hank of Hair and a Piece of Bone

Alan Vanneman

Staircases in Hitchcock's films almost always lead to trouble. For Hitchcock, the simple act of going up a staircase seemed to be a disorienting experience, taking you away from safety towards the unknown. Spiral staircases were particularly threatening. In Hitchcock's films, circular movement—the swirling vortex—implies a loss of control, usually with sexual overtones, and often leading to death.

The staircase in *Notorious* (1946). Note how the chandelier, the urn, and the column at the bottom of the banister all reinforce the circular imagery.

The staircase in the McKittrick Hotel in *Vertigo* is a dead ringer for the one in the Bates' residence in *Psycho*. (The exteriors are equally similar.) This three-shot sequence shows the first floor, the lighting fixture/banister post, and an anticipation of Mrs. Bates. (However, the old lady here is harmless.)

The second set of stairs in *Vertigo*, at the old mission, merge the staircase and vortex images completely. These are steps that drive you crazy.

The staircase in *Psycho* is almost a combination of the two staircases in *Vertigo*, forming a complete spiral, which we can't quite see, because the steps that lead down to the basement are concealed beneath the steps going up to the second story.

All © 1960 Shamley Productions, Inc.

Hitchcock often used banister slats to suggest prison bars and confinement. This framing shot from *Psycho* (in the deputy sheriff's house) achieves a remarkably claustrophobic effect.

In *Psycho*'s climax, Lila Crane (Vera Miles) hides from Norman (Anthony Perkins) underneath the stairs, and then decides to enter the basement, leading her to the heart of the matter.

1. How does the author organize the written and visual text?

2. Why do you think this organizational pattern was used?

3. If you had to "translate" this visual essay into a fully written one, would the organization change? If so, how?

CONNECTING TO YOUR CULTURE

1. What is the purpose of the essay?

2. Is this purpose appropriate based on the readers/audience of the publication?

3. Is this type of essay something you see in publications that you read? If so, what type of publications are they?

4. Is there a range of places where this type of visual essay might be published?

5. Is there a range of audiences that this type of visual essay might appeal to? Are you in that audience?

contemplations in the pop culture zone

1. The movie industry reaps huge profits each year from blockbusters (movies with big budgets that make even more money). Movies like *Star Wars, Jurassic Park, Independence Day,* and *Titanic* have changed the way movies are made nowadays. What have been the positive and negative effects of the blockbuster phenomenon? Are movies better than ever, or have commercial formulas drastically reduced the variety of films released each year?

2. Go back and reread the Genre section and then list the last ten films that you have watched, classifying them into genres. What genre did you watch the most? What does this say about you?

3. Do you judge movies by their pace? Do you prefer fast- or slow-moving films? Chris Driver sees Kubrick's long, slow-moving shots as a positive. Do you? Driver calls *2001* a classic. Do you think its style or pace has affected or even helped create this film's status? If you haven't seen *2001*, focus on a film that used pacing as a prominent feature.

collaborations in the pop culture zone

1. Discuss what films have had the greatest impact on each of you as a viewer. Make a list of at least ten of them and briefly describe how each film affected specific viewers. Compare your list with your group and/or the class.

2. Discuss why movie stars become cultural icons. Think of movie stars from the Hollywood studio era (Bette Davis, Spencer Tracy, Clark Gable, Humphrey Bogart) and stars of more recent years (Tom Hanks, Will Smith, Meg Ryan, John Travolta, Scarlett Johansson, Halle Berry, Brad Pitt, Harrison Ford, Julia Roberts). What do they tell us about American culture? How do they function as symbols? Share your thoughts with your group and/or the class.

3. Form a group and examine and discuss the movie ads in a newspaper, magazine, or website. Think of various categories that the ads could be put in according to movie genre or method of composition. Write a description of the traits of each category. Try to draw some conclusions about the nature of movie advertising.

4. Form a small group and have each member make a list of the first movies he or she remembers seeing. Compare lists. Try to remember whom you saw the films with and what memories and emotions they bring to mind. Draw some conclusions from your discussion about how movies play a role in our development in early life.

start writing essays about films

Reviews or Review Essays

1. Using a film you watched for class or one that you chose on your own, write a film review. Before you get started, though, look at film reviews in different formats and in different publications (for instance, check out reviews for the same film in different magazines or online sites). Choose a specific audience and place of publication before you start writing your film review.

2. Write two film reviews of the same film, one that is slanted in a positive or negative way and one that is more balanced. Be sure to change the organization, the supporting examples, and the language used as you develop these different reviews of the same film.

3. Choose a film that triggers strong emotion in some viewers, such as *The Passion of the Christ*, *The Shawshank Redemption*, or *Bowling for Columbine*. Write a review that is specifically geared toward those viewers who normally would not want to see the film.

Reflection or Response Essays

1. In summer 2006, *Entertainment Weekly* ranked what their writers believe are the top ten high school movies of all time (see the list). If you had to choose one high school film to help describe your time in high school, which film would it be? You can use one of the top ten *EW* films listed or any other film of your choice. Reflect on why the film represents your high school experience, including your thoughts about characters, scenes, storylines, and so on.

The Breakfast Club (1985)	*American Graffiti* (1973)
Fast Times at Ridgemont High (1982)	*Clueless* (1995)
Dazed & Confused (1993)	*Boyz N the Hood* (1991)
Rebel Without a Cause (1955)	*Election* (1999)
Heathers (1989)	*Ferris Bueller's Day Off* (1986)

2. In their essay on *Malcolm X*, Lee and Wiley focus on a time when film and other events in and around Spike Lee's life came together to create an impression of that time. Choose a film that you saw at an important time of your life, and reflect on how the film and the events in and around the film and your life came together to create an important memory.

3. Many times, we see bits and pieces of ourselves in film characters. Choose a character from a recent film who represents part or all of your own personal character. Reflect on how the film character's presence, language use, actions, or storyline echo your own character. Check with your instructor for instructions about using more than just written text for this essay; if you get the go-ahead, experiment with using visuals from the film and your life to support your reflection.

4. Make a list of your favorite films. Which film genre is represented the most? Explore why you watch or enjoy one genre more than others, and write an essay in which you reflect on what it is about this genre that draws you in and why you think you are so attracted to this type of film. Consider using visuals to support your choices.

Analysis Essays

1. Choose a character from a film and write a profile of that character. Your general purpose is to inform the audience about this character and his or her role in the movie; however, your opinion will be presented in the details you choose to include. Use the strategies you have learned to explain this character's significance in the film, and consider using visuals to support this impression.

2. Think about a film you've seen recently. What genre was it? How do you know? Does it follow the genre conventions that are familiar to you? Does it play with or change any of these conventions? What is the result? Do you think this was the director's original intent? How do genre conventions add to or detract from the viewing experience with this film?

3. In this chapter, you read three reviews for *Fahrenheit 9/11*, all of which focused on different aspects of the documentary. Choose a recent film that you have seen and find at least ten reviews for it, including fan reviews posted online and reviews published in more traditional arenas, such as *The Washington Post* or the *Chicago Tribune*. Analyze the different reviews by looking at the authors' reactions to the film, their use of language, their attention to their audience, and their use of effective supporting examples. Write an essay

that divides the reviews you found into different categories (for example, positive vs. negative vs. balanced), explain how you divided the reviews, and support your categories by providing specific examples. Check with your instructor about experimenting with text placement and using visuals in your paper.

4. View a film like *Blade Runner*, which can be seen in several different versions: the original theater version, the director's cut on DVD, the edited television version. Compare and contrast these different versions. What specific changes have been made? What do viewers gain or lose as they move from one version to another? How do the changes affect how the characters are viewed or how the theme is revealed? Which version do you prefer and why? Consider using visuals to support some of the points you make.

Synthesis Essays

1. Marketing surveys show that R-rated movies are likely to draw the largest audiences. Why do you think this is? What does it say about the rating system on movie production? Do you think marketing pressures encourage filmmakers to insert more violence and sex in these films to ensure that the movies receive an R rating? If you were a marketing manager whose major concern was making money, what would you tell moviemakers and why? Consider looking at and using film advertisements (posters, online ads, radio/TV ads) as textual and visual support.

2. Look at some movie posters, ads, or CD soundtrack covers, and write an essay in which you examine the advertising strategies used to sell movies and music. How do they entice consumers to take an interest in their form of expression? How do movies and music overlap? Consider looking at and using film advertisements (posters, online ads, radio/TV ads) as textual and visual support.

3. Write an essay in which you consider and explore the reasons that horror films (*Friday the 13th, Halloween, The Texas Chainsaw Massacre, Scream, Saw, Hostel*) are so popular among teens or another group of viewers.

4. Hollywood continues to remake films or to create films based on TV shows at an astounding rate. Investigate films that have been remade for various reasons: updating the time period, changing the story ending, converting the story from TV to film, changing gender, or changing race. Argue whether or not remakes are a valuable part of our culture. Check this list for some originals and remakes to get you started on your search.

Original	Remake
Guess Who's Coming to Dinner (1967)	*Guess Who* (2005)
Here Comes Mr. Jordan (1941)	*Heaven Can Wait* (1978); *Down to Earth* (2001)
Last Holiday (1950)	*Last Holiday* (2006)
Stepford Wives (1975)	*Stepford Wives* (2004)
Charlie's Angels (1976–1981 TV show)	*Charlie's Angels* (2000)
Firefly (2002–2004 TV show)	*Serenity* (2005)

5. In summer 2006, *Entertainment Weekly* chose the top ten films about high school. Create your own top ten list on a theme of your choice and then explain your choices in an essay that provides reasons and examples that support your list.

6. The following chart compares films that were nominated for awards and those that became blockbusters in the same year. Write an essay that investigates why award-nominated films do not usually become blockbusters. Be sure to support your argument(s) with specific data or examples.

AWARD YEAR	ACADEMY AWARD NOMINATED FILMS	TOP GROSSING FILMS (in parentheses: rank for top-grossing films of all time)
2005	★ *Crash*	*Star Wars: Episode III—Revenge of the Sith* (7)
	Brokeback Mountain	*The Chronicles of Narnia: The Lion, the Witch, and the Wardrobe* (23)
	Capote	*Harry Potter and the Goblet of Fire* (25)
	Good Night, and Good Luck	*War of the Worlds* (44)
	Munich	*King Kong* (51)
2000	★ *Gladiator*	*How the Grinch Stole Christmas* (32)
	Chocolat	*Cast Away* (45)
	Crouching Tiger, Hidden Dragon	*Mission: Impossible 2* (55)
	Erin Brockovich	*Gladiator* (73)
	Traffic	*What Women Want* (82)
1995	★ *Braveheart*	*Toy Story* (75)
	Apollo 13	*Batman Forever* (79)
	Babe	*Apollo 13* (98)
	The Postman	*Pocahontas* (152)
	Sense and Sensibility	*Ace Ventura: When Nature Calls* (279)
1990	★ *Dances with Wolves*	*Home Alone* (26)
	Awakenings	*Ghost* (52)
	Ghost	*Dances with Wolves* (78)
	The Godfather, Part III	*Pretty Woman* (90)
	GoodFellas	*Teenage Mutant Ninja Turtles* (174)
1985	★ *Out of Africa*	*Back to the Future* (59)
	The Color Purple	*Rambo: First Blood Part 2* (138)
	Kiss of the Spider Woman	*Rocky IV* (196)
	Prizzi's Honor	*The Color Purple*
	Witness	*Out of Africa*
1980	★ *Ordinary People*	*Star Wars: Episode V—The Empire Strikes Back* (24)
	Coal Miner's Daughter	*9 to 5* (305)
	The Elephant Man	*Stir Crazy* (317)
	Raging Bull	*Airplane*
	Tess	*Any Which Way You Can*
1975	★ *One Flew over the Cuckoo's Nest*	*Jaws* (33)
	Barry Lyndon	*One Flew Over the Cuckoo's Nest* (275)
	Dog Day Afternoon	*The Rocky Horror Picture Show* (258)
	Jaws	*Shampoo*
	Nashville	*Dog Day Afternoon*
1970	★ *Patton*	*Love Story*
	Airport	*Airport*
	Five Easy Pieces	*M*A*S*H*
	Love Story	*Patton*
	*M*A*S*H*	*The Aristocats*

★ Winner

FOR FURTHER READING

Cavallero, Jonathan J. "Gangsters, Fessos, Tricksters, and Sopranos: The Historical Roots of Italian American Stereotype Anxiety." *JPF&T: Journal of Popular Film and Television* 32 (2004): 50–63.

Clover, Carol J. *Men, Women, and Chain Saws: Gender in the Modern Horror Film*. Princeton, NJ: Princeton UP, 1992.

Dick, Bernard F. *Anatomy of Film*. 5th ed. Boston: Bedford/St. Martin's, 2005.

Documentary Films. <http://www.documentaryfilms.net>.

Jenkins, Henry. *Confessions of an Aca-Fan: The Official Weblog of Henry Jenkins*. <http://www.henryjenkins.org>.

———. *Convergence Culture: Where Old and New Media Collide*. New York: NYUP, 2006.

Kaveney, Roz. *Teen Dreams: Reading Teen Films and Television from* Heathers *to* Veronica Mars. London: I. B. Tauris, 2006.

Lee, Spike. *Spike Lee's Gotta Have It: Inside Guerrilla Filmmaking*. New York: Fireside/Simon & Schuster, 1988.

Maltin, Leonard. *The Disney Films*. 4th ed. New York: Disney Editions, 2000.

Moscowitz, John E. *Critical Approaches to Writing About Film*. 2nd ed. Boston: Pearson, 2006.

Variety. <http://www.variety.com>.

writing about groups, spaces, and places

"In light of these events, America is cancelled. Citizens are asked to choose between Canada and Mexico by 4:00 p.m. tomorrow."

—From *Saturday Night Live*, "Weekend Update"

1 Which of these cultures does not celebrate using tea ceremonies?

    a. Southern U.S. culture
    b. British culture
    c. Asian culture
    d. Cuban culture

TEST YOUR POP CULTURE IQ: GROUPS, SPACES, AND PLACES

2 When David Duke ran for a Louisiana Senate seat in 1991, what association organized a voter turnout that aided in his defeat?

    a. The National Association for the Advancement of Colored People (NAACP)
    b. The Congressional Black Caucus Foundation
    c. Alpha Kappa Alpha and Alpha Kappa Psi
    d. The American Civil Liberties Union (ACLU)

3 Frank Lloyd Wright designed what New York City museum?

    a. The Museum of Modern Art
    b. The Museum of Natural History
    c. The Guggenheim Museum
    d. The Metropolitan Museum of Art

© Goodshot/Jupiter Images

4 Which of these is not a staple of indie fashion?

    a. Adidas track suits
    b. Argyle
    c. Horn-rimmed glasses
    d. Punk-influenced designs

5 Who told more than 900 of his religious followers to drink a cherry-flavored, cyanide-laced fruit drink and murdered those who refused in what was considered one of the largest mass suicides in history?

    a. David Koresh
    b. Marshall Herff Applewhite
    c. Jim Jones
    d. Jose Luis de Jesus Miranda

Chapter opener photo © Robert King/Newsmakers/Getty Images

6 What organization has the purpose: "to take action to bring women into full participation in the mainstream of American society now, exercising all privileges and responsibilities thereof in truly equal partnership with men"?

    a. The Gay and Lesbian Alliance Against Defamation (GLAAD)
    b. The National Organization for Women (NOW)
    c. The National Women's Studies Association (NWSA)
    d. The American Civil Liberties Union (ACLU)

7 Whose New York City loft, known as The Factory, became a hangout for artists, musicians, models, and people famous for being famous?

    a. Lou Reed
    b. Keith Haring
    c. Andy Warhol
    d. Edie Sedgwick

8 What is highly regulated in Yellowstone National Park because it produces thirty-six times more carbon monoxide and ninety-eight times more hydrocarbons than a car?

    a. Snowmobiles
    b. Personal aircraft
    c. SUVs
    d. Four-wheelers

9 Which of these does the Federal Communications Commission (FCC) not regulate?

    a. "Radio Free" nonprofit stations
    b. Local access community television
    c. Satellite radio (XM, Sirius)
    d. None of the above

10 Who was the first female U.S. Supreme Court justice?

    a. Sandra Day O'Connor
    b. Ruth Bader Ginsberg
    c. Evelyn Baker Lang
    d. Beverley McLachlin

© photolibrary.com pty ltd/Index Open

ANSWERS

1 *d. Cuban culture*   2 *a. The National Association for the Advancement of Colored People (NAACP)*   3 *c. The Guggenheim Museum*   4 *b. Argyle*   5 *c. Jim Jones*   6 *b. The National Organization for Women*   7 *c. Andy Warhol*
8 *a. Snowmobiles*   9 *d. None of the above*   10 *a. Sandra Day O'Connor*

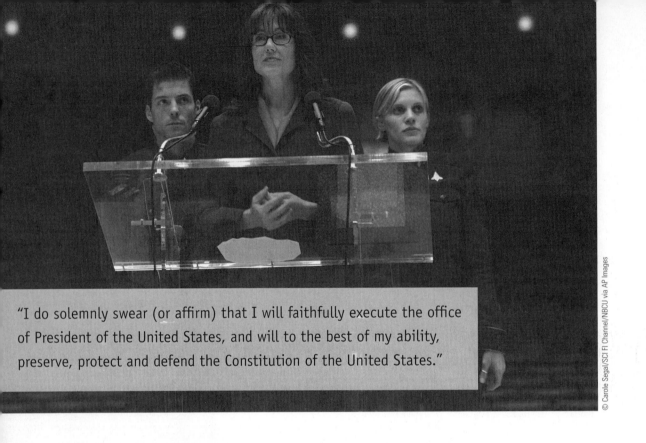

"I do solemnly swear (or affirm) that I will faithfully execute the office of President of the United States, and will to the best of my ability, preserve, protect and defend the Constitution of the United States."

© Carole Segal/SCI FI Channel/NBCU via AP Images

YOU AND GROUPS, SPACES, AND PLACES

Every four years, with hand on the Bible, the U.S. president repeats this pledge after the chief justice of the Supreme Court. The politician who takes this oath is as much a part of American popular culture as Kanye West or the actors on *Law & Order*. The character of the U.S. president is even a popular one on television shows and in films, such as Mary McDonnell's President Laura Roslin on *Battlestar Galactica* (in the above photo) or Bill Pullman's President Thomas J. Whitmore in *Independence Day*. Even so, sometimes it is hard to imagine the extensive role that politics, cultural groups, and our environment play in our pop culture.

Groups and subcultures often represent us and even help us form identities. You are a college student. You are a son or daughter, perhaps a parent or grandparent. You may be a computer science major, a future teacher, or a CEO in training. Perhaps you are working your way through college as a tutor, a waitress, or a computer salesperson. You may be a member of a campus social organization, an intramural sports team, or a religious group. Perhaps you belong to a gym or country club. You might be a Republican, Democrat, Independent, or a member of the Green Party. All of these associations can change the way you view popular culture and the way you are viewed as a potential consumer of pop culture.

Groups and associations often make the news for lobbying the government, filing legislation to promote their issues, or for holding rallies or conferences; however, their role in popular culture is much larger. These organizations often form culture or help it change. For example, Scientology, a religion formed during the last half of the twentieth century, has evolved from a self-help strategy to being known as the religion of celebrities. From members Tom Cruise and John Travolta to its controversial representation on *South Park*, Scientology is both participating in and creating pop culture. Even organizations such as the Popular Culture Association (PCA), whose job is to study the effects and critical implications of pop culture, play a role in validating certain forms of pop culture. For example, at the 2007 Popular Culture Association conference in Boston, nine panel presentations included a discussion of Stephen King's popular fiction. Of course, King is a popular figure, but his repeated inclusion in the program will help to increase the study of his importance as a writer.

Spaces, large areas of literal or figurative geography, and places, more specific locations in a space, are also included in this chapter. Broadly defined, this could include anything as private as your own dorm room or bedroom to public spaces like your favorite store, the Empire State Building, or the state of Texas. The kind of popular culture you experience is often directly related to your environment. For example, in a theater, you will experience films, plays, food, advertisements, and maybe even arcade games. In the Gaslamp Quarter of San Diego, you will experience restaurants, bars, shopping, and art galleries. In a convenience mart, you might see magazine covers, food and cola packaging, lottery ticket sales, and cheap souvenirs. Popular culture can also create environments; Disneyland, for example, is a creation of popular culture. If Disney's films and television series were not popular, the theme park would probably not exist.

The readings and writing suggestions in this chapter should encourage you to explore your identity and your environment. They will also help you to consider economics, class, gender, race, and politics when you think about your own individuality, the groups or subcultures you belong to, and your various daily surroundings.

WHY WRITE ABOUT GROUPS, SPACES, AND PLACES?

Writing about groups, spaces, and places should help you discover new things about yourself and your environment; however, personal insight is not the only reason to write about these subjects. If you are a member of a group or association, you may choose to write about your organization to promote your agenda, to debate your competitors, or to correct misconceptions. For example, a student who is a member of Greenpeace may choose to write a rationale for membership based on the positive activities of the organization rather than the ecoterrorism for which they are most often identified. Or a member of People for the Ethical Treatment of Animals (PETA) may use writing to convince others to boycott fur. You might also research an organization or environment that you are not a part of to learn about a different culture. Perhaps you could interview someone from your hometown who is a couple of generations older than you about the popular hangouts from his or her teen years.

You may also see groups or environments of which you are a part from a more critical viewpoint by writing about them. This critical perspective may help you reconsider your own attachments and the choices you make in life.

grapplingwithideas

- Make a list of the ways you are identified by those around you. What labels are assigned to you? Are you an aunt? A Christian? A liberal? A football player? A princess? A snob? A guitar player? A hipster?

- Make a list of as many labels as you can give yourself.

- Now, choose three of these labels to write a detailed description of yourself. Is it accurate?

- Can you adequately describe yourself through these labels?

- Where did you hang out in high school? Where did you go in the afternoons?
- Which of your friends had open homes where friends were invited in? Which friends did not?
- Where do you hang out now? How does your environment differ from your high school choices? Are you as comfortable?
- Reflect on and discuss these differing environments.

PREPARING TO WRITE ABOUT GROUPS, SPACES, AND PLACES

When you get dressed each morning, you are making a choice, whether conscious or not, about how to present yourself to the world. You know that these choices send messages to those you encounter, whether it is the serious suit needed for your job or a job interview, the flirty top designed to catch someone's attention, or the rainbow jewelry meant to signal a gay or lesbian identity. These markers of present or desired subgroups can be interesting to study and useful to understand. These groups often occupy particular spaces and places, and understanding these places can lend insights to the people who inhabit them. But how do you write about groups, spaces, and places?

One key to writing in this area is to think about the group, space, or place as a text that needs to be read critically and analyzed. Places carry meanings and messages, or signs that can be interpreted and understood, or read, as we do with words on a printed page or screen. For example, when a woman goes to work out at the Curves gym, the bright colors and cartoon drawings of smiling women on the walls send a message that working out will make you happy and carefree. As with any text, you will probably need to read it more than once to really understand it. Asking questions of the text, looking for patterns in the text, examining your own biases and stereotypical thinking in connection to the text, and examining what parts of the text interest you or surprise you will all help you understand the text so you can write about it. Conversing with the text will also help; try interviewing members of a group you are fascinated by, visiting a space you want to know more about, traveling to a place of interest, or collecting artifacts that represent a group, space, or place. All of the prewriting activities discussed in Chapter 2, Writing About Popular Culture, can help you write about groups, spaces, and places, but you may find the following journalistic approach the most viable.

- *Who?* Who are the members of this organization? Who hangs out in this space? Who visits this place?

- *What?* What does this group do or believe in? What happens in this space? What draws people to this place?

- *When?* When was this association formed? When do people gather in this space? When is or was this place popular?

- *Where?* Where does this group meet? Where is this space located? Where is this place located on a map?

- *Why?* Why are people drawn to this group? Why is this space important to others? Why is this place such a draw for tourists?

- *How?* How does this group communicate with its members? How is this space arranged? How is this place connected to a particular culture or way of life?

Asking questions like these should get you started on your journey of exploration and understanding.

Terms to Know

As you explore groups, spaces, and places, there are a few terms you should be aware of, terms that may be useful as you conduct your research or begin your writing.

- **Artifact:** An object, usually of physical substance, that represents or is part of a group of people or a culture, such as a skateboard or a game piece.

- **Culture:** The defining characteristics of a group of people who have connections to each other and share a common language or vocabulary, including behaviors, rules, and rituals—for example, fall rush, with all of its attendant rules and traditions, is part of fraternity and sorority culture.

- **Emic:** This is when the researcher or writer is an insider, a member of the culture or group under study.

- **Ethnography:** The study of people or cultures.

- **Etic:** This is when the researcher or writer is an outsider, not a member of the culture or group under study.

- **Informant:** A person who shares information about his or her culture with a researcher.

- **Reflexivity:** The process of self-study and reflection that comes about after studying others.

Researching and Documenting

Any of the essay types in this textbook can be written without outside research, but often, research will help you expand your topic, support your points, or illustrate to your audience that you are a credible authority on your topic. Research can also help when you are not able to answer your research question on your own.

Areas of research may include the following:

- The history of an organization or a space

- A celebrity's support of an organization

- The culture represented by an association or environment

- The perception of an association or environment in popular culture

- The economic impact of an association or environment

- The intended audience for an organization or environment

- The history or evolution of an ideology, scene, or culture

- An individual's experience with a particular group or place

The event, activity, television broadcast, or podcast, as well as the actual members of a group or association, are your primary, or original, sources; likewise, the actual physical space, even if it is virtual, is a primary source, but your research may lead you to a variety of other primary and secondary sources as well. As discussed in Chapters 2 and 11, secondary sources are limited only by what has actually been published and by your imagination. You may find books, articles, and websites from friends, television, or your own library, but make sure you check out your school's holdings as well as the electronic databases available through your school or public libraries, such as InfoTrac College Edition, LexisNexis, or JSTOR. When researching groups, spaces, and places, you should pay special attention to indexes and databases connected to the social sciences, particularly sociology, anthropology, and geography.

You may have to research nontraditional sources for current and relevant information about groups, spaces, and places. In fact, many groups are located, or at least meet, online, and the space you want to investigate may be as diverse as the local park or shopping mall. When using an Internet source, remember to evaluate the site and its purpose before you trust it as a reliable resource. Check out the following sites to get you started:

American Institute of Philanthropy	http://www.charitywatch.org
Genealogy.com	http://www.genealogy.com
Google Earth	http://www.earth.google.com
History of Cartography	http://www.maphistory.info
iVillage	http://www.ivillage.com
Lonely Planet	http://www.lonelyplanet.com
Mapquest	http://www.mapquest.com
Project for Public Spaces	http://www.pps.org
Project Vote Smart	http://www.vote-smart.org
Writers Write	http://www.writerswrite.com

When writing about groups, spaces, or places, you may find it useful to conduct your own primary research. For example, to write about a particular subculture or association, you may want to talk to members of the group through interviews or surveys, even comparing the stories of different informants. Likewise, you can observe a group in its meeting space, natural habitat, or other key location to see how members act, the language or words they use, and how they dress or represent themselves. You can also study the documents of a particular group, such as brochures, websites, and letters, for insight into how the group presents itself or interacts with others. As with more traditional research, you will want to keep accurate records of who you talk to, when you talk to them, or when you conduct observations, as well as precise records of what is said.

One tool you may find useful is the double-entry notebook or log. The idea is to take your interview and observation notes on one side or half of the page while leaving space to go back and remark on or respond to your entries on the other side. The first entry represents the language of your informants, notes on your observations, or maps of the places you visit. The second entry represents your personal thoughts about what you have recorded, including questions, your readings of the text, the messages presented by the group, space, or place, your conclusions about what you are seeing and hearing, and your working thesis.

Remember, all sources must be listed on a Works Cited page, so you should write down the information (that is, web addresses, authors' names, where you found the source, and the date of publication) for your in-text citations and the bibliography. Always know

Think of a space or place that has lots of rules, perhaps a school or the movie theater.

- Who created these rules? What purpose do these rules serve? Are they designed to protect? To control? What happens when someone breaks or trespasses the rules?

- If you were in charge of the space, would you change the rules? If yes, in what ways? If no, why would you keep the rules?

where you found your information and how to get back to it. Also, be sure to record names and dates of interviews for your Works Cited. Chapter 11 will remind you of specific guidelines, and the Works Cited pages at the ends of chapter readings can provide examples of citations.

WRITING ABOUT GROUPS, SPACES, AND PLACES

Groups, spaces, and places are very broad fields and can be written about in a variety of ways. You may want to investigate a group on campus you have thought about joining or one you are already a part of; you may even want to review it for your classmates so they can check it out, too. A place that was important to your family or your favorite hangout in high school may be worth reflecting on or analyzing. You may be interested in finding out about a new city or the amusement park you want to visit on vacation this summer. Your purposes, or your assignment, will lead you to a variety of rhetorical choices; this chapter will continue to focus on reviews, reflection or response essays, analysis essays, or a combination of these with synthesis essays.

Reviews or Review Essays

A review is a thorough assessment of a particular group, space, or place that often expresses an opinion or evaluation. For example, you might review your school's baseball team and make a prediction about how well they will perform in the upcoming season, or you may want to review the new movie theater that just opened up. The group, space, or place that is the subject of your review essay might be completely new or unfamiliar to your reader, so you will want to give some description of the group or place, including its location. Your review may even help your audience decide whether or not to visit a place or join a group. As you are giving a judgment of the group, space, or place, you will want to provide enough information and examples to support your opinion and illustrate that you are indeed an authority on the subject. Such reviews can be found in local, national, and international magazines and newspapers as well as brochures and websites. In fact, many publications have columns and regular writers devoted to such reviews, such as the travel section in many magazines or the restaurant review column in your local newspaper.

A review essay of a group, space, or place will usually address three or four important aspects of the topic. Your overall evaluation of the group, space, or place is usually phrased as the thesis of the essay and may come at the beginning or end of the essay, or it may be implied. The group review essay often gives a brief description of the group—the people who make up the group, what brings them together or defines them, what activities the group members sponsor or participate in. The space or place review essay usually begins with description as well. It defines the space and the purpose it serves, and it may explain how to get to the location or what it does; it will probably describe what it looks like and how it

keyquestions

Key Questions for a Group/ Association Review Essay

- Have you provided a brief summary of the group's purpose or the people who make up the group?
- Have you mentioned specific elements of the group's activities that support your judgment?
- Have you defined yourself as a credible source by writing clearly and giving support for your arguments?
- Have you qualified your judgment with both positive and negative aspects of the association or the association's activities?
- Have you begun the review with an attention-grabbing opening? Have you concluded it with a final evaluation of the group?
- Did you write in present tense for active organizations but in past tense for those that no longer exist?

keyquestions

Key Questions for a Space/Place Review Essay

- Have you clearly indicated your judgment of the environment's quality, comfort, or purpose?
- Have you provided a brief example of your experience in or with the environment?
- Have you mentioned specific elements that support your judgment? Have you described these quickly and vividly, using concrete language and metaphors?
- Have you defined yourself as a credible source by writing clearly and giving support for your arguments?
- Have you qualified your judgment with both positive and negative aspects of the environment?
- Have you begun the review with an attention-grabbing opening? Have you concluded it with a striking sentence?
- Did you write in present tense for environments that still exist but in past tense for those that no longer exist?

operates as well. The space or place review essay may also tie a place to a particular purpose or group of people—perhaps the audience or potential attendees for the location.

As with anything in life, groups, spaces, or places may have both positive and negative elements, so it is important to present a balanced picture of the topic being reviewed. Balanced reviews are much more believable and make you, as the writer, more credible. Of course, some reviews are slanted in one direction. A group that is trying to recruit new members is much more likely to present only the good side of the organization. The tourist bureau for a given place is going to present the best possible picture as it works to entice vacationers to visit or asks travel agents to represent it. You might also compare groups or places that share similarities or that are after the same people. You may even write a review that ranks spaces, such as the top ten websites for bloggers or the top ten zoos in the United States.

Reflection or Response Essays

Thinking about a group you once belonged to or a place you used to visit may bring up thoughts about your own behavior or identity. Considering a group you would like to be a part of may lead you to reflect on what is important to you and how you can achieve your goals. In these instances, thinking about a group, space, or place becomes a starting point for your reflection or response essay or a discussion of your own feelings in connection to the text of the group, space, or place. This reflection or response essay will probably include some reference to specific elements of the group, space, or place, but you will spend most of your essay relating your own thoughts or responses that have arisen from critically engaging with the group, space, or place. This essay will often resemble personal or narrative writing.

You can begin your reflection or response essay by considering what aspects of the group, space, or place make you think, reflect, ask questions, feel pleasure, or get angry. Do you agree with this group's code of conduct or purposes? Does this place bring back good memories or bad ones? Can you relate to the members of this association? Why do you like to hang out in this place? Why do you refuse to enter this space? After thinking about your personal reaction, you can decide what you would like to share with your audience and the best way to share this information. These decisions will then lead you to a working thesis that can guide the rest of your essay and help you connect your reflection or response to the actual group, space, or place.

Analysis Essays

The analysis essay is more in depth than the review essay and more formal than the reflection or response essay. The analysis essay usually makes a critical judgment about a particular group, space, or place or perhaps a series or combination of several groups, spaces, and places. It can be more argumentative and perhaps even persuasive—for example, asking the audience to rethink a group, try out a space, or vote to protect a place. The analysis essay often includes descriptions of the group, space, or place or perhaps quotes from informants; these references are extensive and are accompanied by an explanation of their significance. Although this explanation may reflect your personal opinion or interpretation of the group, space, or place, it may also be supported by evidence from outside sources.

To write an analysis essay, you can start with your thoughts about the group, space, or place—the idea you want to share with your readers. Then you will use this idea to develop a working thesis that will be either stated or implied in your essay and will guide the points you make as you write. You will want to support this thesis with examples from or about the group, space, or place, as well as any outside research you have done. Because you are writing about popular groups, spaces, or places, you may also include relevant maps, diagrams, or photos that serve as support; you will also want to explain the significance of these references. With the analysis essay, you should still remember that there may be many valid interpretations, or readings, of the group, space, or place you are examining. The members of your audience may have had different experiences with the group, space, or place you are analyzing. You will want to support your own interpretation with specific details about the group, space, or place and its people, purposes, language, artifacts, or actions.

Synthesis Essays

Sometimes, the best rhetorical approach to your topic is a mixture of approaches. You may discuss your own experiences as a member of a choir when you review the local community chorus. Perhaps your analysis of bowling alleys and the role they play for working-class families will also include a review of the two bowling alleys in town. Perhaps an interview with a group informant will lead you to reflect on your own membership in a similar or contrasting group. As you can tell, a synthesis essay combines two or more rhetorical approaches to create the best possible essay for your audience regardless of the topic or argument. If you have been given a specific class assignment, be sure to look closely at the assignment to see if the rhetorical approach has been assigned or if a synthesis essays fits within the parameters of the assignment. You may find it helpful to look over the key questions for each of the types of writing you have decided to use in your essay.

keyquestions

Key Questions for a Reflection or Response Essay

- Have you clearly indicated how you used the group or environment as a springboard for your thesis?
- Have you expressed your personal response to one aspect of the association or space?
- Did you include minimal summary?
- Does your introduction direct your audience into your response?
- Does your concluding paragraph include some reflection on both the organization or environment and your response?
- Are your essay's intentions clear?

Key Questions for an Analysis Essay

- Do you have a clearly stated or implied thesis that is guiding your analysis?
- Do you have a series of reasons or examples supporting the thesis? Are these arranged in a logical and convincing order?
- Are your supporting reasons backed up? Do you provide specific evidence and examples from the group, space, or place for each reason you offer?
- Does your introduction orient your reader to the direction of your argument?
- Does your concluding paragraph reiterate your thesis and leave your reader with something to think about in regard to the group, space, or place you are writing about?

SAMPLE ANNOTATED ESSAY

CONSIDERING IDEAS

1. When you visit a new town, whether for business or pleasure, how do you decide which restaurants to try?

2. Do you read reviews online or in the local paper? Do you ask others who have visited the locale? Do you ask employees at your hotel or perhaps the bus or taxi driver?

3. Do you make recommendations to your friends when you visit a new eatery in town?

Nika Hazelton *was the author of numerous cookbooks.* The International Cookbook, *written in 1967, became a standard for anyone who was serious about the art of cooking. Her bimonthly column in* National Review *titled "Delectations" was unsurpassed in its popularity before her death in 1992. She also wrote her autobiography entitled* Ups and Downs: Memoirs of Another Time. *"You're the Tops" was a 1978 review in* National Review.

YOU'RE THE TOPS

Nika Hazelton

Begins with the author's judgment of her experience.

Includes the name of the specific restaurant, the location, and the name and qualifications of the designer in the introduction.

Recently, I had an outstanding dinner in an extraordinary restaurant—I use both adjectives deliberately. The place is The Cellar in the Sky, part of the restaurant complex on the ground and top floors (and some intermediate floors) of the World Trade Center 1 Tower in New York. When the twin towers of the Trade Center were built, the problem of how to feed the multitudes who'd be working there was an urgent one. The task of solving the problem fell to Joe Baum, without doubt the most influential restaurateur in the United States and a genius in his field—again I use the words deliberately. He was singlehandedly responsible for the vast restaurant revolution of the late Fifties, when he changed what had been the only standard for restaurant elegance—French, with plush banquettes, etc. He created such places as The Four Seasons, The Forum,

La Fonda del Sol, and the Brasserie, unforgettable for their food and surroundings: how I remember the collection of Mexican folk art in La Fonda, museum pieces all. Happily, The Four Seasons, though now in other hands, is carried on in the same spirit in which it was created.

Windows on the World, the collective name of the restaurants on the 107th floor of the building, occupy about one acre of the floor space swathed in glass and with the most spectacular view in New York. The Statue of Liberty is but a toy way down below, the city's skyline an airplane photograph, and, on a clear day, you can see fifty miles. In a snow storm, or when thick clouds swirl by, you get an even more extraordinary feeling of being in space. Starting with this unequaled view, Joe Baum has architecturally so arranged his restaurants that every single diner in the various restaurants, such as the Hors d'Oeuvrerie, the City Lights Bar, and The Restaurant, shares the view, thanks to the terraced tables. I'll write about these restaurants and the ground floor establishment, The Market Place, some other time, because they are all differently priced and wonderfully out of the ordinary (you can also have private dining rooms with the same view).

Today I want to report on The Cellar in the Sky, an inner room off a passage lit by the tall windows of the top floor, whose glass walls house wine stacks stocked with bottles through which comes a dappled light. The place has an intimate, club-like air, with comfortable tables and chairs, Rosenthal china, and various wine glasses. The room seats only 35 people, and the attentive staff is supervised by cellarmaster Kevin Zraly and Pepe Enriquez, the maître d'. Where the Cellar is different from other restaurants is that it offers a *prix fixe* dinner served at a single sitting, whose $45 tab includes five outstanding wines, around which the seven courses are designed. Considering the food and the wine, which are liberally poured, this is a very good deal indeed. Our dinner started with a pale fino sherry from Wisdom and Warter, drawn no less from a 1908 solera and wonderful of its kind; it retails for around $30 a bottle. It was served with a mashed eggplant appetizer seasoned with tahini, olive oil, and lemon juice, and then whipped, which made it deliciously

> Details in this paragraph emphasize the various environments of the World Trade Center's many restaurants.

> Details in this paragraph specifically describe the environment of The Cellar in the Sky.

> Describes the menu and price of this dining experience, emphasizing its uniqueness.

light and creamy. The sherry was suitably continued for a double consommé with field mushrooms and the chicken quenelles that followed. A chilled Muscadet Marquis de Goulaine Magnum 1976 was poured with an elegant seafood flan of scallops, lobster, shrimp, and mussels in a custard flavored with a reduction of seafood essences, and served with a truffle and lobster sauce. For our edification, we tasted an Eltviller Sonnenberg Kabinett Schloss Eltz 1975 along with the Muscadet, an interesting comparison with that course; I preferred the Muscadet, but others like the Rhenish wine better.

Freemark Abbey is a small Napa Valley winery about whose magnificent vines I have written before in this column. Their 1973 Cabernet Sauvignon, a big, round wine with a fine nose, came with roast lamb, a saddle stuffed with a forcemeat of lamb and rosemary and a bit of thyme, and a rack. We were served portions of both rack and saddle, pink and tender meat than which I have never had better. In fact, it was extraordinary meat, both in quality and cooking. Following the entree was a crisp and cooling salad of arugula and red leaf lettuce dressed with walnut oil, vinegar, mustard, chives, thyme, and tarragon. From here we went into a platter of cheeses, Roquefort, Corolle, and the Italian Fontina, all in prime condition. I did not know the Corolle, shaped in a ring, with an outer part softer than the center, and I liked it very much. The wine that was served with the cheese can only be described as glorious: a 1966 Chateau Beychevelle, a St. Julien Bordeaux, noted for its breeding, delicacy and finesse—all of this in an outstanding vintage year. Chateau Beychevelle is an actual, and very picturesque, chateau, dating from 1757, which overlooks the estuary of the Gironde and was once owned by the Grand Admiral of the French Fleet, the Duke of Epernon. The name is said to have come from the French "baisse viole" or "lower sail," a gesture of tribute to the Duke. The wine is classified as a fourth growth, but such is its quality that it now brings higher prices than many second growths; it too was poured liberally.

- Not on the menu were two very good California Cabernet Sauvignons, a Chappellet 1973 and a Robert Mondavi 1973, which cellarmaster Zraly, who is young, and

Wines and foods are reviewed with ingredients, preparation style, and pairings noted to finish the description of the article. The author also mentions that a wine was offered that was not included on the menu.

as polite as he is knowledgeable (and this far beyond his years), poured us as a treat: the French wine was far more elegant and complex. The dinner ended with a Chocolate Strawberry Tart of chocolate pastry, bavarian cream, chocolate genoise, and fresh strawberries, prettied with a ribbon of soft chocolate and tied with a chocolate bow. Its mate was an excellent Niersteiner Auglanger Auslese 1976, one of the great names in German wines from the Rhine south of Mainz. The wine had fine fruit, fragrance, and balance, but I think the dessert was too much for it. All in all, quite a meal, generous both in food and wines, and charmingly served. A guitarist in the back plays soothing—mainly classical—music which contributes to the festive feeling of the place; dining there is indeed an occasion.

As I said, there is just one sitting at 7:30. Reservations are necessary and you can check the menu and the wines, which change weekly or so, by phone. The number is (212) 938-1111.

Remarks on the one negative aspect of the experience.

Author restates overall judgment of the restaurant's service and quality.

Conclusion includes the hours, contact information, and reservation request.

DECODING THE TEXT

1. Twice Hazelton says, "and I use both adjectives deliberately." Why does she call attention to this use of adjectives? Why is, or isn't, it necessary?

2. What is the author's overall opinion of the restaurant The Cellar in the Sky? What leads you to this conclusion?

3. She makes several references to other columns she has written and even to ones she will write in the future. Do these references make you want to read any more of her reviews?

CONNECTING TO YOUR CULTURE

1. Have you ever partaken of a meal like the one Hazelton describes in her review? If yes, what was your experience like? If no, would you like to?

2. How does it affect you as a reader to read a review of a restaurant that was located in the World Trade Center and now no longer exists?

3. Have you ever thought about the planning it takes to create a space as large as the World Trade Center, a space that employed—and needed to feed—thousands of people?

TACKLING TOPICS

1. Think about what you like to do and where you like to go on the weekends. Do you go to the same places every week? Who goes with you? What do you do there? Why do you like this space or these people? What does this hangout say about you?

2. Where is the last place you went just for fun? The last place you took a vacation? How did you find out about these places? Did you read about them before you went? What did you read? Did you talk to others about them? What did you find out? How did this information affect what you did there or when you went?

3. Where did you grow up? Would you classify the area as rural, urban, suburban, or with some other label? How did this location affect you and the choices you have made? Who were the people around you? What were your schools like? What was the shopping like? The arts? The parks? The sports? Other attractions? What did the members of this community have in common?

4. Do you consider yourself a fan of anyone or anything in particular? A sports team? A television show? A musical group? A particular hobby or pastime? What does it mean to be a fan? How are fans different from general participants or enthusiasts? What behaviors do fans exhibit that others don't?

5. When you go online, where do you spend your time? Do you go online to work or shop, to play games, or to just hang out? Do you have a MySpace or Facebook page? Do you like to visit chat rooms or instant message your friends? When you have a research project, do you go to the Internet first? Are there certain sites you visit over and over again? Do you think the Internet has expanded your space or put new limits on it?

READING SELECTIONS

As in previous chapters, the readings that follow are organized into five sections: 1970s, 1980s, 1990s, 2000s, and Across the Decades. The readings in each of the sections may have been written in that particular decade or may discuss a group, space, or place that was popular during the decade—something that still influences pop culture today. For example, in the '70s section, you will find a reminder of the disco phenomenon, which influenced music, dress, hangouts, careers, and even people's health. In the '70s, you will also find David Sedaris's reflection on vacation spots and families and how the two are intertwined. In the '80s, William Severini Kowinski takes us to the mall, and Ralph Nader and Mark Green take us into the world of Reagan-Bush politics. In the '90s, you will have the opportunity to examine black and white sororities on college campuses as well as the suburbs as William Sharpe and Leonard Wallock question suburban ideals and their representations in the media. In the '00s, you can read about the influence of NASCAR and examine who NASCAR fans are; then you can travel to the National Storytelling Festival with a visual essay by Mike Caplanis. You will also have the opportunity to travel to the Florida Keys, as we present a case study on Key West; you will be able to compare stories of Key West from a guidebook writer, a local blogger, the tourist bureau, and an academic's review of the bard of the Keys, Jimmy Buffett. In the Across the Decades section, you will be able to attend a gaming convention and meet the people who play war games for hours on end, and ride in a parade with the Motor Maids, the first female motorcycle organization devoted to owning and riding bikes.

As mentioned previously, the readings in each of the sections may present information for more than one decade because pop culture often carries across time periods and has effects for many years after events have occurred and fads have passed. The readings in this chapter are presented as examples to help you investigate, analyze, and critically respond to pop culture; however, they are also offered as samples of writing reviews, reflections or responses, analyses, and synthesis essays about groups, spaces, and places.

Reading Selections: the '70s

CONSIDERING IDEAS

1. Do you like to dance? What kind of dancing do you enjoy?

2. What kind of music do you dance to? Where do you go to dance? Who do you dance with?

3. Have you ever taken dancing lessons? At a studio? From a friend?

4. Does dancing define any part of your identity?

Janet J. Jasek *is the borrowing supervisor for Baylor University's Interlibrary Services. Jasek's book on disco, from which this excerpt is taken, includes a discotheque guide for various U.S. states, a glossary, and guides for various dances, including the Hustle and the New Yorker.*

DISCO-DANCE

An Introduction

Janet J. Jasek

Disco dancing is the latest national craze. It has been popular in New York, Chicago and on the West Coast ever since its early beginnings; before the 1970's, when informal Sock-Hops and Record Bars provided entertainment for the weekend dancers. Its national popularity was greatly intensified by the movie *Saturday Night Fever*, which inspired even the most conservative New Yorkers to hit the "Disco Scene." Since then, temperatures have been rising everywhere as discotheques have evolved to become the social gathering place for people of all ages and walks of life. Perhaps it was John Travolta's display of excellent precision on the dance floor, or, the magnetic Disco Beat that drew people to discotheques. But whatever the reason, it is obvious that there is today a world-wide disco craze sweeping over all of us.

Because of the overwhelming response to Disco, it is not unusual to find people standing patiently in line for hours, just to gain entrance to their favorite discotheque. Every weekend over 15,000 Americans visit and perform in one of the 10,000 discotheques throughout the United States. With such a powerful interest, the disco scene has developed into a gigantic, and still growing dance industry. During the past several years, the number of discotheques in the U.S. has increased by over 500% with an even greater expansion predicted during the early 1980's. As more and more discotheques enter upon the scene, a bright new architecture style is emerging, with almost every type of building imaginable being converted into refreshing, high intensity, sparkling discotheques.

The Disco Explosion has greatly rewarded the music industries which have reaped an unparalleled profit from their recent 4 billion dollar income year. Disco, today, is greater than all of Broadway, and has helped the record industry surpass even the film and cinema industry in gross sales income. Over 20 million copies of the *Saturday Night Fever* album have been sold; this is nearly three times the number of any other album ever produced (including Sinatra, the Beatles, or Elvis), making it the most popular LP in music history!

Today, the disco scene is also a powerful, creative force in the world of fashion. Already the loosely fitting Disco Dance styles are replacing the ever-popular blue jeans, and soon the common "rural-worker

"Disco-Dance: An Introduction" from DISCO LOVERS GUIDE TO DANCE by Janet J. Jasek, pp. 9–12.

image" will become an urban memory, as we witness a turn-around in fashion, because of the impact of Disco Dance on our society. With this kind of economic influence and the anticipated investments of the entertainment industry in the 1980's, it seems that Disco Dancing will be with us for many years to come.

© Paramount/The Kobal Collection

ROCK vs DISCO

Despite the skeptical view that Disco Dancing is only a recent fad, it has, in fact, remained with us for many years. Its tradition precedes the release of *Saturday Night Fever*, when Disco Dance was in its early infancy at various record-bars, especially in New York, Atlanta and Los Angeles. During these less popular years, Disco was, however, plagued by plenty of bad publicity and controversy. At best, its critics rejected it as simply "just another fad" that would soon reach its apex, become overexposed, fade and then eventually disappear. Meanwhile, more serious critics attacked the very spirit and social creative joy that goes along with Disco Dancing.

The greatest division that emerged during the mid-70's was the Disco-Rock Musical Controversy which worked to separate most music fans into two distinct "music appreciation groups," (1) Disco Fans and (2) Rock Fans. Each claimed a rightful inheritance to modern popular music;

each believed itself both incompatible and exclusive of the other, yet, today in the rear-view mirror of experience, we can see that nothing could have been further from the truth. Like Apples vs. Oranges, the myth of musical superiority was debated and argued, all sadly reminiscent of the mods vs rockers factions in Great Britain during the early 1960's, where much ado was made over the rightful and just solitary heir to modern music.

Numerous highly academic arguments were held over the "compatibility" of rock with disco music. Proponents for each argued by often excluding the other as being somehow "bad" or "unhealthy" to music fans. They spoke in terms of absolutes, claiming that it would never be possible for anyone to be both mentally and physically involved in the two musical genres. For a time during the 1970's this difference may have been true, especially since during the early stages of disco, one could simply and clearly isolate, separate, and identify the two musical forms from one another, for in fact, each was quite different. Disco Music had its own uniquely driving, dance stimulating Beat, while rock was diverse, often cerebral and designed to be "more for listening and less for moving."

The great chasm between rock and disco was highlighted by Dr. John Diamond, psychiatrist and President of the International Academy of Preventative Medicine, who claimed that, according to his studies, Rock Music was physiologically opposed to human body rhythms (heart beat, circulation, respiration, etc). Dr. Diamond claimed that Rock Music's syncopated delayed beat could even cause a temporary loss of two-thirds of our body's muscle strength! On this basis, he warned Rock Music fans to beware, and had a ready explanation for why so many concert fans would just sit motionless and listen to the music, rather than openly express a desire to dance.

Meanwhile, the Rock Music camp also had its share of critics who aimed out against Disco Music. Claims that Disco Music was hollow, unable to offer any systematic, thematic, rhythmic development were often heard from some of the most popular and best respected Rock Music artists, critics, and fans. Some of the otherwise liberal fans maintained that Disco Music "all sounds the same," lacked diversity, subtlety, and artistic creativity.

Musicologists who studied these two forms of modern music were divided amongst themselves concerning the respective values of Rock and Disco Music. For example, Dr. Bruce McLean, Chairman of Modern Musicology at Western State, reported that Rock Music was perhaps the best contemporary expression of Classical Music. He explained that listeners of Rock Music were immobile simply because of their infatuation with the magnificence and splendor of the complex instrumentation. He disputed other studies that revealed that Rock Music could "incapacitate listeners." McLean still maintains that Disco Music, although possibly "more in tune" with the human body rhythms, is by no means the ultimate evolved form of modern music.

Wherever the truth of this debate may lie, few people today would argue that either Disco or Rock Music is clearly separable,

or that they can be assigned to be the property of any kind of opposing music-fan camp. Surely, there will always be an audience of diversified listeners, among whom this question will be important, as there will always be dancers who tend to act spontaneously with what they hear. But to confuse the issue of "good" modern music, with synthetic dribbles of disco or rock being "intrinsically superior," or more righteous is grievously fallacious. In the end, it must always be the Public who will decide what is the best anyway. Today, it appears that Disco Music is on top, as people throughout the world are expressing their passionate interest in learning how to Disco Dance.

DISCO BACKLOG

Because of the sudden and intense increase in the public demand to learn how to dance, many studios, disco clubs, and community recreation centers, park districts, etc., are experiencing a tremendous backlog in Disco Dance Class enrollments. There just aren't enough Disco Dance Instructors to go around! To my knowledge, the primary reason for this shortage is that there are no popular materials available on "how to" professionally learn Disco Dancing.

Of course, there are some very clever dance step-by-step guides and manuals available, but I have discovered that it takes indeed much more than mere "steps" to become a good Disco Dancer. This is the central reason for why this book exists. This book is divided into two major sections. The first section deals with some basic concepts on Disco Dancing; a brief Disco Guide of some popular Discotheques around the U.S., and a series of easy to follow Home Exercise Lesson Plans. The second section is a pictorial, step-by-step photo-guide of many of the more popular Disco Dance steps through which you may learn these by self-study.

I look forward to sharing these techniques and philosophies with you through this book, and sincerely hope that this work will broaden your knowledge of Disco Dancing. May you catch the "Saturday Night Fever" seven days a week.

DECODING THE TEXT

1. Jasek has several positive things to say about disco. List as many as you can. Do these still hold true today?

2. Summarize the fight between disco and rock that the author discusses. Are the debate points valid? Which musicologists won the debate? How can you tell?

CONNECTING TO YOUR CULTURE

1. What do you know about discotheques, especially those that were popular in the 1970s?

2. Where did you learn about these discos? Your own experience? Television? Film?

3. Jasek only discusses the positive aspects of disco. What do you think she left out? Why did she neglect these aspects of disco life?

4. Do people still dance in disco style today? Why or why not?

CONSIDERING IDEAS

1. Why do people name their boats, houses, cars, and other possessions?

2. Have you ever named an inanimate object? What about a living thing such as a plant or a part of your anatomy?

3. What purpose does this naming serve?

David Sedaris, *a recipient of* Time *magazine's Humorist of the Year Award, is known for his satirical wit and humor in his monologues. Along with six books, eight plays, and three comic recordings, Sedaris also authors commentaries for "This American Life" on* National Public Radio *as well as contributing to periodicals such as* Esquire *and* The New Yorker. *"The Ship Shape" was taken from Sedaris's best-selling collection of personal essays* Dress Your Family in Corduroy and Denim, *for which he also received a Grammy nomination for Best Spoken Word Album in 2005.*

THE SHIP SHAPE

David Sedaris

My mother and I were at the dry cleaner's, standing behind a woman we had never seen. "A nice-looking woman," my mother would later say. "Well put together. Classy." The woman was dressed for the season in a light cotton shift patterned with oversize daisies. Her shoes matched the petals and her purse, which was black-and-yellow-striped, hung over her shoulder, buzzing the flowers like a lazy bumblebee. She handed in her claim check, accepted her garments, and then expressed gratitude for what she considered to be fast and efficient service. "You know," she said, "people talk about Raleigh, but it isn't really true, is it?"

The Korean man nodded, the way you do when you're a foreigner and understand that someone has finished a sentence. He wasn't the owner, just a helper who'd stepped in from the back, and it was clear he had no idea what she was saying.

"My sister and I are visiting from out of town," the woman said, a little louder now, and again the man nodded. "I'd love to stay awhile longer and explore, but my home—well, *one* of my homes—is on the garden tour, so I've got to get back to Williamsburg."

I was eleven years old, yet still the statement seemed strange to me. If she'd hoped to impress the Korean, the woman had obviously wasted her breath, so who was this information for?

"My home—well, *one* of my homes": by the end of the day my mother and I had repeated this line no less than fifty times. The garden tour was unimportant, but the first part of her sentence brought us great pleasure. There was, as indicated by the dash, a pause between the words *home* and *well,* a brief moment in which she'd decided, *Oh, why not?* The following word—*one*—had blown from her mouth as if propelled by a gentle breeze, and this was the difficult part. You had to get it just right, or else the sentence lost its power. Falling somewhere between a self-conscious laugh and a sigh of happy confusion, the *one* afforded her statement a double meaning. To her peers it meant "Look at me, I catch myself coming and going!" and to the less fortunate it was a way of saying, "Don't kid yourself, it's a lot of work having more than one house."

The first dozen times we tried it, our voices sounded pinched and snobbish, but by midafternoon they had softened. We wanted what this woman had. Mocking her made it seem hopelessly unobtainable, and so we reverted to our natural selves.

"My home—well, one of my homes . . ." My mother said it in a rush, as if she were under pressure to be more specific. It was the same way she said, "My daughter—well, one of my daughters," but a second home was more prestigious than a second daughter, and so it didn't really work. I went in the opposite direction, exaggerating the word *one* in a way that was guaranteed to alienate my listener.

"Say it like that and people are going to be jealous," my mother said.

"Well, isn't that what we want?"

"Sort of," she said. "But mainly we want them to be happy for us."

"But why should you be happy for someone who has more than you do?"

"I guess it all depends on the person," she said. "Anyway, I suppose it doesn't matter. We'll get it right eventually. When the day arrives, I'm sure it'll just come to us."

And so we waited.

At some point in the mid to late 1960s, North Carolina began referring to itself as "Variety Vacationland." The words were stamped onto license plates, and a series of television commercials reminded us that, unlike certain of our neighbors, we had both the beach *and* the mountains. There were those who bounced back and forth between one and the other, but most people tended to choose a landscape and stick to it. We ourselves were Beach People, Emerald Isle People, but that was mainly my mother's doing. I don't think our father would have cared whether he took a vacation or not. Being away from home left him anxious and crabby, but our mother loved the ocean. She couldn't swim, but enjoyed standing at the water's edge with a pole in her hand. It wasn't exactly what you'd call fishing, as she caught nothing and expressed neither hope nor disappointment in regard to her efforts. What she thought about while looking at the waves was a complete mystery, yet you could tell that these thoughts pleased her, and that she liked herself better while thinking them.

One year our father waited too late to make our reservations, and we were forced to take something on the sound. It wasn't a cottage but a run-down house, the sort of place where poor people lived. The yard was enclosed by a chain-link fence, and the air was thick with the flies and mosquitoes normally blown away by the ocean breezes. Midway through the vacation a hideous woolly caterpillar fell from a tree and bit my sister Amy on the cheek. Her face swelled and discolored, and within an hour, were it not for her arms and legs, it would have been difficult to recognize her as a human. My mother drove her to the hospital, and when they returned she employed my sister as Exhibit A, pointing as if this were not her daughter but some ugly stranger forced to share our quarters.

"*This* is what you get for waiting until the last minute," she said to our father. "No dunes, no waves, just *this*."

From that year on, our mother handled the reservations. We went to Emerald Isle for a week every September and were always oceanfront, a word that suggested a certain degree of entitlement. The oceanfront cottages were on stilts, which made them appear if not large, then at least imposing. Some were painted, some were sided "Cape Cod style" with wooden shingles, and all of them had names, the cleverest being Loafer's Paradise. The owners had cut their sign in the shape of two moccasins resting side by side. The shoes were realistically painted and the letters were bloated and listless, loitering like drunks against the soft faux leather.

"Now *that's* a sign," our father would say, and we would agree. There was The Skinny Dipper, Pelican's Perch, Lazy Daze, The Scotch Bonnet, Loony Dunes, the name of each house followed by the name and hometown of the owner. "The Duncan Clan—Charlotte," "The Graftons—Rocky Mount," "Hal and Jean Starling of Pinehurst"—signs that essentially said, "My home—well, *one* of my homes."

While at the beach we sensed more than ever that our lives were governed by luck. When we had it—when it was sunny—my sisters and I felt as if we were somehow personally responsible. We were a fortunate family, and therefore everyone around us was allowed to swim and dig in the sand. When it rained, we were unlucky, and stayed indoors to search our souls. "It'll clear after lunch," our mother would say, and we would eat carefully, using the place mats that had brought

us luck in the past. When that failed, we would move on to Plan B. "Oh, Mother, you work too hard," we'd say. "Let *us* do the dishes. Let *us* sweep sand off the floor." We spoke like children in a fairy tale, hoping our goodness might lure the sun from its hiding place. "You and Father have been so kind to us. Here, let us massage your shoulders."

If by late afternoon it still hadn't cleared, my sisters and I would drop the act and turn on one another, searching for the spoiler who had brought us this misfortune. Which of us seemed the least dissatisfied? Who had curled up on a mildewed bed with a book and a glass of chocolate milk, behaving as though the rain were not such a bad thing after all? We would find this person, most often my sister Gretchen, and then we would beat her.

The summer I was twelve a tropical storm moved up the coast, leaving a sky the same mottled pewter as Gretchen's subsequent bruises, but the following year we started with luck. My father found a golf course that suited him, and for the first time in memory even he seemed to enjoy himself. Relaxing on the deck with a gin and tonic, surrounded by his toast-colored wife and children, he admitted that this really wasn't so bad. "I've been thinking, to hell with these rental cottages," he said. "What do you say we skip the middleman and just buy a place."

He spoke in the same tone he used when promising ice cream. "Who's up for something sweet?" he'd ask, and we'd pile into the car, passing the Tastee Freeze and driving to the grocery store, where he'd buy a block of pus-colored ice milk reduced for quick sale. Experience had taught us not to trust him, but we wanted a beach house so badly it was impossible not to get caught up in the excitement. Even our mother fell for it.

"Do you really mean this?" she asked.

"Absolutely," he said.

The next day they made an appointment with a real-estate agent in Morehead City. "We'll just be discussing the possibility," my mother said. "It's just a meeting, nothing more." We wanted to join them but they took only Paul, who was two years old and unfit to be left in our company. The morning meeting led to half a dozen viewings, and when they returned, my mother's face was so impassive it seemed almost paralyzed. "It-was-fine," she said. "The-real-estate-agent-was-very-nice." We got the idea that she was under oath to keep something to herself and that the effort was causing her actual physical pain.

"It's all right," my father said. "You can tell them."

"Well, we saw this one place in particular," she told us. "Now, it's nothing to get worked up about, but . . ."

"But it's perfect," my father said. "A real beauty, just like your mother here." He came from behind and pinched her on the bottom. She laughed and swatted him with a towel, and we witnessed what we would later come to recognize as the rejuvenating power of real estate. It's what fortunate couples turn to when their sex life has faded and they're too pious for affairs. A second car might bring people together for a week or two, but a second home can revitalize a marriage for up to nine months after the closing.

"Oh, Lou," my mother said. "What am I going to do with you?"

"Whatever you want, baby," he said. "Whatever you want."

It was queer when people repeated their sentences twice, but we were willing to overlook it in exchange for a beach house. My mother was too excited to cook that night, and so we ate dinner at the Sanitary Fish Market in Morehead City. On taking our seats I expected my father to mention inadequate insulation or corroded pipes, the dark undersides of home ownership, but instead he discussed only the positive aspects. "I don't see why we couldn't spend our Thanksgivings here. Hell, we could even come for Christmas. Hang a few lights, get some ornaments, what do you think?"

A waitress passed the table, and without saying please, I demanded another Coke. She went to fetch it, and I settled back in my chair, drunk with the power of a second home. When school began, my classmates would court me, hoping I might invite them for a weekend, and I would make a game of pitting them against one another. This was what a person did when people liked him for all the wrong reasons, and I would grow to be very good at it.

"What do you think, David?" my father asked. I hadn't heard the question but said that it sounded good to me. "I like it," I said. "I like it."

The following afternoon our parents took us to see the house. "Now, I don't want you to get your hopes up too high," my mother said, but it was too late for that. It was a fifteen-minute drive from one end of the island to the other, and along the way we proposed names for what we had come to think of as our cottage. I'd already given it a good deal of thought but waited a few minutes before offering my suggestion.

"Are you ready?" I said. "Our sign will be the silhouette of a ship."

Nobody said anything.

"Get it?" I said. "The shape of a ship. Our house will be called The Ship Shape."

"Well, you'd have to write that on the sign," my father said. "Otherwise, nobody will get it."

"But if you write out the words you'll ruin the joke."

"What about The Nut Hut?" Amy said.

"Hey!" my father said. "Now there's an idea." He laughed, not realizing, I guess, that there already was a Nut Hut. We'd passed it a thousand times.

"How about something with the word *sandpiper* in it," my mother said. "Everybody likes sandpipers, right?"

Normally I would have hated them for not recognizing my suggestion as the best, but this was clearly a special time and I didn't want to ruin it with brooding. Each of us wanted to be the one who came up with the name, and inspiration could be hiding anywhere. When the interior of the car had been exhausted of ideas, we looked out the windows and searched the passing landscape.

Two thin girls braced themselves before crossing the busy road, hopping from foot to foot on the scalding pavement. "The Tar Heel," Lisa called out. "No, The Wait 'n' Sea. Get it? S-E-A."

A car trailing a motorboat pulled up to a gas pump. "The Shell Station!" Gretchen shouted.

Everything we saw was offered as a possible name, and the resulting list of nominees confirmed that once you left the shoreline, Emerald Isle was sorely lacking in natural beauty. "The TV Antenna," my sister Tiffany said. "The Telephone Pole." "The Toothless Black Man Selling Shrimp from the Back of His Van."

"The Cement Mixer." "The Overturned Grocery Cart." "Gulls on a Garbage Can." My mother inspired "The Cigarette Butt Thrown Out the Window" and suggested we look for ideas on the beach rather than on the highway. "I mean, my God, how depressing can you get?" She acted annoyed, but we could tell she was really enjoying it. "Give me something that suits us," she said. "Give me something that will last."

What would ultimately last were these fifteen minutes on the coastal highway, but we didn't know that then. When older, even the crankiest of us would accept them as proof that we were once a happy family: our mother young and healthy, our father the man who could snap his fingers and give us everything we wanted, the whole lot of us competing to name our good fortune.

The house was, as our parents had promised, perfect. This was an older cottage with pine-paneled walls that gave each room the thoughtful quality of a den. Light fell in strips from the louvered shutters, and the furniture, which was included in the sale, reflected the taste of a distinguished sea captain. Once we'd claimed bedrooms and lain awake all night, mentally rearranging the furniture, it would be our father who'd say, "Now hold on a minute, it's not ours *yet*." By the next afternoon he had decided that the golf course wasn't so great after all. Then it rained for two straight days, and he announced that it might be wiser to buy some land, wait a few years, and think about building a place of our own. "I mean, let's be practical." Our mother put on her raincoat. She tied a plastic bag over her head and stood at the water's edge, and for the first time in our lives we knew exactly what she was thinking.

By our final day of vacation our father had decided that instead of building a place on Emerald Isle, we should improve the home we already had. "Maybe add a pool," he said. "What do you kids think about that?" Nobody answered.

By the time he'd finished wheedling it down, the house at the beach had become a bar in the basement. It looked just like a real bar, with tall stools and nooks for wine. There was a sink for washing glasses and an assortment of cartoon napkins illustrating the lighter side of alcoholism. For a week or two my sisters and I tottered at the counter, pretending to be drunks, but then the novelty wore off and we forgot all about it.

On subsequent vacations, both with and without our parents, we would drive by the cottage we had once thought of as our own. Each of us referred to it by a different name, and over time qualifiers became necessary. ("You know, *our* house.") The summer after we didn't buy it, the new owners—or "those people," as we liked to call them—painted The Ship

Shape yellow. In the late seventies Amy noted that The Nut Hut had extended the carport and paved the driveway. Lisa was relieved when the Wait 'n' Sea returned to its original color, and Tiffany was incensed when The Toothless Black Man Selling Shrimp from the Back of His Van sported a sign endorsing Jesse Helms in the 1984 senatorial campaign. Four years later my mother called to report that The Sandpiper had been badly damaged by Hurricane Hugo. "It's still there," she said. "But barely." Shortly thereafter, according to Gretchen, The Shell Station was torn down and sold as a vacant lot.

I know that such a story does not quite work to inspire sympathy. ("My home— well, *one* of my homes—fell through.") We had no legitimate claim to self-pity, were ineligible even to hold a grudge, but that didn't stop us from complaining.

In the coming years our father would continue to promise what he couldn't deliver, and in time we grew to think of him as an actor auditioning for the role of a benevolent millionaire. He'd never get the part but liked the way that the words felt in his mouth. "What do you say to a new car?" he'd ask. "Who's up for a cruise to the Greek Isles?" He expected us to respond by playing the part of an enthusiastic family, but we were unwilling to resume our old roles. As if carried by a tide, our mother drifted farther and farther away, first to twin beds and then down the hall to a room decorated with seascapes and baskets of sun-bleached sand dollars. It would have been nice, a place at the beach, but we already had a home. A home with a bar. Besides, had things worked out, you wouldn't have been happy for us. We're not that kind of people.

1. This essay is about a beach house, but it is also about Sedaris's family, especially his mother and father. How does he balance the two stories?
2. What does the place say about the group of people, and vice versa?

CONNECTING TO YOUR CULTURE

1. Sedaris refers to the rejuvenating power of real estate. What does he mean by this? How does he show this in the text? What happens when the real estate deal falls through?
2. Why does the family continue to keep tabs on the beach house and the area in which it is located?
3. Has the purchase, plan for purchase, or lack of purchase of an item ever affected you or your family? In what ways?

Reading Selections: the '80s

CONSIDERING IDEAS

1. Have you ever taken a seat or stood around in a public space and simply watched the people go by? What did you notice about the people?
2. Did you make fun of any of them? Envy others? Feel sorry for some?
3. Why do so many of us enjoy people watching?

William Severini Kowinski *is a freelance writer and has written for such magazines as the* Smithsonian, Esquire, Rolling Stone, *and* The New York Times Magazine. *His most recent articles can be found in the* San Francisco Chronicle, Los Angeles Times, *and* The New York Times. *He is best known for his book* The Malling of America—Travels in the United States of Shopping. *"Mallingering" is an excerpt from that 1985 book.*

MALLINGERING

William Severini Kowinski

If you had to pick one thing that would typify civilization in the U.S. in the twentieth century, a front-running candidate would be the suburban shopping mall.

—Tom Walker, business editor
of the *Atlanta Journal*

On low-clouded nights in Greensburg, Pennsylvania, there are two glowing strips in the sky. The one in the west, which is orange, hovers over Greengate Mall. The one in the east, which is white, is the aureole of Westmoreland Mall. These are the signatures written across the darkness, signing the decree of Greensburg's fate.

On a Friday evening, for instance, the crowded flow of cars on Route 30 edged gently into the off-ramp at Westmoreland Mall. The streams of paired white lights cut into the twilight as the cars wound around the perimeter of the parking lot, heading for separate destinations in the wide expanse of asphalt. In the dim light dispersed from high stanchions, the chuffing and coughing of engines stopping and the last blinks of headlights winking out yielded to the smaller sounds of footsteps and muted voices, as people walked quickly through the cool air and the overwhelming quiet.

Inside the mall it was Michael Jackson Night. He wasn't going to be there, of course, but one of the many Michael Jackson look-alikes fanning out to malls across America was on the center-court stage, with the wet-permed hair, the red-and-black jacket, and the silver glove, duplicating the dance moves from the Jackson videos. A crowd watched from both levels, girls screamed, and a few younger children thought they were seeing the real thing. Meanwhile, the National Record Mart was playing the Jacksons at full volume, Camelot Music displayed the albums and videos, clothing stores had racks of the appropriate fashions, the bookstores had the Jackson bios and picture books, and even a furniture store had a wooden Michael Jackson dummy out front holding a sign that said TRY AND BEAT IT—IT'S A THRILLER.

As I got into the foyer at the main entrance, two teenaged girls who seemed to be leaving did an about-face when they saw two of their friends entering behind me. "God, we've already been here *three hours,*" one of them cried. The small court just inside this entrance is where the teenagers first congregate; it's where the swarm gathers, buzzing and swirling with the smell of sweat and hot cologne, the hive in heat. Tonight it was as crowded as a high-school hallway outside the gym at half time of the biggest basketball game of the year.

A little further into the mall itself, two boys were quietly talking about their body-building progress, while one girl sharing a bench with another suddenly shouted emphatically, "I *hate it* when people do that—I *hate it*!" A mixed group of teens in a shifting circle listened to a girl say to a bemused boy, "I *never* said that about her. What did she say about me?"

"Mallingering" from THE MALLING OF AMERICA by William Severini Kowinski, pp. 26–37. Copyright © 1985 by William Severini Kowinski. By permission of the author.

I made my way past the spectators at the second-level railing around center court who were jostling the card table filled with literature on abortion rights and black women in history, sponsored by the National Organization for Women. Two women were sitting there patiently while people bobbed their heads against the ERA NOW! balloons, trying to get a better look at the dancing clone below.

I stopped at the National Record Mart, where a friend of mine had recently become the store manager. "One kid who works here told me why he likes the mall," Jim said. "It's because no matter what the weather is outside, it's always the same in here. He likes that. He doesn't want to know it's raining—it would depress him."

Hearing this, another teenaged boy who worked there added, "It's better for looking at girls, too. They aren't all bundled up in coats and stuff even in the winter."

I told them that Bobbi (a friend of Jim's and mine who worked in one of Westmoreland's women's clothing shops) told me she was convinced that the glass doors at the mall entrance are purposely tinted dark so it always looks gloomy outside, and customers will decide to stay inside the mall.

The young clerk looked amazed. "We have paranoid friends," Jim explained. On the other hand, it was true that I'd just heard a disc jockey on the radio say, "Outside it's cold and rainy—a great day to spend at the mall." Then he announced the malls where other DJs from his rock music station were hosting promo parties.

I walked toward the other end of the mall, past two older men sitting on a bench in front of the organ store requesting their favorite tunes from the woman playing the display model closest to the doorway, as teenagers passed by, worrying aloud about their popularity. I trotted down the stairs at Kaufmann's department store to my favorite place in Westmoreland Mall. It's just under the stairs, where a bench is built into a planter in a kind of sunken patio, a few steps below the mall court. There is a static lawn-sprinkler fountain sending thin layers of spray into a small pool that reflects elements of surrounding light; the silver rods of the sprinkler parse the red neon from the Radio Shack logo with a diffusion of blue from Command Performance. The bricks around it are tinted an oddly glowing shade of dark red. Green branches of small trees hang over the bench, and above it is a skylight, one of the few sources of natural light in this mall. The place is clearly designed to be a kind of retreat, a cool nook away from the bustle, and people sit there silently, as if no one could see them. It is strange that such a small space could seem so set apart, with an aura of peace and isolation, like a garden. It is the best place in the mall to read, and I was not the only one who sought it out for that purpose.

Farther down the first level a buxom middle-aged couple was walking blandly down the court, wearing identical camouflage battle fatigues, complete with berets. The only difference was that he wore combat boots and she wore running shoes. Two girls were sitting on a bench positioned where they could hear music blaring simultaneously from Camelot record store and through the two-way acoustic suspension speakers on sale at Radio Shack next door: ZZ Top mixing with Paul Simon singing "Still Crazy After All These Years."

There was a Friday-night crowd in the court in front of the three-screen cinema, which at Westmoreland is contained within the mall itself. Kids streamed out of the theater lobby, heading for hamburgers and Cokes at Lums, while the older dating crowd checked the movie times. Westmoreland has two game arcades and more restaurants than Greengate, so entertainment is more of a factor here. That makes Westmoreland the mall of choice for family excursions on the weekend—everyone can go to the movies, either the same film or different ones, with the kids making up the extra time at the video arcades, or their parents with shopping. In fact, a divorced father I knew often brought his daughter here during his weekend visitations. He could take her to a movie, have lunch, and buy whatever guilt-gifts he could afford, without wasting time and energy on driving, parking, and getting in and out of cars and coats.

Westmoreland is the newer of the two malls, slightly larger than Greengate and done in the style prevailing in the late seventies—dimly lit dark-brick tile and wood and nostalgic globe lights, contrasted with gleaming high-tech fixtures and a shiny glass elevator as its centerpiece. Westmoreland also has a strip center out back, with a supermarket, Murphy's Mart, and other stores that supposedly have more of a quick-purchase, in-and-out clientele. The enclosed mall is for more leisurely shopping—that, at least, is the theory that now prevails in the mall industry.

Greengate had opened a decade earlier; in the style of an earlier age, it had a supermarket inside it for a long time, and still contains a Murphy's. But Greengate has changed with the times, too. There is

a satellite strip center now, and a cluster of buildings out back that houses its cinemas, a bank, offices, a Lady Venus spa, and a V.I.P. nightclub. Because Greengate had been around so long, it had the greater claim to community loyalty, and it plays up that image. Westmoreland was sponsoring more community events than it used to, especially those of a show biz kind, like the Miss Pennsylvania pageants, personal appearances by soap opera stars, and the regional scholastic cheerleading competitions, where junior-high and high-school girls could be rated by university experts on appearance, cheer execution, creativity, and difficulty, and be introduced by a television game-show host. But Greengate was still "the mall" to many people.

Greengate is only a couple of miles down the highway from Westmoreland Mall, on the other side of Greensburg. Inside on this Friday evening, the parade into Greengate began in the fluorescent latitudes of the side-court entrance. Here, every kind of western Pennsylvania citizen that it is possible to assemble or even imagine poured into the mall in their life-costumes: business suits, or overalls and factory-logo baseball caps, frilly blouses and buckskin jackets; in high-heeled shoes, work boots, ballet slippers, and sneakers. The stream clotted briefly outside the video game arcade, where knots of teenagers pattered restlessly, and then divided to flow around a tall birdcage (the aviary) and the indoor picnic area of the food court.

As soon as they hit the mall itself, a brother and sister separated from their parents and took off, racing each other to the same parental disapproval shouted in different pitches. On one bench near the aviary a three-year-old girl in a red jacket, with matching red barrette in her long brown hair, ate a pink ice-cream cone beside her father, who was eating a yellow one and naming for her the birds she pointed to. To the thinly echoed calls of the birds, a young woman strode past, her blond curls touching the shoulders of her sea-green sweater. She was holding hands with a young man in a gray sweat-shirt and jeans; in their free hands they were both carrying their coats.

The wrought-iron lawn tables and chairs of the food court were interspersed with sparsely green trees growing out of metal grilles in the lacquered brick floor. At one table a family of three generations huddled around soft drinks from Burger King; at another a middle-aged man with a loud voice argued enthusiastically with two women, pausing to acknowledge greetings from numerous passersby. "How do you know all these people?" one of the women demanded.

Across from the Stuft Potato, a middle-aged man in striped jersey and black cap, reminiscent of French sailors in old movies, talked quietly to a woman in a peach blouse. An old man with crew-cut hair and a huge belly sat on a bench glaring off into the forlorn blankness beyond Thrift Drug. A girl of seventeen or so sat alone at a white table leafing through *Cosmopolitan* magazine, chewing gum, and dreaming dreams. At the next table a young woman, maybe eighteen or twenty, wearing a crisp skirt and vest with her store's ID card on her blouse collar, munched fries and gossiped with co-workers, launched on a career at the mall.

A bearded young maintenance man wheeled his dark-blue cart of brooms, cleaning solutions, and canvas refuse-pouch to an empty white table. His girl friend, wearing a black T-shirt with the insignia of R.E.O. Speedwagon, talked to him between mouthfuls of pizza from the Pizza Place. At the farthest table a circle of old men, all wearing hats, passed around sections of the local newspaper, occasionally commenting on the news of the day, what the President and the Pittsburgh Steelers were up to, and what was interesting in the classifieds. Nearby was a mall perennial, a former teenager whose habitual presence at the mall had turned sullen. Once I heard a shop manager refer to him as The Vulture; he leaned against a planter, ready to pounce.

Jeannie is in her early twenties; she purveys monstrous chocolate chip and pea-nut butter cookies, funnel cakes, and other baked goods at the Cookie Cupboard, one of the small storefronts on the food court. She tries to mitigate the general boredom of standing here all day by keeping an eye on what's going on. "There goes the pharmacist from Thrift, over to the flower shop again," she said. "He's going over there a lot. Looks like the latest mall romance."

But Jeannie's main field of vision covers the clusters of teenagers outside the video game room, and their strategic conferences held near the aviary. She's not too charmed by them, but she remembers it wasn't so long ago that she was among them. "But we didn't stand around like that," she said with evident distaste. "They look terrible." Then she laughed.

"Yeah, I used to come to Greengate once a week, on Friday," Jeannie admitted. "And then I started to come on Saturdays, too. And then I started coming on weeknights—I'd call my girl friend or she'd call me and we'd say, 'Want to go to the mall?' We even started coming right after school. We did our homework sitting on a bench." She laughed again.

"But I know somebody who had a real romance here," she added. "A girl friend of my sister Delores met her husband here. They met accidentally on purpose. He'd seen her someplace and he wanted to meet her but he didn't want to ask her out. So they arranged to sort of be at the mall at the same time. I think maybe Delores was the one who arranged it. That kind of thing happened a lot. Anyway, she met the guy at Greengate and now she's married to him."

But not everyone was there for fun and romance. "I went back in the supply tunnel with the trash the other night," Jeannie said, "and I turned a corner and there was this couple on the floor. I sort of jumped and said excuse me, and I was getting out of there when I realized that sex wasn't what they were into. They were putting all this stuff they had shoplifted into a big trash bag. It was their stash. I thought about reporting them but they were probably long gone before I even got back out here."

On the other side of the tables and chairs farther up the side court is the place where older people primarily gather at Greengate. They sit at the tables and on the benches there, though some brave the set of benches closer to the games arcade and the kids. There is bus service to Greengate from surrounding towns now, and some is designated for senior citizens. Some older people are here on doctor's orders: the sheltered, comfortable, con-sistent mall is ideal for walking. There are so many of them, in fact, that Greengate's management has instituted a kind of walker's club for senior citizens, and gives them certificates for the miles they walk. That's become a fairly common practice in malls over the country, and some malls even open their doors a little early to accommodate morning constitutionals.

Greengate's public relations director told me once that the elderly are sometimes frightened by the young, especially when they are rowdy or running. I've heard kids complain about old people being intoler-ant, but the two groups coexist as those who most regularly use the mall for social purposes. In the outside world, each group is usually confined to its own age-segregated institutions and activities, so the mall is also about the only place these days that the old and the young seem to see each other.

On the corner of the side court is Ani-mal Crackers, a card and gift shop that is one of the minority of independently owned stores in the mall. (Greengate, however, has more of these than most malls.) Inside, a young clerk named Lori was helping a shy father select a stuffed animal for his son. Lori's husband works for a chain of jewelry stores. When he was transferred from their home in Ohio to Westmoreland Mall, Lori found a job at Greengate. "I didn't want to work at the *same* mall," Lori said. "This is close enough." Meanwhile, Mary Gilbert, Ani-mal Crackers' owner, was writing up an order for a gorilla to deliver a dozen blue balloons to a birthday party. Mary will be the gorilla. Kate, Mary's eight-year-old daughter, drifted back from Murphy's, where she had been visiting the parakeets.

Near the railing around center court, a grandfather and his grandson consulted a bulletin-board kiosk of tacked-up announcements: craft shows, a quit-smoking class, jazz-ercise, the Elks festival, the Seton Hill College evening degree program, the St. Vincent College lecture series on "The Future," a ballroom and Latin dancing class, the March of Dimes Wine and Cheese Gala, a community medical seminar, black lung clinics, a Pennsylvania State Police recruiting poster, and a number to call to report UFO or Bigfoot sightings.

At the head of the escalator a tall blonde-haired young man in black velvet jacket and jeans leaned against the railing; it is the traditional spot, held for many years by another long-haired boy until he became embarrassingly older, of the mall regular most likely to be peddling drugs. The uniformed security guard passed him, seemingly oblivious as he mildly walked his beat—the neighborhood cop.

At The Athlete's Foot, a young woman clerk named Marina waved hello. She was not looking forward to the weekend here; her store is in a high-traffic location at the head of the stairs and not far from the corner of side and central courts, so people tend to congregate there. "I just hope it isn't as bad as last weekend," she said. "It was a full moon, and all the crazies were out. Right out in front here, a bunch of young guys locked arms and stood across the aisles and wouldn't let anybody pass. We had to call the police."

Marina stared at the guy at the head of the escalators. "Mall rats," she said. As defined by people who work at the mall, the species known as *mall rat* consists of people who seem to do nothing else but hang out at the mall, all day, every day. Mall employees are also there all the time, not always willingly but at least productively, and therefore in a position to notice and disdain them.

Some mall rats are women, but they are the hardest to spot if they look like regular shoppers, Marina said. Eventually they are seen too often and seen buying too infrequently. They are the mall's kempt equivalent of shopping-bag ladies, except that they must be prosperous and together enough to drive. Most mall rats, however, are young men who may have been regulars as teenagers but somehow never graduated from the mall. One of Greengate's most famous was a former mall maintenance and security employee who lost his job but kept coming back anyway. Another was the aforementioned most-likely-to-be-a dope dealer, who also accumulated a measure of fame for always being accompanied by a very young teenaged girl—always a different one, but always a blonde.

Some mall employees count the teenaged regulars themselves as mall rats, but if these kids at least go to school and spend some money in the mall, they may earn a more decorous designation, like "the mallies." According to Marina's definition, the classic mall rat is unable to hold a job and simply comes to the mall as something to do every day. "I thought maybe you were one," Marina says, "until I saw you taking notes."

On the other side of the second level above central court, two teenaged girls noticed they were being casually followed by two teenaged boys; they stopped to inspect Country Hits of the 70s at the National Record Mart entrance, to let the boys catch up. The boys lost their nerve and walked past. Looking at cassettes inside, Chris, not yet sixteen, was waiting for her boyfriend. They were going to a movie at the Greengate theaters out back. Since they are both too young to drive and the mall is midway between their homes, they are each dropped off here. Their choices are limited to the three movies showing; often they see one they've seen before. I said hello to Chris; she's my niece.

At the foot of the escalator on the first level, two veteran mall salesmen from neighboring stores met at the planter in front of Florsheim shoes and complained about the condition of the greenery. "I told him about those plants," one said. "And you know what he said? They grow that way. Can you believe it? They *get* that way, I told him, but they don't *grow* that way. Those plants are *dead*." In Standard Sportswear, David waited on an attractive young woman who was buying a sweater for her boyfriend's birthday. David told me later that he asked her out and she accepted. He claimed this isn't too unusual.

Meanwhile in center court, customers gathered for the evening's attraction: a Hawaiian dance show, apparently sponsored by the mall's travel agency. Men in checked hunting jackets, women holding blonde babies, old men leaning on canes, and couples holding hands sat on benches and folding chairs in front of the stage to watch a woman playing the ukulele and a younger woman dancing in a modest outfit that seemed to owe as much to mainland pom-pon girls as to island conditions. As the performers sang and danced and talked to the crowd, shoppers kept passing by, some joining the audience for a moment or two. Others

were confused about what was going on. "It's *Hawaii,* Ellen," one explained.

The performers asked for volunteers to learn the hula but the only taker was a not entirely self-possessed man in a blue windbreaker who climbed onto the stage and gyrated crazily to the music, grinning at the audience while the performers smiled wan Hawaiian smiles. Meanwhile one of the teenagers watching from above along the second-level railing—a girl wearing a red T-shirt that said SOFT IN THE RIGHT PLACES—did her own dance, a kind of funky hula, for the amusement of her friends. The show ended with the performer's thanks for being invited to "your beautiful mall." The audience applauded, but the reviews by those walking away were mixed. "Not as good as *Love Boat,*" one boy said with a shrug.

There is a strong temptation to concentrate on mall weirdness, since there is plenty of it. Besides the mall rats, there are the mall crazies, like the woman with striking blonde hair cut at a severe angle across her luminous forehead who makes continuous circuits of Westmoreland Mall, clinging to the walls; or the middle-aged woman who suddenly stood up on a bench at Greengate, tore off her clothes, and jumped into the fountain. I also heard at Greengate about an elderly woman at a New Jersey mall who showed up every morning with an urn containing the ashes of her husband and father, which she kept all day in a mall locker.

But for the middle-class patrons (including teenagers and the elderly) who make up its majority, the mall has become normal, and by and large they like it. I heard them say why in basically the same terms all over the country, sometimes in response to my questions, sometimes into the cameras and microphones of media doing stories on the mall and my mall trek, or on the phone to radio call-in shows.

"The mall's the greatest thing to bring families together," one woman said. "Father, mother, children—they've got to talk to each other, even if it's at the mall."

"When I have to buy clothes or shoes for my kids in different age brackets, I can come to one place and just go from store to store without fussing with getting the kids in and out," another woman said. "It's just so much more convenient and pleasant."

"I just come to look around and enjoy myself," said a young mother. "To get away from the house, and sometimes the kid."

"The mall is wonderful for senior citizens with no one in their homes and no places to go," said a middle-aged woman. "They can go and see people and be with people. I think that's the greatest thing that's ever happened."

"We meet our old cronies, we go 'round, spend a couple of dollars here and there," said an old man, laughing. "If I have a stroke at home there's nobody there to help me," another man said. "But at the mall, maybe somebody will help me."

"The reason young kids come to the mall is they're too young to do anything else," said a teenaged girl. "Like in seventh and eighth grade we're old enough to be on our own but not old enough to go to like a bar or anywhere, so we walk the mall with our new jeans and our combs in our back pockets and pretend we're hot."

"We come to play video games and pick up girls," a teenaged boy said. "Sometimes the girls pick up the boys but me and my friends aren't that lucky."

"You can sit in the mall and watch all the strange people go by and make comments on them," said another teenager. "Everything's there—the movies and stuff, and all your friends are there."

"I come to the mall to walk around and get some exercise because I have a heart condition," said a middle-aged man. "But also to keep my wife company, so she doesn't spend too much money."

"Usually you meet somebody," said another middle-aged man. "Some days you meet three or four people, some days nobody. Sometimes I meet somebody I haven't seen in ten, fifteen years."

"Walking around," said a young man, holding his girl friend's hand. "Yeah," she said. "We like to walk around."

That the mall has become not only normal but essential is illustrated in a somewhat crazy way by my favorite Greensburg mall story. It was just a small item in the Police Blotter of the local newspaper, but it said everything. A woman shopper was abducted from Greengate Mall by a young man with a knife, but at a stoplight a few miles away she jumped out of the car and escaped unharmed. Her teenaged assailant fled, but nevertheless he was caught the very next day. This quick triumph of justice was accomplished because the very next day he went back to Greengate Mall and so did the woman he kidnapped. She spotted him, alerted a security guard who called the state police. Since both perpetrator and victim had returned so promptly to the scene of the crime, the police got her identification on the spot, and took the guy away.

But even on a Friday night, for all the fun, romance, craziness, and crime, most of what the mall is about is buying and selling. So through all the entrances the parade continues, as the customers come marching in to the infectious beat of products: the dads shrugged into flannel shirts and down vests, the moms munching yogurt cones, followed by clutches of fiber-filled kids . . . the stringy sophomores in letter jackets and the girls in corduroy gaucho skirts, harness-style boots, and acrylic knit sweater-coats, out on shopping dates . . . the wandering gangs of teenaged girls with identical post-Farrah Fawcett blowy-curl permanents in every imaginable shade . . . the blank-browed men in three-piece suits of polyester or natural blends, their eyes focused somewhere above the crowd . . . the smartly suited businesswomen, their squints ticking off an invisible shopping list, their heels clicking to an internal drummer on the terrazzo tile. . . .

They are all here at the malls, moving brightly through the big bazaar and making the bleep-blip-bleep cash registers sing, and the brap-clack-clack-brraaap money processors burp with satisfaction, ringing up all those electric woks, Coleco Arcade microprocessors, Atari space games, Watta Pizzeria electric pizza-makers, Marie Osmond fashion dolls, tube sox, smoke detectors, leisure slippers, champagne charmeuse tucked-front wing-collar blouses with matching parachute pants, wicker-look bench hampers, microwave popcorn poppers, time/date readout ballpoint pens, black leather bomber jackets, cable knits, sherpa-lined Trailblazers, *Star Wars* digital wristwatches, Barbie Disco radios with special seat for Barbie, handbags "crafted from the finest man-made materials," and ceramic jars of Aramis Muscle Soothing Soak that carry the inscription: "Life is a joy and all things show it/I thought it once but now I know it!"—only $22, soak included.

DECODING THE TEXT

1. At one point, the author says that the mall has become normal. What does he mean by this? How does he support this idea?

2. Later, he says that the mall has become essential to our way of life. What is he saying about Americans, particularly suburbanites?

3. Kowinski conducted his research in the '80s. Do you think the mall is still as important today?

1. What attracts you to the mall? How often do you go there? Do you go alone or with family or friends? What do you do when you get there?

2. Today, numerous open shopping centers, rather than enclosed malls, are being built. How do these new centers compare to the malls of the '80s and '90s? Which do you prefer? Why?

• • • • • • • • • • • • • • • • • • • •

CONSIDERING IDEAS

1. What factors do you consider during a presidential election?

2. What are the most important issues that candidates should address as they campaign? After they take office?

Ralph Nader *is best known for his political endeavors, but he is also a prolific writer. He has authored several books and coauthored many more. He is also known as a consumer advocate, lawyer, and teacher. He believes in working for what he terms "powerless citizens."*

Mark Green *is known for his consumer advocacy. His most recent publication is entitled* Losing Our Democracy: How Bush, the Far Right, and Big Business Are Betraying Americans for Power and Profit *(2006). He has written several Nader group reports as well as coauthored numerous books. This coauthored review essay first appeared in* The Nation *in 1990.*

REAGAN–BUSH AT 9

Passing On the Legacy of Shame

Ralph Nader and Mark Green

In their 1980s retrospectives, conservative pundits like William Buckley, Pat Buchanan, Cal Thomas and Jeffrey Bell have been exceeding the bounds of exuberance (for example, "Reagan won the cold war"). At least such hyperbole raises two useful questions: First, what *are* the real legacies of the Reagan-Bush years so far, nine years after their launch; and second, can—or will—President Bush alter them in any serious way?

Using the framework of measurable cause and effect rather than crediting the rooster for the dawn, how have these two Presidents influenced the quality of our lives? Answer: They have been pursuing policies that have quietly sapped America's long-term strength. Here are ten concrete examples out of hundreds, as well as a hint at whether Bush, based on his performance and trajectory, might yet change these legacies:

Infants and Children. Since 1981 the percentage of children living in poverty soared to almost 20 percent, the worst record in the industrial West; after a decade of decline the rate of low birthweight babies rose last year, especially among African-Americans. Cutting infant nutrition programs, Medicaid and prenatal care further hurt the littlest Americans.

Bush has proposed the largest one-year increase in the Head Start program ever offered, $500 million (which would cover only one in five eligible children). However, he offers no suggestions as to how to reduce this country's dismal infant mortality rate (nineteenth in the world). And the self-proclaimed "Education President" shows little more interest in schooling than his predecessor. Although the United States recently ranked fourteenth out of sixteen industrialized countries in elementary and secondary education spending, Bush proposed only a 1 percent increase (after inflation) in federal education spending.

If this trend continues, students won't even be able to read Bush's lips.

Poverty and Idealism. Homelessness, which had virtually disappeared by the 1970s, grew in significant part only after Reagan cut federal appropriations for low-income subsidized housing by 82 percent. Because funding of discretionary low-income programs fell by 55 percent (after inflation) between 1981 and 1989, there were 3 million more poor Americans at the end of the 1980s than at the start of the decade. Nor did Reagan ever make a major public statement on poverty that tapped the idealism of caring among Americans, as John F. Kennedy did with his Peace Corps address. Indeed, Reagan's principal message to the younger generation was go for the gold, not the golden rule.

President Bush, on the other hand, has laudably talked about citizenship rather than mere commercialism. Consider his now well-worn metaphor about "a thousand points of light" in his inaugural

"Reagan-Bush at 9: Passing On the Legacy of Shame" by Ralph Nader and Mark Green, reprinted with permission from the April 2, 1990 issue of THE NATION. For subscription information, call 1-800-333-8536. Portions of each week's Nation magazine can be accessed at http://www.thenation.com.

address as well as his assertion that "the greatest gift is helping others" in his State of the Union Message. But while Michael Dukakis could have delivered the same State of the Union speech, Reagan would have submitted a budget just as ungenerous to the most vulnerable Americans. A thousand points of blight?

Lost Economic Prominence. In 1981 the United States was the world's leading creditor nation, with a $141 billion net international investment credit; after eight years of Reagan-Bush, it had become the world's largest debtor, with a total debt of more than $700 billion. The nation's personal savings rate plunged by one-half, real wages fell and in nine years the federal debt grew three times as much as it had since the birth of the Republic. As a result of this borrowed prosperity, "America is losing its ability to compete in world markets," said John Young, chairman of a presidential Council on Competitiveness.

Recent world events have made it plain that economic power, not military might, will determine who the superpowers of the 1990s are. How are we doing in Bush's America? Not so hot. Nonfarm productivity growth fell to less than 1 percent in 1989, the lowest since the 1981-82 recession. The huge federal deficit is not significantly lower once the Social Security surplus is discounted—nor is the trade deficit. Based on the location of available capital, Lech Walesa would have been well advised to have skipped Washington and gone straight to Tokyo. So far President Bush hasn't really dealt with, or even mentioned, the long-term implications of these dismal facts.

Investing in Bombs, Not Bridges. Because of tax cuts for the wealthy coupled with a $2.2 trillion military spending binge

(including $30 billion for unneeded spare parts), unpaid bills mounted in the 1980s. In an unprecedented series of reports issued right after the 1988 election, the General Accounting Office documented the deterioration of the nation's infrastructure because of inadequate capital investment. The G.A.O.'s estimated bill for repairing America comes to $500 billion to renovate bridges and the interstate highway system, $150 billion to clean up toxic dumps, $100 billion to $130 billion to decontaminate nuclear weapons facilities, $20 billion for new public housing, and more.

Will the evaporation of the Soviet threat, the ostensible reason for most of our $306.9 billion defense budget, persuade Bush to transfer funds from fighting potential enemies abroad to fighting proven ones at home? Not yet. He seems intent on "beating plowshares into swords," as Richard Gephardt, the House majority leader, said. A President who says we should spend nearly the same amount combating "complacency" as Reagan did in combating Communism is saying that the Defense Department is an entitlement program.

Consumers Away. Promising in his 1980 campaign to "get government off our backs," Reagan got government (read: law and order) off the backs of corporations by sabotaging the health and safety agencies that were supposed to assure safe food, drugs, pesticides and water, and by immobilizing antitrust laws in the midst of the greatest merger wave of the century. Further, the Reagan-Bush Administration rescinded protections such as a tougher crash standard for motor vehicles that was slated to start saving an estimated 11,000 lives a year on the highways in 1981. This delay has directly caused tens of thousands of serious injuries and deaths on the highways.

In his Economic Report to Congress, President Bush signaled a welcome departure from his predecessor when he recognized that "in some cases, well-designed regulation can serve the public interest." And new regulations restricting misleading health claims on food packages were considered a good first step by the Center for Science in the Public Interest. Yet Bush allowed the Consumer Product Safety Commission to slip into a coma by failing to appoint enough commissioners (at least three) to form a governing quorum.

Ecocide. For nine years two Presidents shrugged and said, "Who, us worry?" while acid rain ravaged lakes, waste gases widened the hole in the ozone layer and the greenhouse effect warmed up the earth. The Reagan-Bush Environmental Protection Agency will be remembered largely as a place of scandal and stagnation. (Joel Hirschorn, a senior associate at the Office of Technology Assessment, says "not one major complex toxic waste site has ever been completely cleaned up.")

If George Bush thinks he can reverse the James Watt years merely by quoting Teddy Roosevelt and elevating the head of the E.P.A. to Cabinet rank, he's wrong. Instead, he's shown his true hand by opposing serious action on global warming or on clean-air legislation, and by reneging on his promise to protect wetlands. He didn't even include funds in his 1990 budget for a cleanup of Boston Harbor, to which he devoted so much attention in the 1988 presidential campaign, confirming Governor Dukakis's charge that it was "just a phony campaign issue." Environmental President? Or environmentally hesitant?

S&L and HUD Scandals. In what is probably the largest epidemic of financial criminality in American history, the Reagan-Bush deregulation policies allowed thrift institutions to make reckless or corrupt investments while seeing less of federal auditors. Result: a bailout bill that will amount to more than $3,000 per taxpayer over the next ten years, with no reciprocal rights for taxpayers and depositors or guarantees to prevent future debacles.

The corruption in the Department of Housing and Urban Development showed that it had become an accounts payable for Republican cronies. Conservative columnist James Kilpatrick blames Reagan, who "paid virtually no attention to this huge, costly Department." Meanwhile, the percentage of American families owning their homes actually *fell* in the 1980s for the first time since World War II.

The department has regained visibility and some respectability under Jack Kemp, but not much money. And don't expect too much from the independent prosecutor who will look into the HUD scandal. Dick Thornburgh, the most partisan Attorney General since John Mitchell, has carefully limited the scope of the inquiry to avoid further embarrassment. As for savings and loans, don't expect more than a fraction of these corporate crooks to face trial.

Regressive Redistribution of Wealth. Because Reagan-Bush cut benefits for the poor and at the same time cut taxes for the rich, the income share of the poorest fifth of the nation's households fell to 3.8 percent, the lowest since the 1950s, and the income of the wealthiest fifth rose to 46.3 percent, its highest ever. This trend will deepen if President Bush's capital gains tax cuts are enacted. Escalating Social Security taxes on working families have wiped out any gains from lower income tax rates and have effectively subsidized tax breaks for the richest citizens. Following a proposal by Senator Daniel Patrick Moynihan to reduce Social Security taxes, even the conservative Heritage Foundation admitted that "thanks to hikes in the Social Security payroll tax, the vast majority of middle-income Americans forfeit a larger share of their income to the federal tax collector in 1990 than they did in 1980."

Still, Bush insists on a capital gains tax in which 66 percent of the benefits would flow to the top 1 percent of all taxpayers, including himself. (Citizens for Tax Justice has revealed that Bush personally saved $303,516 in federal income taxes between 1980 and 1986 by using the old capital gains tax break.)

These Presidents are two class acts.

Reign of Error and Sleaze. From David Stockman's early admission that he essentially "cooked" the budget books to President Reagan's initial denial of an arms-for-hostages deal in the Iran/*contra* scandal to Elliott Abrams's documented lies in Congressional testimony, Reagan's two terms showed how routinely tactics conquer truth. And although more than a hundred Reagan appointees either were convicted of crimes or committed ethics violations (Ed Meese's own Justice Department concluded its chief had acted unethically), not once did Messrs. Reagan and Bush reproach the wrongdoers.

The Bush Administration has avoided so deplorable a rap sheet, in part because the Senate kept the ethically suspect John Tower from tainting the Cabinet. But a steady diet of deception (saying Soviet military spending is up when his Pentagon knows it's down; saying there was no quid pro quo to get Honduras to help the *contras* in exchange for aid when documents prove the opposite; denying a secret mission to Beijing so soon after the Tiananmen Square massacre, for example) shows the lingering influence of President Ronald Pinocchio.

Hostile Race Relations. What did Reagan-Bush do when the percentage of African-American and Latino youths attending college fell and the gap in life expectancy between blacks and whites widened during their decade of governance? They grossly reduced antidiscrimination law enforcement, appointed a largely white judiciary and ridiculed civil rights organizations as, in President Reagan's phrase, mere "special-interest" groups.

George Bush has now gone out of his way to change the tone of his Administration (he said all Americans must "confront and condemn racism, anti-Semitism, bigotry and hate"), in the process attracting a 68 percent approval rating among African-Americans. But his actual policies on affirmative action and job discrimination—his executive branch won't support proposed legislation to reverse several recent Supreme Court decisions hostile to civil rights—are vintage Reagan. "Extremely disappointing" is how Ralph Neas, executive director of the Leadership Conference on Civil Rights, rates them.

As the reactionary revisionism of the Reagan-Bush era continues, let's remember mourning in America: the oft-ignored legacies of economic slippage, child poverty, environmental abuse, racial tensions, S&L sleaze.

Will the Bush years bring some real *glasnost* to the White House? So far, not likely. Bush has proved to be, in the phrase of Georgetown University Law Center associate dean Peter Edelman, "the Revlon President," who applies cosmetic rhetoric to national problems.

Ultimately, though, the state of the Reagan-Bush legacy depends not on a speechwriter's cosmetics but on the actual living conditions of the American people. Has this presidential duo performed well or merely postured well? Will drug use be down? the air cleaner? poverty down and ethics up? Will there be more economic well-being for all Americans or only more wealth for the already powerful? And will Washington face up to our problems or look away?

Vaclav Havel, the playwright President of Czechoslovakia, counseled his people that the highest patriotism is the frank admission of serious problems. For Ronald Reagan and, so far, for George Bush, the idea has been to throw a coat of fresh paint over a house with rotting beams.

DECODING THE TEXT

1. Nader and Green list ten examples to support their claim that Reagan and Bush (senior) have "quietly sapped America's long-term strength." Do you agree with their ten supports?

2. How do you think the authors decided on an order for their ten supports or proofs? What is the organizational pattern used?

CONNECTING TO YOUR CULTURE

1. How many of the issues listed by Nader and Green are still problematic today?

2. Has Bush Jr. continued the policies of his father and Reagan? Has he made any important changes?

3. How have these policies affected your life or the lives of your friends and family?

Reading Selections: the '90s

CONSIDERING IDEAS

1. What is your perception of sororities and fraternities? What purpose(s) do they serve?

2. Are you a member of a sorority or fraternity? Does your campus even have sororities or fraternities?

3. Should these organizations be divided by race or other factors?

Alexandra Robbins, *public speaker and journalist, has made numerous appearances on various news and talk shows, including* 60 Minutes *and* The Oprah Winfrey Show. *Her written work has appeared in* The New Yorker, Atlantic Monthly, *and* The Washington Post. *She is the author of* The Overachievers: The Secret Lives of Driven Kids, The Secret Lives of Students: Greek Life and Secret Societies, *and* Pledged: The Secret Life of Sororities, *from which this excerpt was taken.*

PLEDGED

The Secret Life of Sororities

Alexandra Robbins

Tall, bright, pretty, and outgoing, Melody Twilley is leading me on a tour of the University of Alabama's Sorority Row: two streets full of impressive Greek Revival houses framed by manicured lawns, meticulously pruned shrubbery, and flowers planted in each sorority's colors. Rocking chairs and wrought-iron tables line columned porches straight from a southern grandmother's dreams. The front of the Zeta house is festooned with a large banner proudly proclaiming, "Congrats! ZTA Gini Mollohan lavaliered to BΘΠ Jason Hudson."

Melody and I pass the Tri-Delt house. "Old money," she says, gesturing to the fountain in front of the house, surrounded by brick mosaic and orange flowers, and featuring a sculpture of a cherub. On the sidewalk leading up to the house the Tri-Delt letters are inlaid in metal.

We pass the Pi Phi house, where broad windows reflect long Ionic columns tied with yellow ribbons. "New money," Melody points out. She sighs as we continue down Sorority Row. "Ah," she mutters. "Skid Row."

On paper, Melody Twilley is, by anyone's standards, prime sorority material. A graduate of the prestigious Alabama School of Math and Science, Melody won several awards and was chosen to speak at commencement. At the time that she rushed at the University of Alabama, she had a 3.87 GPA and sang first soprano in the campus choir. She was seventeen, having skipped two grades before arriving at college. Her father was known as the largest black landowner in the state.

In the fall of 2000, Melody signed up for fall rush. One of the main reasons she had backed out of going to Rice University at the last minute was that they didn't have sororities. At Alabama, by contrast, sororities practically controlled the student body. The University of Alabama, like many southern schools, runs a segregated rush process: white Greeks rush in the fall for white organizations, while the black Greeks rush in the spring for the black organizations. Melody didn't think anything of joining white rush; she was used to navigating a mostly white community from her time in high school. Many of the more ambitious Alabama students—and a fifth of the campus—join the UA Greek system, which is expected to match them with appropriate future spouses and provide an entree into a powerful state network. Residents who aren't members of the UA Greek system, it has been said, rarely break into the state's political and economic elite. But Melody wasn't motivated by the promise of power and connections. She merely liked the idea of belonging to a sisterhood. It sounded like fun.

So Melody, optimistic and excited, began the year as the only black girl to enter white rush. "I thought I was the greatest. Stupid me. I didn't know they didn't take black people," she explains. The girls seemed nice and Melody looked forward to the social outlet a sorority could offer her. She was especially excited about the Thursday night "swaps," or Greek theme parties—"Pimps and Hos," "Saints and Angels"—in which pledges from sororities and fraternities were matched up. When seven of the sororities invited her back for the second round of rush, she was mildly disappointed that the other eight weren't interested, but didn't think anything more of it.

Only a small group of women were rejected from all fifteen white sororities. Melody was one of them. Over the next year, faculty members and administrators rallied around Melody as a way to encourage the university to desegregate its Greek system and unify its rush process. In the fall of 2001, at the insistent prodding of students, faculty members, and sorority alumnae, Melody rushed again, this time with letters of recommendation from scores of sorority graduates and endorsements from university officials.

"I was glad she was going back through," says Kathleen Cramer, the university's associate vice president for Student Affairs. Cramer, who had been the president of the Kappa Kappa Gamma house when she attended Alabama in the 1970s, gestures in her office with manicured nails and a crisp bob. "I was very optimistic the second time could work. I lined up recommendations, introduced her to alumnae, student, and Panhellenic leaders, and a faculty member and I had a talk with her about rush wardrobe and conversation. We thought we could help her."

Melody wasn't completely willing to believe that she had been rejected the first time around because of her skin color. She still wanted to join a white sorority, and she thought there was a good chance they might take her in. By the third round of rush, only one sorority, Alpha Delta Pi, still had her on its list. Sparkling in an indigo gown, a rhinestone cross necklace and earring set, and smart patent-leather pumps, Melody walked into ADPi, the first house on the corner of Sorority Row. Inside, sisters and rushees were talking one-on-one, mostly about the latest football game. A sister sat Melody down. "There's a rumor going around that you're only going through rush just to prove a point," said the ADPi sister.

Melody was flabbergasted. "You've been through rush—why would anybody go through all of this twice just to prove a point?!" The sister seemed to understand. "I'm here to find sisterhood, fun, and good times, same as everyone else is," Melody continued. "Don't look at me as the black girl going through rush. Look at me as a girl going through rush." They couldn't do it. Once again, every white sorority on campus turned her down.

When I speak about this with Kathleen Cramer, she shakes her head with resignation. "This is a system steeped in tradition, and I think that's part of the problem. Chapters are afraid to go first. I think there's an unarticulated pressure toward sameness, which fosters racism

and a homogeneity they'll never see the rest of their lives," she says. In May 2002, Cramer and the Alabama faculty senate sent to each of the twenty-six historically white national sorority presidents a letter requesting help "eliminating barriers to recruitment of diverse members for fraternity and sorority chapters" by deemphasizing the letter of recommendation requirement. Only Tri-Delt responded. (The Tri-Delt president thanked Cramer and said she would work on this issue.) "Most Nationals don't want to talk about it," Cramer tells me. "Nationals have other priorities. These are women who had a very different sorority experience and are struggling with change. They're more worried about the media attention than they are about doing a progressive thing."

The University of Alabama remains the only Greek system in the country never to knowingly admit an African American. (One sister with a white mother and a black father came forward in 2001 to defend the Greeks, but because she looked like a white girl with a tan, her sorority hadn't known—and she hadn't confessed—her background.) This is a school where many of the alumni, who comprise the largest university alumni association in the world, opposed integration. This is a school where, in the late 1980s—when the campus chapter of Alpha Kappa Alpha, the country's oldest African American sorority, was about to move into what had until then been an all-white Sorority Row—two white students burned a cross on the front lawn of the new house.

"We have one hundred percent illegal segregation here, and the president, vice president, and board of trustees lie about it," says Pat Hermann, a professor at Alabama who has been fighting this issue for twenty years as the liaison to the faculty senate on Greek diversity and the chair of the Student Coalition Against Racism. When I meet with him in his out-of-the-way office on the English department floor, I don't have to prompt him with any questions. He calmly leans forward, eyes flashing through his thin-framed glasses, pale fists clenched in the sleeves of his checked blazer. "There have been a dozen whites in the black system, but there have been and are zero blacks in traditional sororities. This is our third century of total segregation. The administrators would rather support racism and a one hundred percent apartheid policy than take any real steps, steps they claim to be taking."

He points to the current issue of the student daily newspaper, which ran an article about a vice president who had just announced her resignation. "She was one of the very worst vice presidents we ever had. She took no steps. This problem could have been solved in ten minutes, but there is an extreme reluctance to polarize the racist element," he says. "The older Greek alumni are racist and the Panhellenic group here is hard-core racist. They want to make sure there is no desegregation under their watch. They are *not* going to allow a breaking of that line."

Hermann has been an explosive force on the segregation issue on a campus that he says hosts "the most powerful Greek system in America," a system that the sororities control, while the fraternities are "appendages." Hermann has been so vocal that the national office of a white sorority flew in a lawyer from Colorado to discuss cultural diversity with him. "She privately indicated that she supported me, but that her professional obligations required that she represent the other side of the argument." The national president of the sorority, Hermann says, "was very hostile to me simply because we suggested integration. She reacted in a way that, I felt, showed lack of breeding and a cold-hearted commitment to her local chapter's racist policies rather than a civilized, open-minded 'liberal' attitude toward the inevitable integration."

Hermann is disgusted with his university. "I'm pro-Greek, but hard-line racist sororities like all of ours should be disbanded. This is the only social group we allow to discriminate on the basis of race. It's illegal, it's immoral, it's imprudent," he says. This is a school where, Hermann tells me, his tone incredulous, "one of the members of the board of trustees said, 'We're not going to turn our fraternities and sororities into places where just any nigger could get in.'"

"I guess there were too many others saying, 'No, you're not letting that black girl in my sorority,'" Melody tells me now as we continue down Sorority Row. I silently wonder if Hermann ever told her what the trustee said.

"But why would you try again when it seemed those girls didn't want to be your sister?" I ask her.

"That's not what it was," Melody says. "It wasn't that the members didn't want to be my sister. It was pressure from the alumnae saying, 'I don't want a black girl wearing my sorority letters.'"

I give her a skeptical look.

"For the most part I blamed the alumnae, after the second time," she adds. "I can't think that the girls, even after all the pressure, would still not want me. I'm sure it was hard for some of them to agree to turn me down. At least, I would like to think that."

An Alpha Omega Pi sister who works at the library reference desk under Melody's supervision calls out to Melody and crosses the street to greet her. The girls talk about upcoming Formals. "She's a sweet girl," Melody tells me as we walk away. "But we're not allowed to talk about what happened. Rush is a forbidden topic with me. Sorority sisters always change the subject, even my good friends."

I ask her why she didn't consider joining any of the black sororities on campus, one of which expressly told her she'd be welcome. With one exception, the black sororities are housed across campus, far from the venerated Sorority Row. "I didn't know a whole lot about black sororities," Melody says. "And I wouldn't fit in at all. DST, AKA—they'd put me out in two days."

"Why?"

"Because they'd be like, 'You're really a white girl. You're on the wrong row.'"

We watch as, at about ten minutes to the hour, white girls come streaming out of the sorority houses with backpacks and sorority T-shirts, ponytails bouncing as they walk each other to class in small groups. Melody glances at one of the houses, then looks down. "Sometimes I wonder what could have been," she says softly. "It's hardest to see the girls who would have been in my pledge class. Life would have been so much easier if they had just let me in."

* * *

When Melody Twilley found herself without a Greek affiliation, she began researching MSU and dozens of other national multicultural sororities with the aim of founding her own nondiscriminatory multicultural group. At the first open meeting she held on campus for students interested in joining a multicultural society—an entity foreign to the University of Alabama—fifty girls showed up, many of them white. In January 2003, Melody and eight of the girls officially started their own sorority from scratch. For reasons they keep secret, they picked a mascot (the sea horse), colors ("real blue," blush, and silver), a flower (Stargazer Lily), and a jewel (pearl). They came up with a secret group purpose and the letters to stand for it: Alpha Delta Sigma. They wrote rituals, put themselves through an induction ceremony, a pledge period, and initiation, and a sisterhood was born.

Now, as Melody—in jeans, flip-flops, and a T-shirt commemorating a community service event—and I lounge on couches in a student center, coincidentally across from the university's Greek Life Office, she tells me what it's like to be a sister. "We had an ice cream social Tuesday night, Friday night we had a dinner, and we have to fulfill our community service requirement," she says, "We'll rush in the fall. We're trying to be as close to Panhellenic as possible, but there are some differences."

"Like what?" I ask.

"Well, during Panhellenic rush, [rushees] wait in front of each house and suddenly the doors fling open and the sisters do their 'door songs.'"

"They have door songs?"

"Oh, yes!" Melody puts on a phony wide smile and, in a cheesy little-girl voice, sings and claps the chirpy Phi Mu door song. Then she says, "We can't do door songs because we have no door."

The Panhellenic Association, the university's governing body for the white sororities, has yet to reach out to Alpha Delta Sigma. Melody plans to apply for her group to be accepted as a campus Panhellenic sorority; if Panhellenic rejects ADS, Melody will consider suing them.

A thin white girl passes by and taps Melody. "I'm going to come to one of y'all's things, I promise. It's just finals and everything," she says before moving on.

"Potential New Member," Melody explains to me, her face lit up as she uses one of the terms newly instituted by the national white sororities (it is supposed to replace the word "rushee").

I ask her why it is so important to her to be part of a sorority. "Why not just have friends?"

She tells me that sisters are more than friends. "We want to leave a legacy, perpetuate this. We'll be seniors and then the next year all of us are gone," she says. "I wanted to start a sorority so my future daughter can join it. All the other little girls would get to say, 'My mama was a Tri-Delt,' or 'My auntie was a Pi Phi.'" Melody laughs as she mimics the you-go-girl gesture of snapping in the shape of the letter Z. "My daughter will be able to say, 'My mama *founded* Alpha Delta Sigma.'"

DECODING THE TEXT

1. Why did Melody Twilley decide to rush white sororities rather than black ones? What was the result of this decision—for her? The white sororities? The black sororities? School administrators?

2. Whose voices does Robbins incorporate into her essay? What role(s) do these people play in the essay; what is their purpose?

CONNECTING TO YOUR CULTURE

1. Is the popular notion that sororities are only concerned with fashion and social events true in your experience? Why or why not?

2. How are sororities presented in popular film? In television shows, like the 2007 show *Greek*?

3. What is your experience with Greek organizations?

1. What is your idea of the suburbs? Who lives there?

2. What do suburbanites look like? Act like? What jobs do they hold?

3. Can you think of any television shows or movies that depict the suburbs or suburbanites?

William Sharpe *is a professor of English at Barnard College. He focuses on the literature, art, and culture of the modern city, with an emphasis on New York. He has published numerous articles and has a forthcoming book that focuses on the images of New York nightlife in paintings, literature, and photography.*

Leonard Wallock *is currently the associate director of the Walter H. Capps Center for the Study of Ethics, Religion, and Public Life at the University of California, Santa Barbara. At the time this article was published, he was the director of the Urban History Association and a professor at Hunter College of the City University of New York (CUNY). He is the author of* New York: Cultural Capital of the World 1940–1965 *and coauthored two other titles with William Sharpe. "Bold New City or Built-Up 'Burb? Redefining Contemporary Suburbia," from which this excerpt is taken, was first published in* American Quarterly *in 1994.*

BOLD NEW CITY
OR BUILT-UP 'BURB?

Redefining Contemporary Suburbia

William Sharpe and Leonard Wallock

America has created a new form of urban settlement. It is higher, bolder, and richer than anything man has yet called city.

. . . Most Americans still speak of suburbs. But a city's suburbs are no longer just bedrooms. They are no longer mere orbital satellites. They are no longer sub.

—Jack Rosenthal, "The Outer City:
U.S. in Suburban Turmoil," *New York Times,*
May 30, 1971

Postsuburban regions have become the most common form of metropolitan development in this country. And this emergence has undeniably transformed our lives.

—Rob Kling, Spencer Olin, and Mark Poster,
eds., *Postsuburban California,* 1991

In the last few decades, the United States has become a suburban nation. Between 1950 and 1980 the number of people living

Sharpe, William and Leonard Wallock. "Bold New City or Built-Up 'Burb? Redefining Contemporary Suburbia." AMERICAN QUARTERLY 46:1 (1994), 1–30. © The American Studies Association. Reprinted with permission of The Johns Hopkins University Press.

in suburbia nearly tripled, soaring from 35.2 to 101.5 million. By 1990, almost half of all Americans called suburbia home.[1]

* * *

Is Suburban Ideology Dead?

Because critics rely on functional rather than cultural criteria to proclaim the birth of the "new city," they forget that the "old" suburbia represented something more than a bedroom community. Focusing on changes in the suburban infrastructure enables Fishman to declare that "suburbia in its traditional sense now belongs to the past."[83] Similarly, Marsh's emphasis on new patterns in suburban family life—especially "wives holding jobs outside the home"—permits her to assert that "the suburban domestic ideal . . . no longer holds sway."[84] Both conclusions assume that functional and behavioral changes rapidly ensure liberating ideological ones. The patterns of employment and commuting that defined "classic suburbia"—where the white middle-class housewife and mother was sequestered at home while her husband worked in the city—may have evolved. But the fundamental attitudes underlying this way of life remain potent.[85] They include belief in female subordination, class stratification, and racial segregation, all wrapped up in a pastoral mythology. Nearly two hundred years in the making, suburban ideals are still widespread.[86] They continue to influence social behavior, particularly through mass culture media, and must be taken into account when analyzing the status of the suburbs today. As this section will demonstrate, television and film have helped keep the "old" suburbia alive.

Representations that reinforce suburban ideals abound both on television and in the movies. Televised images of suburbia are so prevalent that they now operate simultaneously on many levels. Programs affectionately recalling earlier eras—such as *The Wonder Years* (1988-1993), a sitcom which portrays the white-bread homogeneity of a boy's suburban schooldays in the 1960s—coexist with reruns of the original 1950s celebrations of suburban life—such as *Leave It to Beaver* (1957-1963) and *Father Knows Best* (1954-1962), where dads dispense sage advice to compliant wives and children. These visions of suburban yesteryear are complemented by programs that depict white middle-class life today. Among them are *Growing Pains* (1985-1992), which has been called a *Father Knows Best* for the 1980s, and *Family Ties* (1982-1989), a role-reversal comedy featuring a teenage son who worships William F. Buckley, Jr., espouses Reaganomics, and strives to bring his ex-hippie parents more in line with conventional suburban values. Finally, shows such as *Married . . . with Children* (1987–), *The Simpsons* (1990–), and *Dinosaurs* (1992–) parody the now-classic suburban sitcoms of the 1950s only to recreate in detail for new audiences the very conventions of suburban life they ostensibly subvert.

Cinematic treatments of suburbia offer a similar assortment of takes on a patriarchal world. In the nostalgic *Peggy Sue Got Married* (1986), an unhappily wed suburban mother of the 1980s magically returns to her youth, where she passively reenters the relationship that will entrap her. Films dating from the "golden age" of suburbia, such as *Mr. Blandings Builds His Dream House* (1948) and *The Man in the Gray Flannel Suit* (1956), focus sympathetically on the struggle of commuting husbands to maintain their wives and children in pastoral splendor. Contemporary comedies of domestic crisis, such as

Home Alone (1991) and *Suburban Commando* (1991), shore up the embattled patriarchy by relying on stand-in fathers, whether from grammar school or outer space, to protect the home and community against outsiders. Golden-age suburbia has also been the subject of film parodies like *Edward Scissorhands* (1990), which, in the midst of recounting a cruel fairy tale of suburban ostracism, still fondly reimagines the quaint conformity and rigid gender roles of tract-house life.

Television has played an especially decisive part in the social construction of suburbia. Television came of age during the suburban boom of the 1950s, and, as a home-based form of entertainment, it soon emerged as the perfect vehicle to sell the suburban lifestyle—with its fixation on good housekeeping, the newest appliances, and a late-model car—to a national audience.[87] Television shows and advertisements offered consumer items and behavioral models designed to be attractive to all members of the family. Erasing time as easily as space, television represented consumer-oriented suburbia, with its housebound mothers and commuting fathers, as both perennial and universal; in the early 1960s, the cartoon series *The Flintstones* (1960–1966) and *The Jetsons* (1962–1963) imagined gadget-conscious suburban life as the ultimate human condition, from the stone age to the space age.

To be sure, the effect of television as a socializing agent is much disputed by theoreticians of mass media. While earlier analysts regarded consumers as passive recipients of capitalist brainwashing, more recently, proponents of the "uses and gratifications" approach have contended that television viewers are "actively judging and deciding subjects," who manipulate visual images rather than being manipulated by them.[88] But both of these positions overstate the case. The crux of the matter is, as Stephen Heath points out, that experience and reality "are not separate from but are also determined by television which is a fundamental part of them. . . . [They] are complexly defined, mediated, [and] realized in new ways in which the power of the media is crucial."[89] Thus, rather than regarding the viewer as incapable of resisting or interpreting images, it makes more sense to view television reception as a partly determined, partly determinative process. As Ella Taylor puts it, television images "both echo and participate in the shaping of cultural trends."[90]

Representations of suburban life on television help hold social practices in place by sanctioning classic suburban patterns of consumption, social exclusivity, and familial relations. In the 1990s, many television programs continue to reinforce the myth of suburbia as a haven in which white middle-class families live sheltered from the ills of the city.[91] Not only are suburban-based series overwhelmingly populated by well-to-do whites,[92] but when urban outsiders do appear, their working-class behavior makes them objects of humor and suspicion.[93] Set in Connecticut, *Who's the Boss* (1984–1992) focuses on the class tension between a female advertising executive who works in Manhattan and her live-in male housekeeper from Brooklyn. On the West Coast, *The Fresh Prince of Bel-Air* (1990–) explores a similar situation; a streetwise black teenager from West Philadelphia creates havoc when he goes to live with his rich relatives in an elite suburban-style enclave in Los Angeles. The newcomer's embarrassing presence also signals to viewers how out of place black families seem in this rarified milieu. These series build upon the prime-time tradition that usually restricts minorities and members of the working class to cities: *The Jeffersons* (1975–1985) and *Diff'rent Strokes* (1978–1985) are set in Manhattan; *Amen* (1986–1991) in Philadelphia; *All in the Family [Archie Bunker's Place]* (1971–1983) in Queens; *Laverne and Shirley* (1976–1983) in Milwaukee; and *Roc* (1991–) in Baltimore. Even the black, dual-career, professional family depicted on *The Cosby Show* (1984–1992) resides in Brooklyn, when in reality they would have been more likely to live in the suburbs. Thus television segregates its imaginary suburbs to an even greater degree than suburbs are segregated in real life.[94]

Television's penchant for suburban sameness is coupled with its preference for traditional male-female roles.[95] In particular the suburban middle-class housewife has been stereotyped as consumer, home manager, and sexual object.[96] The "ideal" role of the suburban woman was most thoroughly charted in the situation comedies that originated in the 1950s, such as *The Donna Reed Show* (1958–1966) and *The Adventures of Ozzie and Harriet* (1952–1966). These series provided a "natural" environment in which docile homemakers acted out prescribed rituals of social interaction and material consumption. As Mary Beth Haralovich writes, "the suburban family sitcom indicates the degree of institutional as well as popular support for ideologies which naturalize class and gender identities."[97]

But if in the 1950s television focused on minor family crises which momentarily disrupted the placid domesticity of suburbia, programming in the 1980s explored the threat to familial harmony posed by working women[98] and reiterated the message that they belonged at home. In her 1989 study of "prime-time families," Ella Taylor concludes that many contemporary television shows provide "at best a rehearsal of the costs of careerism for women, at worst an outright reproof for women who seek challenging work."[99] Susan Faludi extensively documents in *Backlash* that "in the mid-'80s, [television] reconstructed a 'traditional' female hierarchy, placing suburban homemakers on the top, career women on the lower rungs, and single women at the very bottom."[100] With a few exceptions, such as *L.A. Law* (1986–) and *Murphy Brown* (1988–), network television featured women like Hope Murdoch in *thirtysomething* (1987–1991), who gave up her career to stay home with the kids, or Elizabeth Lubbock in *Just the Ten of Us* (1988–1990), an outspoken antifeminist who proved her womanhood as a homemaker while her gym-teacher husband struggled to make ends meet.

Many Hollywood films also bolster the idea that women must stay at home to preserve suburban domesticity. Sometimes they elaborate a related theme: that women may need to combat outsiders who menace the security of suburban neighborhoods. Two of the most notorious affirmations of the classic female sequestration pattern are *Fatal Attraction* (1987) and *Presumed Innocent* (1990).[101] In *Fatal Attraction,* a husband's efforts to end a brief affair with a career woman he meets at work in the city lead her to attack his family and home in the suburbs. The spurned woman is presented amid trappings of the horror genre—lurid sunsets, oil-barrel fires outside her apartment—and she brings urban evil into the suburban backyard, schoolground, and colonial-style home. She can only be stopped by a bullet, and only the beleaguered wife is able to pull the trigger, thereby rescuing the nuclear family and shoring up patriarchy.[102] In *Presumed Innocent*, a suburban homemaker makes a preemptive strike; she murders her husband's lawyer mistress and conceals the crime so well that her husband is almost convicted of it. Both films portray wives fighting the dangerous power that urban career women exert over their husbands. What seems at first to be a feminist twist—the wives, not the husbands, seize the initiative and intervene—in fact reinforces the notion that suburban women are vitally needed in the home to defend their marriages and families against other women who have none. The film critic Kathi Maio neatly sums up Hollywood's "anti-feminist punch": "the good/chaste/suburban/wife/homemaker must fend off the attack of the evil/sexy/urban/slut/career woman. When the Mother and the Whore do battle, can the victor be in doubt?"[103]

Films in which women battle to save home, husband, and children belong to a larger, "home-in-danger" genre that exploits suburbanite fears that their way of life is imperiled by the breakdown of exclusivity, the traditional family, and cultural homogeneity. The genre is predicated on the nineteenth-century realization—explored by Poe, Dickens, and others—that since the bourgeois household appears to be the last refuge from social disruption, nothing will be more terrifying than threats to the safety of the family in its own home.[104] *The 'Burbs* (1989), one of the best recent examples, is a comic analysis of suburban paranoia in which bickering neighbors

unite to spy on peculiar new residents with foreign accents, whom they suspect of being body snatchers. Patient, detached wives mother their inept husbands through futile raids on the newcomers' house. Momentary doubts prompt the protagonist to shout, "so they're different—they didn't do anything to us," but his plea for tolerance loses all credibility when he discovers that the trunk of the strangers' car is full of human bones. The film ends with the most aggressive of the vigilantes shouting to television cameras, "I think the message to psychos, fanatics, murderers, nutcases all over the world is: do not mess with suburbanites, because we're just not going to take it anymore." Despite its self-mocking tone, the film vocalizes and validates suburban fears of the immigrant Other.

In films focusing on children and teenagers, the streets and backyards of suburbia belong to kids, who create a microcosmic version of their parents' world. Among the most-watched films of all time, suburban classics such as *E.T. The Extra-Terrestrial* (1982) and *Back to the Future* (I, II, and III) (1985–1990) follow a "kids save the day" plot in which adults are hopeless bumblers or symbols of sinister self-interest.[105] Only the children, by practicing self-reliance and ingenuity, can eventually restore the social order that their parents taught them and thus maintain its gender and class structures. In *E.T.*, children in a tract-house settlement in California befriend a childlike extraterrestrial whose only aim is to "go home." While their sister trails behind, boys on their bikes succeed in foiling representatives of the adult world (the U.S. government and the police) so that domestic harmony can be restored.

The *Back to the Future* trilogy uses its complex chronology to convey a similar message: young males must temporarily assume adult responsibility to protect their suburban world from outsiders. With the aid of a father figure, Doc Brown, a teenager named Marty McFly alters history to provide a better life for his family in their suburban California town, "Hill Valley." In the first film, Marty returns to the 1950s to redirect the course of his parents' relationship by standing up, in the place of his father, to the local bully, Biff. The second film, set in the near future, echoes Frank Capra's *It's A Wonderful Life* (1946) by showing the urban nightmare that would have befallen Hill Valley if Biff's son had succeeded in turning the town over to developers and to organized crime. As in Capra's film, the hero realizes that he can save his town only by remaining in it as a loyal citizen and by raising his children there. The third episode of *Back to the Future* journeys to the Wild West period of the town's history, when Biff's ancestors were also determined to foment crime and vice. Foiling his enemies one last time, Marty returns to the present and rejoins his passive girlfriend, who has slept through most of the story. He reassumes the conventional role of boyfriend and husband-to-be in a now-stable suburb in the 1980s, the best of all possible worlds.[106]

Thus, despite the growth of the "new city," the suburbs are still frequently represented as the same old neighborhood, though now they are besieged by grave new threats—sexual, social, supernatural—that require ever more extreme responses. As these examples indicate, women's opportunity to work in high-rise office parks down the interstate has not brought about the "end of suburbia." Amid a changing landscape, the "suburbanization" of a new generation continues, aided by the long-lived relics of the 1950s suburb. From detergent commercials on daytime television to comic strips such as *The Family Circus, Blondie,* and *Dennis the Menace*, the middle-class housewife still stands at the stove while commuting husband and rambunctious kids dominate the action and create piles of laundry around her.[107] In many representations, children assume parental roles and reestablish domestic order so as to preserve a suburban way of life. Through such *rites de passage,* children are taught to defend and practice the same values as their parents, for the video image performs the same work of socialization on its young audience that it depicts happening to the children onscreen. Thus it comes as no surprise that in 1986 *Newsweek* ran an article on suburbia subtitled "Boomers Are Behaving Like Their Parents" or that in 1987 a suburban rock group's anthem to teen-age alienation concluded:

And the kids in the basement will carry on the
    family name
And the kids in the basement will turn out just
    the same
And the kids in the basement will have more
    kids to blame.[108]

Far from expiring, the ideology of suburbia—as embodied in film, television, and other forms of mass culture—still aggressively perpetuates the stereotypes upon which the traditional suburb was built.

Thus, while some scholars and journalists have declared that suburbia is now "over," its vitality—whether defined in physical, social, or cultural terms—remains undiminished. Indeed, the forces driving suburbanization have grown even stronger in the last few decades. Since World War II, suburban America has changed in substantial and even profound ways. But the rush to identify its new features has obscured something equally important—the underlying continuity in its character. Prematurely declaring the death of traditional suburbia, observers overlook the persistence of its essential features: a continuing resistance to heterogeneity and a desire to remain apart. Even as suburbia evolves, its ethos is likely to endure. Rather than having come to an end, the history of suburbia is still in the making.

NOTES

1. Census figures indicate that by 1990 about 46 percent of the American population resided in suburbs. See Frank Clifford and Anne C. Roark, "Big Cities Hit by Census Data Showing Declining Role," *Los Angeles Times,* 24 Jan. 1991; and Robert Reinhold, "Chasing Votes from Big Cities to the Suburbs," *New York Times,* 1 June 1992.

* * *

82. Stuart M. Blumin, "The Center Cannot Hold: Historians and the Suburbs," *Journal of Policy History,* vol. 2, no. 1 (1990): 119.

83. Fishman, *Bourgeois Utopias,* 205.

84. Marsh, *Suburban Lives,* 187.

85. In 1976, Barry Schwartz argued that the urbanization of the suburbs was not likely to alter their essential character. The "superimposition in the suburbs of drastic population and economic growth upon a stubbornly permanent sociopolitical base," he found, meant that "the 'face' of the suburb is changing" but its "underlying structure—its 'soul,' so to speak—is not." "Images of Suburbia: Some Revisionist Commentary and Conclusions," in *The Changing Face of the Suburbs,* ed. Barry Schwartz (Chicago, 1976), 339.

86. As Mary Corbin Sies writes, the "suburban ideal—the assumption that the proper residential environment was one in which every family resided in a one-family home with plenty of yard within a locally controlled, homogeneous community—is still embraced by many Americans today, having been incorporated into our common understanding of the American dream itself." See "The City Transformed: Nature, Technology, and the Suburban Ideal, 1877–1917," *Journal of Urban History* 14 (Nov. 1987): 83.

87. See Mary Beth Haralovich, "Sitcoms and Suburbs: Positioning the 1950s Homemaker," *Quarterly Review of Film and Video* 11 (1989): 61–83.

88. See Stephen Heath, "Representing Television," in *Logics of Television: Essays in Cultural Criticism,* ed. Patricia Mellencamp (Bloomington, Ind., 1990), 284.

89. Ibid., 289–90.

90. See Ella Taylor, *Prime-Time Families: Television Culture in Postwar America* (Berkeley, 1989), 4. See also Lynn Spigel, "Television in the Family Circle: The Popular Reception of a New Medium," in Patricia Mellencamp, ed., *Logics of Television: Essays in Cultural Criticism* (Bloomington, Ind., 1990), 73–97.

91. Police shows set in the city contribute to this picture by sensationalizing urban crime and violence: cf. *Miami Vice* (1984–1989), *Hill Street Blues* (1981–1987), *Kojak* (1973–1978), *The Equalizer* (1985–1989), and NYPD Blue (1993–). On the "antiseptic model of space" proposed by television's rendition of suburbia, see Lynn Spigel, "The Suburban Home Companion: Television and the Neighborhood Ideal in Postwar America," in *Sexuality and Space,* ed. Beatriz Colomina (New York, 1992), 185–217.

92. Among the prime-time shows set in affluent white suburbs and having few or no black or working-class characters are: *Dallas* (1978–1991); *Family Ties* (1982–1989); *The Golden Girls* (1985–1993); *Alf* (1986–1990); *Parker Lewis Can't Lose* (1990–1993).

93. Urbanites do not necessarily have to be visible to provoke displays of suburban antipathy. In a September 1991 episode of *Growing Pains,* a Long Island schoolteacher who has taken in a homeless boy named Luke rejects the application of would-be foster parents

from the city: "forget about that couple from Brooklyn—I don't want Luke being raised by people who drag their knuckles on the ground."

94. As Mark Crispin Miller argues, prime-time segregation "betrays the very fears that it denies. In thousands of high-security buildings, and in suburbs reassuringly remote from the cities' 'bad neighborhoods,' whites may, unconsciously, be further reassured by watching not just Cosby, but a whole set of TV shows that negate the possibility of black violence with lunatic fantasies of containment." "Cosby Knows Best," *Boxed In: The Culture of TV* (Evanston, Ill., 1988), 74.

95. For an analysis of television's persistent gender stereotyping since the 1950s, see Susan Faludi, *Backlash* (New York, 1991), 140–68.

96. See Elaine Tyler May, *Homeward Bound: American Families in the Cold War Era* (New York, 1988); and Haralovich, "Sitcoms and Suburbs," 61–83.

97. Haralovich, "Sitcoms and Suburbs," 81.

98. Literary views of the suburbs during the 1950s, as exemplified by the works of John Cheever and John Updike, were far more critical of the constricting roles that men and women were expected to play. In the 1980s, such authors as Don DeLillo, Gloria Naylor, and Frederick Barthelme continued to emphasize suburban status-consciousness, sexual anomie, and racial and social stratification.

99. Taylor, *Prime-Time Families,* 159.

100. Faludi, *Backlash,* 148.

101. Other recent Hollywood movies suggesting that women belong in the home, caring for their children, are *Someone to Watch over Me* (1987) and *Baby Boom* (1987).

102. For an extended discussion of the filmmakers' antifeminist intent, see Faludi, *Backlash,* 112–26.

103. Kathi Maio, *Feminist in the Dark: Reviewing the Movies* (Freedom, Calif., 1988), 218.

104. Some examples of the suburban horror genre include *The Amityville Horror* (1979), *Friday the 13th* (1980), *A Nightmare on Elm Street* (1984), and their various sequels.

105. The darker side of this genre is represented by films such as *Over the Edge* (1979), in which alienated suburban kids living in still unfinished tract housing are so disgusted with their environment that they lock their parents in the local school and go on an apocalyptic rampage. An outsider explains to the parents, "you all were in such a hopped up hurry to get out of the city that you turned your kids into exactly what you were trying to get away from."

106. See Maio's incisive analysis of the difference between male and female time-travel in the suburbs: "*Back to the Future* allows a teenage boy, Marty McFly, to go back and change life for the better. He is able to bring his parents together, improve the lives and lifestyle of his entire family, *and* save the life of his friend and mentor, Doc Brown. . . . It is an *empowering* vision of what a young man can do. But in *Peggy Sue Got Married,* where a mother returns to her high-school days in 1960, "a grown woman . . . is totally unable to change even the course of her own life. . . . In a world of happy and successful male time travelers, the female time-traveler is passive in and little enriched by her re-exploration of the past" (*Feminist in the Dark,* 192–93).

107. Although Blondie now has a paying job, Dagwood has yet to assume many of her domestic chores.

108. Raymond Jalbert, quoted in Donna Gaines, *Teenage Wasteland: Suburbia's Dead End Kids* (New York, 1991), 16.

1. According to Sharpe and Wallock, fundamental suburban ideals include belief in "female subordination, class stratification, and racial segregation." How do they illustrate this assertion? Are they convincing?

2. Do you think this has changed since the mid-90s, when this article was published?

CONNECTING TO YOUR CULTURE

1. Sharpe and Wallock credit television with perpetuating myths of the suburb. Are they accurate?

2. Do you identify with any of the suburban families mentioned in the essay? Why or why not?

3. What television shows or movies since the mid-90s have continued this image of suburbia? Have the media changed this image in any way?

• • • • • • • • • • • • • • • • • • • •

Reading Selections: the '00s

CONSIDERING IDEAS

1. How many NASCAR drivers can you name? How many NASCAR sponsors can you name?

2. Have you ever actually watched a NASCAR race?

3. Where have you encountered these various NASCAR personalities?

M. Graham Spann *is an associate professor of sociology at Lees-McRae College. He is interested in issues of community, including the classroom and NASCAR races. The article featured here was first published in* The Journal of Popular Culture *in 2002.*

NASCAR RACING FANS

Cranking Up an Empirical Approach

M. Graham Spann

The death of Dale Earnhardt on the last lap of the 2001 Daytona 500 brought unprecedented media attention to NASCAR fans. Media sources showed fans gathered at racetracks, churches, and other memorial services where they prayed, cried, and talked to each other about what Earnhardt meant to them personally, and to the quality of their lives. Nearly 4,000 people attended a service at the Bristol Motor Speedway in Tennessee, and the Governor of South Carolina declared the week of March 13th, 2001, "Dale Earnhardt Memorial Week." These examples illustrate the connection between NASCAR fans and American popular culture. NASCAR racing fans are some of the most loyal sports enthusiasts and represent a population ready for increased analytical consideration.

Social scientists have paid little attention to fans of automobile racing in the United States. Of particular note is the lack of empirical research on NASCAR fans. On any given weekend from the middle of February to the beginning of November social scientists can find hundreds of thousands of people gathered at automobile race venues across America. The Memorial Day Winston Cup race in Charlotte, North Carolina, for example, typically draws in excess of 180,000 people. NASCAR (National Association of Stock Car Auto Racing) is an organization that governs a set of rules regarding the technical and engineering components of racing cars; as well as race rules, regulations, logistics, marketing, and general business practices of the sport. NASCAR, founded in 1947, held many of its races in the southern part of the United States, but it is no longer constrained by southern consumers or venues (Fielden). In the past five years, construction of racetracks has taken place in decidedly non-southern places like Chicago, Illinois; Las Vegas, Nevada; Loudon, New Hampshire and Fontana, California. Clearly, people from many different geographic regions now go to the races, making racing one of the most attended cultural and sporting events in America (Howell; Lord).

The search for patterns among groups of people is a basic task of social scientists and this paper suggests a five-fold approach for discovering patterns among NASCAR fans. All sports are embedded in the general patterns of social interaction and organization in society, so the premise here is that NASCAR fans are people participating in collective behaviors that have consequences for individuals (Mills, Nixon & Frey). These consequences may range from unwittingly perpetuating inequality to the development of identity in a (racing) social context. As such, this paper suggests gathering data on (1) the demographic composition of NASCAR fans, especially class, race, and gender; (2) the cultural and sub-cultural phenomena of fans including the role of heroes in fans' lives; (3) fans' sense of

"NASCAR Racing Fans: Cranking Up an Empirical Approach" by M. Graham Spann from JOURNAL OF POPULAR CULTURE, Fall 2002, pp. 352–360. Reprinted by permission of Wiley-Blackwell Publishing.

community; (4) how fans create their identities around racing norms and values; and finally, (5) the organizational structure of fans. The hope is that scholars of popular culture, sports sociology, and the like will gain some insight into fans of NASCAR racing that will help them set forth a productive research agenda.

Demographic Composition

Fans are enthusiastic admirers of a person, organization, or movement (Volger & Schwartz). One popular myth about NASCAR fans is that they are all white, working-class males. Concomitantly, some assume that racism and sexism also flourish among these males given that the confederate flag is a widely displayed symbol at race venues. Social scientists need good information about socially sanctioned exclusivity, intentional or otherwise, among NASCAR fans. We need to critically examine the demographic composition of fans. It is not the case that NASCAR fans are only from one social class position. An increasingly large number of dominant group members from higher classes enjoy the sport. Business executives are now using skyboxes at racetracks to entertain clients, just as they do in professional basketball or football. Furthermore, though income is only one proxy measure of class position, it is worth noting that nearly 13% of NASCAR fans have a household income above $75,000 a year (Simmons Market Research Bureau, Inc.; Performance Research).

Most social scientists agree that it is difficult to separate social class descriptions of Americans from their racial composition. That is to say, racial and ethnic minorities disproportionately occupy status positions near the bottom of the class structure. Clearly, an athletes' race is an organizing feature of most professional sports. Some suggest that overt racism exists when whites occupy more leadership positions and blacks occupy more subordinate positions (Myers). The notion of "stacking" comes to mind here. Loy and McElvogue show how racial segregation in professional sports is positively correlated with the centrality of position. Black athletes are often forced to compete among themselves, rather than with members of other racial groups, for team membership and playing time because they do not typically occupy the most powerful positions (Nixon & Frey).

Wendell Scott is one of the few black drivers in NASCAR's history (Howell), but NASCAR teams currently have limited minority representation. This might partially explain the mostly white fan base. Fans of professional sports typically identify with members of their same racial and ethnic background, but NASCAR, as represented by its top series "The Winston Cup," currently has no drivers from underrepresented groups. Crews who work on the racecars are more racially diverse, but crews typically receive less media and promotional attention than drivers do. Ask any NASCAR fan that you know whom their favorite "right tire changer" is and you will likely get a blank look of confusion. If, however, we compare racing drivers to football quarterbacks and racing crews to football linemen, then the stacking hypothesis is useful.

Nixon points out that when elite sports organizations use exclusive social and economic membership criteria, they reinforce historical segregation patterns. The appeal, then, of certain sports to dominant group members may be a basis for boundary maintenance (Schwalbe, Godwin, Holden, Schrock, Thompson, Wolkomir). The social class of sports fans may vary over time within a nation or community, as well as across nations and communities (McPherson, Curtis & Voy). Collecting data on the demographic composition of NASCAR fans should provide some interesting cross-cultural data because other race organizations in other countries (i.e., Formula 1) may have a more diverse fan base in terms of class, race, and gender.

The gender composition of NASCAR fans could also be included in any demographic investigation. Women drivers have historically been a part of NASCAR racing, but currently only Shawna Robinson is a competitive driver. Messner argues that the propensity for men to be more involved in sports than women is part of our socially constructed cognitive images of what men and women are supposed to be and do. Dominant ideologies of what it means to be a woman or a man typically reflect deeper-seated structural arrangements of society, especially patterns of power, status, and social class. Interestingly, nearly 39% of NASCAR fans over 18 are women (Simmons Market Research Bureau, Inc.; Performance Research). Given generally acknowledged differences in socialization practices between females and males, we might partially explain the rather large proportion of female sports fans to changing gender expectations in society (Risman).

About 40% of NASCAR fans have attended college (Simmons Market Research Bureau, Inc.; Performance Research), but investigating how level of education affects NASCAR fan participation, their attitudes and beliefs, or other areas of sociological interest has yet to be empiri-

cally tested. The same is true for political affiliation. There are, of course, many other demographic variables available for our theoretical propositions, but discovering basic demographics like class, race, gender, education, and political affiliation is a start to an empirical approach of NASCAR racing fans.

Cultural and Sub-cultural Phenomena

The second empirical approach suggested by this paper is examining NASCAR racing fans from a cultural standpoint. Culture is all human-made products, either material or nonmaterial, associated with a society. Culture is the framework where society's members construct their way of life (Nixon & Frey). Howell chronicles the cultural history of the NASCAR Winston Cup Series and posits that the "regional strength projected by NASCAR racing history—its ties to southern culture and folklore—creates a stereotypical depiction of drivers" (117). These stereotypes are reinforced in movies like *Thunder Road* (1958), *The Last American Hero* (1973), and more recently *Days of Thunder* (1990) starring Tom Cruise. But whether these images help constitute a real world subculture remains to be discovered.

Is it the case that NASCAR fans constitute a subculture? Doob defines subculture as the "culture of a specific segment of people within a society, differing from the dominant culture in some significant respects, such as in certain norms and values" (66). Two major subcultural patterns may be present among race fans. The first pattern is usually mutually exclusive: fans of General Motors racing cars, fans of Ford racing cars, and fans of Dodge racing cars. Currently, NASCAR teams field Chevrolet, Ford, Pontiac,[1] and Dodge[2] racing cars. This phenomena is of particular cultural and symbolic interest because all of the cars, regardless of make or model, are hand-built, track-specific race cars. Major automobile producers manufacture few of the mechanical parts; rather, fabricators create cars that look like the major automotive brands. Some teams switch brands by simply putting a different body and name on the same chassis. As Berger once said, things "aren't what they seem." Fan loyalty to a particular brand of car may be relevant to the study of NASCAR fans, but we also need to discover if different norms and values exist for fans of the different makes. More importantly, we could discover the boundaries that people maintain which perpetuate the division between fans of the various makes.

Beyond automobile make, the second subcultural pattern among fans is loyalty to, and identification with, a particular driver. This loyalty also takes on symbolic meaning. Readers may have noticed small round window stickers with numbers on people's cars. These numbers correspond to NASCAR drivers' car numbers and are symbolic representations of driver support. For example, the number twenty-eight matches up with the Texaco sponsored Ford of Ricky Rudd and the number twenty-four represents the DuPont sponsored Chevrolet of Jeff Gordon. Most of us have seen sports news reports of Jeff Gordon winning a race, but many drivers have active fan clubs and loyal, lifelong fan followings. Fans of Dale Earnhardt, for example, have already catapulted him to a hero to be worshipped in the folk religion of NASCAR (Lord; Mathisen). As a hero, Earnhardt becomes a symbolic representation of the dominant social myths and values of society (Nixon).

Clearly, sport and culture are interdependent (Luschenn). Sport is bound to society and structured by culture. Connecting symbolic patterns is an important part of an empirical approach to NASCAR fans. Social scientists could discover if patterns exist between types of fans and the driver(s) they follow. Are fans willing to support their favorite driver if he/she switches to a different make of car? By looking at fan automotive brand and driver loyalty, we can better identify cultural and subcultural patterns and discover if NASCAR fans really are a subculture.

Sense of Community
The third empirical approach includes studying fans as members of friendship networks who share a common "sense of community" with other fans (Adams; McMillan and Chavis). Both Tönnies' work on community typologies and Durkheim's insight into social integration (conscience collective) stress the importance of community in human life. Similarly, sense of community ought to be important for NASCAR fans. Sense of community is where people believe their needs can be and are being met by the collective capabilities of the group; feel that they belong; believe that they can exert some control over the group; and have an emotional bond to the group (Sarason; McMillan). Sport spectating is a social activity (Danielson) and if NASCAR fans are a subculture then we should find a higher sense of community among them. Melnick sees sport spectatorship as enhancing people's lives by "helping them experience the pure sociability, quasi-intimate relationships, and sense of belonging that are so indigenous to the stands" (46). Spreitzer and Snyder found that 75% of women and 84% of men viewed sport as a good

way of socializing with others. We might then inquire whether sense of community among NASCAR fans exists only at the track or is it pervasive throughout the fan base.

Identity

Studying identity formation among NASCAR racing fans centers on subcultural norms and values. Identity "refers to who or what one is, to the various meanings attached to oneself by self and others" (Cook, Fine, House, 42). Do NASCAR fans build their sense of self around being a "Chevy" or a "Ford" fan? Fans might reinforce such an identity by cheering for a particular brand, rooting for and belonging to fan clubs associated with a particular driver, and finding themselves in social settings where other people have similar identity characteristics. We could look at how racing fans construct a sense of self and how that sense of self affects behavior.

Organizational Structures

Finally, social scientists could examine NASCAR auto racing fans from an organizational perspective. We can look at the degree of commitment to racing as a determinant of placement within a hierarchy (Yinger; Fox). Examining the cultural and subcultural beliefs of fans, their commitment to particular automotive brands and drivers, their sense of community, and their identity may give us the social organizational "picture" we need to determine a series of outwardly expanding concentric circles; with the most committed fans occupying the core, inner roles (these will probably be family members and friends who make up the actual teams), and the least involved fans composing the periphery.

Conclusion

As Guttmann notes, sport as a social institution includes a number of qualities such as secularism, the ideal of equality of opportunity, specialization of statuses and roles, bureaucracy, quantification of achievement and the keeping of records. By critically examining differences in social class, race, and gender, and by determining cultural and subcultural patterns, we garner insight into the structural foundations of fans' identity, their sense of self, and their sense of community. All of these areas point to the interplay of structural conditions and human action. Why do this? As social science moves into the 21st century, we must study topics people not trained in science can understand. We must continually emphasize the importance of social science and show that the theory and methods of our disciplines can make seemingly ordinary events, like automobile racing, understandable as part of the larger structural and institutional fabric.

Notes

1. Both Chevrolet and Pontiac are GM brand names.

2. Dodge recently re-entered NASCAR racing after a 15-year hiatus.

Works Cited

Adams, Rebecca G. "Inciting Sociological Thought by Studying the Deadhead Community: Engaging Publics in Dialogue." *Social Forces* 77(1) (1998): 1–25.

Berger, Peter. *Invitation to Sociology: A Humanistic Perspective.* Garden City, NY: Doubleday, 1963.

Cook, Karen S., Gary Alan Fine, and S. House, James, eds. *Sociological Perspectives on Social Psychology.* Boston: Allyn and Bacon, 1995.

Danielson, M. N. *Home Team: Professional Sports and the American Metropolis.* Princeton, NJ: Princeton UP, 1997.

Doob, Christopher Bates. *Sociology: An Introduction*. Fifth Edition. New York: The Harcourt Press, 1997.

Durkheim, E. *The Division of Labor in Society*. New York: Free Press of Glencoe, 1893/1964.

Fielden, Greg. *Forty Years of Stock Car Racing*. Revised Edition. Surfside Beach, SC: Galfield Press, 1992.

Fox, Kathryn Joan. "Real Punks and Pretenders: The Social Organization of a Counterculture." *Journal of Contemporary Ethnography* 16(3) (1987): 373–388.

Guttmann, Allen. *From Ritual to Record: The Nature of Modern Sports*. New York: Columbia University Press, 1978.

Howell, Mark D. *From Moonshine to Madison Avenue: A Cultural History of the NASCAR Winston Cup Series*. Bowling Green, OH: Bowling Green State University Popular Press, 1997.

Lord, Lewis. "The Fastest-Growing Sport Loses Its Hero." *U.S. News & World Report* 130(9) (2001): 52.

Loy, John W., and Joseph F. McElvoge. "Racial Segregation in American Sport." *International Review of Sport Sociology* 5 (1970): 5–24.

Luschen, Gunther. "The Interdependence of Sport and Culture." *International Review of Sport Sociology* 2 (1967): 27–41.

Mathisen, James A. "From Civil Religion to Folk Religion: The Case of American Sport." In Shirl J. Hoffman, ed. *Sport and Religion*. Champaign, IL: Human Kinetics, 1992. 17–34.

McMillan, David W. "Sense of Community." *Journal of Community Psychology* 24(4) (1996): 315–325.

McMillan, David W., and David M. Chavis. "Sense of Community: A Definition and Theory." *Journal of Community Psychology* 14 (1986): 6–23.

McPherson, Barry D., Curtis, James E., and John W. Voy. *The Social Significance of Sport*. Champaign, IL: Human Kinetics Publishers, 1989.

Melnick, Merrill J. "Searching for Sociability in the Stands: A Theory of Sports Spectating." *Journal of Sport Management* 7 (1993): 44–60.

Messner, Michael A. *Power at Play: Sports and the Problem of Masculinity*. Boston: Beacon Press, 1992.

Mills, Wright C. *The Sociological Imagination*. New York: Oxford UP, 1959.

Myers, Jim. "Racism is a Serious Problem in Sports." In *Sports in America: Opposing Viewpoints*. San Diego, CA: Greenhaven Press, 1994.

Nixon, Howard L., and James H. Frey. *A Sociology of Sport*. Belmont, CA: Wadsworth, 1996.

Nixon, Howard L. II. *Sport and the American Dream*. Champaign, IL: Human Kinetics/Leisure Press Imprint, 1984.

Performance Research (www.performanceresearch.com)

Risman, Barbara. *Gender Vertigo: American Families in Transition*. New Haven, CT: Yale UP, 1998.

Sarason, Seymour. *The Psychological Sense of Community: Prospects for a Community Psychology*. San Francisco: Jossey-Bass, 1974.

Schwalbe, Michael, Sandra Godwin, Daphne Holden, Douglas Schrock, Shealy Thompson, and Michele Wolkomir. "Generic Processes in the Reproduction of Inequality." *Social Forces* 79(2) (2000): 419–452.

Simmons Market Research Bureau, Inc. (www.smrb.com)

Spreitzer, Elmer, and Eldon E. Snyder. "The Psychosocial Functions of Sport as Perceived by the General Population." *International Journal of Physical Education* 11 (1975): 8–13.

Tönnies, F. *Community and Society*. New York: Harper & Row, 1957.

Volger, Conrad C., and Stephen E. Schwartz. *The Sociology of Sport: An Introduction*. Englewood Cliffs, NJ: Prentice-Hall, 1993.

Yinger, J. Milton. *Countercultures*. New York: Free Press, 1982.

DECODING THE TEXT

1. Spann suggests gathering empirical data about NASCAR fans with a fivefold approach. What are the five areas to investigate?

2. How would you suggest social scientists gather these data?

3. Are there other areas of investigation that you would suggest?

CONNECTING TO YOUR CULTURE

1. The author of this essay suggests that we look at sports and sports fans "by critically examining differences in social class, race, and gender." What does he have to say about the class, race, and gender of NASCAR fans?

2. What sports do you follow? What can you say about the class, race, and gender of the fans in this sport?

CONSIDERING IDEAS

1. What festivals are held in your neighborhood, state, or hometown? Do you attend these festivals?

2. What happens there? What kind of food is served?

3. To whom is the festival marketed? Do people come from other areas to attend?

Mike Caplanis *is an artist who has contributed illustrations to many publications, including* The Washington Post, *the* Los Angeles Times, American History, *and* Oxford American. *His caricature of Hillary Clinton and Condoleezza Rice was featured on the front page of* U.S. News & World Report. *He also illustrated* Drawn to the Civil War, *which features biographies and caricatures of Civil War heroes. This visual essay of* The National Storytelling Festival *first appeared in* Oxford American.

THE NATIONAL STORYTELLING FESTIVAL

SKETCHBOOK

BY MIKE CAPLANIS

The town of Jonesborough (pop: 4,200) is located in a picturesque area between the Blue Ridge and Great Smoky Mountains. Founded in 1779, Jonesborough is the OLDEST town in Tennessee. Since October 1973, it has been the annual site of the National Storytelling Festival. In that first year a total of sixty audience members and storytellers attended the festival (seating was on hay bales; the

The National Storytelling Festival

Jonesborough Tennessee

Oct 4, 5, 6, 2002

stage was a covered wagon). The focus back then was on Southern in particular Appalachian-folk tales stories, jokes and tall tales. The National Storytelling Festival which now averages twelve thousand visitors, has since taken on a more international flavor. This year's featured storytellers included a Cuban American, a Native American, a Québecois man and even somebody from Chicago.

Take the kids. Storytelling is for the whole family.

I love a great Story!

...I tried to warn President Garfield, but did he listen? NO

Composite storyteller:
Bill Winship of Itty Bitty Mississippi Claims to be 137 years old! He tells stories of people who are mostly like you and me but who have the habit of hibernating during the winter months. He himself adopted this practice as a young man and gives hibernation full credit for his long life.

And that is why to this day, my head is no bigger than a softball

Although he was unable to attend this year's festival due to illness, the abiding presence of the great six-foot-seven-inch Appalachian storyteller Ray Hicks (a man designated by our federal government a living HISTORICAL TREASURE) is nonetheless everywhere. Ray, with a voice like a phone call from the 1840's, has an almost saintly manner and tells ancient "Jack Tales" as handed down from his Scotch-Irish FOREBEARS. "I'd give my larynx for that kind of credibility," another storyteller was heard to say.

Some parents ought to be ASHAMED exposing their kids to terrifying Ghost stories told by some of the most physically frightening people that nature ever produced.

1. How do the visuals in this essay identify the people who attend The National Storytelling Festival?
2. What details can you read from the visuals that are not included in the text? What details in the text are not obvious in the visuals?
3. How do the pictures and text work together?

1. In this article, the author describes a festival that celebrates a folk tradition. Consider what local festival you could design if asked. Perhaps it would be hosted by your town, your dorm mates, your sorority or fraternity, your church, or your sports team.
2. What would it celebrate or promote?
3. How would it add to your local community?

Case Study

1. Tourism is a major contributor to many American economies, especially in states such as Florida, Hawaii, and Louisiana. How does tourism impact the industries, businesses, and advertising that are brought into a state or local area?
2. Can tourism be both a positive and negative influence on a location? On the people there? Why or why not?

Joy Williams's *first novel,* State of Grace, *captured the attention of both the critics and the populace and was a finalist for the National Book Award. She has written three other novels, three collections of short stories, a collection of essays, and a travel guide entitled* The Florida Keys: A History and Guide.

PARADISE RUINED

A Guidebook Writer's Lament

Joy Williams

In 1987 I wrote a guide to the Florida Keys. I don't know why I did this. There was little money involved. There was *no* money for expenses. Guidebook writers are supposed to ingratiate themselves with others, develop an ever widening circle of contacts and acquaintances. They're supposed to be charming enough to get a free meal now and then, complimentary tickets and drinks and such. But I never had the requisite persona. I was shy, certainly no gourmand, and kind of unsociable and critical as well. Instead, solitary, I threw myself into the project, followed my interests and put the book together block by block. When finished, it was a little odd and I was told by an editor that it was too "environmental" for a guidebook. But they published it anyway, and over the years, when they asked for revisions, I would insert my changes on strips of paper stapled or paper-clipped to the pages of a previous edition. The book became a gawky perennial, and I realized (as I had in the beginning but I realized it *more*) that I didn't like guidebooks. I've never liked guidebooks.

Le Parc Botanique et Zoologique de Tsimbazaza is a little rundown, but worth a visit. . . . Most of the cages and enclosures within the park are empty, which will please animal liberationists.

— *Madagascar and Comoros*
(Lonely Planet)

May I suggest to *this* cheery guidebook writer that . . . THE ANIMALS ARE DEAD, DUMMY! Starved, neglected. Don't be so chipper and sly. Read your Burroughs! He wrote about your islands in the sad, fantastic screed, "Christ and the Museum of Extinct Species." Of course, he was just fooling around, venting some spleen, taking us on an ugly trip through our comfy attitudes. A hipster whose heart went out to octopi and lemurs, he wasn't trying to show us a good time.

Which is the guidebook writer's intention.

"A little run-down," indeed. Or perhaps overbuilt, luxurious, off the beaten track, inexpensive, welcoming, overambitious, not ambitious enough, a mere shadow of its former self, but, all in all, more or less worth the visit.

The guidebook writer is beneath the travel writer, the nature writer, the journalist, way below the philosopher and poet, of course, probing the bottom, the very bottom of the literary pile. What kind of person would choose the guidebook form to sing one's song, to press one's case, to gawk at wonders, to learn and share? The guidebook writer has to be a sunny optimist, a good mate, a brisk historian, eventempered, tolerant, eager to point out the odd and agreeable, counting only the fulsome, happy hours. Whereas travel writers compose out of a merry darkness (Bowles); an angry darkness (all of D.H. Lawrence); an exhilarating ill-nature (Theroux); a kindly thoroughness (Morris); or even the elitist need to pull an exquisite hoax on a beauty-seeking public (Van Dyke and his remarkable *The Desert*); the guidebook writer has the soul of a gabby concierge who becomes increasingly less nimble in his enthusiasms as the years grind on. (Time is essentially evil as we must, by now, suspect.) For it is the nature of a guidebook to be revised, updated. It cannot enjoy the dignity of a travel book, which exists in an imperfect but essentially realized moment, a moment aware of itself in time. The guidebook attempts to accommodate change, politely, like a sociable sheep trying to reason with a wolf. Unrevised, un-updated, it becomes a quaint and feckless thing, but constantly revised, it becomes less true to its original, modest, and peculiar aims. In my case, I must admit, I'm unsure as to what those aims exactly were. I'm sure they were benign. Maybe as a breed, guidebook writers are a little simple-minded. They wake to find themselves unwitting boosters, pimps for purveyors, commerce's collaborators.

National Geographic's handsome guide to the country's national parks claims that it can be distinguished from other guides because of its "conscience," which pretty much means in this case that the "pressure of progress" is cited and the suggestion is made that we "give nature a little more room to make its choices." Hardly revolutionary rhetoric. Along with tips on the times to avoid bumper-to-bumper traffic, we are assured that "the way we appreciate nature" has changed

(. . . when Yosemite was first established, woodpeckers were routinely shot if their tapping disturbed hotel guests . . .) and might even evolve further, though not to the satisfaction of snowmobiler & snowshoer, hunter & photographer alike, unfortunately. Even in a guide with a conscience, the goal is to be accommodating, to provide accessibility, to open the doors of utilization (if not perception) wider.

Guidebooks of lesser "conscience" abound, obviously, though it has become acceptable even in those breezy tracts to comment briefly and with stoic acceptance on what of nature has been lost before plunging optimistically on. What can a tourist do about it anyway? He's not here to redress old wrongs. History isn't his fault. It's his first time in this place, or maybe his second. He wants to get the gist and enjoy. He doesn't want to drink from the gloomy cup. If he wanted to be depressed he'd read about vast, mysterious places that have existed for thousands of years and disappeared just yesterday before he had a chance to visit.

Like the marshes of Mesopotamia. Those great wetlands of Southern Iraq—the largest freshwater ecosystem in the Middle East since Biblical times—are now gone, never more to be. I had been ignorant of the marsh existence (though a number of British writers, always a bit more enterprising in these matters, have written excellent books about the Marsh Arabs). I learned about them the same time I read of their elimination by Saddam Hussein. (A long article in *The Atlantic Monthly* detailing the man's sins didn't even mention this one.) An ancient human culture dismantled, untold birds, fish, and animals destroyed, unique species now extinct.

Why would Saddam systematically drain thousands of acres of precious marsh in a desert? Everyone knows the fellow's crazy, but apparently he did it for "security reasons." But it's not just nervous dictators who destroy ecosystems; it can be developers and duly elected (or barely elected) world leaders too.

So Iraq's marshes are gone, as are, closer to home, most of the Everglades. The earth is vanishing—blowing, melting, draining away, buried beneath man's stratagems and devices. Some of the attacks on earth are vicious, irrational—acts of technological barbarism—while others are merely arrogantly economic or giddily consumptive. Sustainable development, like smart growth, is just another oxymoron, a sedative, a myth, meant to stroke and stoke a consumer society that is pathologically dynamic. We have accepted our limitations, which are that we don't have the energy or desire to alter our behavior on the scale that's required of us. Better to accept the conclusion of some of the new "population ecologists," which is that "Nature in the twenty-first century will be a nature that we make.'" An authentically artificial Nature which we can experience in an artificially authentic way.

All this is beyond the guidebook writer's purview, of course. A guidebook writer would have to be nuts to dwell on this kind of stuff. Better to sample more pie. (Sinfully delicious!!)

Still, a guidebook writer, simple- or service-minded as he might be, cannot accommodate unsettling, rapid, reckless change in a place which once held his fascinated and devoted interest forever. So it is that the guide I wrote—sixteen years old, and revised ten times, will stop.

In those years, the rough edges of the raggedy Keys have been smoothed away. They are no longer unruly or even vulnerable. The blows of development have been absorbed, the critical mass of a totally tourist-based economy achieved. A business-development oligarchy is firmly in charge despite the promoted carefree image. The health of the waters, the plentitude of its life, is being managed (they hope . . .) precisely along the razor's edge of viability and exploitation. Tourism is an industry, the tourist the resource. The oligarchy would have us believe that only the tourist enables the Keys to be different, to be perceived as being "different." A tourist, though, is a protean thing. Once, twice. To be a tourist a third time in a place is scarcely possible. One moves on.

To be a happy tourist is to remain determinedly ignorant about a great deal. It's preferable to think of the reef as being "fragile" and "learning" about it, rather than acknowledge that it's moribund and there's nothing that can be done to save it. To *think*, to be troubled, is to lose tourist credentials and become an irritant to the industry that only wants to serve you.

The environment's "carrying capacity" for population was reached in the '90s in the Keys. The deer of Big Pine will soon have their own underpass, if they can survive its construction. Failed resorts are being razed and turned into parks, complete with tennis courts, swimming pools, dog playgrounds, jogging trails, and baseball diamonds—'burb amenities. The sinuous Keys have become flabby with growth, while rascally Key West has fallen hard for its own commodification.

In the introduction to his classic misanthropic hymn, *Desert Solitaire,* Edward Abbey said, "This is not a travel guide but an elegy. A memorial. You're holding a tombstone in your hands. A bloody rock." A rock he suggests throwing at "something big and glassy. What do you have to lose?" Abbey would have been amused, though not surprised, to know that today's hip travelers seeking nature-oriented moments in the West are moving away from the typical, and increasingly tainted, wilderness experiences such as river rafting—viruses from sewage treatment plants along the Colorado have spoiled many a tourist's holiday—toward remote natural "shows" like the manmade lightning field in New Mexico. There's a lot that's big and glassy out there and it's all coming closer. And you have nothing to lose by objecting to it because the good stuff has all pretty much been lost. We are losing species, aquifers, open space, forests— so many, so much, every hour, every minute. This isn't the stock market crashing, this isn't money, which is practically imaginary, but the living earth, which can't be recharged, replumbed, restored, restocked, reactivated, reinvested, or reinvented, despite our touching (or cynical) love of that prefix. Environmentally, this country has taken very significant steps in a very wrong direction and that's fine with the majority of us.

The future belongs to crowds, Don DeLillo wrote. Crowds, I posit, who will hunger not so much for bread and freedom but access to spaces. World population is projected to reach 9.5 billion by 2100, only 3.5 billion fewer than what some theorists believe is the planet's maximum limit. Crowds won't need guidebooks to anywhere, for crowds will already be everywhere, all knowing pretty much the same things. There we'll be, part of a crowd, exploiting together our every interest, exercising our every right, indulging our every curiosity—all complicit in the mock worship of vanished paradises we never much believed existed in the first place. And the grudging agreements we made with Nature, the worthless treaties and stingy protective resolves, will be forgotten because we will not want to be reminded that such a remarkable world had once been ours to care for.

This excerpt comes from a forty-six-page brochure for tourists to the Florida Keys. The brochure was published by the **Monroe County Tourist Development Council,** *whose mission is to "provide web cams, videos, downloadable brochures, and seasonal weather information to help you visualize your trip" to the Keys.*

GREETINGS FROM THE FLORIDA KEYS AND KEY WEST

Monroe County Tourist Development Council

fla-keys.com 1-800-FLA-KEYS

KEY WEST

Whether you drive or fly into Key West, one thing's for sure: there's simply no place quite like it. An island city of palm-lined streets boasting Victorian homes, gingerbread conch houses and mansions on the National Register.

John Audubon and Ernest Hemingway lived here. One had a passion for preservation. The other, a great zest for living. And that combination gives Key West its unique personality. The moment you get on world-famous Duval Street, in Old Town Key West, you do more than feel the ambiance. You become a part of it.

Sure, Key West is dive shops and charter boats. And glorious sunsets. But it's also a Bahamian Village. Historic Forts. Lighthouses. Theaters. Museums. Galleries. Festivals. Markets. Sidewalk cafes. Legendary pubs. Even Truman's Little Whitehouse. (For a comprehensive listing, please see Attractions page.)

At Key West you can buy a postcard or a famous handprint. You don't need a car. Tour the city on foot or by trolley. Mingle with some of the world's most fun-loving characters. And find some of the best-made cigars and aloe products anywhere.

Key West is unique. And unspoiled. A feast for your heart and your soul. In short, if you're planning on visiting Key West, plan on staying longer than anticipated.

To learn all about Key West, stop by the Chamber of Commerce at 402 Wall Street in Old Town. Or call 1-800-LAST-KEY. You can also e-mail us at info@keywestchamber.org and visit our web site fla-keys.com/keywest.

DIVING & SNORKELING

The beauty and diversity of the underwater experience in the Florida Keys have made this the world's most popular dive destination. In fact, the Keys have been protected by designation as the nation's only tropical marine preserve, the *Florida Keys National Marine Sanctuary*.

Key Largo is home of the famed *John Pennekamp Coral Reef State Park,* the *Key Largo National Marine Sanctuary* and the 510 foot U.S.S. *Spiegel Grove*—the largest wreck in divable U.S. waters. *Molasses Reef* is the world's most popular dive site for its consistently clear water, amazing hordes of tropical fish and easy access. With

outstretched arms seemingly welcoming scuba enthusiasts, the submerged *Statue of Christ of the Abyss* is a Key Largo icon.

The entire Florida Keys are rich with wreck dive opportunities, including the 327 foot U.S. Coast Guard Cutters *Bibb* and *Duane* off Key Largo, the 287 foot freighter *Eagle* off Islamorada, the 188 foot *Thunderbolt* off Marathon, the 210

foot *Adolphus Busch, Sr.* off the Lower Keys and Key West's favorite wrecks, the 187 foot *Cayman Salvager* and the perfectly upright *Tug.* All of these ships are within easy depth ranges for sport divers and now host incredible resident populations of marine life.

Yet, it is the natural reefs of the Florida Keys that inspire the greatest awe among visiting divers. From the immense schools of grunts and snapper off *Davis Ledge* and *Alligator Reef* in Islamorada, to the dramatic coral canyons of Marathon's *Sombrero Reef* and *Coffin's Patch,* to the lush beauty and incredible diversity of the Lower Keys' famed *Looe Key National Marine Sanctuary,* to the majesty of the spur and groove coral formations decorating Key West's *Sambo Reefs,* the Florida Keys and Key West have it all!

Randy Duncan, *who has a Ph.D. in Communications from Louisiana State University, has taught at Henderson State University since 1987 and serves as chair of the Communication and Theatre Arts Department. He teaches a variety of courses dealing with rhetoric, movies, and comics. He is co-authoring* The Power of Comics, *a college-level textbook on comic books and graphic novels forthcoming in 2009. He is also co-founder of the Comics Arts Conference, which celebrated its 15th anniversary in 2007, and serves on the Editorial Board of the* International Journal of Comic Art. *This excerpt from Jimmy Buffett's biography, which details the influences of his Key West style, appeared in* The St. James Encyclopedia of Pop Culture.

BUFFETT, JIMMY

(1946–)

Randy Duncan

Devoted fans—affectionately dubbed Parrot Heads—find escapism in Jimmy Buffett's ballads, vicariously experiencing through his strongly autobiographical songs Buffett's life of beaches, bars, and boats. Yet Buffett's life has been far more than rum-soaked nights and afternoon naps in beachside hammocks. Even though Buffett relishes his image of "the professional misfit," this millionaire "beach bum" is actually an ambitious and clever entrepreneur.

In his mid-twenties, Buffett found himself broke, divorced, and hating Nashville. Then in 1971, Jimmy Buffett took a trip that changed his life and his music. Fellow struggling singer Jerry Jeff Walker invited Buffett down to his home in Summerland Key, just 25 miles from Key West. It was the beginning of Key West's "decade of decadence," and Buffett quickly immersed himself in the Conch subculture's non-stop party that they referred to as the "full-tilt boogie." To maintain the freedom of his new lifestyle Buffett ran up bar tabs, literally played for his supper, and got involved in the local cottage industry—drug smuggling.

The lifestyle and the local characters became the substance of Buffett's songs. The first of the Key West-inspired songs appeared in 1973 when he landed a record deal with ABC/Dunhill and recorded *A White Sport Coat and a Pink Crustacean.* The tongue-in-cheek "The Great Filling Station Holdup" made it to number 58 on Billboard's country charts. The most infamous song from the album, "Why Don't We Get Drunk (and Screw)," became a popular jukebox selection and the favorite Buffett concert sing-along song.

ABC's rising star, Jim Croce, died in 1973, and the record company looked to Jimmy Buffett to fill his shoes. They even promoted Buffett's next album, 1974's *Living and Dying in 3/4 Time*, with a fifteen-minute promotional film that showed in ABC-owned theaters. "Come Monday" made it all the way to number 30 on the Billboard pop charts. For years, Buffett had been making reference to, even introducing, his mythical Coral Reefer Band. In the summer of 1975 he put together an actual Coral Reefer Band to tour and promote his third ABC/Dunhill album, *A1A*. The album contains "A Pirate Looks at Forty," which became a central tale in the mythos Buffett was spinning, and a virtual theme song for every Buffett fan as they neared middle age. 1976's *Havana Daydreamin'* got good reviews and fed the frenzy of his growing cult following; but it was 1977's *Changes in Latitude, Changes in Attitude* that was the defining moment of his career. The album's hit single, "Margaritaville," stayed in the Billboard Top 40 charts for fifteen weeks, peaking at number eight. That summer "Margaritaville" permeated the radio and Buffett opened for the Eagles tour. The exposure helped *Changes in Latitude, Changes in Attitude* go platinum.

The song "Margaritaville" gave a name to the place fans escaped to when they listened to Jimmy Buffett's music. And Margaritaville was wherever Jimmy Buffett was playing his music, be that Key West, Atlanta, or Cincinnati. Supposedly it was at a concert in Cincinnati in the early 1980s that Eagles bassist Timothy B. Schmidt looked out at the fans in wild Hawaiian shirts and shark fin hats and dubbed them Parrot Heads. By the late 1980s the Parrot Head subculture had grown to the point that Buffett had become one of the top summer concert draws. The concerts were giant parties with colorful costumes, plentiful beer,

and almost everyone singing along out of key with the songs they knew by heart. The concerts were more about the experience than about hearing Jimmy Buffett sing.

Buffett soon found ways to extend the experience beyond the concerts . . . and aggressively marketed the Margaritaville mythos. The Caribbean Soul line of clothing appeared in 1984, and in 1985 he opened Jimmy Buffett's Margaritaville store in Key West. A few months after opening the store, he sent out a 650-copy initial mailing of *Coconut Telegraph*, a combination fan newsletter and advertising flyer for Buffett paraphernalia. By the end of the decade, the newsletter had 20,000 subscribers.

Buffett reasoned that anyone who wanted to read his newsletter would buy a book with his name on it. His first literary effort, in 1988, was *Jolly Mon,* a children's book he co-wrote with his daughter Savannah Jane. The following year, Buffett's collection of short stories, *Tales from Margaritaville*, became a bestseller. His first novel, *Where is Joe Merchant?*, warranted a six figure advance and became a bestseller in 1992. By this time Buffett had opened a Margaritaville café next to the store in Key West. Eventually, he opened Margaritaville clubs and gift shops in New Orleans, Charleston, and Universal Studios in Florida.

More than anything else, Jimmy Buffett is a lifestyle artist. Whether it be a Caribbean meal, a brightly colored shirt, a CD, or a live performance, Buffett transports his fans to the state of mind that is Margaritaville.

Cayo Dave *is the owner and author of the Key West Chronicle Blog. His goal, since 2004, is to give a local perspective on the Keys (http://www.keywestchronicle.blogspot.com). This blog post first ran in the spring of 2007.*

MORE KEY WEST HOTELS GOING OFFLINE

Cayo Dave

Tough days are ahead for Key West tourism.

It is no secret on the island of Key West that tourism is changing. Hotels have been bought up by developers seeking to transform them into condos, time-shares, and higher priced hotels. Most of the properties targeted by developers have been the moderately priced hotel rooms—the bulk of Key West's typical-tourist accommodation.

Many businesses in Key West have been suffering due to nearly 1000 hotel rooms being "off-line" during their reconstruction. It remains to be seen if these projects will be a success, whether tourists of the future will spend $350+ night to stay in Key West, whether "condotels" are a smart investment (I have my doubts), and whether the island will seriously suffer by pricing out the majority of our visitors. It is a risky gamble on the part of developers—rolling the dice with the livelihood and character of Key West.

Unfortunately, things are looking tougher for the future.

One of the largets property owners and developers on the island, the Spottswoods, have announced a massive redevelopment at the west end of Key West—near the entrance from U.S. 1.

The Spottswoods have bought up one of the last remaining stretches of moderately priced Key West hotel rooms and plan to replace it with new expensive hotel rooms and time-share units (along with restaurants, retail, bar, and a huge conference center). Oh, and they'll build 50 affordable housing units on the property.

The hotels that are due to close are the Days Inn (with 133 hotel rooms), the Comfort Inn (with 100 rooms), the Holiday Inn (with 144 hotel rooms) and the Radisson Inn (with 145 rooms). This is a total of 522 hotel rooms that will close. When it reopens, the new hotel will have 417 hotel rooms—a loss of 105 hotel rooms. Even if you add in the time share properties, there is still a loss of 72 hotel rooms!

Maybe most worrying is that the hotels' closings are some of the last moderately priced hotels on the island. So the big question for the future is, will there be enough tourists willing to pay $350+ per night to stay in Key West? My guess is "probably not". In any market, when you double the price of anything, you can expect to receive less buyers. What is yet to be determined is the "price elasticity of demand"—which shows how much demand drops when prices change.

Either way, the difficult times for Key West's tourist businesses are surely not over.

DECODING THE TEXTS

1. How do each of these authors and texts portray the Florida Keys differently?

2. Does the genre of each text control the information given? How?

3. If the blog had been written for an online magazine, what information would need to be changed?

4. If it had been written for a magazine in print, what information would change? Why?

CONNECTING TO YOUR CULTURE

1. How did you view your college campus before attending school there? Did you physically visit the campus before orientation or did you take a virtual tour?

2. How has your perception of the campus changed since you have become a student?

3. What impact does your familiarity have on your perception of an environment?

● ● ● ● ● ● ● ● ● ● ● ● ● ● ● ● ● ● ● ●

Reading Selections:
Across the Decades

CONSIDERING IDEAS

1. What games do you enjoy playing? Do you consider yourself a fan of any particular game or online activity?

2. How often do you play games with family and friends versus online or individual games?

3. What does this say about your personality? About the way you spend your free time?

Shari Caudron *is a former business journalist who became an independent writer. Since then, she has been published in magazines such as* Reader's Digest, The Christian Science Monitor, *and* Traveler's Tales. *She has written two books,* What Really Happened *(2005) and* Who Are You People? A Personal Journey into the Heart of Fanatical Passion in America *(2006), which included this essay on war gamers.*

HITLER DID FINE, I CAN DO BETTER

Shari Caudron

"This war will not be over by the next commercial break."
—News announcer during the Gulf War

Ever had one of those dizzying moments, where you find yourself standing among a crowd of people who are so thoroughly alien to you, so thoroughly Not Like You, that it takes every ounce of willpower you possess not to turn and run screaming home to mommy?

Me too.

In fact, I'm having one right now.

It's a sunny summer morning and I've just arrived at the World Boardgaming Championships being held at the Marriott Hunt Valley Inn in a suburb north of Baltimore. When I first heard about the Boardgaming Championships, I began to skip happily around my bedroom. Boardgames? Now *this* was something I could relate to. I envisioned rooms full of pleasant, well-scrubbed people playing Monopoly, Scrabble, Trivial Pursuit, and other games I've been known to play, enjoy, and gloat a little over winning. I was excited by the potential of finding an interest I could relate to; jazzed by

the thought that maybe here I'd find my tribe—*my* pigeon racers.

I was also way off the mark.

I'm standing inside the doorway of a hotel ballroom named the Maryland Room. Inside, dozens of people are clustered around banquet tables holding board games, the likes of which I've never seen before. Signs on the tables tell me they're playing "Robo Rally," "VINCI: The Rise & Fall of Civilizations," and something called "Merchant of Venus." I find a description of Merchant of Venus and read: "If you like your grease immortal, your sculpture psychotic, and your genes designer, then this is the game for you."

Huh?

Although I've never heard of games like this, it's not the games themselves that have activated my get-to-safety alarm. It's the participants. They are overwhelmingly male, predominantly white, and most look like they haven't shaven, combed their hair, crunched a fresh vegetable, or experienced a good night's sleep in days. Clad in rumpled and untucked T-shirts, the players look like men who, having escaped the civilizing influence of their wives, have

"Hitler Did Fine, I Can Do Better" from WHO ARE YOU PEOPLE? A PERSONAL JOURNEY INTO THE HEART OF FANATICAL PASSION IN AMERICA, by Shari Caudron, 2006, pp. 93–108. Reprinted by permission of Barricade Books.

found themselves descending into pits of slovenliness heretofore only dreamed of.

A few minutes ago, I watched a man with curly black hair thrust half a hamburger into his mouth—using the palm of his hand—while trying to discuss something with his tablemates. Unaided by chewing, the compressed burger sat idly inside the man's mouth, straining his left cheek to the bursting point, making conversation all but impossible. I felt sorry for that burger. All cramped up in the dark with nothing to do but wait for further instructions.

Perhaps recognizing the futility of trying to speak with a burger in his mouth, the man then swallowed it—wholly unchewed—in a feat of guttural capacity that could have merited a cover story in a scientific journal.

It's not the first time I've wondered whether hobbies like this are merely an excuse for men to get out of the house.

In fact, since I've been investigating passion, I've found it far easier to find communities of men devoted to singular interests, especially those that involve balls, pucks, bullets, drills, bait, breasts, engines, and bottles of oxygen. But perhaps I'm simply more intrigued by the male-dominated subcultures because they've always seemed so off-limits.

When I was a little girl, I'd spend summers at the family cabin in Northern California, playing on the Eel River with my five male cousins. They were always jokey and dirt-caked and full of stitches, and their fearless vitality thrilled me. I had no brothers and thus no direct daily experience with dirt bikes or dune buggies or playtime that involved imaginary fox holes and machine-gun fire. And I was fascinated by it all. My cousins spent summers backpacking in Yosemite, while my sisters and I worked on our tans.

As a kid, I yearned to sample a bit of that active male world but whenever I'd talk to my mother about, say, riding a motorcyle or scaling a mountain, I got her emergency room lecture. Mom worked in a hospital emergency room throughout my childhood and she knew from nightly experience what a motorcycle and mountain climbing could do to the human body. At one end of the spectrum: cuts. Stitches. Scrapes. Breaks. Burns. Sprains. At the other: death. Skiers landed in the ER. Daredevils landed in the ER. The *Kennedys* landed in the ER. Tame, sensible families like ours did not.

Appealing to my father was useless. He spent his young, active years teaching ballroom dancing at an Arthur Murray studio in San Francisco.

With the world of male passions off limits, I, of course, craved them all the more. In college, I started camping. I learned to drive a motorcycle. I drank tequila shooters. But somewhere along the line I must have absorbed the message that polite restraint—not unchecked exuberance—was the consummate behavior to strive for. Whenever I forgot that, whenever I got a little stinky and sweaty and *involved,* my mother would reel me back in.

"Honey," she'd say, shaking her head at my silly attempts at tomboy behavior. "Only men and horses sweat."

Reflecting on this, it's no wonder I've been drawn to these secret male worlds with their no-holds-barred behavior. But now, as I look at the board gamers in their rumpled clothing and stale body smells, I believe I may have over-romanticized men and their passions.

And yet . . . I can't seem to pull myself away.

I leave Burger Boy and the Maryland Room behind and enter a hallway where many of the board games being played are on display. I browse their covers.

A game called Battle Cry boasts: "Recreate 15 Epic World War battles. There's just one difference. You are *there*!"

The cover of Cosmic Encounter tells me: "Armed with alien power, you are ready to colonize the galaxy."

Other games include Attila, Air Baron, Acquire, Liberty, Brute Force, Samurai, Attack Sub, Vanished Planet, Squad Leader, Greed, Pay Dirt, and PanzerBlitz.

Given the all-girls family I hail from, I wasn't aware they could build so much testosterone into a board game. The most violent it ever got at our house was when my sisters and I played Feeley Meeley, a game in which players shoved their hands inside holes cut into a cardboard cube and tried to find an object inside, such as a comb or whistle, using only the sense of touch. With four young female hands grasping inside for the same object, we endured our fair share of slapping, jabbing, poking, pulling, threats, tears, and piercing, high-pitched accusations of cheating. I shudder to think what viciousness a game like Air Baron would have unleashed.

Still, looking at the racks of games, I'm mystified by this slash 'n' burn, conquer-and-destroy mentality. Who plays these games anyway? The urge to flee has now given way to curiosity. Asking around for someone to help me, I am connected with Don Greenwood, the convention director.

Greenwood is a large man with a soft belly, oversized glasses, and bushy mustache. He's standing behind a dark wood registration counter, and when I tell him why I'm here, he looks at me and taps his pen on the counter without saying a word. I can't help but think it's because he sees me for what I am: Someone who is acting politely interested in boardgamers, but actually sees herself as a teensy bit superior to them—primarily because feeling superior is preferable to feeling left out. If I was Mr. Greenwood, I don't know if I'd talk to me.

His pen continues to tap.

"Okay," he says, finally, "but I have just ten minutes."

He steps from behind the counter and tells a woman standing nearby he'll only be a minute. Unlike other people I've visited with, Don doesn't seem particularly interested in recruiting me.

We begin chatting and he tells me that 1,100 people from around the world have come here to the fifth annual World Boardgaming Championships. This weekend, about 140 games are being played as part of the competition, but hundreds more are being played during open gaming.

"What do the winners receive?" I ask. "Money?"

"There's no prize money. That brings out the daggers."

I wait for Don to tell me what, exactly, they do receive. The silence lengthens.

"So . . . what *do* they play for?"

"Woods."

"Woods?"

"Yeah. Woods. Plaques." Don is no longer tapping his pen, but he might as well be.

"I see," I reply, although of course I don't see anything at all.

Don must sense my discomfort for he takes a deep breath, exhales slowly, and decides that since I'm not going away he might as well answer my questions.

"Okay," he says. "This is how it works."

Don explains that players get points for winning individual events. These points are called laurels. The more competitive the game, the more people who play, the more laurels you get. At the end of a game, the person with the most laurels gets a plaque showing he is the winner of that game. At the end of the convention, the person with the most laurels overall is named the Caesar, the reigning king of the World Boardgaming Championships.

"We do it this way 'cause if there was prize money it would bring out the pros and we'd have to worry about cheating. This way, people play for honor and bragging rights only. This conference is for purists."

I tell Don that I'd expected to encounter more popular board games like Scrabble and Monopoly and maybe—ha-ha—Chutes and Ladders.

Don does not find this amusing.

"There are not party or social games like *you* might be familiar with," he says. "These are niche games. They are highly *involved* games that have *intricate* rules and are heavy on strategy. These games require a *significant* investment of time. They are *not* for the general populace."

Well then.

Don removes his ball cap and scratches his bald head. He has two puffs of curly hair over each ear and smoothes these down before replacing his cap.

I soldier on.

I ask Don why he is attracted to boardgames, and he tells me it's because niche games are tense and exciting, and they allow players to stay involved. In Monopoly, if you get the right real estate, you push everyone else into poverty. In Scrabble, wordsmiths can out-vocabularize their opponents in no time. But niche games allow people to remain emotionally engaged and strategically involved throughout the length of the game. Plus, he adds, they offer a great intellectual challenge.

"Intellectual challenge?" I ask, thinking about the man with the hamburger.

"Absolutely. Many of these games simulate historic, real-world events. I especially like games where you set the parameters so historical events can occur the way you create them."

"So players need some knowledge of history?"

"That's good to have," he agrees, "but math is more important. In fact, most of the people here are extremely well-educated. There are lots of engineers."

I'll be honest. For the last several minutes I've been trying to convince myself that burger-eating boardgamers have nothing to teach me. It's just so foreign here, so *male,* even for my voyeuristic tastes. Plus, the whole gamey gaming environment just makes me want to shower.

But Don's comment about the educational level of participants reels me back in, especially since I had so recently concluded that pigeon racers did what they did because of the lack of intellectual challenge in their jobs. In fact, to date, most of the people I've been with have been predominantly working class. This has made it easy for me to conclude I don't have passions because I've got two master's degrees and thus am simply too educated (she says, head lifted with a misplaced bit of hubris) to bother with them.

But if what Don says is true, fanaticism is not the province of the underemployed, and the people here might have something to teach me after all.

Don looks toward his berth at the registration desk, and I suspect he's about to call time on our conversation. "Um, can I ask one more favor?" I ask.

He exhales again.

I tell him I'm researching passion and would like to talk with some of the most zealous gamers here. "Any suggestions?"

"Head over to the Worthington Room," he says.

"The Worthington Room?"

"Yeah. It's what, Saturday now? The guys in there have been playing the same game since Tuesday."

"The *same* game?"

"You said you wanted passion."

I believe Don Greenwood was telling the truth when he proclaimed niche games were tense and exciting, but I've been standing in the Worthington Room for the last ten minutes and have yet to spot evidence of the action-packed, zip-a-dee-doo-da adventure he referred to.

Inside the room, clusters of men are gathered around large round tables covered by incongruously pink tablecloths. Like the players downstairs, these guys look rumpled and tired, and the room smells like adult male bodies that haven't seen the tiled interior of a shower stall for days. Most are quietly staring at game boards on the tables in front of them. The atmosphere feels heavy, like a room full of students straining to complete their college entrance exams.

A large man with four days' worth of white chin stubble notices me.

"How're you doing?" he asks.

His voice is craggy like that of a lifelong smoker. I walk over to his table, on which sits a game board the size of a hood from a small sedan. He introduces himself.

Steve Voros, he says. Former material control specialist. Ford Motor Company. Now retired. He extends his hand.

I tell Steve that I'm investigating fanatical passion, and he tells me that boy-howdy, have I come to the right place.

"You have to be nuts to play this," he says. "I've been playing for twenty-five years and I'm *still* learning the game."

"*That's* for sure," says the man who's sitting across the table from him.

"Yeah, you wish," Steve replies.

"Are you two playing against each other?" I ask.

"Yeah," Steve says. "We've played four games since Tuesday. We're not like the guys over there." He cocks his head toward the table behind me.

I look over at the table. Steve tells me the men there are playing A World At War, which takes sixty or seventy hours of play time. He's playing its predecessor, Advanced Third Reich, which is not only easier, he says, but also requires a scant twelve hours to complete.

"*Only* twelve?"

"Yeah. We don't go as long, so it doesn't get as tense."

There's that word again. "Tense how?"

"I'll tell you how. You should've been here this morning at about three o'clock. There was a group of guys playing at that table in the corner." He points to a table that now sits vacant. "They'd been playing for about twenty hours straight without sleep when they got into a fight about the rules. One of the guys got so mad he picked up the game and overturned it. You do that, and the game's over."

"Did you see it?"

"Nah, I left about 1 A.M. I just heard the rumors this morning. But I know they're true. You take a bunch of guys who haven't slept, put 'em around a table where the Second World War is going on, and you can expect a few disagreements. Everyone here's pretty smart, so they all think they're right all the time. Just look around."

Steve turns and starts pointing toward the other players in the room. "That guy's a lawyer. That guy's got a Ph.D. in tree hugging. And see that sublime guy over there? He's a neurologist."

I gaze in the direction Steve's pointing but fail to find someone I would characterize as sublime. Still, I'm impressed. Don was right—brainiacs play these games.

Steve turns back to his own table and gestures toward his opponent, a small, slim man with wire-rim glasses. "And this guy here, he knows world leaders."

"Not quite," his opponent says. He has a thick German accent.

We chat, and I learn Steve's opponent is Herbert Gratz from Vienna, Austria. Herbert has attended the World Board-gaming Championships every year since 1991 and, when he's not playing games, he works at the International Monetary Fund at the Central Bank in Vienna. "It sounds impressive, but I'm just a policy advisor to management."

I ask Herbert why he comes to Maryland all the way from Austria every year. "Can't you play these games at home?"

"Oh, no. All the serious conflict-resolution games are published in English," he says. For a small man, he sounds eerily like Arnold Schwarzenegger. "In Germany, you can be legally prosecuted if you publish a game with a swastika on the package. That's why all the games Germans publish are about saving the environment. They all have funny little bunnies skipping through the forest."

Herbert says this with such disdain that I've no need to ask him why he prefers conflict games. Instead, I ask him specifically what it is about Advanced Third Reich that causes him to cross the Atlantic every year to play it for several days on end.

"Because I want to be like the Americans. I want to be like the maniacs that rule the world."

Herbert laughs in a manner that's intended to suggest he's kidding.

"But," he adds, "I also like eating the ribs they serve at the hotel. Of course, in Austria, we have ribs. But they're not as good as the Marriott."

Steve interjects. "You *do* like your ribs."

"I tell you, I do."

Herbert looks around the room at the other players and then turns his attention back to me.

"Okay, seriously," he says. "I started playing this game because I like complicated strategy games. When I was younger, I played chess and bridge. I liked the competition. But now it's not so much about competition. It's about companionship. Like with this guy," he says, pointing to Steve.

I look back and forth between the two men. The unexpected retreat of Herbert's Third Reich swagger takes me by surprise, and I find myself touched by his confession.

"It's true," Steve adds. "We've played together for years."

The two men start bickering over exactly how many years it's been. Five? Four? Six? Watching them, I'm once again struck by the unlikely friendships that form around common interests. How else would a retired autoworker from Detroit come to fraternize with an international money manager from Vienna? Although their interests may be the same, their lives aren't.

"So, tell me," I ask, in an attempt to stop their squabbling, "what is the aim of the game?"

"The victory conditions are not clearly win or lose," Herbert says. "There are shades of winning. You play to lose by only a little. Of course, if the other guy whines . . ." he pauses and looks across the table at Steve, "that is also very positive and rewarding."

"Oh, brother," Steve says.

"You said you were on the fourth game?" I ask Steve.

"That's right," he says.

"Have you lost each one?"

"Oh, most certainly."

I leave to let Steve resume his happy losing streak and I walk over to a table where four men are sitting curved over a game board. I stand beside a man wearing a St. Johns ball cap. He's staring intently at the game board and chewing his thumbnail. The other players around the table are conversing. But their conversation is slow, as if their responses are time-delayed because of great distance.

"In my last Euro scenario, the Russians had rockets."

Pause.

"I hate it when they do that."

Pause.

"You going for pizza?"

Pause.

"I *said* are you going for pizza?"

"Nah, I'm gonna hang around here, because it looks like my brother is going to toast Japan."

Pause.

"Yeah. Japan is getting hot."

Pause.

"Will you be hitting me with the bomb?"

Pause.

"I dunno."

As the game proceeds, one of the players sitting close to me attempts to give me a brief, entry-level overview of A World at War. He tells me the game is a World War II strategy game in which two teams—one serving as the Axis powers, the other as the Allies—compete to gain world control. The game is designed to allow players to pursue their own wartime strategies. They build navies to suit their strategic requirements. They deploy armies and air force pools based on projected need. They worry about oil reserves, their nation's economies, and diplomatic alliances with other nation-states. All of these factors have an impact on the war strategies they can eventually put into place, and the options are endless. Japan could choose to invade Australia or India, for example. Germany could develop the atomic bomb. The British position in the Middle East could crumble.

"It sounds complicated," I say, capitalizing on my highly refined journalistic ability to state the obvious.

"Oh, it takes a good ten years to get to proficiency level," he says.

I continue to watch them play and realize that unlike the pigeon racers, these guys have not chosen a passion that utilizes untapped skills and talents. Instead, they are turning up the dial on intellectual strengths they use every day in their professional lives. As lawyers and doctors and academics, they've already developed the ability to synthesize information, think strategically, and create workable strategies. What A World at War appears to do is allow them to fully test these skills in a more intense environment. The fact that they don't have to sleep or shave or shower is merely an added bonus.

During one of the many long pauses, I ask the players how much they've slept over the past four nights and learn they've only broken for three-to-five hours a night—tops.

"And it's not restful sleep, either. You're tossing and turning and thinking about the game. Your adrenaline gets stuck in one mode."

"Yeah. I can't even imagine going back to work on Monday. It'll be like coming back from outer space."

The other players lean forward and appear to grow energized by the discussion of their extreme gaming accomplishments.

"We're like Navy Seals. They train like this too. A whole week without sleep."

"My philosophy is this. If we're gonna do this all week, we're *gonna do this all week.*"

"I totally agree. I had to play all the chits with the wife to come here. Hey . . . wait a minute! Did you bomb him?"

"Naaa."

"Come on. This game is called A World at War, but there's not much fighting going on. It should be called A World at Peace."

This last comment brings their attention back to the game. I watch them for a while seeking clues as to what they're doing. On a nearby chair, I spot the game's rulebook and lean over to pick it up. It's 196 full-sized pages, 8.5 point type, single spaced.

The man with the St. Johns ball cap sees me looking at it. "You ought to talk to the guy who wrote that."

"Who's that?"

"Over there, in the corner." He points to a man wearing a T-shirt from the National Air and Space Museum that features illustrations of World War II bombers. "That's Bruce Harper. He designed the game."

Bruce Harper is a forty-eight-year-old lawyer from Vancouver, British Columbia, who prosecutes tax offenses. He's got pale skin, short reddish hair, and deep purple circles under his eyes. He reminds me of Woody Allen, minus the glasses. He's sitting at the same corner table that was allegedly vacated at three o'clock this morning by the group of angry, overtired players.

In the last fifteen years, Bruce has designed four games: Wrasslin', Advanced Civilization, Advanced Third Reich, and Empire of the Rising Sun. He combined the last two games into A World at War,

which—although it officially debuted only four days ago at the World Boardgaming Championships—has been under development for years.

Bruce got into game designing because he understands the importance of rules to a good game and how to write rules that people understand. In 1981, he was playing a game with friends when a question arose about the proper play procedure. He wrote a note to the company making a suggestion about how to improve the rules so as to eliminate such confusion.

"They put my suggestion in the next rule book and before I knew it, I'd become the Q-and-A guy for that particular game," he explains. "You see, for most people rules are sacrosanct. If the rules say that pigs fly, well then, pigs fly. For a game to be successful, the rules have to be clear. You don't want to spend your play time arguing about them."

Bruce speaks the way you'd expect a person who is concerned about the interpretation of rules to speak. He looks me directly in the eye. He prefaces each sentence with long, thoughtful pauses. And although he is eating a Marriott-issue hamburger much like the one compacted earlier by the man downstairs, Bruce takes time to carefully chew every bite before speaking.

"Why are strategy games like A World at War so popular here?"

Chew. Swallow.

"If you read a book about history, say, about World War II, you know how it will end," he explains. "But games like this are interactive. The players themselves decide the outcome based on their own strategic moves. People can say to themselves, 'Hitler did fine up until this point. I can do better.' The challenge of the game is not to recreate actual events, but to respond to different what-if scenarios.

For example, what if Japan didn't bomb Pearl Harbor? If all the assumptions are reasonable, and all the rules make sense, then the game proceeds without a problem. But if you get a rule wrong, it can wreck the game."

"Do your skills as a lawyer help you design games?" I know the answer to this, but I have to ask anyway.

Chew. Swallow. Napkin dab.

"Probably. I've learned to write clearly because I understand the problems caused by a lack of clarity. There's an old law from England that's only one page long and has been massively litigated. There's been something like twenty thousand decisions on that one single law. But when a law is clearly written, the need for litigation is diminished. There's far less litigation with a long law than a shorter one because the answer is in the writing. Game designers who don't take time to clarify the rules so that people understand how to follow them, well, to me, that shows an astounding misinterpretation of human nature."

Bruce is clearly not a person I want to be caught jaywalking around.

"What other games do you play?" I ask.

"I haven't played many games besides my own over the last few years. It seems self-indulgent to play when so many people are waiting for my rules." Bruce says this as if the rules he's been working on hold the key to everlasting world peace. Which they might, for all I know.

"So playing games is your passion?"

"Definitely.

"When I'm playing a game like this, I'm totally focused. I'm not thinking about work, or anything else. It's the way I relax. My wife relaxes by reading trashy novels. I relax by coming here. Really, there's no other way I'd rather spend a week than by playing games, acting like an idiot and not sleeping and eating."

Sensing Bruce will have an opinion on the subject, I ask him why it seems there are so many male-dominated subcultures.

"Because guys have to be doing something to get together. Women form social groups easily, but men need an excuse. One guy never calls up another guy and says, 'Hey, let's go have a few beers and talk.'"

"But isn't locking yourself in a hotel for a week pretty obsessive?"

"Obsessive, passionate. Whatever. They both describe the same kind of behavior. I'm proud that I've designed a game that might cause some loner to come out of his house and interact with others. I like to think that I've prevented some crazy guy from heading out onto the street with a rifle.

"I tell you who I feel sorry for," he adds. "I feel sorry for those people who don't have any passions at all. Passion is a great thing in life."

Sheepishly, I say nothing.

"I mean what harm does all this do anyway?" Bruce sweeps his hand from right to left in a room-encompassing gesture. "We're all old friends here, even the people who met just four days ago."

I thank Bruce for his time and walk through the tables to the exit. And as I do, I feel the familiar stab of envy return.

DECODING THE TEXT

1. At the end of the reading, the author states that obsession and passion both lead to the same kind of behavior. How does the author characterize her obsession and passion throughout the text?

2. What details does she give or what language does she use that leads the reader to think of her as obsessed?

CONNECTING TO YOUR CULTURE

1. What is your major obsession or passion? What actions do you take as a result of this passion? How did it develop?

2. Do your friends and family members know about this obsession? Do they share your passion? If not, do they understand your interest?

CONSIDERING IDEAS

1. Should members of a group or organization conform to fit in? Is this part of the price members pay for being a part of the group?

2. What is the meaning behind the old saying "never say never"?

Dianna Baldwin's research interests include cultural studies and composition pedagogy. A doctoral student at Middle Tennessee State University, she is currently investigating the positive and negative effects of teaching writing in the virtual world of Second Life, an online community built by its members, with hopes of publishing a book on the topic. She works as the associate director of The Writing Center at Michigan State University. Her work on the Motor Maids has been presented at numerous pop culture and women's studies conferences.

LADIES OF THE WHITE GLOVES

Riding with Pride

Dianna Baldwin

As Zoe sat astride her BMW K1200LTC and watched other Motor Maids pull into position for the upcoming parade, she could feel the sweltering heat of the pavement seeping through the soles of her shoes and sweat began to soak her skull cap underneath her black half helmet. She unfastened it, took it off, and realized that even over the sound of booming motorcycles she could still hear the rumble of thunder in the distance. She glanced to the evening sky and wondered if the nightly thunder storms would hold off until after the parade was finished.

As she sat there in the discomfort of the heat and motorcycle exhaust fumes, she began to realize that there was a strange sense of pride slowly growing in her that, to be quite honest, had not been expected. It was July the 5th, 2005, the first official day of the annual Motor Maids Inc. convention, and thus far, it had been a hot and humid day in Hagerstown, Maryland. She had ridden over 600 miles through intense heat and humidity as well as dangerous thunder storms to get there, and she found herself sitting at about midpoint in a parade formation that she had sworn she would never be in. At this position, she knew there was time to sit and reflect on what was about to take place, namely, her first parade with the Motor Maids, and exactly how she had arrived at this point in time.

Zoe had joined the Motor Maids in June of 1999; her first convention was that July. At that time, she declined to participate in the official opening parade, using the excuse that there had been no opportunity to purchase the required uniform. Even now, sitting and waiting for the parade to begin, she cringed at the thought of what she was wearing and what it must look like. The slacks were gray—supposedly, they were to be slate gray but hers were much closer to white than any shade of gray she had ever seen—and her shirt was an official Motor Maid blue shirt complete with her name embroidered on the front; actually, she had borrowed the shirt and it read "Bertha" across the upper left hand side and on the back a rocker stating "Motor Maid North Carolina." She also wore a little white tie that was, quite frankly, beyond description—not resembling a bow tie, nor a regular tie. The ensemble was completed with white gloves and white boots, but she actually wore white Keds. Zoe now recalled that at the first convention several people had offered to lend her a shirt and tie, and she was also told that white tennis shoes could be worn instead of boots. That was what most members wore anyway because getting white boots was tough enough, but white boots with a good non-slick sole for motorcycling was next to impossible and costly. So the group overlooked the use of white sneakers just as they overlooked having the exact correct shade of gray slacks. Of course white gloves could be found with little trouble. Still, Zoe declined their offers, and not

"Ladies of the White Gloves: Riding with Pride" by Dianna Baldwin. Written for presentation at the Popular Culture Association/American Culture Association Conference in San Diego, CA, 2005 and revised for THE POP CULTURE ZONE: WRITING CRITICALLY ABOUT POPULAR CULTURE, 2006.

without reasons; reasons that as a brand new member she was not quite willing to spout off about at her first convention. She somehow knew that the time for spouting would come soon enough.

And so it did. In January of 2000 came an invitation to attend the annual officers' meeting, where the executive board, all of the district directors, and their assistants came together and discussed what business needed to be brought before the entire membership at the annual convention, allowing only the issues that concern a majority of the members to be on the agenda and weeding out or settling the small stuff. One of the major issues this particular year was the current uniform, which, by all accounts, had really not changed much since the beginning of the club back in the 1940s. Many young members wanted a newer, sharper look, while many of the older ones and some of the younger ones who were traditionalists wanted to keep the current look. They broke off into small groups for discussion. After listening to arguments from both sides in her group, Zoe was asked for her opinion. Well, she thought, they asked; so she frankly, and admittedly, without much finesse, told them, "I will never, as long as I am a Motor Maid, wear this uniform. It is uncomfortable, hot, and quite honestly, ugly. Having come out of the Navy just four years ago," she told this small group, "I will never wear such a uniform, and to be honest, it will have to go through some drastic changes before I would ever consider it." Her comments were not favorably received.

One of the older members, whom Zoe was not familiar with, attacked her criticism; "Well, then why did you join the Motor Maids?" she demanded.

Zoe thought it over for a couple of minutes and replied, "Because this is the first group of women motorcyclists I have ever met that take riding seriously and that is what I want to be a part of. Many of these other women's groups will allow women to join who do not even own a motorcycle. Not to mention the fact that they seem to rarely ride. I didn't join the Motor Maids for their uniform, but because they know how to ride."

"Well," she stormed back, "if you refuse to wear the uniform you cannot participate in parades or end-of-convention banquets, which means you will not be able to personally receive any awards you might earn and you will miss out on the Motor Maids' biggest social event of the year."

Zoe quietly stared at what had become her adversary and then with a sly grin on her face, and in an attempt to lighten the now tension-ridden atmosphere, she simply said, "I guesses I just won't participates then!" One lady laughed out loud but was quickly silenced with a death glare from the all-too-serious woman, and Zoe quickly began to realize just how intense this debate over uniforms really was.

When all of the smaller groups came together to discuss the issues as one large group, the topic of uniforms was definitely the hottest debated subject. The group as a whole could not come to any consensus; therefore, it was decided that the matter would be tabled for another year. In Zoe's opinion, that pretty much sealed her fate as a Motor Maid when it came to conventions. If she couldn't parade and couldn't attend the banquets, why bother going? The important thing was not whether or not she went to conventions, but rather what the Motor Maids were known for: riding. And the Motor Maids in her area were especially good at this, so she shrugged off the disappointment of no uniform changes and went back home knowing that the pleasure of riding with these women and others was really all that mattered.

The sound of firing motorcycle engines quickly jerked Zoe back from her stroll down memory lane to the reality that here she sat astride her mammoth motorcycle wearing exactly what she had sworn five years ago to never put on. She shook her head in disbelief and thought to herself, "Never say never!"

With that thought, she donned her helmet, straightened up her bike, retracted the kick stand, and fired the engine. Balty, the name the bike earned when first bought because of its calming ability, like the sound of the ocean, started on the first attempt and purred almost silently when compared to the Harley Davidsons surrounding her, which sounded more like booming thunder during tornado season. She looked around and realized that there were still bikes falling into formation in the rear, so she put the kick stand back down and contemplated what had occurred after that meeting in 2000.

She had remained true to her promise of never attending a convention, while participating in many of the local rides and events that took place throughout the years. At the yearly January meeting of 2003, which Zoe attended, the officers decided to put together a uniform committee that would be responsible for coming up with a new uniform that the club would vote on at that year's convention in Chico, California. She was excited about some of the suggestions being made, including adopting a NASCAR style shirt to

be worn with jeans and black boots, but by convention time, the uniform debate had really become heated. Zoe learned from friends who attended this convention that the uniform introduced by the committee was shot down and that the club decided to table the discussion for three years, making the next vote at the convention in 2006. She began to think there was no chance of the current blue and gray ever being replaced.

As she contemplated, she realized that motorcycles were beginning to move in front of her, so she pulled up the kick stand once more, squeezed the clutch, stomped the gear lever into first, and slowly eased on the throttle. As the double lines began to move forward, a dim understanding of why these women would argue so fervently over a uniform that was at the least outdated, and at the most dangerous, began to dawn in Zoe's mind. Brake lights started to flash ahead, and Zoe realized they weren't ready to go, but had simply been tightening up the formation to allow more bikes to line up in the rear.

She placed her bike in neutral and looked around her, really looked around her. There were women of every shape, size, and age surrounding her, but the one thing they all had in common was the way they were dressed. The different shades of gray in the slacks and blue in the shirts didn't really seem to show up so much anymore. Even those who had put on white tube socks over their black boots seemed to fit right in. How could this be? She had just thought, not 30 minutes ago, how out of sync everyone looked with their different variations of a very old uniform. Some women still had shirts they purchased in the 60s when they were made of a heavy polyester material. Zoe silently thanked God that Bertha had bought a shirt that was made of 100% cotton and the gray slacks she had found were actually made of denim. Still, she had to admit that the sense of pride that had begun when she entered the formation was, in part, about this uniform and the way these women looked wearing it.

She suddenly became aware that bikes were moving again, and she figured this had to be the real deal this time. She went through the ritual of placing her bike in gear and pulled out when her turn came. The local police had blocked traffic for them, and they slowly made their way from the convention hotel in downtown, Main Street, Hagerstown. Over 100 women motorcyclists were riding in a staggered formation, or side-by-side, at about 30 miles an hour, waving their white-gloved hands at the crowds that were gathering on the streets. Little kids were pointing and waving back while many adults stopped in their tracks to stare: some open-mouthed. Zoe found that the sense of pride that had been growing in small stages suddenly exploded inside of her as she grinned from ear to ear and blared Balty's air horns at the waving kids. She even found herself performing the Motor Maid wave that everyone joked about and she had never fully understood until now.

As the parade continued, Zoe had no more time to reflect on why or how she had gotten to this place; she simply relished the feelings of pride and excitement that she was experiencing. However, once the parade returned to the hotel and she had parked and dismounted Balty, she quietly returned to her room to continue reliving this journey.

Zoe attended that 2003 officers' meeting not because she had any interest in the uniforms, but because she had a new commitment to research and cultural studies. She needed information from these women for one of her projects dealing with the myths surrounding women and motorcycling. Partially from that project, but more from her love and respect of these motorcycle-riding women, she decided to pursue her research on this group in more depth, and as a direct result of that, she had learned that the uniform had always been a popular topic for discussion among these women.

Zoe, at first, had little luck in determining exactly when a uniform made an official appearance, but in a 1947 edition of *American Motorcycling* she found a piece on a new uniform that stated, "They are considered by the best fashion designers as being very attractive and practical, being made of good quality grey serge and trimmed with royal blue, the Motor Maid colors" ("The Girl Riders: The New MMA Uniform" 29). Then in a 1948 edition of this magazine, she found a group photo of 27 members, but none were in uniforms. Further research, however, turned up a website called *Motorcycle Goodies* that claimed that the first convention, which was held in Columbus, Ohio in 1944, was when the group decided on a uniform. According to this site "Out of this meeting came the club colors—Royal Blue and Silver Gray—and the Motor Maid emblem in the form of a shield. . . . Initially the uniforms were tailor-made of silver-gray gabardine with royal blue piping. It evolved into a uniform consisting of gray slacks, royal blue over-blouse with white boots and tie" ("Motor Maids History"). She also learned that the Motor Maids earned the nickname "Ladies of the White

Gloves" by parading at the Charity News-ies races in the uniform, wearing white gloves as if they were ladies out for an afternoon tea. These gloves soon became a permanent addition. Zoe found evidence of what the 1947 uniform might have looked like in a picture of Dot Robinson, the original president, in a 1950 copy of *American Motorcycling,* but very little of the shirt could be seen.

Zoe then found the evidence she had been looking for in the very next month's edition of the magazine, where she found a group photo of Maids and recognized the uniform that one member was wearing as the current one. The only difference was that the shirt was tucked in, which she had been told by many members was about the only change the uniform had gone through in years: whether to tuck or un-tuck. That this was indeed the current uniform was confirmed by the August edition that same year with a picture of 26 Maids, most of whom were in what could be considered the present uniform.

It became obvious to Zoe from the pictures in the magazines that the women were proud of their uniform because they wore it at more events than just conventions and parading. After that group photo in August of 1950, it seemed that Zoe found Maids in uniform in practically every monthly installment. She began to understand what really got her into this Motor Maid uniform she had sworn to never wear; she had thought it was her desire to gain access into the heart and the soul of this group to further her research, when in reality it was her desire to be a part of the pride that these women feel when they don these uniforms and parade for all the world to see and, yes, admire. As Zoe sat and considered all of this, she wondered if the same pride would be felt without a uniform; she somehow doubted it. She had ridden in a huge motorcycle parade for Toys for Tots with Wynonna Judd as the grand marshal and not felt the pride that she had experienced in the Motor Maid parade. It had been a five-year journey getting to where she was, but she was quite glad to have made it, and even though she hadn't changed her mind about the uniform itself—it still needed drastic changes to attract new members into the club—she understood the reason why many of the older members fought so vehemently to keep it as it was.

Zoe wondered if she would feel the same thrill of excitement if she ever paraded again, and her answer soon came. Only six weeks after the Motor Maid convention, she found herself in Sturgis, South Dakota, for Bike Week where the Motor Maids were asked to parade around the race track to kick off the motorcycle races that week. It was a completely different venue than the convention parade, but the same feelings of pride and joy enveloped her as she guided Balty around the dirt track to the cheers of the racing fans. It was then that she realized that regardless of the uniform she would always be proud to wear the Motor Maid blue and gray and be known as one of the "Ladies of the White Gloves."

Works Cited

"Our Girl Riders: Order Your MMA Uniform." *American Motorcycling* (Jan. 1948): 21.

"Motor Maid History." *Motorcycle Goodies.* 05 July 2005 <http://www.motorcyclegoodies.com/>.

1. Why does Zoe object to the Motor Maid uniform? What changes her mind?
2. Why does the author use flashbacks?
3. Baldwin uses descriptive details to place the reader at the parade. What did you learn about the parade or the Motor Maids from her descriptions? What images stood out to you as you read the essay?

1. If you were in Zoe's position, would you conform? Why or why not?
2. Have you ever belonged to a group where you willingly did something you did not want in order to fit in? What were the consequences of conforming?
3. How do the Motor Maids compare to your perception of bikers?
4. What other women's organizations can you name?

contemplations in the pop culture zone

1. Have you ever worn a uniform? What was it for? What did it look like? Did it reflect a specific group or a specific place? How did this type of dress affect your mood? Did you feel proud to wear it? Ashamed?
2. Think about your own tattoo or a tattoo of a friend or family member. Describe the tattoo and consider its implications. What does it mean to you? Does it identify a particular culture? Why do mainly young Americans get tattoos? Why is tattooing a popular way to memorialize someone's death?
3. Describe the first time you felt a sense of belonging. Perhaps it was with your parents at a family reunion or in a children's worship service. What gave you that feeling? In what circumstances has the feeling been replicated since then?
4. Recently, digital billboards have been placed on busy thoroughfares across the United States; these signs change based on the demographics of your car. What does your car say about you? What would your billboard advertise?

collaborations in the pop culture zone

1. Each group member should identify his or her favorite space and tell the group what makes it so special. How is it decorated? Did you choose the décor? As a group, consider why people often identify so closely with their surroundings. Comfort? Familiarity? What does each group member's space say about him or her?
2. To your group, describe a tradition from your hometown. Compare the characteristics of your various traditions. Perhaps you have a local festival, sporting event, or parade that is held annually. What does this event say about your community to your group members?
3. What hats do you wear or have you worn in your life? Each group member should make a list of the figurative hats that you wear. How do your lists differ? Does age, gender, race, or sexuality affect your many roles? What about religion, politics, or family?
4. As a group, create a postcard for your composition class to send to a friend you haven't talked to in a while. What is on the front? A picture or drawing? A poem or excerpt from an essay? What would you write on the other side to explain your choice? Now, still in your group, create a postcard for your class to send to your parents, grandparents, or guardians. How does the front of the card change? Why does it change?
5. Anonymously, make a list and describe five personal items in your wallet, purse, or school bag using pictures, patterns, brand names, and colors. Then, place these lists at the front of the room. As someone reads from the front of the room, guess who made each list. What assumptions do you make about your peers? About their marketing choices?
6. Get together with a group in class and write a constitution for your class. If a number of you belong to the same subculture or are members of the same campus or community organization, you could write your constitution for that group. Your constitution can be humorous or serious, but you will need to consider the format of a constitution, the characterisitics of the groups, and what you want to share with your members as well as outsiders.

start writing essays about groups, spaces, and places

Reviews or Review Essays

1. Review the ease of access, safety, and popularity of a local attraction or theme park. You must visit the attraction to complete this essay.
2. Write a review of your favorite restaurant. Describe the ethnicity, the décor, the patrons, and the location. What is the best item on the menu? What would you change about the restaurant if you could? Is the restaurant locally owned or operated? Does this affect your review or patronage?
3. Many organizations sponsor campus events that are open to the student body. Attend one of these events (of which you are not a host) and write an objective review. Briefly describe the hosting organization or association, the purpose of the event, and the success in achieving this purpose. (You may want to read a review of a larger event, such as a Heart Walk for the American Heart Association, as a model.)
4. Review the effect of a devoted fan or fandom on a television series, song, film, or work of popular literature. Where and how has the fan community built itself? Is there a structure? A name or title for the community? Are there known leaders of this community? What is the intention or purpose of the fan community? Does this fandom help or hurt the original work, group, or place? (See Hillary Robson's essay in Chapter 8 for an explanation of fandom and fan fiction.)
5. Find a virtual space (such as a chat room, an ongoing blog, or an open forum) and review the effectiveness of this space. What is the intended purpose of the space? Is this purpose achieved? Who are the participants in these conversations? Would you recommend this source to a friend or family member?

Reflection or Response Essays

1. Reflect on your idea of love or spirituality by describing one event in your life that reflects the way that you view either emotion. For example, the day of your bar/bat mitzvah might symbolize your personal spirituality, or the night that you got engaged may encompass your feelings about love.
2. Describe the first hour of an experience you had as you entered a new culture, community, association, or group *and* a new space. This example could include your first day in a new school, your first day on the job, or moving into the freshman dorm.
3. Find a photo, either personal or from the Internet, of a space, place, or landscape and respond to the photo. Have you been there? What does it make you think about or remind you of? What do other people do there? Does it signify a certain place in popular culture?
4. Reflect on an experience you have had with an animal, family pet, or animal lover by describing an event in your life when an animal (or animal lover) has played a major role. Describe the experience and respond to the significance of this animal, or animal lover, in your life.

Analysis Essays

1. Misconceptions about health and disease are often propagated in popular culture. Examine the way that the AIDS epidemic has been exposed or hidden in popular culture. How is it portrayed in the media? Where did you learn facts and details about HIV/AIDS? Research headlines on the subject and draw your own conclusions.

2. Research the cultural practices of a specific community and analyze the consequences of these practices. You may want to interview a member of the Southern Baptist Convention, Greenpeace, or your city council. What rituals or rites do they practice? When do they meet? What is the significance of their individual roles?

3. Analyze the intended purpose of a controversial association. What do the participants wish to gain through their membership? Is the association effective in achieving its goals? What is the historical background or effectiveness of the association? How is this association depicted in popular culture?

4. Discuss prison culture. How are prisons portrayed in film? In song lyrics? On television? Research the history or basis of popular prison myths.

Synthesis Essays

1. Review a spot where you have vacationed and consider the cost to you or to your family. Through your own experience, reflect on the way this locale advertised. Who is the local tourism council trying to attract? Does this spot appeal to a certain age, class, or gender? How did it appeal to you or to your family?

2. Choose a specialized word from one of your cultures (the culture of your academic major, of your religious affiliation, of your favorite genre of music, of your virtual community) and define this word. How is this word used within the culture? What does it say about you or your community? Describe this culture and its implications in popular culture.

3. In March 2007, the Delta Zeta sorority at DePauw University, called the "Dog House" by other students, was kicked off campus for allegedly evicting twenty-three members who were not considered attractive enough to promote the sorority's exclusive image. Consider other stories like this that you have heard. How are sororities portrayed in popular culture? In the news? On film or television? How are fraternities portrayed? Is their representation different? Why or why not?

4. Several news stories by entertainment journalists have blamed the "Trash Pack" (Britney Spears, Paris Hilton, Lindsay Lohan, Nicole Richie, and so on) for the rise of "prostitots," or young girls—usually tweens—who dress and act promiscuously. Respond to your own choices in music, film, and television as a tween. What appealed to you? Analyze today's tween choices and compare your culture to theirs.

FOR FURTHER READING

Browning, Dominique, ed. *House of Worship: Sacred Spaces in America.* New York: Assouline, 2006.

Calmes, Anne M., ed. *Community Association Leadership: A Guide for Volunteers.* Alexandria, VA: CAI Press, 1997.

Caudron, Shari. *Who Are You People? A Personal Journey into the Heart of Fanatical Passion in America.* Fort Lee, NJ: Barricade Books, 2006.

Gray, Jonathan, and Cornel Sandvoss. *Fandom: Identities and Communities in a Mediated World.* New York: NYUP, 2007.

Hills, Matthew. *Fan Cultures.* London: Routledge, 2002.

Jenkins, Henry. *Fans, Bloggers, and Gamers: Media Consumers in a Digital Age.* New York: NYUP, 2006.

Kennedy, David Daniel. *Feng Shui for Dummies.* Indianapolis, IN: John Wiley, 2000.

Low, Setha M., and Denise Lawrence-Zuaniga. *The Anthropology of Space and Place: Locating Culture.* Boston: Blackwell Publishing, 2003.

Zachary, Lois J. *Creating a Mentoring Culture: An Organization's Guide.* San Francisco: Jossey-Bass, 2005.

The first top 10 debut to bullet in its second chart week since Eden's Crush's "Get Over Yourself" in April 2001. Downloads increase to 163,000 (up 20%).

With album now at retail, digital downloads for set's top radio single triple to 30,000. It's No. 21 on Adult Top 40.

Singer teams up with producer/writer Bill Bottrell for the first time since her debut album. Their last Hot 100 hit together was 1995's "Can't Cry Anymore."

CHAPTER 7

writing about music

"I feel like I'm in the prime of my life, physically, emotionally, spiritually—and musically. And, knowing there is still love for me in the marketplace, that gives me energy."

—From UsherWorld.com: The Official Website of Usher

1 The "Beef: It's What's for Dinner" ad campaign uses a score by what composer?

    a. Beethoven
    b. Gershwin
    c. Bach
    d. Copland

TEST YOUR POP CULTURE IQ: MUSIC

© HBO/The Kobal Collection

2 The song "Memory" is from what long-running Broadway play?

    a. *The Phantom of the Opera*
    b. *Joseph and the Amazing Technicolor Dreamcoat*
    c. *Cats*
    d. *Rent*

3 The song "We Are the World" was recorded in 1985 to raise money for what charitable fund?

    a. Famine in Ethiopia
    b. The American Foundation for AIDS Research
    c. Comic Relief
    d. Sport Aid

4 The president of the United States is introduced using what instrumental song?

    a. "Peaches"
    b. "The Naval Hymn"
    c. "Hail to the Chief"
    d. "The President's Song"

5 Which 2006 television soundtrack was the first to debut at number one on Billboard's Top 200?

    a. Fox's *American Idol*
    b. Disney's *Hannah Montana*
    c. NBC's *Saturday Night Live: 25 Years of Music*
    d. CMT's *Crossroads: Hank Williams Jr. and Kid Rock*

6 Which icon of country music boasted, "It takes a lot of money to look this cheap"?

    a. Patsy Cline
    b. Dolly Parton
    c. Reba McEntire
    d. Tammy Wynette

7 What was the first major rap single to reach as high as number thirty-six on the Billboard charts?

    a. "Rapper's Delight," The Sugarhill Gang
    b. "The Message," Grandmaster Flash
    c. "Walk This Way," Run-DMC/Aerosmith
    d. "(You Gotta) Fight for Your Right to Party," The Beastie Boys

© AP Photo/KEYSTONE/Steffen Schmidt

8 The Rolling Stones chose their name because of

    a. Bob Dylan's "Like a Rolling Stone"
    b. *Rolling Stone* magazine
    c. Muddy Waters's "Rollin' Stone"
    d. The proverb, "A rolling stone gathers no moss"

9 Which of these is not a disco lyric?

    a. "So now go. Walk out the door. Don't turn around now 'cause you're not welcome anymore."
    b. "Voulez-vous coucher avec moi ce soir."
    c. "You can get yourself cleaned. You can have a good meal. You can do whatever you feel."
    d. "Que sera sera. Whatever will be, will be."

10 What character in 1999's *Office Space* despises the musician with whom he shares a name?

    a. Michael Bolton
    b. John Tesh
    c. Kenny G
    d. Michael McDonald

ANSWERS

1 *d. Copland*   2 *c. Cats*   3 *a. Famine in Ethiopia*   4 *c. "Hail to the Chief"*   5 *b. Disney's* Hannah Montana

6 *b. Dolly Parton*   7 *a. "Rapper's Delight," The Sugarhill Gang*   8 *c. Muddy Waters's "Rollin' Stone"*   9 *d. "Que sera sera. Whatever will be, will be."*   10 *a. Michael Bolton*

Video killed the radio star.

Video killed the radio star.

In my mind and in my car, we can't rewind we've gone too far

Oh-a-aho oh,

Oh-a-aho oh

—From "Video Killed the Radio Star" by The Buggles

YOU AND MUSIC

With the introduction, "Ladies and Gentlemen, Rock 'n' Roll," and these lyrics performed by The Buggles on August 1, 1981, MTV debuted as the first television channel devoted to music and music programming. Now, more than twenty-five years later, the programming of MTV and the many cable channels, such as BET, VH1, GAC, and MHD, which promote music and music videos, is less about the actual lyrics and arrangements of popular songs and more about the youth culture that popular music often represents.

Not only is music entertaining and culturally relevant, but it is also a way to express emotion, to gain support for a product, thought, or idea, and some people even use it to help them learn or memorize facts. The readings and writing prompts in this chapter should help you think about the popular music you like and listen to, as well as introduce some music and musicians you may be less familiar with.

Whether you are an avid musician or merely a bystander in the world of popular music, you are constantly bombarded with melodies and lyrics from a variety of sources. The tunes on your iPod, the songs on the radio, the songs you sing in church, the concerts you attend, the soundtrack of your favorite movie or television show, and the jingles on television, the Internet, or radio advertising are all valid examples of popular music. Because pop music is so easily accessible, from downloading songs to buying CDs at the mall, it is often the focus of writing assignments or classroom activities. The crossover between music and the subjects of other chapters in this text is common and may be useful when you decide to write about pop music.

Music can be a common space for personal, social, and political experiences. Music is (or is not) a reflection of the culture that surrounds it. For example, Bob Dylan's songs from the 1960s give the impression that they reflect the world at that time.

grappling with ideas

- Who is your favorite musician or band? How did you hear about him, her, or them? Did a friend introduce them to you? Did you see their video on MTV or hear them on the radio? Or are they a local act?

- Think about how much money a record company or promoter might have spent to get this musician or band to your ears and eyes. How much have you spent on their albums, concerts, and merchandise?

His songs are often about protests or are themselves protests. Today, gansta rap also seemingly tells the stories of the disadvantaged. Although songwriters sometimes have social aims that go along with their music, this isn't always the case. However, unintended messages still can come from the music itself, whatever the writer's intentions. Because music is a creative endeavor and a direct form of expression, you need to think not only about your personal response to music but also about the means by which music gets to its audience, who the audience is, and the ways in which music is interpreted and used by listeners in a variety of contexts.

Music is produced and created for both financial and artistic reasons. Even music produced solely for artistic reasons usually depends on expensive promotional techniques to become popular. Musicians and bands make money from touring and merchandise sales, whereas record companies make money from CDs, downloadable albums or singles, and selling music for advertising and soundtracks. Artists appear in videos, on awards shows, and even involve themselves in elaborate stunts—such as New Kids on the Block member Donnie Wahlberg setting a carpet on fire at the historic Seelbach Hotel in Louisville, Kentucky, at the height of their early 1990s success—to sell albums and to gain celebrity status. Musicians often cross over to acting, just as actors often promote themselves as musicians.

WHY WRITE ABOUT MUSIC?

Using music as the subject of your writing can help you discover much about yourself, your interests, and your prejudices of classes, cultures, or tastes. Although it is hard to be completely objective about a song, album, or musician whom you already like or listen to, it is important to choose essay topics that you can relate to and learn from. Choosing to write about the music used in a film or commercial to set a mood or develop a theme can also be a learning experience. Becoming a critical listener can deepen your enjoyment of popular music and may even open your ears to music with which you were not previously familiar.

PREPARING TO WRITE ABOUT MUSIC

When listening to music, viewing a music video, or watching an artist perform as part of a writing assignment, you must think critically about the subject. Again, it is important that you take a step back from your own interests and try to see the subject from the perspective of your audience, even if you are using a song or album that you are familiar with.

grapplingwithideas

- What type of popular music is the most foreign to you? Country or bluegrass? Acid jazz or blues? Contemporary folk or indie rock?

- How could you learn more about this type of music? Whom would you talk to or interview? What publications could you read?

- Why haven't you explored this type of music in the past? Why don't you enjoy listening to this type of music now?

Listening, Watching, and Thinking

When you listen to music, you are affected by your environment, by those around you, by the quality of the system playing the music, and by your prior experiences with the song, album, artist, or genre. View the video or listen to the song several times to become more familiar with your subject, and try to adjust your situation to remove distractions.

keyquestions

Key Questions for Listening to Music

- How does the title relate to the album or song?
- How does the album, song, or concert start? Are the production credits displayed or revealed?
- How does the packaging affect your interpretation of the music?
- When was the song recorded? The video filmed? The concert staged?
- What is the concluding song on the album? Concluding performance recorded? Concluding shot on the video? Do you think its placement is deliberate?
- Is this song or album similar to or different from others that are in the same genre?
- Is there anything different or special about the production techniques such as connecting loops between tracks, orchestral contributions, or unusual effects?
- How does your prior knowledge affect your experience?
- What cultural beliefs underlie the lyrics of the song or album?

To prepare, ask questions about what you expect. What instruments (if any) do you expect to hear? What do you already know about the artist, song, or album? Who is the intended audience for this album? What initially attracted you to or repelled you from this music? What are people saying about it? Make some notes as you answer these questions so that you can go back and review your initial thoughts.

If possible, take notes about themes, production, and quality as you listen to the music. After you listen to it a few times, reassess the answers to your initial questions. Did anything challenge your original expectations? Look for discrepancies between the preliminary notes you made and the notes you took during the experience. Did you enjoy what you heard? Why or why not?

Now, consider the context of the recording or the performance. Think about historical value (Does it identify a particular time period?), timelessness (Does it mean something different to another generation than it does to you? Will it have meaning or appeal to future generations?), and convention versus invention (What is new? What is traditional to the genre?), as mentioned in Chapter 3, Defining Popular Culture. Again, consider your experience. Were you alone or did you listen over someone else talking? Any part of your environment—from what you are looking at while you listen to a song to the way your speakers are arranged—has the potential to affect your experience.

Remember that details are important when you write about music, so make descriptive notes and answer your questions fully through prewriting activities before you start composing.

Listening, Watching, Analyzing, and Understanding

As with all popular culture, music is a text that can be analyzed; music contains readable elements that contribute to the listener's experience. It is a medium that you are already reading actively (by simply listening to the lyrics or a particular instrument) and passively (by connecting to the sounds and to the tone). As you actively read a song or album, several elements, including the lyrics and the instruments used, should be your focus.

Music has terminology that may be important in writing about the subject. However, it is not necessary for you to be an expert on music theory to write a compelling essay. The following are some basic terms and ideas for you to consider when writing a music essay.

SONG PATTERN. The patterns that follow are a sample only and may not be found in some genres of music such as jazz or classical.

> **Introduction:** The intro, which is usually music or lyrics only, catches the listener's attention with a short refrain or a sample of the song's rhythmic pattern.

Verse: Vocal melody and lyrics. Verses tell the story or develop an idea, as in the chapters of a book or the paragraphs of an essay; each verse often focuses on a separate but related idea. The verses develop the songwriters' main ideas and prepare the listener for the chorus. For some listeners, they can give value to a song, or verses may be completely ignored for a catchy chorus.

Prechorus: A vocal and/or melodic foreshadow of the chorus through tone, melody, or both.

Chorus: The chorus, sometimes called a *hook* or *refrain,* can most easily be described as that part of the song that is most often repeated and, because of this, usually garners the most focus both lyrically and musically. Musically speaking, the chorus is often the most dynamic part of the song.

Bridge: The purpose of the bridge is to break up the monotony of the verse/chorus, chorus/verse musical pattern. A bridge is typically an entirely new melody of music and words or even drums and bass only (sometimes called a *breakdown* or *jam*). The bridge reaches for the highest level of energy in the song, and it often rivals the chorus in its dynamics.

grappling with ideas

Choose your favorite song, or a song that you are familiar with, and identify the different sections of the song's pattern as listed in the sample.

- Is the song similar to the sample pattern? In what way?
- If it is different, in what way?
- In what way does the song's similarity or difference add to or take away from the quality or value of the song?

LYRICS.   Most songwriters concentrate on expressing a message to listeners, and they often try to connect with the most basic human emotions. Although some lyrics are only meant to entertain, this is not a less important purpose than emotional connection, only different. Lyrics are poetic and can contain some of the same elements that we see when we analyze literature or poetry. For more examples of literary terms, see Chapter 8, Writing About Popular Literature.

Alliteration: The repetition of sounds at the beginning of words or in stressed syllables, such as the hard "D" sound in the phrase "Dirty deeds, done dirt cheap" by AC/DC.

Meter: The measured arrangement of words and syllables in poetry. One type, ballad meter, is even named after a common syllabic arrangement in hymns and other songs; "Amazing Grace" is an example of this—a line of iambic tetrameter followed by a line of iambic trimeter:

"I once/was lost/but now/I'm found/
Was blind/but now/I see."

Parallelism: The repetition of phrases, sentences, or lines that are similar in meaning or structure, such as the repeated use of the word "low" in the song "Low" by FloRida. The repeated chorus of a song is a form of parallelism.

Rhyme Scheme: The arrangement of rhyming words or syllables in a song or stanza, such as the rhyming of "spoon" and "lagoon" in the lines "protected by a silver spoon" and "by the banks of her own lagoon" in the song "She Came in Through the Bathroom Window" by Sir Paul McCartney.

Stanza: A section of song lyrics composed of two or more lines. A verse is often one or more stanzas.

Structure: The way that a lyric is composed, consisting of line, stanza, and parallelism.

INSTRUMENTATION. The elements of instrumentation can combine to form a cohesive unit—a song or a movement in classical or jazz music. Consider each element individually and as part of the larger song and album to analyze the tone, mood, and purpose of both the lyrics and the music.

> **Instruments:** Musicians use countless instruments, from their own voice to a piano, an electric guitar, drums, violins, harmonicas, and even old washboards. When analyzing the instruments, consider what instruments the band uses, whether or not they use them effectively, and if their use symbolizes anything outside normal use.

> **Mood:** The mood of a song can be shown in many different ways, such as using particular instruments; using a major key, which often implies happiness, or a minor key, which implies sadness; playing different tones; keeping or changing the speed of the rhythm; sharing lyrics; and using or not using countless other elements. Through the mood of the song, listeners hear and feel what the songwriter(s) are attempting to convey.

> **Electric versus Acoustic:** Electric performances create energy and are perceived as more impersonal, whereas acoustic performances, often referred to as unplugged, may convey a more intimate connection between artist and audience. The artist's use of electric or acoustic instruments may enhance the mood and message of the song or album, and an electric song can seem very different if heard in an acoustic setting.

> **Live Performance versus Studio Performance:** Many artists choose to record their live performances, complete with the audience cheering in the background, while some prefer to record studio performances. The moods that these performances convey can completely change the listener's perception of a song or album.

> **Technology:** Artists have more technological options in music than ever before. Artists are now able to digitally enhance their voices, dub additional tracks over their songs, loop musical interludes throughout the song electronically (such as sampling), or even add a digital audience to a recording. These techniques may also apply to concert performances.

PRODUCTION. Many components exist outside the music itself, including the artist's image, the band name, the album or song name, and the album cover. These external details may add more to a song, album, or performance.

> **Artist's Image:** The way musicians present themselves is crucial to our perception of them and of their music. Hairstyles, clothing, body art, and other deliberate or even accidental choices can influence our perception of the musician and the music.

> **Album Cover:** Packaging can enhance or interfere with the listening experience. The packaging of music might reflect the band's or the record company's purpose, and it has an effect on the way you view music.

> **Genre:** Music can be divided by type, style, form, content, or technique. Some large categories of genres include top forty, pop, rap, hip hop, alternative, new country, classic country, and alt country. Songs, artists, albums, or performances can often be categorized. Although there is some

need by popular radio to classify songs so that they can be marketed, many songs and artists resist this classification. Also, many artists and songs may cross between genres. For example, Wilco's *Yankee Hotel Foxtrot* includes songs that are definitively alt country and songs that fit into the pop genre.

How and Where It Is Heard: Whether you hear songs in a car, in a dance club, in an elevator, on a date, on TV, in film, in a doctor's office, or at church, this experience changes your perception of the music.

Concept Album: An album that has one basic theme, tone, mood, or purpose that is consistent throughout. The Beatles' *Sgt. Pepper's Lonely Hearts Club Band* and Pink Floyd's *Dark Side of the Moon* are two popular examples.

VIDEOS/MUSICAL PERFORMANCES. Musical performances can be seen on MTV and subsequent music channels, on formulaic "high school dance" episodes of television shows or teen movies, at halftime of the Super Bowl, on variety shows such as *Late Night with David Letterman* or *Jimmy Kimmel Live*, and even on comedy series like *Chappelle's Show*. These performances can, again, add to or detract from a musical experience. For more help analyzing videos and live performances, see the chapters on film, television, and sports.

Production: Videos and performances are often produced by an entire team of musical and technical artists. Where and how the production was designed and filmed, how much money and time were spent, and where the performance or video will be aired or sold are all important considerations.

Technical and Artistic Features: These features include the language; the video techniques, such as sound, lighting, and camera shots; and the musical techniques, such as tone, rhythm, and presentation used. The actors or extras hired may also address the band's or producer's intended audience, mood, and purpose for the song. All of these are technical and artistic choices that a band, producer, or director make before and during the performance or shooting of a video.

Audience: Performances or videos usually target a specific audience. Your social position, race, gender, sexual preferences, background, or academic achievement may play a part in your recep-tion of the performance. Videos and performances may serve a social, economic, or political interest or may address, reinforce, or subvert any beliefs, values, or attitudes. These are impor-tant considerations when analyzing a performance/video or an album/song.

Listening, Watching, Researching, and Documenting

If you are writing a reflection or response essay, you may not need to do any outside research. However, you may need to do some outside research to write a convincing and well-supported review or analysis essay.

Areas of research may include the following:

- The artist's life
- The artist's or producer's body of work
- The historical background of the music
- The culture or cultural ideas represented or presented in the lyrics or video
- The reception of the song by others
- The economic history or budget of the album or tour
- The writer of the song, particularly if different from the performer
- The history or development of techniques used
- The evolution of particular genres or conventions

The research you do will be guided by the questions that you want answered and by the assumed expectations of your audience. See the introduction to each content chapter and Chapter 11 for more information about researching within popular culture topics.

For writing about music, your primary text is the song, album, artist, or concert you have chosen to write about, and it may include the album, CD, or DVD packaging. For secondary sources within music, you may use popular publications, such as *Rolling Stone, Spin,* or *Magnet.* You might turn to Internet sources, such as *Billboard.com.* Academic journals such as *The Journal of Popular Music* are another place to turn for reliable information. Start with the information in your school's library (especially with your school's online databases), but do not be afraid to expand your search to the Internet, a great source for older recordings and all lyrics, and to your own collection of books, magazines, and CDs.

Song lyrics are quoted within your essay in the same style as poetry. See Chapter 11, Researching and Documenting in the Pop Culture Zone, for more assistance with this.

Some sites to check out, whether for basic facts, reviews, archives, or analyses, include the following:

Billboard magazine	http://www.billboard.com
The Blues Foundation	http://www.blues.org
Country Music Hall of Fame	http://www.countrymusichalloffame.com
The Grammy Awards	http://www.grammy.com
The History of Rock Music	http://www.historyofrockmusic.com
Lyrics.com	http://www.lyrics.com
The Rock 'n' Roll Hall of Fame	http://www.rockhall.com
Rolling Stone magazine	http://www.rollingstone.com
SoundtrackNet	http://www.soundtrack.net
Yahoo! Music	http://music.yahoo.com

Do not forget to record the citation information you will need for your Works Cited page and for your in-text citations to remember where you found your information and how to get back to it should you need to. See Chapter 11 for specific guidelines and investigate the Works Cited at the end of each sample essay for examples of citations for specific sources.

WRITING ABOUT MUSIC

Music as an artistic medium can be written about in many ways; however, this chapter focuses on the four main essay types as discussed in the previous chapters. Whether you focus on the mood that "Jaan Pehechaan Ho" creates in *Ghost World,* Beyoncé's celebrity status after leaving Destiny's Child, or how

Guns N' Roses' "Welcome to the Jungle" promotes *Grand Theft Auto: Vice City*, music topics often overlap with other subjects, so look at the suggestions and advice for film, television, gaming, advertising, or celebrity culture in the other content chapters for more advice.

Music Reviews or Review Essays

A listening report on an album or song or a screening report on a concert is usually called a music review. Though descriptive, opinions about quality are often included. An evaluation of some sort is necessary. These judgments about the album, song, or concert are usually written for magazine, newspaper, or website articles and columns. Music review essays differ from music reviews mainly in purpose. A review essay is typically written for a more academic audience and, therefore, may include different kinds of details than a review written for a magazine or blog. However, the strategies for writing a review essay are similar.

For a music review, some objectivity is important. All artistic media have some good and some bad qualities, so try to examine both. When you write a review for a class, your overall evaluation is usually phrased as the thesis or main idea of the essay.

Music reviews differ in the characteristics they possess. For an album or CD review, a writer typically discusses the overall theme of the album, some background of the artist or the album's production, the strongest and/or weakest songs on the album, and perhaps comments on the overall look and design of the album's packaging. Song reviews are much more specific. Although some commentary on the artist or the background of the song's production may be necessary, more detail is significant when discussing the strengths and weaknesses of the song, the lyrics, and the melody. Concert reviews may discuss the music, the sound, the lighting, the songs the artist chose to play or perform (or the songs that they did not play), and the production as a whole. Remember that you could also review a book about a musician, a music writer, or an album.

A review may also compare the song or album to others in the same genre or to others made by the same artist. With concert reviews, it is valid to compare it to others you have attended or watched on DVD. Most important, make sure your experience is obvious to the reader so that your opinion is taken seriously.

Reflection or Response Essays

The main purpose of a reflection or response essay is to use music as a jumping-off point for your own discussion. You may reflect on a song that was playing at an important moment in your life or respond to the way an album made you feel the first time you listened to it. Although the essay will mostly be personal, it is still

keyquestions

Key Questions for an Album/Song/Concert Review or Review Essay

- Have you clearly indicated your judgment of the album's/song's/concert's quality?
- For a song or album, did you mention any background information about the artist, previous recordings, or production? For a concert, did you mention the artist's success?
- Have you provided a brief synopsis of the music and lyrics of a song/album or the lighting, backup singers, band, dancers, and stage video for a concert?
- Have you defined yourself as a credible source? Have you mentioned specific elements of the album/song/concert that support your judgment?
- Have you described these quickly and vividly, using concrete language and metaphors?
- Have you qualified your judgment with both positive and negative aspects of the song/album/concert?
- If reviewing a song or album, did you discuss the appearance and packaging?
- If reviewing a concert, did you discuss the music that the artist chose (or did not choose) to play or perform?
- If a song or album, did you discuss the medium? Is it a download or a CD? From a soundtrack? Is the song part of an album? Part of a concept album?
- Have you begun the review with an attention-grabbing opening? Have you concluded it with a striking sentence?
- Did you write in present tense?

Key Questions for a Reflection or Response Essay

- Have you clearly indicated how you used the album, song, artist, or concert as a springboard for your thesis?
- Have you expressed your personal response to one aspect of the album, song, artist, or concert?
- Did you include too much summary (instead of more reflection)?
- Does your introduction direct your audience into your response?
- Does your concluding paragraph include some reflection on both the music and your response?
- Did you write about the song or album in present tense but any past life experiences in past tense?
- Are your essay's intentions clear?
- Did you explain the significance or effectiveness of your experience?

important to use evidence from the song, concert, album, or artist to explain why you are making your specific point.

A reflection or response essay can be written about a song, an album, a band, or a concert that means something to you, that sparks an emotion, or that triggers a memory. Then, think about who your audience is and what you would like him or her to know about this experience. When you are writing about a personal subject, a solid thesis statement may help keep you on topic.

Analysis Essays

There are many reasons to write an analysis of music; most significantly, this type of writing may help you reach a deeper, more critical appreciation of a song, album, or concert experience. To analyze music in an essay, you must first describe what you are analyzing. These descriptive details are important because your purpose is to explain their relation to one another, to the audience, or to you to support your main point. Your thesis will explain to your audience what you are analyzing and the major idea you are offering or judgment you are making about your subject. Also, remember that the key terms from this chapter may give you a vocabulary from which to write about a specific song, album, performance, or video.

When analyzing music, remember that you may be more familiar with the subject than your audience. Identify your audience and do not assume that they listen to the same music that you do or that they agree with your basic assumptions about music. For example, a teenager in 2008 may have a different take on Prince's "1999" than an adult who was a teenager when the song was originally released in 1983.

Synthesis Essays

These preceding essay types are not the only ways that you may write about music, and they may often be used in combination. Your needs or those of your audience may be best served by combining the skills used to analyze, respond to, and review an album, song, or concert. Music lends itself to essays that combine review and response or analysis and reflection. Examples of synthesis writing that you may be familiar with include album reviews in *Rolling Stone* that both analyze and review an album or MySpace blogs that review and personally respond as well.

keyquestions

Key Questions for an Analysis Essay

- Do you have a clearly stated thesis or main point or one that is obvious to the reader?
- Do you have a series of reasons supporting the thesis or main point? Are these arranged in a logical and convincing order?
- Are your supporting reasons backed up? Do you provide specific evidence and examples from the song, album, artist, or concert for each reason you offer?
- Does your introduction orient your reader into the direction of your argument?
- Does your concluding paragraph express the effectiveness or significance of your analysis and provide a vivid ending?
- Did you write in literary present tense if referring to an album or song?
- Did you avoid too much summary?
- Did you consider your audience?

SAMPLE ANNOTATED ESSAY

1. Folk music is not often placed in the category of popular music; however, crossover artists such as Bob Dylan, Johnny Cash, and Emmylou Harris have given the genre more radio play. Can you think of other genres that have revived in popularity by the support of popular artists?

2. Has folk music crossed into popular music in other ways?

Based in Kansas City, Missouri, **David Cantwell** *has written music reviews and analyses for* Oxford American, Salon, *the* Nashville Scene, The Journal of Country Music, *and* No Depression. *Coauthor of* Heartaches by the Number: Country Music's 500 Greatest Singles, *Cantwell also hosts the blog* Living in Stereo. *This article first appeared in* Oxford American *in 2000.*

THE TRIPLE-THREAT FOLK HERO

David Cantwell

First sentence introduces Cash's legacy as well as the author's bias.

If Johnny Cash had performed and recorded in the first half of the twentieth century, he would likely have achieved, like Babe Ruth or Pretty Boy Floyd, the status of folk hero. Coming to prominence in an era of electronic media, Cash has instead become something more modern. His booming yet humble salutation ("Hello, I'm Johnny Cash") and sartorial simplicity (The Man in Black) represent an honest-to-God icon. Cash owes much of this visibility to timing. Though he is, in sensibility, a country artist to the core, he arrived on the scene in that brief 1950s moment when his twangy, thumping music could also be heard as rockabilly. That entrance, teamed with his occasional pursuit of rock songwriting and self-destructive behavior, has made him one of the few country acts ever appropriated by

"The Triple-Threat Folk Hero" from OXFORD AMERICAN MAGAZINE, July/August 2000, p. 62 by David Cantwell.

a larger pop audience. A member of both the country and rock halls of fame, Cash has always been, in other words, a little bit country and a little bit rock 'n' roll. The new *Love God Murder* triple-CD set (Columbia/American/Legacy) chooses, refreshingly, to emphasize the former. Neither a greatest-hits set nor a rarities collection—just four songs here were ever released as singles, and only three more are previously unreleased in the U.S.—*Love God Murder* offers forty-eight songs, available as four separate titles or as a three-disc box set. Selected by the man himself, the collection showcases Johnny Cash, country singer. Whether begging a lover to let him down easy (as on 1962's "A Little at a Time," from *Love*), praising the Lord (on a camp-meeting-inspired Sun Records–era cut, "It Was Jesus," on *God*), or attempting to silence the jealous voices in his head (the Harlan Howard–penned ballad "The Sound of Laughter" from 1966 on *Murder*), Cash rarely rocks out here. Instead he has chosen songs that tend to frame his Southern tales with acoustic guitar, piano, and white gospel choirs. Covering forty years, *Love God Murder* is a marvelous way for fans to expand their Cash collections beyond essential albums like *The Sun Years* and *At Folsom Prison*.

Still, there is a hint of missed opportunity about the project. Some problems are little more than annoying. Shuffling the titles to read *Love Murder God,* for instance, would have righted the emotional chronology and also given the last word to the chapter of the story Cash clearly sees as the real climax. Other choices are more troubling. A gushing goof like 1964's "My Old Faded Rose" is tossed off with considerable charm, but a few other cuts merely sound tossed off, period. "What on Earth Will You Do (For Heaven's Sake)," from 1974, is a clever idea but one that remains unrealized, while a devotional to Jesus called "The Greatest Cowboy of Them All" was probably doomed from the start. In fact, consisting largely of Cash's second-string material, *Love God Murder* occasionally feels less like a career overview than an extended press release for Cash's much-anticipated album of new material due later this summer.

To that end, June Carter Cash contributes an essay to the *Love* disc that is sweet if not exactly revealing.

Conclusion adds
new, but pertinent,
information, and
it addresses the
effectiveness of
the packaging and
the significance of
this release.

- • The other guest-star liner notes here (Bono contributes an essay to *God,* Quentin Tarantino to *Murder*), are well-meaning but overwritten and unnecessary. To hear Cash's honest, trembling instrument strive to hit a note at the top of his humble range on one line, then tumble to Southern-gospel bass in the next, is all the testimony anyone needs to understand that this is one twentieth-century voice that will resound well into the twenty-first century.

DECODING THE TEXT

1. The author is obviously a fan of Cash's earlier work. Does this color his review?

2. How would the tone of the article have changed if the author had been unfamiliar with Cash's storied career?

CONNECTING TO YOUR CULTURE

1. What band, artist, musician, or producer do you feel this strongly impressed by? What characteristics make this person or group so significant in your mind? What weaknesses does this person or group hold?

2. Is your opinion shared by others? Why or why not?

THE READING ZONE

TACKLING TOPICS

1. Think about the musicians whom you consider icons. Why do you assign them this iconic status? Do popular critics, reviews, and music writers agree with you? Do people outside your generation agree with you?

2. What do you know about the history of rock 'n' roll? Research the first number one rock 'n' roll hit on the charts, the first singer classified as rock 'n' roll, and the influences on the genre to find out more.

3. Country music has gone through many changes since its early roots in folk and gospel melodies. What similarities can you see in current country or bluegrass hits to the music of its origins?

4. How are women portrayed in rock, R&B, hip hop, country, and rap music? How do their portrayals differ across genres and across generations?

5. What songs do you know that you would not consider "popular"? Perhaps a Broadway tune or a song you sang in choir? A hymn or a kid's song? What would it take for this music to become more popular? You may want to consider the way rap uses such songs.

READING SELECTIONS

The readings that follow are organized into five sections: 1970s, 1980s, 1990s, 2000s, and Across the Decades. The familiar decades organization that underpins all content chapters for this textbook is used, and the readings in each of the sections are not isolated to that decade or section because pop culture is not only what happened at the time but also how the same item or idea is received or remembered later on.

The readings here are presented as a way for you to become more versed in investigating music as pop culture; however, they are also offered as samples of writing reviews, responses, analyses, and synthesis essays. In the '70s section, Michael A. Stusser reviews and analyzes Bob Marley's life and career as a reggae artist and political activist. The Velvet Underground's album, *The Velvet Underground Loaded*, is reviewed in "Beyond Warhol." The influence of black music on American 1980s mainstream pop and top forty is analyzed by Kevin Phinney in "Controversy." George Plasketes responds to the 1990s rise in vinyl records' popularity from *The Journal of Popular Culture*. Also in the '90s section, *Billboard* magazine writers analyze the evolution of rap music in TV and film. Guitar players search for spiritual meaning in the '00s section, along with a student essay comparing war-inspired music from the '70s and the '00s and an essay examining music piracy published in *Studies in Popular Culture*. Across the Decades offers three essays that overview music from the past few decades. First, Gregory McNamee reviews an influential text by Lester Bangs, America's most famous rock critic. Theodore Matula offers commentary and review on the life of punk legend Joe Strummer, and Kalene Westmoreland addresses women's issues in music with her response to Meredith Brooks's "Bitch" lyrics and to the Lilith Fair. This article is paired with The Rolling Stones' "Bitch" lyrics for comparison.

These readings might inspire you to analyze your own music tastes or to listen to and review an artist, band, or album you are currently unfamiliar with; however, their main purpose is to inspire your response to the vast landscape of popular music over the decades.

Reading Selections: the

CONSIDERING IDEAS

1. Think of a current musician, or celebrity, who has been involved in the political spectrum. How has this person been treated in entertainment circles?
2. Has he or she been celebrated or ignored?
3. Has it hindered or helped his or her career?

Michael A. Stusser *is a freelance writer for many publications, including* mental_floss, Law & Politics, *and* Seattle *magazines, and he also writes a regular column, "Accidental Parent," for* ParentMap. *Stusser has also coauthored several screenplays along with* Twisted Scholar, *an educational television series. "Bob Marley: Music Man, Man with a Mission" was published in* mental_floss *in 2006.*

BOB MARLEY

Music Man, Man with a Mission

Michael A. Stusser

*"We come from Trench Town, Trench Town . . .
We free the people with music, sweet music."*

—from "Trench Town"

Born on February 6, 1945, Robert Nesta Marley grew up in Jamaica's West Kingston ghetto, often passed between a variety of caretakers and family friends. His father was a white man long estranged from the family, and his mother was a black Jamaican woman who'd picked up and left for America when Bob was just a youngster. Effectively abandoned, Marley spent most of his time in Trench Town, the worst of Jamaican slums, where he got to see firsthand the world of crime, shanty towns, and impoverished gangs. Even the name of his band, The Wailers, was inspired by hardship. "We started out cryin' . . ." Marley once said.

But oppression and poverty were only two cornerstones in Marley's life and music. The other foundation was his Rastafarian faith—a way of life that included studying the Old Testament, smoking copious quantities of ganja (in a sacred communion with Jah, or God), growing one's hair out into dreadlocks (tresses are seen as a part of the spirit), and worshiping the Ethiopian emperor Haile Selassie I. Most Rastas consider His Imperial Majesty Selassie, who died in 1975, to be the Messiah of the African race—a representative divine connection with the holy land. (For those needing a family tree to understand the Rasta picture, Selassie was believed to be the direct descendent of Sheba and Solomon.)

Hokey as it sounds, playing music and smoking marijuana were actually a religion to Marley. He believed both were ways of communicating with Jah—a way to be spiritual and offer your musical gift to a higher place. Marley wanted people who listened to his music to understand his own beliefs, hoping it would bring salvation through one love for all mankind.

"Open your eyes and look within / Are you satisfied with the life you're living?"

—from "Exodus"

The "one love" theory is great on paper (and in song), unfortunately, Jamaican politics has been filled with violence since the country's independence from Britain in 1962. When general elections were held in February 1967, the two major political parties—the People's National Party (PNP) and the Jamaica Labour Party (JLP)—were ruthless in their tactics. Opposition members were intimidated, threatened, and even murdered. A political culture had been born, and the craziness never stopped.

The Rastas called it "politricks." They'd seen their share of the corruption, broken promises, and violence that had come with reform and elections. And Marley was right there with them. He distrusted

"Bob Marley: Music Man, Man with a Mission" by Michael Stusser from MENTAL FLOSS MAGAZINE, November/December 2006, pp. 70–72. Reprinted by permission of Mental Floss. www.mentalfloss.com.

the process and avoided out-and-out campaigning.

Fortunately, some progressive changes began being made after the PNP won a majority in the 1972 election. The party had campaigned on a job growth platform, and it was the better option for any Jamaican who didn't own a swank tourist hotel or a coffee plantation. Further, its elected prime minister, Michael Manley, was a left-winger who bore the slogan "politics of participation." Once in office, Manley implemented social reforms welcomed by the masses, which included reducing government censorship and eliminating the crackdown on civil liberties. Marley may not have been a registered member of the PNP, but with its emphasis on reducing illiteracy, he was clearly on its side. Unfortunately, the party's economic plan never gained traction—in part because businesses and conservatives dug in their heels and in part because of strikes, shortages, and a lack of cash to fund its social agenda.

Despite his nonpartisan nature, Marley wound up in the political crossfire— mainly because, by the mid-1970s, he'd become a national celebrity. Marley (and his Wailers) had been recording songs since 1961 with some success, but it took more than a decade for their ska-based style to catch fire with a broader audience. Helped along by legendary producer Lee "Scratch" Perry, the band developed a more mainstream, reggae-rock sound. As a result, Bob Marley and the Wailers gained worldwide popularity, finally hitting it big with their 1973 album *Catch a Fire* and Marley's song "I Shot the Sheriff" (recorded the following year by Eric Clapton).

Marley's status as a leader and prophet in Jamaica also bloomed, not only with the kids in Trench Town, but also with the population at large. In other words: If you had Bob on your side, you might very well win an election. So, when campaigning time for the 1976 election came around, Marley got pulled into a political fight he wanted no part of. Scheduled to perform at the nonpartisan Smile Jamaica Concert (more for party animals than party faithful), Prime Minister Manley used the government's sponsorship of the event to his advantage, making it look as if the PNP was orchestrating the concert, and announcing there'd be an election shortly after the big show. The conservative opposition candidate, Edward Seaga of the JLP, had a few choice words to say about Manley's deceptive tactics. Death threats flew, and Marley got caught in the middle.

On December 3, just two days before the Smile Jamaica Concert, a group of thugs ambushed Marley and his bandmates at his compound on Hope Road in Kingston. (Ironically, Marley had designed his Hope Road home to be a safe haven for youth to escape the shootings and crime on the streets.) Marley's wife, Rita, was shot in the head, Bob was nailed in the arm and chest, and Marley's manager was hit several times—but they all somehow survived. The shooters were never caught, though it's assumed the violence was a political attempt on his life from the JLP camp to stop Marley and Manley from going ahead with their Smile Jamaica concert.

Amazingly, Marley was undeterred, and he played the concert two nights later in front of 80,000 strong. Rita sang with bandages on her head, and although Marley couldn't play guitar due to his injuries, he blew away the crowd with a 90-minute set. It began, aptly, with his song "War," and continued with him exiting the stage doing a ritualistic hunter dance and pantomiming a gunslinger's quick draw. After the show, Marley and his wife left Jamaica, and he spent the next 14 months in England crafting his famed album *Exodus*. But back in Jamaica, the PNP won the election, and the violence got worse.

"If you listen carefully now you will hear . . . Things are not the way they used to be,
Don't tell no lie;
One and all got to face reality now."

—from "Natural Mystic"

Whereas most folks might have avoided politics after being shot, Marley did just the opposite. In an attempt to promote a cease-fire between Jamaica's political parties—not to mention the gangs on the street and the Rastafari factions—Marley returned to his native land in 1978 to headline the "One Love" Peace Concert. The show was performed at the National Stadium in Kingston before tens of thousands of proud Jamaicans. Among them were both Michael Manley and rival Edward Seaga. On stage during the event, Marley grabbed their hands, clasped them with his own, and held them high in a show of solidarity and hope for a new era of peace in Jamaica.

Sadly, peace did not prevail. During the bitter elections of 1980, more than 700 people were killed in the streets. And in the following years, several influential members of the Jamaican music community were murdered, including close Marley friend Claudie Massop in 1979, peacemaker Aston "Bucky Marshall"

Thompson in 1980, and both Rasta leader Peter Tosh and Wailer drummer Carlton Barrett in 1987.

IN HIS OWN WORDS

On Having a White Father and Black Mother
"I don't have prejudice against myself. My father was a white and my mother was black. Them call me half-caste or whatever. Me don't dip on nobody's side. Me don't dip on the black man's side nor the white man's side. Me dip on God's side, the one who create me and cause me to come from black and white."

On How He Began Singing
"During school break, de teacher she say, 'Who can talk, talk, who can make anything, make, who can sing, sing.' And me sing."

On Political Lyrics
"De government is tramplin' over de people's sweat and tears. Comin' down hard, hard. We're oppressed, so we sing oppressed songs and sometime people find themselves guilty. And dey can't stand de terrible weight of it."

On the Power of Music
"One good thing about music, when it hits you, you feel no pain." (from "Trench Town Rock")

"Emancipate yourself from mental slavery;
None but ourselves can free our minds."
—from "Redemption Song"

Asked if he was a political figure, Marley always denied it. "We're not talkin' bout burnin' and lootin' for material goods," he told *The New York Times Magazine* in 1977.

"We want to burn capitalistic illusions. Me no deal with politics. Me sing and deal with detrot' (downtrodden) de best I can. Me sing de song and hope de people catch de tune and mark de words. People have plenty misunderstanding, mon. No ting is important dat much. Love life and live it. Dat's all."

Look at his accolades, though, and they suggest otherwise. In 1978, the Senegalese Delegation to the United Nations gave Marley the Third World Peace Medal for helping to inspire Zimbabwe to independence. (The line *"One love, one heart, let's get together and feel all right"* inspired freedom fighters during Zimbabwe's struggle with Britain.) And in 1981, the Jamaican government awarded their native son the Order of Merit for his international recognition in the arts. Sadly, Marley died only one month after this honor, on May 11, 1981. In 1977, he'd discovered a wound on his right big toe that he thought was a soccer injury but was later diagnosed as a malignant melanoma. Despite doctors' warnings, Marley refused amputation saying, "Rasta no abide amputation. I don't allow a man to be dismantled." The cancer spread through his body and took his life when he was just 36 years old.

Bob, of course, lives on, not only in the minds and spirits of all he inspired, but on their iPods and CD players, too. His retrospective collection, *Legend,* is the bestselling reggae album of all time, with sales of more than 15 million. A legend indeed, Marley's music always carried a message. And even though his music often dealt with hardships and revolution, it always did so in a positive way that guided the world to a better place.

DECODING THE TEXT

1. The author uses the adjectives "hokey" and "spiritual" to characterize Marley's drug use and many others to characterize his political activities. However, he offers very little description of his music. What does this say about the article's purpose?

2. What does it say about Marley's legacy?

CONNECTING TO YOUR CULTURE

1. How does Marley's legacy, music, and Jamaican culture affect your perceptions of popular culture?

2. Have you heard his music on the radio or seen students at your school in Rastafarian garb?

3. In your opinion and based on your reading, why is he such an icon?

1. How did Andy Warhol's factory, and the bands and artists who performed there, influence American popular culture of the 1970s through today?

2. Can you think of other visual artists who impacted the music community in such a powerful way? How?

Danny Goldberg *is a former rock critic, publicist, and manager for such talents as Nirvana, the Beastie Boys, and Bonnie Raitt. He was also the founder and CEO of Artemis Records, home to Steve Earle, Warren Zevon, and Better Than Ezra. Goldberg also helped to form the Musical Majority in collaboration with the ACLU; the group challenged the movement to put warning labels on albums. A freelance writer for* The Village Voice *and* Rolling Stone, *Goldberg also served as managing editor for* Circus *magazine.*

BEYOND WARHOL

Danny Goldberg

The Velvet Underground are famous for their association with Andy Warhol, for singing songs about heroin and sex, for having rock's first female drummer, for being mysterious and remote, for being perverse and esoteric, for having a banana on their first album cover and for being written about with love by Lenny Kaye.

Like the Grateful Dead they remained the darlings of a relatively small set, either un-willing or unable to pierce the needle hole of hit record radio, and like the Dead, in spite of their long tenure as everybody's favorite starving superstars, their basic in-born instinct for rock and roll has driven them, albeit gradually, to the ranks of the finest and most popular American rock bands. The reasons have to do with their talent and perseverance (the band has been together more or less for five years!), with their vision and their integrated style, but mainly with the Mick Jagger of the group, its song-writer, lead singer, guitar-ist, pianist, and sex symbol, Lou Reed.

The Velvets' history is well known. They got together in Syracuse, surfaced in New York in 1966 playing the Café Bizarre where they met and fell in love with Andy Warhol, who was then at the peak of his pop art success. They teamed up with Nico, a Warhol superstar beauty, sang songs with lyrics that made the Rolling Stones look like prudes, and made history as part of a multimedia event (the first and best . . .) called the Plastic Explod-ing Inevitable [*sic*] where they turned their back to the audience, and played very very loud. A legend of decadence evolved about the group as well as one of mind expanding music. They were the first and only East Coast acid rock band of the period. They released three excel-lent albums on Verve and now MGM has released a "Best of" collection.

"Beyond Warhol" by Danny Goldberg, as appeared in ALL YESTERDAY'S PARTIES edited by Clinton Heylin, pp. 206–210. New York: DaCapo. 2005.

But the point of this article is not to further rehash what New York City acid was like in 1967 (an adorable but rather over reported square inch in the many acred farm of contemporary American consciousness). The point is to tell you about a new Atlantic album by the very same Velvets. It is an LP which neither imitates nor forgets the past. It's called *The Velvet Underground Loaded,* has a nondescript cover, and conveys the wonderful feeling that the Stones have in the past exclusively reserved: unforeseeable growth, immediate excitement and memorable new material.

Typically, *Loaded* is the completion, not the beginning, of another Velvet chapter; the album changed producers in midstream, resulted in some group dissension and ended an all summer engagement at Max's Kansas City where Lou Reed had returned rock joy to the sweaty cynical summer empire city. It's hard to tell what caused what—who left whom if at all, or what will happen in the months to come. Suffice it to say that the summer of 1970 has become instant Velvet Underground history as sure as 1967 was—and luckily for the present and future, *Loaded* exists as a lasting relic of the recent time.

Rock and roll, as we all know, went through somewhat of a plateau most of this summer. Festivals were plagued by government fear and quick buck promoters, and no revolutionary supergroup seemed on the horizon. New York, more than any other part of the country, craves freshness from its entertainers. Charles Manson could have been talking about New York when he wrote "Restless people from the sick city— but they're home now to make the sky look pretty. What can I do—I'm just a person?— this is the line we always seem to hear—you just sit—things get worse—watch TV and drink your beer." And if things are difficult for the average person, the imagined woes of the large core of avant garde are even worse. The Velvets were one of the first genuine rock groups to win the affection of the New York City art crowd. In June, Danny Fields, the young Atlantic Records savant who brought the group to the label, arranged for them to play the upstairs room at Max's Kansas City, the sprawling "in crowd" center of Gotham. Within the red lit walls of Max's, stars from Brian Jones to Bob Dylan, from Janis Joplin to Penny Arcade, have whiled away their late night hours.

The upstairs room is usually a "discotheque" but for the Velvets it became a concert hall. And for their opening night of a one week engagement—their first in native New York for close to two years— uncountable hundreds squeezed together at midnight hoping for a glimpse into the recent past that more had read about (or written about) than lived through.

But Lou Reed was too soulful to be an ivory tower golden oldie. There were changes from the old days. John Cale, producer of the first few albums, had left the group and was replaced on bass and organ by Doug Yule. Maureen Tucker was back with the group and played on the album.

The old Velvet sound combined a Dylanesque vocal with an eastern rock freak backing. In the old days Reed had concocted complex feedback systems where he would get dozens of notes for every string he touched. The new Velvets were unpretentious, tight, throbbing hard hard rock and roll, blistering with Reed's super voice of pleasure/pain which sang songs no one had ever heard before. "Dance," he demanded, raising his left hand with an intensity and grace which made him appear some beautiful combination of Frank Sinatra and Mick Jagger. And dance they did, even the most hardcore wallflowers. The diehard spectators and the impassioned table sitters could not help but move to the driving beat that the new Velvet Underground produced, driven by Sterling Morrison's lead guitar. It was Reed's show and no one would dispute it. In black tee shirt, his veins bulging from his muscular neck, he played two sets a night—and not for the one week that had been originally scheduled but for the entire summer.

The Velvets' old professor Delmore Schwartz once wrote, "a cup of coffee can destroy your sadness," and the Velvet Underground were New York's cup of coffee throughout the summer smog. It must be observed that New York is one of the most performed-in cities in the nation—in addition to the always busy Fillmore East there is Unganos, the Bitter End, the Village Gaslight, and a dozen lesser known stages where pop music is offered. Yet it was Max's that led the most sophisticated rock audience in the world to dance as if they were in high school. And to return night after night because they actually enjoyed the music, not merely the social mannerism of a single viewing. Not since the early Lovin' Spoonful days had a rock band in New York continued to draw crowds for such a long period of time. Quite literally everyone of musical importance came to hear Lou belt out with exquisite contempt: "Oh sweet nothing/you ain't got nothing at all."

Naturally a scene sprang up. The group performed a couple of their old classics like "Heroin" or "I'm Waiting for My Man" each night, but they played them the new rock way—commanding respect and a love for their new style. Meanwhile rumors

developed. Reed would appear to hate the gig on some nights, or to be at his happiest on another. He gave interviews saying things like, "A rock band can be a form of yoga." And he exuded genuine rock—not an imitation of the fifties, or of the sixties—it was a timeless dynamite feeling that made people dance—and smile.

Meanwhile the Velvets were cutting the record *Loaded* in an involved and confusing manner. At first Adrian Barber, producer of the Iron Butterfly, was to be their producer—then Atlantic staffer Shel Kagen. Also involved was Geoffry Halsam, who did the final mix, and the group itself. The album is overall softer than their Max's sets; but the songs are the same and the album is a monument in rock history. Like Dylan, Lou Reed is an artist who changes faster than machines can record him.

At this writing there were rumors that the group had broken up and that Reed was in seclusion writing new songs. But with this group there is no telling what, if anything, the future will bring. The Velvets, thank God, are still unpredictable in an age of rock which revolves around record buying seasons and press releases more often than it does around the artist. Let us be thankful for *Loaded,* an inadequate but potent expression of that summer of 1970.

If nothing else, the album is concrete evidence of what the Velvet fans have always maintained: the group's early decadence and its continuing hassles do not change the fact that they are among the most complex, inventive and musical musicians in the world. They express the scathing, often nightmarish reality of the physical world, yet sing of inner love with a sensitivity that beckons angels. And in their most recent stage they combined their lyricism with their most centered rock music to date, maintaining their position in the dwindling handful of groups who perform rock as the divine momentary celebration it can be.

As Lou Reed passionately sings in "Rock and Roll," "Despite all that amputation you could just go out and listen to a rock and roll station." Or better still, get *Loaded*.

DECODING THE TEXT

1. Why does the author spend much of the article on background information and on the live performances of songs from the album? What purpose does that serve for his audience?

2. How does Goldberg add his own voice to the essay through specific details? Vocabulary? Background information?

CONNECTING TO YOUR CULTURE

1. What bands/artists do you listen to who are "unable to pierce the needle hole of hit record radio"? Why does the band/artist not appeal to a mass audience?

2. The author writes that *Loaded* was "an inadequate but potent expression of that summer of 1970." What album identifies a certain period of time for you? A certain event?

Reading Selection: the '80s

CONSIDERING IDEAS

1. In the 1980s, dance music—often considered a shallow genre—was very popular. However, rap, alternative rock, and grunge music were also on the rise. What assumptions can you make about '80s popular culture based on these facts?

2. What assumptions can you make about '80s subcultures based on these facts?

Kevin Phinney *is an entertainment journalist from Austin, Texas. His early morning radio show on KGSR-FM, "Kevin & Kevin," premiered in 1988 but ended with his move to Seattle in 2005. Souled American: How Black Music Transformed White Culture, Phinney's first book, follows the history of popular music through race relations. "Controversy" is an excerpt from this book.*

CONTROVERSY

Kevin Phinney

America nursed its disco-induced hang-over in the lingering months separating Jimmy Carter from Ronald Reagan, and in the interim the cash cow of American pop music gave but grudgingly. After reaping unprecedented profits through most of the 1970s with revenues doubling in just five years, the record industry suffered its first recession in more than a quarter century. The numbers said it all: between 1978 and 1979, revenues slid eleven per-cent, tumbling from $4.1 billion to $3.7 billion. Some seven hundred jobs were lost in the waning months of 1979, and downsizing continued through much of the 1980s. CBS alone cut seven thousand jobs in the years from 1980 through 1986.

Billboard talent editor Paul Grein says the industry had one collective scapegoat for their misfortune. "The more specific reason for the slump in crossover," he explained, "was that disco had such a negative association for white people that any kind of music would remind people of the dreaded disco phenomenon. That's the reason a lot of people blamed the record slump on disco itself."

Conversely, music critic Ed Ward saw the downturn as a microcosm of a larger eco-nomic process at work. "It's something you see in American business in general," he said in 1985. "When expansion stops happening at a rate that seems to indi-cate growth, people start to scream. They call it a slump or a depression, which is not really true. There was a lot of dead wood in the industry, and people suddenly saw their jobs being threatened. They expected to sell millions and millions every time out of the box."

Panic set in. During the 1970s, it had been simple enough to gauge public interest because given previous buying trends, what music buyers really wanted was more: more tuneful pop from relative newcomers Boston and Billy Joel, and more classics on demand from the titans of the 1960s—Bob Dylan, Diana Ross, Barbra Streisand, and Jefferson (Airplane) Starship. They wanted more roots rock from Bruce Springsteen, Linda Ronstadt, and the Eagles, and more quirky new wave music from the likes of The Cars, Blondie, Elvis Costello, and Devo. And, of course, the public wanted more and more and more disco . . . until suddenly, they didn't.

While big band swing took nearly half a decade to disappear from the airwaves,

"Controversy" from SOULED AMERICAN: HOW BLACK MUSIC TRANSFORMED WHITE CULTURE by Kevin Phinney, pp. 268–76 (Billboard Books, 2005).

disco vanished like a gaudy new super-store caught in a flash fire. In the first half of 1979, almost half the pop records tracked by *Billboard* registered on the R&B charts, too. But six months into 1980, that number had fallen to twenty-one percent, and by the winter of 1982, the trend bottomed out at seventeen percent black, urban, or R&B in origin. In October of 1982, just as Michael Jackson's *Thriller* was shipping to stores, not a single black artist was represented among *Billboard*'s Top 20 singles or albums.

It seemed no one wanted to remember anything about the decade just ended: not the leisure suits or the smiley faces; not *Roots* or school busing; and neither urban decay nor the victory of the Viet Cong. In the aftermath of disco, the humiliation of the Iranian hostage crisis, and the emergence of a strange new disease communicated by sex, Americans joined together in penitence and a shared longing for someone who could tell them how everything would be all right and that society as a whole could ease back into an imagined past of moral certitude.

Ronald Reagan agreed to do that, and more. As the GOP's 1980 candidate for president, he told supporters that the country's problems stemmed not from too little compassion, but from too much money wasted being compassionate. According to the Reagan scenario, "trickle-down economics" guaranteed eventual prosperity for all, if only his plan could be given time to work. As Nelson George writes in *The Death of Rhythm and Blues,* "Reaganomics—more guns, less butter, and the failure to enforce civil rights legislation—just stone cold stopped black progress in this country. For the first time since the New Deal, the government, including Congress and the Supreme Court,

didn't support the civil rights agenda, and, in fact, did much to dismantle the laws on the books and encourage a resurgence of racism."

Urban blue-collar workers found themselves competing in a shrinking market as local businesses yielded to national companies and those companies mushroomed into international corporations that outsourced jobs to the lowest bidder. The proliferation of crack and angel dust were decimating the inner cities, leaving many families short not only a principal wage earner, but also an indispensable role model.

"Hard times for healing," Craig Werner echoed in *A Change Is Gonna Come: Music, Race & the Soul of America,* "the worst period in race relations since the 1890s." Werner cites the murder of Yusef Hawkins in Bensonhurst—killed for walking with a white woman—and the Ku Klux Klan murders of five participants in a North Carolina anti-Klan rally in 1979. Incredibly, candidate Reagan began his presidential quest in the same Mississippi county where civil rights workers Michael Schwerner, Andrew Goodman, and James Chaney were murdered in 1964. With contenders seeking the nation's highest office either unconscionably callous or shockingly oblivious, how could anyone even think that singing and dancing together might bridge the racial divide?

So many changes, observed semiretired songwriter Bill Withers; yet so little change. "Those are things that really make people stop and think," he intones. "A lot of people have never seen that real hate. I've *seen* it. It was all over me, Jack. When you're in Mississippi, man, and you see that kind of hate. I remember seeing that, and looking at that, and seeing those faces, and thinking, *Man*. That hate look. They ain't even listening to no music you made. How in the hell you gonna change their minds with music?"

The unblinking eye of cable TV put the country on 24-hour alert with calamities instantly available via satellite hookups from CNN. And the news never failed to disappoint. By the end of summer in 1981, audiences had witnessed attempts to fell a Pope and a president, as well as the killings of John Lennon and Egyptian peace advocate Anwar Sadat. Network television programmers conversely set about reinforcing middle class mythology through *The Cosby Show* and *Family Ties*.

What did any of that have to do with life in what Hollywood now calls "the flyover states"—that vast expanse of America between the high-rises of Manhattan and Los Angeles? Not much, concluded the kids growing up in New York area ghettos at the turn of the decade. Just as punk and new wave provided respite from the ear candy of REO Speedwagon, Styx, and Supertramp, black youth from the boroughs devised an alternative to the trashy flash of disco. Out of the detritus of crack dens, hock shops, and rehab centers, hip-hop culture was born, bringing with it a graffiti style known for its color and braggadocio known as "tagging," the whirligig athleticism of breakdancing, and rap. Once again, black Americans were taking twenty-five cents and making it look like a dollar.

THE BREAKS

When a power blackout plunged New York City into darkness in 1977, hundreds of area businesses were sacked by the same regulars who had shopped there for years. After nearly a decade of neglect and middle-class flight, residents of the South Bronx accepted that their home had become emblematic of every failure and vice attributed to city life. They even had a nickname for it: "Vietnam." Moralists ready to pass judgment on the failings of modern society could always point to New York in general—the city President Ford refused to bail out with federal assistance in the mid-1970s—and the South Bronx in particular, as the nadir of civilization. But deep in the heart of the ghetto, something was rising up through the grates that eluded statisticians, doomsayers, and Hollywood's myth machine.

In the 1981 film *Fort Apache, the Bronx*, filmmakers somehow managed to wade hip deep through the community's lawlessness and devastation without stumbling over the creative impulses of the youth culture taking root there. The hip-hop renaissance coalesced in relative obscurity even as decay enveloped the scene's pioneers. As early as 1973, youngsters interested in urban art began to gravitate toward the Youth Organization at Adlai Stevenson High School. Under the supervision of Afrika Bambaataa, an ex-gang leader familiar with the teachings of Malcolm X, these kids and their associates—mostly black, Puerto Rican, and Jamaican—began to explore new ways to express themselves. Some chose creative application of magic markers and spray paint, others drifted behind the turntables to spin records, while the most daring grabbed a microphone to lead the revelers in chants. The playlists at these gatherings typically depended on funk staples from James Brown, Wilson Pickett, and Rick James, but were recombined with samples cannibalized from elsewhere, often lifting a riff or vocal hook from the hits of yesteryear. Frequent targets included bands which first appealed almost exclusively to white youth:

Grand Funk, the Monkees, Chicago, and Led Zeppelin.

These were unconventional choices perhaps, but they paled by comparison to the liberties deejays took with the mechanics of record playing. Where disco mixmasters sought to segue seamlessly from one vinyl source into the next, hip-hop deejays grew fixated on "the break," that optimal moment containing a track's percussion breakdown, guitar solo, or horn fanfare. With two turntables and twin copies of the same track, "spinners" (as they became known) could sustain their breaks indefinitely. Rhythmic accents were added by rapidly tugging the vinyl back and forth beneath the stylus—all while the song continued to play over the speakers. "Scratching," they called it. In disrespecting the record and the turntables (neither was made to weather such abuse), deejays not only found a new way to present music, they discovered an uncharted universe of sound locked within. This "break-beat" music quickly attracted adventurous dancers who dubbed themselves b-boys and b-girls, who responded by inventing an entirely new dance lexicon. They developed the rudiments of breakdance, which eventually included popping and locking (moves in which various body parts appear to "lock" into position before "popping" out again).

Nothing like it had been seen or heard before. Still, breakdancers had to depend on music provided by the deejays, and in turn the deejays received second billing to the records they played. But when various "MCs" (from "emcee") began taking turns at the microphone either to exhort the dancers or to demonstrate their own rhyming skills, the result was an immediate and visceral connection to the audience. And, whether they knew it or not, these MCs were revisiting practices that predated slavery.

As far back as the 1600s, explorer Richard Jobson logs journal entries that describe the griots as a roving assortment of West African troubadours renowned for their storytelling skill. Rap has early American roots, too. In the 19th century, the practice of "patting juba" (or the hambone) was often accompanied by a vocalist who would repeat an existing rhyme or invent verses on the spot. Antecedents of rap are strewn about black culture, in fact, from the hepcat jive of Cab Calloway and Shirley Ellis' word-warping novelty, "The Name Game," to the social commentaries of performance artist Gil Scott-Heron.

But rap's most obvious precursor is the venerated black tradition called "playing the dozens," an informal competition where players inflate their own assets while denigrating those of an opponent. Whites have engaged in similar games for years. Consider the "tall tales" of America's frontier days, including Davy Crockett's boast that he could swallow a black man whole—if he was buttered and had his ears pinned back. Antecedents are strewn throughout the blues ("I'm a back door man," Willie Dixon told the world. "The men don't know . . . but the little girls understand"), and then white rock 'n' roll arrived, and with it came Elvis Presley's warning, "I'm evil, so don't you mess around with me." Of course, no one played the dozens like Muhammad Ali, the boxing legend whose grandstanding raised trash talk to a sport all its own. (Before his upcoming 1974 bout with George Foreman, Ali told reporters he'd "float like a butterfly, sting like a bee, his hands can't hit what his eyes can't see. Now you see me, now you don't. George thinks he will, but I know he won't.")

Even 1970s folkie James Taylor dabbled in the dozens, jokingly referring to himself in "Steamroller" as "a napalm bomb, stone guaranteed to blow your mind."

Like rap, hip-hop culture also claims international origins. When the Jamaican government refused to air politically charged reggae on its stations in the early 1970s, fans of the music took to the streets with sound systems assembled on flatbed trucks. Inevitably, crowds would gather around for a spontaneous party, where "dub" versions (in which songs are tweaked to elongate and enhance their rhythmic qualities, while other melodic elements weave in and out of the mix) of current favorites would leave plenty of room for MCs to engage in oral cutting contests, typically for bragging rights, and sometimes for prizes or cash. Because these battles (known by the locals as "toasting") escalated back and forth to the triumph of a winner, dual turntables and records were used to draw out the drama. And, as immigrants made their way into the United States, many of their techniques survived largely intact. Several of hip-hop's original deejays hailed from Jamaica, including Grandmaster Flash (whose given name was Joseph Saddler) and DJ Kool Herc (born Clive Campbell), who arrived in the Bronx from the Jamaican capital of Kingston at the age of twelve.

In October 1979, rap first demonstrated commercial potential when the Sugarhill Gang's "Rapper's Delight," a disco/rap hybrid with no political axe to grind, began shipping 75,000 copies a day. Eventually, it slipped into the Top 40 pop charts and sold two million copies. Major record labels still feeling the sting of disco's spectacular flameout took notice, but no action. Meanwhile, as rap gathered momentum in Harlem and then moved into Manhattan's downtown scene through the Danceteria, Peppermint Lounge, Ritz, and Roxy nightclubs, MCs began to diversify in topics and style. Just as rock 'n' roll marked a departure from the swing and crooner eras that went before, rap now drew a line between the music of baby boomers and generations X and Y. Everything about rap—its sound, its dances, its politics, its fashion—telegraphed one overarching message: *This Is Not Your Parents' Music.*

Everything about hip-hop sprang from the street. Pop, rock, and the burgeoning heavy metal scene belonged to big business; it had become the stuff of arena shows for the fans and life behind limo glass for its stars. Punk had more attitude, but less music. Rhythm and blues was tainted by association with disco, and besides, the idea that there "Ain't No Stoppin' Us Now" or that we'd board a "Love Train" seemed absurdly naïve for inner city adolescents growing up in the Reagan Age.

Todd Boyd's 2003 book, *H.N.I.C.: The Death of Civil Rights and the Reign of Hip Hop* opens with a preface attributed to "The Notorious D.O.C." (H.N.I.C., by the way, refers to "Head Niggas in Charge.") "Hip-hop has rejected and now replaced the pious, sanctimonious nature of civil rights as the defining moment of blackness. In turn, it offers new ways of seeing and understanding what it means to be black at this pivotal time in history."

By the time Grandmaster Flash and the Furious Five issued a manifesto of their own called "The Message" in 1982, it was also clear that this music had unique identifiers setting it apart from disco and that hip-hop wasn't going to be some momentary diversion on the way to something else. Where "Rapper's Delight" really was a novelty record—albeit a key one for introducing hip-hop into the mainstream—"The Message" was seeded with the same dread and menace that would eventually typify the most confrontational rap music. Rapper Melle Mel's assortment of urban terrorscapes run the gamut, from repossessed cars and bill collectors who "scare my wife when I'm not home" to people pissing on the stairs and baseball bat–wielding junkies crouched in the alleys nearby. To it all, he adds his own chilling admonitions, "It's like a jungle sometimes, it makes me wonder how I keep from going under." Just as Stevie Wonder's "Living for the City" showed the bigotry directed at America's working poor, "The Message" visits the same territory and concludes with a staged police–artist altercation reminiscent of Wonder's classic. With conditions substantially worse and a hip-hop generation coiled to strike back, Mel says he's reached the point of no return. "Don't push me," he warns, "cause I'm close to the edge."

Harsh as it may seem, rap's rejection of the civil rights mentality was essential to the creation of a new identity for the young and disaffected. They knew better than anyone how the brilliant sunshine of Dr. King's vision refused to penetrate the places they slept, played, and went to school.

British musicians embraced their dissident expressions long before hip-hop earned notice stateside, and, just as predictably, they helped America get comfortable with its own music. By 1981, the Police had already scored several Top 40 hits with their Jamaican-tinged pop (the group's album *Regatta de Blanc* translates

to "White Reggae") and England's ska-influenced agitprop band the Clash had Grandmaster Flash and the Furious Five open for them the same year, when they appeared at a New York City club called Bond's. Unfortunately, the crowd still held the opinion that if it wasn't rock, it wasn't right. Long before the end of their set, Flash and crew fled the stage under a hail of plastic cups.

CROSSING OVER

Black rockers received even less respect than black rappers. In the 1970s, it had become commonplace for white rock artists to appropriate elements of the black burden (witness John Lennon's "Woman Is the Nigger of the World," Lou Reed's "I Wanna Be Black" or his drag queen opus, "Walk on the Wild Side," and Patti Smith's "Rock 'n' Roll Nigger"), so long as the lyrics implied solidarity. Mick Jagger made himself an exception when he groused on "Some Girls" in 1978 that black girls "only want to get f**ked all night," adding sourly, "I don't have that much jam." Even though his jibe was equal parts satire and satyr, the comment kindled a firestorm in the media. For months Jesse Jackson publicly lobbied Atlantic, the band's parent label, to have the song banned and the Stones sanctioned. True to their image as jet-set reprobates, the Stones refused to capitulate to either Jackson or Atlantic. "I've always been opposed to censorship of any kind," Jagger demurred, "especially from conglomerates. I've always said, 'If you can't take a joke, it's too f**king bad.'"

White artists could claim immunity from African-American approval by invoking freedom of expression. Conversely, either by choice or by playing to the lowest common commercial denominator, black artists continued to write from a palate limited to dance, romance, or oppression. One Los Angeles outfit, the Bus Boys, managed to work against those conventions. With an assortment of tunes lampooning black stereotypes, the group (who charted with "The Boys Are Back in Town" from the 1983 film *48 Hrs.*) pointed out how blacks remained marginalized in a genre that wouldn't exist without them. The cover of their 1980 LP *Minimum Wage Rock & Roll* presents a Norman Rockwell-esque rendering of an Afro-wearing waiter rushing toward a customer with serving tray held high in hand. Call it Steppin Fetchit meets Ike Turner. Among the tracks were "There Goes the Neighborhood" ("the whites are moving in, they'll bring their next of kin, oh boy"), "Johnny Soul'd Out" ("he's into rock and roll and he's given up the rhythm and blues"), and "KKK," in which the singer longs to "be an All-American man . . . join the Ku Klux Klan and play in a rock 'n' roll band."

Through the Bus Boys, Los Angelinos had some experience with contemporary rock music played from a black perspective. But they were caught unawares Friday, October 9, 1981, when a young black artist from one of the flyover states appeared to open shows on the Los Angeles leg of the Rolling Stones tour. Jagger himself handpicked the Minneapolis-bred Prince Rogers Nelson to warm up the L.A. Memorial Coliseum, and it made perfect sense—in theory. Prince freely told reporters he wished his band could become a "black Rolling Stones." He and his sidemen grew up loving and recycling everything they heard on the radio, from psychedelic Temptations and Sly and the Family Stone hits to the gospel according to Al Green and the Staple Singers. They were as likely to turn out to see Black

Sabbath as Tower of Power or Weather Report. But for Warner Brothers Records, Prince's talented and eye-catching band was mere icing on the cake. The label wanted Prince, knowing he was a studio prodigy and multi-instrumentalist, and as such he was granted the rare opportunity to produce himself from the outset.

Trouble was, neither of his first two records made much of an impact on the hit parade, although the early singles "Soft and Wet" (#92 pop and #12 R&B hits in 1978) and "I Wanna Be Your Lover" (#11 pop and #1 R&B hits, 1979) are now regarded among his first great songs. His third LP, *Dirty Mind,* was considered a freak show—the front cover presenting Prince in androgynous drag, and the back peddling such aural delights as "Head," "Do It All Night," and a zippy ode to incest called "Sister." The tune provides a good indicator of the album's direction: "I was only sixteen but I guess that's no excuse," coos the narrator, who describes his sister as "thirty-two, lovely and loose." Then it gets nasty. "She don't wear no underwear," he tattles, "she says it only gets in her hair." Synthesizers race the giddy vocal to cross paths at the punchline: "and it's got a funny way of stopping the juice."

Not that this was anything new. Josephine Baker danced in a skirt made of bananas and T-Bone Walker had his table-in-teeth twirling routine. Little Richard piled his perm high and wore three times as much makeup as most hookers twice his age, and Jimi Hendrix liked to dry-hump his amplifier. All were exemplary talents, but they understood, as did Prince, that the First Commandment of show business is to captivate the public. Love him or hate him, no one was going to ignore Prince.

Percussionist Sheila Escovedo recalled meeting Prince around this time. "I heard about this kid from Minneapolis doing all his own writing, playing, and producing," she reflected in 1987, "and even now record people won't let anybody do something like that. I saw him backstage; it was at an Al Jarreau concert. He turned and saw me; I knew it was him, and then I saw him a couple of months later onstage in San Francisco wearing a pair of bikini bottoms and leg warmers."

It was this incarnation of Prince who strolled out to greet the Rolling Stones' throng of Los Angeles diehards. Guitarist Dez Dickerson recalled the gig in an interview with Dave Hill for the British journalist's 1989 book, *Prince: A Pop Life*. They opened with the title track from the about-to-be released album, *Controversy*. Next, according to Dickerson, the group launched into "a fairly metallic" rendering of "Why You Wanna Treat Me So Bad."

A roar of approval washed across the stage, Dickerson remembers. "I'd never heard so huge an ovation in my life. But the next song we played—I don't remember what it was—was a bit too black for that part of the audience that harbored ill feelings toward black people." Objects, cups mostly, began landing on the stage. "I had seen many, many shows where the headlining act got pelted with things out of admiration," the guitarist tells Hill.

"That's rock 'n' roll. Culturally, it's a different thing. Black audiences generally don't throw things unless they don't like what's going on." Prince left the arena, left the city, and ultimately had to be coaxed back to California from Minneapolis to fulfill his contract two days later.

After the Friday set, promoter Bill Graham lectured the Stones' fans about treating others with respect. The crowd responded with catcalls, and word spread that Prince was a prima donna poseur who'd been booed from the stage, although that wasn't the case. By the time he returned, Los Angeles was primed to give this Prince the royal treatment. The band was pelted with spoiled chicken parts, shoes, and a full bottle of Jack Daniels. Dickerson recalls that their newfound bassist, still in his teens, was hit by "a half-gallon jug of orange juice. It was pretty wild."

In less than five years, Prince would have many of those same Stones fans paying top dollar to buy his records, watch him onscreen, or see him perform live. The performer they jeered that night in Los Angeles was simply sketching out his formula for stardom—a wedding of pop melodies to James Brown funk and Hendrixian theatrics with just enough Little Richard sexual ambiguity to titillate. And, by adding claims of mixed race parentage to the mix, Prince soon set an image translucent enough for every music lover to project upon regardless of color.

1. Does the author make generalizations or stereotype either "white" or "black" music or people to make his argument?

2. If so, is this necessary?

3. If not, how does he avoid this?

4. Can you write about race, gender, or class without making some generalizations? How can you overcome this challenge?

CONNECTING TO YOUR CULTURE

1. Consider the music you prefer to listen to. What are its roots?

2. Who are your favorite artists' main influences?

3. Can you trace your favorite genre back to threads of pop music in the 1960s? The '40s? The '20s?

Reading Selections: the '90s

CONSIDERING IDEAS

1. Many music enthusiasts assert that analog sound—that of vinyl records—is the only way to listen to music. However, others argue that the clear digital sound of CDs and some quality downloads is the best way to hear your favorite tunes. What is your take on this debate?

2. Have you ever listened to vinyl? Do the pops and cracks add warmth to the sound?

Writer **George Plasketes** *is a professor of communications and journalism at Auburn University. He is the author of two books on the influence of Elvis Presley on American culture, and he regularly contributes to publications, including* Popular Music and Society *and* The Journal of Popular Culture, *where "Romancing the Record" was published in 1992.*

ROMANCING THE RECORD

The Vinyl De-evolution and Subcultural Evolution

George Plasketes

History is an Angel . . . But there is a storm blowing from Paradise and the storm keeps blowing the angel backwards into the future. And this storm, this storm is called progress.

> —Laurie Anderson, "The Dream Before"
> Copyright 1989 Difficult Music BMI

To die-hard aficionados of long-playing records, [the compact disc] is nothing less than a Faustian struggle between humanism and technocracy for music's soul . . . A contest that pits the past against the future.

> —Michael Walsh (66)

Technology and economics are among the primary forces which determine or contribute to cultural transitions and movements. Innovations routinely shape and define our cultural experience and consumption patterns. Whether referred to as a "revolution," or simply "progress," advancements are characterized by a cause and effect process—a simultaneous evolution of one form and de-evolution of another. In the current age of cable television, VCRs, and the multi-screen cineplexes, outdoor drive-ins are left standing as weed covered landmarks, and once-thriving art movie houses are filled with empty seats, both victims of the obsolescence principle. The passage of cultural icons such as these, and their accompanying artifacts and products, can often result in the emergence—or submergence—of a subculture, made up of those who, for various reasons, resist technology or progress and determinedly cling to the artifact, collecting or presenting a part of it because of the meaning and experience contained within.

One of the significant cultural transitions during the 1980s involved the popular music industry and the record buying audience. The technology and economics of the Compact Disc (CD) redefined a long established cultural product—the vinyl record—and simultaneously laid the foundation for a new subculture of vinyl collectors.

The Vinylogical Time Clock
Make room for my 45s / Along beside your 78s Nothing survives.

> —Jackson Browne, "Daddy's Tune"
> Copyright 1976 Swallow Turn Music ASCAP

The year 1988 marked a turning point in the music industry. For the first time since its arrival in the market in 1983, compact disc sales surpassed vinyl revenues. Record sales declined 33%, leveling off at 15% of the market, while CDs increased 31%. On April 2, for the first time, all 200 records on the charts were available on CD.

Vinyl's decline has been a gradual process, a slow death. Between 1978 and 1988, the number of vinyl units (LPs and EPs) shipped by manufacturers dropped nearly 80%, from 341 million to 72 million, according to the Recording Industry Association of America (RIAA).

"Romancing the Record: The Vinyl De-evolution and Subcultural Evolution" by George Plasketes from THE JOURNAL OF POPULAR CULTURE, 1992, pp. 109–119. Reprinted by permission of Wiley-Blackwell Publishing.

Conversely, the number of CDs shipped went from zero in 1978 to 149.7 million in 1988. Cassette shipments rose to 450 million in the same period. By the first six months of 1989, vinyl had dropped to 6% of recorded music sales, a fall of 50% over the same period during 1988. CD sales went up 37.5%, while cassette sales were flat, rising only 1.5%.

The vinylogical clock was ticking, winding louder, clearer, and closer to the compact disc alarm. While the numbers pointed to the inevitable, other signs and sounds of the CD takeover were becoming uncomfortably common to record collectors, creeping deeper into their consciousness and threatening the existence of their cherished black artifact. To them, CD meant "certain death."

During the 1980s, record inventories at many major chains, especially at malls, diminished. In stores, CDs outnumbered records by as much as 6 to 1; cassettes outnumbered vinyl by 12 to 1. An increasing number of new releases, including popular artists such as Phil Collins, Rod Stewart, and Milli Vanilli, were available only on CD and cassette. Any remaining vinyl stock was usually exiled to the back of stores or handled by special order. Some stores (Record Bar chain) and labels (Elektra) even changed their names from "Record" to "Tracks," "Music," or "Entertainment" in order to drop the "waxy implications."

With record companies limiting editions of albums and deleting their vinyl catalogs, many pressing plants were forced to close down. In addition, audio component manufacturers such as Dual and Ortofon trimmed their lines of turntables, cartridges and styluses.

The extra cuts on CDs as incentive to change formats frustrated many hardcore record collectors, who were torn between their loyalty to vinyl and the CD "bonus track." They also heard radio stations promote the new format by increasingly identifying songs with the tag—"on compact disc," and more subtly noticed that vinyl was relegated to being listed third in the fine print on music ads— "available on Compact Discs, cassettes and records wherever music is sold."

Historically, music format changes are nothing new. And every advance in recording has been accompanied by the cries of those whom technology has left behind. No doubt there were those who bemoaned the loss of their Edison cylinders when shellac became available. In 1949, one year after Peter Goldmark's Long Play (LP) 33 1/3 record was introduced, a British critic complained:

I ask readers if they want to feel that their collections of records are obsolete, if they really want to spend money on buying discs that will save them the trouble of getting up to change them, and if they really want to wait years for a repertory as good as what is available to them. (Walsh 66)

The critic was defending 78s against the encroachments of the new 33s in much the same terms that LP defenders cast their arguments today.

The current situation with LPs, cassettes, and CDs competing in the music market parallels that of the late 1940s when the 33 joined the 45 and 78 as the available formats. After the confusion among consumers settled, the 33 accommodated musicals, symphonies, operas, and soundtracks; the 45 proved ideal for hit singles and jukeboxes; and the 78 was crowded out of the market and into a box in the attic, where its thick black surface would collect dust as an artifact of days gone by.

There were other marks on the music format time line as well. In the 1960s, stereophonic sound replaced monaural records, with a slight price increase. The 8-track tape was popular through the 1970s before becoming a snarled roadside relic. And by the late 1980s, the obsolescence principle was well at work: 7-inch vinyl 45s had all but disappeared, giving way to "cassingles"; CDs and cassettes squeezed LPs out; and the newest format, Digital Audio Tape (DAT), was ready to enter the market.

Although cassettes are the primary music format, the CD has pinched the LP more quickly. "It took 18 years and the Walkman for cassettes to break through," said Lou Dennis, vice-president of sales for Warner Brothers. The fast acceptance rate of the CD should not be that surprising. As a culture, we have grown to be much more comfortable with technology as computers, cable, satellites, VCRs, and FAX machines are a part of our daily routines. Not only have we come to expect innovations, we are aware that changes take place at a more accelerated pace. Advancements are less threatening or overwhelming, and consumers are more willing to adopt them into their lifestyles and experience more quickly than they were five or ten years ago.

The technological superiority of the CD has been hyped since the laser format was introduced in the market in 1983. The unprecedented audio clarity, disc durability, and storage capacity made the CD a more attractive format than vinyl. And in keeping with the design of most

new technologies, CDs featured certain conveniences that transcended the other available modes. CD players could be programmed to play random tracks off multiple discs, while the less automated turntable demanded some listener involvement and decisions, if only to flip the record or select a particular song. The only disadvantages of the CD are the high costs, which are characteristics of most new technologies, and the inability to record on discs, a constraint which may only be a temporary condition.

The new technological advantages of the CD often overshadowed one of the most significant factors contributing to the LPs demise—mobility. To a generation raised on "boom boxes" and the Sony Walkman, music mobility is a necessity. And, vinyl does not travel. While the tendency is to attribute vinyl's decline almost exclusively to compact discs, cassettes have quietly been a contributing factor. "You want to know what really killed the LP?" asks Jarid Neff, Southern marketing manager for Warner/Reprise. "I think the cassette started the demise, the whole mobile music thing—the boom box, the car cassette player. The CD just basically delivered the knockout punch" (Thomas C-4).

The vinyl phaseout has been handled with great indecision and confusion by the music industry. One executive characterized it as "near panic," as there has been no consensus as to how to manage the transition. "I assume the death knell has been sounded and there's not much we can do about it," says Joe Smith, president of Capitol EMI. "But the industry has approached the problem with all the organization, planning, and communication of a Three Stooges movie" (Ressner 15). Arguably, the industry's response during the conversion has been no different than any other time as its standard mode of operation is profit motivated. However, many feel in this case greed is a more appropriate characterization, as charges of collusion between labels, retailers, and manufacturers have surfaced. The result has been considerable finger pointing at everyone's hasty marketing moves. Manufacturers blame retailers for not stocking LPs; dealers criticize manufacturers for phasing out vinyl too rapidly. When all else fails, everyone involved declares "the consumer has made the final decision; we're responding to what they want." "Both sides are making it happen, but no one wants to take the credit or blame," says *Billboard*'s Los Angeles bureau chief, Dave Di Martino.

Record company executives say they do not want to speed the LPs demise when a significant market for the configuration still exists, but most labels have adopted sales programs that encourage retailers not to buy heavily into vinyl albums. "We certainly don't want people buying what they can't sell," said Warner Brothers' Lou Dennis. As a disincentive to ordering LPs, record companies have increased returns penalties by charging retailers more when they return unsold LPs than when they return unsold units of other formats. This policy discourages stores from ordering titles considered "marginal."

The primary force behind such policies is economic. Record companies receive at least one dollar per disc more from CD sales than from albums. By holding back LP inventories, buyers are "gently manipulated" into buying discs, which allows companies to recover costs more quickly. "Everyone's minimizing LP inventories more so than necessary," argues Russ

Solomon, head of the 53-store Tower Records chain. "If this were being done sensibly, vinyl LPs could last a couple more years than they're going to" (Ressner 15).

Just how much longer companies will continue vinyl manufacturing has been a much speculated date, with prognosis ranging anywhere between 1990 to 1993. Although an increasing number of new releases are unavailable on LP, some major companies like Polygram and Warner Brothers say they still have a solid commitment to vinyl. Companies continue to press albums, but in smaller editions, with decisions frequently made on a case-by-case basis. "The real catalyst will be when a Bob Dylan album comes out and there's no vinyl behind it, because he's still the best vinyl seller in the country," says Jack Eugster, whose Musicland group is the largest American record chain. "When a new Dylan comes out without an LP, you'll know the LP is really dead" (Ressner 16).

Sociologist/music industry analyst R. Serge Denisoff senses a collective apprehension in the industry to end vinyl.

When you get a *Thriller* selling 35 million units, LP sales go crazy. Granted, that's really a rarity, but the numbers seem to show that the bigger the units, the more LP sales are. That alone scares the industry about burying vinyl. Besides, no one wants to be the first. When Columbia or Warners pulls the plug, that will be it; the rest will follow.

Sentiment has also contributed to the industry's hesitation in ending vinyl completely. "Our little flat friend the record is what drove the business for a long time," said Bob Sherrod, senior vice-president of Columbia records. Adds David Steffen, senior vice-president of sales and distribution for A&M, "Most people I know in the business are emotionally attached to vinyl. I don't want to picture the day of the record industry without records" (Hochman E-3).

Generation, Gender, and Genre: Defining the Vinyl Subculture

RIAA surveys offer solid evidence of vinyl's plummeting sales, hints of extinction, and the format's inevitable demise. Yet there are many record industry executives and LP sentimentalists who prefer to point to other signs and figures which indicate that vinyl remains viable; and that although forces have combined to squeeze records from the mainstream to the fringe or the underground, the subcultural movement for the exiled format is a strong one.

With vinyl accounting for five to eight percent of the record industry's total sales, that $600 million in gross revenues is substantial. Other figures cast doubt on the widely held belief that the record player is also about to become obsolete. In 1988, although 5 million new CD players were sold, consumers also bought 4.2 million new turntables. There are currently 20 million CD players in homes, compared to 90 million turntables. These figures seem to refute the suggestion by Steve Bennett, vice-president of marketing for the 135-store Record Bar chain, that "90% of those turntables never get turned on. It's a bunch of inactive hardware."[1]

There are other facts which may provide some momentary comfort to ease the vinyl junkies' anxiety. Rykodisc, which prided itself in being the only all-CD company, began manufacturing LPs in 1988. Other "all-CD" companies such as Dun-

hill Compact Discs and Mobile Fidelity are also now dealing in vinyl.

And who are the vinyl junkies who define this subculture of collectors? A general profile of the group usually begins with generational distinctions, those marked by who grew up listening to music on albums, and have remained devoted through the years. This group commonly includes those individuals who "came of age during the 1960s." MCA vice-president Walt Wilson reinforces this view: "About the only reason we're doing vinyl is for critics and for Canada, where there are lots of hippies and draft dodgers from the Sixties who still buy vinyl" (Ressner 16).

Gender-wise, surveys indicate that the core-LP buyer is male, over the age of 24, and often older than 35. Those numbers are perhaps one of the primary reasons larger record chains in malls have eliminated vinyl, as that demographic is less likely to frequent the mall than the younger teenage-to-24 group.

In addition to generation and gender, music genre helps characterize the composition of the vinyl subculture. Pop, rock, and classical listeners have almost entirely switched to cassettes and CDs, but R&B, folk, Blues, and other genres are still holding their own on wax.

"We love vinyl," says Ken Irwin, co-founder of Rounder Records, the independent roots music label based in Cambridge, Massachusetts. "LPs still account for 50% of our overall sales and about 80% of our mail order business." Alligator Records, the Chicago based blues and folk label, does one-third of its total business in LPs, according to the company's president, Bruce Iglauer. He adds that vinyl sales "have dropped off some, but not nearly as much as the industry says they should" (Ressner 16).

Sales also remain strong in Soul, due in part to rappers who use records for "scratching," and the popularity of the 12-inch dance single. "The dance records and ethnic markets are very strong for LPs," says Tony Van Veen of Discmakers. "For ethnic labels there is not such a high penetration of CD players in those markets—Reggae, Calypso, Latin, African—so you see considerably fewer people doing CDs" (Unterberger, 1: 14).

The vinyl subculture is not entirely made up of an older generation of hippies or hard-core collectors. One of the strongest places for the vinyl album is the rock underground, which features music from the college and alternative/progressive radio formats. Although many artists from this axis are on independent labels, the majors are also well represented. According to Mark Kates, director of alternative A&R at Geffen Records, many major labels have had to reassess their position on vinyl before forsaking LP editions of their fringe titles. Their vinyl pressing decisions are usually done on a case-by-case basis. Geffen Records recently announced that the new record by the British group Fuzzbox would only be released on CD and cassette, but reversed the decision after complaints from Kates' department. "It's true that vinyl isn't selling in a lot of formats," Kates concedes. "It happens to be selling 10% in alternative music, which is why I made a big stink about the Fuzzbox record."

Supporting Kates' view are Warner, Elektra Asylum's (Geffen's distributor) unit sales figures from 1989, which indicate that alternative music is still selling more than most formats on vinyl. For all WEA products, vinyl totaled 5%, ranging from zero in Classical (which is what brings the average down), to 15.3% in Black; 11.1% in Jazz; 9.8% in Alternative; 7.3% in Pop; 7.3% in Country; and 5.6% in Metal. In the month of August, three WEA records which received airplay on the college/alternative formats—Peter Case's *The Man With the Blue Postmodern Fragmented Neo-Traditionalist Guitar,* Maria McKee's self-titled debut, and XTC's double album *Oranges and Lemons*—netted a combined average of 12%. Peter Case alone sold 22% vinyl during the year, a figure which is in Kates' terms "ridiculously high." He adds, "There's going to be people out there selling vinyl forever, and I just want to make sure that the big artists in my department continue to be pressed on vinyl—The Creatures, Sonic Youth. I don't see alternative buyers walking away from vinyl that quickly" (Unterberger 1: 14).

The scarcity of vinyl in the mainstream has forced collectors to walk a little farther, look a little harder, and at times pay a little more money. During the late 1980s, the underground market revealed a greater availability of records at flea markets, a rise in mail order and import business, and overflowing crowds at the increasing number of Record conventions and shows. According to Todd Ploharski of Rock 'N' Roland, an Atlanta based record collector organization which sponsors conventions at least six times a year, the vinyl trade, though forced underground, is stronger than ever.

The record crowd has always been a devoted, passionate bunch of collectors; as intense as any group I've ever been associated with, including the comic book freaks. Within the past few years, attendance at our shows has been phenomenal. Whether it's CD anxiety, desperation, the usual obsessive behavior, or more people unloading their record collections; but people have just come out of the woodwork. There seems to be a very special bond, some sense of purpose, among the record collectors, like a little community.

Perhaps the most significant shift result from diminishing vinyl can be seen in the movement to smaller stores. Specialty shops and used record stores have become havens, or museums, for the vinyl subculture. In a survey of several major metropolitan LP-only and used record stores, owners indicated that their sales have increased—not decreased—during the past three years.[2] "With the few remaining chains that stock vinyl, it's new-release business. Buyers anticipate new records and blitz stores the first week. After that, sales drop off the cliff," explains "Record Ron," whose two used record stores are located in New Orleans' French Quarter district. "Our sales are steady. We're like some record refuge for collectors."

Jim Richardson of Atlanta's Chapter 3 Records, whose music inventory is 80 percent vinyl, comments, "When they totally phase out vinyl, people will be screaming for albums. Right now, we probably average two or three calls a day from larger chains like Turtles or Metronome asking if we have one LP or another."

The boom in the used record store business can largely be attributed to the growing number of CD converts selling their entire record collections on their way to buying their first disc player. LP devotees are the beneficiaries as they can pick up some real gems for their own collections. "People come back for what they grew up with," says Richardson. "You

see their faces light up and they say, 'God, I can't believe I found this!' Half the fun is searching for that rare album, and the love of the music is the other half that makes recording collecting so motivational" (Yandel E-5).

Much of the used inventory also includes promotional copies of records, many of which are filtered down from radio stations. Although large chains provide the volume sales for the industry, record companies are increasingly recognizing the value of the used and specialty market. WEA's Kates explains:

I have a big problem in a record being serviced to college radio on CD, because a lot of stations still need vinyl. On an alternative artist you can break even on a pressing of 5000 pieces of vinyl when at least 1000 of those are going to be promos. Through the Warner Bros. alternative marketing people, we've learned that it's better to sell a promo than not sell anything at all. The person who buys it will probably buy their next record clean. (Unterberger Part I, 14)

Many predict the vinyl specialty store and used record business will "explode" and be a fairly large industry during the 1990s. "And there will be a large market for a specialty manufacturer who's going to go to labels and license titles and pay a small royalty," says A&M Records' David Steffen (Hochman). Others in the industry also believe that as LPs become more scarce, buyers will have to pay a premium for them. "What I see for the LP is manufacturers continuing to make sure they don't get hurt by pressing them, so they'll charge more and more for them," says retailer Howard Applebaum. "That means retail LP prices will go up while CD prices come down." Rounder Records' Bruce Iglauer agrees. "I think there'll be big bucks made in selling old albums. There's going to be a lot of stuff that will never show up on CD and people will want to have it" (Ressner). Danny Beard, both co-owner of Wax 'N' Facts, Atlanta's most successful used record store, and president of DB Records, the South's most successful independent label (early B-52's, Swimming Pool Q's), expresses similar concerns: "Much of the music that would be routinely issued on vinyl, such as recordings by little known bands on independent labels, and classic reissues of early R & B and country recordings by the majors probably won't come out on CD."

In some cases, the price increase has been self-imposed by vinyl devotees who choose to pay for their passion. One trend store owners have reported is the significant increase in special orders for imports, as many records unavailable in vinyl on domestic labels can be ordered as an import, which usually doubles the price. "It shows what people will do just to have a record on vinyl," comments Beard. "They insist. Cost doesn't matter. It may be a bit extreme, especially when you consider they could get a CD for the same price, or less. But I find that loyalty to the album very admirable."

Compact Discontent and the Passing of a Cultural Icon

Things in CD land ain't what they appear to be, folks, but why be surprised? You've got to be suspicious of any-thing or anyone who succeeds during the Reagan years, be it Madonna, the Boss, Nutra Sweet, or CDs.

—Michael Fremer, editor, *The Absolute Sound*

The vinyl transition is more than business and technology; it marks the passing of a cultural icon. To those who grew up with the LP and 45s, it has been bittersweet how the various forces have redefined a cultural product which defined a generation. "Rock and roll was born to the LP and now the format is dying. That's hard to take," says Pat Schweiterman, a buyer for Tower Records. To that generation who lived through an era when vinyl transformed rock and roll from a singles-oriented medium to the more ambitious and conceptual art form that albums like *Sgt. Pepper's Lonely Hearts Club Band* showed it could be, vinyl represents a part of history, both cultural and personal.

With that sense of history comes an emotional attachment to the artifact. And emotion alone has made parting with the valued configuration difficult for vinyl junkies. With stubborn ears, and even more stubborn hearts, many appear unwilling to concede to the CD generation, that is, only until they have to. "I still haven't bought a CD player," said record collector Bruce Barham, who bought his first album in 1964—*Meet the Beatles*—and has since added more than 12,000 records. "I think I can hold out another year. I sort of feel like the CD is being forced on me. And that really bothers me."

Accompanying the record reverence is a simultaneous resistance as vinyl devotees have expressed their compact discontent in various ways. In 1987, the California based Rhino Records distributed buttons, sweatshirts, and other items in a "Save the LP" campaign. The crusade also appeared in print as vinyl advocates have frequently used column space of audio magazines as sounding boards to attack the threatening new technology. In editorial fashion, articles question the CD's "perfect sound forever" and point out flaws such as laser rot. An example is a commentary by Michael Fremer, senior music editor of *The Absolute Sound*. The article appeared in *Music Connection* (22 August 1988), and months later was reprinted in the record collector's publication, *Goldmine*. Fremer writes:

CDs are to records what videos are to movies: sampled, scanned, and coarse, missing huge chunks of information. If your CD player sounds better than your turntable, you have a lousy turntable . . . If you want fake, processed, artificial, lifeless, dimensionless sound from all your music, if you want one-note "bass" where you can't tell a Hoffner from a Precision from a Jazzmaster, a pick from a thumb, go spend $15 for the privilege and buy CDs. If you want what is still the finest way to enjoy music in the home, buy LPs and invest in a good belt-drive turntable.

Other responses to the conversion have a less resentful tone. In a column in *Stereo Review*, William Livingston offers a preservation point of view. "I've just bought not one, but two turntables. Much as I am intrigued by the Compact Disc, I want to be sure that my treasured LPs are there to sustain me" (6).

In perhaps the most reactionary move against the CD takeover, Steve Fallon of Coyote Records, Bob Mould, formerly of Husker Du, and Nicholas Hill have started the Singles Only Label. Fallon explains:

"A lot of independent record companies can't afford CDs, or CD singles. We just do it so that bands can get some exposure and some kind of foundation going. Not only was it done for the CD reason, but also because I don't think bands can afford to make albums any more. The sales have gone down so badly because of the overtaking of the independent market by the majors' alternative companies. It makes it virtually impossible to recoup what the initial investment was, or come close to that. I don't think these 45s are going to make us any easier to get played; I think it's more of a comment." (Unterberger 2: 14)

One of the most unusual cases of "CD anxiety" was shared by one die-hard who insists on skipping the letters "C" and "D" when teaching his two-year-old daughter the alphabet. "I'm hopeful my children will appreciate vinyl; maybe even understand what 'sounds like a broken record' means," said the collector. "For the upcoming generation, that phrase, like the album, will fade from the language."

Although written tirades, hoarding components destined for obsolescence, and eliminating CD from the alphabet may be viewed as desperate, futile responses in a losing struggle against technology, these acts of resistance are also indications of the collector's emotional attachment to the vinyl LP.

Another focus of the vinylists' lament is the size of their treasured black artifact. Collectors speak passionately about artsy album covers and graphics, insightful liner notes, and distinctive label packaging. In the format transition, that form of creative expression is reduced to the size of a baseball card on cassettes, and only slightly larger on the 5-inch by 5-inch album length shiny compact discs. "The main loss in all of this is the artwork and just the feel of the record," says Pat Schweiterman of Tower Records.

"You just can't get the same image, or feeling, on a CD package," agrees collector Barham, illustrating his point with an album cover portrait of jazz great John Coltrane. "When you buy a record you feel like you're buying something substantial. It's big. The difference between buying a small pizza and a large pizza."

Retailers, of course, prefer the advantages of the small compact disc. They take up less display space in stores and require less freight expense. Yet some in the industry like the album's size. "From a marketing standpoint, the LP was incredible. Browsing through bins, it's a hell of a lot easier with an album," said M.C. Kostek, co-owner of the 50 Skidillion Watts label. Kostek's partner, Kate Messer, also prefers LPs. "I don't like the sound of CDs and I think the packaging sucks. I'm an LP cover fan and it's just horrible seeing that stuff translated down to that size" (Unterberger 1: 14).

The movement away from vinyl LPs and 45s toward cassettes and compact discs also reflects a broader cultural trend toward miniaturization. This is the first time such "shrinkage" and scaling down has revealed itself in music with such an impact. This progression, no doubt, will continue, as technology's relationship with music evolves. New modes of presentation will be emphasized, while the "old" will be de-emphasized, perhaps fading to the point of obsolescence. Already the cycle may be set to repeat itself as Digital Audio Tape—CD quality sound on a palm-sized cassette—is ready to challenge the existing formats in the music market.

"Some of my real world jobs were in educational media, and I saw the trickle down of technology," said Kate Messer. "I saw a lot of deliberate holding back of technology basically to milk the market.

I just have this really cruddy feeling that that's what's happening with CDs, and there's going to be a more efficient carrier and format in the future. I think this is a transitional format" (Unterberger 2: 12).

Record Bar's Barry Bergmen agrees. "Ten or fifteen years from now, there will be something new. We'll be selling little silicone chips. You'll be able to encode a whole album on a chip the size of your fingernail and carry a whole record library in your pocket" (Haight 24).

For the Record:
From CD to Shining CD, the Vinyl Days
A lot of people grew up with vinyl. To take it away you take away a part of their history. It's more than music . . . it's an era.

> —Don Radcliffe, President,
> Justin Entertainment (Thomas 4)

The CD establishes the future. It's like the Monsanto House of the Future Exhibit at Disneyland.

> —Jeff Ayeroff, co-president,
> Virgin America (Pond 117)

The vinyl LP, and its phaseout, signals a cultural moment that is marked by the redefining of a product and the formation of a subculture of collectors. The significance of vinyl records extends beyond the sounds in its grooves, or the technological, economic, and cultural forces which have contributed to its demise.

Like other artifacts of an age, or icons, vinyl records contain meaning derived from human experience. The revolutions per minute—whether 78, 33 1/3, or 45—embody meanings that are social, cultural, historical, personal, and now with vinyl's passing, sentimental. To collectors, vinyl is an experience that embraces emotion, passion, and romance. From decorating rooms with colorful album covers, or playing with the zipper on the Rolling Stones' *Sticky Fingers* LP to the personal pride in thinking how impressive a record library looks stacked on the wall. The vinyl experience is that box of 78s a collector will never get rid of, or being able to relate a story or experience for every record in the collection. Or the quirky post-purchase appeal of having to wait to get home to a turntable before hearing a new record, rather than pop-ping a cassette into the car stereo. The feeling of holding an album, removing the 12-inch records from its sleeve, holding the edges careful not to fingerprint the vulner-able black surface, then placing it down on the turn-table, activating the tonearm until the stylus softly sets down in the grooves. The "intermission" between changing-sides. And the sound of vinyl—a crack, pop, or hiss from a record that has worn from ex-tensive play; or worse, a record that some- one borrowed and returned scratched up, never to be lent again. And the sight of vinyl—a 78 turning on the Victrola; a stack of 45s, the next single ready to drop down to play; or the colored label of a 33 encircled by black, spinning around and around and around. The record speaks for itself.

And it is because of the meaning and experience, the investment of passion, emotion, and romance, that makes the vinyl record so difficult to part with. Vinyl is biography. Vinyl is culture and subculture. And vinyl is history.

Notes

1. Quoted in Fred Goodman, "Record Industry Prepares to Bury the LP," *Rolling*

Stone 10 March 1988, 24. Among industry executives, Bennett has been one of the most outspoken advocates against vinyl. For several years he has expressed his indifference toward prolonging LPs. "If they don't want to make the LP, that's fine with me," he said.

2. Store owners surveyed included Wazoo in Ann Arbor, MI; Vintage Vinyl in St. Louis, MO; Record Ron's in New Orleans, LA; Eat More Records, Wax 'N' Facts, Chapter 3, and Fantasyland in Atlanta, GA; and Second Hand Tunes, Reckless Records, The Turntable, Record Swap, and Wax Tracks in Chicago; and Peter Dunn's Vinyl Museum in Toronto, Ontario, Canada.

3. Although manufacturers have been commonly criticized for "cutting corners," "skimping" and leaving out information on CD packages, there have also been several recordings available in higher priced, limited edition, CD-only packages. As an example, Keith Richards' *Talk Is Cheap* was marketed in a "Keith in a Can" package. By 1990, "skimping" was more common in vinyl packaging. Record labels routinely chose to print musician's credits and song lyrics only on CDs and cassettes, not on album sleeves. In some cases, such as Roger McQuinn's *Back from Rio* (1991) on Arista, the album jacket noted that credits and lyrics were available by writing the company. "As if vinyl dying isn't bad enough, they've got to punish us for sticking with albums," objected one collector. "It's not surprising, no doubt it's economics. Yet an album and cassette cost the same, so why not include the liner notes on the LP? Let vinyl die with dignity. But the way things are now, I guess we should just be grateful the company put the record out on vinyl."

Works Cited

Fremer, Michael. "What's Wrong with Compact Discs?" *Goldmine* 2 Dec. 1988: 23.

Goodman, Fred. "Record Industry Prepares to Bury the LP." *Rolling Stone* 10 Mar. 1988: 24.

Haight, Kathy. "Vinyl's Final Days." *Charlotte (NC) Observer* 24 July 1988: 24.

Hochman, Steve. "Will Those Vinyl Records Be All Played Out by 1988?" *Los Angeles Times* 8 Oct. 1988: E3.

Livingston, William. "Speaking My Piece." *Stereo Review* Oct. 1984: 6.

Pond, Steve. "The Industry in the Eighties." *Rolling Stone* 15 Nov. 1990: 117.

Ressner, Jeffrey. "Going, Going, Gone?" *Rolling Stone* 20 Apr. 1989: 15.

Thomas, Keith L. "Many Die-Hard Record Lovers Spinning from Vinyl's Demise." *Atlanta Constitution* 27 Feb. 1990: C4.

Unterberger, Richie. "Issue by Issue: The CD Takeover." *Option* Nov./Dec. 1989: 14.

———. "Issue By Issue: The CD Takeover (part two)." *Option* Jan./Feb. 1990: 14.

Walsh, Michael. "The Great LP vs. CD War." *Time* 25 Aug. 1986: 66.

Yandel, Gary. "Facing the Music: Retailers Say LPs Won't Be Playing Much Longer." *Atlanta Journal* 25 Oct. 1988: E5.

DECODING THE TEXT

1. How does the author's choice to include specific sales figures on the decline of vinyl add to his argument? Is this research necessary to convince his academic journal audience?

2. How would this essay change for a national magazine publication, such as *Rolling Stone*?

CONNECTING TO YOUR CULTURE

1. Do you agree that "technology and economics are among the primary forces which determine or contribute to cultural transitions and movements"?

2. Think of an example to support or oppose this statement.

CONSIDERING IDEAS

1. Consider the Oscar won by Three Six Mafia for "It's Hard Out Here for a Pimp" in 2006. Has rap reached its pinnacle of popularity and respect?

2. Are there still music enthusiasts that do not embrace rap as a legitimate musical form? Who and why?

Havelock Nelson *is the coauthor of* Bring the Noise: A Guide to Rap Music and Hip-Hop Culture. *A contributor to* Billboard *magazine and* Entertainment Weekly, *Nelson is a premier journalist in the field of rap criticism.*

Gerrie E. Summers *writes for* Billboard *magazine,* Rapsheet, *and* Rock & Soul. *She also adds to musical conversations through the* Village Voice. *"Rap of the Ages" was published in* Billboard *in 1993.*

RAP OF THE AGES

Tracking the Highs and Lows of Nearly 20 Years

Havelock Nelson and Gerrie E. Summers

1975

DJ Kool Herc hosts shows at Hevalo in the Bronx, where he spins brief rhythmic sections of records called breaks. The dancers at the nightclub are known as break boys or B-boys.

1978

Disco Fever, "hip-hop's first home," opens in the Bronx.

1979

Brooklyn group The Fatback Band releases "King Tim III (Personality Jock)" on Spring Records. Many in the rap community regard it as the first rap record.

The Sugarhill Gang releases "Rapper's Delight" on Sylvia Robinson's Sugar Hill Records, ushering rap into the commercial age.

J.B. Ford and former Billboard reporter Robert Ford Jr. write and produce Kurtis Blow's "Christmas Rappin'," which gets picked up by a major label, Mercury.

Seminal female rap crew Sequence enters the male-dominated world of recorded

The Sugarhill Gang

rap and drops "Funk Your Head Up" (Sugar Hill).

Mr. Magic's "Rap Attack," which aired on WHBI then WBLS New York, plays an integral part in giving rap exposure outside of clubs; Whodini pays homage to Magic on its track "Mr. Magic's Wand."

1980

With "Rapture," Blondie becomes the first mainstream artist to be involved with rap, referring to Grandmaster Flash and Fab 5 Freddy.

Kurtis Blow, the first rapper signed to a major label, Mercury, releases the gold single, "The Breaks."

Grandmaster Flash & the Furious Five

Kurtis Blow

Afrika Bambaataa and Soul Sonic Force

1981

In business for six months, Profile releases "Genius Rap," by Dr. Jeckyll (Andre Harrell, now the president of Uptown Enterprises) and Mr. Hyde (Alonzo Brown).

Grandmaster Flash's "Grandmaster Flash On the Wheels of Steel," the first record to capture the excitement of turntable scratching, is released.

1982

Trouble Funk's "Drop The Bomb" brings go-go beats to rap.

Tommy Boy establishes itself on the rap map with Afrika Bambaataa & Soul Sonic Force's "Planet Rock," a funky concept built around Kraftwerk-like electro blips.

Grandmaster Flash & the Furious Five puts out "The Message," a landmark reality rap track.

Herbie Hancock collaborates with turntable musician Grandmixer DST and producer Bill Laswell to record "Rockit" (Columbia), perhaps the first summit between a jazzman and a hip-hopper.

Malcolm McLaren records "Buffalo Gals" (Island), a track that combines rap with new-wave aesthetics.

Profile Records releases "Sucker MCs" by Run-DMC. This blast of rhythmic mini-malism establishes rap's "new school."

Herbie Hancock

1984

Grandmaster Flash & the Furious Five split with Melle Mel, leave Sugar Hill Records and sign with Elektra.

KDAY Los Angeles debuts the first all-rap radio format.

UTFO drops "Roxanne Roxanne," and the 12-inch inspires an unprecedented amount of answer records.

With "Run-DMC," Run-DMC becomes the first rap group to be certified gold.

The Wall Street Journal dubs Def Jam CEO Russell Simmons "the mogul of rap." Today, Simmons' ventures include Rush Management, the Phat Farm clothing line and HBO's *Def Comedy Jam*.

1985

Def Jam forms a landmark distribution pact with Columbia Records. LL Cool J's "Radio" is the first release under the agreement.

LL Cool J

Boogie Down Productions releases the classic blueprint for gangsta rap, "Criminal Minded."

On his own label, Schoolly-D releases "PSK What Does It Mean," a seminal hardcore release about a Philadelphia gang.

"Krush Groove," the film starring Run-DMC, the Fat Boys, Kurtis Blow, and others, comes out.

Run-DMC

1986

Uptown Records, specializing in R&B-style rap, is launched with a compilation featuring Heavy D. & the Boyz and others.

Run-DMC's "Raising Hell" album, which includes the breakthrough collabora-

Public Enemy

1987

With his Marley Marl-produced single "Raw," Big Daddy Kane becomes hip-hop's man-of-the-moment.

16-year-old MC Lyte makes the first hardcore rap record by a female, "I Cram to Understand U (Sam)."

Public Enemy debuts with "Yo! Bum Rush the Show," an album that emphasizes Afrocentric music.

1988

Ruthless Records drops Eazy E's "Eazy Duz It" and, more importantly, NWA's "Straight Outta Compton," two recordings at the leading edge of West Coast gangsta rap.

De La Soul's "3 Feet High & Rising" is released by Tommy Boy, ushering in "the D.A.I.S.Y. age." It opened the door for alternative acts like PM Dawn, Mo Phi Mo, Arrested Development, etc.

Kitted-up Jumps become urban America's new status symbol.

Public Enemy's masterful "It Takes A Nation of Millions To Hold Us Back" comes out.

Rick Rubin leaves his post at Def Jam and forms Def American.

tion with Aerosmith, "Walk This Way," is unleashed.

The Beastie Boys' "Licensed to Ill" sells 4 million units.

Scott La Rock, from Boogie Down Productions, is shot to death.

DJ Jazzy Jeff & the Fresh Prince's "Parents Just Don't Understand" is a huge crossover hit.

Four platinum rappers—Run-DMC, the Beastie Boys, Whodini, and LL Cool J—go on tour.

DECODING THE TEXT

1. How do the visuals contribute to the timeline of rap "highs and lows"?

2. What do they signify about the progressing culture of rap music and of the rap industry?

1. What songs or albums have defined the highs and lows of your musical life?

2. Think about the first song you remember and the year you heard it; continue your path through high school or into college. You might include pictures and share this with friends or family.

• •

CONSIDERING IDEAS

1. How do music stores identify their "spiritual" or "religious" selections? Are they labeled by the production company and shipped as such?

2. What makes any one song more fitting in the "spiritual" or "religious" section of the store than another?

3. How is this music marketed to the consumer?

Chris Gill *is the editor in chief for The Museum of Musical Instrument's website as well as a former senior editor of* Guitar Player *and* Guitar World. *Gill owns a guitar collection with more than forty instruments, and he coauthored "Within You, Without You" for* Guitar Player *in 1995.*

James Rotondi *is editor in chief of* Future Music Magazine, *a former editor of* Guitar World, *and a contributing writer to* Guitar Player, Spin, Rolling Stone, *and* Remix *magazines, and Amazon.com as well as many other music industry publications. Rotondi is also a former member of the bands Air and Mr. Bungle.*

Jas Obrecht *has written about the blues, heavy metal, and rock for publications such as* Rolling Stone *and* Blues Review. *A senior editor of* Guitar Player, *Obrecht coauthored a book on the memoirs of James A. Hendrix,* My Son Jimi. *Obrecht is also a recipient of the Blues Foundation's Keeping the Blues Alive Award.*

WITHIN YOU, WITHOUT YOU

The Guitarist's Search for Spiritual Meaning

Chris Gill, James Rotondi, and Jas Obrecht

Few forces are more powerful than music. It can make people smile, cry, fight, or fall in love. It can influence people to drink Coca-Cola, vote Republican, or drive a Chevrolet. It's a language that needs no interpreter. Regardless of whether the motivation is to heal listeners or make the musician rich, music has a unique capability to profoundly affect people's lives. From the moment the very first note was sounded, music has remained an expression of its creator's soul. But this primary function of music is also one of its least understood properties. Many guitarists can define their music in great detail in technical and theoretical terms, but when it comes to explaining the emotional impetus of their music, most give the simple explanation, "I just play from the heart." What they are saying, whether they realize it or not, is that the act of making music is fundamentally a spiritual experience.

Although music has always been a central element of religion—the Bible contains more than 50 references to music or musicians, and the gods and goddesses in Indian religion and myth are all musicians—spiritual music is not necessarily religious music. Spirituality may often be related to or channeled by religion, but the two are not unconditionally intertwined. "Spirituality is like an ocean," says Carlos Santana. "When you put your toe in one ocean, you've touched all of them. Religion is like Muslim or Christian. Spirituality is only one love—a love supreme."

The essence of spirituality is an awareness of a higher form of inspiration, one that comes both from within and without. Religion may help a person achieve a heightened state of spirituality, but a person can be spiritual without being religious. "Religion is politics, not spirituality," observes Celtic/blues guitarist Martin Simpson. "Whatever you're doing, if you're getting into the spirit of the thing, you're being spiritual. People say, 'I'm not a spiritual person,' but you can't *not* be a spiritual person. You can define what spirituality means, and you can not like what somebody else has defined for you, but you can't help being a spiritual person."

New York avant-guitarist Elliot Sharp warns that it's dangerous to talk about spirituality, especially if you are trying to define it. "For me a spiritual feeling is one that *can't* be defined," he says. "There are as many definitions as there are people. Maybe it's that part of the brain that we haven't quite integrated into our consciousness. That's the great thing about it—you can't really know. I know that there's this other feeling that comes in with certain kinds of music, but it's hard to be very exact when you're speaking about these things. In the ancient Hebraic bible, even spelling out the name of God was the worst thing you could do, and I see that as cutting to the essence of the thing—as soon as you start to define spirit, you lose it."

"Within You, Without You: The Guitarist's Search for Spiritual Meaning" by Chris Gill, James Rotondi, and Jas Obrecht from GUITAR PLAYER MAGAZINE, May 1995, pp. 49–56.

Steve Tibbetts, a progressive jazz guitarist who records for ECM Records, expresses similar concerns: "You run into all these problems when you talk about music and spirituality, because you don't know what you're talking about. Some people can be clear about it, but it's real treacherous ground when you talk about spirituality and art, because if your art isn't spiritual, then there's nothing to talk about; if it is, there's *still* nothing to talk about. I really don't want to hear about other people's spiritual awakenings, because it's their *pure expression* that wakes up my spiritual longing. When you talk about that spiritual element, you invite the danger of spiking the drink that people are getting. I'd rather let electricity be electricity and not have to trace it back to some power plant."

Though their approaches differ, many players argue that to become a truly effective musician, it is necessary to devote as much effort to developing the spiritual side of music as to mastering the technical aspects. Santana feels that musicians can develop spiritually once they recognize the difference between playing to complement and playing to impress. "'That's the spiritual path in a nutshell," Carlos explains. "You can play to bring people together, or you can play to say, 'Check this out!' In order to experience spirituality, you need to illumine your ego, because your ego is like a horse. You don't have to kill him, but you have to enlighten him so he doesn't run away and throw himself off a cliff with you on him. Basically the ego is a good thing—it's pure dynamism. Why don't you make it work for you and with you?"

Because spirituality is inherently personal, one of the primary steps towards achieving spiritual awareness is to look inward instead of relying on external sources for approval. "It's better that we try to feel secure about ourselves," says Eric Johnson, "rather than looking to an external thing to tell us what we're supposed to be. When you turn on the TV and see a perfume commercial—that's 100% externalization: 'Oh, we're not quite as pretty as that person. We don't smell quite as nice, and we're not glamorous and living on the French Riviera.' All of a sudden we're subtracting from the internal. Time and time again it's been shown that the real spiritual building blocks are inside of us. If we have a little bit of self-love and self-esteem, we get messages from within of what intuitively feels right. Then we can say, 'I love playing rock and roll, but maybe I want to say something a little different. I don't have to say what these other guys are saying. I don't have to chase that carrot.'"

Looking inward does not mean withdrawing from others and becoming self-centered. Steve Vai feels that by looking inward a person can develop a meaningful relationship with God, which in turn can greatly affect how he views the external world. "Whether you believe in God or not, your relationship with God is extremely personal," he comments. "Probably more personal than you can even imagine, and more so than any relationship you can have with another individual. In the search for this elusive God, we reach towards all these things in the world that might help us to reunite with this *thing*. We express ourselves through this desire, and it comes out in love, anger, art, and music, in the way we relate to our friends and family, and the way we feel about ourselves—whether we have a happy life or we put a bullet in our head.

"The true path to spirituality is to get closer to that spark or God, whatever it is. There are a lot of different realms, religions, and so-called spiritual worlds out there, but they could be deterrents to our real spirituality, just like other things in this world are. Just because things exist in other planes of existence doesn't necessarily mean that they're good for us. The greatest thing that we can achieve is that single-pointedness of mind to go within."

The act of making music is a remarkably effective manner of looking inward. Concentrating, focusing, and listening, which are requirements for becoming a good musician, are necessary for exploring the inner being. For many, the act of playing is a form of meditation that allows separation from thought. "Meditating and playing are very similar kinds of concentration, and you even get similar physical reactions," notes David Torn. "Playing is my only regular form of meditation, and there's definitely something in it that's completely out of my hands. For me the whole thing is spirituality—this is how I better myself, how I have a positive effect on the world. It's beyond the limitations of my thinking and my own agenda."

The connection between music and meditation is timeless. According to Indian violin virtuoso L. Shankar, who accompanied John McLaughlin in Shakti and currently plays with Peter Gabriel, many of India's ancient Vedic texts describe music as the highest form of meditation. "Learning and acquiring the skills to play music is important," he comments, "but when the real thing comes, you are like a medium for what is passing through you. Your state of mind, your physical state, and your spiritual state have to be fit enough in the highest sense to receive that. There

must be a balance between those three things. You have to be very clear. There is a life in every note, and to achieve that is a matter of learning concentration, not simply practicing. To be able to let things go and concentrate on nothing—that is the ultimate thing. Meditation helps you to listen, and also to stop listening."

One way that guitarists achieve a meditative state is to let go of their inhibitions and concerns and simply play. Musicians who do this often describe the sensation as "becoming the instrument," as opposed to playing the instrument themselves. "When I walk out onstage, I want inspiration to take everything that I have, everything that is me," John McLaughlin describes. "If I can get out of the way, if I can be pure enough, if I can be selfless enough, and if I can be generous and loving and caring enough to abandon what I have and my own preconceived, silly notions of what I think I am—and become truly who in fact I am, which is really just another child of God—then the music can really use me. And therein is my true fulfillment. That's when the music starts to happen. And that's part of my process in my own spiritual life—to become more selfless, because it's selfish to impose myself on the music."

Robert Fripp feels that the best way of letting go is to take the attention away from the act of playing and simply relax. "I try to be in a place where music can more freely play the human instrument," he remarks. "There is a creative impulse, and if I were insensitive, I wouldn't be aware of it. So I have to develop my sensitivity. If I were tight and tense, I wouldn't be able to respond to that impulse, so I train my hands to respond very quickly to an impulse."

For some musicians, the act of letting go has enabled them to have transcendental experiences. "One time I was playing at a festival in Northern England," recalls Martin Simpson. "The moment that I started to play, all the nonsense went away, and I felt really able to focus. The next thing I knew, I was actually in mid-air above the stage watching myself perform. I was really aware of the separation. I was going, 'Wow! Look at him go. What an incredible job that guy is doing.' I don't know how long it went on. It was astonishing. It never happened before, and I don't know if it will ever happen again. I'd like it if it would."

"I lose myself at some point during almost every musical performance," says Torn. "There's some point of struggle and super self-consciousness, but I always get lost at some point. If I don't, I have a really bad time. While I'm playing, there's a pattern of struggling through something and then cracking through it by a weird combination of willpower and letting go. That's the most enjoyable thing for me: 'Uh-oh, he's gone! Finally, the guy can't talk!'"

For Carlos Santana, playing from the heart is a means of achieving transcendence: "When you play from your heart, all of a sudden there's no gravity. You don't feel the weight of the world, of bills, of anything. That's why people love it. Your so-called insurmountable problems disappear, and instead of problems you get *possibilities*."

Sometimes the experience can be transcendental for the audience as well, as people who are not musicians often encounter spiritual enlightenment while listening to music. "Not all of us have experience in forms of organization or producing music or singing," Robert Fripp says. "But we all have access to the quality of music, the spirit of music."

David Torn has had transcendental experiences while listening to records or watching other performers. "When I listen to certain records, I'm transformed and moved to places that I wouldn't normally go," he remarks. "I certainly don't get that from watching television or a movie or trying hard to make money. The first time I saw the Mahavishnu Orchestra, I was so high on the music that I was barely in my body; I could barely contain myself. Something evolved, my forward path shifted, and I felt better."

The psychological effect that music can have on an audience places the performer in a unique position of power. John McLaughlin feels that music's beautiful, spiritual, and unifying powers should be used for affecting people in a positive manner. "It's such a mysterious and wonderful thing," he says. "People love it everywhere, so why don't we use it to bring a greater understanding to the people of the planet? If music can remind people where they truly belong in the consciousness of love and kindness—which is truly God-consciousness—then it might be a small contribution, but at least it's a positive one. All we can do is help each other, to remind ourselves that in the midst of all this anguish there is a sanctuary, that everything is all right. Music can do that. It is a healing force in the world."

There has been a great amount of study into music's healing properties, but no one has been able to pinpoint a particular form of music that is more effective than another, probably because music is a highly individualized experience. The same music affects different people in different ways. But most musicians agree that if the intent is positive, the outcome will be positive.

"If our motive is to instill good, positive, healing force in our music—something that will elevate the listener—then people can pick up on it on a sublime level," says Eric Johnson. "It doesn't matter what kind of music it is—it can be the most raucous thing in the world or just a couple of notes on a classical guitar."

"Nouveau flamenco" guitarist Ottmar Liebert has talked to many people who thanked him for the pleasure his records brought them while they were hospitalized. "It's so nice that people still have that awe that music can do so much," he marvels. "I know that much of my life has been formed by certain pieces of music, and to be able to do that for somebody else is wonderful. If you can move people, that's what it's all about."

Pops Staples comments that his main effort as a musician is to try to help people. "I'm trying to make my music do something constructive," he explains. "Music is healing to the soul, a healing to the feeling of the people. I'm trying to get peace here between the United States and the people. I can't figure out why there's a difference in people. Some have and some have not. I'm trying to sing a song that says together we stand and divided we fall. If you're keeping one nationality down, sooner or later you're going to be down there with them. The only time you should look down on a person is when you're lookin' to pick him up. Everybody is somebody. If you're a president or a drunk walkin' the street, everybody is a human being. God loves all of us the same."

But music can also affect people in a negative manner. Although playing the blues can help musicians exorcise the demons of everyday life, for many decades the blues was viewed by a large segment of society as inherently evil. Historically, many African Americans in the South found it prudent to denounce the blues as "the devil's music," a notion that goes back nearly a century. "When I was a kid," said Delta bluesman Johnny Shines, "if people heard you singing the blues and recognized your voice, you couldn't go down their house, around their daughters."

Early blues recording artists such as Robert Johnson and Peetie Wheatstraw, a.k.a. "The Devil's Son-In-Law," worked the devil angle for self-promotional purposes, while other early blues recording artists such as Rube Lacy and Robert Wilkins denounced blues altogether and became preachers. Near the end of his career, Son House, the inspiration for Muddy Waters and Robert Johnson, was able to reconcile playing both blues and gospel. "I'm sitting here playing the blues, and I play church songs too," he reported in 1967, "but you can't take God and the devil along together. Them two fellows, they don't communicate together so well. They don't get along so well. The devil believes in one way, and God believes in a different way. Now, you got to separate them two guys. How you gonna do it? You got to follow one or the other. You can't hold God in one hand, the devil in the other one. You got to turn one of them loose. Which side do you think is the best?"

Because music can affect an audience so deeply in positive and negative ways, many feel that musicians must take responsibility for the emotions they evoke. This controversy has taken many musicians off the stage and into courtrooms and Senate hearings to defend their music. (This dilemma is not new. Many classical composers' works were deemed "too terrifying" for children. At the premiere of Stravinsky's *Le Sacré du Printemps* in 1913, the audience became so riled up by the music that a riot broke out. More recently, musicians have been accused of influencing people to murder, commit suicide, kill police officers, and become drug addicts.)

Martin Simpson believes that a musician has considerable responsibility to an audience willing to surrender to the music. "A dictator desires to create the same effect as a good musician," he explains. "When I get onstage with a guitar, whether I'm alone or with a band. I can create the most astonishing feelings in people. I can make entire audiences literally weep, shout, or think. In performance, there is a conduit where the energy that you give the audience comes back to you. It is magnetized greatly and truly becomes an exchange of spirit."

The musician, he feels, is ultimately responsible for his own actions, not those of the audience. "My responsibility is to try to be true and genuine and express what I feel are important matters that can perhaps make a difference. All of what I do is my best expression, my best musicality, my best communication. That is my spiritual path."

Nevertheless, the musician's spiritual role is a source of disagreement among guitarists. Some feel that musicians are today's priests, whereas others think that a musician is no more important than a doctor, waiter, or street sweeper. "The cobbler's

beautiful pair of shoes shouldn't be any different than a great work of music by Penderecki or Stravinsky," says Eric Johnson. "I used to think that maybe music would work on a more grandiose level, but ultimately it's not a savior. And that's good, because it puts everything into more of a soulful, human perspective. Although art might give us chills and make us think more of wonderful things, if we spent our whole life delved into it and then expected it to solve our whole human existence, it would be elusive."

Guitarists in particular are often perceived as spiritual figures, largely due to players like George Harrison, Pete Townshend, and John McLaughlin, who have closely and publicly aligned themselves with spiritual gurus. "It's become such a cliché," comments Steve Tibbetts. "All these guitar players turn into such spiritual guys—it doesn't happen to bass players! A lot of guitar players embrace a teacher or religion or sect, and then they give all these interviews, and it comes out like some weird salamander."

Martin Simpson states that this perception has a great deal to do with the guitarist's role in the band. "Guitarists tend to attract more attention," he illustrates. "Bass players and drummers don't get interviewed as much; they don't stand in the front of the stage and become the focus. Guitarists and singers are usually the ones who direct the spirit of the band. A lot of selection goes into putting a band together, trying to create unity and something that is a functional machine. A good band has a focus of spirit, and each band member is equally important in projecting that spirit."

Steve Vai thinks that spiritually oriented people are drawn to the guitar because of the instrument's nature. "The guitar is an extremely emotional instrument," he reasons. "There's no other instrument that allows you to bend the notes or manipulate sound like this. There's something about the vibrations of the guitar that attracts certain people. We tortured souls who are trying to express ourselves in the spiritual realm, and don't know how to do it, may naturally gravitate to the guitar. We may think that we believe in something or not, but ultimately we're searching. When I look back, it seems like the guitarists who had a real effect on me were people who, in a sense, were very driven—maybe centered, or maybe tortured—but seeking souls, searching souls."

Many people who are searching for meaning in life often turn to music for answers. In turn, they often become musicians. But can existence as a musician provide insight into the meaning of life? "The world is craving spirituality so much right now," says Carlos Santana. "If they could sell it at McDonald's, it would be there. But it's not something you can get like that. You can only wake up to it, and music is the best alarm."

DECODING THE TEXT

1. How does the authors' choice of personal response and reflection strengthen their discussion of music and spirituality?

2. Which of these musicians makes the most convincing argument? Why does this argument convince you? Which of the musicians makes the least convincing argument? How would it have needed to change to appeal to you?

3. Who is the audience for this article? Does this audience include or exclude you? How can you tell?

CONNECTING TO YOUR CULTURE

1. How do music and spirituality connect in your life? Perhaps you were in the church choir, or maybe a certain song always gives you a calm, peaceful feeling.

2. Do you see this music as a part of your popular culture? Why or why not?

Reading Selections: the '00s

1. In 2003, when the Dixie Chicks' Natalie Maines criticized George W. Bush's presidency, The Chicks lost radio play on country stations across the United States. They have since bounced back but will be known for both Maines's remark and the political and musical aftermath, especially since Maines sings in her 2006 song, "I'm Not Ready to Make Nice." Should musicians play to their demographic audiences? Should they speak their minds?

2. Why do live audiences buy tickets? Is it the experience? The music? The thrill of seeing a celebrity?

John Vandenberg *is a criminal justice major at Middle Tennessee State University, working as a correctional officer for the Davidson County Sheriff's Office in Nashville, Tennessee. A sophomore at the time of writing "Static Minds," Vandenberg enjoys reading and karate.*

STATIC MINDS

John Vandenberg

People have used music to express themselves throughout all of history. Some of these people are telling us about their lives, while others are telling us what they think about the world. Many people, however, will take what a popular music artist says about world events quite seriously, even when the artist is no more skilled, qualified, or knowledgeable in political matters than an average person. It often seems that to persuade people to listen to you, you do not need political knowledge or real life experience; you just need a charismatic personality and a good singing voice. This has led many music artists to use the power that their influence grants them to try to sway the minds of their fans to their own side of the political fence. This has never been truer than during the times that our country goes to war. Edwin Starr's "War" is an example of a song made to strongly oppose not only the Vietnam War, but war in general. Toby Keith's "Courtesy of the Red, White, and Blue" was written in support of not only the war in Iraq, but also any other military campaign that the United States of America chooses to

"Static Minds" by John Vandenberg. Written for Expository Writing at Middle Tennessee State University with Professor Stacia Watkins, 2006.

undertake. There are many parallels that one can draw between the war in Iraq and the Vietnam War. One major parallel is the American attitude towards sending our soldiers overseas to fight and die for a nation that few people in our country could quickly find on a map. Some groups of people fully support this, while other groups believe that this is the worst thing that this country could possibly do. This attitude has not changed with time; instead, this attitude changes with demographics. Whether it is the 1960's or the 2000's, the same groups of people will have the same things to say.

Edwin Starr was an R&B artist that wrote the well-known song "War." He wrote this song as a protest to the Vietnam War. This song was not responsible for all of the American protests of the Vietnam War, it only added fuel to the fire. His disposition in the song is unwavering. His first three lines show this quite clearly. "War, huh, yeah / what is it good for / Absolutely nothing." He gives no alternative to the view of war being a monstrous idea and that there is never a reason to fight it. Starr continues to speak in absolutes throughout his song. On lines 29 through 31, he states, "War, it ain't nothing / But a heartbreaker / War, friend only to the undertaker." Again, he tells us how bad war is by saying that the only people to benefit from it are those that prosper from death. He appeals to our sympathy throughout the song, but more so at certain points. On lines 16 through 19 he sings, "War means tears / To thousands of mothers eyes / When their sons go to fight / and lose their lives." He does this again in lines 63 through 65 when he says "Ooooh, war, has shattered / Many a young mans dreams / Made him disabled, bitter and mean." He is trying to reach to more than one audience with these lyrics.

He reaches out to the parents of soldiers by telling them that their sons will die. He then reaches out to the soldiers themselves by telling them that going to fight will ruin their lives forever. Edwin Starr's message seems quite clear, that war is an extremely horrible thing and we should never take part in it.

This song is far too black and white to convey the message properly. The Vietnam War was not a popular war. It was fought for ambiguous reasons and many in this country had good reason to despise that particular conflict. However, Edwin Starr does not address the Vietnam War. Instead he states, with absolute certainty, that war is bad and should never be fought. This idea, in and of itself, is ludicrous. Even though war can be one of the most horrific things that mankind can inflict upon itself, there are still times when people must fight. The Revolutionary War, World War I, and World War II are perfect examples of conflicts that this country could not have avoided without trading its freedom and way of life for peace. Edwin Starr says in lines 81 through 84, "Peace, love and understanding / Tell me, is there no place for them today / They say we must fight to keep our freedom / But Lord knows there's got to be a better way." In those lines, Starr insists that we should never have a need to fight, but he fails to offer an alternative to those times when there seems to be no other option.

On the opposite end of the spectrum would be Toby Keith's "Courtesy of the Red, White, and Blue." This song was written in response to our retaliation on the Middle Eastern countries after the events of September 11, 2001. Instead of telling us how horrible war is, Toby Keith glorifies our bombing campaigns, telling these other countries that they are getting what they deserve because they messed with America. On lines 15 through 22, Keith explains this solution:

Now this nation that I love
Has fallen under attack
A mighty sucker punch came flying in
From somewhere in the back
Soon as we could see clearly
Through our big black eye
Man we lit up your world
Like the 4th of July

Keith again tells us what happens when you mess with America in lines 35 through 40. "This big dog will fight / When you rattle his cage / And you'll be sorry that you messed with / The U.S. of A. / 'Cause we'll put a boot in your ass / It's the American Way." Keith is trying to tell us that America does not pick fights, nor do we want conflict. According to Keith, we fight only when we are attacked. And when we fight, we fight hard.

Just like Edwin Starr, Toby Keith makes an attempt to appeal to American sympathies. In lines 5 through 7, Keith tells us, "There's a lot of men dead / So we can sleep in peace at night / When we lay down our head." Keith is trying to make us sympathize by telling us about all of the Americans that have died to protect our freedom. He is careful to tell us about the "American men" that died, instead of the "American boys." Keith then tries to draw out our sympathy by speaking of his family in lines 8 through 11. "My daddy served in the Army / Where he lost his right eye / But he flew a flag in our yard / Until the day that he died." Considering that this part of the song is in the beginning, Keith is trying to soften us up before he tells us how great it is that we are raining hell down upon those that would dare attack the United States.

"Courtesy of the Red, White, and Blue" is, obviously, a very patriotic song. Keith portrays America as a sleeping giant that would not take up arms unless it was for self-defense. In this song, America does no wrong. This can easily be argued as not true, but Keith is careful not to use too many absolutes in his song. It comes across as what he thinks and feels, instead of what he knows. This makes his message a little easier to swallow.

Edwin Starr's "War" is no more or less true than Toby Keith's "Courtesy of the Red, White, and Blue." Both songs appeal to different crowds. Both songs are one man's opinion. Both songs agree with the fans of their particular genre. Toby Keith is a country music artist. You will find few fans of contemporary country music that are not patriotic to some degree. Edwin Starr, meanwhile, was an R&B singer. His fans were anti-government and anti-war before he ever wrote his song. These music artists do not always sway the hearts and minds of their fans. Their fans have often already made up their minds when they got to them. This fact makes one question whether or not these artists truly feel the way they say they do in their music. It is difficult to see if they actually want to spread their message to the world, or if they just want to appeal to their fans to sell records. The end result is the same, however. When someone, regardless of who they are or what they know, sings a message that people want to hear, they take it as gospel and treat it as evidence.

Works Cited

Keith, Toby, performer and lyricist. "Courtesy of the Red, White, and Blue." Dreamworks, 2003.

Starr, Edwin, performer. "War." *War and Peace.* Norman Whitfield and Barrett Strong, lyricists. 1969.

1. Why is the author so concerned with Keith's and Starr's emotional appeals?
2. How can these lyrics affect the listener? Are either of these lyrics emotionally convincing enough to sway a listener who may not have originally agreed with the songwriter?

CONNECTING TO YOUR CULTURE

1. Persuade a classmate to agree with you on a contemporary social issue by comparing two songs or musical compositions—one contemporary and one from the past.
2. How do the cultures of each decade differ in their musical compositions? In lyrics? In rhythm? In instrumentation?

CONSIDERING IDEAS

1. From sheet music played live or over the radio, to musical performances on TV and film, to vinyl records, to eight tracks, to audiocassettes, to compact discs, to downloads, music has become more and more accessible over time. How has music's accessibility affected its marketing?
2. How has this accessibility affected its audience?

Don Cusic *is a professor of music business at Belmont University. Cusic was the host of The Nashville Network's* The Music Biz, *and he has written liner notes for country musicians such as Dolly Parton and Willie Nelson. He has also worked in the music industry at Monument Records as the head of artist development and international relations and as a staff writer for the Country Music Association.*

Gregory K. Faulk *is an associate professor of business at Belmont University who researches and writes on the financial aspects of the music industry. He has coauthored articles in* Studies in Popular Culture, *the* Journal of Nonprofit and Public Sector Marketing, *and the* Journal of Financial Education.

Robert P. Lambert *is a professor of marketing at Belmont University. He has written on subjects as varied as music finance and copyright protection to identity theft. Lambert also coauthored articles for* Studies in Popular Culture *and the* Journal of Nonprofit and Public Sector Marketing. *The coauthored "Technology and Music Piracy" was published in* Studies in Popular Culture *in October 2005.*

TECHNOLOGY AND MUSIC PIRACY

Has the Recording Industry Lost Sales?

Don Cusic, Gregory K. Faulk, and Robert P. Lambert

The recording industry asserts that the introduction of technology facilitating home recording, most notably cassette tapes and peer-to-peer file sharing, has reduced sales of recordings. This issue of piracy is relatively new and dates back to the introduction of cassettes as a major format for recorded music in the early 1970s. The primary technology used as a recording industry format prior to this time was the record, either the 78, the 45 or the 33 1/3 rpm disk. The 78 and 45 were both single song formats (with a song on each side) while the 33 1/3 or Long Playing (LP) record, was generally marketed with ten to twelve songs on each disk.

In order to create the disks, a manufacturing plant was needed to process and stamp the vinyl with the recorded music. The barriers to entry (cost of a plant, cost of production, and so forth) were such that piracy of records was almost non-existent. That changed with the introduction of the tape, first eight track and then cassette, because setting up a manufacturing facility was relatively inexpensive, and thus pirated recordings flooded the market. Also, with the advent of home cassette recorders, it became easy for an individual to make a copy of a favorite group of songs, or copy an album, and thus "home taping" became a major concern of the recording industry as blank cassettes soon rivaled the sales of pre-recorded cassettes.

To combat this piracy the recording industry used legislation, the court system, and introduced non-recordable technology. Ironically, with the introduction of the Compact Disc (CD) in the early 1980s, the recording industry thought it had finally solved the problem of piracy. There were few CD manufacturing plants in the world at that time (and none in the United States), the cost of building one was prohibitive, and the widespread availability and use of computers was just in its infancy. Only the truly visionary saw the potential for computers on office desks and in homes, in CD burning software on these computers, and on a World Wide Web, which was not created until the early 1990s.

The major breakthrough with Internet file sharing occurred in 1999 when Shawn Fanning created Napster, a web site where users stored and retrieved songs stored in a central computer server with no payments to copyright holders. In other words, those savvy to the Napster system could obtain unlimited copies of recordings "free." The recording industry asserted that Napster was a party to piracy and sued Napster, effectively putting it out of business.

Soon after Napster's demise other Internet portals (web sites) evolved that allowed individuals to swap songs freely over the Internet; however these web sites utilized software that allowed users to

"Technology and Music Piracy: Has the Recording Industry Lost Sales?" by Don Cusic, Gregory K. Faulk, and Robert P. Lambert from STUDIES IN POPULAR CULTURE, October 2005, 28.1. Popular and American Culture Associations in the South.

send and retrieve songs and movies from one user's personal computer to another's, thus circumventing web site host computer song storage that was Napster's legal downfall. This time around the recording industry went after all parties involved. The Recording Industry Association of America (RIAA) sued the Internet Service Provider Verizon for a list of users who had illegally posted songs on the Internet. In addition the RIAA sued individual users of Internet song swapping portals (*RIAA vs. John Doe*). The most significant legal action taken by the recording industry was when it joined forces with the movie industry and sued the major peer-to-peer (P2P) Internet portals using the song and movie file sharing software (*Metro-Goldwyn-Mayer Studios et. al. vs. Grokster Ltd, StreamCast Networks Inc., et. al.*). The entertainment industry claimed that up to 90% of the songs and movies copied on the Internet were downloaded illegally. This case reached the United States Supreme Court and was decided in favor of the entertainment industry. Grokster and StreamCast's defense, that they were not liable because it was the system users who violated copyright law by transferring songs and movies, was vitiated by the Supreme Court on the grounds that Grokster and StreamCast took active steps to encourage copyright infringement. The court ruling is certainly a deterrent to P2P file sharing, but not necessarily a harbinger of its demise. P2P networks that do not overtly espouse copyright infringement appear to be protected by the court ruling. In addition consumers might seek out file-sharing services based outside the United States.

The alleged economic loss caused by copyright infringement gave the recording industry grounds for pursuing the above cited court cases. The RIAA currently estimates that the recording industry loses about $4.2 billion annually to piracy worldwide. BigChampagne, a site that tracks illegal downloads, claims that one billion songs are illegally downloaded every month, more music than is being purchased in any format.

Although the recording industry insisted that piracy hurt the sales of recordings, some critics and fans insisted that it did not; their argument tended to be either (1) the heaviest copiers were the heaviest buyers of music, (2) the spread of music increased sales by creating a demand for purchases, and (3) the free downloads were not "lost" sales because consumers would never have bought these songs/albums if they had had to pay, thus the music lost nothing but gained some valuable promotion. These counterclaims suggest that the recording industry's claim that piracy affects revenues should be independently validated.

Several studies examine RIAA's contention that downloading affected record sales. Liebowitz (2003) studies the effects on annual trends in national record sales from 1973 to 2002 of various factors: the macroeconomy, demographics, changes in recording format and playback equipment, album prices and changes in music distribution. Analyzing pattern changes and regressions he finds these factors cannot fully explain declines in record sales over the period and concludes, based on 1999 to 2003 data, that digital file sharing (MP3) has reduced aggregate record sales. Professors Felix Oberholzer-Gee of Harvard Business School and Koleman S. Strumpf of the University of North Carolina at Chapel Hill come to a different conclusion. They analyze sample data of music downloads over a seventeen-week period in the fall of 2002 and compare that activity with a sample of United States released albums over that time period. They use an econometric model that compares downloaded songs to the sales of the album containing the songs, with adjustments for the effects of track length (download time), network traffic conditions, and track length of albums in the same music category. They conclude that it would take 5,000 downloads to reduce album sales by one copy. This implies a yearly sales loss of two million albums, equivalent to rounding error given the sale of 803 million records in 2002. The professors conclude: "While downloads occur on a vast scale, most users are likely individuals who would not have bought the album even in the absence of file sharing."

Both of these studies focus on the effect on record sales of digital downloading, a phenomenon that became significant with the appearance of Napster in 1999. These studies shed no light on the long-term effects of piracy. The recording industry was concerned with piracy as far back as 1971, when it convinced Congress to strengthen copyright protection law. From this date forward there have been periods where technology allowing pirating was readily available to consumers (cassettes and P2P) as well as periods when the predominant forms of recorded music were not easily susceptible to piracy (LPs and CDs).

In addition to gauging the effects of piracy over time, changes in record sales over time should be measured against personal consumption expenditures. RIAA's claims of revenue losses due to piracy are based on downward trends of recording revenues. However, record sales went from $75 million in 1929 to $6 million in 1933. During the same time frame personal consumption fell from $77.4 billion to $45.9 billion. The downward trend in record sales was caused by an overall reduction in personal consumption in the United States during the Depression. In order to put RIAA's claims of the effect of piracy loss on revenues into perspective recording revenues should be measured as a percentage of personal consumption.

This paper extends our knowledge of the effect (if any) of piracy on record sales by addressing issues not covered in previous studies of the topic. More specifically, this paper encompasses the period from 1972 to 2003 and separates the sale of recorded music into eras categorized by the predominant technology (LPs, cassette tapes, CDs and P2P). These categorizations allow the comparison over time of record sales in periods of home recording friendliness (when music was delivered on cassettes or available through P2P) to periods not amenable to home recording (music formatted on LPs and CDs). In addition, this study measures record sales as a percentage of consumer expenditures. In any given year a certain percentage of consumer expenditures will be on pre-recorded music. This percentage will naturally vacillate from year to year as economic conditions change, the population expands or contracts, and the percentage of the population of members of different age and ethnic groups (with possibly different propensities to purchase pre-recorded music) changes. Expressing record sales as a percentage of personal consumption will account for these factors. Any remaining changes in record sales as a percentage of personal consumption will be caused by other factors (for example, the effect of piracy on record sales). The percentages during periods when technology facilitated consumer home recording capability (i.e. when cassettes and P2P file sharing were the dominant form of pre-recorded music releases and copying technology was easily accessible) can then be compared to percentages in periods when the prevalent technology to deliver songs wasn't easily recordable (LPs, CDs). Finding a significant difference in recording revenues as a percentage of personal consumption in periods where home recording was readily available compared to periods where it was not, would be consistent with RIAA's contention that consumer piracy hurt revenues. If there is no significant difference, then, although piracy existed, it likely had no material effect on recording revenues.

Data are available on annual record sales beginning in 1921. The United States Bureau of Economic Analysis has annual data on personal consumption starting in 1929. During this period commercially recorded music formats included 33 1/3, 45 and 78 rpm records, 4 and 8 track tapes, cassette tapes, CDs, music videos, DVD audios and videos, SACDs, and digital music transferred on the Internet. However, since the focus of this study is on home-based piracy in the United States, the relevant time span is from 1972 to the present. Prior to 1972, there was no national standard for enforcing copyright infringement; that infraction was covered by individual state statutes and case law. In 1971 Congress amended the 1909 copyright law and specifically prohibited the actual copying of a copyright protected sound recording. The amendment became effective on February 15, 1972. Thus 1972 is selected as the beginning year of

the study since that is when a national benchmark for prosecuting piracy became effective.

During this period, from the perspective of consumer piracy, four predominant forms of pre-recorded song delivery existed: LPs, cassette tapes, CDs, and peer-to-peer file swapping. LPs were introduced in the late 1940s. Cassette tapes were introduced in 1963, but it was 1983 before they replaced long-playing vinyl albums (LPs) as the predominant form of pre-recorded music sales. The relatively inexpensive, flexible and portable cassette player/recorder enabled individuals to copy songs, albeit with sound quality degradation, from LPs, 8 tracks and other cassettes and bring their newly captured music with them wherever they went. To combat the inherent piracy capabilities of cassettes, the recording industry introduced CDs in 1983. CDs enhanced song quality through digital technology and, more importantly from the perspective of the recording industry, couldn't be copied. However, the equipment needed to play CDs was expensive, and early models of the CD players installed in automobiles tended to skip tracks. Reduced equipment cost and more reliability enabled the sales of CDs to surpass cassettes in 1992. During the same time frame that CDs began rocking along as the major form of music delivery, the Internet rolled onto the scene as a major form of mass communication. Since the digital technology for recording music on CDs was the same used in personal computers that were linked by the Internet, it wasn't long before Napster appeared (1999) allowing individuals to share songs on the Internet (P2P). The recording industry's relatively short period of copyright protection evaporated, replaced by consumer recording capabilities exponentially larger than existed with cassette recorders. Initially record labels were unable to utilize the Internet as a delivery mechanism since they had no way to prohibit online consumers from freely sharing purchased songs with others. Although record labels eventually began authorizing third parties to sell recorded music online, CDs remain their preponderant method of sales.

To characterize eras where record sales were most susceptible to home piracy, record sales are stratified by period based on the medium that was the predominant delivery mechanism of pre-recorded music as well as the period where P2P file sharing was readily accessible. The periods selected for comparison in this study are: LPs (1972–1982), cassettes (1983–1991), CDs (1992–1998) and P2P (1999–2003).

The Mann-Whitney procedure is employed to test the hypotheses of differences in record sales as a percentage of personal consumption between the periods. If record sales as a percentage of personal consumption are higher during the LP and CD eras (when equivalent sound quality recording capability was not readily available) than during the cassette and P2P eras (when equivalent sound quality recording capability was readily available) and the differences between the percentages of the eras being compared are statistically significant, these results would be consistent with RIAA's contention that consumer piracy hurt record sales.

The percentage of record sales to personal consumption during the LP era is higher than the percentage in the cassette era and the difference is statistically significant. Likewise, LP record sales as a

percentage of personal consumption are higher than record sales in the P2P era and the difference is statistically significant. These results support the view that record sales significantly dropped in the home recording friendly cassette and P2P eras when compared to the LP era. The percentage of record sales to personal consumption during the CD era is higher than the percentage in the cassette era and statistically significant. The CD percentage is also higher than record sales in the P2P era and the difference is statistically significant. These results are consistent with the proposition that record sales percentages during the CD era were higher than during the cassette and P2P eras. Using data from 1972 (when piracy prosecution under copyright law was standardized nationally) to 2003 this study finds record sales as a percentage of personal consumption to be statistically higher during the LP and CD eras, when equivalent sound quality recording equipment was not readily available to consumers, than the cassette tape and peer-to-peer Internet song swapping eras, when equivalent sound quality recording capability was readily available.

The reduction of relative album sales revenues in the digital era gives credibility to the interpretation that it was piracy induced due to the ease of illegal distribution of copyrighted songs on the Internet. However, alternative explanations are possible. Economic downturns, competition from electronic games and DVDs and changes in consumer patterns of identifying and obtaining music (shifts in the exposure of new music to the Internet from the radio, digital purchases of single songs) may also contribute to the decline in record sales. However, the relative reduction of album sales in the cassette era is not as easily explained by some of the alternative explanations. During this period Internet marketing was non-existent, copy degradation occurred, and distribution had physical limitations. Interpreted together, it seems reasonable to deduce that piracy was a significant component in the reduction of relative album sales in both the cassette and digital eras.

Mann-Whitney Test and CI: LPs, Cassettes

LPs   N = 11   Median = 0.23570
Cassettes   N = 9   Median = 0.17960
Point estimate for ETA1-ETA2 is 0.05610
95.2 Percent CI for ETA1-ETA2 is (0.03471, 0.07721)
W = 160.0
Test of ETA1 = ETA2 vs ETA1 > ETA2 is significant at 0.0004

Mann-Whitney Test and CI: LPs, P2P

LPs   N = 11   Median = 0.23570
P2P   N = 5   Median = 0.20670
Point estimate for ETA1-ETA2 is 0.03350
95.9 Percent CI for ETA1-ETA2 is (-0.00108, 0.07872)
W = 111.0
Test of ETA1 = ETA2 vs ETA1 > ETA2 is significant at 0.0271

Mann-Whitney Test and CI: CDs, Cassettes

CDs   N = 7   Median = 0.23270
Cassettes   N = 9   Median = 0.17960
Point estimate for ETA1-ETA2 is 0.05410
95.9 Percent CI for ETA1-ETA2 is (-0.03770, -0.07190)
W = 45.0
Test for ETA1 = ETA2 vs ETA1 > ETA2 is significant at 0.0005

Mann-Whitney Test and CI: CDs, P2P

CDs   N = 7   Median = 0.23270
P2P   N = 5   Median = 0.20670
Point estimate for ETA1-ETA2 is 0.03170
96.5 Percent CI for ETA1-ETA2 is (0.00049, 0.07998)
W = 59
Test of ETA1 = ETA2 vs ETA1 > ETA2 is significant at 0.0174

Works Cited

Faulk, Greg, Robert Lambert, and Clyde Rolston, "The Effects of Changing Technology and Government Policy on the Commercialization of Music." *Government Policy and Program Impacts on Technology Development, Transfer, and Commercialization: International Perspectives.* Ed. Kimball P. Marshall, William Sanford Piper and Walter W. Wymer. Binghamton, NY: Hayworth Press, 2004. 75–91.

Garofalo, Reebee, "From Music Publishing to MP3: Music and Industry in the Twentieth Century." *American Music* 17.3 (1999): 318–354.

Leibowitz, Stan, "Will MP3 Downloads Annihilate the Record Industry? The Evidence so Far." *Advances in the Study of Entrepreneurship, Innovation, and Economic Growth.* Ed. Gary Libecap. Amsterdam: JAIP, 2003. 229–260.

Oberholzer, Felix, and Koleman Stumpf, "The Effect of File Sharing on Record Sales: An Empirical Analysis." Harvard Business School working paper, March 2004.

Recording Industry Association of America (RIAA) web site: http://www.riaacom/ issues/piracy/default.asp

1. The authors allege that piracy has become easier for listeners as recording and producing have become cheaper for labels. What strategies do the authors use to connect these two ideas?
2. Do these strategies work for you? What other strategies would you recommend?

1. How many songs have you downloaded in the past six months?
2. How much money have you spent? How many of them were free?
3. If you had bought the CD versions of these songs, how much money would you have spent?
4. Is the industry losing out on money because of your downloads?

• • • • • • • • • • • • • • • • • •

Reading Selections:
Across the Decades

1. What critic, publication, or friend do you trust when deciding whether or not to buy an entire album or whether to download just one or two songs?
2. Or do you always make this decision on your own?

Gregory McNamee *is the author or editor of more than twenty-five books and 3,000 periodical publications, including many on music and the music industry. Literary critic for* The Hollywood Reporter *and a contributing editor for* Encyclopaedia Britannica, *McNamee is also a research associate at the Southwest Center of the University of Arizona. This book review was published in* Tucson Weekly *in 1998.*

THE WRITINGS OF LESTER BANGS RISE AGAIN IN *PSYCHOTIC REACTIONS*

Gregory McNamee

He called himself "a contender if not now then tomorrow for the title Best Writer in America." He might even have seized the crown, had not a hard, 15-year campaign of steady drugging and boozing taken him out of the ring (at the suitably legendary age of 33) before he could duke it out with the likes of Bellow and Updike and Burroughs. Lester Bangs rewrote the rules of pop-music criticism, and the millions of words that sprang from his typewriter, many into the pages of *Rolling Stone* and *Creem,* set standards for writing about popular culture that have not been matched since Bangs drifted into glory.

When Bangs died in 1982—from the flu, of all things—he left behind a mountain of record reviews, essays, short stories, novels, and book proposals as his literary legacy. Fellow critic Greil Marcus took on the task of sorting the tens of thousands of manuscript pages and printed pieces into a manageable reader. *Psychotic Reactions and Carburetor Dung,* the result of Marcus' work, is a fine testimonial to Bangs' talent, and every page reminds discophiles just how lost they are without him all these years later.

The title essay—its name combines those of two albums, circa 1967, by the now all-but-forgotten protopunk band Count Five—illustrates the qualities for which Bangs will most be missed: a quick wit, a wandering style, and a gift for coining flawless phrases. In that essay, and he deserves a plaque in the Rock and Roll Hall of Fame for this alone: Bangs invented the name "punk rock" 10 years before the Sex Pistols, the Ramones, and the Damned would make it a household expression. (Bangs used it to describe The Troggs, of "Wild Thing" fame.) He meant it as a compliment, for Bangs was always a champion of punks and the grunge-rock they screamed out: the Fugs, the Godz, Iggy Pop and the Stooges, Richard Hell and the Voidoids, The Clash. In fact, Bangs penned a few grungy classics himself, among them "Please Don't Burn My Yo-yo" and "He Gave You the Finger, Mabel"—tunes that never made the airwaves, and that some enterprising band should one day cover.

Reserving his praise for those unlikely to get it (or an audience) elsewhere, Bangs savaged all the right people for bringing down the average in rock and roll: Chicago, the Eagles, Paul McCartney ("the only rock-and-roller in *A Hard Day's Night*," Bangs rightly observed, "was Paul's grandfather"); and the post-*Madman Across the Water* Elton John, whose current decline would make Bangs scream. Never afraid to shoot fish in a barrel, he nourished a special hatred for the wimps who took over popular music in the early- and mid-'70s, one of them above all:

"The Writings of Lester Bangs Rise Again in *Psychotic Reactions*" from TUCSON WEEKLY, March 5, 1998 by Gregory McNamee.

If I ever get to Carolina I'm gonna try to figure out a way to off James Taylor. I hate to come off like a Nazi, but if I hear one more Jesus- walking- the- boys- and- girls- down- a- Carolina- path- while- the- dilemma- of- existence- crashes- like- a- slab- of- hod- on- J.T.'s- shoulders song, I will drop everything . . . and hop the first Greyhound to Carolina for the signal satisfaction of breaking off a bottle of Ripple . . . and twisting it into James Taylor's guts until he expires in a spasm of adenoidal poesy.

James Taylor is probably a very nice guy, but it's always a pleasure to see someone uphold standards. The pages of Bangs' book, true to its name, overrun with even harsher judgments of right and wrong, and thank the heavens for that.

Marcus chose not to include in this collection any of Bangs' sharp-tongued reviews from *Rolling Stone* (for which Bangs was fired for not being sufficiently "respectful" to such acts as Rod Stewart, the Bee Gees, and the aforementioned Mr. Taylor). Those reviews, along with Joe Esterhaz's journalism back when Esterhaz served the forces of good, offered some of the only things worth reading in the magazine for many years. The book could have used a good selection from them.

And Marcus devotes a full tenth of the book to Bangs' reporting on Lou Reed, the ex-Velvet who perpetrated *Metal Machine Music*—which Bangs called "the greatest album of all time," ranking it over even Blue Cheer's peerlessly loud, peerlessly wonderful *Vincebus Eruptum*—only to grow up to shill American Express cards and Honda scooters. Any number of much better pieces could have taken the place of the five long, repetitive essays on Reed that Marcus includes.

"A very great man (I think it was the Isley Brothers) once said," wrote Bangs, "that the bottom truism re life on the planet is that it is merely a process of sequential disappointments." The faults of *Psychotic Reactions* aren't serious enough to make the book one of them. Lester Bangs' greatness as a critic lay in his drawing the right moral lessons from popular music and culture and choosing the right friends and enemies, excoriating millionaire rock stars for their arrogance and mediocrity while championing artists whom less imaginative critics ignored.

Marcus' collection gathers Bangs' work as he would surely wish it to be remembered: the product of a skillful, opinionated writer with an endless appetite for aural stimulation, a short temper, and no patience for the hype and posturing that defines so much of what passes today for rock and roll.

1. In this review, the author uses a selection of the text to give readers a taste of Bangs's style. What other methods does the author use to convey Bangs's personality and writing style?
2. Is the author reviewing the book or the author? Both?

CONNECTING TO YOUR CULTURE

1. What music text have you read most recently? Perhaps an album review online or in *Spin* magazine? A celebrity profile of Justin Timberlake on *E!*? Briefly review this text or source. What were its strengths and weaknesses?
2. Will you use this source to get information in the future?

CONSIDERING IDEAS

1. Music halls of fame often have regulations for eligibility; for example, artists become eligible for induction into the Rock 'n' Roll Hall of Fame twenty-five years after the release of their first single. Is this fair? Many musicians have not lived to see their induction into the Rock Hall.
2. What eligibility requirements would you recommend?

Theodore Matula *is an assistant professor of composition and rhetoric at the University of San Francisco's College of Arts and Sciences. He has published in* Communication Studies *and* Popular Music and Society, *where this obituary for Joe Strummer was printed in 2003.*

JOE STRUMMER

1952–2002

Theodore Matula

Joe Strummer's death this past December was not a rock and roll death; there was no suicide, no blaze of glory, no drug overdose, no airplane missing in a snowstorm over the heartland. The punk legend (whose real name was John Mellor) apparently collapsed in his Somerset home after walking the dog. His wife, Linda, was unable to revive him.

Strummer's death produced a relatively mild response in the media and popular culture world, including a few memoirs in places like the *New York Times* and *Rolling Stone,* and a tribute performance at the Grammys, where Bruce Springsteen, Elvis Costello, and Dave Grohl performed the Clash song "London Calling." (Unaccompanied by any explanation or context, other than Strummer's image at the conclusion of the "year of deaths in the music world" segment, the performance prompted *Chicago Tribune* music critic Greg Kot to ask how any of the musicians responsible for the song's "slaughter"—aside from fellow Brit, Costello—had anything to do with Strummer.) The underwhelming response to Strummer's death should not lead social critics and scholars of popular music to overlook the significance of Strummer's career, though. Strummer's career is noteworthy not only to those who appreciate the Clash's strident political lyrics, but also to those interested in music's ability to articulate social critique, and to those intrigued by the amazing range of musical innovation sparked by punk.

Strummer's contributions both to the music world and to the pursuit of social change continued up to his death, and his influence surpasses his involvement with the Clash.

Strummer—and, in a larger sense, the band he fronted, the Clash—shows how problematic and contradictory the standard myths of punk can be—particularly those associated with the idea of punk as an authentic voice of social rebellion. While the Sex Pistols were promoting a mindless anarchic punk—the ascendancy of a new and particularly shocking breed of rock and roll "bad boys"—the Clash was producing Marxist-inflected social critique on albums like *Give 'em Enough Rope* and *Sandinista* and cranking out great anthems with titles like "I'm So Bored with the USA" and "White Riot," all of which made them a frequent object of attention and affection, heroes among left-leaning academics and popular music fans. Yet, they labored for Columbia Records, filling the coffers of large corporations even as they complained about the corporate control of music on songs like "Complete Control," "Hitsville, UK," and "Capital Radio One." Their songs were also used to sell blue jeans and automobiles, showing how easily coopted punk could be even as it was celebrated for its capacity to articulate social rebellion through violation of the norms of taste and decency, and by breaking expectations of genre. The Clash is a symbol of

"Joe Strummer" by Theodore Matula from POPULAR MUSIC AND SOCIETY, 2003, pp. 523–528. Reprinted by permission of Routledge via Copyright Clearance Center.

rock music as a politics of resistance as well as perfect proof that anything—even explicitly anticapitalist revolutionary messages—can be readily coopted in the service of consumerism and the interests of powerful corporations. In fact, their oft-repeated slogan—"the only band that matters"—is the product of the marketing efforts of Columbia Records. ("Ha, you think it's funny," sings Strummer on one Clash song, "turning rebellion into money?")

Strummer himself also confounds the myths of punk: in particular, the social realist assumptions visited by music critics and popular culture academics who connect the authenticity of punk to its putative origins in the "the street." Strummer has often been considered one of the most influential political spokesmen from the "punk street." (The myth is that he removed Mick Jones from the band in the wake of decidedly nonpolitical hit singles like "Train in Vain" and "Should I Stay or Should I Go?".) Yet, John Mellor was born the son of a diplomat and worked as a prefect in an upper-class school. In an interview shortly before his death, he chafed at being called the "voice of his generation" and often claimed, even while being involved in Rock against Racism and recording songs whose lyrics skewered Thatcherite policies and the British caste system, that he was apolitical.

Despite this seeming political ambivalence, Strummer's career shows us how punk, even if easily coopted and reanimated in the service of capitalism, can shape the way its listeners approach political realities of everyday life. Punk finds the "cracks and fissures" in capitalism and oppressive social relations (even if it sometimes spackles them over with its own variety of sexism and domination), encapsulating a moment, or a grievance, or a fault and amplifying it and turning our rage towards it. My own experience serves as testimony: I began listening to the Clash as an undergrad in the 1980s, and their music played no small role in transforming my adolescent critique of freedom into a more coherent view that focused on the inequities of social class and political power. If punk is easily appropriated by capitalist forces, it is also sometimes effective in articulating a critique of capitalism with a protreptic energy capable of positioning its audience in struggles over justice and social change.

But aside from its debatable role as an instrument of political and social change, punk has had an undisputed effect on the evolution of popular music esthetics. The Clash was a big part of this influence—for example, introducing dub, reggae, and world music to three-chord rock in the late 1970s. Strummer continues this fusion on two albums released in the last four years. If you haven't been paying attention, then you may not have noticed that, after a decade-long hiatus, Strummer returned to recording in 1999, fronting a new band, the Mescaleroes, who released two thoroughly satisfying records—*Rock Art and the X-Ray Style* (1999) and *Global a-go-go* (2001)—that blend worldly folk with dance grooves, punkish vocalist and straight-up rock. This kind of hybrid style can easily come off as cliché or careless cultural appropriation, but Strummer and the Mescaleroes use it to make the world sound like both a smaller place and a bigger place than most would consider it.

This convergence of the local and the global—the recognition that people's struggles are *the people's struggles,* even if they are articulated in ways in different contexts—seems to be the most prevalent theme on these two records, both politically and musically. In this way, these records tell us something about the significance of hybridity and intertextuality in contemporary popular music. Like the Clash before them (as well as Rancid, Ani DiFranco, the Mekons, and others), the Mescaleroes blend these musics not only to make a new sound, but to make a politics of connection imaginable.

The most obvious case is on one of the best songs from these recent efforts, "Bhindi Bhaghee," in which Strummer recounts an actual event in which a "kiwi" (New Zealander) accosted him, looking for "mushy peas." Strummer tells him that they "haven't really got any around here" and then launches into a catalog of the local delicacies this stranger may find in his "humble neighborhood," a list that ranges from "dal" to "humus" to "rocksoul okra" to "exotic avocados and toxic empenadas." Later, when the stranger asks him what the music in his band is like, Strummer struggles to find an answer. He stammers over several bars: "Umm . . . umm . . . . It's sort of like . . . and it's got a bit of . . ." and finally, with African guitars, flutes, a synthesized beat, and a Wurlitzer organ

flailing away behind him, he finds his words: "ragga, bhangra, two-step tanga, mini-cab radio, music on the go!/umm, surfbeat, backbeat, frontbeat, backseat, there's a bunch of players and they're really letting go!/We got brit pop, hip hop, rockabilly lindy hop, gaelic heavy metal fans fighting in the road."

Combined with the more overtly political offerings on these records, the overall effect is one in which music constitutes a common forum that celebrates "the people" by revealing how implicated we are in each other's struggles. If punk could never establish a politics of freedom and equality because it imagined and practiced these values through a radical individualism, Strummer and the Mescaleros come a little closer by linking these values to interdependence and a dialogic awareness that is wrapped into the music itself.

In a divisive political climate marked by a lack of responsiveness to the marginalized and the critics of powerful interests, where an imperial United States moves unilaterally on the world, Strummer's music summons a space that feels tonic. This message doesn't belong to any one generation, and he may not be the voice of his generation, but his is a voice that will be sorely missed.

DECODING THE TEXT

1. How biased or unbiased is the author of this tribute about the significance of Strummer's musical contributions?

2. What details in the article support your interpretation?

1. An obituary is often a review of someone's life, giving specific details and general evaluations. Are obituaries important in American popular culture?

2. Write an obituary for your favorite living musician. What details do you already know? What would you have to research?

Case Study

1. Name as many female music groups and bands as you can think of throughout the history of popular music. Do you think there are fewer bands made up of female musicians? If so, why?

2. Are females more likely to be solo acts? If so, why?

Kalene Westmoreland *is an instructor of English at the University of Alabama. She enjoys watching, writing on, and researching many areas of popular culture, including* Buffy the Vampire Slayer. *"'Bitch' and Lilith Fair" was published in* Popular Music and Society *in 2001.*

"BITCH" AND LILITH FAIR

Resisting Anger, Celebrating Contradictions

Kalene Westmoreland

Feminism has moved away from a struggle for equality toward an engagement with difference, an assertion that girls can have the best of both worlds (that they, for example, can be both violently angry and vampily glamorous). [Third wave] feminism owes much to the struggles of second wave, yet it differs in many ways, especially in the way it is defined by contradiction.
—Klein 207–08

I'm a bitch, I'm a lover, I'm a child, I'm a mother, I'm a sinner, I'm a saint, I do not feel ashamed . . .
—Meredith Brooks, "Bitch"

"Bitch," a top ten hit song by singer/songwriter/guitarist Meredith Brooks, illustrates the inherent contradictions of third-wave feminism while it celebrates emotion and anger from a feminist perspective. "Bitch" draws on feminism, music, and anger; as an anthem for the commodified commemoration of women through Lilith Fair, the song reclaims femininity by celebrating traditional feminine qualities and tenets. Lilith Fair, a rock music festival that toured the nation from 1997 until 1999, drew on musical variety, feminist carnival, and political consciousness to critical and popular acclaim. Lilith Fair and "Bitch" represent a restrained, moderate anger, which highlights a "celebratory" message; the song and festival can be read as responses to the Riot Grrrl movement, which relied on visceral anger to reject rigid gender roles. Responding to the Riot Grrrl movement's use of anger, "Bitch" and Lilith Fair promote more tempered feminist solutions and praxis—solutions voiced in "Bitch" and manifest throughout Lilith Fair.

"Bitch" and Lilith Fair promote a feminist message by revising the less mainstream feminist message of Riot Grrrls. The Riot Grrrl movement appropriated the term "girl" (among others, such as "bitch," "whore," and "slut") in order to critique and challenge patriarchal definitions of women. Similarly, by reclaiming the connotations of the word "bitch," Brooks uses a sexist term to criticize sexism. Brooks expands the list of possibilities for women while subversively alerting listeners to complex gender issues by embracing and appropriating the negative connotations of the word. In a similar manner, Lilith Fair promotes Brooks and other female artists; it operates as a proactive medium for feminism to reach and affect masses, a necessary goal in a postfeminist era when many young women either passively accept or blindly reject the advances made by their foremothers. As progressive representations of feminism's developing third wave, "Bitch" and Lilith Fair neither completely accept nor reject second-wave feminism. Instead, much like third-wave feminism, the focus and goals of Lilith Fair and "Bitch" are multifaceted and multistrategic, fusing useful and diverse feminisms together. Leslie Heywood and Jennifer Drake, editors of *Third Wave Agenda: Being Feminist, Doing Feminism,* explain third wave feminism and its inherent reliance on contradiction: "Because our lives have been shaped by struggles between various feminisms as well as by cultural backlash against feminism and activism, we argue that contradiction . . . marks the strategies and desires of third wave feminists" (2). Heywood and Drake carefully position third-wave feminism as the alternative to conservative postfeminism, which pits second- and third-wave's tenets ("victim feminism" vs. "power feminism," respectively) against one another, in favor of the "power feminism" of third-wave which "serves as a corrective to a hopelessly outmoded 'victim feminism' (2). For Heywood and Drake, however, the "second and third waves of feminism are neither incompatible nor opposed" (2). Instead, they define third-wave feminism "as a movement that contains elements of second wave critique of beauty culture, sexual abuse, and power structures while it also acknowledges and makes use of the pleasure, danger, and defining power of those structures" (3).

Unlike postfeminism, third-wave feminism treats personal empowerment and political activism equally and interdependently; Lilith Fair, for example, has the potential to turn a personal experience, such as attending a concert, into an opportunity for activism through its emphasis on feminist charities and activity booths. Fans may peruse the political booths and wonder about the political structures that have prevented such a commercially successful, female-rostered show before. Further, "Bitch" and Lilith Fair focus on the woman writer—a strategy of second-wave feminism—in their use of the singer-songwriter by featuring performers like Brooks. In this new formulation, third-wave feminism tends to fuse "the confessional mode of earlier popular feminisms with the more analytic mode that has predominated the academy" (Heywood and Drake 2). Nowhere does third-wave feminism more explicitly perform this fusion than in the confessional singer-songwriter tradition.

Brooks and her Lilith Fair cohorts belong to what Simon Reynolds and Joy Press, authors of *The Sex Revolts,* call a tradition of confessional singer-songwriters, which distinguishes them from other categories, such as "tough rock chicks."[1] However, through its variety of musical acts, Lilith Fair's musical diversity seems to fuse the myriad categories which Reynolds and Press explore, such as "tomboys," "tough rock chicks," and "confessional singer-songwriters," among others. Taken together, the artists of Lilith Fair exemplify third-wave feminist praxis as they use the "personal" to achieve a political end—to enlighten audiences into engagement with some form of feminist activism. Lilith Fair and "Bitch" answer questions of structural and aesthetic rebellion that Reynolds and Press pose, such as when they ask, "Is it better to sacrifice aesthetic power for the sake of political explicitness, or to opt for purity of artistic expression,

at the expense of being understood?" (384). Though diversity is key to Lilith Fair's appeal and success, and contradiction is fundamental to "Bitch," these two examples of third-wave praxis offer a negotiation of the seemingly oppositional choices which Reynolds and Press question, a negotiation which diminishes the distance between the artists—both as individuals and, as in Lilith Fair, a collective of voices, "presenting a strong, unified front . . . or exploring their inner turmoil" (355). The categories which Reynolds and Press discuss are easily deconstructed, yet their description of confessional artists is pertinent to examining the messages of Lilith Fair and "Bitch" (233-34). "Bitch" and Lilith Fair exhibit a "soul-baring" which "turns suffering into an affirmation: a kind of strength through vulnerability. For a particular breed of female singer songwriters, personal candor and political concern are different sides of the same coin . . . they believe wrongs can be righted in both private and public realms, if only the truth can be uttered—if the tissue of the lies is torn apart and an 'authentic' reality revealed" (249).

This "strength through vulnerability" can be seen in the lyrics of "Bitch." If we view the contradictions embedded in the collective feminine voice as feminist stories, we will encounter more than a text or song. Instead we will encounter what Patricinio Schweickart refers to as a "'subjectified object': the 'heart and mind' of another woman . . . who comes into close contact with an interiority—a power, a creativity, a suffering, a vision—that is not identical with her own . . . To understand a literary work, then, is to let the individual who wrote it reveal [herself] to us in us" (212-13). "Bitch" exemplifies interiority as Brooks reveals herself through her lyrics: she catalogues traditional concepts of womanhood—lover, child, mother, goddess—embraces each temporarily, and finally, rejects them by embracing and redefining a negative stereotype of femininity, the bitch.[2]

"Bitch" offers listeners a reflexive discourse, in part due to Brooks's voice and image as artist/woman. "Bitch" not only transcends semantic realignment through its lyrics; the tone of the song—gutsy, guitar-driven, and passionately discontent—enables Brooks to assert her femininity as well. Brooks's version of femininity appeals to listeners through her lyrics, authoritative guitar playing, and assertive voice. As Brooks vacillates between contradictory labels and definitions, framing her rant against patriarchal limitations with a confessional tone, she creates a believable voice and compelling subjectivity. Brooks's song fulfills the call of critics like Neil Nehring, who states that "emotion . . . supplies a missing link . . . between tactile vocality and meaning" (133). This theory of reflexivity and authentic subjectivity is closely related to Schweickart's concept of interiority. Through her explicit emotional connection with audience, Brooks also fulfills Schweickart's call for an exploration of symbolic self-definition; "Bitch" explores a "symbolic self-definition" for both Brooks and her female listeners. Thus, rock music and feminist theories work in concert in "Bitch," altering the definition of what it means to be a "bitch," to play feminist rock music, and to be considered a success in a patriarchal industry.

Although Brooks's "Bitch" and other songs, such as Missy Elliott's "She's a Bitch," have improved the image of women-in-rock, feminist advancement within the patriarchal rock industry is still slow. In the introduction to *Angry Women in Rock,* Andrea Juno states "We are currently at an interesting stage in the history of rock with the recent influx of women entering as a steady and unstoppable force. Perhaps, like a Trojan horse or a mutating virus, they can't help but change the status quo in, as yet, unknown ways" (5). Juno wrote this in 1996, one year before "Bitch" was released and spread a message of appropriation, one year before Lilith Fair was conceived and spawned its message of feminist rebirth and community. While Juno's skepticism was warranted in 1996, her ideas must now be reassessed in light of "Bitch" and Lilith Fair. The success of "Bitch," along with the success of Lilith Fair, solidifies what once seemed only a trend, the importance of female performers. Andy Steiner, a reporter for *Ms.*, notes the sweeping change in the music industry in an article that reveals Lilith Fair's importance, "The Last Days of Lilith":

Just three years ago, it was common practice for radio DJs to refuse to play two songs by women artists back to back. Too many girl singers kill the buzz, the theory went. You need to throw a guy in the mix or the estrogen will pollute the air. . . . Then, suddenly, everything changed. Lilith Fair [drew] large crowds at each stop that first summer and [made] a strong and sassy statement about the commercial power of women artists. The message spread to other corners of the industry and, poof, the format changed to all Lilith, all the time. The Grammys became a regular girlfest, radio stations put more women in their lineups, and sales of recordings by Lilithians hit record highs. For women in music (and their fans), things never looked better. (61)

Although "things never looked better" in 1999, as Steiner reflected on Lilith Fair's cumulative effects, Juno's suspicion of rock's patriarchy is still warranted. While Steiner's analysis of the current status of women-in-rock is accurate and invigorating, Juno's preemptive warnings about complacency are appropriate, especially since Lilith Fair, the most important feminist vehicle in recent years, has drawn to a close.

"Bitch" exemplifies the progressive feminist message Lilith Fair promotes, in part because it celebrates personal empowerment.[3] Through her song's lyrics, Brooks contradicts a masculine perspective by compromising with her discontent male companion, who is exasperated with Brooks's contradictory nature; by social standards, this complex construction of femininity justifies the term "bitch." Schweickart incorporates Judith Fetterly's analysis of "immasculation" to explore the complex process of disqualifying a male point of view in terms which are applicable to Brooks's song:

notwithstanding the prevalence of the castrating bitch stereotype, the cultural reality is not the emasculation of men by women, but the *immasculation* of women by men. As readers and teachers and scholars, women are taught to think as men, to identify with a male point of view, and to accept as normal and legitimate a male system of values, one of whose central principles is misogyny. (205)

The process of overcoming immasculation is complex and difficult, yet images of immasculation as a process in "Bitch" highlight anger as a healthy emotion.

Significantly, Brooks does not rail at the male character in the song; rather, we hear her character overcoming immasculation by alternately soothing and challenging him to embrace her self-definition as a "bitch." She begins the song with temperate understanding: "I hate the world today/You're so good to me /I know but I can't change/tried to tell you/ but you look at me like maybe/ I'm an angel underneath /Innocent and sweet/Yesterday I cried/Must have been relieved to see/The softer side/I can understand how you'd be so confused/I don't envy you/I'm a little bit of everything all rolled into one." As the first verse builds toward the anthemic chorus ("I'm a bitch, I'm a lover/I'm a child, I'm a mother/ I'm a sinner, I'm a saint/I do not feel ashamed/I'm your hell, I'm your dream/I'm nothing in between/You know you wouldn't want it any other way"), Brooks identifies and categorizes feminine traits that play into typically masculine perspectives, such as using the term "bitch" to refer to any assertive woman.

Thus, the speaker in the song overcomes immasculation while simultaneously overtly and subversively exploring confining gender roles. Using a generic male partner, one who is intimidated and confused by the speaker's complexity, Brooks challenges patriarchal assumptions about women: "So take me as I am/This may mean you'll have to be a stronger man/ Rest assured that when I start to make you nervous/ And I'm going to extremes/ Tomorrow I will change and today won't mean a thing." The process of immasculation nears its end in "Bitch" as the chorus is repeated and then altered to allow for a celebration of self and reclamation of the term: "I'm a bitch, I'm a tease/I'm a goddess on my knees . . . I've been numb, I'm revived/Can't say I'm not alive/You know I wouldn't want it any other way." This final catalogue of terms is paradoxical: the speaker equates "bitch" with being a "goddess," which suggests ultimate power, yet she is also on her knees. The speaker challenges what it means to be a bitch, concluding for herself and her audience that she must embrace all connotations of the term. "Bitch" provides a space where residual anger about the difficult process of overcoming immasculation is explored as a celebration.

Brooks's image as artist/woman is central to her message of empowerment and appropriation; Brooks successfully creates dialectic between listeners and creators of feminist music. For example, Brooks creates two positions as writer and speaks to two audiences. On the surface, Brooks sings to her lover ostensibly about her multifaceted nature; however, in the chorus, she catalogues and reclaims the larger paradoxes of femininity. Her assertions extend beyond the context of the lover who serves as the tentative audience of her song; instead, to her larger audience—demographically similar to Lilith Fair's audience, which was composed largely of women who might identify themselves as third-wave feminists—she makes strong claims about the inner struggle of self-definition and acceptance as a feminist. "Bitch" emphasizes feelings and ideology harmonizing in a feminist resistance and challenges postmodern, cynical listeners to embrace feminist rock. Brooks's song performs a tolerant feminist position as articulated by Nehring: "'Just because someone is not resisting in the same way you are'—because he or

she values feelings over your ideology, for instance—does not mean they are not resisting" (171).

In addition to Brooks's feminist voice and image, her resistance is informed by her status as guitarist. Resistance and interiority in feminist music is informed by musicianship and production; we must understand more than the lyrics of these critical and popular reassessments of feminism by letting the writer, as Schweickart invites us to do, reveal herself to us in us. Brooks achieved this intimate revelation in the first stage of the songwriting process by cowriting the song with a female friend, Shelly Peiken, who Brooks thanks in the cover of her album: "for making me laugh my ass off and pushing the edge with me . . . you bitch." In this vein of recognizing and celebrating the process of songwriting and production, Brooks proudly identifies herself first as a guitarist. Brooks's online bio at www.Meredith Brooks.com notes that

She can stand tall when noting that she played every lick of guitar on Blurring the Edges, including glass slide, some e-bow, wah-wah, and a canny layering of vintage and high-tech Stones-inspired rhythms. "If I had listed a guy as a guitarist in the liner notes, everyone would've thought that he played all the cool stuff. So I decided to do it all myself just to prove that I could. Now I want all those 13 year olds—especially the girls who don't have role models—to look at me with confidence and say 'I can do that,' and go pick up a guitar. When I was growing up, I didn't have many female guitarists to look up to." (paragraph 6)

Brooks defines herself as a guitarist, reveling in a form of artistic and feminist resistance unavailable to singer/songwriters. For a female artist to identify herself primarily with her instrument and secondly through her voice is a critical difference between artists like Brooks, many of whom have not been heard since the heyday of the Riot Grrrl movement, and performers like Alanis Morissette, who constitute the majority of female representation in music today. Gillian Gaar notes the reluctant progress of female guitarists in *She's a Rebel: The History of Women in Rock and Roll*. She points out that the "non-traditional" role of female lead or solo guitarist was always deemed unusual because of its rarity, but it was assumed (by many in the 1970s) that "as more women became rock musicians the idea of women-in-rock would lose its validity . . . [but] women are still by and large defined in that order—as women first, and rock performers second" (xi-xii).

Although her guitar-playing is a central part of her feminism, Brooks's voice is also crucial to the song's ability to incite communication with its listeners. She says, "I really believe in the beauty of scratch tracks. The lead vocal and guitars on 'Bitch' are scratches—the vocal was recorded as I was playing a Martin acoustic, live to tape. Of course, we later set up to record the 'real' vocals, but we never could beat the rawness of it and innocence of those scratch tracks. They were just 'it'" (Molenda 24). Although Brooks is not by any means the only solo female guitarist performing today, her voice and message in "Bitch," when combined with her solo guitarist status, are parts of what Nehring sees as an "important achievement" in feminist music. "For women to play and sing through the same forms dominated by men is inherently a form of

resistance, refusing to accept the definition of woman as the male's subordinate "Other" (164).

Brooks's capacity to become a role model for her audience is part of her feminist achievement. In a topic thread entitled "Role Model" on the official Meredith Brooks website, which Brooks herself moderates, a young fan named Laura, posting as "grace," states that Brooks is a role model for her, specifically because "I never really had many women guitarists to look up to until blurring the edges [with the single for "Bitch"] came out. When I heard that I realized that it was possible to be a female guitarist and to play rocking music" (Grace, paragraph 2). Not only does Brooks appropriate the term "bitch," she also reclaims for herself and for audience members such as Laura the instrument which signifies "male power and virtuosity, the legitimate expression of phallic sexuality, perversity . . . and violence" (Nehring 164).

The success of "Bitch" as an accessible rejection of the "castrating bitch stereotype" shows how second-wave theories of feminist reader response apply to third-wave feminist rock, how the "dialectic of reading" becomes a dialectic of listening and resistance (Schweickart 213). Brooks's audience encounters the subjectified object through her image and through the inversion of the word bitch, a dichotomously personal and generic term, one which all women at one point fear and must come to terms with before they can invert its larger cultural meaning. In "Appropriating the Bitch," Jim Roderick discusses the distinction between the patriarchal, oppressive meaning of the word and the empowered, subversive meaning which Brooks is illustrating: "'Bitch' [is] someone who doesn't support the patriarchal-ruled relationship. . . . [There is a] power of being a bitch, [or] a woman who subverts the patriarchy, leaves and stays away from the physical, mental, emotional, and spiritual oppression of patriarchy" (2). Brooks's appropriation of "bitch" is a step in changing or eradicating its subjugating meaning, but it is also a continuance of the more radical appropriation which the Riot Grrrl movement began. Nehring assesses this process:

Any sensate, honest male knows full well that supposedly wild-eyed radical feminists are absolutely right about our culture: Women are on constant display, everywhere, as semen receptacles. The "gaze," when it comes to women, is real; Riot Grrrls write BITCH, RAPE, SLUT and WHORE on their bodies because that's what a lot of men *already* see there. Beyond actual physical assault, though, as well as pornography and the whole sex industry, the problem is how "normal" guys have learned to look at women—as well as how *not* to hear them, a problem women in punk rock are obviously working on. (153)

Brooks's emphasis on temperance may be crucial to understanding a more persuasive feminism that Riot Grrrls reject. "Bitch" may not be a revolutionary statement but Brooks can perhaps reach more male listeners as well as female. Brooks says that "men completely get [the song's meaning] and are so relieved that somebody's saying it; all they want us to do is admit that we can be irrational and illogical sometimes, and then it's their job to put up with it" (Willman 65). Indeed, male listeners, whether in passive consumption or as active fans, must engage the term in new ways, both in general attitudes toward women and in the context of personal relationships with them.

Brooks's message in "Bitch" moves towards balancing aggression and compassion in the context of a "healthy" relationship wherein gender differences are capable of being understood and affirmed by both partners; more importantly, the message defies the patriarchal systems which still dominate self-formation and socialization. This dual message, which focuses on public and personal self-formation, is common in confessional feminist rock music. The liberating nature of Brooks's song becomes a subversive strategy for listeners, who identify with multiple readings of the song, allowing potential essentializing to become more personally suited to individual listeners. What Schweickart sees as interiority is obvious in the community of Brooks's listeners and fans, who have contributed to the "Meanings" portion of "Meredith Brooks Mania," a website devoted to her music. Although only a few examples are available on the "meanings" page, and few of them are credited to anyone in particular (though there are perhaps more female contributors than male), the messages are nonetheless important for reading the song as an open dialectic. The collection begins with one listener responding somewhat naïvely: "This is such a cheerful song. It starts from a depressing place 'I hate the world today' and carries the listener to a very happy state 'I wouldn't want it any other way!' It's hard to still be depressed by the time the song ends" ("Meanings" paragraph 1). Recognizing the uplifting nature of the song is an important contribution to its meaning—for this listener, female solidarity is achieved through an emotional connection to the performer and the optimistic mood the song creates.

The website offers more aggressive, critical feminist responses, exemplifying how reader response criticism applies to a third-wave feminist song. One listener suggests that an open community is implied in the song's meaning, commenting that "'Bitch' is not just a song, it's a revelation. After listening to this song, it got me to thinking; I'm many different people inside. I'm sure you can relate" ("Meanings" paragraph 4). Another listener, seeking adaptation from the inherently emotional and personal text of the song, comments on the song's effect on feminism and popular culture. Her comment reinforces Brooks's artistic and feminist intent: "Meredith is trying to perform 'semantic realignment' to change the world's perception of the word 'bitch.' Instead of condemning the less pleasant parts of ourselves, let's honour each of those many parts instead" ("Meanings" paragraph 3). Inverting the definition of "bitch," along with viewing the scope of the song as moving beyond the narrative between the two primary audiences of lover and solitary listener, shows that Brooks's fans are aware of her optimistic brand of feminism.

Comparing Brooks's use of "bitch" to a more recent appropriation reveals a compelling praxis of the song's celebration of contradiction. While "Bitch" uses emotion, ideology, and guitar-driven assertiveness to form resistance, Missy Elliott, one of the most successful female rap artists, approaches appropriation of "bitch" through overt philosophies about female aggression and power.

Like Brooks, Elliott resists patriarchal ideology through her appropriation of the term "bitch." Just as Brooks appropriates the signifier of "male power and virtuosity," by proudly playing the guitar, Elliott's role as producer reclaims the term's meaning in a positive manner (Nehring 164). Whereas Brooks emphasizes emotional and psychological healing through appropriating "bitch," Elliott emphasizes practical perspectives of being a "bitch," relating her experiences in the music industry to women's life experiences. Elliott has released the single "She's a Bitch" from her sophomore effort, *Da Real World,* and she frequently discusses the term in interviews. In an interview with *Ms.,* Elliott proclaims, "I think sometimes you have to be a bitch in this business to get where you want to go. Sometimes you have to put your foot down because it is a male-dominated field. If you don't, people will walk all over you. I think bitch is a strong word. I feel like I'm a bitch in power" (McDonnell 82). Although Elliott's opinions on a feminist reclamation of the term are pertinent, her ethics of production prove her stance. Devoting more time to production than performance (Elliott was a featured performer on 1998's Lilith Fair tour), she has "traded fame for power" in the industry. She says that she "became a bitch in power because when I walked in, I asked for what I wanted. At the end of the day, if this is the way I want, this is the way I'm going to have it" (84).

Elliott's blunt, unequivocal assertion of power shows another side to the "bitch" persona, presenting a practical image for audiences. While Brooks's song is confessional and soul baring and achieves "a kind of strength through vulnerability,"

Elliott's efforts belong to what Reynolds and Press have called the "tough rock chick category" (249). Her inclusion on the Lilith Fair tour in 1998 added to the variety of performances and the depth of the tour's feminist message. Elliott's credentials as producer/rapper, combined with her aggressive attitude, enable her to resist the term as a negative description of feminist success. In fact, it is Elliott's overtly aggressive attitude as rapper and producer that distinguishes her effort to reclaim "bitch." Although Brooks and Elliott achieve appropriation of "bitch" differently, they successfully reclaim the term while using celebratory messages to create a daring, aggressive feminist stance.

The potential to create more aggressive feminisms is borne out in Lilith Fair, the ongoing tour which started in 1997. If "Bitch" is anthem, Lilith Fair is praxis of the tenets of the song's embedded contradictions which help define femininity and third-wave feminism. Just as "Bitch" may be heard as appropriation which is more accessible to a larger audience than its Riot Grrrl predecessors may be, Lilith Fair, too, adapts Riot Grrrl anger and transforms the carnival to affect its audience on progressive feminist issues and identity. Lilith Fair embodies and has the potential to rectify the anxiety over feminist identity, the "I'm not a feminist, but . . ." syndrome—or turning it around to "I am a feminist, but . . ."—because it celebrates women's roles without anger, though it does not deny the "energy" which emotion may invoke.

Lilith Fair and Brooks's use of "bitch" created anger within feminist circles. Founder Sarah McLachlan found herself embroiled in a less than harmonious feminist discourse with critics who charged she was bringing female artists together with little concern for their talent or their musical diversity. *Ms.* berated McLachlan "for her reluctance to use the word 'feminist'" because of its negative connotations; in order to accomplish her goal, she later explained, she felt it necessary to say that Lilith Fair wasn't about "chopping anyone's dick off" (Childerhose 71). She later responded "I'm sure *Ms.* was upset by what I had said . . . but if I took every opportunity to spout feminism then, sadly, men would be terrified of the tour. And in order for Lilith to achieve our goals, we couldn't have it be marginalized" (71). While McLachlan takes "the ghettoization of women" and subverts it—"turning it in to something positive"—as spokesperson she must contend with the remnants of the anger associated with feminism, as well as reassess her own understanding of feminism. Andy Steiner interviewed McLachlan for *Ms.* during Lilith Fair's third and final tour: "'Yes, I'm a feminist . . . Lilith doesn't have anything to do with men in a negative sense. It's about bringing women up'"(83).

McLachlan has since become more comfortable with her role as feminist leader; Steiner describes her response—she says "'yes, I'm a feminist,' with some exasperation"—in the same terms as Buffy Childerhose in *From Lilith to Lilith Fair* (Steiner 83). Childerhose concentrates on the press coverage these issues received and McLachlan's exasperated reactions to popular (mis)readings of feminism:

She's quick to point out that she's never denied being a feminist. "Absolutely, I'm a feminist," she says. "And I don't hate men. I know that it's ridiculous that I have to say those things in the same breath, and I don't want to have to. Yet," she explains, "many people still equate feminism with man-hating. I tried to diffuse that thinking because I don't think that's what feminism is. But," she concedes, "I can't escape what many people still believe it to be." (71)

While she didn't "spout" feminism to the press, McLachlan and fair organizers made feminism accessible, at least, in any given venue on any particular date, through its music, the alley of informative, political booths, and the celebratory atmosphere; thus, Lilith Fair alters (but does not contrast) the type of celebration which Riot Grrrl concerts offered. Nehring cites Angela McRobbie as he develops his argument that Riot Grrrls are a reincarnation of punk's spirited political resistance and anarchy, but her words apply to Lilith Fair's less vitriolic conception and celebration:

. . . especially from a feminist point of view stressing the importance of feelings in themselves, "perhaps [politics] is not what we should be looking for in any case." What it may be more realistic to look for, suggests Angela McRobbie, "are cultural forms and expressions which seem to suggest new or emergent 'structures of feeling,'" especially among young women. In exploring "a greater degree of fluidity about what femininity means," the Riot Grrrls, for example, are significant for trying to change how feeling itself is valued, especially anger—no longer something to be ashamed of and repressed but to celebrate. (xxviii)

Anger may not be one of the many emotions which the Lilith Fair experience invokes—in fact, Lilith Fair is often lauded specifically because it offers a contrast to the testosterone-driven festivals it competes with—but anger is nonetheless a muted source in its genesis.

The festival is the brainchild of Sarah McLachlan, a Canadian singer/songwriter whose music is ethereal and sentimentally cathartic. The idea for Lilith Fair began for her as an alternative to "alternative" music; McLachlan's vision for a feminist music fair rejected the andro-centric music that derived from mainstream pop and the reactive feminism of the Riot Grrrl movement. She writes in the foreword of *From Lilith to Lilith Fair,* acknowledging her indebtedness to her angry predecessors: "The fact that there have been women's festivals happening all over North America for years, even though my knowledge of them was sadly limited, helped to create a space where my idea could be heard, accepted and brought into mainstream" (xii). Lollapalooza, an alternative music national tour that generated and reflected early '90s music trends, offered variety, but it lacked adequate female presence. When McLachlan approached her manager several years ago about possibly headlining with Paula Cole, the promoters railed against the idea, telling her simply to forget it, but "Sarah angrily pushed for an explanation. 'Nobody wants to pay to see two women in one night,' they declared" (Childerhose 19).

The blatant sexism of the patriarchal record industry, which included radio programmers who refused to add more than one female act during a week and would not play women artists back to back, angered McLachlan. The industry exploits complacency among female performers, who typically do not push for more airtime and publicity, yet female artists dominate the charts. This hegemonic paradox frustrated McLachlan into action as she began to formulate the idea for an all-women tour and music festival. The tour began with trial dates in late 1996; those dates proved to McLachlan that the patriarchal system of musical promotion was hopelessly inaccurate and unjust and could easily be toppled, at least within the context of her tour and her attempts at mainstream feminism. Plans for a full-scale, 35-date tour were soon under way. By the time the tour wrapped up, Lilith Fair was the most successful tour of the summer.

McLachlan's decision to use the Lilith myth to promote the tour exemplifies how "Bitch" and Lilith Fair consistently rewrite traditional feminine stereotypes and stories. These revisions exclude the negative connotations of anger and denigrating terms while they simultaneously celebrate femininity and feminism. In the foreword of *From Lilith to Lilith Fair,* McLachlan pieces together the Lilith myth, the story of Adam's first wife who refused to be subservient to him; after Adam refused to keep her as his wife, she began birthing hundreds of the devil's spawn daily. The angels who were sent to find her warned her that "if she didn't return, God would kill one hundred of her children a day (not very PC of him—funny how God never got a bad rap about that . . .). Despite the dire consequences, Lilith never went back to a subservient life with Adam" (xiii). In her revision of the story, McLachlan chooses the "parts that can guide us in our lives" and discards the elements that displease her. McLachlan's version, which informs the masses of Lilith Fair attendees, ignores the parts of the story that vilify her or call her a demon, because these alterations are "surely only the rantings of terrified men who were trying to keep other women from getting any silly ideas" (xiii).

The National Liberty Journal, a product of Jerry Falwell Ministries, illustrates

the alarm felt among conservatives as McLachlan revises the Lilith story. A recent article in the *NLJ,* entitled "Parents Alert," warns that "to alter the content of the Bible in even the smallest way results in man attempting to create God in his image. This is the false hope of Lilith who has been concocted in order to create politically-correct image of equality" (Smith paragraph 12). "Parents Alert" adamantly opposes Lilith Fair, despite its positive message and concerns: "Christian parents are advised to consider the Lilith legend should their children become interested in the concerts . . . [while] Lilith Fair does donate a portion of earnings to the worthy Breast Cancer Fund . . . it also supports Planned Parenthood" (paragraph 17). McLachlan's feminist revision of the myth reforms and appropriates negative connotations, just as "Bitch" does for the opprobrious term it revises. Through this revision, along with the celebratory atmosphere of Lilith Fair, Schweickart's theory of interiority moves beyond feminist literary theory and into a more tangible realm of a live audience.

Lilith Fair's tempered version of feminism does not emphasize anger. We must question whether this lack of emphasis suppresses the full range of emotion possible and if such cathartic moments that attendees speak of are complete. Neil Nehring makes a strong case for the need for anger in feminist music and the Riot Grrrl movement. Reacting against innumerable recent self-help manuals which teach consumers how to suppress anger, Nehring suggests through his study of emotion that "the problem with psychotherapy that stresses catharsis is its notion that feelings require discharge not to seek their social causes but because they're unhealthy symptoms of individual dysfunction that reason must gain control over, to have done with them" (111). By seeing Lilith Fair as a medium for a feminist message, a medium that exists along the same continuum as Riot Grrrls, I am not suggesting that the full range of human emotion must be present in order for the fair's goals to be achieved. However, I suggest Lilith Fair presents an opportunity for the audience to undergo a simultaneous personal and social catharsis. As Buffy Childerhose recounts her initial Lilith Fair experience, she seems to be describing undergoing a mystical catharsis as she realizes what she has previously missed as a feminist and music lover: "When the crowd joined in to help the women of Lilith sing 'Closer to Fine' with the Indigo Girls, all the distance created by rock venues and star systems became a dim memory. I actually felt like I was a part of what was happening on the stage and in the crowd. People throughout the stadium exchanged genuine smiles with on another" (Childerhose 2). Lilith Fair empowers attendees by participating in social causes and charities as it convenes in each city on the tour, donating to community shelters and empowering attendees with knowledge of various feminist and humanist causes. The tempered anger plays a role in catharsis, but anger does not necessarily have to enter into the equation as Nehring's analysis of anger suggests and requires. Instead, the catharsis from complacency and apathy towards empowerment and interiority can be channeled through the "love and respect" McLachlan aims for (Childerhose 70).

A moderate feminist message is an effective strategy for a top ten hit and a music festival; the celebration of femininity which "Bitch" and Lilith Fair have stimulated challenges traditional ideas of women in rock. Neil Nehring states "the best female artists are fully aware at all times that they are parodying conventions of female representation and the processes by which various media propagate them. (Whether the audience gets the joke, of course, is always a sticking point" [170].) "Bitch" and Lilith Fair encourage the audience to get the joke because they reveal progressive feminist strategies that ironically employ anger and female solidarity to promote women in rock; both engage with difference and contradiction, offering listeners possibilities for self-acceptance and social change. Brooks's and Lilith Fair's use of "Bitch" draws the audience's attention to stereotypes of femininity, and in so doing, exemplifies third-wave feminism's positive effect on rock.

Notes

1. Press and Reynolds offer categories to describe threads of feminist music history, yet acknowledge that artists often overlap these strategies (233).

2. While vulnerability is an inherent factor in the concept of interiority, as well as in "Bitch" and Lilith Fair, it does not equate to the "victim feminism" which helped to define second-wave feminism. See Leslie Heywood and Jennifer Drake's analysis and rejection of conservative postfeminism in *Third Wave Agenda: Being Feminist, Doing Feminism,* 2-3.

3. Many of Brooks's listeners have expressed their appreciation for the personal empowerment that "Bitch" promotes. See the following websites for message boards and fan input: http://www.musicfanclubs.org/meredithbrooks/mblinks.html, http://www.hollywoodandvine.com/meredithbrooks/, where fans can read posts from Meredith Brooks and post their thoughts on her

message board, and http://www.angelfire
.com/ca2/umbx2/stories.html, where fans
have posted personal stories about "Bitch"
and Brooks.

Works Cited

Brooks, Meredith. "Bitch." *Blurring the Edges*.
Los Angeles, 1997.

Childerhose, Buffy. *From Lilith to Lilith Fair*. New
York: St. Martin's Griffin, 1998.

"Fan Stories." A Site Dedicated to Meredith
Brooks: Prepare to be Mesmerized." http://
www.angelfire.com/ca2/umbx/index.html.
27 April 2000.

Gaar, Gillian. *She's a Rebel: The History of Women
in Rock and Roll*. Seattle: Seal, 1992.

Grace. "Role Model." Hollywood and Vine
Bulletin Boards: Meredith Mondays. 14 April
2000. http://www2.hollywoodandvine
.com/UBB/Forum9/HTML/000050.html

Heywood, Leslie, and Jennifer Drake. Introduction. *Third Wave Agenda: Being Feminist, Doing
Feminism*. Minneapolis: U of Minnesota P,
1997. 1–20.

Juno, Andrea. *Angry Women in Rock*. New York:
Juno, 1996.

Klein, Melissa. "Duality and Redefinition:
Young Feminism and the Alternative Music
Community." *Third Wave Agenda: Being Femi-
nist, Doing Feminism*. Ed. Leslie Heywood and
Jennifer Drake. Minneapolis: U of Minne-
sota P, 1997. 207–25.

McDonnell, Evelyn. "Missy in Action." *Ms.*
June–July 1999: 82+.

"Meanings." *Meredith Brooks Mania*. Home Page.
27 Feb 1999. (http://www.musicfanclubs
.org/meredithbrooks/bitscub.html).

Molenda, Michael. "Songcraft: Meredith
Brooks." *Guitar Player* June 1998: 24.

Nehring, Neil. *Popular Music, Gender, and
Postmodernism: Anger Is an Energy*. Thousand
Oaks, CA: Sage, 1997.

Press, Joy, and Simon Reynolds. *The Sex Revolts:
Gender, Rebellion, and Rock 'n' Roll*. Cambridge, MA: Harvard UP, 1995.

Roderick, Jim. "Appropriating the Bitch."
Paper. Louisiana State University, 1996.

Schweickart, Patricinio. "Reading Ourselves:
Toward a Feminist Theory of Reading."
Contemporary Literary Criticism. Ed. Robert
Con Davis and Ronald Schliefer. 4th ed.
New York: Longman, 1998. 197–219.

Smith, J. M. "Parents Alert: Secrets of the Lilith
Fair." http://www.liberty. edu/chancellor/
June1999/lilith.htm

Steiner, Andy. "The Last Days of Lilith." *Ms.*
June–July 1999: 60+.

"Up Close and Personal." *Pollyanne* 2 May
1999. http://www.meredithbrooks.com/
upclose/bio.html

Willman, Chris. "Meredith, She Rolls Along."
Entertainment Weekly 13 June 1997: 65.

Mick Jagger *is the lead singer for The Rolling Stones.* **Keith Richards** *is the group's lead guitarist. Their album* Sticky Fingers, *from which this song is taken, was released in 1971.*

BITCH

Mick Jagger and Keith Richards

I'm feeling so tired, can't understand it
Just had a fortnights sleep
I'm feeling so tired, Ow!, so distracted
Ain't touched a thing all week

I'm feelin' drunk, juiced up and sloppy
Ain't touched a drink all night
Feeling hungry, can't see the reason
Just had a horsemeat pie

Yeah when you call my name
I salivate like a Pavlov dog
Yeah when you lay me out
My heart starts beating like a big bass
   drum, alright

Yeah you got to mix it child
Ya got to fix it must be love
It's a bitch

You got to mix it child
Ya got to fix it must be love
It's a bitch alright

Sometimes I'm sexy, move like a stud
Kicking the stall all night
Sometimes I'm so shy, got to be worked on
Don't have no bark or bite

Yeah when you call my name
I salivate like a Pavlov dog
Yeah when you lay me out
My heart starts beating like a big bass
   drum

DECODING THE TEXTS

1. Does Westmoreland's use of only one song's lyrics, by a singer who is often considered a one-hit wonder, weaken her argument?

2. Would the inclusion of the "Bitch" lyrics by the all-male group The Rolling Stones have helped or hurt her main thesis?

CONNECTING TO YOUR CULTURE

1. Think of your favorite female songwriter. Is she seen as a feminist or are her song lyrics viewed in this light? Is this a fair assumption to make?

2. Now, consider your favorite male artist. Are any such assumptions made about him? About male songwriters in general?

contemplations in the pop culture zone

1. Rewrite the lyrics to your favorite song as a parody. Think of examples by "Weird Al" Yankovic or the cast of *Saturday Night Live*.
2. Look at the cover of an album or CD you have never heard before and describe the cover in detail. Then, make assumptions about the artist and/or songs on the album. What does the artwork tell you?
3. Make a list of the top five songs that relate to your major area of study. For example, for a science list you might include "The Planets" by Gustav Holst, "Sounds of Science" by The Beastie Boys, and "Love Potion No. 9" by The Clovers. What can these songs add to your field? Do they detract from the reality of the field?

collaborations in the pop culture zone

1. Develop a soundtrack for your writing class. What music would start out each class, play while you freewrite, or serenade you as you leave the room?
2. In a group, make a list of as many *American Top Forty* songs, broadcast as a countdown in the past by Casey Kasem and more recently by Ryan Seacrest on radio stations across the country and online, as you can think of from the past three months. If students from another country or planet were to hear these songs only, what judgments would they make about the United States and its culture?
3. Collaborate with a classmate to convince each other to listen to an album, song, or artist he or she is otherwise unfamiliar with. Find out from your partner what details are important in the music he or she considers and listens to. Make a list of these details and answer his or her questions about your song or artist. How do your lists differ? Can his or her questions be answered for your artist, and vice versa, or do your details work more appropriately for the music choices you have already made?

start writing essays about music

Reviews or Review Essays

1. Review one of your favorite songs or albums from high school. Think back on the reasons that you liked the song then and on the way your opinions have changed when writing your overall evaluation.
2. Consider your favorite film or TV show. How does the soundtrack add to or detract from the action? Describe and evaluate the soundtrack and its contributions, while also considering why producers chose the music. For an example, look at the following list of songs from the *Forrest Gump* soundtrack; the soundtrack contained more than fifty musical selections and became a big contributor to the buzz around the film.

> "Hound Dog," performed by Elvis Presley
> "Pomp and Circumstance," written by Sir Edward Elgar
> "Blowin' in the Wind," written by Bob Dylan
> "Fortunate Son," performed by Creedence Clearwater Revival
> "Respect," performed by Aretha Franklin
> "All Along the Watchtower," performed by The Jimi Hendrix Experience
> "California Dreamin'," performed by The Mamas and the Papas

"Hello, I Love You," written and performed by The Doors

"Mrs. Robinson," written and performed by Simon & Garfunkel

"On the Road Again," written and performed by Willie Nelson

3. Read an article or book on your favorite musician. Then, review its assessment of him or her. What was the author's thesis? Remember to include your opinion of the author's writing style, purpose, and effectiveness.

Reflection or Response Essays

1. *American Idol* winner and country singer Carrie Underwood credits several '80s hair bands among her biggest musical influences. Can you see this influence in her music? Her performance style? Her "look"? How has the music you listen to impacted your culture, fashion, activities, friends, and so on? Reflect on your musical choices and their influence on your life.

2. Tell the story of the first song you remember. Who was singing it? Where were you when you heard it? How do you feel when you hear the song now? Was it an appropriate song for someone your age? Try to remember the feeling the song gave you as a child, too.

3. What song do you listen to when you are angry? Hurt? Sad? Happy? When you want to celebrate? What makes these songs perfect for your many moods? Reflect on the characteristics of these songs that allow you to revel in your own emotions.

4. In the soundtrack of your life, which song is the most significant and why? Address a letter to someone important to you and explain the meaning of this song.

Analysis Essays

1. Write an essay in which you analyze what type of music appeals to the different generations of your family or a friend's family. Try not to overgeneralize but to learn what appeals to your parents, grandparents, children, or even older brothers and sisters and why.

2. Analyze the advantages and disadvantages of downloading music. Does it affect the music industry? Does it affect your finances, time, or convenience or those of your friends? Is paying for downloads the solution to piracy problems?

3. At what age should children or teenagers be allowed to listen to anything they choose? Should a thirteen-year-old listen to Marilyn Manson or a ten-year-old listen to the band Judas Priest? Remember to consider a child's psychological development in your research and writing.

Synthesis Essays

1. Compare the way that sexuality is treated in two different genres. Is rap music really more offensive to women than rock music? Or than 1920s jazz? This may include both the review of and response to two songs or artists.

2. In a season fourteen episode of *The Simpsons*, "How I Spent My Strummer Vacation," Elvis Costello's glasses are accidentally knocked off, and he cries, "My image!" How does the appearance of your favorite musician affect his or her image or audience? What does he or she normally wear? How would you describe his or her style? Review the effectiveness of this person's public image and analyze the importance of image on the marketing, production, and consumption of his or her music.

3. Write lyrics to describe the most significant aspect of one friend or family member's life. Then, use the chosen aspect to define his or her importance to you.

FOR FURTHER READING

Azerrad, Michael. *Our Band Could Be Your Life: Scenes from the American Indie Underground 1981–1991*. London: Little, Brown, 2001.

Escott, Collin. *Good Rockin' Tonight: Sun Records and the Birth of Rock 'n' Roll*. New York: St. Martin's, 1992.

Jackson, Blair. *Garcia: An American Life*. Boston: Penguin, 2000.

MacDonald, Ian. *Revolution in the Head: The Beatles' Records and the Sixties*. New York: Holt, 1995.

McNeil, Legs. *Please Kill Me: The Uncensored Oral History of Punk*. London: Grove, 2006.

Palmer, Robert. *Deep Blues: A Musical and Cultural History of the Mississippi Delta*. New York: Penguin, 1982.

Smith, Richard D. *Can't You Hear Me Callin': The Life of Bill Monroe, Father of Bluegrass*. London: Little, Brown, 2000.

Werner, Craig. *A Change Is Gonna Come: Music, Race, and the Soul of America*. New York: Penguin, 1999.

writing about popular literature

Favorites from Oprah's collection at home: "*The Grapes of Wrath* . . .
Steinbeck. Anything Steinbeck. All of Toni Morrison—*The Bluest Eye* and
Sula are all-time favorites. *The Power of Now*. Of course, *I Know Why the
Caged Bird Sings* by Maya. *White Oleander* by Janet Fitch . . . "

—From "Oprah's Bookshelf," Oprah.com

1 Which two of the following comics did *not* become a major motion picture?

    a. *Ghost Rider*
    b. *Dilbert*
    c. *Garfield*
    d. *The Hulk*
    e. *Calvin and Hobbes*
    f. *Spider-Man*

TEST YOUR POP CULTURE IQ: POPULAR LITERATURE

2 Which of these writers is not a romance novelist?

    a. Julia Quinn
    b. Patricia Cornwell
    c. Nora Roberts
    d. Janette Oke

3 What is a *blog*?

    a. An online place to meet friends
    b. An online chat room
    c. An online diary/journal
    d. A really swampy place to avoid

4 Of the following Stephen King novels, which one is not considered in the genre of horror?

    a. *Christine*
    b. *The Eyes of the Dragon*
    c. *Salem's Lot*
    d. *It*

5 True or False: In hard-boiled detective fiction, part of the detective "code" means that the detective may break the rules when dealing with the "bad" people to solve the crime and protect the innocent.

6 Which four of these movies were books first?

    a. *The War of the Roses*
    b. *Mission: Impossible*
    c. *Guardian*
    d. *Freedom Writers*
    e. *Star Trek*
    f. *The Aviator*
    g. *Jurassic Park*

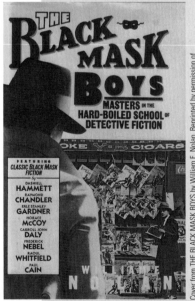

Cover from THE BLACK MASK BOYS by William F. Nolan. Reprinted by permission of HarperCollins Publishers.

7 The term *smushing* in fan fiction refers to what?

    a. Comparing the original work to a piece of fan fiction
    b. Negatively critiquing a piece of fan fiction
    c. Combining the names of two characters who are seen romantically in the original fiction to create a new name
    d. Spoofing or making fun of the original work in a piece of fan fiction

8 Where was J. K. Rowling when the idea for Harry Potter came to her?

    a. Driving to Manchester
    b. At home with her daughter Jessica
    c. On a train to London
    d. In the park with her daughter Jessica

Harry Potter book series by J.K. Rowling, published by Bloomsbury

9 The term *chick lit*, which refers to fiction written primarily about young, career-oriented women, became popular in what decade?

    a. '70s
    b. '80s
    c. '90s
    d. '00s

10 *Archy and Mehitabel* by Don Marquis is what genre of popular fiction?

    a. Satire
    b. Horror
    c. Fantasy
    d. Western

ANSWERS

1 *b. Dilbert and e. Calvin and Hobbes*　2 *b. Patricia Cornwell*　3 *c. An online diary/journal*　4 *c. The Eyes of the Dragon*
5 *True*　6 *a. The War of the Roses, d. Freedom Writers, f. The Aviator, and g. Jurassic Park*　7 *c. Combining the names of two characters who are seen romantically in the original fiction to create a new name*　8 *c. On a train to London*　9 *c. '90s*
10 *a. Satire*

YOU AND POPULAR LITERATURE

How does Oprah Winfrey do it? And why does no one else—TV pundit, critic, or retailer—have anything like her influence among book readers? On Sept. 22 [2005], Winfrey announced that the next pick for her television book club would be James Frey's *A Million Little Pieces*, a memoir of alcohol, drug addiction, and detoxification. Within four days, club aficionados bought 85,000 copies, reckons publisher Anchor Books. . . . Winfrey provides what's missing in stores and online. She also creates communities of readers, ensuring that no one need face brain benders like William Faulkner's *The Sound and the Fury* all alone. The books often contain "something so amazing you can't wait to share it," says Rachel Bensadia of New York City, whose book club reads Winfrey's picks. "Reading is a solitary experience, but it can also be very much about creating a community." No one has been able to single-handedly connect readers and sell books quite like Oprah has. (Green)

Popular literature is an integral part of our lives. Mass-produced books and magazines, as well as independently published texts like fan fiction and blogs, are now more readily available than at any time in history. You find these texts online, at your local grocery store, pharmacy, and chain department store, as well as the more traditional bookstores. Many readers get their books through online booksellers and peruse numerous online booklists for advice and previews; some readers even read their books, newspapers, and magazines online. According to *Publishers Weekly*, "In 2004, the Association of American Publishers conservatively estimated total book publishing revenues at $23.7 billion, which was 152% more than the total box-office gross for all movies in theatrical release, 76% more than all the dollars generated by AM and FM radio stations, 60% more than the net dollar value of all recorded music shipments and North American concert revenues, and 39% more than the entire video and portable gaming industry, according to their respective trade associations" (Grabois 84). Despite cries that people do not read anymore, it seems that Americans are buying and reading a variety of texts on a regular basis.

So, what are people reading? What authors do you like? What book trends have you been a part of? What makes a book or magazine popular? Does popularity make a text good by literary standards? What are these literary standards? How are particular books and periodicals sold to consumers? What political and social ideologies are being espoused in these texts? Are any of these texts being censored? And if so, by whom? For what reasons? What are alternative methods of producing and distributing texts, magazines, newspapers, and books? These are just some of the questions you will explore in this chapter; your responses will get you started as you write about popular literature and the authors and genres you like to read. The reading and writing assignments provided will help you see how others have questioned and analyzed the texts that Americans have been consuming over the past forty years and get you started asking your own insightful questions and writing your own answers.

grappling with ideas

- What texts do you like to read? Books? Magazines? Online fan fiction? Blogs?
- How do you decide what to read? What texts are on your bookshelf right now? In your magazine rack? Stacked on your floor?
- Besides textbooks for classes, how much money do you spend on reading materials each year?
- Do you use your local library for pleasure reading?

WHY WRITE ABOUT POPULAR LITERATURE?

Reading and writing about popular literature are much like reading and writing about traditional or canonical literature, the literature of high culture as defined in Chapter 3; it is only the object of analysis that has changed. Of course, the line between the two is very blurry as more and more popular texts are studied by academics and classes like the ones using this text. Many texts that are now labeled canonical were once considered popular texts, including Shakespearean plays and Jane Austen novels. You may study and write about popular books and magazines for many reasons: for new and different perspectives on a variety of issues; to spark your imagination, giving insight into people, experiences, and worlds beyond your own; even as a way to see the familiar through another's eyes. Likewise, reading, studying, and writing about popular literature can reinforce a theme or issue, like loss of innocence or the environment, that is the focus of your course while also helping you learn to become a better writer. Thus, you may be asked to read like a writer, reading a text for its qualities of good writing, such as originality, coherence, clarity, precision, persuasiveness, and voice. Finally, reading and writing about popular literature, authors, and genres can inspire your own creative expression—perhaps putting your own thoughts, feelings, and experiences into a creative text.

grapplingwithideas

- What makes a book good to you? Action? Mystery? Romance?
- Characters who look and act like you? Characters who are completely different from you?
- Settings that are familiar or foreign and perhaps exotic?
- Lots of dialogue? First-person narratives?
- Texts that play with format—perhaps written as a series of letters or journal entries?

PREPARING TO WRITE ABOUT POPULAR LITERATURE

As previously stated, popular literature is an ever-growing part of our culture. Although it is hard to draw a definitive line between popular literature and more traditional or highbrow literature, the way it is read is often a key factor. When you read a traditional novel for a class, such as Nathaniel Hawthorne's *The Scarlet Letter*, you probably read more slowly, take more notes, and pay more attention to literary elements, such as symbolism or imagery, and character development. When reading popular texts, like the newest thriller from Patricia Cornwell or the latest romance from Nora Roberts, people often read quickly, even skimming the text at times, and people read in more relaxed settings—on the subway, at the beach, in the bathtub. However, if you are going to write about these novels, you will have to adopt many of the reading habits used with more formal literature for reading popular literature—for example, taking notes as you read or looking up unfamiliar words. Likewise, you will have to do more than just flip through a magazine if you are going to review or analyze it. The following sections will review elements of literature and literary study that you have probably seen before but may not have considered in conjunction with popular literature.

Literary Genres

Genre, a French word that means "kind" or "type," applies to the classification of many types of media, not just literature. These categories are based on factors such as **form** (how the text is set up or arranged), **content** (what the text is about), and **purpose** (the goal or primary message of the text). Generally, literature is divided into four broad genres or types—drama, fiction, nonfiction prose, and poetry—and each genre can be categorized further into a variety of subgenres. For example, fiction is divided into numerous subgenres, and some of these are divided even further.

- Adventure/Suspense   Tom Clancy, *The Hunt for Red October*
- Christian Fiction   Tim LaHaye and Jerry Jenkins, *Left Behind*
- Crime and True Crime   Vincent Bugliosi, *Helter Skelter*
- Fantasy   Robert E. Howard, *Conan the Barbarian*
- Graphic Novels   Art Spiegelman, *Maus: A Survivor's Tale*
- Historical   Charles Frazier, *Cold Mountain*
- Horror   Stephen King, *Cujo*
- Mystery/Detective   Mickey Spillane, *The Killing Man*
- Romance   Susan Elizabeth Phillips, *It Had to Be You*
- Science Fiction   Madeleine L'Engle, *A Wrinkle in Time*
- Thriller   James Patterson, *Along Came a Spider*
- Western   Louis L'Amour, *The Riders of Lost Creek*

Depending on your instructor's purposes, you may be asked to read a specific genre or even subgenre, or you may be able to choose for yourself. Likewise, depending on your own interests and experiences, you may only read texts in one or two areas. Researching and looking at the characteristics of a particular genre or subgenre are one way you might analyze popular literature. How well does this text meet the requirements of the genre? For example, does your fantasy novel include magic, monsters, gods, and heroes? You may look at how the author plays with or even subverts the form, and if so, you may question the reason or purpose behind this modification. Likewise, you may consider how or why the author or text combines two or more different genres.

Helpful Literary Terms

The following terms are often used to discuss the elements of a literary text regardless of genre. They are indicative of some of the ways you might choose to analyze a popular literature text. For more extensive definitions and examples, see one of the dictionaries or glossaries listed at the end of this chapter.

- **Alliteration:** the repetition of sounds at the beginning of words or in stressed syllables, such as Donald Duck, the Pixelgirl Presents website, or Beavis and Butt-head.
- **Characters:** the fictional or nonfictional people in a story or play, such as Romeo and Juliet, John F. Kennedy, or Garfield.
- **Diction:** choice and use of words as well as sentence structures; for example, Chief Brenda Lee Johnson of *The Closer* is known for her southern sayings and pronunciations (diction), such as "aggervatinest" for annoying and "walking on a slant" for drunk.

grappling with ideas

- How do you read for pleasure? For school?
- Do you have a favorite place to read? Do you want music in the background or total quiet?
- Do you make notes in the book margins, write on sticky notes, in a notebook?
- Do you argue with the text, characters, or author as you read?
- How could you improve your reading habits?

- **Imagery:** the use of vivid or figurative language; an appeal to the five senses; for example, consider the different senses Kathy Reichs engages in this short selection from her novel *Bare Bones:* "As I secured the tub in an evidence locker, the memory cells floated an image of Gideon Banks. Wrinkled brown face, fuzzy gray hair, voice like ripping duct tape."
- **Metaphor:** words or phrases used to compare two relatively unlike things, such as this example from the Metaphor Observatory: "rate freeze to cool mortgage meltdown," which compares the economy to nuclear fallout.
- **Meter:** the measured arrangement of words, sounds, rhythms, and stresses in poetry or music; can also be applied to dialogue. For example, Dr. Seuss books have a recognizable beat and rhythm (or meter) to them.
- **Parallelism:** the repetition of phrases, sentences, or lines that are similar in meaning or structure; for example, Martin Luther King, Jr.'s famous "I Have a Dream Speech" is known for its set of parallel clauses beginning with "I have a dream that . . ."
- **Plot:** the events that take place in a narrative or story. The plot can be divided into three parts—rising action, climax, and falling action. The plot builds up to the climax, where something important happens that changes the sequence of events or something about the character; after this change, at the climax, the action falls or leads to the final conclusion.

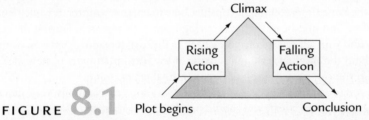

FIGURE 8.1

- **Rhyme Scheme:** the arrangement of rhymes in a poem, song, or other text.
- **Setting:** where the action takes place; for example, the main setting for the Harry Potter books is Hogwarts School of Witchcraft and Wizardry.
- **Simile:** a comparison of two relatively unrelated things using *like* or *as*; for example, the title of this recent book by Bill and Pam Farrel includes two similes, *Men Are Like Waffles—Women Are Like Spaghetti: Understanding and Delighting in Your Differences.*
- **Speaker:** the person who is assumed to be talking (not necessarily the author) or narrating the story or poem or even song. For example, Princess Mia is the speaker in Meg Cabot's *Princess Diaries* series.
- **Stanza:** one of the divisions of a poem (or song), composed of two or more lines; may also be referred to as a verse.
- **Structure:** the way that a poem or story is composed or arranged; for example, many novels are divided into chapters; in addition, these chapters may be arranged into sections; likewise, a typical song structure has verse one, then the chorus, then verse two and the chorus, then a bridge followed by verse three and the chorus one or more times.
- **Symbolism:** representing things by symbols or attributing symbolic meanings or significance to objects, events, or ideas; for example, in pop culture colors often symbolize a number of different values: green often symbolizes spring or new life, red symbolizes blood and sacrifice, white symbolizes innocence or purity, while black often symbolizes evil or sin.
- **Theme:** the significance or meaning of the work; for example, many critics claim that Superman comic books have a central theme of good versus evil.
- **Tone:** the general quality, effect, or atmosphere of a work; for example, a work might be formal or informal, it might be serious or humorous, it might be casual or sophisticated.

Researching and Documenting Popular Literature

Oftentimes, research is not needed to complete your essay, especially if you are relying on personal response or reflection. However, sometimes, research will help you present a more convincing analysis or review of a popular literature text or meet assignment requirements.

Areas of research in popular literature may include the following:

- The history of the book, series, or subgenre
- The biography of the author
- The reception of the book: sales figures, other reviews, other analyses, protests
- Marketing strategies for the text
- The history or development of techniques used in the text
- The cultures or subcultures represented in the book

Start by analyzing your assignment and by asking yourself what you want to know, what you want to share with your reader, and what you need to know to complete your essay. You may want to look at your initial notes and reading responses. Where are the holes? What else do you need to know? Where can you find that information? At the same time, you might consider how to narrow your focus while remaining open to new ideas, responses, and questions that may spring from your research. During the research process, you will probably find yourself repeatedly going back to the text, rereading passages, comparing what others have to say about the original text, and looking at the text for support of new ideas. Take notes during this process so you can use what you find in your final paper.

Your research can lead you to a variety of primary and secondary sources. Naturally, your first source is the text itself. If you like to mark up a text, you should purchase your own copy, but low- or no-cost alternatives include your school, city/county, or state library and e-books online. Many people like to share their books with friends, but remember to treat a borrowed book with care. Unless you have the owner's permission, don't write in it, dog-ear the pages, or crack the spine.

As with any research project, secondary sources can be found in a variety of places, so be open to the possibilities shared with you by your instructor, classmates, or librarian. You may find books, articles, and websites about your particular book or author or about the genre or subgenre you're researching. Make sure you check out your library's holdings as well as the electronic databases available through your school or public libraries. You may also want to check out the databases and indexes specifically related to literary analysis—for example, The Literature Resource Center, MLA International Bibliography, and LION (Literature Online), as well as general humanities databases like JSTOR and Project MUSE. Likewise, you can check out databases connected to the sociological examination of books and their impact on U.S. culture. For book reviews, use databases like InfoTrac College Edition and LexisNexis that contain magazine and newspaper articles because so many of these periodicals run regular book review columns, as well as *Book Review Index, Book Review Digest,* and *What Do I Read Next?* When applicable, use the tables of contents and the indexes in the sources you find to make sure they have relevant information. With any source, but particularly with Internet sites, remember to evaluate and test its credibility before using it in your research. For example, an author's home page is usually designed to sell books; bookseller sites are also trying to sell books, so the reviews they list will more often be favorable. Likewise, some sites are slanted by politics or religion, among other things, and their reviews will contain this slant, whether positive or negative.

As you conduct your research, remember to write down the citation information you'll need for your Works Cited page and for your in-text citations. Record information about any books, articles, or websites you read. You will want to know where you found your information and how to get back to it in case you need it again. See Chapter 11, Researching and Documenting in the Pop Culture Zone, for specific guidelines; you can also review the Works Cited at the end of essays in this chapter for sample citations.

WRITING ABOUT POPULAR LITERATURE

Popular literature can be analyzed and written about in a variety of ways. You may want to look at a particular genre or subgenre and analyze how it is written, how it targets a particular audience, or what effect it has had on the general population. For example, you might examine how the Harry Potter books captured the attention of so many readers or how *Gone with the Wind* renewed interest in the Civil War. You may want to look at what different texts have to say about a specific issue or how they present a particular ideology or political stance, as seen with *The Wonderful Wizard of Oz* versus *Wicked: The Life and Times of the Wicked Witch of the West*. You may want to consider the general reception of a particular book or author or analyze trends in the bookselling market. Although there are many formats for writing about popular literature, this chapter focuses on the four main assignments you have seen throughout this text: reviews, reflection or response essays, analysis essays, or synthesis essays, which can be a combination of any of the preceding types.

Book Reviews or Review Essays

A book review is basically a close examination of a specific book. You could also review a series or collection of books on a similar topic, a number of texts within a genre, or a particular author. Likewise, you can review other types of texts such as magazines and newspapers or specific pieces of these texts such as editorials, columns, or obituaries. Online texts are also open to review—blogs and wikis, fan fiction, and e-zines. In the review essay, evaluation is the guiding principle, so you will express an opinion about what is interesting or useful about the text. Because your reader may not have read what you are reviewing, you will have to give at least some description of the content, plot, characters, or author. In fact, readers often peruse reviews to decide whether or not to read a new book, buy a magazine, or check out a website. You are giving a judgment about the quality and purpose of the text, backed up with enough information to indicate that your judgment is based on good reasoning. These close readings may be found in newspapers, in magazines, and on many websites. Various newspapers and magazines have regular columns devoted to reviews, and a few periodicals are designed specifically to give reviews; for example, *Publishers Weekly* and *The New York Times Book Review*. For a class, your review will most likely be about a book or other text you were asked to read as a class or a text you were asked to choose within stated parameters and read independently.

<aside>
key questions

Key Questions for a Book Review or Review Essay

- Have you given the reader an overall outline or summary of the text? Have you introduced the main character(s) or purpose of the text?
- Have you clearly indicated your judgment of the text's quality?
- Have you noted specific elements of the text that support your judgment? Have you described these clearly or used brief quotes from the text to illustrate? Have you documented your quotes?
- Have you shown yourself to be a credible source?
- Have you qualified your judgment with both positive and negative aspects of the text?
- Have you begun the review with an attention-grabbing opening? Have you concluded it with a recommendation for your reader?
- Did you write in literary present tense?
</aside>

keyquestions

Key Questions for a Reflection or Response Essay

- Have you clearly indicated how your essay connects to at least one aspect of the text you read?
- Does your introduction lead your reader into your response?
- Does your concluding paragraph include some reflection on both the text and your response?
- Did you write about the book in present tense but any past life experiences in past tense?
- Does your essay have a clearly stated or implied thesis that connects your reflection to the text you read?

A review essay will usually address three or four key issues about the text. Your overall evaluation is usually phrased as the thesis of the essay and may come at the beginning or end of the essay. The essay often gives a brief summary of the text (usually without giving away the ending), outlines the main purpose of the text, the characters, or the basic plot, and is written in present tense. The essay will also identify the audience(s) for the text and might then discuss how the book is designed to appeal to the audience(s) identified, including the genre of the text.

Remember that most texts have both good and bad elements, so you want to present a balanced picture of the text under review. Do note, however, that some reviews are slanted in one direction, either because they want everyone to read the text or because they want everyone to avoid the book—perhaps for political or religious reasons. For example, when *The Da Vinci Code* by Dan Brown became popular in 2004, it also received a lot of criticism from the Catholic community because they felt that Brown misrepresented their history. If you are reviewing a book, you might also compare the book to other books in the same genre, to other books written by the same author, or to books that have similar themes. You may even write a review that ranks a list of texts, like the top ten serial killer novels or the twenty all-time best children's books. Because you want your reader to trust your evaluation, it will help your credibility if your review illustrates that you are familiar with a wide range of books or texts, especially within the genre being reviewed.

Reflection or Response Essays

The main purpose of a reflection or response essay is to use the text as a starting point for your own discussion, your own feelings, or your own reactions to the text(s). Although you will probably make some references to specific elements of the text, you will spend more time reflecting on your own personal feelings that have arisen through critically reading the book, or you will respond to some personal issue or emotion that has arisen during your encounter with the magazine or author. It is important to use evidence from the text to explain why you are making your specific point, but the essay will have more in common with personal writing. You may have encountered this type of writing before in a literature class, especially if your professor or textbook followed the reader response criticism movement, which focuses on the reader's reactions to a given text when it is read or experienced.

To start your reflection or response essay, you can reflect on the aspect of the book or other text that grabs your attention, sparks your interest, or perhaps triggers your anger or disgust. Do you agree or disagree with the author's view? Can you relate to one or more of the characters? Have you ever experienced a similar event or had to make a similar choice? Using these starters, you can then decide what you would like to say to your audience. It will help your writing stay focused if you decide on a solid thesis statement that explains the purpose of your essay and how it connects to the text you are considering.

Analysis Essays

An analysis essay presents more of an argument about some element of a book or text, whether it is the author's use of dialogue to make the characters realistic, the role of children in the genre to symbolize the move from innocence to adulthood, or the importance of new, original drawing styles to make the comic book stand out (see The Reading Zone for these examples). The analysis essay often includes descriptions or quotes from the text, but these references are more extensive and are accompanied by an explanation of their significance. This explanation may reflect your own personal opinion or reading, but it may also be supported by evidence from outside sources.

When writing an analysis essay, you will usually start with an idea you have about the text, author, genre, or a specific literary element or writing technique. You will turn this idea into an argument or thesis that will be stated or implied in your essay; this is the statement that your essay will explain and support. This thesis may offer your opinion, but it will also help other readers understand the magazine, book, series, genre, or author—perhaps the genre's purpose, the magazine's effects on readers, or the book's meaning, as well as how the author achieved any one of these. To maintain credibility, you will want to support your thesis throughout the paper with specific evidence and examples from the book and possibly from outside resources. Analysis requires close reading of the book and explanations of what the book is doing, not just a summary of the plot or descriptions of the characters.

When analyzing a book or magazine, remember that there may be many valid interpretations of what you read or see. Every reader experiences a text differently. If you experienced a fire in your childhood home, you may have a different reaction to Stephen King's *Firestarter* than someone who loves to be scared. You need to support your interpretation of the book or author with specific details from the book or about how the author uses specific literary elements. Pay particular attention to patterns you notice in the book or the genre. You may also need to support your argument with research about the book's reception (did people love it or hate it?), the author's intention (is she trying to sell you something?), or the book's design (is the whole story told through letters?). Likewise, you may research and analyze patterns you have noticed in a collection of books that address similar issues or have comparable characters.

key questions

Key Questions for an Analysis Essay

- Do you have a clearly stated or implied thesis?
- Do you have a series of reasons supporting the thesis? Are these arranged in a logical and convincing order?
- Are your supporting reasons backed up? Do you provide specific evidence and examples from the book for each reason you offer? Have you properly documented direct quotes from the text?
- Have you presented yourself as a credible authority by writing clearly and giving support for your arguments?
- Does your introduction grab the reader's attention and then orient your reader into the direction of your argument?
- Does your concluding paragraph provide a thoughtful ending?
- Did you avoid simple description or plot summary?
- Have you written in literary present tense?

Synthesis Essays

At times, you will want to mix the types of essays just discussed to produce the best essay you can. Perhaps your analysis will begin with a personal reflection or another reader's review; likewise, your review may include an element of personal response or an analysis of the author's use of imagery. A synthesis essay combines two or more types of essays or rhetorical approaches to create the strongest possible writing for your reader, whatever the specific topic or thesis. For example, you might decide to review a list of books that were important to you in high school; this essay would include personal response as you explain why the books were important to you as well as reviews of the texts on your list. When writing for a specific class assignment, be sure to look over the assignment instructions and speak to your instructor if this type of mixture does not fit strictly into the directions for the essay. When you choose to use a mixture of rhetorical strategies, be sure to look over the key questions for each of the essay types you are including in your paper.

SAMPLE ANNOTATED ESSAY

1. What makes a book timeless or able to appeal to readers year after year?

2. What books have you read that would be considered timeless? Did you find this to be true of the book? Why or why not?

3. What is a coming-of-age story? What events would you expect such a story to address?

Meg Cabot *is the author of over fifty books for adults and teens, many of which have appeared on the The New York Times Bestseller List. Two books from her* Princess Diaries *series have been made into Disney movies, and her* 1-800-Where-R-You *series was the basis for the Lifetime series* Missing. *She is presently working on two new series.* "Cry, Linda, Cry" *first appeared in the collection* Everything I Needed to Know About Being a Girl I Learned from Judy Blume, *an anthology of personal essays about the unforgettable influence of Judy Blume, still one of our most censored authors.*

CRY, LINDA, CRY

Meg Cabot

> Notice the various techniques Cabot uses to describe Shoshona and to grab the reader's attention.

• She had big brown eyes, an elfin smile, soft, curly brown hair, and go-go boots . . . the kind of boots Julie on *Mod Squad* wore. The kind of boots none of our mothers would get for us, no matter how much we pleaded, because they were too expensive and too grown up for us. Even her T-shirt was new and differ-ent—*TNT,* it read across the budding mounds of what were destined (possibly at any moment) to become actual boobs: *Talent, Not Talk.*

• Her name was as exotic as the place from which she'd moved—Shoshona. And she'd transferred into Mrs. Hunter's fourth-grade class at Elm Heights Elementary School in Bloomington, Indiana, all the way from Canada.

• And she was about to make my existence a living hell.

I didn't know it, of course. And if someone had told me, I wouldn't have believed it. Everyone knew that bullies didn't come in four-foot, sixty-pound packages, with brand-new solid gold post earrings and Goody barrettes.

Everyone, that is, except for Judy Blume.

Too often in books, schools are depicted as nurturing, caring environments where bullies either don't exist, or on the rare occasions when they do crop up, they come from troubled homes. They're "victims" just like the children they've terrorized. Eventually, when the child the bully has been tormenting comes to understand that her bully doesn't have a daddy or lives in a trailer park instead of middle-class suburbia, she forgives and even eventually befriends the bully, and everyone gets along.

Yeah. Right.

Judy Blume is careful not to give *Blubber* that kind of *After-School Special* ending. True to life, the victim and the bully in *Blubber* do *not* become friends, the bully is never even punished for her crimes, nor is there any obvious lesson learned. While the protagonist, through becoming a target of bullying herself, comes to understand that by tolerating the bullying of others, she did something wrong, this is portrayed subtly, so subtly that the careless—or youthful—reader might miss it entirely.

Still, even if in the fourth grade I'd known there was such a thing as pretty female bullies, I was hardly the victim type. Like *Blubber*'s heroine, Jill, I was as average as a kid could be—not too smart but not too dumb; not too fat but not too skinny; not too short but not too tall. I was completely normal . . . a little shy, maybe, but I got along with all my peers and had a tight group of friends, some of whom I am still in touch with today, thirty years later.

Sure, my family wasn't the most well off, and my mom made a lot of my clothes. But I attended a school populated by children of academics—college professors who valued books over designer jeans and had successfully shielded their children from the knowledge that they might be missing out on current trends, as the

Internet hadn't been invented yet, and the only channels any of us got were the three major networks and
PBS (and *Cowboy Bob* on local station 4).

There was nothing physically to set me apart from my
peers—just as Judy Blume is careful to point out there
is nothing physical that sets her bully's victim, Linda,
apart from the other children in her class. Linda is
slightly overweight. But there are other children in the
class who are larger—who could even be classified as
fat—and Wendy, the book's antagonist, doesn't pick
on them. Perhaps because of the title, I've often seen
Blubber categorized as a book about a fat girl who gets
tormented by her peers. But the discerning reader soon
realizes that the reason Linda is picked on has nothing
to do with her weight (although her weight is the subject
about which Linda is most sensitive and therefore the
subject on which Wendy chooses to focus the majority
of her taunts) and that the term *blubber* doesn't have
as much to do with Linda's size as it does her personality—or lack thereof.

• No, Linda is picked on by Wendy for the same reason
  that my bully, Shoshona, picked on me.

• We, the victims, allow it to happen.

Oh, yes. I went there. I, like Judy Blume, am putting
the blame—well, part of it, anyway—on the victim
herself. In today's society—thirty years post-*Blubber* and
Shoshona—it may be considered politically incorrect to
say these girls asked for it. But Jill's mother's suggestion—that her daughter "laugh off" the taunts that
are making her life so hellish—is still the best advice a
parent can give to a child in such a situation (although
obviously a call to the teacher who has allowed such
bullying to go on under her very nose is also recommended). Judy Blume herself, when describing *Blubber*
on her Web site, writes:

A person who can laugh at herself will be respected, right?

But Linda doesn't laugh. And maybe that's the problem.

*There's something about her that makes Jill and a lot of kids in her
fifth-grade class want to see how far they can go.*

> Cabot uses short paragraphs, even one-sentence paragraphs, to emphasize important, stand-out points.

Bullying is about power. And those who wield power can quickly turn on others, even those who once considered them friends—especially those who lack the inner resources to laugh at or stand up for themselves. I considered Shoshona a friend, although truthfully we had nothing in common. At ten years old, I still considered playing with Barbies the height of amusement, a pastime Shoshona looked down upon, although she didn't seem to have any better suggestions as to what else we might do while playing together. Drawing, reading, and board games were all "dumb" to her. One memorable playdate included Shoshona asking me to sit in a desk chair that spun, then twirling me around and around in it until I begged her to stop (true to form, when I asked her to stop, she wouldn't . . . until I threw up, that is. Shoshona, disgusted, stomped home, not even apologizing for making me sick . . . or, as my parents later discovered, for breaking the chair).

You might think an afternoon that ended in vomit would have dampened my enthusiasm about pursuing a friendship with a person who disdained the pursuits I enjoyed yet could think of no alternative activities, save those that caused me to lose my lunch and ruined my parents' furniture.

But that was the power Shoshona held over me—the same power Wendy, in *Blubber*, holds over Jill. I was shy. Shoshona was not. I was willing to let others have their way in an effort to get them to like me. Shoshona was not. I, along with the rest of the girls in my class, worshipped Shoshona the way Jill, in *Blubber*, worships Wendy—the way any ten-year-old worships a natural leader—even though it turned out her T-shirt had lied: Shoshona had no discernible talents. She couldn't sing, for instance, like my friend Becky, or do backflips, like my friend Erika, or do fractions in her head, like Barbara. In fact, Shoshona was almost *No Talent* and *All Talk*.

The desk chair incident was devastating to me. Shoshona had come to my house, and she had a bad time! How would I ever live it down? How would I get back in her good graces?

I felt even worse when my attempt to redeem myself in Shoshona's eyes by having a "cool" birthday party with a *Freaky Friday* theme—everyone was to come dressed as their mother—fell flat. My friends Becky, Erika, and Barbara arrived dressed like me, in long trailing gowns with white gloves, loaded down with rhinestone jewelry, giggling like mad. Shoshona, however, didn't dress in her mother's clothes. She wore an exact replica of her mother's clothes—but in her own size: business attire for the busy ten-year-old executive. She narrowed her eyes at the rest of us in our floppy hats and too-big high heels and told us we looked like a "bunch of babies."

We were only too ready to agree with her. Being Canadian, Shoshona seemed hopelessly cosmopolitan. She had some very fancy ways compared to us Hoosiers. It was Shoshona who introduced our class to the titillating concept of "going together." She and Jeff Niehardt were going together by the end of Shoshona's first day at Elm Heights. It didn't take much longer than that for most of the rest of the class to pair up.

Everyone except for me and my friends. Like Becky, Erika, and Barbara, I didn't want to "go with" anyone.

Still, most of the talking Shoshona did was about boys. Though I had no particular interest in boys at the time, it was clear from the way Shoshona carried on that the interests I did have—Barbies and *The Boxcar Children*— were babyish and that I needed to "grow up."

This was news to me. Things had seemed to be going swimmingly for me in Mrs. Hunter's fourth-grade class until Shoshona came along and pointed out that in actual truth they were not. My friends—particularly sensitive Erika, who cried when her science experiment involving glucose didn't turn out, and beanpole brain Barbara, whose main offense, according to Shoshona, was that she was good in math, a trait that would certainly never win her any dates—were as babyish as I was. If I ever wanted to grow up, I needed to be more like Shoshona.

And I needed to get a boyfriend, pronto.

Notice Cabot's use of dashes to weave in descriptive information and to make her sentences more sophisticated and varied.

It was my reluctance to go with anybody that really horrified Shoshona. She suggested I go with Joey Meadows, a fifth grader, and even got him to ask me to go with him. Nice as I found Joey, I wasn't ready for that kind of commitment. So I gently turned down his kind (read: terrified. He was as scared of Shoshona as the rest of us were) offer.

Little did I know how this simple act would enrage Shoshona. The very next day when I arrived at school, I was no longer Meggin Cabot. According to Shoshona, I was now Maggot Cabbage and would remain so until I changed my mind, stopped being so babyish, and accepted Joey Meadows's request to go with him.

Suddenly I had gone from being Shoshona's "friend" to being the object of her scorn and antipathy. I was mortified.

I didn't cry in front of her. I had more pride than that. But I spent plenty of hours in my bedroom closet weeping as if my heart would break. I didn't want to be called Maggot Cabbage for the rest of my life. But then, I didn't want to go with anybody, either.

It didn't take long for my parents to catch on that something was wrong, primarily because most nights I wouldn't come out of the closet. Finally, one evening my father crawled in there with me and asked what was the matter. I explained about Maggot Cabbage and Shoshona. I listed the myriad ways Shoshona had taken over the class—swinging classmates Muffy and Monique (the only names that have been changed in this essay are those of the innocent) to her side; making faces at me and rude remarks, if when the class split into groups, I tried to join my old friends Becky, Barbara, and Erika, who liked and accepted me just the way I was; calling me a baby when I wouldn't play "chase the boys" on the playground at recess; making fun of my homemade clothes and nondesigner jeans; laughing at the fact that I was forbidden from watching *Starsky and Hutch*.

My father, a computer science professor who was the first in his family to go to college—on a basketball scholarship, no less—was not particularly versed in

> Note how Cabot uses concrete nouns—proper names—to give specific details.

psychology, let alone child psychology. And he seemed to know next to nothing about women, having dated exactly one in his entire life—my mother.

His desire to help with my situation, however, was heartfelt. He showed me—right there in the closet—how to make a fist (never tuck the thumb on the inside. You might break it) and always to aim for the nose (if you aim for the mouth, you might cut your knuckles on your opponent's teeth).

Yes. My father advised that the next time Shoshona called me a baby or Maggot Cabbage, I should punch her in the face.

I was horrified. I had never punched anyone before in my life (not counting my brothers. But I had never hit them in the face, preferring the more sisterly practices of "Indian rubs" and pinching).

The situation had clearly progressed to a point where something needed to be done. But what, to my father, indicated a need for fisticuffs, to my mother showed a need for something else entirely. Always a woman of action, Mom placed a single phone call and purchased a single book. The phone call was to my teacher (though I begged Mom not to tell Mrs. Hunter what was going on, certain that word would get out that Maggot Cabbage was such a baby, she couldn't handle her own affairs), and the book was for me. The book was called *Blubber*.

I don't remember if I recognized myself in its pages. Certainly I, a timid child, had never been so bold as to egg anyone's house (whether or not they deserved it) as Jill, the narrator, does. Nor had I ever participated as actively in tormenting another student as Jill does at one point in the novel.

But there had been a certain girl—I'll call her R.—at a school I'd attended previous to attending Elm Heights, whom I, along with everyone else in the class, had found insufferable.

And though I myself had never joined in on teasing her, I had certainly never done anything to stop it, some-

Since this is a personal response essay, Cabot clearly connects her experience to the novel that has inspired this essay.

what relishing R.'s comeuppance (she was incredibly bright, and like many bright children, came off to those of us who were more of an average intelligence as a horrible know-it-all).

What I took away from *Blubber* during that first reading, at the age of ten, was that doing nothing to stop the tormenting of a classmate was, in its own way, every bit as bad as if I had been one of the ringleaders. Certainly Linda was as obnoxious and deserving of mocking as R. had been, but that didn't make what had been done to her or to R. right . . .

. . . any more than what Shoshona was doing to me was right.

I knew that I, like Jill in *Blubber,* was going to have to learn not to punch Shoshona but to laugh off her taunts. At the very least, I was going to have to stop letting them bother me.

And that wasn't going to be as hard as it sounded. I had gotten to a point where I no longer wanted Shoshona as a friend. I no longer cared if she liked me. I found her, in fact, boring. What fun is spinning around in a chair when you could mutilate Ken (who had already permanently lost an arm in a tragic war accident) or read a book?

So the very next day during art, while Mrs. Hunter's fourth-grade class was gathered around the clay table and I said something to Erika that cracked her up—but caused Shoshona to raise her eyebrows and go, "God, Maggot, could you be more of a baby?"—I did it.

Oh, I didn't punch her in the face (though, thanks to my father, I knew how). Instead, I said the phrase I'd been rehearsing since finishing *Blubber.*

"Look Shoshona," I said. "You be you, and I'll be me. If you think what I like and what I do is babyish, that's fine. You don't have to like them or do them. But don't expect *me* to stop liking them just because *you* don't. Because I'm not you."

Shoshona, blinking in astonishment at this mild statement—which was, given that it had come from me, one

Using direct quotations is common in a narrative; however, Cabot waits until this point in the essay to use a full quotation, effectively highlighting an important point.

of the shyest girls in the class, quite an outburst—said, "God. Okay. You didn't have to yell."

It's no coincidence that Mrs. Hunter dropped the bomb later that day that she understood there were children in her class who were going together. Never, Mrs. Hunter said, had she heard of anything more ridiculous. Fourth graders, she said, do not "go together." She added that if she heard any more reports of children going together, she would send the offenders to Mrs. Harrigan, the principal, a fate—needless to say—worse than death. When Shoshona raised a hand to protest, Mrs. Hunter looked her dead in the eye and said simply, "Shoshona. *Don't.*"

Shoshona made a face to show how unfair she thought Mrs. Hunter was being, and I watched as Jeff Niehardt sadly erased his beloved's name from the inside of his pencil box. Shoshona swore at recess that when she and Jeff turned eighteen, no one, not even Mrs. Harrigan, would stop them from going together.

I'm not sure if that actually happened, because Shoshona moved back to Canada at the end of the school year, and I personally never saw her again. All I know was, after that day, no one—not even Shoshona—called me Maggot Cabbage again.

But I've thought of Shoshona—and *Blubber*—often over the past thirty years. Not even one year later, a girl named—ironically—Judy became the target of some of Shoshona's bullies-in-training, Muffy and Monique, for wearing blue eyeshadow and sleeping during social studies. When Judy didn't bother to come to her own defense, I did, making sure Judy had someone to sit with at lunch and someone to swing with at recess. Muffy and Monique, not being anywhere near as vicious as Shoshona, soon lost interest.

Middle school followed, with a whole new batch of social misfits who were targeted by a whole new batch of bullies. The tears in the girls' room flowed freely and copiously—sometimes from Muffy and Monique, who in turn became victims themselves and eventually my friends.

But I myself was never again a victim. *Blubber* had taught me how to stand up for myself and even—

Cabot repeatedly comes back to the idea of the victim—who is a victim? Why is this person a victim? How can he or she stop being a victim? This recurring idea helps tie the pieces of the essay together and provides consistency and cohesion.

amazingly—how to defuse situations for others. Soon I found myself coming to the defense of R.—the girl from my previous elementary school—when we met again in high school. R. had lost none of her insufferable know-it-allness in the years since I'd last seen her. She had, if anything, become worse. Brilliant academically but socially inept, not a day passed when her books weren't scattered from one end of the hall to the other by some smirking jock.

But this time I wouldn't stand by and watch as others taunted her. And I certainly didn't laugh at her. I invited her to eat with me at lunch (to the chagrin of my other friends), attended slumber parties at her house, invited her to the movies, and occasionally still see her, to this day. As with Jill and Linda, I can't say we became best friends . . . but I felt for her. I'd stood in R.'s shoes. I knew how it felt.

And if there was a way I could help her not sit in her closet and cry every night, I was willing to try it.

Today, whenever I need to remind myself about the massive disconnect between adulthood and childhood, I go to Amazon.com and look up the reviews for Judy Blume's *Blubber.* I can't think of another children's book that is more polarizing—parents are "appalled" at the behavior of the children in the book and at the way the parents in the book handle the situation (Jill's mother's suggestion that her daughter "laugh it off" seems to raise parental hackles, though, if you ask me, it's way better than advising her to punch Wendy in the face), while children—the ones who aren't "appalled" by the number of times Jill's mother says the D word—accept what happens to Linda and Jill as a matter of course.

Because it *is* a matter of course. I don't know if there's something that happens to some adults—especially once they've had children of their own—where they selectively forget what being a kid is really like, or if these people really grew up in such a sheltered environment that bullying never went on in their schools. I sort of think it's the former. Only Judy Blume, despite having children of her own, never lost sight of the fact that girls are *not* made of sugar and spice and everything nice.

Years after the Shoshona incident, I found comfort in a cartoon by Matt Groening (creator of the *Simpsons*) in his book *Life in Hell*. It's a simple line drawing of a group of little girls surrounding another little girl, who is weeping. The girls are chanting, "Cry, Debbie, cry." The cartoon is called "The Cruelest Thing in the World: A Roving Gang of Fourth-Grade Girls."

Unsensational and unsentimental, *Blubber* is this cartoon exemplified. Judy Blume understands that there have always been bullies and there have always been victims, and until the victim learns to stand up for herself, the bullies won't quit torturing her. No amount of parental or teacher interventions will save her.

She has to save herself.

That's what Judy allows Jill to do, and in doing so, she allowed me to save myself.

DECODING THE TEXT

1. Cabot says, "Judy Blume is careful not to give *Blubber* that kind of *After-School Special* ending." What does this description say to you as the reader? Are such comparisons effective as a form of imagery? Why or why not?

2. "Maggot Cabbage" gets very different advice about how to handle Shoshona from her mother and father. What is this advice? Why do you think the advice is so different? Could you predict which advice Cabot was going to follow? Why or why not?

CONNECTING TO YOUR CULTURE

1. Describe the bully or bullies at your elementary school. What did they do as bullies? How do they compare to the bully in this essay? To bullies on current television shows?

2. List popular literature, television shows, or movies that include teen bullies. What do these bullies have in common? How are they different? Do male and female bullies act in the same or different ways? How would Cabot's and Blume's ways of dealing with bullies work with the bullies you have just described?

3. Have you ever been the victim of a bully or acted as the bully? What were the circumstances? What happened? How did it make you feel?

THE READING ZONE

TACKLING TOPICS

1. Consider what kinds of books you like to read. Are these genres or styles connected to your gender in any way? Your race? Your socioeconomic or class status? Your religion or belief system? Your sexuality? Why are these factors important to authors, readers, and publishing houses?

2. Check out what kinds of book or reading clubs exist in your community. Who are the members of these clubs? What do they read? Where do they meet? What purposes do the clubs serve? Do you belong to a book club? If not, would you join one?

3. What is your definition of a comic? A comic book? A graphic novel? Do you consider any of these (popular) literature? Is the artist who draws a comic an author? Why or why not? Should comic books be used in school? In what ways? Have you ever created a comic yourself?

4. How many books have you read that were later turned into films? What about books that were inspired by films or television shows? Have you ever read a book because you saw the film or television show? How do the books and films compare? Which do you prefer?

READING SELECTIONS

The readings that follow are organized into the now-familiar five sections: 1970s, 1980s, 1990s, 2000s, and Across the Decades, which help organize the sample essays and give a broader picture of what popular culture is and how it affects our daily lives.

In the '70s section, an anthropologist discusses the role of romance magazines in recording and dictating interpersonal relationships; then we have an excerpt from Maxine Hong Kingston's memoir *The Woman Warrior*. In the '80s section, you will explore the role of "terrible" children in a literary analysis of several Stephen King novels as well as a review that details the history of lesbian mystery fiction. The '90s and '00s sections look at popular literature aimed at young adults, from the influence of R. L. Stine's *Goosebumps* horror series to comic books to Harry Potter novels and the controversies they have created—book burnings and witch hunts. The '00s section also presents a personal response to the phenomenon of writing fan fiction, particularly online; for Hillary Robson, this form of popular literature often intersects with films and television shows. The Across the Decades section returns to the art of graphic writing with a review of Gary Larson's popular and financially successful comic *The Far Side*. The reading selections conclude with a case study about romance novels: Ann Barr Snitow's essay from the '70s discusses Harlequin romance novels and the apparently large communication gap between men and women, and Janice A. Radway's article from the '80s uses interviews to illustrate the important role that romance novels play in middle-class women's lives; the case study closes with an article from the '00s that examines the importance of food and eating in modern romance novels.

The readings in each of the sections are not isolated to that decade or section because pop culture is not only what happened in a specific decade or time period but also how the same medium or idea is received or remembered later on or even how it has affected later writers and readers. The readings in this chapter are presented as a way for you to become more versed in investigating and analyzing popular literature as both a creator and reflector of pop culture; however, they are also offered as samples of writing reviews, responses, analyses, and synthesis essays about popular literature, authors, and trends.

Reading Selections: the  '70s

CONSIDERING IDEAS

1. What kinds of magazines do you like to look at and read?

2. How do the stories in these magazines affect the way you view the world or the way you act in the world?

3. What other elements of the magazine carry cultural weight or influence?

David Sonenschein *is the author of four books dealing with the topic of pedophiles and homosexual men. He worked for the Institute for Sex Research at Indiana University and was with the Department of Anthropology at the University of Texas. He now resides in Austin, Texas. The sociological study "Love and Sex in the Romance Magazines" appeared in* The Journal of Popular Culture *in 1970.*

LOVE AND SEX IN THE ROMANCE MAGAZINES[1]

David Sonenschein

It is fairly common to say that the mass media and popular culture contain suggestions as to many of our culture's values. There may be some disagreement as to the exact boundaries of these systems, but a general consensus among social scientists on this seems to exist. The anthropologist in particular is prone to examine textual material for value and symbolic content, for it is within this realm that he sees the very essence of culture. This area is our concern here.

Two major interests have motivated the present analysis: one in cultural conceptions of "pornography" and the other in forces of cultural socialization. A great deal of the mass media has been identified with, even defined as, "pornography," "obscenity," or "objectionable" material. Hard-core erotica (the sole, specific depiction of sexual action) has been referred to as "the mass media of sex," but now we find sex permeates much of the media around us; items readily available on the market that deal directly (girlie magazines) or indirectly (advertising) in erotica have been called "soft-core" pornography. Thus, the traditional and perennial question of obscenity—what are its effects?—is asked of a far wider range of material than before; in fact, many are asking that question of what they see to be no less than their total environment ("it's all around us!").

In addition, however, to the mere mention of acts, an extremely crucial aspect of erotica is the way in which sex is described with attendant values. It is this total configuration that becomes the major variable in socialization. Through this process of "social scripting"[2] acts, contexts, and consequences are spelled out as behavioral alternatives in various interpersonal settings. It is this that determines for the observer or reader whether the sex is arousing or not, moral or immoral, and consequently, pornographic or not.

Beyond the immediate action in the stories, we find that sexual behaviors and attitudes are inseparably linked to broader cultural symbol systems, and it is within these that we begin to find and understand what it is that may be "wrong" with certain kinds of activities. We know that sexuality, previously thought of as a monolithic "drive" that motivates and determines a number of behaviors and dispositions, is in fact much more diffuse in human personalities and social systems.[3] We may gain a sense of this linkage in the ways sex is connected to nonsexual values and activities in the lives and thoughts of people in the magazine stories.

With regard to socialization interests, it is known that many of the readers of confession magazines are adults, usually younger married lower-middle or lower class housewives, living in the Midwestern United States.[4] On the other hand, there are indications from initial observations by this author that many readers of the

"Love and Sex in the Romance Magazines" by David Sonenschein from JOURNAL OF POPULAR CULTURE, Vol. 4, No. 2, 1970, pp. 398–409. Reprinted by permission of Wiley-Blackwell Publishing.

magazines are of a different sort: younger girls of preteen years, usually from ages 9 to 12, are also attracted to the magazines. This population needs further definition in terms of its motivations and characteristics, but the need for socialization considerations for an age group younger than previously thought is established.

Eight different romance or confession magazines with a total of 73 fictional stories form the basis of the analysis. They were purchased from a downtown Austin newsstand and represent *all* of the magazines available on the stand at that time (one month's availability). While they are a "universe" of material at that point in time and space, they are a "sample" of a larger universe of published magazines. In 1966, there were 32 different confession magazines available; total readership was about 13 ½ million.[5] The magazines used here were published by five different publishers though there seems to be little difference among them with regard to editorial policies. Each magazine averaged about nine stories per issue.

An initial survey of their content was made by coding for aspects of format, characteristics of the narrator and main partner, sexual events and situations, and other factors that figures in the plots of the stories.

For those who have seen the magazines, it is clear that the most salient characteristic of them is sex. Throughout all of the format features, the themes of sex and the physical nature of people are heavily played upon. The immediate and initial appeal, however, is to the femininity of the potential buyer, an image with which she may most readily identify. For example, six of the eight magazines carry cover pictures of young females of a very wholesome sort; even those depicted in a "seductive" kind of pose (i.e., facial expressions, body postures, clothing arrangements and types suggesting eroticism) may still retain a look of innocence.

Surrounding the picture are the titles of the magazine itself and of the stories for that month, but, upon inspection, one is struck by the apparent incongruities of the two sets of images. The names of some of the magazines in the sample were such ones as REAL CONFESSIONS, SECRETS, INTIMATE STORY, DARING ROMANCES, and so on. The titles imply what is to be the nature of the stories. They promise to be stories of an intensely personal sort, the kind that one would confide only to one's closet friend. There is a strong element of wickedness and even sinfulness about the relationships to be described inside. Such large-type statements as

One Night A Week We Were Wicked— We Were Single Girls on the Prowl For Men! I Lost My Virginity—And Reputation— In The Boys' Locker Room! He Left Sex Out Of Our Dates—If He Loved Me, Why Didn't He Show It?!

all serve to heighten the anticipation for sex in a way that finds some correspondence with many popular judgments of what is seen to be "obscene:" *illicit* sex. Such activities as abortion, premarital sex, incest, and adultery are explicitly mentioned on the covers of the magazines.

In the table of contents, the stories are listed with a short statement of what is to be the basic theme, a kind of "abstract" of the story. Again, these statements serve to set up the reader for access to an illicit affair of the narrator. Some examples are:

"When I Say It Baby, You Do It—Anything
    And Everything!" His Vile Commands
Ring In My Ears, and There Is Nothing I
    Can Do To Escape His Ugly Desires!

"My Stepfather Taught Me Sex!" It's My
    Wedding Night—I'm In My Bridal Bed.
        But The Arms That Hold Me,
    The Lips That Seek Mine, Belong
        To My Mother's Husband!

There begins to appear a message that the narrator seems to have little control over the situations she finds herself in. All in all, however, 77% of the story titles directly implied some sort of *sexual* activity as the *main* theme for the story.

For each story, there is an accompanying photograph supposedly depicting some main event in the story. These were coded in a broad way for the kind and style of posing in the picture. Photos of couples predominate, with 22% involving kissing (some with partial undress), and 15% depict the couple in a situation that can be described as "erotic," that is, there is a salient sexual intent between the two individuals. In most of these latter cases, the couple is touching or is in some kind of physical contact. Consequently, 37% of the format pictures involve a sexual or at least a physical relationship. Thirty-three percent of the pictures represent some kind of fight, argument, or anguish, usually between a couple or in a family setting. This latter theme becomes significant as we shall see in the content of the stories.

Advertising was also coded for simple content and kind of appeal. Ads selling material of a mail-order dime store variety comprised a large category, 37% of all ads. However, the general category of "improvement" was the largest and most significant. In this there were two varieties. One was labeled "appearance improvement," and included such things as bust development, weight losing aids, fashions, and beauty aids; this comprised 36% of all the ads. Other kinds of ads based on a direct appeal to the improvement of one's self and position, such as loans, medicine, and religion, comprised 27%. In total, "improvement" advertising amounted to 63%.

The values of oneself as a physical being, more so as an appealing and in some ways a marketable physical being, are thus played upon heavily from the beginning. But we also start to get a sense of some of the risks that simply being a woman may entail. The relationships that await one, and the path through them that one must necessarily take, begins to seem more and more difficult. To what extent merely living life and being a woman means enduring punitive experiences are themes further elaborated upon in the texts of the stories.

Story types were classified into four general categories according to a classification set up by the editors of *TRUE STORY* magazine (one from 1958—not included in the sample) as a guide to potential authors. The resultant distribution on this basis was as follows:

Marriage story types   36%
Love story types   30%
Family story types   20%
Teenage story types   14%

It may be noted that the stories that deal with home life, marriage and family stories, total over half of the sample: 56%. The contextualization of the activities in the stories (recall the titles) are not as exotic, or erotic, as originally anticipated; they turn out to be settings that involve the basic values and symbols in our culture: the Home, Family, and Love.

Overwhelmingly, the narrator is female (90%), young in age (teenage, 36%, or in her twenties, 22%), fairly religious (34% of the narrators mentioned a Christian affiliation or a "general belief in God"), and usually a housewife, 41% (other occupations are secretarial/clerical/sales: 22%, or student, usually high school, at 16%). Race was, with one exception, unspecified but implied white. Fifty-one percent were married, 38% were single with no previous marriage. Married women usually had a small family of one or two children. The settings of the stories were usually in small towns, but if set in a large city, the narrator was mentioned as having come from a small town or rural area. The depiction of the narrator then is that she is just "average." Even her physical appearance is not especially gorgeous, but she is explicitly described many times as being "pretty." She is at the same time like all other girls, yet like all other girls want to be.

The life of the narrator is also "average," with problems that arise in any family which are not of a totally disabling sort. Money problems, for example, occur in 25% of the stories, housing problems in 21%, health difficulties in 16%, and occupational troubles in 14%. The complications in the lives of the narrators, however, derive not from aspects of a larger world or "society" (indeed, there is little that can be called social consciousness in the stories), but rather problems

come from the people in life, especially those close to the narrator, and from within the narrator herself. Life is a series of personal involvements, the management of which constitutes "life" or "living," and the existence of which "makes life worthwhile." Satisfaction comes from having a loving mate and having a supportive environment of "people you can get along with."

To return to the characters of the stories, the main partner of the narrator usually had fewer specified qualities. The main "other" was usually a male (69%), older in age, either the narrator's spouse (34%) or a previously unmarried single male (25%). His religion and race are unspecified but he appeals less to religion or the name of God, and no question ever arises over miscegenation. His occupation is given in general terms but usually set in skilled jobs or middle class office work.

Given the anticipation for sex as set up by the format, the actual incidence of activities was not as frequent as expected. Coitus is the most frequently occurring singular activity (63% of all stories) but more diffuse in its setting, "scripting," and consequences. Kissing occurs in second place (60%) but with more partners than coitus. Heavy petting is mentioned least of all in its specifics but occurs in 18% of the stories. Other kinds of sexual activity are rare. Incest is mentioned in only a few of the stories, homosexuality hinted at only once, and oral-genital activity never considered. Extra-marital sex occurs in less than 5% of the married cases. It is of note that the partners with whom the narrator has sex are either the spouse (27% for coitus) or a single male (i.e., only one: 25%). In most of the cases, therefore, sex takes place within the boundaries of an emotional relationship with one male. Despite the lure of the titles, promiscuity in the sense of frequent and indiscriminate sexual behavior does not occur as a behavioral mode. In those few cases where it does happen, the punishments for indiscriminate sex are swift and severe; they are dealt out in an almost destructive fashion so as to indicate that those kinds of consequences were what was to be expected anyway.

The disruptive troubles that beset the stories are those that have personalistic references; that is, as we indicated before, "people" are the causes of trouble and the kinds we see in the stories are of a particularly damaging sort. Relationships are volatile, hostile, and even dangerous; in contrast to male-oriented erotica, it is trauma, rather than sex, which is "just around the corner." In those relationships where sex occurs, the results for the people involved were destructive. In relations where sex occurred, 54% of the relationships worsened because of the event. Much of this, of course, happened in the case of premarital sex, but even in many instances of marital sex the message was that when sex is attempted to be used as a solution for a problem, or the basis for forming a relationship, it became evident very quickly that it was not the answer. According to the stories, then, guilt, anxiety, and personal difficulties for the narrator as well as damages to others are the costs of misusing or even just having sex.

Other themes of disruption occur significantly and regularly. Some are as follows:

Fight or argument in stories	70%
Mention of violence of any kind	53%
Loss of partner	36%
Guilt felt by narrator for coitus	34%
Loss of virginity by narrator	33%

Each of these, of course, may be elaborated upon separately, but we may mention here only how they cumulatively contribute to the feelings of uneasiness underlying each story. In nearly all the stories, the narrator goes through some sort of crisis; the crux of each, and the attraction for the readers, seemingly, is the *consequences* of events and their resolutions. This is in itself a separate topic for investigation, but story endings give us a clue. Forty-eight percent end on a note of the narrator having mixed feelings of guilt and hope, punishment and salvation. This derives from the narrator having gone through a basic and fundamental crisis that seems to involve one's psychological self, particularly as felt through the emotions of love and sex. Nineteen percent of the stories end on a completely sad tone, where punishment has come about with the tacit admittance by the narrator that she deserved what she got in the end. Even though others are in the environment who will, perhaps by their very nature, take advantage of the narrator, the burden of villainy is assumed by her. She has misused or misapplied herself and her sex in a way that brings not only punishment but retribution.

We noted that the crucial and emotionally involving aspect of the stories is not so much the sex itself but the "social scripting" of the sex, the perception of the partner and the narrator as "responsible" (as opposed to "responsive") beings, and the consequences of interpersonal commitment. The emphasis in the stories is that the purpose of life is the establishment of a series of dependable and stable sets of interpersonal relations, ideally to be founded upon that most stable and enduring of all forces, Love. To this, sex is only secondary; sex can be generated by love but love may be degenerated by sex. When we spoke of the "misuse" of sex, we were referring to the settings in the stories where relationships were attempted to be founded and sustained by sex. It couldn't be done.

We spoke of sex as being "diffuse" in both personality and sociocultural systems. We wish to place particular emphasis upon the latter and suggest that in addition to sex being connected to such things as roles, preferences, and activities, sex is at least distributed through, and at most generated by, a broader system of values which contains views of the world and the social order.[6] It is this latter set of orientations that determines the place and propriety of sex. From the scriptings in the romance magazines, a very explicit sense of what that value and symbolic order is can be obtained.

The basic theme of each story is the stabilization of one's personal life. This may occur in a variety of settings (as with our story types on marriage, etc.) and with a variety of results (getting married, getting divorced, getting pregnant, etc.), but the essence of life is the search for continuity through dependable relationships. It is very obvious in the stories that the most desired manifestations of this essential quality for life are marriage, a family, and love. These are the stable blocks on which daily life, and hence our culture and society, is built. These institutions are the resources for the relationships that allow for the expression of our "real nature." The crises in our stories all seem solvable by recourse only to love; love is the over-riding context of sex and any use of sex beyond this is taboo and destructive.

Here are the links between the values of legitimate versus illegitimate behavior. The condemnation of sexual activities and relationships is discussed not so much in terms of themselves but in terms of their consequences. Thus, activities and attitudes that threaten or violate the symbols and values of love, marriage, and the family are acts which endanger their very existence. The stability of these institutions is threatened by the volatile nature of sex itself and the enduring values of the institutions are threatened by sexual and emotional exploitation, "taking" rather than "giving." Sex cannot occur without love; by itself it is immoral, illicit, and even "obscene." Outside the institutions of family and marriage, it is even worse: it is "unnatural."

What we are led to is the conclusion that the condemnation and negative sanctioning of sex occurs when the continuity and stability of basic cultural institutions is perceived to be threatened or denied as valid and necessary. "Obscenity" and "pornography" in this sense are those acts and attitudes which violate fundamental and symbolic realms in our culture. We know historically the perception of this has varied with time and place, but we may explain the great variety of judgments that have occurred in the past on this basis.

The issues of obscenity and pornography are basically symbolic issues; they are connected to what is perceived to be the essential traditions of our society in its cultural values and social structures. Violations of these are what call forth the cries of the impending End of Civilization

As We Now Know It. Judgments of obscenity and pornography can be applied to a wider variety of things and behaviors, many of them non-sexual in nature. It is believed that widespread and continued indulgence in "obscene" and illicit acts creates a "moral collapse" and social destruction. The family is the fundamental sociocultural unit and the institution of marriage through love is necessary for its origin and continuance. "When these go, what else is there?" ask the magazines.

Contrary to our initial expectations, then, the romance magazines really appear to be paragons of virtue, arguing with a traditional, cultural morality for the necessity of love and the family and the minimizing of sex if one is to survive personally or socially. The effects and consequences of acting outside these values are spelled out in a fashion that explicitly details the risk. For the reader, the result is not a pretty picture.

Contained in the romance magazines and their explicit treatments of sex is the argument for the continuity of the American mode of life. Obviously, one of the main ways of establishing cultural continuity is to define the borders of deviance and state the consequences for going over. This is done by imbuing specific areas of interpersonal relations with an aura of heavy negative sanctioning. If a young female reader acquires the language of sex in the punitive terms that are portrayed in the magazines, we may wonder what the cost is of maintaining cultural continuity. The alternatives are limited for us in the media and the penalties are severe for the wrong choices. Yet the social order continues to be questioned and challenged. The problem is one that is demanding attention by its very protestations.

Notes

1. A revised version of a paper presented to a special session on "The Issue of Obscenity and Pornography in the Contemporary Media" for the American Association for Public Opinion Research (May, 1969). This paper is preparatory to a larger study of mass media erotica and popular culture funded by the Commission on Obscenity and Pornography. In operationalizing this, I am grateful to the following people who commented critically on earlier drafts: Eva Hunt, Nancy O. Lurie, Nancy L. Gonzalez, H. C. Dillingham, Brenda E. F. Beck, Alice Marriott, Carole Rachlin, Edward Sagarin, W. Cody Wilson, James L. Mathis, M. D., J. W. Mohr, Gunther Schmidt, and Roger Abrahams. Co-workers Mark J. M. Ross, Richard Bauman, and Morgan Maclachlan join in colleagueship in the newer project.

2. William Simon and John Gagnon, "Pornography—Raging Menace or Paper Tiger?" *Transaction IV* (1967), 41–48.

3. William Simon and John Gagnon, "On Psychosexual Development," in D. Goslin (ed.), *Handbook of Socialization Theory and Research* (Chicago: Rand McNally, 1969), 733–752; John Gagnon and William Simon, "Sex Education and Human Development," in P. Fink and V. Hammett (eds.), *Sexual Function and Dysfunction* (Philadelphia: Davis, 1969), 133–126.

4. Fawcett Publications, Inc., *Reader Characteristics* (New York, 1953); *Look* Magazine, *The Audiences of Nine Magazines: A National Study* (New York: Politz Research, 1955).

5. *Standard Periodical Directory* (2nd. ed., New York, 1967). A larger number of magazines for the new study has been obtained. However, due in part to the formalized nature of the stories, the present sample sufficed in yielding significant themes in proper proportions. General agreement was also found in the present study with two earlier surveys. See George Gerbner, "The Social Role of the Confession Magazine," *Social Problems* V (1958), 29–40; and Wilbur Schramm, "Content Analysis of the World of Confession Magazines," in J. C. Nunnall (ed.), *Popular Conceptions of Mental Health* (New York: Holt, Rinehart & Winston, 1961), 297–307.

6. David Sonenschein, "Pornography: A false Issue," *Psychiatric Opinion* VI (1969), 10–17; *ibid.,* "Pornography and Erotica in America," in E. Sagarin (ed.), *Sex and the Contemporary American Scene* (New York: Dell, 1970), in press.

1. Sonenschein questions whether or not romance magazines cross the line into obscenity. What purpose does this question serve for the research? For the written essay?

2. Sonenschein also notes that the "social scripting" of sex is more important than the actual sex in the magazines. How does he describe and/or illustrate social scripting?

CONNECTING TO YOUR CULTURE

1. Sonenschein determines that elements of popular culture, such as the romance magazine, serve to "define the borders of deviance" and to outline the consequences of breaking societal rules. What elements of popular media have defined societal rules for you?

2. What are these rules? What areas of your life are affected by these rules?

CONSIDERING IDEAS

1. Have you ever felt silenced because of your language, dialect, or speech patterns?

2. Have you ever felt that no one was listening to you? What made you feel this way?

3. How did you overcome this inability to communicate, if you did?

Maxine Hong Kingston *is a prolific fiction/nonfiction author with such titles as* Tripmaster Monkey: His Fake Book, *published in 1989, and her most recent title published in 2006 titled* The Fifth Book of Peace. *The excerpt included here is from her most famous book,* The Woman Warrior, *which won the National Book Critics Circle Award for Nonfiction and reflects her Chinese American cultural heritage.*

MEMOIRS OF A GIRLHOOD AMONG GHOSTS

Excerpt from The Woman Warrior

Maxine Hong Kingston

Long ago in China, knot-makers tied string into buttons and frogs, and rope into bell pulls. There was one knot so complicated that it blinded the knot-maker. Finally an emperor outlawed this cruel knot, and the nobles could not order it anymore. If I had lived in China, I would have been an outlaw knot-maker.

Maybe that's why my mother cut my tongue. She pushed my tongue up and sliced the frenum. Or maybe she snipped it with a pair of nail scissors. I don't remember her doing it, only her telling me about it, but all during childhood I felt sorry for the baby whose mother waited with scissors or knife in hand for it to cry—and then, when its mouth was wide open like a baby bird's, cut. The Chinese say "a ready tongue is an evil."

I used to curl up my tongue in front of the mirror and tauten my frenum into a white line, itself as thin as a razor blade. I saw no scars in my mouth. I thought perhaps I had had two frena, and she had cut one. I made other children open their mouths so I could compare theirs to mine. I saw perfect pink membranes stretching into precise edges that looked easy enough to cut. Sometimes I felt very proud that my mother committed such a powerful act upon me. At other times I was terrified—the first thing my mother did when she saw me was to cut my tongue.

"Why did you do that to me, Mother?"

"I told you."

"Tell me again."

"I cut it so that you would not be tongue-tied. Your tongue would be able to move in any language. You'll be able to speak languages that are completely different from one another. You'll be able to pronounce anything. Your frenum looked too tight to do those things, so I cut it."

"But isn't 'a ready tongue an evil'?"

"Things are different in this ghost country."

"Did it hurt me? Did I cry and bleed?"

"I don't remember. Probably."

She didn't cut the other children's. When I asked cousins and other Chinese children whether their mothers had cut their tongues loose, they said, "What?"

"Why didn't you cut my brothers' and sisters' tongues?"

"They didn't need it."

"Why not? Were theirs longer than mine?"

"Why don't you quit blabbering and get to work?"

If my mother was not lying she should have cut more, scraped away the rest of the frenum skin, because I have a terrible time talking. Or she should not have cut at all, tampering with my speech. When I went to kindergarten and had to speak English for the first time, I became silent. A dumbness—a shame—still cracks my voice in two, even when I want to say "hello" casually, or ask an easy question in front of the check-out counter, or ask directions of a bus driver. I stand frozen, or I hold up the line with the complete, grammatical sentence that comes squeaking out at impossible length. "What did you say?" says the cab driver, or "Speak up," so I have to perform again, only weaker the second time. A telephone call makes my throat bleed and takes up that day's courage. It spoils my day with self-disgust when I hear my broken voice come skittering out into the open. It makes people wince to hear it. I'm getting better, though. Recently I asked the postman for special-issue stamps; I've waited since childhood for postmen to give me some of their own accord. I am making progress, a little every day.

My silence was thickest—total—during the three years that I covered my school paintings with black paint. I painted layers of black over houses and flowers and suns, and when I drew on the blackboard, I put a layer of chalk on top. I was making a stage curtain, and it was the moment before the curtain parted or rose. The teachers called my parents to school, and I saw they had been saving my pictures, curling and cracking, all alike and black. The teachers pointed to the pictures and looked serious, talked seriously too, but my parents did not understand English. ("The parents and teachers of criminals were executed," said my father.) My parents took the pictures home. I spread them out (so black and full of possibilities) and pretended the curtains were swinging open, flying up, one after another, sunlight underneath, mighty operas.

During the first silent year I spoke to no one at school, did not ask before going to the lavatory, and flunked kindergarten. My sister also said nothing for three years, silent in the playground and silent at lunch. There were other quiet Chinese girls not of our family, but most of them got over it sooner than we did. I enjoyed the silence. At first it did not occur to me I was supposed to talk or to pass kindergarten. I talked at home and to one or two of the Chinese kids in class. I made motions and even made some jokes. I drank out of a toy saucer when the water spilled out of the cup, and everybody laughed, pointing at me, so I did it some more. I didn't know that Americans don't drink out of saucers.

I liked the Negro students (Black Ghosts) best because they laughed the loudest and talked to me as if I were a daring talker too. One of the Negro girls had her mother coil braids over her ears Shanghai-style like mine; we were Shanghai twins except that she was covered with black like my paintings. Two Negro kids enrolled in Chinese school, and the teachers gave them Chinese names. Some Negro kids walked me to school and home, protecting me from the Japanese kids, who hit me and chased me and stuck gum in my ears. The Japanese kids were noisy and tough. They appeared one day in kindergarten, released from concentration camp, which was a tic-tac-toe mark, like barbed wire, on the map.

It was when I found out I had to talk that school became a misery, that the silence became a misery. I did not speak and felt bad each time that I did not speak. I read aloud in first grade, though, and heard the barest whisper with little squeaks come out of my throat. "Louder," said the teacher, who scared the voice away again. The other Chinese girls did not talk either, so I knew the silence had to do with being a Chinese girl.

Reading out loud was easier than speaking because we did not have to make up what to say, but I stopped often, and the teacher would think I'd gone quiet again. I could not understand "I." The Chinese "I" has seven strokes, intricacies. How could the American "I," assuredly wearing a hat like the Chinese, have only three strokes, the middle so straight? Was it out of politeness that this writer left off strokes the way a Chinese has to write her own name small and crooked? No, it was not politeness; "I" is a capital and "you" is lower-case. I stared at that middle line and waited so long for its black center to resolve into tight strokes and dots that I forgot to pronounce it. The other troublesome word was "here," no strong consonant to hang on to, and so flat, when "here" is two mountainous ideographs. The teacher, who had already told me every day how to read "I" and "here," put me in the low corner under the stairs again, where the noisy boys usually sat.

When my second grade class did a play, the whole class went to the auditorium except the Chinese girls. The teacher, lovely and Hawaiian, should have under- stood about us, but instead left us behind in the classroom. Our voices were too soft or nonexistent, and our parents never signed the permission slips anyway. They never signed anything unnecessary. We opened the door a crack and peeked out, but closed it again quickly. One of us (not me) won every spelling bee, though.

I remember telling the Hawaiian teacher, "We Chinese can't sing 'land where our fathers died.'" She argued with me about politics, while I meant because of curses. But how can I have that memory when I couldn't talk? My mother says that we, like the ghosts, have no memories.

After American school, we picked up our cigar boxes, in which we had arranged books, brushes, and an inkbox neatly, and went to Chinese school, from 5:00 to 7:30 P.M. There we chanted together, voices rising and falling, loud and soft, some boys shouting, everybody reading together, reciting together and not alone with one voice. When we had a memo- rization test, the teacher let each of us come to his desk and say the lesson to him privately, while the rest of the class practiced copying or tracing. Most of the teachers were men. The boys who were so well behaved in the American school played tricks on them and talked back to them. The girls were not mute. They screamed and yelled during recess, when there were no rules; they had fistfights. Nobody was afraid of children hurting themselves or of children hurting school property. The glass doors to the red and green balconies with the gold joy symbols were left wide open so that we could run out and climb the fire escapes. We played capture-the-flag in the auditorium, where Sun Yat-sen and Chiang Kai-shek's pictures hung at the back of the stage, the

Chinese flag on their left and the American flag on their right. We climbed the teak ceremonial chairs and made flying leaps off the stage. One flag headquarters was behind the glass door and the other on stage right. Our feet drummed on the hollow stage. During recess the teachers locked themselves up in their office with the shelves of books, copybooks, inks from China. They drank tea and warmed their hands at a stove. There was no play supervision. At recess we had the school to ourselves, and also we could roam as far as we could go—downtown, Chinatown stores, home—as long as we returned before the bell rang.

At exactly 7:30 the teacher again picked up the brass bell that sat on his desk and swung it over our heads, while we charged down the stairs, our cheering magnified in the stairwell. Nobody had to line up.

Not all of the children who were silent at American school found voice at Chinese school. One new teacher said each of us had to get up and recite in front of the class, who was to listen. My sister and I had memorized the lesson perfectly. We said it to each other at home, one chanting, one listening. The teacher called on my sister to recite first. It was the first time a teacher had called on the second-born to go first. My sister was scared. She glanced at me and looked away; I looked down at my desk. I hoped that she could do it because if she could, then I would have to. She opened her mouth and a voice came out that wasn't a whisper, but it wasn't a proper voice either. I hoped that she would not cry, fear breaking up her voice like twigs underfoot. She sounded as if she were trying to sing though weeping and strangling. She did not pause or stop to end the embarrassment. She kept going until she said the last word, and then she sat down. When it was my turn, the same voice came out, a crippled animal running on broken legs. You could hear splinters in my voice, bones rubbing jagged against one another. I was loud, though. I was glad I didn't whisper. There was one little girl who whispered.

1. Kingston says her "silence was thickest—total—during the three years [she] covered [her] school paintings with black paint." How does she then explain, or show, what she means?

2. Which of Kingston's word choices give clues as to the time period she attended school? When do you think she went to school?

3. Kingston uses numerous metaphors and similes—"fear breaking up voice like twigs underfoot," for example. What do these add to her writing?

1. Kingston refers to herself and others by racial and ethnic labels—for example, Chinese, Japanese, Negro, and Hawaiian. Why are these labels so important to her and her story? If she was writing this today instead of the mid-'70s, would she use the same terminology?

2. How do the differences in teaching styles affect the students' learning? Their self-images?

3. Kingston asks her mother to tell her the same story over and over again. Why? What purpose does the repetition serve?

4. Do you have any family stories you ask for over and over again? Why do you want to hear them repeatedly? What is their significance?

Reading Selections: the '80s

CONSIDERING IDEAS

1. Do you like to read horror novels or watch horror films?

2. Do you like the experience of being scared? What frightens you the most?

3. What scared you when you were a child?

Tony Magistrale *is an expert when it comes to the genre of gothic and horror fiction. His primary focus is on the works of Stephen King as evidenced by the five books Magistrale has written about the horror author. He has also written several articles for popular periodicals dedicated to the study of horror fiction. He is currently an associate professor and associate chair of the English Department at the University of Vermont. "Inherited Haunts" was first published in* Extrapolation *in 1985.*

INHERITED HAUNTS

Stephen King's Terrible Children

Tony Magistrale

On March 25, 1984, in Boca Raton, Florida, Stephen King delivered the closing address at the International Conference on the Fantastic in the Arts. Following a discussion about King's childhood readings in the horror genre, someone in the audience asked the author the question, "What terrifies you the most?" King's reply was emphatic and immediate: "Opening the door of my children's bedroom and finding one of them dead."

King's dread that his offspring could be harmed has not inhibited his use of infantile and adolescent characters throughout his writing, which has achieved wide notoriety and brought a degree of untoward fame on its author. It is a fiction centering on excursions into terror, surreal fantasies which spring suddenly to life, the dark spirits that inhabit a deserted town or hotel. His stories are populated with demons and ghosts, monsters and phantoms. And his youthful protagonists are besieged by a variety of these creatures. This siege is in keeping with the foreword to his collection of short tales in *Night Shift,* where King insists that a requisite for a successful horror story is its ability to "hold the reader or listener spellbound for a little while, lost in a world that never was, never could be." Yet one of the major reasons for King's commercial and critical success as a horror writer is his uncanny ability to blend and convolute the artifacts of everyday reality, replete with brand names and actual geographical locations, with the incongruous and startling details of an imagined realm. In creating this blend, King displays no neglect for the humans who inhabit his works, be they children, many of whom appear to be endowed with either supernatural powers or an uncommon trait, or adult protagonists, the majority of whom are, by and large, middle-class men and women eking out a living in contemporary America. For varied reasons (sometimes accidental, usually deliberate) these characters find themselves suddenly and helplessly enmeshed in the Gothic machinery of a nightmare from which they will not awaken. King's people are not superhuman, but ordinary, flawed, and vulnerable. In his tales, good must struggle against evil, and from the encounter become less good. Behind this moral backdrop, he invests the majority of his protagonists with a persuasive sympathy: we care about these people, hope they will somehow discover a way to survive, and continue reading about the unfolding of their fates with a curious mixture of fascination and apprehension, because in many ways his literary characters represent our own fears and values.

King's most memorable and important characters, and the ones to whom we as readers grow increasingly attached, are his children. Frequently they form the moral centers of his books, and from

"Inherited Haunts: Stephen King's Terrible Children" from EXTRAPOLATION 26.1 (Spring, 1985) by Tony Magistrale, pp. 43–49. Reprinted by permission of American Library Assosiation.

them all other actions seem to radiate. In King's fiction, children embody the full spectrum of human experience; they are identified with the universal principles of ethical extremes. Some represent the nucleus for familial love. They are often healing forces, as in *Cujo* and the first halves of *The Shining* and *Pet Sematary,* enabling parents in unstable marriages to forgive one another's human failings. On this level of being, many of King's children represent the principle of good in a corrupt world; they seem both divinely inspired and painfully cursed with prophetic knowledge. Danny Torrance in *The Shining*, Carrie White in *Carrie,* and Charlie McGee in *Firestarter* possess superhuman abilities that trigger death and destruction, and yet these children elicit our sympathy because they appear more often in the role of victim than victimizer. It is not really the children who are responsible for their various acts of destruction, but the adults who mislead and torment them.

At the other moral pole are the adolescent hunters—the denim fascists in "Sometimes They Come Back," *Christine,* and *Carrie,* who portray ambassadors from an immoral world, their sole purpose being to wreak destruction on anyone or anything weaker than or different from themselves. These "children" have completely severed their bonds with innocence; in their vicious lust to exploit sex, alcohol, and violence, they model their behavior on an extreme conception of adulthood. They want all the pleasures of worldly experience, with none of the responsibilities. Thus, they are simply young versions of the corruption which animates King's adult society. If they manage to live long enough, they will become the Jack Torrances (*The Shining*), John Rainbirds

(*Firestarter*), and Greg Stillsons (*Dead Zone*) of the next generation.

The adults in King's world act frequently as children; they explore places where they have no business going, their behavior is often immature and without conscience, and their institutions—the church, the state's massive bureaucratic system of control, the nuclear family itself—barely mask an undercurrent of violence that is capable of manifesting itself at any given moment. The daily interactions in their marriages and neighborhoods bring out the worst in King's adult characters; they revert to the meanness of adolescence, acknowledging their selfish urges only after they have set in motion a series of events which lead to catastrophe. Throughout the novel *Carrie,* for example, Carrie White is forced into the role of persecuted outsider. Her first and greatest impediment to a normal life is her mother, a woman indoctrinated with a fierce religious fanaticism who refuses to teach Carrie the adjustment skills necessary for survival in the real world. Consequently, Carrie's discovery of her menstrual period—the initial event associated with the emergence into womanhood—brings her only fear and loathing. Her mother translates the biological function into a symbol of corruption sent by God to punish women. As a direct result of her mother's negative sermonizing, and motivated by the final humiliation of having a bucket of pig's blood dropped on her head at the senior prom, Carrie uses her telekinetic powers to destroy everything in sight. Since no one is either willing to, or capable of, guiding Carrie through the difficult transition from adolescence to adulthood, distinctions between good and evil lose their significance for her, and Carrie's night of carnage includes those who are innocent along with those who are culpable. Her only introductions to adulthood are presented through images of violence and pain, and all of Carrie's subsequent reactions become a grotesque reflection of what she has experienced personally. As King himself explains the novel in *Danse Macabre,* "Carrie can only wait to be saved or damned by the actions of others. Her only power is her telekinetic ability, and both book and movie eventually arrive at the same point: Carrie uses her 'wild talent' to pull down the whole rotten society."

The theme of innocence betrayed is at the heart of *Carrie.* Indeed, this concept unifies the major work of King's canon: throughout his fiction, the power of evil to malign and pervert innocence is omnipresent. Louis Creed (*Pet Sematary*), Jack Torrance (*The Shining*), and Arnie Cunningham (*Christine*), sacrifice their families and sanities when they succumb to the lure of evil. Evil becomes a pervasive force that these characters cannot resist. Creed

© United Artists/The Kobal Collection

is attracted to the power of the Micmac burial ground despite its obvious dangers; Torrance probes the history of decadence and violence in the Overlook hotel and yearns to become part of it; and in his automobile from hell, Arnie Cunningham surrenders both his personality and his soul to avenge a lifetime of frustration. In King's novels and stories, there are few heroes; at best his major characters endure, but they seldom prevail. Like the young protagonist in the tale "Graveyard Shift," his men and women are usually (and often literally) overwhelmed by the legions of the underworld.

The most effective dramatization of King's dark vision occurs through the interaction of adults and children. His children, in spite of their goodwill and special gifts, are shaped and motivated by adults who are enmeshed in a personal struggle with evil. Most often, his young protagonists—Gage Creed, Danny Torrance, Charlie McGee—are forced to pay for their fathers' sins of curiosity; their innocence is the price for an intimate examination of evil.

The short story "Children of the Corn" is one of the more sophisticated illustrations of this formula. A young couple, their marriage in disarray, stumble upon Gatlin, Nebraska, a town where time has apparently stopped. Instead of August 1976, Burt and Vicki discover calendars and municipal records that go no further than 1964: "Something had happened in 1964. Something to do with religion, and corn . . . and children." Moreover, there are no adults in this town, only children under the age of nineteen.

The time period is certainly of crucial importance to the story's meaning. But King never completely explains its mystery. Nor is it clear immediately why all the adults have been killed and why no child is permitted to survive past the age of nineteen. Like Vicki and Burt, the reader is supplied only with information about an Old Testament Jehovah whom the children worship in the corn fields. In return for their human sacrifices, he invests the crop with a special purity: "In the last of the daylight [Burt] swept his eyes closely over the row of corn to his left. And he saw that every leaf and stalk was perfect, which was just not possible. No yellow blight. No tattered leaves, no caterpillar eggs, no burrows."

Reading King's best fiction is like visiting a city with innumerable corners of intriguing complexity and atmospheres that reward lingering absorption. "Children of the Corn" encourages the reader to linger over multiple interpretations. On the most obvious level, it is a story of religious fanaticism dedicated to a malevolent deity. But such a reading does not, however, explain the significance of the 1964 time setting—the initial period of active involvement by American forces in Vietnam—and its relationship to the fertility of the Nebraska corn. Both appear irrevocably linked. Listening to the radio outside the town, Vicki and Burt hear a child's voice: "There's some that think it's okay to get out in the world, as if you could work and walk in the world without being smirched by the world." And later in the story, after he has learned the awful secret of the town, Burt wonders if human sacrifices were ordained because the corn was dying as a result of too much sinning.

Although King is cautious to avoid so overt a nexus, the reader with any sense of history will recall the violation of the land in Vietnam by such toxic chemicals as Agent Orange. Man's technology carried the poisoning of the soil, not to mention the levels of death and carnage, to the point at which the land itself (the allegorical corn god) demanded repentance. If we place the events of this story in such a context, it becomes possible to understand why all the adults past the (draft?) age of nineteen are sacrificed. These are the individuals who were most responsible for the war, for the "adult sins" that defiled and destroyed acres of Vietnamese landscape, thousands of American and Vietnamese lives, and, finally, what was left of America's innocence. For Vietnam was, among other things, America's collective cultural emergence into the "adult world" of sin and error. Our loss of innocence and our recognition of self-corruption is what gave impetus to the antiwar movement. In trying to decide whose side God favored in this war we were shown with painful certitude that life is a more complicated mixture of good and evil than we earlier had assumed. King's own view on the immorality of the Vietnam experience, as expressed in *Danse Macabre*, corresponds precisely with such an inter- pretation: "By 1968 my mind had been changed forever about a number of fundamental questions. . . . I did and do believe that companies like Sikorsky and Douglas Aircraft and Dow Chemical and even the Bank of America subscribed more or less to the idea that war is good business."

Burt and Vicki are therefore sacrificed because they are adult representatives of fallen, post-Vietnam America. Both have strayed from any sense of a belief in God, their marriage is in disharmony; both appear as selfish, stubborn, and unforgiving individuals, they are anxious to pass through Nebraska and travel on to "sunny, sinful California"; and Burt is a Vietnam veteran. References to this last point are made on three separate occasions, but the most significant reference occurs immediately after Burt discovers the 1964 time setting. While standing on a sidewalk in the town, he smells fertilizer. The odor had always reminded him of his childhood in rural upstate New York, "but somehow this smell was different from the one he had grown up with. . . . There was a sickish sweet undertone. Almost a death smell. As a medical orderly in Vietnam, he had become well versed in that smell." The association between Vietnam and Nebraska and its corn fields, and the disenchantment inherent in adult experience, is maintained on similar symbolic levels throughout the story. Nebraska and its corn are in the "heartland" of America, its moral center, and out of an effort to reestablish the purity and innocence of an earlier era, both the corn and the land itself seem to be demanding adult penance for a sin that originated in 1964.

King's corn god is furious with the adult world, demanding blood in exchange for reclaiming the land from its state of spiritual and physical barrenness. Burt discovers the god's maxim written on the cover of the town's registry: "Thus let the iniquitous be cut down so that the ground may be fertile again saith the Lord God of Hosts." The very fact that the ground needs to be made "fertile again" suggests that it has suffered from some kind of pestilence. And the "disease of the corn" in this tale, while ambiguous throughout, can be interpreted in terms of American defoliation of the Vietnamese landscape, as well as the more symbolic

cultural "illness" of moral guilt and spiritual taint that accompanied American war involvement.

The human sacrifices in "Children of the Corn" have been successful; vitality has been restored to the American soil. The corn itself grows in flawless rows. Moreover, as Burt discovers while running wounded through the open fields, the soil even contains a mysterious recuperative power: "The ache in his arm had settled into a dull throb that was nearly pleasant, and the good feeling was still with him." The corn deity has made the land, and all that comes in contact with it, into an agrarian Arcadia, a neo-Eden of pristine perfection and harmony. But to maintain this environment, the corn deity exacts from this symbolic American community in Nebraska a never-ending cycle of adult penance and revenge. In fact, at the conclusion of the story the corn god lowers the age of sacrifice from nineteen to eighteen, suggesting that the inherited guilt and shame of Vietnam will never be completely exorcised.

In *Danse Macabre*, on the other hand, King states that he has "purposely avoided writing a novel with a 1960's time setting . . . . But those things did happen; the hate, paranoia, and fear on both sides were all too real." King may not have directed his energies into a full-length novel, but in "Children of the Corn" he has provided us with a frightening little allegory of the decade's major historical event. It is also interesting, given the time setting for "Children of the Corn," that the "adult world" is interpreted as sinful and in need of punishment. In the sixties, American youth were in the streets directing a cultural critique of the mores and values of their parents. The adults were the enemy; they had perpetuated the war in Vietnam and had sent America's children to perform the killing and the dying.

In Stephen King's Gothic landscape, horror often springs from social reality: the failure of love and understanding triggers disaster. King's world is a fallen one, and evil is perpetuated through legacies of sin, based in social, cultural, mythical, and historical contexts, and handed down from one generation to the next. Adulthood, because of its litany of selfish mistakes, broken marriages, cruel machinations, and drunken excesses, fully embodies this legacy of human corruption; adults show themselves capable of betrayal at any point. The inevitable violence and cruelty which are the usual end results of adult values and behavior force King's adolescent protagonists to relinquish their tentative hold on innocence and sensitivity. Gage Creed, the young boy in *Pet Semetary,* becomes a grotesque extension of The Wendigo, a creature from the pre-Christian world, because the human adults, Louis Creed and Jud Crandall, avail themselves of the unholy power within the Micmac burial ground. Charlie McGee's childhood in *Firestarter* is abruptly and hideously fragmented by the government's manipulation of her parents' chromosomes and the Shop's desire to extend the experiment. The child is caught in a conflict over the morality of using her superhuman powers. Knowing her confusion, the Shop engages in psychic blackmail, forcing her to refine her abilities and use them for destructive purposes. Although she cooperates with their devious methods, Charlie loses both parents, is betrayed by a surrogate father, and faces an uncertain future of fear and flight. In the short story "Last Rung on the Ladder," an attorney becomes so involved with his career and his reputation in the world that he fails to heed the plea for help issued from his misdirected younger sister. As a child, he was always there to protect her and lend his support, but as an adult he is too preoccupied. When she finally commits suicide, in large measure because of his failure to become involved, he is left with the enormous burden of responsibility.

Finally, King's novella, *Apt Pupil,* from the collection *Different Seasons,* works with a similar set of suppositions. Todd Bowden, a precocious adolescent fascinated with the grisly details of Nazi Germany, discovers an aging war criminal, Dussander, sharing his suburban American neighborhood. Over a period of years the child's fascination deepens into obsession, as he practices more devious and intricate methods of extracting a personal history from the Nazi officer. Through the course of their long relationship, the boy is slowly transformed into a version of the Nazi adult: his interest in schoolwork and sports is abandoned in favor of stalking and butchering helpless drunks and indigent street people. It is a complex, albeit overwritten, study of negative adult influence and the corrupting fusion of evil: the Nazi's oral history of death camp atrocities exacts an intimate, active response from the high school student. Todd may never have been a paragon of moral purity or innocence (in fact his psychological torment of the officer suggests quite the opposite), but steady contact with Dussander pushes him into a deeper, more serious, and personal participation in evil. By the conclusion of the novella, the child relinquishes all control over his own life; he is forged from the same furnace of hate that created the Nazi.

King's children, like those found in Dickens' novels, illustrate the failings of adult society. The destruction of their innocence accomplishes more than a simple restating of the universal theme of the Fall from Grace; it enlarges to include a specific critique of respective societies and cultures as well. Like Todd Bowden in *Apt Pupil,* the children in "Children of the Corn" are neither symbols of purity nor sensitivity. Yet, similar to many of King's other, more sympathetic adolescents—Carrie, Charlie McGee, Danny Torrance, Gage Creed—they are victimized by the inherited sins of an older world. In each of these examples, the children are constrained to pay for the mistakes of their elders; they do so, significantly, at the expense of their own transition into adulthood.

DECODING THE TEXT

1. In this analysis essay, does it matter if you, the reader, know all of the characters discussed?

2. Does Magistrale give enough information to make his point even if you haven't read King's novels (or seen films based on his stories)? Does he give away too much of the texts?

3. Does his analysis interest you in reading any of King's texts?

CONNECTING TO YOUR CULTURE

1. According to Magistrale, King's children "illustrate the failings of adult society." What failings does he describe? What failings would you add to the list?

2. How does the children's loss of innocence help them move past these failings? What cultural events have led to the loss of innocence in U.S. society?

3. What events in your life have led to the loss of your innocence?

CONSIDERING IDEAS

1. The term *coming out* is often used in connection to gay and lesbian identity, but in reality, people "come out" about a variety of lifestyle issues and experiences. Have you ever come out to your friends, family, or co-workers about some issue in your life?

2. How did it make you feel—before and after?

3. Is coming out necessary? Why or why not?

Sally R. Munt, *a professor of media and cultural studies at the University of Sussex, focuses her research on cultural formations. She has authored three books, including* Murder by the Book? Feminism and the Crime Novel, *and edited several others. She has also written numerous book chapters and journal articles.* "Mystery Fiction" *was first published online in* GLBTQ: An Encyclopedia of Gay, Lesbian, Bisexual, Transgender, and Queer Culture *in February 2007.*

MYSTERY FICTION

Lesbian

Sally R. Munt

Although most lesbian mystery fiction reflects a political stance, the most effective lesbian crime novels have been those that have most enthusiastically embraced the need to entertain the reader.

The lesbian mystery novel has its origins in the ubiquitous lesbian pulp fictions of the 1950s and early 1960s. A paradigm of deviance, drugs, and urban decay located these literary lesbians in lonely antithesis to the security of the law-abiding suburban American dream.

Such popular potboilers constituted a plethora of splendidly sordid sensationals blessed with such titles as *Strange Sisters, The Shadowy Sex,* and *Lesbians in Black Lace.* These books were primarily about sex, supposedly written for prurient heterosexual males, but lesbian readers loved them.

The thrilling glimpse into an underworld of intrigue and suspense is redelivered in the lesbian crime novels of the present, which allow us to step into, relish, and then render safe a quagmire of sex, violence, and death.

The Lesbian Feminist Crime Novel
The first lesbian feminist crime novel was M. F. Beal's *Angel Dance* (1977). Its angry, complex, visionary indictment of heterosexual and patriarchal capitalism is steaming with the peculiar energy of 1970s protest culture. The Chicana detective and first-person narrator Kat Guerrera is a subversive. The character embodies the way class, race, gender, and sexuality interface to uphold the hegemonic order of law. The corrupt power of the state is represented as being so extensive that concepts of "justice" can no longer be invoked.

This figure of the lesbian guerrilla was an icon of 1970s resistance culture, as distilled by French materialist philosopher Monique Wittig in her 1971 novel *Les Guérillères.* This invention of a new, militant category of lesbian, inspired by the myth of the Amazon, invigorated a whole community of women to declare war on the political institution of heterosexuality. The lesbian detectives reproduced this figure in the 1980s and 1990s.

The traditional crime novel is a site for the expression of anxieties about society in which the enemy is named and destroyed. In the lesbian and feminist crime novel, the terms often become inverted so that the state is identified as the corrupt enemy, and the lesbian sleuth, normally the feared and hated Other, is the victor.

The narrative resolution of the mystery is resolved in two stages: First, by using the process of individuation intrinsic to the thriller mode, the lesbian hero achieves self-determination; second, she becomes integrated into a community. The first phase is often represented by coming out, the second frequently by finding love or discovering the lesbian community, in a movement toward politicized integration.

Forming an Identity through Solving a Crime

These structures are to be found in other lesbian literary genres, but in mystery novels the formation of an identity happens through the solution of a crime. The central narrative device and locus of readerly pleasure is discovery.

For example, in an early feminist bestseller, *Murder in the Collective* by Barbara Wilson (1984), we meet Pam Nilsen, thinly disguised Proto-Dyke. Her hands sweat and her body is wracked by erotic fevers as she gulps and swallows in the presence of Hadley. They eventually manage to consummate their lust; however, the romantic tension is yoked to the crime fiction hermeneutic of alternate disclosure and disappointment.

Pam's new identity gives her individuality through a sense of difference, not just from her (heterosexual) twin, but in the series of dialectical oppositions set up by the text around race, class, gender, and sexuality.

"Identity" is seen as a transitional process of discovery involving contradictory states of desire—for sex and for a new "self."

Identities that Change to Fit the Times

The new identities offered to the reader of the lesbian mystery novel are dependent upon the possible political alternatives presented by any given cultural period or context. Thus, texts of the 1970s offer different models of sexuality from texts of the 1980s or 1990s.

Early lesbian feminist crime novels of the 1980s tended to be inflected by the specific countercultural discourses of that time, structuring men as the enemy and making lesbian feminism a heroic principle. The signposts of lesbian feminism—sisterhood, collectivism, "wimmin's" energy, and "wombyn's" anger—are smattered throughout these texts.

By the mid-and late-1980s, however, the prerogative of identity politics had seemingly superseded the earlier lesbian feminism, and consequently, a complex critique of diverse social forces began to emerge.

A British attempt to disrupt racial and gender stereotypes can be found in Claire Macquet's *Looking for Ammu* (1992). The cover-blurb promises "A film noir world where distinctions between saints and sinners become devastatingly uncertain," thus invoking the urban dystopian tradition of the hard-boiled crime novel in which perception itself, intrinsic to investigation, is at best unstable, at worst morally flawed.

Looking for Ammu breaks with feminist crime convention by rejecting the model of a supersleuth. White nursing tutor Harriet Weston, a prissy, conceited, repressed, self-righteous narrator, pursues her mythologized mentor, Black Dr. Ammu Bai. As Harriet tries to find the missing Ammu, the investigative trajectory incisively deconstructs the sign of Black-Woman-As-Mystical-Enigma, signaling how sexualized and racist this dominant narrative construction is.

Thus, a formally noble act of discovery is revealed—through some viciously satiric writing—as self-interest. That the narrator is in love with her idol is plain from the first chapter. Evoking the classic way White Westerners have fantasized the Black Other, the text lays bare the eroticism in this White gaze. The text manipulates the generic certainties of both detective and romance fiction to leave the reader questioning the representation of desire.

Problematizing the Heroic
Lesbian mystery fiction has consistently problematized the use of the heroic in the crime novel. A swathe of novels predominant in the mid-1980s self-consciously appropriated the image of the avenging knight, proferring a sexy superdyke striding the city streets in her steel-capped Doc Martens, swinging her double-headed axe, dispensing slain patriarchs in her wake. This was one form of transgressing the genre.

Later manifestations made more explicit the legacy of butch-femme roles in this image. These literary figures made more acceptable pre-Women's Liberation lesbian sexual identities, which were becoming reintegrated and reformed for the new sexual cultures of the 1980s and 1990s.

However, is the fact that so many dyke detectives appeared as *butch* fantasies due to the regrettably intransigent masculine conventions of the genre? Or is the effect on the representation of the heroic rather more destabilizing, more parodic? The

figure of the detective is crucially a fantasy of agency, which is culturally conflated with masculinity in both the dominant culture and within feminism itself. Could a femme detective focus our desires so effectively?

As a subcultural stereotype, the butch detective works at two levels of identification for the reader. Not only does the reader desire the butch, she also wants to *be* the butch. In her outlaw status, the butch detective promises a romantic, forbidden fantasy and the incarnation of a felt alienation that is fictionally empowered. The convention of the detective hero is appropriated and destabilized by the parodic acknowledgment that the complex sign "butch" can encapsulate a field of contradictions, primarily dependent on readerly projections.

Detective Fiction as Satire
In genre theory, detective fiction has been most likened to satire. Menippean satire, in its simplest form, consists of a dialogue between stylized characters who merely mouth ideas. The two speakers are an eiron, the hero, and an alazon, someone usually revealed to be a deluded and pompous fool. The alazon's self-delusion is continually confirmed in inverse relation to the eiron's discernment.

The lesbian crime fiction detective's dramatic function is to expose alazons using her ratiocinative powers, thus leading the reader into a changed and enlightened consciousness. The feminist ideological project presents patriarchy and heterosexism as synonymous with alazony, thus "false consciousness" is revealed by an investigation into gender relations.

It is a persuasive structure that artfully seduces the proto-feminist reader. The protagonist or eiron is able to scrutinize the hysterical excesses of masculinity with a deflationary gaze. Masculinity, in these narratives, usually ends up shooting itself in the foot.

Interweaving Suspense with Pleasure

The novels that achieve the most convincing critique of patriarchy, heterosexism, and masculinity have not done it through "political correctness" or even through the simple moral dualism that lesbian equals good and patriarch equals bad. The most effective lesbian crime novels have been those that have most enthusiastically embraced the need to entertain the reader, to interweave suspense with pleasure.

Those, such as *She Came Too Late* (1986) and *She Came in a Flash* (1988) by Mary Wings, which reproduce most faithfully the classic element of satire, succeed most as popular novels. The defining glance of the detective is to reveal the real and sordid nature of the world, but this revelation is achieved obliquely, through the sideways glance of satire.

Novels that are consciously satiric employ a heroine who tends to undermine her own transcendence. Sarah Dreher's serial antihero Stoner is a case in point: She humorously incarnates the misfit motif pandemic to lesbian identity; she is a detective outlaw who can reassuredly exorcise the reader's internalized homophobia. Like the classical fool, she attracts the laughter of self-recognition; she is the awkward, soft-hearted butch who parodies back to ourselves our inflated desires for a heroine.

The Parodic Reinvention of Roles

Urban sexual identities during the 1980s were inflected with a self-conscious irony expressed through the parodic reinvention of roles for sexual interaction. Lesbians as a group are highly self-conscious and ironically self-deferential; along with other minority cultures, they have recognized the destabilizing potential of parody. Having a sense of humor is an essential survival tool for lesbians, necessary to deflect some of the damage dominant homophobic and misogynistic discourses inflict on us.

Thus lesbian crime novels, by their double deflationary gaze—at the sex-gender system and at ourselves—swing the two-headed axe liberally not just to destroy, but also to carve out and recombine new kinds of identities for us to inhabit.

For example, Barbara Wilson's *Gaudi Afternoon* (1990) is symptomatic of the shifting debates that see gender and sexual identities as, in the words of Judith Butler, "performative strategies of insubordination." Seeing gayness as being a "necessary drag," Butler regards the sense of play and pleasure so prevalent in the production of homosexuality as fundamentally destabilizing the seriousness and "naturalness" of heterosexuality.

Gaudi Afternoon concerns Cassandra Reilly, a translator who is hired by Frankie from San Francisco to find her gay husband in Barcelona in order that he might sign some family papers. But the novel soon degenerates into comic gender picaresque. Cassandra's task is to chase a circling chaos of individuals involved in a custody contest where each claims to be the real mother.

Frankie, the "wife," is actually a male-female transsexual; Ben, the "husband," is a radical feminist bulldagger; April, her New Age cultural feminist "girl"friend, is an Earth Mother who dislikes children and a male-female transsexual, but Ben doesn't know it; April's "friend" is her gay closet-cross-dressing stepbrother with whom she shares "shame issues."

In this world where there is no grounding reality of the physical, there is no final recourse to the body either, as in the nature-culture opposition. All is "up for grabs," and the only conclusion to draw from this parodic cacophony is the rejection of "true sexualities" in favor of the hilarious creativity of inventing new ones. The fun is in the performance—the process—not the end result.

The Influence of Postmodernist Aesthetics
The more literary of the lesbian crime novels have experimented with a kind of parodic inventiveness infused by postmodernist aesthetics. Sarah Schulman's works most clearly exhibit this confluence of interest. Every literary form evolves, and even during the short period of time in which this subgenre has developed, identifiable trends toward a more metafictional awareness can be detected.

Many of the earlier novels such as Vicki P. McConnell's *Mrs. Porter's Letter* (1982), *The Burnton Widows* (1984), and *Double Daughter* (1988) were little more than pulp romances, published by the highly popular Naiad Press, renowned for producing the lesbian sentimental "quickie"; but the form also soon diversified into the various permutations to be found in the mainstream and traditional detective genre.

For example, the classic Golden Age format of the country house murder exemplified by Dorothy L. Sayers and Agatha Christie structures *Something Shady* (1986) by Sarah Dreher, and a North American

interpretation of the small town mystery is the format of Dreher's later novel *A Captive in Time* (1990).

A related British subgenre—one that allows for the inclusion of lesbian "teenage crushes"—is the girl's school mystery, such as *Report for Murder* (1987) by Val McDermid and *Hallowed Murder* (1989) by Ellen Hart.

The police procedural that has been popular in mainstream U.S. crime fiction since the 1960s is rewritten with a lesbian cop-hero in *Amateur City* (1984), *Murder at the Nightwood Bar* (1987), and *The Beverly Malibu* (1989), all by established lesbian genre author Katherine Forrest. *Lessons in Murder* (1988), *Fatal Reunion* (1989), and *Death Down Under* (1990) are Australian versions by Claire McNab.

The Urban Dystopia
The urban dystopia allows the exploration of gender and sexuality in the city and particularly stresses themes of the urban oppression of women; examples are *Death Strip* (1986) by Benita Kirkland, *Sisters of the Road* (1986) by Barbara Wilson, and *Jumping the Cracks* (1987) by Rebecca O'Rourke.

The hard-boiled private eye is the essence of the American form; a masculinized hero alienated from the urban jungle is turned into a lesbian in *She Came Too Late* (1986) and *She Came in a Flash* (1988) by Mary Wings and *A Reason to Kill* (1978), *Work for a Million* (1986), and *Beyond Hope* (1987) by the Canadian writer Eve Zaremba.

The supernatural chiller, such as *The Crystal Curtain* (1988) by Sandy Bayer, improvises themes of spirituality from cultural feminism—indeed almost all of

Camarin Grae's novels contain these mysterious elements.

The Amateur Investigator

Crime fiction has a long tradition of female investigators, but the lesbian mystery novels that proffer an amateur investigator are unimaginable without the kinds of interventions into the workplace that feminism made in the 1970s. *Cass and the Stone Butch* (1987) and *Skiptrace* (1988) by Antoinette Azolakov and *In the Game* (1991) by Nikki Baker all offer ironic versions of the lone woman supersleuth.

In the British novels *Report for Murder* (1987), *Common Murder* (1989), and *Final Edition* (1991), she is dressed as the journalist-investigator.

The Political Thriller

Finally, lesbian mystery fiction has also appropriated the political thriller in *Blood Sisters* (1981) by Valerie Miner and *The Providence File* (1991) by Amanda Kyle Williams. Both works deal with terrorism, but from opposite ends of the political spectrum. Lesbian mystery fiction has exploited a variety of formula fictions, and a diversity of ideological belief is represented in them.

Conclusion

Many of these books are enjoyable as pulp fictions. They exploded into the new markets created by gay consumerism during the 1980s. Gay and lesbian publishing enterprises have flourished in the post-Stonewall era in "out and proud" purchasing communities.

In creating our own popular culture, we have inevitably drawn on the mainstream models offered to us, and the resultant combinations vary in form and content. The crime novel, with its legacy of socialist critique (Dashiell Hammett, for example, was a communist), its formal relationship to parody, and its tendency to produce antiheroic narratives, contains elements favorable to countercultural appropriation.

But the lesbian crime novel had its heyday under the individualistic era of Reaganism and Thatcherism. It often posed answers to crime and social problems in the form of personal rather than structural acts of justice. Its *modus operandi,* in a decade when television was inundating us with programs that fictionalized the upholding of—rather than the resistance to—hegemonic versions of the law, must cause us to consider what readerly needs were being satisfied.

Popular narratives are never wholly reactionary nor wholly radical because despite their offering us dominant reading positions to occupy, readers will always find a way to read "other-wise," to put their own particular needs and interpretations into the text. This is how we can read Hitchcock's film *Rebecca* (1940) as a lesbian thriller.

With the lesbian crime novel, we can speculate why it proliferated during a decade of individualistic identity politics, in the aftermath of the liberation movements of the 1970s. We can observe that lesbian feminist science fiction—the literature of utopian vision, of hope and social possibilities—was the favorite form of the 1970s but became passé by the 1980s.

Crime fiction allows us to express anxieties about a period of conformity, conventionalism, and crackdown, but did it give us any impetus for new formulations of the law?

1. Munt uses subheadings throughout her essay. What purpose do they serve?

2. Who is Munt's primary audience for this essay? How does awareness of this audience affect her writing style or word choice? How else does it affect the essay?

CONNECTING TO YOUR CULTURE

1. Munt discusses the intersections of race, class, gender, and sexuality. How do these identity markers affect the novels she is discussing? The readers of the novels? The readers of the essay?

2. How can solving a crime or some other problem lead to self-discovery and identity formation?

3. Can you identify a time in your life when solving a problem helped you learn something about yourself? Can problem solving help you learn about others as well?

Reading Selections: the

CONSIDERING IDEAS

1. What series books were popular when you were in elementary, middle, and high school?

2. Did you read these texts? Why or why not?

3. What is the appeal of a series rather than individual novels?

Sally Lodge *is a contributing editor for* Publishers Weekly *and has written a vast number of articles dealing with children and youth literature. She also regularly contributes to PublishersWeekly.com's "TalkBackPost," where readers are allowed to comment on the topic presented. "Life After Goosebumps" was first published in* Publishers Weekly *in 1996.*

LIFE AFTER GOOSEBUMPS

In the Wake of R. L. Stine's Sizzling Chiller Series, the Kids' Horror Genre Assumes Monstrous Proportions

Sally Lodge

"WARNING: MONSTERS INSIDE! . . . Wherever you go, they will find you." "Welcome to the next level of terror." "No one hears your screams!" Splashed across the covers of three current children's paperbacks, these tag lines may well prove off-putting to unsuspecting bookstore browsers. But countless kids are willing victims, thrilled to be chilled by what lurks within.

Typical of horror-series hype, such pitches are snaring millions of middle-graders and teens whose idea of a good read is a tale that gives them, well, goose bumps.

And *Goosebumps*—R. L. Stine's spooky, spectacularly successful series from Scholastic—appears to be largely responsible for getting this gargantuan ball rolling. *Goosebumps* boasts an astounding 160 million copies in print, and titles in the series (now numbering 50) sell at the rate of more than four million a month. Created by packager Parachute Press and launched in July 1992, Stine's series now has incarnations on TV, CD-ROM and videocassette, and has spawned an array of products from more than 40 licensees, who offer everything from *Goosebumps* bike helmets and skateboards to boxer shorts and sneakers.

A glance at the paperback lists of children's publishers offers a broader picture of what is available. There are a handful of obvious—and admitted—imitators, as well as some series with different, and sometimes inventively warped, twists. In an attempt to determine the extent, nature and fate of publishers' offerings in this genre, PW spoke with some of the players in the kids' thriller-horror publishing game.

The Source of the Scares

Though Dracula, Frankenstein, the Headless Horseman and other creepy creatures have given young readers the shivers for many generations, *Fear Street*, the first mass market horror series for kids, appeared less than a decade ago from Pocket Books' Archway imprint. Also penned by R. L. Stine, *Fear Street* was created for a young adult audience. Jane Stine, the author's wife and executive v-p of Parachute Press (which she and president Joan Waricha founded 13 years ago), recalled *Fear Street*'s precedent-setting conception. "The prevailing wisdom at the time was that one couldn't publish horror as a series," she said. "Christopher Pike and others had of course written individual horror titles, but it was hard to imagine how one could craft a whole series, since it was thought that a series needed to have the same characters reappearing. Then we came up with the idea of setting stories on *Fear Street*—a place where strange things happen—

which gave the books a continuity and a basis for a series."

The Stines' *Fear Street* proposal landed on the desk of Pat MacDonald, Pocket Books' v-p and editorial director of Archway and Minstrel, through "serendipity" according to MacDonald. Having signed up and edited Christopher Pike's *The Last Act* and *Spellbound*, MacDonald was not only knowledgeable about the genre, but she had herself been mulling over the possibility of publishing a horror series. When Archway released the first *Fear Street* book, *The New Girl*, in 1989, she recalled, "some people in the business weren't at all convinced that the series would work, but I was willing to take the chance."

With the 70th title due this month and more than 41 million copies in print, *Fear Street* has proved a chance worth taking. And, as often happens when publishers of children's series strike gold (remember *Sweet Valley Twins* and *Baby-sitters Little*

It's a field of screams!

THE SCARECROW WALKS AT MIDNIGHT
SCHOLASTIC

Cover from GOOSEBUMPS #20: THE SCARECROW WALKS AT MIDNIGHT by R.L. Stine. © 1994 by Scholastic Inc. Reprinted by permission of Scholastic Inc.

Sister), the horror series concept was soon adapted for a younger audience. Devising some less frightening, fatality-free plots, R. L. Stine wrote the first *Goosebumps* novels for Scholastic. Then in 1995, the author took middle-grade readers for a stroll down the less scary side of Fear Street with the debut installment of *The Ghosts of Fear Street*, whose 16 volumes now have an in-print total of more than eight million copies.

Veteran thrillmeister Pike also began publishing for the eight-to-12-year-old crew in fall '95, when Minstrel Books released the initial titles in his relatively tame *Spooksville* series. With this month's release of its 13th book, this series has more than 2.5 million copies in print.

Going After *Goosebumps*

It took very little time for others in the industry to recognize how much younger kids wanted books for themselves like the ones spooking their siblings. And it seems that Bob Stine was just the writer to nourish this interest, given his inimitable knack for concocting just the right brew for his audience, adding enough that is funny to take the edge off what is frightening. This, and his ability to snag the ever-elusive middle-grade boy reader, has played a large role in *Goosebumps*' enviable domination of the genre.

Four years after the initial *Goosebumps* releases were shipped to stores, at least three dozen similarly themed series are crowding booksellers' shelves, and publishers have pulled the plug on at least a half-dozen others that suffered from sluggish sales. Virtually every editor contacted who has a program competing with Stine's line freely gave *Goosebumps* credit for setting the standard. Wryly referring to "the 'G' word," Jessica Lichtenstein, senior editor of Harper Paperbacks, who oversees its *Bone Chillers* series, commented that *Goosebumps* "gave everyone in this business a frame of reference and a sales handle. As much as we're all competing with *Goosebumps*, we owe its creators special thanks for making the middle-grade horror genre easier to classify and to market."

Evidently opting not to tinker with something that is not broken, several publishers have shaped series that, in their view, compete directly with *Goosebumps*. "We're not looking for a new angle—we're taking *Goosebumps* head-on," said Roy Wandelmaier, v-p and publisher of Troll, whose *Deadtime Stories* debuted in September. Aided by Troll's presence in the school book fair and book club markets, the series is off to a rousing start: by year's end, Wandelmaier estimates, there will be two million copies of the first seven titles in print. Sisters Annette and Gina Cascone (who use the pen name of A. G. Cascone) have contracts to write 17 *Deadtime Stories*, which will be published monthly through December '97. "We signed this series up last year when we saw how popular *Goosebumps* had become," Wandelmaier candidly stated. "We're confident we have a good formula, though we obviously have a long way to go before we match *Goosebumps*' sales."

Similarly, former Bantam chairman Lou Wolfe made no bones about the model for *Shivers*, the new series his Lake Worth, Fla.-based River Publishing has developed for Paradise Press. "Are we copycats?" he asked. "Sure! But book for book, we think ours are as good or better. But let's let nine-year-old readers be the true judges." Though Wolfe didn't rule out the possibility that the series will eventually be distributed through other channels, *Shivers* titles are currently found only in such outlets as Dollar Stores, Odd Lots and Target. Written by a team of authors under the pseudonym of M. D. Spenser, the series has 2.5 million copies of its inaugural 12 titles, released in September, in print. Another 12 books are due in January.

New Twists on Terror

Craig Virden, v-p and publisher of Bantam Doubleday Dell Books for Young Readers, captured the sentiments of most publishers queried when he said: "It seems that most of us have pretty much given up competing with *Goosebumps* on its own turf. I believe these days the key is to find the new thing that will engage kids, to psych out the market for the next stage." Among Bantam's entries in the kids' horror genre are the *Graveyard School* series by Tom B. Stone and the *Choose Your Own Nightmare* series, a spin on the publisher's popular reader-interactive format.

Goosebumps' own publisher is banking on the allure of a horror-SF hybrid in its *Animorphs* series by Catherine Applegate, which started up in June. Jean Feiwel, Scholastic's senior v-p and editor in chief, called the concept "an *X-Files*-type of idea for middle-graders; anything can happen here—and it does." Sales are certainly happening: as the fifth title, *The Predator*, shipped early this month, there were more than two million *Animorphs* titles in print. And the genuine *X-Files* article, licensed by Harper Trophy, is faring well in stores, obviously bolstered by the successful TV show on which the books are based. Begun in June '95, the middle-grade series has sold 1.25 million copies of its first eight titles. Trophy will debut a line of YA tie-ins to the adventure program next June.

Also exploring SF territory is a brand-new Bullseye series titled *The Web*, Tom Hughes's tale of ancient, giant spiders who return to reclaim the earth. Ruth Koeppel, senior editor for Random House Children's Publishing, explained: "It's very hard to compete with *Goosebumps* when the books are written at the same level. We wanted to strike out in a new direction, and this sci-fi angle seemed to make sense. These books have a horror edge but also cash in on the current interest in big bugs." Another Bullseye series, launched in August, is Carol Ellis's *Fangs*, which Koeppel described as "vampire-specific."

This company is taking a classic tack with its newly renamed Random House *Chillers* line, which plans to issue such timeless eerie tales as Monica Kulling's adaptation of Robert Louis Stevenson's *The Bodysnatcher*, due next spring. And Koeppel also mentioned a recent conservative tide among publishers of kids' horror-related books, some of whom are showing an interest in "starting small" rather than launching a series with multiple titles and pricey fanfare. As an example, the editor pointed out a single volume, *Phantom Trucker*, by newcomer Jason Friedman. "This is a book that could definitely spawn a series," she remarked. "But we're going to wait and watch the response to it."

At Harper Paperbacks, Lichtenstein talked of how a well-respected author can give a series a "leg up." Fitting that description is Betsy Haynes, whose *Bone Chillers*, launched in spring '94; now has 12 titles

and 1.5 million copies in print. "In this case," Lichtenstein said, "the author's voice immediately created a buzz about the series and has been key to its success." And the buzz is likely to amplify, since ABC-TV has recently begun airing a live-action Saturday morning show based on *Bone Chillers* plots. The publisher plans to advertise its books during the episodes, each of which concludes with an appearance by Haynes.

Taking a different approach to the issue of author recognition is Avon's *Spine-tinglers* series, whose 16 releases have been created by various writers, though all carry the pseudonym M. T. Coffin. Editor Stephanie Siegel pointed out the advantage of having a range of authors contribute to the series, noting that "the writers have no specs to follow. Each book has a different voice and a brand new plot angle." The publisher is promoting *Spinetinglers*, which has more than one million copies in print, with a forthcoming contest for youngsters, the winner of which will serve as a model for a character in a future book.

Pushing the Age Limits
Not surprisingly, those series aimed at beginning readers de-emphasize the horror aspect in favor of humor so as not to, in the words of Ellen Krieger, Aladdin's v-p and editorial director, "send seven-year-olds screaming into the night." Acting on the belief that there was an open slot in the market for youngsters whose older siblings were hooked on *Goosebumps*, Aladdin last spring issued the first in its *Scaredy Cats* series, which, Krieger quipped, "we actually referred to as 'Gosling Bumps' in its early stages." The publisher plans at least 12 titles for the series.

Lightheartedly likening *Goosebumps* to "the Blob, sucking up everything in its path," Grosset & Dunlap president Jane O'Connor also opted to start up a series for younger readers rather than compete with the omnipresent beast on its home ground. Aimed at children six to eight, *Eek! Stories to Make You Shriek* will include eight volumes by spring '97. An outgrowth of a single title which O'Connor herself wrote and published in 1992, the series showcases the work of a number of authors and illustrators.

The Black Cat Club, an early chapter-book series from Harper Trophy introduces a girl ghost who joins a club of young ghostbusters. The two debut books by Susan Saunders are speedily moving through their 25,000-copy first printings, reports Stephanie Spinner, Trophy's editorial director, who called Saunders "a very strong writer who came up with a wonderful premise for a series."

Luring Teen Readers
Some publishers hope to snare *Goosebumps* graduates before they move on to Stephen King. Pat MacDonald noted three recent Archway series that aim for older readers: Pike's *Fear Street Sagas*, which delivers "historical horror"; *Night World* by L. J. Smith, offering "romantic horror, where your soulmate becomes your enemy"; and M. C. Sumner's *Extreme Zones*, "terrifying supernatural tales."

A project from the Random House Cyber Fiction imprint has a multimedia handle—and perhaps presages things to come. Spun off from a "cyber serial" launched in March on a World Wide Web site, the *Lurker Files* by Scott Ciencin presents novelizations of online stories that evolved from the author's interaction with thousands of teenage keyboarders. In September, the publisher shipped 50,000 copies of each of the series' two inaugural releases, *Know Fear* and *Faceless*, and packaged the latter with a disk containing information about the characters and clues to the whereabouts of the Lurker (a menace who is controlling the minds of students on a college campus). The books are selling briskly, primarily to readers between the ages of 15 and 25, Ruth Koeppel reported, adding that *Lurker Files* releases are scheduled through 1997.

"Catch the blockbuster book series that gives you more than just goose bumps" urges the in-Scholastic's-face promotional copy for another venture that boasts its own Web page. Written by Marty Engle and Johnny Ray Barnes Jr., the 22 volumes in the *Strange Matter* series are supernatural plots involving such legendary characters as the Loch Ness monster and the Abominable Snowman. Released by San Diego–based Montage Publications, this series has a follow-up series, *Strange Forces*, for slightly older readers. Laura Hill—who, as "director of strange things," has the liveliest title we encountered—described it as intended for "readers a half-step above *Goosebumps*, but not yet ready for *Fear Street*." Also created by Engle and Barnes, *Strange Forces*, a sequential series based on characters introduced in *Strange Matters*, has its own Web page as well. Hill reported a combined in-print figure of two million copies for the two series.

Accepting No Substitutes
On the basis of booksellers' reports, it's evident that *Goosebumps'* pervasive popularity has led to a resolute brand-name loyalty on the part of young readers, who do the monster's share of the buying themselves. "It's the *Goosebumps* name

that has hooked them, not the genre," noted Pamela Kempf, assistant manager for children's books at Borders' Rockville, Md., store. "Kids head right for the *Goosebumps* display and don't look to the right or the left at any other series."

Lorna Ruby, buyer for Lauriat's in Canton, Mass., remarked, "Our YA and middle-reader paperback sections are at least 50% horror, but the spinoffs don't fare nearly as well. When you look at sales of *Goosebumps* and *Fear Street*, you realize that R. L. Stine has magic in his name."

Happily under Stine's spell, ardent young fans admit to largely ignoring the competition. Conversations with several *Goosebumps* aficionados revealed that, though some read an occasional horror title by other authors, their allegiance to Stine (who is, youngsters unanimously proclaim, "much funnier" than other horror writers) is unwavering. Their parents, who said they are likely to help fund but don't initiate their kids' *Goosebumps* purchases, echoed booksellers' comments that this series has attained the status of "way cool" among kids, who compete with each other to amass the greatest number of titles—even if some spines remain uncracked. "I've heard from at least one parent," Kempf said, "that their children don't actually read every book—they just want to collect them to keep up with their friends."

BDD's Craig Virden believes that the children's paperback business has a relatively new focus on what he called "kid-initiated purchases."

"Instead of appealing to parents and teachers," Virden said, "we are now marketing to kids. We're all going after a share of their pocket money, which gives young readers a power they didn't have 20 years ago." He acknowledged how difficult it is to lure strong-willed young purchasers away from their favorite brand, noting that this, along with what he perceives as an overcrowded market, has been responsible for the demise of a number of *Goosebumps*-inspired horror series, including Bantam's *Doomsday Mall*, which met its own doom after six releases.

And, despite reported millions-plus in-print figures, five out of six independent booksellers responded that they stock but a single one. "Middle-grade kids don't want the rip-offs, so I don't stock any of them," said Collette Morgan, co-owner of Wild Rumpus in Minneapolis, who reported brisk sales of *Goosebumps* titles and success with several new beginning-reader series, especially *The Black Cat Club* and *Scaredy Cat* titles. Likewise, Kim White at Crocodile Pie in Libertyville, Ill., stocks no other middle-grade horror series, explaining that "R. L. Stine does such a good job that my customers want only his books."

Similarly, Borders' Celeste Risko reported that though she stocks a fairly extensive selection of kids' thrillers, the majority have failed to "take off for us." Calling publishers' output "definitely overkill," Risko believes that there are too many competitors for too little shelf space and, given kids' magnetic attraction to *Goosebumps*, it is, in her words, "almost impossible to introduce another series that will sell well, given the instant name recognition of *Goosebumps* and the fact that tie-in product is everywhere. Though we try most new series from major publishers, none is even in the same field as *Goosebumps* in terms of sales."

Risko did point to Montage's *Strange Matters* and Scholastic's *Animorphs* as two bright spots on the sales horizon, and she predicts that the latter may well mutate into the next kids' series craze. "We're seeing a slight slippage in *Goosebumps* sales, which may mean that the horror genre in general is slowing down. I think a lot of the imitators started up too late and it may be a series in a related but slightly different genre—*Animorphs*—that is the next big wave."

The Bottom Line

Despite some stores' *Goosebumps*-only stance, kids' diehard loyalty to Stine and the general consensus that there's a glut of ghouls and gore in the market, publishers are obviously still willing to take a stab at the genre.

Though editors commonly acknowledged that kids' horror shelves are indeed groaning, none voiced serious concern that the current slew of series are strangling each other, but rather alleged that their entries in the field are living up to expectation and bringing in respectable revenue—though admittedly not to the point of giving *Goosebumps* a scare. Virtually all concurred that Stine is a nearly impossible act to follow, yet publishers are obviously willing to follow in its wake. And to Stine's credit, *Goosebumps*' would-be audience-snatchers betrayed no sour grapes. Instead, many expressed their resounding admiration for the author's inexhaustible imagination and deftly delivered humor, echoing Jane O'Connor's belief that such success "couldn't happen to a nicer guy."

Stine's *Goosebumps* was not an overnight success, a point Scholastic's Feiwel is quick to make. *Goosebumps*' popularity evolved as kids became more involved in the stories and spread the word. It wasn't a planned marketing strategy or effort to capitalize on a perceived mania.

Jane Stine at Parachute Press isn't at all razed by the slew of spinoffs. "Truthfully, we're not sitting around gnashing our teeth about imitators," she said. "The way we look at it, if *Goosebumps* and *Fear Street* have inspired other series, this means that kids have even more reason to go into a bookstore and greater incentive to develop the habit of reading for pleasure. We're proud that we've created this niche—and something magical that has captured the imagination of kids. This is what's important."

1. According to Lodge, how did the *Goosebumps* series become so popular with young adult readers? What has been the result of Stine's success?

2. This essay also uses subheadings. Do they serve the same purpose(s) as the subheadings in Munt's essay?

3. Likewise, Lodge plays with words throughout the essay—for example, the subheading The Bottom Line for the conclusion. What effect does she create with this wordplay?

1. Lodge discusses the publishers' marketing of books to children's expendable income. Do all children and young adults have expendable income? How does this affect what kinds of books are written?

2. Research shows that women purchase more books than men. Do you think this is true for male and female children as well?

3. What reading and book-buying patterns have you observed?

CONSIDERING IDEAS

1. The top ten list is a common phenomenon in U.S. culture, occurring in a variety of different contexts. Why are making lists and ranking so important?

2. Why do these lists often start at the bottom and move to number one?

3. When creating a top ten list, what factors do you need to consider?

Andy Smith *is a staff writer for Sequart.com and an avid comic fan who reads comics from across the spectrum of the genre. He often writes under the pseudonym Andrew Daniels to avoid being confused with the artist Andy Smith. "The Ten Most Important Comic Books of the 1990s" is on* The Comic Book Bin *website and first appeared in 2007.*

THE TEN MOST IMPORTANT COMIC BOOKS OF THE 1990s

Andy Smith

The 1990s was an incredible decade for comics. More people were buying and reading them than ever before and, in turn, more new publishers and new titles came into being. We had the formation of the superstar independent in Image Comics and the birth of the still un-equaled VALIANT Universe, a high water mark in storytelling, as well as a host of others trying to imitate the two. Gimmick covers and variants were all the rage, but we loved them and (don't tell Marvel) we still do. We were all going to be rich because the generic hot book of the week was going to be the next big thing. Well hindsight is 20/20 and with that in mind, let's chart the Ten Most Important Comic Books of the 1990s.

Number 10 - *Authority* #1

Authority #1 is very similar to the number one book on this list. Both books changed the way superhero teams are written, they both caused a storm when they were released, and they both brought a modern reality to comics. So, why isn't this book Number 1? Well, while the impact of the *Authority* in all three aspects is not as great as the Number 1 book, there is also one additional and very telling difference. In re-creating *Stormwatch* for the *Authority,* Warren Ellis fashioned characters who took matters into their own hands, cutting through the politics dealt with by the *JLA* and the *Avengers.* Both of those books, and a host of others, have adopted this approach since Ellis pioneered it, but that's where the innovation ends. The *Authority* is a really fun comic book that looks and feels like a blockbuster movie—something enjoyable like *Bad Boys 2*—but not a piece of art, and certainly, not a masterpiece. Nevertheless, the innovations in illustrations and writing, and the subsequent influence on similar books, make *Authority* #1 a worthy entry at Number 10.

Number 9 - *Daredevil* #1

Produced under the Marvel Knights banner, *Daredevil* #1 was a harbinger of things to come. Joe Quesada proved he had the skills required to innovate the production process, reimagine an ailing icon, and still keep fans happy. *Daredevil* #1 was a key moment on his journey to the top of Marvel's creative mountain and a forerunner for the *Ultimate* line. But, even more important, is the other half of the book's creative team. Long time comic book fan and successful filmmaker, Kevin Smith, blazed a trail for writers from outside the medium. Before Joss Whedon, Bryan Singer, Brad Meltzer and Orson Scott Card could make waves, Kevin Smith had to prove that fans would accept an outsider. Smith was also crucial to the formation of Hollywood's current love affair with comics. He showed studios and the world that comics were cool, both through his work writing the book, and in associating himself with the medium.

Number 8 - *Solar* #0

The best single issue of the decade and number four on *Wizard's* list of the top ten best comics over the last fifteen years. Jim Shooter, Barry Windsor-Smith and Bob Layton, all at the peak of their powers, tell the story of the birth and death, and then birth again of the VALIANT Universe. Originally serialized in the first ten issues of *Solar Man of the Atom,* the story set the tone for every science fiction and superpowered book that has come since. Shooter used real science, and even explained complex ideas, to firmly ground his epic. But, the real genius of the book is its focus on one man, Phil Seleski, and his struggle to come to terms with waking up to find he has the power of a god. Barry Windsor-Smith provides his best work since the final issue of his *Conan* run, while Jim Shooter only had to wait six months to top this (but we'll get to that).

Number 7 - *Astro City* #1

In *Astro City,* Kurk Busiek created a series based on good writing and accessibility. It sparked a trend in which collectors started reading Image books for the first time and, more importantly, brought a new audience into comics. *Astro City* made fans of those who had never, and probably would never, have read a comic otherwise. Core titles such as *Spider-Man, X-Men* and *Superman* have a steep learning curve for new readers due to their lengthy histories and the inaccessibility of the comic book medium. In *Astro City,* each issue is a new beginning and is presented without many of the visual and narrative shortcuts that are conventions of the comic book medium but confusing for many first-time comic readers.

Number 6 - *Magnus* #1

The first superhero book published by VALIANT Comics marks the birth of the only publisher to have ever seriously given Marvel and DC a run for their money. VALIANT did what Image was supposed to do: Create a roster of completely original characters under a shared universe, and they succeeded with both style and swagger. VALIANT came out of the gate with a winning formula—a top quality product with great storytelling. The VALIANT name soon became associated with quality and everything they did turned out golden. VALIANT was the Gucci of the comics industry.

Jim Shooter began the famous *Steel Nation* story line in *Magnus* #1 and it ranks among the best of all time (#17 according to *Wizard's Top 100 Trade Paperbacks*). *Magnus* #1 would have placed higher but it only set in motion what would eventually spark a revolution.

Number 5 - *Marvels* #1

Marvel gave this mini-series the royal treatment with high quality paper and a transparent acetate cover, but the real quality was from the creative team. Following the approach pioneered by VALIANT Comics, Kurk Busiek chronicled the beginnings of the Marvel universe in a distinctly real setting. We see the first Marvel heroes interact with a world that isn't used to superpowers or heroism. More interestingly, and probably more importantly, this

book was fully painted by (and marks the break-out of) Alex Ross. Ross has since gone on to define comics for a generation of readers and creators with his vividly realistic paintings. Like the greats before him (Kirby, Steranko, Miller, etc.), Ross has since become a public figure and a respected artist throughout the world—but it all started right here.

Number 4 - *X-Men* #1

Marvel found a winning formula with *Spider-Man* #1 and repeated it less than a year later, but this time they pulled out all the stops. They united one of the hottest artists in the field, Jim Lee, with one of the hottest properties, the *X-Men,* in a new series with five different covers on the first issue. The comic had one of the biggest marketing campaigns in comics history: Marvel was aiming to break records, and break records they did. *X-Men* #1 still stands as the highest print-ordered comic in history with more than eight million copies in all versions.

Among collectors, the pairing of Lee and the *X-Men* further established the mental association of a big talent on a popular book equaling a good product, which led to a string of new short-lived titles with big-name creators. More importantly, it proved the power of the industry's superstar artists and set the stage for their eventual departure and the formation of Image Comics.

Number 3 - *Superman* #75

As the story goes, the day *Superman* #75 hit the stands there were lines outside comic shops across the country. *The Death of Superman* was a major news story that was covered by the likes of CNN and *Time* magazine. It was the death of an icon— probably the most famous character in all of comicdom. In hindsight, it was nothing more than a publicity stunt by DC, but it worked spectacularly. *Superman #75* had one of the largest audiences in comics' history, and in turn, one of the largest print runs. Suddenly everybody was collecting comics and the hobby was flooded with speculators. Sports card dealers (who had just suffered a huge crash in their own market) shifted their attention to comics, creating a vast new audience. The entire industry benefited, but at a great cost: Event books and gimmicks were all the rage, and *The Death of Superman* was soon followed by major changes to almost every character conceivable—most memorably *Batman, Green Lantern* and *Daredevil.* The flashy covers and excessive hype got old quickly and much of the new audience moved onto the next hottest craze, sending the industry into a low it's still struggling to overcome. Eventually, *Superman* did return, but *Superman #75* still stands as a unique moment in the decade—when the eyes of the world were focused on comic books, a feat not repeated until the opening weekend of the first *Spider-Man* movie.

Number 2 - *Spawn* #1

At the height of his popularity, Todd McFarlane left Marvel and *Spider-Man* behind to create his own character. *Spawn*'s inaugural issue was one of the top selling comics in history, and unlike a number of other Image creations, has stood the test of time—the book just reached its 150th issue. But, McFarlane did more than create a hit book with *Spawn.* *Spawn #1* is the book that built an empire. MacFarlane has since added to his publishing wing by forming a major toy company built on the *Spawn* characters and a multimedia division that has produced a *Spawn* animated series and a movie.

Often recognized as one of the most important characters created since Stan Lee and Jack Kirby created the Marvel icons, *Spawn* might have nabbed the number one spot on this list had the character been a more exceptional creation. But the book's writing was never a big part of its success. As part of the first wave of books released under the Image Comics banner, *Spawn #1* is a marker of an event that changed the face of the comics industry. Image comics is the creator-owned start-up founded by the seven, now famous and, in some cases infamous, superstar artists of the comics world. Image was supposed to break up the monopoly of Marvel and DC, and for a while it looked like it might. Today, Image continues to provide creators with an alternative publishing route for their properties and remains a symbol of independence for the industry.

And the comic book of the decade is . . .

Number 1 - *Harbinger* #1

In the editorial, VALIANT's Editor in Chief, Jim Shooter, tells us that *the book we hold in our hands is the most important since* Avengers #1. Thirteen years later and I'm still not sure that he was wrong. When this book was first released it was a national sensation. Every kid worth his polybag and backing board just had to have one, and the resulting frenzy sent the book to the top of *Wizard's Top Ten Hottest Books List* for a then-record four months. What's more, the demand didn't stop even when the book began selling for well over $100. When it was good, *Harbinger* was without a doubt one of the best written books in comics history.

The first story line (*Children of the Eighth Day*) deserves to be uttered in the same

© 2008 VALIANT Entertainment, Inc.

breath as the masterpieces of the art form; *Watchmen, Maus, Dark Knight Returns,* etc.

The book's creative team reinvented the genre popularized by the *X-Men.* The good guys did unforgivable things, the bad guys were usually more right than the good guys, and best of all, they behaved like real people would—in the VALIANT Universe, when you want to kill your enemy, you don't challenge him to a stand-off at your base on the moon (this is actually a plot involving the *X-Men*), you send someone he trusts to shoot him in the back of the head. Things happen in *Harbinger* that would never happen in an *X-Men* book (for those that know *Harbinger* think Torque), but happen all the time in the movies and other arts, and definitely in real life. Most importantly, *Harbinger* was the book that sparked a revolution in comics. *Harbinger* was the *Pulp Fiction* of the comics industry—an indie critical and

commercial smash hit that changed all the rules and broke down the door for a host of independent talent. Without *Harbinger,* VALIANT wouldn't have become the third largest publisher as quickly as it did. Without *Harbinger,* there wouldn't have been an Ultraverse Universe or a Crossgen Universe. Without *Harbinger,* there wouldn't have been a wake-up call for the rest of the industry to move away from gimmicks and hype, and back to quality story-telling.

Twenty more that almost made the list:

Adventures of Superman #500 (DC)—The sequel to *Superman #75* with equally high orders, the book's poor quality left a bad taste in readers mouths' and set the ball rolling that would crash the industry.

Bloodshot #1 (VALIANT)—The day *Death of Superman* hit the stands there wasn't one line outside comic shops across the country, there were two—one for *Superman* and one for *Bloodshot.*

Bone #1—The biggest consistently successful independent book and the second independent book to achieve success after *Cerebus.*

Dark Horse Presents 5th Anniversary Special (Dark Horse)—The first appearance of *Sin City.* Miller's creation has shown outsiders that comics are more than superheroes.

Death, the High Cost of Living #1 (Vertigo)—The first book published under the Vertigo Comics banner.

Gen 13 #1 (Image)—The second hoorah of the bad girl craze and the beginning of a new slate of successful Image books.

Harbinger #0 Pink Cover (VALIANT)—The most sought-after variant of the decade and the hardest book to find from the most sought-after story-line of the decade.

Kingdom Come #1 (DC)—Cemented Alex Ross as the artist of the decade and pushed the back-to-basics writing approach into overdrive.

Lady Death #1 (Chaos)—The start of the Bad Girl craze. Although predated by the *Vamperilla* mini-series, the success of *Lady Death* came first.

New Mutants #87 (Marvel)—The first appearance of Cable, a major *X-Men* character and one of the most sought-after books of the decade.

Next Men #21 (Image)—The first appearance of Hellboy. A fan favorite, critical darling and blockbuster movie star.

Preacher #1 (Vertigo)—The most popular book from the Vertigo line. *Preacher* made writer Garth Ennis and his writing style famous.

Prime #1 (Ultraverse)—From the success of Image comics, Malibu formed Ultraverse and spent millions on marketing. *Prime* #1 was the flagship title and ultimately led to the computer coloring revolution.

Rai #0 (VALIANT)—Innovations galore (enough for its own article), the bible of the VALIANT Universe and possibly the best cover of the decade. This was one of the most sought-after books from *Rai*, one of the most famous characters of the decade, and a strong contender for the ten most important comic books of the decade.

Spider-Man #1 (Marvel)—Paired together, Todd McFarlane and *Spider-Man* broke a number of sales records, and set the stage for Image Comics.

Turok #1 (VALIANT)—One of the top ten largest print runs in history, a runaway video game success that brought gamers into the fold, and the first real sign that comic properties were viable for licensing.

Unity #0 (VALIANT) – The first chapter in one of the greatest company-wide crossovers in history.

Witchblade #1 (Top Cow)—The flagship and most successful book by Top Cow. Has since become a television series, animated series and is gearing up for a feature film.

X-O Manowar #1 (VALIANT)—X-O Manowar is one of the most popular characters created in the past 15 years and issue #1 is his first appearance.

Youngblood #1 (Image)—The first book published under the Image Comics banner.

DECODING THE TEXT

1. According to Smith, what factors are important when evaluating comic books? Does Smith use these factors consistently throughout his list?

2. Smith says that number seven "*Astro City* made fans of those who have never, and probably would never, have read a comic otherwise." What clues does Smith give to define who reads comics and who creates comics?

1. Do you read comics? Do you watch them when they are turned into feature films? Why or why not?

2. Smith talks about the writing and the artistry of comics; in fact, he refers to his top picks as masterpieces as well as bestsellers. Is there a connection between art and sales? Should there be?

3. What do comic books tell us about our culture? About what we value?

Reading Selection: the '00s

Hillary Robson's primary research interest while a student at Middle Tennessee State University was cultural and fan studies with an emphasis on Buffy the Vampire Slayer. She was also instrumental in creating the book Unlocking the Meaning of Lost: An Unofficial Guide and is coeditor of the collection Saving the World: A Guide to "Heroes." She is a web designer and is currently involved in several projects dealing with fan fiction and its cultural effects.

TAKING WRITING "SERIOUSLY"

(Or How Fan Fiction Taught Me to Write)

Hillary Robson

Recently, a friend of mine asked when I started considering myself a "serious" writer. I answered that while I'd always had writerly aspirations, I never really considered myself a *writer* until about seven years ago when I wrote my first novel. Curiosity piqued, she pressed me for more information; I explained the set-ting (a post-apocalyptic world where alien disease ravaged the population) and how two unlikely heroes (F.B.I. agents) were charged with protecting a girl capable of saving the world.

"Sounds interesting," she responded, "whatever happened?"

"Taking Writing 'Seriously' (Or How Fan Fiction Taught Me to Write)" by Hillary Robson. Written for THE POP CULTURE ZONE: WRITING CRITICALLY ABOUT POPULAR CULTURE. 2006.

"I published it," I shrugged. "It wasn't popular. I consider it more of a learning experience."

"Really?" She assumed I was joking, so I pulled out my laptop and went to an internet archive site to show her the first chapter of *Darkness Ascending*.

"Oh, that's not real writing," she laughed. "That's fan fiction. That's just for fun!"

Now it was my turn to laugh. Writing fan fiction can be fun, sure, in the way *all* writing can be fun. The excitement of generating ideas, free-writing, drafting; the adrenaline rush of publishing and thrill of reader feedback: those were great. Despite the *fun*, there is a large amount of hard work involved. Eager to explain my perspective, I looked, smiled, and replied: "Writing fan fiction isn't just fun; it taught me how to write."

When I was twelve years old, I wrote my first novella during a summer spent devouring the "Desire" series of Harlequin paperbacks and watching taped episodes

of the 1991 revival of *Dark Shadows*. This uncanny marriage inspired the creation of a rather static storyline involving a modern-day heroine, Victoria, who was transported back in time following a tragic head injury caused by a brick. She awakens in the Victorian age with amnesia (of course) to soon fall head-over-heels in love with—and I kid you not—a vampire named Barnabus. Barnabus and Victoria were undoubtedly influenced by characters with the same names in *Dark Shadows,* and the rest of the story's inclusions of passionate sighs and heaving bosoms were owed to Harlequin. To add my own twist, the story concluded with Barnabus claiming Victoria as his vampire bride. My narrative was by no means original, in fact, the accompanying illustrations I had drawn by hand (complete with colorful subtitles such as "Victoria, here, hit by a brick") are the only contributions I can claim as mine and mine alone.

That story inspired what became a personal manifest-destiny-style-pipe-dream of becoming a Writer, capital "W"—as in esteemed, published, world-renowned writer. Famous like Danielle Steel, John Grisham, Stephen King, with mass market paperbacks sold at grocery stores and airports, covers featured on *Booklist,* and novels that spent weeks at the top of the *New York Times* bestseller list. I occupied every moment of my spare time hacking out a variety of what I felt to be sure-fire bestsellers based upon content inspired by my favorite daytime television series or other works of fiction. I started a notebook to stuff full of ideas, penned realms of sloppy, angst-filled poetry and waited for an unsolicited publishing contract to land in my mailbox offering a million dollar deal and confiming my inherent skills as a future Pulitzer-prize-winning novelist.

Screen shot printed courtesy of MuggleNet.com's Fan Fiction site, MuggleNet Fan Fiction. Design and layout by Haley Keim.

I saw my favorite television shows, films, and books as vehicles for personal inspiration, but I was writing in a vacuum: I had no audience. Despite piles of composition notebooks stacked in my closet there was no other proof of my creative effort. At this time, I had no idea what fan fiction was, or that there were others out there writing like me.

After high school, I began to question whether or not I had what it took to be a famous writer. After all, I'd replaced short stories with college-entrance essays and felt as though I'd run out of inspiration. I boxed up my old notebooks and decided that I was an adult now: I'd grown out of manifest-destiny style pipe dreams. But the summer of 1998 proved pivotal in a change of heart. As a long-term fan of the supernatural drama *The X-Files* I'd grown apprehensive during the fifth-season hiatus and impatiently waited for the release of the feature film. Surfing the internet for any kind of news about the series, I stumbled upon the auto-archive site, *Ephemeral,* where fan fiction based on the show was published.

Somehow, I had managed to stumble upon my very own heaven. Here, writers were free to have Scully and Mulder confess their love for one another, even amidst massive alien invasions, colonizations, and apocalypses. What's more, the writing was *good*! I became, in short order, a fan fiction addict. I fell in love with the stories and their authors, and impatiently waited for new chapters in fan-penned novels or a new story from a favorite writer.

By the end of summer, I had found my missing inspiration: a spark fueled by other writers and their creative interpretations. I admired their skills of playing with

opportunities afforded to and denied the audience. They compelled me to pick up my own pen and start to write, again. I bought a new notebook and tried my hand at writing fanfic, bringing my own voice and ideas to the world of *The X-Files.*

Despite enthusiasm, I still lacked the courage to let anyone else read my stories. I saw my writing as private: it was a form of *personal* expression. I didn't feel worthy of an audience and was plagued with nervousness. The fan fiction authors I read and admired left me in awe of their skill with words, their lack of errors in logic or grammar, and preservation of the canon of the series and its characters. I felt incapable of challenging their unspoken authority, and so for two years, I didn't: I remained locked in my own world of writing.

Eventually, though, the lack of audience proved a deafening sort of silence. I grew curious about what someone else might think of my writing, and so I worked up enough courage to seek out a beta reader. A beta reader is a type of "test" reader or editor that offers feedback and constructive criticism about a writer's prose. Through a website designed to pair writers with beta readers, I nervously filled out a request, asking for feedback on plot, characterization, dialogue, and overall readability.

A week later my chapter returned to my inbox bleeding red-typed text. I gaped at the screen in abject horror. My beta reader had noticed—with a sadistic proficiency—every single typo, grammatical error, and sticky plot point imaginable. I skimmed through the first page, apprehension and anxiety filling my stomach, until I came to a type-written comment that read: "I really like the start of this, and I'm interested in reading more, but as a reader I have to admit that the grammatical errors are distracting."

I burst into tears. Made silent by the technological distance between us, I could not defend my writing or articulate that I'd always been a good student in the past, that run on sentences, tense, and passive voice had never been a problem. Jess's criticism deflated an ego built on a lack of constructive criticism about my writing from teachers that had applauded the five-paragraph essay format and my verbose sentence structures. My institutionalized style and adherence to direction had awarded "A" -level achievement in high school, but creative writing was a different species entirely. In five minutes, I'd received confirmation that I was not a natural, my form lacked function, and I needed to learn the benefits of proofreading, editing, and revision.

While grammar was the first thing I noticed in the response, it was not the primary focus of Jess's beta reading. Once I recovered from my wounded pride, I continued to read. She pointed out the errors I had made in narrative flow, places where characterization was lacking and spots where the narrative was ill-developed. She showed me where my dialogue was choppy and my transitions were rocky. Her comments were constructive, offering guidance and recommendations for improvement, and at the conclusion of the chapter she invited me to revise and resend for another once over.

Darkness Ascending is, by far, my most flawed piece of writing. Even after the seemingly countless hours I spent in revision, every time I revisit it, I see places that could be strengthened and improved.

This is the case with every thing that a writer writes: everything can *always* stand for improvement and nothing is permanently perfect. When I published my story, I received a small amount of feedback from readers that liked my narrative and encouraged me to keep writing, and I did. I went on to write ten fan fictions based on *The X-Files,* and when I read those stories today I feel a sense of pride and amazement at what I have accomplished as a writer.

While it might be my least perfect, *Darkness Ascending* proved pivotal in teaching me some of the most important lessons about writing, beginning with the concept that it really is all about revision. In writing classrooms we hear that phrase a lot, and might not take it very seriously, but believe me, it's true. The hardest thing in the world is writing down *exactly* what you mean the first time you write it. Successful revision, however, can't happen without an audience, one that provides a writer with a separate perspective.

Fan fiction showed me that audiences— and revision—are *hard*. Becoming a better writer means putting forth effort to develop skills in becoming a better reader. It takes having skin thick enough to admit your writing is never perfect, in fact, nothing is; you have to develop the skills necessary to take a draft from fledgling to adult form. Having the courage to really listen to audience feedback is important, and a good writer is willing to consider positive and negative feedback.

There was one reader that hated everything I ever wrote, and made it a point to tell me about it, through pointing out every flaw, typo, or implausible plot point. Listening to audience feedback means taking in what someone has to say, but also creating the distance you need to know that audiences are subjective—no one opinion is the one best opinion. Fan fiction helped me to learn that perspective, and I take it with me every time I invite anyone to share their thoughts with me about my writing, or whenever I sit down to edit and revise.

After detailing my history with the writing process and fan fiction to my friend, I showed her another story. I explained that it was one of my favorites and how I'd spent a particularly grueling time in revision and editing, because I became so focused on wanting the final draft to be as close to flawless as possible.

The story, "Absentee Logic," proves particularly fitting for my journey of self-discovery about writing: "Seven years is a long time, for anything. It deserves revelations, catastrophes, question marks and exclamations."

I then pointed out to her all the things that were still wrong with it. When I was finished, she asked, "So, then, what makes fan fiction *real* writing?"

"Real writing," I answered, "is a process."

I explained how fan fiction showed me that becoming a Writer isn't just a jaunt down a perfectly paved path: it's a journey. A long, hard, painful journey—where you have to fall and scrape your knees a few times before you know where you're going. In the world of fan fiction, I wrote, beta read, opened archival websites, and composed at least a thousand e-mails of feedback to fellow writers. I became an advocate for the benefits of revision, of not writing within a vacuum, and the importance of listening to my audience. Those experiences are the basis for my views about writing today. It's how I'm able to advise writers to not fear giving feedback about the writing they love and to not to be afraid of receiving constructive criticism from others. Above all else, fan fiction has helped me to encourage writers to *write,* to try their hands at creative expression, to see their writing as a process where nothing happens overnight and hard work is always a basis.

When I was twelve, I saw writing as some inherent skill that came naturally and didn't take development. Fan fiction changed my perspective, and taught me how to write—a lesson I'll continue to build on for the rest of my life.

Now, if that multi-million dollar publishing contract would just show up in my mailbox . . .

DECODING THE TEXT

1. Robson's friend does not consider fan fiction real writing. How does Robson show that it is real writing? Is her argument convincing?

2. Robson says that writing takes courage. In what ways does it take courage? How does Robson show this? Do you agree with her?

3. How do you feel about the help provided by Robson's beta reader?

1. Becoming a writer is a dream for Robson. What steps does she take to make her dream come true?

2. What are your dreams? What steps have you taken to make them come true?

3. Is hard work enough? What other factors affect our goals and our ability to reach our goals?

Case Study

CONSIDERING IDEAS

1. What is censorship? When is censorship appropriate?

2. Who should make decisions about whom, what, and when to censor items in the world? Whom should they protect?

3. What happens when people have different values and belief systems?

Will Manley, *a former librarian, is currently the city manager of Tempe, Arizona. He has written nine books, including* Unprofessional Behavior: The Confessions of a Public Librarian, *which he coauthored with Gary Handman, and more than 350 magazine and journal articles. "In Defense of Book Burning" was first published in* American Libraries *in 2002.*

IN DEFENSE OF BOOK BURNING

Will Manley

If you want to make a strong statement about something, it's hard to find a stronger image to use than fire. When God revealed himself to Moses, he did so as a burning bush. When Jesus attempted to describe the pain of hell, he conjured up a terrifying portrait of eternal flames. When the white-hooded thugs of the Ku Klux Klan rode menacingly through the rural South to stir up the hatred of racism, they burned crosses on people's front yards. When anti-war dissidents protested U.S. involvement in the Vietnam War, they burned the American flag. When Buddhist monks protested the corrupt Diem regime in South Vietnam, they burned themselves. When the Nazis wanted to rid Germany of dangerous and undesirable ideas, they burned piles and piles of books.

Unfortunately, book burning is back in business, but not in Germany. It's happening right here in the U.S., and, oddly, it has nothing to do with our worldwide war on terrorism. In fact, there's probably been a book burning at a church or school near you. The target is Harry Potter, hero of millions of children. Harry is a fictional young boy who can perform extraordinary feats of magic. The fact that he has captured the hearts and imaginations of children has driven some clerics and parents into fits of frustration and rage. It's the kind of rage that bursts into fire.

The whole book-burning phenomenon is actually quite difficult to understand. You would think that Harry would be a cause for celebration by anyone sincerely interested in young people. With a wave of a wizard's wand he has done the utterly impossible. He has turned kids away from television, videos, and computer games and back into books. I never thought I'd see the day when kids would line up outside of a bookstore just to buy a book! Miraculously, that is what happens whenever a new Potter title is released, and that is precisely why Harry is driving his enemies crazy.

He's so popular that they think that he might mesmerize young children, turning them away from God and toward the black arts. Never mind the fact that Harry is a force of goodness and courage in a world that is creeping with evildoers. It's actually hard to think of a character in all of children's literature that is more a Goody Two-shoes than young, innocent Harry. In fact from a literary perspective, the only thing that I don't like about Harry is that he seems too good to be true. His sidekicks, Ron and Hermione, are much more appealing because they do have some minor character flaws.

So, how do you deal with a wizard who is mesmerizing your children? If you're really clueless about the magical arts, you will do something stupid like trying to burn him in hopes that he will instantly vanish. Anyone who knows anything about wizards or sorcerers however, recognizes that this approach is probably the worst thing that you can do. Wizards have a way of miraculously reappearing stronger than ever, and in Harry's case that is exactly what is happening. It's actually quite magical—the more you burn Harry, the more he multiplies. As a result, his creator, J. K. Rowling, is laughing all the way to the bank. I wonder how the book burners feel about helping finance her new castle in Scotland.

Book burnings bring big publicity. Nothing provokes public interest more than a fire, and nothing helps to sell books more than public interest. Book burners, therefore, are playing right into Harry's wily hands. He's not a wizard for nothing.

Not only are they clueless about wizards, the book burners are equally clueless about kids. What's the old expression— "don't tell kids not to put beans up their nose because that's exactly what they will do as soon as you turn your back." The same thing holds true here. If you burn a book because you don't want your child to read it, don't you think the kid will make it his first order of business to seek the book out on his own? He might even go to the public library to read it.

Oh, I get it—these book burnings are really a ruse to get kids back into libraries.

Robert Boston *serves as the assistant director of communications for Americans United for Separation of Church and State (AU) as well as the organization's monthly magazine entitled* Church & State. *He is considered an expert researcher and writer on topics of church and state. He has written three books, including* Close Encounters with the Religious Right: Journeys Into the Twilight Zone of Religion and Politics, *and numerous articles for* Church & State, *where this essay first appeared in 2002.*

WITCH HUNT

Why the Religious Right Is Crusading to Exorcise Harry Potter Books from Public Schools and Libraries

Robert Boston

Robert Fichthorn had decided to take a stand.

Fichthorn, captain of the Penryn, Pa., "fire police," a volunteer body that provides traffic control services during fires, auto accidents and civic events, declared in late January that his officers would not help cordon off streets during a YMCA-sponsored triathlon scheduled for this September.

Fichthorn's reason surprised many in the community. Despite its Christian roots, Fichthorn asserted, the YMCA is in fact supporting witchcraft by allowing students taking part in an after-school program to read the popular "Harry Potter" books. The fire police would do nothing, he insisted, to aid this nefarious behavior.

"I don't feel right taking our children's minds and teaching them [witchcraft]," Fichthorn told the *Lancaster New Era*. "As long as we don't stand up, it won't stop."

Fichthorn's declaration hit the local papers and promptly sparked an uproar in the tiny central Pennsylvania community. But things really got interesting after the story was circulated nationally by the Associated Press and spread worldwide over the Internet. Irate residents squared off in letters to the editor. YMCA officials were swamped with messages from all over the country and even overseas as people offered to stand in for the fire police.

Newspaper columnists blasted Fichthorn and the rest of his department as narrow-minded and silly. *Sports Illustrated* cited the flap as "This Week's Sign of the Apocalypse." *The Denver Post* gave Fichthorn its "Doofus of the Month" award.

Many in the community and surrounding area were not pleased with the attention. "Yes, all across the country, people are reading about the Penryn Fire Police decision to spurn the triathlon because Harry Potter goes against their Christian morals," groused Gil Smart, a columnist with the *Lancaster Sunday News*. "And all across the country, people are thinking: What bumpkins."

But if the Penryn Fire Police are bumpkins for hating Harry Potter, they are not the only ones. All over the country, Religious Right groups and local activists have put the Potter series in their theological crosshairs. The Penryn incident captured national headlines, but it is in no way an aberration.

According to the American Library Association (ALA), the Potter series, authored by Scottish writer J. K. Rowling, now holds the dubious distinction of being the most censored books in America. Public schools and libraries in many communities are under siege as far-right forces demand that the books be removed outright or placed on restricted access.

At first glance, the books look like unlikely candidates for all this fuss. Designed for pre- and early teens, the series recounts the adventures of Harry Potter, an orphan growing up in London. Verbally abused and forced to live in a dingy space at his domineering uncle's house, Potter's fortunes take a dramatic turn for the better when he learns he is descended from a long line of wizards and is invited to attend Hogwarts, a private academy for wizards in training.

The series is phenomenally popular, and the four books so far have sold in the millions worldwide. Late last year, a movie based on the first book, *Harry Potter and the Sorcerer's Stone*, opened to long lines and generally favorable reviews.

But not everyone is wild about Harry. Religious Right forces, including TV preacher Pat Robertson's *700 Club*, James Dobson's Focus on the Family, the Rev. Louis P. Sheldon's Traditional Values Coalition and a host of far-right lesser lights are convinced that the books promote evil and the occult—and they are spurring local activists to drive the books from public schools and libraries.

A sampling of recent incidents includes:

- York, Pa.: Led by a local pastor who is also an elementary school teacher, a handful of parents demanded that the Harry Potter books be removed from the Eastern York schools, asserting that the tomes promote witchcraft. "It's against my daughter's constitution, it's evil and it promotes witchcraft," parent Deb Eugenio told reporters. "I'm not paying taxes to teach my child witchcraft."

The school board voted 7-2 in January to allow teachers to continue to use the Potter books provided that parents first sign permission slips. Sixth-grade teacher Ed Althouse had been using the first book, *Harry Potter and the Sorcerer's Stone*, during a unit on fantasy literature. The parents of four students declined to sign the permission slips, and their children were given an alternate assignment.

- Alamogordo, N.M.: In an incident that captured headlines worldwide, Pastor Jack Brock of the Christ Community Church led a mass burning of Harry Potter books Dec. 30. Brock told reporters that the books "encourage our youth to learn more about witches, warlocks and sorcerers, and those things are an abomination to God and to me." For good measure, Brock also tossed a copy of *The Collected Works of William Shakespeare* on the bonfire.

- Duvall County, Fla.: Parent Mendy Robinson challenged the Potter books at Thomas Jefferson Elementary School, insisting that they are "turning children to lies & falsehoods of this present world." A committee of teachers, parents and librarians in October spurned a request that the Potter books be removed from school library shelves. Students had to get parental permission to read the books while the committee deliberated the matter.

• Oskaloosa, Kan.: The board of directors of the local public library voted to cancel a Harry Potter-themed event after some fundamentalists complained. The library had planned a reading program in June for "aspiring young witches and wizards" featuring a storyteller who had appeared at other Kansas libraries. The board voted to cancel the program after a handful of residents complained that the program promoted witchcraft.

• Fargo, N.D.: Officials at Agassiz Middle School in November cancelled a planned field trip to the Harry Potter movie after a few parents, backed by a local right-wing radio talk-show host, denounced the outing. School officials took the action even though all of the students, aged between 12 and 15, had received parental permission.

"It's a little bizarre," Fargo School Superintendent David Flowers said. "We believe that we were on firm ground in letting the kids go, but [the school] made the decision . . . that they would just as soon not be embroiled in controversy."

• Copley Township, Ohio: Library Coordinator Cathy Hall of the Copley-Fairlawn School District recommended in January that the district stop buying books in the Potter series. The system's library currently has two of the four Potter books, and Hall said she believes no more titles from the series should be added.

Hall told the *Akron Beacon Journal* that she made the recommendation primarily on the basis of financial concerns but then went on to say she was "also keeping in mind those things that are being said about the book."

• Modesto, Calif.: The Rev. B. Joseph Mannion has called on "religious parents" to keep the Potter books out of local public schools. In a Dec. 29 letter to the *Modesto Bee*, Mannion wrote, "The Harry Potter books are evil. They are based on evil: witchcraft, wizardry and the occult."

• Lewiston, Maine: The Rev. Doug Taylor announced plans to hold a book burning of the Potter tomes in a community park in November. Taylor, head of a local organization called the Jesus Party, applied for a permit to hold a bonfire in the park but was turned down by the Lewiston Fire Department. Instead, he cut up a Potter book with a pair of scissors and tossed it into a trashcan.

Maine newspapers reported that a minister from Portland who attended the event to support Taylor confronted members of a pro-Potter contingent mounting a counter-protest. "Some of you young people," the minister said, "should take a look at where you're going. Hell is a very bad place."

• Jacksonville, Fla.: Officials with the city's public library system dropped a plan to distribute "Hogwarts certificates" to encourage youngsters to read after a local resident, John Miesburg, complained that the books promoted "the evil of witchcraft." Librarians at the Regency Library did distribute some of the certificates in July of 2000 but stopped after attorneys with the Liberty Counsel, a Religious Right legal group affiliated with the Rev. Jerry Falwell, threatened to sue. Mathew Staver, head of the Liberty Counsel, insisted that the library's plan violated church-state separation.

• Zeeland, Mich.: A long-running dispute over the Potter books has culminated in the resignation of a school board president. Tom Bock stepped down after repeatedly butting heads with Mary Dana, a middle school teacher who protested a 1999 vote by the board to ban the Potter books.

The restrictions were later lifted, but Bock and Dana continued sparring over the matter. Bock resigned after school administrators turned down his demands that Dana be removed from her position as a mentor to new teachers, reported the *Grand Rapids Press*.

These incidents are just a few of the recent challenges to the Potter books. According to the ALA, which tracks incidents of censorship nationwide, Rowling's books have been the most challenged works in public school libraries and public libraries for three years running.

Beverly Becker, associate director of the ALA's Office of Intellectual Freedom, has noticed a common theme among the complaints. "It's always witchcraft," Becker told *Church & State*. "Occasionally they throw something else in, but ultimately these challenges are all about witchcraft."

Becker points out that the ALA noted a dramatic upswing in the challenges in October of 1999, when *Harry Potter and the Prisoner of Azkaban* was published. Becker said this was probably due to increased media attention.

"When the third book came out," she said, "the publicity went crazy. I think that's when every adult heard about the books, not just the ones who had a 10- or 12-year-old at home." Becker notes that more public schools began using the books at that time as well.

As sales climbed, Religious Right groups went into a frenzy. Some of the charges they have lobbed against the books seem too fantastic to believe, but millions of Religious Right activists around the country are now apparently convinced that the Potter series is part of a plot to lure youngsters into Wiccan groups.

High-profile TV preacher Robertson launched a full-scale assault on the Potter books late last year. On the Dec. 5 *700 Club*, cohost Terry Meeuwsen interviewed Caryl Matrisciana, identified as an "expert on the occult" and producer of a video titled "Harry Potter: Witchcraft Repackaged."

In fact, Matrisciana is the wife of Pat Matrisciana, a long-time far-right political operative who made his living during much of the 1990s peddling conspiracy-theory videos attacking President Bill Clinton, most notably "The Clinton Chronicles." During the CBN interview, Caryl Matrisciana asserted that Rowling had based the books on "the religions of Celtic, druidic, Satanic, Wiccan and pagan roots and written them into her fiction books for children."

Asserted Matrisciana, "The harm is first of all that witchcraft is being normalized to our children. For the first time in the history of the world, witchcraft is being given to children in a children's format, and children are seeing other children practicing it and say it's all right."

Following the interview, Robertson felt moved to offer his own comments. Glaring sternly into the cameras, Robertson told the audience that God will turn his back on nations that tolerate witchcraft—with dire consequences.

"Now, ladies and gentlemen, we have been talking about God lifting his anointing and his mantle from the United States of America," Robertson said. "And if you read in Deuteronomy or Leviticus, actually, the eighteenth chapter, there's certain things that he says that is going to cause the Lord, or the land, to vomit you out. At the head of the list is witchcraft. . . . Now we're welcoming this and teaching our children. And what we're doing is asking for the wrath of God to come on this country. . . . And if there's ever a time we need God's blessing it's now. We don't need to be bringing in heathen, pagan practices to the United States of America."

(Strangely enough, a series of anti-Potter articles on the CBN website disappeared not long after Robertson's outburst. This may be due to the fact that ABC/Disney, which now owns the cable channel that carries the *700 Club*, recently purchased the rights to broadcast the first Potter movie on television.)

Other Religious Right groups were quick to join the anti-Potter bandwagon.

"Is Harry Potter a Harmless Fantasy or a Wicca Training Program?" blared a recent press released issued by Sheldon's Traditional Values Coalition. Sheldon, one of the Religious Right's most vociferous gay bashers, even tried to link the Potter series to homosexuality, writing, "While the themes in Harry Potter books do not expressly advocate homosexuality or abortion, these are the philosophical beliefs deeply embedded in Wicca. The child who is seduced into Wicca witchcraft through Harry Potter books will eventually be introduced to these other concepts."

TV preacher D. James Kennedy of Coral Ridge Ministries is also promoting the alleged Potter-Wicca connection. In late October, Kennedy interviewed Richard Abanes, a self-proclaimed "expert on the occult" and author of the anti-Potter tome *Harry Potter and the Bible*.

Appearing on Kennedy's "Truths That Transform" radio show, Abanes asserted that as a result of the Potter books, Wiccan groups in England are flooded with new members. The leading Wiccan group in the United Kingdom, Abanes told Kennedy, has had to hire a youth minister.

Series author Rowling, Abanes asserted, "has had a fascination with the occult and witchcraft and wizardry ever since she was a little girl. And so, her creativity, her talent, when she wrote something, that came out on the page—I'm not sure she actually meant to draw kids into the occult, but that's indeed what's already happening, especially in England."

The Rev. Donald Wildmon's American Family Association has also attacked Rowling's books and the film version of the first volume. In November the AFA's website (www.afa.net) posted an article by "contributing columnist" Berit Kjos, whose ministry has made attacking Potter into a cottage industry. The article, titled "Twelve Reasons Not to See the Harry Potter Movie," asserted that the film presents witchcraft as an appealing alternative lifestyle.

Wrote Kjos, "This pagan ideology comes complete with trading cards, computer and other wizardly games, clothes and decorations stamped with [Harry Potter] symbols, action figures and cuddly dolls and audio cassettes that could keep the child's minds [sic] focused on the occult all day and into night. But in God's eyes, such paraphernalia become little more than lures and doorways to deeper involvement with the occult."

(Wildmon, whose AFA is based in Tupelo, Miss., is best known for attempting to censor television programs. Last month he joined 14 other groups in petitioning the Federal Communications Commission to demand the removal of an award-winning drama series, *Boston Public*, from the Fox Network.)

Falwell has also recommended caution. Falwell's *National Liberty Journal* noted late last year "that there does appear to be a legitimate reason to be cautious in regard to Harry Potter" and asserted, "Even if the author's intent is anything but evil, the attractive presentation of witchcraft and wizardry—both ultimately godless pursuits—may desensitize children to important spiritual issues."

The unbylined piece, however, does note that some conservative Christians see no danger in the Potter books and adds, "Harry Potter is not worth causing a major schism within the church." (Falwell may have good reasons for not launching a full-scale assault on the Potter series. In 1999, he became the target of international ridicule after warning parents that a character named Tinky Winky from the PBS children's series *Teletubbies* is gay.)

Rowling, who wrote the first Potter book while struggling to keep her head above water as a single mom, has called the assertions that her books seek to lure

youngsters into the occult "absurd." In one interview she observed, "I have met thousands of children now, and not even one time has a child come up to me and said, 'Ms. Rowling, I'm so glad I've read these books because now I want to be a witch.'"

Many experts on education and children's literature agree that the books are unlikely to draw children into the occult. They note that witches, fairies, dragons and other mythical beasts have a long lineage in stories aimed at young readers. Witches are a staple in Grimm's Fairy Tales, which date back to the Middle Ages and remain popular today. In the Grimm Brothers' tales, as in the Potter books today, good triumphs over evil in the end. Such stories usually end up teaching simple moral lessons that youngsters can readily understand.

None of this has slowed down the censors one iota. And, with three more books in the Potter series on the horizon—and more film adaptions on the way—anti-censorship activists expect to see more efforts to ban the Potter series and others. (According to the ALA, the most common targets of censorship in America for the period 1990-2000 include *The Adventures of Huckleberry Finn* by Mark Twain, John Steinbeck's *Of Mice and Men*, *The Catcher in the Rye* by J. D. Salinger, Harper Lee's *To Kill a Mockingbird*, *The Witches* by Roald Dahl and *A Wrinkle in Time* by Madeleine L'Engle.)

Officials at the ALA recommend that both public school libraries and public libraries have clear policies in place for dealing with censorship attempts. They advocate review committees that can examine challenged books and say it's essential that everyone involved in the committee and the larger effort actually read the book under challenge. These policies, ALA staffers say, can avoid a rush to judgment.

"That allows for a fair hearing, so everyone can cool down," says the ALA's Becker. "The decision is not made in such an emotional moment."

Given time, many censorship efforts collapse in the face of counter mobilization by concerned community members or just fail because the charges against a book are preposterous. This was often the case 100 years ago when efforts were made to censor another children's book featuring witches—L. Frank Baum's *The Wizard of Oz*. Outraged *Oz* fans stepped forward to defend the book, turning back some censorship efforts. (See "Lions And Tigers And Censors—Oh, My!".)

An echo of that long-ago struggle was heard in central Pennsylvania recently during the incident in Penryn. Laura Montgomery Rutt, director of the Alliance for Tolerance and Freedom in Lancaster, which keeps tabs on the Religious Right locally, said community sentiment is running solidly against the fire police. Many people in the area, she said, think the fire police are being silly.

"People here are not supporting the decision of the fire police," she said. "And their actions have helped the YMCA. People are volunteering and saying they want to help. No one knew about the triathlon before this happened. Now they are volunteering to help run it—even people from other states."

Lancaster County is a conservative area, Rutt said, but that doesn't mean residents support censorship. "The community has seen and learned that extremism is not going to win," Rutt told *Church & State*. "This shows that even the guys in the fire police are going beyond what Lancaster County is willing to put up with. We've also seen that the community is willing to rally when an organization shows it is intolerant. So many have spoken out on behalf of the Potter books. A lot of people have a tendency to stay in their shells, but this was just too much. All in all, this was kind of a good thing. It really rallied the troops."

DECODING THE TEXTS

1. What is Boston's stance on censorship in regard to Harry Potter books? What clues in the text reveal his position?

2. What is Manley's attitude toward censorship? How does he show his position in the essay?

3. What similarities do the two authors and essays share? Where do they differ? Where do you stand on the issue?

1. Manley says we should celebrate the Harry Potter books because they have "turned kids away from television, videos, and computer games and back into books." What values are revealed by this statement? Do you share these values?

2. Boston quotes a reporter from Pennsylvania who is concerned that the rest of the world views the people in his community as "bumpkins." What values are revealed here?

3. What other beliefs are discussed in Boston's essay? Who holds these various beliefs?

Reading Selection:
Across the Decades

CONSIDERING IDEAS

1. How would you describe your sense of humor?
2. What do you find funny? What do you find gross or offensive?
3. Do you think of scientists as funny people? Why or why not?

Kelly Ferguson *writes for* mental_floss *magazine, where the essay "A Walk on* The Far Side*" first appeared in 2006. She is an aspiring creative nonfiction writer at the University of Montana in Missoula. Her blog is located at http://www.charmschoolreject.com.*

A WALK ON *THE FAR SIDE*
The Life and Times of Gary Larson

Kelly Ferguson

From the Primordial Suburban Ooze
As a kid growing up in Tacoma, Wash., Gary Larson never dreamed that a knack for doodling amoebas would one day score him a place in history. After all, he was merely a simple life form, born into a working-class family. His father, Vern, worked as a car salesman, and his mother, Doris, was a secretary—but both moonlighted as the Best Parents Ever. From an

"A Walk on *The Far Side*: The Life and Times of Gary Larson" by Kelly Ferguson from MENTAL FLOSS MAGAZINE, 2006, pp. 59–65. Reprinted by permission of Mental Floss. www.mentalfloss.com.

early age, Gary spent a lot of time studying nature, reading science books, and drawing dinosaurs and whales. Fortunately, his folks kept their son's crayon caddy well stocked. And when Larson wanted a pet snake instead of a beagle? Well, that was OK too.

All evidence points to a childhood of nerdy bliss, but many of Larson's cartoons have caused people to think, "That boy ain't right." So what about the creatures that go bump in the night? If fans want to credit someone for tweaking the artist's brain, thanks go to Larson's older brother, Dan. Knowing Gary had a crippling fear of monsters under the bed, Dan was the kind of brother who hid in Gary's closet for hours, just waiting for the golden opportunity to scare his sibling sick. Indeed, Larson would later claim that Dan's continuous series of pranks contributed to his "unusual" world perspective.

Of course, Larson also acknowledges Dan as having inspired his wacky investigative spirit and love for science. Growing up, the brothers used the family basement to build elaborate terrariums for all the animals they caught around Puget Sound. They even took over one of the rooms and turned it into a miniature desert ecosystem. Instead of freaking out, however, Mr. and Mrs. Larson reportedly invited the neighbors to join them in gawking.

In 1968, Larson left his terrariums behind and headed to Washington State University. To nobody's surprise he started out as a biology major, but then switched to communications because he "didn't know what you did with a biology degree." At the time, he wanted to bring humor to the world of advertising—an idea he later regretted. When graduation rolled around in 1972, Larson rejected the briefcase and tie, opting instead to follow the well-blazed trail of disenchanted youth. In other words, he played guitar and banjo in a duo called Tom & Gary and worked in a retail music shop.

From High Fidelity to High Finance

Larson's transformation from music store clerk to internationally famous cartoonist follows a sequence of random decisions, sporadic efforts, and lucky breaks. At least, that's how Larson tells it. Ask the newspaper editors who first discovered Larson, and you're more likely to hear a tale about finally finding cartoon work that stood out from the drudgery of "Mary Worth."

Either way, the story of "The Far Side" begins in 1976. One day, after a long afternoon of hawking instruments, Larson realized just how much he hated his job, so he took a weekend off to "find himself." After wracking his brain for 48 hours straight, he entered that special mental zone that exists somewhere between breakdown and epiphany. And in that zone, Larson drew six single-panel cartoons.

Fortunately, the reticent Larson mustered up enough pluck to submit them to a few area newspapers. Not only was he able to sell them (with ease) to a regional science magazine called *Pacific Search*, he also earned a quick 90 bucks in the process. Suddenly, the lightbulb dinged: Maybe it was possible to make a living doing something he actually enjoyed! And just like that, Larson quit his job, moved back home, and began drawing full time. (Thanks again, Vern and Doris.)

Pretty soon, he was raking in the dough—$5 a week—from a Tacoma suburb paper called *The Summer News Review*. But things changed in 1979, after a reporter he'd met convinced him to approach *The Seattle Times*. To Larson's astonishment, they bit, and he soon began earning a whopping $15 a week for a quirky cartoon he called "Nature's Way."

In "Nature's Way," the basics of Larson's work emerged. He had his cast of characters (the mad scientists, the aliens, and the bovines), and he had a point to his punch lines. Larson always derived great joy from humbling *Homo sapiens*, and he reveled in reminding audiences that we're just another species. One cartoon, for instance, simply showed a rabbit wearing a human foot on a necklace for good luck.

Humor like this, while becoming Larson's trademark, also made "Nature's Way" a quick source of controversy. Strangely, the cartoon ran adjacent to the paper's "Junior Jumble," a puzzle aimed at children. Undoubtedly, when kids came to their parents with questions like, "Why do spider mommies eat their babies?" some parents weren't thrilled, and angry letters ensued.

A few disgruntled readers aside, Larson enjoyed moderate success. Still, full-time drawing hadn't translated into full-time cash, and in 1979 he decided to embark on a cartoon job quest in San Francisco. Mustering up his nerve, he squared his round shoulders, pushed his glasses up his nose, and stalwartly puttered south in his Plymouth Duster.

Larson had a list of papers to target in the area, but after getting lost a few times, he found himself on Market Street, home of *The San Francisco Chronicle*. He didn't have an appointment, but he went ahead and left his portfolio with the secretary, who was less than encouraging. The thing is,

Larson hadn't thought to bring multiple copies of said portfolio, so *The Chronicle* shaped up to be his one lottery ticket to cartoon success.

Several days later, the prospects weren't looking good. Larson had heard nothing, and he felt like he was irritating the secretary with his calls. But just as his Rice-a-Roni stash was running low, he got a call from the paper's editor. He told Larson he was sick—as in twisted—but in a good way. Then he offered him a spot in the paper and worked out a syndication deal to boot. It was a cartoonist's equivalent of Charlie Brown making contact with the football. Editors renamed Larson's comic "The Far Side," and the panel started running in 30 papers nationwide.

Ironically, just days after Larson received the news from *The Chronicle*, he returned to Seattle to find a letter from *The Seattle Times* saying they were dropping him from the paper.

Survival of the Fittest

While Larson eventually became the page-a-day-calendar king, success wasn't instantaneous. After all, it took time for audiences raised on "Marmaduke" to appreciate a world where squids say the darndest things. Not everyone related to cartoon panels where the end of the world is nigh, people do aerobics in hell, and there are definitely, always, monsters in every closet.

Interestingly, while Larson's "sick" humor riled, what really worked the public into a lather was when they didn't get the joke. Lightning rod in point: a seemingly innocuous 1982 edition of "The Far Side" that featured a cow standing behind an assortment of amorphous objects on a table.

The caption: "Cow tools." Larson's intent was to parody the tools used by early man, and more specifically, how even archaeologists are often baffled by their purpose.

Admittedly, the cartoon was a bit esoteric. But was it worth a national outcry? Apparently so. For reasons unknown, a population comfortable with being baffled by "Hi and Lois" day after day just couldn't handle a tool-wielding cow. Letters poured in from readers across the country, reporters and radio stations called with inquiries, and newspaper columnists had a field day.

The media barrage overwhelmed Larson, who, after all, had only gotten into this line of work to escape a dead-end retail job. Now, here he was, faced yet again with cranky customers. All the hoopla made him cringe with embarrassment, and he became convinced "The Far Side" would be canned. Yet, as mail continued to deluge his desk, he came upon a realization. People cared. Actually, *lots* of people cared. If this many readers felt the need to write, maybe he didn't just have a job, he had a career.

Larson was right. "The Far Side" contingency grew, and by 1983, the panel appeared in 80 papers nationwide. By 1985, it was in 200. Before all was said and done, the cartoon would run in 1,900 newspapers and be translated into 17 languages—lest we forget the book series, the calendars, the animated films, and the greeting cards.

Lab Partners
While denouncers found "The Far Side" base, devotees (especially scientists and researchers) loved its highbrow humor. After all, getting a Larson joke sometimes required knowledge of praying mantis mating habits, or a basic understanding of evolutionary theory. And when Larson made heroes out of ichthyologists and found humor in the antics of dung beetles? Well, it sent the white coats into fits of egghead bliss. They gleefully snorted and wheezed, smothering their office doors and metal file cabinets one panel at a time.

Of course, the same fan base that loved Larson for his scientific accuracy also felt the need to point out the occasional blooper—like when he featured a male mosquito coming home from work (it's the female who does the biting) or when he committed the zoological faux pas of commingling polar bears and penguins (they live in separate poles). According to interviews with Larson, these sorts of errors drove him crazy. A perfectionist—and a scientist—by nature, he did not take his gaffes lightly.

THE FAR SIDE®   **BY GARY LARSON**

© 1984 FarWorks, Inc. All Rights Reserved/Dist. by Creators Syndicate

The Far Side® by Gary Larson © 1984 FarWorks, Inc. All Rights Reserved. The Far Side® and the Larson® signature are registered trademarks of FarWorks, Inc. Used with permission.

"And now Edgar's gone. ... Something's going on around here."

Whether or not Larson has ever forgiven himself, the scientists haven't been able to stay mad at him for long. In fact, one time, out of love, they turned Larson's comedic fiction into scientific fact. While it's common knowledge that dinosaurs and cavemen never co-existed, Larson blatantly disregarded this fact in a cartoon that showed a primitive hominid pointing to a picture of the spiky tail of a Stegosaurus. In it, the caveman explains, "Now this end is called the thagomizer . . . after the late Thag Simmons." Well, these days, paleontologists actually recognize that "spiky thingy" as a Thagomizer.

In 1989, scientists decided to honor Larson in an even more special way. The Committee on Evolutionary Biology at The University of Chicago named a newly discovered species after him—the *Strigiphilus garylarsoni,* a louse found only on owls. Later, Larson's name was also given to a butterfly—the *Serratoterga larsoni,* a native of the Ecuadorian rain forest. Quite the hallmark of success for a man who once described entomology as the "fantasy road not taken."

Extinction

While we might prefer to believe that Gary Larson exists for the sole purpose of drawing us cartoons, he has decided otherwise. In 1988, he went on sabbatical for 14 months, then put the pen down at the beginning of 1995. And because it's been over a decade now, we might have to consider that he really means it this time. Irritatingly, he seems perfectly content enjoying his royalties, rather than sitting at his desk six days a week in a panic trying to finish his next panel before the Federal Express truck arrives.

"The Far Side" withdrawal is undoubtedly a bummer, but admittedly, it would have been more depressing to watch the cartoon devolve into the realm of the "unfunnies," or as Larson termed it, the "Graveyard of Mediocre Cartoons." Larson felt he was starting to repeat himself and wanted to quit while he thought the panel held up. For this, we might consider forgiving him for retiring wealthy at the age of 44.

These days, Larson enjoys the spoils of his success with his wife, anthropologist Toni Carmichael, while pursuing his love of jazz guitar. There are rumors he moonlights as a wedding crasher—only, in true nerd fashion, he doesn't pick up bridesmaids but jams with the band. On a tragic note, his brother Dan died of a sudden heart attack at the age of 46. That is, unless he's just lying in the dirt, waiting to grab his little brother's ankle.

Since his retirement, Larson has tossed us a few crumbs. In 1998, he published *There's Hair in My Dirt! A Worm's Story,* a naturalist morality tale told in an illustrated book. And in 2003, he released *The Complete Far Side,* a massive collection of his work containing all 4,337 of his panels. To promote the effort, Larson also gave a few promotional interviews, and pointed out that the two-volume set doubles neatly as a murder weapon. But other than that, he's managed to keep out of the public eye. Meanwhile we imagine his fans will simply have to wait, hoping one day Larson will emerge from retirement—just long enough to draw a python that strangles "The Family Circus."

1. Throughout the essay, Ferguson refers to Larson as a nerd. Is this meant to be ridicule or praise or something else?

2. *The Far Side* is called highbrow humor. What does the author mean by this? Does she show support for this claim? Do you agree? Can something be highbrow and popular at the same time?

CONNECTING TO YOUR CULTURE

1. Why does Ferguson point out that Gary Larson was born to working-class parents? What difference does this make?

2. Ferguson says that scientists and researchers in particular like *The Far Side*. Why do you think this is true?

3. Why does Ferguson hope Larson will emerge from retirement "long enough to draw a python that strangles 'The Family Circus'"?

4. Do you like Larson's "warped mind"? Do you know anyone like Larson?

Reading Selections: A Case Study Across the Decades

CONSIDERING IDEAS

1. What do you know about the women's movement of the 1970s? What was the agenda of '70s feminists?

2. How has that movement affected the life you live today?

3. Is the movement still alive? If so, what are its present goals?

4. Do you consider yourself a feminist?

Ann Barr Snitow *is professor of gender studies and literature at The New School for Social Research at New York University. She is the author of* Ford Madox Ford and the Voice of Uncertainty *(1984), and she coedited* The Feminist Memoir Project: Voices from Women's Liberation *(1998) and* Powers of Desire: The Politics of Sexuality *(1983).*

MASS MARKET ROMANCE

Pornography for Women Is Different

Ann Barr Snitow

. . . What is the Harlequin romance formula? The novels have no plot in the usual sense. All tension and problems arise from the fact that the Harlequin world is inhabited by two species incapable of communicating with each other, male and female. In this sense these Pollyanna books have their own dreamlike truth: our culture produces a pathological experience of sex difference. The sexes have different needs and interests, certainly different experiences. They find each other utterly mystifying.

Since all action in the novels is described from the female point of view, the reader identifies with the heroine's efforts to decode the erratic gestures of "dark, tall and gravely handsome"[1] men, all mysterious strangers or powerful bosses. In a sense the usual relationship is reversed: woman is subject, man, object. There are more descriptions of his body than of hers ("Dark trousers fitted closely to lean hips and long muscular legs . . .") though her clothes are always minutely observed. He is the unknowable other, a sexual icon whose magic is maleness. The books are permeated by phallic worship. Male is good, male is exciting, without further points of reference. Cruelty, callousness, coldness, menace, etc. are all equated with maleness and treated as a necessary part of the package: "It was an arrogant remark, but Sara had long since admitted his arrogance as part of his attraction."[2]

She, on the other hand, is the subject, the one whose thoughts the reader knows, whose constant re-evaluation of male moods and actions make up the story line.

The heroine is not involved in any overt adventure beyond trying to respond appropriately to male energy without losing her virginity. Virginity is a given here; sex means marriage and marriage, promised at the end, means, finally, there can be sex.

While the heroine waits for the hero's next move, her time is filled by tourism and by descriptions of consumer items: furniture, clothes, and gourmet foods. In *Writers Market* (1977) Harlequin Enterprises stipulate: "Emphasis on travel." (The exception is the occasional hospital novel. Like foreign places, hospitals offer removal from the household, heightened emotional states, and a supply of strangers.) Several of the books have passages that probably come straight out of guide books, but the particular setting is not the point, only that it is exotic, a place elsewhere.[3]

More space is filled by the question of what to wear. "She rummaged in her cases, discarding item after item, and eventually brought out a pair of purple cotton jeans and a matching shift. They were not new. She had bought them a couple of years ago. But fortunately her figure had changed little, and apart from a slight shrinkage in the pants which made them rather tighter than she would have liked, they looked serviceable."[4] Several things are going on here: the effort to find the right clothes for the occasion, the problem of staying thin, the problem of piecing together outfits from things that are not new. Finally, there is that shrinkage, a signal to the experienced Harlequin reader that the heroine, innocent as her intent may be in putting on jeans that are a little too tight, is wearing something revealing and will certainly be seen and noted by the hero in this vulnerable, passive act of self-exposure. (More about the pornographic aspects later. In any other titillating novel one would suspect a pun when tight pants are "serviceable" but in the context of the absolutely flat Harlequin style one might well be wrong. More, too, about this style later on.)

Though clothes are the number one filler in Harlequins, food and furniture are also important and usually described in the language of women's magazines:[5] croissants are served hot and crispy and are "crusty brown,"[6] while snapper is "filleted, crumbed and fried in butter" and tomato soup is "topped with grated cheese and parsley"[7] (this last a useful, practical suggestion anyone could try).

Harlequins revitalize daily routines by insisting that a woman combing her hair, a woman reaching up to put a plate on a high shelf (so that her knees show beneath the hem, if only there were a viewer), a woman doing what women do all day, is in a constant state of potential sexuality. You never can tell when you may be seen and being seen is a precious opportunity. Harlequin romances alternate between scenes of the hero and heroine together in which she does a lot of social lying to save face, pretending to be unaffected by the hero's presence while her body melts or shivers, and scenes in which the heroine is essentially alone, living in a cloud of absorption, preparing mentally and physically for the next contact.

The heroine is alone. Sometimes there is another woman, a competitor who is often more overtly aware of her sexuality than the heroine, but she is a shadow on the horizon. Sometimes there are potentially friendly females living in the next bungalow or working with the patient in the next bed, but they, too, are shadowy, not important to the real story which consists entirely of an emotionally isolated woman trying to keep her virginity and her head when the only person she ever really talks to is the hero, whose motives and feelings are unclear: "She saw his words as a warning and would have liked to know whether he meant [them] to be."[8]

The heroine gets her man at the end, first, because she is an old-fashioned girl (this is a code for no premarital sex) and, second, because the hero gets ample opportunity to see her perform well in a number of female helping roles. In the course of a Harlequin romance, most heroines demonstrate passionate motherliness, good cooking, patience in adversity, efficient planning, and a good clothes sense, though these are skills and emotional capacities produced in emergencies, and are not, as in real life, a part of an invisible, glamourless work routine.

Though the heroines are pliable (they are rarely given particularized character traits; they are all Everywoman and can fit in comfortably with the lifestyle of the strong-willed heroes be they doctors, lawyers, or marine biologists doing experiments on tropical islands), it is still amazing that these novels end in marriage. After one hundred and fifty pages of mystification, unreadable looks, "hints of cruelty"[9] and wordless coldness, the thirty-page denouement is powerless to dispel the earlier impression of menace. Why should this heroine marry this man? And, one can ask with equal reason, why should this hero marry this woman? These endings do not ring true, but no doubt this is precisely their strength. A taste for psychological or social realism is unlikely to provide a Harlequin reader with a sustaining fantasy of rescue, of glamour, or of change. The Harlequin ending offers the impossible. It is pleasing to think that appearances are deceptive, that male coldness, absence, boredom, etc. are not what they seem. The hero *seems* to be a horrible roué; he *seems* to be a hopeless, moody cripple; he *seems* to be cruel and unkind; or he *seems* to be indifferent to the heroine and interested only in his work; but always, at the end, a rational explanation of all this appears. In spite of his coldness or preoccupation, the hero really loves the heroine and wants to marry her.

In fact, the Harlequin formula glorifies the distance between the sexes. Distance becomes titillating. The heroine's sexual inexperience adds to this excitement. What is this thing that awaits her on the other side of distance and mystery? Not knowing may be more sexy than finding out. Or perhaps the heroes are really fathers—obscure, forbidden objects of desire. Whatever they are, it is more exciting to wonder about them than to know them. In romanticized sexuality the pleasure lies in the distance itself. Wait-

ing, anticipation, anxiety—these represent the high point of sexual experience.

Perhaps there is pleasure, too, in returning again and again to that breathless, ambivalent, nervous state *before* certainty or satiety. Insofar as women's great adventure, the one they are socially sanctioned to seek, is romance, adventurousness takes women always back to the first phase in love. Unlike work, which holds out the possible pleasures of development, of the exercise of faculties, sometimes even of advancement, the Harlequin form of romance depends on the heroine's being in a state of passivity, of not knowing. Once the heroine knows the hero loves her, the story is over. Nothing interesting remains. Harlequin statements in *Writers Market* stress "upbeat ending essential here" (1977). Here at least is a reliable product that reproduces for women the most interesting phase in the love/marriage cycle and knows just when to stop. . . .

Are Harlequin Romances Pornography?

She had never felt so helpless or so completely at the mercy of another human being . . . a being who could snap the slender column of her body with one squeeze of a steel clad arm.

No trace of tenderness softened the harsh pressure of his mouth on hers . . . there was only a savagely punishing intentness of purpose that cut off her breath until her senses reeled and her body sagged against the granite hardness of his. He released her wrists, seeming to know that they would hang helplessly at her sides, and his hand moved to the small of her back to exert a pressure that crushed her soft outlines to the unyielding dominance of his and left her in no doubt as to the force of his masculinity.[10]

In an unpublished talk,[11] critic Peter Parisi has hypothesized that Harlequin romances are essentially pornography for people ashamed to read pornography. In his view, sex is these novels' real *raison d'être*, while the romance and the promised marriage are primarily salves to the conscience of readers brought up to believe that sex without love and marriage is wrong. Like me, Parisi sees the books as having some active allure. They are not just escape; they also offer release, as he sees it, specifically sexual release.

This is part of the reason why Harlequins, so utterly denatured in most respects, can powerfully command such a large audience. I want to elaborate here on Parisi's definition of *how* the books are pornography and, finally, to modify his definition of what women are looking for in a sex book. . . .

Parisi sees Harlequins as a sort of poor woman's D. H. Lawrence. The body of the heroine is alive and singing in every fiber; she is overrun by a sexuality that wells up inside her and that she cannot control. ("The warmth of his body close to hers was like a charge of electricity, a stunning masculine assault on her senses that she was powerless to do anything about."[12]) The issue of control arises because, in Parisi's view, the reader's qualms are allayed when the novels invoke morals, then affirm a force, sexual feeling, strong enough to override those morals. He argues further that morals in a Harlequin are secular; what the heroine risks is a loss of social face, of reputation. The books uphold the values of their readers who share this fear of breaking social codes, but behind these reassuringly familiar restraints they celebrate a wild, eager sexuality which flourishes and is finally affirmed in "marriage," which Parisi sees as mainly a code word for "f**k."

Parisi is right: *every* contact in a Harlequin romance is sexualized:

Sara feared he was going to refuse the invitation and simply walk off. It seemed like an eternity before he inclined his head in a brief, abrupt acknowledgement of acceptance, then drew out her chair for her, his hard fingers brushing her arm for a second, and bringing an urgent flutter of reaction from her pulse.[13]

Those "hard fingers" are the penis; a glance is penetration; a voice can slide along the heroine's spine "like a sliver of ice." The heroine keeps struggling for control but is constantly swept away on a tide of feeling. Always, though, some intruder or some "nagging reminder" of the need to maintain appearances stops her. "His mouth parted her lips with bruising urgency and for a few delirious moments she yielded to her own wanton instincts." But the heroine insists on seeing these moments as out of character: She "had never thought herself capable of wantonness, but in Carlo's arms she seemed to have no inhibitions."[14] Parisi argues that the books' sexual formula allows both heroine and reader to feel wanton again and again while maintaining their sense of themselves as not that sort of woman.

I agree with Parisi that the sexually charged atmosphere that bathes the Harlequin heroine is essentially pornographic (I use the word pornographic as neutrally as possible here, not as an automatic pejorative). But do Harlequins actually contain an affirmation of female sexuality? The heroine's condition of passive receptivity to male ego and male sexuality is exciting to readers, but this is not necessarily a free or deep expression of the female potential for sexual feeling. Parisi says the heroine is always trying to humanize the contact between herself and the apparently undersocialized hero, "trying to convert rape into love-making." If this is so, then she is engaged on a social as well as a sexual odyssey. Indeed, in women, these two are often joined. Is the project of humanizing and domesticating male sexual feeling an erotic one? What is it about this situation that arouses the excitement of the anxiously vigilant heroine and of the readers who identify with her?

In the misogynistic culture in which we live, where violence towards women is a common motif, it is hard to say a neutral word about pornography either as a legitimate literary form or as a legitimate source of pleasure. Women are naturally overwhelmed by the woman-hating theme so that the more universal human expression sometimes contained by pornography tends to be obscured for them.

In recent debates, sex books that emphasize both male and female sexual feelings as a sensuality that can exist without violence are being called "erotica" to distinguish them from "pornography."[15] This distinction blurs more than it clarifies the complex mixture of elements that make up sexuality. "Erotica" is soft core, soft focus; it is gentler and tenderer sex than that depicted in pornography. Does this mean true sexuality is diffuse while only perverse sexuality is driven, power hungry, intense, and selfish? I cannot accept this particular dichotomy. It leaves out too much of what is infantile in sex—the reenactment of early feelings, the boundlessness and omnipotence of infant desire and its furious gusto. In pornography all things tend in one direction, a total immersion in one's own sense experience, for which one paradigm must certainly be infancy. For adults this totality, the total

sexualization of everything, can only be a fantasy. But does the fact that it cannot be actually lived mean this fantasy must be discarded? It is a memory, a legitimate element in the human lexicon of feelings.

In pornography, the joys of passivity, of helpless abandonment, of response without responsibility are all endlessly repeated, savored, minutely described. Again this is a fantasy often dismissed with the pejorative "masochistic" as if passivity were in no way a pleasant or a natural condition.

Yet another criticism of pornography is that it presents no recognizable, delineated characters. In a culture where women are routinely objectified it is natural and progressive to see as threatening any literary form that calls dehumanization sexual. Once again, however, there is a more universally human side to this aspect of pornography. Like a lot of far more respectable twentieth-century art, pornography is not about personality but about the explosion of the boundaries of the self. It is a fantasy of an extreme state in which all social constraints are overwhelmed by a flood of sexual energy. Think, for example, of all the pornography about servants f**king mistresses, old men f**king young girls, guardians f**king wards. Class, age, custom—all are deliciously sacrificed, dissolved by sex.

Though pornography's critics are right— pornography *is* exploitation—it is exploitation of *everything*. Promiscuity by definition is a breakdown of barriers. Pornography is not only a reflector of social power imbalances, sexual pathologies, etc., but it is also all those imbalances run riot, run to excess, sometimes explored *ad absurdum*, exploded. Misogyny is one content of pornography; another content is a universal infant desire for complete, immediate gratification, to rule the world out of the very core of passive helplessness.

In a less sexist society, there might be a pornography that is exciting, expressive, interesting, even, perhaps, significant as a form of social rebellion, all traits which, in a sexist society, are obscured by pornography's present role as escape valve for hostility towards women, or as metaphor for fiercely guarded power hierarchies, etc. Instead, in a sexist society, we have two pornographies, one for men, one for women. They both have, hiding within them, those basic human expressions of abandonment I have described. The pornography for men enacts this abandonment on women as objects. How different is the pornography for women, in which sex is bathed in romance, diffused, always implied rather than enacted at all! This pornography is the Harlequin romance.

I described above the oddly narrowed down, denatured world presented in Harlequins. Looking at them as pornography obviously offers a number of alternative explanations for these same traits: the heroine's passivity becomes sexual receptivity and, though I complained earlier about her vapidity, in pornography no one need have a personality. Joanna Russ observed about the heroines of gothic romances something true of Harlequin heroines as well: they are loved as babies are loved, simply because they exist.[16] They have no particular qualities, but pornography bypasses this limitation and reaches straight down to the infant layer where we all imagine ourselves the center of everything by birthright and are sexual beings without shame or need for excuse.

Seeing Harlequins as pornography modifies one's criticism of their selectivity, their know-nothing narrowness. Insofar as they are essentially pornographic in intent, their characters have no past, no context; they live only in the eternal present of sexual feeling, the absorbing interest in the erotic sex object. Insofar as the books are written to elicit sexual excitation, they can be completely closed, repetitive circuits always returning to the moment of arousal when the hero's voice sends "a velvet finger"[17] along the spine of the heroine. In pornography, sex is the whole content; there need be no serious other.

Read this way, Harlequins are benign if banal sex books, but sex books for women have several special characteristics not included in the usual definitions of the genre pornography. In fact, a suggestive, sexual atmosphere is not so easy to establish for women as it is for men. A number of conditions must be right.

In *The Mermaid and the Minotaur,* an extraordinary study of the asymmetry of male and female relationships in all societies where children are primarily raised by women, Dorothy Dinnerstein discusses the reasons why women are so much more dependent than men on deep personal feeling as an ingredient, sometimes a precondition, for sex. Beyond the obvious reasons, the seriousness of sex for the partner who can get pregnant, the seriousness of sex for the partner who is economically and socially dependent on her lover, Dinnerstein adds another, psychological reason for women's tendency to emotionalize sex. She argues that the double standard (male sexual freedom, female loyalty to one sexual tie) comes from the asymmetry in the way the sexes are raised in infancy. Her argument is too complex to be entirely recapitulated here but her conclusion seems crucial to our understanding of the mixture of sexual excitement and anti-erotic restraint that characterizes sexual feeling in Harlequin romances:

Anatomically, coitus offers a far less reliable guarantee of orgasm—or indeed of any intense direct local genital pleasure—to woman than to man. The first-hand coital pleasure of which she is capable more often requires conditions that must be purposefully sought out. Yet it is woman who has less liberty to conduct this kind of search: . . . societal and psychological constraints . . . leave her less free than man to explore the erotic resources of a variety of partners, or even to affirm erotic impulse with any one partner. These constraints also make her less able to give way to simple physical delight without a sense of total self-surrender—a disability that further narrows her choice of partners, and makes her still more afraid of disrupting her rapport with any one partner by acting to intensify the delight, that is, by asserting her own sexual wishes. . . .

What the double standard hurts in women (to the extent that they genuinely, inwardly, bow to it) is the animal center of self-respect: the brute sense of bodily prerogative, of having a right to one's bodily feelings. Fromm made this point very clearly when he argued, in *Man for Himself,* that socially imposed shame about the body serves the function of keeping people submissive to societal authority by weakening in them some inner core of individual authority. . . . On the whole . . . the female burden of genital deprivation is carried meekly, invisibly. Sometimes it cripples real interest in sexual interaction, but often it does not: indeed, it can deepen a woman's need for the emotional rewards of carnal contact. What it most reliably cripples is human pride.[18]

This passage gives us the theoretical skeleton on which the titillations of the Harlequin formula are built. In fact, the Harlequin heroine cannot afford to be only a mass of responsive nerve endings. In order for her sexuality, and the sexuality of the novels' readers, to be released, a number of things must happen that have little to do directly with sex at all. Since she cannot seek out or instruct the man she wants, she must be in a state of constant passive readiness. Since only one man will do, she has the anxiety of deciding, "Is this *the* one?" Since an enormous amount of psychic energy is going to be mobilized in the direction of the man she loves, the man she sleeps with, she must feel sure of him. A one-night stand won't work; she's only just beginning to get her emotional generators going when he's already gone. And orgasm? It probably hasn't happened. She couldn't tell him she wanted it and couldn't tell him *how* she wanted it. If he's already gone, there is no way for her erotic feeling for him to take form, no way for her training of him as a satisfying lover to take place.

Hence the Harlequin heroine has a lot of things to worry about if she wants sexual satisfaction. Parisi has said that these worries are restraints there merely to be deliciously overridden, but they are so constant an accompaniment to the heroine's erotic feelings as to be, under present conditions, inseparable from them. She feels an urge towards deep emotion; she feels anxiety about the serious intentions of the hero; she role plays constantly, presenting herself as a nurturant, passive, receptive figure; and all of this is part of sex to her. Certain social configurations feel safe and right and are real sexual cues for women. The romantic intensity of Harlequins—the waiting, fearing, speculating—are as much a part of their functionings as pornography for women as are the more overtly sexual scenes.

Nor is this just a neutral difference between men and women. In fact, as Dinnerstein suggests, the muting of spontaneous sexual feeling, the necessity which is socially forced on women of channeling their sexual desire, is in fact a great deprivation. In *The Mermaid and the Minotaur* Dinnerstein argues that men have a number of reasons, social and psychological, for discomfort when confronted by the romantic feeling and the demand for security that so often accompany female sexuality. For them growing up and being male both mean cutting off the passionate attachment and dependence on woman, on mother. Women, potential mother figures themselves, have less need to make this absolute break. Men also need to pull away from that inferior category, Woman. Women are stuck in it and naturally romanticize the powerful creatures they can only come close to through emotional and physical ties.

The Harlequin formula perfectly reproduces these differences, these tensions, between the sexes. It depicts a heroine struggling, against the hero's resistance, to get the right combination of elements together so that, for her, orgasmic sex can at last take place. The shape of the Harlequin sexual fantasy is designed to deal women the winning hand they cannot hold in life: a man who is romantically interesting—hence, distant, even frightening—while at the same time he is willing to capitulate to her needs just enough so that she can sleep with him not once but often. His intractability is exciting to her, a proof of his membership in a superior

class of beings but, finally, he must relent to some extent if her breathless anticipation, the foreplay of romance, is to lead to orgasm.

Clearly, getting romantic tension, domestic security, and sexual excitement together in the same fantasy in the right proportions is a delicate balancing act. Harlequins lack excellence by any other measure, but they are masterly in this one respect. In fact, the Harlequin heroine is in a constant fever of anti-erotic anxiety, trying to control the flow of sexual passion between herself and the hero until her surrender can be on her own terms. If the heroine's task is "converting rape into love-making," she must somehow teach the hero to take time, to pay attention, to feel, while herself remaining passive, undemanding, unthreatening. This is yet another delicate miracle of balance which Harlequin romances manage quite well. How do they do it?

The underlying structure of the sexual story goes something like this:

1. The man is hard (a walking phallus).
2. The woman likes this hardness.
3. But, at the outset, this hardness is *too hard*. The man has an ideology that is anti-romantic, anti-marriage. In other words, he will not stay around long enough for her to come, too.
4. Her final release of sexual feeling depends on his changing his mind, *but not too much*. He must become softer (safer, less likely to leave altogether) but not too soft. For good sex, he must be hard, but this hardness must be *at the service of the woman*.

The following passage from Anne Mather's *Born Out of Love* is an example:

His skin was smooth, more roughly textured than hers, but sleek and flexible beneath her palms, his warmth and maleness enveloping her and making her overwhelmingly aware that only the thin material of the culotte suit separated them. He held her face between his hands, and his hardening mouth was echoed throughout the length and breadth of his body. She felt herself yielding weakly beneath him, and his hand slid from her shoulder, across her throat to find the zipper at the front of her suit, impelling it steadily downward.

"No, Logan," she breathed, but he pulled the hands with which she might have resisted him around him, arching her body so that he could observe her reaction to the thrusting aggression of his with sensual satisfaction.

"No?" he probed with gentle mockery, his mouth seeking the pointed fullness of her breasts now exposed to his gaze. "Why not? It's what we both want, don't deny it." . . .

Somehow Charlotte struggled up from the depth of a sexually-induced lethargy. It wasn't easy, when her whole body threatened to betray her, but his words were too similar to the words he had used to her once before, and she remembered only too well what had happened next. . . .

She sat up quickly, her fingers fumbling with the zipper, conscious all the while of Logan lying beside her, and the potent attraction of his lean body. God, she thought unsteadily, what am I doing here? And then, more wildly: Why am I leaving him? *I want him!* But not on his terms, the still small voice of sanity reminded her, and she struggled to her feet.[19]

In these romantic love stories, sex on a woman's terms is romanticized sex. Romantic sexual fantasies are contradictory. They include both the desire to be blindly ravished, to melt, and the desire to be spiritually adored, saved from the humiliation of dependence and sexual passivity through the agency of a protective male who will somehow make reparation to the woman he loves for her powerlessness.

Harlequins reveal and pander to this impossible fantasy life. Female sexuality, a rare subject in all but the most recent writing, is not doomed to be what the Harlequins describe. Nevertheless, some of the barriers that hold back female sexual feelings are acknowledged and finally circumvented quite sympathetically in these novels. They are sex books for people who have plenty of good reasons for worrying about sex.

While there is something wonderful in the heroine's insistence that sex is more exciting and more momentous when it includes deep feeling, she is fighting a losing battle as long as she can only define deep feeling as a mystified romantic longing, on the one hand, and as marriage, on the other. In Harlequins the price for needing emotional intimacy is that she must passively wait, must anxiously calculate. Without spontaneity and aggression, a whole set of sexual possibilities is lost to her just as, without emotional depth, a whole set of sexual possibilities is lost to men.

Though one may dislike the circuitous form of sexual expression in Harlequin heroines, a strength of the books is that they insist that good sex for women requires an emotional and social context that can free them from constraint. If one dislikes the kind of social norms the heroine seeks as her sexual preconditions, it is still interesting to see sex treated not primarily as a physical event at all but as a social drama, as a carefully modulated set of psychological possibilities between people. This is a mirror image of much writing more commonly labeled pornography. In fact one can't resist speculating that equality between the sexes as child rearers and workers might well bring personal feeling and abandoned physicality together in wonderful combinations undreamed of in either male or female pornography as we know it.

The ubiquity of the books indicates a central truth: romance is a primary category of the female imagination. The women's movement has left this fact of female consciousness largely untouched. While most serious women *novelists* treat romance with irony and cynicism, most women do not. Harlequins may well be closer to describing women's hopes for love than the work of fine women novelists. Harlequins eschew irony; they take love straight. Harlequins eschew realism; they are serious about fantasy and escape. In spite of all the audience manipulations inherent in the Harlequin formula, the connection between writer and reader is tonally seamless; Harlequins are respectful, tactful, friendly towards their audience. The letters that pour in to their publishers speak above all of involvement, warmth, human values. The world that can make Harlequin romances appear warm is indeed a cold, cold place.

Notes

1. Lindsay (1977, p. 10).
2. Stratton (1977, pp. 56, 147).
3. Here is an example of this sort of travelogue prose: "There was something to appeal to all age groups in the thousand-acre park in the heart of the city—golf for the energetic, lawn bowling for the more sedate, a zoo for the children's pleasure, and even secluded walks through giant cedars for lovers—but Cori thought of none of these things as Greg drove to a parking place bordering the Inlet"

(Graham, 1976, p. 25).
4. Mather (1977, p. 42).
5. See Russ (1973).
6. Mather (1977, p. 42).
7. Clair (1978, p. 118).
8. Lindsay (1977, p. 13).
9. Stratton (1977, p. 66). The adjectives "cruel" and "satanic" are commonly used for heroes.
10. Graham (1976, p. 63).
11. Delivered, April 6, 1978, Livingston College, Rutgers University.
12. Stratton (1977, p. 132).
13. Stratton (1977, p. 112).
14. Stratton (1977, pp. 99, 102, 139).
15. See Gloria Steinem (1978) and other articles in the November 1978 issue of *Ms.* An unpublished piece by Brigitte Frase, "From Pornography to Mind-Blowing," MLA talk, 1978, strongly presents my own view that this debate is specious. See also Susan Sontag's "The Pornographic Imagination," in *Styles of Radical Will* and the Jean Paulhan preface to *Story of O*, "Happiness in Slavery."
16. Russ (1973, p. 679).
17. Stratton (1977, p. 115).
18. Dinnerstein (1976, pp. 73–75).
19. Mather (1977, pp. 70–72).

References

Clair, C. (1978). *A streak of gold*. Toronto: Harlequin.

Dinnerstein, D. (1976). *The mermaid and the minotaur: Sexual arrangements and human malaise*. New York: Harper & Row.

Graham, E. (1976). *Mason's ridge*. Toronto: Harlequin.

Lindsay, R. (1977). *Prescription for love*. Toronto: Harlequin.

Mather, A. (1977). *Born out of love*. Toronto: Harlequin.

Russ, J. (1973). Somebody's trying to kill me and I think it's my husband: The modern gothic. *Journal of Popular Culture, 6*(4), 666–691.

Sontag, S. (1991). The pornographic imagination. In S. Sontag, *Styles of radical will*. New York: Doubleday.

Steinem, G. (1978, November). Erotica and pornography: A clear and present difference. *Ms.*

Stratton, R. (1977). *The sign of the ram.* Toronto: Harlequin.

NOTE: Excerpts reprinted from *Radical History Review* (Summer 1979), by permission of Cambridge University Press and Ann Barr Snitow.

Janice A. Radway *is the Francis Fox Professor of Literature at Duke University. She is currently interested in the history of literacy and reading in the United States and how it pertains to the lives of women. She has published two books, including* Reading the Romance: Women, Patriarchy, and Popular Literature, *and is the editor of* American Quarterly. *"Women Read the Romance" was first published in* Feminist Studies *in 1983.*

WOMEN READ THE ROMANCE

The Interaction of Text and Context

Janice A. Radway

By now, the statistics are well known and the argument familiar. The Canadian publisher, Harlequin Enterprises, alone claims to have sold 168 million romances throughout the world in the single year of 1979.[1] In addition, at least twelve other paperback publishing houses currently issue from two to six romantic novels every month, nearly all of which are scooped up voraciously by an audience whose composition and size has yet to be accurately determined.[2] The absence of such data, however, has prevented neither journalists nor literary scholars from offering complex, often subtle interpretations of the meaning of the form's characteristic narrative development. Although these interpreters of the romance do not always concur about the particular ways in which the tale reinforces traditional expectations about female-male relationships, all agree that the stories perpetuate patriarchal attitudes and structures. They do so, these critics tell us, by continuing to maintain that a woman's journey to happiness and fulfillment must always be undertaken in the company of a protective man. In the words of Ann Snitow,

Radway, Janice A., "Women Read the Romance: The Interaction of Text and Context" was originally published in FEMINIST STUDIES, Volume 9, Number 1 (Spring 1983): 53–78, by permission of the publisher, Feminist Studies, Inc.

romances "reinforce the prevailing cultural code" proclaiming that "pleasure for women is men."[3]

The acuity of interpretations such as those developed by Snitow, Ann Douglas, and Tania Modleski certainly cannot be denied.[4] Indeed, their very complexity lends credence to the secondary, often implicit claim made by these theorists of the romance that their proposed interpretations can also serve as an adequate explanation of the genre's extraordinary popularity. However, a recent ethnographic study of a group of regular romance readers clustered about a bookseller, who is recognized by authors and editors alike as an "expert" in the field, suggests that these explanations of reading choice and motivation are incomplete.[5] Because these interpreters do not take account of the actual, day-to-day context within which romance reading occurs, and because they ignore romance readers' own book choice and theories about why they read,

they fail to detect the ways in which the activity may serve positive functions even as the novels celebrate patriarchal institutions. Consequently, they also fail to understand that some contemporary romances actually attempt to reconcile changing attitudes about gender behavior with more traditional sexual arrangements.

The particular weaknesses of these interpretations as *explanations* of reading behavior can be traced to the fact that they focus only on the texts in isolation. This reification of the literary text persists in much practical criticism today which continues to draw its force from the poetics of the New Criticism and its assertion that the text, as a more or less well-made artifact, contains a set of meanings that can be articulated adequately by a trained critic.[6] Interpretive reading is an unproblematic activity for these students of the romance because they too assume that the text has intrinsic power to coerce all cooperative readers into discovering the core of meaning that is undeniably *there* in the book. Moreover, because their analysis proceeds under the assumption that a literary work's objective reality remains unchanged despite differences among individual readers and in the attention they devote to the text, these critics understandably assume further that their own reading of a given literary form can stand as the representative of all adequate readings of it. Finally, they assume also that their particular reading can then become the object of further cultural analysis that seeks to explain the popularity of the form and its appeal to its audience. In the end, they produce their explanation merely by positing a desire in the reading audience for the specific meaning they have unearthed.

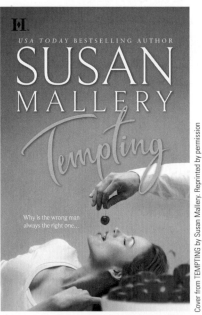

Cover from TEMPTING by Susan Mallery. Reprinted by permission of Harlequin Enterprises Limited.

New theories of the literary text and the reading process have been advanced, however, the basic premises of which call for a modification of this standard explanatory procedure. Although the myriad forms of reader-theory and reader-response criticism are too diverse and too complicated to review in any depth here, all acknowledge, to a greater or lesser degree, that the reader is responsible for what is made of the literary text.[7] Despite their interest in the *making* of meaning, reader-theorists do not believe that literary texts exert no force at all on the meaning that is finally produced in a given reading. Rather, most argue that literary meaning is the result of a complex, temporally evolving interaction between a fixed verbal structure and a socially situated reader. That reader makes sense of the verbal structure by referring to previously learned aesthetic and cultural codes. Literary meaning, then, in the words of Stanley Fish, perhaps the most prominent of reader-theorists, is "the property neither of fixed and stable texts nor of free and independent readers but of interpretive communities that are responsible both for the shape of the reader's activities and for the texts those activities produce."[8]

Clearly, the reader-theory emphasis on the constitutive power and activity of the reader suggests, indeed almost demands, that the cultural critic who is interested in the "meaning" of a form and the causes of its popularity consider first whether she is a member of a different interpretive community than the readers who are her ostensible subjects. If she is, she may well produce and evaluate textual meaning in a manner fundamentally different from those whose behavior she seeks to explain. None of the early

students of the romance have so foregrounded their own interpretive activities. Because of their resulting assumption of an identity between their own reading and that of regular romance readers, they have severed the form from the women who actually construct its meaning from within a particular context and on the basis of a specific constellation of attitudes and beliefs. This assumption has resulted, finally, in an incomplete account of the particular ideological power of this literary form, in that these critics have not successfully isolated the particular function performed through the act of romance reading which is crucially important to the readers themselves. In ignoring certain specific aspects of the romance readers' daily context, they have also failed to see how the women's selection and construction of their favorite novels addresses the problems and desires they deem to be characteristic of their lives.

To guard against the ever-present danger of advancing a theory about the meaning of a text for a given audience on the basis of a performance of that text, which no individual in the group would recognize, one must investigate exactly what the entire act of romance reading means to the women who buy the books. If the romance is to be cited as evidence testifying to the evolution or perpetuation of cultural beliefs about women's roles and the institution of marriage, it is first necessary to know what women actually understand themselves to be doing when they read a romance they like. A more complete cultural analysis of the contemporary romance might specify how actual readers interpret the actions of principal characters, how they comprehend the final significance of the narrative resolution and, perhaps most important, how the act of repetitively encountering this fantasy fits within the daily routine of their private lives. We need to know not what the romantic text objectively means—in fact, it never means in this way—but rather how the *event* of reading the text is interpreted by the women who engage in it.[9]

The interpretation of the romance's cultural significance offered here has been developed from a series of extensive ethnographic-like interviews with a group of compulsive romance readers in a predominantly urban, central midwestern state among the nation's top twenty in total population.[10] I discovered my principal informant and her customers with the aid of a senior editor at Doubleday whom I had been interviewing about the publication of romances. Sally Arteseros told me of a bookstore employee who had developed a regular clientele of fifty to seventy-five regular romance readers who relied on her for advice about the best romances to buy and those to avoid. When I wrote to Dot Evans, as I will now call her, to ask whether I might question her about how she interpreted, categorized, and evaluated romantic fiction, I had no idea that she had also begun to write a newsletter designed to enable bookstores to advise their customers about the quality of the romances published monthly. She has since copyrighted this newsletter and incorporated it as a business. Dot is so successful at serving the women who patronize her chain outlet that the central office of this major chain occasionally relies on her sales predictions to gauge romance distribution throughout the system. Her success has also brought her to the attention of both editors and writers for whom she now reads manuscripts and galleys.

My knowledge of Dot and her readers is based on roughly sixty hours of interviews conducted in June 1980, and February 1981. I have talked extensively with Dot about romances, reading, and her advising activities as well as observed her interactions with her customers at the bookstore. I have also conducted both group and individual interviews with sixteen of her regular customers and administered a lengthy questionnaire to forty-two of these women. Although not representative of all women who read romances, the group appears to be demographically similar to a sizable segment of that audience as it has been mapped by several rather secretive publishing houses.

Dorothy Evans lives and works in the community of Smithton, as do most of her regular customers. A city of about 112,900 inhabitants, Smithton is located five miles due east of the state's second largest city, in a metropolitan area with a total population of over 1 million. Dot was forty-eight years old at the time of the survey, the wife of a journeyman plumber, and the mother of three children in their twenties. She is extremely bright and articulate and, while not a proclaimed feminist, holds some beliefs about women that might be labeled as such. Although she did not work outside the home when her children were young and does not now believe that a woman needs a career to be fulfilled, she feels women should have the opportunity to work and be paid equally with men. Dot also believes that women should have the right to abortion, though she admits that her deep religious convictions would prevent her from seeking one herself. She is not disturbed by the Equal Rights Amendment and can and does converse eloquently about the oppression women have endured for years at the hands of men. Despite her opinions, however, she believes implicitly in the value of true romance and thoroughly enjoys discovering again and again that women can find men who will love them as they wish to be loved. Although most of her regular customers are more conservative than Dot in the sense that they do not advocate political measures to redress past grievances, they are quite aware that men commonly think themselves superior to women and often mistreat them as a result.

In general, Dot's customers are married, middle-class mothers with at least a high school education.[11] More than 60 percent of the women were between the ages of twenty-five and forty-four at the time of the study, a fact that duplicates fairly closely Harlequin's finding that the majority of its readers is between twenty-five and forty-nine.[12] Silhouette Books has also recently reported that 65 percent of the romance market is below the age of 40.[13] Exactly 50 percent of the Smithton women have high school diplomas, while 32 percent report completing at least some college work. Again, this seems to suggest that the interview group is fairly representative, for Silhouette also indicates that 45 percent of the romance market has attended at least some college. The employment status and family income of Dot's customers also seem to duplicate those of the audience mapped by the publishing houses. Forty-two percent of the Smithton women, for instance, work part-time outside the home. Harlequin claims that 49 percent of its audience is similarly

employed. The Smithton women report slightly higher incomes than those of the average Harlequin reader (43 percent of the Smithton women have incomes of $15,000 to $24,999, 33 percent have incomes of $25,000 to $49,999—the average income of the Harlequin reader is $15,000 to $20,000), but the difference is not enough to change the general sociological status of the group.

In one respect, however, Dot and her customers may be unusual, although it is difficult to say for sure because corroborative data from other sources are sadly lacking. Although almost 70 percent of the women claim to read books other than romances, 37 percent nonetheless report reading from five to nine romances each week. Even though more than one-half read less (from one to four romances a week), when the figures are converted to monthly totals they indicate that one-half the Smithton women read between four and sixteen romances a month, while 40 percent read more than twenty. This particular group is obviously obsessed with romantic fiction. The most recent comprehensive survey of American book readers and their habits has discovered that romance readers tend to read more books within their favorite category than do other category readers, but these readers apparently read substantially fewer than the Smithton group. Yankelovich, Skelly, and White found in their 1978 study that 21 percent of the total book reading public had read *at least* one gothic or romance in the last six months.[14] The average number of romantic novels read by this group in the last six months was only nine. Thus, while it is probably true that romance readers are repetitive consumers, most apparently do not read as consistently or as constantly as Dot and her customers. Romances undoubtedly play a more significant role, then, in the lives of the Smithton women than they do in those of occasional romance readers. Nevertheless, even this latter group appears to demonstrate a marked desire for, if not dependency upon, the fantasy they offer.

When asked why they read romances, the Smithton women overwhelmingly cite escape or relaxation as their goal. They use the word "escape," however, both literally and figuratively. On the one hand, they value their romances highly because the act of reading them literally draws the women away from their present surroundings. Because they must produce the meaning of the story by attending closely to the words on the page, they find that their attention is withdrawn from concerns that plague them in reality. One woman remarked with a note of triumph in her voice: "My body may be in that room, but I'm not!" She and her sister readers see their romance reading as a legitimate way of denying a present reality that occasionally becomes too onerous to bear. This particular means of escape is better than television viewing for these women, because the cultural value attached to books permits them to overcome the guilt they feel about avoiding their responsibilities. They believe that reading of any kind is, by nature, educational.[15] They insist accordingly that they also read to learn.[16]

On the other hand, the Smithton readers are quite willing to acknowledge that the romances which so preoccupy them are little more than fantasies or fairy tales that always end happily. They readily admit in fact that the characters and events discovered in the pages of the typical romance do not resemble the people and occurrences they must deal with in their daily lives. On the basis of the following comments, made in response to a question about what romances "do" better than other novels available today, one can conclude that it is precisely the unreal, fantastic shape of the story that makes their literal escape even more complete and gratifying. Although these are only a few of the remarks given in response to the undirected question, they are representative of the group's general sentiment.

Romances hold my interest and do not leave me depressed or up in the air at the end like many modern day books tend to do. Romances also just make me feel good reading them as I identify with the heroines.

The kind of books I mainly read are very different from everyday living. That's why I read them. Newspapers, etc., I find boring because all you read is sad news. I can get enough of that on TV news. I like stories that take your mind off everyday matters.

Different than everyday life.

Everyone is always under so much pressure. They like books that let them escape.

Because it is an escape, and we can dream. And pretend that it is our life.

I'm able to escape the harsh world a few hours a day.

It is a way of escaping from everyday living.

They always seem an escape and they usually turn out the way you wish life really was.

I enjoy reading because it offers me a small vacation from everyday life and an interesting and amusing way to pass the time.

These few comments all hint at a certain sadness that many of the Smithton women seem to share because life has not given them all that it once promised. A deep-seated sense of betrayal also lurks behind their deceptively simple expressions of a need to believe in a fairy tale. Although they have not elaborated in these comments, many of the women explained in the interviews that despite their disappointments, they feel refreshed and strengthened by their vicarious participation in a fantasy relationship where the heroine is frequently treated as they themselves would most like to be loved.

This conception of romance reading as an escape that is both literal and figurative implies flight from some situation in the real world which is either stifling or overwhelming, as well as a metaphoric transfer to another, more desirable universe where events are happily resolved. Unashamed to admit that they like to indulge in temporary escape, the Smithton women are also surprisingly candid about the circumstances that necessitate their desire. When asked to specify what they are fleeing from, they invariably mention the "pressures" and "tensions" they experience as wives and mothers. Although none of the women can cite the voluminous feminist literature about the psychological toll exacted by the constant demand to physically and emotionally nurture others, they are nonetheless eloquent about how draining and unrewarding their duties can be.[17] When first asked why women find it necessary to escape, Dot gave the following answer without once pausing to rest:

As a mother, I have run 'em to the orthodontist, I have run 'em to the swimming pool. I have run 'em to baton twirling lessons. I have run up to school because they forgot their lunch. You know, I mean really. And you do it. And it isn't that you begrudge it. That isn't it. Then my husband would walk in the door and

he'd say, "Well, what did you do today?" You know, it was like, "Well, tell me how you spent the last eight hours, because I've been out working." And I finally got to the point where I would say, "Well, I read four books, and I did the wash and got the meal on the table and the beds are all made and the house is tidy." And I would get defensive like, "So what do you call all this? Why should I have to tell you because I certainly don't ask you what you did for eight hours, step by step."

But their husbands do do that. We've compared notes. They hit the house and it's like "Well, all right, I've been out earning a living. Now what have you been doin' with your time?" And you begin to be feeling, "Now, really, why is he questioning me?"

Romance reading, as Dot herself puts it, constitutes a temporary "declaration of independence" from the social roles of wife and mother. By placing the barrier of the book between themselves and their families, these women reserve a special space and time for themselves alone. As a consequence, they momentarily allow themselves to abandon the attitude of total self-abnegation in the interest of family welfare which they have so dutifully learned is the proper stance for a good wife and mother. Romance reading is both an assertion of deeply felt psychological needs and a means for satisfying those needs. Simply put, these needs arise because no other member of the family, as it is presently constituted in this still-patriarchal society, is yet charged with the affective and emotional reconstitution of a wife and mother. If she is depleted by her efforts to care for others, she is nonetheless expected to restore and sustain herself as well. As one of Dot's customers put it, "You always have to be a Mary Poppins. You can't be sad, you can't be mad, you have to keep everything bottled up inside."

Nancy Chodorow has recently discussed this structural peculiarity of the modern family and its impact on the emotional lives of women in her influential book, *The Reproduction of Mothering*,[18] a complex re-formulation of the Freudian theory of female personality development. Chodorow maintains that women often continue to experience a desire for intense affective nurturance and relationality well into adulthood as a result of an unresolved separation from their primary caretaker. It is highly significant, she argues, that in patriarchal society this caretaker is almost inevitably a woman. The felt similarity between mother and daughter creates an unusually intimate connection between them which later makes it exceedingly difficult for the daughter to establish autonomy and independence. Chodorow maintains, on the other hand, that because male children are also reared by women, they tend to separate more completely from their mothers by suppressing their own emotionality and capacities for tenderness which they associate with mothers and femininity. The resulting asymmetry in human personality, she concludes, leads to a situation where men typically cannot fulfill all of a woman's emotional needs. As a consequence, women turn to the act of mothering as a way of vicariously recovering that lost relationality and intensity.

My findings about Dot Evans and her customers suggest that the vicarious pleasure a woman receives through the nurturance of others may not be completely satisfying, because the act of caring for them also makes tremendous demands on a woman and can deplete her sense of self. In that case, she may well turn to romance reading in an effort to construct a fantasy-world where she is attended, as the heroine is, by a man who reassures her of her special status and unique identity.

The value of the romance may have something to do, then, with the fact that women find it especially difficult to indulge in the restorative experience of visceral regression to an infantile state where the self is cared for perfectly by another. This regression is so difficult precisely because women have been taught to believe that men must be their sole source of pleasure. Although there is nothing biologically lacking in men to make this ideal pleasure unattainable, as Chodorow's theories tell us, their engendering and socialization by the patriarchal family traditionally masks the very traits that would permit them to nurture women in this way. Because they are encouraged to be aggressive, competitive, self-sufficient, and unemotional, men often find sustained attention to the emotional needs of others both unfamiliar and difficult. While the Smithton women only minimally discussed their husbands' abilities to take care of them as they would like, when they commented on their favorite romantic heroes they made it clear that they enjoy imagining themselves being tenderly cared for and solicitously protected by a fictive character who inevitably proves to be spectacularly masculine and unusually nurturant as well.[19]

Indeed, this theme of pleasure recurred constantly in the discussions with the Smithton women. They insisted repeatedly that when they are reading a romance, they feel happy and content. Several commented that they particularly relish moments when they are home alone and can relax in a hot tub or in a favorite chair with a good book. Others admitted that they most like to read in a warm bed late at night. Their association of romances with contentment, pleasure, and good feelings is apparently not unique, for in conducting a market research study, Fawcett discovered that when asked to draw a woman reading a romance, romance readers inevitably depict someone who is exaggeratedly happy.[20]

The Smithton group's insistence that they turn to romances because the experience of reading the novels gives them hope, provides pleasure, and causes contentment raises the unavoidable question of what aspects of the romantic narrative itself could possibly give rise to feelings such as these. How are we to explain, furthermore, the obvious contradiction between this reader emphasis on pleasure and hope, achieved through vicarious appreciation of the ministrations of a tender hero, and the observations of the earlier critics of romances that such books are dominated by men who at least temporarily abuse and hurt the women they purportedly love? In large part, the contradiction arises because the two groups are not reading according to the same interpretive strategies, neither are they reading nor commenting on the same books. Textual analyses like those offered by Douglas, Modleski, and Snitow are based on the common assumption that because romances are formulaic and therefore essentially identical, analysis of a randomly chosen sample will reveal the meaning unfailingly communicated by every example of the genre. This methodological procedure is based on the further assumption that category readers do not themselves perceive variations within the genre, nor do they select their books in a manner significantly different from the random choice of the analyst.

In fact, the Smithton readers do not believe the books are identical, nor do they approve of all the romances they read. They have elaborated a complex distinction between "good" and "bad" romances and they have accordingly experimented with various techniques that they hoped would enable them to identify bad romances before they paid for a book that would only offend them. Some tried to decode titles and cover blurbs by looking for key words serving as clues to the book's tone; others refused to buy romances by authors they didn't recognize; still others read several pages *including the ending* before they bought the book. Now, however, most of the people in the Smithton group have been freed from the need to rely on these inexact predictions because Dot Evans shares their perceptions and evaluations of the category and can alert them to unusually successful romantic fantasies while steering them away from those they call "disgusting perversions."

When the Smithton readers' comments about good and bad romances are combined with the conclusions drawn from an analysis of twenty of their favorite books and an equal number of those they classify as particularly inadequate, an illuminating picture of the fantasy fueling the romance-reading experience develops.[21] To begin with, Dot and her readers will not tolerate any story in which the heroine is seriously abused by men. They find multiple rapes especially distressing and dislike books in which a woman is brutally hurt by a man only to fall desperately in love with him in the last four pages. The Smithton women are also offended by explicit sexual description and scrupulously avoid the work of authors like Rosemary Rogers and Judith

Krantz who deal in what they call "perversions" and "promiscuity." They also do not like romances that overtly perpetuate the double standard by excusing the hero's simultaneous involvement with several women. They insist, one reader commented, on "one woman—one man." They also seem to dislike any kind of detailed description of male genitalia, although the women enjoy suggestive descriptions of how the hero is emotionally aroused to an overpowering desire for the heroine. Their preferences seem to confirm Beatrice Faust's argument in *Women, Sex, and Pornography* that women are not interested in the visual display characteristic of male pornography, but prefer process-oriented materials detailing the development of deep emotional connection between two individuals.[22]

According to Dot and her customers, the quality of the *ideal* romantic fantasy is directly dependent on the character of the heroine and the manner in which the hero treats her. The plot, of course, must always focus on a series of obstacles to the final declaration of love between the two principals. However, a good romance involves an unusually bright and determined woman and a man who is spectacularly masculine, but at the same time capable of remarkable empathy and tenderness. Although they enjoy the usual chronicle of misunderstandings and mistakes which inevitably leads to the heroine's belief that the hero intends to harm her, the Smithton readers prefer stories that combine a much-understated version of this continuing antagonism with a picture of a gradually developing love. They most wish to participate in the slow process by which two people become acquainted, explore each other's foibles, wonder about the other's feelings,

and eventually "discover" that they are loved by the other.

In conducting an analysis of the plots of the twenty romances listed as "ideal" by the Smithton readers, I was struck by their remarkable similarities in narrative structure. In fact, all twenty of these romances are very tightly organized around the evolving relationship between a single couple composed of a beautiful, defiant, and sexually immature woman and a brooding, handsome man who is also curiously capable of soft, gentle gestures. Although minor foil figures are used in these romances, none of the ideal stories seriously involves either hero or heroine with one of the rival characters.[23] They are employed mainly as contrasts to the more likable and proper central pair or as purely temporary obstacles to the pair's delayed union because one or the other mistakenly suspects the partner of having an affair with the rival. However, because the reader is never permitted to share this mistaken assumption in the ideal romance, she knows all along that the relationship is not as precarious as its participants think it to be. The rest of the narrative in the twenty romances chronicles the gradual crumbling of barriers between these two individuals who are fearful of being used by the other. As their defenses against emotional response fall away and their sexual passion rises inexorably, the typical narrative plunges on until the climactic point at which the hero treats the heroine to some supreme act of tenderness, and she realizes that his apparent emotional indifference was only the mark of his hesitancy about revealing the extent of his love for and dependence upon her.

The Smithton women especially like romances that commence with the early marriage of the hero and heroine for reasons of convenience. Apparently, they do so because they delight in the subsequent, necessary chronicle of the pair's growing awareness that what each took to be indifference or hate is, in reality, unexpressed love and suppressed passion. In such favorite romances as *The Flame and the Flower, The Black Lyon, Shanna,* and *Made For Each Other,* the heroine begins marriage thinking that she detests and is detested by her spouse. She is thrown into a quandary, however, because her partner's behavior vacillates from indifference, occasional brusqueness, and even cruelty to tenderness and passion. Consequently, the heroine spends most of her time in these romances, as well as in the others comprising this sample, trying to read the hero's behavior as a set of signs expressing his true feelings toward her. The final outcome of the story turns upon a fundamental process of *reinterpretation,* whereby she suddenly and clearly sees that the behavior she feared was actually the product of deeply felt passion and a previous hurt. Once she learns to reread his past behavior and thus to excuse him for the suffering he has caused her, she is free to respond warmly to his occasional acts of tenderness. Her response inevitably encourages him to believe in her and finally to treat her as she wishes to be treated. When this reinterpretation process is completed in the twenty ideal romances, the heroine is always tenderly enfolded in the hero's embrace and the reader is permitted to identify with her as she is gently caressed, carefully protected, and verbally praised with words of love.[24] At the climactic moment (pp. 201–2) of *The Sea Treasure,* for example, when the hero tells the heroine to put her arms around him, the reader is informed of his gentleness in the following way:

She put her cold face against his in an attitude of surrender that moved him to unutterable tenderness. He swung her clear of the encroaching water and eased his way up to the next level, with painful slowness. . . .When at last he had finished, he pulled her into his arms and held her against his heart for a moment. . . .Tenderly he lifted her. Carefully he negotiated the last of the treacherous slippery rungs to the mine entrance. Once there, he swung her up into his arms, and walked out into the starlit night.

The cold air revived her, and she stirred in his arms.

"Dominic?" she whispered.

He bent his head and kissed her.

"Sea Treasure," he whispered.

Passivity, it seems, is at the heart of the romance-reading experience in the sense that the final goal of the most valued romances is the creation of perfect union in which the ideal male, who is masculine and strong, yet nurturant, finally admits his recognition of the intrinsic worth of the heroine. Thereafter, she is required to do nothing more than exist as the center of this paragon's attention. Romantic escape is a temporary but literal denial of the demands these women recognize as an integral part of their roles as nurturing wives and mothers. But it is also a figurative journey to a utopian state of total receptiveness in which the reader, as a consequence of her identification with the heroine, feels herself the passive *object* of someone else's attention and solicitude. The romance reader in effect is permitted the experience of feeling cared for, the sense of having been affectively reconstituted, even if both are lived only vicariously.

Although the ideal romance may thus enable a woman to satisfy vicariously those psychological needs created in her by a patriarchal culture unable to fulfill them, the very centrality of the rhetoric of reinterpretation to the romance suggests also that the reading experience may indeed have some of the unfortunate consequences pointed to by earlier romance critics.[25] Not only is the dynamic of reinterpretation an essential component of the plot of the ideal romance, but it also characterizes the very process of constructing its meaning because the reader is inevitably given more information about the hero's motives than is the heroine herself. Hence, when Ranulf temporarily abuses his young bride in *The Black Lyon,* the reader understands that what appears as inexplicable cruelty to Lyonene, the heroine, is an irrational desire to hurt her because of what his first wife did to him.[26] It is possible that in reinterpreting the hero's behavior before Lyonene does, the Smithton women may be practicing a procedure which is valuable to them precisely because it enables them to reinterpret their own spouse's similar emotional coldness and likely preoccupation with work or sports. In rereading this category of behavior, they reassure themselves that it does not necessarily mean that a woman is not loved. Romance reading, it would seem, can function as a kind of training for the all-too-common task of reinterpreting a spouse's unsettling actions as the signs of passion, devotion, and love.

If the Smithton women are indeed learning reading behaviors that help them to dismiss or justify their husbands' affective distance, this procedure is probably carried out on an unconscious level. In any form of cultural or anthropological analysis in which the subjects of the study cannot reveal all the complexity or covert significance of their behavior, a certain amount of speculation is necessary. The analyst, however, can and should take account of any other observable evidence that might reveal the motives and meanings she is seeking. In this case, the Smithton readers' comments about bad romances are particularly helpful.

In general, bad romances are characterized by one of two things: an unusually cruel hero who subjects the heroine to various kinds of verbal and physical abuse, or a diffuse plot that permits the hero to become involved with other women before he settles upon the heroine. Since the Smithton readers will tolerate complicated subplots in some romances if the hero and heroine continue to function as a pair, clearly it is the involvement with others rather than the plot complexity that distresses them. When asked why they disliked these books despite the fact that they all ended happily with the hero converted into the heroine's attentive lover, Dot and her customers replied again and again that they rejected the books precisely because they found them unbelievable. In elaborating, they insisted indignantly that *they* could never forgive the hero's early transgressions and they see no reason why they should be asked to believe that the heroine can. What they are suggesting, then, is that certain kinds of male behavior associated with the stereotype of male machismo can never be forgiven or reread as the signs of love. They are thus not interested *only* in the romance's happy ending. They want to involve themselves in a story that will permit them to enjoy the hero's tenderness *and* to reinterpret his momentary blindness and cool indifference as the marks of a love so intense that he is wary of admitting it. Their delight in both these aspects of the process of romance reading and their deliberate attempt to select books that will include "a gentle hero" and "a slight misunderstanding" suggest that deeply felt needs are the source of their interest in both components of the genre. On the one hand, they long for emotional attention and tender care; on the other, they wish to rehearse the discovery that a man's distance can be explained and excused as his way of expressing love.

It is easy to condemn this latter aspect of romance reading as a reactionary force that reconciles women to a social situation which denies them full development, even as it refuses to accord them the emotional sustenance they require. Yet to identify romances with this conservative moment alone is to miss those other benefits associated with the act of read-ing as a restorative pastime whose impact on a beleaguered woman is not so simply dismissed. If we are serious about feminist politics and committed to reformulating not only our own lives but those of others, we would do well not to condescend to romance readers as hopeless traditionalists who are recalcitrant in their refusal to acknowledge the emotional costs of patriarchy. We must begin to recognize that romance reading is fueled by dissatisfaction and disaffection, not by perfect contentment with woman's lot. Moreover, we must also understand that some romance readers' experiences are not strictly congruent with the set of ideological propositions that typically legitimate patriarchal marriage. They are characterized, rather, by a sense of longing caused by patriarchal marriage's failure to address all their needs.

In recognizing both the yearning and the fact that its resolution is only a vicarious one not so easily achieved in a real situation, we may find it possible to identify more precisely the very limits of patriarchal ideology's success. Endowed thus with a better understanding of what women want, but often fail to get from the traditional arrangements they consciously support, we may provide ourselves with that very issue whose discussion would reach many more women and potentially raise their consciousnesses about the particular dangers and failures of patriarchal institutions. By helping romance readers to see why they long for relationality and tenderness and are unlikely to get either in the form they desire if current gender arrangements are continued, we may help to convert their amorphous longing into a focused desire for specific change.

The strategic value of recognizing both the possibility that romance reading may have some positive benefits and that even its more conservative effects actually originate in significant discontent with the institutions the books purport to celebrate becomes even clearer when one looks more carefully at the Smithton readers' feelings about heroine/hero interactions in ideal romances. Those feelings also indicate that small changes are beginning to occur in women's expectations about female and male behavior. Dot and her customers all emphatically insist that the ideal heroine must be intelligent and independent, and they particularly applaud those who are capable of holding their own in repartee with men. In fact, three-fourths of the Smithton women listed both "intelligence" (thirty-three women) and "a sense of humor" (thirty-one women) as being among the three most important characteristics of a romantic heroine. Although "independence" was chosen less often, still, twenty of these readers selected this trait from a list of nine as one of three essential ingredients in the heroine's personality. These readers value romance writers who are adept at rendering verbal dueling because, as one woman explained, "it's very exciting and you never know who's going to come out on top."

Their interest in this characteristic aspect of romantic fiction seems to originate in their desire to identify with a woman who is strong and courageous enough to stand up to an angry man. They remember well favorite heroines and snatches of dialogue read several years before in which those heroines managed momentarily to best their antagonists.[27] Dot and her customers are quite aware that few women can hope to subdue a man physically if he is determined to have his way. As a consequence, they believe it essential for women to develop the ability to use words adroitly if they are to impose their own wills. The Smithton women reserve their greatest scorn for romances with "namby-pamby" heroines and point to Barbara Cartland's women, whom they universally detest, as the perfect example of these. Their repeated insistence on the need for strong and intelligent heroines attests to their wish to dissociate themselves from the stereotype of women as weak, passive, and foolish individuals. Clearly, their longing for competence could be encouraged by showing such women how to acquire and to express it more readily in the world beyond the home.

However, the ideal heroine who temporarily outwits the hero often symbolically "pays for" her transgression later in the same chapter when he treats her brusquely or forces his sexual attention upon her. This narrative may well betoken ambivalence on the part of writers and readers who experience a certain amount of guilt over their desire to identify with a woman who sometimes acts independently and with force. Still, I have placed the "pays for" in quotation marks here because neither the books, nor apparently do the readers, consciously construct the interaction in this particular manner. When questioned closely about such a chronology of events, instead of admitting reservations about the overly aggressive nature of a heroine's behavior, Dot and her customers focused instead on the unjustified nature of the hero's actions. Not only did they remember specific instances of "completely blind" and "stupid" behavior on the part of romantic heroes, but they also often went on at length about such instances, vociferously protesting this sort of mistreatment of an innocent heroine. Given the vehemence of their reaction, it seems possible that the male violence that does occur in romances may actually serve as an opportunity to express anger which is otherwise repressed and ignored.

Although I did not initially question the Smithton women about their attitudes toward the commonplace mistreatment of the heroine, principally because I assumed that they must find it acceptable, the women volunteered in discussions of otherwise good stories that these kinds of scenes make them very angry and indignant. They seem to identify completely with the wronged heroine and vicariously participate in her shock and outrage. When I did wonder aloud about this emotional response to the hero's cruelty, Dot's customers indicated that such actions often lead them to "hate" or "detest" even especially memorable heroes for a short period of time. The scenes may function, then, as a kind of release valve for the pent-up anger and resentment they won't permit themselves in the context of their own social worlds.

However, it is also likely that in freely eliciting feelings of displeasure and even rage, the romance defuses those sentiments in preparation for its later explanation of the behavior that occasioned them in the first place. Having already imaginatively voiced her protest, the reader is emotionally ready to accept the explanation, when it is formally offered, of the hero's offensive treatment of the heroine. Like the heroine herself, she is then in a position to forgive his behavior, because what she learns is that his actions were the signs of his deep interest in her. It is because the ideal hero is always persuaded to express his love with the proper signs that the Smithton women interpret his discovery that he actually loves the heroine as the heroine's triumph. The power, they believe, is all hers because he now recognizes he can't live without her. In actuality, what is going on here, as I have noted before, is that active process of justification whereby the reader is encouraged to excuse male indifference and cruelty if it can be demonstrated that these feelings are also accompanied by feelings of love. The romance may therefore recontain any rebellious feelings or impulses on the part of its heroines or readers precisely because it dramatizes a situation where such feelings prove unnecessary and unwarranted. The reader of the ideal romance closes her book, finally, purged of her discontent and reassured that men can indeed learn how to satisfy a woman's basic need for emotional intensity and nurturant care within traditional marriage.

The reassurance is never wholly successful, however. That reader almost inevitably picks up another romance as soon as she puts her last one down. If we can learn to recognize, then, that the need for this repeated reassurance about the success of patriarchal gender arrangements springs from nagging doubt and continuing resentment, we will have developed a better picture of the complex and contradictory state of mind that characterizes many women who, on the surface, appear to be opposed to any kind of change in female-male relations. Strengthened by such comprehension, we might more successfully formulate explanations, arguments, and appeals that will enable at least some women to understand that their need for romances is a function of their dependent status as women and of their acceptance of love and marriage as the only routes to female fulfillment. If they can be persuaded of this, they may find it within themselves to seek their fulfillment elsewhere, to develop a more varied array of their abilities, and to demand the right to use them in the public sphere ordinarily controlled by men.

Although romances provide their readers with a good deal more than can be delineated here, again, the dynamic surrounding their status as both a figurative and a literal escape from present reality indicates that romance reading may not function as a purely conservative force. In fact, it appears to be a complex form of behavior that allows incremental change in social beliefs at the same time that it restores the claim of traditional institutions to satisfy a woman's most basic needs. It is true, certainly, that the romantic story reaffirms the perfection of romance and marriage. But it is equally clear that the constant need for such an assertion derives not from a sense of security and complete faith in the status quo, but from deep dissatisfaction with the meager benefits apportioned to women by the very institutions legitimated in the narrative. When romances are used to deny temporarily the demands of a family, when they are understood as the signs of a woman's ability to do something for herself alone, when they are valued because they provide her with the opportunity to indulge in positive feelings about a heroine and women in general, then their popularity ought to be seen as evidence of an unvoiced protest that important needs are not being properly met. It is the *act* or *event* of romance reading that permits the Smithton woman to reject those extremely taxing duties and expectations she normally shoulders with equanimity. In picking up her book, she asserts her independence from her role, affirms that she has a right to be self-interested for a while, and declares that she deserves pleasure as much as anyone else.

To be sure, this kind of defiance is relatively mild, because the woman need not pit herself against her husband and family over the crucial issues of food preparation, childcare, financial decisions, and so on. But for women who have lived their lives quiescently believing that female self-interest is exactly coterminous with the interest of a husband and children, the ability to reserve time for the self, even if it is to read a romance, is a significant and positive step away from the institutional prison that demands denial and sublimation of female identity. It is unfortunate, of course, that this temporary assertion of independence is made possible only because the manifest content of the novels holds out the promise of eventual satisfaction and fulfillment in the most conventional of terms. As a consequence, the

Smithton women materially express their discontent with their restricted social world by indulging in a fantasy that vicariously supplies the pleasure and attention they need, and thereby effectively staves off the necessity of presenting those needs as demands in the real world. Simultaneously, the romance short-circuits the impulse to connect the desire to escape with the institution of marriage or with male intolerance precisely because it demonstrates that a woman like the heroine can admit the truth of the feminist discovery that women *are* intelligent and independent and yet continue to be protected paternally by a man.

At this particular historical moment, then, romance reading seems to permit American women to adopt some of the changing attitudes about gender roles by affirming that those attitudes are compatible with the social institution of marriage as it is presently constituted. This is not to say, however, that its success at papering over this troublesome contradiction is guaranteed to last forever. Perhaps it will not if we begin to admit the extent of romance readers' dissatisfaction and to point out that discontent not only to ourselves, but also to the women who have made the romance business into a multimillion dollar industry. If we do not take up this challenge, we run the risk of conceding the fight and of admitting the impossibility of creating a world where the vicarious pleasure supplied by romance reading would be unnecessary.

Notes

I would like to thank all of the participants at the November 1981 American Studies Association Session in Memphis on Remembering the Reader for their perceptive comments and questions about an earlier version of this article. Their remarks were immensely helpful to me as I tried to refine the logic of my argument about romance reading. I would also like to express my gratitude to Peter Rabinowitz and to two anonymous reviewers for *Feminist Studies* for their written responses to that same early draft. Their thoughtful readings have helped me to improve both the argument and expression of this article.

1. Harlequin Enterprises Limited, Annual Report 1979, 5. Can be obtained from Harlequin Corporate Office, 220 Duncan Mill Road, Don Mills, Ontario, Canada M3B 3J5.

2. Although Harlequin Enterprises, Fawcett Books (CBS Publications), and Silhouette Books (Simon & Schuster) have conducted market research analyses of their prospective audience, none of these companies will disclose any but the most general of their findings. For descriptions of the three studies, see the following articles: on Harlequin, Phyllis Berman, "They Call Us Illegitimate," *Forbes* 121 (6 Mar. 1978): 38; on Fawcett's study, see Daisy Maryles, "Fawcett Launches Romance Imprint with Brand Marketing Techniques," *Publishers Weekly* 216 (3 Sept. 1979): 69–70; on the Silhouette study, see Michiko Kakutani, "New Romance Novels Are Just What Their Readers Ordered," *New York Times,* 11 Aug. 1980, C13.

3. Ann Barr Snitow, "Mass Market Romance: Pornography for Women is Different," *Radical History Review* 20 (Spring/Summer 1979): 150.

4. Ann Douglas, "Soft-Porn Culture," *The New Republic,* 30 Aug. 1980, 25–29; Tania Modleski, "The Disappearing Act: A Study of Harlequin Romances," *Signs* 5 (Spring 1980): 435–48.

5. The complete findings of this study are summarized and interpreted in my forthcoming book, *Reading the Romance: Women, Patriarchy, and Popular Literature.*

6. For a discussion of the lingering influence of New Criticism poetics, see Jane P. Tompkins, "The Reader in History: The Changing Shape of Literacy Response," in a volume she also edited, *Reader-Response Criticism: From Formalism to Post-Structuralism* (Baltimore: Johns Hopkins University Press, 1980), 201–26; see also Frank Lentricchia, *After the New Criticism* (Chicago: University of Chicago Press, 1980).

7. Two good collections of essays that survey recent work on the theory of the reader have recently appeared. See the volume edited by Tompkins mentioned in note 6 and Susan Suleiman and Inge Crosman, *The Reader in the Text: Essays on Audience Interpretation* (Princeton: Princeton University Press, 1981).

8. Stanley Fish, *Is There A Text in This Class?: The Authority of Interpretive Communities* (Cambridge: Harvard University Press, 1980), 322. It was Fish's work that persuaded me of the necessity of investigating what real readers do with texts when the goal of analysis is an explanatory statement about why people read certain kinds of books.

9. I do not believe that attention to the way real readers understand their books and their reading activities obviates the need for further critical probing and interpretation of potential unconscious responses to the texts in question. I also do not believe that an adequate cultural analysis should stop at such an account of their conscious behavior. What careful attention to that conscious response can produce, however, is a more accurate description of the texts to which the women do in fact consciously and unconsciously respond. In possession of such a description, the critic can then subject it to further analysis in an effort to discern the ways in which the text-as-read might also address unconscious needs, desires, and wishes which she, the critic has reason to believe her reader may experience. This procedure is little different from that pursued by an anthropologist whose goals are not merely the description and explanation of a people's behavior, but understanding of it as well. As Clifford Geertz has pointed out, descriptions of cultural behavior "must be cast in terms of the constructions we imagine Berbers, Jews or Frenchmen . . . place upon what they live through, the formulae they use to define what happens to them." Descriptions of romance reading, it might be added, should

be no different. See Clifford Geertz, "Thick Description: Toward an Interpretive Theory of Cultures," in his *The Interpretation of Cultures* (New York: Basic, 1973), 14.

10. All information about the community has been taken from the 1970 U.S. Census of the Population *Characteristics of the Population,* U.S. Department of Commerce, Social and Economic Statistics Administration, Bureau of the Census, May 1972. I have rounded off some of the statistics to disguise the identity of the town.

11. Table 1. Select Demographic Data: Customers of Dorothy Evans

Category	Responses	Number	%
Age	(42) Less than 25	2	5
	25–44	26	62
	45–54	12	28
	55 and older	2	5
Marital Status	(40) Single	3	8
	Married	33	82
	Widowed/ separated	4	10
Parental Status	(40) Children	35	88
	No children	4	12
Age at Marriage	Mean–19.9 Median–19.2		
Educational Level	(40) High school diploma	21	53
	1–3 years of college	10	25
	College degree	8	20
Work Status	(40) Full or part time	18	45
	Child or home care	17	43
Family Income	(38) $14,999 or below	2	5
	15,000–24,999	18	47
	25,000–49,999	14	37
	50,000 +	4	11
Church Attendance	(40) Once or more a week	15	38
	1–3 times per month	8	20
	A few times per year	9	22
	Not in two (2) years	8	20

Note: (40) indicates the number of responses per questionnaire category. A total of 42 responses per category is the maximum possible. Percent calculations are all rounded to the nearest whole number.

12. Quoted by Barbara Brotman, "Ah, Romance! Harlequin Has an Affair for Its Readers," *Chicago Tribune,* 2 June 1980. All other details about the Harlequin audience have been taken from this article. Similar information was also given by Harlequin to Margaret Jensen, whose dissertation, "Women and Romantic Fiction: A Case Study of Harlequin Enterprises, Romances, and Readers" (Ph.D. dissertation, McMaster University, Hamilton, Ontario, 1980), is the only other study I know of to attempt an investigation of romance readers. Because Jensen encountered the same problems in trying to assemble a representative sample, she relied on interviews with randomly selected readers at a used bookstore. However, the similarity of her findings to those in my study indicates that the lack of statistical representativeness in the case of real readers does not necessarily preclude applying those readers' attitudes and opinions more generally to a large portion of the audience for romantic fiction.

13. See Brotman. All other details about the Silhouette audience have been drawn from Brotman's article. The similarity of the Smithton readers to other segments of the romance audience is explored in greater depth in my book. However, the only other available study of romance readers which includes some statistics, Peter H. Mann's *The Romantic Novel: A Survey of Reading Habits* (London: Mills & Boon, 1969), indicates that the British audience for such fiction has included in the past more older women as well as younger, unmarried readers than are represented in my sample. However, Mann's survey raises suspicions because it was sponsored by the company that markets the novels and because its findings are represented in such a polemical form. For an analysis of Mann's work, see Jensen, 389–92.

14. Yankelovich, Skelly and White, Inc., *The 1978 Consumer Research Study on Reading and Bookpurchasing,* prepared for the Book Industry

Study Group, October 1978, 122. Unfortunately, it is impossible to differentiate from the Yankelovich study findings what proportion of the group of romance readers consumed a number similar to that read by the Smithton women. Also, because the interviewers distinguished between gothics and romances on the one hand and historicals on the other, the figures are probably not comparable. Indeed, the average of nine may be low since some of the regular "historical" readers may actually be readers of romances.

15. The Smithton readers are not avid television watchers. Ten of the women, for instance, claimed to watch television less than three hours per week. Fourteen indicated that they watch four to seven hours a week, while eleven claimed eight to fourteen hours of weekly viewing. Only four said they watch an average of fifteen to twenty hours a week, while only one admitted viewing twenty-one or more hours a week. When asked how often they watch soap operas, twenty-four of the Smithton women checked "never," five selected "rarely," seven chose "sometimes," and four checked "often." Two refused to answer the question.

16. The Smithton readers' constant emphasis on the educational value of romances was one of the most interesting aspects of our conversations, and chapter 3 of Reading the Romance discusses it in depth. Although their citation of the instructional value of romances to a college professor interviewer may well be a form of self-justification, the women also provided ample evidence that they do in fact learn and remember facts about geography, historical customs, and dress from the books they read. Their emphasis on this aspect of their reading, I might add, seems to betoken a profound curiosity and longing to know more about the exciting world beyond their suburban homes.

17. For material on housewives' attitudes toward domestic work and their duties as family counselors, see Ann Oakley, The Sociology of Housework (New York: Pantheon, 1975) and Woman's Work: The Housewife, Past and Present (New York: Pantheon, 1975); see also Mirra

Komorovsky, Blue Collar Marriage (New York: Vintage, 1967) and Helena Znaniecki Lopata, Occupation: Housewife (New York: Oxford University Press, 1971).

18. Nancy Chodorow, The Reproduction of Mothering: Psychoanalysis and the Sociology of Gender (Berkeley: University of California Press, 1978). I would like to express my thanks to Sharon O'Brien for first bringing Chodorow's work to my attention and for all those innumerable discussions in which we debated the merits of her theory and its applicability to women's lives, including our own.

19. After developing my argument that the Smithton women are seeking ideal romances which depict the generally tender treatment of the heroine, I discovered Beatrice Faust's Women, Sex, and Pornography: A Controversial Study (New York: MacMillan, 1981) in which Faust points out that certain kinds of historical romances tend to portray their heroes as masculine, but emotionally expressive. Although I think Faust's overall argument has many problems, not the least of which is her heavy reliance on hormonal differences to explain variations in female and male sexual preferences, I do agree that some women prefer the detailed description of romantic love and tenderness to the careful anatomical representations characteristic of male pornography.

20. Maryles, 69.

21. Ten of the twenty books in the sample for the ideal romance were drawn from the Smithton group's answers to requests that they list their three favorite romances and authors. The following books received the highest number of individual citations: The Flame and the Flower (1972), Shanna (1977), The Wolf and the Dove (1974), and Ashes in the Wind (1979), all by Kathleen Woodiwiss; The Proud Breed (1978) by Celeste DeBlasis; Moonstruck Madness (1977) by Laurie McBain; Visions of the Damned (1979) by Jacqueline Marten; Fires of Winter (1980) by Joanna Lindsey; and Ride the Thunder (1980) by Janet Dailey. I also added Summer of the Dragon (1979) by Elizabeth Peters because she was heavily cited as a favorite author although none of her titles were specifically singled out. Three more titles were added because they

were each voluntarily cited in the oral interviews more than five times. These included *The Black Lyon* (1980) by Jude Deveraux, *The Fulfillment* (1980) by LaVyrle Spencer, and *The Diplomatic Lover* (1971) by Elsie Lee. Because Dot gave very high ratings in her newsletter to the following, these last seven were added: *Green Lady* (1981) by Leigh Ellis; *Dreamtide* (1981) by Katherine Kent; *Made For Each Other* (1981) by Parris Afton Bonds; *Miss Hungerford's Handsome Hero* (1981) by Noel Vreeland Carter; *The Sea Treasure* (1979) by Elisabeth Barr; *Moonlight Variations* (1981) by Florence Stevenson; and *Nightway* (1981) by Janet Dailey.

Because I did not include a formal query in the questionnaire about particularly bad romances, I drew the twenty titles from oral interviews and from Dot's newsletter reviews. All of the following were orally cited as "terrible" books, labeled by Dot as part of "the garbage dump," or given less than her "excellent" or "better" ratings: *Alyx* (1977) by Lolah Burford; *Winter Dreams* by Brenda Trent; *A Second Chance at Love* (1981) by Margaret Ripy; *High Fashion* (1981) by Victoria Kelrich; *Captive Splendors* (1980) by Fern Michaels; *Bride of the Baja* (1980) by Jocelyn Wilde; *The Second Sunrise* (1981) by Francesca Greer; *Adora* (1980) by Bertrice Small; *Desire's Legacy* (1981) by Elizabeth Bright; *The Court of the Flowering Peach* (1981) by Janette Radcliffe; *Savannah* (1981) by Helen Jean Burn; *Passion's Blazing Triumph* (1980) by Melissa Hepburne; *Purity's Passion* (1977) by Janette Seymour; *The Wanton Fires* (1979) by Meriol Trevor; and *Bitter Eden* (1979) by Sharon Salvato. Four novels by Rosemary Rogers were included in the sample because her work was cited repeatedly by the Smithton women as the worst produced within the generic category. The titles were *Sweet Savage Love* (1974), *Dark Fires* (1975), *Wicked Loving Lies* (1976), and *The Insiders* (1979).

22. See Faust, passim.

23. There are two exceptions to this assertion. Both *The Proud Breed* by Celeste DeBlasis and *The Fulfillment* by LaVyrle Spencer detail the involvement of the principal characters with other individuals. Their treatment of the subject, however, is decidedly different from that typically found in the bad romances. Both of these books are highly unusual in that they begin by detailing the extraordinary depth of the love shared by hero and heroine, who marry early in the story. The rest of each book chronicles the misunderstandings that arise between heroine and hero. In both books the third person narrative always indicates very clearly to the reader that the two are still deeply in love with each other and are acting out of anger, distrust, and insecurity.

24. In the romances considered awful by the Smithton readers, this reinterpretation takes place much later in the story than in the ideal romances. In addition, the behavior that is explained away is more violent, aggressively cruel, and obviously vicious. Although the hero is suddenly transformed by the heroine's reinterpretation of his motives, his tenderness, gentleness, and care are not emphasized in the "failed romances" as they are in their ideal counterparts.

25. Modleski has also argued that "the mystery of male motives" is a crucial concern in all romantic fiction (p. 439). Although she suggests, as I will here, that the process through which male misbehavior is reinterpreted in a more favorable light is a justification or legitimation of such action, she does not specifically connect its centrality in the plot to a reader's need to use such a strategy in her own marriage. While there are similarities between Modleski's analysis and that presented here, she emphasizes the negative, disturbing effects of romance reading on readers. In fact, she claims, the novels "end up actually intensifying conflicts for the reader" (p. 445) and cause women to reemerge feeling "more guilty than ever" (p. 447). While I would admit that romance reading might create unconscious guilt, I think it absolutely essential that any explanation of such behavior take into account the substantial amount of evidence indicating that women not only *enjoy* romance reading, but feel replenished and reconstituted by it as well.

26. Jude Deveraux, *The Black Lyon* (New York: Avon, 1980), 66.

Susan Wise Bauer *is a professor of English at the College of William and Mary and a prolific writer. Her most popular title is* The Story of the World Series, *a textbook for grades kindergarten through sixth. She has also published many articles in magazines like* Beliefnet, Christianity Today, *and* Books & Culture. *"The Secret Life of Chick Lit (Food Porn)" was first published in* Books & Culture *in 2004.*

THE SECRET LIFE OF CHICK LIT (FOOD PORN)

Susan Wise Bauer

Twentysomething reporter Jemima Jones is bright, funny, warm, caring, kind—and overweight. Despite her extra pounds, Jemima still hopes to snare the man of her dreams, studly deputy editor Ben Williams. If she's funny and charming enough, Ben might notice her wit and intelligence; he might forget about her cellulite and instead be drawn to "the emerald green of her eyes . . . the fullness of her ripe lips . . . the shiny swinginess of . . . her ever so glossy hair." Will Ben finally see past Jemima's unfashionable waistline, to the real Jemima?

Fat chance.

Jemima J., a glossy trade paperback with a pair of legs on the cover, is "chick lit," part of a genre spawned by Helen Fielding's megabestseller *Bridget Jones's Diary*. Chick-lit heroines—urban twenty- and thirty-somethings searching for love—are sharp, independent, frustrated working women. The women who buy chick lit, according to British chick-lit author Jenny Colgan, have grown up "with financial independence; with living on our own and having far too many choices about getting married (while watching our baby boomer parents fall apart) . . . [with] hauling ourselves up through the glass ceiling." Chick lit readers don't want to entertain themselves with old-fashioned romances starring "women with long blonde hair [who] built up business empires from harsh beginnings using only their extraordinary beauty." They want heroines just like themselves.

At 204 pounds, Jemima Jones is one of the heaviest characters in chick lit. But Cannie Shapiro (*New York Times* bestseller *Good in Bed*) wears a size 16; in chapter 1, she discovers that her ex-boyfriend Bruce has just written a magazine column called "Loving a Larger Woman." ("I loved . . . her size, her amplitude, her luscious, zaftig heft," Bruce sighs. "Loving a larger woman is an act of courage in this world.") When we meet sharp, ambitious lawyer Kate (*Did You Get the Vibe?*), she's standing in front of a mirror mourning her rounded stomach: "Brokenhearted women are supposed to lose weight. So why was she getting so fat?" (Kate starts lifting weights, loses 20 pounds, dumps law to become a personal trainer, and hooks a weightlifter.)

Plump Minerva Dobbs (*Bet Me*) longs to hear her boyfriend say, "You're beautiful, you're thin," but the closest he gets before breaking up with her is "You'd make a wonderful mother."

Even when weight isn't central to the plot, the scale is never far away. In *The Devil Wears Prada*, Andrea gets a prime job at the fashion magazine *Runway*, thanks to a 20-pound weight loss brought on by a bout of amoebic dysentery. Now 5´10˝ and 115 pounds, Andrea soon realizes that she is "the troll of the group, the squattest and widest." When the magazine's fashion consultant brings Andrea a bagful of designer clothes, he remarks, "Every few months or so I clean out the Closet and give this stuff away, and I figured you, uh, might be interested. You're a size six, right? . . . Yeah, I could tell. Most everyone is a two or smaller, so you're welcome to all of it."

Natalie Miller, senior press officer for the London Ballet (Anna Maxted's *Running in Heels*) is surrounded by tiny, fine-boned dancers. "I feel bloated, huge," Natalie thinks, eyeing herself in the mirror. (She's gained two pounds, giving her a "new portly figure.") Halfway through *Running in Heels*, Natalie realizes that she's anorexic, thanks to some plain talking from her best friend Babs, an "Amazonian" (read: size 12) woman who works as a firefighter.

In Marian Keyes' *Sushi for Beginners*, London fashion editor Lisa Edwards gets exiled to Dublin to launch a new magazine called *Colleen*. There she shops in the local market, where her new assistant editor Ashling sees her for the first time: "In fascination, Ashling checked out the contents of the woman's basket. Seven cans of strawberry Slim-Fast, seven baking potatoes, seven apples, and four . . . five six . . . seven individually wrapped little squares of chocolate from the pick 'n' mix. . . . Some irresistible instinct told Ashling that this paltry basketful constituted the woman's weekly shop." Indeed it is: Lisa, exiled in Dublin, still keeps up her high-fashion eating habits. ("She coiled in an armchair, slowly removed the paper, and ran her teeth along the side of the chocolate, shaving away tiny curl after tiny curl, until it was all gone. It took an hour.")

As it turns out, Lisa Edwards isn't the real heroine of *Sushi For Beginners*. Even though she tries to seduce the handsome manager of *Colleen*, Ashling—who is described as having "no waist"—gets him instead.

She isn't alone. Although chick lit is filled with calorie counting, there's a moral in all of these books: Don't try to be as thin as a fashion model. Sometimes, the heavy girl gets the guy.

Unfortunately, "heavy" turns out to be a relative term; chick-lit heroines have an unnerving tendency to lose 20 pounds and then declare their independence from society's obsession with weight. In *The Devil Wears Prada*, Andrea finally quits her job at *Runway*, goes home, and gains ten pounds: "Now that I no longer had to resort to gulping down a bowl of soup or subsisting on cigarettes and Starbucks alone, my body had adjusted itself accordingly and gained back the ten pounds I'd lost while working at *Runway*. And it didn't even make me cringe; I believed it when . . . my parents told me I looked healthy, not fat." (Unless my math is even worse than my calorie intake, Andrea went from 115 pounds to

105 and then back to 115, which means that she still has the circumference of a toothpick.) In *Jemima J.*, size-20 Jemima meets a gorgeous guy named Brad on the Internet and tells him that she's thin and beautiful. When he insists on meeting her, she loses 97 pounds, exercises herself into sleekness, gets blond highlights, and flies to California. Unfortunately, it turns out that Brad is having a fling with his enormously fat personal assistant; he wants Jemima around only as a trophy, because he owns a gym and needs a California-thin girlfriend to improve his public profile. ("Is it possible that men would have found me attractive then, despite being hugely overweight?" Jemima gasps.) Enlightened, Jemima allows her weight to soar back up: "Jemima is no longer skinny," the epilogue tells us, "no longer hardbodied, no longer obsessed with what she eats. Jemima Jones is now a voluptuous, feminine, curvy size 10 who is completely happy with how she looks." (A "voluptuous" size 10?)

Even the occasional author who breaks this mold displays an unseemly preoccupation with food. Jennifer Crusie's *Bet Me* makes a valiant effort to demonstrate that size-14 Minerva Dobbs is truly attractive. "Her lips were full and soft," Crusie writes, chronicling the gradual realization of hero Cal Morrisey that big is beautiful, ". . . smooth milky skin, wide-set dark eyes, a blob of a nose, and that lush, soft, full, rosy mouth." But while *Bet Me* insists that eating is good, Min and Cal still treat food like something illicitly delicious, an ecstatic but anarchic pleasure, as naughty and luscious as . . .

Er, well, as sex. In chick lit, a startling number of carnal liaisons actually take place in restaurants (lobbies, coatrooms, kitchens, and—in one memorable instance—under the table while the waiter is in the middle of listing the chocolate-and-cream-laden dessert specials). And *Bet Me*'s descriptions of Minerva eating come awfully close to food porn. When Cal takes Minerva to his favorite Italian restaurant and tempts her with carbs, he "broke the bread open and the yeasty warmth rose and filled her senses. . . . She closed her eyes and her lips tight, which was useless. . . . Cal watched her tear off a piece of the bread and bite into it. 'Oh,' she breathed, and then she chewed it with her eyes shut and pleasure flooding her face. . . . Her face flushed."

Well, you get the idea. Cal and Min's first kiss involves Krispy Kreme doughnuts ("He popped another piece of doughnut in her mouth and watched as her lips closed over the sweetness. Her face was beautifully blissful, her face soft and pouted, her full lower lip glazed with icing, and as she teased the last of the chocolate from her lip, Cal heard a rushing in his ears. . . . before she could open her eyes, he leaned in and kissed her, tasting the chocolate"), and later on there's even more explicit stuff involving two dozen Krispy Kremes and a sofa. "I like eating," Natalie's large friend Babs announces in *Running In Heels*. "Spaghetti with bolognese sauce so rich and thick it glitters—the joy of slurping it, sucking it up from the plate . . . the juiciness, the chewy satisfaction, my teeth ache just to think of it!"

Naughty indeed. Slurping down food is supposed to demonstrate the heroine's evolution into a woman independent of warped social mores. The choice to unwrap a bar of chocolate becomes a kind of conversion to a new world view—one in which weight doesn't matter. So why is eating still so . . . transgressive?

Behind the rejection of the size-two mentality is a vague groping toward a counterculture existence. All of these writers really want their heroines to live authentically, reject society's false messages, and march to a different drummer. "Looks are nothing!" Natalie's Amazonian friend Babs shouts at her, while Natalie's mouth drops open. "Estee Lauder and her zilliondollar cosmetics dynasty . . . all our cosmetically perfect film stars . . . a million airbrushed cover girls . . . nothing!" But although Natalie and her chick-lit sisters are supposed to be evolving into truly independent women—mature, adult women with minds of their own, who aren't slavishly copying cover models—chick lit doesn't seem to have any idea what they're supposed to be instead.

These hapless heroines could ask their mothers what a grown woman is supposed to be like. Unfortunately, chicklit mothers are almost universally evil: fashion-obsessed, bitter, unloving weight police. Jemima's mother "never seems to ask about Jemima's work, her friends, her social life. She always asks about her weight. . . . Her mother wants a slim beautiful daughter who will be the envy of all her neighbors. . . . What she doesn't want is what she's got. A daughter . . . of whom she's ashamed." Finally Jemima has an epiphany: "I will never make her happy. . . . Nothing I ever do is destined to please her." So much for Mom, who never reappears in the book. In *Bet Me*, we learn right up front (page 5) that the only thing Min has ever done to please her mother is get the flu and lose ten pounds; when Min's mother finally makes an appearance in the book, she points an

"imperious, French-manicured hand" at Min's flab and reminds her not to eat any butter before the wedding. By page 26 of *Sushi For Beginners*, Lisa's mother has been called "an interfering old cow" (and worse). "My mother's satisfaction at seeing me eat while she abstains makes me want to slap her," snaps anorexic Natalie in *Running In Heels*.

So What Do Women Want to Be?

They don't want to be fat, although they'd like to be muscular. They don't want to be skeletally thin, although life tends to be better toward that end of the spectrum. They don't want to be obsessed with designer shoes, although they'd like to have a pair or two in the closet for special occasions. They don't want to be their mothers, although they'd like to get married and have children while being as little like their parents as possible. Missing any model of what a grown woman can be, these novels are stuck with a list of negatives. The result is a pathetic attempt to give women a positive self-image by chronicling (in vivid detail) everything society wants them to be and then scolding, "No, no, no." As a result, chick lit is about as life-affirming as a penal code—the entertainment equivalent of evangelizing by telling prospective converts all the things God doesn't want them to do any more.

Chick lit authors may be trying to resist, but they don't know what to put in the place of that skeletal fashion-magazine cover model. The cover-model ideal is warped and twisted, but they can't manage to unwarp it. I'm reminded of J. R. R. Tolkien's orcs, who (according to the *Silmarillion*) were modeled on elves by the dark powers; they were fashioned "by slow arts of cruelty . . . in envy and mockery," because dark powers can only warp and twist, not create afresh. If you've never seen an elf, and you try to work backwards from an orc to its model, you're darn well not going to end up with Orlando Bloom.

The great rejecting-false-society scenes in chick lit are almost laughable in their failure. In *The Devil Wears Prada*, Andrea finally realizes how "delusional" the world of fashion writing is, defies her boss, and goes home to become a writer. At the book's end, she gets her heart's desire: the editor of *Seventeen* falls in love with her prose and hires her. (I think we're maybe supposed to think of *Seventeen* as a huge step up from a fashion magazine, but as far as I'm concerned we're still trying to make elves out of orcs here.) "Jemima Jones," announces Jane Green in the epilogue to *Jemima J.*, ". . . never dared to believe that one of these days fate would actually take the time and trouble to pick her out from the crowd and smile upon her. But fairy tales can come true. . . . If we trust in ourselves, embrace our faults, and brazen it out with courage, strength, bravery, and truth, fate may just smile upon us too." Well, actually, Jemima Jones went on a water fast, bleached her hair, and was rewarded with marriage to a TV star. Far from rejecting society's twisted standards, Jemima gets exactly what she wants by playing society's game, and then announcing (once she's won the game) that she's superior to the rules. That's not countercultural behavior. It's just plain bad manners.

Like the dark powers of Middle Earth, these novelists can't create life; they have no picture of Eve before the fall. And they're not very good at unwarping, either. After reading 15 chick-lit novels in a row, I had a mental itch; Eve-like, I was pathetically aware of all of those things which I had just been told, sternly (and in great detail), that I really shouldn't think about. Andrea's shallow coworkers laugh at her Nine West shoes! (Now I'm embarrassed to wear mine to New York for my next editorial meeting.) You can still be beautiful even if you're a size ten! (I went on a diet halfway through my fourth chick-lit tome.)

According to recent news articles in *Publishers Weekly* and *The Christian Science Monitor*, Christian publishers are just getting ready to jump on the tail-end of the chick lit bandwagon as it disappears into the distance. Will Christian chick lit manage to unwarp its secular model? The books haven't yet hit the stores, but early reports are not encouraging. "Imagine a Bridget Jones who tallies calories, but not sex partners," the *Monitor* reports, and quotes Zondervan editor Karen Ball: "There are a lot of readers who like these books but prefer [their chick lit] to be tamer. "If Christians can learn anything from chick lit, it ought to be that lists of negatives never produce good original work. Authors and editors who haven't yet figured this out should be sentenced to read the *Silmarillion* (the whole thing) before eating any more chocolate.

DECODING THE TEXTS

1. Each of these three authors takes a different approach toward understanding the genre of the romance novel. Describe these three approaches or attitudes. How are each of these attitudes revealed in the essays?

2. How do the essays reflect the decade in which they were written?

CONNECTING TO YOUR CULTURE

1. Have you ever read romance novels or chick lit? Why or why not?

2. Several of these authors imply that romance novel reading is a secret indulgence. Why do some women feel the need to make this reading habit a secret?

3. Are there other reading habits that people keep a secret? What are they? Are these habits affected by socioeconomic status, as Radway discusses? How are they affected by size or weight, as Bauer discusses?

4. How do reading habits change over time? What factors affect this change?

contemplations **in the pop culture zone**

1. A number of these essays address issues connected to our personal and/or cultural values. Why is popular literature so connected to values or belief systems? What do the books or magazines you read say about your values? Are your values shaped by or influenced by what you read? How does this tie into the practice of censorship?

2. Stephen King fears something happening to his children but then writes about children who suffer and perpetuate terrible horrors. Hillary Robson dreams of being a writer but is also afraid of harsh reviews when she publishes her work. Some citizens are scared that the Harry Potter books will turn our children into witches, whereas others celebrate the role the books have played in getting kids to read. Love and fear seem to be staples of popular literature. How did two such different emotions or psychological responses become so important to what we read and write? Is this also happening through media we listen to or watch? Do you think love and fear operate out of the same place?

3. When the readings in this chapter are taken as a whole, what do they tell us about good writing and popular literature? Are they necessarily the same thing? What are the characteristics of a good novel? A good magazine? A good fan fiction story? What makes a piece of literature popular? What makes a book sell? Does celebrity endorsement make a book good?

4. If you were a popular fiction writer, what type of books or articles would you write? Do your name and personality fit the writing you want to do? Come up with a pseudonym and alter ego that fit your writing style, genre, and audience. You may want to consider where your chosen name would come on the shelf at the bookstore or library.

collaborations **in the pop culture zone**

1. Spend ten minutes writing your observations of and responses to a given text. Then spend five minutes writing in your journal about what knowledge, situations, and experiences you have had that you think influenced your observations and responses. As a group, discuss your various observations and responses. Next discuss how individual knowledge, situations, and experiences create different responses to the text. Did anyone in your group have similar reactions? Were these reactions or responses a result of similar experiences?

2. In 2006, Allan Karlan Lazar and Jeremy Salter published a list of the 101 most influential people who never lived, including characters from fiction, myths, and legends. Included in the top ten were Big Brother, King Arthur, Santa Claus, Hamlet, and Sherlock Holmes. Lower on the list appear Bambi, Barbie, Nancy Drew, and The Cat in the Hat. With your group, create your own top ten list of fictional characters who have affected you in some way.

3. Choose a character from a text you have all read and come up with as many ways as you can think of to describe a character. Create a profile of the character using the various description methods your group discussed. Present the profile to the class without naming the character and see if your peers can guess who the character is, based on your descriptions.

4. As a group, design a list of questions to find out about people's popular literature reading habits. Then take your lists and conduct interviews with your family members, friends, other classmates, instructors, or some other population your group chooses. Bring in your results and compare them. Look for patterns and interesting anomalies.

5. Create your own visual essay in the style of a comic or graphic novel. Perhaps your visual essay could be a review of something you have read in class. It might be a way to create your own top ten list. It could also reveal what you learned from your interviews about people's reading habits. If you do not have an artist in your group, you may want to use Comic Creator at the following educational website, http://www.thinkwritelearn.org.

start writing essays about popular literature

Reviews or Review Essays

1. Choose a text you have read recently and write a review of it. To help you get started, you may want to look at some additional reviews in a magazine or newspaper you trust. To help you focus, write your review for a specific publication. Remember that you can review books, magazines, various online texts, newspapers, or pieces of any of these.
2. Choose a book or magazine that you really like or one that you strongly dislike. Write a letter to the author of the book or the editor of the magazine; share with the author your review of the text and why you like or dislike it. Be sure to give specific details from the text itself to support your opinion.
3. Create your own top ten review list of some aspect of popular literature. You may rank works by one author, texts in a particular subgenre, general works, periodicals produced in a particular year or decade, or you may use another set of factors that are important to you. Publish your list online—on your website or MySpace page, on Amazon.com, or on a bulletin board connected to a particular genre or author. You may want to check out some of the numerous top ten lists published online, including those on Amazon.
4. Check out a fan fiction site online and then write a review of it. Who is writing for the site? What kinds of stories are they writing? Do you like these additional stories? What do they add to the original? You may want to compare a couple of different sites.

Reflection or Response Essays

1. Based on an event in a text of your choosing, write about an event in your life that had as much of an impact on you as it did on the character(s) of the text. You may want to compare and contrast your experience with that of the characters in the book.
2. Discuss the books that were popular when you were in elementary school, middle school, or high school. Why were these books popular? How did they affect you or the people around you? Did you dress like a character from a book or try to act like one? Did you want to visit the same places or play the same games as the characters in your favorite novel?
3. When you read a popular book or magazine, do you see yourself or your life in the text? If yes, describe a book or magazine that represents you and explain how this makes you feel. If no, why not? Why do you think you are being left out? What would a book or magazine that represents you look or read like?
4. In the style of Maxine Hong Kingston or Meg Cabot, write about a story you heard in your childhood or an experience you had at school that had a profound effect on your

life. What happened? Who was involved? Did you tell anyone about it at the time? Later? How has the story changed over time? In what ways did this story or event affect you?

Analysis Essays

1. Analyze the intended audience(s) of a given book, magazine, author, or genre and how well the author or editor addresses the intended audience. How do you know who the audience is? How does the author write (or not write) for this audience? How do the images in the magazine give you a clue to the intended audience? Has the audience been stereotyped? How can you tell?

2. Go to the American Library Association's website (http://www.ala.org) and look at their list of censored books. How many of these censored texts have you read? Do you notice any patterns to the books being censored? What are the top reasons for censorship? Who is asking for the censorship? Choose one of the texts on the list and then pick a side: The text should be censored because. . . . The text should not be censored because. . . . Be sure to support your argument using specific examples from the text. You might also consider the intended audience of the text, the availability of the text, and how this text fits into a specific genre.

3. Using one or more of the literary elements discussed in this chapter, write a literary analysis of a popular literature text, or set of texts, that you have read recently. For example, you might discuss the author's use of symbolism or how the author developed the characters in the text.

4. Analyze a text that was published as the result of a film or television show, such as the *Star Trek* novels, the Mary-Kate and Ashley mystery books, or the *Buffy the Vampire Slayer* comic books. How was the written text influenced by the original visual text? Did it control descriptions in the book? Did the book choose to depart from the original? If so, in what ways? How did these choices affect the final text for readers?

Synthesis Essays

1. Do some research about the reception of a book you have read recently. What do reviewers say about the text? How were the book's sales? Compare this public reception to your responses. Do you agree with the popular view of the text? Does this view have any effect on your reading of the book? In what ways? Would you recommend this text to other readers? Why or why not?

2. Interview people about their reading habits. What do they read? When do they read it? How do they read it? See if you can find any patterns. How do these reading habits compare to your own? How did it start for you? For your friends and family? For your teachers and colleagues? How does the beginning affect present reading habits? Is there anything you'd like to change about your own reading habits?

3. Try writing (and publishing) your own fan fiction story. First, you'll have to pick a book, show, or cast of characters you want to explore. You can check out fan sites that already exist for the program. What are people writing and saying? Then you can try freewriting or listing to get you started with your new take on the story or characters. You may also want to chat with other fan fiction writers to get a better idea of the community. After you have researched and planned, write your story—then share your story. Get feedback like Hillary Robson did and make your story the best you can.

4. Write an obituary for your favorite fictional character. Consider how the character died, what and whom the character is leaving behind, and what the character accomplished before he or she died. You may also want to look at some obituaries as models for your writing.

5. Consider presenting any of the preceding as a graphic novel. What are the special challenges of a graphic novel or visual essay compared to a more traditional essay?

FOR FURTHER READING

Abrams, M. H., ed. *A Glossary of Literary Terms.* 8th ed. Boston: Thomson/Wadsworth, 2005.

Bear, John. *The #1 New York Times Bestseller: Intriguing Facts About the 484 Books That Have Been #1 New York Times Bestsellers Since the First List in 1942.* Berkeley, CA: Ten Speed Press, 1992.

Gelder, Ken. *Popular Fiction: The Logics and Practices of a Literary Field.* New York: Routledge, 2005.

Korda, Michael. *Making the List: A Cultural History of the American Bestseller, 1990–1999.* New York: Barnes and Noble Books, 2001.

Mandell, Judy. *Magazine Editors Talk to Writers.* Hoboken, NJ: John Wiley, 1996.

Murfin, Ross C., and Supryia Ray, eds. *The Bedford Glossary of Literary and Critical Terms.* 2nd ed. New York: Bedford/St. Martin's, 2003.

Walker, Nancy. *Shaping Our Mothers' World: American Women's Magazines.* Studies in Popular Culture. Jackson: UP of Mississippi, 2000.

2007 NCAA FINAL FOUR ATLANTA

Men's Division I Basketball Championship

1 Florida	112		
16 Jackson State	69	1 Florida	74

New Orleans

	1 Florida	65
8 Arizona	63	
9 Purdue	72	9 Purdue	67

		1 Florida	85
5 Butler	57	5 Butler	62
12 Old Dominion	46		

Buffalo, N.Y.

		5 Butler	57
4 Maryland	82	4 Maryland	59
13 Davidson	70		

MIDWEST

		1 Florida	76
6 Notre Dame	64		
11 Winthrop	74	11 Winthrop	61

St. Louis

Spokane, Wash.

		3 Oregon	76
3 Oregon	58	3 Oregon	75
14 Miami-Ohio	56		

		3 Oregon	77
7 UNLV	67	7 UNLV	74
10 Georgia Tech	63		

Atlanta

Chicago

		7 UNLV	72
2 Wisconsin	76	2 Wisconsin	68
15 Texas A&M-CC	63		

		1 Florida	84
1 Kansas	107	1 Kansas	88
16 Niagara	67		

1 Florida Gators

Chicago

		1 Kansas	61
8 Kentucky	67	8 Kentucky	76
9 Villanova	58		

Ohio State 75 1

		1 Kansas	55
5 Virginia Tech	54	5 Virginia Tech	48
12 Illinois	52		

Columbus, Ohio

		4 Southern Illinois	58
4 Southern Illinois	61	4 Southern Illinois	63
13 Holy Cross	51		

San Jose, Calif.

WEST

		2 UCLA	66
6 Duke	77	11 VCU	79
11 VCU	79		

Buffalo, N.Y.

		3 Pittsburgh	55
3 Pittsburgh	58	3 Pittsburgh OT 84
14 Wright State	58		

		2 UCLA	68
7 Indiana	70	7 Indiana	49
10 Gonzaga	57		

Dayton, Ohio

		2 UCLA	64
2 UCLA	70	2 UCLA	54
15 Weber State	42		

Niagara 16

Florida A&M 69 ···· Niagara 77

North Carolina 81 1		
	North Carolina 74 1	

		North Carolina 86 1
		E. Kentucky 65 16

Winston-Salem, N.C.

Michigan State 67 9	
Marquette	
	Michigan S...

North Carolina 84 1

Southern Cal 87 5		
Southern Cal 64 5		Southern...
		Arkans...

EAST

Spo...

Texas 68 4		Texas ... 4
		N. Mex... 13

Georgetown 60 2 — East Rutherford, N.J.

Vanderbilt 78 6		Vanderb... 6
Vanderbilt 65 6		G. Washi...

Sacramento...

Wash. St. 2OT 74 3		Washington Stat...
		Oral Roberts 54 ...

Georgetown 96 2

Boston College 55 7		Boston College 84 7
		Texas Te... 5 10

Georgetown 66 2

Winston...

Georgetown 62 2		Georgetow...
		Belmont

Ohio State 78 1		Ohio State 78 ...
Ohio State 85 1		Cent. Conn. St. 57 16

Lexington, Ky.

Xavier OT 71 9		BYU 77 8
		Xavier 79 9

Ohio State 92 1

Tennessee 77 5		Tennessee 121 5
		Long Beach State 86 12

Tennessee 84 5

Columbus, Ohio

Virginia 74 4		Virginia 84 4
		Albany, N.Y. 57 13

Ohio State 67 1 — San Antonio

Louisville 69 6		Louisville 78 6
		Stanford 58 11

Texas A&M 64 3

Lexington, Ky.

Texas A&M 72 3		Texas A&M 68 3
		Pennsylvania 52 14

Memphis 76 2

Nevada 62 7		Nevada 77 7
		Creighton OT 71 10

Memphis 65 2

New Orleans

Memphis 78 2		Memphis 73 2
		North Texas 58 15

SOUTH

AP

"Surely, the NCAA basketball tournament has such special appeal because it is, of all our great championships, so quintessentially illustrative of our national contradictions. It manages to be the perfect mix of illusion and reality alike, of democracy and privilege side by side."

—From Frank Deford, as quoted in *Sports Illustrated*

CHAPTER 9

writing about sports and leisure

1 Who said, "If I weren't earning $3 million a year to dunk a basketball, most people on the street would run in the other direction if they saw me coming"?

    a. Wilt Chamberlain
    b. Charles Barkley
    c. Yao Ming
    d. Dennis Rodman

TEST YOUR POP CULTURE IQ: SPORTS AND LEISURE

Top left: © Image Source Black/Jupiter Images; Top right: © Brand X Pictures/
Jupiter Images; Bottom left: © Image Source Pink/Jupiter Images; Bottom right:
© LWA/Dann Tardif/Blend Images/Jupiter Images

2 According to most polls, what is commonly the most popular leisure activity that is shared between sexes?

    a. Fishing
    b. Cooking
    c. Playing card games
    d. Gardening

3 In the American Film Institute's "100 Years, 100 Films," what sports movie was ranked closest to the top?

    a. *Raging Bull*
    b. *Rocky*
    c. *Hoosiers*
    d. *Rudy*

4 After the 2005–2006 NHL season, who held the record as the all-time leading total points scorer?

    a. Wayne Gretzky
    b. Mark Messier
    c. Gordie Howe
    d. Ron Francis

5 How many NBA championships did the Chicago Bulls win in the 1990s? How many World Series did the New York Yankees win in the 1990s?

    a. 2, 1
    b. 4, 2
    c. 6, 3
    d. 8, 4

Chapter opener image © AP Graphics

6 Which sports reporter was ranked both the most liked and most hated journalist in America?

    a. Harry Caray
    b. Howard Cosell
    c. Bob Uecker
    d. Dick Vitale

7 Which college team has won the most NCAA 1-A Division championship football games?

    a. Oklahoma
    b. Alabama
    c. Ohio State
    d. Notre Dame

8 Who said, "I never thought of losing, but now that it's happened, the only thing is to do it right. That's my obligation to all the people who believe in me. We all have to take defeats in life"?

    a. Mike Tyson
    b. Evander Holyfield
    c. Muhammad Ali
    d. George Foreman

9 Which gold medal-winning athlete was nicknamed "Jordan" by her teammates at the University of North Carolina?

    a. Sheryl Swoops
    b. Mia Hamm
    c. Jackie Joyner-Kersee
    d. Chris Evert

10 Which of these was a game made for the original Nintendo game system?

    a. *Base Wars: Cyber Stadium Series*
    b. *Bases Loaded*
    c. *Baseball*
    d. *Baseball Stars*

ANSWERS

1 b. Charles Barkley   **2** d. Gardening   **3** a. Raging Bull   **4** a. Wayne Gretzky   **5** c. 6, 3   **6** b. Howard Cosell

7 d. Notre Dame   **8** c. Muhammad Ali   **9** b. Mia Hamm   **10** c. Baseball

YOU AND SPORTS AND LEISURE

Whether you are a player or a spectator, sports play at least a minor role in your popular culture. Both athletics and athletes are common topics of discussion and venues for entertainment. Sports are often portrayed as shallow in American society because of the emphasis on money and entertainment that professional leagues promote, but realistically, sports contribute a lot to the health of Americans and to people around the world and their cultures. Athletes often serve as ambassadors for and to the countries in which they compete. Think about the Olympic Games or World Cup Soccer; these events bring the world together and allow the smallest of countries to share the international stage with world powers. Of course, not all athletes are role models, but many of those players who are in the public eye are looked up to by their young fans.

Sports are also important at the local or community level. Children play Little League to learn sportsmanship and teamwork, and to practice skills for healthy living that they will, ideally, carry with them throughout their lives. High school athletics are another example of how sports can build community and enrich the grade school experience for students who may or may not be academically inclined.

University sports, though, may be the unique sporting experience in American culture. Although college athletes are sometimes treated like professionals, they are also expected to be students. The National Collegiate Athletic Association (NCAA) sets many rules and regulations from the number of classes from which a player may be excused to the GPA required for eligibility. At many universities and colleges, athletic programs are well funded, and players are recruited based on the talent and experience they have displayed in high school. At smaller schools, though, team play is often voluntary. From the smallest divisions to NCAA-1A, college and university sports can inspire unmatched enthusiasm, devotion, and support from alumni and fans. The income generated from large college sporting events can even help fund other projects at universities, with the money trickling down to academic programs.

Of course, this chapter is also about American popular leisure and recreation activities. These can include sporting events such as sailing, hiking, or mountain climbing and less adventurous activities like gardening, fishing, knitting, scrapbooking, or photography. Most of your hobbies probably fit into either the sports or leisure categories. Your leisure activities may cross over into other chapters of this text; perhaps you prefer to watch films, read, or hang out with your friends in your spare time. The readings in this chapter may inspire you to write about not only the products in popular culture that you know well but also to research the activities that you enjoy.

grappling with ideas

- Why is the championship tournament of Major League Baseball called the *World* Series? Or, why are some of the most prestigious cheerleading competitions hosted by the *World* Cheerleading Association? Canada and the United States are the only countries represented by teams in either sport, even though players and teammates often represent other countries.
- Are these names appropriate? Why or why not?

WHY WRITE ABOUT SPORTS AND LEISURE?

Writing about sports and leisure can allow participants to share their stories and teach from experience. Viewers can analyze a player's chances or the outcomes of a season and review games and matches. Those who are not sports enthusiasts can respond to the influence and impact that sports have on their everyday environment. Sports-writers and sports journalists are often former players or coaches with valuable experience but sometimes have entered the field with no experience and only a serious interest in athletics. Perhaps more than in other forms of popular culture, sportswriting must convey the physical and mental aspects of a game or event. From the strategies used in training and practice, to the sights, sounds, and smells of the arena, to the final score, there are many characteristics of sports-writing to consider, and a writer's choice to include or exclude these details can be more telling about the writer than about the athletics. However, your level of involvement in sports may not affect your ability to write about it. An outsider's point of view is often just as interesting, sometimes even more interesting, than that of a sports or leisure expert.

Leisure activities are a popular subject for student essays as well as for professional writers. Travel writers, for example, use their vacation experiences to tell a story, to teach a lesson, to review a location or event, or to analyze and identify common and varied experiences between cultures. Sports and leisure activities may be appreciated on a higher level when a writer can explain an event or experience to his or her reader from a more critical standpoint.

Following is only a sampling of some sports and leisure activities that may trigger writing assignments or prompt you to write about a personal experience. Obviously, these activities may blur the boundaries of the categories they are in; for example, sailing is considered an Olympic sport, and dancers are definitely athletes. They also might cross over into other chapters; for instance, watching a film is such a popular leisure activity that it warrants its own chapter.

grappling with ideas

- Which games or major events are you sure to watch every year? The Super Bowl? The final game of March Madness? The Academy Awards?

- If you miss a game or event, how do you find out who won "Best Supporting Actress" or the final score? Do you watch or read the news? Do you ask friends or classmates? Do you check on the team's or film's official website?

Individual Sports	Team Sports	Leisure Activities
Archery	Badminton	Arts and Crafts/Ceramics
Badminton	Baseball	Attending Sporting Events
Bowling	Basketball	Auto Repair
Boxing	Bowling	Bird Watching
Canoe/Kayak	Cricket	Bowling
Cup Stacking	Curling	Camping/Backpacking/Hiking
Cycling	Field Hockey	Coin Collecting
Equestrian	Football	Conversing
Fencing	Gymnastics	Cooking
Frisbee	Handball	Dancing/Singing
Golf	Ice Hockey	Flower Arranging/Woodworking
Ice Skating	Lacrosse	Gardening
Rollerblading	Luge/Bobsled	Hacky Sack/Juggling
Rope Skipping	Martial Arts	Hunting
Running	Polo	Jogging
Shooting	Roller Derby	Listening to/Playing Music
Skiing	Rowing	Painting

Squash	Rugby	Photography
Swimming/Diving	Sailing	Playing Cards/Games/Puzzles
Table Tennis	Soccer	Reading
Tennis	Softball	Sailing
Unicycling	Synchronized Swimming	Scuba Diving
Walking	Team Handball	Sewing/Knitting/Quilting
Weight Training	Track and Field	Shuffleboard
Wrestling	Volleyball	Taking Walks

PREPARING TO WRITE ABOUT SPORTS AND LEISURE

Sports are ever present in American culture. However, you do not need to have personal experience playing sports or even watching sporting events to have a broad knowledge about sports and leisure and to be successful at these types of writing assignments. Films about sports, songs that provide the soundtracks for sports footage, the advertising and marketing of sporting events and leisure products, television series and networks devoted to sports and leisure, and athletic magazines, columns, and websites are all fodder for sport and leisure writing assignments. These connections require critical thinking; the way that you think about sports when completing an assignment may be different from the way that you usually discuss them with your friends.

grapplingwithideas

- How do you spend your leisure time?

- Do you enjoy crafting or playing games? Do you enjoy working out or traveling?

- What do your leisure choices say about you?

- What influences your leisure choices? Your family? Your social class? Your race? Your gender?

- Have you ever felt inhibited from joining or participating in a leisure activity because of one of these classifications?

Participating, Watching, and Thinking

Many different writing assignments and modes of essay writing may fit into the category of sports and leisure, but the way that you experience sports, sporting events, leisure activities, hobbies, and products may influence the way that you present them in your writing. As you have already discovered, there are many different reasons to write about sports and leisure and many ways to present your writing. Think about these questions as you prepare to write: Where and when did you watch, participate in, or experience the event or activity—your own big-screen TV, a DVD of highlights from ESPN, at the stadium or arena, in a classroom, your own backyard, a recording borrowed from a friend, a do-it-yourself instructional guide? How much did you pay? Who was with you? Why did you go, participate, or view the event? Is the activity or experience one of your favorites?

When you view a sport or participate in an activity to gain experience for a writing assignment, make sure that you are prepared for the experience. Continue to ask questions and take notes about your initial thoughts and answers so that you can compare them with your analysis: What experience have others had with the event or activity? What do you already know about the rules of the game, the production of the event, the skills or talents required, or the intended audience? Is the activity or event a specific interest of yours? If not, what can you gain from the experience? What would you like to learn? What interest of yours could it compare to? What are your expectations for the outcome of the game? Enjoyment? Success?

As you participate in an activity or watch a game, listen to the commentary around you. Are sportscasters completely unbiased? Are your friends or teammates making informed or educated judgments? What is different about this experience from others you have had? How or why is this experience different or what makes this experience similar to those you have had in the past? Look for the climax of the activity or event. Does it come at the end of the event (a sixty-yard game-winning field goal) or at the very beginning (running the ball back for a touchdown on the first play of the game)? How does this affect your viewing or participation?

Because sports and leisure subjects often merge with other chapters of this book, it may be important for you to follow the guidelines in other chapters as well. For example, if you choose to write an essay about watching the X Games on ESPN2, you may want to read the suggestions from Chapter 10, Writing About Television, as well as this chapter. Or if you are writing about your last high school rugby match or "crop"—a popular name for group scrapbooking sessions—Chapter 6, Writing About Groups, Spaces, and Places, may help you better express your ideas about your peers or the environment in which the event took place or the game was played.

Take notes as you watch an event you plan to write about. When actually participating in an activity about which you are planning to write, taking notes may not be a possibility, but you should make notes as soon as possible on the highlights and details of your experience. The blank page can be intimidating, and these notes may remind you of certain characteristics or steps that will not be as memorable when you sit down to write. Another option is to use your cell phone or iPod to snap pictures or to record ideas that might help you later as you begin to write.

Before you write, look at the notes you made prior to your viewing or participation. How did your expectations change? Were you correct about the intended audience? About rules and regulations? How did your previous experiences affect this activity? Was the activity as fun or educational as expected? Did your beliefs, background, politics, or value systems affect your viewing or participation? What conclusions can you draw about yourself in relation to this experience?

Context is also important when reflecting on your experience. First, the context of your own situation should be considered. Were you talking with a friend as you watched the game or planted jalapeños? Did someone's cell phone conversation make you miss the ref's penalty explanation at the end of the third quarter or make you miss a stitch? Were you reading the instruction manual for your

keyquestions

Key Questions for Television Sports Viewing or Analysis

- How is the game introduced? As two rivals taking the field? As the biggest game of the season?

- How are the sportscasters introduced? Do you know their credentials?

- When was the game played? Is it live? On a thirty-second delay? Is it being replayed because of its popularity?

- Where was the game played?

- What is the concluding image of the broadcast? The winning fighter? An aerial shot of the stadium?

- What happens before and after commercial breaks? When are commercial breaks taken?

- Look at the advertisements in the arena or stadium. Are they visible to all audiences?

- Is this game similar to or different from your own sporting experiences?

- Did you notice anything about the camera footage? Who is shown in the crowd at the beginning of the game? At the end? Are these fans particularly emotional?

- How does the soundtrack contribute to the broadcast? What type of music is used at the beginning? At the end?

key questions

Key Questions for Sports and Leisure Participation and Analysis

- How was the activity arranged? Is it a pickup game with friends? A regular knitting circle? Do you play for a college team where games are determined by a conference schedule?
- Who serves as the authority? Who makes the rules? The conference? The refs? The person who invited you to participate?
- Who is the expert? The announcers? A teacher? The coach?
- When is the activity taking place? Morning? Night? Summer? Winter? Does it matter?
- Where is the activity taking place? Your living room? Yankee Stadium? The park? A class?
- If this is a regular event or activity, when did it begin? Is it popular? With whom?
- When will the event end? When the game is over? When someone leaves for work?
- Are there advertisements around you? Are they for products you are interested in?
- Is this experience similar to or different from your past experiences?
- Is music being played? How does the soundtrack contribute to the environment?

new sewing machine while sewing? Were you too hot in the sun or sitting in snow on the metal bleachers? What distractions should you address? The context of the game or event is also important. What is the historical background of the game? Is this relevant to your assignment? How have the rules and regulations changed over time? Why? Is there specific political relevance to the game, activity, or event?

These questions should not all be answered in your essay, but they may help you to determine which facts, details, and examples are the most relevant to the assignment and to you. Though you may find that some outside reading or research may be required, prewriting, with good notes, can move you quickly on to drafting the assignment with confidence that you fully understand your sports or leisure review, reflection, response, or analysis.

Participating, Watching, Analyzing, and Understanding

Some analysis will be necessary to write any assignment involving sports and leisure. You, as the writer, must determine what you want your reader to gain from your essay. What could your reader learn from the 2006 Cardinals–Bears *Monday Night Football* game in which the Bears won without scoring a single offensive touchdown? What was the most important set of tennis in the 1994 U.S. Open? What items are essential for a stocked pantry? How did your life change when you started training for the Boston Marathon? When you began making jewelry? What did you learn from your research? From your experience? What can you teach your audience?

From this analysis, you must first gain an understanding of your subject before you can expect your reader to do the same. Perhaps the purpose of an essay about the Cardinals–Bears game would be to explain that defense can win a football game, that quarterbacks are not necessarily the most important players on the field, or that the score of a game is an ineffective way of determining which team played better. Sometimes, an understanding of your purpose comes as you consider your notes—and your interests—during prewriting; you may find the purpose of your essay and write the first draft with a complete grasp of your subject. Writing about sports and leisure or writing in general is not always that simple, though. You may begin to understand your subject more and more as you draft and revise your essay. Or you may finish the second or third draft of your essay and realize that the last sentence of the last body paragraph actually suggests the strongest, most effective, or most successful point that you can make. These realizations may require major revisions, but they are worth the effort to successfully address your subject, to find your purpose, and to express yourself effectively to your audience.

Participating, Watching, Researching, and Documenting

A review or a reflection or response essay may not require outside research. But to make sure that you come across as an authority, some research may benefit any essay topic.

Areas of research may include the following:

- The history of the game or the activity
- A team's, coach's, or athlete's record
- An athlete's life history
- The culture represented by a sporting event or leisure activity
- The perception of the sport or activity in popular culture
- The economic impact of a sport or activity
- The reception of a game, sport, or event by its intended audience
- The history or development of techniques, skills, or talents
- The evolution of particular rules and regulations

The questions you want answered will determine what type of research you do, so it is best to start with the intended purpose of your essay. What do you need to know to successfully write to your audience? What might your audience need to know to understand your initial purpose? Would a brief history of the Bears' losing seasons help your audience to understand the impact of their 1985 Super Bowl win? Use research to fill in your notes and observations, to narrow your focus, and to help you become more of an authority on your subject. Remember to remain open to new ideas and interpretations you may discover in your research and be willing to revise your original idea if necessary. If you get too far off track from your original idea, go back to your preliminary notes and decide if your original purpose or your new information better meets your expectations and the assignment.

The event, activity, or broadcast is your primary source, but your research may lead you to a variety of other primary and secondary sources. As you learned in previous chapters, secondary sources are only limited by what has actually been published and by your imagination. You may find books, articles, and websites from friends, television, or your own library, but make sure you check out the school's holdings as well as the electronic databases available through your school or public libraries, such as InfoTrac College Edition, Lexis-Nexis, JSTOR, or the MLA International Bibliography.

Most popular culture subjects require that you research nontraditional sources for current and relevant information. The Internet has numerous worthwhile sites and zines, but remember to evaluate the site and its purpose before you trust it as a reliable source Of course, the Miami Dolphins' website may provide up-to-date information about the team, but a site with an educational or analytical

Lance Armstrong overcame doping allegations, negative criticism from European cycling fans about his domination of the Tour de France, and cancer to win seven Tours. As of 2007, Tiger Woods has overcome racism and the trauma of his father's death to win twelve major golf titles. Figure skater Nancy Kerrigan overcame an attack at the 1994 U.S. Figure Skating Championships in Detroit that injured her knee, and she went on to win the silver medal at the Olympics one month later. What is the significance of stories like these in American popular culture?

- Can you think of other athletes who have had similar experiences?
- Do you have friends or family members who have overcome illness, discrimination, or criminal behavior to become even more successful?
- Can you think of celebrities in television, film, or music who have similar stories?

focus on NFL history will provide more balance in its review, analysis, and history of the team. For facts, reviews, archives, or analyses, check out the following:

American Automobile Association	http://www.aaa.com
Artist Trading Cards	http://www.artist_trading_cards.ch/
CBS Sports Line	http://sportsline.com
DIY Network	http://diynetwork.com
ESPN Network	http://espn.go.com
GetCrafty	http://getcrafty.com
International Olympic Committee	http://olympic.org
Knitgrrl	http://knitgrrl.com
Major League Baseball	http://mlb.com
National Basketball Association	http://www.nba.com
National Collegiate Athletics Association	http://www.ncaa.org
National Football League	http://www.nfl.com
National Hockey League	http://www.nhl.com
Sports Illustrated	http://sportsillustrated.cnn.com
World Tourism Organization	http://www.unwto.org

Remember, all sources must be listed on a Works Cited page, so you should write down the information (that is, web addresses, authors' names, where you found the source, and the date of publication) for your in-text citations and the Works Cited. Always know where you found your information and how to get back to it. Chapter 11, Researching and Documenting in the Pop Culture Zone, will remind you of specific guidelines, and the Works Cited at the end of each sample essay can provide examples of citations for specific sources.

WRITING ABOUT SPORTS AND LEISURE

Sports and leisure are written about in many ways. Sportswriting may focus on a specific game or match, an athlete's celebrity status, or a spectator's response to a team's success. Leisure writing is equally diverse, focusing on the process of choosing a fishing lure, the best place to buy camera equipment, or an economic analysis of organic farming. As explained in Chapter 1, four main assignments are used in composition classes to help you learn to write about sports and leisure: reviews, reflection or response essays, analysis essays, and synthesis essays, which combine essay types.

Sports and Leisure Reviews or Review Essays

A review is complicated when discussing both sports and leisure, and some distinctions must be made. For a sports review, a writer typically will describe what happened during a game or match. From the players walking onto the court to the last-minute shot at the buzzer, details are important. Of course, game reviews can also include details about outside events that could affect a player's state of mind or quotes from players, coaches, or fans about the outcome of the game. Most sports articles in newspapers or on the Internet are reviews of a game, season, or a player's career. A thesis statement toward the beginning of the review usually suggests a writer's overall evaluation of a game.

Most often, game reviews are written objectively, with the writer equally describing the play of both teams; however, university news writers may show a bias for the school's team just as a writer for the *Chicago Sun-Times* may obviously root for the White Sox or the Cubs over the Mets and the Yankees. A game review is typically a chronological description of a game, match, or event that builds to the climax in which the final score is given. In the case of a news story, it discloses the final score at the beginning of the article before explaining what happened. Unlike a literary analysis, past tense is used. A game, once it has been played, can never be reenacted.

Leisure writing presents a different type of review essay. For example, a travel writer may review a hotel, a restaurant, or a tour package. A fisher may review the potential for catching large-mouth bass in a certain lake. A quilter may review a certain brand of needles. These types of reviews demand assertions of opinion or quality. An experience is typically not completely good or completely bad, and your reader will expect an honest assessment of quality, service, and value. Though opinionated, the evaluation that you make in this kind of essay should still be balanced, objective, and fair. A mean-spirited review typically has the opposite of its intended effect.

Comparison is an important characteristic of both sports and leisure reviews. A reader may garner more about a football player's running game if you compare him to Jerome Bettis or more about a digital camera lens when compared to the analog version of the same model from previous years. Some experience is required for a reviewer's opinion to matter to the reader.

A sports or leisure review essay may be organized differently from a regular review and might include details that would appeal to a more academic audience; more analysis of the event or activity is necessary to support your opinion. For example, you might start out with a brief summary of the game to catch the audience's attention or end with the significance or effectiveness of a particular team's play.

Reflection or Response Essays

Reflection or response essays written about subjects within sports and leisure will require mostly personal writing. However, some summary or description of a game, activity, or event may be more important than in other areas within popular culture because of accessibility issues. Your reader may not have access to watch film of a game you are writing about, to travel to that small inn outside Dublin, or to hike in Great Smoky Mountains National Park. Therefore, it is important that your reflection or response gives the reader the information needed to understand your experience and inspiration for writing.

keyquestions

Key Questions for a Sports Review Essay

- Have you provided a brief summary of the game or match?
- Have you mentioned specific elements of the game or match that support your judgment? Have you described these quickly and vividly, using concrete language?
- Have you defined yourself as a credible source? How?
- Have you qualified your judgment with both positive and negative aspects of the game or match?
- Have you given the final outcome of the game or match? Of the player or team?
- Have you begun the review with an attention-grabbing opening? Have you concluded it with a striking sentence?
- Did you write in past tense?

Key Questions for a Leisure Review Essay

- Have you clearly indicated your judgment of the subject's quality?
- Have you provided a brief example of your experience with the subject?
- Have you mentioned specific elements that support your judgment? Have you described these quickly and vividly, using concrete language and metaphors?
- Have you defined yourself as a credible source? How?
- Have you qualified your judgment with both positive and negative aspects of the subject?
- Have you begun the review with an attention-grabbing opening? Have you concluded it with a striking sentence?

Key Questions for a Reflection or Response Essay

- Have you clearly indicated how you used the subject as a springboard for your thesis?
- Have you expressed your personal response to one aspect of the game, match, event, or activity?
- Did you include minimal summary?
- Does your introduction direct your audience into your response?
- Does your concluding paragraph include some reflection on both the activity and on your response?
- Are your essay's intentions clear?

Key Questions for an Analysis Essay

- Do you have a clearly stated thesis?
- Do you have a series of reasons supporting the thesis? Are these arranged in logical and convincing order?
- Are your supporting reasons backed up? Do you provide specific evidence and examples from the activity for each reason you offer?
- Does your introduction orient your reader into the direction of your argument?
- Does your concluding paragraph show the effectiveness or significance of your analysis and provide a vivid ending?
- Did you provide only minimal summary?

Inspiration is the key for a successful reflection or response. Whether it is a beautiful sunset you saw while windsurfing, a masterful three-pointer that won the game, or your award-winning rosebush, sports and leisure have an uncanny ability to spark discussion and narrative, which are both important parts of reflection. In a response, a writer does simply that—he or she responds to a situation, event, or game, whether as a spectator or participant. The response will be mainly about his or her place within the situation, though. In a reflection, the writer thinks back on a past experience with new eyes. This type of writing usually leads the writer, and possibly the reader, to learn something new about himself or herself or about the event that he or she participated in or viewed.

Analysis Essays

An analysis essay within sports and leisure is similar to a review essay. Some summary is crucial for the audience to access your subject. Fortunately, the purpose of the analysis essay—to identify a subject you see as significant, to explain your view, and to defend your view with evidence from the game, match, or experience—should eliminate the need for extensive initial description. Instead, the description will be integrated throughout the essay to adequately discuss its meaning and significance.

An analysis essay is often an argument, and a thesis is necessary to clarify the point you are making as a writer. A thesis gives your essay purpose, and it may help you identify the support needed to convince your reader. A sports analysis will often analyze the functions, effects, or meaning of a sporting event or leisure activity. Your thesis must be supported with examples and evidence from the event or activity and/or from outside resources. Analysis requires more observations about significance and cultural meaning than simple description.

Synthesis Essays

An assignment will not always specify that you should write a review essay, reflection or response essay, or analysis essay. More often than not, an assignment asks you to combine and synthesize the writing strategies just described into one essay. Personal response may strengthen the attention-grabbing value of the introduction to your analysis essay, or a brief review may call for some analysis of the details you chose to include. Synthesis essays, those that combine different essay strategies, often produce the strongest writing because of the lack of limitations.

The most important aspect of interpreting an assignment is to listen to the guidelines given by your instructor and to talk with your instructor about your prewriting ideas. If you know that you will be combining two types of essays, look over the guidelines for each to help you. For example, a sports synthesis essay assignment may ask you to discuss the life of a college athlete; this assignment may demand both analysis of his or her life and your own reflection on your role in the university. If you write the essay first and then realize that you have reviewed a Wimbledon match, reflected on a Caribbean scuba-diving lesson, or analyzed your first Little League tee-ball game, look back over the guidelines as a revision strategy.

SAMPLE ANNOTATED ESSAY

CONSIDERING IDEAS

1. Is any sport more "American" than others? What Americans call soccer is actually "football" throughout the international sports community. Baseball, football, and basketball are all American inventions, but other countries have joined the games.

2. What about the phrase "As American as baseball and apple pie . . . "? Does this have any impact on the way baseball is viewed by the average citizen?

3. Is the popularity of these sports affected by their American roots?

Nicholas X. Bush, *a student at Middle Tennessee State University, wrote his master's thesis on baseball in literature in which he discusses, among other things, the role of the baseball star as a nouveau American hero. Bush has published in* COMPbiblio: Leaders and Influences in Composition Theory and Practice *and* The Blue Writer. *This article is an excerpt from his ongoing research.*

HISTORY AT THE PLATE

The Value of Baseball in American Culture

Nicholas X. Bush

Intro sentence tells the reader that the essay is about sport and the concept of sport in literature.

Sports and literature are two entities that can easily be married: both reflect aspects of the culture that produce them in ways unique to themselves, both can act as aesthetic entertainment and both can reveal metaphorical truths about how people interact. Depending on the culture, sports can take on a myriad of roles. And it is within this wide array of spaces where the significance of sport plays itself out, not just on the pages of books or in pictures through a camera, but also on the stage of history. For example, we get a glimpse into Roman society by studying and understanding the circumstances surrounding the manufactured conflicts involving gladiators, lions, prisoners, and slaves that took place in their coliseums. For America, perhaps the most important sport that can be viewed in this cultural context is baseball. Admittedly, baseball is only a game, and even though the influence of a game is limited, so is any other aspect of society. But in combination with context, circumstance, and other cultural activities, a game can have a large impact on the shaping and perception of a society. Baseball is a worthy subject of study because it acts as an icon for the country as a whole while also shaping the ever-changing idea of the American individual.

Introduction clarifies the purpose of the essay as well as the background information about sport and culture.

First example: sport as collective American consciousness.

By studying American sport, much about the country can be revealed. Thus, baseball has, at times, acted as a litmus test of Americanness. Do not misunderstand; knowing baseball is not crucial to being American, but understanding the game's place in United States history can provide insight into American culture. Baseball surfaces so much in American society because it is interlaced so much with the country's growth. We can see this point illustrated in the lives of individuals. Children who grow up doing a particular craft or hobby, even if they pick up other interests in adult-

"History at the Plate: The Value of Baseball in American Culture" by Nicholas X. Bush. Written as part of his Master's Thesis and revised for THE POP CULTURE ZONE: WRITING CRITICALLY ABOUT POPULAR CULTURE, 2006.

hood have, as a point of reference, this particular ability that's part of their consciousness. Similarly, baseball is so much a part of our country's makeup because "its history is irrevocably entwined with the rise of industrialization, urbanization, and the technological coming-of-age" (Riess 2). In short, the game was there with America as it went through puberty and developed its identity as a country. The history of the game, from its beginnings as an upper class genteel sport to its evolution as an avenue for the Americanization of immigrants, reflects closely the changes in the nation that invented and modernized it. In the past 40 years, other sports have joined baseball in terms of reflecting American consciousness. By studying these, an outsider can come to understand certain aspects of the country. But from 1880 to midway through the twentieth century, baseball performed what football, basketball, hockey, and NASCAR, in conjunction with baseball, do today. Each provide a microcosm of American life through sport. In his book *Making the Team: The Cultural Work of Baseball Fiction,* Timothy Morris says that "sport and sports fiction are players in the marketplace of ideas" (14). Sports, and baseball in particular, are not the only representation of the American mindset. But make no mistake about it: baseball is a prominent avenue through which American awareness or American identity can be traced.

This American identity can be examined collectively, but it can also be studied from an individual perspective by looking at the development and role of the baseball star. Critic Debra A. Dagavarian goes on to talk about how baseball "illustrates our exaltation of individualism, patriotism, and nationalistic pride" (2). Sports, in this instance baseball, provide an avenue through which these concepts of the American hero can continue. After 1880, frontier heroes became less common, and as early American experiences such as settling unknown parts of the continent began "turning ever more into elements of nostalgia and fantasy," sports began to act as "a surrogate frontier where the athletic hero played out the role of pathfinder/pioneer [who] overcame obstacles with talent and determination" (Levy 52 and Dorinson 79). Therefore, the athlete became someone to be honored, not just for his physical skills but for the echo of the past that he represents. This connection between historic and

> Topic sentence transitions to the idea of sport's significance to individuals.

present day heroes has roots in a "mythic imagination" that allows people to attach themselves to "cultural meanings, entities, and stories bigger and older" than themselves (Oliver 294). In baseball, this awareness of the past helps create a dialogue that is acted out by its players, which combines the classical story ("someone went on a long journey") and the American story ("a stranger came to town") (Simmons 4). Players who can represent these images well, whether they be real life figures such as Hank Greenberg or Derek Jeter, or fictional ones like Henry Wiggen in *Bang the Drum Slowly* or Roy Hobbs in *The Natural,* fit into a hero-by-proxy role that was once filled by pioneers, soldiers, and adventurers.

Refutation identifies arguments against baseball's cultural importance.

Despite the apparent symbolism of the baseball star, some critics see the game and its players as little more than a snapshot of American popular culture that holds no more significance than the entertainment value it possesses at a given moment. For how can a children's game played by grown-ups contain the ingredients needed for a well-cooked slice of news or literature? Author and baseball fan Wilfrid Sheed once intimated that baseball does not count as representational art and that it does not remind him of anything else (Orodenker 5). Scholar Stephen Jay Gould agrees, saying that "the silliest and most tendentious of baseball writing tries to wrest profundity from the spectacle or grown men hitting a ball with a stick by suggesting linkages between the sport and deep issues of morality, parenthood, history, lost innocence, gentleness, and so on *ad infinitum*" (qtd. in Orodenker 5). Admittedly, there is an air of triviality about even the most important sporting events. Whether it is Game 7 of the World Series, a Little League scrimmage, or sandlot stickball, baseball, for all its metaphors, remains a game, a contrived situation constructed by rules and circumstances. Despite the finality of any ball game, there is always a next game or a next year. And it is this tacit knowledge that makes the metaphors of baseball, and all sports for that matter, appear second-rate when compared with the actual sacrificial heroics and struggles of real people from real life.

Transition sentence leads to dispute the validity of the opposing argument.

It is arguments such as these that all baseball writing, whether criticism, literature, or journalism must answer. If those who study baseball cannot handle these issues or can only handle them poorly, then its place as good subject matter is limited to mediocre stories, sub-standard poetry, and second-class journalism. However, critics like Wilfrid Sheed must realize that baseball, like any topic, is merely a medium to something else. For instance, writer David Carkeet observes that "the only book that is about baseball and nothing else is the rule book," meaning that every baseball novel, short story, essay, or poem is merely using baseball as a prism through which to view other aspects of life (Horvath *et al* 186). Mark Harris, author of the baseball novel *Bang the Drum Slowly,* expounds on this idea by pointing out that people engaged in the illumination of ideas cannot just talk about baseball in terms of "grown men hitting a ball with a stick." This desire to look beyond the face value of things is true about any field. For example, people interested in politics are not satisfied with simply talking about who wins or loses an election; they also discuss the implications of those results and how those outcomes connect to the past and affect the future. Similarly, sports fans who have intellectual mindsets observe what they see on the field and intertwine them with their ideas about culture, literature, psychology or any other field (Horvath *et al* 193). Baseball is a game, but when framed within a specific context, it can act as a vehicle through which to wrestle any number of themes: history, morality, comedy, even tragedy.

In a 1913 article for *Outlook* magazine, writer H. Addington Bruce described baseball as "'something more than the great American game—it is an American institution having a significant place in the life of the people" (218). It would be a gross exaggeration to say that baseball is or ever was important to every American. But baseball is one of many symbols of America. Like the country that founded it, baseball has British roots but has evolved into its own thing and has come to represent the country's culture. In the Ken Burns documentary *Baseball*, writer Gerald Early says that "years from now, when historians study America, it will be remembered for three things: the Constitution, jazz music, and baseball." The veracity of that statement remains to be seen, but his words point to the fact that baseball is very American. And perhaps, centuries from now, the baseball field, like the Roman

The author uses quotes from popular critics to support his claim and to wrap up the argument more creatively.

stadiums before it, will provide insight into a diverse and complex culture for future generations.

Works Cited

Bruce, H. Addington. "Baseball and the National Life." *Major Problems in American Sports History*. Steven A. Riess ed. New York: Houghton Mifflin Company, 1997: 218–220.

Dagavarian, Debra A. *Saying It Ain't So: American Values as Revealed In Children's Baseball Stories 1880–1950*. New York: Peter Lang Publishing Inc., 1987.

Dorinson, Joseph. "Baseball's Ethnic Heroes: Hank Greenberg and Joe DiMaggio." *The Cooperstown Symposium on Baseball and American Culture 2001*. William M. Simons ed. North Carolina: McFarland and Company, 2001: 66–82.

Early, Gerald, perf. *Baseball: A Film by Ken Burns*. Dir. Ken Burns. PBS, 1994.

Horvath, Brooke K., and William J. Palmer. "Three On: An Interview with David Carkeet, Mark Harris, and W. P. Kinsella." *Modern Fiction Studies* 33.1 (1987): 183–94.

Levy, Alan H. "The Right Myths at the Right Time: Myth Making and Hero Worship in Post Frontier Society—Rube Waddell and Christy Mathewson." *The Cooperstown Symposium on Baseball and American Culture 2001*. William M. Simmons ed. North Carolina: McFarland and Company, 2001: 30–50.

Morris, Timothy. *Making the Team: The Cultural Work of Baseball Fiction*. Urbana: Illinois UP, 1997.

Oliver, Phil. "Baseball, Transcendence, and the Return to Life." *The Cooperstown Symposium on Baseball and American Culture 2001*. William M. Simmons ed. North Carolina: McFarland and Company, 2001: 291–306.

Orodenker, Richard. *The Writers' Game*. New York: Twayne Publishers, 1996.

Riess, Steven A. "What Is Sports History?" *Major Problems in American Sports History*. Steven A. Riess ed. New York: Houghton Mifflin Company, 1997: 1–2.

Simmons, William M. "Searching for Hank Greenberg: Aviva Kempner's Mythic Hero and Our Fathers." *The Cooperstown Symposium on Baseball and American Culture 2001*. William M. Simmons ed. North Carolina: McFarland and Company, 2001: 83–102.

1. What support does the author give in opposition to the essay refutation? Is this an effective argument?

2. What additional support would you recommend?

1. Do you participate in a sport or leisure activity that is symbolic of a "culture" that you are a part of? A church culture, a school culture, a racial culture, and so on?

2. Perhaps you are on a step team that represents your African American heritage or a Christian softball league that supports living a healthy and active lifestyle. Describe both the activity and the culture it represents.

THE READING ZONE

TACKLING TOPICS

1. How are sports represented in popular culture? Think about popular opinions of NASCAR versus soccer or hockey versus football. How do these opinions and representations differ? Why do they differ? How do class and race affect these representations? The exclusion or inclusion of gender differences?

2. How does the American idea of the underdog affect American sport? What makes a team an underdog? Do you ever root for the underdog in a one-on-one sport such as tennis or boxing?

3. How have your leisure activities changed since you started college? Are there activities that you enjoyed in high school that you are not as involved in now? How do life-changing events (that is, marriage, children, moving, a new job, graduation) affect the way your leisure time is spent?

4. The idea of a "Renaissance person" suggests that an individual should enjoy both athletic and artistic activities as part of a complete life. Many leisure activities are also athletic events (sailing, hiking, jogging), but others are more artistic or aesthetic (painting, knitting, taking photographs). Which category do you most often fit into? What does this say about you? About your life?

5. Do you have a team or player that you always support? How did you become a fan? Did geography or family connections determine your favorites? Did this connection play a role in your college choices? Do you actively support your college team?

READING SELECTIONS

As in previous chapters, the readings that follow are organized into five sections: 1970s, 1980s, 1990s, 2000s, and Across the Decades. The readings in each of the sections are either from the decade or about that decade. The readings in this chapter are also samples of writing reviews, responses, analyses, and synthesis essays about sports and leisure.

Two articles represent the '70s. First, Roger Kahn discusses the need for sport outside commercialism. Then, Larry Schwartz, writer for ESPN.com, reviews the life of Billie Jean King and her contributions to sports in the '70s and beyond. In the '80s section, a *Time* magazine article highlights the lack of leisure time available in that decade and the predictions for leisure in future decades. The '90s are represented by an article about the University of Kentucky–Duke basketball game in 1992, considered one of the top ten sports moments by most polls. There is also a visual essay identifying trends in skateboard art. A case study about doping in baseball fills the '00s section. These articles and essays all fit together around the central theme, but each tells a different part of the story. The Across the Decades readings include an article from *Smithsonian* about the significance of quilting in American society and the recognition of the leisure activity as a bona fide art form. Finally, an essay by Felicia Paik describes the changing American leisure landscape and the role that scrapbooking has played in this change.

These readings should inspire you to write about the things you love and to research areas of sports and leisure that you may not know as much about. Use the readings as starting points for your own discussion.

Reading Selections: the '70s

CONSIDERING IDEAS

1. There are several levels and types of sports play—children's games, Little League, pickup games, middle and high school sports, college and university sports, intramural team play, professional sports, and exhibitions. How does each of the levels differ from the others?

2. How does love for the game factor into high school basketball versus the NBA? Does professional play always require a passion for the game? Are professional players more passionate than those weekend, pickup-game athletes?

Born in Brooklyn, **Roger Kahn** *rose through the ranks of journalism to become known as the dean of American sportswriting; his 1972 book about baseball,* The Boys of Summer, *is in its eighty-fifth printing. Kahn has written for* Sports Illustrated, Esquire, *and* The Saturday Evening Post *along with many other well-known publications, and he is the former sports editor for* Newsweek *magazine.* "The Joy of Deprogramming Sport" *was published in* Time *in 1977.*

THE JOY OF DEPROGRAMMING SPORT

Roger Kahn

On a warm August night in a southern Ontario town called Guelph, a dozen Americans are playing hockey. There are no commercial interruptions. There is no crowd.

Don Rife, 41, a child psychiatrist from Vermont, reacts quickly at one end of the Victoria Road Arena and makes a save with his gloved hand. Jon Reiff, 38, a law professor from Ohio, spins twice chasing a puck but does not fall. George Wolbert, 56, an attorney for Shell Oil, narrowly misses a body check. These men have made their way to the Can/Am Hockey School in Guelph to play for the unvarnished joy of sport. They earn no money playing. Indeed, they pay tuition to hone their skills.

The Guelph sky has been a high, clean blue, the way boyhood skies appear in memory, and at the rink one feels a sense of boyhood. Of course, the men have me mix it with them. In full hockey gear—was any errant knight more burdened?—I skate till my back smarts and my thighs are lead. It is good to leave customary places and remember. This is how sport ought to be: play some, watch some, give pain, take pain, exult.

Most days for most Americans, sport is a narrower experience. Sit in the living room. Tug the TV button. Heralded by an announcer-salesman, canned sport pops up on the color screen.

This is an era of sophisticated canned goods. Old-fashioned lemonade arrives canned. Presidential memoirs come canned. American sport is canned and packaged, produced and directed until naturalism and spontaneity are fled. Sport appears in the living room marketed as fun and games. More deeply, big-time sport is profit and loss. It is a lode for the television industry.

The American Broadcasting Co., probably the most cynical of networks, regularly brings us something called The Wide World of Sports, which includes Demolition Derby. I cannot follow the rules of Demolition Derby. The idea seems to be to drive automobiles into each other until all but one are broken. The apostle of this glorious venture, Roone Arledge, has lately been elevated to direct ABC news.

The Columbia Broadcasting System offers endless, some would say interminable,

hours of football and basketball, without either a sense of humor or a sense of proportion. The last is just as well for CBS. Football players have been fed and exercised into gargantuan size. Basketball players have been crossbred with giraffes. CBS announcers suggest we identify with football and basketball stars. I identify more easily with King Kong (in the original black-and-white version).

Baseball once held a lovely sway. There were 16 major league teams, eight to a league. Below that, hundreds of minor league teams and town teams were flourishing. In Oklahoma, you could root for the Ponca City Eagles. In Brooklyn, you could pull for the Dodgers or, more parochially, for the Nine representing the Union Gas Co. Now, assisted by favorable tax laws and network money from NBC, the major leagues have carved the country into 26 franchises. No one can follow the casts of 26 separate teams, scattered from Seattle to Atlanta, but the networks focus on the teams that win. Everywhere, town baseball is dead.

Lest we doze through a $75,000 commercial, television addresses us in a chronic forte. One team is best. One man is No. 1. One sport is better than it has ever been before. The salesmanship is skillful, and I am always finding myself persuaded.

I admire Chris Evert's consistency and dedication. She makes a perfect cross-court smash. The picture flickers. Evert reappears selling a brand of sneakers. Damn, I think, why do they have to package Evert? But the truth is that the package and person are one.

In Guelph, George Wolbert, the Shell Oil lawyer, has spent four hours on ice. He is white-haired and balding. "What do you get here?" I say.

"Complete relaxation. An absolute change in my life. A chance to work off hostilities. Discipline." Wolbert puffs and smiles. "At my age, I'm not going to get faster, so I'd better try and get better."

George Wolbert is not No. 1, or the best or even as good as he used to be. He just wants to play hockey as long and as well as he can. We sit alone in a dressing room within an empty arena. The networks are not here. It is fine to savor sport this way, without packages, cans and nonsense.

"I'm 56," Wolbert says, "but there is no reason why I can't play competitive hockey until I'm 60 years old." We begin, George and I, to define sport.

DECODING THE TEXT

1. Why does the author refer to sports as "canned"?

2. How are sports sold to their target audiences?

3. How are athletes marketed or used to market other goods?

CONNECTING TO YOUR CULTURE

1. How do you define sport?

2. Is sport best defined by professionals, occasional players, or spectators?

3. What characteristics of sporting events appeal to you?

4. What sports do you play? What characteristics of these sports appeal to you?

CONSIDERING IDEAS

1. How are women's sporting events different from men's events?

2. Should there be differences in court size, rules, or uniforms?

3. Should women and men play on the same teams in middle school? High school? College? Professional? Why or why not?

Larry Schwartz *is a contributor to ESPN.com. His articles have covered many great athletes from Billie Jean King to Jackie Robinson to Muhammad Ali. He is also an Emmy-winning producer of SportsCentury on ESPN Classic. The article "Billie Jean Won for All Women" can be found at ESPN.com.*

BILLIE JEAN WON FOR ALL WOMEN

Larry Schwartz

Billie Jean King won six Wimbledon singles championships and four U.S. Open titles. She was ranked No. 1 in the world five years. She defeated such magnificent players as Martina Navratilova, Chris Evert and Margaret Court.

Yet of all her matches, the one that is remembered most is her victory against a 55-year-old man.

History has recorded all King accomplished in furthering the cause of women's struggle for equality in the 1970s. She was instrumental in making it acceptable for American women to exert themselves in pursuits other than childbirth. She was the lightning rod in starting a professional women's tour. She started a women's sports magazine and a women's sports foundation.

But what is remembered most about her is that she humbled Bobby Riggs.

Let's get that match out of the way. Riggs, a 1939 Wimbledon champion turned hustler, had already massacred Court on Mother's Day 1973. So King, who previously had rejected Riggs' advances for a match, accepted his latest challenge.

"I thought it would set us back 50 years if I didn't win that match," she said. "It would ruin the women's tour and affect all women's self esteem."

The "Battle of the Sexes" captured the imagination of the country, not just tennis enthusiasts. On Sept. 20, 1973 in Houston, she was carried out on the Astrodome court like Cleopatra, in a gold litter held aloft by four muscular men dressed as ancient slaves. Riggs was wheeled in on a rickshaw pulled by sexy models in tight outfits, "Bobby's Bosom Buddies."

King, then 29, ran the con man ragged, winning 6-4, 6-3, 6-3 in a match the London *Sunday Times* called "the drop shot and volley heard around the world."

"Most important perhaps for women everywhere, she convinced skeptics that a female athlete can survive pressure-filled situations and that men are as susceptible to nerves as women," Neil Amdur wrote in *The New York Times*.

But King was much more than the woman who undressed the self-proclaimed "male chauvinist pig" before a worldwide television audience estimated at almost 50 million. Above all, even more significant than her winning 39 Grand Slam singles, doubles and mixed-doubles titles, she was a pioneer.

"She has prominently affected the way 50 percent of society thinks and feels about itself in the vast area of physical exercise," Frank Deford wrote in *Sports Illustrated*.

"Moreover, like (Arnold) Palmer, she has made a whole sports boom because of the singular force of her presence."

Navratilova said, "She was a crusader fighting a battle for all of us. She was carrying the flag; it was all right to be a jock."

It was for King's crusading that *Life* magazine in 1990 named her one of the "100 Most Important Americans of the 20th Century." Not sports figures, but Americans. She was the only female athlete on the list, and one of only four athletes (Babe Ruth, Jackie Robinson and Muhammad Ali were the others).

She was born Billie Jean Moffitt on Nov. 22, 1943 in Long Beach, Calif., the daughter of a firefighter father and homemaker mother. Her younger brother Randy would become a major-league pitcher.

She developed into a star softball shortstop before her parents decided that she should pursue a more "ladylike" sport and give up playing baseball and football. Her father suggested tennis, because it involved running and hitting a ball.

"I knew after my first lesson what I wanted to do with my life," she said.

Developing her game on the Long Beach public courts, the pudgy adolescent first gained international recognition as a 17-year-old in 1961 by winning with Karen Hantze the doubles championship at Wimbledon. It was the first of her 20 titles (10 doubles and four mixed to go with the six singles) on the hallowed English grass.

In 1966, King (by now she had married law student Larry King) won her first singles Wimbledon title and was ranked No. 1, the first of three straight years at the top. The next year, the myopic pepper pot repeated at Wimbledon and won her first U.S. championship.

After having to get by on $100 a week as a playground instructor and student at Los Angeles State College while at the same time shining at Wimbledon, King became a significant force in opening tennis to professionalism. She carried a deep sense of injustice from her amateur days.

With the birth of the "Open" era in 1968, King turned pro. This time she received more than a trophy for winning Wimbledon. She was on her way to earning $1,966,487 in career prize money.

In those days, women players received much less money than men earned. King's voice was heard loudest in the quest for equality. When a new women's tour was started, with Philip Morris sponsoring a new brand of cigarette, King was perceived as a "radical" heading a breakaway group. The Virginia Slims Tour was marketed with the slogan "You've Come a Long Way, Baby."

Things improved financially. King became the first woman athlete to earn $100,000 in prize money in a year (1971), and President Richard Nixon called to congratulate her.

She convinced her colleagues to form a players' union, and the Women's Tennis Association was born. King was its first president in 1973. King, who received $15,000 less than Ilie Nastase did for winning the U.S. Open in 1972, said if the prize money wasn't equal by the next year, she wouldn't play, and she didn't think the other women would either. In 1973, the U.S. Open became the first major tournament to offer equal prize money for men and women.

The next year, King founded *Women Sports* magazine, started the Women's Sports Foundation, an organization dedicated to promoting and enhancing athletic opportunities for females, and with her husband, formed World Team Tennis.

In 1975, *Seventeen* magazine polled its readers and found that King was the most admired woman in the world. Golda Meir, who had been Israel's prime minister until the previous year, finished second.

Despite her promotions and activities away from the court, the 5-foot-4 King still played outstanding tennis. The same aggressive, hard-hitting net rusher she had been, she hated to lose. "Victory is fleeting," she said. "Losing is forever."

When she hit the perfect shot, she would become ecstatic. "My heart pounds, my eyes get damp, and my ears feel like they're wiggling, but it's also just totally peaceful," King said. "It's almost like having an orgasm — it's exactly like that."

Unlike most athletes, King's sexual preference became a matter of public record. Two decades ago, having a lover of the same sex was viewed quite unkindly, and was sensational news. In 1981, King admitted her bisexuality amid a palimony suit brought by a former woman lover.

While King's former personal assistant lost the suit, King estimated the episode cost her and her husband millions in endorsements. Eventually, King and her husband were divorced.

After retiring from competitive tennis, she remained in the game — as an announcer, coach and author. She gave clinics, became director of World Team Tennis, and played on a Legends tour. Her legs might have given out, but not her passion for the game.

King believes that she was born with a destiny to work for gender equity in sports and to continue until it's achieved.

"In the '70s we had to make it acceptable for people to accept girls and women as athletes," she said. "We had to make it OK for them to be active. Those were much scarier times for females in sports."

1. The King–Riggs matchup is only a supporting point for the author's thesis. How does the author's glossing over of this match demonstrate assumptions about his audience?

2. Who is the audience for this article?

CONNECTING TO YOUR CULTURE

1. Have you ever played on a coed team?

2. If so, how did this experience differ from your previous sporting activities? If not, would you consider playing on a coed team? What accommodations would need to be made?

3. Would it depend on the sport being played? Tackle football or touch football? Full-court or half-court basketball? Why or why not?

Reading Selection: the '80s

CONSIDERING IDEAS

1. How do class, race, age, and gender help to determine leisure activities?

2. What can your, your family's, or your friends' leisure activities tell you about your background?

Nancy Gibbs, *a native New Yorker, has held several positions at* Time *magazine from a columnist in the mid-1980s to editor at large, a position she assumed in 2002. Gibbs has written several cover stories in her twenty-plus years at the publication, including "The Columbine Tapes" and "The Right to Die." The following article, "How America Has Run Out of Time," was printed in 1989.*

HOW AMERICA HAS RUN OUT OF TIME

Nancy Gibbs

All my possessions for a moment of time.
—Queen Elizabeth I,
with her dying breath, 1603

If you have a moment to read this story with your feet up, free of interruption, at your leisure . . . put it down. It's not for you. Congratulations.

If, like almost everyone else, you're trying to do something else at the same time—if you are stuck in traffic, waiting in the airport lounge, watching the news, if you're stirring the soup, shining your shoes, drying your hair . . . read on. Or hire someone to read it for you and give you a report.

There was once a time when time was money. Both could be wasted or both well spent, but in the end gold was the richer prize. As with almost any commodity, however, value depends on scarcity. And these are the days of the time famine. Time that once seemed free and elastic has grown tight and elusive, and so our measure of its worth is dramatically changed. In Florida a man bills his ophthalmologist $90 for keeping him waiting an hour. In California a woman hires somebody to do her shopping for her—out of a catalog. Twenty bucks pays someone to pick up the dry cleaning, $250 to cater dinner for four, $1,500 will buy a fax machine for the car. "Time," concludes pollster Louis Harris, who has charted America's loss of it, "may have become the most precious commodity in the land."

This sense of acceleration is not just a vague and spotted impression. According to a Harris survey, the amount of leisure time enjoyed by the average American has shrunk 37% since 1973. Over the same period, the average workweek, including commuting, has jumped from under 41 hours to nearly 47 hours. In some professions, predictably law, finance and medicine, the demands often stretch to 80-plus hours a week. Vacations have shortened to the point where they are frequently no more than long weekends. And the Sabbath is for—what else?—shopping.

If all this continues, time could end up being to the '90s what money was to the '80s. In fact, for the callow yuppies of Wall Street, with their abundant salaries and meager freedom, leisure time is the one thing they find hard to buy. Their lives are so busy that merely to give someone the time of day seems an act of charity. They order gourmet takeout because microwave dinners have become just too much trouble. Canary sales are up (low-maintenance pets); Beaujolais nouveau is booming (a wine one needn't wait for). "I gave up pressure for Lent," says a theater director in Manhattan. If only it were that easy.

More seriously, this shortcut society is changing the way the family functions.

"How America Has Run Out of Time" by Nancy Gibbs from TIME, 1989, pp.58–63.

Nowhere is the course of the rat race more arduous, for example, than around the kitchen table. Hallmark, that unerring almanac of American mores, now markets greeting cards for parents to tuck under the Cheerios in the morning ("Have a super day at school," chirps one card) or under the pillow at night ("I wish I were there to tuck you in"). Even parents who like their jobs and love their kids find that the pressure to do justice to both becomes almost unbearable. "As a society," warns Yale University psychology professor Edward Zigler, "we're at the breaking point as far as family is concerned."

The late Will Durant, the Book-of-the-Month Club's ubiquitous historian, once observed that "no man who is in a hurry is quite civilized." Time bestows value because objects reflect the hours they absorb: the hand-carved table, the handwritten letter, every piece of fine craftsmanship, every grace note. But now we have reached the stage at which not only are the luxuries of time disappearing—for reading meaty novels, baking from scratch, learning fugues, traveling by sea rather than air, or by foot rather than wheel—but the necessities of time are also out of reach. Family time. Mealtime. Even mourning time. In 1922 Emily Post instructed that the proper mourning period for a mature widow was three years. Fifty years later, Amy Vanderbilt urged that the bereaved be about their normal business within a week or so.

So how did America become so timeless? Those who can remember washing diapers or dialing phones may recall the silvery vision of a postindustrial age. Computers, satellites, robotics and other wizardries promised to make the American worker so much more efficient that income and GNP would rise while the workweek shrank. In 1967 testimony before a Senate subcommittee indicated that by 1985 people could be working just 22 hours a week or 27 weeks a year or could retire at 38. That would leave only the great challenge of finding a way to enjoy all that leisure.

And not only would the office be transformed. The American household soaked up microwaves, VCRs, blow dryers, mix 'n' eat, the computerized automobile that announces that all systems work and it is getting 23 miles to the gallon. The kitchen was streamlined with so much labor-saving gadgetry that meals could be prepared, served and cleaned up in less time than it took to boil an egg. Thus freed from household chores, Mom could head off to a committee meeting on social justice, while Dad chaired the men's-club clothing drive, and the kids went to bed at 10:30 after watching a PBS special on nuclear physics.

Sure enough, the computers are byting, the satellites spinning, the Cuisinarts whizzing, just as planned. Yet we are ever out of breath. "It is ironic," writes social theorist Jeremy Rifkin in *Time Wars*, "that in a culture so committed to saving time we feel increasingly deprived of the very thing we value." Since leisure is notoriously hard to define and harder to measure, sociologists disagree about just how much of it has disappeared. But they do agree that people feel more harried by their life-styles. "People's schedules are more ambitious," says John Robinson, who heads up the Americans' Use of Time project at the University of Maryland. "There just isn't enough time to fit in all the things one feels have to be done."

A poll for TIME and CNN by Yankelovich Clancy Shulman found this sense especially acute among women in two-income families: 73% of the women complain of having too little leisure, as do 51% of the men. Such figures produce no end of questions for sociologists, and everyone else, to stew over. Why do we work so hard? Why do we have so little time to spare? What does this do to us and our children? And what would we give up in order to live a little more peaceably?

Experts tracking the cause and effect are coming to see how progress has carried hidden costs. "Technology is increasing the heartbeat," says Manhattan architect James Trunzo, who designs "automated environments." "We are inundated with information. The mind can't handle it all. The pace is so fast now, I sometimes feel like a gunfighter dodging bullets." In business especially, the world financial markets almost never close, so why should the heavy little eyes of an ambitious baby banker? "There is now a new supercomputer that operates at a trillionth of a second," says Robert Schrank, a management consultant in New York City. "What's a trillionth of a second? Time is being eaten up by all these new inventions. Even leisure is done on schedule. Golfing is done on schedule. My son is on the run all the time. I ask him, 'Are you having fun?' He says, 'Hell, I don't know.'"

The pace of change and the explosion of information mean that professionals are swamped with too many new facts to absorb. Meanwhile, the drill-press operator discovers that the drill comes with a computer attached to it. Workers find that it takes all the energy they have just to remain qualified for their jobs, much less have time to acquire new skills

that might allow for promotion. "There is no question that the half-life of most job skills is dropping all the time," says Edward Lawler, University of Southern California professor of management. People are falling by the wayside, just as companies are."

There is an additional irony: all the time-saving devices may actually make people work harder. Sometime in the early '80s, suggests futurist Selwyn Enzer, Americans came to worship career status as a measure of individual worth, and many were willing to sacrifice any amount of leisure time to get ahead. "Social scientists underestimated the sense of self-esteem that came with having a career," he observes. These days, if an entrepreneur has not made his first million by the time he is 30, his commitment to capital accumulation is suspect. And in the transition from an industrial to a global service economy, many of the white-collar "servants"— lawyers, bankers, accountants—are pushing harder than ever to meet their clients' inexhaustible needs.

For these hardy souls, there is no longer any escape from the office. Simply to remain competitive, professionals find that their lives are one long, continuous workday, bleeding into the wee hours and squeezing out any leisure time. "My wife and I were sitting on the beach in Anguilla on one of our rare vacations," recalls architect Trunzo, "and even there my staff was able to reach me. There are times when our lives are clearly leading us." There are phones in the car, laptops in the den, and the humming fax machine eliminates that once peaceful lull between completing a document and delivering it. "The fax has destroyed any sense of patience or grace that existed," says

Hollywood publicist Josh Baron. "People are so crazy now that they call to tell you your fax line is busy."

Add to that a work ethic gone mad. "Work has become trendy," observes Jim Butcher, a management consultant for the Boston Consulting Group. But he and other professionals acknowledge the toll that such a relentless pace takes on creativity. No instrument, no invention, can emit an utterly original thought. "I flew 80,000 miles last year," says economist James Smith of the Rand Corp. "You start losing touch with things. My work is research, which at its best is contemplative. If you get into this mode of running around, you don't have time to reflect."

The risk is that the unexamined life becomes self-sustaining. Attention spans may be richly elastic, but little in this rapid life-style conspires to stretch them. In fact the reverse is true, as TV commercials shrink to 15-second flashes and popular novels contain paragraphs no longer than two sentences. "I do things in a lot of 3½-minute segments," muses UCLA anthropologist Peter Hammond. "Experience just sort of rolls by me. I think it affects the quality of my work."

Technology alone, however, bears only part of the responsibility for the time famine. All the promises of limitless leisure relied on America's retaining its blinding lead in the world's markets and unfolding prosperity at home. No one quite bargained for the Middle-Class Squeeze, what Paula Rayman, a sociologist at Wellesley College's Stone Center, calls "falling behind while getting ahead." The prices of houses have soared, inflation erodes paychecks, wages are stagnant,

and medical and tuition costs continue to skyrocket. So now it can take two paychecks to fund what many imagined was a middle-class life. "The American Dream is very much intact," says Rayman. "It's just more expensive."

Keeping a home and raising 2.4 children, as anyone who has ever done it knows, is a full-time job. The increasing rarity of the full-time homemaker has done more to eat away everyone's leisure time than any other factor. If both mother and father are working to make ends meet, as is the case in 57% of U.S. families, someone still has to find the time to make lunches and pediatrician appointments, shop, cook, fix the washer, do the laundry, take the children to choir practice. Single-parent households are squeezed even more.

On the surface, families are coping by teaching children to put the roast in the oven after school, enrolling them in day care, hiring nannies, making play dates, sending out laundry and ordering in pizza. "We spend a lot of time buying time," observes economist Smith. "What we're doing is contracting out for family care," notes Rand demographer Peter Morrison, "but there's a limit. If you contract out everything, you have an enterprise, not a family."

Like the ever expanding white-collar workday, this stage of family evolution defies all the expectations of a generation ago. For years, stress research tended to focus on men, and so the office or factory floor was viewed as the primary source of tension. The home, on the other hand, was a sanctuary, a benign environment in which one recuperated from problems at work. The experts know better now.

Listen to the families:

—"Tired is my middle name," says Carol Rohder, 41, a single mother of three in Joliet, Ill. She works days as a medical technician and four nights a week as a waitress. "I'm exhausted all the time. I didn't think it would be this hard on my own. I thought once I was divorced the pressure would be off."

—"You get addicted to overworking," says Nancy Baker-Velasquez, a partner in an insurance brokerage in California, whose husband is a sheriff's deputy on the night shift. "At the same time, you have so many more obligations as a parent now. These days, you have to start brushing their teeth even before they have teeth."

—"It's not so much that we need to make ends meet," says Jon Hilliard, his three-year-old at his side. Hilliard works for the Street Department in Crown Point, Ind., and as a self-employed carpenter. His wife Sharron is a gym teacher, and together they earn something over $60,000 a year. "It's the way we get extra things. I grew up in a poor family with four kids, and we had no extras. There's no way my kids are going to be like that. We want to make sure that if they're not good athletes or smart academically, they can still go to college."

—"The most precious commodity to us is time," agree architect Trunzo and his wife Candace, both 41 and parents of two. "We have tried to simplify our lives as much as possible." Candace believes she and her husband are living "better lives than our parents. More hectic. But fuller." James wonders about that. "It's dangerous to use the word fuller. Where is that sense of spirituality that we talked about in the '60s? Where is the time to go up to the mountaintop? Technology is a diversion from life. You can be transfixed. I'm not sure that technology doesn't remove us from each other, isolate us. In architecture we're seeing demands for media rooms. What ever happened to the kitchen as a gathering place?"

—Lynne Meadow and Ron Shechtman, both 42, dote on their son Jonathan, 4. "And there's maybe 30 minutes every day," says Ron, "when we don't discuss having another child. But where would the extra minutes come from?" Lynne runs the red-hot Manhattan Theater Club; Ron is a partner in a midsize law firm. They live in a home where the telephone cords stretch into every room, and the nanny starts work at 7:30 A.M. "You can imagine what getting out the door in the morning is like," says Ron. Are there regrets? He ponders, "Can we take the added pressure that a second child would bring?" For the moment, the answer is no.

Parents know all too vividly the effects of the stress they endure in order to keep up with their lives. Addiction to a speeded-up schedule can lead to a physical breakdown from hypertension, ulcers, heart disease, or dependence on alcohol, cocaine and cigarettes. The effect on the psyche is subtler and more insidious. People find themselves growing impatient and restless, and it seems harder to think logically about a problem. Even if two hours miraculously open up one evening, they may be spent watching TV, since people are too tired to do much else.

More ominous are the effects on children. "Making an appointment is one way to relate to your child," says UCLA anthropologist Hammond, "but it's pretty desiccated. You've got to hang around with your kids." Yet hanging-around time is the first thing to go. The very culture of children, of freedom and fantasy and kids teaching kids to play jacks, is collapsing under the weight of hectic family schedules. "Kids understand that they are being cheated out of childhood," says Edward Zigler at Yale. "Eight-year-olds are taking care of three-year-olds. We're seeing depression in children. We never thought we'd see that 35 years ago. There is a sense that adults don't care about them."

Adults may care a lot, but in ways that are often distorted by their own zealous professional lives. Eager parents arrive home late and pour a day's stored attention onto a child who is more ready to be tucked in than talked at. "It may be that the same loss of leisure among parents produces this pressure for rapid achievement and overprogramming of children," argues Allan Carlson, president of the conservative Rockford Institute, an Illinois think tank. If parents see parenting largely as an investment of their precious time, they may end up viewing children as objects to be improved rather than individuals to be nurtured at their own pace.

Children are scuttling from karate classes to play dates scheduled by Mommy's secretary. Their social lives out of nursery school may rival those of their parents in complexity. Meanwhile, the parents must work even harder to pay for it all. When Arlie Hochschild studied working couples in the San Francisco area for a forthcoming book, *Second Shift*, she found that "a lot of people talked about sleep. They talked about sleep the way a hungry person talks about food."

Thus for many exhausted American families, the premium placed on free time is bringing about both subtle and sweeping changes. In some cases, it means a new division of labor between husband and wife, parents and kids; a search for more flexible professional schedules; or an outright rebellion against the rat race. Any or all of these may force a family to make some hard and intriguing choices. Which is most important? A challenging and fulfilling job? A bigger house? A college education for a gifted child? A life in the big city?

The glib answer most often boils down to women withdrawing from the work force and returning home, thereby easing the time crunch for the whole family. But it is almost never that easy. After 20 years of studying women and stress, Wellesley College researcher Rosalind Barnett has found that alcoholism and depression in women are less frequent among those who work. Nor could most families afford to have one spouse give up working. And the American economy could not stand the hemorrhage of so much talent from its work force.

So the interesting reactions of families and individuals are more daring than simply "dropping out." In 1986 the advertising firm of D'Arcy Masius Benton & Bowles released a poll: If you could have your dream job, it asked, what would it be? The most popular choice among men was to own or manage their own company, followed by being a professional athlete, the head of a large corporation, a forest ranger and a test pilot. The favorite among women? To own and manage their own business, but in their case followed by tour guide, flight attendant, novelist and photographer.

"Running your own business means you are controlling your own destiny," says M.I.T. research director David Birch, who has studied entrepreneurship. While starting a company rarely means more free time, it can promise greater satisfaction, autonomy and flexible working conditions. Freedom-minded men and women alike have recognized that technology and the restructuring of the economy, which so often work against individual peace of mind, can actually work for the small entrepreneur. The same computers and fax machines that torment corporate drudges allow small businesses access to world markets.

Some fast-lane veterans who are fed up with their harried working conditions are trying other escape routes, including climbing down the corporate ladder. Trading in a big salary for a lower-level job with more vacation time, flexible hours, improved maternity or paternity leave, even weekends off may seem a luxury, but it is one that many people are choosing. Dann Pottinger, 42, nephew and grandson of Florida bank presidents, was CEO of Commercial State Bank of Orlando, one of the most profitable independent banks in central Florida. This winter he chaired the search committee to select his replacement. "It is all too time-consuming," he says of his job. Pottinger has spent a total of eight days out of the office in the past year. So he will give up a six-figure salary to go on commission for State Farm Insurance Companies. "I'm not naïve enough to say that money doesn't matter," Pottinger says. "But I want my children to know me as something besides their provider."

Such sentiments help explain why the high-draw cities in the U.S. are not the metropolises of New York and Los Angeles but the smaller and more habitable climes of Albuquerque, Fort Worth, Providence and Charlotte, N.C. To many working families, a higher quality of life, and more

of it, compensate nicely for the absence of the Metropolitan Opera or the Hollywood Bowl. When Equitable Life Assurance Society summoned Jim Crawford, 43, back to Manhattan from its Des Moines office, he would not relinquish his Iowa life-style. "We based that decision on the quality of the environment," he says. "People do work hard here, and there is a deep appreciation for family life." He traded a higher salary and a two-hour commute for better schools and more free time. "We wonder how we did it, went through the routine," he says now.

For families who cannot handle such a radical departure, there are alternatives. What was once a cottage industry of people providing household services is currently a booming business in cities all across the country. Anyone who can protect a family's free time is a sure success. "The hot new family commodity is 'off time,'" says Heloise, the syndicated oracle of household hints. "If I can give them another 20 minutes, even if it costs them $4 in dry cleaning, then I'm successful."

Four dollars for 20 minutes is cheap. Two corporate dropouts, Glenn Partin and Richard Rogers, founded At Your Service last year in Winter Park, Fla. They are typical of the growing number of entrepreneurs who will perform any service within their expertise, for anywhere between $25 and $50 an hour. They chauffeur people to airports, return video tapes, cater parties. "I can pick up the phone and ask them to do anything," says Debbie Findura, 35, a part-time real estate agent who has called them to fix a light bulb that broke off in the socket, remove a live lizard she found in her oven, and deliver a package of hot-dog buns for one of her family picnics. "We charged $20 to deliver

59 cents worth of hot-dog buns," says Rogers, "but she had them there, and that's what these people expect."

Professional organizers are also in demand. Stephanie Culp of Los Angeles is a pleasant, schoolmarmish woman who seven years ago turned her personal inclinations ("I was neurotically organized") into a career. "If I said I was a professional organizer seven years ago, people would have laughed," she says. "Now the idea is accepted." Culp's golden rule is to set priorities, and she's not kidding. "When you die, what do you want people to say at your funeral?" she asked California businesswoman Baker-Velasquez. Answer: "I didn't want my children to say, 'My mother was a wonderful businesswoman.'"

Among the tactics Culp's clients are testing: watching less TV, shopping by phone, buying low-maintenance clothes and appliances, screening calls on the answering machine and taking a more lax atti-tude toward housekeeping. "I'm not so immaculate anymore," Baker-Velasquez explains. "There are spots on the carpet, and things are broken. But I'd rather sacrifice my home than my husband's or children's needs."

No combination of innovations, inventions or timely hints will restore the American household to its imagined bygone tranquillity. Only a dramatic change in both attitudes and economics would offer a genuine respite. And, anyway, who hasn't felt the exhilaration of running this race, which many might actually miss if they slowed to a trot. But at some point individuals must find the time to consider the price of their preoccupation and the toll on the spirit exacted by exhaustion. With too little sleep there are too few dreams. And for children, especially, being eight years old should include some long, ice-creamy afternoons of favorite stories and grassy feet. Some things are just worth the time.

DECODING THE TEXT

1. Consider these questions from the text: "Why do we work so hard? Why do we have so little time to spare? What does this do to us and our children? And what would we give up in order to live a little more peaceably?" Now, compare your answers and those included in the article.

2. How has leisure culture changed since this article was written?

CONNECTING TO YOUR CULTURE

1. How many leisure hours do you spend per week?

2. How often do you go on vacation?

3. How often do you see your family?

4. Are these things priorities for you?

5. What advancements have allowed you to save a few more seconds for leisure?

Reading Selections: the '90s

CONSIDERING IDEAS

1. A "fish tale" is a story that continues to change, grow, or evolve as it is retold. Many sporting events lend themselves to this kind of retelling. Have you ever experienced an event or activity that has become legendary?

2. How have the details changed as the story became more popular?

A senior writer for ESPN.com, **Pat Forde** *spent seventeen years at* The Courier-Journal *in Louisville, Kentucky—the last twelve covering sports. Forde, the recipient of many honors from the Associated Press Editors and a Pulitzer Prize nominee, is also a frequent contributor to National Public Radio (NPR). "'92 Loss to Duke Proved UK Could Win Again" was published in 1997 and is archived on ESPN.com.*

'92 LOSS TO DUKE PROVED UK COULD WIN AGAIN

Pat Forde

> *"Oh, my God. People always remind me of that game. I compare it to when President Kennedy got shot. Everybody remembers exactly where they were, who they were with, and what they were doing when Christian Laettner hit that shot."*
>
> —Richie Farmer, Kentucky guard 1988–92

At first glance, what Farmer said above might easily be construed as utterly lacking perspective. Comparing reactions to a basketball game with a presidential assassination? Please.

Except that in Farmer's home state of Kentucky, it's true. That is exactly the way people remember Duke 104, Kentucky 103, on March 28, 1992—acclaimed by many the greatest college basketball game ever played.

In Kentucky, at least, it is certainly the most vividly remembered game ever played. You could take a poll on a busy street corner in Louisville, or on a rural road in Farmer's tiny hometown of Manchester, and just about everybody can give you immediate and exact recall.

The impact of Laettner's 17-foot jump shot at the final horn was that percussive. The emotions were that raw. The stakes were that high. And the Kentucky team was that revered.

"People have told me numerous stories about where they were at the time, and the funny thing is they always remember the little details," Farmer said.

I remember where I was. Courtside in The Spectrum in Philadelphia. Awestruck. And trying to write about it on deadline.

After that game, the NCAA selection committee realized that matching up Duke and Kentucky was a brilliant stroke. So they tried to do it again in 1994. Kentucky didn't keep its side of the bargain, being upset by Marquette in the second round. Last year was another near-miss—in Philly, no less—when the Wildcats were upset by Southern California, ruining a reincarnated East Regional final with Duke.

But the committee did successfully engineer another classic Duke-Kentucky March moment, in 1998. That time, the Wildcats won an incredible regional final on the way to a national title, coming from 17 points down with less than 12 minutes to play to win 86–84.

The basket that wiped out the last of that lead and put the Cats ahead for the first time, 80–79, came on a 3-pointer by senior Cameron Mills—a slow-footed, walk-on shooting specialist from Lexington whose daddy, Terry, played for Adolph Rupp. Framed panoramic photos of Mills

hitting that shot, autographed by the shooter, are big sellers in Kentucky malls this Christmas season at $195 apiece.

The ball wound up in Mills' hands after a furious battle for a rebound, as Kentucky forward Heshimu Evans swatted it back to the top of the key in desperation. Mills did what came naturally: caught and shot. Today, his only recollection of that moment comes from watching tapes of the game. He can't remember it happening.

"I did a little pirouette at midcourt and pumped my fist," he said. "I don't remember that, either."

Interesting, because he can recall the 1992 Duke–Kentucky climax vividly. Cameron Mills is one of those people Richie Farmer was talking about.

Mills watched the game at home alone, "sitting in my dad's old recliner." He clearly recalled "hitting the floor" when Sean Woods' banker went in for a 103–102 Kentucky lead.

"I called one of my friends and just screamed 'We're going to do it! We're going to do it! We're going to do it!'" Mills recalled. "Then on the next play, Christian hit that shot and I just sat there, stunned."

Which is why providing the payback to Duke six years later really did matter to Mills and fellow from-the-crib Kentucky fan Scott Padgett, who also hit a huge 3 in the final minute.

"I think when we look back down the road, Cam and I can say we did this for our state, our fans and our school," Padgett says proudly today.

Duke and Kentucky have played just one other time since then, in December 1998. The Blue Devils won that one handily, 71–60, with a huge game from Elton Brand.

Tuesday night in the Meadowlands, they meet again. It's hard to believe that the latest Duke-Kentucky game comes in the 10th anniversary of that 1991–92 season.

It was a watershed year in college basketball.

That season saw Duke become the first repeat champion since the John Wooden dynasty at UCLA. It saw Duke ranked No. 1 every single week of the season. We haven't had a repeat champ or a wire-to-wire No. 1 team since.

The season saw Bob Knight make his last Final Four appearance at Indiana. It saw the Fab Five make its first Final Four appearance, materializing as brazen Michigan freshmen and shaking the game to its foundation—without winning a national title, or even a Big Ten crown. And it saw Kentucky make a fairy-tale return from the ash heap of scandal and probation, a rag-tag group playing its way into history.

The story behind the story is this: the path to that game actually began four years earlier, in Springfield, Mass. The first college game and the last college game Farmer and fellow Kentuckians John Pelphrey and Deron Feldhaus ever played were against Duke.

"They beat the fire out of us," Farmer said of Duke 80, Kentucky 55 in the Tip-Off Classic in Springfield, Mass.

Sports Illustrated's story on that game ran under the headline, "Blue Devils vs. Devil Blue." Dick Vitale went on the air before the game and called for Wildcats coach Eddie Sutton to resign.

Kentucky was beginning the bleakest season in its history, a 13–19 disaster completed with one of the most infamous NCAA scandals ever hanging over its head. It began the previous spring, when an overnight envelope from the Kentucky basketball office to recruit Chris Mills popped open, revealing $1,000 dollars in cash.

Pelphrey, Feldhaus and Farmer were lost boys, playing for a lost cause. Recruited as afterthoughts, it was their lifelong dream to play at Kentucky—but not this Kentucky.

But the worst thing that ever hit Kentucky turned out to be one of the best things that ever hit Kentucky. The scandal led to Sutton resigning at the end of the season and the school hiring Rick Pitino in May 1989, setting in motion the rejuvenation of a tarnished program.

A rejuvenation that came full circle in The Spectrum.

By then, Pelphrey, Feldhaus, Farmer and Indianapolis product Woods had become the foundation of a spectacular success story. The four seniors who stuck it out in Lexington—through mass transfers, and a probation that denied the Wildcats postseason play for two years—brought Kentucky back. (With an admittedly large assist from sophomore Jamal Mashburn, the best player on that team.)

The Wildcats entered that game 29–6. And seemingly without a chance against 31–2 Duke.

The Blue Devils performed as expected, sprinting to a 67-55 lead in the second half. Duke sliced up a Kentucky zone Pitino had employed to offset severe matchup problems, and the Blue Devils appeared to be pulling away toward the Final Four.

That's when Pitino called a timeout and unleashed the hounds, throwing his team's trademark full-court pressure at junior point guard Bobby Hurley. The Cats came back, and the game began to take on the feel of a classic.

The final few minutes of regulation and overtime produced some of the finest offensive basketball ever seen. Mashburn at one end, Laettner at the other, basket after basket in an exceptional game of can-you-top-this?

In the closing seconds of OT, it finally appeared that Kentucky had the shot that couldn't be topped. Following a UK timeout with 7.8 seconds to play, Woods curled off a wicked Pelphrey screen that flattened Hurley, drove from the top of the key to just inside the foul line and flung a one-handed shot, high over the 6-foot-11 Laettner. The ball shot off the backboard and through the net in flukish fashion.

(Pitino had put the ball in Woods' hands at the end of a half or a game many times in three seasons, with uniformly disappointing results. The one shot he did make was in the final seconds at Mississippi State in 1991—a driving layup when the Cats were down three, as he lost track of the score. Against Duke, the hard-luck kid finally got it right, in the biggest moment of his career.)

Duke called timeout with 2.1 seconds left.

Mike Krzyzewski immediately told his players, "We're going to win the game." Not sure whether he believed it, but it needed to be said. Then he drew up the most famous play in college basketball history.

Grant Hill's 75-foot baseball pass was aided and abetted by Pitino's fateful decision not to put any pressure on Hill. Instead, he had Pelphrey and Feldhaus double-team Laettner.

Pelphrey went for the pass, and to this day can't understand how he missed it. But the ball wound up in Laettner's hands, and after lightly bumping Laettner, Pelphrey backed away, not wanting to risk a foul. Feldhaus also kept his distance.

Laettner's exceptional internal clock told him he had time for a stabilizing dribble before turning to his right and launching a high, arcing shot through the exhausted Spectrum air.

Laettner had taken 19 other shots in the game, nine from the field and 10 from the foul line. He had made all of them, and this one made him a mythic 20 for 20. From where I sat on press row, you knew it was good the instant it left his hand.

The immediate aftermath illustrated how much had been invested in the game. Laettner made his victory dash back upcourt before being swallowed by his delirious teammates. Woods sprawled under the basket, face-down. Pelphrey put his hands to his red hair in shock. On the Duke bench, Thomas Hill also put his hands on his head, as tears streamed down his face.

And his team won.

Krzyzewski showed remarkable composure, class and empathy. He consoled Farmer, then went over to legendary Kentucky radio broadcaster Cawood Ledford. As Ledford was ending a peerless career and signing off from his final Kentucky game, Krzyzewski asked for his headset and expressed his admiration for the Wildcats directly to their fans.

Duke, of course, went on to beat Indiana and Michigan to win the national title. Kentucky went home to a hero's welcome, and a surprise honor for Woods, Farmer, Feldhaus and Pelphrey from athletic director C. M. Newton shortly after the season.

"Today, our program is back on top, due largely to four young men who persevered, who weathered the hard times, and who brought back the good times to Kentucky basketball," Newton said, as they raised the players' jerseys to the rafters in Rupp.

They're remembered as "The Unforgettables" in Kentucky lore. Their final game has proven truly unforgettable for everyone who saw it.

DECODING THE TEXT

1. The author of this story is obviously a Kentucky fan. How would this story change from a Duke fan's point of view?

2. What language in the article shows a specific bias?

CONNECTING TO YOUR CULTURE

1. Have you ever been part of a team that worked so well together that the individual became less important than the group?

2. How do team dynamics transfer to other parts of your life? In the classroom? With your family?

Sport and art are not often thought of in the same category, but skateboard design is one example that combines sport and art.

1. What other interests combine a love of sport or leisure activities and aesthetics?

2. Have you ever been involved in any activity that combined art and athletics, such as ballet?

Writer and graphic designer **Steven Brower** *is the author or coauthor of several books on visual design, including* 2D: Visual Basics for Designers. *Based in New York, Brower has been a creative director for* Print *and art director for* The New York Times *and* Nation.

John Gall, *vice president and art director for both Vintage and Anchor Books, coauthored* 2D: Visual Basics for Designers *with Steven Brower. Gall is best known for designing innovative book covers. The coauthored visual essay "Skateboard Art" was published in* Print *magazine in 1996.*

SKATEBOARD ART

Steven Brower and John Gall

It's the underside of design, it comes in many artistic styles, and it all began (surprise!) in Southern California.

Here's a test: What are "nosepick," "face plant," and "Wilson"? If you know, read no further. If not, welcome to the world of the skateboard artist.

Ripping through the collected motifs of popular art with total disregard for esthetic rules or copyright protection, skateboard artists turn out work that comes on like a blast of beer-scented air in the face of the design establishment. Working for companies with names like Fuct and Anti-Hero, these designers are often unschooled, they are usually riders themselves, and they are a part of a subculture with a verbal and visual language that only insiders can understand.

With their youthful hubris, skateboarders are one of the few groups to have been co-opted by the mainstream, and subsequently reappropriated by the true teen trust. This is no mean feat. Imagine, if you will, the Beats surviving Maynard G. Krebbs or hippiedom lasting past *Love American Style* and *Dragnet*. Though skateboards are visible everywhere these days in films like *Clueless* and *Kids*, the members of this private club continue to develop their own means of communication.

"Skateboard Art" by Steven Brower and John Gall from PRINT MAGAZINE, 1996, pp. 52–56.

Not surprisingly, it all began in Southern California. According to vintage-skateboard collector Eric "Arab" Groff, the first skateboards developed from the scooters of the '30s, '40s, and '50s. "Some of the earliest known skateboards were made by cutting the wheel assembly and mounting it on two-by-fours," he says. "The first manufactured skateboards were from the late '50s." The board and the motion were closely related to surfing, and many a surfer would "ride these contraptions when the waves went flat," says Ed Templeton, a contemporary skateboard designer based in Huntington Beach, California.

The origins of skateboard art can be traced back to the mid-1950s, when a group of rubber-burning outlaws, Ed "Big Daddy" Roth, Von Dutch, and Robert Williams, began customizing hot rods with decorative pinstripes and monster cartoons. Throughout the 1960s, the boards, unlike the cars, were unadorned. By the '70s, however, with the advent of skateboard parks and skate teams with corporate sponsorship, logos began to appear on the underside of the boards. Concurrently, a pioneering group of skaters from an area in Los Angeles known as Dogtown adopted a ganglike attitude and used skateboard graphics as a means of identification. Although kids had always personalized their boards with stickers and drawings, it wasn't until the 1980s, with the emergence of second-generation punk bands like Black Flag and Circle Jerks, whose DIY esthetic and anti-establishment stance appealed to like-minded skaters, that this artwork began to take on a broader connotation. "Skate punks," as these riders were labeled, used skateboards not only to cruise around town but also to display—with artwork—their allegiance to the insider culture. As designer and

Left: Stereo/Ethan Fowler/by Thomas Campbell/1996. Image courtesy of Sean Cliver/www.disposablethebook.com.
Left center: Powell Peralta/Longboard/by John Keester/1990. Image courtesy of Sean Cliver/www.disposablethebook.com.
Right center: Powell Peralta/Bucky Lasek/by Sean Cliver/1990. Image courtesy of Sean Cliver/www.disposablethebook.com.
Right: Toy Machine/Jamie Thomas/by Ron Cameron/1996. Image courtesy of Sean Cliver/www.disposablethebook.com.

skateboard authority Mike Mills notes, "Skating was becoming an activity for people who didn't want, or couldn't fit into, mainstream ideals. The graphics and style functioned as a way for skateboarders to tell the [upholders of the] status quo they were different and to tell other skaters they were the same."

By the '90s, skateboarding had moved to more densely populated areas, and skaters abandoned the suburbs and skate parks in favor of urban street skating. Small, bedroom-based skateboard companies with a heavy emphasis on visuals began popping up. The new esthetic combined the "in your face" attitude of punk with the street wisdom of hip-hop.

Flirting with taboo subject matter and deliberately eschewing good taste, skateboard art covers a vast range of artistic styles and media, including "sick" comic art, parodies of well-known logos, Surrealist sculptures, '50s beatnik kitsch, and cool Swiss moderne graphics. The repertoire is endless. And all of this is meant to attract "an ever-changing group of violence- and sex-crazed skateboarders aged 13 to 18," says Templeton.

To keep their looks fresh, or at least stay one step ahead of the copyright police, skateboard companies revise their board graphics at a blinding rate. The average company creates six new board designs a month, each one reproduced on about a thousand boards. Because the previous month's designs become obsolete so fast, and because the new ones are ridden to destruction, individuals like Aaron Rose, who runs the Alleged Gallery in New York and is also responsible for mounting exhibitions of skateboard art throughout the world, have begun to preserve this ephemeral art.

Left: World Industries/Chico Brenes/by Marc McKee/1993. Image courtesy of Sean Cliver/ www.disposablethebook.com.
Left center: Anti Hero/Team/by Chris Johanson/1997. Image courtesy of Sean Cliver/ www.disposablethebook.com.
Right center: Plan B/Sean Sheffey/by Jeff Tremaine/1993. Image courtesy of Sean Cliver/ www.disposablethebook.com.
Right: Toy Machine/Ed Templeton/by Ed Templeton/1994. Image courtesy of Sean Cliver/ www.disposablethebook.com.

Though some skateboard-related artists like Spike Jonz (much-in-demand skateboard photographer turned video director), David Carson (erstwhile art director of *Transworld Skateboarding* magazine), and Mark Gonzales (the subject of a recent *Wall Street Journal* profile) have transcended the field, skateboarding art itself seems in little danger of becoming mainstream. "I don't think it will ever happen," says Rose. "There is just too much destruction—destruction of property, destruction of boards, and destruction of the skater's body. I don't think it'll ever become a yuppie sport; it's just too rough. It'll never make it into the Olympics."

Oh, by the way:

Nosepick: Any skateboarding trick where your front truck (wheel assembly) hits the curb.

Face plant: Total facial contact with the skating surface.

Wilson: As in the TV show *Dennis the Menace*, when Mr. Wilson unwittingly steps on Dennis's board and falls on his backside—"Hellooo, Mr. Wilson." Any time you get out of control with one foot on and one foot off. Also "shackle," "slam," "dump," "chow," "pizza," "lites out," and "Beefaroni."

Got it?

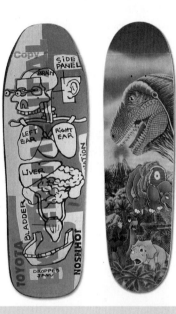

Left: Blind/Rudy Johnson/by Mark Gonzales/1991. Image courtesy of Sean Cliver/ www.disposablethebook.com.
Right: World Industries/Daewon Song/by Sean Cliver/1993. Image courtesy of Sean Cliver/www.disposablethebook.com.

DECODING THE TEXT

1. The authors of this visual text give examples of the artistry of skateboard design. Is this essay an argument? A position paper?

2. What is the thesis of this essay?

3. Could any of these pictures make a stronger or weaker argument for the thesis you have chosen?

CONNECTING TO YOUR CULTURE

1. Look at the definitions given for "nosepick," "face plant," and "Wilson." What specialized terms are used in your favorite sports or leisure activities?

2. List three terms that your classmates may not be familiar with and write their definitions.

Reading Selections:
A Case Study from the

Doping has become a major scandal in baseball, cycling, and several Olympic sports.
However, it has also been a problem in high schools and colleges around the United States.

1. How has the infamous baseball steroid scandal affected high school and college athletes?

2. Has this steroid scandal affected fans? If so, in what way?

Frank Deford *is a senior writer at* Sports Illustrated, *a correspondent for* RealSports *with Bryant Gumbel, and a commentator for NPR's* Morning Edition. *The author of more than fourteen books, Deford has been honored six times as U.S. Sportswriter of the Year by the National Sportscasters and Sportswriters Association. You can listen to the audio file of this commentary at NPR.org.*

CLEMENS' DENIAL OF STEROID USE HARD TO BELIEVE

Frank Deford

Most of you never heard of Ralph Beard, or if you did, had forgotten him by the time he died a few weeks ago just short of age 80. But back in the 1940s, Beard was a terrific All-American, who led Kentucky to two national championships and the United States to a gold medal in the 1948 Olympics. He was already a first-team NBA All-Star when it was revealed that he had taken money from gamblers to shave points in games at Kentucky.

Beard, like so many other players of that era, was summarily banned for life from the game. He admitted his guilt, too, saying that he had simply grown up poor and just couldn't resist taking the money. He lost it all for only about $700—branded forever as a fixer.

We tend to be more critical of athletes, like Ralph Beard, who conspire to lose, rather than those, like steroid users, who cheat trying to win.

But the fact is, that it makes no difference in which direction an athlete cheats; either way he is distorting fairness, which is the very essence of sport. Ralph Beard's transgressions cost his own team victory.

"Clemens' Denial of Steroid Use Hard to Believe" by Frank Deford from NPR, 2008.

If Roger Clemens—or any other player named in the Mitchell Report—is guilty as charged, then he cost other teams their fair due. What, pray, is the difference?

Now, of course, Clemens has taken a refrain from so many other guilty athletes' lyrics by claiming that he didn't know that he was being given a banned substance. Barry Bonds swore he thought it was all just flaxseed oil. Remember?

But here Clemens is, disputing his trainer, Brian McNamee, who testified—under threat of jail if he was caught lying—that he injected Clemens with steroids and HGH.

The sad and bizarre phone call with McNamee that Clemens taped last Friday and then played in public seemed only—to me—to confirm the pitcher's guilt.

McNamee was distraught for having testified against his old friend and meal ticket.

Time and again, he pleaded: "What do you want me to do, Roger?"

Wouldn't an innocent man, with the tape secretly running, say: "Just tell the truth, Brian." And never did McNamee volunteer that he had lied. He seemed only to regret that the truth had hurt so.

All right, I'm sorry. Perhaps I'm just too cynical. Perhaps I have just heard it all too often—even emotionally, to my face—from athletes claiming, with just as much dramatic insistence as Clemens, that they were innocent, only to be convicted later.

Even after he told the truth, Ralph Beard spent more than 50 years of his life in shame. If Roger Clemens is guilty, then he deserves no better. Let's put the right word on it. Any player who took steroids is a fixer. He fixed games.

A survivor of World War II in Poland and winner of the 1981 Nobel Prize in Chemistry, **Roald Hoffmann** *is now the Frank H. T. Rhodes Professor of Humane Letters at Cornell University. As a chemist, poet, and playwright, he has written several books, including* Chemistry Imagined *and* New Flasks: Reflections on Science and Jewish Tradition, *and he has published many collections of poetry and several plays, including 1987's* The Metamict State.

FOR A FEW ATOMS MORE

Roald Hoffmann

To enhance our appearance we will do terrible things to our bodies. And when there is money—or its correlate, fame—to be gained, athletes will seek to enhance their performance in sometimes ter-rible ways, using chemicals, natural and synthetic, to make themselves stronger, faster, leaner. With consequences that may be terrible.

"For a Few Atoms More" by Roald Hoffmann from AMERICAN SCIENTIST, March/April 2008, pp. 104–106.

This has probably been true for millennia. I recently passed pedestals hailing the athletes of ancient Ephesus, now in Turkey; I am sure they tried diets and herbs to get their statues on those pedestals. It's not just professional athletes who are responsible: Nations (such as the former German Democratic Republic), and we ourselves share the blame, with our gladiatorial instincts and (male dominated?) dependence on the forces of fandom and partisanship.

In the recently released "Report to the Commissioner of Baseball of an Independent Investigation into the Illegal Use of Steroids and Other Performance Enhancing Substances by Players in Major League Baseball," former Senator George J. Mitchell says, "For more than a decade, there has been widespread anabolic steroid use," and "the illegal use of anabolic steroids, human growth hormone, and similar drugs poses a serious threat to the integrity of the game of baseball." Barry Bonds has been indicted for perjury and obstruction of justice in connection with his testimony denying anabolic steroid use; his trainer has been convicted of distributing steroids. Marion Jones has admitted to lying about her use of a steroid before the Olympics in which she won five gold medals.

What is going on? How and why did our athletes come to use "the clear" and "the cream," as Bonds and Jones called the substances their trainers gave them? What are these substances? And how do we detect them? In an approach to this sordid story, in which no one comes out clean, let us go back to the sport regrettably tied most closely to doping in the public imagination, competitive cycling.

Turning Wheels

The 2006 Tour de France winner, Floyd Landis, was reported to have failed a testosterone drug test. More of what was actually found in his urine in just a while. Race officials collected a sample after his comeback victory in a critical stage of bicycling's premier race. A second sample confirmed the problem, and eventually Landis's victory was disallowed. Appeals followed; as the case stands now, Landis has appealed to the Court of Arbitration for Sport to overturn the decision against him.

Testosterone is the principal male sex hormone, produced mainly where you would expect from its name. It is also made in the ovaries of females. Testosterone is an *anabolic* compound, so-called because it promotes the growth of tissues such as muscle and bone; testosterone is also a steroid, member of a class of molecules that gives us a continuing lesson that almost the same is not the same.

All the steroids have the same atomic framework—four all-carbon rings, fused together. Three are hexagons, the third ring going off at an angle to the other two. Fused to that last ring is a pentagon of carbon atoms. Call the rings *A* (6 carbons), *B* (6), *C* (6) and *D* (5). Testosterone has an oxygen and a hydrogen (OH) attached to ring *D* and two CH_3 (methyl) groups, one at the juncture of rings *C* and *D*, the other at the juncture of *A* and *B*. Ring *A* contains a double bond and has an oxygen attached to it as well.

Testosterone is responsible for the secondary sex changes that occur in male puberty—facial and pubic hair, oily skin, body odor, all that teenage-boy stuff.

But the molecule is also produced by human females, albeit in one twentieth of the amount in males. In both sexes, testosterone affects energy levels and protects against osteoporosis. Nothing is simple in the real world—only human beings want it black or white, male or female.

Four Atoms Make the World Go 'Round

Remarkably enough, the biochemical precursor of testosterone in both sexes is progesterone, a female sex hormone. The difference between progesterone and testosterone is all of four atoms—two carbons and two hydrogens—on the five-membered D ring. Two other female sex hormones, estradiol and estrone, differ from testosterone by the loss of CH_3 and an H from the former plus two more hydrogens from the latter. Small changes, indeed, but ones with major consequences.

Other molecular family members with the same 6:6:6:5 fused-ring pattern include ecdysone, the molting hormone of insects; cholesterol, an essential, abundant part of our bodies; cortisones, which are important anti-inflammatory drugs; and bile acids. A pretty incredible set of biological functions, *n'est-ce pas*? All made distinctive with one less atom here, one more atom there.

Chemical Detective Work

It's fun to figure out this exquisite biological diversity, but why should a biker take testosterone? And how did the testers find out that Landis did?

Testing for abuse is not simple. Blood concentrations of testosterone vary widely between individuals and within one individual over time. So one cannot conclude from just an elevated level of testosterone that the molecule has been supplemented!

Enter epitestosterone, a *stereoisomer* of testosterone. In other words, it contains all the same atoms as testosterone, attached to each other in similar ways, but with a different disposition in space. In particular, the OH group of epitestosterone points "down" . . . instead of "up" toward us, as it does in testosterone. It turns out that epitestosterone has no apparent physiological effect (the same and not the same redux). Both testosterone and epitestosterone are produced in the body in similar amounts, by distinct biochemical pathways. So whereas there may be a higher absolute concentration of testosterone (and epi-testosterone) in one person compared with another, the ratio of testosterone to epitestosterone is close to 1 for both of them.

This is the clue to detecting abuse. Supplementing testosterone, the only isomer that has the desired physiological effects, doesn't change the biological production of epitestosterone. So the sports-medical bodies settle on the testosterone:epitestosterone ratio as an indicator of foul play. Ideally, one should have a profile of that ratio for every individual. In the absence of this profile, one makes liberal assumptions for the entire population: near 1:1 is normal, 4:1 is when the red card is shown. Landis's samples apparently had an 11:1 ratio.

I know, I know—you will tell me that the dopers, making big bucks, are not stupid. They'll give not only testosterone, but also some epitestosterone, so as to keep the ratio of testosterone:epitestosterone under 4:1. The sports "doctors" in the GDR did this 25 years ago.

With good science, this strategy too can be countered. Natural testosterone differs from the synthetic material in its ratio of carbon-12 to carbon-13 isotopes. The synthetic molecules are made from precursors derived from steroids found in certain plant oils, such as soybean. These plants biosynthesize their steroids from smaller building blocks of three carbons, somewhat different from those found in many of the plants we consume (and which then go into our testosterone), which form C_4 molecules. A consequence of the different biochemical mechanisms is an isotope effect, a slight difference in the way ^{12}C and ^{13}C (present naturally in small amounts) are incorporated. The net result is that our testosterone is ever so slightly (and detectably) richer in ^{13}C than synthetically derived steroids.

What is puzzling in this story is why any bicyclist would take testosterone on one isolated occasion (Landis was tested at other stages of the race, and nothing showed up in those samples). Anabolic, muscle-mass-building processes require the prolonged use of testosterone. Perhaps its use was an act of desperation by a superb cyclist who was behind. The irony is that it may have functioned not because of what it was, but as a placebo.

The Clear and the Cream

The Bay Area Laboratory Cooperative (BALCO) had a good business going. It provided athletes and their trainers with a variety of performance-enhancing substances. Several BALCO principals have been convicted of various crimes connected with distributing, among other things, anabolic steroids. Two of these substances are of particular interest—"the clear" and "the cream." Barry Bonds received both from his trainer Greg Ander-son; Bonds has said he was told the former was flaxseed oil, the latter a rubbing balm for arthritis. Marion Jones said similar things about the substances she got from her trainer, Trevor Graham. Jones said she noticed changes in her body after she stopped using the products and admits "Red flags should have been raised in my head when he [Graham] told me not to tell anyone. . . ." Bonds apparently noticed nothing.

What are these substances, which BALCO principal Victor Conte obtained from chemist Patrick Arnold (more on Arnold below)? Well, it turns out that "the clear" is a solution of a steroid, tetrahydrogestrinone (THG). The skeleton should look familiar. The drug was banned internationally in 2003, but not until a trainer (the above-mentioned Trevor Graham; that's another story) sent a syringe of the stuff to the United States Anti-Doping Agency. Prior to that, no one tested for it—because they didn't know it existed. And "the cream"? That turns out to be mainly our old friend, a mixture of testosterone and epitestosterone, in a ratio that will not trigger an alarm.

Some of the rotten apples in this story are chemists, my own clan. Patrick Arnold pleaded guilty to a count of selling controlled substances (he actually supplied much of the BALCO material). A prosteroid website lauds this "father of prohormones" as "a chemist who is responsible for the introduction of androstenedione [another anabolic compound] to the market as well as other second and third generation prohormone products." It continues, "Always supporting the industry, Arnold is also the President of the Prohormone Research Organization (PRO), a lobby group assembled from some of the most influential members in the supplement industry as well as the antiaging community. PRO is committed to providing legislators and government officials with truthful, scientific information about prohormones and other dietary supplements." The scientific information that exists (and much work needs to be done) points to long-range biological harm in nonmedical, excessive use of anabolic steroids. But good science is not what Arnold had in mind. Arnold "cut his Ph.D. studies short to pursue his own busi-ness venture."

Will There Be Other Ones?

THG is a "designer steroid." With so many sites for substitution on that skeleton of four fused rings, there are many ways to change this structure—medicinal chemists have been doing it for years. Many of the resulting molecules will have no physiological effect at all (remember epitestosterone?), others will be poisonous, and still others will prove to be anabolic and really harmful in large doses.

How harmful? The problem is that these drugs have seldom been studied in detail (excepting testosterone, of course). When used illegally by athletes, there is no standard dosage. Anecdotal evidence indicates that athletes are reaching steroid concentrations 5 to 30 times greater than the natural level of testosterone in the body. The list of potential effects begins with acne, hirsutism, changes in body shape and voice, and increased sebaceous gland activity. The list goes on to include permanent muscle fiber damage, breast enlargement in men, breast diminution in women, effects on sexual organs, and liver damage.

Asking the question "Why would anyone risk doing that to themselves?" ignores human nature and shifts the blame away from ourselves. Our gladiatorial (spectator!) instincts and our own active glorification of athletic prowess are important parts of what makes young people do such foolish things.

It is relatively easy to make new steroids and test, in a rough way, which are anabolic. An average chemist (as you see, no Ph.D. needed) can do it. The chemistry, like that involved in the transformation of cold-medicine pseudoephedrine to street-drug methamphetamine (another dismal story), is really simple. The making of some steroids may require skillful hands. But they too can be hired.

So is this a losing battle? To the extent that we are struggling against ourselves, to the extent that our clamor for sports victory perversely encourages the formation of muscle at any cost (*voilà!* 300-pound football players in high school), it's hard to think that anything will change. A few will maim themselves for the dream of money or fame. The market to supply them, to think up ever more ingenious ways of subverting the doping tests, will not disappear. And chemists somewhere will do the dirty work. Of course, the institutions we create, that one might think would control unfair and illegal use, are no better. The reaction of the executive director of the Major League Baseball Players Association to the Mitchell report was shamefully evasive and legalistic.

The hope is that there is a strong place in the human dream for a level playing field. And a special feeling for the disastrous effect steroid use can have on children, whose aspirations are focused on athlete-heroes and heroines. The national and international anti-doping agencies can also hire good chemists, and develop tests for potential new anabolic steroids.

We can relearn to see the action in our softball teams, instead of the "major" leagues (for a kid who lived on Bedford Avenue, the world ended anyway when the Dodgers left Ebbets Field). And I will keep on cycling, on my own Tour de Ithaca.

The following article, "Bush Calls for Anti-Doping Effort," was posted on CNN.com in 2004.

BUSH CALLS FOR ANTI-DOPING EFFORT

CNN.com

U.S. President George W. Bush used his annual State of the Union address to urge athletes and sports leagues to tackle the use of performance-enhancing drugs.

American athletics has been damaged by a rash of positive tests for THG, while four players with the Oakland Raiders NFL team have also tested for the banned steroid.

"To help children make right choices, they need good examples," President Bush told Congress.

"Athletics play such an important role in our society, but, unfortunately, some in professional sports are not setting much of an example," said President Bush, a former owner of the Texas Rangers baseball team.

"The use of performance-enhancing drugs like steroids in baseball, football, and other sports is dangerous, and it sends the wrong message—that there are shortcuts to accomplishment, and that performance is more important than character.

"So tonight I call on team owners, union representatives, coaches and players to take the lead, to send the right signal, to get tough, and to get rid of steroids now."

President Bush's remarks were welcomed by Craig Masback, the chief executive of U.S. Track and Field.

"I think it's especially important he focused on young athletes and that cheating by star athletes sends the wrong message," said Masback.

"In order for America to confront this issue, it needs to be raised to a level of importance, and having the president of the United States talk about it can't help but do that. The battle can never be won unless it becomes an important American issue."

Dave Sheinin is a staff writer covering sports for The Washington Post. He also writes for The Sporting News.

BASEBALL HAS A DAY OF RECKONING IN CONGRESS

McGwire Remains Evasive During Steroid Testimony

Dave Sheinin

On an extraordinary day of words and images, a House committee investigating steroids in baseball forced the sport to confront its past and rethink its future—encountering resistance on both counts—and the most extraordinary image of all was that of Mark McGwire, once the game's most celebrated slugger but now the face of the steroid scandal, reduced to a shrunken, lonely, evasive figure whose testimony brought him to the verge of tears.

During the course of an all-day, nationally televised hearing, the House Government Reform Committee fulfilled its goal of examining baseball's oft-criticized drug-testing program and its impact on steroid use among teenagers. Committee members said baseball's policy was full of holes and threatened to legislate tougher testing policies if the sport doesn't come up with them itself.

In the process, however, the committee also ripped wide open the sport's most tender wound. Asked repeatedly by committee members whether he had used steroids in achieving unprecedented power numbers before his retirement in 2001, McGwire deflected each question—his non-answers standing in stark contrast

Baseball Has a Day of Reckoning in Congress: McGwire Remains Evasive During Steroid Testimony, by Dave Sheinin, from THE WASHINGTON POST, March 18, 2005. Reprinted by permission.

to the unabashed frankness of Jose Canseco, McGwire's former Oakland Athletics teammate and an admitted steroid user.

While McGwire acknowledged "there has been a problem with steroid use in baseball," he responded to questions about his own involvement by saying, "I'm not here to discuss the past," or, "I'm here to be positive about this subject."

The hearing came as baseball struggles to come to terms with what it admits is a steroid problem. In the past few months, leaked grand jury testimony by sluggers Jason Giambi and Barry Bonds showed them acknowledging steroid use and Canseco's book fingered some of the game's biggest stars as steroid users. Pressure from President Bush and Sen. John McCain (R-Ariz.), among other national figures, forced baseball to strengthen its steroid policy this winter.

Rep. Thomas M. Davis III (R-Va.), the committee chairman, opened the hearing at 10 A.M. and brought it to a close more than 11 hours later. Throughout the day, the panel threatened congressional action to bring the sport's testing program closer in line to the Olympic testing program, which includes regular testing and swift, tough sanctions.

Committee members grilled baseball's leadership—Commissioner of Baseball Bud Selig, league officials Rob Manfred and Sandy Alderson and union chief Donald Fehr—over what they saw as flaws in the sport's drug-testing policy, which was instituted for the 2003 season and strengthened this winter to include, for the first time, penalties for first-time offenders. However, baseball's current policy calls for a 10-day suspension for first offenses, as opposed to two years under the Olympics policy.

Selig, Fehr and the other baseball officials implored committee members to understand their policy in the context of a collective-bargaining agreement in which items such as drug testing must be bargained.

By the end of the hearing, the lawmakers seemed mostly unmoved by baseball's arguments.

"I have not been reassured one bit by the testimony I have heard today," said Rep. Stephen F. Lynch (D-Mass.). The testing program "has so many loopholes in this, it is just unbelievable." McGwire, whose Ruthian feats on the field in the late 1990s made him a national folk hero, sat on the same panel but never made eye contact with Canseco, whose recent tell-all book gave voice to the long-rumored view that McGwire's accomplishments—along with those of many other contemporaries—were done with the help of steroids.

Steroids, Canseco said, were "as prevalent in . . . the late 1980s and 1990s as a cup of coffee." Canseco's audacious claims and admissions set him apart from the other players who appeared yesterday—McGwire, Baltimore Orioles stars Rafael Palmeiro and Sammy Sosa, and Boston Red Sox pitcher Curt Schilling. Schilling and the Chicago White Sox's Frank Thomas, who gave a statement via video conference, were invited because of outspoken views against steroid use. The others had all been connected to or accused of steroid use.

Giambi had been excused from testifying because of his involvement in the grand jury inquiry into the Bay Area Laboratory Co-Operative (BALCO), a California nutritional supplements company, while Bonds was never invited to attend because, according to the committee's leaders, his presence would have overshadowed the substance of the hearing.

Palmeiro denied having used steroids, while Sosa—or his lawyers—crafted an opening statement in which he said he has never used "illegal performance-enhancing drugs," has never "injected myself or had anyone inject me with anything," and has not "broken the laws of the United States or the laws of the Dominican Republic."

"Let me start by telling you this," Palmeiro said in his opening statement, looking directly at Davis and pointing at the committee chairman with his index finger. "I have never used steroids, period."

McGwire's testimony, meantime, was noteworthy for what it did not say. "Asking me or any other player to answer questions about who took steroids in front of television cameras," he said, "will not solve the problem. . . . My lawyers have advised me that I cannot answer these questions without jeopardizing my friends, my family and myself. I intend to follow their advice."

McGwire, who has been estimated to be 30 to 40 pounds lighter than at the end of his career, appeared on the verge of tears at least twice as he read his opening statement. The first time came as he referred to some of the participants of an earlier panel—the parents of two amateur baseball players whose suicides were attributed to steroid use.

The tone of the day was set by Sen. Jim Bunning (R-Ky.), whose previous career was as a Hall of Fame pitcher in the 1950s and '60s.

Apparently referring to modern sluggers like McGwire and Bonds, whose physiques expanded and whose home run totals began skyrocketing in their mid- to late-thirties, Bunning told the panel: "When I played with Henry Aaron, Willie Mays and Ted Williams, they didn't put on 40 pounds . . . and they didn't hit more home runs in their late thirties as they did in their late twenties. What's happening in baseball is not natural, and it's not right."

Bunning went a step beyond those who say the records of steroid users should be marked by an asterisk, arguing that the records should be thrown out of the book. "If they started in 1992 or '93 illegally using steroids," Bunning said, "wipe all their records out. Take them away. They don't deserve them."

The following news story, posted on The Onion.com in 2006, is a satire of the preceding articles.

BARRY BONDS TOOK STEROIDS, REPORTS EVERYONE WHO HAS EVER WATCHED BASEBALL

The Onion

With the publication of a book detailing steroid use by San Francisco Giants superstar Barry Bonds, two *San Francisco Chronicle* reporters have corroborated the claims of Bonds' steroid abuse made by every single person who has watched or even loosely followed the game of baseball over the past five years.

In *Game Of Shadows,* an excerpt of which appeared in *Sports Illustrated* Wednesday, authors Mark Fainaru-Wada and Lance Williams claim that more than a dozen people close to Bonds had either been directly informed that Bonds was using banned substances or had in fact seen him taking the drugs with their own eyes. In addition to those witnesses, nearly 250 million other individuals nationwide had instantly realized that Bonds was using banned substances after observing his transformation from lanky speedster to hulking behemoth with their own eyes.

According to hundreds of thousands of reports coming out of every city in the U.S., Bonds' steroid use has been widely reported and well-documented for years, with sports columnists, bloggers, people attending baseball games, memorabilia collectors, major ballpark popcorn and peanut vendors, groundskeepers, room-mates, significant others, fathers-in-law, next-door neighbors, fellow fitness club members, bartenders, mailmen, cowork-ers, teachers, doormen, parking-lot attendants, fellow elevator passengers, Home Depot clerks, servicemen and women serving in Iraq, former baseball players, Congressmen, second-tier stand-up comics, *Sports Illustrated*'s Rick Reilly, and random passersby all having stated at some point in the last five years that Bonds was obviously taking some sort of performance-enhancing drugs.

Many of those eyewitnesses came forward following Wednesday's revelation with their own accounts of Bonds' seven-year history of steroid use.

"I originally heard that Barry Bonds was on steroids during a Giants game in 2001, when my buddy Phil, who was on the couch next to me, said, 'Dude, that Barry Bonds guy is definitely on steroids,'" said Chicago resident Mitch Oliveras. "After 10 seconds of careful observation, and performing a brief comparison of Bonds' present neck width with that on Phil's old 1986 Bonds rookie card, I was convinced."

"I can see how some people might be shocked about Bonds' doping, but this has been an open secret for years among

Barry Bonds Took Steroids, Reports Everyone Who Has Ever Watched Baseball, from THE ONION, Issue 4–10. Reprinted with permission of THE ONION. Copyright © 2008, by ONION, INC. www.theonion.com.

the people in my industry," said air-conditioner repairman Mike Damus. "I'm sure it's an even more widely known fact in baseball."

"Everyone in our front office has known about Bonds since the 2001 season," said San Francisco–area accounts-receivable secretary Mindy Harris of McCullers and Associates, Ltd. "People in our ninth-floor office, too, and all seven branch offices. None of us were sure exactly which *kind* of steroids he was on, but we were pretty sure it was the kind that causes you to gain 30 pounds of muscle in one off-season, get injured more easily, become slow-footed, shave your head to conceal your thinning hair, lash out at the media and fans, engage in violent and abrupt mood swings, grow taut tree-trunk-like neck muscles, expand your hatband by six inches, and hit 73 home runs in a single season."

"Come to think of it, we're all fairly certain he's on all of them," Harris added.

"My 6-year-old son and I bonded over our mutual agreement that Bonds was obviously juicing up," San Francisco–area construction worker Tom Frankel said. "I hope that, one day, little Davey will have kids of his own, and that they will be able to easily glean the knowledge that Bonds was a cheater just by looking at the remarkable shift in his year-by-year statistics on his Hall of Fame plaque."

In light of the most recent accusations, which echo what any idiot with a pair of eyes and even the most fundamental knowledge of how the human body works has said in recent years, MLB Commissioner Bud Selig issued a statement Wednesday to address the issue.

"It is unfair to judge Mr. Bonds based solely on the fact that everyone says he has taken some sort of performance-enhancing drug for the past five years," Selig said. "I myself think Bonds has been taking steroids—I'm not blind, after all—but nothing, even an admission by Bonds himself, can conclusively prove that he took steroids, as he has not tested positively in an MLB-sanctioned drug test. Unless that is somehow made to happen, we must all accept his recent unfathomable accomplishments as one of the truly exciting and continuing storylines of this great sport."

When reached for comment, Bonds insisted that he "[doesn't] have time to deal with all these charges."

"I'm not going to respond to these 228 million allegations," Bonds said. "I don't care what every last person in the entire world thinks. As long as my fans believe me, that's the most important thing."

1. How do the preceding texts differ in their audience and purpose?

2. What type of article is *The Onion*'s piece satirizing?

3. What language suggests that it is a satire?

CONNECTING TO YOUR CULTURE

1. What jurisdiction does Congress have over Major League Baseball? Should the president and Congress have intervened in the controversy?

2. In what other ways are government and sport intertwined? For example, think about the funding of professional ballparks and arenas.

Reading Selections: Across the Decades

CONSIDERING IDEAS

1. Quilting is often considered a dying art because so few people in younger generations have learned the craft. How can quilting survive the next generation?

2. What about this expressive art would interest young people?

Amei Wallach *is the chief art critic for* New York Newsday. *The author of several essays and articles published in magazines and newspapers across the country, including* The New York Times *and* Smithsonian, *and three books, Wallach was also the on-air art essayist for the* MacNeil/Lehrer Newshour. *"Fabric of Their Lives" was published in* Smithsonian *in 2006.*

FABRIC OF THEIR LIVES

Amei Wallach

Annie Mae Young is looking at a photograph of a quilt she pieced together out of strips torn from well-worn cotton shirts and polyester pants. "I was doing this quilt at the time of the civil rights movement," she says, contemplating its jazzy, free-form squares.

Martin Luther King Jr. came to Young's hometown of Gee's Bend, Alabama, around that time. "I came over here to Gee's Bend to tell you, You are somebody," he shouted over a heavy rain late one winter night in 1965. A few days later, Young and many of her friends took off their aprons, laid down their hoes and rode over to the county seat of Camden, where they gathered outside the old jailhouse.

"We were waiting for Martin Luther King, and when he drove up, we were all slappin' and singin'," Young, 78, tells me when I visit Gee's Bend, a small rural community on a peninsula at a deep bend in the Alabama River. Wearing a red turban and an apron bright with pink peaches and yellow grapes, she stands in the doorway of her brick bungalow at the end of a dirt road. Swaying to a rhythm that nearly everyone in town knows from a lifetime of churchgoing, she breaks into song: "We shall overcome, we shall overcome. . . ."

"We were all just happy to see him coming," she says. "Then he stood out there on the ground, and he was talking about how we should wait on a bus to come and we were all going to march. We got loaded on the bus, but we didn't get a chance to do it, 'cause we got put in jail," she says.

Many who marched or registered to vote in rural Alabama in the 1960s lost their jobs. Some even lost their homes. And the residents of Gee's Bend, 60 miles southwest of Montgomery, lost the ferry that connected them to Camden and a direct route to the outside world. "We didn't close the ferry because they were black," Sheriff Lummie Jenkins reportedly said at the time. "We closed it because they forgot they were black."

Six of Young's quilts, together with 64 by other Gee's Bend residents, have been traveling around the United States in an exhibition that has transformed the way many people think about art. Gee's Bend's "eye-poppingly gorgeous" quilts, wrote *New York Times* art critic Michael Kimmelman, "turn out to be some of the most miraculous works of modern art America has produced. Imagine Matisse and Klee (if you think I'm wildly exaggerating, see the show), arising not from rarefied Europe, but from the caramel soil of the rural South." Curator Jane Livingston, who helped organize the exhibition with collector William Arnett and art historians John Beardsley and Alvia Wardlaw, said that the quilts "rank with the finest abstract art of any tradition." After stops in such cities as New York, Washington, D.C., Cleveland, Boston and Atlanta, "The Quilts of Gee's Bend" will end its tour

"Fabric of Their Lives" by Amei Wallach from SMITHSONIAN MAGAZINE, October 2006, pp. 66–75.

at the Fine Arts Museums of San Francisco's de Young Museum December 31.

The bold drama of the quilt Young was working on in 1965 is also found in a quilt she made out of work clothes 11 years later. The central design of red and orange corduroy in that quilt suggests prison bars, and the faded denim that surrounds it could be a comment on the American dream. But Young had more practical considerations. "When I put the quilt together," she says, "it wasn't big enough, and I had to get some more material and make it bigger, so I had these old jeans to make it bigger."

Collector William Arnett was working on a history of African-American vernacular art in 1998 when he came across a photograph of Young's work-clothes quilt draped over a woodpile. He was so knocked out by its originality, he set out to find it. A couple of phone calls and some creative research later, he and his son Matt tracked Young down to Gee's Bend, then showed up unannounced at her door late one evening. Young had burned some quilts the week before (smoke from burning cotton drives off mosquitoes), and at first she thought the quilt in the photograph had been among them. But the next day, after scouring closets and searching under beds, she found it and offered it to Arnett for free. Arnett, however, insisted on writing her a check for a few thousand dollars for that quilt and several others. (Young took the check straight to the bank.) Soon the word spread through Gee's Bend that there was a crazy white man in town paying good money for raggedy old quilts.

When Arnett showed photos of the quilts made by Young and other Gee's Bend-ers to Peter Marzio, of the Museum of Fine Arts, Houston (MFAH), he was so impressed that he agreed to put on an exhibition. "The Quilts of Gee's Bend" opened there in September 2002.

The exhibition revived what had been a dying art in Gee's Bend. Some of the quilters, who had given in to age and arthritis, are now back quilting again. And many of their children and grandchildren, some of whom had moved away from Gee's Bend, have taken up quilting themselves. With the help of Arnett and the Tinwood Alliance (a nonprofit organization that he and his four sons formed in 2002), fifty local women founded the Gee's Bend Quilters Collective in 2003 to market their quilts, some of which now sell for more than $20,000. (Part goes directly to the maker, the rest goes to the collective for expenses and distribution to the other members.)

Now a second exhibition, "Gee's Bend: The Architecture of the Quilt," has been organized by the MFAH and the Tinwood Alliance. The show, which opened in June, features newly discovered quilts from the 1930s to the 1980s, along with more recent works by established quilters and the younger generation they inspired. The exhibition will travel to seven other venues, including the Indianapolis Museum of Art (October 8–December 31) and the Orlando Museum of Art (January 27–May 13, 2007).

Arlonzia Pettway lives in a neat, recently renovated house off a road plagued with potholes. The road passes by cows and goats grazing outside robin's-egg blue and brown bungalows. "I remember some things, honey," Pettway, 83, told me. (Since my interview with her, Pettway suffered a stroke, from which she is still recovering.) "I came through a hard life. Maybe we weren't bought and sold, but we were still slaves until 20, 30 years ago. The white man would go to everybody's field and say, 'Why you not at work?'" She paused. "What do you think a slave is?"

As a girl, Pettway would watch her grandmother, Sally, and her mother, Missouri, piecing quilts. And she would listen to their stories, many of them about Dinah Miller, who had been brought to the United States in a slave ship in 1859. "My great-grandmother Dinah was sold for a dime," Pettway said. "Her dad, brother and mother were sold to different people, and she didn't see them no more. My great-grandfather was a Cherokee Indian. Dinah was made to sleep with this big Indian like you stud your cow. . . . You couldn't have no skinny children working on your slave master's farm." In addition to Pettway some 20 other Gee's Bend quiltmakers are Dinah's descendants.

The quilting tradition in Gee's Bend may go back as far as the early 1800s, when the community was the site of a cotton plantation owned by a Joseph Gee. Influenced, perhaps, by the patterned textiles of Africa, the women slaves began piecing strips of cloth together to make bedcovers. Throughout the post-bellum years of tenant farming and well into the 20th century, Gee's Bend women made quilts to keep themselves and their children warm in unheated shacks that lacked running water, telephones and electricity. Along the way they developed a distinctive style, noted for its lively improvisations and geometric simplicity.

Gee's Bend men and women grew and picked cotton, peanuts, okra, corn, peas and potatoes. When there was no money to buy seed or fertilizer, they borrowed one or both from Camden businessman E. O. Rentz, at interest rates only those without any choice would pay. Then came the Depression. In 1931 the price of cotton plummeted, from about 40 cents a pound in the early 1920s, to about a nickel. When Rentz died in 1932, his widow foreclosed on some 60 Gee's Bend families. It was late fall, and winter was coming.

"They took everything and left people to die," Pettway said. Her mother was making a quilt out of old clothes when she heard the cries outside. She sewed four wide shirttails into a sack, which the men in the family filled with corn and sweet potatoes and hid in a ditch. When the agent for Rentz's widow came around to seize the family's hens, Pettway's mother threatened him with a hoe. "I'm a good Christian, but I'll chop his damn brains out," she said. The man got in his wagon and left. "He didn't get to my mama that day," Pettway told me.

Pettway remembered that her friends and neighbors foraged for berries, hunted possum and squirrels, and mostly went hungry that winter until a boat with flour and meal sent by the Red Cross arrived in early 1933. The following year, the Federal Emergency Relief Administration provided small loans for seed, fertilizer, tools and livestock. Then, in 1937, the government's Resettlement Administration (later the Farm Security Administration) bought up 10,000 Gee's Bend acres and sold them as tiny farms to local families.

In 1941, when Pettway was in her late teens, her father died. "Mama said, 'I'm going to take his work clothes, shape them into a quilt to remember him, and cover up under it for love.'" There were hardly enough pants legs and shirttails to make up a quilt, but she managed. (That quilt—jostling rectangles of faded gray, white, blue and red—is included in the first exhibition.) A year later, Arlonzia married Bizzell Pettway and moved into one of the new houses built by the government. They had 12 children, but no electricity until 1964 and no running water until 1974. A widow for more than 30 years, Arlonzia still lives in that same house. Her mother, Missouri, who lived until 1981, made a quilt she called "Path Through the Woods" after the 1960s freedom marches. A quilt that Pettway pieced together during that period, "Chinese Coins," is a medley of pinks and purples— a friend had given her purple scraps from a clothing factory in a nearby town.

"At the time I was making that quilt, I was feeling something was going to happen better, and it did," Pettway says. "Last time I counted I had 32 grandchildren and I think between 13 and 14 greatgrands. I'm blessed now more than many. I have my home and land. I have a deepfreeze five feet long with chicken wings, neck bones and pork chops."

The first exhibition featured seven quilts by Loretta Pettway, Arlonzia Pettway's first cousin. (One in three of Gee's Bend's 700 residents is named Pettway, after slave owner Mark H. Pettway.) Loretta, 64, says she made her early quilts out of work clothes. "I was about 16 when I learned to quilt from my grandmama," she says. "I just loved it. That's all I wanted to do, quilt. But I had to work farming cotton, corn, peas and potatoes, making syrup, putting up soup in jars. I was working other people's fields too. Saturdays I would hire out; sometimes I would hire out Sundays, too, to give my kids some food. When I finished my

chores, I'd sit down and do like I'm doing now, get the clothes together and tear them and piece. And then in summer I would quilt outside under the big oak." She fingers the fabric pieces in her lap. "I thank God that people want me to make quilts," she says. "I feel proud. The Lord lead me and guide me and give me strength to make this quilt with love and peace and happiness so somebody would enjoy it. That makes me feel happy. I'm doing something with my life."

In 1962 the U.S. Congress ordered the construction of a dam and lock on the Alabama River at Miller's Ferry just south of Gee's Bend. The 17,200-acre reservoir created by the dam in the late 1960s flooded much of Gee's Bend's best farming land, forcing many residents to give up farming. "And thank God for that," says Loretta. "Farming wasn't nothing but hard work. And at the end of the year you couldn't get nothing, and the little you got went for cottonseed."

Around that time, a number of Gee's Bend women began making quilts for the Freedom Quilting Bee, founded in 1966 by civil rights worker and Episcopalian priest Francis X. Walter to provide a source of income for the local community. For a while, the bee (which operated for about three decades) sold quilts to such stores as Bloomingdale's, Sears, Saks and Bonwit Teller. But the stores wanted assembly-line quilts, with orderly, familiar patterns and precise stitching—not the individual, often improvised and unexpected patterns and color combinations that characterized the Gee's Bend quilts.

"My quilts looked beautiful to me, because I made what I could make from my head," Loretta told me. "When I start I don't want to stop until I finish, because if I stop, the ideas are going to go one way and my mind another way, so I just try to do it while I have ideas in my mind."

Loretta had been too ill to attend the opening of the first exhibition in Houston. But she wore a bright red jacket and a wrist corsage of roses to the opening of the second show last spring. Going there on the bus, "I didn't close my eyes the whole way," she says. "I was so happy, I had to sightsee." In the new show, her 2003 take on the popular "Housetop" pattern—a variant of the traditional "Log Cabin" design—is an explosion of red polka dots, zany stripes and crooked frames within frames (a dramatic change from the faded colors and somber patterns of her early work-clothes quilts). Two other quilts made by Loretta are among those represented on a series of Gee's Bend stamps issued this past August by the U.S. Postal Service. "I just had scraps of what I could find," she says about her early work. "Now I see my quilts hanging in a museum. Thank God I see my quilts on the wall. I found my way."

Mary Lee Bendolph, 71, speaks in a husky voice and has a hearty, throaty laugh. At the opening of the new exhibition in Houston, she sported large rhinestone earrings and a chic black dress. For some years, kidney disease had slowed her quiltmaking, but the first exhibition, she says, "spunked me to go a little further, to try and make my quilts a little more updated." Her latest quilts fracture her backyard views and other local scenes the way Cubism fragmented the cafés and countryside of France. Her quilts share a gallery with those of her daughter-in-law, Louisiana Pettway Bendolph.

Louisiana now lives in Mobile, Alabama, but she remembers hot, endless days picking cotton as a child in the fields around Gee's Bend. From age 6 to 16, she says, the only time she could go to school was when it rained, and the only play was softball and quiltmaking. Her mother, Rita Mae Pettway, invited her to the opening in Houston of the first quilt show. On the bus ride home, she says, she "had a kind of vision of quilts." She made drawings of what would become the quilts in the new exhibition, in which shapes seem to float and recede as if in three dimensions.

"Quilting helped redirect my life and put it back together," Louisiana says. "I worked at a fast-food place and a sewing factory and when the sewing factory closed, I stayed home, being a housewife. You just want your kids to see you in a different light, as someone they can admire. Well, my children came into this museum, and I saw their faces."

To Louisiana, 46, quiltmaking is history and family. "We think of inheriting as land or something, not things that people teach you," she says. "We came from cotton fields, we came through hard times, and we look back and see what all these people before us have done. They brought us here, and to say thank you is not enough." Now her 11-year-old granddaughter has taken up quiltmaking; she, however, does her drawings on a computer.

In Gee's Bend not long ago, her great-grandmother Mary Lee Bendolph picked some pecans to make into candy to have on hand for the children when the only store in town is closed, which it often is. Then she soaked her feet. Sitting on her screened-in porch, she smiled. "I'm famous," she said. "And look how old I am." She laughed. "I enjoy it."

1. In the reading, the author gives an example of how cultural opinions of folk art have changed. Now, many crafts, such as quilting, have found their place in museums around the world. What other crafts or leisure activities are still struggling to be accepted as significant to American culture?
2. Would these examples strengthen or weaken the author's thesis? How?

CONNECTING TO YOUR CULTURE

1. Many people use arts and crafts to relax, to express their creativity, and to pass traditions from generation to generation. Do you have any similar traditions in your family?
2. Do your friends have any similar traditions?

CONSIDERING IDEAS

1. Why is scrapbooking so popular?
2. Do you think that the ease and simplicity of digital photography has played a role in its development?
3. Consider the money spent on scrapbooking tools and supplies. What benefit do these materials provide over typical photo albums?

Felicia Paik *is a former senior editor for Forbes.com, a leading Internet media company focused on business and accruing wealth, and she is a former editor of the* Pasadena Star News. *Paik has written for* The Wall Street Journal, *the* Dow Jones News Service, The New York Times, *and* The Saturday Evening Post, *in which this article was reprinted. "A Cruise for Glue and Scissors" was published in the September/October 2007 issue.*

A CRUISE FOR GLUE AND SCISSORS

Felicia Paik

In the sun-drenched Mexican port of Ensenada, lighthearted passengers from yet another cruise ship bounced down the gangway for a much-anticipated adventure ashore. Decked out in floppy sun hats, smelling of sunscreen and armed with water bottles, they clustered on the pier around waiting tour guides who wore wide, fixed smiles. After 15 hours on the *Monarch of the Seas,* a Royal Caribbean International ship, the travelers had reached their only stop on a three-day cruise from Los Angeles.

Ushered into a squadron of tour buses, they set off for the short ride into town, a living postcard of mom-and-pop stores crammed with dangling piñatas, colorful ceramics, leather belts and silver jewelry. A mariachi band struck its first chord.

Back inside the ship, about 40 passengers, all women, had stayed behind. In a cramped conference room lighted by fluorescent bulbs, they sat hunched over folding tables piled full of scissors, adhesive strips, stickers, colorful ribbon, photographs and paper in many shapes and sizes and tints. Intently, they arranged, shaped and glued. Not even a warm sun and the Baja California breezes could beckon them away.

For them, this trip was a scrapbooking cruise, an organized shipboard workshop and getaway for enthusiasts of the increasingly popular hobby of making elaborate albums to preserve memories and tell personal stories.

A survey in 2004 by *Creating Keepsakes,* a magazine about scrapbooking, reported that about 25 percent of American households includes someone who participated in it, supporting a $2.5 billion industry that supplies acid-free paper, durable adhesives, tools and all manner of decorative accessories. Scrapbook stores have opened around the country, Target and Wal-Mart carry scrapbook merchandise, and EK Success, a New Jersey company, says it has a Martha Stewart line of scrapbook products in the works.

Women—and scrapbookers are nearly always women—describe the crafting of their books as a creative outlet, a stress reliever, and a gift to their families. It is also a social activity, fueled by the camaraderie of classes, workshops, conventions and retreats—and now the scrapbook cruise.

Scrapbooking and ships are an unlikely pair, and not only because of the disconnect of huddling over a project while the sea sparkles and deck chairs sit empty. A rocking boat doesn't provide a level working surface; it can be hard even to cut a straight line, some scrapbookers said. Shipboard conference rooms, designed for the laid-back passenger who wants to play hooky, are often poorly lighted and inadequately ventilated for 18-hour work stints.

Yet since their first appearance about six years ago, scrapbook cruises have caught on. Joan Levicoff, vice president of group sales for the Carnival Cruise Line, said her line does more than 20 scrapbooking cruises annually, with groups ranging in size from 30 to 200.

On the *Monarch of the Seas* cruise in 2006, there were about 2,500 passengers, 81 of them scrapbookers (and half of those obsessive enough to skip the offshore excursion), all luxuriating in uninterrupted scrapbook time.

"It's like a drug, being able to scrapbook all night and not have to worry about going home," said Lisa Baldwin, a 39-year-old mother of four who taught scrapbook-technique classes to pay her way onto the cruise.

Deloris Saams-Hoy, 39, who left her husband, children and job behind to join the cruise, had similar sentiments. "I can sleep when I'm at home," she said as she finally headed to her cabin at 4:30 A.M. the first night on board. "I'm determined to get these pages done."

Scrapbook cruises cropped up as part of a trend of theme cruises of various kinds.

"It's a phenomenon that has taken hold across the industry," said Brian Major, a spokesman for the Cruise Lines International Association (CLIA), a trade organization in New York. "Whether it's people interested in Harley-Davidsons, knitting or scrapbooking, there is a trend toward organizing a trip around a common interest."

Theme cruises may have helped the cruise industry's recent growth. Mr. Major's association, whose members are 24 cruise lines responsible for 97 percent of the cruise capacity marketed in North America, reports more than 12 million people in 2006 took a cruise. CLIA predicts one-half million more will cruise this year.

According to Ms. Levicoff, scrapbook cruises on Carnival have left from Galveston, Texas, as well as Los Angeles. She said the cruises were usually organized and marketed by a local travel agent, who then approached the cruise line for accommodations and services like reserving conference rooms and providing tables. "We can make arrangements on any of our vessels to do a scrapbook cruise," she said. "And we make an effort to make it a great experience for everyone."

Scrapbooking cruise destinations have included Mexico, Alaska, the Caribbean, Eastern Canada, and the New England states. Debbie Haas, an author of the forthcoming *Chicken Soup for the Scrapbooker's Soul,* led a group on a seven-day cruise to Southampton, England, from New York on the *Queen Mary 2. Creating Keepsakes* sponsored a Mediterranean cruise with stops in Barcelona and Rome.

The scrapbook cruise to Ensenada was organized by Anita Pagliasso-Balamane, a travel agent in San Jose, California, and Picture Passion, a store in nearby Campbell that sells scrapbooking items from rubber stamps to colored staples.

Many of the scrapbookers on the cruise had carried their materials aboard in specially designed scrapbook luggage with brand names like Cropper Hopper and Crop in Style. Beri Anderson, 40, of Elizabeth, Colorado, packed so many materials for the cruise that her baggage was 27 pounds overweight at the Denver International Airport when she set off for Los Angeles. She had to pay a $25 penalty.

"It was definitely my scrapbooking stuff," Mrs. Anderson said. "I brought very few clothes."

During the scrapbooking sessions, the chatty talk often veered away from the hobby itself and into stories of weddings and divorces, bosses and children, triumphs and tragedies—a normal pattern at scrapbooking events.

"Everyone has a story to tell," said Veronica Hugger, a founder of the National Scrapbooking Association in Katy, Texas, near Houston. "Scrapbooking is like writing an autobiography."

And there is always the topic of husbands, who have sometimes been known to have trouble comprehending the scrapbook mania. "Both my husband and 15-year-old son are hard sells," Mrs. Saams-Hoy said.

But she added that she had little guilt about going off alone on the cruise. "My biggest dilemma about leaving," she said, "was that I was going to miss the opening day of my younger son's T-ball and the last day of soccer, because I won't be there to take the pictures."

Pictures that she will need, of course, for future scrapbooks.

DECODING THE TEXT

1. Does the author support her assumption that scrapbooking is primarily for women? Does she need to support this assumption, or did you already agree with that statement before you read the article?

2. What techniques of travel writing does the author use to talk about both the cruise aspect and the scrapbooking aspect of this article? What techniques are different than those in your typical travel article?

CONNECTING TO YOUR CULTURE

1. Consider Chapter 6: Writing About Groups, Spaces, and Places as you think about the trend of scrapbooking; do you fit into any specific groups because of your leisure hobbies? Do these groups organize events together? Have meetings? Go on trips?

2. If you answered yes, define your group. What makes you similar to one another? Different from one another? Are you a "demographic"? Could a company market to you? If you answered no, how would a company market to the group of scrapbookers featured in this article?

contemplations in the pop culture zone

1. Why are sports bars such a part of the sporting world? These businesses pay the major leagues to show every game. What is the connection between eating, drinking, and smoking and athletic events?
2. Make a list of your five most common leisure activities. Then, make a list of your five most enjoyable leisure activities. Compare the lists. How do they differ and why? Can you rearrange your priorities or daily schedule to have more time for the activities you enjoy?
3. As more male athletes come out of the closet, media analysts often devote entire segments to discussion and debate. However, the same cannot be said for female athletes who do the same. Is homosexuality in sports most often only an issue for men?
4. Video-game programming is now a major at several universities across the United States. How will this evolution affect the gaming world? How will it affect game design and character design?

collaborations in the pop culture zone

1. Make a list of the last three sporting events you attended or watched. Work together in a peer group of three or four to make a list of "fan" characteristics. What makes a fan? How do your definitions differ?
2. After reading this news release from the American College of Emergency Physicians, consider in groups the implications of this study. What do these results imply about gender differences? Are these differences accurate based on your experiences? What other reasons could there be for these results?

   > Dr. David Jerrard, associate professor of emergency medicine at the University of Maryland Medical Center in Baltimore, conducted the study over three years and examined emergency department registration patterns at his hospital following 796 sporting events, including professional and college football, professional baseball and college basketball. According to the study, the number of men checking into the emergency department increased following all of the sporting events in the study. There were approximately 50 percent more men in the emergency department following a professional football game, than during the contest. Thirty to 40 percent more men sought care following a baseball game.

3. In 1985, the Chicago Bears won the Super Bowl. The team released a chart-topping rap called "The Super Bowl Shuffle." Search for lyrics on the Web, or search for the music video on your favorite video-sharing website as a model, and then, as a group, write a song, poem, or story about a team of your choice.

start writing essays about sports and leisure

Reviews or Review Essays

1. Watch a game or match, specifically making notes on one player's behavior, talents, skills, and actions. Review his or her contributions to the team, the match, and the fans' reactions.
2. Review the accommodations of where you live now. Write a review of your dorm/dorm room, your apartment/complex, or your home/your parents' home. Act as though it is a spot where your audience of peers might consider living. Look at articles by travel writers for inspiration, and remember to include both positive and negative details.
3. Report on fan attendance for a sporting event sponsored by your college or university. Review the percentage of students who attend the game, their enthusiasm, their support for the team, and their activities during the game. Remember to make an overall evaluation of the fan support at this event, and consider comparing the fandom to that at other events you have attended.

Reflection or Response Essays

1. Perhaps your high school team made it to the state championship or won your senior homecoming game by one touchdown in overtime. Describe your role in an important game that you attended while in high school. Were you a participant, a band member, a cheerleader, or a fan in the bleachers? What details do you remember? Was the game important to you or was it merely a social event? Describe the event from your perspective.
2. Are you involved in collecting, trading, or playing any card games, such as "Artist Trading Cards," "Dungeons and Dragons" cards, or baseball cards? If so, how does this hobby connect to other parts of your life? Do you play online games, paint, or watch baseball on television? If not, why not? Is card culture stereotyped? Does the stereotype depend on the type of card being collected or traded?
3. Consider the influential people in your life and the hobbies they enjoyed. Perhaps your grandmother was a gardener or your fifth-grade teacher shared his stamp collection with the class. Reflect on the role of important people in your life through leisure activities. Perhaps you enjoy photography because of your uncle or hiking because of your mother. Describe this person through his or her influence on your leisure activities. How have they molded your interests?
4. In 1985, California gay activist Cleve Jones came up with the idea for an AIDS quilt, supporting gay rights and causes. As of 2006, 46,000 squares had been donated for the quilt. Identify a cause you feel this strongly about. Design your own quilt square. Then, describe your personal relationship to the cause and the meaning of your design.
5. Reflect on your representation in video games. Is your culture represented? Your class? Your gender? Your race? Are you represented? In what context do characters of minority races or classes appear? Respond to the way you are portrayed or to the way you are excluded.

Analysis Essays

1. Consider how race or nationality is viewed differently in various sporting events. For example, why is it news for an African American golfer to play well or for a Chinese player to make an NBA team? Why are certain nationalities expected to play certain sports well but to stay out of others? Find news stories that support or oppose your assumptions. You might also consider this concept with gender differences.

2. Write a letter to convince a friend or family member to participate in an activity with you. Perhaps you want to join a team, to go on a vacation, or to take a cooking class. Analyze your audience. Which details about the event will be the most convincing for your audience?

3. Investigate politics' relation to sports. Former professional wrestler Jesse "The Body" Ventura was the governor of Minnesota, former Mr. Olympia Arnold Schwarzenegger became governor of California, and even President Ronald Reagan began his career as a sports announcer. What do these connections say about American culture? About our political culture?

4. Many sportswriters and analysts argue that women's sports are often more fundamentally proficient because fewer marketing dollars are spent on merchandise promotion, individual personalities, and athletic stunts. Research this assumption and analyze its truth or deception.

Synthesis Essays

1. Choose a sporting event on television about which you do not know all of the rules. Watch the game and take notes. Next, research the rules and regulations of the game and then review the game based on the differences between your initial thoughts and your newly researched knowledge.

2. Interview your advisor, major professor, or resident assistant about his or her leisure activities; then, assess whether these activities fit in with the academic persona of your mentor. Finally, analyze the relationship between your own academic and career choices and your leisure choices. Are these choices similar? In what way? Why or why not?

3. CBSNews.com released this statement in October 2006:

   "Major League Baseball has a marketing deal with a company called Eternal Image. It'll put team logos on caskets and urns. The effort begins next season with the Yankees, Red Sox, Tigers, Phillies, Cubs and Dodgers. It could eventually include all 30 teams. Each urn will be stamped with a message saying Major League Baseball officially recognizes the deceased as a lifelong fan of that team. After starting with baseball, Eternal Image hopes to branch out by making similar deals with the NFL, the NHL and NASCAR."

   Respond to this type of fandom by comparing your own merchandise purchases in sports or leisure. Then, research the eccentric ways that other fans in your area of interest show their loyalty.

FOR FURTHER READING

Beacham, Sally, and Lori J. Davis. *Digital Scrapbooking*. Boston: Course Technology PTR, 2004.

BestTravelWriting.com. 2007. 19 Feb. < http://www.besttravelwriting.com/>.

Halberstam, David, ed. *The Best American Sports Writing of the Century*. Boston: Houghton Mifflin, 1999.

Lonely Planet Guide to Travel Writing. Los Angeles: Lonely Planet Publishing, 2005.

Rosen, Wendy. *Crafting as a Business*. New York: Sterling, 1998.

Stoller, Debbie. *Stitch 'N Bitch: The Knitter's Handbook*. New York: Workman, 2004.

Wilstein, Steve. *Associated Press Sports Writing Handbook*. London: Schaum, 2001.

writing about television

"Television is an invention that permits you to be entertained in your living room by people you wouldn't have in your home."

—From David Frost, as quoted in *A Companion to Television*

© AP Photo/Jason DeCrow

THE DAILY SHOW
WITH JON STEWART

TEST YOUR POP CULTURE IQ: TELEVISION

Match the catchphrase with the television show.

1 "If it weren't for you meddling kids!" a. *Star Trek*

2 "Elizabeth, I'm coming!" b. *South Park*

3 "Live long and prosper." c. *Scooby Doo*

4 "No soup for you!" d. *The X-Files*

5 "Here it is, your moment of Zen." e. *Sanford and Son*

6 "Oh my God! They killed Kenny!" f. *The Daily Show*

7 "The tribe has spoken." g. *Good Times*

8 "The truth is out there." h. *The Apprentice*

9 "You're fired!" i. *Survivor*

10 "Dynomite!" j. *Seinfeld*

© 20th Century Fox/Getty Images

ANSWERS

1 *c.* Scooby Doo **2** *e.* Sanford and Son **3** *a.* Star Trek **4** *j.* Seinfeld **5** *f.* The Daily Show **6** *b.* South Park

7 *i.* Survivor **8** *d.* The X-Files **9** *h.* The Apprentice **10** *g.* Good Times

YOU AND TELEVISION

Television influences us every day of our lives whether we acknowledge it or not. The most recent census shows that Americans now own 2.4 televisions per household, and the A. C. Nielsen Co. reports that the average American watches more than four hours of television each day—the equivalent of two months of nonstop watching per year ("10"). You can now even easily carry your television shows with you on cell phones, iPods, and wireless computers. Television entertains and engages us just as much as it invades and shapes many aspects of our culture and world. It influences elections, it provides access to worldwide events, and it never sleeps. And because of this accessibility, even though some may not own or watch television, they still cannot completely avoid the influences of television, whether it is on themselves, their family and friends, or the culture at large.

WHY WRITE ABOUT TELEVISION?

Reading and then writing about television help us investigate exactly how television plays a role in our lives. For some, television does not play any role or a minor role at best; for others, television is a major part of everyday experiences. Even if you do not watch much television yourself, how television may or may not affect the lives and cultures of those around you is very important. Television is around us all the time, whether it is in the room and turned on or not. One of the most interesting aspects of writing about television is keying into exactly how influenced you and the people around you are by it. Think of how our clothing and hairstyles are affected by the styles worn by television characters. Do you remember the "Rachel" haircut? Or how our conversations use new words made popular by television characters or news anchors, as in "yadda-yadda-yadda" from *Seinfeld* and "sound byte" used to describe a synopsis of news.

PREPARING TO WRITE ABOUT TELEVISION

Most of us have spent a considerable amount of our time as children and adults watching television. For some of us, television has been a babysitter, a companion, or our only source for entertainment and news. Depending on your relationship with television, you may have to watch it differently when you are planning to write about it. Some of the strategies given in previous chapters may help you, especially those in Chapter 5, Writing About Film, which focus on analyzing the parts of a film. However, here are some strategies that are particular to viewing and writing about television that might assist you.

grappling with ideas

Think about the past week and what you watched on television.

- How many hours did you watch?
- Did you watch programs on commercial TV? Cable TV? A DVR system? DVD? Videotape? iPod? Cell phone?
- Create a list of the shows you watched and the venue. Are you surprised by how much or how little TV you watched? Compare your answers with others in the class.

Watching and Thinking

You will probably have to watch a television show differently from the way you have before, focusing on the parts that you want to use as supporting examples in your writing. Whenever you write a review or a reflection, you will want to find those parts of a show that trigger your reaction to it. When you analyze a character or a scene, you will need to watch parts of a show multiple times to take your analysis to a deeper level. And if you want to combine some reflection and analysis into a synthesis essay, you will want to combine these methods. For instance, if you are asked to analyze the change in family comedies across the past few decades, your analysis could focus on your personal reaction to how characters such as Archie Bunker from *All in the Family,* Dr. Huxtable from *The Cosby Show,* and Homer Simpson from *The Simpsons* react when their children get into trouble. This personal reaction could also focus on how your own father treated you and how these television characters relate to what happened in your home.

Because there are many reasons you watch television, your particular reason for watching may relate directly to how you react. Why did you view this show? Were you required to watch? Did you have to pay to watch—pay-per-view, cable movie channel, iPod, DVD rental? Did you watch by yourself? How and why you watched may influence your overall impression of a show or a character or an assignment, and you should take this into consideration as you begin to think critically about what you are watching.

Just as with any other topic that you may analyze, when you watch television specifically for the purpose of writing about it, you may want to prepare yourself by using some of the key questions that follow. Take notes. Question what you see and hear. Watch for key characters or moments. And be prepared to watch more than once.

If you are watching a television show because you have a writing assignment, try to watch the show straight through at first without taking notes or doing anything that is out of the ordinary for your regular viewing. Then, go back and watch the episode again and take notes on technical aspects, key characters or scenes, or things you want to focus on and return to. If that is not possible, try to use an effective shorthand system for note taking so the flow of the show is not interrupted. After you have viewed the show each time, try to fill in your notes by elaborating with examples, noting key points that you want to research a bit more, or connecting to other shows or characters or episodes from your own life.

After viewing the show, ask yourself these additional questions to expand your critical thinking and writing options. Answering these questions about your viewing experience will help you figure out what you want to write about and also help you find the details needed to support your argument(s) or conclusion(s).

keyquestions

Key Questions for Television Viewing

- How does the title relate to the television show?
- How does the show start? How are the opening credits displayed or revealed?
- When was the television show created? How long has it been on?
- Where was the television show created?
- What type of show is it?
- What kinds of characters inhabit the world of the show?
- Did you notice anything about the camera movements? Were they jumpy? Close-up? Slowly fading in or out?
- What is the concluding image of the television show?
- Is this television show similar to or different from other television shows?

Watching, Analyzing, and Understanding

For technical analysis, writing about television is similar to writing about film; refer back to Chapter 5, Writing About Film, for ways to focus on and write about characters, cinematography, composition, critical approaches, genre, mise-en-scène, setting, sound, and subject. One of the first ways you can begin to analyze television shows is by trying to categorize the show into a television genre.

TELEVISION GENRES. Due to television's similarities with film, you will find that many genres, including subgenres, may exist across various categories, such as drama, comedy, and action. Television has also developed a specialty that is unique to this medium—the series. Established genres and subgenres include the following television programs and series from recent decades.

keyquestions

Key Questions after Preliminary Viewing

- How did the television show match or not match your pre-viewing expectations?
- How did this episode or show compare with others in the same series or other series?
- What is the historical background of the show?
- How does your own belief or value system affect how you experienced the show?
- How do your political beliefs or the beliefs of those close to you or the politics of the time period of the show affect your viewing?

Television Genres	1970s	1980s	1990s	2000s
Action/Adventure	Kung Fu	Hart to Hart	Baywatch	24
Animated	The Flintstones	The Simpsons	Daria	The Boondocks
Anthology	Night Gallery	Mystery!	Red Shoe Diaries	Masters of Horror
Cartoons	The Pink Panther Show	She-Ra: Princess of Power	Pokemon	SpongeBob SquarePants
Children's	The Muppet Show	Sesame Street	Barney & Friends	The Wiggles
Cop/Detective	Starsky and Hutch	Cagney & Lacey	NYPD Blue	Monk
Courtroom Drama	The Bold Ones: The Lawyers	L.A. Law	Judging Amy	Boston Legal
Crime Drama	Mannix	The Equalizer	Oz	The Sopranos
Drama	Dallas	China Beach	Northern Exposure	Desperate Housewives
Family Drama	The Waltons	Father Murphy	Seventh Heaven	Everwood
Family Sitcom	Good Times	The Cosby Show	Roseanne	The George Lopez Show
Game Show	Family Feud	Hollywood Squares	Who Wants to Be a Millionaire?	Deal or No Deal
Horror/ Supernatural	The Addams Family	Friday the 13th	Angel	Lost
Hospital Drama	Marcus Welby, M.D.	St. Elsewhere	Chicago Hope	Grey's Anatomy
Miniseries	Roots	North and South	Stephen King's The Stand	Into the West
News	60 Minutes	20/20	The O'Reilly Factor	The Colbert Report

(continued)

Television Genres	1970s	1980s	1990s	2000s
Procedurals	Police Story	Murder, She Wrote	Law & Order	CSI
Reality	An American Family	That's Incredible	The Real World	Laguna Beach: The Real Orange County
Reality/ Competition	The Dating Game	Dance Fever	America's Funniest Home Videos	American Idol
Sci-Fi/Fantasy	Wonder Woman	Beauty and the Beast	Highlander	Heroes
Sitcom	Maude	The Cosby Show	Friends	The Office
Soap Opera	All My Children	Knots Landing	Melrose Place	Passions
Sports	Sports Challenge	SportsCenter	NFL Monday Night Football	Cold Pizza
Talk	The Phil Donahue Show	The Oprah Winfrey Show	The Arsenio Hall Show	Ellen: The Ellen Degeneres Show
Teen	Welcome Back, Kotter	Fame	My So-Called Life	The O.C.
Television Movie	My Sweet Charlie	The Day After	If These Walls Could Talk	Broken Trail
Variety	The Richard Pryor Show	Saturday Night Live	In Living Color	Chappelle's Show

There are some very popular genres shown on American television, including the following general types.

© Hulton Archive/Getty Images

CHILDREN'S TELEVISION—Feeling too grown-up to write about children's television? You may want to reconsider, because children's programs offer a seemingly endless supply of challenging topics. How does television fulfill its mission as America's number one babysitter? How many children's television networks or channels are there? Don't forget to count all the different branches of a children's network, such as the multiple cable channels owned by the Nickelodeon network. What patterns can you detect concerning gender roles, race relations, and environmental issues? What products are advertised in the commercial breaks? What are the possible effects on the adults of tomorrow—as voters, consumers, and critical thinkers?

COMEDY SHOWS—Presenting real life in a humorous, often satirical way, comedy shows frequently mock everyday life and everyday people. Consider the sketch comedy in *Saturday Night Live,* stylish sitcoms like *Friends,* animated characters like those in *The Simpsons* or *Family Guy,* or even cable networks such as Comedy Central dedicated to showing comedy shows day and night. Comedy shows usually address a number of important issues, such as gender, race, sexuality, and class. The exploration of these shows can tell you and your audience a lot about U.S. society.

DOCUMENTARIES AND REALITY TELEVISION—The documentary is more than an educational supplement for school. Most documentaries teach us about issues we otherwise might never encounter: foreign cultures, unfamiliar customs, wild and strange animals, and natural disasters. Television documentaries are available in many forms and venues, such as those seen on *Frontline, NOVA,* and the Documentary Channel and the History Channel on cable. Reality television shows, such as *Survivor* or *American Idol,* are often placed in the documentary category as well, but rarely are any shows considered as credible as most television documentaries. Many questions raised about these shows are of an ethical nature and are well worth developing in an essay. How real are reality television shows? Do contestants forfeit their right to privacy when they participate? How do technology and computer animation influence the reality of documentaries—for example, shows about extinct species? What is the appeal in watching people like the Osbourne family?

DRAMA—Drama, especially in series format, is probably one of the most dominant genres on television. Its subgenres are plentiful and popular. You will notice that dramas can be presented as either serial shows (*24* or *Grey's Anatomy*) or shows that open a story or multiple stories and close them within one episode (*CSI*). Television dramas and film dramas have much in common and can be analyzed in similar ways on the technical, artistic, and story levels. Some sample drama subgenres are given here.

- The Action Series (*Alias*)
- Hospital Drama (*ER*)
- The Miniseries (*Band of Brothers*)
- The Police Series (*CSI*)
- Postmodern Drama (*Lost*)
- Science Fiction (*Battlestar Galactica*)
- The Teen Series (*Veronica Mars*)
- The Western (*Deadwood*)

NEWS—We may not like to think of it, but in reality, news shows and programs have become a profitable business just like any other to the point that twenty-four-hour news channels proliferate across the airwaves. In this context, the question of objectivity might strike you as the most intriguing. How does the competition among different channels influence the presentation of the news? What are the different political agendas of broadcasting stations, and what effect does that have on their coverage? What has become of journalistic integrity? What are the differences between news coverage in the United States and, for example, in a European country?

POPULAR ENTERTAINMENT—The category of popular entertainment shows describes a number of shows that, like all other programs, strive to entertain the viewer, but its concept does not follow any of the genres mentioned so far. The most obvious difference is probably the absence of actors, although not necessarily of acting. Examples include game shows, such as *Jeopardy!;* talk shows hosted by people like Oprah Winfrey and David Letterman; and also sports and music broadcasts, such as those on ESPN and MTV. These productions usually appeal to an audience's unrefined or even crude tastes, and analyzing this supposedly uncultured audience alone provides a rich subject. In fact, today, it is quite easy to find each of these types of popular entertainment shows because most of them have their own channel on cable.

SOAP OPERAS—The soap opera is a typical television genre that began on radio. Its short, half-hour to one-hour format is ideal to promote a number of products in commercial breaks and make even busy people feel that they can squeeze soap operas into their full day. The audience's fascination with this genre is a topic as intriguing to analyze as the programs themselves. People sometimes even plan their work or school days around their favorite soap or catch up on a week's worth of shows by watching SoapNet or the Soap City channel on cable or satellite. Soap opera characters and shows can become very popular.

grapplingwithideas

- In general, what is your favorite television genre?
- What are some of your favorite television shows that make up that genre?
- What is it about these television shows that you enjoy? Give examples.
- Do these shows play at a certain time of day or on particular channels? Do you always watch HBO or HGTV? Perhaps you usually watch late night talk shows or early morning game shows?

In fact, one of the highest-rated shows in soap opera, or even television, history was the wedding of Luke and Laura on *General Hospital* on November 16, 1981, with 30 million viewers tuning in.

Watching, Researching, and Documenting

You may not need to do any outside research for a response or reflection essay because this type of writing usually uses your own life as its central focus. However, if you are writing a review or an analysis of a television show, you may need to do some outside research to create an effective and well-supported essay.

Areas of research may include the following:

- The writer's or director's life
- The writer's or director's body of work
- The backgrounds of the cast
- The historical background of the television episode or show itself, the events portrayed in the program, television production codes at the time, technology at the time the television show was made, and so on
- The culture represented or presented in the television show
- How the television show is or was received by others
- The economic history or budget of the television show
- The original source for the script
- The history or development of filming or televising techniques
- The evolution of particular genres or recognized storyline or character conventions

Since this type of research hinges on what you want answered, one of the best places to start is with a list of questions. Create your own list, try to answer as many questions as you can, and then start your outside research. Check out Chapter 11, Researching and Documenting in the Pop Culture Zone; it suggests helpful strategies and sources for you to use. For research on television, in particular, you may find reference sources helpful. Look for dictionaries and encyclopedias devoted to television, such as *The Television Encyclopedia* or *The Complete Television Dictionary*. Look for online sources as well, but be sure to look for reliable and balanced information. Most networks and television shows now have websites, and many shows also have fan fiction sites. Some of the more reliable online sources are listed here.

Academy of Television Arts and Sciences	http://www.emmys.tv/
The American Television Institute	http://www.earlytelevision.org/ati.html
Brilliant but Cancelled	http://www.brilliantbutcancelled.com/
FanFiction.net	http://www.fanfiction.net/tv/
FlowTV: A Critical Forum on Television and Media Culture	http://flowtv.org
The International Federation of Television Archives	http://www.fiatifta.org/cont/index.aspx

The Internet Movie Database	http://www.imdb.com
Museum of Broadcast Communications	http://www.museum.tv/museumsection.php
Rotten Tomatoes	http://www.rottentomatoes.com/
Screensite	http://www.screensite.org

WRITING ABOUT TELEVISION

Writing about television in a composition class offers many opportunities to investigate your reactions and the reactions of those around you to television and how it shapes us and our culture. You and your peers may want to talk or write about your reactions or responses to particular shows you watch together or to shows that only interest you. Since most students have different viewing schedules or interests, the wealth of topics is never ending.

Writing about television can be much like writing about film or literature because it shares many similarities with these other types of media. However, since television is available to a much greater number of people than film or literature, your knowledge of how television shapes your world may be even more developed. Just as with film or literature, some critics would argue that picking apart characters, scenes, or language may destroy the beauty of the whole for the viewer. However, analyzing television programs or television in general can help you become more aware of the elements that make up the whole. It might allow you to appreciate aspects of television that you may never have appreciated before or push you to clearly see how television affects our culture in many ways.

You may want to investigate the structure of *Family Guy* or the theme music of *Grey's Anatomy*. Your investigation could focus on how these make you reflect on your own life or interests or how these technical aspects compare with other television shows. If you are more interested in social and cultural phenomena, television is ideal for investigating its positive or negative influences on you or your culture, whether that culture is the culture of a local community as seen in *Scrubs* or the culture of an ethnic background as focused on in *Ugly Betty*. Whatever way you choose to use television in your writing, the wealth of channels, agendas, voices, and programming is what makes television an exciting medium for critical thinking and writing.

Just like film, television is considered an artistic medium and can usually be interpreted or analyzed in many ways. Though there are many options to choose from when you are writing about television, four main types of assignments are common: television reviews or review essays, reflection or response essays, analysis essays, and synthesis essays.

keyquestions

Key Questions for a Television Review Essay

- Have you clearly indicated your judgment of the television show's quality?
- Have you provided a brief plot synopsis while avoiding plot summary?
- Have you mentioned specific elements of the television show that support your judgment? Have you described these quickly and vividly, using concrete language and metaphors?
- Have you defined yourself as a credible source by writing clearly and giving support for your arguments?
- Have you qualified your judgment with both positive and negative aspects of the television show?
- Have you begun the review with an attention-grabbing opening? Have you concluded it with a striking sentence?
- Did you write in literary present tense?

Television Reviews or Review Essays

Just as with film, a review of a television episode, show, or genre is basically a screening report; however, it is not just a synopsis of the plot of the show or the series. Some kind of evaluative opinion is expected, along with description that supports your judgments or opinions. These are the types of essays normally found in journals such as *The Journal of Popular Film and Television,* in magazines such as *Entertainment Weekly,* and on online review sites such as *Salon.* Just as with film reviews, television reviews usually follow particular conventions. Your overall evaluation is often the thesis or argument of the essay, such as in this thesis: "Although *Ugly Betty* focuses on a main character who is Latina, the show continues to perpetuate cultural stereotypes." However, instead of giving an explicit thesis or argument at the beginning of their review, some review writers build up their description of different aspects of what they are reviewing and then lead their readers to the final evaluation at the end of the essay.

Reflection or Response Essays

Remember that reflection or response essays usually include some description of the television show as a way to begin your discussion. However, this description should not be overwhelming or the only information given to the reader. Reflection or response essays are quite personal in nature, so be sure that you reflect on your own personal feelings or ideas that came about due to watching the show. The show should ignite something personal that you are excited or impelled to share with your audience. For instance, writers watching an episode of *Survivor* might discuss how one participant's lies to the other castaways reminded them of how they were lied to by a friend at one time.

Analysis Essays

When you write an analysis essay about a television episode or series, you are giving a strong opinion or an argument about an idea you have about the television show. You want to come across to the reader as an expert, providing a strong argument and supporting this argument with evidence from the show. Analyzing a television show usually means that you are focused on one or more particular aspects of the show's structure(s), meaning(s), or effect(s). For instance, you could write about how the structure of *The Simpsons* often follows the same structure as a nonanimated comedy. Or you could delve into the meanings behind certain key elements of scenery in *Lost* or *Heroes* or investigate the effects that violence on television has on elementary schoolchildren. You are trying to convince the reader that your take on the show is true, and you do this by using specific and effective evidence either from the show or from the viewers. Remember, you are not just describing; you are arguing that your analysis is true, so when you use descriptive information, be sure it supports your argument rather than just shares an interesting part of the show. Strong supportive detail can include specific descriptions of scenes or specific details about characters or locations, outside research about the writer or director and the choices he or she makes, or the context or culture that surrounds the show.

keyquestions

Key Questions for a Reflection or Response Essay

- Have you clearly indicated how you used the television show as a springboard for your thesis?
- Have you expressed your personal response to one aspect of the television show?
- Did you avoid plot summary?
- Does your introduction direct your audience into your response?
- Does your concluding paragraph include some reflection on both the television show and your response?
- Did you write about the television show in literary present tense but any past life experiences in past tense?
- Are your writing intentions clear?

Synthesis Essays

As a genre, synthesis essays are just that—they synthesize other approaches into one essay or take a broad view across multiple shows or time periods. Although a review usually involves stating whether or not you liked a show, it might be made stronger by using some analysis, or an analysis might be more effective with some personal reflection in it. The essay writing described here is not given to restrict you but to help guide you when asked to write specific types of assignments. However, the type of assignment you are given or choose to write will help you determine whether you need to break out of just one type of essay writing. If you choose to write using a combination of strategies, be sure to check with your instructor and then look over the key questions for the types of writing you are including.

keyquestions

Key Questions for an Analysis Essay

- Do you have an implied or explicit thesis?
- Do you have a series of reasons supporting the thesis? Are these arranged in logical and convincing order?
- Are your supporting reasons backed up? Do you provide specific evidence and examples from the television show for each reason you offer?
- Does your introduction orient your reader into the direction of your argument?
- Does your concluding paragraph provide a vivid ending?
- Did you write in literary present tense?
- Did you avoid plot summary?

SAMPLE ANNOTATED ESSAY

CONSIDERING IDEAS

Make a list of at least ten television shows that depict the lives of teenagers.

1. How realistic are these shows?

2. Is it necessary for teen comedies and dramas on television to be realistic for the shows to become hits?

To help you process ideas for writing about television, **Andrew Coomes**'s *essay comparing* Dawson's Creek *with* My So-Called Life *is included here. Coomes could have written a review of either show or a personal response that focused on how one or the other show affected or changed his life. However, he chose to write an analysis essay that uses outside sources to support his arguments and conclusions. Note where he supports his ideas and how he incorporates outside sources into his prose.*

Coomes wrote this essay as a student at Middle Tennessee State University. He is now a high school English teacher whose writing interests include film and television studies. "Timing Is Everything" was published in Dear Angela: Remembering My So-Called Life *(2007).*

TIMING IS EVERYTHING

The Success of *Dawson's Creek* and the Failure of *My So-Called Life*

Andrew Coomes

> Note how Coomes highlights or blueprints the types of relationships that are the focus of the rest of the essay.

Created and written by Kevin Williamson, the first season of *Dawson's Creek* (WB, 1998–2003) bears an uncanny resemblance to Winnie Holzman's *My So-Called Life,* which ran for only one year on ABC (1994–1995). Although *My So-Called Life* and *Dawson's Creek* deal with many of the same issues, the former was ahead of its time, and the latter is more self-aware and gives the issues more life and panache. The two shows have nearly identical characters, plots, and soundtracks, but viewer interest (or lack thereof) caused *My So-Called Life* to be cancelled and *Dawson's Creek* to thrive. *My So-Called Life* and the first season of *Dawson's Creek* both portray the lives of high school sophomores and their relationships—friendly, romantic, and family. In his 1994 review of *My So-Called Life,* James Martin states, "Perhaps the best part of the show is the dead-on portrait of high school life, with its moments of learning and love as well as boredom and lunacy. In this arena, *My So-Called Life* is as clever as any mainstream film satire of high school" (24). The same words could have been used to describe *Dawson's Creek* just four years later.

Both shows revolve around a central character, Angela Chase (Claire Danes) in *My So-Called Life* and Dawson Leery (James Van Der Beek) in *Dawson's Creek.* Angela's viewpoint is constantly revealed though her voice-over narration; however, because there is no voice-over in *Dawson's Creek,* we learn about Dawson's through his conversations with his best friend Joey Potter (Katie Holmes) and his actions. In Michael Krantz's article "The Bard of Gen-Y: Hot-wired into Today's Teens, Kevin Williamson is Giving Hollywood Something to Scream About," Van Der Beek asserts, "'[Williamson's] characters are incredibly honest. They say things teen-agers are thinking but don't necessarily say, especially about sexuality'" (106). While Angela's honesty is in her mind, which audiences are privy to through her voice-over, Dawson's honesty is revealed to the audience (and the characters surrounding him) through his speech and actions.

In addition to the similar main characters, Angela's parents and Dawson's parents also share similar characteristics. Graham and Patty Chase (Tom Irwin and Bess Armstrong) are essential elements of *My So-Called Life,* partly because they help attract adult viewers, but mostly due to the influential role of parents in a teenager's life. Mitch and Gail Leery (John Wesley Shipp and Mary-Margaret Humes) have the same purpose in *Dawson's Creek,* serving as role models, albeit not always the best role models. The pilot episodes of both series unveil a marital affair when Angela sees her father talking to another woman late at night, and Joey sees Dawson's mother kissing another man late at night. While Graham calls off his affair in the second episode, "Dancing in the Dark," the temptation of another affair appears with Hallie Lowenthal (Lisa Waltz) in the "Self-Esteem" episode. The threat and temptation of an affair is constantly present, but Graham never actually cheats on Patty. *Dawson's Creek*, on the other hand, is more aggressive with the affair subplot, devoting much more time and excitement to the affair. Gail actually does cheat on Mitch with her co-worker Bob Collinsworth (Ric Reitz), and Mitch eventually finds out about it in the "Hurricane" episode. The remainder of the first season shows Dawson trying to cope with his parents' possible divorce and Mitch and Gail struggling to keep a 20-year marriage alive.

The relationships of the younger characters in both series are just as complex and complicated as the

Note the use of a transition to another point of comparison.

adults'. Love triangles and unreciprocated love are key elements in both *Life* and *Dawson's*. Although Angela is oblivious to the fact, her friend Brian (Devon Gummersall) wants to be much more than friends, but she is too infatuated with Jordan Catalano (Jared Leto) to notice. Likewise, Joey is in love with Dawson, but he is in love with Jen Lindley (Michelle Williams). In the "Betrayal" episode, Angela is enraged when her friend Rayanne Graff (A. J. Langer) sleeps with Jordan just as Dawson is upset when his friend Pacey Whitter (Joshua Jackson) kisses Jen in the "Detention" episode. The betrayal of the central characters' best friends causes ripples in the friends' relationships and the love interests' relationships as well. Because Pacey only kisses Jen as part of a game of Truth or Dare, Dawson is quick to forgive his friend, but Angela is not as forgiving. Rayanne is not playing a game, and having sex with Jordan completely demolishes her friendship with Angela. In the last episode of *My So-Called Life*, "In Dreams Begin Responsibilities," Brian confesses his love to Angela, but she leaves with Jordan before she can respond. If a second season had followed "In Dreams Begin Responsibilities," this cliffhanger may have been resolved, or at least developed further. Unfortunately, ABC cancelled the series due to poor ratings, leaving its audience with no sense of closure. *Dawson's Creek* ends its first season with the "Decisions" episode in which Joey, like Brian, confesses her love to the main character. *Dawson's Creek* goes a step beyond *My So-Called Life* when Dawson tells Joey that he shares her feelings and kisses her, providing some closure to the season.

Life and *Dawson's* also shared a love for music. In her essay on "The Teen Series," Rachel Moseley observes that, "At the imaginative center of the teen drama, as in soap, are place, character and relationships, and emotional drama is often heightened through the use of close-up and (generally romantic pop) scoring (for example, *My So-Called Life* and *Dawson's Creek*)" (41–42). The soundtracks from both shows often comment on the actions taking place during a scene. For example, in the pilot episode of *My So-Called Life*, Angela cries because she sees her father talking to his female co-worker in the middle of the night, and R.E.M.'s "Everybody Hurts" begins to play. Likewise, in the pilot episode of *Dawson's Creek*, The Pretenders' "I'll Stand

Coomes includes names of characters, actors, and episodes, and he also gives full descriptions of all of these to give support to his claims.

Coomes connects two types of pop culture media here.

By You" is playing as Dawson confesses to Joey that their friendship will last through the tough adolescent years. The correlating songs and scenes continue as both series progress. In "The Zit" episode of *My So-Called Life,* Enigma's "Return to Innocence" plays as Angela watches young girls with their mothers and ponders the significance of beauty and appearances of women in society. The song reflects the idea that children don't think about outward appearances, and Angela's desire to return to this innocence of childhood is signified in her words, "People are so strange and complicated that they're actually beautiful—possibly even me." In the "Dance" episode of *Dawson's Creek*, Jann Arden's "You Don't Know Me" plays as Joey watches Dawson dance outside with Jen. The significance of the song is twofold: Dawson is falling in love with Jen, but he doesn't yet know Jen's history of sex, drugs, and alcohol in New York; and Joey is falling in love with Dawson, but he doesn't yet know her true feelings for him. Throughout many of the episodes of both *My So-Called Life* and *Dawson's Creek,* the music follows along with story, and the songs' lyrics help relate the significance of images on screen.

Both shows also have controversial gay teenage characters, Rickie Vasquez (Wilson Cruz) on *Life* and *Dawson's* Jack McPhee (Kerr Smith). Frank DeCaro addresses these similarities in his article "In With the Out Crowd," noting that *My So-Called Life* was criticized for its focus on the gay community, but *Dawson's Creek* and other teen dramas on The WB made the exploration of the gay lifestyle more acceptable (44). Kevin Williamson states in "Outings on the Creek" that he 'didn't want to make it an open-and-shut one-episode situation. I wanted to explore the complexities of a young boy coming to terms with his homosexuality, very much the way I did in a small town'" (Epstein 46). Both Rickie and Jack openly express their homosexuality and have male love interests that are discussed overtly as well.

Both *My So-Called Life* and the first season of *Dawson's Creek* explore the reality of gay teachers as well. Mr. Katimpski (Jeff Perry), the drama teacher in *My So-Called Life*, connects with Rickie and even offers him a place to stay when Rickie becomes homeless in the "Resolutions" episode. In the days before *Will and Grace*

> Coomes uses secondary sources to support his own ideas.

(NBC, 1998–2006), *Queer as Folk* (Showtime, 2000–2005), and *Queer Eye for the Straight Guy* (Bravo, 2003–present), Mr. Katimpski and Rickie were two of the very few gay characters on television, and they offered realistic portrayals of gay men. They both have a lot to lose if people found out they are gay: Mr. Katimpski stands to lose his job, and Rickie always risks being beaten, as he often is. Likewise, Mr. Gold (Mitchell Laurance), the film teacher in *Dawson's Creek*, hides his homosexuality in the first season of *Dawson's Creek* until the aptly named episode "Discovery." Rickie and Mr. Katimpski helped pave the way for Jack, Mr. Gold, and the number of other gay television characters that have appeared since *My So-Called Life*.

With so many similarities between the two series, why did one thrive and the other get cancelled? The main reason *Dawson's Creek* succeeded and *My So-Called Life* failed was not their respective homosexual characters as the previous paragraph may suggest; it was the number of people watching the shows. *Dawson's Creek* was able to attract more viewers partially because of its popularity on a new television netlet, The WB. In Bruce Fretts' article "High School Confidential: *Dawson's Creek*," Joshua Jackson explains that by airing on The WB, "we can avoid *My So-Called Life*-itis, (36)" which, of course, is the medical condition of a short-lived television series. Another reason for *Dawson's Creek*'s success was its audience's acceptance and desire to see the world, both the good and bad parts, from the viewpoint of a 15-year-old. *My So-Called Life,* though still offering the same realistic viewpoint of a 15-year-old, was simply not able to keep an audience. In "Please Remember, *Dawson's Creek* is Fiction," Ken Parish Perkins says, "For *Life* to have succeeded then—and for any series dealing honestly with teenagers to gain an audience now—there must be an acceptance of their interpretation of the world as a scary, sometimes depressing place" (219). *Dawson's Creek,* just three years after *My So-Called Life,* was able to accomplish this feat, giving a realistic portrayal of teen life and doing so for an audience that was finally willing to accept the bad with the good.

My So-Called Life was merely three or four years ahead of its time. Dealing with so many of the same issues, plots,

Note that Coomes does not give a list of similarities and then a list of differences. He fleshes out the previous paragraphs of similarities and then starts to wonder why and how these two shows met such different receptions.

and character types, the main difference between *My So-Called Life* and *Dawson's Creek* was the years they were released and the television networks on which they debuted. Unlike *My So-Called Life*, *Dawson's Creek* had other television series to help pave the way to make its content more acceptable to viewers. *Buffy the Vampire Slayer* (1997–2003) and *Felicity* (1998–2002), both on The WB, and even *My So-Called Life* itself set the stage for *Dawson's Creek*. In his 1995 review of *My So-Called Life,* Ken Tucker declares,

There was nothing else like this on the air last season—no show at once so serious and so entertaining, so insightful yet so much fun. Had the series continued for another season, who knows what sort of dramatic miracles lead actress Claire Danes might have performed as Angela, what twists there might have been in the marriage between Patty and Graham? (50)

We are left with even more questions after *My So-Called Life*'s finale: "What happens when the central character actually falls in love with the best friend who has secretly desired her the entire season?" and "Does a marriage last after it has battled the infidelity of one of the spouses?" *My So-Called Life* could not provide the answers, but *Dawson's Creek* had the narrative time, the will, and the audience and could address similar questions.

Another reason for *Dawson's Creek*'s first season success was its postmodern self-awareness as a teen drama, an ability Williamson had already exhibited in blatantly self-aware horror films *Scream* (1996) and *I Know What You Did Last Summer* (1997). *Dawson's Creek* and *My So-Called Life* were both teen dramas, but *Dawson's Creek* overtly recognizes itself as a teen drama through its writing, characters, and plotlines. Between *My So-Called Life*'s cancellation and *Dawson's Creek*'s debut, this self-awareness became an acceptable style. In the "Dance" episode, Dawson asks Joey at the end of a drama-filled night, "What did we learn from tonight's 90210 evening?" Referencing Aaron Spelling's teen drama from the 1990s, Dawson draws attention to his own actions and experiences resembling a television teen drama. "My So-Called Soap: The Creator of *Scream* Goes 90210; Scary" describes the cast of *Dawson's*

Coomes starts to reach his conclusions here about why *My So-Called Life* did not meet the same reception as *Dawson's Creek*. Note how the similarities of the shows have been presented first and in much more length than his conclusions. Why doesn't this weaken the essay?

Creek: "Improbably self-aware"; "this hyperverbal Party of Four all speak in the same jaded mix of pop-culture referencing and therapyspeak" (68). Dawson and Joey even go so far as to discuss cliffhangers of television shows in the final episode of the first season. In their introduction to *Teen TV: Genre, Consumption and Identity*, Glyn Davis and Kay Dickinson describe scenes like this flawlessly:

> Witty, knowing and slightly mawkish, such dialogue highlights key elements of the texture of *Dawson's Creek:* a use of language which is too sophisticated for the ages of the characters; frequent intertextual references; recourse to a sense of community based on generation; a blunt, somewhat melodramatic use of emotion and aphoristic psychological reasoning; and a prominent pop music soundtrack. (1)

While the lack of self-awareness was probably not part of the reason *My So-Called Life* was cancelled, the postmodern characteristic quickly became an essential element of contemporary television in the late 1990s, contributing to *Dawson's Creek*'s success.

- Holzman's *My So-Called Life* and Williamson's *Dawson's Creek* were both milestones in teenage television dramas, providing opportunities for the genre to flourish. However, timing and ratings were the downfall of *My So-Called Life* and, eventually, *Dawson's Creek.* Surviving six seasons, *Dawson's Creek* was cancelled due to poor ratings. In *"Dawson's Creek:* 'Quality Teen TV' and 'Mainstream Cult'?," Matt Hills defines the series as quality television because of its "status both textually (via its representations of relationships and character reflexivity) and intertextually (by aligning itself with Williamson's other, high-profile work in teen horror cinema)" (54). Though *My So-Called Life* did not have the same "high-profiled" connection with Holzman's work, the series easily falls into the same textual and cult TV categories that Hills describes as evidence of quality television. Additionally, in their introduction to *Quality Popular Television,* Mark Jancovich and James Lyons state that "contemporary television has witnessed the emergence of 'must see TV', shows that are not simply part of a habitual flow of television programming but, either through design or audi-

A secondary conclusion is reached here—both shows were quality television. Why is this an effective conclusion to the entire essay? Why do you think Coomes chose to include this rather than just listing similarities and differences of the two shows?

ence response, have become 'essential viewing' " (2). Again, both *Dawson's Creek* and *My So-Called Life,* through their design as eminent teenage television dramas, fit Jancovich and Lyons' description of quality television. Although *My So-Called Life* was short-lived and *Dawson's Creek* eventually died as well, both series are the epitome of quality television and provide viewers with insightful comments on the reality of adolescence.

Works Cited

Davis, Glyn, and Kay Dickinson, ed. *Teen TV: Genre, Consumption and Identity.* London: British Film Institute, 2004.

Dawson's Creek: The Complete First Season. Perf. James Van Der Beek, Michelle Williams, Joshua Jackson, and Katie Holmes. 1998. DVD. Columbia Tristar, 2003.

DeCaro, Frank. "In With the Out Crowd." *TV Guide.* 1 May 1999: 44–46.

Epstein, Jeffrey. "Outings on the Creek." *The Advocate.* 16 Mar. 1999: 46.

Fretts, Bruce. "High School Confidential: *Dawson's Creek.*" *Entertainment Weekly.* 9 Jan. 1998: 34–37.

Hills, Matt. "*Dawson's Creek:* 'Quality Teen TV' and 'Mainstream Cult'?" *Teen TV: Genre, Consumption and Identity.* Ed. Glyn Davis and Kay Dickinson. London: British Film Institute, 2004. 54–67.

Jancovich, Mark, and James Lyons, ed. *Quality Popular Television.* London: British Film Institute, 2003.

Krantz, Michael. "The Bard of Gen-Y: Hot-wired into Today's Teens, Kevin Williamson is Giving Hollywood Something to Scream About." *Time.* 15 Dec. 1997: 105–106.

Martin, James. "My So-Called Life." *America.* 17 Sep. 1994: 24.

Moseley, Rachel. "The Teen Series." *The Television Genre Book.* Ed. Glen Creeber. London: BFI Publishing, 2001. 41–43.

My So-Called Life: The Complete Series. Perf. Claire Danes, Bess Armstrong, Wilson Cruz, Jared Leto, and Devon Gummersall. 1994–95. DVD. BMG, 2002.

"My So-Called Soap: The Creator of *Scream* Goes 90210; Scary." *Newsweek.* 19 Jan. 1998: 68.

Perkins, Ken Parish. "Please Remember, Dawson's Creek is Fiction." *Knight Ridder/Tribune News Service.* 19 Feb. 1998: 219. *InfoTrac.* James E. Walker Library, Murfreesboro. 3 May 2003 <http://80-web6.infotrac.galegroup.com.ezproxy.mtsu.edu/itw/infomark.

Tucker, Ken. "*My So-Called* Death." *Entertainment Weekly.* 16 June 1995: 50–51.

DECODING THE TEXT

1. How many similarities does Coomes use to compare the two teen dramas?

2. If Coomes had to drop one of the similarities, which one do you think should be deleted? Why?

3. What is the disease Coomes calls *My So-Called Life*-itis?

4. What are some of the questions viewers were left with when *My So-Called Life* was cancelled?

CONNECTING TO YOUR CULTURE

Both of the teen dramas Coomes discusses in this essay play heavily in syndication, especially on channels owned by Nickelodeon.

1. How familiar are you with these shows?

2. Does Coomes's essay make you want to watch them?

3. Teen dramas supposedly represent the lives of real teens. Based on Coomes's description and what you've seen of these two shows, do they represent the life of the average teen? Of you as a teen?

4. What teen dramas are playing on television this season?

5. Do they represent your life as a teen? Why or why not?

TACKLING TOPICS

1. In what ways does television enrich your life? Negatively impact your life?

2. What are some of the stereotypical characters that are depicted in television dramas, comedies, or reality shows? Why do you think that writers and producers continue to create television shows that include such stereotypical or stock characters?

3. If you had to choose the top three television shows that you have ever seen, what would they be? Why would you choose these three and leave others off your list?

4. Every once in a while, television characters break stereotypical boundaries on television. Consider Roseanne or Archie Bunker or Ugly Betty—all of these characters were new to television; however, they are quite stereotypical people. Why do characters such as these become so popular with the viewing audience?

5. Are there certain groups that are constantly portrayed on television in a negative manner? What are these groups? Why do writers or producers bring these characters to television?

6. Is your culture—whatever culture or subcultures you belong to—portrayed accurately on television or even portrayed at all?

READING SELECTIONS

Using the decades approach, the readings about television are divided into five sections: 1970s, 1980s, 1990s, 2000s, and Across the Decades. Essays are placed into these sections based on many factors, including when the essay was written and what the author is writing about, and they are presented here as thought-provoking samples of popular culture writing. In the '70s section, five writers review *Roots,* a 1977 miniseries that dramatized the life of Alex Haley—author of the book by the same name—and his family line. The miniseries celebrated its thirtieth anniversary in 2007 with a newly packaged DVD set, making these reviews relevant once again. Next in the '70s, Michael Novak discusses how television can help shape the soul of the viewer, asking you to question what you are viewing and its influences on you. In the '80s section, Kathleen Rowe Karlyn looks at how Roseanne brought feminism to television in the form of the unruly woman. In the '90s section, Douglas Kellner discusses how Beavis and Butt-Head brought postmodern youth into our living room. Elana Levine begins the '00s section with a look at what she calls docu-soaps, a mixture of reality television and soap operas. Next, Rebecca Traister shows how sweet *Ugly Betty* is really subversive television at its best, and Mark I. Pinsky proposes that cartoons can teach many things, including faith. The '00s section ends with Lynn Spigel's investigation into how media influence behavior, and vice versa. Richard Butsch begins the Across the Decades section by looking at television buffoons from the 1950s to now. And finally, Across the Decades presents a case study on how homosexuality is represented on television, including a satiric essay from *The Onion,* a *Time* magazine essay on characters coming out on television, and an *Entertainment Weekly* essay on (lack of) tolerance and what Mark Harris calls the "Official Entertainment Remorse Machine."

Reading Selections: the '70s

Roots was a thirteen-hour miniseries broadcast in 1977 and watched by millions.

1. How familiar are you with this miniseries and its theme?

2. How much do you know about African American history and culture?

Since 1969, The Black Scholar *has become one of the leading journals of black cultural and political thought. After ABC broadcast the thirteen-hour mini-series* Roots *in 1977, the editors at Black Scholar, in keeping with their interest in publishing topics of concern to the African American community, asked a number of "black intellectuals, media workers and scholars" to comment on their reactions to* Roots *in a special edition of* The Black Scholar Forum. *Five of those reviews and responses follow.*

THE BLACK SCHOLAR FORUM:

A Symposium on *Roots*

(*Roots* marked such a major event in the history of television and its treatment of the black experience, that the impact has seriously been examined by many who viewed *Roots*. The success and controversy of the television producton and the book *Roots* has taken many forms.

One notable development is that Alex Haley is suing his publisher, Doubleday & Co., for allegedly failing to sell or promote the book properly. In other developments, the National Book Awards gave *Roots* a special citation of merit, and most recently, the authenticity of the African section of *Roots* has been questioned by British journalist Mark Ottaway of the *London Times*.

Particular concern has been raised by the black community over the extent to which the recent television sequence of 13 hours broadcast by ABC-TV during the last week of January 1977 accurately reflects the plot, characters or intentions of Alex Haley's epic treatment of the black experience. *The Black Scholar* asked a number of black intellectuals, media workers and scholars to comment on the television production of *Roots*. We have published their responses in this symposium. We welcome remarks, ideas and criticism from our readers.)

The Black Scholar Forum: A Symposium on *Roots* by Robert Allen, pp. 36–42, 1977. Reprinted by permission of THE BLACK SCHOLAR.

Robert Staples *is professor emeritus of the University of California, San Francisco, where he taught sociology. He is the author of* The Black Woman in America *(1973) and* Introduction to Black Sociology *(1976). He has contributed more than 100 articles and reviews to sociology journals and various magazines.*

ROOTS

Melodrama of the Black Experience

Robert Staples

It is not easy to sort out one's feelings about the television production of *Roots*. On the one hand it is tempting to succumb to the flattery bestowed upon blacks by the national attention paid to a television show in which we are the major, and in most cases positive, protagonists. As a scholar and critic it would be equally convenient for me to conclude that it gave the black masses a feeling of pride and militancy and hence, its overall impact was beneficial to our cause. Upon further reflection I find it hard to settle for just those conclusions.

Unlike some critics I will not dwell upon any unique racial motives behind the showing of *Roots* at this juncture in our history. I assume that as is true of most television productions they made this one for profit without regard for any higher value. The fact that the television show did not conform strictly to the book is no different than other TV or movie adaptations of books or plays. That it was not historically accurate is again a typical way that the mass media takes liberties with historical and contemporary facts. In essence *Roots* was a typical television melodrama played out in a prosaic fashion which attracted the attention of the American public due to a combination of socio-psychological factors.

For whites it confirmed their view of blacks as victims of an institution which none of them created or feel responsible for. It imbedded in the public consciousness a view of black problems as deriving chiefly from historical forces which in turn have fashioned an incapacity of Afro-Americans to adjust to the imperatives of Euro-American culture. The blacks who witnessed the television show may have a greater, if inaccurate, awareness of their past. But, the tragic consequence of *Roots* for many blacks is that it has chained them to a fictional past without explaining where and why they are today. *Roots* told us little about how our use as human capital shored up a fledgling industrial order in the South nor did it explain our use as a scapegoat for all of America's problems.

To wit, *Roots* set in motion blacks trying to find out who and where their ancestors are while we do not know where in the pecking order our children will be. Its markedly apolitical character did not describe how the modern political state continues to exploit us with its oppressive

The Black Scholar Forum: A Symposium on *Roots* by Robert Staples, p. 37, 1977. Reprinted by permission of THE BLACK SCHOLAR.

machinery in order to maintain this society's equilibrium. In short, *Roots* was like the proverbial Chinese dinner: we feel satisfied when eating it but are still hungry a few hours later. Someday we may be diners at the freedom table but the television production of *Roots* was nothing more than an ephemeral episode in a saga that is still being played out.

Clyde Taylor *is professor in Africana studies at New York University and at NYU's Gallatin School. His publications include* Vietnam and Black America *(1973) and* The Mask of Art: Breaking the Aesthetic Contract—Film and Literature *(1998).*

ROOTS

A Modern Minstrel Show

Clyde Taylor

The serious questions black people have to direct to the TV version of *Roots*, or any dramatic presentation, begin with authorship and direction. Can it be *black* drama (drama *for* black people) when neither author nor director is black? *Roots* on television fails this test on all counts except for one hour directed by Gilbert Moses.

In the white artistic control behind ABC's televising of *Roots* lies a clue to one very important possible motive behind the production (not forgetting other possibilities, like money, mind-manipulation, etc.). The motives of white artists in dealing with black reality are usually couched, more deeply than we generally realize, in the obscure, complex, self-serving impulses of minstrelsy. *Roots* televised was yet another offering of black images in animation, enacting the perception of white creative controllers as to what it must be like to be black in America.

We should not be deflected from recognizing the minstrel motive by the comparatively high quality of the production or the scraps of good intentions displayed. The historical fact is that many of the original minstrel shows contained liberal, even anti-slavery, sentiments. The recent dramatization of *Minstrel Man* was excellent in many ways and surpassed some episodes of *Roots* in skill and subtlety. (Some of the worst aspects of *Roots* on TV came in sequences not in the book, that degenerated into the "they-went-thataway" modes of *Gunsmoke*.) But artistic skill and liberal sentiments are misleading barometers when assessing the impact of the varieties of minstrelism.

If *Roots* on video has elevated the creative possibilities of television, that fact is in harmony with American cultural history, which owes (but seldom pays for) some of its greatest leaps to either the presence of black creativity or to the curious

The Black Scholar Forum: A Symposium on *Roots* by Clyde Taylor, pp. 37–38, 1977. Reprinted by permission of THE BLACK SCHOLAR.

impetus that the black presence has on white American imagination. ABC's television spectacular should be seen in continuity with the phenomenally successful nineteenth century minstrel shows and also with the enormous influence that *Shuffle Along*, a *black* musical, had on subsequent American musical comedy.

In cases like *Roots*, what must be weighed is the *total* gain or loss, not just the artistic. Harriet Beecher Stowe's *Uncle Tom's Cabin* may have helped to end slavery, but we are right to remember the later mythic and cultural damage its images of black people effected, too. If, in the area of politics, the ultimate measure is freedom, in esthetics the comparable measure must be total truth. Sterling Brown says "they take two steps forward, then one step back" of the white productions that, in my opinion, *Roots* is heir to. And as Malcolm pointed out,

why should we be grateful to a man who pulls his knife *half-way* out of our backs?

Chinweizu *is a Nigerian poet and critic. In the 1970s, he was associate professor at San Jose State University. He is the author of many works, including the historical study* The West and the Rest of Us: White Predators, Black Slavers, and the African Elite *(1975) and* Energy Crisis and Other Poems *(1978).*

ROOTS

Urban Renewal of the American Dream

Chinweizu

That *Roots-TV* was produced and massively promoted is not difficult to understand when it is seen as supplying one of the finishing touches to the imperial reformation which the American establishment undertook, seriously, but with all deliberate speed, after the Korean no-win war. Having racially integrated various parts of American society, the liberal establishment had to buttress its exercise in internal decolonization and neo-colonization of Afro-America with a reshaped popular memory of American history. Since the history of Afro-America could no longer be profitably slandered and distorted, or treated as problematic, unique, and apart, there developed a need to integrate the American saga of those who were brought with the American saga of those who came, making them mere variants of the quintessential American saga in pursuit of the American Dream. Therefore, a suitably rehabilitated portrait of slavery had to be inserted into the national historical memory. Given this clue to the question, why now?, still, why the choice of *Roots* for this role? But what would have been the alternatives?

Haley's *Roots* is unquestionably a saga of vast scope, and about indomitable human spirit. But still, *Chicken George was*

The Black Scholar Forum: A Symposium on *Roots* by Chinweizu, pp. 38–39, 1977. Reprinted by permission of THE BLACK SCHOLAR.

no Nat Turner. Given its objectives, what sort of story would the establishment pick up and project? One which would compel a more radical or a less radical questioning of the system? Imagine a film, *Nat Turner*, made with even so mild a treatment as that in the movie *Spartacus*. Would any network pick it up and risk having all those young and impressionable all-American kids who rooted for Chicken George root instead for Nat Turner? But, leaders of slave revolts aside, where were the field hands in *Roots-TV*? As a brief review in *Rumble* points out: "Anyone who knows anything about the nature of slavery in this country knows . . . (that *Roots-TV*) was understated. This is not to say that Haley's book is anything but authentic. But only to point out that the life of the field hand was much more severe than what we saw in the production."

Now, put yourself in the position of the establishment's manipulators of the national memory. If you were concerned with grounding a program of neo-colonial racial integration upon a shared national memory of slavery, and were on the lookout for the best possible material, and along came a highly researched historical saga about an Afro-American family which survived and made good, a saga that most Afro-Americans, as survivors of slavery and as a people fed up with Jim Crow travesties, could identify with, but nevertheless a saga which, by the particular historical circumstances it faithfully treats, does not provide as radical a criticism of slavery as some others might do, would you not snap it up and give it maximum exposure? I would say that an establishment would have to be, not asleep, but rather too busy surrendering its power in order for it to pass up such a grand opportunity.

On the matter of its content and impact, clearly, the view from *Roots-TV* is not the whole picture of Afro-American enslavement. Muted and inauthentic as it may be in comparison to Haley's *Roots*, still, as a saga of survival, *Roots-TV* is significant for, and fundamentally representative of, Afro-America today. (After all, did the Nat Turners bequeath progeny to the Bicentennial? Not very likely.) At the very least, it ought to retire from the minds of its viewers the old stereotypes invented to serve segregation; it ought to indelibly stamp upon the popular American mind the historical fact that the USA is much more the rightful patrimony of Afro-America than it is that of any immigrant groups who arrived after the Civil War. It ought to drive it home that the oppression and degradation which Kunta Kinte's family, and all Afro-American families, survived were not due to biology, but were social, and entirely man-made. It ought also to impress upon all blacks that, besides family cohesiveness, their survival required contributions from the entire spectrum of the enslaved population, from those who died in revolts, whether on slave ship or on plantations, as well as from those who would be considered Toms. The importance of, and lessons from such contributions, should never be minimized, for group-survival is a many-sided business.

It should, however, still be stressed that this partial rehabilitation of Afro-American history was not done for the primary benefit of Afro-America, but rather for the present purposes of the Euro-American establishment. One should not allow oneself to be conned into gratitude. After all, what they have done through *Roots-TV* is to help Haley to rectify in the national mind some of the distortions they had deliberately concocted and enforced for centuries. To reinforce and supplement the positive impact of *Roots* and of *Roots-TV*, Afro-America needs to produce more corrective books and films on Afro-American history. Otherwise, when the establishment turns desperately and unabashedly fascist, under pressures from the disintegration of its global empire, the positive impressions from *Roots-TV* will be eroded and replaced, with little, if any, difficulty. Besides, *Roots-TV* should not be allowed to become another example of the one-star tokenism system. Shall the networks be allowed to wait another century before they correctly present other periods of Afro-American history, such as Reconstruction, the Great Betraying Compromise of 1877, the Afro-American experience in the labor unions, in the ghettos, etc., and so put *Roots-TV* in its larger historical context? What about a film of *Invisible Man*, for instance? Or of Malcolm X, or even Nat Turner, each done from the point of view of others besides the winners? After all, the networks cannot claim anymore that there is no audience for authentic Afro-Americana!

Charles (Chuck) Stone *has been a journalist, a novelist, a political speechwriter, and a professor. He was a columnist and the senior editor for* The Philadelphia Daily News. *His books include* Black Political Power in America *(1968),* King Strut *(1970), and the children's book* Squizzy the Black Squirrel *(2003).*

ROOTS

An Electronic Orgy in White Guilt

Chuck Stone

It was an electronic orgy in white guilt successfully hustled by white TV literary minstrels.

With incredulous docility, some 80 million Americans sat transfixed in their separate but equal sanctuaries for the final two-hour episode of the eight-part black historical soap opera, *Roots*, trying to winnow the screen's message from conflicting images in color of black good and white bad.

But images are not carved in the Gibraltars of antiquity. Ideas are. For its literary gracefulness, *Roots*, the book, will stand in solitary preeminence, distinguished by its narrative sweep, historical detail and elo-quent craftsmanship. Alex Haley is the Thucydides of our day, interpreting the Black Diaspora as majestically as the Greek historian catalogued the Peloponessian War.

He labored hard for his people. From the Afro-Caribbean island of Jamaica, my Afro-American friend, Haley, wrote me on June 4, 1974, that "the book aspires to be the symbol saga of all of us of African ancestry." The griot from Tennessee succeeded, painstakingly unraveling the umbilical cord that had stretched a tortured distance from Africa to America.

But *Roots*, the television drama, was aimed at a white market. Television executives

The Black Scholar Forum: A Symposium on *Roots* by Chuck Stone, pp. 39–41, 1977. Reprinted by permission of THE BLACK SCHOLAR.

rarely produce shows aimed solely or primarily at blacks, even if 24 million blacks watch TV 21 percent more than whites. Nor are blacks hired to do anything more than entertain.

One of the cruel paradoxes of the TV show, *Roots*, was the lily-white cast of writers. "We were not involved in the production or the writing," said Robert Hooks, one of America's most together black actors.

Given those exclusions, why, then, would a major network set aside eight consecutive nights budgeted at $6 million to document this electrifying black experience?

For the same reasons, we would like to conclude, Harriet Beecher Stowe wrote *Uncle Tom's Cabin*. And that's what the television version of *Roots* was—an electronic *Uncle Tom's Cabin*. But an essential difference distinguishes the two artistic expressions.

Uncle Tom's Cabin, which sold an incredible 300,000 copies (the bestseller of its day in 1851), was written to sell the American people on the emancipation of black slaves by raising the public conscience. ABC-TV's *Roots*, which was watched by one-third of all Americans, was produced to sell advertising for the enrichment of white TV executives by raising network ratings. There was an added dividend. A convenient one-shot expiation of white guilt accumulated over 200 years.

The one-third of all Americans who were mesmerized by this epochal event—and despite its flaws, the television showing of *Roots* was one of the great emotional experiences of all time—was probably the same percentage which clung to the evening news on August 28, 1963, and heard the beloved prophet, Rev. Martin Luther King Jr., "go tell it on the mountain."

The combined outpouring of black and white humanity for the "March on Washington" capped by King's soul-wrenching exhortation seemed a natural watershed for black economic and educational empowerment. Instead, the "March" disemboweled the civil rights movement. Blacks did eke out some symbolically spectacular political gains, but the economic condition of blacks has actually worsened disproportionally since then.

The televised *Roots* has fertilized similar expectations of racial progress. Many black and white social critics are convinced this remarkable black soap opera will somehow modulate the racist conscience of America. Will it? Will we move from a second post-Reconstruction retrogression toward *Plessy vs. Ferguson* to a progressive "era of *Roots*"?

I doubt it. Television is a therapeutic catharsis, not a social engineer. Fashion—not faith—is its food. There will be no new jobs created, slums rebuilt, criminal justice made more fair, white police assassinations of blacks prevented, or ghetto schools transformed merely because *Roots* was shown on television.

What the televised *Roots* did accomplish, however, was to give many blacks who had not known who they were—or who had not read the book, *Roots*—an ennobling sense of their pastness. At last, they could unshackle a subliminal Tarzan mentality and boldly bind a blessed tie of American Negroness to African antiquity.

For whites, *Roots* was another fascinating, but powerful, evening of entertainment. Many were shocked, appalled, even angered, by this accurate depiction of their tawdry past. In that the televised *Roots* seared many white consciences for the first time, the drama achieved a magnificent landmark in entertainment, and, I'm almost tempted to add, educational history. Yet, so far it's still business as usual as television networks—not only ABC-TV, but CBS-TV and NBC-TV—continue to merchandise a vast wasteland of Negro minstrels.

In the cold sobriety of several weeks later, was the televised *Roots* faithful to the quintessence of the black experience? Moderately so. Even an all-white stable of TV writers can not emasculate that much black history.

But there's a basis for comparison. *This Far by Faith* is an hour-long television documentary on the black church, conceived by a black advertising executive and narrated by Brock Peters, one of our black artistic luminaries.

Sensitively written, it explores emotional nuances that only an inhabitant in the

black ethos could describe. Near the end of the film, Peters embraces the enormity of the black church's liberating ethic as defined by a triad of black prophets. First, he mentions Adam Clayton Powell and Malcolm X (what white writer could deal with that?).

Then, the film cuts to a church window pane and we hear once again those heart-throbbing cadences of the black Baptist preacher . . . "I have a dream today . . . Free at last, free at last, thank God a-mighty, I'm free at last."

Peters pauses, looks aside and murmurs with gentle reverence: "The voice of the griot."

That one exquisitely poignant moment which chills my spine even now as I now recapitulate it was what ABC-TV's white writers spend eight episodes of *Roots* trying to say.

Robert Chrisman *founded* The Black Scholar: Journal of Black Studies and Research *in 1969. He has also published two collections of his poetry:* Children of Empire *(1981) and* Minor Casualties *(1993). He has served as visiting professor at the University of California, Berkeley, and chair of the Black Studies Department of the University of Nebraska at Omaha.*

ROOTS

Rebirth of the Slave Mentality

Robert Chrisman

Like many black viewers of the epic film *Roots,* I watched the series with mixed emotions—anger, disgust, exhilaration, and, in the main, extraordinary identifi-

cation with the fate of Kunta Kinte and his family. Superbly acted, the first three sections of the *Roots* film provided a view of the despicable slave trade and the

The Black Scholar Forum: A Symposium on *Roots*: "Roots: Rebirth of the Slave Mentality" by Robert Chrisman from THE BLACK SCHOLAR, 1977, pp. 41–42. Reprinted by permission.

subsequent brutalization of black people in the United States that burned like a blowtorch.

But despite its artistry, its candor, *Roots*' end effect upon me was irritation, bemusement, frustration, not for what it said, but for all the things it did not say.

Perhaps that frustration has its basis in the final lessons of the *Roots* film, which seem to be "survival by any means necessary." In the case of Kunta Kinte and his descendants, this meant submission to floggings, rape, murder, the destruction of the family, and the brutality of forced labor. A mood of resignation to any kind of calamity pervades the *Roots* film and whatever the atrocity be (the breaking of Kunta, the cutting off of his foot, the heart-rending sale of Kunta's daughter Kizzy) the response of the blacks is muffled outrage, canny calculation, and voluntary debasement of themselves to soften the inevitable blow from their white oppressors.

Tomming is first presented as a tactic used by the slaves to assuage the guilt, fear, and suspicion of whites, but as *Roots* unfolds, it becomes the way of life for black peoples, their primary response to critical situations. While tomming is a basic strategy for survival, it is not a strategy for liberation. Had blacks during slavery been interested only in survival, the slave system would have lasted much longer than it did.

But blacks did not comply, they resisted. The varied and active resistance of black slaves took the form of arson, theft, sabotage, and over 130 documented slave rebellions, including Nat Turner's uprising; further, the successful Haitian revolution and *Amistad* rebellion helped make the slavery system costly, dangerous, and untenable. The vigorous activity of the black underground railroad subverted the security of the plantation system; and the heroic resistance organized in the Northern states by escaped slaves like Frederick Douglass, Harriet Tubman, Sojourner Truth, and free men like Martin Delaney, David Walker, and Henry Highland Garnet clearly establish active black resistance to enslavement.

While *Roots* was primarily the story of a particular family, it is nonetheless regrettable that it bypasses these larger social dimensions, that it does not firmly establish the fact that many black and white people were actively engaged in a struggle to destroy the slave system, for a complex of reasons.

Even the immediate social dimensions of black life are lacking in *Roots*. Rarely do we see the community of blacks at work, church, or other collective activity. Rather, the focus, indeed the obsession, of the series is events that disrupt, torment, and test the integrity of the *Roots* family—rape, mutilation, sale, miscegenation. Even manumission becomes a calamity.

In this respect, *Roots* is a soap opera, for the main thematic concern of that genre is the disruption of domestic life through a series of crises and confrontations and problems besetting the principal characters. Soap opera excludes social, political, and economic realities; its universe is the family home; its concerns are infidelity, incest, romance, rape, abortion, and bastardy. So it is with *Roots*. Though this film spans a period of great political activity from 1750 through the late 1860s, it is anchored in the feral passions of the plantation, the dialectic of the house on the hill and the shack in the back.

Roots' mixture of helpless blacks and brutal whites recalls *Uncle Tom's Cabin* which, after its success as an abolitionist novel, became the most successful, longest running play in U.S. history, being performed continuously in various ways from the 1860s on into the early twentieth century. It is an ironic possibility that after emancipation *Uncle Tom's Cabin* served to entrench those racist stereotypes that had sustained the vanquished institution of slavery—that of the meek, frightened and submissive slave, and in this fashion had a reactionary as well as a progressive propaganda function.

Because *Roots* is a confession, and one volunteered by the criminal, the nature of the crime is necessarily distorted. The whites in *Roots* are savage, sadistic, and brutal with an intensity that, consciously intended or not, has the effect of intimidation upon the contemporary audience. While *Roots* is most graphic in displaying the sexual activity that occurred between white males and black females ("I always did like a lively nigger gal," says Chuck Connors at one point), no mention whatever is made of sexual activity between black males and white females. Yet the obsession with relations between black males and white females was a cornerstone of white terrorism against

blacks, the ideological linchpin of the night rider. In addition to this dishonesty *Roots* also exposes the need whites have to view blacks as superior to themselves and at the same time impotent and relegated to quiet survival, to being a source of wisdom and solace to benighted white men and women in the tradition of the hundreds of patient, understanding and enduring blacks that populate the white American mind.

The 1960s demonstrated that black people had not only survived slavery but transcended its deleterious effects in the continuing drive for complete equality and freedom from racism, and the 1970s continue to enrich the black consciousness with new perspectives and understandings being gained from the struggle in Southern Africa, the Watergate revelation, the Cointelpro scandals.

But *Roots*'s image of hapless blacks is a regression to a less heroic, less dignified, black image than that we saw and projected during the 1960s.

Much of our struggle during that period was to destroy the slave mentality so graphically resurrected in the *Roots* film.

That struggle still continues.

DECODING THE TEXTS

1. Based on the authors' reviews of *Roots,* why was it not only a successful miniseries but also a controversial one? Give specific examples.

2. The multiple reviewers in *The Black Scholar* presented different viewpoints about the same miniseries, but all of the reviews shared a common thread. What was that common thread? Why do the authors choose different aspects of the miniseries and African American history or culture to support their points of view?

3. Why does Chinweizu call *Roots* a "partial rehabilitation of Afro-American history"?

4. In his review of *Roots,* Robert Chrisman calls the miniseries a soap opera and considers this its biggest fault. What support does he provide for this claim?

CONNECTING TO YOUR CULTURE

Roots portrays a time that many in the United States know nothing about or have forgotten. In fact, until the thirtieth anniversary of the miniseries, many people had forgotten the miniseries as well.

1. Are there times in your life—within your culture or subculture—that others know nothing about?

2. Is this due to ignorance or deliberate forgetfulness or some other cause?

3. Even though they share a common overall thread, the five reviewers share different views and perspectives about the same miniseries. Describe a recent television show (episode or series) that inspired differing perspectives among you and your friends or family. Where did the differences lie?

4. Both Coomes in the earlier sample annotated essay and the *Roots* reviewers say that the television programs in question do not necessarily depict the cultures—teen culture or early African American culture—accurately. When have you felt like you have been depicted in a way that does not accurately reflect who you are or what your culture is?

CONSIDERING IDEAS

1. How does television help shape the souls of its viewers?

2. What are some of the positive and negative forces that may help create or modify our views?

3. Can you think of any television shows that have modified how you view the world or how you respond to others in the world?

Michael Novak *is an author, philosopher, and theologian. He is director of social and political studies at the American Enterprise Institute in Washington, D.C. His publications include* The Open Church *(1964),* The Joy of Sports *(1976, 1994), and* On Two Wings: Humble Faith and Common Sense at the American Founding *(2003). This is an excerpt from "Television Shapes the Soul," which first appeared in 1977 in the anthology* Mass Media Issues.

TELEVISION SHAPES THE SOUL

Michael Novak

For twenty-five years we have been immersed in a medium never before experienced on this earth. We can be forgiven if we do not yet understand all the ways in which this medium has altered us, particularly our inner selves: the perceiving, mythic, symbolic—and the judging, critical—parts of ourselves.

Media, like instruments, work "from the outside in." If you practice the craft of writing sedulously, you begin to think and perceive differently. If you run for twenty minutes a day, your psyche is subtly transformed. If you work in an executive office, you begin to think like an executive. And if you watch six hours of television, on the average, every day . . . ?[1]

Innocent of psychological testing and sociological survey, I would like to present a humanist's analysis of what television seems to be doing to me, to my students, and to my children, and in general, to those I see around me (including those I see on television, in movies, in magazines, etc.). My method is beloved of philosophers, theologians, cultural critics: try to *perceive,* make *distinctions, coax into the light* elusive moments of consciousness. It goes without saying that others will have to verify the following observations; they are necessarily in the hypothetical mode, even if some of the hypotheses have a cogency that almost bites.

* * *

---

[1] There is no discernible variation between the hours spent watching television by the college-educated, or by professors and journalists, and the public as a whole.

TELEVISION AND REALITY

Television is a molder of the soul's geography. It builds up incrementally a psychic structure of expectations. It does so in much the same way that school lessons slowly, over the years, tutor the unformed mind and teach it "how to think." Television *might* tutor the mind, soul, and heart in other ways than the ways it does at present. But, to be concrete, we ought to keep in view the average night of programming on the major networks over the last decade or so—not so much the news or documentaries, not so much the discussions on public television or on Sundays, not so much the talk shows late at night, but rather the variety shows, comedies, and adventure shows that are the staples of our prime-time viewing. From time to time we may allow our remarks to wander farther afield. But it is important to concentrate on the universe of primetime network programming; that is where the primary impact of television falls.

It is possible to isolate five or six ways in which television seems to affect those who watch it. Television series represent genres of artistic performance. They structure a viewer's way of perceiving, of making connections, and of following a story line. Try, for example, to bring to consciousness the difference between the experience of watching television and the experience of learning through reading, argument, the advice of elders, lectures in school, or other forms of structuring perception. The conventions of the various sorts of

"Television Shapes the Soul" by Michael Novak, from Leonard L. Sellars and Wilbur C. Rivers, eds., MASS MEDIA ISSUES (New York: Prentice-Hall, 1977). Reprinted by permission of Michael Novak.

television re-create different sorts of "worlds." These "worlds" raise questions—and, to some extent, illuminate certain features of experience that we notice in ourselves and around us as we watch.

1. Suppose that you were a writer for a television show—an action-adventure, a situation comedy, even a variety show. You would want to be very careful to avoid "dead" spots, "wooden" lines, "excess" verbiage. Every line has a function, even a double or triple function. Characters move on camera briskly, every line counts, the scene shifts rapidly. In comedy, every other line should be a laugh-getter. Brevity is the soul of hits.

Television is a teacher of expectations; it speeds up the rhythm of attention. Any act in competition with television must approach the same pace; otherwise it will seem "slow." Even at an intellectual conference or seminar we now demand a swift rhythm of progressive movement; a leisurely, circular pace of rumination is perceived as less than a "good show."

2. But not only the pace is fast. Change of scene and change of perspective are also fast. In a recent episode of *Kojak,* action in three or four parts of the city was kept moving along in alternating sequences of a minute or less. A "principle of association" was followed; some images in the last frames of one scene suggested a link to the first frames of the new scene. But one scene cut away from another very quickly.

The progression of a television show depends upon multiple logics—two or three different threads are followed simultaneously. The viewer must figure out the connections between people, between chains of action, and between scenes. Many clues are *shown,* not *said.* The viewer must detect them.

The logic of such shows is not sequential in a single chain. One subject is raised, then cut, and another subject is picked up, then cut. Verbal links—"Meanwhile, on the other side of the city . . ."—are not supplied.

In teaching and in writing I notice that for students one may swiftly change the subject, shift the scene, drop a line of argument in order to pick it up later—and not lose the logic of development. Students understand such a performance readily. They have been prepared for it. The systems of teaching in which I learned in my student days—careful and exact exegesis proceeding serially from point to point, the careful definition and elucidation of terms in an argument and the careful scrutiny of chains of inference, and the like—now meet a new form of resistance. There has always been resistance to mental discipline: one has only to read the notebooks of students from medieval universities to recognize this well-established tradition of resistance. But today the minds and affections of the brighter students are teeming with images, vicarious experiences, and indeed of actual travel and accomplishments. Their minds race ahead and around the flanks of lines of argument. "Dialectics" rather than "logic" or "exegesis" is the habit of mind they are most ready for. I say this neither in praise nor in blame; pedagogy must deal with this new datum, if it is new. What are its limits and its possibilities? What correctives are needed among students—and among teachers?

3. The periodization of attention is also influenced by the format of television. For reasons of synchronized programming the ordinary television show is neatly divided into segments of approximately equal length, and each of these segments normally has its own dramatic rhythm so as to build to dramatic climax or subclimax, with the appropriate degree of suspense or resolution. Just as over a period of time a professor develops an instinct for how much can be accomplished in a fifty-minute lecture, or a minister of religion develops a temporal pattern for his sermons, so also the timing of television shows tutors their audience to expect a certain rhythm of development. The competitive pressures of television, moreover, encourage producers to "pack" as much action, intensity, or (to speak generally) entertainment into each segment as possible. Hence, for example, the short, snappy gags of *Laugh-In* and the rapid-fire developments of police shows or westerns.

Character is as important to successful shows as action; audiences need to "identify" with the heroes of the show, whether dramatic or comic. Thus in some ways the leisure necessary to develop character may provide a counter-tendency to the melodramatic rapidity. Still, "fast-paced" and "laugh-packed" and other such descriptions express the sensibility that television both serves and reinforces.

4. Television tutors the sensibilities of its audience in another way: it can handle only a limited range of human emotions, perplexities, motivations, and situations. The structure of competitive television seems to require this limitation; it springs from a practiced estimation of the capacity of the audience. Critics sometimes argue that American novelists have a long tradition of inadequacy with respect to the creation of strong, complicated women and, correspondingly, much too simple and superficial a grasp of the depths and complexities of human love. It is, it is said, the more direct "masculine" emotions, as well as the relations of comradeship between men, that American artists celebrate best. If such critical judgments may be true of our greatest artists working in their chosen media, then, a fortiori, it is not putting down television to note that the range of human relations treated by artists on television is less than complete. The constraints under which television artists work are acute: the time available to them, the segmentation of this time, and the competitive pressures they face for intense dramatic activity. To develop a fully complicated set of motivations, internal conflicts, and inner contradictions requires time and sensitivity to nuance. The present structure of television makes these requirements very difficult to meet.

This point acquires fuller significance if we note the extent to which Americans depend upon television for their public sense of how other human beings behave in diverse situations. The extent of this dependence should be investigated. In particular, we ought to examine the effects of the growing segregation of Americans by age. It does not happen frequently nowadays that children grow up in a household shared by three generations, in a neighborhood where activities involve members of all generations, or in a social framework where generation-mixing activities are fairly common. I have many times been told by students (from suburban environments, in particular) that they have hardly ever, or never, had a serious conversation with adults. The social world of their parents did not include children. They spent little time with relatives, and that time was largely formal and distant. The high schools were large, "consolidated," and relatively impersonal. Their significant human exchanges were mostly with their peers. Their images of what adults do and how adults think and act were mainly supplied by various media, notably television and the cinema. The issue such comments raise is significant. Where *could* most Americans go to find dramatic models of adult behavior? In the eyes of young people does the public weight of what is seen on television count for more than what they see in their private world as a model for "how things are done"? Indeed, do adults themselves gain a sense of what counts as acceptable adult behavior from the public media?

If it turns out to be true that television (along with other media like magazines and the cinema) now constitutes a major source of guidance for behavior, to be placed in balance with what one learns from one's parents, from the churches, from one's local communities, and the like, then the range of dramatic materials on television has very serious consequences for the American psyche. While human behavior is to a remarkable extent diverse and variable, it tends to be "formed" and given shape by the attraction or the power of available imaginative materials: stories, models, symbols, images-in-action. The storehouse of imaginative materials available to each person provides a sort of repertoire. The impact of new models can be a powerful one, leading to "conversions," "liberations," or "new directions." The reservoir of acquired models exerts a strong influence

both upon perception and upon response to unfamiliar models. If family and community ties weaken and if psychic development becomes somewhat more nuclearized or even atomized, the influence of television and other distant sources may well become increasingly powerful, moving, as it were, into something like a vacuum. Between the individual and the national source of image-making there will be little or no local resistance. The middle ground of the psyche, until recently thick and rich and resistant, will have become attenuated.

The point is not that television has reached the limit of its capacities, nor is it to compare the possibilities of television unfavorably with those of other media. It is, rather, to draw attention to television as it has been used in recent years and to the structures of attention that, by its presentations, it helps to shape.

The competitive pressures of programming may have brought about these limits. But it is possible that the nature of the medium itself precludes entering certain sorts of depths. Television may be excellent in some dimensions and merely whet the appetite in others.

5. Television also seems to conceive of itself as a national medium. It does not favor the varieties of accent, speech patterns, and other differences of the culture of the United States. It favors a language which might be called "televisionese"—a neutral accent, pronunciation, and diction perhaps most closely approximated in California.

Since television arises in the field of "news" and daily entertainment, television values highly a kind of topicality, instant reflection of trends, and an effort to be "with it" and even "swinging." It values the "front edge" of attention, and it dreads being outrun by events. Accordingly, its product is perishable. It functions, in a way, as a guide to the latest gadgets and to the wonders of new technologies, or, as a direct contrary, to a kind of nostalgia for simpler ways in simpler times. Fashions of dress, automobiles, and explicitness "date" a series of shows. (Even the techniques used in taping may date them.)

Thus television functions as an instrument of the national, mobile culture. It does not reinforce the concrete ways of life of individual neighborhoods, towns, or subcultures. It shows the way things are done (or fantasized as being done) in the "big world." It is an organ of Hollywood and New York, not of Macon, Peoria, Salinas, or Buffalo.

I once watched television in a large hut in Tuy Hoa, South Vietnam. A room full of Vietnamese, including children, watched Armed Forces Television, watched Batman, Matt Dillon, and other shows from a distant continent. Here was their glimpse of the world from which the Americans around them had come. I wanted to tell them that what they were watching on television represented *no place,* represented no neighborhoods from which the young Americans around them came. And I began to wonder, knowing that not even the makers of such shows lived in such worlds, whose real world does television represent?

There are traces of local authenticity and local variety on national television. *All in the Family* takes the cameras into a neighborhood in Queens. The accents, gestures, methods and perceptions of the leading actors in *Kojak* reflect in an interesting and accurate way the ethnic sensibilities of several neighborhoods in New York. The clipped speech of Jack Webb in *Dragnet* years ago was an earlier break from "televisionese." But, in general, television is an organ of nationalization, of homogenization—and, indeed, of a certain systematic inaccuracy about the actual, concrete texture of life in the United States.

This nationalizing effect also spills over into the news and the documentaries. The cultural factors which deeply affect the values and perceptions of various American communities are neglected; hence the treatment of problems affecting such communities is frequently oversimplified. This is especially true when matters of group conflict are involved. The tendency of newsmen is subtly to take sides and to regard some claims or behavior as due to "prejudice," others as rather more moral and commendable.

The mythic forms and story lines of the news and documentaries are not inconsonant with the mythic forms represented in the adventure stories and Westerns. "Good" and "evil" are rather clearly placed in conflict. "Hard-hitting" investigative reporting is mythically linked to classic American forms of moral heroism: the crimebuster, the incorruptible sheriff. The forces of law and progress ceaselessly cut into the jungle of corruption. There is continuity between the prime-time news and prime-time programming—much more continuity than is detected by the many cultivated Cyclopses who disdain "the wasteland" and praise the documentaries. The mythic structure of both is harmonious.

It should prove possible to mark out the habits of perception and mind encouraged by national television. If these categories are not decisive, better ones can surely be discerned. We might then design ways of instructing ourselves and our children in countervailing habits. It does not seem likely that the mind and heart tutored by many years of watching television (in doses of five or six hours a day) is in the same circumstance as the mind and heart never exposed to television. Education and criticism must, it seems, take this difference into account.

DECODING THE TEXT

1. Why does Novak say that television can only handle a limited range of emotions?

2. Do you agree with his view on this? If so, why? If not, why not?

3. Novak suggests that education and criticism must take into account how television affects everyone. How and why should this be done?

4. How do the numbered points affect your reading of the essay? Why did Novak choose to organize his essay this way?

CONNECTING TO YOUR CULTURE

1. How do you believe television has shaped your own soul or the view you have of yourself in relation to others in your world?

2. Are there particular television shows that have influenced your development more than others? Why those shows?

3. What other popular culture influences might play a role in shaping your soul or identity? How so?

4. Novak states that television has a homogenizing effect, creating a national identity that ignores individuals and communities. What does it mean to be an American? What other communities or cultures are there to which you belong? How are these similar to or different from being an American?

Reading Selection: the '80s

1. Think of some recent popular sitcoms. What roles do the lead female characters play or hold?

2. Do you think that females are stereotyped in sitcoms? If so, in what way? If not, explain how the roles that lead female characters play do not fall into stereotypical descriptions.

Kathleen Rowe Karlyn *teaches film studies at the University of Oregon. Her interests include film history, genre studies, and feminist theory. She has been published in several journals and is the author of* The Unruly Woman: Gender and the Genres of Laughter *(1995). This essay is an excerpt of "Roseanne: Unruly Woman as Domestic Goddess," which originally appeared in 1990 in the journal* Screen.

ROSEANNE

Unruly Woman as Domestic Goddess

Kathleen Rowe Karlyn

The episode I'm going to talk about (7 November 1989) is in some ways atypical because of its stylistic excess and reflexivity. Yet I've chosen it because it so clearly defines female unruliness and its opposite, the ideology of the self-sacrificing wife and mother. It does so by drawing on and juxtaposing three styles: a realist sitcom style for the arena of ideology in the world of the working-class wife and mother; a surreal dream sequence for female unruliness; and a musical sequence within the dream to reconcile the "real" with the unruly. Dream sequences invariably signal the eruption of unconscious desire. In this episode, the dream is linked clearly with the eruption of *female* desire, the defining mark of the unruly woman.

The episode begins as the show does every week, in the normal world of broken plumbing, incessant demands, job troubles. Roseanne wants ten minutes alone in a hot bath after what she describes as "the worst week in her life" (she just quit her job at the Wellman factory). But between her husband Dan and her kids, she can't get into the bathroom. She falls asleep while she's waiting. At this point all the

"Roseanne: Unruly Woman as Domestic Goddess" by Kathleen Rowe Karlyn, originally published in SCREEN 31.4 (1990): 408–19. Reprinted by permission of the author.

marks of the sitcom disappear. The music and lighting signal "dream." Roseanne walks into her bathroom, but it's been transformed into an opulent, Roman-esque pleasure spa where she is pampered by two bare-chested male attendants ("the pec twins," as Dan later calls them). She's become a glamorous redhead.

Even within this dream, however, she's haunted by her family and the institution that stands most firmly behind it—the law. One by one, her family appears and continues to nag her for attention and interfere with her bath. And one by one, without hesitation, she kills them off with tidy and appropriate means. (In one instance, she twitches her nose before working her magic, alluding to the unruly women of the late 60s/early 70s sitcom *Bewitched*.) Revenge and revenge fanta-sies are of course a staple in the feminist imagination (Marleen Gorris's *A Question of Silence* (1982), Nelly Kaplan's *A Very Curious Girl* (1969), Cecilia Condit's *Possibly in Michigan* (1985), Karen Arthur's *Lady Beware* (1987)). In this case, however, Roseanne doesn't murder for revenge but for a bath.

Roseanne's unruliness is further chal-lenged, ideology reasserts itself, and the dream threatens to become a nightmare when she is arrested for murder and brought to court. Her family really *isn't* dead, and with her friends they testify against her, implying that because of her shortcomings as a wife and mother she's been murdering them all along. Her friend Crystal says: "She's loud, she's bossy, she talks with her mouth full. She feeds her kids frozen fish sticks and high calorie sodas. She doesn't have proper groom-ing habits." And she doesn't treat her husband right even though, as Roseanne

explains, "The only way to keep a man happy is to treat him like dirt once in a while." The trial, like the dream itself, dra-matizes a struggle over interpretation of the frame story that preceded it: the court judges her desire for the bath as narcissis-tic and hedonistic, and her barely sup-pressed frustration as murderous. Such desires are taboo for good self-sacrificing mothers. For Roseanne, the bath (and the "murders" it *requires*) are quite pleasurable for reasons both sensuous and righteous. Everyone gets what they deserve. Coinci-dentally, ABC was running ads during this episode for the docudrama *Small Sacrifices* (12–14 November 1989), about a real mother, Diane Downs, who murdered one of her children.

Barely into the trial, it becomes apparent that Roseanne severely strains the court's power to impose its order on her. The rigid oppositions it tries to enforce begin to blur, and alliances shift. Roseanne defends her kids when the judge—Judge Wapner from *People's Court*—yells at them. Roseanne, defended by her sister, turns the tables on the kids and they repent for the pain they've caused her. With Dan's abrupt change from prosecutor to crooner and character witness, the courtroom becomes the stage for a musical. He breaks into song, and soon the judge, jury, and entire cast are dancing and singing Roseanne's praises in a bizarre production number. Female desire *isn't* monstrous; acting on it "ain't misbehavin'," her friend Vanda sings. This celebration of Roseanne in effect vindicates her, although the judge remains unconvinced, finding her not only guilty but in contempt of court. Dream-work done, she awakens, the sound of the judge's gavel becoming Dan's hammer on the plumbing. Dan's job is over too, but the kids still want her attention. Dan jokes that there's no place like home but Roseanne answers "Bull." On her way, at last, to her bath, she closes the door to the bathroom to the strains of the chorus singing "We Love Roseanne."

The requirements for bringing this fantasy to an end are important. First, what ultimately satisfies Roseanne isn't an escape from her family but an acknowledgement from them of *her* needs and an expression of their feeling for her—"We love you, Roseanne." I am not suggesting that Roseanne's series miraculously transcends the limitations of prime-time television. To a certain degree this ending does represent a sentimental co-opting of her power, a shift from the potentially radical to the liberal. But it also indicates a refusal to flatten contradictions. Much of Roseanne's appeal lies in the delicate balance she maintains between individual and institution and in the impersonal nature of her anger and humour, which are targeted not so much at the people she lives with as at what makes them the way they are. What Roseanne *really* murders here is the ideology of "perfect wife and mother," which she reveals to be murderous in itself.

The structuring—and limits—of Roseanne's vindication are also important. Although the law is made ludicrous, it retains its power and remains ultimately indifferent and immovable. Roseanne's "contempt" seems her greatest crime. More important, whatever vindication Roseanne does enjoy can happen only within a dream. It cannot be sustained in real life. The realism of the frame story inevitably reasserts itself. And even within the dream, the reconciliation between unruly fantasy and ideology can be brought about only deploying the heavy artillery of the musical and its conventions. As Rick Altman has shown, few forms embody the utopian impulse of popular culture more insistently than the musical, and within musicals, contradictions difficult to resolve otherwise are acted out in production numbers. That is what happens here. The production number gives a fleeting resolution to the problem Roseanne typically plays with: representing the unrepresentable. A fat woman who is also sexual; a sloppy housewife who's a good mother; a "loose" woman who is also tidy, who hates matrimony but loves her husband, who hates the ideology of "true womanhood" yet considers herself a domestic goddess.

There is much more to be said about Roseanne and the unruly woman: about her fights to maintain authorial control over (and credit for) her show; her use of the grotesque in the film *She Devil* (1989); her performance as a stand-up comic; the nature of her humour, which she calls "funny womanness;" her identity as a Jew and the suppression of ethnicity in her series; the series' move toward melodrama and its treatment of social class. A more sweeping look at the unruly woman would find much of interest in the Hollywood screwball comedy as well as feminist avant-garde film and video. It would take up questions about the relation between gender, anger, and Medusan laughter—about the links Hélène Cixous establishes between laughing, writing, and the body and their implications for theories of female spectatorship. And while this article has emphasized the oppositional potential of female unruliness, it is equally important to expose its misogynistic uses, as in, for example, the Fox sitcom *Married . . . With Children* (1988). Unlike Roseanne, who uses female unruliness to push at the limits of acceptable female behaviour, Peg inhabits the unruly woman stereotype with little distance, embodying the "male point of view" Roseanne sees in so much television about family.

Roseanne points to alternatives. Just as "domestic goddess" can become a term of self-definition and rebellion, so can spectacle-making—when used to seize the visibility that is, after all, a precondition for existence in the public sphere. The ambivalence I've tried to explain regarding Roseanne is evoked above all, perhaps, because she demonstrates how the enormous apparatus of televisual star-making can be put to such a use.

DECODING THE TEXT

1. What is the metaphor of the unruly woman that the author describes?

2. Why does she say that this metaphor both fits and doesn't fit Roseanne Barr?

3. Do you agree with the author?

4. Do you see unruly women in any current ongoing television series? If so, how do these women compare to Roseanne?

5. What does the author mean by "the male point of view" within television series? Does your favorite television series fit her definition?

CONNECTING TO YOUR CULTURE

1. Have you ever been labeled as something you do not think you are? What was the label? Why did others think it fit you? Why did you think it didn't?

2. The author mentions the sitcom family of *Roseanne* in her essay. How does Roseanne's family resemble or not resemble your own family? Why?

3. Many comedians such as Dave Chappelle and Sarah Silverman speak and behave similarly to Roseanne, often using rude language and addressing taboo subjects. What is the appeal of these comedians to you? To your friends? To college students overall?

Reading Selection: the '90s

Television often offers "loser" characters—those who can't get anything right, can't get the girl, the guy, or the job, or just can't make it in the so-called normal world.

1. What television losers do you know?

2. What makes them losers?

3. How do their wardrobes, actions, or speech label them as losers?

Douglas Kellner *is professor of philosophy at Columbia University. He is the author of several books about philosophy, popular culture, and politics, including* Grand Theft 2000 *(2001) and* Media Spectacle and the Crisis of Democracy *(2005). "Beavis and Butt-Head: No Future for Postmodern Youth" is an excerpt of a chapter from Kellner's book,* Media Culture, *published in 1995.*

BEAVIS AND BUTT-HEAD

No Future for Postmodern Youth

Douglas Kellner

Animated cartoon characters Beavis and Butt-Head sit in a shabby house much of the day, watching television, especially music videos, which they criticize in terms of whether the videos are "cool" or "suck." When they leave the house to go to school, to work in a fast food joint, or to seek adventure, they often engage in destructive and even criminal behavior. Developed for MTV by animated cartoonist Mike Judge, the series spoofs precisely the sort of music videos played by the music television channel. *Beavis and Butt-Head* quickly became a cult favorite, loved by youth, yet elicited spirited controversy when some young fans of the show imitated typical Beavis and Butt-Head activity, burning down houses, and torturing and killing animals.

The series provides a critical vision of the current generation of youth raised primarily on media culture. This generation was possibly conceived in the sights and sounds of media culture, weaned on it, and socialized by the glass teat of television used as pacifier, baby sitter, and educator by a generation of parents for whom media culture, especially television, was a natural background and constitutive part of everyday life. The show depicts the dissolution of a rational subject and perhaps the end of the Enlightenment in today's media culture. Beavis and Butt-Head react viscerally to the videos, snickering at the images, finding representations of violence and sex "cool," while anything complex which requires interpretation "sucks." Bereft of any cultivated taste, judgment, or rationality, and without ethical or political values, the characters react in a literally mindless fashion and appear to lack almost all cognitive and communicative skills.

The intense alienation of Beavis and Butt-Head, their love for heavy metal culture and media images of sex and violence, and their violent cartoon activity soon elicited heated controversy, producing a "Beavis and Butt-Head" effect that has elicited literally thousands of articles and heated debates, even leading to U.S. Senate condemnations of the show for promoting mindless violence and stupid behavior. From the beginning, there was intense media focus on the show and strongly opposed opinions of it. In a cover story on the show, *Rolling Stone* declared them "The Voice of a New Generation" (August 19, 1993) and *Newsweek* also put them on its cover, both praising them and damning them by concluding: "The downward spiral of the living white male surely ends here: in a little pimple named Butt-Head whose idea of an idea is, 'Hey, Beavis, let's go over to Stewart's house and

light one in his cat's butt'" (October 11, 1993). "Stupid, lazy, cruel, without ambitions, without values, without futures" are other terms used in the media to describe the characters and the series (*The Dallas Morning News,* August 29, 1993) and there have been countless calls to ban the show.

Indeed, a lottery prize winner in California began a crusade against the series, after hearing about a cat that was killed when kids put a firecracker in its mouth, imitating Beavis and Butt-Head's violence against animals and a suggestion in one episode that they stick a firecracker in a neighbor boy's cat (*The Hollywood Reporter,* July 16, 1993). Librarians in Westchester, New York ranked *Beavis and Butt-Head* high "on a list of movies and television shows that they think negatively influence youngsters' reading habits," because of their attacks on books and frequent remarks that books, or even words, "suck" (*The New York Times,* July 11, 1993). Prison officials in Oklahoma banned the show, schools in South Dakota banned clothing and other items bearing their likeness (*Times Newspapers Limited,* October 11, 1993), and a group of Missouri fourth graders started a petition drive to get the program off the air (*Radio TV Reports,* October 25, 1993).

Yet the series continued to be highly popular into 1994, and it spawned a best-selling album of heavy metal rock, a popular book, countless consumer items, and movie contracts in the works. *Time* magazine critic Kurt Anderson praised the series as "the bravest show ever run on national television" (*The New York Times,* July 11, 1993) and there is no question but that it has pushed the boundaries of the permissible on mainstream television to new extremes (some critics would say to new lows).

In a certain sense, *Beavis and Butt-Head* is "postmodern" in that it is purely a product of media culture, with its characters, style, and content almost solely derivative from previous TV shows. The two characters Beavis and Butt-Head are a spin-off of Wayne and Garth in *Wayne's World,* a popular *Saturday Night Live* feature, spun off into popular movies. They also resemble the SCTV characters Bob and Doug McKenzie, who sit around on a couch and make lewd and crude remarks while they watch TV and drink beer. Beavis and Butt-Head also take the asocial behavior of cartoon character Bart Simpson to a more intense extreme. Their comments on the music videos replicate the popular Comedy Central channel's series *Mystery Science Theater 3000,* which features two cartoon stick figures making irreverent comments on god-awful old Hollywood movies and network television shows. And, of course, the music videos are a direct replication of MTV's basic fare.

Beavis and Butt-Head is interesting for a diagnostic critique because the main characters get all of their ideas and images concerning life from the media and their entire view of history and the world is entirely derived from media culture. When they see a costumed rapper wearing an eighteenth-century-style white wig on a music video, Butt-Head remarks: "He's dressed up like that dude on the dollar." The 1960s is the time of hippies, Woodstock and rock 'n' roll for them; Vietnam is ancient history, collapsed into other American wars. Even the 1950s is nothing but a series of mangled media clichés: on Nelson, the twins of 1950s teen idol Ricky Nelson, Butt-Head remarks that: "These chicks look like guys." Beavis responds: "I heard that these chicks' grandpa was Ozzy Osbourne." And Butt-Head rejoins:

"No way. They're Elvis's kids."

The figures of history are collapsed for Beavis and Butt-Head into media culture and provide material for salacious jokes, which require detailed knowledge of media culture:

Butt-Head: What happened when Napoleon went to Mount Olive?

Beavis: I don't know. What?

Butt-Head: Popeye got pissed.

Moreover, Beavis and Butt-Head seem to have no family, living alone in a shabby house, getting enculturated solely by television and media culture. There are some references to their mothers and in one episode there is a suggestion that Butt-Head is not even certain who his father is, thus the series presents a world without fathers. School is totally alienating for the two, as is work in a fast-food restaurant. Adult figures who they encounter are largely white conservative males, or liberal yuppies, with whom they come into often violent conflict and whose property or goods they inevitably destroy.

There is a fantasy wish-fulfillment aspect to *Beavis and Butt-Head* that perhaps helps account for its popularity: kids often wish that they had no parents and that they could just sit and watch music videos and go out and do whatever they wanted to (sometimes we *all* feel this way). Kids are also naturally disrespectful of authority and love to see defiance of social forces that they find oppressive. Indeed, Beavis and Butt-Head's much maligned, discussed, and imitated laughter ("Heh, heh, heh" and "Huh, huh") may signify that in their space *they rule,* that Beavis and Butt-Head are sovereign, that they control the television and can do any damn thing that they want. Notably, they get in trouble in school and other sites of authority with their laugh, but at home they can laugh and snicker to the max.

And so the series has a utopian dimension: the utopia of no parental authority and unlimited freedom to do whatever they want when they want to. "Dude, we're there" is a favorite phrase they use when they decide to see or do something—and they never have to ask their (absent) parents' permission. On the other hand, they represent the consequences of totally unsocialized adolescent behavior driven by aggressive instincts. Indeed, their "utopia" is highly solipsistic and narcissistic with no community, no consensual norms or morality to bind them, and no concern for other people. The vision of the teenagers alone in their house watching TV and then wreaking havoc on their neighborhood presents a vision of a society of broken families, disintegrating communities, and anomic individuals, without values or goals.

Beavis and Butt-Head are thus left alone with the TV and become couch-potato critics, especially of their beloved music videos. In a sense, they are the first media critics to become cult heroes of media culture, though there are contradictions in their media criticism. Many of the videos that they attack are stupid and pretentious, and in general it is good to cultivate a critical attitude toward culture forms and to promote cultural criticism—an attitude that can indeed be applied to much of what appears on *Beavis and Butt-Head*. Such critique distances its audience from music video culture and calls for making critical judgments on its

products. Yet Beavis and Butt-Head's own judgments are highly questionable, praising images of violence, fire, naked women, and heavy metal noise, while declaring that "college music," words, and any complexity in the videos "suck."

Thus, on one level, the series provides sharp social satire and critique of the culture and society. The episodes constantly make fun of television, especially music videos, and other forms of media culture. They criticize conservative authority figures and wishy-washy liberals. They satirize authoritarian institutions like the workplace, schools, and military recruitment centers and provide critical commentary on many features of contemporary life. Yet, the series undercuts some of its social critique by reproducing the worst sexist, violent, and narcissistic elements of contemporary life, which are amusing and even likeable in the figures of Beavis and Butt-Head.

Consequently, *Beavis and Butt-Head* is surprisingly complex and requires a diagnostic critique to analyze its contradictory text and effects. There is no denying, however, that the *Beavis and Butt-Head* effect is one of most significant media phenomena of recent years. Like [Richard] Linklater, Judge has obviously tapped into a highly responsive chord and created a media sensation with the characters of Beavis and Butt-Head serving as powerfully resonant images. In 1993, while lecturing on cultural studies, wherever I would go audiences would ask me what I thought of *Beavis and Butt-Head* and so I eventually began to watch it and to incorporate remarks on the series into my lectures. If I was critical or disparaging, young members of the audience would attack me and after a lecture at the University of Kansas, a young man came up, incredulous that I would dare to criticize the series, certain that Mike Judge was a great genius who understood exactly how it was for contemporary youth, with no prospects for a job or career, and little prospect for even marriage and family and a meaningful life. In this situation, I was told, what else can young people do except watch MTV and occasionally go out and destroy something?

In a sense, the series thus enacts youth and class revenge against older, middle-class and conservative adults, who appear as oppressive authority figures. Their neighbor Tom Anderson—depicted as a conservative World War II and Korean war veteran—is a special butt of their escapades and they cut down trees in his yard with a chain saw, which, of course, causes the tree to demolish his house, assorted fences, power lines, and cars. They put his dog in a laundromat washing machine to clean it; they steal his credit card to buy animals at the mall; they lob mud baseballs into his yard, one of which hits his barbecue; and otherwise torment him. Beavis and Butt-Head also blow up an Army recruiting station with a grenade, as the officer attempts to recruit them; they steal the cart of a wealthy man, Billy Bob, who has a heart attack when he sees them riding off in his vehicle; and they love to put worms, rats, and other animals in the fast food that they are shown giving to obnoxious male customers in the burger joint where they work.

Beavis and Butt-Head also love to trash the house of their "friend" Stewart whose yuppie parents indulgently pamper their son and his playmates. Stewart's permissive liberal parents are shown to be silly and ineffectual, as when his father complains that Stewart violated his parents'

trust when he let Beavis and Butt-Head in the house after they caused an explosion which blew the wall out. The mother gushes about how cute they are and offers them lemonade—in fact, few women authority figures are depicted.

The dynamic duo also torment and make fun of their liberal hippie teacher, Mr. Van Driessen, who tries to teach them to be politically correct. They destroy his irreplaceable eight-track music collection when he offers to let them clean his house to learn the value of work and money. When he takes them camping to get in touch with their feelings and nature, they fight and torment animals. In fact, they rebel against all their teachers and authority figures and are thus presented in opposition to everyone, ranging from conservative males, to liberal yuppies, to hippie radicals.

Moreover, the series presents the revenge of youth and those who are terminally downwardly mobile against more privileged classes and individuals. Like the punk generation before them, Beavis and Butt-Head have no future. Thus, while their behavior is undeniably juvenile, offensive, sexist, and politically incorrect, it allows diagnosis of underclass and downwardly mobile youth who have nothing to do, but to destroy things and engage in asocial behavior.

From this perspective, *Beavis and Butt-Head* is an example of media culture as popular revenge. Beavis and Butt-Head avenge youth and the downwardly mobile against those oppressive authority figures who they confront daily. Most of the conservative men have vaguely Texan, or Southwestern, accents, so perhaps the male authority figures represent oppressive males experienced by Judge in his own youth in San Diego, New Mexico and Texas. Moreover, Beavis and Butt-Head's violence is that of a violent society in which the media present endless images of the sort of violent activities that the two characters regularly engage in. The series thus points to the existence of a large teenage underclass with no future which is undereducated and potentially violent. The young underclass Beavis and Butt-Heads of the society have nothing to look forward to in life save a job: the local 7-Eleven, waiting to get held up at gunpoint. Consequently, the series is a social hieroglyphic which allows us to decode the attitudes, behavior, and situation of large segments of youth in contemporary U.S. society.

DECODING THE TEXT

Kellner uses the term *postmodern* to describe the '90s television show *Beavis and Butt-Head*.

1. How does Kellner define postmodern?

2. How does *Beavis and Butt-Head* work as an example of his definition?

3. Using Kellner's definition, choose another postmodern television show and explain why it can be called that.

4. How does the satire Kellner describes in *Beavis and Butt-Head* compare to that in the *Onion* article "Letter D Pulls Sponsorship" (page 726)?

CONNECTING TO YOUR CULTURE

1. Do you find anything in the daily life of Beavis and Butt-Head that appeals to you?

2. They are supposed to represent our culture's idea of postmodern youth. Do they represent anyone you know?

3. Which fictional character(s) would you choose to represent your generation? What qualities would you use to define your generation?

4. If shows such as *Beavis and Butt-Head* reflect '90s youth, what television shows, films, or songs represent other generations?

Reading Selections: the '00s

CONSIDERING IDEAS

1. Are you a fan of reality shows? If so, which ones? If not, why don't you enjoy them?

2. What are some of the most popular reality shows on television currently?

3. Who do you think is watching these shows? Describe who you think the audience is.

Elana Levine *is assistant professor at the University of Wisconsin–Madison, where she teaches in the areas of mass media and gender studies. Her publications include* Wallowing in Sex: The New Sexual Culture of 1970s American Television *(2007) and* Undead TV: Essays on *Buffy the Vampire Slayer (2007). "The New Soaps?" was published in the online journal* Flow *(http://www.flowtv.org) on September 8, 2006.*

THE NEW SOAPS?

Laguna Beach, The Hills, and the Gendered Politics of Reality "Drama"

Elana Levine

In the last column I wrote for *Flow*, I talked about the many developments in today's U.S. daytime soap operas and the rich material these neglected texts offer for television scholarship. In this column, I want to consider a variant on the conventional soap opera, a contemporary television genre that may offer similar, serialized pleasures but that also has significant differences from daytime soaps. Reality soaps, also known as docu-soaps, are best represented by MTV's *Laguna Beach* and *The Hills*. These programs have proven appealing to MTV's young viewers, unlike the daytime soap operas on the U.S. broadcast networks, which have seen drop-offs in youth audiences in recent years. In this column, I explore some of the similarities and differences between these two genres, including their gendered politics and pleasures.

The premise of *Laguna Beach* is simple. The show captures the lives and loves of high school students in the affluent eponymous town. The first two seasons have relatively clear narrative arcs—most of the cast are seniors and they are enjoying their last months together before graduating and moving on to new lives. *The Hills* is a sequel to *Laguna.* It follows one of the earlier program's original "characters," Lauren "LC" Conrad, as she moves to L.A. to attend fashion school and intern at *Teen Vogue.* This gives *The Hills* a fundamentally different premise than *Laguna,* more akin to *The Mary Tyler Moore Show* or *Sex and the City* than to *The O.C.* (the subtitle for *Laguna* is "The Real Orange County"—the parallels to *The O.C.* are a deliberate marketing point).

Both series employ a similar structure. Much like daytime soaps, the "plot" may not really advance in any given episode. Instead, each episode revolves around "drama" (the kids' favorite word, with the exception, perhaps, of "random"), which has the vague meaning of some kind of conflict or emotional upheaval. Although there are specific occurrences in the characters' lives—high school graduation, Lauren's internship—the "drama" primarily revolves around romantic relationships. This is a key difference between these series and reality shows such as *The Amazing Race* or *Big Brother,* which certainly represent interpersonal relationships but make them the context, the background, for the contests that move the narratives forward. In any given episode of *Laguna* and *The Hills,* the cast discusses the "drama," much as multiple members of fictional daytime soap communities talk about each other's lives.

In the soaps, these conversations are meant to reveal the implications of plot developments for a host of complexly intertwined characters. On *Laguna* and *The Hills,* these conversations conversely work to force a plot around a sequence of somewhat disconnected events and characters. On the first season of *Laguna,* for instance, passing mentions of the time Lauren spends with Stephen during the gang's trip to Cabo function to develop the not-entirely-there triangle of Lauren, Stephen, and Stephen's sort-of girlfriend, Kristin. We get that there is a rivalry between the girls over Stephen because we are privy to every catty remark the girls make about each other, because others talk about Lauren and Stephen or Kristin and Stephen, and because we see a shots of Lauren looking off-screen, followed by shots of Stephen (the Kuleshov effect at work!). In this sort of storytelling, the show follows soap opera conventions without the narrative content or character development to flesh them out.

Although the appeal of these programs is rooted in part in their "reality," they forego many of the conventions of reality programs. First, there is no justification for the cameras' attention to these characters, no transformations of home decor, self-display, or lifestyle and no monetary prize for victory. Even these programs' most likely progenitor in "observational" reality, MTV's *The Real World,* offers a reality manufactured around its "seven strangers picked to live in a house" set-up. This makes *Laguna* and *The Hills* (as well as ABC's blink-and-you-missed-it *One Ocean View*) more like fictional, scripted television than reality TV and more like soaps than like most prime-time fare.[1] After all, soaps present the "trials

---

[1] CBS has just contracted *Laguna*'s producers to create reality TV-like scripted programming, the logic being that they have already successfully produced scripted programming-like reality TV.

and tribulations of the Bauer, Lewis and Spaulding families," as my TiVo describes *Guiding Light,* much as *Laguna Beach* presents the trials and tribulations of Lauren, Stephen, Kristin, and their classmates (and much unlike the higher-concept situations facing Jack Bauer or even Meredith Grey). MTV's reality soaps also emphasize the ongoing existence of their worlds, their independence from a manufactured premise, by eliminating the direct-address interviews, the "confessionals," that are standard to so much reality TV. As a result, the fourth wall is never broken, making the shows more soap-like but also enhancing their reality claims—these events are just happening, we are encouraged to believe, they are not being set-up by producers.

Of course, these shows are meticulously crafted by producers; their choices literally create conflict, "drama," narrative

out of the thinness of the shows' premises. In one such choice, the producers use musical montages to tell stories; the frequency of these montages makes the series more akin to MTV's original bread and butter—music videos—than to most reality programming. On *Laguna,* the luxurious homes, pristine beaches, vivid sunsets, and swimsuit-clad bodies of the high school cast make these montages delicious eye candy. These montages may well be the show's primary pleasure.

Another key trick the producers use is their liberal inclusion of long close-ups of the characters' relatively blank faces, much like the "egg"—the shot at the end of many daytime soap scenes in which an actor holds an expression for several beats until the scene fades out. The egg is an effective technique in soaps because viewers spend so much time with the characters that they learn to read into their faces, to understand that Sonny's blank look actually displays his fear of hurting his children or his anger at his mafia rival. On the reality soaps, however, viewers spend much less time with the characters, the characters are not nearly as clearly drawn or as complexly represented. We know that Lauren has led a sheltered, privileged life, that she wants to work in fashion, that she cares about her boyfriend even though he has hurt her in the past, that she's generally a nice person (we know this chiefly because her *Laguna* rival, Kristin, is constructed as LC's opposite—a somewhat bitchy tramp). But we don't really understand what motivates her, what she fears or what she hopes. Most soap viewers could write a 10,000-word essay on what any given soap character wants, hopes, fears, etc. This in-depth knowledge of character history is essential to making meaning of a soap, as anyone who attempts to watch one without such background knowledge will attest. But MTV's reality soaps can be meaningful without this sort of back-story, as they draw so heavily—in their musical montages and soap-like "eggs"—on pop culture clichés. We get that Lauren is unsure about getting back together with Jason, her philandering ex-boyfriend, because the music and her smile-free face communicate it. But we understand this not so much because we understand who Lauren is but because we've seen enough music videos and soap-like scripted drama to read the codes.

This meaning-without-meaning spills over into these shows' gender politics, particularly when it comes to the politics of heterosexuality. On *The Hills,* Lauren and Jason reunite when he declares that he misses her and wants her back. In the succeeding episodes, however, Jason repeat-edly treats Lauren like crap, clearly disappointing her. This is communicated by her somber expressions and the music that accompanies her scenes. Yet she also continues to take him back, usually in response to his patented apologies, always accompanied by flowers for her. Daytime soaps tell stories about men who treat women poorly, too. Such stories tend to develop in one of two ways: either the woman breaks free of the jerk and establishes a new sense of self (and, eventually, a new romance with someone who treats her better) or the man undergoes a substantial transformation, realizing the error of his ways and truly changing—at least in his behavior toward the woman he loves. But the first season of *The Hills* did not conclude with either of these potential outcomes. Instead, Lauren turns down a summer internship in Paris to stay with Jason at the Malibu beach house they are renting. Although we are urged to think that Lauren has agonized over her decision, we are also encouraged to believe that she has made the right choice. The season ends with Lauren in Jason's arms, the Malibu sunset affirming the happily-ever-afterness of her choice. She has not left him and found herself; he is not about to change.

Here is where the differing gender and sexual politics of the reality soaps and the daytime soaps are most clear. With its ongoing storytelling and consequent need for character developments, a daytime soap would have to introduce one of the above turns of events in a story such as Lauren's and Jason's. Sure, we'd have watched a multitude of instances just like those on *The Hills,* in which the man behaves badly and the woman takes him back anyway, but these events would be building toward something that would ultimately generate a substantive change. On *The Hills,* because it purports to be "real," and because it has a limited amount of time to tell its story (it's a half-hour weekly series with an eleven-episode season), Lauren and Jason's relationship gets a happy ending. They may face lots of "drama" along the way, but that "drama" is offered as a given of hetero-sexual romance, not as a problematic situation that should change, not only for the sake of storytelling but also for the well-being of those involved. On *The Hills,* this means Lauren's well-being, as she is treated disrespectfully, even abusively, and yet seems resigned to a life in which this kind of "drama" is the only reality that counts. Are these the gendered pleasures to which a new generation of viewers are being drawn?

DECODING THE TEXT

Levine calls MTV's *Laguna Beach* and *The Hills* docu-soaps.

1. Why does she give these shows that name?

2. How are the shows organized?

3. What characters do the shows focus on?

4. What is the appeal of these types of reality shows or docu-soaps?

5. According to Levine, how do the docu-soaps differ from traditional soap operas? From other reality shows? Does she present these differences as positive or negative?

6. Levine primarily focuses on the female characters in these shows. How does she describe these female characters? Why does she focus on females when discussing these shows?

CONNECTING TO YOUR CULTURE

Levine is concerned about the representations of gender that MTV docu-soaps depict, especially because focusing on the unhappiness brought to the female characters is a key plot point of this type of reality show.

1. Do docu-soaps like the ones on MTV actually depict the reality of young people's lives today?

2. Do they depict your life or the lives of those in your circle of friends?

3. Do you watch scripted prime-time shows that feature teenagers or young adults? How would you compare these shows with the docu-soaps that Levine describes? Are the docu-soaps more realistic? What themes or character types do they share?

1. How many shows with Latinos as main characters have appeared on television in the last few decades?

2. How are these characters usually defined or depicted?

3. Are there stereotypical descriptions given, or are you familiar with a range of descriptions used for Latinos on television comedies and dramas?

Rebecca Traister *is a staff writer for* Salon, *where she often writes on the issues of politics and gender in the media. She has also contributed to publications such as* The New York Times, GQ, *and* Elle. *"Class Act" first appeared on http://www.salon.com on November 4, 2006.*

CLASS ACT

Rebecca Traister

You've probably heard a lot about *Ugly Betty,* ABC's new hourlong comedy-soap opera about a supposedly hideous young woman who scores a job as assistant to a foxy male fashion magazine editor. The show's tidily uplifting premise—she is a beast in the beauty industry who in fact brings beauty to a beastly world—along with its crack cast, cuspidate humor and sudsy plot, has helped turn *Ugly Betty* into a rare bona fide hit on fall's television slate. It garners around 16 million viewers a night and is one of only a few new shows to have received orders for a full season.

Ugly Betty's mostly laudatory notices have covered the wan irony of its unlovely title and winning appeal: "Ugly Betty Is a Beauty" and all that. Many critics have also pointed out that Betty, played by America Ferrera, is not ugly. She is merely encumbered by a mouth full of blue metal, one hellacious poncho and a wonky eye for color coordination. The show should be called *Badly Styled Betty*. (And naturally, within a month of *Ugly Betty*'s premiere, newspaper style sections fell predictably in line, touting a new "ugly chic" inspired by the program.)

But those who have taken the title's bait and examined only the aesthetics of the show have missed the point. *Ugly Betty* is not about being unattractive, or at least not simply about being unattractive. It's about class. And ethnicity. Its smart take on cultural and economic differences, enmeshed as it is in a fresh, funny package, makes it positively subversive television.

Betty Suarez is the 22-year-old daughter of Mexican immigrants. She lives in Queens with her widowed father; older sister, Hilda; and Hilda's son, Justin, a fashion-obsessed preteen. But when we first meet Betty, it's in the marble lobby of Meade Publications, where she's awaiting a job interview with an H.R.-bot who needs only an eyeful of her metal-mouthed grin to shut the door in her face. But Betty catches the eye of company founder Bradford Meade, who hires her to assist his son, Daniel (Eric Mabius), recently installed as editor in chief at fashion-bible *Mode* after the untimely departure of *Mode*'s legendary nuclear winter of an editor, Fey Summers. Daniel is the family f**k-up, a playboy who generally prefers his assistants under his desk, administering fellatio.

Bradford hires Betty because he assumes his son will never look twice at a not-anorexic Mexican woman in braces, red spectacles and polymer-fabric cardigans. As far as the lily-white Meades are concerned, Betty might as well not have secondary sexual characteristics: She's so "ugly" that she's not even female. But she is capable and smart, and as it turns out, that's what Daniel needs most in an assistant. He's under siege from *Mode*'s creative director, Wilhelmina (Vanessa Williams), who was passed over for the editor-in-chief post. If this seems convoluted . . . remember folks, it's a soap.

Ugly Betty's debut so soon after this summer's *The Devil Wears Prada* makes it easy to assume that it was inspired by Lauren Weisberger's epic lament of fashion servitude. (The pilot even nodded to the movie by ending with its catchy theme song, "Suddenly I See.") In fact, *Ugly Betty* is the American adaptation of the Colombian telenovela *Yo soy Betty, la fea,* which began airing in 1999 and has since been translated and remade around the world.

Unlike *Prada, Ugly Betty* is not driven by the traumas of the boss-lackey dynamic. This heroine doesn't flinch when she has to put cream cheese on her boss's bagel or get him tickets to the Harvard-Yale game. Betty has serious professional ambitions, but she's sanguine about starting at the bottom of the ladder, happy to be working at a major magazine straight out of college. When compared to her tasks at home—like trying unsuccessfully to persuade the HMO to refill her ailing father's heart medication—ordering a town car doesn't seem quite such an affront to anyone's sensibilities.

Betty la fea's creator, Fernando Gaitán, who is also a producer on *Ugly Betty,* told the *Guardian* in 2000 that telenovelas "are all about the class struggle. They're made for poor people in countries where it's hard to get ahead in life. Usually the characters succeed through love. In mine, they get ahead through work." The U.S. version of *Betty* offers a bracing look at how those class struggles are further fraught by cultural diversity and intolerance, thanks to *Betty* producers Salma Hayek and Silvio Horta, who insisted that it retain a Latina heroine.

The scorn with which Betty is treated at *Mode* has less to do with her looks than with her place of economic and cultural origin. "Are you DE-LIV-ER-ING something?" enunciates receptionist Amanda when Betty first arrives, assuming that a brown girl in a bad outfit could only be a messenger. "Sale at the 99-cent store?" she later remarks when Betty misses a party. When Daniel frets because Betty has taken the "book" home to Queens, Amanda purrs, "You're going to get it back and there's going to be chimichurri sauce *all* over it."

Most egregious is the treatment of the stuffed bunny on Betty's desk, a gift to mark her graduation from Queens College. "One of America's best value colleges!" sneers Wilhelmina's assistant Mark. Betty, like most people in the United States, probably considered value when choosing a college. And the bunny, which endures a toilet-bowl odyssey after being swiped by Betty's colleagues, isn't a Tiffany tennis bracelet or a car or whatever Ross or Rachel probably received when they graduated from college.

With the chimichurri sauce and the stuffed rabbit, *Ugly Betty* has joined shows like *All in the Family, Roseanne, The George Lopez Show, Everybody Hates Chris* and the prematurely axed *Lucky Louie* in the very narrow pantheon of television that has explored what it's like not to be rich and/or white in America.

What makes it extra electric is that unlike those other shows, *Betty* also explores the forbidding traverse to the other side of the class spectrum. The Bunkers didn't leave Queens any more frequently than Roseanne and Dan's brood left their cramped home. But Betty crosses the class ravine daily, hopping from the skyscraping heights of Manhattan to the spicier climes of her home turf.

In this, she shows us a New York City we haven't seen for a while. The myth of shows like *Sex and the City* or *Friends* was that simply living in Gotham put you in close proximity to some glama-glama heartbeat: Cross a bridge and you'll

promptly be waxed, liposuctioned and handed a cosmopolitan. It's a fantasy that still propels the bus tours to Tao and Magnolia Bakery.

Betty lives in New York, but for her familiarity with pink drinks, she might as well be from Cleveland. Her neighborhood isn't made of high-rises or brownstones, but of aluminum-sided row homes. Betty's Queens is a Latina version of Woody Allen's Brooklyn; the Manhattan skyline gleams just across the river like Gatsby's green light, but it is a world away. Where Allen's childhood homes were shaken by roller coasters and populated by relatives glued to radio plays, the Suarez house is engrossed in never-ending telenovelas and shaken by the beat of the Dance-Dance-Revolution video game.

Betty's life at home, where she is stuffed with food and frets about her family's health, plays out in sharp contrast to her life at *Mode,* where no one eats and colleagues fret about wearing 2-year-old Manolo Blahniks. "Sometimes I feel like the E train dropped me off on Mars," Betty confesses in a recent episode.

But part of what's biting is just how true some of even the most outlandish send-ups of the fashion world ring. In one episode, the *Mode* team proposes a fiery-car-crash photo spread to a diva designer with grotesquely inflated lips, forgetting that she recently backed her SUV into 12 pedestrians in front of a club. The whole thing looks like a Brenda Starr strip until you remember: The lips *exist;* the violent fashion spreads *exist;* the celebrity pedestrian-mangler *exists.* The cartoon that is *Mode* is not, in fact, much of a cartoon.

Then there are the comparative preoccupations of the wealthy in contrast to the far less wealthy. Wilhelmina dresses to impress her senator father, who arrives late and sneers, "So you're still *just* a creative director?" Daniel complains to Betty about his dad's favoritism toward his dead brother, while Mama Meade, played with scenery-chewing zeal by Judith Light, is in rehab, where her perfume has been confiscated, forcing her "to smell like . . . people." They're all keeping secrets about extramarital affairs and probably murder.

But one of the lovely things about *Ugly Betty* is that, while it veers precipitously close to finding savage nobility in economic hardship, life in Queens is nearly as dysfunctional as life with the rich and moderately famous. After all, Betty's boyfriend Walter is cheating on her with trampy neighbor Gina Gambaro, who spent a year in juvy and tries to extort Betty for $4,000. Walter is a bizarro-world take on a Manhattan catch; every woman wants him because of his sweet employee discount at the local electronics store. Then there is Betty's dad's own long-kept secret, and the reason Betty's having so much trouble with the HMO: He's been using another man's Social Security number because he's in the country illegally. "Everybody's got problems," Daniel tells Betty. That's true. But *Ugly Betty* puts them in perspective.

Betty's family is not thrilled about the merging of worlds. Her supportive father grumbles that there are no Latina pictures in *Mode* magazine. Walter is horrified when she comes home from "networking night" to "tamale night" having had one mango margarita. Hilda is even more suspicious of her sister's gig, worried that this new world will never admit her. "Why do you do this to yourself," she scolds one night after Betty has been turned away from a work party at a hot club. "I keep telling you those places aren't for people like us."

But the show again escapes the too-good-to-be-true trap by making clear that Betty is not *above* wanting to belong or look good. In Episode 3, at Hilda's urging, she undergoes a makeover. "You want to fit in with these people? They're not going to change. *You* have to," says her sister. "The hair, the face, the clothes. You gotta look it to be it." She whisks Betty to Choli, a local beauty technician who works her magic on Betty's hair, nails and wardrobe.

Betty's transformation is dramatic. With hair piled on top of her head, an outfit of jangling jewelry, a tight skirt and heels, Betty becomes a goddess to the men who catcall her ("She's hot!" exclaims one) as she walks to the subway the next morning. But the look doesn't translate in Manhattan, and it provokes the most scathing round of jeering she's yet received. The other assistants photograph her as if she's a zoo animal, and Wilhelmina scoffs, "It looks like Queens threw up." The message is clear: Queens pretty is not Manhattan pretty. Poor pretty is not rich pretty. Latina pretty is not white pretty.

Ugly Betty is preoccupied with difference—the ways we acknowledge or punish or misinterpret it. Wilhelmina mischaracterizes Betty's work friend, the seamstress Christina, as a "drunken Irish woman." When told that Christina is Scottish, Wilhelmina replies: "Don't care." But she gets ruffled during a discussion of winter holidays, incredulously asking Daniel, "Did you just gesture at me when you said Kwanzaa?" Openly gay Mark advises Betty's fashion-loving nephew Justin, who's admitted that the kids at school don't get him: "Be who you are; wear what you want. Just learn to run real fast."

In exploring the ways we negotiate chasms in status and experience, *Ugly Betty* provides a compelling counterpoint not to *The Devil Wears Prada* but to Sofia Coppola's *Marie Antoinette*. Both are campy, brightly colored candy things. If Coppola's film has politics (and that is still being debated) they are in its portrait of end-of-empire excess that looks familiar at the same time it looks contrived and mildly nauseating. *Ugly Betty*'s depiction of wealth offers something similar. An early scene in which Wilhelmina reclines next to a pyramid of oranges as Mark fills her forehead with Botox might be ripped from the opening credits of *Marie Antoinette*, in which the doomed queen languorously reclines into a foot massage while trawling a finger through an iced cake.

But Coppola's confection has come in for criticism for its unwillingness to visit the angry masses behind the barricades. One of those proles is actually our guide to *Ugly Betty*'s urban Versailles. We see the world of underfed women, racial and economic insularity, and overconsumption of material goods through her eyes, and in counterpoint if not to the starving poor, then at least to the Queens family where you get a stuffed bunny for graduating from college.

But like *Marie Antoinette, Betty* hides its class tensions beneath an effortlessly fun surface. It's a real romance, and Ferrera's tremendous sex appeal is so apparent that she generates sparks with every man with whom she shares the screen, whether it's Daniel or the nerd from accounting who recently introduced her to sushi.

Whatever happens in Betty's love life, for unadulterated television joy it will be hard to beat a scene from the show's fourth episode in which Walter ingratiates himself by serenading Betty with help from a discounted karaoke machine. Temporarily persuaded, she joins him outside, where they sing "Bittersweet and strange, finding you can change," from Betty's favorite movie, *Beauty and the Beast,* sitting on her front stoop as Manhattan glitters in the distance.

DECODING THE TEXT

1. Why does Traister consider *Ugly Betty* subversive television?

2. Do you agree with her?

3. What other television shows fit Traister's definition of subversive television? Why?

4. The essay includes several lines of dialogue from the series. How does this dialogue support Traister's thesis? If you are not familiar with the series, does Traister's description make you want to watch?

Ugly Betty focuses on the problems of both the rich and poor and how each group deals with them.

1. Even if you have never seen an episode of *Ugly Betty,* how can you relate to some of the problems Traister describes in her description of the show and its characters?

2. Is Betty a role model? In what ways is she an ideal character? A realistic character?

3. What communities or cultures does Betty also represent? What communities or cultures do other characters in *Ugly Betty* represent?

CONSIDERING IDEAS

1. How do religion and entertainment coexist on television?

2. How does religion influence television?

3. How does television influence religion?

Mark I. Pinsky *is a former journalist who writes about the issues of faith, media, and popular culture. In addition to his contributions to* Christianity Today, The Columbia Journalism Review, *and* The New York Times, *he is the author of* The Gospel According to *The Simpsons:* The Spiritual Life of America's Most Animated Family *(2001) and* The Gospel According to Disney: Faith, Trust and Pixie Dust *(2004).* "Cartoons (Seriously) Can Teach Us About Faith" *was published in* USA Today *on November 27, 2006.*

CARTOONS (SERIOUSLY) CAN TEACH US ABOUT FAITH

Mark I. Pinsky

Do television's Homer and Bart Simpson have anything to teach us about eternal questions such as how God wants us to worship him, or whether there is one true faith? What does the controversial cable cartoon show *South Park* have to say about the nature of the soul, or how the founders of the world's great religions might get along with each other in the hereafter? Nowhere on the small screen are these weighty issues dealt with on a more regular basis than in edgy, animated comedies.

For some reason, many who might shun such serious topics when presented by

"Cartoons (Seriously) Can Teach Us About Faith" by Mark Pinsky, p. 21 from USA TODAY, November 27, 2006. Reprinted by permission of Mark Pinsky.

religious and educational leaders will listen to debates about theology if they are presented in the context of a cartoon. Over the years, *The Simpsons* has broken long-running TV taboos by including religious plots, themes and characters. My survey of nearly 300 episodes confirms at least one academic study that religion is a staple of the show's plots, jokes and images. Like most Americans (but unlike most live characters on TV), the Simpsons say grace at meals, attend church regularly, read the Bible and pray aloud. For almost 20 years, the show's gifted, highly literate writers, producers and directors have drawn on the divine in ways that animate sincere faith and belief—without caricaturing them.

These days, apart from Billy Graham or Jerry Falwell, America's best-known evangelical is probably Ned Flanders, the Simpsons' goodhearted next-door neighbor. Christians on college campuses have adopted the affectionate, if overdrawn, character as a mascot. As early as 1996, Gerry Bowler, professor of history at the University of Manitoba, called Flanders "television's most effective mortal (i.e., non-angelic) exponent of a Christian life well-lived." *The Simpsons* has been the subject of more than a score of academic papers, including some at Christian colleges and universities, and for good reason.

"The satiric *Simpsons* program takes religion's place in society seriously enough to do it the honor of making fun of it," Bowler wrote in one of the earliest papers. Evangelist and long-time fan Tony Campolo writes that the show "can easily be mistaken for an assault that ridicules middle-class Christianity. It is not! What the show is really depicting through the antics of the Simpsons is the character

of some of the people who are in our churches, and the ways they choose to live out their faith. . . . As an evangelical Christian, I find that *The Simpsons* provides me with a mirror that reflects my own religious life."

Bart, Lisa and the Soul

In one episode dealing with moral dilemmas, bad boy Bart sells his soul to his friend for $5. His sister Lisa is appalled. "How could you do that?" she asks. "Your soul is the most valuable part of you. . . . Whether or not the soul is physically real, Bart, it's the symbol of everything fine inside us. . . . Bart, your soul is the only part of you that lasts forever." In his DVD commentary on this episode, *Simpsons* creator Matt Groening observes, "I love these religious shows, these spiritual shows," which often critique organized religion while honoring sincere faith, "because they please both the Christians and the atheists. Each has their own belief or non-belief system."

Increasingly, *The Simpsons* is not alone in integrating religion and entertainment. Other shows have walked through this door Groening has opened (or kicked in), including *Futurama, King of the Hill, Family Guy, American Dad* and, yes, even Comedy Central's *South Park*. Together, these shows reach millions of viewers— mostly teens and young adults—and millions more through DVD sales and fan websites. Some fans of these shows might spend more time watching them than they do attending weekly religious services.

While the post-*Simpsons* shows deal with faith less frequently, and with considerably less respect, the grappling can be deep, even on a series as nasty, naughty and nihilistic as *South Park*. In one episode, Eric Cartman, the show's pint-size, potty-mouthed villain, cries out to God in despair. After his friends decide to ignore him, Cartman believes he has died and become a living ghost. "How can my own God forsake me?" he asks. Cartman concludes his spirit is trapped on earth, blocked from going to heaven because of his unforgiven sins. So the venal and cynical fourth-grader goes to everyone he has offended in life to ask for forgiveness, and to atone for his sins.

South Park is that part of TV Land where the profane regularly head butts the sacred, a show that has stirred up controversy over episodes about Scientology and Islam. But another episode, devoted to the history and modern practice of Mormonism, was recently the subject of an academic paper and a panel in Salt Lake City. No doubt many Mormons were outraged by the episode's snarky portrayal of their religion—at least if they heard about it, if not saw it. But those attending the symposium on religion and popular culture, sponsored by the liberal Sunstone Education Foundation, were serious and appreciative of the treatment their faith received.

Why this growing interest in religion in cartoons? Why are young viewers willing to accept it and take it seriously? And is this a good thing? As someone who spends a lot of time in houses of worship, where young people are often scarce, I think it is.

Encouraging Dialogue

Some critics may dismiss the discussion of religion in cartoons. But when people, especially young people, sit in a sanctuary pew or a lecture hall to hear someone discuss religion, a veil of skepticism often descends over their minds, filtering what follows. Yet when they are at home or in their dorm rooms, on their couches, watching an animated comedy, their minds tend to remain more open. While few viewers are likely to be spiritually transformed by watching these shows, they can be exposed to aspects of faith, and to critical issues of religion they know nothing about, in a non-threatening way. Serious dialogue can grow out of silly situations.

As hapless Homer Simpson puts it, "It's funny 'cause it's true."

DECODING THE TEXT

1. Are you surprised that Ned Flanders from *The Simpsons* is cited by Pinsky as one of the best-known evangelical Christians on television? If so, why?

2. What details does Pinsky use to support this argument?

3. Do you agree or disagree with Pinsky's main argument?

4. Pinsky discusses the connection of the sacred to the profane. What subjects do you consider sacred? Where do you draw the line in how these subjects can be presented?

1. Pinsky believes that serious dialogue can come out of silly situations, including the silly situations that occur on animated shows. Do you agree?

2. Is there something in your life or the lives of those close to you that might be resolved or at least discussed if the first attempt at discussion was part of a silly situation?

3. Is humor good medicine for serious thoughts or problems?

1. What stories do you tell about yourself? Your family? Your culture?

2. Do these stories change with the type of media you use (for example, audiotape, videotape, websites, Facebook) because of time limits or media limitations?

3. Do these same stories change depending on your audience?

Lynn Spigel *is department chair and professor in the Department of Radio/Television/Film at Northwestern University. Her interests include media and U.S. cultural history, gender and media, and cultural theory. She is the author of* Make Room for TV: Television and the Family Ideal in Postwar America *(1992) and* Welcome to the Dreamhouse: Popular Media and Postwar Suburbs *(2001). "Osama bin Laden Meets the* South Park *Kids" is an excerpt from "Entertainment Wars: Television Culture After 9/11," which was originally published in the journal* American Quarterly *in 2004.*

OSAMA BIN LADEN MEETS THE *SOUTH PARK* KIDS

Lynn Spigel

In the introductory pages of his essay "The Uncanny," Sigmund Freud discusses the intellectual uncertainty he faced during World War I when he found it impossible to keep up with the flow of international publications.[44] In the world of electronic "instant" histories, these problems of intellectual uncertainty are compounded in ways that Freud could never have imagined. The "uncanny" seems an especially appropriate trope for the current situation, as nothing seems to be what it was and everything is what it wasn't just minutes before it happened. In this context, the literate pursuit of history writing seems slow to the point of useless-

Spigel, Lynn. "Entertainment Wars: Television Culture After 9/11." 56:2 (2004), 13 (c) The Johns Hopkins University Press. Reprinted with permission of The Johns Hopkins University Press.

ness. This is, of course, compounded by the fact that the publishing industry is painfully behind the speed of both war and electronic media. So rather than partake of either historical "conclusions" or future "predictions," I want to open up some questions about television and nationalism vis-à-vis the changing economies of industrially produced culture.

Given the political divisions that have resurfaced since 2001, it seems likely that the grand narratives of national unity that sprang up after 9/11 were for many people more performative than sincere. In other words, it is likely that many viewers really did know that all the newfound patriotism was really just a public performance staged by cameras. Still, after 9/11 many people found it important to "perform" the role of citizen, which included the performance of belief in national myths of unity. And if you didn't perform this role, then somehow you were a bad American. In this respect, no matter what they thought of the situation, in the wake of 9/11 stars had to perform the role of "love it or leave it" citizen to remain popular (a lesson that Bill Maher learned with a vengeance when his TV show *Politically Incorrect* was canceled).[45]

But did the performance really work? Just days after the attacks, the limits of performative nationalism were revealed in the televised celebrity telethon *America: A Tribute to Heroes* when, in the final sequence, everyone gathered 'round Willie Nelson to sing "America the Beautiful." Now, this was certainly a bad performance. Most of the celebrities were either too embarrassed to sing, or else they just didn't know the words to this show tune turned national anthem.[46] Some stars were visibly squinting at teleprompt-

ers with consternation, hoping to sing a verse. Yet, because the telethon was foremost aimed at baby boom and post-baby boom generations, most audiences would have known the popular ballads that were directly aimed at these niche generations. Clearly pop songs like John Lennon's "Imagine" (sung by Neil Young), Bob Marley's "Redemption Song" (sung by Wyclef Jean), or Paul Simon's "Bridge over Troubled Water" have more historical meaning to these taste publics than any national anthem does.

More generally, I think the post-9/11 performance of nationalism will fail because it really does not fit with the economic and cultural practices of twenty-first-century U.S. media society. The fact that there is no longer a three-network broadcast system means that citizens are not collected as aggregate audiences for national culture. As we all know, what we watch on TV no longer really is what other people watch—unless they happen to be in our demographic taste culture. The postnetwork system is precisely about fragmentation and narrowcasting. While the new five-hundred-channel cable systems may not provide true diversity in the sense of political or cultural pluralism, the postnetwork system does assume a culture that is deeply divided by taste, not one that is unified through national narratives.[47] In a multinational consumer culture it becomes difficult for media to do business without addressing the niche politics of style, taste, and especially youth subcultures that have become central to global capitalism. In the end, the new media environment does not lend itself to unifying narratives of patriotism, if only because these older forms of nationalism have nothing to do with the "return to normalcy" and normal levels of consumption. While nationalist popular culture does, of course, exist (and obviously rose in popularity after 9/11), it appears more as another niche market (those people who hang flags on their cars) than as a unifying cultural dominant.[48]

The actual cultural styles in these new narrowcast media markets are increasingly based on irony, parody, skepticism, and "TV-literate" critical reading protocols. For people who grew up watching *The Simpsons'* hilarious parodies of mass culture and national politics; for people who fell asleep to Dave Letterman or Conan O'Brien; and for viewers who regularly watched *Saturday Night Live, In Living Color, The Daily Show,* and *Mad TV*'s political/news parodies, a sudden return to blind patriotism (and blind consumerism) is probably not really likely.

In the first week after the September 11 attacks, the cable operators and networks all did cover the same story—and for a moment the nation returned to something very much like the old three-network system.[49] Yet, the case of 9/11 also demonstrates that in the current media landscape it is hard to sustain the fantasy of utopian collectivity that had been so central to previous media events. Comparing media coverage of 9/11 with the coverage of the Kennedy assassination, Fredric Jameson argues that back in 1963 a utopian fantasy of collectivity was in part constructed through news reporters' "clumsiness [and] the technological naiveté in which they sought to rise to the occasion." But, he claims, the media are now so full of orchestrated spectacle and public violence on a daily basis that many people had a hard time seeing media coverage of 9/11 as documents of

anything sincere, much less as any kind of intersubjective, utopian communication. As Jameson puts it, despite the many claims that America lost its innocence on 9/11, it was "not America, but rather its media [that had] . . . definitively lost its innocence."[50]

Certainly, for industry executives who work in the competitive environment of narrowcasting, sentiments of national belonging and utopian collectivity quickly gave way to the "bottom line." In fact, even in the "good will" climate of September 2001, the industry was still widely aware of the competitive realities of the postnetwork marketplace. CNN, which then had an exclusive deal with the Al Jazeera network, tried to block other news outlets from broadcasting its satellite transmissions of bin Laden's video address.[51] Even the celebrity telethon was a source of industry dispute. Worried that cable telecasts would undercut audience shares for broadcasters, some network affiliates and network-owned-and-operated stations tried to stop a number of cable channels from simulcasting *America: A Tribute to Heroes.* According to *Variety,* upon hearing of possible cable competition, "some of the vocal managers at the Big Four TV stations . . . went bananas and threatened to cancel the telethon and schedule their own local programming."[52] So much for humanitarianism in the postnetwork age!

Given this competitive media marketplace, it comes as no surprise that industry insiders quickly revised their initial predictions about the fate of American popular culture. By October 4, the front page of the *New York Times* proclaimed, "In Little Time Pop Culture Is Back to Normal," stating that the industry was backtracking on its initial predictions that the events of September 11 would completely change culture. David Kissinger, president of the USA Television Production Group, told the *Times* that the industry's initial reaction to the attacks may have been overstated and that because most industry people were "terror stricken" on September 11, "we shouldn't be held accountable for much of what we said that week."[53]

In fact, within a month, even irony was back in vogue, especially on late-night TV, but increasingly also on entertainment programs. By early November, Comedy Central's *South Park*—a cartoon famous for its irreverence—ran an episode in which the *South Park* kids visit Afghanistan. Once there, Cartman (*South Park*'s leading bad boy) meets bin Laden, and the two engage in an extended homage to Warner Bros. cartoons. Bin Laden takes the roles of the wacky Daffy Duck, the dull-headed Elmer Fudd, and even the lovesick Pepe La Pew (he is shown romancing a camel much as Pepe romances a cat that he thinks is a skunk). Meanwhile, Cartman plays the ever-obnoxious Bugs Bunny (like Bugs, he even does a drag performance as a harem girl wooing a lovesick bin Laden, whose eyes, in classic Tex Avery cartoon style, pop out of his head).

Although the episode was the usual "libertarian" hodgepodge of mixed political messages (some seemingly critical of U.S. air strikes, others entirely Orientalist), its blank ironic sensibility did at least provide for some unexpected TV moments. In one scene, when the *South Park* kids meet Afghan children in a war-torn village, American claims of childish innocence (promoted, for example, in *The West Wing*'s fictional

classroom) are opened up for comic interrogation. Dodging a U.S. bomb attack, the Afghan children tell the *South Park* kids, "Over a third of the world hates America." "But why?" ask the *South Park* kids, "Why does a third of the world hate us?" And the Afghan kids reply, "Because you don't realize that a third of the world hates you." While the episode ends with an over-the-top cartoon killing of bin Laden and an American flag waving to the tune of "America the Beautiful," the program establishes such a high degree of pastiche, blank irony, and recombinant imagery that it would be difficult to say that it encourages any particular "dominant" reading of the war. The laughter seems directed more at semiotic breakdowns, perhaps mimicking the way in which news coverage of the war seems to make people increasingly incapable of knowing what's going on—a point that one of the *South Park* characters underscores at the end of the show, when he says, "I'm confused."

To be sure, programs like *South Park* and the niche cable channels on which they appear might not translate into the old enlightenment dream of "public service" TV with a moral imperative for its national public. Television studies is, of course, riddled with debates over the question of whether these new forms of narrowcasting and multichannel media outlets will destroy what some critics call common culture. In response to the increasing commercialization and fragmentation of European electronic media, scholars like Jostein Gripsrud, Graham Murdock, and James Curran champion European public service broadcast models, and even while they do not advocate a simplistic return to paternalistic models of "cultivation" and taste, they seek a way to reformulate the ideal of an electronic democratic culture.[54] In the United States the situation is somewhat different. The "public interest" policy rhetoric on which the national broadcast system was founded has been woefully under-achieved; broadcasters did not engage a democratic culture of diverse interests, but rather for the most part catered to the cultural tastes of their target consumers (which for many years meant white middle-class audiences). Moreover, the networks often interpreted public service requirements within the context of public relations and the strengthening of their own oligopoly power.[55] Meanwhile, the underfunded Public Broadcasting System grew increasingly dependent on corporate funding. And, as Laurie Ouellette argues, by relying on paternalistic notions of "cultivation" and catering to narrow-minded taste hierarchies, the network has alienated audiences.[56]

Still, I am not saying that the new multichannel and multiplatform system of niche culture is necessarily better. Instead, we need to ask exactly what the new fragmented niche networks, as well as the proliferation of Internet sites, provide. What do the new forms of multinational media outlets offer beyond the proliferation of products and styles? The question is even more complex when we consider the fact that cable and broadcast networks, Internet sites, search engines, television producers/distributors, movie studios, radio stations, newspapers, and publishing companies are increasingly part of global conglomerate media structures (Disney, Rupert Murdock's News Corp., Viacom, Time-Warner, etc.).[57] In the media industries, as in other postindustrial modes of capitalism, there is both fragmentation and centralization at the same time. Any attempt to consider the political effects of the multiplication of channels (and fragmentation of audiences) still has to be considered within the overall patterns of consolidation at the level of ownership.[58]

Perhaps I am a bit overly optimistic, but I do want to end by suggesting some alternative possibilities within the highly consolidated, yet also fragmented, global mediasphere. As Daniel Dayan and Elihu Katz argue, although media events may be hegemonically sponsored and often function to restore consensual values, they always also "invite reexamination of the status quo." Following Victor Turner, Dayan and Katz claim that media events put audiences in a "liminal" context, outside the norms of the everyday. Even if media events do not institutionalize new norms, they do "provoke . . . mental appraisal of alternative possibilities."[59] In this sense, although I have focused primarily on media myths of reunification and nationalism, it is also true that 9/11 provoked counternarratives and political dialogues. In particular, 9/11 made people aware of new prospects for communication in a rapidly changing media environment.

Certainly, the Internet allowed for a collective interrogation of mainstream media and discussions among various marginalized groups. According to Bruce A. Williams, while "mainstream media reiterated themes of national unity, the chat rooms allowed different groups of Americans to debate what the impact of the attacks was for them specifically."[60] Internet sites like Salon.com—as well as access to a host of international news outlets—provided alternative views and global discussions. Convergence platforms opened up venues for expression. For example, after 9/11 a chat room hosted by the Black Entertainment Television network included conversations about whether it was possible to reconcile black beliefs about racist police and fire departments with the heroic images of police and firefighters after 9/11. Resistance groups from around the globe used the Internet as a forum for antiwar e-mails, virtual marches, and group organizing. The Social Science Research Council's Web site allowed scholars to weigh in on the events at Internet speed. The "low-tech" medium of radio (especially National Public Radio) likewise provided alternative voices.

That said, my point here is not that "new" media or "alternative media" are categorically "better" than TV. Certainly, many Internet sites and talk radio stations were filled with right-wing war fever. As Williams suggests, because the Internet allows for insular conversations, some message boards (such as "Crosstar") discussed ways to draw clear ideological boundaries and to keep "dissident voices" (i.e., liberals) off the board.[61] In this respect, we should not embrace the Internet in some essentialist sense as a pure space of pluralism which is always already more democratic than "old" media. Instead, it seems more accurate to say that the presence of multiple media platforms holds out hopeful possibilities for increased expression, but what this will amount to in terms of democracy and citizenship remains a complex historical question.

In addition to the Internet, the presence of the Al Jazeera news network had a destabilizing effect on the status of information itself. Al Jazeera officials defy the democratic legacy of the "free press" that had been so crucial to U.S. Cold War politics. Whereas the United States used to claim that its so-called free press was a reigning example of "free world" democracy, Al Jazeera now has taken up the same public pose, claiming that it will present all sides of the story from a Middle Eastern vantage point. In their book on Al Jazeera, Mohammed El-Nawawy and Adel Iskandar discuss how the network's post-9/11 coverage—especially its graphic coverage of the U.S. bombings in Afghanistan and the circulation of bin Laden's videotapes—quickly became a public relations crisis for the Bush administration.[62] Troubled by the bad PR, the Bush administration formed a Hollywood summit to discuss the role the industry might play in the war on terrorism. The military also met with Hollywood talent at the University of Southern California's Institute for Creative Technologies, a military/Hollywood alliance that Jonathan Burston aptly terms "militainment."[63] By late November 2001 President Bush had signed an initiative to start the Middle East Radio network (which strives to counterbalance anti-Americanism in the Arab world and is aimed especially at youth audiences).[64] As such federally sponsored efforts suggest, the proliferation of news outlets, entertainment networks, and Internet sites, as well as the mounting synergy between Hollywood and the military, has changed the nature of semiotic warfare, and the United States is certainly keen to play by the new rules of the game.[65]

Back to Normal?

On the one hand, as I have suggested, much of the TV landscape looks like a continuation of the same kinds of programs that aired prior to 9/11, and for this reason it is tempting to say that television's "return to normal" transcended the events of 9/11 and that everything is as it was before. On the other hand, 9/11 haunts U.S. commercial television.[66] The memory of 9/11 now—in 2004—circulates in ways that disrupt the kind of historical narratives and nationalist logic that had been so central to the initial return to the normal TV schedule.

Since 2001 the history and memory of 9/11 have in fact become a national battleground—not only in the notorious fights over Ground Zero's reconstruction but also in the electronic spaces of television. By March of 2002 major networks had begun to feature commemorative documentaries that told the story of 9/11.[67] By March of 2004 President Bush launched a presidential campaign with TV ads that show historical footage of the firefighters, implicitly equating their heroism with his presidency. But whereas nationalist historical pedagogy initially served to solidify consent for the Bush administration, now the history and memory of 9/11 are not so simply marshaled. On March 5, 2004, just one day after the ads began to circulate, CNN interviewed a woman who had lost her husband on 9/11. Unlike the speechless pregnant widows on *Oprah* back in 2001, this woman had regained her voice and spoke quite articulately of her disgust for the President's use of 9/11 footage for political ends.

In the end, I suspect that the current situation is ripe for new visions of apocalyptic techno-futures, with satellites, guided missiles, surveillance cameras, and communication media of all kinds at the core of an ongoing genre of techno-warfare criticism waged by Jean Baudrillard, Paul Virilio, and many others.[68] But it seems to me that, as forceful and perceptive as this

kind of work has been, this is really just the easy way out. Instead of engaging in yet another stream of doom-and-gloom technological disaster criticism, it seems more useful to think about how cultural studies and media studies in particular might hold on to a politics of hope. What I have in mind is in no way the same as utopian claims to transcendence and unity (whether local, national, or global) through new media technologies. Rather, this politics of hope is situated in a confrontation with the actually existing historical divisions around us. This materialist politics of hope should embrace the new global media environment as an opportunity to listen to "the third of the world that hates us" rather than (to use Bush's formulation) clutter the globe with messages about "how good we are." The world has heard enough about America. Time now to tune in elsewhere.

Notes

44. Sigmund Freud, "The Uncanny," in *Studies in Parapsychology* (1919; New York: Collier Books, 1963), 19–60. Freud discusses his lack of bibliographical references vis-à-vis the war in Europe on page 20.

45. When I delivered this paper at a conference at the University of California, Berkeley, Ratiba Hadj-Moussa pointed out that this dynamic of national performance doesn't necessarily suggest that people don't in some way believe in the performance. I want to thank her for this observation. Clearly, through the act of national performance, it is possible to actually to believe in the role you are playing—and even to believe in it more than ever!

46. Note, too, that "America the Beautiful" replaced the actual national anthem after 9/11 because no one seemed to be able to remember the words to the "Star-Spangled Banner."

47. Even news is now a matter of taste and "branded" by networks in ways that appeal to consumer profiles. For example, the news on Fox (especially its markedly conservative

talk shows) attracts one of cable TV's most loyal publics, but many on the left mock its pretense of "Fair and Balanced" reporting. Al Franken's best-seller *Lies and the Lying Liars Who Tell Them: A Fair and Balanced Look at the Right* (New York: E. P. Dutton, 2003) and his lawsuit with Fox obviously drew on the more left-associated taste publics that define themselves in distinction—in Bourdieu's sense—not only to Fox News but also to the viewers who (they imagine) watch it. For his discussion of taste as social distinction, see Pierre Bourdieu, *Distinction: A Social Critique of the Judgement of Taste,* trans. Richard Nice (Cambridge: Harvard University Press, 1984).

48. Even before the attacks, patriotic symbols were re-emerging as a fashion fad. Corporations such as Tommy Hilfiger, Polo Ralph Lauren, and Gap Inc.'s Old Navy sported the flag trend, while European haute couture designer Catherine Malandrino unveiled her flag-motif fall collection in the summer of 2001 (which included a skirt that Madonna wore on her concert tour). See Teri Agins, "Flag Fashion's Surging Popularity Fits with Some Fall Collections," *Wall Street Journal,* September 19, 2001, B5. According to Agins, the post-9/11 flag fashions were an extension of this trend, not an invention of it.

49. In 1992 Dayan and Katz speculated on the fate of television, nationalism, and media events in what they saw to be an increasingly multichannel and segmented television system. They argued that while the old three-network or public broadcast systems "will disappear," television's previous functions of "national integration may devolve upon" media events. Their speculation now seems particularly apt. They also predicted that with new technologies and possible erosion of the nation state, "media events may then create and integrate communities larger than nations." See Dayan and Katz, *Media Events,* 23.

50. Fredric Jameson, "The Dialectics of Disaster," *South Atlantic Quarterly* 101 (Spring 2002): 300.

51. According to *Variety,* news organizations were "furious that CNN wouldn't forego competition" and "rallied against exclusives,

saying that they don't serve the public's interest during a time of national crisis." ABC News spokesperson Jeffrey Schneider disputed any exclusivity deal by arguing fair use. He said, "There was no question in anybody's mind that these images from Al Jazeera were of compelling national interest," and "We felt we had a duty to broadcast them to the American people which far outweighed whatever commercial agenda CNN was attempting to pursue in this time of war." Meanwhile, Walter Isaacson, CEO of CNN News Group, told *Variety* that CNN had a "reciprocal affiliate deal" with Al Jazeera and that "it's Al Jazeera's material and we don't have a right to give it away." Isaacson did admit, however, that "in a time of war, we won't make a big deal about this sort of thing." See Paul Bernstein and Pamela McClintock, "Newsies Fight over Bin Laden Interview," *Variety.com,* October 7, 2001, 1–2.

52. John Dempsey, "Invite to Cablers to Join Telethon Irks Affils," *Variety.com,* September 20, 2001, 1. The underlying reasons for the broadcasters' concern had to do with issues of East Coast–West Coast transmission times. The big four networks—ABC, CBS, NBC, and Fox—aired the telethon at 9 p.m. eastern time, and because they wanted to make it seem like a simultaneous nationwide event, they also showed it taped via a dual feed at 9 p.m. on the West Coast. Some single-feed cable networks such as TBS and the National Geographic Channel, however, planned to show the telethon live at 6 p.m. on the West Coast, and thereby preempt the 9 p.m. taped West Coast network broadcast. Some network affiliates and owned and operated stations were simply unhappy that any cable networks were airing the telethon, even if cablers showed it simultaneously (at 9 p.m.) with the Big Four.

53. David Kessinger, cited in Rick Lyman with Bill Carter, "In Little Time Pop Culture Is Almost Back to Normal," *New York Times,* October 4, 2001.

54. See, for example, Jostein Gripsrud, ed., *Television and Common Knowledge* (New York: Routledge, 1999), esp. Graham Murdock, "Rights and Representations," 7–17;

James Curran, "Mass Media and Democracy Revisited," in *Mass Media and Society,* ed. James Curran and Michael Gurevitch, 2nd ed. (London: Arnold, 1996), 81–119.

55. See, for example, Vance Kepley Jr., "The Weaver Years at NBC," *Wide Angle* 12 (April 1990): 46–63, and "From 'Frontal Lobes' to the 'Bob and Bob Show': NBC Management and Programming Strategies, 1949–65," in *Hollywood in the Age of Television,* ed. Tino Balio (Boston: Unwin-Hyman, 1990), 41–62; Lynn Spigel, "The Making of a Television Literate Elite," in *The Television Studies Book,* ed. Christine Geraghty and David Lusted (London: Arnold, 1998), 63–85.

56. Laurie Ouellette, *Viewers Like You? How Public TV Failed the People* (New Brunswick, N.J.: Rutgers University Press, 2002).

57. ABC is now owned by Disney (which owns, for example, the Disney theme parks, radio stations, cable networks like ESPN and Lifetime, retail outlets, feature film companies, newspapers, and magazines); the multiple-system operator Comcast has recently bid for the now-struggling Walt Disney Company; CBS is owned by Viacom (which also owns, for example, Paramount Studios as well as cable networks like MTV and Nickelodeon, theme parks, and radio stations); NBC is owned by General Electric (which entered into a joint venture with Microsoft and owns MSNBC); and Fox is owned by Rupert Murdock's News Corp. (which owns, for example, Fox Broadcasting; Fox News Channel; Fox Sports Net; motion picture companies; magazines like *TV Guide, Elle,* and *Seventeen;* book publishers; and numerous newspapers and delivers entertainment and information to at least 75 percent of the globe). Meanwhile, media conglomerate Time-Warner owns a large number of cable channels, production companies, home video, magazines, music companies, and book publishers (for example, HBO, Cinemax, TNT, Comedy Central, E! Entertainment, Black Entertainment Television, Time-Life Video, Warner Bros. Television, Book of the Month Club, and its notorious deal with America Online). With telephone and cable operators acquiring and partnering with media corporations

and moving into content, the synergy among these sectors is even more pronounced. These ownership structures make these media organizations more like vertically integrated movie studios of the classical period, as they have controlling stakes in all sectors of their industry—production, distribution, and exhibition—in addition to obvious benefits of owning multiple and related companies that reduce risk and increase opportunities for synergy between different companies in the umbrella corporation. Note, however, that the great instability of the technologies market (including, of course, the fate of AOL and the AOL–Time Warner merger) begs us to ask new questions regarding the future of media conglomeration and convergence.

58. Media conglomerates often say that consolidation of ownership leads to more choice (for example, some media conglomerates claim that consolidation of business holdings allows them to use income from their mainstream media outlets to launch minority channels). A variety of media activists, industry executives, media scholars, and government officials have, however, sharply attacked conglomeration and questioned the degree to which freedom of speech and diversity of representation can exist in a deregulated media system in which just a few major corporations own most of the media sources. See, for example, Patricia Aufderheide, *Communications Policy and the Public Interest: The Telecommunications Act of 1996* (New York: Guilford Press, 1999); Patricia Aufderheide, ed., *Conglomerates and the Media* (New York: New Press, 1997); Robert McChesney, *Corporate Media and the Threat to Democracy* (New York: Seven Stories Press, 1997); Ben H. Bagdikian, *The Media Monopoly,* 6th ed. (Beacon Press, 2000); Dean Alger, *Megamedia: How Giant Corporations Dominate Mass Media, Distort Competition, and Endanger Democracy* (New York: Rowman and Littlefield, 1998).

59. Dayan and Katz, *Media Events,* 20.

60. Bruce A. Williams, "The New Media Environment, Internet Chatrooms, and Public Discourse after 9/11," in Thussu and Freedman, eds., *War and the Media,* 183. It should

be noted that the Pew Research Center found that nine out of ten Americans were getting their news primarily from television after the 9/11 attacks. See "Troubled Times for Network Evening News," *Washington Post,* March 10. Citing an ABC News poll, however, Williams claims that "almost half of all Americans now get news over the Internet, and over a third of them increased their reliance on online sources after September 11" ("New Media Environment," 176).

61. Williams, "New Media Environment," 182. Although Williams cites various online attempts to draw ideological boundaries, he doesn't necessary view this as a bad thing. While he admits that some such attempts were disturbing, he also argues that "insular conversations that are not easily accessible to the wider public play a positive role by allowing marginalized groups to clarify their distinct values in opposition to those of the society-at-large within the safety of a sympathetic and homogeneous group" (184). Despite his pointing to the insular nature of the Web and the desire of some groups to draw ideological boundaries, Williams also argues that there was a general air of civility on the Internet (188–89).

62. The administration viewed the presence of Al Jazeera's graphic war footage and bin Laden's videotapes (which were aired around the world) as a grave problem. On October 3, 2001 (a few days before the bombings began), Secretary of State Colin Powell asked the Qatari emir, Sheikh Hamad bin Khalifa, to "tone down" Al Jazeera's inflammatory rhetoric, and the Bush administration specifically requested that the tapes be taken off the network. The International Press Institute sent a letter to Colin Powell, stating that Powell's tactics had "serious consequences for press freedom" (176–77). Al Jazeera journalists defended their coverage of graphic images by stating that they were trying to cover the war objectively, from both sides (Mohammed El-Nawawy and Adel Iskandar, *Al Jazeera: The Story of the Network That Is Rattling Governments and Redefining Modern Journalism,* updated ed. [Cambridge, Mass.: Westview Press, 2002], 176–81). See

also El-Nawawy and Iskandar's discussion of Europe's and Al Jazeera's coverage of Afghanistan (ibid., 186–89).

63. Jonathan Burston, "War and the Entertainment Industries: New Research Priorities in an Era of Cyber-Patriotism," in Thussu and Freedman, eds., *War and the Media,* 163–75. For more, see James Der Derian, *Virtuous War: Mapping the Military Industrial Media Entertainment Network* (Boulder, Colo.: Westview, 2001). At ICT, technologies such as immersive simulation games are being developed simultaneously for entertainment and military uses.

64. A member of the Bush administration met with Hollywood studio chiefs and network executives in Beverly Hills on October 18 to discuss efforts to "enhance the perception of America around the world." See Peter Bart, "H'wood Enlists in War," *Variety.com,* October 17, 2001, 1–3. A few weeks later, they gathered in what was referred to as a "summit" to discuss more detailed plans for Hollywood's participation in the war effort. See Rick Lyman, "White House Sets Meeting with Film Executives to Discuss War on Terrorism," *Variety.com,* November 8, 2001, 1–3. See also Pamela McClintock, "Nets Rally Stars around Flag," *Variety.com,* December 3, 2001, 1–2.

65. Meanwhile, in a connected fashion, Al Jazeera's presence also threatens the hegemony of Western global news sources. Driven by fierce competition for Arab audiences, in January 2002 CNN officially launched its Arabic Web site, CNNArabic.com. See Noureddine Miladi, "Mapping the Al Jazeera Phenomenon," in Thussu and Freedman, eds., *War and the Media,* 159. Note that CNN launched the Web site at the same time (January 2002) that Al Jazeera withdrew its exclusivity agreement with CNN because of the dispute over a tape CNN aired without its approval.

66. In a provocative thesis, Bret Maxwell Dawson argues that while TV returned to much of its previous content, television's temporal and narrational forms were "traumatized" by 9/11. He argues that the effects of this trauma can be seen in the way that elements of catastrophe television (e.g., live broadcasts, an aura of authenticity, and an

obsession with time) have appeared with increasing popularity in reality TV and programs like Fox's *24*. See his "TV since 9/11" (master's thesis, University of New South Wales, Sydney, Australia, 2003). While I would not posit such deterministic notions of trauma, it does seem useful to think about how 9/11 relates to a particular historical conjuncture in aesthetic ideals of TV realism, and in particular TV's obsession with the reality genre and real time (which, as Dawson admits, began before 9/11).

67. This cycle of memorializing documentaries began with CBS's *9/11* (aired March 10, 2002), which was followed by *Telling Nicholas* (HBO, May 12, 2002), *In Memoriam: New York City, 9.11* (HBO, May 26, 2002), and others. For a seminar I taught at UCLA, Sharon Sharp wrote a very interesting paper "Remembering 9/11: Memory, History, and the American Family," which considers how these documentaries used sentimental images of the family in crisis to tell histories of 9/11.

68. Baudrillard and Virilio both have published monographs on 9/11. See Jean Baudrillard, *The Spirit of Terrorism and Requiem for the Twin Towers,* trans. Chris Turner (London: Verso, 2002); Paul Virilio, *Ground Zero,* trans. Chris Turner (London: Verso, 2002).

DECODING THE TEXT

Spigel argues that many people gave performances of being a good citizen after 9/11.

1. What are some of these performances that she describes?

2. Do you agree with the idea that these are performances and not just something else?

3. What word choice does Spigel use to represent how she feels about these performances?

4. How does Spigel organize the essay? How does this organization affect your reading?

CONNECTING TO YOUR CULTURE

1. Where do you get your news stories from—what type of media?

2. Do you look at more than one medium when you are interested in a story? Why would this be a good idea?

3. What effect do you think the events of 9/11 had on America? On popular culture? How were you affected personally?

Reading Selection:
Across the Decades

CONSIDERING IDEAS

1. How is the working class depicted or described on television in general?

2. How about in sitcoms?

3. Think of the working-class families or characters you know from television. What do these families or characters have in common?

4. Are they depicted or described in stereotypical ways?

Richard Butsch *is professor of sociology and American studies at Rider University. His publications include* For Fun and Profit: The Transformation of Leisure into Consumption *(1990) and* The Making of American Audiences from Stage to Television, 1750–1990 *(2000). This essay is an excerpt from "Ralph, Fred, Archie, and Homer," which was published in* Gender, Race, and Class in Media: A Text-Reader, *2nd edition, in 2003.*

RALPH, FRED, ARCHIE, AND HOMER

Why Television Keeps Re-creating the White Male Working-Class Buffoon

Richard Butsch

Strewn across our mass media are portrayals of class that justify class relations of modern capitalism. Studies of 50 years of comic strips, radio serials, television drama, movies, and popular fiction reveal a very persistent pattern, an underrepresentation of working-class occupations and an overrepresentation of professional and managerial occupations among characters.[1]

My own studies of class in prime-time network television family series from 1946 to 1990 (Butsch, 1992; Butsch & Glennon, 1983; Glennon & Butsch, 1982) indicate that this pattern is persistent over four decades of television, in 262 domestic situation comedies, such as *I Love Lucy, The Brady Bunch, All in the Family,* and *The Simpsons.* In only 11% of the series were heads of house portrayed as working class, that is, holding occupations as blue-collar, clerical, or unskilled or semiskilled service workers. Blue-collar families were most underrepresented: only 4% (11 series) compared with 45% of American families in 1970.

Widespread affluence was exaggerated as well. More lucrative, glamorous, or prestigious professions predominated over more mundane ones: 9 doctors to 1 nurse, 19 lawyers to 2 accountants, 7 college professors to 2 schoolteachers. Working wives were almost exclusively middle class and in pursuit of a career. Working-class wives, such as in *Roseanne,* who have to work to help support the family, were very rare. Particularly notable was the prevalence of servants: one of every five series had a maid or butler.

The working class is not only underrepresented; the few men who are portrayed are buffoons. They are dumb, immature, irresponsible, or lacking in common sense. This is the character of the husbands in almost every sitcom depicting a blue-collar (white) male head of house, *The Honeymooners, The Flintstones, All in the Family,* and *The Simpsons* being the most famous examples. He is typically well-intentioned, even lovable, but no one to respect or emulate. These men are played against more mature, sensible wives, such as Ralph against Alice in *The Honeymooners.*

In most middle-class series, there is no buffoon. More typically, both parents are wise and work cooperatively to raise their children in practically perfect families, as in *Father Knows Best, The Brady Bunch,* and *The Cosby Show.* In the few middle-class series featuring a buffoon, it is the dizzy wife, such as Lucy. The professional/managerial husband is the sensible, mature partner. Inverting gender status in working-class but not middle-class sitcoms is a statement about class.

How Does It Happen?
The prevalence of such views of working class men well illustrates ideological hegemony, the dominance of values in mainstream culture that justify and help to maintain the status quo. Blue-collar workers are portrayed as requiring supervision, and managers and professionals as intelligent and mature enough to provide it. But do viewers, and particularly the working class, accept these views? Only a handful of scattered, incidental observations (Blum, 1969; Gans, 1962; Jhally & Lewis, 1992; Vidmar & Rokeach, 1974) consider how people have responded to portrayals of class.

And why does television keep reproducing these caricatures? How does it happen? Seldom have studies of television industries pinpointed how specific content arises. Studies of production have not been linked to studies of content any more than audience studies have. What follows is an effort to make that link between existing production studies and persistent images of working-class men in domestic sitcoms. In the words of Connell (1978), "No evil-minded capitalistic plotters need be assumed because the production of ideology is seen as the more or less automatic outcome of the normal, regular processes by which commercial mass communications work in a capitalist system" (p. 195). The simple need to make a profit is a structural constraint that affects content (see also Ryan, 1992).

Let us then examine how the organization of the industry and television drama production may explain class content in television series. I will look at three levels of organization: (a) network domination of the industry, (b) the organization of decisions within the networks and on the production line, and (c) the work community and culture of the creative personnel. I will trace how these may explain the consistency and persistence of the portrayals, the underrepresentation of the working class, and the choice of the particular stereotypes of working-class men in prime-time domestic sitcoms.

Network Domination and Persistent Images

For four decades ABC, CBS, and NBC dominated the television industry. Of all television audiences, 90% watched network programs. The networks accounted for over half of all television advertising revenues in the 1960s and 1970s and just under half by the late 1980s (Owen & Wildman, 1992). They therefore had the money and the audience to dominate as almost the sole buyers of drama programming from Hollywood producers and studios.[2]

During the 1980s, the three-network share of the audience dropped from about 90% to 60%; network share of television ad revenues declined from 60% to 47% (Owen & Wildman, 1992). These dramatic changes have generated many news stories of the demise of the big three. Cable networks and multistation owners (companies that own several local broadcast stations) began to challenge the dominance of the big three. They became

alternative markets for producers as they began purchasing their own programs.

But program development is costly; even major Hollywood studios are unwilling to produce drama programs without subsidies from buyers. Nine networks have sufficient funds in the 1990s to qualify as buyers of drama programming: the four broadcast networks (ABC, CBS, Fox, and NBC) and five cable networks (Disney, HBO, Showtime, TNT, and USA Network) (Blumler & Spicer, 1990). But ABC, CBS, and NBC still account for the development of the overwhelming majority of new drama series, the programming that presents the same characters week after week—and year after year in reruns.

This is the case in part because the broadcast networks still deliver by far the largest audiences. Even in 1993, the combined ratings for the 20 largest cable audiences would still only rank 48th in ratings for broadcast network shows. The highest rated cable network, USA Network, reached only 1.5% of the audience, compared to an average of 20% for ABC, NBC, and CBS. The larger audiences translate into more dollars for program development.

And producers still prefer to work for the broadcast networks. When sold to broadcast networks, their work receives much broader exposure, which enhances their subsequent profits from syndication after the network run and increases the likelihood for future purchases and employment.

Moreover, whether or not dominance by the big three has slipped, many of the same factors that shaped their programming decisions shape the decisions of their competitors as well. The increased number of outlets has not resulted in the innovation and diversity in program development once expected. Jay Blumler and Carolyn Spicer (1990) interviewed more than 150 industry personnel concerned with program decision making and found that the promise of more openness to innovation and creativity was short-lived. The cost of drama programming limits buyers to only a handful of large corporations and dictates that programs attract a large audience and avoid risk. How has this affected content?

Using their market power, the networks have maintained sweeping control over production decisions of even highly successful producers from initial idea for a new program to final film or tape (Bryant, 1969, pp. 624–626; Gitlin, 1983; Pekurny, 1977, 1982; Winick, 1961). Their first concern affecting program decisions is risk avoidance. Popular culture success is notoriously unpredictable, making decisions risky. The music recording industry spreads investment over many records so that any single decision is less significant (Peterson & Berger, 1971). Spreading risk is not a strategy available to networks (neither broadcast nor cable), because only a few programming decisions fill the prime-time hours that account for most income. Networks are constrained further from expanding the number of their decisions by their use of the series as the basic unit of programming. The series format increases ratings predictability from week to week. Each decision, then, represents a considerable financial risk, not simply in production costs but in advertising income. For example, ABC increased profits from $35 million in 1975 to $185 million in 1978 by raising its average prime-time ratings from 16.6 to 20.7 (personal communication, W. Behanna, A. C. Nielsen Company, June 1980).

Because programming decisions are risky and costly and network executives' careers rest on their ability to make the right decisions, they are constrained, in their own interest, to avoid innovation and novelty. They stick to tried-and-true formulas and to producers with a track record of success (Brown, 1971; Wakshlag & Adams, 1985). The result is a small, closed community of proven creative personnel (about 500 producers, writers, directors) closely tied to and dependent on the networks (Gitlin, 1983, pp. 115, 135; Pekurny, 1982; Tunstall & Walker, 1981, pp. 77–79). This proven talent then self-censor their work on the basis of a product image their previous experience tells them the networks will tolerate (Cantor, 1971; Pekurny, 1982; Ravage, 1978) creating an "imaginary feedback loop" (DiMaggio & Hirsch, 1976) between producers and network executives.

These same conditions continue to characterize program development in the late 1980s (Blumler & Spicer, 1990), as the new buyers of programming, cable networks, operate under the same constraints as broadcast networks.

To avoid risk, network executives have chosen programs that repeat the same images of class decade after decade. More diverse programming has appeared only in the early days of an industry when there were no past successes to copy—broadcast television in the early 1950s and cable in the early 1980s—or when declining ratings made it clear that past successes no longer worked (Blumler

& Spicer, 1990; Turow, 1982b, p. 124). Dominick (1976) found that the lower the profits of the networks, the more variation in program types could be discerned from season to season and the less network schedules resembled each other. For example, in the late 1950s, ABC introduced hour-long western series to prime time to become competitive with NBC and CBS (Federal Communications Commission [FCC], Office of Network Study, 1965, pp. 373, 742). Again, in 1970, CBS purchased Norman Lear's then controversial *All in the Family* (other networks turned it down) to counteract a drift to an audience of undesirable demographics (rural and over 50). Acceptance by the networks of innovative programs takes much longer than conventional programs and requires backing by the most successful producers (Turow, 1982b, p. 126). *Roseanne* was introduced by Carsey-Werner, producers of the top-rated *Cosby Show,* when ABC was trying to counter ratings losses (Reeves, 1990, pp. 153–154). Hugh Wilson, the creator of *WKRP* and *Frank's Place,* described CBS in 1987 as desperate about slipping ratings; "Consequently they were the best people to work for from a creative standpoint" (Campbell & Reeves, 1990, p. 8).

Network Decision Making—Program Development

The second factor affecting network decisions on content is the need to produce programming suited to advertising. What the audience wants—or what network executives imagine they want—is secondary to ad revenue. (Subscriber-supported, pay cable networks, which do not sell advertising, also do not program weekly drama series.) In matters of content, networks avoid that which will offend or dissatisfy advertisers (Bryant, 1969). For example, ABC contracts with producers in 1977 stipulated that

no program or pilot shall contain . . . anything . . . which does not conform with the then current business or advertising policies of any such sponsor; or which is detrimental to the good will or the products or services of . . . any such sponsor. (FCC, Network Inquiry, 1980, Appendix C, p. A-2)

Garry Marshall, producer of several highly successful series, stated that ABC rejected a story line for *Mork & Mindy,* the top rated show for 1978, in which Mork takes TV ads literally, buys everything, and creates havoc. Despite the series' and Marshall's proven success, the network feared advertisers' reactions to such a story line.

An advertiser's preferred program is one that allows full use of the products being advertised. The program should be a complimentary context for the ad. In the 1950s, an ad agency, rejecting a play about working-class life, stated, "It is the general policy of advertisers to glamourize their products, the people who buy them, and the whole American social and economic scene" (Barnouw, 1970, p. 32). Advertisers in 1961 considered it "of key importance" to avoid "irritating, controversial, depressive, or downbeat material" (FCC, Office of Network Study, 1965, p. 373). This requires dramas built around affluent characters for whom consuming is not problematic. Thus, affluent characters predominate, and occupational groups with higher levels of consumer expenditure are overrepresented.

A third factor in program decisions is whether it will attract the right audience.

Network executives construct a product image of what they *imagine* the audience wants, which surprisingly is not based on actual research of audiences in their homes (Blumler & Spicer, 1990; Pekurny, 1982). For example, Michael Dann, a CBS executive, was "concerned the public might not accept a program about a blue collar worker" when offered the pilot script for *Arnie* in 1969 (before *All in the Family* proved that wrong and after a decade in which the only working-class family appearing in prime time was *The Flintstones*). On the other hand, in 1979 an NBC executive expressed the concern that a couple in a pilot was too wealthy to appeal to most viewers (Turow, 1982b, p. 123).

With the exception of the few anecdotes I have mentioned, almost no research has examined program development or production decisions about class content of programs. My research found no significant differences between characters in sitcom pilots and series from 1973 to 1982, indicating that class biases in content begin very early in the decision-making process, when the first pilot episode is being developed (Butsch, 1984). I therefore conducted a mail survey of the producers, writers, or directors of the pilots from 1973 to 1982. I specifically asked how the decisions were made about the occupation of the characters in their pilot. I was able to contact 40 persons concerning 50 pilots. I received responses from 6 persons concerning 12 pilots.

Although this represents only a small portion of the original sample, their responses are strikingly similar. Decisions on occupations of main characters were made by the creators and made early in program development, as part of the program idea. In no case did the occupation become a matter of debate or disagreement with the networks. Moreover, the choice of occupation was incidental to the situation or other aspect of the program idea; thus, it was embedded in the creator's conception of the situation. For example, according to one writer, a character was conceived of as an architect "to take advantage of the Century City" location for shooting the series; the father in another pilot was cast as owner of a bakery after the decision was made to do a series about an extended Italian family; in another pilot, the creator thought the actor "looked like your average businessman." The particular occupations and even the classes are not necessitated by the situations that creators offered as explanations. But they do not seem to be hiding the truth; their responses were open and unguarded. It appears they did not think through themselves why this *particular* class or occupation; rather, the occupations seem to them an obvious derivative of the situation or location or actors they choose. The choice of class is thus diffuse, embedded in their culture.

This absence of any awareness of decisions about class is confirmed by Gitlin's (1983) interviews with industry personnel about social issues. Thus, the process of class construction seems difficult to document given the unspoken guidelines, the indirect manner in which they suggest class, and the absence of overt decision about class. Class or occupation is not typically an issue for discussion, as are obscenity or race. To examine it further, we need to look at the organization of the production process and the culture of creative personnel.

The Hollywood Input—Program Production

Within the production process in Hollywood studios and associated organizations, and in the work culture of creative personnel, we find factors that contribute to the use of simple and repetitious stereotypes of working-class men.

An important factor in television drama production is the severe time constraint (Lynch, 1973; Ravage, 1978; Reeves, 1991 p. 150). The production schedule for series requires that a finished program be delivered to the networks each week. Even if the production company had the entire year over which to complete the season's 22 to 24 episodes, an episode would have to be produced on the average every 2 weeks, including script writing, casting, staging, filming, and editing. This is achieved through an assembly line process in which several episodes are in various stages of production and being worked on by the same team of producer, writers, directors and actors, simultaneously (Lynch, 1973; Ravage, 1978; Reeves, 1990).

Such a schedule puts great pressure on the production team to simplify the amount of work and decisions to be made as much as possible. The series format is advantageous for this reason: When the general story line and main characters are set, the script can be written following a simple formula. For situation comedy, even the set and the cast do not change from episode to episode.

The time pressures contribute in several ways to the dependence on stereotypes for characterization. First, if ideas for new series are to be noticed, they cannot be "subtle ideas and feelings of depth," but rather, "have to be attention getters—loud farts," in the words of a successful director (Ravage, 1978, p. 92).

Also, time pressure encourages type-casting to obtain casts quickly. The script is sent to a "breakdown" agency, which reads the script and extracts the description of characters that need to be cast. One such agency, employing six persons, provides this service for the majority of series (Turow, 1978). These brief character descriptions, not the script, are used by the casting agency to recommend actors, particularly for minor characters. Not surprisingly, the descriptions are highly stereotyped (Turow, 1980). Occupation—and by inference, class—was an important part of these descriptions, being identified for 84% of male characters.

Producers, casting directors, and casting agencies freely admit the stereotyping but argue its necessity on the basis of time and dramatic constraints. Type-casting is much quicker. They also argue that to diverge from stereotypes would draw attention away from the action, the story line, or other character and destroy dramatic effect. Thus, unless the contradiction of the stereotype is the basic story idea—as in *Arnie,* a blue-collar worker suddenly appointed corporate executive—there is a very strong pressure, for purpose of dramatic effect, to reproduce existing stereotypes.

The time pressures also make it more likely that the creators will stick to what is familiar to them whenever possible. Two of the most frequent occupations of main characters in family series were in entertainment and writing, that is, modeled on the creators' own lives (Butsch & Glennon, 1983).

The vast majority of producers grew up in middle-class homes, with little direct experience of working-class life (Cantor, 1971; Gitlin, 1983; Stein, 1979; Thompson & Burns, 1990). Moreover, the tight schedule and deadlines of series production leave no time for becoming familiar enough with a working-class lifestyle to be able to capture it realistically. Those who have done so—for example, Jackie Gleason, Norman Lear—had childhood memories of working-class neighborhoods to draw on.

Thus, the time pressure encourages creative personnel to rely heavily on a shared and consistent product image—including diffuse and undifferentiated images of class—embedded in what Elliott (1972) called "the media culture." The small, closed community of those engaged in television production, including Hollywood creators and network executives (Blumler & Spicer, 1990; Gitlin, 1983; Stein, 1979; Tunstall & Walker, 1981; Turow, 1982a) shares a culture that includes certain conceptions of what life is like and what the audience finds interesting. According to Norman Lear, the production community draws its ideas from what filters into it from the mass media (Gitlin, 1983, p. 204). From this, they try to guess what "the public" would like and formulate images of class they think are compatible (Gitlin, 1983, pp. 225–226).

Although the consistency of image, the underrepresentation of the working class, and the use of stereotypes can be explained by structural constraints, the particular stereotypes grow from a rather diffuse set of cultural images, constrained and framed by the structure of the indus-try. Any further specification will require a close examination of the construction of the consciousness of the program creators and network executives from, among other things, their exposure to the same media they create—a closed circle of cultural reproduction. Whether one can indeed extract the process of class image making from the totality of this occupational culture remains a challenge to researchers.

Notes

1. Subordinate statuses, generally, race and gender as well as class, are underrepresented and/or presented negatively.

2. The sellers, the production companies, on the other hand, are not an oligopoly. Market concentration is low compared to the buyers (broadcast and cable networks); there was high turnover in the ranks of suppliers and great year-to-year fluctuation in market share; and collusion between suppliers is very difficult (FCC Network Inquiry Special Staff, 1980; Owen & Wildman, 1990).

References

Barnouw, E. (1970). *The image empire: A history of broadcasting in the U.S. from 1953.* New York: Oxford University Press.

B'cast, cable: Trading places. (2000, April 24). *Variety,* p. 6l.

Blum, A. (1969). Lower class Negro television spectators. In A. Shostak (Ed.), *Blue collar world* (pp. 429–435). New York: Random House.

Blumler, J., & Spicer, C. (1990). Prospects for creativity in the new television marketplace. *Journal of Communication, 40*(4), 78–101.

Brown, L. (1971). *Television: The business behind the box.* New York: Harcourt Brace Jovanovich.

Bryant, A. (1969). Historical and social aspects of concentration of program control in television. *Law and Contemporary Problems, 34,* 610–635.

Butsch, R. (1984, August). *Minorities from pilot to series: Network selection of character statuses and traits.* Paper presented at the annual meeting of the Society for the Study of Social Problems, Washington, DC.

Butsch, R. (1992). Class and gender in four decades of television situation comedy. *Critical Studies in Mass Communication, 9,* 387–399.

Butsch, R. (2000). *The making of American audiences.* Cambridge, UK: Cambridge University Press.

Butsch, R., & Glennon, L. M. (1983). Social class: Frequency trends in domestic situation comedy, 1946–1978. *Journal of Broadcasting, 27*(1), 77–81.

Campbell, R., & Reeves, J. (1990). Television authors: The case of Hugh Wilson. In R. Thompson & G. Burns (Eds.), *Making television: Authorship and the production process* (pp. 318). New York: Praeger.

Cantor, M. (1971). *The Hollywood TV producer.* New York: Basic Books.

Connell, B. (1978). *Ruling class, ruling culture.* London: Cambridge University Press.

DiMaggio, P., & Hirsch, P. (1976). Production organization in the arts. *American Behavioral Scientist, 19,* 735–752.

Dominick, J. (1976, Winter). Trends in network prime time, 1953–1974. *Journal of Broadcasting, 26,* 70–80.

Elliott, P. (1972). *The making of a television series: A case study.* New York: Hastings.

Federal Communications Commission, Network Inquiry Special Staff. (1980). *Preliminary reports.* Washington, DC: Government Printing Office.

Federal Communications Commission, Office of Network Study. (1965). *Second interim report: Television network program procurement* (Part 2). Washington, DC: Government Printing Office.

Gans, H. (1962). *The urban villagers.* New York: Free Press.

Genre-ation gap hits sitcoms. (1999, April 26). *Variety,* p. 25.

Gitlin, T. (1983). *Inside prime time.* New York: Pantheon.

Glennon, L. M., & Butsch, R. (1982). The family as portrayed on television, 1946–78. In National Institute of Mental Health, *Television and social behavior: Ten years of scientific progress and implications for the eighties* (Vol. 2, Technical Review, pp. 264–271). Washington, DC: Government Printing Office.

Gomery, D. (1999). The television industry. In B. Compaine & D. Gomery, *Who owns the media?* Mahwah, NJ: Lawrence Erlbaum.

James, C. (1995, December 3). Dysfunctional wears out its welcome. *New York Times,* p. H1.

Jhally, S., & Lewis, J. (1992). *Enlightened racism: The Cosby Show, audiences and the myth of the American dream.* Boulder, CO: Westview.

Lynch, J. (1973). Seven days with *All in the Family:* A case study of the taped TV drama. *Journal of Broadcasting, 17*(3), 259–274.

Meisler, A. (1997, February 2). Paul Reiser's balancing act. *New York Times,* p. H42.

Owen, B., & Wildman, S. (1992). *Video economics.* Cambridge, MA: Harvard University Press.

Pekurny, R. (1977). *Broadcast self-regulation: A participant observation study of NBC's broadcast standards department.* Unpublished doctoral dissertation, University of Minnesota.

Pekurny, R. (1982). Coping with television production. In J. S. Ettema & D. C. Whitney (Eds.), *Individuals in mass media organizations.* Beverly Hills, CA: Sage.

Peterson, R. A., & Berger, D. (1971). Entrepreneurship in organizations: Evidence from the popular music industry. *Administrative Science Quarterly, 16,* 97–107.

Ravage, J. (1978). *Television: The director's viewpoint.* New York: Praeger.

Reeves, J. (1990). Rewriting culture: A dialogic view of television authorship. In R. Thompson & G. Burns (Eds.), *Making television: Authorship and the production process* (pp. 147–160). New York: Praeger.

Ryan, B. (1992). *Making capital from culture: The corporate form of capitalist cultural production.* New York: Walter de Gruyter.

Stein, B. (1979). *The view from Sunset Boulevard.* New York: Basic Books.

Thompson, R., & Burns, G. (Eds.). (1990). *Making television: Authorship and the production process.* New York: Praeger.

Tunstall, J., & Walker, D. (1981). *Media made in California.* New York: Oxford University Press.

Turow, J. (1978). Casting for TV parts: The anatomy of social typing. *Journal of Communication, 28*(4), 18–24.

Turow, J. (1980). Occupation and personality in television dramas. *Communication Research, 7*(3), 295–318.

Turow, J. (1982a). Producing TV's world: How important is community? *Journal of Communication, 32*(2), 186–193.

Turow, J. (1982b). Unconventional programs on commercial television. In J. S. Ettema & D. C. Whitney (Eds.), *Individuals in mass media organizations.* Beverly Hills, CA: Sage.

TV tosses kiddie litter. (1999, December 6). *Variety,* p. 1.

Upscale auds ease b'casters. (1999, August 23). *Variety,* p. 34.

Vidmar, N., & Rokeach, M. (1974). Archie Bunker's bigotry: A study in selective perception and exposure. *Journal of Communication, 24,* 36–47.

Wakshlag, J., & Adams, W. J. (1985). Trends in program variety and prime time access rules. *Journal of Broadcasting and Electronic Media, 29*(1), 23–34.

Webs' final answer: Reality. (1999, November 8). *Variety,* p. 27.

Winick, C. (1961). Censor and sensibility: A content analysis of the television censor's comments. *Journal of Broadcasting, 5*(2), 117–135.

Young auds seek Web, not webs. (1999, January 4). *Variety,* p. 65.

Zook, K. B. (1999). *Color by Fox: The Fox network and the revolution in black television.* New York: Oxford University Press.

DECODING THE TEXT

Butsch argues that working-class families and middle-class families are depicted in significantly different ways on television.

1. What are some of the differences Butsch describes in his essay?

2. Do you agree or disagree with him? Why?

3. In addition to the differences Butsch mentions, are families of other socioeconomic statuses represented differently on television?

4. How do the statistics that Butsch includes in the essay affect your reading?

Describe a situation when you felt that you were expected to behave in a certain way because of your family background, job, race, ethnicity, or gender.

1. Who had the expectations?

2. How do you think these expectations developed?

3. Are there ways to counter this type of stereotyping or discrimination?

4. Do you see the buffoon husband–sensible wife dynamic presented in other areas of popular culture? How are married couples presented in film?

Reading Selections: A Case Study Across the Decades

CONSIDERING IDEAS

1. Describe some situations in which particular television characters or television shows have been boycotted or censored by groups. What were the boycotts about? What action did the boycotting group want the television network or studio to take? Do you think that television boycotts are effective?

2. Do you believe that gay characters on television shows represent an accurate view of gay culture? What is gay culture anyway? Is there such a culture?

3. What power do words have? Are there words that people might use to describe you but that you find uncomfortable or offensive? If you were called these words, how would you feel? What would you do?

The Onion is a widely read national print publication and website (http://www.theonion.com) that offers a satirical take on traditional news outlets. It was founded in 1988 by two students at the University of Wisconsin–Madison. "Letter D Pulls Sponsorship from Sesame Street" was posted on December 7, 1997.

LETTER D PULLS SPONSORSHIP FROM *SESAME STREET*

The Onion

A spokesperson for the letter D announced Monday that the consonant is withdrawing sponsorship from *Sesame Street* following a Children's Television Workshop announcement that a homosexual muppet will soon join the show's cast.

"The letter D is proud to have brought you many wonderful *Sesame Street* episodes throughout the program's 28-year history," said Patricia Willis, public-relations director for D. "But the letter D does not condone the sort of morally questionable lifestyles that *Sesame Street* is advocating with the introduction of this new character. It can no longer in good conscience associate itself with the show."

Willis said D's withdrawal is effective immediately, and applies to both capital and lower-case versions of the letter.

The gay muppet, "Roger," will be introduced on *Sesame Street* Dec. 23, CTW director Leslie Charren said. Thus far, no other sponsors have pulled out, though the number seven has requested an advance tape of the episode before it makes a decision.

Many public-television insiders believe D's withdrawal was motivated by a desire not to alienate religious conservatives, a section of the population that employs the letter frequently.

"D is for, among other things, demagoguery, dogma and doctrine, words crucial to right-wing groups like the Christian Coalition," said Yale University political-science professor J. Wright Franklin. "It is likely that D felt it could ill afford to offend such a large segment of its users."

While a long-term replacement for D has not yet been secured by *Sesame Street,* the number three will temporarily fill in for it in a number of the show's animated shorts. Other pieces will simply skip from C to E, with vocalists stretching out C into two syllables to match the rhythm of the alphabet song.

Sesame Street is stung by the sudden departure of its longtime supporter. Speaking to reporters, cast member Cookie Monster said: "Me disappointed letter D choose to end relationship with *Sesame Street* due to pressure from extremely vocal minority. We accused of endorsing deviant lifestyle. Me say homosexuality natural, not immoral. Diversity and enrichment. That's good enough for me."

James Poniewozik *is a television and media critic for* Time (*http://www.time.com*), *where he also writes the* Culture Complex *column and* Tuned In: A Blog About Television (*http://www.time-blog. com/tuned_in*). *He has contributed to publications such as* Fortune *and* Rolling Stone, *and he is a regular radio commentator for NPR's "On the Media" and "All Things Considered."*

Jeanne McDowell *is a reporter for* Time.

"TV's Coming-out Party" was first published in Time *on October 25, 1999.*

TV'S COMING-OUT PARTY

James Poniewozik and Jeanne McDowell

The first Tuesday of his second season on the air was a big day for Will Truman. Will, the male half of NBC's *Will & Grace*, went on a date, after spending last year setting an endurance record for getting over a painful breakup. The date was with a hunky bookstore clerk we saw for all of five teasing seconds, but it was a date nonetheless. His other accomplishment: the Top-20 *W&G* beat its straight-couple neighbor, ABC's *Dharma & Greg*, in the first round of a pitched battle for ratings.

And there you have the state of gayness on television in 1999: TV has come out, within fuzzily defined but undeniable limits. Since the much touted coming out of Ellen DeGeneres in 1997—and the much noted rapid demise of her sitcom in the following season—prime time has seen an influx of popular, prominent and well-rounded gay characters without Ellen-esque audience or advertiser cavils. Indeed, there's so much cachet in being gay that even straight characters are trying it. On Fox's *Action*, scheming movie producer Peter Dragon received oral sex from a star to whom he passed himself off as gay, and in what promises to be a head-turning second episode of Fox's *Ally McBeal* on Nov. 1, Ally engages in steamy lip-wrestling with another woman.

That straight characters are getting more on-screen same-sex action than gay ones speaks to the bizarre rules surrounding gay sexuality on TV. The first strange rule: gay men are more lovable than gay women. But girl kisses are better than boy kisses—and it's best if at least one girl is straight. Straight actors playing gay (as in Eric McCormack, who plays lawyer Will Truman) go over better than openly gay actors (DeGeneres), and so on. Thus

"TV's Coming-Out Party" from TIME, 10/25/99 by James Poniewozik and Jeanne McDowell, pp. 116–118.

America is apparently ready for implicit fellatio as a punch line or for a foxy hetero babe's experimentation, while actual gay characters such as Will—though enjoying increasingly substantial roles—still have libido restrictions.

There are nearly 30 gay or lesbian characters in prime time (depending on how you count and categorize them). Most are post-Ellen additions, and they are no longer limited to bit roles and punch lines (though TNT dropped a stereotypically gay "character" from *World Championship Wrestling* after receiving complaints about gay bashing). ABC's *Oh Grow Up* and *Wasteland* feature gay leads with actual, if tentative, love lives (Ford, a lawyer who's just left his marriage, and Russell, a closeted soap actor). *Action* has two gay regulars; one is Bobby G., a ruthless studio head whose massive male endowment symbolizes his show-biz power and the hetero fear of gay sexuality (literally striking dumb straight men who witness it).

Interestingly, in a season of protest over the underrepresentation of racial minorities, series creators have managed to add gay characters without getting much pressure to do so. One factor is that while coming out is still daunting to actors, there are a number of openly gay TV writers and producers, including *Wasteland*'s Kevin Williamson (who worked a regular character's coming-out story line into *Dawson's Creek* last season), *Oh Grow Up*'s Alan Ball and *W&G*'s co-creator and co-executive producer Max Mutchnick. In addition, the pioneering DeGeneres is developing a show for CBS. The network says it's unknown whether she'll play a gay character but contends she's free to.

Gay writers and producers "realize it's their responsibility [to create gay characters] because the straight guy down the hall isn't going to," says Scott Seomin, entertainment-media director for the Gay and Lesbian Alliance Against Defamation (GLAAD).

Gay characters still account for only about 2% of TV's roster, and with scant exceptions, we generally see a lone gay character associating largely with straights, viewing pals' sexcapades from the sidelines with what-fools-these-breeders-be amusement. But if nothing else, gay and straight characters show a new openness, sophistication and realism, sometimes with the help of consultants; GLAAD worked with McCormack to refine Will after the show's pilot. ("No gay man had hair like Will's, really long in the back," jokes Seomin. "He looked like Jerry Seinfeld.") Certainly much of the biting banter and in-jokes of *W&G*—"I haven't seen a kiss that uncomfortable since Richard Gere and Jodie Foster in *Sommersby*"—would be unimaginable in the era of *Three's Company*'s fairy jokes. Some shows even cultivate what you might call a gay sensibility. HBO's heterosexual (and how) sitcom *Sex and the City* regularly broaches sexual gray areas, taking the perspective, less broadly embraced among straights, that sexuality isn't either-or but a continuum. The *Ally McBeal* same-sex kiss episode, for all its easy titillation, takes the same view.

Gay content and gay characters—increasingly common accessories on shows aimed at trendy young adults—serve as a sort of coolness shorthand, bestowing hipness on their shows and audience, serving as a conduit to cred for the majority group, just as racial minorities have in the past. From Norman Mailer's White Negro we've gone to the Gay Hetero. As a side benefit, these characters allow networks to put affluent white boys on the air and call it diversity. (Indeed, the elderly animated pair Wally and Gus on the WB's *Mission Hill* are notable not so much for making out in the show's premiere as for proving that gay men don't vaporize after age 30.) But *Spin City*'s Carter Heywood is the networks' only gay person of color, and we've scarcely seen working-class gays or bisexuals since Sandra Bernhard on *Roseanne*. Speaking of which, anybody remember lesbians? Judy Wieder, editor in chief of the gay-and-lesbian magazine *The Advocate,* says that although gay men's sexuality "seems to be more threatening to society in general than [that of] gay women," lesbians have largely been left out of TV's gay renaissance.

Mutchnick, Ball and Williamson are mum on how much of their characters' love lives audiences will see this season, and network execs' willingness to show air kisses among actual gay characters is vague and jittery at best. Weirdly, both *Wasteland* and *Oh Grow Up* have sent their gay men on dates with men who turned out to be straight. Williamson says Russell will have an active love life, but Ball and Mutchnick say they're not that interested in entering the bedrooms of their straight or gay characters. True,

that's convenient. But in a sense, to focus on the Kiss Question casts the issue in terms of the schoolyard obsessions of homophobes: What do they do together? Do they kiss on the lips? Ironically, dialing down the sexual controversy has allowed *W&G*'s writers to nurture the title pair's "sexless marriage," one of TV's richest male-female relationships. "We were interested in exploring what happens between a man and a woman when sex isn't a factor," says Mutchnick. It has also enabled the writers to develop the wonderful bipolar characters of straitlaced Will and his unapologetically flaming pal Jack (it's as if you spun one gay man's personality into two in a centrifuge) and to show that physical love is not the sum of a gay person's identity.

Of course, physical love ain't chopped liver, either. Avoiding all one-on-one contact is a lacuna that will become all the more glaring as babes like Will and Ford remain unattached. Even actor McCormack said this summer that he felt Will was ready for an on-air kiss. As Ford tells his estranged wife, "Sooner or later, I'm going to end up naked, in bed, with another man." But when he does, he may be bound by TV's answer to the military's fumbling version of tolerance. Go ahead and ask, and please do tell. Just, for the love of God, don't show.

Mark Harris *is a writer and former executive editor of* Entertainment Weekly, *where he has published many articles on film, television, books, and music. "Sorry Situation" first appeared on http://www .ew.com on January 25, 2007.*

SORRY SITUATION

Mark Harris

For a while, Isaiah Washington was actually going to get away with it. I'm talking about how things felt before the Official Entertainment Remorse Machine kicked in—the denial, then the half-baked small apology, then the more impressive, bigger, "I'm scared" apology (the one that goes, "I have sinned, I must look deep inside myself and deal with my issues, I shall summon leaders of the offended community to meet with me") with a side order of official corporate rebuke, presumably followed by regret-soaked on-air interviews and a group hug. For three months, all the evidence suggested that everyone—Washington, *Grey's Anatomy* creator Shonda Rhimes, Touchstone TV, and ABC—had decided it was no big deal for an actor to refer to a gay colleague as a "faggot" on the set and that if everyone just averted their eyes, the word would become a tiny speed bump that a show could bounce over without looking back.

Forgive my skepticism, but I'm not a huge fan of apologies that come only after an evident threat to one's livelihood; I have difficulty believing that they spring spontaneously from a troubled soul. After all, it wasn't until Washington used the word again (during his "denial" at a press session after the Golden Globes), and two of his castmates called him on it, that a public outcry forced the issue. After Mel Gibson's Driving While Anti-Semitic bust, he was probably still looking for a post-mug-shot clean shirt when acts of contrition started flying out of his publicist's fax machine. And Michael Richards still had his own racist slurs ringing in his ears when he threw himself on the mercy of David Letterman. So why did it take a producer, a show, a network, and a corporation such an unconscionably long time to locate their sense of the right thing to do?

If I sound grudging about Washington's apology, it's not because I don't believe him (I suppose time will tell if he's sincere). It's because now that he's started the Machine, everyone is reading from the same script, and we already know how this trite old plot plays out. Pop culture (and that includes all of us who are pop culture consumers) has become addicted to a cycle of misbehavior followed by regret followed by a warm wallow in forgiveness in which we agree to pretend that saying you're sorry undoes whatever was done. And anyone who isn't willing to play that game gets labeled a bad sport or a sore winner.

"Sorry Situation" by Mark Harris from ENTERTAINMENT WEEKLY, 1/25/07.

© AP Photo/Matt Sayles

So, at the risk of sounding uncharitable, let me hold off on accepting that apology for a moment. Considering that everyone in a position to do something about it was content to let the word *faggot* hang in the air all winter, I'm sure they'll indulge me if I mention a few regrets of my own. I'm sorry that the first time this happened, Shonda Rhimes, whose commitment to on-air diversity is evident (even if the evidence stops short of including an actual gay staffer at Seattle Grace), thought it was okay to write this off as a private affair rather than immediately let the many offended fans of her show know how hateful she thought that epithet was. I'm sorry that T. R. Knight, the target of Washington's slur who came out following the incident, didn't have the instant, unqualified, and loudly public (because that matters) support of every one of his colleagues. I'm sorry that the overall non-reaction to Washington's behavior helped to reinforce a perception that some quarters of the African-American community tolerate homophobia, a stereotype that is only going to divide us more unless both groups fight it at every turn. I'm sorry that it took ABC half the TV season to remind itself of its corporate responsibility. I'm sorry that not a single sponsor of *Grey's Anatomy* had the guts to speak up, even last week. I'm sorry that we in the gay community didn't make a lot more noise about this a lot sooner. I'm sorry that so many actors choose—and it is, whatever they tell themselves, a self-serving choice—to stay in the closet, since the more out actors there are, the less okay homophobia in entertainment becomes. I'm sorry that there aren't more gay characters on television: I don't want quotas or tokens, but I do think that shows like *Grey's Anatomy* and *Lost* and *Heroes*, which pride themselves on the variety of their ensembles, could expand their vision to better reflect their world, since series ranging from *The Office* to *The Wire* have shown that it's not so hard. Most of all, I'm sorry that the rerun ritual that Washington's apology invites us to watch is likely to obscure all this.

Anyone who calls a colleague a faggot and manages not to get fired should count himself lucky. But Washington's use of the word didn't break anything that wasn't already broken, and his apology won't fix it any more than his dismissal. For all the progress that has been made fighting homophobia, and for all the ways in which the entertainment industry has led that fight, we clearly have miles to go. The problem is a lot bigger than Isaiah Washington, and the solution doesn't come gift-wrapped in the words "I'm sorry."

1. Poniewozik and McDowell say that "Gay Hetero" characters in 1999 were allowed to have more same-sex scenes on television than characters who were actually gay. What is the "Gay Hetero" that the authors describe? Do you agree with their argument and supporting examples?

2. *The Onion* is a very well-known satirical online newspaper around college campuses, and this "Letter D" piece is an excellent example of satire or parody. What makes this piece satirical or a parody? Is there a special tone, organization, or structure that makes this piece work?

3. What does Harris mean when he uses the term "Official Entertainment Remorse Machine" to describe how celebrities handle significant lapses in their behavior? What other instances of the Official Entertainment Remorse Machine have you seen recently?

4. How would you describe the tone of the three essays that make up this case study? How does tone relate to how you read the essays?

1. Are there any characters in your real life who are underrepresented on television? If so, why do you think television studios do not find it necessary to depict these characters on the screen?

2. Think of the people who are your closest friends. For what reason would they want to boycott something or someone? Would you agree with the boycott? Would you take an active or inactive part? Why?

3. Harris talks about the lack of true remorse that celebrities have when they have lapses in their behavior; however, the idea of the remorse machine can also be transferred into our own noncelebrity lives as well. How have you or someone close to you acted when you, he, or she was remorseful for bad behavior? Is there a certain script or set of conventions you follow with your family? With your friends? With your peers at school or colleagues at work?

contemplations in the pop culture zone

1. What exactly do you like about watching television? Consider the television shows that appeal to you the most and compare them to the ones that you do not enjoy. Make a list of reasons you like the shows you do, considering the following topics: the visuals that television provides in comparison to other information forms, the content that television focuses on, the availability of television compared to other media, and the format of television shows themselves, along with their commercials.
2. When we open a magazine or book to read, we have certain expectations about the format, the organization, and the content. What kind of expectations do you have when you turn on a television show (choose one type of show) and read/watch it?
3. What are the different ways you view/read a television episode or show when you are just an audience member versus being asked to be a critic of that episode or show? Is there a difference in your level of attention or level of pleasure?
4. In what ways can television be educational? Consider the different genres and subgenres.

collaborations in the pop culture zone

1. Television is not only entertainment, but it is also big business. To keep making money, networks need to keep viewers, especially during commercial breaks. What types of commercials are on regular networks (ABC, CBS, NBC, FOX)? How about on cable networks (Lifetime, USA, TNT, TBS, FX)?
2. Many television series now offer website content for their shows, and some shows offer special content online that regular viewers who do not go to the website miss out on. Investigate some of these shows and categorize the type of information that networks are offering online. Whom are they trying to attract with this type of information? Are they successful?
3. Choose a particular time of day and flip through all the channels offered on your network or cable system. Note what programs are playing on each channel and how many of the programs are of interest to you. Compare your lists with others in the class, and answer these questions and others that your group might have.
   - Can you always find something to watch on television? Why or why not?
   - What types of shows are more prevalent at the time of day you chose for flipping through the channels?
   - How much of a difference in availability does having cable make?
4. What is the first television viewing that you can remember? What kind of show was it? How old were you? Has that show influenced your life in any way? Why or why not?

start writing essays about television

Reviews or Review Essays

1. Choose two shows that you believe are completely different in at least one way and write a review essay that compares and contrasts the two shows. Consider the content, the audience, the actors, the direction, and the time period of the shows as you structure and expand your essay.

2. Choose one of your favorite television series and take a fresh look at it by pretending to be someone who dislikes the series. Write a review of the series, taking care to stay within this new persona throughout the essay.
3. Write a review essay that focuses on stereotypical depictions of a particular American subculture (for instance, skateboarders, African Americans, white middle-class working women, intelligent high school students). In your essay, make a judgment about your enjoyment of multiple television series by using stereotypical characters from each series.

Response or Reflection Essays

1. Reflect on which television series depicts or represents you and your life the best. Write an essay that details out the different shows and explains how and why these shows define or describe you.
2. If you have ever been bothered by the depiction of a character or scene on a television series, write an essay about why you were bothered. Give details from the show or series to support your argument(s).
3. What is your favorite television program of all time? In an essay, reflect on why this is your favorite, explaining how this program is different from all the other ones you have watched in your lifetime.
4. In "Television Shapes the Soul," Michael Novak argues that television can help shape the souls of viewers. Has television affected you in a deep way? Reflect on whether television has helped shape you into who you are today.

Analysis Essays

1. Videotape or audiotape a five-minute conversation on a sitcom and a five-minute conversation from a type of drama (for instance, a family drama like *Brothers and Sisters* or a mystery/thriller show like any of the *CSI* series). Write out the conversations fully and then look for ways the language on the sitcom differs from the language on the drama. In an essay, analyze the differences and propose an argument about how writers and audiences view these types of programs differently with regard to the language used.
2. Some television programs incite deep emotions, sometimes to the point where groups or organizations will initiate boycotts. Research an instance of television boycotting, and either analyze why the boycott was organized or argue that the boycott was necessary or unnecessary.
3. Animated television shows often include overblown or stereotypical characters. Choose one animated television character, explain how the character is defined through his or her actions and words, and decide whether the depiction of the character is stereotypical.
4. In the following quotation, writer Carl Sagan encapsulates a conundrum that is commonly discussed with regard to violence on television. Do you think that violence on television makes children more violent? Investigate some outside sources and write a nonbiased essay on the different sides of this complicated issue.

> There is a report that says that kids who watch violent TV programs tend to be more violent when they grow up. But did the TV cause the violence, or do violent children preferentially enjoy watching violent programs? (Sagan 203)

Synthesis Essays

1. Just like with films, popular television shows rarely win awards (see the list below). What is it about these popular television shows that those who vote for Emmy Awards are unwilling to notice or reward? Reflect on which type of show—popular or award winning—you watch more often and consider why this is true.

Emmy

Outstanding Comedy Series

2005	*Everybody Loves Raymond*
2000	*Will & Grace*
1995	*Frasier*
1990	*Murphy Brown*
1985	*The Cosby Show*
1980	*Taxi*
1975	*M*A*S*H*
1970	*My World and Welcome to It*

Outstanding Drama Series

2005	*Lost*
2000	*The West Wing*
1995	*NYPD Blue*
1990	*L.A. Law*
1985	*Cagney & Lacey*
1980	*Lou Grant*
1975	*Masterpiece Theatre: Upstairs, Downstairs*
1970	*Marcus Welby, M.D.*

Nielsen: Highest Average Rating No. 1

2005	*American Idol*
2000	*Who Wants to Be a Millionaire?*
1995	*Seinfeld*
1990	*Roseanne*
1985	*Dynasty*
1980	*60 Minutes*
1975	*All in the Family*
1970	*Rowan and Martin's Laugh-In*

Source: Alex McNeil. *Total Television*. New York: Penguin, 1996.

2. *Cocooning* was a term coined in the 1980s for staying at home and watching television instead of going out to see movies or doing some other activity outside the house. Do you consider yourself someone who cocoons at times? If so, describe how you cocoon, when you do it, and why. Investigate the cocooning practices of your family, friends, peers, and colleagues by developing a survey with questions that will help you define cocooning and explain the practices that can be associated with it.

3. Write an essay in which you consider and explore the reasons one genre (for instance, children's television, comedy shows, or soap operas) is so popular among college students or another group of viewers.

4. Create a visual essay that uses the new "science" of bracketology, which is based on the final-four system used in sports (see Figure 10.1). Fill in your favorite sixteen TV shows, narrow them down to eight, narrow them down to four, narrow them down to two, and then narrow them down to one, explaining each step of your narrowing process in your essay. This essay requires you to reflect on your reactions and analyze a specific theme

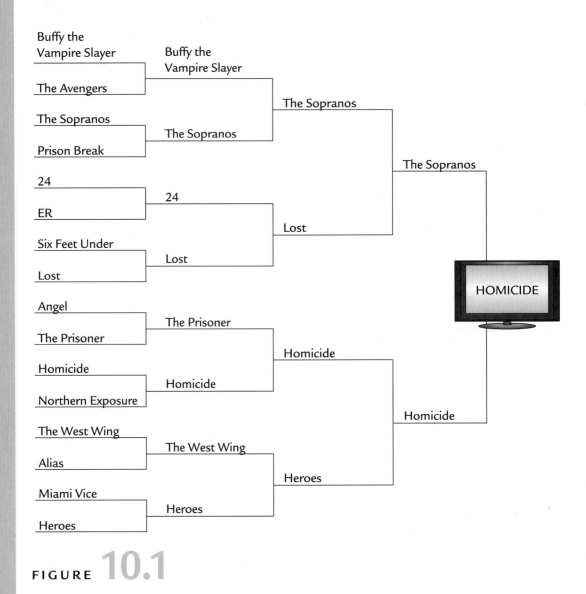

FIGURE 10.1

or item across many television programs. You can then compare your winner with others in class. Here are some ideas for topics (some adapted from *The Enlightened Bracketologist: The Final Four of Everything,* edited by Mark Reiter and Richard Sandomir):

Bloodiest, smartest, or scariest horror scene ever shown on television
Best one-liners on a television comedy
Smartest presidential character ever depicted on a television show
Most stereotypical character ever
Television shows that make you cry the most

FOR FURTHER READING

Allen, Robert C., and Annette Hill, eds. *The Television Studies Reader.* London: Routledge, 2004.

Edgerton, Gary R., and Brian G. Rose, eds. *Thinking Outside the Box: A Contemporary Television Genre Reader.* Lexington: UP of Kentucky, 2005.

Fiske, John. *Television Culture.* London: Methuen, 1987.

Jenkins, Henry. *Textual Poachers: Television Fans and Participatory Culture.* New York: Routledge, 1992.

Joyrich, Lynne. *Re-Viewing Reception: Television, Gender, and Postmodern Culture.* Bloomington: Indiana UP, 1996.

McNeil, Alex. *Total Television: The Comprehensive Guide to Programming from 1948 to the Present.* 4th ed. New York: Penguin, 1996.

Miller, Toby, ed. *Television Studies.* London: BFI, 2002.

Modleski, Tania. *Loving with a Vengeance: Mass Produced Fantasies for Women.* Hamden, CT: Archon Books, 1982.

The Museum of Broadcast Communications. <http://www.museum.tv>.

Simon, Ron, Robert J. Thompson, Louise Spence, and Jane Feuer. *Worlds Without End: The Art and History of the Soap Opera.* New York: Abrams, 1997.

Spigel, Lynn. *Make Room for TV: Television and the Family Ideal in Postwar America.* Chicago: U of Chicago P, 1992.

researching and documenting in the pop culture zone

Giles: "Um, I've not found any creature as yet that strikes terror in a vampire's heart."

Buffy: "Try looking under things that can turn their heads all the way around."

Giles: "Nothing human can do that."

Buffy: "No, nothing human. There are some insects that can. Whatever she is, I'm gonna be ready for her."

Giles: "What are you going to do?"

Buffy: "My homework. Where are the books on bugs?"

—From *Buffy the Vampire Slayer*, "Teacher's Pet," Season 1

© Columbia Tristar/
The Kobal Collection

1 All of the following movies have a form of plagiarism. Match the movie title to the plagiarist.

1. *A Murder of Crows*
2. *Bring It On*
3. *Secret Window*
4. *Good Will Hunting*

a. Lindsay Sloan as Big Red
b. Scott William Winters as Clark
c. Cuba Gooding Jr. as Larson Russell
d. Johnny Depp as Mort Rainey

TEST YOUR POP CULTURE IQ: RESEARCHING AND DOCUMENTING

2 Which of the following bands or artists did not use the drum introduction from Led Zeppelin's "When the Levee Breaks" in their own songs?

a The Beastie Boys
b. Tone-Loc
c. Mike Oldfield
d. Erasure

3 Match the following forensic scientists with the cities where they conduct their research.

1. Gill Grissom
2. Jordan Cavanaugh
3. Kay Scarpetta
4. R. Quincy

a. Los Angeles, CA
b. Las Vegas, NV
c. Richmond, VA
d. Boston, MA

4 Many modern movies are retellings or paraphrases of classic novels and plays. Match the modern film title with the classic work.

1. *Clueless*
2. *Ten Things I Hate About You*
3. *Scrooged*
4. *She's the Man*

a. *A Christmas Carol*
b. *Twelfth Night*
c. *Emma*
d. *The Taming of the Shrew*

5 Name the authors of the classic works in the previous question.

6 Many rap songs use samples of music (lyrics and/or melodies) from songs recorded by other artists. Match the following rap songs with the original artists the samples were taken from.

1. "Pretty Woman"
2. "You Can't Touch This"
3. "If"
4. "Fergalicious"

a. Diana Ross and the Supremes
b. Salt-N-Pepa
c. Roy Orbison
d. Rick James

7 In the previous question, which group's use of sampling sparked a debate over the legality of the practice?

8 Which of the following television shows does not require research as a key element of the plot?

a. *Heroes*
b. *Veronica Mars*
c. *Desperate Housewives*
d. *Law and Order: Criminal Intent*

9 Name the character names or actor names for the librarians in the following films and television shows.

a. *The Mummy*
b. *Buffy the Vampire Slayer*
c. *The Librarian: Quest for the Spear*

10 Which of the following Internet sources does not include a dictionary?

a. m-w
b. Bartleby
c. IMDb
d. Onelook

ANSWERS

1 1. *c. Cuba Gooding, Jr., 2. a. Lindsay Sloan, 3. d. Johnny Depp, 4. b. Scott William Winters* **2** *b. Tone-Loc* **3** *1. b. Las Vegas, NV, 2. d. Boston, MA, 3. c. Richmond, VA, 4. a. Los Angeles, CA* **4** *1. c. Emma, 2. d. The Taming of the Shrew, 3. a. A Christmas Carol, 4. b. Twelfth Night* **5** *a. Charles Dickens, b. William Shakespeare, c. Jane Austen, d. William Shakespeare* **6** *1. c. Roy Orbison, 2. d. Rick James, 3. a. Diana Ross and the Supremes, 4. b. Salt-N-Pepa* **7** *2 Live Crew's "Pretty Woman"* **8** *c. Desperate Housewives* **9** *a. The Mummy—Evelyn Carnahan (Rachel Weisz); b. Buffy the Vampire Slayer (television series)—Rupert Giles (Anthony Head); c. The Librarian: Quest for the Spear—Flynn Carsen (Noah Wyle)* **10** *c. IMDb*

YOU AND THE RESEARCH PROCESS

When writing about pop culture, you may rely on your own personal knowledge, evaluations, experiences, and reactions. In addition, you may draw upon primary and secondary research to give background information, to illustrate or back up what you have to say, to support your conclusions, or to provide various reactions and points of view. Primary research includes the actual show, book, group, or event you are writing about as well as data you collect yourself, perhaps through surveys or interviews. Secondary sources include all of the material related to your topic—for example, a *Rolling Stone* review of the film you intend to analyze, an argumentative essay in *Time* online about the subculture you are studying, and a presentation at the local library about the book you just read. When you use information from any source in your essay, you need to verify that the information is accurate and trustworthy and then document the source, usually parenthetically (inside the essay) and in a Works Cited page at the end of the essay. Using source information without documentation is one type of plagiarism and a quick way to receive an F on an assignment and suffer other ramifications in any class. Consequently, this section provides information about how to

- Find reliable source material, particularly when working with pop culture topics
- Summarize, paraphrase, and/or properly quote source material
- Document source material using Modern Language Association (MLA) or American Psychological Association (APA) guidelines

Your instructor may have specific requirements for the number and type of sources you may use, so always check with him or her or consult your assignment sheet.

grapplingwithideas

- Where do you start when you need to research something? Do you visit the library? Turn to the Internet? Talk with a friend? Make lists? Search randomly?
- How does research change when the topic is pop culture? How is it the same as any other research process?
- What types of pop culture research have you done in the past, whether for school projects or personal interest?

KNOWING YOUR RESOURCES ON CAMPUS

Researching an idea takes time; most projects will require many hours of research before you even begin writing and perhaps more research after you begin the writing process. Random researching will sometimes turn up information about your chosen topic but more often results in wasted effort. On the other hand, a purposeful search will usually yield more useful results. Once you have a topic, you must know where to find information for your project. This involves first knowing what resources are available on your campus. Most campuses have a central library; others may also have specialized libraries devoted to particular topics, times periods, or media—for example, a music library or a law library. Likewise, many campuses now have database or online subscriptions that can be accessed from computers anywhere on or off campus. Don't forget your local city, county, or state libraries; they may also have materials you can use and databases you can access. When conducting research on pop culture, it is especially important to know where to look because many primary and secondary resources in the field may be found outside the traditional venues and sources you have used in the past. For example, you may visit the archives at the local television station or talk to people on your intramural sports team when conducting your research.

RESEARCHING A TOPIC

Once you have determined a general topic through the use of brainstorming techniques (see Chapter 2 for an explanation of various approaches to brainstorming), you can begin looking up materials to help you expand your points, to support your ideas if you need more information, or narrow your ideas if you have too much. If you are unfamiliar with the topic, then it is always a good idea to consult a basic reference such as an encyclopedia or dictionary to get some general knowledge of your subject. However, you should note that such general works, although useful for helping you get started or narrow down your topic, may not be appropriate as a final source for your essay, especially when writing analysis and synthesis essays. You should find out what your instructor allows.

Suppose, for example, you have been asked to analyze the popular novel you just read, and your assignment sheet asks you, or even requires you, to use outside sources. You might begin by looking up the author in a biographical dictionary, or you might research the genre in a literary dictionary; both of these will help you get started. In addition, you might look up published book reviews, the sales record for your book, interviews with the author, and/or reviews and critiques of previous works by the same author. This information might lead you to write about how the author develops his or her characters. You may even want to narrow your topic still further to one particular character, such as the heroine. Following are some places to start with your research.

The Reference Section

The reference section of your brick-and-mortar library, as well as its online resources, is often a good place to start for background information and for help narrowing your topic and understanding research terms. Check your library for the following resources.

ENCYCLOPEDIAS. Encyclopedias are a good resource for getting general information about a topic. They often include lists of works on a topic, which can cut down research time. Examples of general encyclopedias include *Compton's Encyclopedia, Encyclopaedia Britannica,* and *World Book Encyclopedia;* many of these can be found in print and online. When researching pop culture, you may also want to look at encyclopedias about specific topics such as music, art, or business—for example, *The Encyclopedia of Popular Music* or the *African Music Encyclopedia.* A useful online tool to get you started is *Wikipedia.* **Caution:** Because *Wikipedia* entries can be written and edited by anyone, including you, it should not be considered a valid source to cite in your paper, but it can provide general definitions and a direction to get you started.

DICTIONARIES. Besides dictionaries of the English language, libraries often have dictionaries for numerous other languages. Libraries also have specialized dictionaries with topics such as slang, aphorisms (short, pithy statements expressing a general truth such as "Believe nothing you hear, and only half of what you see" by Mark Twain), slogans, clichés, and other phrases. You might use one of these when you want to better understand the lyrics to a popular song or the dialogue in your favorite television show. One well-known example of this type of dictionary is *Bartlett's Familiar Quotations* (http://www.bartleby.com/reference). Many of these dictionaries can be found online as well, either through library subscriptions or free to the general public.

HISTORICAL DICTIONARIES. Historical dictionaries document not only a word's meaning but also how its meaning has changed over time. The most comprehensive English historical dictionary is *The Oxford English Dictionary* (often called the *OED*), which is available in hard copy, on CD-ROM, and through subscriptions. The *OED* would be useful if you wanted to trace the use of a word being adopted by a particular group of people or a subculture or a word newly coined by the news media.

BIOGRAPHICAL DICTIONARIES. Biographical dictionaries contain short biographies of various individuals who have some characteristic in common. For instance, *The Dictionary of American Biography* contains short biographies of famous American artists, authors, scientists, and others. The library and various online databases have numerous *Who's Whos* and still others that are extremely specialized—for example, *Grove's Dictionary of Music and Musicians* and *The Dictionary of Victorian Painters*.

SCIENTIFIC ABSTRACTS. The Reference Section contains numerous abstracts of various scientific experiments, articles, and observations. *Chemical Abstracts* is one such work. Perhaps you want to know how violence in films affects young teens; you can look at studies in psychology, sociology, nursing, and anthropology, just to name a few areas.

Internet Sources

Often, the quickest way to find information on many topics is to use the Internet; however, the Internet has advantages and disadvantages for writing academic essays. While an hour surfing the net can yield a great deal of information, not all of it is accurate or from a reliable source. Many companies put misleading information into their meta tags or indexes, which are used by search engines such as Google, so their site will appear more often in basic searches and thus increase traffic to their site. More traffic means more advertising dollars.

Government websites (.gov sites) usually contain reliable information. If a website is sponsored by a university (.edu), journal, well-known organization (.org or .net), or other established corporate entity (.com), then information from these sites is probably usable. In addition, much of the information

[CARS Checklist

You can use the CARS checklist to help you establish the validity of a website. These questions are not guarantees, but they will help you eliminate unauthoritative websites.

- **Credibility:** Is the information from a trustworthy source? What are the author's credentials? Is there evidence of quality control? Is the author a known or respected authority? Is there organizational support for this work? Can the author be contacted through this website?
- **Accuracy:** Is the information up to date, factual, detailed, exact, and comprehensive? Do the links work? Are there obvious grammatical or spelling errors?
- **Reasonableness:** Is the account fair, balanced, objective, and reasoned? Are there any conflicts of interest? Is it free of fallacies or slanted tone? Who is the site's intended audience?
- **Support:** Are supporting sources listed? Is there contact information? Is corroboration or a bibliography available? Are all claims supported and is documentation supplied?

found on such sites can also be found in printed sources, many of which are available in the library. Of course, although the information at such sites may be accurate, it may still be one-sided.

Websites sponsored by individuals (these can also be .com, .edu, .net, or .org) can be useful ways of gathering information, but for the most part, unless the individual is an acknowledged authority in the field, these sites are considered unreliable or at least biased. Always look at who created the site and for what purpose, as well as what their credentials are.

Listed next are some resources to get you started (check our companion website, http://academic .cengage.com/english/SmithPopCulture, for the most up-to-date links). You should also look at the sources that have been approved (and probably linked to) by your own librarians; many of these sources are available online through subscriptions, so check out what your local libraries have to help your research.

ARTS

Dance Heritage Coalition	http://www.danceheritage.org
The Getty Online (info about art, artists, and architects)	http://www.getty.edu

BUSINESS

Consumer.gov	http://www.consumer.gov
Consumer World	http://www.consumerworld.org

GENERAL

Commercial Portals

GovSpot	http://www.govspot.com
LibrarySpot	http://libraryspot.com
The Library of Congress (check for their spoken word audio, music, and video titles free to download)	http://loc.gov
New York Public Library	http://www.nypl.org
Publications.com	http://www.publications/factbook/index.html
U.S. Census Bureau (maintained by the U.S. Census Bureau, the guide to government resources on the web)	http://www.census.gov/
The World Factbook (maintained by the CIA)	https://www.cia.gov/library/publications/ the-world-factbook/

HEALTH/NUTRITION

Health Resources and Services Administration	http://www.hrsa.gov/
National Library of Medicine	http://www.nlm.nih.gov/
USDA Food and Nutrition Information Center	http://fnic.nal.usda.gov

LITERATURE

Books in Print, Book Review Index, and *Book Review Digest* (for short reviews, periodicals that contain book reviews)

Movies

Internet Movie Database   http://www.imdb.com
> (for basic information about film producers, characters, actors, and release dates, but be aware that this site is maintained by self-proclaimed "movie fans" and is maintained by commercial sponsors)

Movie Review Query Engine   http://www.mrqe.com
> (this site collects and indexes published reviews, but it also provides space for users to post their own reviews, so pay attention to the various sources on this site and their reliability)

Music

Grove Dictionary of Music and Musicians or *Grove Music Online*
> (these are usually subscription sites, so check your library's holdings)

Periodicals

Ulrich's Periodical Directory, LexisNexis, and InfoTrac College Edition
> (for many newspapers and magazines, you can also go directly to their sites; some will require a personal login; others may require a subscription for full access)

Science/Technology

National Science Foundation—Statistics   http://www.nsf.gov/statistics/

National Science Resources Center   http://www.nsrconline.org/

Wired   http://www.wired.com

Quick Search Example

A popular general database available in most libraries is InfoTrac College Edition, which contains access to a variety of online databases, including InfoTrac OneFile, Expanded Academic Index, and Business and Company ASAP. These databases are similar in the way they are searched and are much like other commercial or subscription databases. Following is a brief guide for a basic search in InfoTrac OneFile, which is often a good starting place for research about popular culture because it indexes numerous magazines and newspapers, as well as more academic journals and even podcasts in the multimedia section.

Notice that the start page in Figure 11.1 is set up for a basic search and that it defaults to the *keyword* search. Keywords are words and short phrases that indicate the subject matter of the article; they can be chosen by the author or by the indexers. You can also search by subject, broader categories used by InfoTrac for organizing materials; in addition, you can search for words that appear anywhere in a document. Searching the entire document is not very useful unless your research question lends itself to such a search—for example, if you are trying to determine how many different authors make reference to Harry Potter. Another search option to be aware of is the advanced search, which allows you to narrow your search using more than one keyword and/or putting in the author's name or the publication name. It also lets you put in date parameters or search for articles of a certain type, such as full text or peer reviewed.

Now, suppose you want to know more about football fans. Where would you start your search? You can put the word *football* into your basic search and see what you get (Figure 11.2).

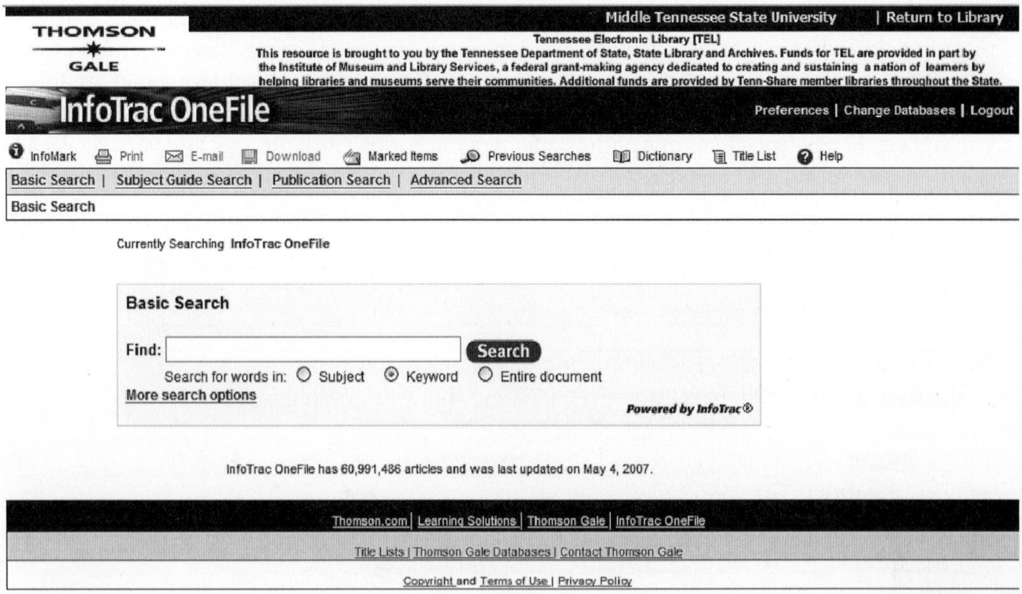

THOMSON
*
GALE

Middle Tennessee State University | Return to Library

Tennessee Electronic Library [TEL]

This resource is brought to you by the Tennessee Department of State, State Library and Archives. Funds for TEL are provided in part by the Institute of Museum and Library Services, a federal grant-making agency dedicated to creating and sustaining a nation of learners by helping libraries and museums serve their communities. Additional funds are provided by Tenn-Share member libraries throughout the State.

InfoTrac OneFile   Preferences | Change Databases | Logout

InfoMark   Print   E-mail   Download   Marked Items   Previous Searches   Dictionary   Title List   Help

Basic Search | Subject Guide Search | Publication Search | Advanced Search

Basic Search

Currently Searching InfoTrac OneFile

Basic Search

Find: [   ]   Search

Search for words in: ○ Subject   ● Keyword   ○ Entire document

More search options   Powered by InfoTrac®

InfoTrac OneFile has 60,991,486 articles and was last updated on May 4, 2007.

Thomson.com | Learning Solutions | Thomson Gale | InfoTrac OneFile

Title Lists | Thomson Gale Databases | Contact Thomson Gale

Copyright and Terms of Use | Privacy Policy

FIGURE 11.1

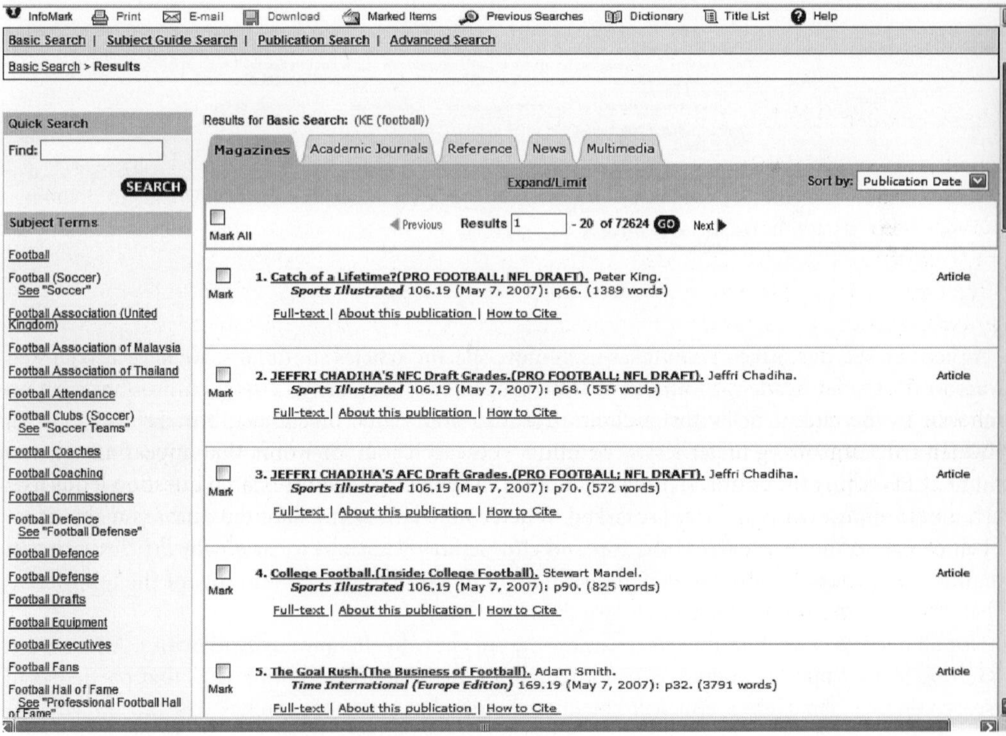

InfoMark   Print   E-mail   Download   Marked Items   Previous Searches   Dictionary   Title List   Help

Basic Search | Subject Guide Search | Publication Search | Advanced Search

Basic Search > Results

Quick Search

Find: [   ]

SEARCH

Subject Terms

Football

Football (Soccer)
See "Soccer"

Football Association (United Kingdom)

Football Association of Malaysia

Football Association of Thailand

Football Attendance

Football Clubs (Soccer)
See "Soccer Teams"

Football Coaches

Football Coaching

Football Commissioners

Football Defence
See "Football Defense"

Football Defence

Football Defense

Football Drafts

Football Equipment

Football Executives

Football Fans

Football Hall of Fame
See "Professional Football Hall of Fame"

Results for Basic Search: (KE (football))

Magazines | Academic Journals | Reference | News | Multimedia

Expand/Limit   Sort by: Publication Date ▼

☐ Mark All   ◀ Previous   Results 1 - 20 of 72624 GO   Next ▶

☐ Mark 1. **Catch of a Lifetime?(PRO FOOTBALL; NFL DRAFT).** Peter King.   Article
          Sports Illustrated 106.19 (May 7, 2007): p66. (1389 words)
          Full-text | About this publication | How to Cite

☐ Mark 2. **JEFFRI CHADIHA'S NFC Draft Grades.(PRO FOOTBALL; NFL DRAFT).** Jeffri Chadiha.   Article
          Sports Illustrated 106.19 (May 7, 2007): p68. (555 words)
          Full-text | About this publication | How to Cite

☐ Mark 3. **JEFFRI CHADIHA'S AFC Draft Grades.(PRO FOOTBALL; NFL DRAFT).** Jeffri Chadiha.   Article
          Sports Illustrated 106.19 (May 7, 2007): p70. (572 words)
          Full-text | About this publication | How to Cite

☐ Mark 4. **College Football.(Inside; College Football).** Stewart Mandel.   Article
          Sports Illustrated 106.19 (May 7, 2007): p90. (825 words)
          Full-text | About this publication | How to Cite

☐ Mark 5. **The Goal Rush.(The Business of Football).** Adam Smith.   Article
          Time International (Europe Edition) 169.19 (May 7, 2007): p32. (3791 words)
          Full-text | About this publication | How to Cite

FIGURE 11.2

According to the search on this particular day, the keyword *football* gets 72,624 hits, or articles in the magazines indexed for InfoTrac OneFile. This large number of articles is not very useful, so you may want to narrow your search. On the left-hand column, you can see the subject terms that are linked to the keyword *football*; these are narrower categories already set up by the database. As you go down the list, you will see that *football fans* is one of the database's categories. Click this link and you will get a New Results page using this more specific term (Figure 11.3).

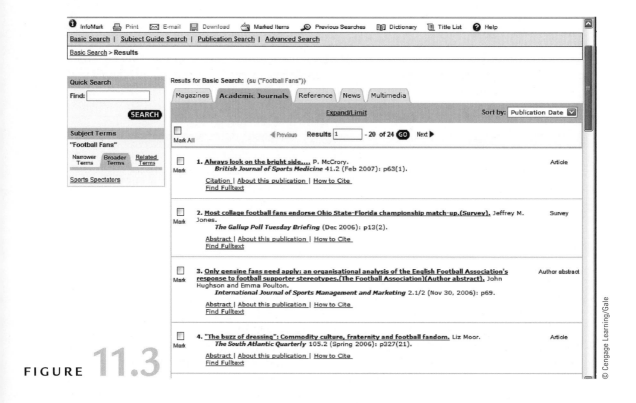

FIGURE 11.3

As you can see, this subject term takes us to more specific articles about fans. We have also clicked the tab across the top for Academic Journals to show that this option gives you more choices but is set up the same way. Twenty-four articles are much more manageable. Now you can read through the abstracts to see which articles might be of use to you or which ones catch your attention. When you find articles you want to hold on to, you can mark them by clicking the mark box next to the title of the article; a check mark should appear when an essay is marked. When you have marked all of the essays you are interested in, you can go to the menu across the top and choose how you want to save your articles: print them, e-mail them to yourself, or download and save them to a disk. In the second row of the top menu, you will also find options for starting a new search.

Not all databases work in the exact same way, but they do share many similarities. All have a Help or Getting Started option, where you can learn about the basics of searching with that particular index or search engine. The Help menu will usually tell you what kinds of searches you can do, what kinds of search limits or Boolean logic you can use (for example, AND, OR, NOT), and how to retrieve the resources you have found. Some also have lists of subject or index terms as well as lists of periodicals and other sources indexed in the database. It is usually worth your time to look at the Help section and learn how to conduct a useful search instead of just scrolling through pages of resources or settling for the first few articles that appear, which may or may not be relevant for your project. Also, do not forget to use your local librarian as a resource.

ANALYZING AND USING RESEARCH MATERIALS

It is important to analyze your sources and decide which books, articles, or sites have the most information about your topic. In most cases, entire books are not devoted to narrow topics such as those found in a first-year composition essay; therefore, use the indexes or table of contents to locate topics within books. Abstracts of journal articles will usually give necessary information for determining the value of the source. Internet sources that come from a guided search often are useful sources. If the website has a lot of information, it can be helpful to break this down into notes about various aspects of your topic.

Now you can read or view the materials in the order of their value, starting with the most useful. You will probably want to take notes, being sure to include bibliographic information (see the sections for MLA or APA citation guidelines). Be sure to follow your instructor's guidelines for recording notes and turning in note files (whether on cards, papers, or electronic files), as well as the documentation style necessary for the class, assignment, or discipline you are working in. As you read and take notes, think about the most useful way to organize your annotations, using some system that works for you and your writing project: chronological order, points in your argument, or sources. Once your notes are categorized and organized, you may be ready to start writing.

When writing about pop culture, your primary source is the movie, song, television show, artwork, novel, group, location, event, website, or advertisement that you are writing about. Many writers find it useful to read and analyze the primary source multiple times throughout the brainstorming, researching, and writing process. For example, if you were writing about an episode of *Buffy the Vampire Slayer*, perhaps "Teacher's Pet," the episode quoted at the beginning of this chapter, you would want to watch the episode numerous times. Each time you watch it, you should take notes about important details. Perhaps you can ask some questions about what is happening in the episode: Why do Buffy and Willow think the biology teacher is a predator? Or you can ask why characters act in particular ways: This is the first of Xander's demon love interests; does this episode foreshadow other crushes or relationships in later episodes? As you watch, you would probably find it useful to record important quotes or pieces of dialogue that support your argument points. Once you have a working thesis and perhaps an outline or web of your analysis, you might find yourself watching the episode again to test your ideas or to look for additional support. After finishing a draft of the paper, it would be a good idea to watch the episode one more time just to make sure you have not missed any important details or misrepresented anything. You would also want to properly document this source within your text and on your Works Cited page because, as mentioned previously, documentation is important for avoiding plagiarism.

TIPS FOR AVOIDING PLAGIARISM

1. *Know what plagiarism is.* Although definitions of plagiarism vary slightly, they all usually contain the same basic ideas. Plagiarism occurs when a student tries to present another's words or ideas as his or her own, using them in some parts of the paper or for the entire paper. The most common types of plagiarism occur from Internet use: Either the student cuts and pastes from one or more documents/websites, or the student purchases the entire paper from a website that sells documents.

Although the Internet has become the most common source of plagiarism, plagiarism can also occur when a student incorrectly uses print sources in part or in their entirety. Additionally, a student who copies a paper topic, point, or wording from a peer, a parent, or some other source is generally subject to the same consequences as a student who plagiarizes from an Internet or print source. Be sure to check your school's rules about what constitutes plagiarism. You might be surprised at how some actions—such as turning the same paper in for two different assignments in two different classes—can also be considered plagiarism.

2. *Decide in advance that all of your work will be your own.* A paper that is weak, a late paper (if accepted by the instructor), or a zero on the assignment is better than the consequences of plagiarism.

3. *Give yourself sufficient time to write the paper* so that you do not become desperate and resort to plagiarism.

4. *Learn to properly document your sources.* If you are unclear about citing sources, consult your instructor, your textbook, your school writing center, or a librarian at the reference desk. If you do not take the initiative to ensure that your source material is documented correctly, you have *intentionally* plagiarized.

5. *Take careful notes as you research.*
   a. Make photocopies of your sources and write down all of the bibliographic information, including the URL and date of access if researching online.
   b. If you take notes instead of making photocopies, write down the information in direct quotes and give the necessary information, such as page numbers, as well as the bibliographic information.
   c. Save paraphrasing and summarizing for the actual writing process. Do not paraphrase or summarize in the note-taking stage of research; otherwise, you may inadvertently plagiarize later on.

6. *To write a paraphrase, use your own words and sentence structure;* pretend that you are explaining the material to someone else. However, be careful: The intent of the original passage must remain the same, which means that you do not distort the author's meaning with your own opinions. Also, a paraphrase should be approximately the same length as the original.

EXAMPLE OF PARAPHRASING

• **Original Quote:** "Most teachers believe that violence occurs in hallways or under staircases, in the lunchroom or cafeteria, or in unattended classrooms. Students concur that most acts of violence occur in these places, but add the gym and locker room as prime sites" (Futrell and Powell).

• **Paraphrase:** According to a study by Futrell and Powell, both teachers and students agree that violence occurs in places within the school where there are many students and where there is not as much adult supervision, such as empty classrooms, the hallway, the gym, and the cafeteria.

7. Like a paraphrase, a summary puts the original passage into your own words and sentence structure without changing the meaning. Since a summary shortens the original passage and

focuses on its main points, partial quotes may be used along with your own words to highlight the most important information.

EXAMPLES OF SUMMARIZING

- **Original Quote:** "America's children are exposed to a steady diet of verbal and physical violence that begins early and continues throughout their lives. . . . Most of what children watch, including cartoons, is unsupervised and much of it is filled with scene after scene of unadulterated sex and violence. All too often children who behave violently are themselves victims of an overdose of violence" (Futrell and Powell).
- **Summary without Quotes:** Too much television watching exposes children in the United States to violence, which may be a factor in their own violent behavior (Futrell and Powell).
- **Summary with Partial Quote:** Too much television watching makes children in the United States "victims of an overdose of violence," which may contribute to their own violence (Futrell and Powell).

8. Take your essay and the copies of your sources to your instructor or your school writing center if you have one. Ask for help double-checking whether or not you have properly used and cited your sources within the essay as well as in the Works Cited.

DOCUMENTATION

As you take courses in a variety of fields or disciplines, you will encounter and use a number of different documentation styles. This range of styles exists to govern the research, writing, and documentation of various genres and disciplines. For example, in a psychology, business, or nursing class, you might be asked to use APA style; these rules have been set up by the American Psychological Association. In an engineering or math class, you might be asked to use the Institute of Electrical and Electronics Engineers (IEEE) style, or your biology class might ask for the Council of Science Editors (CSE) style. A journalism class will want you to follow *The Chicago Manual of Style* for a magazine article and the Associated Press (AP) guidelines for a newspaper article, which often does not include a Works Cited or References page.

In most English classes, you will be asked to use The Modern Language Association (MLA) style; consequently, many writing classes also use MLA. All of these documentation styles are designed to inform your reader about what the field finds important about source materials, including a record of the original research you have conducted with both primary and secondary sources.

In *Listening to the World: Cultural Issues in Academic Writing,* Helen Fox explains to a teacher upset about plagiarism, "This student [from Korea] comes from a system where the relationship between the student and the authority of teachers and texts is very different from what it is here. . . . In our culture, children are trained to think of themselves as separate individuals from the time they are born. . . . But in most cultures, children have grown up much more connected to other human beings, so it's hard for them to feel convinced that it is all that important to delineate whose ideas are whose . . ." (123–24).

- What is your response to Fox?
- What have you been taught, at home or at school, about referencing famous people, quoting aphorisms, or developing original ideas and arguments?
- Why is plagiarism such an important issue for Western academics?

MLA GUIDELINES

The Modern Language Association offers specific guidelines for formatting texts and for crediting sources used in your research. MLA style uses a type of cross-referencing that includes in-text, or parenthetical, citations and a Works Cited list. In this section, you will find a general overview of MLA style rules, especially as they apply to common pop culture resources. For more specific questions, you should consult the most recent edition of *The MLA Handbook for Writers of Research Papers* or the MLA section of your grammar or writing text. We do not recommend using online citation services to generate Works Cited material, as many of these sites are inaccurate, and citing correctly is a skill you are expected to have as an academic writer.

Citing Sources in Your Text

When you make reference to someone else's idea, either through paraphrasing, summarizing, or quoting, you should

- Give the author's name (or the title of the work) and the page (or paragraph) number of the work in a parenthetical citation.
- Provide full citation information for the source in your Works Cited.

Remember that paraphrasing and summarizing involve putting a source's information into your own words and sentence structures, whereas quoting is copying the author's words and structures exactly as written or spoken.

Parenthetical Citations

MLA style uses an author–page method of citation. This means that the author's last name and the page number(s) from which the quotation or paraphrase was taken should appear in the text. The author's name may appear either in the sentence itself or in parentheses following the quotation or paraphrase, and the page number(s) always appears in parentheses. The period goes after the parentheses, and you need a space, and only a space, between the author's last name and the page number of the source. Also notice that the quotation mark goes before the parentheses and has no ending punctuation mark.

EXAMPLE: AUTHOR'S NAME IN TEXT

Yu claims that Tiger Woods's move from amateur to professional in 1996 "said much about the current situation of race, ethnicity, and capitalism in the United States" (197).

Hague and Lavery have explained this concept in detail (2).

EXAMPLE: AUTHOR'S NAME IN REFERENCE

"The strange career of Tiger Woods said much about the current situation of race, ethnicity, and capitalism in the United States" (Yu 197).

This concept has already been explained in detail (Hague and Lavery 2).

When quoting verse, such as poetry or song lyrics, use a slash (/) to indicate line breaks and put the line numbers in your parenthetical citation rather than a page number.

EXAMPLE: QUOTING TWO LINES OF A SONG IN THE TEXT

Pink indicts many of George Bush's actions in "Dear Mr. President." For example, she asks, "What do you feel when you see all the homeless on the street? / Who do you pray for at night before you go to sleep?" (6–7).

If the work you are making reference to has no author, use an abbreviated version of the work's title or the name that begins the entry in the Works Cited.

EXAMPLE: NO AUTHOR GIVEN

In a leaflet passed out at a number of gay pride parades in the '90s, a group of anonymous homosexuals argue that being "queer is not about a right to privacy; it is about the freedom to be public, to just be who we are" ("Queers Read This" 138).

At times, you may have to use an indirect quotation—a quotation you found in another source that was quoting from the original source. Use "qtd. in" to indicate the source.

EXAMPLE: INDIRECT QUOTATION

Eco says that parody "must never be afraid of going too far" (qtd. in Hague and Lavery 1).

Your parenthetical citation should give enough information to identify the source that was used for the material as the source that is listed in your Works Cited. If you have two or more authors with the same last name, you may need to use first initials or first names as well—for example, (R. Wells 354). If you use more than one work from the same author, you may need to include a shortened title for the particular work from which you are quoting—for example, (Morrison *Bluest Eye* 58).

Long or Block Quotations

Sometimes, you will want to use long quotations. If your quotation is longer than four typed lines, you will omit the quotation marks and start the quotation on a new line. This block quote should be indented one inch (ten spaces or two tabs) from the left margin throughout, should extend to the right margin, and should maintain double spacing throughout. With a block quote, your period will come at the end of the quotation, before the parenthetical citation. If you are quoting poetry, song lyrics, or dialogue from movies, television shows, or plays, you will use a block quote for more than three lines and should maintain the original line breaks.

EXAMPLE: BLOCK QUOTE OF PROSE

In "A New Vision of Masculinity," Thompson calls for a change in the socialization of young boys:

> In his first few years, most of a boy's learning about masculinity comes from the influences of parents, siblings, and images of masculinity such as those found on television. Massive efforts will be needed to make changes here. But at older ages, school curriculum and the school environment provide powerful reinforcing images of traditional masculinity. This reinforcement occurs through a variety of channels, including curriculum content, role modeling, and extracurricular activities, especially competitive sports. (209)

Example: Block Quote of Poetry

In "What Hurts the Most," Rascal Flatts explores the pain of unspoken words:

What hurts the most
Was being so close
And havin' so much to say
And watchin' you walk away
And never knowin'
What could've been (1–6)

Citing Online Sources

Online sources, particularly websites, often lack specific page numbers. If the author has not assigned clear page numbers to the text, do not assign page numbers to online material yourself because page numbers for a website, which are assigned if you print the material, can differ among computers; what appears on page 3 of one printout may appear on page 5 of another. If the creator or author of the source numbers the paragraphs of the source, you can use paragraph numbers in the parenthetical citation as follows: (par. 1). Only cite by paragraph number if the author of the source numbers the paragraphs. Do not assign numbers to the paragraphs yourself.

There is a difference between a parenthetical citation for a print source and an online source. In the citation for the online source, there is a comma between the author's last name and the page or paragraph number.

Example: Author in Parenthetical Citation

"We miss *Buffy the Vampire Slayer*. We really do. The kicks. The quips. And Willow. Wonderful, wonderful Willow" (Jensen).

Adding or Omitting Words in Quotations

If you find it necessary to add a word or words in a quotation, you should put square brackets around the words to indicate that they are not part of the original text. However, be sure that the words do not change the original meaning of the text.

Example: Adding Words to a Quotation

In "Code 2.0," Lawrence Lessig describes the advent of Second Life: "[It is a] virtual world in the sense that the objects and people are rendered by computers. [It has been] built by its residents [Second Life users] in the sense that Second Life merely provided a platform upon which its residents built the Second Life world" (108).

If you find it necessary to omit a word or words in a quotation, you should use points of ellipsis—three periods in a row with spaces in between—to indicate the deleted words. If information is deleted between sentences, use four periods (the final period of the first sentence and the points of ellipsis).

Example: Omitting Words in a Quotation

Lessig writes, "On any given day, 15 percent of Second Life residents are editing the scripts that make Second Life run. . . . Residents acquired land in that world, and began building structures" (108).

PREPARING YOUR WORKS CITED

The Works Cited should appear at the end of your essay. It provides readers with the necessary information to locate and read any sources you cite in your text. Each source you use in your essay *must* appear in your Works Cited; likewise, each source in your Works Cited *must* have been cited in the text of your essay. Remember: Make sure your header (containing your last name and page number) appears on your Works Cited page as well as in your essay.

Basic Guidelines for Works Cited

- Begin your Works Cited on a separate page at the end of your essay. The Works Cited page has one-inch margins on all sides and a header with your last name and the page number one-half inch from the top, just like all the other pages of your essay.
- This page should have the title Works Cited centered at the top (with *no* italics, quotation marks, or underlining).
- Make the first line of each entry flush left with the margin. Subsequent lines in each entry should be indented one-half inch. This pattern is called a *hanging indent*.
- Maintain double spacing throughout your Works Cited with no extra spaces between entries.
- Alphabetize the Works Cited by the first major word in each entry (usually the author's last name). Do not use articles for determining alphabetical order.

Basic Guidelines for Citations

- Author's names are inverted (last name first, e.g., Presley, Elvis). If a work has more than one author, invert the first name only, follow it with a comma, then continue listing the rest of the authors (e.g., Lennon, John, and Paul McCartney).
- If you have cited more than one work by the same author, order the works alphabetically by title, and use three hyphens in place of the author's name for every entry after the first.
- If a cited work does not have a known author, alphabetize by the title of the work, and use a shortened version of the title in the parenthetical in-text citation.
- Capitalize each word in the titles of essays, books, films, and other works. This rule does not apply to articles, short prepositions, or conjunctions unless one of these is the first word of the title or subtitle (e.g., *Race, Class and Gender: An Anthology*).
- Italicize the titles of books, journals, magazines, newspapers, films, television shows, and album or game titles.
- Place quotation marks around the titles of articles or essays in journals, magazines, newspapers, and web pages, as well as short stories, book chapters, poems, songs, and individual episodes of a television series.
- For works with more than one edition, give the edition number and the abbreviation directly after the title of the work (e.g., *Feminist Frontiers*. 5th ed.).

- What experiences have you had with creating Works Cited lists in the past?
- What particular challenges does the use of pop culture create when conducting and citing research? How can these be overcome?
- Why is it important to include an accurate Works Cited List? What's the difference between a Works Cited list and a For Further Reading list?

- For numbers with more than two digits, use only the last two digits of the number (e.g., if you refer to a magazine article that appeared on pages 150 through 175, list the page numbers on your Works Cited citation as 150–75; 201 through 209 would be listed as 201–09).
- Give URLs or database names (e.g., InfoTrac College Edition or LexisNexis) for websites and other online sources, which will be indicated by angled brackets in your citation (e.g., <http://www.newyorktimes.com>). You should also give the date of access for online sources.

BASIC MLA FORMS FOR ALL MEDIA

1. ADVERTISEMENTS

Name of Product, Company, or Institution. Descriptive label (Advertisement). Publisher date. page numbers, if applicable.

Sony. Advertisement. *People* 30 Dec. 2002: 42–43.

America Online. Advertisement. NBC. 14 Feb. 2003.

NOTE: This same format is used for documenting such items as product labels, billboards, rebate/refund forms, and posters.

2. ANTHOLOGY OR COLLECTION

Editor's Name(s), ed. *Title of Book*. Place of Publication: Publisher, date.

Hague, Angela, and David Lavery, eds. *Teleparody: Predicting/Preventing the TV Discourse of Tomorrow*. London: Wallflower P, 2002.

3. ANTHOLOGY: WORK WITHIN

Author's Name. "Title of Work." *Title of Anthology*. Ed. Editor's Name(s). Place of Publication: Publisher, date. pages.

Yu, Henry. "How Tiger Woods Lost His Stripes: Post-Nationalist American Studies as a History of Race, Migration, and the Commodification of Culture." *Popular Culture: A Reader*. Ed. Raiford Guins and Omayra Zaragoza Cruz. London: Sage, 2005. 197–209.

4. ARTICLE IN A SCHOLARLY JOURNAL WITH CONTINUOUS PAGINATION

Author's Name. "Title of Article." *Journal Title* volume number (year of publication): pages.

Robinson, Bobbie. "Playing Like the Boys: Patricia Cornwell Writes Men." *The Journal of Popular Culture* 39 (2006): 95–108.

5. ARTICLE IN A SCHOLARLY JOURNAL THAT PAGINATES EACH ISSUE SEPARATELY

Author's Name. "Title of Article." *Journal Title* vol. issue (date of publication): pages.

Silbergleid, Robin. "'The Truth We Both Know': Readerly Desire and Heteronarrative in *The X-Files*." *Studies in Popular Culture* 25.3 (Apr. 2003): 49–62.

6. BOOKS (INCLUDES BROCHURES AND PAMPHLETS)

Author's Name. *Title of Book*. Place of Publication: Publisher, date of publication.

Kaku, Michio. *Hyperspace: A Scientific Odyssey Through Parallel Universes, Time Warps, and the Tenth Dimension*. New York: Oxford UP, 1994.

Strauss, William, and Neil Howe. *Millennials and the Pop Culture*. Great Falls, VA: LifeCourse, 2006.

EXAMPLE: TWO BOOKS BY THE SAME AUTHOR

King, Stephen. *Dreamcatcher: A Novel*. New York: Scribner, 2001.

---. *Misery*. New York: Viking, 1987.

7. COMIC OR COMIC STRIP

Artist's Name. "Comic or Comic Strip Title, if any." Label Comic or Comic strip. *Publication Title* date: page number.

Byrnes, P. Cartoon. *The New Yorker* 27 Nov. 2006: 131.

Walker, Greg, and Mort Walker. "Beetle Bailey." Comic strip. *The Tennessean* [Nashville] 28 Nov. 2006: 4D.

8. Film

Title. Dir. Director's Name. Medium. Distributor, year of release.

The Princess Bride. Dir. Rob Reiner. Videocassette. MGM/UA, 1987.

The Usual Suspects. Dir. Bryan Singer. Perf. Kevin Spacey, Gabriel Byrne, Chazz Palminteri, Stephen Baldwin, and Benicio del Toro. DVD. Polygram, 1995.

NOTE: You may include other relevant data, such as the names of the writer, performers, and producer, between the director's name and the medium. Note that fan films also follow this format.

9. Interview

Name of Person Being Interviewed. If published, "Title" of interview; if unpublished, label Interview and type (e.g., personal or e-mail). Interviewer's Name if pertinent. Appropriate bibliographic information.

Waits, Tom. Interview with Jon Stewart. *The Daily Show*. Comedy Central. New York. 28 Nov. 2006.

Smith, Kevin. Personal interview. 8–12 Mar. 2002.

10. Lecture, Speech, Address, or Reading

Speaker's Name. "Title of Presentation." Meeting and Sponsoring Organization if applicable. Location. Date.

Cofer, Judith Ortiz. "Judith Ortiz Cofer in the Classroom." The Compleat Teacher: Bringing Together Knowledge, Experience, and Research. NCTE 96th Annual Convention. Opryland Convention Center, Nashville, TN. 18 Nov. 2006.

11. Library Subscription Service, such as InfoTrac College Edition or LexisNexis: Article

Author's Name. "Title of Article." *Journal Title* vol. issue date of publication: pages. Name of Database or other relevant information. Library Name, Location. Date of access. URL if applicable.

Ornstein, Aviva. "MY GOD!: A Feminist Critique of the Excited Utterance Exception to the Hearsay Rule." *California Law Review* 85.1 Jan. 1997: 161–223. InfoTrac. Walker Library, Murfreesboro, TN. 22 Apr. 2003.

NOTE: Only give URLs if the reader can get back to the original source using the URL you have given; omit URL addresses when they stop making sense to the reader.

12. Liner Notes

Author's Name. Title of Material. Description of material. *Album Title*. Manufacturer, date.

Cady, Brian. Liner notes. *My Generation*. Decca Records, 1965.

13. Music Videos

Music videos should follow the television format in example 23 and should include performer information along with a note that this is a music video.

Stefani, Gwen. "Hollaback Girl." *Love.Angel.Music. Baby*. Universal, 2004. Music video. MTV Hits. 12 Nov. 2006.

14. Newspaper Article

Author's Name. "Title of Article." *Newspaper Title* day Month year: pages.

Berger, Leslie. "Quest for Male 'Pill' Is Gaining Momentum." *New York Times* 10 Dec. 2002: F5.

Lederman, Douglas. "Athletic Merit vs. Academic Merit." *Chronicle of Higher Education* 30 Mar. 1994: A37–38.

Tagliabue, John. "Cleaned Last Judgment Unveiled." *New York Times* 9 Apr. 1994: 13.

15. Online Newspaper or Magazine

Author's Name. "Title of Article." *Newspaper Title* date: pages. Date of access <URL>.

Quindlen, Anna. "Getting Rid of the Sex Police."
Newsweek 13 Jan. 2003. 28 Mar. 2003 <http://
www.msnbc.com/news/NW-front_Front.asp>.

Berger, Leslie. "Quest for Male 'Pill' Is Gaining
Momentum." *New York Times* 10 Dec. 2002: F5.
18 Mar. 2003 <http://nytimes.com>.

16. ONLINE JOURNAL ARTICLE

Author's Name. "Title of Article." *Title of Journal*
vol. issue (year or date): pages. Date of
access <URL>.

Whithaus, Carl. "Think Different/Think
Differently: A Tale of Green Squiggly Lines,
or Evaluating Student Writing in Computer-
Mediated Environments." *The Writing
Instructor* 2.5 (1 Jul. 2002): 42 pages.
21 Apr. 2003 <http://www.writinginstructor.
com>.

17. PAINTING, SCULPTURE, OR PHOTOGRAPH

Artist's Name. *Title*. Name of Institution that
houses the work or the Individual who owns
the work, City.

Leibovitz, Annie. *Nicole Kidman*. National Portrait
Gallery, London.

O'Keeffe, Georgia. *Sky Above White Clouds I*. 1962.
National Gallery of Art, Washington D.C.

NOTE: You may add the creation date of a work
immediately after the title.

18. PERFORMANCE

Title. Performer, Director, other pertinent data.
Performance Site including City. date.

Be a Candle of Hope. Nashville in Harmony,
Director Don Schlosser. First Unitarian
Universalist Church, Nashville, TN. 5 Dec. 2006.

19. RELIGIOUS WORKS

Title of Work. Name of Author or Editor, Title (e.g.,
gen. ed.) Place of Publication: Publisher, date.

Bhagavad-Gita: As It Is. A. C. Bhaktivedanta Swami
Prabhupada. Australia: McPherson's Printing
Group, 1986.

The Holy Bible. Thomas Scofield, gen. ed.
Nashville, TN: Thomas Nelson, 1983.

NOTE: You can give the title of the book within
the Bible as well as chapter and verse information
in your parenthetical citation (e.g., *The Holy Bible*
John 3:16 or *Bhagavad-Gita: As It Is* 6.26).

20. REVIEW

Reviewer's Name. "Title of Review." Rev. of *Title
of Work*, by Name of Author (Editor, Director,
etc.). *Journal* date: pages.

Franklin, Dana Kopp. "*Bend It Like Beckham
Goooooal!*" Rev. of *Bend It Like Beckham*,
by Dir. Gurinder Chadha. *The Rage: All
Entertainment* 17 Apr. 2003: 95–96.

21. SOFTWARE OR OTHER NONPERIODICAL PUBLICATION ON CD-ROM (OR DVD)

Author's (or Producer's, etc.) Name. *Title*. Name
of Editor, Compiler, etc. Format (CD-ROM).
Edition. Publication information (Place,
Name, and date).

Down, Chris, producer. *Ultimate Yahtzee*.
Developer PCA. CD-ROM. Beverly, MA:
Hasbro Interactive, 1996.

22. SOUND RECORDING

Artist. "Song Title." *Title of Album*. Manufacturer,
date.

Coolio. "Kinda High, Kinda Drunk." *Gangsta's
Paradise*. Tommy Boy Music, 1995.

23. TELEVISION OR RADIO PROGRAM

"Title of Episode or Segment." *Title of Program*.
Name of Network. Call Letters, City of the
local station (if applicable). Broadcast date.

"The Blessing Way." *The X-Files*. Fox. WXIA,
Atlanta. 19 Jul. 1998.

24. TELEVISION ON DVD

"Title of Episode or Segment." *Title of Program*.
Season or edition (if applicable). Name of
Network. Distributor, date.

"Man of Science, Man of Faith." *Lost.* Season 1. ABC. Buena Vista, 2005.

NOTE: With television programming, directors and/or performers can be added if relevant.

25. WEBSITE

Author's Name. *Name of Page.* Date of posting/revision. Name of Institution or Organization associated with the website. Date of access <URL>.

Irvine, Martin, and Deborah Everhart. *The Labyrinth: Resources for Medieval Studies.* 1994–2002. Georgetown University. 21 Jun. 2001 <http://www.georgetown.edu/labyrinth/labyrinth-home.html>.

NOTE: This same format can be used for blogs and any fan fiction found online.

26. WEBSITE: ARTICLE

Author's Name. "Article Title." *Name of Website.* Date of posting/revision. Name of Institution or Organization associated with the website. Date of access <URL>.

Stanley, Sally. "Sabotaging a Child's Education: How Parents Undermine Teachers." *Teacher-Parent Connections.* 2003. Disney Learning. 22 Apr. 2003 <http://disney.go.com/disneylearning/family-school/relationship/articles.html>.

SAMPLE WORKS CITED

Here is an example of how a completed Works Cited would look at the end of your essay. The Works Cited is part of the essay and should contain the same header (usually your name and the page number) as the rest of your essay.

Works Cited

Berger, Leslie. "Quest for Male 'Pill' Is Gaining Momentum." *New York Times* 10 Dec. 2002: F5.

Quindlen, Anna. "Getting Rid of the Sex Police." *Newsweek* 13 Jan. 2003. 28 Mar. 2003 <http://www.msnbc.com/news/NW-front_Front.asp>.

Robinson, Bobbie. "Playing Like the Boys: Patricia Cornwell Writes Men." *The Journal of Popular Culture* 39 (2006): 95–108.

Strauss, William, and Neil Howe. *Millennials and the Pop Culture.* Great Falls, VA: LifeCourse, 2006.

Yu, Henry. "How Tiger Woods Lost His Stripes: Post-Nationalist American Studies as a History of Race, Migration, and the Commodification of Culture." *Popular Culture: A Reader.* Ed. Raiford Guins and Omayra Zaaragoza Cruz. London: Sage, 2005. 197–209.

APA GUIDELINES

APA style uses a type of cross-referencing that includes in-text, or parenthetical, citations and a References list. In this section, you will find a general overview of APA style rules. For more specific questions, you should consult the most recent edition of the *Publication Manual of the American Psychological Association* or the APA section of your grammar or writing text. We do not recommend using online citation services to generate Reference list material, as many of these sites are inaccurate, and citing correctly is a skill you are expected to have as you write in a variety of courses.

Citing Sources in Your Text

When you make reference to someone else's idea, either through paraphrasing, summarizing, or quoting, you should

- Give the author's name (or the title of the work), the year of publication, and the page (or paragraph) number of the work in a parenthetical citation.
- Provide full citation information for the source in your References section.

Remember that paraphrasing and summarizing involve putting a source's information into your own words and sentence structures, whereas quoting is copying the author's words and structures exactly as written or spoken.

Parenthetical Citations

APA style uses an author–year–page method of citation. This means that the author's last name, year of publication, and the page number(s) from which the quotation or paraphrase was taken should all appear in the text. The author's name and publishing year always accompany one another and may appear either in the sentence itself or in parentheses following the quotation or paraphrase. When multiple authors appear in parentheses, an ampersand (&) replaces *and*. The page number(s) always appears in parentheses. The period goes after the closing parentheses. Within the parentheses, the order should be: the author's name, a comma and a space, the year of publication, another comma and space, and the abbreviation "p." (page) followed by a space and the Arabic numeral page number(s). If a citation occurs across multiple pages, you should instead use "pp." and a dash (with no spaces) between the beginning and ending pages—for example (pp. 202–205). Also notice that the quotation mark goes before the parentheses and has no ending punctuation mark.

EXAMPLE: AUTHOR'S NAME IN TEXT

Yu (2005) claims that Tiger Woods's move from amateur to professional in 1996 "said much about the current situation of race, ethnicity, and capitalism in the United States" (p. 197).

Hague and Lavery (2002) have explained this concept in detail (p. 2).

EXAMPLE: AUTHOR'S NAME IN REFERENCE

"The strange career of Tiger Woods said much about the current situation of race, ethnicity, and capitalism in the United States" (Yu, 2005, p. 197).

This concept has already been explained in detail (Hague & Lavery, 2002, p. 2).

If the work you are referencing has no author, cite in the text the first few words from the References list entry. If the work is an article or chapter, capitalize the first word only (unless the title contains a proper noun or adjective) and do not put it in quotation marks. If it is a book, periodical, brochure, or report, italicize the title and capitalize as you would for the References list.

EXAMPLE: NO AUTHOR GIVEN

In a leaflet distributed at a number of gay pride parades in the '90s, a group of anonymous homosexuals argue that being "queer is not about a right to privacy; it is about the freedom to be public, to just be who we are" (Queers read this, 1990, p. 1).

Note that if the author is specifically given as anonymous, you should use the format (Anonymous, 2002) or (Anonymous, 2002, p. 1).

At times, you may have to use an indirect quotation—a quotation you found in another source that was quoting from the original source. Use "as cited in" to indicate the source.

EXAMPLE: INDIRECT QUOTATION

Eco says that parody "must never be afraid of going too far" (as cited in Hague & Lavery, 2002, p. 1).

Your parenthetical citation should give enough information to identify the source that was used for the material as the source that is listed in your References list. If you have two or more authors with the same last name, you need to use each author's initials in each citation—for example, (R. Wells, 2002, p. 354).

Long or Block Quotations

Sometimes, you will want to use long quotations. If your quotation is longer than forty words, you will omit the quotation marks and start the quotation on a new line. This block quote should be indented one-half inch (five spaces or one tab) from the left margin throughout, should extend to the right margin, and should maintain double spacing throughout. With a block quote, your period will come at the end of the quotation, before the parenthetical citation.

EXAMPLE: BLOCK QUOTE OF PROSE

In "A New Vision of Masculinity," Thompson (1999) calls for a change in the socialization of young boys:

In his first few years, most of a boy's learning about masculinity comes from the influences of parents, siblings, and images of masculinity such as those found on television. Massive efforts will be needed to make changes here. But at older ages, school curriculum and the school environment provide powerful reinforcing images of traditional masculinity. This reinforcement occurs through a variety of channels, including curriculum content, role modeling, and extracurricular activities, especially competitive sports. (p. 209)

Citing Online Sources

Online sources, particularly websites, often lack specific page numbers. If the author or site has not assigned specific page numbers, do not assign page numbers to online material yourself because page numbers for a website, which are assigned if you print the material, can differ among computers; what appears on page 3 of one printout may appear on page 5 of another. If the creator or author of the source numbers the paragraphs of the source, you can use paragraph numbers in the parenthetical citation as follows: (para 1) or (¶ 1). If the author does not number the paragraphs, give the heading title and the paragraph of the citation after that heading.

EXAMPLE: AUTHOR IN PARENTHETICAL CITATION

"We miss *Buffy the Vampire Slayer.* We really do. The kicks. The quips. And Willow. Wonderful, wonderful Willow" (Jensen, 2007, ¶ 1).

Adding or Omitting Words in Quotations

If you find it necessary to add a word or words in a quotation, perhaps for explanation or clarification, you should put square brackets around the words to indicate that they are not part of the original text. However, be sure that the words do not change the original meaning of the text.

EXAMPLE: ADDING WORDS TO A QUOTATION

In "Code 2.0," Lawrence Lessig (2006) describes the advent of Second Life: "[It is a] virtual world in the sense that the objects and people are rendered by computers. [It has been] built by its residents [Second Life users] in the sense that Second Life merely provided a platform upon which its residents built the Second Life world" (p. 108).

If you find it necessary to omit a word or words in a quotation, you should use points of ellipsis—three periods in a row with spaces in between—to indicate the deleted words. If information is deleted between sentences, use four periods (the final period of the first sentence and the points of ellipsis).

EXAMPLE: OMITTING WORDS IN A QUOTATION

Lessig (2006) writes, "On any given day, 15 percent of Second Life residents are editing the scripts that make Second Life run. . . . Residents acquired land in that world, and began building structures" (p. 108).

PREPARING YOUR REFERENCES LIST

The References list should appear at the end of your essay. It provides readers with the necessary information to locate and read any sources you cite in your text. Each source you use in your essay *must* appear in your References list; likewise, each source in your References list *must* have been cited in the text of your essay. Remember: Make sure your header (containing the short two- to three-word version of your title and page number) appears on your References list page as well as in your essay (top right corner of each page).

grappling with ideas

- What experiences have you had with creating References lists in the past?
- What particular challenges does the use of pop culture create when conducting and citing research? How can these be overcome?
- Why is it important to include an accurate References list? What is the difference between a References list and a For Further Reading list?

Basic Guidelines for a References List

- Begin your References list on a separate page at the end of your essay. The References list page has one-inch margins on all sides.
- This page should have the title References centered at the top (with *no* italics, quotation marks, or underlining).
- Make the first line of each entry flush left with the margin. Subsequent lines in each entry should be indented one-half inch. This pattern is called a *hanging indent*.
- Maintain double spacing throughout your References list with no extra spaces between entries.
- Alphabetize the References list by the first major word in each entry (usually the author's last name). Do not use articles for determining alphabetical order.

Basic Guidelines for Citations

- Author's names are inverted (last name first, e.g., Presley, E.) and list only first and middle (if available) initials, not first and middle names. If a work has more than one author, invert all names, follow each with a comma, and precede the final name with ", &" (e.g., Lennon, J., & McCartney, P.).
- If you have cited more than one work by the same author, order the works sequentially by year of publication, the earliest first.
- If a cited work does not have a known author, alphabetize by the first significant word in the title of the work. Use Anonymous as an author if, and only if, the work lists the author as Anonymous.
- Capitalize the first word in the titles of essays, books, films, and other works.
- Capitalize all major words in periodical titles, including journals, magazines, and newspapers.

- Italicize the titles of books, journals, magazines, newspapers, films, television shows, and album or game titles.
- Do not place quotation marks around the titles of articles or essays in journals, magazines, newspapers, or web pages.
- For works with more than one edition, give the edition number and the abbreviation directly after the title of the work—for example, *Feminist frontiers* (5th ed.).
- For periodicals, give the volume number, but only give the issue number if each volume starts over with the number 1.
- Give URLs or database names (e.g., InfoTrac College Edition or LexisNexis) for websites and other online sources. You should also give the date of retrieval for online sources (e.g., Retrieved December 11, 2003, from http://www.newyorktimes.com or Retrieved March 23, 2003, from the LexisNexis database). Note that URLs are not followed by periods so they won't be mistaken as part of the Internet address.

BASIC APA FORMS FOR ALL MEDIA

1. ANTHOLOGY OR COLLECTION

Editor's Name(s), (Ed.). (year). *Title of book*. Place of Publication: Publisher.

Hague, A., & Lavery, D. (Eds.). (2002). *Tele-parody: Predicting/preventing the TV discourse of tomorrow*. London: Wallflower Press.

2. ANTHOLOGY: WORK WITHIN

Author's Name. (year). Title of Work. In Editor's Name(s) (Ed.), *Title of anthology* (page numbers). Place of Publication: Publisher.

Yu, H. (2005). How Tiger Woods lost his stripes: Post-nationalist American studies as a history of race, migration, and the commodification of culture. In R. Guins & O. Z. Cruz (Eds.), *Popular culture: A reader* (pp. 197–209). London: Sage.

3. ARTICLE IN A SCHOLARLY JOURNAL

Author's Name. (year). Title of article. *Journal Title, volume number,* pages.

Robinson, B. (2006). Playing like the boys: Patricia Cornwell writes men. *The Journal of Popular Culture, 39,* pp. 95–108.

4. BOOKS

Author's Name. (year). *Title of book*. Place of Publication: Publisher.

Kaku, M. (1994). *Hyperspace: A scientific odyssey through parallel universes, time warps, and the tenth dimension*. New York: Oxford University Press.

Strauss, W., & Howe, N. (2006). *Millennials and the pop culture*. Great Falls, VA: LifeCourse.

EXAMPLE: TWO BOOKS BY THE SAME AUTHOR

King, S. (1987). *Misery*. New York: Viking.

King, S. (2001). *Dreamcatcher: A novel*. New York: Scribner.

5. CD-ROM ARTICLE

Name. (pub. year). Title. *Publication*, volume, page. Retrieved from Database Name (CD-ROM Item: item no. if available).

Down, C. (Producer). (2006). Ultimate Yahtzee. *Developer PCA*. Retrieved from Hasbro Interactive (CD-ROM).

6. COMIC, COMIC STRIP, OR ADVERTISEMENT

Name. (Artist or Producer). (date). Comic or comic strip title, if any. [medium]. *Publication Title*. page number.

Byrnes, P. (Artist). (2006, November 28). [Cartoon]. *The New Yorker*. p. 131.

Walker, G., & Walker, M. (2006, November 28). Beetle Bailey. [Comic strip]. *The Tennessean.* p. 4D.

Yves Saint Laurent. (Producer). (2007, September). [Advertisement]. *Out.* p. 17.

7. LIBRARY SUBSCRIPTION SERVICE, SUCH AS INFOTRAC COLLEGE EDITION OR LEXISNEXIS: ARTICLE

Author's Name. (pub. year). Title of article. *Journal Title, vol. issue*, pages. Retrieved Date from Name of Database, Location, or URL.

Ornstein, Aviva. (2003). MY GOD!: A feminist critique of the excited utterance exception to the hearsay rule. *California Law Review, 85.1*, pp. 161–223. Retrieved April 22, 2003 from InfoTrac.

NOTE: Only give URLs if the reader can get back to the original source using the URL you have given; cut off lengthy URL addresses at the point where they stop making sense to the reader.

8. NEWSPAPER ARTICLE

Author's Name. (pub. date). Title of article. *Newspaper Title*, pages.

Berger, L. (2002, December 10). Quest for male "pill" is gaining momentum. *The New York Times*, p. F5.

Lederman, D. (1994, March 30). Athletic merit vs. academic merit. *The Chronicle of Higher Education*, pp. A37–38.

Tagliabue, J. (1994, April 9). Cleaned last judgment unveiled. *The New York Times*, p. 13.

9. NONPRINT MEDIA (INCLUDING MOTION PICTURES, RECORDINGS, TELEVISION SHOWS, RADIO BROADCASTS, LIVE SPEECHES, CONCERTS, ETC.)

MOTION PICTURE

Person or Persons primarily responsible for the product or program. (Person's Title). (year). *Title* [medium]. Location (country of origin): Studio.

Reiner, R. (Director). (1987). *The princess bride* [Motion picture]. Los Angeles: MGM/UA.

Singer, B. (Director). (1995). *The usual suspects* [Motion picture]. New York: Polygram.

TELEVISION BROADCAST OR SERIES

Name of Producer. (Producer). (Date of broadcast, year for a series). Title of program [Television series]. City where distributor located: Name of Distributor.

Cohen, D. S. (Executive Producer). (1993). *Living single* [Television series]. Burbank, CA: Warner Brothers Burbank Studios.

SINGLE EPISODE OF A TELEVISION PROGRAM

Writer's Name, & Director's Name. (date of broadcast). Title of episode [Television series episode]. In Producer's Name, *Name of television series*. City where distributor located: Name of Distributor.

Edlund, B. (Writer), & Grabiak, M. (Director). (2002, October 18). Jaynestown [Television series episode]. In J. Whedon (Producer), *Firefly*. Los Angeles: 20th Century Fox Studios.

RADIO BROADCAST

Name of Originator or Primary Producer. (Date of broadcast). Title of radio program. [Radio broadcast]. City where distributor located: Name of Distributor.

Glass, I. (Host). (2002, December 27). *This American life* [Radio broadcast]. Chicago: WEBZ.

LIVE CONCERT OR SPEECH

Name of Artist or Producer. (Date of event). *Title of event* (if any). [Type of event]. Location of event.

Lennox A. (Singer). (2007, October 22). *Annie Lennox Songs of Mass Destruction Tour* [Musical concert]. Detroit, MI: Music Hall Center.

MUSIC RECORDING

Writer's Name. (date of copyright). Title of song [Recorded by if Artist differs from Writer]. On *Title of album* [Medium: CD, record, cassette, etc.]/ Location: Label. (Recording date if different from copyright date).

Coolio. (1995). "Kinda high, kinda drunk." On *Gangsta's paradise* [CD]. New York: Tommy Boy Music.

NOTE: Do not reference in-person interviews in your References list; only cite interviews within the text itself. For television or multi-media interviews, just cite the episode in normal format and then mention in the text who was interviewed.

10. Online Periodical Article

Author's Name. (pub. date). Title of article. *Newspaper Title*, page numbers (if applicable). Retrieved Date from URL.

Quindlen, A. (2003, March 28). Getting rid of the sex police. *Newsweek* [Online serial]. Retrieved April 2, 2003, from http://www.msnbc.com/news/NW-front_Front.asp

Berger, L. (2002, December 10). Quest for male "pill" is gaining momentum. *The New York Times* [Online serial]. Retrieved March 18, 2003, from http://nytimes.com

Whithaus, C. (2002, July 1). Think different/think differently: A tale of green squiggly lines, or evaluating student writing in computer-mediated environments. *The Writing Instructor, 2.5* [Online serial]. Retrieved April 21, 2003, from http://www.writinginstructor.com

11. Review

Reviewer's Name. (review pub. date). Title of review. [Review of the medium *Work title*]. *Journal, volume*, pages.

Franklin, D. K. (2003, April 17). *Bend it like Beckham* goooooal! [Review of motion picture *Bend it like Beckham*]. *The Rage: All Entertainment*, pp. 95–96.

12. Software

Product/Software Name (Version) [Computer software]. (year). Place: Manufacturer.

Macintosh OSX (Version 10.4) [Computer software]. (2006). Cupertino, CA: Apple Computer.

13. Website

Author's Name. (pub. date). *Name of page*. Retrieved from URL.

Irvine, M., & Everhart, D. (2002). *The laby-rinth: Resources for medieval studies*. Retrieved June 21, 2002, from http://www.georgetown.edu/labyrinth/labyrinth-home.html

NOTE: This same format can be used for blogs and any fan fiction found online.

SAMPLE REFERENCES LIST

Here is an example of how a completed References list would look at the end of your essay. The References list is part of the essay and should contain the same header (a short two- to three-word version of your title and the page number) as the rest of your essay.

References

Cohen, D. S. (Executive Producer). (1993). *Living single* [Television series]. Burbank, CA: Warner Brothers Burbank Studios.

Franklin, D. K. (2003, April 17). *Bend it like Beckham* goooooal! [Review of motion picture *Bend it like Beckham*]. *The Rage: All Entertainment*, 95–96.

Quindlen, A. (2003, March 28). Getting rid of the sex police. *Newsweek* [Online serial]. Retrieved April 2, 2003, from http://www.msnbc.com/news/NW-front_Front.asp

Robinson, B. (2006). Playing like the boys: Patricia Cornwell writes men. *The Journal of Popular Culture, 39,* 95–108.

Strauss, W., & Howe, N. (2006). *Millennials and the pop culture.* Great Falls, VA: LifeCourse.

Tagliabue, J. (1994, April 9). Cleaned last judgment unveiled. *New York Times,* p. 13.

FOR FURTHER READING

Bogle, Donald. *Blacks in American Films and Television: An Encyclopedia.* New York: Garland, 1988.

Boorstin, Daniel. *The Image: A Guide to Pseudo-Events in America.* 1961; rpt. New York: Vintage, 1992.

Cawelti, John. *Adventure, Mystery, and Romance: Formula Stories as Art and Popular Culture.* Chicago: U of Chicago P, 1976.

Cultural Studies Central. <http://www.culturalstudies.net/index.html>.

Dunne, Michael. *Metapop: Self-Referentiality in Contemporary American Popular Culture.* Jackson: UP of Mississippi, 1992.

Ewen, Stuart. *All Consuming Images: The Politics of Style in Contemporary Culture.* New York: Basin Books, 1988.

Fiske, John. *Understanding Popular Culture.* Boston: Unwin Hyman, 1989.

Gabler, Neal. *Life: The Movie: How Entertainment Conquered Reality.* New York: Knopf, 1998.

Gibaldi, Joseph. *MLA Handbook for Writers of Research Papers.* 6th ed. New York: Modern Language Association, 2003.

Hague, Angela, and David Lavery, eds. *Teleparody: Predicting/Preventing the TV Discourse of Tomorrow.* New York: Wallflower Press, 2002.

Harris, Joseph, Jay Rosen, and Gary Calpas. *Media Journal: Reading and Writing About Popular Culture.* 2nd ed. New York: Longman, 1998.

Hebdige, Dick. *Subculture: The Meaning of Style.* New York: Routledge, 1979.

Jenkins, Henry. *Textual Poachers: Television Fans and Participatory Culture.* New York: Routledge, 1992.

Johnson, Steven. *Everything Bad Is Good for You: How Today's Popular Culture Is Actually Making Us Smarter.* New York: Penguin, 2005.

Kaplan, E. Ann. *Rocking Around the Clock: Music Television, Postmodernism, and Consumer Culture.* New York: Methuen, 1987.

Marc, David. *Comic Visions: Television Comedy and American Culture.* Malden, MA: Blackwell, 1997.

McLuhan, Marshall, and Quentin Fiore. *The Medium Is the Message: An Inventory of Effects.* 1967; rpt. New York: Genko, 2005.

Modleski, Tania. *Loving with a Vengeance: Mass-Produced Fantasies for Women.* Hamden, CT: Shoestring, 1982.

---. *Studies in Entertainment: Critical Approaches to Mass Culture.* Bloomington: Indiana UP, 1986.

Mukerju, Chandra, and Michael Schudson, eds. *Rethinking Popular Culture: Contemporary Perspectives in Cultural Studies.* Berkeley: U of California P, 1991.

Nye, Russell. *The Unembarrassed Muse: The Popular Arts in America.* New York: Dial Press, 1970.

Publication Manual of the American Psychological Association. 5th ed. Washington, D.C.: APA, 2001.

Radner, Hilary. *Shopping Around: Feminine Culture and the Pursuit of Pleasure.* New York: Routledge, 1995.

Research Channel. <http://www.researchchannel.org>.

Simon, Richard Keller. *Trash Culture: Popular Culture and the Great Tradition.* Berkeley: U of California P, 1999.

Stark, Steven D. *Glued to the Set: The 60 Television Shows and Events That Made Us Who We Are Today.* New York: Free Press, 1997.

University of Chicago Press. *Chicago Manual of Style.* 15th ed. Chicago: U of Chicago P, 2003.

Wolf, Naomi. *The Beauty Myth: How Images of Beauty Are Used Against Women.* New York: Anchor, 1992.

CHAPTER 1: THE POP CULTURE ZONE

The Breakfast Club. Dir. John Hughes. A&M Films, 1985.

Pratt, Mary Louise. "Arts of the Contact Zone." *Profession* (1991): 33–40.

CHAPTER 2: WRITING IN THE POP CULTURE ZONE

Bozell, L. Brent, III. "Fifty Ways to Leave the Liberal Spin." *Media Research Center.* 25 Oct. 2000. 30 Sept. 2007 <http://www.mediaresearch.org/BozellColumns/newscolumn/2000/col20001025.asp>

Harper, Stephanie. "Freewrite Assignment." June 2006.

Shakespeare in Love. Dir. John Madden. Universal Pictures, 1998.

Tipton, Holly. "Ethical Issues in *Se7en* (Essay 2 Assignment)." Feb. 2007.

---. "Journal Assignment." Feb. 2007.

CHAPTER 3: DEFINING POPULAR CULTURE

Browne, Ray B., ed. *Mission Underway: The History of the Popular Culture Association/American Culture Association and the Popular Culture Movement, 1967–2001.* Bowling Green, OH: PCA/APA, 2002.

---, ed. *Popular Culture Studies Across the Curriculum.* Jefferson, NC: McFarland, 2005.

"The Long Lead Story." *Studio 60 on the Sunset Strip.* Warner Bros. Television. 16 Oct. 2006.

"1985." Lyrics by John Allen, Kenneth Lowe, Jaret Ray Reddick and Mitchell Allan Scherr. Universal Music, 2004.

Storey, John. *Cultural Studies and the Study of Popular Culture.* 2nd ed. Athens: Georgia UP, 2003.

CHAPTER 4: WRITING ABOUT ADVERTISEMENTS

Browne, David. "Licensed to Shill." *Entertainment Weekly* 12 Jan. 2001. 9 Dec. 2006 <http://www.ew.com/ew/article/commentary/0,6115,279404_4_0_,00.html>.

Cortese, Anthony J. *Provocateur: Images of Women and Minorities in Advertising.* 2nd ed. Lanham, MD: Rowman and Littlefield, 2004.

Fowles, Jib. "Advertising's Fifteen Basic Appeals." *Etc.: A Review of General Semantics* 39.3 (1982).

"'Got Milk? Turns 10: Ad Campaign Becomes an American Icon." 19 June 2003. *FashionWindows.com.* 6 May 2008 <http://www.fashionwindows.com/visualprofiles/2001/skip.asp>.

Smith, Dianne. "Advertising Notebook." *For Journalism Teachers Only.* 28 Feb. 2007. 5 Apr. 2007 <http://www.jteacher.com/adnotebook.html>.

SuperBowl-Ads.com 2008. 21 Mar. 2008 <http://www.superbowl-ads.com>.

"Top Ten Advertising Icons of the Century." *Advertising Age.* 2005. 16 Dec. 2006 <http://adage.com/century/ad_icons.html>.

Yankelovich Partners. *Yankelovich.* 1999–2007. 18 Aug. 2007 <http://www.yankelovich.com>.

CHAPTER 5: WRITING ABOUT FILM

Ferris Bueller's Day Off. Dir. John Hughes. Paramount Pictures, 1986.

"The 50 Best High School Movies." *Entertainment Weekly* 15 Sept. 2006. 17 Sept. 2006 <http://www.ew.com/ew/report/ 0,6115,1532588_1|17765|249578|1_0_,00.html>.

"$100 Million Movies." *The Washington Post* 16 May 2005. 14 Sept. 2006 <http://www.washingtonpost.com/wp-srv/style/daily/movies/100million/article.htm>.

"Search." *Hollywood Foreign Press Association.* 2006. 14 Sept. 2006 <http://www.hfpa.org/browse/years>.

CHAPTER 6: WRITING ABOUT GROUPS, SPACES, AND PLACES

"DePauw Cuts Ties to Sorority Accused of Discrimination." *WashingtonPost.com CNN.com.* 13 Mar. 2007. 13 Mar. 2007 <http://www.washingtonpost.com/wp-dyn/content/article/2007/03/13/AR2007031300229.html> <http://www.cnn.com/2007/EDUCATION/03/12/troubled.sorority.ap/index.html>.

"Val Kilmer/U2." *Saturday Night Live.* NBC Studios. 9 Dec. 2000.

CHAPTER 7: WRITING ABOUT MUSIC

Costello, Elvis, voice actor. "How I Spent My Strummer Vacation." *The Simpsons.* Fox, 10 Sept. 2002.

The Forrest Gump Soundtrack. Sony Music, 1994.

Nash, Alanna. "Carrie Underwood Is Atop a *Carnival Ride.*" *Los Angeles Times* 23 Oct. 2007: online ed.

"She Came In Through the Bathroom Window." Lyrics by John Lennon and Paul McCartney. Sony Music, 1969.

UsherWorld.com. 2008. 10 February 2008 <http://www.usherworld.com>.

"Video Killed the Radio Star." Lyrics by Geoffrey Downes, Trevor Horn, Bruce Woolley. Carbert Music, Inc., 1979.

CHAPTER 8: WRITING ABOUT POPULAR LITERATURE

Grabois, Andrew. "These Are the Good Old Days: U.S. Book Publishing Has Become the World's Greatest Enabler of Reading." *Publishers Weekly* 20 June 2005: 84.

Green, Hardy. "Why Oprah Opens Readers' Wallets." *Business Week Online* 10 Oct. 2005. 30 Mar. 2007 <http://www.businessweek.com>.

Lazar, Allan Karlan, and Jeremy Salter. *The 101 Most Influential People Who Never Lived: How Characters of Fiction, Myth, Legends, Television, and Movies Have Shaped Our Society, Changed Our Behavior, and Set the Course of History.* New York: Harper, 2006. 253–55.

"Oprah's Bookshelf." *Oprah.com.* 6 May 2008 <http://www.oprah.com/books/favorite/books_favorite_main.jhtml>.

CHAPTER 9: WRITING ABOUT SPORTS AND LEISURE

Deford, Frank. "Mythical No More: George Mason Made the Impossible Possible." *Sports Illustrated Online.* 29 March 2006. 10 February 2008 <http://sportsillustrated.cnn.com/2006/writers/frank_deford/03/28/gm/index.html>.

Greenfeld, Karl Taro. "A Wider World of Sports." *Time* 9 Nov. 1988. 24 Mar. 2008 <http://www.time.com/time/magazine/printout/0,8816,989525,00.html>.

"Men Delay Going to the Emergency Department Until After Sporting Events: New Study Presented at ACEP's Scientific Assembly." *The American College of Emergency Physicians Website.* 11 Oct. 2006. 31 Jan. 2007 <www.acep.org/webportal/newsroom/nr/general/2006/101106b.htm>.

Walters, Patrick. "Coffins to Bear Logos of Baseball Teams." *CBSNews.com.* 18 Oct. 2006. 31 Jan. 2007 <http://www.cbsnews.com/stories/2006/10/18/ap/strange/mainD8KR9QVO1.shtml> .